American Casebook Series
Hornbook Series and Basic Legal Texts
Black Letter Series and Nutshell Series

of

WEST PUBLISHING COMPANY
P.O. Box 64526
St. Paul, Minnesota 55164–0526

Accounting

FARIS' ACCOUNTING AND LAW IN A NUTSHELL, 377 pages, 1984. Softcover. (Text)

FIFLIS, KRIPKE AND FOSTER'S TEACHING MATERIALS ON ACCOUNTING FOR BUSINESS LAWYERS, Third Edition, 838 pages, 1984. (Casebook)

SIEGEL AND SIEGEL'S ACCOUNTING AND FINANCIAL DISCLOSURE: A GUIDE TO BASIC CONCEPTS, 259 pages, 1983. Softcover. (Text)

Administrative Law

BONFIELD AND ASIMOW'S STATE AND FEDERAL ADMINISTRATIVE LAW, 826 pages, 1989. (Casebook)

GELLHORN AND BOYER'S ADMINISTRATIVE LAW AND PROCESS IN A NUTSHELL, Second Edition, 445 pages, 1981. Softcover. (Text)

MASHAW AND MERRILL'S CASES AND MATERIALS ON ADMINISTRATIVE LAW—THE AMERICAN PUBLIC LAW SYSTEM, Second Edition, 976 pages, 1985. (Casebook) 1989 Supplement.

ROBINSON, GELLHORN AND BRUFF'S THE ADMINISTRATIVE PROCESS, Third Edition, 978 pages, 1986. (Casebook)

Admiralty

HEALY AND SHARPE'S CASES AND MATERIALS ON ADMIRALTY, Second Edition, 876 pages, 1986. (Casebook)

MARAIST'S ADMIRALTY IN A NUTSHELL, Second Edition, 379 pages, 1988. Softcover.

(Text)

SCHOENBAUM'S HORNBOOK ON ADMIRALTY AND MARITIME LAW, Student Edition, 692 pages, 1987 with 1989 pocket part. (Text)

Agency—Partnership

FESSLER'S ALTERNATIVES TO INCORPORATION FOR PERSONS IN QUEST OF PROFIT, Second Edition, 326 pages, 1986. Softcover. Teacher's Manual available. (Casebook)

HENN'S CASES AND MATERIALS ON AGENCY, PARTNERSHIP AND OTHER UNINCORPORATED BUSINESS ENTERPRISES, Second Edition, 733 pages, 1985. Teacher's Manual available. (Casebook)

REUSCHLEIN AND GREGORY'S HORNBOOK ON THE LAW OF AGENCY AND PARTNERSHIP, Second Edition, Approximately 750 pages, October, 1989 Pub. (Text)

SELECTED CORPORATION AND PARTNERSHIP STATUTES, RULES AND FORMS. Softcover. Approximately 700 pages, 1989.

STEFFEN AND KERR'S CASES ON AGENCY-PARTNERSHIP, Fourth Edition, 859 pages, 1980. (Casebook)

STEFFEN'S AGENCY-PARTNERSHIP IN A NUTSHELL, 364 pages, 1977. Softcover. (Text)

Agricultural Law

MEYER, PEDERSEN, THORSON AND DAVIDSON'S AGRICULTURAL LAW: CASES AND MATERIALS, 931 pages, 1985. Teacher's Manual available. (Casebook)

Alternative Dispute Resolution

KANOWITZ' CASES AND MATERIALS ON ALTER-

Alternative Dispute Resolution—Cont'd

NATIVE DISPUTE RESOLUTION, 1024 pages, 1986. Teacher's Manual available. (Casebook)

RISKIN AND WESTBROOK'S DISPUTE RESOLUTION AND LAWYERS, 468 pages, 1987. Teacher's Manual available. (Casebook)

RISKIN AND WESTBROOK'S DISPUTE RESOLUTION AND LAWYERS, Abridged Edition, 223 pages, 1987. Softcover. Teacher's Manual available. (Casebook)

TEPLE AND MOBERLY'S ARBITRATION AND CONFLICT RESOLUTION, (The Labor Law Group). 614 pages, 1979. (Casebook)

American Indian Law

CANBY'S AMERICAN INDIAN LAW IN A NUTSHELL, Second Edition, 336 pages, 1988. Softcover. (Text)

GETCHES AND WILKINSON'S CASES AND MATERIALS ON FEDERAL INDIAN LAW, Second Edition, 880 pages, 1986. (Casebook)

Antitrust—see also Regulated Industries, Trade Regulation

FOX AND SULLIVAN'S CASES AND MATERIALS ON ANTITRUST, Approximately 1100 pages, 1989. (Casebook)

GELLHORN'S ANTITRUST LAW AND ECONOMICS IN A NUTSHELL, Third Edition, 472 pages, 1986. Softcover. (Text)

HOVENKAMP'S BLACK LETTER ON ANTITRUST, 323 pages, 1986. Softcover. (Review)

HOVENKAMP'S HORNBOOK ON ECONOMICS AND FEDERAL ANTITRUST LAW, Student Edition, 414 pages, 1985. (Text)

OPPENHEIM, WESTON AND MCCARTHY'S CASES AND COMMENTS ON FEDERAL ANTITRUST LAWS, Fourth Edition, 1168 pages, 1981. (Casebook) 1985 Supplement.

POSNER AND EASTERBROOK'S CASES AND ECONOMIC NOTES ON ANTITRUST, Second Edition, 1077 pages, 1981. (Casebook) 1984–85 Supplement.

SULLIVAN'S HORNBOOK OF THE LAW OF ANTITRUST, 886 pages, 1977. (Text)

Appellate Advocacy—see Trial and Appellate Advocacy

Architecture and Engineering Law

SWEET'S LEGAL ASPECTS OF ARCHITECTURE, ENGINEERING AND THE CONSTRUCTION PROCESS, Fourth Edition, 889 pages, 1989. Teacher's Manual available. (Casebook)

Art Law

DUBOFF'S ART LAW IN A NUTSHELL, 335 pages, 1984. Softcover. (Text)

Banking Law

LOVETT'S BANKING AND FINANCIAL INSTITUTIONS LAW IN A NUTSHELL, Second Edition, 464 pages, 1988. Softcover. (Text)

SYMONS AND WHITE'S TEACHING MATERIALS ON BANKING LAW, Second Edition, 993 pages, 1984. Teacher's Manual available. (Casebook) 1987 Supplement.

Business Planning—see also Corporate Finance

PAINTER'S PROBLEMS AND MATERIALS IN BUSINESS PLANNING, Second Edition, 1008 pages, 1984. (Casebook) 1987 Supplement.

See also Selected Corporation and Partnership Statutes, Rules and Forms

SELECTED CORPORATION AND PARTNERSHIP STATUTES, RULES AND FORMS. Approximately 700 pages, 1989. Softcover.

Civil Procedure—see also Federal Jurisdiction and Procedure

AMERICAN BAR ASSOCIATION SECTION OF LITIGATION—READINGS ON ADVERSARIAL JUSTICE: THE AMERICAN APPROACH TO ADJUDICATION, 217 pages, 1988. Softcover. (Coursebook)

CLERMONT'S BLACK LETTER ON CIVIL PROCEDURE, Second Edition, 332 pages, 1988. Softcover. (Review)

COUND, FRIEDENTHAL, MILLER AND SEXTON'S CASES AND MATERIALS ON CIVIL PROCEDURE, Fifth Edition, Approximately 1280 pages, 1989. Teacher's Manual available. (Casebook)

COUND, FRIEDENTHAL, MILLER AND SEXTON'S CIVIL PROCEDURE SUPPLEMENT. Approximately 450 pages, 1989. Softcover. (Casebook Supplement)

FEDERAL RULES OF CIVIL PROCEDURE—EDUCATIONAL EDITION. Softcover. Approximately 600 pages, 1989.

Civil Procedure—Cont'd

FRIEDENTHAL, KANE AND MILLER'S HORN-BOOK ON CIVIL PROCEDURE, 876 pages, 1985. (Text)

KANE AND LEVINE'S CIVIL PROCEDURE IN CALIFORNIA: STATE AND FEDERAL Approximately 500 pages, 1989. Softcover. Casebook Supplement.

KANE'S CIVIL PROCEDURE IN A NUTSHELL, Second Edition, 306 pages, 1986. Softcover. (Text)

KOFFLER AND REPPY'S HORNBOOK ON COMMON LAW PLEADING, 663 pages, 1969. (Text)

MARCUS, REDISH AND SHERMAN'S CIVIL PROCEDURE: A MODERN APPROACH, 1027 pages, 1989. Teacher's Manual available. (Casebook)

MARCUS AND SHERMAN'S COMPLEX LITIGATION–CASES AND MATERIALS ON ADVANCED CIVIL PROCEDURE, 846 pages, 1985. Teacher's Manual available. (Casebook) 1989 Supplement.

PARK'S COMPUTER-AIDED EXERCISES ON CIVIL PROCEDURE, Second Edition, 167 pages, 1983. Softcover. (Coursebook)

SIEGEL'S HORNBOOK ON NEW YORK PRACTICE, 1011 pages, 1978, with 1987 pocket part. (Text)

Commercial Law

BAILEY AND HAGEDORN'S SECURED TRANSACTIONS IN A NUTSHELL, Third Edition, 390 pages, 1988. Softcover. (Text)

EPSTEIN, MARTIN, HENNING AND NICKLES' BASIC UNIFORM COMMERCIAL CODE TEACHING MATERIALS, Third Edition, 704 pages, 1988. Teacher's Manual available. (Casebook)

HENSON'S HORNBOOK ON SECURED TRANSACTIONS UNDER THE U.C.C., Second Edition, 504 pages, 1979, with 1979 pocket part. (Text)

MURRAY'S COMMERCIAL LAW, PROBLEMS AND MATERIALS, 366 pages, 1975. Teacher's Manual available. Softcover. (Coursebook)

NICKLES' BLACK LETTER ON COMMERCIAL PAPER, 450 pages, 1988. Softcover. (Review)

NICKLES, MATHESON AND DOLAN'S MATERI-ALS FOR UNDERSTANDING CREDIT AND PAYMENT SYSTEMS, 923 pages, 1987. Teacher's Manual available. (Casebook)

NORDSTROM, MURRAY AND CLOVIS' PROBLEMS AND MATERIALS ON SALES, 515 pages, 1982. (Casebook)

NORDSTROM, MURRAY AND CLOVIS' PROBLEMS AND MATERIALS ON SECURED TRANSACTIONS, 594 pages, 1987. (Casebook)

RUBIN AND COOTER'S THE PAYMENT SYSTEM: CASES, MATERIALS AND ISSUES, Approximately 885 pages, 1989. (Casebook)

SELECTED COMMERCIAL STATUTES. Softcover. Approximately 1600 pages, 1989.

SPEIDEL'S BLACK LETTER ON SALES AND SALES FINANCING, 363 pages, 1984. Softcover. (Review)

SPEIDEL, SUMMERS AND WHITE'S COMMERCIAL LAW: TEACHING MATERIALS, Fourth Edition, 1448 pages, 1987. Teacher's Manual available. (Casebook)

SPEIDEL, SUMMERS AND WHITE'S COMMERCIAL PAPER: TEACHING MATERIALS, Fourth Edition, 578 pages, 1987. Reprint from Speidel et al., Commercial Law, Fourth Edition. Teacher's Manual available. (Casebook)

SPEIDEL, SUMMERS AND WHITE'S SALES: TEACHING MATERIALS, Fourth Edition, 804 pages, 1987. Reprint from Speidel et al., Commercial Law, Fourth Edition. Teacher's Manual available (Casebook)

SPEIDEL, SUMMERS AND WHITE'S SECURED TRANSACTIONS: TEACHING MATERIALS, Fourth Edition, 485 pages, 1987. Reprint from Speidel et al., Commercial Law, Fourth Edition. Teacher's Manual available. (Casebook)

STOCKTON'S SALES IN A NUTSHELL, Second Edition, 370 pages, 1981. Softcover. (Text)

STONE'S UNIFORM COMMERCIAL CODE IN A NUTSHELL, Third Edition, Approximately 540 pages, 1989. Softcover. (Text)

UNIFORM COMMERCIAL CODE, OFFICIAL TEXT WITH COMMENTS. Softcover. 1155 pages, 1987.

WEBER AND SPEIDEL'S COMMERCIAL PAPER IN A NUTSHELL, Third Edition, 404 pages,

Commercial Law—Cont'd

1982. Softcover. (Text)

WHITE AND SUMMERS' HORNBOOK ON THE UNIFORM COMMERCIAL CODE, Third Edition, Student Edition, 1386 pages, 1988. (Text)

Community Property

MENNELL AND BOYKOFF'S COMMUNITY PROPERTY IN A NUTSHELL, Second Edition, 432 pages, 1988. Softcover. (Text)

VERRALL AND BIRD'S CASES AND MATERIALS ON CALIFORNIA COMMUNITY PROPERTY, Fifth Edition, 604 pages, 1988. (Casebook)

Comparative Law

BARTON, GIBBS, LI AND MERRYMAN'S LAW IN RADICALLY DIFFERENT CULTURES, 960 pages, 1983. (Casebook)

GLENDON, GORDON AND OSAKWE'S COMPARATIVE LEGAL TRADITIONS: TEXT, MATERIALS AND CASES ON THE CIVIL LAW, COMMON LAW AND SOCIALIST LAW TRADITIONS, 1091 pages, 1985. (Casebook)

GLENDON, GORDON AND OSAKWE'S COMPARATIVE LEGAL TRADITIONS IN A NUTSHELL. 402 pages, 1982. Softcover. (Text)

LANGBEIN'S COMPARATIVE CRIMINAL PROCEDURE: GERMANY, 172 pages, 1977. Softcover. (Casebook)

Computers and Law

MAGGS AND SPROWL'S COMPUTER APPLICATIONS IN THE LAW, 316 pages, 1987. (Coursebook)

MASON'S USING COMPUTERS IN THE LAW: AN INTRODUCTION AND PRACTICAL GUIDE, Second Edition, 288 pages, 1988. Softcover. (Coursebook)

Conflict of Laws

CRAMTON, CURRIE AND KAY'S CASES—COMMENTS—QUESTIONS ON CONFLICT OF LAWS, Fourth Edition, 876 pages, 1987. (Casebook)

HAY'S BLACK LETTER ON CONFLICT OF LAWS, Approximately 325 pages, 1989. Softcover. (Review)

SCOLES AND HAY'S HORNBOOK ON CONFLICT OF LAWS, Student Edition, 1085 pages, 1982, with 1989 pocket part. (Text)

SEIGEL'S CONFLICTS IN A NUTSHELL, 470

pages, 1982. Softcover. (Text)

Constitutional Law—Civil Rights—see also Foreign Relations and National Security Law

ABERNATHY'S CASES AND MATERIALS ON CIVIL RIGHTS, 660 pages, 1980. (Casebook)

BARRON AND DIENES' BLACK LETTER ON CONSTITUTIONAL LAW, Second Edition, 310 pages, 1987. Softcover. (Review)

BARRON AND DIENES' CONSTITUTIONAL LAW IN A NUTSHELL, 389 pages, 1986. Softcover. (Text)

ENGDAHL'S CONSTITUTIONAL FEDERALISM IN A NUTSHELL, Second Edition, 411 pages, 1987. Softcover. (Text)

FARBER AND SHERRY'S HISTORY OF THE AMERICAN CONSTITUTION, Approximately 476 pages, August, 1989 Pub. Softcover. (Text)

GARVEY AND ALEINIKOFF'S MODERN CONSTITUTIONAL THEORY: A READER, Approximately 494 pages, 1989. Softcover. (Reader)

LOCKHART, KAMISAR, CHOPER AND SHIFFRIN'S CONSTITUTIONAL LAW: CASES—COMMENTS—QUESTIONS, Sixth Edition, 1601 pages, 1986. (Casebook) 1989 Supplement.

LOCKHART, KAMISAR, CHOPER AND SHIFFRIN'S THE AMERICAN CONSTITUTION: CASES AND MATERIALS, Sixth Edition, 1260 pages, 1986. Abridged version of Lockhart, et al., Constitutional Law: Cases—Comments—Questions, Sixth Edition. (Casebook) 1989 Supplement.

LOCKHART, KAMISAR, CHOPER AND SHIFFRIN'S CONSTITUTIONAL RIGHTS AND LIBERTIES: CASES AND MATERIALS, Sixth Edition, 1266 pages, 1986. Reprint from Lockhart, et al., Constitutional Law: Cases—Comments—Questions, Sixth Edition. (Casebook) 1989 Supplement.

MARKS AND COOPER'S STATE CONSTITUTIONAL LAW IN A NUTSHELL, 329 pages, 1988. Softcover. (Text)

NOWAK, ROTUNDA AND YOUNG'S HORNBOOK ON CONSTITUTIONAL LAW, Third Edition, 1191 pages, 1986 with 1988 pocket part. (Text)

ROTUNDA'S MODERN CONSTITUTIONAL LAW:

Constitutional Law—Civil Rights—Cont'd

CASES AND NOTES, Third Edition, 1085 pages, 1989. (Casebook) 1989 Supplement.

VIEIRA'S CIVIL RIGHTS IN A NUTSHELL, 279 pages, 1978. Softcover. (Text)

WILLIAMS' CONSTITUTIONAL ANALYSIS IN A NUTSHELL, 388 pages, 1979. Softcover. (Text)

Consumer Law—see also Commercial Law

EPSTEIN AND NICKLES' CONSUMER LAW IN A NUTSHELL, Second Edition, 418 pages, 1981. Softcover. (Text)

SELECTED COMMERCIAL STATUTES. Softcover. Approximately 1600 pages, 1989.

SPANOGLE AND ROHNER'S CASES AND MATERIALS ON CONSUMER LAW, 693 pages, 1979. Teacher's Manual available. (Casebook) 1982 Supplement.

Contracts

CALAMARI, AND PERILLO'S BLACK LETTER ON CONTRACTS, 397 pages, 1983. Softcover. (Review)

CALAMARI AND PERILLO'S HORNBOOK ON CONTRACTS, Third Edition, 1049 pages, 1987. (Text)

CALAMARI, PERILLO AND BENDER'S CASES AND PROBLEMS ON CONTRACTS, Second Edition, approximately 846 pages, 1989. Teacher's Manual Available. (Casebook)

CORBIN'S TEXT ON CONTRACTS, One Volume Student Edition, 1224 pages, 1952. (Text)

FESSLER AND LOISEAUX'S CASES AND MATERIALS ON CONTRACTS—MORALITY, ECONOMICS AND THE MARKET PLACE, 837 pages, 1982. Teacher's Manual available. (Casebook)

FRIEDMAN'S CONTRACT REMEDIES IN A NUTSHELL, 323 pages, 1981. Softcover. (Text)

FULLER AND EISENBERG'S CASES ON BASIC CONTRACT LAW, Fourth Edition, 1203 pages, 1981 (Casebook)

HAMILTON, RAU AND WEINTRAUB'S CASES AND MATERIALS ON CONTRACTS, 830 pages, 1984. (Casebook)

JACKSON AND BOLLINGER'S CASES ON CONTRACT LAW IN MODERN SOCIETY, Second Edition, 1329 pages, 1980. Teacher's Manual

available. (Casebook)

KEYES' GOVERNMENT CONTRACTS IN A NUTSHELL, 423 pages, 1979. Softcover. (Text)

SCHABER AND ROHWER'S CONTRACTS IN A NUTSHELL, Second Edition, 425 pages, 1984. Softcover. (Text)

SUMMERS AND HILLMAN'S CONTRACT AND RELATED OBLIGATION: THEORY, DOCTRINE AND PRACTICE, 1074 pages, 1987. Teacher's Manual available. (Casebook)

Copyright—see Patent and Copyright Law

Corporate Finance

HAMILTON'S CASES AND MATERIALS ON CORPORATION FINANCE, Second Edition, approximately 1177 pages, 1989. (Casebook)

Corporations

HAMILTON'S BLACK LETTER ON CORPORATIONS, Second Edition, 513 pages, 1986. Softcover. (Review)

HAMILTON'S CASES ON CORPORATIONS—INCLUDING PARTNERSHIPS AND LIMITED PARTNERSHIPS, Third Edition, 1213 pages, 1986. Teacher's Manual available. (Casebook) 1986 Statutory Supplement.

HAMILTON'S THE LAW OF CORPORATIONS IN A NUTSHELL, Second Edition, 515 pages, 1987. Softcover. (Text)

HENN'S TEACHING MATERIALS ON THE LAW OF CORPORATIONS, Second Edition, 1204 pages, 1986. Teacher's Manual available. (Casebook)

See Selected Corporation and Partnership Statutes

HENN AND ALEXANDER'S HORNBOOK ON LAWS OF CORPORATIONS, Third Edition, Student Edition, 1371 pages, 1983, with 1986 pocket part. (Text)

SELECTED CORPORATION AND PARTNERSHIP STATUTES, RULES AND FORMS. Softcover. Approximately 650 pages, 1989.

SOLOMON, SCHWARTZ AND BAUMAN'S MATERIALS AND PROBLEMS ON CORPORATIONS: LAW AND POLICY, Second Edition, 1391 pages, 1988. Teacher's Manual available. (Casebook)

See also Selected Corporation and Partnership Statutes

Corrections

KRANTZ' CASES AND MATERIALS ON THE LAW OF CORRECTIONS AND PRISONERS' RIGHTS, Third Edition, 855 pages, 1986. (Casebook) 1988 Supplement.

KRANTZ' THE LAW OF CORRECTIONS AND PRISONERS' RIGHTS IN A NUTSHELL, Third Edition, 407 pages, 1988. Softcover. (Text)

POPPER'S POST-CONVICTION REMEDIES IN A NUTSHELL, 360 pages, 1978. Softcover. (Text)

ROBBINS' CASES AND MATERIALS ON POST-CONVICTION REMEDIES, 506 pages, 1982. (Casebook)

Creditors' Rights

BANKRUPTCY CODE, RULES AND FORMS, LAW SCHOOL EDITION. Approximately 820 pages, 1989. Softcover.

EPSTEIN'S DEBTOR-CREDITOR RELATIONS IN A NUTSHELL, Third Edition, 383 pages, 1986. Softcover. (Text)

EPSTEIN, LANDERS AND NICKLES' CASES AND MATERIALS ON DEBTORS AND CREDITORS, Third Edition, 1059 pages, 1987. Teacher's Manual available. (Casebook)

LoPUCKI'S PLAYER'S MANUAL FOR THE DEBTOR-CREDITOR GAME, 123 pages, 1985. Softcover. (Coursebook)

NICKLES AND EPSTEIN'S BLACK LETTER ON CREDITORS' RIGHTS AND BANKRUPTCY, 576 pages, 1989. (Review)

RIESENFELD'S CASES AND MATERIALS ON CREDITORS' REMEDIES AND DEBTORS' PROTECTION, Fourth Edition, 914 pages, 1987. (Casebook)

WHITE'S CASES AND MATERIALS ON BANKRUPTCY AND CREDITORS' RIGHTS, 812 pages, 1985. Teacher's Manual available. (Casebook) 1987 Supplement.

Criminal Law and Criminal Procedure—see also Corrections, Juvenile Justice

ABRAMS' FEDERAL CRIMINAL LAW AND ITS ENFORCEMENT, 866 pages, 1986. (Casebook) 1988 Supplement.

AMERICAN CRIMINAL JUSTICE PROCESS: SELECTED RULES, STATUTES AND GUIDELINES. Approximately 700 pages, 1989. Softcover.

CARLSON'S ADJUDICATION OF CRIMINAL JUSTICE: PROBLEMS AND REFERENCES, 130 pages, 1986. Softcover. (Casebook)

DIX AND SHARLOT'S CASES AND MATERIALS ON CRIMINAL LAW, Third Edition, 846 pages, 1987. (Casebook)

GRANO'S PROBLEMS IN CRIMINAL PROCEDURE, Second Edition, 176 pages, 1981. Teacher's Manual available. Softcover. (Coursebook)

HEYMANN AND KENETY'S THE MURDER TRIAL OF WILBUR JACKSON: A HOMICIDE IN THE FAMILY, Second Edition, 347 pages, 1985. (Coursebook)

ISRAEL, KAMISAR AND LaFAVE'S CRIMINAL PROCEDURE AND THE CONSTITUTION: LEADING SUPREME COURT CASES AND INTRODUCTORY TEXT, Approximately 735 pages, Revised 1989 Edition. Softcover. (Casebook)

ISRAEL AND LaFAVE'S CRIMINAL PROCEDURE—CONSTITUTIONAL LIMITATIONS IN A NUTSHELL, Fourth Edition, 461 pages, 1988. Softcover. (Text)

JOHNSON'S CASES, MATERIALS AND TEXT ON CRIMINAL LAW, Third Edition, 783 pages, 1985. Teacher's Manual available. (Casebook)

JOHNSON'S CASES AND MATERIALS ON CRIMINAL PROCEDURE, 859 pages, 1988. (Casebook) 1989 Supplement.

KAMISAR, LaFAVE AND ISRAEL'S MODERN CRIMINAL PROCEDURE: CASES, COMMENTS AND QUESTIONS, Sixth Edition, 1558 pages, 1986. (Casebook) 1989 Supplement.

KAMISAR, LaFAVE AND ISRAEL'S BASIC CRIMINAL PROCEDURE: CASES, COMMENTS AND QUESTIONS, Sixth Edition, 860 pages, 1986. Softcover reprint from Kamisar, et al., Modern Criminal Procedure: Cases, Comments and Questions, Sixth Edition. (Casebook) 1989 Supplement.

LaFAVE'S MODERN CRIMINAL LAW: CASES, COMMENTS AND QUESTIONS, Second Edition, 903 pages, 1988. (Casebook)

LaFAVE AND ISRAEL'S HORNBOOK ON CRIMINAL PROCEDURE, Student Edition, 1142 pages, 1985, with 1988 pocket part. (Text)

LaFAVE AND SCOTT'S HORNBOOK ON CRIMINAL LAW, Second Edition, 918 pages, 1986.

Criminal Law and Criminal Procedure— Cont'd

(Text)

LANGBEIN'S COMPARATIVE CRIMINAL PROCEDURE: GERMANY, 172 pages, 1977. Softcover. (Casebook)

LOEWY'S CRIMINAL LAW IN A NUTSHELL, Second Edition, 321 pages, 1987. Softcover. (Text)

LOW'S BLACK LETTER ON CRIMINAL LAW, 433 pages, 1984. Softcover. (Review)

SALTZBURG'S CASES AND COMMENTARY ON AMERICAN CRIMINAL PROCEDURE, Third Edition, 1302 pages, 1988. Teacher's Manual available. (Casebook) 1989 Supplement.

UVILLER'S THE PROCESSES OF CRIMINAL JUSTICE: INVESTIGATION AND ADJUDICATION, Second Edition, 1384 pages, 1979. (Casebook) 1979 Statutory Supplement. 1986 Update.

VORENBERG'S CASES ON CRIMINAL LAW AND PROCEDURE, Second Edition, 1088 pages, 1981. Teacher's Manual available. (Casebook) 1987 Supplement.

Decedents' Estates—see Trusts and Estates

Domestic Relations

CLARK'S CASES AND PROBLEMS ON DOMESTIC RELATIONS, Third Edition, 1153 pages, 1980. Teacher's Manual available. (Casebook)

CLARK'S HORNBOOK ON DOMESTIC RELATIONS, Second Edition, Student Edition, 1050 pages, 1988. (Text)

KRAUSE'S BLACK LETTER ON FAMILY LAW, 314 pages, 1988. Softcover. (Review)

KRAUSE'S CASES, COMMENTS AND QUESTIONS ON FAMILY LAW, Third Edition, approximately 1200 pages, October, 1989 Pub. (Casebook)

KRAUSE'S FAMILY LAW IN A NUTSHELL, Second Edition, 444 pages, 1986. Softcover. (Text)

KRAUSKOPF'S CASES ON PROPERTY DIVISION AT MARRIAGE DISSOLUTION, 250 pages, 1984. Softcover. (Casebook)

Economics, Law and—see also Antitrust, Regulated Industries

GOETZ' CASES AND MATERIALS ON LAW AND ECONOMICS, 547 pages, 1984. (Casebook)

Education Law

ALEXANDER AND ALEXANDER'S THE LAW OF SCHOOLS, STUDENTS AND TEACHERS IN A NUTSHELL, 409 pages, 1984. Softcover. (Text)

Employment Discrimination—see also Women and the Law

JONES, MURPHY AND BELTON'S CASES AND MATERIALS ON DISCRIMINATION IN EMPLOYMENT, (The Labor Law Group). Fifth Edition, 1116 pages, 1987. (Casebook)

PLAYER'S CASES AND MATERIALS ON EMPLOYMENT DISCRIMINATION LAW, Second Edition, 782 pages, 1984. Teacher's Manual available. (Casebook)

PLAYER'S FEDERAL LAW OF EMPLOYMENT DISCRIMINATION IN A NUTSHELL, Second Edition, 402 pages, 1981. Softcover. (Text)

PLAYER'S HORNBOOK ON EMPLOYMENT DISCRIMINATION LAW, Student Edition, 708 pages, 1988. (Text)

Energy and Natural Resources Law—see also Oil and Gas

LAITOS' CASES AND MATERIALS ON NATURAL RESOURCES LAW, 938 pages, 1985. Teacher's Manual available. (Casebook)

SELECTED ENVIRONMENTAL LAW STATUTES— EDUCATIONAL EDITION. Softcover. Approximately 850 pages, 1989.

Environmental Law—see also Energy and Natural Resources Law; Sea, Law of

BONINE AND McGARITY'S THE LAW OF ENVIRONMENTAL PROTECTION: CASES—LEGISLATION—POLICIES, 1076 pages, 1984. Teacher's Manual available. (Casebook)

FINDLEY AND FARBER'S CASES AND MATERIALS ON ENVIRONMENTAL LAW, Second Edition, 813 pages, 1985. (Casebook) 1988 Supplement.

FINDLEY AND FARBER'S ENVIRONMENTAL LAW IN A NUTSHELL, Second Edition, 367 pages, 1988. Softcover. (Text)

RODGERS' HORNBOOK ON ENVIRONMENTAL LAW, 956 pages, 1977, with 1984 pocket

Environmental Law—Cont'd
part. (Text)

SELECTED ENVIRONMENTAL LAW STATUTES—
EDUCATIONAL EDITION. Softcover. Approximately 850 pages, 1989.

Equity—see Remedies

Estate Planning—see also Trusts and Estates; Taxation—Estate and Gift

LYNN'S AN INTRODUCTION TO ESTATE PLANNING IN A NUTSHELL, Third Edition, 370 pages, 1983. Softcover. (Text)

Evidence

BROUN AND BLAKEY'S BLACK LETTER ON EVIDENCE, 269 pages, 1984. Softcover. (Review)

BROUN, MEISENHOLDER, STRONG AND MOSTELLER'S PROBLEMS IN EVIDENCE, Third Edition, 238 pages, 1988. Teacher's Manual available. Softcover. (Coursebook)

CLEARY, STRONG, BROUN AND MOSTELLER'S CASES AND MATERIALS ON EVIDENCE, Fourth Edition, 1060 pages, 1988. (Casebook)

FEDERAL RULES OF EVIDENCE FOR UNITED STATES COURTS AND MAGISTRATES. Softcover. 378 pages, 1989.

GRAHAM'S FEDERAL RULES OF EVIDENCE IN A NUTSHELL, Second Edition, 473 pages, 1987. Softcover. (Text)

KIMBALL'S PROGRAMMED MATERIALS ON PROBLEMS IN EVIDENCE, 380 pages, 1978. Softcover. (Coursebook)

LEMPERT AND SALTZBURG'S A MODERN APPROACH TO EVIDENCE: TEXT, PROBLEMS, TRANSCRIPTS AND CASES, Second Edition, 1232 pages, 1983. Teacher's Manual available. (Casebook)

LILLY'S AN INTRODUCTION TO THE LAW OF EVIDENCE, Second Edition, 585 pages, 1987. (Text)

MCCORMICK, SUTTON AND WELLBORN'S CASES AND MATERIALS ON EVIDENCE, Sixth Edition, 1067 pages, 1987. (Casebook)

MCCORMICK'S HORNBOOK ON EVIDENCE, Third Edition, Student Edition, 1156 pages, 1984, with 1987 pocket part. (Text)

ROTHSTEIN'S EVIDENCE IN A NUTSHELL: STATE AND FEDERAL RULES, Second Edition,

514 pages, 1981. Softcover. (Text)

Federal Jurisdiction and Procedure

CURRIE'S CASES AND MATERIALS ON FEDERAL COURTS, Third Edition, 1042 pages, 1982. (Casebook) 1985 Supplement.

CURRIE'S FEDERAL JURISDICTION IN A NUTSHELL, Second Edition, 258 pages, 1981. Softcover. (Text)

FEDERAL RULES OF CIVIL PROCEDURE—EDUCATIONAL EDITION. Softcover. Approximately 600 pages, 1989.

REDISH'S BLACK LETTER ON FEDERAL JURISDICTION, 219 pages, 1985. Softcover. (Review)

REDISH'S CASES, COMMENTS AND QUESTIONS ON FEDERAL COURTS, Second Edition, 1122 pages, 1989. (Casebook)

VETRI AND MERRILL'S FEDERAL COURTS PROBLEMS AND MATERIALS, Second Edition, 232 pages, 1984. Softcover. (Coursebook)

WRIGHT'S HORNBOOK ON FEDERAL COURTS, Fourth Edition, Student Edition, 870 pages, 1983. (Text)

Foreign Relations and National Security Law

FRANCK AND GLENNON'S FOREIGN RELATIONS AND NATIONAL SECURITY LAW, 941 pages, 1987. (Casebook)

Future Interests—see Trusts and Estates

Health Law—see Medicine, Law and

Human Rights—see International Law

Immigration Law

ALEINIKOFF AND MARTIN'S IMMIGRATION PROCESS AND POLICY, 1042 pages, 1985. (Casebook) 1987 Supplement.

WEISSBRODT'S IMMIGRATION LAW AND PROCEDURE IN A NUTSHELL, 345 pages, 1984, Softcover. (Text)

Indian Law—see American Indian Law

Insurance Law

DEVINE AND TERRY'S PROBLEMS IN INSURANCE LAW, Approximately 230 pages, 1989. Softcover. Teacher's Manual available. (Course book)

Insurance Law—Cont'd

DOBBYN'S INSURANCE LAW IN A NUTSHELL, Second Edition, approximately 285 pages, 1989. Softcover. (Text)

KEETON'S CASES ON BASIC INSURANCE LAW, Second Edition, 1086 pages, 1977. Teacher's Manual available. (Casebook)

KEETON AND WIDISS' INSURANCE LAW, Student Edition, 1359 pages, 1988. (Text)

WIDISS AND KEETON'S COURSE SUPPLEMENT TO KEETON AND WIDISS' INSURANCE LAW, 502 pages, 1988. Softcover. (Casebook)

YORK AND WHELAN'S CASES, MATERIALS AND PROBLEMS ON GENERAL PRACTICE INSURANCE LAW, Second Edition, 787 pages, 1988. Teacher's Manual available. (Casebook)

International Law—see also Sea, Law of

BUERGENTHAL'S INTERNATIONAL HUMAN RIGHTS IN A NUTSHELL, 283 pages, 1988. Softcover. (Text)

BUERGENTHAL AND MAIER'S PUBLIC INTERNATIONAL LAW IN A NUTSHELL, 262 pages, 1985. Softcover. (Text)

FOLSOM, GORDON AND SPANOGLE'S INTERNATIONAL BUSINESS TRANSACTIONS—A PROBLEM-ORIENTED COURSEBOOK, 1160 pages, 1986. Teacher's Manual available. (Casebook) 1989 Documents Supplement.

FOLSOM, GORDON AND SPANOGLE'S INTERNATIONAL BUSINESS TRANSACTIONS IN A NUTSHELL, Third Edition, 509 pages, 1988. Softcover. (Text)

HENKIN, PUGH, SCHACHTER AND SMIT'S CASES AND MATERIALS ON INTERNATIONAL LAW, Second Edition, 1517 pages, 1987. (Casebook) Documents Supplement.

JACKSON AND DAVEY'S CASES, MATERIALS AND TEXT ON LEGAL PROBLEMS OF INTERNATIONAL ECONOMIC RELATIONS, Second Edition, 1269 pages, 1986. (Casebook) 1989 Documents Supplement.

KIRGIS' INTERNATIONAL ORGANIZATIONS IN THEIR LEGAL SETTING, 1016 pages, 1977. Teacher's Manual available. (Casebook) 1981 Supplement.

WESTON, FALK AND D'AMATO'S INTERNATIONAL LAW AND WORLD ORDER—A PROBLEM-ORIENTED COURSEBOOK, 1195 pages, 1980. Teacher's Manual available. (Casebook)

Documents Supplement.

Interviewing and Counseling

BINDER AND PRICE'S LEGAL INTERVIEWING AND COUNSELING, 232 pages, 1977. Teacher's Manual available. Softcover. (Coursebook)

SHAFFER AND ELKINS' LEGAL INTERVIEWING AND COUNSELING IN A NUTSHELL, Second Edition, 487 pages, 1987. Softcover. (Text)

Introduction to Law—see Legal Method and Legal System

Introduction to Law Study

DOBBYN'S SO YOU WANT TO GO TO LAW SCHOOL, Revised First Edition, 206 pages, 1976. Softcover. (Text)

HEGLAND'S INTRODUCTION TO THE STUDY AND PRACTICE OF LAW IN A NUTSHELL, 418 pages, 1983. Softcover (Text)

KINYON'S INTRODUCTION TO LAW STUDY AND LAW EXAMINATIONS IN A NUTSHELL, 389 pages, 1971. Softcover. (Text)

Jurisprudence

CHRISTIE'S JURISPRUDENCE—TEXT AND READINGS ON THE PHILOSOPHY OF LAW, 1056 pages, 1973. (Casebook)

Juvenile Justice

FOX'S CASES AND MATERIALS ON MODERN JUVENILE JUSTICE, Second Edition, 960 pages, 1981. (Casebook)

FOX'S JUVENILE COURTS IN A NUTSHELL, Third Edition, 291 pages, 1984. Softcover. (Text)

Labor Law—see also Employment Discrimination, Social Legislation

FINKIN, GOLDMAN AND SUMMERS' LEGAL PROTECTION OF INDIVIDUAL EMPLOYEES, (The Labor Law Group). Approximately 1000 pages, December, 1989 Pub. (Casebook)

GORMAN'S BASIC TEXT ON LABOR LAW—UNIONIZATION AND COLLECTIVE BARGAINING, 914 pages, 1976. (Text)

GRODIN, WOLLETT AND ALLEYNE'S COLLECTIVE BARGAINING IN PUBLIC EMPLOYMENT, (The Labor Law Group). Third Edition, 430 pages, 1979. (Casebook)

Labor Law—Cont'd

LESLIE'S LABOR LAW IN A NUTSHELL, Second Edition, 397 pages, 1986. Softcover. (Text)

NOLAN'S LABOR ARBITRATION LAW AND PRACTICE IN A NUTSHELL, 358 pages, 1979. Softcover. (Text)

OBERER, HANSLOWE, ANDERSEN AND HEINSZ' CASES AND MATERIALS ON LABOR LAW—COLLECTIVE BARGAINING IN A FREE SOCIETY, Third Edition, 1163 pages, 1986. (Casebook) Statutory Supplement.

RABIN, SILVERSTEIN AND SCHATZKI'S LABOR AND EMPLOYMENT LAW: PROBLEMS, CASES AND MATERIALS IN THE LAW OF WORK, (The Labor Law Group). 1014 pages, 1988. Teacher's Manual available. (Casebook) 1988 Statutory Supplement.

Land Finance—Property Security—see Real Estate Transactions

Land Use

CALLIES AND FREILICH'S CASES AND MATERIALS ON LAND USE, 1233 pages, 1986. (Casebook) 1988 Supplement.

HAGMAN AND JUERGENSMEYER'S HORNBOOK ON URBAN PLANNING AND LAND DEVELOPMENT CONTROL LAW, Second Edition, Student Edition, 680 pages, 1986. (Text)

WRIGHT AND GITELMAN'S CASES AND MATERIALS ON LAND USE, Third Edition, 1300 pages, 1982. Teacher's Manual available. (Casebook) 1987 Supplement.

WRIGHT AND WRIGHT'S LAND USE IN A NUTSHELL, Second Edition, 356 pages, 1985. Softcover. (Text)

Legal History—see also Legal Method and Legal System

PRESSER AND ZAINALDIN'S CASES AND MATERIALS ON LAW AND JURISPRUDENCE IN AMERICAN HISTORY, Second Edition, approximately 1092 pages, 1989. Teacher's Manual available. (Casebook)

Legal Method and Legal System—see also Legal Research, Legal Writing

ALDISERT'S READINGS, MATERIALS AND CASES IN THE JUDICIAL PROCESS, 948 pages, 1976. (Casebook)

BERCH AND BERCH'S INTRODUCTION TO LEGAL

METHOD AND PROCESS, 550 pages, 1985. Teacher's Manual available. (Casebook)

BODENHEIMER, OAKLEY AND LOVE'S READINGS AND CASES ON AN INTRODUCTION TO THE ANGLO-AMERICAN LEGAL SYSTEM, Second Edition, 166 pages, 1988. Softcover. (Casebook)

DAVIES AND LAWRY'S INSTITUTIONS AND METHODS OF THE LAW—INTRODUCTORY TEACHING MATERIALS, 547 pages, 1982. Teacher's Manual available. (Casebook)

DVORKIN, HIMMELSTEIN AND LESNICK'S BECOMING A LAWYER: A HUMANISTIC PERSPECTIVE ON LEGAL EDUCATION AND PROFESSIONALISM, 211 pages, 1981. Softcover. (Text)

KELSO AND KELSO'S STUDYING LAW: AN INTRODUCTION, 587 pages, 1984. (Coursebook)

KEMPIN'S HISTORICAL INTRODUCTION TO ANGLO-AMERICAN LAW IN A NUTSHELL, Second Edition, 280 pages, 1973. Softcover. (Text)

REYNOLDS' JUDICIAL PROCESS IN A NUTSHELL, 292 pages, 1980. Softcover. (Text)

Legal Research

COHEN'S LEGAL RESEARCH IN A NUTSHELL, Fourth Edition, 452 pages, 1985. Softcover. (Text)

COHEN, BERRING AND OLSON'S HOW TO FIND THE LAW, Ninth Edition, approximately 800 pages, October, 1989 Pub. (Coursebook)

Legal Research Exercises, 3rd Ed., for use with Cohen, Berring and Olson, 229 pages, 1989. Teacher's Manual available.

COHEN, BERRING AND OLSON'S FINDING THE LAW, approximately 565 pages, 1989. Softcover reprint from Cohen, Berring and Olson's How to Find the Law, Ninth Edition. (Coursebook)

ROMBAUER'S LEGAL PROBLEM SOLVING—ANALYSIS, RESEARCH AND WRITING, Fourth Edition, 424 pages, 1983. Teacher's Manual with problems available. (Coursebook)

STATSKY'S LEGAL RESEARCH AND WRITING, Third Edition, 252 pages, 1986. Softcover. (Coursebook)

TEPLY'S PROGRAMMED MATERIALS ON LEGAL RESEARCH AND CITATION, Third Edition, ap-

Legal Research—Cont'd

proximately 450 pages, 1989. Softcover. (Coursebook)

Student Library Exercises, 3rd ed., 391 pages, 1989. Answer Key available.

Legal Writing

CHILD'S DRAFTING LEGAL DOCUMENTS: MATERIALS AND PROBLEMS, 286 pages, 1988. Softcover. Teacher's Manual available. (Coursebook)

DICKERSON'S MATERIALS ON LEGAL DRAFTING, 425 pages, 1981. Teacher's Manual available. (Coursebook)

FELSENFELD AND SIEGEL'S WRITING CONTRACTS IN PLAIN ENGLISH, 290 pages, 1981. Softcover. (Text)

GOPEN'S WRITING FROM A LEGAL PERSPECTIVE, 225 pages, 1981. (Text)

MELLINKOFF'S LEGAL WRITING—SENSE AND NONSENSE, 242 pages, 1982. Softcover. Teacher's Manual available. (Text)

PRATT'S LEGAL WRITING: A SYSTEMATIC APPROACH, Approximately 412 pages, 1989. Teacher's Manual available. (Coursebook)

RAY AND RAMSFIELD'S LEGAL WRITING: GETTING IT RIGHT AND GETTING IT WRITTEN, 250 pages, 1987. Softcover. (Text)

SQUIRES AND ROMBAUER'S LEGAL WRITING IN A NUTSHELL, 294 pages, 1982. Softcover. (Text)

STATSKY AND WERNET'S CASE ANALYSIS AND FUNDAMENTALS OF LEGAL WRITING, Third Edition, 424 pages, 1989. (Text)

WEIHOFEN'S LEGAL WRITING STYLE, Second Edition, 332 pages, 1980. (Text)

Legislation

DAVIES' LEGISLATIVE LAW AND PROCESS IN A NUTSHELL, Second Edition, 346 pages, 1986. Softcover. (Text)

ESKRIDGE AND FRICKEY'S CASES AND MATERIALS ON LEGISLATION: STATUTES AND THE CREATION OF PUBLIC POLICY, 937 pages, 1988. Teacher's Manual available. (Casebook)

NUTTING AND DICKERSON'S CASES AND MATERIALS ON LEGISLATION, Fifth Edition, 744 pages, 1978. (Casebook)

STATSKY'S LEGISLATIVE ANALYSIS AND

DRAFTING, Second Edition, 217 pages, 1984. Teacher's Manual available. (Text)

Local Government

FRUG'S CASES AND MATERIALS ON LOCAL GOVERNMENT LAW, 1005 pages, 1988. (Casebook)

McCARTHY'S LOCAL GOVERNMENT LAW IN A NUTSHELL, Second Edition, 404 pages, 1983. Softcover. (Text)

REYNOLDS' HORNBOOK ON LOCAL GOVERNMENT LAW, 860 pages, 1982, with 1987 pocket part. (Text)

VALENTE'S CASES AND MATERIALS ON LOCAL GOVERNMENT LAW, Third Edition, 1010 pages, 1987. Teacher's Manual available. (Casebook) 1989 Supplement.

Mass Communication Law

GILLMOR AND BARRON'S CASES AND COMMENT ON MASS COMMUNICATION LAW, Fifth Edition, approximately 1068 pages, September 1989 Pub. Teacher's Manual available. (Casebook)

GINSBURG'S REGULATION OF BROADCASTING: LAW AND POLICY TOWARDS RADIO, TELEVISION AND CABLE COMMUNICATIONS, 741 pages, 1979 (Casebook) 1983 Supplement.

ZUCKMAN, GAYNES, CARTER AND DEE'S MASS COMMUNICATIONS LAW IN A NUTSHELL, Third Edition, 538 pages, 1988. Softcover. (Text)

Medicine, Law and

FURROW, JOHNSON, JOST AND SCHWARTZ' HEALTH LAW: CASES, MATERIALS AND PROBLEMS, 1005 pages, 1987. Teacher's Manual available. (Casebook)

KING'S THE LAW OF MEDICAL MALPRACTICE IN A NUTSHELL, Second Edition, 342 pages, 1986. Softcover. (Text)

SHAPIRO AND SPECE'S CASES, MATERIALS AND PROBLEMS ON BIOETHICS AND LAW, 892 pages, 1981. (Casebook)

SHARPE, FISCINA AND HEAD'S CASES ON LAW AND MEDICINE, 882 pages, 1978. (Casebook)

Military Law

SHANOR AND TERRELL'S MILITARY LAW IN A NUTSHELL, 378 pages, 1980. Softcover.

Military Law—Cont'd

(Text)

Mortgages—see Real Estate Transactions

Natural Resources Law—see Energy and Natural Resources Law, Environmental Law

Negotiation

GIFFORD'S LEGAL NEGOTIATION: THEORY AND APPLICATIONS, 225 pages, 1989. Softcover. (Text)

PECK'S CASES AND MATERIALS ON NEGOTIATION, (The Labor Law Group). Second Edition, 280 pages, 1980. (Casebook)

WILLIAMS' LEGAL NEGOTIATION AND SETTLEMENT, 207 pages, 1983. Softcover. Teacher's Manual available. (Coursebook)

Office Practice—see also Computers and Law, Interviewing and Counseling, Negotiation

HEGLAND'S TRIAL AND PRACTICE SKILLS IN A NUTSHELL, 346 pages, 1978. Softcover (Text)

STRONG AND CLARK'S LAW OFFICE MANAGEMENT, 424 pages, 1974. (Casebook)

Oil and Gas—see also Energy and Natural Resources Law

HEMINGWAY'S HORNBOOK ON OIL AND GAS, Second Edition, Student Edition, 543 pages, 1983, with 1989 pocket part. (Text)

KUNTZ, LOWE, ANDERSON AND SMITH'S CASES AND MATERIALS ON OIL AND GAS LAW, 857 pages, 1986. Teacher's Manual available. (Casebook) Forms Manual. Revised.

LOWE'S OIL AND GAS LAW IN A NUTSHELL, Second Edition, 465 pages, 1988. Softcover. (Text)

Partnership—see Agency—Partnership

Patent and Copyright Law

CHOATE, FRANCIS, AND COLLINS' CASES AND MATERIALS ON PATENT LAW, INCLUDING TRADE SECRETS, COPYRIGHTS, TRADEMARKS, Third Edition, 1009 pages, 1987. (Casebook)

MILLER AND DAVIS' INTELLECTUAL PROPERTY—PATENTS, TRADEMARKS AND COPYRIGHT IN A NUTSHELL, 428 pages, 1983. Softcover.

(Text)

NIMMER'S CASES AND MATERIALS ON COPYRIGHT AND OTHER ASPECTS OF ENTERTAINMENT LITIGATION ILLUSTRATED—INCLUDING UNFAIR COMPETITION, DEFAMATION AND PRIVACY, Third Edition, 1025 pages, 1985. (Casebook) 1989 Supplement.

Products Liability

FISCHER AND POWERS' CASES AND MATERIALS ON PRODUCTS LIABILITY, 685 pages, 1988. Teacher's Manual available. (Casebook)

NOEL AND PHILLIPS' CASES ON PRODUCTS LIABILITY, Second Edition, 821 pages, 1982. (Casebook)

PHILLIPS' PRODUCTS LIABILITY IN A NUTSHELL, Third Edition, 307 pages, 1988. Softcover. (Text)

Professional Responsibility

ARONSON, DEVINE AND FISCH'S PROBLEMS, CASES AND MATERIALS IN PROFESSIONAL RESPONSIBILITY, 745 pages, 1985. Teacher's Manual available. (Casebook)

ARONSON AND WECKSTEIN'S PROFESSIONAL RESPONSIBILITY IN A NUTSHELL, 399 pages, 1980. Softcover. (Text)

MELLINKOFF'S THE CONSCIENCE OF A LAWYER, 304 pages, 1973. (Text)

PIRSIG AND KIRWIN'S CASES AND MATERIALS ON PROFESSIONAL RESPONSIBILITY, Fourth Edition, 603 pages, 1984. Teacher's Manual available. (Casebook)

ROTUNDA'S BLACK LETTER ON PROFESSIONAL RESPONSIBILITY, Second Edition, 414 pages, 1988. Softcover. (Review)

SCHWARTZ AND WYDICK'S PROBLEMS IN LEGAL ETHICS, Second Edition, 341 pages, 1988. (Coursebook)

SELECTED STATUTES, RULES AND STANDARDS ON THE LEGAL PROFESSION. Softcover. Approximately 450 pages, 1989.

SUTTON AND DZIENKOWSKI'S CASES AND MATERIALS ON PROFESSIONAL RESPONSIBILITY FOR LAWYERS, Approximately 800 pages, 1989. Teacher's Manual available. (Casebook)

WOLFRAM'S HORNBOOK ON MODERN LEGAL ETHICS, Student Edition, 1120 pages, 1986. (Text)

Property—see also Real Estate Transactions, Land Use, Trusts and Estates

BERNHARDT'S BLACK LETTER ON PROPERTY, 318 pages, 1983. Softcover. (Review)

BERNHARDT'S REAL PROPERTY IN A NUTSHELL, Second Edition, 448 pages, 1981. Softcover. (Text)

BOYER'S SURVEY OF THE LAW OF PROPERTY, Third Edition, 766 pages, 1981. (Text)

BROWDER, CUNNINGHAM, NELSON, STOEBUCK AND WHITMAN'S CASES ON BASIC PROPERTY LAW, Fifth Edition, approximately 1200 pages, 1989. (Casebook)

BRUCE, ELY AND BOSTICK'S CASES AND MATERIALS ON MODERN PROPERTY LAW, Second Edition, 953 pages, 1989. Teacher's Manual available. (Casebook)

BURKE'S PERSONAL PROPERTY IN A NUTSHELL, 322 pages, 1983. Softcover. (Text)

CUNNINGHAM, STOEBUCK AND WHITMAN'S HORNBOOK ON THE LAW OF PROPERTY, Student Edition, 916 pages, 1984, with 1987 pocket part. (Text)

DONAHUE, KAUPER AND MARTIN'S CASES ON PROPERTY, Second Edition, 1362 pages, 1983. Teacher's Manual available. (Casebook)

HILL'S LANDLORD AND TENANT LAW IN A NUTSHELL, Second Edition, 311 pages, 1986. Softcover. (Text)

KURTZ AND HOVENKAMP'S CASES AND MATERIALS ON AMERICAN PROPERTY LAW, 1296 pages, 1987. Teacher's Manual available. (Casebook) 1988 Supplement.

MOYNIHAN'S INTRODUCTION TO REAL PROPERTY, Second Edition, 239 pages, 1988. (Text)

UNIFORM LAND TRANSACTIONS ACT, UNIFORM SIMPLIFICATION OF LAND TRANSFERS ACT, UNIFORM CONDOMINIUM ACT, 1977 OFFICIAL TEXT WITH COMMENTS. Softcover. 462 pages, 1978.

Psychiatry, Law and

REISNER'S LAW AND THE MENTAL HEALTH SYSTEM, CIVIL AND CRIMINAL ASPECTS, 696 pages, 1985. (Casebook) 1987 Supplement.

Real Estate Transactions

BRUCE'S REAL ESTATE FINANCE IN A NUTSHELL, Second Edition, 262 pages, 1985. Softcover. (Text)

MAXWELL, RIESENFELD, HETLAND AND WARREN'S CASES ON CALIFORNIA SECURITY TRANSACTIONS IN LAND, Third Edition, 728 pages, 1984. (Casebook)

NELSON AND WHITMAN'S BLACK LETTER ON LAND TRANSACTIONS AND FINANCE, Second Edition, 466 pages, 1988. Softcover. (Review)

NELSON AND WHITMAN'S CASES ON REAL ESTATE TRANSFER, FINANCE AND DEVELOPMENT, Third Edition, 1184 pages, 1987. (Casebook)

NELSON AND WHITMAN'S HORNBOOK ON REAL ESTATE FINANCE LAW, Second Edition, 941 pages, 1985 with 1989 pocket part. (Text)

OSBORNE'S CASES AND MATERIALS ON SECURED TRANSACTIONS, 559 pages, 1967. (Casebook)

Regulated Industries—see also Mass Communication Law, Banking Law

GELLHORN AND PIERCE'S REGULATED INDUSTRIES IN A NUTSHELL, Second Edition, 389 pages, 1987. Softcover. (Text)

MORGAN, HARRISON AND VERKUIL'S CASES AND MATERIALS ON ECONOMIC REGULATION OF BUSINESS, Second Edition, 666 pages, 1985. (Casebook)

Remedies

DOBBS' HORNBOOK ON REMEDIES, 1067 pages, 1973. (Text)

DOBBS' PROBLEMS IN REMEDIES. 137 pages, 1974. Teacher's Manual available. Softcover. (Coursebook)

DOBBYN'S INJUNCTIONS IN A NUTSHELL, 264 pages, 1974. Softcover. (Text)

FRIEDMAN'S CONTRACT REMEDIES IN A NUTSHELL, 323 pages, 1981. Softcover. (Text)

LEAVELL, LOVE AND NELSON'S CASES AND MATERIALS ON EQUITABLE REMEDIES, RESTITUTION AND DAMAGES, Fourth Edition, 1111 pages, 1986. Teacher's Manual available. (Casebook)

MCCORMICK'S HORNBOOK ON DAMAGES, 811 pages, 1935. (Text)

Remedies—Cont'd

O'CONNELL'S REMEDIES IN A NUTSHELL, Second Edition, 320 pages, 1985. Softcover. (Text)

YORK, BAUMAN AND RENDLEMAN'S CASES AND MATERIALS ON REMEDIES, Fourth Edition, 1029 pages, 1985. Teacher's Manual available. (Casebook)

Sea, Law of

SOHN AND GUSTAFSON'S THE LAW OF THE SEA IN A NUTSHELL, 264 pages, 1984. Softcover. (Text)

Securities Regulation

HAZEN'S HORNBOOK ON THE LAW OF SECURITIES REGULATION, Student Edition, 739 pages, 1985, with 1988 pocket part. (Text)

RATNER'S MATERIALS ON SECURITIES REGULATION, Third Edition, 1000 pages, 1986. Teacher's Manual available. (Casebook) 1989 Supplement.

See Selected Securities and Business Planning Statutes

RATNER'S SECURITIES REGULATION IN A NUTSHELL, Third Edition, 316 pages, 1988. Softcover. (Text)

SELECTED SECURITIES AND BUSINESS PLANNING STATUTES, RULES AND FORMS. Softcover. 493 pages, 1987.

Social Legislation

HOOD AND HARDY'S WORKERS' COMPENSATION AND EMPLOYEE PROTECTION IN A NUTSHELL, 274 pages, 1984. Softcover. (Text)

LAFRANCE'S WELFARE LAW: STRUCTURE AND ENTITLEMENT IN A NUTSHELL, 455 pages, 1979. Softcover. (Text)

MALONE, PLANT AND LITTLE'S CASES ON WORKERS' COMPENSATION AND EMPLOYMENT RIGHTS, Second Edition, 951 pages, 1980. Teacher's Manual available. (Casebook)

Sports Law

SCHUBERT, SMITH AND TRENTADUE'S SPORTS LAW, 395 pages, 1986. (Text)

Tax Practice and Procedure

GARBIS, STRUNTZ AND RUBIN'S CASES AND MATERIALS ON TAX PROCEDURE AND TAX FRAUD, Second Edition, 687 pages, 1987. (Casebook)

Taxation—Corporate

KAHN AND GANN'S CORPORATE TAXATION, Third Edition, approximately 978 pages, 1989. Teacher's Manual available. (Casebook)

WEIDENBRUCH AND BURKE'S FEDERAL INCOME TAXATION OF CORPORATIONS AND STOCKHOLDERS IN A NUTSHELL, Third Edition, 309 pages, 1989. Softcover. (Text)

Taxation—Estate & Gift—see also Estate Planning, Trusts and Estates

MCNULTY'S FEDERAL ESTATE AND GIFT TAXATION IN A NUTSHELL, Fourth Edition, 496 pages, 1989. Softcover. (Text)

PENNELL'S CASES AND MATERIALS ON INCOME TAXATION OF TRUSTS, ESTATES, GRANTORS AND BENEFICIARIES, 460 pages, 1987. Teacher's Manual available. (Casebook)

Taxation—Individual

DODGE'S THE LOGIC OF TAX, Approximately 330 pages, September, 1989 Pub. Softcover. (Text)

GUNN AND WARD'S CASES, TEXT AND PROBLEMS ON FEDERAL INCOME TAXATION, Second Edition, 835 pages, 1988. Teacher's Manual available. (Casebook)

HUDSON AND LIND'S BLACK LETTER ON FEDERAL INCOME TAXATION, Second Edition, 396 pages, 1987. Softcover. (Review)

KRAGEN AND MCNULTY'S CASES AND MATERIALS ON FEDERAL INCOME TAXATION—INDIVIDUALS, CORPORATIONS, PARTNERSHIPS, Fourth Edition, 1287 pages, 1985. (Casebook)

MCNULTY'S FEDERAL INCOME TAXATION OF INDIVIDUALS IN A NUTSHELL, Fourth Edition, 503 pages, 1988. Softcover. (Text)

POSIN'S HORNBOOK ON FEDERAL INCOME TAXATION, Student Edition, 491 pages, 1983, with 1989 pocket part. (Text)

ROSE AND CHOMMIE'S HORNBOOK ON FEDERAL INCOME TAXATION, Third Edition, 923 pages, 1988, with 1989 pocket part. (Text)

SELECTED FEDERAL TAXATION STATUTES AND REGULATIONS. Softcover. Approximately 1550 pages, 1990.

SOLOMON AND HESCH'S PROBLEMS, CASES AND MATERIALS ON FEDERAL INCOME TAXATION OF INDIVIDUALS, 1068 pages, 1987.

Taxation—Individual—Cont'd

Teacher's Manual available. (Casebook)

Taxation—International

DOERNBERG'S INTERNATIONAL TAXATION IN A NUTSHELL, 325 pages, 1989. Softcover. (Text)

KAPLAN'S FEDERAL TAXATION OF INTERNATIONAL TRANSACTIONS: PRINCIPLES, PLANNING AND POLICY, 635 pages, 1988. (Casebook)

Taxation—Partnership

BERGER AND WIEDENBECK'S CASES AND MATERIALS ON PARTNERSHIP TAXATION, 788 pages, 1989. Teacher's Manual available. (Casebook)

Taxation—State & Local

GELFAND AND SALSICH'S STATE AND LOCAL TAXATION AND FINANCE IN A NUTSHELL, 309 pages, 1986. Softcover. (Text)

HELLERSTEIN AND HELLERSTEIN'S CASES AND MATERIALS ON STATE AND LOCAL TAXATION, Fifth Edition, 1071 pages, 1988. (Casebook)

Torts—see also Products Liability

CHRISTIE'S CASES AND MATERIALS ON THE LAW OF TORTS, 1264 pages, 1983. (Casebook)

DOBBS' TORTS AND COMPENSATION—PERSONAL ACCOUNTABILITY AND SOCIAL RESPONSIBILITY FOR INJURY, 955 pages, 1985. Teacher's Manual available. (Casebook)

KEETON, KEETON, SARGENTICH AND STEINER'S CASES AND MATERIALS ON TORT AND ACCIDENT LAW, Second Edition, approximately 1307 pages, 1989. (Casebook)

KIONKA'S BLACK LETTER ON TORTS, 339 pages, 1988. Softcover. (Review)

KIONKA'S TORTS IN A NUTSHELL: INJURIES TO PERSONS AND PROPERTY, 434 pages, 1977. Softcover. (Text)

MALONE'S TORTS IN A NUTSHELL: INJURIES TO FAMILY, SOCIAL AND TRADE RELATIONS, 358 pages, 1979. Softcover. (Text)

PROSSER AND KEETON'S HORNBOOK ON TORTS, Fifth Edition, Student Edition, 1286 pages, 1984 with 1988 pocket part. (Text)

ROBERTSON, POWERS AND ANDERSON'S CASES

AND MATERIALS ON TORTS, 932 pages, 1989. Teacher's Manual available. (Casebook)

Trade Regulation—see also Antitrust, Regulated Industries

McMANIS' UNFAIR TRADE PRACTICES IN A NUTSHELL, Second Edition, 464 pages, 1988. Softcover. (Text)

OPPENHEIM, WESTON, MAGGS AND SCHECHTER'S CASES AND MATERIALS ON UNFAIR TRADE PRACTICES AND CONSUMER PROTECTION, Fourth Edition, 1038 pages, 1983. Teacher's Manual available. (Casebook) 1986 Supplement.

SCHECHTER'S BLACK LETTER ON UNFAIR TRADE PRACTICES, 272 pages, 1986. Softcover. (Review)

Trial and Appellate Advocacy—see also Civil Procedure

APPELLATE ADVOCACY, HANDBOOK OF, Second Edition, 182 pages, 1986. Softcover. (Text)

BERGMAN'S TRIAL ADVOCACY IN A NUTSHELL, 402 pages, 1979. Softcover. (Text)

BINDER AND BERGMAN'S FACT INVESTIGATION: FROM HYPOTHESIS TO PROOF, 354 pages, 1984. Teacher's Manual available. (Coursebook)

CARLSON AND IMWINKELRIED'S DYNAMICS OF TRIAL PRACTICE: PROBLEMS AND MATERIALS, 414 pages, 1989. Teacher's Manual available. (Coursebook)

GOLDBERG'S THE FIRST TRIAL (WHERE DO I SIT? WHAT DO I SAY?) IN A NUTSHELL, 396 pages, 1982. Softcover. (Text)

HAYDOCK, HERR, AND STEMPEL'S FUNDAMENTALS OF PRE-TRIAL LITIGATION, 768 pages, 1985. Softcover. Teacher's Manual available. (Coursebook)

HEGLAND'S TRIAL AND PRACTICE SKILLS IN A NUTSHELL, 346 pages, 1978. Softcover. (Text)

HORNSTEIN'S APPELLATE ADVOCACY IN A NUTSHELL, 325 pages, 1984. Softcover. (Text)

JEANS' HANDBOOK ON TRIAL ADVOCACY, Student Edition, 473 pages, 1975. Softcover. (Text)

MARTINEAU'S CASES AND MATERIALS ON AP-

Trial and Appellate Advocacy—Cont'd

PELLATE PRACTICE AND PROCEDURE, 565 pages, 1987. (Casebook)

NOLAN'S CASES AND MATERIALS ON TRIAL PRACTICE, 518 pages, 1981. (Casebook)

SONSTENG, HAYDOCK AND BOYD'S THE TRI-ALBOOK: A TOTAL SYSTEM FOR PREPARATION AND PRESENTATION OF A CASE, 404 pages, 1984. Softcover. (Coursebook)

Trusts and Estates

ATKINSON'S HORNBOOK ON WILLS, Second Edition, 975 pages, 1953. (Text)

AVERILL'S UNIFORM PROBATE CODE IN A NUT-SHELL, Second Edition, 454 pages, 1987. Softcover. (Text)

BOGERT'S HORNBOOK ON TRUSTS, Sixth Edition, Student Edition, 794 pages, 1987. (Text)

CLARK, LUSKY AND MURPHY'S CASES AND MATERIALS ON GRATUITOUS TRANSFERS, Third Edition, 970 pages, 1985. (Casebook)

DODGE'S WILLS, TRUSTS AND ESTATE PLAN-NING–LAW AND TAXATION, CASES AND MATERIALS, 665 pages, 1988. (Casebook)

KURTZ' PROBLEMS, CASES AND OTHER MATER-IALS ON FAMILY ESTATE PLANNING, 853 pages, 1983. Teacher's Manual available. (Casebook)

MCGOVERN'S CASES AND MATERIALS ON WILLS, TRUSTS AND FUTURE INTERESTS: AN INTRODUCTION TO ESTATE PLANNING, 750 pages, 1983. (Casebook)

MCGOVERN, KURTZ AND REIN'S HORNBOOK ON WILLS, TRUSTS AND ESTATES–INCLUDING TAXATION AND FUTURE INTERESTS, 996 pages, 1988. (Text)

MENNELL'S WILLS AND TRUSTS IN A NUT-SHELL, 392 pages, 1979. Softcover. (Text)

SIMES' HORNBOOK ON FUTURE INTERESTS, Second Edition, 355 pages, 1966. (Text)

TURANO AND RADIGAN'S HORNBOOK ON NEW YORK ESTATE ADMINISTRATION, 676 pages, 1986. (Text)

UNIFORM PROBATE CODE, OFFICIAL TEXT WITH COMMENTS. 578 pages, 1987. Softcover.

WAGGONER'S FUTURE INTERESTS IN A NUT-SHELL, 361 pages, 1981. Softcover. (Text)

WATERBURY'S MATERIALS ON TRUSTS AND ES-TATES, 1039 pages, 1986. Teacher's Manual available. (Casebook)

Water Law—see also Energy and Natural Resources Law, Environmental Law

GETCHES' WATER LAW IN A NUTSHELL, 439 pages, 1984. Softcover. (Text)

SAX AND ABRAMS' LEGAL CONTROL OF WATER RESOURCES: CASES AND MATERIALS, 941 pages, 1986. (Casebook)

TRELEASE AND GOULD'S CASES AND MATERI-ALS ON WATER LAW, Fourth Edition, 816 pages, 1986. (Casebook)

Wills—see Trusts and Estates

Women and the Law—see also Employment Discrimination

KAY'S TEXT, CASES AND MATERIALS ON SEX-BASED DISCRIMINATION, Third Edition, 1001 pages, 1988. (Casebook)

THOMAS' SEX DISCRIMINATION IN A NUT-SHELL, 399 pages, 1982. Softcover. (Text)

Workers' Compensation—see Social Legislation

CASES AND MATERIALS ON
ANTITRUST

By

Eleanor M. Fox
Professor of Law
New York University

Lawrence A. Sullivan
Professor of Law
University of California, Berkeley

AMERICAN CASEBOOK SERIES®

WEST PUBLISHING CO.
ST. PAUL, MINN., 1989

COPYRIGHT © 1989 By WEST PUBLISHING CO.
            50 West Kellogg Boulevard
            P.O. Box 64526
            St. Paul, Minnesota 55164–0526

Library of Congress Cataloging-in-Publication Data

Fox, Eleanor M.
   Cases and materials on antitrust / by Eleanor M. Fox and
Lawrence A. Sullivan.
      p.   cm. — (American casebook series)
   Includes index.
   ISBN 0–314–53319–2
   1. Antitrust law—United States—Cases. I. Sullivan, Lawrence
Anthony. II. Title. III. Series.
   KF1648.F69   1989
   343.73'0721—dc20
   [347.303721]
                                                    89–9001
                                                     CIP

ISBN 0–314–53319–2

    (Fox & Sullivan) Antitrust ACB

*To Byron, Douglas, Margot
and Randall*

E.M.F.

*To Larry, Mark, Neil, Mara,
Marcus and Amy*

L.A.S.

*

Preface and Acknowledgments

Antitrust law once reflected broad, value-based policy, informed by the enacting Congresses' distrust of bigness and power and their concern for economic opportunity on the merits. But in the mid to late 1970s, the Supreme Court put a cap on the growing body of antitrust constraints, and in the early 1980s, a new Administration turned the old antitrust on its head. In 1981 the Justice Department, taking a leaf from Chicago School economics, proclaimed that the sole role for antitrust is to stop inefficient transactions; and it asserted that few transactions are inefficient because the market is a robust check on inefficient behavior. Government enforcement since 1981 has focused almost entirely on blatant cartelization. As this book goes to press, minimal antitrust is still the rule of thumb amid speculation about what changes further time may bring.

There are compelling reasons to study antitrust. First, antitrust is a unique blend of intellectual theory, social policy, political economy, microeconomics and law. Thus, to study antitrust law is to engage in an interdisciplinary enterprise that informs the study of law, legal institutions, and social policy. Second, the study of antitrust prepares the student for the practice of antitrust law, which is a field of great intellectual and practical interest and excitement; it may involve one in government service, counselling, practice before an administrative agency, analytical discussions and negotiations with the Justice Department, and federal court litigation. Moreover, the practice of antitrust law provides the constant challenge of learning facts about the functioning of whole industries. Third, as we approach the centennial of the Sherman Antitrust Law, antitrust is at a cusp where different social forces meet; future developments will be interesting to observe, and perhaps even to shape.

In this book of history, economics, politics, and law, we have steered an eclectic course. Our goal is to provide the student with sufficient background to understand the intellectual history, the evolution, and the state of the law of antitrust; to excite the student to question the path the law has taken and to consider the paths it might take. We also hope to give the student a simple introduction to economic thinking and to illuminate the process of choosing the assumptions that shape economic analysis, so that the emerging antitrust lawyer or scholar can ask the right questions and, as well, appreciate the policy choices that underlie competing styles of antitrust economics.

We are deeply indebted to Jed Davis, Randall M. Fox, Katharine Lauer, Vickie Saker and Anita Stork for their indispensable research assistance, to Rita Tidwell and Simpson Thacher & Bartlett for aid and assistance in preparing the manuscript, and to the Filomen D'Agostino and Max E. Greenberg Research Fund, New York University and to the

Committee on Research, University of California, Berkeley, for their generous research support.

ELEANOR M. FOX
LAWRENCE A. SULLIVAN

New York City, New York
Berkeley, California
June 1989

Summary of Contents

Table of Contents

Table of Cases

The principal cases are in bold type. Cases cited or discussed in the text are roman type. References are to pages. Cases cited in principal cases and within other quoted materials are not included.

*

Table of Statutes

CASES AND MATERIALS ON
ANTITRUST

*

Chapter 1

THE ANTECEDENTS OF MODERN ANTITRUST

A. INTRODUCTION

We start our study of antitrust with a look at history, economics, and law. Part A is an introduction; Part B looks at common law antecedents. Part C examines the political, social and economic history that gave rise to antitrust; Part D observes the legal and political developments that marked the early years of this body of law.

1. ANTITRUST AND HISTORY

Antitrust is an elliptical term. It refers to a set of national policies that responded to the emergence of big business and the changing role of business in modern life. These policies have evolved over time and even now continue to develop. We want you to learn not only about what the law is but also about how it came to be that way—what it used to be, what forces changed it, and what destabilizing and inertial forces are presently at work. This approach will add dimension and interest. It will also help you to develop a feel for what is canonical in today's law and what is or may be subject to change. Of course, one must be cautious in predicting even the direction, let alone the magnitude, of future developments; but the chance of error would be greater if one assumed that, as things now are, so they shall remain.

Changes in antitrust policy occur with changes in the world of business. Changes in business structure and business conduct are in turn related to technological development and to a range of cultural developments. For example, changes occurred in merger law as the nature and character of merger activity changed and as popular and theoretical views about the consequences of mergers evolved. The character and pace of merger activity has itself been conditioned both by developments in technology and by developments in the culture of business decisionmaking.

Changes in antitrust policy occur also in response to shifting modes in theoretical thinking about economic problems. Early on, economists

1

tended to ignore antitrust.[1] In the 1930s, economists began to engage in serious work regarding antitrust issues, and an approach called structural analysis began to dominate. This analysis looks centrally at the size and shape of the firms in particular markets. Recently, neoclassical price theory has made gains as a mode of analysis. This mode looks centrally at the relationship of price to costs and uses theoretical models to consider optimal antitrust outcomes. Much antitrust doctrine put in place between 1940 and the mid 1970s has been under siege from theorists who identify themselves with the Chicago School of Economics such as professors and judges Bork, Easterbrook and Posner. Chicago School is a form of neoclassicism which places strong faith in markets and business freedom.

We will explain all of these theories and modes of analysis as our narrative continues. Moreover, as we will show, structural analysis remains viable. There are non-Chicagoans that focus on transactions costs, information deficiencies, and strategic interactions. Other economists are harbingers of behavioral and evolutionary theories. This theoretical ferment adds interest as antitrust analysis reacts to and sometimes assimilates new developments, albeit slowly.

Finally, changes in policy occur in response to changing national concerns and values. During the 1960s, Americans were self-confident. They regarded government as a useful device for solving social problems. In those years Americans thought they could use law and government to eradicate poverty, revitalize cities, and fine-tune the economy. But by the 1980s Americans had been buffeted by Vietnam, OPEC, Watergate, hostage crises and the Asian and European economic resurgence; they were less confident of themselves and were growing timid about their capacity to use law or government to bring about social and economic change. Given such differences in national mood and self-perception, one would expect antitrust to be different today from what it was in 1960—and, of course, it is.

In 1960 any catalog of antitrust concerns would have reflected a variety of values. Economic values—efficiency, progress, stability, equitable distribution—dominated. But dispersion of economic power was also prominently mentioned as a goal with its own merits. Ideally, there should be enough firms in a market so that socially important decisions— what to make, where to make it, what technology to utilize—would not become discretionary calls for managers of powerful firms. Fairness and economic mobility were also relevant values. Markets should be open to

---

1. "The historians of American antitrust policy have emphasized the lack of enthusiasm, and often downright hostility, with which economists greeted the Sherman Act." G. Stigler, The Economist vs. Preacher, and Other Essays 41–42 (1982); W. Letwin, Law and Economic Policy In America 73 (1965) (hereinafter Law and Economic Policy). Perhaps because of this lack of interest, some scholars have apparently supposed that much early antitrust thinking was pragmatic or political, little informed by general theory of any kind. E.g., Bork, The Antitrust Paradox: A Policy At War With Itself 30, 33, 35 (1978) (hereinafter Antitrust Paradox). It has been effectively argued, by contrast, that early judicial approaches were informed by general economic theory, though of a different kind from that adhered to by scholars like Bork. May, Antitrust Practice and Procedure in the Formative Era: The Constitutional and Conceptual Reach of State Antitrust Law, 1880–1918, 135 U.Pa.L.Rev. 495, 541–93 (1987) (hereinafter Antitrust Practice and Procedure).

entry by anyone with capital to risk. And once small traders entered a market, they ought to be able to make decisions for themselves; they should be protected from undue intrusion by powerful business bureaucracies as well as from intrusive governmental bureaucracies.

Today, by contrast, American productivity has been falling and American hegemony fading. We talk less of market failure, more of regulatory failure and governmental excesses. In such a world, economic efficiency looms large as an antitrust value; some now say it should be the sole concern. The sixties and the eighties, then, stand in sharp contrast. Be mindful of these changes in historical context as you read the cases.

2. ANTITRUST AND ECONOMICS

We have identified economic theory as one of many policy sources that influence antitrust. Today, antitrust discussion cannot be carried on without engaging in economic thinking. We will draw on economic theory throughout the book. Here, we make a few introductory comments.

Theoretical thinking is a way of seeking to understand, to explain, to attribute meaning to certain phenomena. Economics provides one body of theory. Economics is frequently described as a science. In a sense it is. But in another sense it is an art. As an effort to understand, to explain, to give meaning to human activities, it shares characteristics with disciplines as different from itself as literature and even poetry. And although there are similarities, the differences between literature and economics are vitally important. It is not just that the novelist and the economist look at different human activities; they look at those activities through different ends of the lens. The novelist seeks to signify much through intensive treatment of the particular; especially, through the feelings of the individual. The novelist normally begins with the idiosyncratic human being.[2] The economic theorist, like the physicist or sociologist, seeks to signify much through generalizations. The economist conceives of human behavior in terms of predictable responses to market signals.

When the economist addresses a policy issue, she attempts a daunting task. You should understand how she goes about it, what of her output you can accept with confidence and what you cannot, and how you can begin to differentiate the one from the other. In 1984, Robert M. Solow, a prominent economist, reviewed a book by Leonard Silk, economics columnist for the New York Times. In a few terse paragraphs, Solow innoculated his readers against an all too rampant social disease—thinking that economic theory is the source of all wisdom for policy issues:

> Thinking precisely and systematically about something as complex and irregular as a modern economy is very difficult, maybe impossible. The same could be said about any other very complicated object, like the earth's atmosphere or the population of sea turtles off the Georgia coast. The only way to make progress is to make simplifying assumptions, that is, to invent a simplified world. Here are a few examples of the sorts of

2. But see M. Jevons, Murder at the Margin (1978).

assumptions economists sometimes like to make: there are only a few goods being produced, maybe only two or even one; the firms producing them are so small and numerous they have no discretion over price but can only meet the market; all consumers have the same tastes.

No one believes those assumptions to be true. The point is that it may be possible to understand how such a simplified world works. The art of good economics . . . is to sense when it is not seriously misleading to extrapolate from the simplified world to the real world and when it is dangerous. Most analytical economists spend their time puzzling out the properties of one simplified world or another, but when they argue fiercely with one another, it is usually over the utility of some particular simplified world as a model of the real world.

This sort of method is not peculiar to economics, of course. Galileo discovered that all bodies, no matter what their weight and density, fall at the same speed when they fall freely under the influence of gravity. The legend is that he tested his theory by dropping a feather and a cannonball from the top of the Leaning Tower of Pisa. Maybe. Try dropping a page of The New York Times and a tennis ball from a high window on a windy day. Of course, Galileo's proposition applies only to a simplified world, to objects falling in a vacuum in which gravity is the only significant force at work. No one would apply it in a real gale. One of Mr. Silk's points, although he does not elaborate it, is that economists go wrong when they put too much strain on their simplifying assumptions. They sure do.

The second way economists lose touch with reality is more prosaic but probably more important for good or evil. Even when economic analysis can successfully see its way through a real problem and propose effective corrective policy, it often runs afoul of the primacy of politics over economics. In the real world, an idea that is useful and practical in narrowly economic terms may be a sure loser politically. History is littered with clever economic ideas that didn't fly, couldn't fly, ideas as dead as dodos and for the same reason.[3]

Remember Solow's words when you look at price theory models of competition and monopoly. The most powerful price theory models posit a theoretical world of pure competition and a very different theoretical world of single firm monopoly. But few, if any, real markets display the characteristics of either model world. In most real markets there are several sellers, differentiated products, information gaps and at least some psychologically driven agendas that do not have to do solely with maximizing stockholder profits. Although economists have also developed oligopoly models, which are simplified worlds of few sellers, those models are more useful to identify problems than to supply bases for predictions. Many of them simplify reality so severely that one cannot rely on their having any predictive force. Others incorporate the complications, but cease providing determinate solutions.

Remember, too, Solow's comment that useful economic ideas can be political losers. Useful economic ideas can also be losers legally. The economic idea works as a legal solution only when the value to which the legal rule responds is identical with the value that informs the economic idea. For example, if an economist testifying in support of a particular merger convinces a court that the risk that the merger will result in inefficiencies is small, the court may still enjoin the merger if the court is convinced that Congress intended to forbid mergers tending toward high concentration, regardless of their efficiency effects.

Now that you've been warned against excessive reliance on economic theory, we ourselves can generalize about economic phenomena. We shall begin by introducing some of the issues that economic thinking must address.

There are functions every economy must perform. It must allocate available and always limited resources among possible productive uses. Guns or butter? Skateboards or computers? Consumption goods or capital goods? Current goods or research that may lead in the future to new and better consumer goods, or to more efficient production methods? The economy cannot provide all that people want of all of these. Should some be given up to assure more of others? If all are to be provided, how much of each?

Every economy must also distribute among members of society the (limited) output achieved. What principle should govern? To each according to need? To each according to productivity? Equally? By lottery or the accidents of birth? By wealth? Beyond selecting a principle, by what mechanism should the principle be carried out? Or is a principle really at work? Perhaps the distributive mechanisms are set in motion independently of any principle.

The economy must stabilize productive activity. For centuries we accepted the ideal of continuous, steady growth. Today, even that ideal is subject to debate. More and more people have accepted the concept of a "space ship earth"; we share a celestial vehicle with limited and non-renewable supplies packed aboard. Should people choose policies that increase productivity or policies that conserve irreplaceable resources?

Allocation, distribution, and stabilization, then, are the major functions of the economic system. To perform them, societies have developed three basic types of economic systems. The oldest, the "customary economy," predominated in pre-industrial times. It is typified, perhaps, by the 18th century English village. One's status signified one's economic role and economic entitlements; one was born to a station in life and occupied that station, either with dignity or without, either happily or not, but seldom with social mobility.

The "command economy," by contrast, is characterized by planning and thus incorporates the concept of conscious development and change. It is also marked by an egalitarian ideology. The socialist economies—the U.S.S.R., China, Hungary—are examples.

The third type is the "market economy." Its defining characteristics are private ownership and contractual freedom. It thus differs from each of the others in the way production and allocation decisions are made.

The economies of the United States, Western European nations, Japan, and South Korea are examples.

All systems existing today are mixed. The American, Western European, and Japanese economies typify relatively high reliance on the market to determine production levels and distribution methods. The Soviet economy emphasizes relatively high reliance on centralized planning to carry out these functions. But there are elements of planning in Western economies—in some, high degrees of planning. There are also customary elements in these economies—especially in Japan. So also, markets are used to some extent even in the Soviet economy, and to a greater extent in other eastern European nations, such as Hungary. The new commitment of China to the use of markets is noteworthy.

Any complex market economy has several different types of markets. In capital markets demand comes from businesses looking for funds supplied by savers and investors. There are also labor markets and, of course, markets for goods and services. These may be intermediate (e.g., a market for nuts and bolts), or final (e.g., a market for washing machines).

The central feature of a market is the concept of a voluntary exchange. A deal is made. Both parties regard themselves as better off than they were before. If they didn't, they would not have made the exchange. Central features of the model for competitive markets are: large numbers of buyers and sellers, adequate information about reasonably available alternatives on both sides, a sole goal of business to maximize its profits, and a single goal of consumers to maximize satisfaction. Note that under this model there would be no market power and therefore there would be equal bargaining positions. The voluntary character of exchange suggests a relationship between the economic and political concerns that influence attitudes toward economic matters. Americans favor "free markets" because they think markets work well economically to move resources to where they are wanted and needed. They also favor "free markets" because they value "freedom"—mobility, individual responsibility, choice, and the prospect of self-improvement.

How well does the American market economy perform its numerous functions? Let's think first about the task of allocating resources among the innumerable production functions the economy performs. It's perfectly clear that our market economy gets the allocation job done—not flawlessly, but well enough and surely more expeditiously than alternatives. If you want a quart of milk or a sports car, you know or can quickly learn where to go and you know you'll find one waiting when you get there. This statement applies not only to millions of consumers and tens of thousands of consumer goods and services, but also to countless producers and their needed inputs. Allocation is done through the interaction of hundreds of thousands of market decisions by producers, distributors and consumers. This contrasts sharply with the "visible hand" allocation in command or customary economies. And there is ample evidence that in many ways markets allocate better than alternative mechanisms in terms of serving demand.

How about the distribution function in the American market economy? Does the market system distribute wealth in a direction that society chooses? The price system provides a theoretical relation between each participant's relative contribution to society to the extent that is measured by earnings, and relative return from it. If a laborer earns $20,000 he presumably produces that much in value—he is "worth" his hire. If an executive earns $100,000 her production is presumably worth five times as much as the laborer's. That is what the labor market is saying about their relative contributions. If you invest in making widgits, and your investment yields a return, you are earning what your investment activity produced. Consumers valued that production; that's why your investment was profitable.

Of course a person's capacity to earn and capacity to invest are both influenced by his "station in life." The executive's education, social capacities and "connections" influenced her career. Your work status and perhaps your inheritance will, in turn, influence your investments. Thus returns depend on where one starts out in the economic game. Initial distribution—wealth and station—which may or may not be justifiable on ethical or pragmatic grounds, influence future distribution.

The distribution function of markets can be looked at also through another lens. If markets are truly competitive (which they seldom are) both producers and consumers get a fair share of the gains from the trades they make. If, however, producers have market power, by definition they have power to exploit consumers; the producers get most of the gains from trade. Thus, market imperfections interfere with the distribution function of markets.

We do not rely solely on the market for distribution of goods, services, and wealth. Governmental interventions of various kinds alter the distribution that the market effects. As an example, markets for agricultural crops are often said to be competitive because no single seller, acting alone, can influence price. But farmers as a political force have influenced government which carries out a range of programs aimed at giving farmers more (and consumers less) than wholly free markets would yield.

Next, consider the stabilization function: markets, if working well, operate as would a pendulum. They tend toward the never achieved equilibrium of supply and demand at market-clearing prices. Business cycles, inflation, recession—all are indications that the stabilization function never works perfectly. No western nation relies solely on the market. Here, as elsewhere, government intervenes.

Markets, then, seem to work quite well to achieve allocative and modest distributive goals and certain (changing) political goals, such as choice, opportunity, power dispersion, and a general state of governance. But in various respects there are "market failures." Antitrust as a system assumes that markets can work well with minimum governmental intervention. But antitrust is not the product of laissez-faire philosophy. Antitrust presupposes what might be called the "liberal state." By that we mean a political consensus to leave markets alone when they are working well to achieve agreed-upon goals, but to intervene when failures have been identified and seem capable of being corrected by state action.

Note that there are at least three possible governmental responses to identified market failures. For one, government may do nothing on the assumption that the failure will correct itself, or that any state action might make it worse. For another, government might encourage voluntary private (individual or concerted) responses. Thirdly, government itself might take action. It might impose price and entry regulation; it might establish and enforce conduct standards; it might take action to alter the structure of the market; it might respond through fiscal, monetary or tax policy.

Let us note some types of market failure and the kinds of interventions that may be used to mitigate them. Instability (depression/inflation) is an omnipresent market failure. The government responds mainly through fiscal and monetary policy, but may also provide employment, unemployment insurance or a "dole" when the market is depressed, and may control prices and/or ration goods when the market is overheated.

Another perceived failure may be a socially unsatisfactory distribution of resources. Government may respond through social security, welfare, graduated taxation, affirmative action, and the like. There are, of course, ebbs and flows in the extent of corrective governmental action. Currently we are in a stage of relatively high reliance on laissez faire. But there remains a social safety net.

Next, consider "indivisibilities" ("indivisible goods" or "public goods"). Police protection is an example. It must be at the ready, and if it is, everyone shares; it cannot readily be provided through market transactions only to those who pay; and we would not want to limit its benefits to those who can afford to pay. There are many goods and services having this characteristic. The lighthouse, the park, are other examples. Government responds to indivisibilities through socialized activity to provide parks, highways, bridges, and defense.

Investment in public goods results in "externalities." An externality is any cost for which the investor does not pay or any benefit in which the investor does not share. For example, a chemical plant pollutes the air, thus imposing on others one of the costs of its production. Because the plant does not pay the cost of pollution, the producer operates on the basis of costs that are lower than actual costs and thus will invest more than is economically optimal in producing this product. An example of a positive externality is the orchard and the bees. You operate an orchard. Owning the adjacent land, I keep bees. I benefit, economically, from your investment; you cannot charge me through the market for what you contribute to my bees because you cannot keep my bees away from your trees. Government responds to negative externalities to some extent—for example, through environmental and health and safety regulations, and through nuisance law.

Also, "information problems" affect markets. For example, consumers select doctors, lawyers, automobiles and even bleaches without much comparative information about characteristics or price. Government responds to deficient or asymmetrically deployed information through consumer protection laws, truth-in-lending laws, federal securities disclosure laws, blue sky laws, and the like. It may also encourage private responses—for example, through trade associations. This has been the briefest of summaries of market failures and governmental responses to them. Harris and Carmen, Public Regulation of Marketing Activity, 3, 4 and 6 J. of Micromarketing (Spring, 1983, 1984 and 1986) provides a comprehensive topology.

The central concern of antitrust is with yet another important kind of market failure—failures of competition. As we shall see in Chapters Two and Three, both monopoly and cartelization result in a less than optimal allocation of resources to the monopolized or cartelized industry, and also result in a distributional shift, from consumers to monopolists or cartelists. How does government respond to competitive failures? Such failures may be structural (e.g., a monopoly or long-lasting cartel) or may be matters of conduct (e.g., predatory pricing or exclusion). There are three conventional responses. One is antitrust (government seeks to improve structure or inhibit anticompetitive conduct). Another is price and entry (public utility) regulation. A third is regulation to encourage cooperation to produce countervailing power (for example, through labor law).

Both antitrust and public utility regulation are particularly American institutions. Most market-oriented nations socialize their utilities rather than regulate them; and though several other nations have pro-competition laws, few have developed their antitrust concepts as fully as has the United States.

Price and entry (public utility) regulation is used when an industry is regarded as a "natural monopoly." This occurs when there are ever increasing economies of scale, and thus one firm can provide service at a lower unit cost than could two or more. Railroads are an example, as are electric and gas utilities. If one company runs gas mains down a street and serves all adjacent customers, unit costs will be lower than if each of two companies runs mains but they share the business. The conventional regulatory pattern is to exclude all but one designated firm (or a select few), to require universal service, and to regulate its rates and service.

Antitrust differs markedly from entry and rate regulation. It is designed to promote and protect a market economy made up of sufficient firms to produce effective competition. Historically, antitrust has had several goals. Greater efficiency has always been an important one. Both monopolization and cartelization can lead to output restriction, higher prices, and sluggishness, and to socially wasteful "rent chasing" activity (e.g., activities aimed at reducing the likelihood of competitive entry, or to policing the cartel). Antitrust also aims for better distribution. Output restrictions and monopoly prices transfer wealth from consumers to monopolists or cartelists; antitrust seeks to stop such transfers.

Note that both utility regulation and a competitive economy (protected by antitrust) are supposed to result in "fair prices"—a distributive goal. A "fair price" means a price closely related to cost. A price greatly in excess of cost is sometimes called "unfair" or "unreasonable." Wider distribution of economic opportunity and economic power is yet another antitrust goal. Related to this may be a wider distribution of political power.

3. ANTITRUST AND LAW

Thus far we have talked of antitrust as though it might be free-form regulation—as though those making antitrust policy could draw upon theory to manipulate the economy to suit their political agendas. That is not so. Congress decided in 1890 to maintain competition through rights and obligations enforced by courts, a decision reinforced from time to time by additional statutes. Law is a system of norms, announced in advance. It has its own values, however imperfectly achieved. They include certainty, predictability, continuity and consistency.

Of course, law can change over time through reasoned judicial elaboration. Indeed, when dealing with antitrust statutes, which are broad, almost constitutional in concept and language, the ongoing process of interpretation can more appropriately extend beyond the original Congressional purpose than could the construction of less spacious statutes. An antitrust court passes Congressional values through the prism of current economic information and current economic understanding. It may perhaps go further and introduce into concepts like "restraint of trade" values that have over time taken on a higher order of significance. And, of course, Congress can change the rules applicable to the future. Sometimes an enforcer such as the Antitrust Division of the Department of Justice purports to speak prospectively. Must it do so within the confines of a tradition about prosecutorial discretion? Or can it properly advocate to the courts that they impose new constraints on economic actors, or jettison old ones, when an agency's current thought and analysis suggests to it that existing norms should be changed?

The relationship between law and economics can be seen as clearly in antitrust as anywhere. Courts draw on economic knowledge. Sometimes they view the economist much as they might any other expert—the accountant, the physician, the geologist. They treat what the expert has to say as relevant to their fact-finding function. But courts also draw on their own economic thinking, often influenced by their perspectives on political economy, when they articulate or apply the law. You will see one example when you study market definition in Chapter 2.

Are there appropriate limits to the judicial use of "economic" thinking? Suppose a court incorporates its view of current economic thought into a legal norm. Suppose a court says that if a firm has 90% of a market it is a monopolist. Suppose that a later court becomes convinced by economic views then current that defining a market and computing shares is not a reliable way to evaluate monopoly power. Is the later court free to adopt the "new thinking"? Does it matter whether the "new thinking" enjoys the consensus of economists?

Note that questions like these can be asked not only about economic theory but also about social priorities and social or political wisdom drawn from sources other than economics. Suppose the courts shaped a relevant legal norm that favored an economy organized in small units—not because they thought such an organization efficient but because they thought an economy so organized would be socially and politically more consistent with American traditions. Can a later court change the law if it thinks efficiency a more important value than did earlier courts, and also thinks that the existing rule may have efficiency costs? Does the answer depend on what the court thinks that the Congress that passed the law valued? Does it, or should it, turn on whether the court thinks that there is a new social consensus valuing efficiency more and non-bureaucratic organization of society less? Questions like this arising in the common law context are perceptively explored in M. Eisenberg, The Nature of the Common Law (1988), especially at pages 26–37 and 104–127. Is common law tradition an appropriate source of guidance for antitrust courts facing claims that policy bases of prior decisions have become obsolete?

These and other issues arise because antitrust regulates economic structure and economic conduct through law, and because at least part of the substantive content of antitrust is based upon economic thinking. Innumerable substantive and procedural problems await solution. Be alert to them as you examine the course materials.

B. MONOPOLIES AND RESTRAINTS OF TRADE IN ENGLAND

1. MONOPOLIES AND THE COMMON LAW

Early England was more a customary than a market economy: Markets were controlled by kings, queens, parliaments and tradition. The sixteenth century economy was mercantilist and was dominated by monopolies. Royalty and parliaments conferred exclusive trading rights, often in the form of patents, on favored individuals. Parliaments and mayors conferred exclusive powers on town guilds—groups of competitors that controlled training, competency standards, and entry. The guilds kept out foreign traders and goods and they fixed prices. For years, custom favored regulation [4] and tolerated privilege. Law and custom discouraged restraints that would keep an individual from practicing his trade in his own home town, lest he and his family become charges on the public. But there was as yet no conception of freedom of trade to achieve ideals of economic liberty or efficiency.[5]

Not until the end of the sixteenth century did British common law begin to disfavor privilege conferred by the crown. The *Case of Monopolies* reflects this change.

4. Economic regulation in mercantile England included common law crimes of forestalling, regrating and engrossing. These were laws against middlemen or speculators who bought up staple foodstuffs before these reached an established market, or gained control of these goods after they reached market, or cornered markets to resell the goods at high prices. The laws protected the guilds, which had the right to control the marketplace. In the name of free trade, these laws were abolished by several statutes, the first of which was passed in 1772. In 1844 Parliament passed a law abolishing all that remained of these common law crimes. See Letwin, The English Common Law Concerning Monopolies, 21 Chi.L.Rev. 355, 368, 373–74 (1954) (hereinafter English Common Law).

5. Id. at 373–74.

CASE OF MONOPOLIES
11 Coke 84, 77 Eng.Rep. 1260 (K.B. 1603).

. . . And in this case two general questions were moved and argued at the Bar, arising upon the two distinct grants in the said letters patent, *viz.* 1. If the said grant to the plaintiff [Edward Darcy, a groom of the Privy Chamber to Queen Elizabeth] of the sole making of cards within the realm was good or not? 2. If the license or dispensation to have the sole importation of foreign cards granted to the plaintiff, was available or not in law? . . .

As to the first question it was argued on the plaintiff's side, that the said grant of the sole making of playing cards within the realm, was good for three reasons. 1. Because the said playing cards were not any merchandize, or thing concerning trade of any necessary use, but things of vanity, and the occasion of loss of time, and decrease of the substance of many, the loss of the service and work of servants, causes of want, which is the mother of woe and destruction, and therefore it belongs to the Queen (who is *parens patriae, et paterfamilias totius regni* . . .) to take away the great abuse, and to take order for the moderate and convenient use of them. 2. In matters of recreation and pleasure, the Queen has a prerogative given her by the law to take such order for such moderate use of them as seems good to her. 3. The Queen, in regard of the great abuse of them, and of the cheat put upon her subjects by reason of them, might utterly suppress them, and by consequence without injury done to any one, might moderate and tolerate them at her pleasure. . . .

As to the second, it was argued, and strongly urged, that the Queen by her prerogative may dispense with a penal law, when the forfeiture is popular, or given to the King, and the forfeiture given by the statute of 3 E. 4. cap. 4 in case of importation of cards is popular.

As to the first, it was argued to the contrary by [counsel for defendant, T. Allein, a London Haberdasher who made and sold cards], and resolved by Popham, Chief Justice, *et per totam curiam*, that the said grant to the plaintiff of the sole making of cards within the realm was utterly void, and that for two reasons:—1. That it is a monopoly, and against the common law. 2. That it is against divers Acts of parliament. Against the common law for four reasons:—1. All trades, as well mechanical as others, which prevent idleness (the bane of the commonwealth) and exercise men and youth in labour, for the maintenance of themselves and their families, and for the increase of their substance, to serve the Queen when occasion shall require, are profitable for the commonwealth, and therefore the grant to the plaintiff to have the sole making of them is against the common law, and the benefit and liberty of the subject, and therewith agrees Fortescue in *Laudibus legum Angliae, cap.* 26.

. . . 2. The sole trade of any mechanical artifice, or any other monopoly, is not only a damage and prejudice to those who exercise the same trade, but also to all other subjects, for the end of all these monopolies is for the private gain of the patentees; and although provisions and cautions are added to moderate them, yet . . . it is mere folly to think that there is any measure in mischief or wickedness: and, therefore, there are three inseparable incidents to every monopoly against the commonwealth, *sc.* 1. That the price of the same commodity will be raised, for he who has the sole selling of any commodity, may and will make the price as he pleases. . . . The 2d incident to a monopoly is, that after the monopoly granted, the commodity is not so good and merchantable as it was before: for the patentee having the sole trade, regards only his private benefit, and not the common wealth. 3. It tends to the impoverishment of divers artificers and others, who before, by the labour of their hands in their art or trade, had maintained themselves and their families, who now will of necessity be constrained to live in idleness and beggary; *vide* Fortescue *ubi supra:* and the common law, in this point, agrees with the equity of the law of God, as appears in Deut. cap. xxiv. ver. 6 . . . you shall not take in pledge the nether and upper millstone, for that is his life; by which it appears, that every man's trade maintains his life, and therefore he ought not to be deprived or dispossessed of it, no more than of his life: and it agrees also with the civil law. . . . 3. The Queen was deceived in her grant; for the Queen, as by the preamble appears, intended it to be for the weal public, and it will be employed for the private gain of the patentee, and for the prejudice of the weal public; moreover the Queen meant that the abuse should be taken away, which shall never be by this patent, but *potius* the abuse will be increased for the private benefit of the patentee. . . . 4. This grant is *primae impressionis,* for no such was ever seen to pass by letters patent under the Great Seal before these days, and therefore it is a dangerous innovation, as well without any precedent, or example, as without authority of law, or reason. And it was observed, that this grant to the plaintiff was for twelve years, so that his executors, administrators, wife, or children, or others inexpert in the art and trade, will have this monopoly. And it cannot be intended, that Edward Darcy an Esquire, and a groom of the Queen's Privy Chamber, has any skill in this mechanical trade of making cards; and then it was said, that the patent made to him was void; for to forbid others to make cards who have the art and skill, and to give him the sole making of them who has no skill to make them, will make the patent utterly void. . . . And as to what has been said, that playing at cards is a vanity, it is true, if it is abused, but the making of them is neither a vanity nor a pleasure, but labour and pains. . . . And therefore it was resolved, that the Queen could not suppress the making of cards within the realm, no more than the making of dice, bowls, balls, hawks' hoods, bells, lures, dog-couples, and other the like, which are works of labour and art, although they serve for pleasure, recreation, and pastime, and cannot be suppressed but by Parliament, nor a man restrained from exercising any trade, but by Parliament. . . .

As to the 2d question it was resolved, that the dispensation or licence to have the sole importation and merchandizing of cards (without any limitation or stint) notwithstanding the said Act of 3 E. 4. is utterly against the law. . . . [W]hen the wisdom of the Parliament has made an Act to restrain *pro bono publico* the importation of many foreign manufactures, to the intent that the subjects of the realm might apply themselves to the making of the said manufactures, & c. and thereby maintain themselves and their families with the labour of their hands;

now for a private gain to grant the sole importation of them to one, or divers (without any limitation) notwithstanding the said act, is a monopoly against the common law, and against the end and scope of the Act itself; for this is not to maintain and increase the labours of the poor cardmakers within the realm, at whose petition the act was made, but utterly to take away and destroy their trade and labours, and that without any reason of necessity, or inconveniency in respect of person, place, or time, and *eo potius,* because it was granted in reversion for years, as hath been said, but only for the benefit of a private man, his executors and administrators, for his particular commodity, and in prejudice of the commonwealth. . . .

And *nota,* reader, and well observe the glorious preamble and pretence of this odious monopoly. . . . And our lord the King that now is, in a book which he in zeal to the law and justice commanded to be printed *anno* 1610, intituled, "A Declaration of His Majesty's "Pleasure, & c." p. 13. has published, that monopolies are things against the laws of this realm; and therefore expressly commands, that no suitor presume to move him to grant any of them. . . .

Questions and Comments

In the view of the court, why was the grant of monopoly to Darcy against the common good? Was this because of the source of the grant (the crown) or the effects of the grant? Is there a link between the source and the effects? Is the crown more likely to grant a monopoly for private gain at the expense of the public, and Parliament more likely to grant a monopoly only when it will enhance the public good?

How strong is the argument that, if the use of playing cards tends towards idleness, scarcity is in the public interest? Who should decide whether scarcity is in the public interest?

After the Case of Monopolies, the Queen could not lawfully ban foreign imports for the gain of her groom or others, but Parliament could do so to protect the trade and labors of the people of England and thus to protect their livelihoods and the source of support for their families. Would the effect on consumers be the same in either case? Was anyone thinking about consumers?

Does the *Case of Monopolies* imply anything about private monopolies secured other than by grant of the crown or Parliament? Suppose someone became the sole seller of a product without any governmental protection—for example, because he "built a better mousetrap"? Would such a monopoly contravene the common law?

 Two decades later, in 1624, Parliament passed the Statute of Monopolies, 21 Jas. I. c. 3. The statute declared void all monopolies, grants and patents "of or for the sole buying, selling, making, working, or using of any thing, . . . or of any other monopolies." The statute, however, contained expansive exceptions for grants, charters or customs of cities or towns, or to "any corporations, companies, or fellowships of any art, trade, occupation or mystery, or to any companies or societies of merchants within this realm, erected for the maintenance, enlargement or ordering of any trade of merchandize. . . ." Thus, while forbidding crown-granted monopolies, the statute probably touched little else.

As time went on, a transition from a customary economy to a market economy began. By the end of the eighteenth century British society valued freedom of trade for both libertarian and economic reasons. But the law protected society against governmental interference, not against exclusion of traders by other market actors. Indeed, by the end of the nineteenth century British law protected monopolistic combinations that excluded competitors, and it did so in the name of defendants' freedom of trade.[6]

2. RESTRAINTS OF TRADE AT COMMON LAW

From Britain there also emerged an early body of law that prohibited certain restraints of trade. This law is of limited relevance to United States problems, however, for the early British holdings were not based on public benefits of competition; they were based on the role of guilds, municipalities, and custom in governing social status and in ordering the production and distribution of goods and services.[7]

In the classic *Dyer's Case,* Y.B. 2 Hen. V, f. 5, pl. 26 (1414), the court held void an undertaking by a dyer, as a condition to a bond, to refrain from carrying on his trade in the town for six months. The court was offended by the presumptuousness of the dyer in disabling himself from practicing his trade by private contract, but it evidenced no concern that the parties had interfered with market forces in a way that might cause prices to rise.[8]

Nearly two centuries later, in *Davenant v. Hurdis,* Moore * 576 (K.B.1599), the court addressed a bylaw of the London Tailor's Guild that required every merchant member that sent out cloth for finishing to send at least half of the work to fellow members of the guild. The clothworkers resented the clause, because they wanted a fair chance to do the work. The court held the bylaw void. The later *Case of Monopolies* cites *Davenant* to uphold the "liberty [of every subject] to put his cloth to be dressed by what clothworker he pleases"; but the *Davenant* case itself reflects merely a jurisdictional dispute among guilds as to which one should control the trade.[9]

A separate line of authority developed for the law on conspiracy. The old common law prohibited persons from combining to interfere with the property or affairs of another. The courts applied this law to attempts by traders to exclude other traders, and it subjected conspirators to criminal as well as civil sanctions.[10] Beginning in the late seventeenth century, the courts extended the conspiracy law to invalidate producers' agreements to limit supply or raise prices.[11]

6. Mogul Steamship Co. v. McGregor (1892) App.Cas. 25. See English Common Law at 382–84 (denying the victim the right to recover, although stating that the combination was unlawful in the sense that it could not be enforced by the courts).

7. See generally Levi, The Antitrust Laws and Monopoly, 14 U.Chi.L.Rev. 153–54 (1947); Law and Economic Policy at 23–26, 31.

8. Accord: King v. Alderman Sterling and Seventeen Others, 83 Eng.Rep. 331 (1664).

9. English Common Law at 366.

10. King v. Alderman Sterling and Seventeen Others, 83 Eng.Rep. at 331; The Poulterer's Case, 77 Eng.Rep. 813 (K.B.1611); Queen v. Daniell, 87 Eng.Rep. 856 (Q.B.1704).

11. Law and Economic Policy at 31. Letwin stresses the development in the following cases: Anonymous, 88 Eng.Rep. 1297 (K.B.1699) (combination of plate-button makers who agreed to a minimum price for their wares; confederacies to raise rates should be suppressed); Cousins v. Smith, 33 Eng.Rep.

In time, England moved from a mercantile society to an economy dominated by relatively small traders, middle class merchants. Adam Smith's book, The Wealth of Nations, published in 1776, gave strong intellectual support to the view that tradespeople, left free to pursue their own profit-maximizing activity, would bring about the best economic result for the public. This book, as well as the writing of other political economists such as Bentham and James Mill, facilitated and probably accelerated the movement toward a market economy; yet it is important to note that the free-market world of Adam Smith was premised upon the existence of many individual traders; big business was beyond imagination. As laissez faire theory gained prominence, it generated some extreme policy reponses. They included the contention that the law should not interfere with the freedom of traders even when they got together to raise prices. As long as an agreement was voluntary, as long as no one was coerced, the market would cure any distortion.[12] By the second half of the nineteenth century, these extreme laissez faire policies were guiding English common law development. The British courts backed away from opposition to price fixing, and also gave greater scope to the traders' right to agree not to practice their trade.[13]

397 (Ch. 1807) (all fruit dealers in city compelled to purchase from a committee; although this was not forestalling, regrating or engrossing, it had evils of all three and was an illegal contract that the court would not enforce); King v. De Berenger, 105 Eng. Rep. 536 (K.B.1814) (conspiracy to raise price of government securities by false rumors illegal). There is, however, at least one earlier cartel case, dating, indeed, to the turn of the fourteenth century, where the concern may have been solely with the effect on price. In Leet Jurisdiction in the City of Norwich During the XIIIth and XIVth Centuries 52 (W. Hudson, ed. 1892) there is reported from the Leet roll of 1299/1300 for Nedham and Manecroft a case against "all of the chandlers for making an agreement amongst themselves—to wit, that none of them should sell a pound of candle at less than another."

12. This was not Smith's view. His model assumed numerous, small independent entrepreneurs, none of whom could possibly control the market by individual decisions as to how much to produce and what price to charge, and all of whom acted independently. Indeed, Smith feared that any meetings of competitors would result in agreements to raise prices and thus would harm the public. A. Smith, The Wealth of Nations ch. x (1776). Cf. Lochner v. New York, 198 U.S. 45 (1905).

13. The following cases are illustrative: Mogul Steamship Co. v. McGregor, App.Cas. 25: A combination to control all trade by offering rebates to exclusive customers is legal because the combination is not for the purpose of injuring excluded individuals who cannot compete, but rather to obtain bene-

fits for the group, a legitimate goal. Id. at 60. Adopting low rates to drive competitors out of business is legal because such rates benefit consumers. Id. at 49.

Hearn v. Griffin, 2 Chitty 407 (1815): An agreement between two coach service owners to charge the same price is not illegal. Similarly, an agreement to divide the market by operating on different days and times is a convenience that prevents each from ruining the other. Id. at 408. Illegality would require a prohibition that prevents others from entering the market and competing. Id. at 408–09.

Wickens v. Evans, 148 Eng.Rep. 1201 (Ex. 1829): A territorial division of market and minimum price agreement among three trunk and box makers is not illegal; it constitutes only a partial restraint on trade. No monopoly results because others may enter and these three do not comprise the entire market. Id. at 1206. Other boxmakers will compete and public will benefit from reduced costs.

Jones v. North, L.R.—Eq. 426 (1875): Agreement among four quarry owners to split a contract to purchase rather than compete on bids is not void because it affects only a small part of total market.

Collins v. Locke, App.Cas. 674 (P.C.1879): An agreement to divide the stevedore business is only a partial restraint of trade and not unlawful.

Urmston v. Whitelegg, 7 T.L.R. 295 (C.A.1891): An agreement fixing the minimum price of mineral water for ten years is unreasonable and the court will not enforce it. The length and scope of agreement are

During the nineteenth century, United States common law on restraints of trade was developing independently of British law. Unlike the British, the American law (all of it state law) generally prohibited price fixing and market divisions as well as coercive and exclusionary restraints.[14] The American law was more sharply focused on maintaining competitive markets than was the English law, and American courts were more ready to intervene for that purpose than were the English courts. One can only speculate about the reason for this difference. Perhaps it was because American law began to develop only after the classical conception of the value of markets was widely accepted, whereas the English law had earlier served very different notions about the social functions of markets.

Three often-cited British common law restraint of trade cases are presented below, one from the fifteenth century and two from the eighteenth. We selected them less to invite generalization about principles prevailing prior to passage of the Sherman Act than to invite thought about competition policy. As you will see, the outcomes of the cases can be justified by competition theory, even though their holdings were not necessarily based on it. Consider the effect of each of the challenged practices on competition, consider the court's rationale for the decision, and reflect upon these three different modes for protecting the public interest.

KING v. NORRIS

2 Kenyon 300.
96 Eng.Rep. 1189 (K.B.1758).

This was a motion for leave to file an information against the defendants, who were separate proprietors of salt-works in *Droitwich,* for a conspiracy to raise the price of salt there, by entering into an article, whereby they bound themselves, under a penalty of 200 pounds, not to sell salt under a certain price, which exceeded the price then received for it.

The articles were now cancelled, and destroyed: but, notwithstanding that, the court were unanimous for making the rule absolute; and Lord Mansfield declared, that if any agreement was made to fix the price of salt, or any other necessary of life (which salt emphatically was), by people dealing in that commodity, the court would be glad to lay hold of an opportunity, from what quarter soever the complaint came, to shew their sense of the crime; and that at what rate soever the price was fixed, high or low, made no difference, for all such agreements were of bad consequence, and ought to be discountenanced. . . .

Questions and Comments

Whose trade was restrained by the agreement of the salt producers to raise the price of salt? What, do you think, was the effect on salt production?

more than was necessary for protection of the parties.

14. See, e.g., Craft v. McConoughy, 79 Ill. 346 (1875); Morris Run Coal Co. v. Barclay Coal Co., 68 Pa. 173 (1871); Stanton v. Allen, 5 Denio 434 (1848).

Why did the salt producers raise the price of salt by agreement, rather than by independent action?

Lord Mansfield declared it a crime to make any agreement to fix the price of a necessity of life; the level, "high or low, made no difference." Why was the direction of the price fix unimportant? Should it be important?

THE SCHOOLMASTERS' CASE
11 Hen. IV, f.47, pl. 21 (1410).

Two masters of a grammar school brought a writ of trespass against another master and counted that *whereas* the appointment to the grammar school of Gloucester has belonged to the Prior of Lantony, near Gloucester, since the time from which memory does not run etc., and the said Prior has made the appointment to the said plaintiffs to have the governance of scholars and to teach children and others etc., the defendant has raised a school in the town because of which, where the plaintiffs were able to take 40d. or 2s. from a child for a quarter, now they can take only 12d., to their damage etc.

Horton made full defense.

Hill: His writ is worth nothing.

Skrene: It is a good action on the case, and the plaintiffs have shown sufficient matter here how they are damaged, by which etc.

Hank[ford]: Damnum [may be] absque iniuria. As, if I have a mill and my neighbor raises another mill through which the profit of my mill is diminished, I have no action against him and yet it is damage to me as *Thirning* conceded and said that the teaching of children is a spiritual thing and if a man retains a master in his house to teach children, he will do damage to the common master of the town and yet I believe that he [the common master] will not have an action.

Skrene: The Masters of Paul's claim that there will be no other masters in all the city of London except for themselves.

* * *

And then *Horton* demurred that the action was not maintainable.

Skrene: Inasmuch as we wish to aver the title of the Prior, as above, and that we are damaged because he has drawn away our scholars and also where we were able to take from a scholar 40d. or 2s. a quarter now we take only 12d., we demand judgment and pray our damages.

Hill: There lacks basis in this case to maintain an action, because the plaintiffs have no estate but a ministry for the time [being]; and although another, who is as well learned as the plaintiffs, comes to teach children, that is a virtuous and charitable thing and a help to the people, so that he cannot be punished by our law. . . .

Skrene: If a market is raised to the nuisance of my market, I will have an assize of nuisance, and in a common case if those coming to my market are disturbed or beaten, by which I lose my toll, I will have a good enough action of trespass on the case; also here.

Hank[ford]: It is not the same, because in your case you have a free tenement and inheritance in the market, but here the plaintiffs have no estate in the schoolmastership etc. but for an uncertain time, and it would be against reason, that a master be disturbed from holding a school where he pleases, unless in the case of a university corporation and a school founded in ancient times; and in the case of a mill (as I said before), if my neighbor raises a mill so that they who were accustomed to grind at my mill go to the other mill, by which my toll is diminished, I shall not have an action for that reason. But if a miller disturbs the water from running to my mill, or does such manner of nuisance, I shall have an action such as the law gives. And the opinion of the Court was that the writ does not lie; by which it was awarded that they should take nothing etc.

Questions and Comments

What was the effect of the new masters' initiative to start a school in Gloucester? Did the entry help anyone?

Of what did the Masters of Paul's complain? What right did they assert? By what were they injured? Since they were concededly injured, why no cause of action?

Is the entry of the new school unambiguously in the public interest? What if twelve pence per pupil was not sufficient to cover the costs of running a school in Gloucester? How do we know how much is sufficient to support a school?

Competition may cause injury. At a later point we will ask, what is antitrust injury? (That is, what is compensable injury, under the antitrust laws?) Distinguish injury caused by competition itself and injury caused by restraints on competition.[15] Compare the harm caused to the buyers of salt in Droitwich, and the harm caused to the Masters of Paul's in Gloucester.

MITCHEL v. REYNOLDS
1 P. Wms. 181.
24 Eng.Rep. 347 (K.B.1711).

Debt upon a bond. The defendant prayed . . . that whereas the defendant had assigned to the plaintiff a lease of a messuage [dwelling house] and bakehouse in *Liquorpond Street,* in the parish of *St. Andrew's Holborn,* for the term of five years: now if the defendant should not exercise the trade of a baker within that parish during the said term, or, in case he did, should within three days after proof thereof made, pay to the plaintiff the sum of fifty pounds, then the said obligation to be void. . . . [H]e pleaded, that he was a baker by trade, that he had served an apprenticeship to it, *ratione cujus* the said bond was void in law, *per quod* he did trade, *prout ei bene licuit.* Whereupon the plaintiff demurred in law.

Parker, C.J., delivered the resolution of the court.

The general question upon this record is, whether this bond, being made in restraint of trade, be good?

---

15. Restraints on competition may be public or private. Public restraints may arise from direct government intervention or from government grant or recognition of a right or license. Note Judge Hankford's distinction between inheritance of a market and mere operation of a mill.

And we are all of opinion, that a special consideration being set forth in the condition, which shews it was reasonable for the parties to enter into it, the same is good; and that the true distinction of this case is, not between promises and bonds, but between contracts *with* and *without* consideration; and that wherever a sufficient consideration appears to make it a proper and an useful contract, and such as cannot be set aside without injury to a fair contractor, it ought to be maintained; but with this constant diversity, *viz.* where the restraint is general not to exercise a trade throughout the kingdom, and where it is limited to a particular place; for the former of these must be void, being of no benefit to either party, and only oppressive, as shall be shewn by and by.

* * *

Where a contract for restraint of trade appears to be made upon a good and adequate consideration, so as to make it a proper and useful contract, it is good.

* * *

Noy, 98; W. Jones, 13; Cro.Jac. 596. In that case, all the reasons are clearly stated, and, indeed, all the books, when carefully examined, seem to concur in the distinction of restraints general, and restraints particular, and with or without consideration, which stands upon very good foundation: *Volenti non fit injuria;* a man may, upon a valuable consideration, by his own consent, and for his own profit, give over his trade; and part with it to another in a particular place.

I come now to make some observations that may be useful in the understanding of these cases. And they are—

1st, That to obtain the sole exercise of any known trade throughout *England,* is a complete monopoly, and against the policy of the law.

2dly, That when restrained to particular places or persons (if lawfully and fairly obtained), the same is not a monopoly.

3dly, That since these restraints may be by custom, and custom must have a good foundation, therefore the thing is not absolutely, and in itself, unlawful.

4thly, That it is lawful upon good consideration, for a man to part with his trade. . . .

. . . The law is not so unreasonable, as to set aside a man's own agreement for fear of an uncertain injury to him, and fix a certain damage upon another; as it must do, if contracts with a consideration were made void. . . .

But here it may be made a question, that suppose it does not appear whether or no the contract be made upon good consideration, or be merely injurious and oppressive, what shall be done in this case?

* * *

[The court concludes that the law presumes the contract void in such a case.]

To conclude: In all restraints of trade, where nothing more appears, the law presumes them bad; but if the circumstances are set forth, that presumption is excluded, and the Court is to judge of those circumstances, and determine accordingly; and if upon them it appears to be a just and honest contract, it ought to be maintained.

For these reasons we are of opinion, that the plaintiff ought to have judgment.

Questions and Comments

In National Society of Professional Engineers v. United States, 435 U.S. 679 (1978), the United States Supreme Court took the occasion to interpret *Mitchel v. Reynolds.* The Court said:

> This principle [that antitrust analysis "focuses directly on the challenged restraint's impact on competitive conditions"] is apparent in even the earliest of cases applying the Rule of Reason, *Mitchel v. Reynolds.* *Mitchel* involved the enforceability of a promise by the seller of a bakery that he would not compete with the purchaser of his business. The covenant was for a limited time and applied only to the area in which the bakery had operated. It was therefore upheld as reasonable, even though it deprived the public of the benefit of potential competition. The long-run benefit of enhancing the marketability of the business itself—and thereby providing incentives to develop such an enterprise—outweighed the temporary and limited loss of competition.[16]

Did the decision in *Mitchel v. Reynolds* turn on the restraint's impact in the bakery market and on the price of baked goods in the parish of St. Andrews Holborn? Did it turn on the extent to which a covenant not to compete enhances the marketability of a business and thus provides incentives to develop business enterprises? Did it turn on anything else?

Why does the court in *Mitchel v. Reynolds* declare that restraints are void unless reasonable? What does the court mean by "reasonable"? Is a restraint reasonable if, despite the restraint, the bakery or other market to which it applies continues to have a large number of sellers? What harm does such a restraint inflict, and on whom?

Compare the agreement between the proprietors of saltworks in Droitwich (which was a crime) and the agreement between Mitchel and Reynolds (which was valid). Did both restrain trade or competition? How much and in what respects? Did either facilitate trade or competition? How? Is the consumer of salt or of bakery products made better off, worse off, or neither, by the agreement?

The above cases can be read to support principles highly relevant to American competition jurisprudence; namely: (1) Agreements among competitors to fix price are illegal. (2) A business firm that gets to a market first has no private right to restrain subsequent entry. (3) Not all restraints of trade are illegal; they may be reasonable and thus permissible.

---

16. 435 U.S. at 688–89.

C. THE AMERICAN SCENE: POLITICAL AND JUDICIAL REACTIONS TO INDUSTRIAL TRANSFORMATION

1. THE TRANSFORMATION OF AMERICAN INDUSTRY AND THE BIRTH OF THE TRUSTS

Before 1850, American industrial structure was simple. The typical business was owned and managed by an individual or partners who worked and provided employment in the community where they lived. Traders specialized in particular goods and used a single production process. Tiers of independent middlemen linked the initial producer with the final consumer. Most factories were small, drawing labor from family members or local young people training to become independent producers. Although industrialization increased during the twenty years before the Civil War, factors such as international competition and periodic shortages of labor and capital prevented advancement on any grand scale.[17]

Between 1865 and 1910, industrial structures and conventional ways of doing business were dramatically and rapidly altered. Changes in corporate structure, first through cartelization and then through consolidation and vertical integration, transformed chains of small firms into complex networks of oligopolies and monopolies. Moreover, by 1920, an urban, wage-earning labor force had taken the place of the independent artisan.[18] First in railroads, then in extractive and manufacturing industries, big, bureaucratic corporations emerged.

Several characteristics distinguished these new businesses from the old. They were in corporate form; they had millions of dollars in capital; they had vast assets in land, buildings, and machinery; they did business throughout wide geographic areas; they performed a variety of vertically related functions; and the separation of ownership and control made technocratic skills and bureaucratic organization prerequisites for competent management.

The modern business enterprise is typically a large, hierarchical corporation run by managers rather than owners. It may be regional, national, or even multi-national in scope. It seldom needs middlemen of the earlier kind, for it consolidates within one entity several distinct tasks previously done in separate firms.[19] How did this transformation happen and what were the reactions to it?

17. For a detailed description of the traditional business enterprise, see A.D. Chandler, The Visible Hand: The Managerial Revolution in American Business (1977), ch. 1–2 (hereinafter Visible Hand). For a general description of the growth of big business, see G. Porter, The Rise of Big Business, 1860–1910 (1973) (hereinafter Rise of Big Business), and H. Scheiber, H. Vatter, and H. Faulkner, American Economic History 159–161 (1976) (hereinafter American Economic History).

18. S.P. Hays, The Response to Industrialism, 1885–1914 11 (1957).

19. Visible Hand at 285.

2. ALTERNATIVE HISTORICAL THEORIES

Historians have variously explained this transformation. Three of the better-known theories focus alternatively on the individual actor, on the internal dynamics of industrial organization, and on the facilitative role of government. Stress upon the individual was the earliest approach. Historians such as Henry Demarest Lloyd viewed big business as the creation of unscrupulous, money-hungry speculators, typified by railroad mogul Jay Gould and oil magnate John D. Rockefeller.[20] Later, progressive historians elaborated on this view, producing the "robber baron thesis." [21] Still other historians gave admiring accounts of the achievements of individuals in big business. Some made "industrial statesmen" of the individual capitalists whom they credited with generating wholesome industrial growth.[22] While some of the writing from these two traditions is engaging, much of it reads like a morality play. The lack of objective attention to personality and social context obscures the motives and circumstances at work. The effect may be to sensationalize the historical record without explaining it.

After the turn of the century, a less lively but more analytical approach developed, variously referred to as "institutional history," the "organizational synthesis," or "amoral history." [23] The institutional approach, as it will be called here, borrows from economic and sociological theories about industrial organization. As elaborated by Alfred D. Chandler, Jr. it views change in industrial structure largely as a response to technological and organizational innovation. Political, demographic and social developments are included "only as they impinge directly on the ways in which the enterprise carried out the processes of production and distribution." [24]

The third group of historians concentrates on the influence of government—legislatures, courts, and agencies—on the growth of private enterprise. Led by J. Willard Hurst, these historians focus on the economic impact of the formal legal regimes that governments establish (e.g., the particulars of contract and corporation law), the direct economic subsidies given to business, governmental policies designed to stimulate growth indirectly, and the extent to which government efforts to mitigate market failures affect market conduct and structure.[25]

These three seemingly contradictory perspectives may be understood as different emphases each of which helps to explain economic and technological development. Individual entrepreneurs, the businesses they built, and political institutions all interacted with and facilitated the development and application of new technologies. Individuals used imagi-

20. H.D. Lloyd, The Story of a Great Monopoly, in Lords of Industry 1–46 (1910) (hereinafter Lords of Industry).

21. See, e.g., M. Josephson, The Robber Barons: The Great American Capitalists, 1861–1901 (1934).

22. See, e.g., H.C. Livesay, Andrew Carnegie and the Rise of Big Business (1975).

23. For a review of the literature taking this approach, see Galambos, The Emerging

Organizational Synthesis in Modern American History, 44 Bus.Hist.Rev. 279–290 (1970).

24. Visible Hand at 6.

25. See, e.g., J.W. Hurst, Law and the Conditions of Freedom in the Nineteenth-Century U.S. 3–32 (1956) (hereinafter Law and Freedom).

nation and ingenuity both to advance technical knowledge and to bring new products and technologies to market. Changes in economic institutions both fueled and were fueled by technological progress. Finally, government encouraged economic change through aid to scientific research and development and through a legal structure that favored the new ways of exploiting natural and human resources. The complex relationships among individuals, institutions, and the American legal system all emerge from what we call an ecclectic approach.

3. AMERICAN INDUSTRIALIZATION AFTER 1865

The process of industrialization began well before the Civil War. What makes the post-war era so remarkable is the nation's rapid rise to the status of the world's industrial leader, which was achieved during the period 1865–1900. American entrepreneurs took advantage of abundant resources, developed new production technologies, and expanded commercial markets. These developments expanded the nation's total economic output.[26] The availability of natural resources impelled settlement westward across the continent. Federal homesteading programs opened the frontier to agriculture, mining, petroleum, lumber, and water development.[27]

The invention of alloys speeded the process of mechanization in both extractive industries and in the manufacture of finished goods.[28] Companies eager to secure sources of raw materials provided markets for and steady infusions of capital into increasingly mechanized extraction industries. Production of alloys in turn advanced the standardization of manufacturing because tools could be made to exact dimensions and specifications.[29] With the greater availability of natural resources, new sources of energy—electric power and petroleum—not only became industries in their own right but also fueled growth in almost every other sector of the economy.[30] Mass production became commonplace with the advances in metallurgy and machine tools.[31] The advantages of mass production—assembly, interchangeability, and standardization—crowded out individual artisans and helped initiate new industries in consumer goods such as bicycles, typewriters, coaches, carriages, and cars. Advances in food processing, spearheaded by the dressed beef and canning industries, opened up new avenues for further commercialization of agriculture. The factory system thrived. The growth of mass markets, as a result of population increases and urbanization, provided adequate demand for the high volume required to make mass production profitable. The innovation of the assembly line contributed to vertical integration as firms spanned the entire process from securing raw materials to turning out finished goods. Innovations in communication and transportation provided the infrastructure necessary to enable business to respond to

26. American Economic History at 193–94, 221.

27. L.E. Davis, et al., American Economic Growth: An Economist's History of the U.S. 106–09 (1972) (hereinafter American Economic Growth); see generally P.W. Gates, History of Public Land Law Development (1968).

28. See American Economic Growth at 233–279.

29. American Economic History at 224.

30. Id. at 196.

31. Id. at 225.

growing urban markets. Railroad mileage doubled between 1865 and 1873. The national network was nearly completed by the early 1890s. Businesses could ship goods more quickly, cheaply and dependably throughout the year. The modernization of the telegraph and the invention of the telephone in 1876 made available more rapid, accurate information about the market and further increased the volume of possible business transactions.[32]

Demographic change, particularly the influx of almost thirty million immigrants after 1865, was a vital factor in American industrialization. The stream of people to the cities provided a labor force for the new factories and, as cities became population centers, a relatively reliable source of demand for agricultural and industrial products. While the rate of immigration was sensitive to cyclical fluctuations in the economy, it was steady enough to contribute to the two-fold increase in U.S. population. The presence of the immigrant labor force enabled a middle class with rising income levels to emerge as the primary purchasers of new consumer products.[33]

4. CHANGES IN BUSINESS STRUCTURE

During the first half of the nineteenth century, the forms of economic organization were simple. The individual proprietorship and the simple partnership were low-capital ventures and easily established. But these forms of business carried significant legal risks that investors were unwilling to assume as industrialization progressed and capital needs grew. Most significantly, the simpler forms could not be easily adapted to take advantage of mass markets, improved production processes, and large-scale employment of both laborers and managers.[34] Business entrepreneurs and investors turned to a historically tried and legally sound form of organization—the corporation—in order to exploit the advantages of the industrial revolution.

a. The Rise of Incorporation

i. The Old Conception

Using the corporation, industrialists sought to avoid the liabilities and shortfalls of partnerships. The corporate form dated back to Roman times, and the formal practice of incorporation was employed, albeit sparingly, in continental and English common law.[35] Long before the age of industrialization, special charters abounded and some general incorporation laws existed among the states of the United States.

The corporation was linked to the role of the state in public life and in the economy. Despite the Supreme Court's ruling in the *Dartmouth College* case in 1819,[36] legislatures continued to alter the terms of charters

---

32. Id. at 195–97.

33. E.C. Kirkland, Industry Comes of Age: Business, Labor, and Public Policy, 1860–1897 at 237–38, 264 (1961) (hereinafter Industry Comes of Age).

34. Handlin and Handlin, Origins of the American Business Corporation, in Public

Policy and the Modern Corporation 3–24 (D. Grunewald and H.L. Bass, eds. 1966) (hereinafter Public Policy).

35. Id. at 5.

36. 17 U.S. (4 Wheat.) 518 (1819).

already granted in order to retain state control over corporations' activities. The prevailing view of corporations as extensions of the state, not as distinct, autonomous legal agents, kept them constantly subject to legislative restraint.[37]

Structural changes in the economy caused investors to look anew at the corporation. Seen as a vehicle for the management of capital rather than as the proxy of the state in the construction of public works, the corporation's "attributes of peculiar economic efficiency, limited liability, and of perpetual freedom from state interference" helped alter the meaning of private enterprise after 1865.

ii. The New Conception

Industrialists adapted the new corporate form to meet the structural needs of the emerging business system. Capital (ownership) and management could be separated; investors could extend their sphere of interest to include more aspects of production and to include related enterprises.

> Judged in terms of its economic usefulness, the corporation had what the partnership lacked: the death or withdrawal of a shareholder did not terminate its existence; the individual investor might have his liability for a corporation's debt limited to the amount of his own investment; owners could easily give, sell, or otherwise transfer their shares. In short, the corporation possessed a possible permanence which was one aspect of that stability upon which the age was so insistent.[38]

These legal and economic advantages paved the way for the great accumulations of capital that became commonplace after 1865.[39]

After the Civil War, the states' role in promoting and regulating enterprise differed in kind from prior experience. Special charters, the primary method of incorporation before mid-century, were gradually replaced by general incorporation laws. The states possessed the power to "determine the very structure of the corporate enterprises doing business within their jurisdiction," [40] but they did not anticipate the speed and scale of the new incorporation movement that would take place during the 1880s and 1890s. Businesses intent on capturing larger shares of the markets for their goods not only took advantage of general incorporation laws and other new legal devices but often evaded remaining state-imposed legal restraints as well.[41] The old concept of the state as controlling private decisions about the economy faded.

b. Manipulation of the New Corporate Form

The changing legal status of the corporation was but one factor in a much larger, ongoing process: the movement to centralize many or all aspects of production, marketing, and distribution. Several incentives existed for combining horizontal consolidation and vertical integration of

37. Public Policy at 23–24.

38. Id. at 23.

39. Industry Comes of Age at 196–98.

40. McCurdy, The Knight Sugar Decision of 1895 and the Modernization of American Corporation Law, 1869–1903, 53 Bus.Hist. Rev. 304–305 (1979) (hereinafter Knight Sugar Decision).

41. McCurdy, American Law and the Marketing Structure of the Large Corporation, 1875–1890, 38 J.Econ.Hist. 637–41 (1978).

units engaged in production and marketing. First, some businesses (the Singer Sewing Machine Company, for example) manufactured new, complex products that required special marketing services such as demonstrations and maintenance.[42] Second, traditional outlets were sometimes not able to dispose of the great volume of manufactured goods. Lastly, and most importantly, corporations wanted to escape from ruinous competition and declining prices.

The railroads—the nation's first "big business," according to Chandler—were first to confront the problem of ruinous competition. Railroads required a high initial investment for construction of fixed assets and their maintenance. To offset the high capital and operating costs, railroad companies sought a large volume of business at low rates. Often, railroads set differential rates for certain large volume shippers and localities and charged less for long hauls than for short hauls. During the construction boom competing roads were forced to lower rates to stay in business.[43]

Responding to these conditions, railroads formed pools or cartels. These were horizontal, loosely structured combinations of competitors that joined forces to create large, regionally dominant systems.[44] Initially, pools or cartels were formed simply to control output and prices without any other elements of integration. They attempted to fix industry-wide price schedules and production quotas, and urged individual firms to comply for the good of all. In a sense they were defensive moves, for they were designed to control unstable competitive conditions within the industry, and few reduced the costs of production.

Pools were unstable, however. Schemes to apportion the petroleum transportation among the railroads collapsed. When oil refiners and shippers refused to participate, railroads either cheated by giving secret rebates, or withdrew from the pool. Likewise, a pool formed to allocate coal production and establish shipping rates favorable to the railroads was short-lived due to fluctuations in the economy during the 1880s and 1890s. The railroads lobbied for legislation to give pools legal sanction, but the pools remained legally unenforceable and under pressure they quickly fell apart.[45]

Because of the widespread cheating in pools several prominent corporations turned to the trust. The trust, a tighter form of combination than the pool, was created when a number of corporations, erstwhile pool members, "turned their stock over to a board of trustees receiving in return trust certificates of equivalent value."[46] Each participating corporation retained its individual state charter, but all participants were subject to the control of the newly formed, unincorporated entity that held their stock. While the trustees could set prices and outputs for all participants, the trust and its members escaped state law limitations on corporate size, scope of enterprise, and requirements for public disclo-

42. Visible Hand at 402–03.

43. G. Miller, Railroads and the Granger Laws 16–23 (1971) (hereinafter Granger Laws); Visible Hand at 140–42, 148–51, 156–64.

44. Visible Hand at ch. 5.

45. Industry Comes of Age at 199–203.

46. Visible Hand at 319.

sure.[47]   Also, the trust made central administration possible.[48]   Some corporations combined vertically, integrating the entire production and distribution process from obtaining raw materials to providing structured marketing systems.   As markets gradually expanded, despite recurring periods of overcapacity and depression, vertical integration permitted businesses to knock out unintegrated rivals by reducing costs and prices. Vertical combinations were more successful than purely horizontal pools in reducing costs, increasing productivity, and eliminating competition.[49]

Standard Oil, the best known of the great trusts, was formed in 1882. It successfully captured the petroleum industry and maintained its control for many years.   Other refining and distilling companies imitated this new form of organization.[50]   After consolidating horizontally, trusts would often attempt to gain control over the input resources and the marketing system needed for their particular industry.[51]   Again, Standard Oil was the model that many imitated.

c. Law and Policy as a Facilitator

The laissez faire image of nineteenth-century America is in large part a myth.   To paraphrase J. Willard Hurst, government was not a passive bystander—it actively encouraged rapid, economic development and it facilitated the "release of entrepreneurial energy." [52]   Federal and state government provided the institutional structure necessary for growth and gave direct subsidies to sectors which could best stimulate economic activity.

For example, the national banking system, established during the Civil War, and the federal government's debt-management and currency policies, encouraged investment and the accumulation of capital.   Eastern and northern manufacturers expanded rapidly toward the end of the Civil War due to generous war contracts and liberal protective tariff acts passed by Congress.[53]   The government's public land and immigration policies encouraged the settlement of the West and the creation of new markets for trade.   The federal government also quickened the development of a national market by giving generous land grants to railroads.[54]   Business also received indirect support through postal and lighthouse systems, sponsorship of scientific surveys and expeditions, and improvements in river navigation.[55]

States intervened more directly than the federal government.   Before 1840, they often subsidized or owned canals, turnpikes, and railroad construction projects.   After 1840, the states encouraged private corporations to undertake these projects by giving them eminent domain powers. Though originally invoked by corporations undertaking transportation

47. A. Eichner, The Emergence of Oligopoly 16 (1969) (hereinafter Emergence of Oligopoly).

48. Visible Hand at 319.

49. Id. at 285–289.

50. Id. at 320.

51. Id. at 315.

52. See Law and Freedom at 6.

53. H. Thorelli, The Federal Antitrust Policy 55–56 (1955) (hereinafter Federal Antitrust Policy).

54. See Goodrich, Internal Improvements Reconsidered, 30 J.Econ.Hist. 289 (1970).

55. Broude, The Role of the State in American Economic Development, 1820–1890, in The State and Economic Growth 4–22 (H. Aitken ed. 1959).

projects, the power of eminent domain was later given to some manufacturers as well. Direct cash subsidies, low taxes, and municipal investments also supported corporate growth.[56]

Market activities thus occurred, as they always do, in an institutional setting based on law. Indeed, it is the legal fabric—the law's assignment of entitlements and the law's means of protecting expectations and setting limits on strategic market conduct—that make markets possible. During the period of industrial transformation, statutory and judge-made law encouraged new economic enterprises by reducing the risks of ventures, providing legal instruments for organizing enterprises, and allocating resources to corporations. Government support, however, did not insure the growth that in fact occurred. As Hurst notes, "law merely guaranteed the framework of opportunity; it was science, technology, the invention of financial procedures, the massing of capital which supplied the dynamic force to occupy these broad areas of economic maneuver."[57] But as Hurst records, the legal developments were important to corporate growth.[58]

5. POLITICAL AND SOCIAL REACTIONS TO ECONOMIC CHANGE

a. *The Economic and Political Power of the Trusts*

The trust movement grew out of the problems of overcapacity caused by the industrial revolution.[59] Large-scale, commercialized agriculture and a comprehensive transformation in the means of production helped the nation prosper as never before, but overcapacity and overproduction revealed structural flaws in the economy. As the pools and cartels collapsed, business leaders increasingly viewed the trust as a solution to these structural flaws. Using combinations and mergers, they hoped to solidify their control over the market and to reduce competition.[60] While it may be difficult to tell the extent to which the trust movement led to monopoly, "many of the combines came close enough to inspire widespread public concern about the trust movement."[61]

The rise of trusts in the oil, steel, electric power, and other public utility industries during the 1880s fed widespread fears about the economic implications of the combination movement. Economic change during this period had wrought a new social order. Traditional values had been upended. The individual worker and independent artisan were displaced by a specialized, wage-earning industrial labor force. The nature of private enterprise required redefinition, prompting public reaction and regulatory responses from government.

56. Scheiber, Property Law, Expropriation, and Resource Allocation by Government: the United States, 1789–1910, 33 J.Econ.Hist. 232 (1973).

57. Law and Freedom at 78.

58. J.W. Hurst, The Legitimacy of the Business Corporation in the Law of the U.S.: 1780–1970 at 159 (1970) (hereinafter Legitimacy of the Business Corporation).

59. T. McCraw, Rethinking the Trust Question, in Regulation in Perspective: Historical Essays 1 (T. McCraw ed. 1981).

60. Industry Comes of Age at 211.

61. L. Galambos, The Public Image of Big Business in America, 1880–1940: A Quantitative Study in Social Change 9 (1975).

The new order carried both advantages and disadvantages. On the one hand, the industrial economy expanded at a rapid rate, bringing a general increase in wealth and productivity. Many people believed in a bright future of even higher production levels, incomes, and standards of living. In the decades after the Civil War, however, this optimism was coupled with sense of "increasing inequities in the distribution of wealth, a drift toward monopoly, railway abuses of various sorts, unemployment on an unprecedented scale, and health and housing problems in the rapidly growing cities." [62] "The promised land," said social commentator Henry George, "flies before us like a mirage."

> [I]n factories where laborsaving machinery has reached its most wonderful development, little children are at work; wherever the new forces are anything like fully utilized, large classes are maintained by charity or live on the verge of recourse to it; amid the great accumulations of wealth, men die of starvation, and puny infants suckle dry breasts, while everywhere the greed of gain, the worship of wealth, shows the force of the fear of want.[63]

During the 1880s, people began to look to law and government to remedy what they perceived had gone wrong in the economy.

To many, the trust became a symbol of the new order. To its supporters, it signified wealth, cooperation, and progressive development. To its detractors, the trust was a monolithic, impersonal, centrally administered organization that represented greed, inhumanity, and economic stratification. Despite the fact that only eight industrial consolidations during the 1880s actually took the form of trusts,[64] the term "trust" came to denote more than a specific legal device for corporate combination. Rather, it became the catchphrase in a public debate over the course of economic growth and the distribution of wealth.

The belief that free competition was essential to a thriving, efficient economy was widely held in the nineteenth century. Business people argued that competition was the "great regulator"; it led to economic natural selection, the survival of the most efficient. Because competition was thought to be governed by natural laws, any attempts to impose "artificial" restraints would hinder progress.[65] But there was a contradiction: large businesses were consolidating to avoid the rigors of the assertedly immutable law of competition.

Business people and economists resolved the contradiction in favor of the trusts. Primarily, they argued that trusts were inevitable growths, dictated by the same forces that governed the evolution of the biological world. The evolutionary argument affirmed the positive nature of the trust. The appearance of the trust signaled that social evolution had reached a new stage. In this schema, the trust was a way of eliminating excessive competition and restoring balance and efficiency to the economic

---

62. S. Fine, Laissez–Faire and the General Welfare State 289 (1956) (hereinafter Laissez–Faire).

63. H. George, Progress and Poverty 8 (1953 ed.) (originally published in 1879).

64. Visible Hand at 320.

65. Laissez–Faire at 100–03. For an interesting review of economic views during this period, and for a useful bibliography, see Antitrust Practice and Procedure at 561–71.

order. Indeed, to some the trust augured the decline of the reign of competition and the rise of a new age of cooperation.[66]

Many people—consumers, farmers, laborers, small business owners—rejected these justifications. Newspapers published exposés of the unscrupulous methods used by trusts' leaders to quash their competitors and to force smaller businesses to cooperate with them. Henry Demarest Lloyd argued that the trusts had achieved their size and power through secret, illegal means. He fueled the growing antitrust movement with tales of the corrupt methods used by the leaders of the most infamous trust—the Standard Oil Company.[67]

Also, opponents of the trust directly challenged the natural-growth conception. Populist leader William Jennings Bryan maintained that trusts were unnatural growths. "Every trust rests upon a corporation and every corporation is a creature of law." [68] Opponents of trusts also rejected the classical theorists' claim that when a business services its own interest it inevitably serves the public.[69] Others observed that the threat of potential competition did not constrain trusts; merely, the trusts responded to the threat by acquiring the potential competitors and continuing to restrict entry.[70]

Public opinion quickly turned against the trusts. Small business owners viewed the expansion of big business with apprehension, fearing that the trusts would either absorb them or drive them out of business. Small retailers, jobbers, and traveling salespeople found their businesses severely challenged by the new chain stores and mail-order firms.[71] Many shippers, angered by the discriminatory railroad rates, agitated for local and national government regulation.[72] Farmers were plagued by the high costs of consumer products and the low prices of their crops. They complained that their situation was "aggravated by . . . trusts . . . that sold farmers bags and bought their linseed oil and cottonseed," [73] and by "middlemen and commodity speculators who handled their crops." [74] The Grange and the Farmers Alliance rallied around proposals to control big business. The emergence of national labor unions by the 1880s and the more frequent occurrence of strikes attested to the economic problems of the new industrial workers.[75]

The trust's ability to obtain favorable political treatment rekindled the traditional American hostility towards monopoly and special privilege. As William Letwin has commented, "Hatred of monopoly is one of the oldest American political habits . . . ." [76] After the Civil War, general incorporation laws resulted from accusations that granting special char-

66. See generally, Laissez–Faire at 110–11, 221–25, 338; and Law and Economic Policy at 75–77.

67. Lords of Industry at 1–46.

68. Chicago Conference on Trusts, 510 (1900).

69. Lloyd, Wealth Against Commonwealth, in The Populist Mind 496, 501–02 (N. Pollack ed. 1967).

70. Emergence of Oligopoly at 124.

71. Visible Hand at 233.

72. L. Benson, Merchants, Farmers and Railroads 13 (1955); see also Granger Laws at 16–23.

73. Law and Economic Policy at 59.

74. American Economic History at 214.

75. D. Brody, Steelworkers in America: The Nonunion Era 159–60 (1960); A. Paul, Conservative Crisis and the Rule of Law: Attitudes of Bar and Bench 1887–1895 at 128–30 (1960).

76. Law and Economic Policy at 59.

ters conferred special, monopolistic status on corporations.[77] Though Americans did not resist subsidies and legal privileges for corporations, Hurst argues that they believed that the corporate legitimacy depended upon responsible use of such grants.[78] The movement leading to the Sherman Antitrust Act was a forceful attempt to remind trusts of their obligation to be responsive and accountable to society.

b. Regulating the Trusts

Identifying the economic and political repercussions of consolidation was only part of the debate. Even when people agreed about the diagnosis they disagreed about whether and how the problems caused by trusts could be solved. The reforms proposed were inextricably linked to the way in which people defined the problems. The first point of contention was whether the trust could be regulated at all. This issue raised two questions: Was it possible to control trusts? And, who had the authority to impose restraints—the states or the federal government?

The pro-trust "evolutionists" were divided into two camps. Business people believed that the regulation of trusts and corporations was both impractical and improper. In The Gospel of Wealth, for example, Andrew Carnegie wrote: "[T]his overpowering irresistible tendency toward aggregation of capital and increase of size . . . cannot be arrested or even greatly impeded." [79] James B. Dill aptly captured the flavor of the evolutionists' arguments in remarks made to Lincoln Steffens:

> Trusts are natural, inevitable growths out of our social and economic conditions . . . .. You cannot stop them by force, with laws. They will sweep down like glaciers upon your police, courts, and states, and wash them into flowing rivers.[80]

These individuals argued that it was neither within the role or the power of the government to regulate trusts.

Other evolutionists accepted the existence of the trust but not their imperviousness to social responsibility. They embraced the idea of the "general welfare state" in opposition to the concept of the laissez-faire state.[81] They thought that "private self-interest is too powerful, too ignorant, or too immoral to promote the common good without compulsion." [82] While "monopoly . . . presents the possibility of cheap and efficient operation, . . . some means must be devised to ensure that the potential advantages of monopoly will actually be realized by society." [83] The state, they thought, not only had the ability but also the duty to interfere to promote "greater comfort in the community." [84]

For many people, however, none of the proposed solutions,[85] not even public ownership, would reach far enough. No reform that allowed trusts to exist could assure a free competitive economy or a fair distribution of

77. Id. at 65–66.

78. Law and Freedom at 27–28.

79. A. Carnegie, The Gospel of Wealth and Other Essays (1900), quoted in Laissez–Faire at 101.

80. L. Steffens, The Autobiography of Lincoln Steffens 196 (1931).

81. Laissez–Faire at 167–68.

82. Id. at 205.

83. Id. at 223.

84. Id. at 208.

85. Id. at 338–39.

wealth and power in the industrialized order. Increasingly, pressure mounted to break up the trusts. Two means were proposed. First, trusts could be attacked under state law as "ultra vires." Second, Congress or the states could enact antitrust legislation. On the first theory, states could revoke the charters of corporations in "quo warranto" proceedings by proving that the corporations had assumed powers not granted by the state. Because states did not authorize corporations to sell their franchises to other corporations (which is, in effect, what happened when trusts were formed) the states could dissolve the constituent firms of the trust. Several states initiated and succeeded in dissolving corporations through "quo warranto" suits. Suits were filed in New York against the Sugar Trust, in Louisiana against the Cottonseed–Oil Trust, and in Illinois against a public utilities holding company.[86]

Quo warranto suits to dissolve trusts proved to be a limited remedy, however. First, New Jersey gave the combination movement new life in 1888 when it legalized holding companies. This meant a corporation could hold stock in other corporations within and outside of the state.[87] In effect, the law protected corporations from prosecution in other states. Second, although many states enacted antitrust statutes, these laws were hard to enforce against multistate or national businesses.[88] Third, most states did not invoke the common and statutory law against the trusts because they feared negative economic repercussions.[89]

Most of the relevant state antitrust cases involved cartels. Some of the states developed law on monopolies.

Legal historians still debate whether the "trust problem" could have been handled through state law. But state law responses [90] certainly neither checked the pace nor greatly altered the form or direction of economic activity. Economic opportunities still seemed endless. Individuals still invested and reinvested. They drilled oil wells, constructed steel mills, and built more railroads. Overinvestment induced fierce competition. Competing firms joined forces with the small group of trustees who controlled the combining firms for their common gain. Thus, the trusts grew bigger and more powerful.

6. PASSAGE OF THE SHERMAN ACT

By the election of 1888, which brought William Henry Harrison to the presidency, it was commonly acknowledged that "the public had found the trusts to be a growing and intolerable evil." [91] In view of the strong public feeling, the candidates of all three political parties supported a national antitrust law. Even big business advocates reconciled themselves to a law against the trusts, perhaps convinced that Congress would not vote for the tariff they wanted unless domestic competition was protected.

86. Knight Sugar Decision at 321–23.

87. Id. at 322–23; Visible Hand at 319.

88. Knight Sugar Decision at 322–23.

89. Scheiber, Federalism and the American Economic Order, 1789–1910, 10 L.Soc'y Rev. 57, 100 (1975).

90. See, e.g., Richardson v. Buhl, 77 Mich. 632 (1889).

91. See W.H. Taft, The Anti–Trust Act and the Supreme Court 2 (1914); see also Federal Antitrust Policy at 129.

In 1889, Senator John Sherman introduced the Sherman Antitrust Act, which was redrafted largely through the efforts of Senators Edmunds and Hoar. During Congressional debate, Senator Sherman reiterated that the purpose of the bill was to contain the concentration of economic power. For example, he said:

> The popular mind is agitated with problems that may disturb social order, and among them all none is more threatening than the inequality of condition, of wealth, and opportunity that has grown within a single generation out of the concentration of capital into vast combinations to control production and trade and to break down competition. These combinations already defy or control powerful transportation corporations and reach State authorities. They reach out their Briarean arms to every part of our country. They are imported from abroad. Congress alone can deal with them, and if we are unwilling or unable there will soon be a trust for every production and a master to fix the price for every necessity of life.[92]

The legislative history of the act is replete with such rhetoric. As Robert H. Bork has written:

> In looking to the legislative history, one discerns repeated concern for the welfare of consumers and also for the welfare of small business and for various other values—a potpourri of other values. So far as I'm aware, Congress, in enacting these statutes, never faced the problem of what to do when values come into conflict in specific cases. Legislators appear to have assumed, as it is most comfortable to assume, that all good things are always compatible.[93]

Little in the legislative history illuminates what Congress meant by "restraint of trade" in Section 1 of the Sherman Act. Virtually every reference says, in effect, that this is a common law concept which the courts should interpret in the context of specific cases. Regarding the specific offense of monopolization, the act says even less. Letwin argues that the law's vagueness reflects a very loosely conceived policy aim: to preserve competition without destroying the trusts.[94] This illustrative exchange, among others, occurred during debate in the Senate:

> MR. GRAY. . . . I shall offer . . . [an] amendment now. It is to strike out of section 2, in lines 1 and 2, the words 'monopolize, or attempt to monopolize or,' so that the section shall read:

> 'Every person who shall combine or conspire with any other person or persons to monopolize any part of the trade or commerce among the several States, etc.'

> We will avoid by that amendment the [problem that we] do not know what definition the courts of the United States have ever given to the word 'monopoly' or 'monopolize.' . . .

> MR. HOAR. . . . I had that precise difficulty [about the meaning of 'monopolize'] in the first place with this bill, but I was answered, and I think all the other members of the committee agreed in the answer, that

92. 21 Cong.Rec. 2,460 (1890).

93. Bork, The Role of the Courts in Applying Economics, 54 Antitrust L.J. 21, 24 (1985).

94. Law and Economic Policy at 16.

'monopoly' is a technical term known to the common law, and that it signifies—I do not mean to say that they stated what the signification was, but I became satisfied that they were right and that the word 'monopoly' is a merely technical term which has a clear and legal signification, and it is this: It is the sole engrossing to a man's self by means which prevent other men from engaging in fair competition with him.

Of course a monopoly granted by the king was a direct inhibition of all other persons to engage in that business or calling or to acquire that particular article, except the man who had a monopoly granted him by the sovereign power. I suppose, therefore, that the courts of the United States would say in the case put by the Senator from West Virginia that a man who merely by superior skill and intelligence, a breeder of horses or raiser of cattle, or manufacturer or artisan of any kind, got the whole business because nobody could do it as well as he could was not a monopolist, but that it involved something like the use of means which made it impossible for other persons to engage in fair competition, like the engrossing, the buying up of all other persons engaged in the same business.

MR. KENNA. If the Senator will permit me, I should like to ask him whether a monopoly such as he defines is prohibited at common law. I ask the Senator from Massachusetts whether a monopoly coming within the definition which he gives is prohibited at common law.

MR. HOAR. I so understand it.

MR. KENNA. Then why should this bill proceed to denounce that very monopoly?

MR. HOAR. Because there is not any common law of the United States.

MR. KENNA. There is a common law in nearly every State in the Union.

MR. HOAR. I know. The common law in the States of the Union of course extends over citizens and subjects over which the State itself has jurisdiction. Now we are dealing with an offense against interstate or international commerce, which the State cannot regulate by penal enactment, and we find the United States without any common law. The great thing that this bill does, except affording a remedy, is to extend the common-law principles, which protected fair competition in trade in old times in England, to international and interstate commerce in the United States.

MR. EDMUNDS. I have only to say, in regard to the amendment suggested by my friend from Delaware and the suggestions of the Senator from West Virginia, that this subject was not lightly considered in the committee, and that we studied it with whatever little ability we had, and the best answer I can make to both my friends is to read from Webster's Dictionary the definition of the verb 'to monopolize.'

'1. To purchase or obtain possession of the whole of, as a commodity or goods in market, with the view to appropriate or control the exclusive sale of; as, to monopolize sugar or tea.'

Like the sugar trust. One man, if he had capital enough, could do it just as well as two.

'2. To engross or obtain by any means the exclusive right of, especially the right of trading to any place, or with any country or district; as, to monopolize the India or Levant trade.'

The old definition. So I assure my friends that although we may be mistaken (we do not pretend to know all the law) we were not blind to the very suggestions which have been made, and we thought we had done the right thing in providing, in the very phrase we did, that if one person alone instead of two, by a combination, if one person alone, as we have heard about the wheat market in Chicago, for instance, did it, it was just as offensive and injurious to the public interest as if two had combined to do it.

21 Cong.Rec. 3,152 (1890).

MR. CULBERSON gave the following explanation in the House of Representatives:

It is provided by the bill that any person who shall monopolize or attempt to monopolize, or combine or conspire with any other person or persons to monopolize any part of the trade or commerce among the several States, or with foreign nations, shall be deemed guilty of a misdemeanor. This is a very important and far-reaching provision. I will read to the House what appears to be Webster's definition of a monopoly:

'To engross, to obtain by any means exclusive right of trade to any place or within any country or district, as to monopolize the trade.'

That is the definition as given by Webster. Every person, therefore, who shall attempt to monopolize, to engross, or to obtain by any means exclusive control of interstate trade to any place, or within any country or district, will be guilty of a misdemeanor under the provisions of the bill. I need only say that there are many cases within our observation in which combinations have succeeded in monopolizing, in part at least, trade between localities in different States. It is to be hoped that if this measure becomes a law an end may be put to such practices and the people relieved of extortion which the destruction of competition always produces.

21 Cong.Rec. 4,090 (1890).

———

Despite doubts about precisely what the statute meant or would accomplish, on July 2, 1890 Congress passed the Sherman Antitrust Act. Sections 1 and 2 read as follows: [95]

"An act to protect trade and commerce against unlawful restraints and monopolies.

"SEC. 1. Every contract, combination in the form of trust or otherwise, or conspiracy, in restraint of trade or commerce among the several States, or with foreign nations, is hereby declared to be illegal. Every person who shall make any such contract or engage in any such combination or conspiracy, shall be deemed guilty of a misdemeanor, and, on conviction thereof, shall be punished by a fine not exceeding five thou-

95. Relevant portions of the Sherman Act, as amended, appear in Appendix A.

sand dollars, or by imprisonment not exceed one year, or by both said punishments, in the discretion of the court.

"SEC. 2. Every person who shall monopolize, or attempt to monopolize, or combine or conspire with any other person or persons, to monopolize any part of the trade or commerce among the several States, or with foreign nations, shall be deemed guilty of a misdemeanor, and, on conviction thereof, shall be punished by fine not exceeding five thousand dollars, or by imprisonment not exceeding one year, or by both said punishments, in the discretion of the court."

The act reflected a complex range of ideals, goals and practical necessities. It was one of several proposals aimed at maintaining the rate of economic growth, while containing the economic and political power of big business and distributing more evenly the material benefits of the industrialized economy. That it was passed at all is a tribute to the widely held antitrust sentiment. The act embodied this sentiment in an official statement of public policy and set the direction for future policy.

D. ANTITRUST: THE FIRST FEW DECADES

1. EARLY ELABORATION OF THE STATUTORY CONCEPT, RESTRAINT OF TRADE

During its first decade, the act was not used to challenge any of the great trusts. Some enforcement against cartels, however, was effective. The Supreme Court first considered the meaning of "restraint of trade" in a railroad price-fixing case. As you read this case and the ones that follow, evaluate the extent to which the Court found guidance in the common law tradition to which Congress had pointed.

UNITED STATES v. TRANS–MISSOURI FREIGHT ASSOCIATION
166 U.S. 290 (1897).

. . . On the 15th day of March, 1889, all but three of the defendants, the railway companies named in the bill, made and entered into an agreement by which they formed themselves into an association to be known as the "Trans–Missouri Freight Association," and they agreed to be governed by the provisions contained in the articles of agreement.

The memorandum of agreement . . . stated [that f]or the purpose of mutual protection by establishing and maintaining reasonable rates, rules, and regulations on all freight traffic, both through and local, the subscribers . . . agree to be governed by the following provisions:

* * *

Section 3 provides that "a committee shall be appointed to establish rates, rules, and regulations on the traffic subject of this association, and to consider changes therein, and make rules for meeting the competition of outside lines. Their conclusions, when unanimous, shall be made effective when they so order, but if they differ the question at issue shall be referred to the managers of the lines parties hereto; and if they disagree it shall be arbitrated in the manner provided in article 7."

* * *

"Sec. 5.   At each monthly meeting the association shall consider and vote upon all changes proposed, of which due notice has been given, and all parties shall be bound by the decisions of the association, as expressed, unless then and there the parties shall give the association definite written notice that, in ten days thereafter, they shall make such modification notwithstanding the vote of the association:

*   *   *

"Sec. 6.   Notwithstanding anything in this article contained, each member may, at its peril, make at any time, without previous notice, such rate, rule, or regulations as may be necessary to meet the competition of lines not members of the association, giving at the same time notice to the chairman of its action in the premises.   If the chairman, upon investigation, shall decide that such rate is not necessary to meet the direct competition of lines not members of the association, and shall so notify the road making the rate, it shall immediately withdraw such rate.   At the next meeting of the association held after the making of such rate, it shall be reported to the association, and if the association shall decide by a two-thirds vote that such rate was not made in good faith to meet such competition, the member offending shall be subject to the penalty provided in § 8 of this article.   If the association shall decide by a two-thirds vote that such rate was made in good faith to meet such competition, it shall be considered as authority for the rate so made.

*   *   *

"Sec. 8.   It shall be the duty of the chairman to investigate all apparent violations of the agreement, and to report his findings to the managers, who shall determine, by a majority vote (the member against whom complaint is made to have no vote), what, if any, penalty shall be assessed, the amount of each fine not to exceed $100, to be paid to the association.

*   *   *

On the 6th of January, 1892, the United States . . . [sued, seeking to have] the agreement between the defendant railroad companies set aside and declared illegal and void, and to have the association dissolved.

*   *   *

Justice Peckham:

. . . The next question to be discussed is as to what is the true construction of the statute, assuming that it applies to common carriers by railroad.   What is the meaning of the language as used in the statute, that "every contract, combination in the form of trust or otherwise, or conspiracy, in restraint of trade or commerce among the several states or with foreign nations is hereby declared to be illegal?"   Is it confined to a contract or combination which is only in unreasonable restraint of trade or commerce, or does it include what the language of the act plainly and in terms covers—all contracts of that nature?

We are asked to regard the title of this act as indicative of its purpose to include only those contracts which were unlawful at common law, but which require the sanction of a Federal statute in order to be dealt with in a Federal court.   It is said that when terms which are known to the common law are used in a Federal statute those terms are to be given the same meaning that they received at common law, and that when the language of the title is "to protect trade and commerce against unlawful restraints and monopolies," it means those restraints and monopolies which the common law regarded as unlawful, and which were to be prohibited by the Federal statute. We are of opinion that the language used in the title refers to and includes and was intended to include those restraints and monopolies which are made unlawful in the body of the statute. It is to the statute itself that resort must be had to learn the meaning thereof, though a resort to the title here creates no doubt about the meaning of and does not alter the plain language contained in its text.

It is now with much amplification of argument urged that the statute in declaring illegal every combination in the form of trust or otherwise, or conspiracy in restraint of trade or commerce, does not mean what the language used therein plainly imports, but that it only means to declare illegal any such contract which is in *unreasonable* restraint of trade, while leaving all others unaffected by the provisions of the act; that the common-law meaning of the term "contract in restraint of trade" includes only such contracts as are in *unreasonable* restraint of trade, and when that term is used in the Federal statute it is not intended to include all contracts in restraint of trade, but only those which are in unreasonable restraint thereof.

The term is not of such limited signification. Contracts in restraint of trade have been known and spoken of for hundreds of years both in England and in this country, and the term includes all kinds of those contracts which in fact restrain or may restrain trade. Some of such contracts have been held void and unenforceable in the courts by reason of their restraint being unreasonable, while others have been held valid because they were not of that nature. A contract may be in restraint of trade and still be valid at common law. Although valid, it is nevertheless a contract in restraint of trade, and would be so described either at common law or elsewhere. By the simple use of the term "contract in restraint of trade," all contracts of that nature, whether valid or otherwise, would be included, and not alone that kind of contract which was invalid and unenforceable as being in unreasonable restraint of trade. When, therefore, the body of an act pronounces as illegal every contract or combination in restraint of trade or commerce among the several states, etc., the plain and ordinary meaning of such language is not limited to that kind of contract alone which is in unreasonable restraint of trade, but all contracts are included in such language, and no exception or limitation can be added without placing in the act that which has been omitted by Congress.

Proceeding, however, upon the theory that the statute did not mean what its plain language imported, and that it intended in its prohibition to denounce as illegal only those contracts which were in unreasonable restraint of trade, the courts below have made an exhaustive investigation as to the general rules which guide courts in declaring contracts to be void as being in restraint of trade, and therefore against the public policy of the country. In the course of their discussion of that subject they have shown that there has been a gradual though great alteration in the extent of the liberty granted to the vendor of property in agreeing, as part consideration for his sale, not to enter into the same kind of business for a certain time or within a certain territory. So long as the sale was the bona fide consideration for the promise, and was not made a mere excuse for an evasion of the rule itself, the later authorities, both in England and in this country, exhibit a strong tendency towards enabling the parties to make such a contract in relation to the sale of property, including an agreement not to enter into the same kind of business, as they may think proper, and this with the view to granting to a vendor the freest opportunity to obtain the largest consideration for the sale of that which is his own. A contract which is the mere accompaniment of the sale of property, and thus entered into for the purpose of enhancing the price at which the vendor sells it, which in effect is collateral to such sale, and where the main purpose of the whole contract is accomplished by such sale, might not be included, within the letter or spirit of the statute in question. But we cannot see how the statute can be limited, as it has been by the courts below, without reading into its text an exception which alters the natural meaning of the language used, and that, too, upon a most material point, and where no sufficient reason is shown for believing that such alteration would make the statute more in accord with the intent of the lawmaking body that enacted it. . . .

To the question why competition should necessarily be conducted to such an extent as to result in this relentless and continued war, to eventuate only in the financial ruin of one or all of the companies indulging in it, the answer is made that if competing railroad companies be left subject to the sway of free and unrestricted competition the results above foreshadowed necessarily happen from the nature of the case; that competition being the rule, each company will seek business to the extent of its power, and will underbid its rival in order to get the business, and such underbidding will act and react upon each company until the prices are so reduced as to make it impossible to prosper or live under them; that it is too much to ask of human nature for one company to insist upon charges sufficiently high to afford a reasonable compensation, and while doing so to see its patrons leave for rival roads who are obtaining its business by offering less rates for doing it than can be afforded and a fair profit obtained therefrom. Sooner than experience ruin from mere inanition, efforts will be made in the direction of meeting the underbidding of its rival until both shall end in ruin. The only refuge, it is said, from this wretched end lies in the power of competing roads agreeing among themselves to keep up prices for transportation to such sums as shall be reasonable in themselves, so that companies may be allowed to save themselves from themselves, and to agree not to attack each other, but to keep up reasonable and living rates for the services performed. It is said that as railroads have a right to charge reasonable rates it must follow that a contract among themselves to keep up their charges to that extent is valid. Viewed in the light of all these facts it is broadly and confidently asserted that it is impossible to believe that Congress or any other intelligent and honest legislative body could ever have intended to include all contracts or combinations in restraint of trade, and as a consequence thereof to prohibit competing railways from agreeing among themselves to keep up prices for transportation to such a rate as should be fair and reasonable.

These arguments, it must be confessed, bear with much force upon the policy of an act which should prevent a general agreement upon the question of rates among competing railroad companies to the extent simply of maintaining those rates which were reasonable and fair.

There is another side to this question, however, and it may not be amiss to refer to one or two facts which tend to somewhat modify and alter the light in which the subject should be regarded. If only that kind of contract which is in unreasonable restraint of trade be within the meaning of the statute, and declared therein to be illegal, it is at once apparent that the subject of what is a reasonable rate is attended with great uncertainty. What is a proper standard by which to judge the fact of reasonable rates? Must the rate be so high as to enable the return for the whole business done to amount to a sum sufficient to afford the shareholder a fair and reasonable profit upon his investment? If so, what is a fair and reasonable profit? That depends sometimes upon the risk incurred, and the rate itself differs in different localities. Which is the one to which reference is to be made as the standard? Or is the reasonableness of the profit to be limited to a fair return upon the capital that would have been sufficient to build and equip the road, if honestly expended? Or is still another standard to be created, and the reasonableness of the charges tried by the cost of the carriage of the article and a reasonable profit allowed on that? And in such case would contribution to a sinking fund to make repairs upon the roadbed and renewal of cars, etc., be assumed as a proper item? Or is the reasonableness of the charge to be tested by reference to the charges for the transportation of the same kind of property made by other roads similarly situated? If the latter, a combination among such roads as to rates would, of course, furnish no means of answering the question. It is quite apparent, therefore, that it is exceedingly difficult to formulate even the terms of the rule itself which should govern in the matter of determining what would be reasonable rates for transportation. While even after the standard should be determined there is such an infinite variety of facts entering into the question of what is a reasonable rate, no matter what standard is adopted, that any individual shipper would in most cases be apt to abandon the effort to show the unreasonable character of a charge, sooner than hazard the great expense in time and money necessary to prove the fact, and at the same time incur the illwill of the road itself in all his future dealings with it. To say, therefore, that the act excludes agreements which are not in unreasonable restraint of trade, and which tend simply to keep up reasonable rates for transportation, is substantially to leave the question of reasonableness to the companies themselves.

* * *

. . . Upon the subject now under consideration it is well said by Judge Oliver P. Shiras, United States district court judge, northern district of Iowa, in his very able dissenting opinion in this case in the United States circuit court of appeals, as follows:

". . . It may be entirely true that as we proceed in the development of the policy of public control over railway traffic, methods will
be devised and put in operation by legislative enactment whereby
railway companies and the public may be protected against the evils
arising from unrestricted competition and from rate wars which
unsettle the business of the community, but I fail to perceive the force
of the argument that because railway companies *through their own
action cause evils to themselves* and the public by sudden changes or
reductions in tariff rates they must be permitted to deprive the
community of the benefit of competition in securing reasonable rates
for the transportation of the products of the country. Competition,
free and unrestricted, is the general rule which governs all the
ordinary business pursuits and transactions of life. Evils, as well as
benefits, result therefrom. In the fierce heat of competition the
stronger competitor may crush out the weaker; fluctuations in prices
may be caused that result in wreck and disaster; yet, balancing the
benefits as against the evils, the law of competition remains as a
controlling element in the business world. That free and unrestricted
competition in the matter of railroad charges may be productive of
evils does not militate against the fact that such is the law now
governing the subject. No law can be enacted nor system be devised
for the control of human affairs that in its enforcement does not
produce some evil results, no matter how beneficial its general purpose may be. There are benefits and there are evils which result
from the operation of the law of free competition between railway
companies. The time may come when the companies will be relieved
from the operation of this law, but they cannot, by combination and
agreements among themselves, bring about this change. . . ."

The arguments which have been addressed to us against the inclusion
of all contracts in restraint of trade, as provided for by the language of the
act, have been based upon the alleged presumption that Congress, notwithstanding the language of the act, could not have intended to embrace
all contracts, but only such contracts as were in unreasonable restraint of
trade. Under these circumstances we are, therefore, asked to hold that
the act of Congress excepts contracts which are not in unreasonable
restraint of trade, and which only keep rates up to a reasonable price,
notwithstanding the language of the act makes no such exception. . . .

This we cannot and ought not to do. . . .

It may be that the policy evidenced by the passage of the act itself
will, if carried out, result in disaster to the roads and in a failure to secure
the advantages sought from such legislation. Whether that will be the
result or not we do not know and cannot predict. These considerations
are, however, not for us. If the act ought to be read as contended for by

defendants, Congress is the body to amend it and not this court, by a
process of judicial legislation wholly unjustifiable. . . .

. . . In the view we have taken of the question, the intent alleged by
the government is not necessary to be proved. The question is one of law
in regard to the meaning and effect of the agreement itself, namely: Does
the agreement restrain trade or commerce in any way so as to be a

violation of the act? We have no doubt that it does. The agreement on its face recites that it is entered into "for the purpose of mutual protection by establishing and maintaining reasonable rates, rules, and regulations on all freight traffic, both through and local." To that end the association is formed and a body created which is to adopt rates, which, when agreed to, are to be the governing rates for all the companies, and a violation of which subjects the defaulting company to the payment of a penalty, and although the parties have a right to withdraw from the agreement on giving thirty days' notice of a desire so to do, yet while in force and assuming it to be lived up to, there can be no doubt that its direct, immediate, and necessary effect is to put a restraint upon trade or commerce as described in the act.

For these reasons the suit of the Government can be maintained without proof of the allegation that the agreement was entered into for the purpose of restraining trade or commerce or for maintaining rates above what was reasonable. The necessary effect of the agreement is to restrain trade or commerce, no matter what the intent was on the part of those who signed it. . . .

JUSTICE WHITE, dissenting: . . .

The plain intention of the law was to protect the liberty of contract and the freedom of trade. Will this intention not be frustrated by a construction which, if it does not destroy, at least gravely impairs, both the liberty of the individual to contract and the freedom of trade? If the rule of reason no longer determines the right of the individual to contract or secures the validity of contracts upon which trade depends and results, what becomes of the liberty of the citizen or the freedom of trade? Secured no longer by the law of reason, all these rights become subject, when questioned, to the mere caprice of judicial authority. Thus, a law in favor of freedom of contract, it seems to me, is so interpreted as to gravely impair that freedom. Progress and not reaction was the purpose of the act of Congress. The construction now given the act disregards the whole current of judicial authority and tests the right to contract by the conceptions of that right entertained at the time of the year books instead of by the light of reason and the necessity of modern society. To do this violates, as I see it, the plainest conception of public policy, for, as said by Sir G. Jessel, Master of the Rolls, in *Printing & N. Registering Co. v. Sampson,* L.R. 19 Eq. 465, "if there is one thing which more than another public policy requires it is that men of full age and competent understanding shall have the utmost liberty of contracting, and their contracts when entered into freely and voluntarily shall be held sacred and shall be enforced by courts of justice." . . .

Questions and Comments

According to Justice Peckham, what is a restraint of trade? What was the role of the common law in informing construction of the words "restraint of trade"? What restraints were legal? Were there exceptions?

In *Trans–Missouri*, what was the nature of the railroads' agreement on rates? Did the member railroads agree to charge the same rates? Did they have a right, under their agreement, not to do so? Under what circumstances? What was the consequence of failing to follow the rules?

Why did the member railroads care if any one of them deviated from the established rates? Would you expect the members to follow the rules? Would you expect them to deviate from the association rates under the procedures outlined by the rules? How do you think this agreement would probably affect shippers? How would it affect the railroads themselves?

What was the purpose of the agreement? Does purpose matter? Whatever their purpose, did the railroads intend to fix rates? Did they intend to fix reasonable rates? What is a "reasonable" rate? Did they have any incentive to fix "unreasonable" rates?

The railroads claimed that they set reasonable rates, and that it was necessary, in the public interest,[96] for them to do so. What was the public interest in rate-fixing? Who, according to the railroads, would be benefited? Would the buyers of the railroads' services (shippers) be benefited? Should the Court have attempted to measure the benefits to buyers? Should a court approve agreements if buyers get a net benefit?

While the Court rejected a rule of reason, it nonetheless considered many factors and values in the process of devising a rule of law. How important to the Court was each of the following: (1) Governance of the market by competition rather than by private agreement. (2) The independence and opportunity of "small dealers and worthy men." (3) The freedom of action of the railroads. (4) The price of transportation and the shipper's freedom of choice. (5) Prices and freedom of choice of the ultimate consumer. (6) The extent to which the shipper and derivatively the ultimate consumer may be exploited by the railroads by a price significantly above the railroads' costs. (7) Judicial administrability of the Sherman Act. What were the sources of these values? Were they part of the common law tradition evoked by the phrase, "restraint of trade"? Were they validated by the legislative history? By the "politics of antitrust," that is, the amorphous range of concerns that led to the statute? How important (or irrelevant) were each of these considerations to Justice White?

What value do *you* put on each of the considerations? Speaking as legislator (or a philosopher-king), which would you identify as important underpinnings of, or considerations to be addressed by, antitrust policy? Speaking as a judge interpreting the Sherman Act, would you apply the considerations or values you have identified as paramount? On what basis do you think you can properly do so?

Trans–Missouri involved an open and notorious agreement by railroads to regulate themselves. The railroads entered into this agreement before the Sherman Act was passed. If price-fixing was initiated after passage of the Sherman Act, it was likely to be done secretly. Shortly after the decision in *Trans–Missouri*, a case involving a secret iron pipe cartel came before a panel of the Court of Appeals for the Sixth Circuit. Judge (later President, and later still, Chief Justice) William Howard Taft wrote the Court's opinion.

---

96. The Interstate Commerce Act was enacted in 1887, but the Interstate Commerce Commission (ICC) did not then have the power to fix and enforce rates.

UNITED STATES v. ADDYSTON PIPE & STEEL CO.

85 F. 271 (6th Cir.1898), *modified* and *aff'd,* 175 U.S. 211 (1899).

JUDGE TAFT:

. . . The argument for defendants is that their contract of association was not, and could not be, a monopoly, because their aggregate tonnage capacity did not exceed 30 per cent. of the total tonnage capacity of the country; that the restraints upon the members of the association, if restraints they could be called, did not embrace all the states, and were not unlimited in space; that such partial restraints were justified and upheld at common law if reasonable, and only proportioned to the necessary protection of the parties; that in this case the partial restraints were reasonable, because without them each member would be subjected to ruinous competition by the other, and did not exceed in degree of stringency or scope what was necessary to protect the parties in securing prices for their product that were fair and reasonable to themselves and the public; that competition was not stifled by the association because the prices fixed by it had to be fixed with reference to the very active competition of pipe companies which were not members of the association, and which had more than double the defendants' capacity; that in this way the association only modified and restrained the evils of ruinous competition, while the public had all the benefit from competition which public policy demanded.

From early times it was the policy of Englishmen to encourage trade in England, and to discourage those voluntary restraints which tradesmen were often induced to impose on themselves by contract. Courts recognized this public policy by refusing to enforce stipulations of this character. The objections to such restraints were mainly two. One was that by such contracts a man disabled himself from earning a livelihood with the risk of becoming a public charge, and deprived the community of the benefit of his labor. The other was that such restraints tended to give to the covenantee, the beneficiary of such restraints, a monopoly of the trade, from which he had thus excluded one competitor, and by the same means might exclude others.

* * *

The inhibition against restraints of trade at common law seems at first to have had no exception. See language of Justice Hull, Year Book, 2 Hen. V., folio 5, pl. 26. After a time it became apparent to the people and the courts that it was in the interest of trade that certain covenants in restraint of trade should be enforced. It was of importance, as an incentive to industry and honest dealing in trade, that, after a man had built up a business with an extensive good will, he should be able to sell his business and good will to the best advantage, and he could not do so unless he could bind himself by an enforceable contract not to engage in the same business in such a way as to prevent injury to that which he was about to sell. It was equally for the good of the public and trade, when partners dissolved, and one took the business, or they divided the business, that each partner might bind himself not to do anything in trade thereafter which would derogate from his grant of the interest conveyed to his former partner. Again, when two men became partners in a business, although their union might reduce competition, this effect was only an incident to the main purpose of a union of their capital, enterprise, and energy to carry on a successful business, and one useful to the community. Restrictions in the articles of partnership upon the business activity of the members, with a view of securing their entire effort in the common enterprise, were, of course, only ancillary to the main end of the union, and were to be encouraged. Again, when one in business sold property with which the buyer might set up a rival business, it was certainly reasonable that the seller should be able to restrain the buyer from doing him an injury which, but for the sale, the buyer would be unable to inflict. This was not reducing competition, but was only securing the seller against an increase of competition of his own creating. Such an exception was necessary to promote the free purchase and sale of property. Again, it was of importance that business men and professional men should have every motive to employ the ablest assistants, and to instruct them thoroughly; but they would naturally be reluctant to do so unless such assistants were able to bind themselves not to set up a rival business in the vicinity after learning the details and secrets of the business of their employers.

* * *

For the reasons given, then, covenants in partial restraint of trade are generally upheld as valid when they are agreements (1) by the seller of property or business not to compete with the buyer in such a way as to derogate from the value of the property or business sold; (2) by a retiring partner not to compete with the firm; (3) by a partner pending the partnership not to do anything to interfere, by competition or otherwise, with the business of the firm; (4) by the buyer of property not to use the same in competition with the business retained by the seller; and (5) by an assistant, servant, or agent not to compete with his master or employer after the expiration of his time of service. Before such agreements are upheld, however, the court must find that the restraints attempted thereby are reasonably necessary (1, 2, and 3) to the enjoyment by the buyer of the property, good will, or interest in the partnership bought; or (4) to the legitimate ends of the existing partnership; or (5) to the prevention of possible injury to the business of the seller from use by the buyer of the thing sold; or (6) to protection from the danger of loss to the employer's business caused by the unjust use of the part of the employe of the confidential knowledge acquired in such business.

* * *

It would be stating it too strongly to say that these five classes of covenants in restraint of trade include all of those upheld as valid at the common law; but it would certainly seem to follow from the tests laid down for determining the validity of such an agreement that no conventional restraint of trade can be enforced unless the covenant embodying it is merely ancillary to the main purpose of a lawful contract, and necessary to protect the covenantee in the enjoyment of the legitimate fruits of the contract, or to protect him from the dangers of an unjust use of those fruits by the other party. . . .

This very statement of the rule implies that the contract must be one in which there is a main purpose, to which the covenant in restraint of trade is merely ancillary. The covenant is inserted only to protect one of the parties from the injury which, in the execution of the contract or enjoyment of its fruits, he may suffer from the unrestrained competition of the other. The main purpose of the contract suggests the measure of protection needed, and furnishes a sufficiently uniform standard by which the validity of such restraints may be judicially determined. In such a case, if the restraint exceeds the necessity presented by the main purpose of the contract, it is void for two reasons: First, because it oppresses the covenantor, without any corresponding benefit to the covenantee; and, second, because it tends to a monopoly. But where the sole object of both parties in making the contract as expressed therein is merely to restrain competition, and enhance or maintain prices, it would seem that there was nothing to justify or excuse the restraint, that it would necessarily have a tendency to monopoly, and therefore would be void. In such a case there is no measure of what is necessary to the protection of either party, except the vague and varying opinion of judges as to how much, on principles of political economy, men ought to be allowed to restrain competition. There is in such contracts no main lawful purpose, to subserve which partial restraint is permitted, and by which its reasonableness is measured, but the sole object is to restrain trade in order to avoid the competition which it has always been the policy of the common law to foster.

Much has been said in regard to the relaxing of the original strictness of the common law in declaring contracts in restraint of trade void as conditions of civilization and public policy have changed, and the argument drawn therefrom is that the law now recognizes that competition may be so ruinous as to injure the public, and, therefore, that contracts made with a view to check such ruinous competition and regulate prices, though in restraint of trade, and having no other purpose, will be upheld. We think this conclusion is unwarranted by the authorities when all of them are considered.

* * *

It is true that there are some cases in which the courts, mistaking, as we conceive, the proper limits of the relaxation of the rules for determining the unreasonableness of restraints of trade, have set sail on a sea of doubt, and have assumed the power to say, in respect to contracts which have no other purpose and no other consideration on either side than the mutual restraint of the parties, how much restraint of competition is in the public interest, and how much is not.

The manifest danger in the administration of justice according to so shifting, vague, and indeterminate a standard would seem to be a strong reason against adopting it.

* * *

In Wickens v. Evans [3 Younge & J. 318] three trunk manufacturers of England, who had competed with each other throughout the realm to their loss, agreed to divide England into three districts, each party to have one district exclusively for his trade, and, if any stranger should invade the district of either as a competitor, they agreed "to meet to devise means to promote their own views." The restraint was held partial and reasonable, because it left the trade open to any third party in either district. In answer to the suggestion that such an agreement to divide up the beer business of London among the London brewers would lead to the abuses of monopoly, it was replied that outside competition would soon cure such abuses,—an answer that would validate the most complete local monopoly of the present day. It may be, as suggested by the court, that local monopolies cannot endure long, because their very existence tempts outside capital into competition; but the public policy embodied in the common law requires the discouragement of monopolies, however temporary their existence may be. The public interest may suffer severely while new competition is slowly developing. The case can hardly be reconciled with later cases, hereafter to be referred to, in England and America. It is true that there was in this case no direct evidence of a desire by the parties to regulate prices, and it has been sometimes explained on the theory that the agreement was solely to reduce the expenses incident to a business covering the realm by restricting its territorial extent; but it is difficult to escape the conclusion that the restraint upon each two of the three parties was imposed to secure to the other a monopoly and power to control prices in the territory assigned to him, because the final clause in the contract implies that, when it was executed, there were no other competitors except the parties in the territory divided.

* * *

Upon this review of the law and the authorities, we can have no doubt that the association of the defendants, however reasonable the prices they fixed, however great the competition they had to encounter, and however great the necessity for curbing themselves by joint agreement from committing financial suicide by ill-advised competition, was void at common law, because in restraint of trade, and tending to a monopoly. But the facts of the case do not require us to go so far as this, for they show that the attempted justification of this association on the grounds stated is without foundation.

The defendants, being manufacturers and vendors of cast-iron pipe, entered into a combination to raise the prices for pipe for all the states west and south of New York, Pennsylvania, and Virginia, constituting considerably more than three-quarters of the territory of the United States, and significantly called by the associates "pay territory." Their joint annual output was 220,000 tons. The total capacity of all the other cast-iron pipe manufacturers in the pay territory was 170,500 tons. Of this, 45,000 tons was the capacity of mills in Texas, Colorado, and Oregon, so far removed from that part of the pay territory where the demand was considerable that necessary freight rates excluded them from the possibility of competing, and 12,000 tons was the possible annual capacity of a mill at St. Louis, which was practically under the same management as that of one of the defendants' mills. Of the remainder of the mills in pay territory and outside of the combination, one was at Columbus, Ohio, two in northern Ohio, and one in Michigan. Their aggregate possible annual capacity was about one-half the usual annual output of the defendants' mills. They were, it will be observed, at the extreme northern end of the pay territory, while the defendants' mills at Cincinnati, Louisville, Chattanooga, and South Pittsburg, and Anniston, and Bessemer, were grouped much nearer to the center of the pay territory. The freight upon cast-iron pipe amounts to a considerable percentage of the price at which manufacturers can deliver it at any great distance from the place of manufacture. Within the margin of the freight per ton which Eastern manufacturers would have to pay to deliver pipe in pay territory, the defendants, by controlling two-thirds of the output in pay territory, were practically able to fix prices. The competition of the Ohio and Michigan mills, of course, somewhat affected their power in this respect in the northern part of the pay territory; but, the further south the place of delivery was to be, the more complete the monopoly over the trade which the defendants were able to exercise, within the limit already described. Much evidence is adduced upon affidavit to prove that defendants had no power arbitrarily to fix prices, and that they were always obliged to meet competition. To the extent that they could not impose prices on the public in excess of the cost price of pipe with freight from the Atlantic seaboard added, this is true; but, within that limit, they could fix prices as they chose. The most cogent evidence that they had this power is the fact, everywhere apparent in the record, that they exercised it. The details of the way in which it was maintained are somewhat obscured by the manner in which the proof was adduced in the court below, upon affidavits solely, and without the clarifying effect of cross-examination, but quite enough appears to leave no doubt of the ultimate fact. The defendants were, by their combination, therefore able to deprive the public in a large territory of the advantages otherwise accruing to them from the proximity of defendants' pipe factories, and, by keeping prices just low enough to prevent competition by Eastern manufacturers, to compel the public to pay an increase over what the price would have been, if fixed by competition between defendants, nearly equal to the advantage in freight rates enjoyed by defendants over Eastern competitors. The defendants acquired this power by voluntarily agreeing to sell only at prices fixed by their committee, and by allowing the highest bidder at the secret "auction pool" to become the lowest bidder of them at the public letting. Now, the restraint thus imposed on themselves was only partial. It did not cover the United States. There was not a complete monopoly. It was tempered by the fear of competition, and it affected only a part of the price. But this certainly does not take the contract of association out of the annulling effect of the rule against monopolies. In U.S. v. E.C. Knight Co., 156 U.S. 1, 16, Chief Justice Fuller, in speaking for the court, said:

> "Again, all the authorities agree that, in order to vitiate a contract or combination, it is not essential that its result should be a complete monopoly. It is sufficient if it really tends to that end, and to deprive the public of the advantages which flow from free competition."

It has been earnestly pressed upon us that the prices at which the cast-iron pipe was sold in pay territory were reasonable. A great many affidavits of purchasers of pipe in pay territory, all drawn by the same hand or from the same model, are produced, in which the affiants say that, in their opinion, the prices at which pipe has been sold by defendants have been reasonable. We do not think the issue an important one, because, as already stated, we do not think that at common law there is any question of reasonableness open to the courts with reference to such a contract. Its tendency was certainly to give defendants the power to charge unreasonable prices, had they chosen to do so. But, if it were important, we should unhesitatingly find that the prices charged in the instances which were in evidence were unreasonable. The letters from the manager of the Chattanooga foundry written to the other defendants, and discussing the prices fixed by the association, do not leave the slightest doubt upon this point, and outweigh the perfunctory affidavits produced by the defendants. The cost of producing pipe at Chattanooga, together with a reasonable profit, did not exceed $15 a ton. It could have been delivered at Atlanta at $17 to $18 a ton, and yet the lowest price which that foundry was permitted by the rules of the association to bid was $24.25. The same thing was true all through pay territory to a greater or less degree, and especially at "reserved cities." . . .

* * *

Questions and Comments

Does Judge Taft accept the reasoning, or some it, of Justice Peckham? Of Justice White? What refinements does he bring to the law?

In *Addyston Pipe*, Judge Taft introduces the concept of "the covenant in restraint of trade [that] is merely ancillary." What does he mean? The concept of the ancillary restraint has survived and plays an important role in modern analysis.

According to Judge Taft, if a restraint of trade is not ancillary to a legitimate main purpose and its central and sole object is to avoid competition, it is a "naked" restraint of trade. How does the law treat naked restraints, according to Judge Taft? Was the pipe producers' agreement to curb competition among themselves a naked or an ancillary restraint? Did the Court inquire into the purpose and effect of this agreement? Why?

Note the Court's economic analysis. After 1893, when Alfred Marshall's book first appeared, most economists viewed cartels as contractual arrangements that yielded results substantially equivalent to monopoly. Is the Court's opinion consistent with this theoretical view?

What was the market (the area within which defendants allegedly exercised power to raise price above costs)?[97] In this market, what was the relationship between supply and demand? Why does the Court use as a basis for comparison capacity of non-member producers and output of member producers? If member producers raised price above cost, what would (did) happen? Did geographically distant sellers face any barriers? Was there a lid on member producers' ability to charge supracompetitive prices? How did the lid come about? Did it adequately protect the consumer?

After the Taft opinion in *Addyston Pipe*, the Supreme Court decided its second railroad price-fixing case. The members of the Joint Traffic Association (railroads east of the Mississippi River) had a rate-fixing agreement similar to that in *Trans–Missouri*, except that a member company could

---

97. "Costs" includes a return on investment sufficient to draw capital to the market.

deviate from the association's rate schedule if its board of directors adopted a resolution to do so and served notice on the association. While defendants claimed this right to deviate to be material, the eastern railroads' principal argument did not depend upon factual distinctions. Their principal argument was that the Supreme Court could not have meant what it said in *Trans–Missouri*. The principle of *Trans–Missouri*, they argued, unreasonably interfered with liberty and property and with most normal business transactions.

Justice Peckham again wrote for the Supreme Court. The Court reaffirmed *Trans-Missouri*, with Justice White and others again dissenting. The Court, however, softened its dictum that all restraints are illegal, stating that the formation of corporations, partnership agreements, joint sales agencies, and sales or leases with ancillary covenants not to compete, have never been regarded as contracts in restraint of trade.

The Court addressed once again the defense of ruinous competition.

UNITED STATES v. JOINT TRAFFIC ASSOCIATION
171 U.S. 505 (1898).

JUSTICE PECKHAM: . . . [I]t is contended that agreements between railroad companies of the nature of that now before us are promotive instead of in restraint of trade.

This conclusion is reached by counsel after an examination of the peculiar nature of railroad property and the alleged baneful effects of competition upon it and also upon the public. It is stated that the only resort open to railroads to save themselves from the effects of a ruinous competition is that of agreements among themselves to check and control it. A ruinous competition is, as they say, apt to be carried on until the weakest of the combatants goes to destruction. After that the survivor, being relieved from competition, proceeds to raise its prices as high as the business will bear. Commerce, it is said, thus finally becomes restrained by the effects of competition, while at the same time otherwise valuable railroad property is thereby destroyed or greatly reduced in value. There can be no doubt that the general tendency of competition among competing railroads is towards lower rates for transportation, and the result of lower rates is generally a greater demand for the articles so transported, and this greater demand can only be gratified by a larger supply, the furnishing of which increases commerce. This is the first and direct result of competition among railroad carriers.

In the absence of any agreement restraining competition, this result, it is argued, is neutralized, and the opposite one finally reached by reason of the peculiar nature of railroad property which must be operated and the capital invested in which cannot be withdrawn, and the railroad managers are therefore, as is claimed, compelled to, not only compete among themselves for business, but also to carry on the war of competition until it shall terminate in the utter destruction or the buying up of the weaker roads, after which the survivor will raise the rates as high as is possible. Thus, the indirect but final effect of competition is claimed to be the raising of rates and the consequent restraint of trade, and it is urged that this result is only to be prevented by such an agreement as we have here. In that way alone it is said that competition is overcome, and general uniformity and reasonableness of rates securely established.

The natural, direct and immediate effect of competition is, however, to lower rates, and to thereby increase the demand for commodities, the supplying of which increases commerce, and an agreement whose first and direct effect is to prevent this play of competition restrains instead of promoting trade and commerce. Whether, in the absence of an agreement as to rates, the consequences described by counsel will in fact follow as a result of competition, is matter of very great uncertainty, depending upon many contingencies and in large degree upon the voluntary action of the managers of the several roads. Railroad companies may and often do continue in existence and engage in their lawful traffic at some profit, although they are competing railroads and are not acting under any agreement or combination with their competitors upon the subject of rates. It appears from the brief of counsel in this case that the agreement in question does not embrace all of the lines or systems engaged in the business of railroad transportation between Chicago and the Atlantic coast. It cannot be said that destructive competition, or, in other words, war to the death, is bound to result unless an agreement or combination to avoid it is entered into between otherwise competing roads.

It is not only possible, but probable, that good sense and integrity of purpose would prevail among the managers, and while making no agreement and entering into no combination by which the whole railroad interest as herein represented should act as one combined and consolidated body, the managers of each road might yet make such reasonable charges for the business done by it as the facts might justify. An agreement of the nature of this one, which directly and effectually stifles competition, must be regarded under the statute as one in restraint of trade, notwithstanding there are possibilities that a restraint of trade may also follow competition that may be indulged in until the weaker roads are completely destroyed and the survivor thereafter raises rates and maintains them. . . .

Questions and Comments

Did the Court treat the railroads' argument too cavalierly? Can the Court's position be sustained even if the railroads' prediction is credible? Suppose there is too much capital in the industry. Is price cutting a good way to shake some of it out? Is it likely to result in withdrawal of the least efficient capital? Might a cartel be a socially better solution? Suppose the over-capitalization is temporary—the problem is a short-term downturn in demand. Can cartelization be defended as a way of holding capacity in the market until demand rises again? Some European and Asian antitrust systems have some means for authorizing "crisis cartels." Should the United States? Who should decide when and how competition should be moderated?

In 1906 the Interstate Commerce Commission initiated railroad rate regulation.[98] In 1948, Congress passed the Reed–Bulwinkle Act, allowing

98. The ICC was given power to fix rates in 1906. In 1920, the ICC was authorized to fix minimum as well as maximum prices.

railroads to fix rates collectively through rate bureaus and giving them antitrust immunity for doing so. Moreover, as a result of numerous railroad mergers, the potential for destructive competition among railroads has greatly diminished. What public policy reasons favor regulation of railroad rates? What forces of supply and demand exert downward pressure on these rates? In recent years the scope of Reed–Bulwinkle antitrust immunities have been restricted by legislation.[99]

In *Addyston Pipe & Steel* defendants appealed to the Supreme Court from the judgment against them. They argued that Congress had no power under the Commerce Clause to prohibit their agreement; they claimed that the exercise of such power would impair their constitutional guarantee of liberty of contract. They also argued that their arrangement had no direct effect on interstate commerce. The Supreme Court rejected all of these contentions. In another opinion by Justice Peckham, the Court quoted approvingly from Judge Taft's lower court opinion. It affirmed the judgment for plaintiff, modifying it only to exclude wholly intrastate activities.

The following excerpt from the Supreme Court's opinion responds to defendants' argument that their agreement to select one of their number to make the lowest bid among themselves could not operate as a restraint of trade because its purpose was to obtain a contract, not to limit the number and extent of contracts.

ADDYSTON PIPE & STEEL CO. v. UNITED STATES
175 U.S. 211 (1899).

JUSTICE PECKHAM: . . . This [argument] takes no heed of the purpose and effect of the combination to restrain the action of the parties to it so that there shall be no competition among them to obtain the contract for themselves.

We have no doubt that where the direct and immediate effect of a contract or combination among particular dealers in a commodity is to destroy competition between them and others, so that the parties to the contract or combination may obtain increased prices for themselves, such contract or combination amounts to a restraint of trade in the commodity, even though contracts to buy such commodity at the enhanced price are continually being made. Total suppression of the trade in the commodity is not necessary in order to render the combination one in restraint of trade. It is the effect of the combination in limiting and restricting the right of each of the members to transact business in the ordinary way, as well as its effect upon the volume or extent of the dealing in the commodity, that is regarded. All the facts and circumstances are, however, to be considered in order to determine the fundamental question— whether the necessary effect of the combination is to restrain interstate commerce.

If iron pipe cost $100 a ton instead of the prices which the record shows were paid for it, no one, we think, would contend that the trade in it would amount to as much as if the lower prices prevailed. The higher

99. The Staggers Rail Act of 1980, P.L. 96–448, 94 Stat. 1895, virtually eliminated antitrust immunities for certain types of collective ratemaking, encouraging carriers instead to rely on individual rate revisions. Dun's Business Month, Jan. 1984, at 105.

price would operate as a direct restraint upon the trade, and therefore any contract or combination which enhanced the price might in some degree restrain the trade in the article. It is not material that the combination did not prevent the letting of any particular contract. Such was not its purpose. On the contrary, the more contracts to be let the better for the combination. It was formed not for the object of preventing the letting of contracts, but to restrain the parties to it from competing for contracts, and thereby to enhance the prices to be obtained for the pipe dealt in by those parties. And when by reason of the combination a particular contract may have been obtained for one of the parties thereto, but at a higher price than would otherwise have been paid, the charge that the combination was one in restraint of trade is not answered by the statement that the particular contract was in truth obtained and not prevented. The parties to such a combination might realize more profit by the higher prices they would secure than they could earn by doing more work at a much less price. The question is as to the effect of such combination upon the trade in the article, and if that effect be to destroy competition and thus advance the price, the combination is one in restraint of trade.

* * *

Thus, at the turn of the century, all agreements among competitors that had the "direct and immediate" effect of restraining trade were banned by Section 1 of the Sherman Act, whereas agreements reasonably collateral to legitimate business transactions were not. The Taft opinion in *Addyston Pipe* convincingly argues that this development is generally consistent with the American common law tradition, to which Congress was apparently pointing. A divided Court had rejected the view that all agreements must be tested by the standard of reasonableness.

2. POST–SHERMAN ACT CONSOLIDATION

a. *The Business Climate*

During the first decade or so the Sherman Act may have discouraged cartelization and certainly precluded open cartels. But none of the great trusts was directly challenged, and the further concentration of business was not checked. In fact, most of the twentieth century's giant firms emerged in the 1890s. The large integrated industrial firm had been the exception in 1890, but by the end of the post-Sherman Act merger wave, "the modern multiunit industrial enterprise became a standard instrument for managing the production and distribution of goods in America." [1]

The merger movement, or the "trustification" process as historian Hans Thorelli calls it, came in two spurts, one lasting from 1890 to 1893 and the other, much larger wave beginning in 1895 and ending about 1904.[2] The high point of the merger activity was in 1899 when 1,208 firms disappeared as the result of mergers.[3] In 1897, only eight industrial companies had more than $50 million in capital, but by 1903, there were

1. Visible Hand at 345.

2. R. Nelson, Merger Movements in American Industry, 1895–1956 34 (1959) (hereinafter Merger Movements). Periodization is by no means standard; it varies among historians.

3. Id. at 37.

40 such companies.[4] By the end of the merger movement in 1904, 318 corporations owned 40% of all manufacturing assets.[5]

The shift was so marked and rapid that the second merger wave has been labeled "the corporate revolution." [6] Businesses combined to stabilize prices in order to control entry, and to create new marketing systems to serve their unique needs. These motives alone, however, cannot explain the tremendous merger activity in the late 1890s. Three other factors encouraged business combination: 1) the economic success of the trusts formed in the 1880s; 2) the maturation of the industrial finance system, and 3) the favorable legal and political climate for consolidation, as opposed to pooling.

The success of the 1800s trusts strongly influenced the "consolidation craze." At the time the Sherman Act was passed, according to Chandler, only eight trusts actually existed.[7] In part, the low number of trusts was due to the conservative nature of many business people. Business leaders hesitated to adopt an organizational device that had yet to prove economically sound. The early trusts, reorganized as holding companies under accommodating state law, proved their resiliency in the 1893–1895 depression. As independent businesses and loose combinations fell by the wayside, business leaders "could not help but notice that prices fell less rapidly and that their fellow capitalists suffered less severely in those industries that had been successfully consolidated." [8] The apparent success of the trusts prompted many businesses to combine when the economy began to recover.[9]

The maturation of certain financial institutions—the securities market in particular—provided the means, and often the motive, for combination during the 1890s. By the mid- to late 1890s, a system for organizing and financing consolidation was firmly in place. About a dozen large investment banking houses financed the mergers and marketed securities to "retail outlets" such as banks, trust companies, and brokerage houses.[10] The financiers were intimately connected with the operations of the newly formed mergers. Because the merger could only offer non-liquid collateral to secure its financing, financiers had a greater incentive to monitor the continuing welfare of the company.[11] Thus, the financier's power over the operations of the corporation greatly increased "until by 1900, he was conceived to be the most important figure in a stage called finance capitalism." [12]

b. The Political and Legal Climate

Those keeping a nervous eye on antitrust enforcement in the first few years soon discovered that, except for challenging blatant cartels, the government was doing little to preserve competition. As historian Arthur

4. T. Cochran, The American Business System 58–59 (1957) (hereinafter American Business System).

5. Emergence of Oligopoly at 16.

6. Id. at 2.

7. Visible Hand at 320.

8. Emergence of Oligopoly at 17.

9. Id.; L. Hacker, The Course of American Economic Growth and Development 247 (1970) (hereinafter Course of American Economic Growth).

10. American Business System at 80.

11. Federal Antitrust Policy at 178.

12. American Business System at 79.

Johnson puts it, the government followed a "policy of drift" because it was generally well-disposed towards business and did not want to impede growth.[13] President Harrison was no trust buster; under his administration, only seven Sherman suits were prosecuted. Cleveland and later McKinley were also indifferent, if not hostile, to antitrust. Their Justice Departments filed eight and three Sherman Act suits, respectively. It is emblematic that Richard Olney, the attorney general in the Cleveland administration, had defended the whiskey trust against the government's prosecution the year before he took office. The McKinley administration's ties to business help to explain why, at the height of the merger movement and renewed opposition to trusts, the government prosecuted the fewest cases of any administration during the 1890s.[14]

Congress tolerated the weak enforcement during the 1890s. Many members apparently preferred not to pursue the issue once the Sherman Act had passed and the "trust busters" had been temporarily appeased. Even those less favorably disposed towards big business apparently thought private enforcement of the Act would suffice. At any rate, Congress failed to allot additional money to the Department of Justice to implement the law. In reality, however, private parties instigated few antitrust suits, and the lack of government funding hampered the prosecution of the few cases the Department of Justice did pursue. During election years, the political parties usually wrote an obligatory pro-antitrust statement into their platforms, but their real concerns were tariffs, free silver, the poor state of the economy, and the Spanish–American War.

The Supreme Court, too, facilitated the "policy of drift" by its narrow construction of antitrust and other regulatory legislation.[15] Relying on the freedom of contract doctrine and an elaboration of the due process clause, the Court consistently protected private enterprise from state interference throughout the 1890s.[16] The Court's early antitrust decisions tended to encourage businesses to abandon loose combinations like price-fixing agreements and pools—especially after *Addyston Pipe*—but it did little to discourage combinations into single legal enterprises.[17]

13. Johnson, Antitrust Policy in Transition, 1908: Ideal and Reality, 48 Miss.Valley Hist.Rev. 415, 416 (1961) (hereinafter Antitrust Policy in Transition).

14. Federal Antitrust Policy at 398–410; W.H. Harbaugh, Power and Responsibility: The Life and Times of Theodore Roosevelt 158 (1961) (hereinafter Power and Responsibility).

15. Federal Antitrust Policy at 254; Law and Freedom at 34–70.

16. For example, in 1890 the Court retreated from Munn v. Illinois, 94 U.S. 113 (1876), which held that a state could regulate the rates of business that were "clothed with the public interest." The Court ruled in

Chicago, Milwaukee & St. Paul Railway v. Minnesota, 134 U.S. 418 (1890), that the reasonableness of rates was ultimately a matter for judicial review, thus weakening the states' regulatory power. For further analysis, see A. Paul, Legal Progressivism, the Courts, and the Crisis of the 1890s, in American Law and the Constitutional Order 283 (L. Friedman and H. Scheiber eds. 1978) (hereinafter American Law and Constitutional Order); McCurdy, Justice Field and the Jurisprudence of Government Business Relations, 61 J.Am.Hist. 970, 971–73 (1975).

17. Visible Hand at 332–33.

c. The Knight Case and Nonenforcement Against Tight Combinations

The first Sherman Act case to reach the Supreme Court was *United States v. E.C. Knight Company.*[18] The government had challenged the American Sugar Refining Company's acquisition of four major sugar refiners, giving the company control over almost all of U.S. domestic sugar refining. By these acquisitions, the government alleged, the American Sugar Refinery Company monopolized the manufacture and sale of refined sugar in the United States.

The district court, however, dismissed the complaint, and the Supreme Court affirmed its judgment. According to Chief Justice Fuller, who spoke for the Court, the Sherman Act prohibited only restraints of interstate or international trade or commerce. Because the acquired refineries were all located in Pennsylvania, defendants' sugar monopoly was held not to restrain interstate or international trade or commerce but "only" manufacture.

Chief Justice Fuller wrote:

> In the view which we take of the case, we need not discuss whether because the tentacles which drew the outlying refineries into the dominant corporation were separately put out, therefore there was no combination to monopolize; or, because, according to political economists, aggregations of capital may reduce prices, therefore the objection to concentration of power is relieved; or, because others were theoretically left free to go into the business of refining sugar, and the original stockholders of the Philadelphia refineries after becoming stockholders of the American Company might go into competition with themselves, or, parting with that stock, might set up again for themselves, therefore no objectionable restraint was imposed.

> The fundamental question is, whether conceding that the existence of a monopoly in manufacture is established by the evidence, that monopoly can be directly suppressed under the act of Congress in the mode attempted by this bill.

> It cannot be denied that the power of a State to protect the lives, health, and property of its citizens, and to preserve good order and the public morals, "the power to govern men and things within the limits of its dominion," is a power originally and always belonging to the States, not surrendered by them to the general government, nor directly restrained by the Constitution of the United States, and essentially exclusive. The relief of the citizens of each State from the burden of monopoly and the evils resulting from the restraint of trade among such citizens was left with the States to deal with . . . .

Historian Charles McCurdy has characterized the *Knight* decision as consistent with earlier cases which strictly maintained the division between the state's power over manufacturing and the federal government's power over interstate commerce.[19] Thorelli, however, suggests that Attorney General Olney carried the *Knight* case to court with a noticeable lack of preparation. In general, says Thorelli, "the lack of a well-integrated judicial interpretation of the Sherman Act" stemmed from a lack of a

---

18. 156 U.S. 1 (1895). **19.** Knight Sugar Decision at 319–23.

coherent plan of prosecution.[20] Whether or not the Court deserves the blame some have heaped upon it for eviscerating the Sherman Act,[21] the *Knight* decision did tend to weaken antitrust regulation and to sanction implicitly the use of the holding company, a trend that continued at least until the *Northern Securities* decision in 1903.[22]

If the national administration and the court aided the "corporate revolution" with relatively inactive antitrust enforcement, state legislatures paved the way for mergers by liberalizing corporation laws. A study of merger movements indicates a strong correlation between liberalization of corporation laws and high levels of merger activity.[23] The economic advantages to states hosting huge consolidations became quickly apparent after New Jersey, in 1888, increased its revenue by authorizing holding companies. New York and Delaware soon followed this lead and state competition for revenue through liberalized corporate law began.[24]

The New Jersey law offered the most useful form of corporate organization. Aside from the legal advantage it had over the trust or the cartel, the holding company was also a relatively inexpensive mechanism that allowed for a significant amount of control. The option of buying another company outright, i.e., "complete fusion," required a great deal of capital and usually required the prior agreement of the stockholders. By simply acquiring enough stock in the other company to control its operations, the holding company avoided the necessity of stockholders' agreements, the expense of incorporation, and the restrictions of some regulatory measures. Reorganization into a holding company also facilitated the effort to increase capital, since the parent company could issue stocks against the securities of its subsidiaries.[25]

Legislatures aided the growth of corporations by removing statutory restrictions on the size and purpose of corporations. They also broadened the types of possible investments by differentiating the kinds of stock that could be sold. For example, some state legislatures allowed corporations to sell non-voting stock. Such differentiation of stock provided corporations with a larger market for their securities while often reducing stockholder control over corporate policy.[26]

The Court's early holding that manufacture was not part of commerce and that restraint of manufacture was not restraint of trade might have presupposed, or even have been intended to encourage, greater responsibility of states for the form and direction of enterprise. When the states failed to bear the burden of enforcing antitrust laws against manufacturing monopolies, the Court gradually abandoned the distinction between commerce and manufacturing. Ultimately it effectively overruled *E.C.*

20. Federal Antitrust Policy at 595.

21. See, e.g., American Law and Constitutional Order at 287.

22. Although the Court did not declare holding companies to be illegal in the Northern Securities decision, it destroyed the belief that holding companies were exempted from the Sherman Act. See Visible Hand, supra note 17, at 333–34.

23. Merger Movements at 64.

24. For contemporaneous discussion of the liberalization of corporation law, see Keasbey, New Jersey and the Great Corporations, 13 Harv.L.Rev. 198, 264 (1899–1900).

25. Federal Antitrust Policy at 255–57.

26. Legitimacy of the Business Corporation at 84.

Knight by 1948.[27] But in the late nineteenth century, *E.C. Knight* constituted an open invitation to consolidate. Indeed, the contrast between the government's failure in *Knight* when it challenged a close-knit arrangement and its success in cartelization cases like *Trans–Missouri, Addyston Pipe* and *Joint–Traffic,* may well have served to encourage mergers and other tightly structured, trust-building activities. *Knight,* then, though transitory as law, left a lasting impact on American industrial structure.

Note that the scope of the commerce clause—which in *E.C. Knight* precluded an antitrust challenge to a close-knit integration in manufacturing—did not present a problem in the early cartelization cases. The distinction between *Knight* and the railroad cartel cases is clear enough, perhaps; but what was the distinction between *Knight* and *Addyston Pipe* that justified jurisdiction over the pipe cartel but not the sugar monopoly? Is combining to increase the prices at which pipe will be sold in commerce (in the future) really distinguishable from combining to control the manufacture of sugar so that, after manufacture, it can be sold at higher prices? Does *Addyston Pipe,* then, suggest that by 1899 the view of the commerce clause taken in *Knight* was already eroding?

3. THE NEW CENTURY: TRUST BUSTING IN EARNEST?

a. *Progressivism and Changing Political Attitudes*

The new industrial state carried inherent limitations that early twentieth century reformers sought to expose. The legal system's apparent indulgence of corporate misconduct and the legislative proclivity to subsidize certain industries galvanized concern of the Progressives after 1900. To address the trust problem, the Progressives looked to institutional reform.

Ten years after the passage of the Sherman Act, trusts continued to thrive. Progressives took advantage of the newly changed political climate to call for more vigorous antitrust enforcement. Their ultimate aim was to secure additional antitrust legislation, for the Sherman Act had done little to stop the merger juggernaut. The social costs of industrial consolidation had been enormous. Unanticipated disruptions in the economy caused unemployment, poor return on investment, and loss of stability. These fluctuations could not be anticipated, much less controlled, in an unregulated, free-market economy that placed a premium on individual autonomy and property rights.

The election of 1900 again brought the antitrust issue before the public. Both the candidates and national political parties again took stands in opposition to industry-dominating firms. The Democratic Party denounced the trusts for robbing producers and consumers, reducing employment, dictating arbitrary terms of employment, and benefiting the few at the expense of the many. Its platform pledged "an increasing warfare in nation, state, and city against private monopoly in every

27. See Mandeville Island Farms, Inc. v. American Crystal Sugar Co., 334 U.S. 219, 229–30 (1948).

form." [28]   Less adamant in its stance, the Republican Party stated that it recognized

> [t]he necessity and propriety for honest cooperation of capital to meet new business conditions, and especially to expand our rapidly increasing foreign trade; but we condemn all conspiracies and combinations intended to restrict business, to create monopolies, to limit production, or to control prices.[29]

The Republicans were elected and upon the assassination of President McKinley a few months after his inauguration, the vice-president, Theodore Roosevelt, took office. Roosevelt was by all accounts an adroit politician who understood the importance of the antitrust issue. He was especially attuned to the widespread fear of the non-economic power possessed by the large corporations. With passionate rhetoric he sought to assure the public of the government's power to control the trusts.[30] Roosevelt is sometimes characterized as a shrewd opportunist, primarily interested in antitrust for its political mileage; but other historians, while recognizing his political motivations, credit him with inciting the nation into a state of indignation.[31]

b. *Government–Business Relations During the Roosevelt Administration*

Despite his rhetoric Roosevelt was no enemy of big business. He did not want to antagonize people who had contributed to his campaign and who were vital to his future political ambitions.[32] More fundamentally, he believed in the "good intentions and social value of the vast majority of businessmen." [33] This, paired with his recognition of the need in principle to attack abusive trusts, led him to a simple and vivid dichotomy. While roundly condemning the unscrupulous tactics of certain "bad" trusts, Theodore Roosevelt balanced his attack with praise for "good" trusts. Good trusts made possible great material development, and they increased the nation's international prestige. The nation, he thought, should accept "bigness" as an unavoidable characteristic of the new economy.

At the same time, Roosevelt argued, government should break up the bad trusts—those that grew not from inevitable economic forces but from unconscionable business practices.[34] Outlining his criteria for antitrust offenses, Roosevelt said, "The line of demarcation we draw must always be on conduct, not on wealth; our objection to any given corporation must be, not that it is big, but that it behaves badly." [35] Indeed, Roosevelt criticized both the Sherman Act and Court decisions interpreting the act for

---

28. K. Porter & D. Johnson, National Party Platforms: 1840–1956 at 114 (1961) (hereinafter National Party Platforms).

29. Id. at 122. This brief statement might well have been an antitrust plank for the Reagan Presidency.

30. R. Hofstadter, What Happened to the Antitrust Movement? in The Paranoid Style in American Politics 203, 204 (1965) (hereinafter Paranoid Style).

31. G. Kolko, The Triumph of Conservatism 65–67 (1963); cf. A. Link, Woodrow

Wilson and the Progressive Era: 1910–1917 at 2 (1954) (hereinafter Woodrow Wilson).

32. Antitrust Policy in Transition at 416.

33. Course of American Growth at 263.

34. T. Roosevelt, 1st Annual Message to Congress, in R. Hofstadter, The Progressive Movement 1900–1915 141–44 (R. Hofstadter ed. 1963) (hereinafter Progressive Movement). See also Power and Responsibility at 163.

35. Quoted in Triumph of Conservatism at 127–28.

failing to distinguish between good and bad trusts and for endangering efficient businesses. He claimed:

> Very many of the antitrust laws which have made their appearance on the statute-books of recent years have been almost or absolutely ineffective because they have blinked the all-important fact that much of what they thought to do away with was incidental to modern industrial conditions, and could not be eliminated unless we were willing to turn back the wheels of modern progress . . . ." [36]

But to accept bigness did not mean to accept badness. Rather, in the view of the Roosevelt administration, the country "must recognize concentration, supervise it, and regulate it." [37]

c. Roosevelt's Legislative Reform Program

Roosevelt's desire to strengthen the federal government and especially the position of the executive guided his antitrust policy. Reforms he sponsored placed primary power in the hands of the executive, either directly or through an administrative agency that he thought he could influence, if not control. Unlike Taft, who admired and trusted courts, Roosevelt wanted to limit judicial discretion. He wanted to place the authority to decide which trusts were good and bad in the hands of his administration.[38]

Roosevelt's proposed program combined several approaches. The investigation and publication of corporate affairs was one of Roosevelt's favorite methods of controlling illegal and unethical corporate practices. Roosevelt thought publicity could be used both as a punitive and a deterrent device against errant businesses. In 1903, Roosevelt created an executive agency, the Bureau of Corporation, to help him root out bad trusts and practices. The Bureau undertook investigations; it reported its findings to the President, who then decided whether to make them public.

Mere publicity, however, was not sufficient to curb bad trusts. Federal corporation laws were also needed, according to the President, to curb the abuses stemming from ineffective, disjointed state laws. Federal corporation laws would narrow loopholes and make supervision of corporate practices easier and more effective. Historians have noted that many large businesses supported a uniform federal incorporation law in the hope that they could avoid the stringent, diverse laws of antagonistic states. Federal law would be easier to comply with and regulation by one, federal regime would provide efficiencies for business.[39]

For Roosevelt, these federal laws would include precise, detailed antitrust provisions to eliminate discretion and clarify distinctions between good and bad trusts.[40] For example, laws could specifically prohibit "such practices as 'unhealthy competition' (instanced by cut-throat pric-

36. Quoted in Law and Economic Policy at 199.

37. Quoted in id. at 247.

38. Antitrust Policy in Transition at 417–27.

39. See Triumph of Conservatism at 69–70, 73–74; Antitrust Policy in Transition at 425. For an example of the type of reasoning supporting federal incorporation, see Dill, National Incorporation Laws for Trusts, 11 Yale L.J. 273 (1902).

40. Antitrust Policy in Transition at 419.

ing), stock-watering, and exclusive dealing arrangements." Also, laws could be more precise in allowing " 'reasonable agreements between, or combinations of, corporations . . . provided they are submitted to and approved by some appropriate government body.' " [41]

Finally, Roosevelt advocated a new federal regulatory agency to administer such laws. The agency would be staffed with experts who would decide if a trust was in compliance with the laws. Such an agency would " 'avoid the chaos and inefficiency necessarily produced' " when courts administer antitrust laws.[42] Roosevelt urged that these reforms would create a cooperative relationship between the government and the trusts, with government the stronger partner.[43]

Although a variety of groups pushed for antitrust reform Congressional conservatism blocked most of Roosevelt's legislative efforts. Historian George Mowry attributes this legislative inaction to the conservative Republicans who, since the McKinley administration, had controlled both the House and the Senate.[44] Also, the reformers were a motley coalition. Progressive muckrakers desired more stringent regulations; organized labor sought exemptions from prosecution, and moderates wanted to protect "good" businesses from strict antitrust laws. Their divergent interests made agreement on any particular bill hard to command. Finally, Roosevelt's desire to limit judicial discretion in statutory interpretation and to expand executive authority in antitrust enforcement cost him the support of many moderates in Congress.

In addition to legislative reform, Roosevelt sought to create a spirit of cooperation between business and government. Rather than prosecuting the members of an errant industry, Roosevelt favored informal resolution. The President would invite corporate leaders and lawyers to the White House and negotiate "gentlemanly agreements" delimiting the future activities of a suspect combination.[45] Consequently, the decision whether or not to prosecute was sometimes based upon idiosyncratic judgment, if not political considerations. Indeed, Roosevelt's decision not to prosecute International Harvester is sometimes attributed to the support the Morgan group gave to Roosevelt's campaign.[46]

Despite Roosevelt's benevolence towards big business, its leaders did not trust him completely.[47] His occasional but well-publicized attacks on some of the combinations made business executives cautious.

d. Roosevelt, Trust Buster

Roosevelt's prosecution record reflects his desire to maintain a vigorous antitrust image in the public mind and, at the same time, to remain a friend of business (at least of "good" business). Roosevelt, the so-called

---

41. Quoted in Law and Economic Policy at 246–47.

42. Antitrust Policy in Transition at 419.

43. Business leaders who hoped that the government would be sympathetic to them were among Roosevelt's political supporters. Triumph of Conservatism at 129; R. Wiebe, Businessmen and Reform 44 (1962) (hereinafter Businessmen and Reform).

44. G. Mowry, The Era of Theodore Roosevelt 118 (1958) (hereinafter Era of Roosevelt).

45. Businessmen and Reform at 45–47.

46. Antitrust Policy in Transition at 418.

47. Era of Roosevelt at 120.

"trust buster," prosecuted fewer cases than one might expect. Still, his attorney general, Philander C. Knox, initiated more suits than preceding administrations and deliberately targeted some of the bigger, better-known combinations. During Roosevelt's eight-year administration, the Justice Department brought eighteen suits in equity and twenty-five indictments under the Sherman Act. This was more than twice as many as were brought during the entire period from 1890 to 1901, but only half as many as Taft would subsequently prosecute during a single term in office.[48] By suing trusts with poor public reputations, the Roosevelt administration could maximize the symbolic effect of prosecutions and assert the administration's executive authority over the enforcement of the antitrust law.

In 1902 by suing the *Northern Securities* railroad combination, Roosevelt altered the government-business relationship that had characterized national policy throughout the period of trustification. Through a vigorous application of the Sherman Act, Roosevelt aimed to assert his own Presidential style, win middle-class support for the Republican Party, and persuade Congress to drop its opposition to his legislative program.[49] Letwin describes the prosecution as a staged performance, carefully chosen for its ability "to arouse public interest":

> It was the first antitrust case in which those cast as villains were celebrities. . . . James J. Hill, the swashbuckling railroad man who had built the Great Northern . . . and J. Pierpont Morgan, the Goliath of bankers. Each was accompanied by a host of minor moguls. . . . The drama was staged . . . as a conflict between Reason and Extravagance, between the respectable requirements of the common good and the wilfulness of colorful, but dangerous, buccaneers.[50]

The *Northern Securities* case may indeed have been staged, but it also gave the Supreme Court an important opportunity to influence national policy during the Progressive era. If Roosevelt's strategy of federal lawsuits seemed uncharacteristic, his choice of a defendant engaged in interstate commerce gave the Court clear grounds for upholding national authority to regulate the economy without having to intrude on production. How the Court decided Roosevelt's first antitrust case thus would have major political repercussions as well as legal ramifications.

NORTHERN SECURITIES CO. v. UNITED STATES
193 U.S. 197 (1904).

JUSTICE HARLAN: [By 1901, J.P. Morgan and James J. Hill had acquired majority interests in three regionally dominant railroad companies: The Northern Pacific, the Great Northern, and the Chicago, Burlington, and Quincy. E.H. Harriman, owner of the Union Pacific, initiated a bitter, costly fight to obtain complete control of the Northern Pacific,

---

48. Power and Responsibility at 340, 404–07. See also Keller, The Pluralist State: American Economic Regulation in Comparative Perspective, 1900–1930, in Regulation in Perspective: Historical Essays 67 (McCraw ed. 1981) (hereinafter Regulation in Perspective).

49. Power and Responsibility at 161.

50. Law and Economic Policy at 182. For a more complete history of the Northern Securities case, see id. at 182–95, 200–37.

his primary competitor. The threat of cut-throat competition and substantial losses in investments to all three industrialists led to a settlement, in the form of a holding company, the Northern Securities Company. Chartered in New Jersey, the corporation held the stock of the Northern Pacific, Great Northern, and Burlington lines in order to protect against other hostile takeover attempts. Suit was brought to dissolve the combination on grounds that it violated the Sherman Act.]

. . . Necessarily by this combination or arrangement the holding company in the fullest sense dominates the situation in the interest of those who were stockholders of the constituent companies; as much so, for every practical purpose, as if it had been itself a railroad corporation which had built, owned, and operated both lines for the exclusive benefit of its stockholders. Necessarily, also, the constituent companies ceased, under such a combination, to be in active competition for trade and commerce along their respective lines, and have become, practically, one powerful consolidated corporation, by the name of a holding corporation the principal, if not the sole, object for the formation of which was to carry out the purpose of the original combination under which competition between the constituent companies would cease. . . . No scheme or device could more certainly come within the words of the act—"combination in the form of a trust or otherwise . . . in restraint of commerce among the several States or with foreign nations,"—or could more effectively and certainly suppress free competition between the constituent companies. This combination is, within the meaning of the act, a "trust;" but if not, it is a *combination in restraint of interstate and international commerce;* and that is enough to bring it under the condemnation of the act. The mere existence of such a combination and the power acquired by the holding company as its trustee, constitute a menace to, and a restraint upon, that freedom of commerce which Congress intended to recognize and protect, and which the public is entitled to have protected. If such combination be not destroyed, all the advantages that would naturally come to the public under the operation of the general laws of competition, as between the Great Northern and Northern Pacific Railway companies, will be lost, and the entire commerce of the immense territory in the northern part of the United States between the Great Lakes and the Pacific at Puget Sound will be at the mercy of a single holding corporation, organized in a State distant from the people of that territory.

* * *

[F]rom the former opinions of this court . . . certain propositions are plainly deducible and embrace the present case. Those propositions are: . . .

That *every* combination or conspiracy which would extinguish competition between otherwise competing railroads engaged in *interstate trade or commerce,* and which would *in that way* restrain *such* trade or commerce, is made illegal by the act; . . .

That the natural effect of competition is to increase commerce, and an agreement whose direct effect is to prevent this play of competition restrains instead of promotes trade and commerce;

That to vitiate a combination, such as the act of Congress condemns, it need not be shown that the combination, in fact, results or will result in a total suppression of trade or in a complete monopoly, but it is only essential to show that by its necessary operation it tends to restrain interstate or international trade or commerce or tends to create a monopoly in such trade or commerce and to deprive the public of the advantages that flow from free competition. . . .

Many suggestions were made in argument based upon the thought that the Anti–Trust Act would in the end prove to be mischievous in its consequences. Disaster to business and wide-spread financial ruin, it has been intimated, will follow the execution of its provisions. Such predictions were made in all the cases heretofore arising under that act. But they have not been verified. It is the history of monopolies in this country and in England that predictions of ruin are habitually made by them when it is attempted, by legislation, to restrain their operations and to protect the public against their exactions. In this, as in former cases, they seek shelter behind the reserved rights of the States and even behind the constitutional guarantee of liberty of contract. But this court has heretofore adjudged that the act of Congress did not touch the rights of the States, and that liberty of contract did not involve a right to deprive the public of the advantages of free competition in trade and commerce. . . .

———

Two dissenting opinions were written. Justice White, joined by Chief Justice Fuller and Justices Peckham and Holmes, dissented on grounds that Congress had no power to regulate the acquisition and ownership of stock, regulation of which was (said to be) entrusted to the states.

Justice Holmes, joined by the Chief Justice and Justices White and Peckham, also wrote a dissenting opinion.

JUSTICE HOLMES, dissenting: . . . This act is construed by the Government to affect the purchasers of shares in two railroad companies because of the effect it may have, or, if you like, is certain to have, upon the competition of these roads. If such a remote result of the exercise of an ordinary incident of property and personal freedom is enough to make that exercise unlawful, there is hardly any transaction concerning commerce between the States that may not be made a crime by the finding of a jury or a court. . . .

The first section [of the Act] makes "Every contract, combination in the form of trust or otherwise, or conspiracy in restraint of trade or commerce among the several States, or with foreign nations" a misdemeanor, punishable by fine, imprisonment or both. Much trouble is made by substituting other phrases assumed to be equivalent, which then are reasoned from as if they were in the act. The court below argued as if maintaining competition were the expressed object of the act. The act says nothing about competition. I stick to the exact words used. The words hit two classes of cases, and only two—Contracts in restraint of trade and combinations or conspiracies in restraint of trade, and we have to consider what these respectively are. Contracts in restraint of trade are dealt with and defined by the common law. They are contracts with a stranger to the contractor's business, (although in some cases carrying on a similar one,) which wholly or partially restrict the freedom of the contractor in carrying on that business as otherwise he would. The objection of the common law to them was primarily on the contractor's own account. The notion of monopoly did not come in unless the contract covered the whole of England. *Mitchel v. Reynolds,* 1 P.Wms. 181. Of course this objection did not apply to partnerships or other forms, if there were any, of substituting a community of interest where there had been competition. There was no objection to such combinations merely as in restraint of trade, or otherwise unless they amounted to a monopoly. Contracts in restraint of trade, I repeat, were contracts with strangers to the contractor's business, and the trade restrained was the contractor's own.

Combinations or conspiracies in restraint of trade, on the other hand, were combinations to keep strangers to the agreement out of the business. The objection to them was not an objection to their effect upon the parties making the contract, the members of the combination or firm, but an objection to their intended effect upon strangers to the firm and their supposed consequent effect upon the public at large. In other words, they were regarded as contrary to public policy because they monopolized or attempted to monopolize some portion of the trade or commerce of the realm. See *United States v. E.C. Knight Co.,* 156 U.S. 1. All that is added to the first section by § 2 is that like penalties are imposed upon every single person who, without combination, monopolizes or attempts to monopolize commerce among the States; and that the liability is extended to attempting to monopolize any part of such trade or commerce. It is more important as an aid to the construction of § 1 than it is on its own account. It shows that whatever is criminal when done by way of combination is equally criminal if done by a single man. That I am right in my interpretation of the words of § 1 is shown by the words "in the form of trust or otherwise." The prohibition was suggested by the trusts, the objection to which, as every one knows, was not the union of former competitors, but the sinister power exercised or supposed to be exercised by the combination in keeping rivals out of the business and ruining those who already were in. It was the ferocious extreme of competition with others, not the cessation of competition among the partners, that was the evil feared. . . .

What I now ask is under which of the foregoing classes this case is supposed to come, and that question must be answered as definitely and precisely as if we were dealing with the indictments which logically ought to follow this decision. The provision of the statute against contracts in restraint of trade has been held to apply to contracts between railroads, otherwise remaining independent, by which they restricted their respective freedom as to rates. This restriction by contract with a stranger to the contractor's business is the ground of the decision in *United States v. Joint Traffic Association,* 171 U.S. 505, following and affirming *United States v. Trans–Missouri Freight Association,* 166 U.S. 290. I accept those decisions absolutely, not only as binding upon me, but as decisions which I have no desire to criticise or abridge. But the provision has not been

. . . [applied] to an arrangement by which competition is ended through community of interest—an arrangement which leaves the parties without external restriction. That provision, taken alone, does not require that all existing competitions shall be maintained. It does not look primarily, if at all, to competition. It simply requires that a party's freedom in trade between the States shall not be cut down by contract with a stranger. So far as that phrase goes, it is lawful to abolish competition by any form of union. It would seem to me impossible to say that the words "every contract in restraint of trade is a crime punishable with imprisonment," would send the members of a partnership between, or a consolidation of, two trading corporations to prison—still more impossible to say that it forbade one man or corporation to purchase as much stock as he liked in both. Yet those words would have that effect if this clause of § 1 applies to the defendants here. . . .

If the statute applies to this case it must be because the parties, or some of them, have formed, or because the Northern Securities Company is, a combination in restraint of trade among the States, or, what comes to the same thing in my opinion, because the defendants, or some or one of them, are monopolizing or attempting to monopolize some part of the commerce between the States. But the mere reading of those words shows that they are used in a limited and accurate sense. According to popular speech, every concern monopolizes whatever business it does, and if that business is trade between two States it monopolizes a part of the trade among the States. Of course the statute does not forbid that. It does not mean that all business must cease. A single railroad down a narrow valley or through a mountain gorge monopolizes all the railroad transportation through that valley or gorge. Indeed every railroad monopolizes, in a popular sense, the trade of some area. Yet I suppose no one would say that the statute forbids a combination of men into a corporation to build and run such a railroad between the States.

. . . [T]he act of Congress makes no discrimination according to size. Size has nothing to do with the matter. A monopoly of "any part" of commerce among the States is unlawful. The supposed company would have owned lines that might have been competing—probably the present one does. But the act of Congress will not be construed to mean the universal disintegration of society into single men, each at war with all the rest, or even the prevention of all further combinations for a common end.

There is a natural feeling that somehow or other the statute meant to strike at combinations great enough to cause just anxiety on the part of those who love their country more than money, while it viewed such little ones as I have supposed with just indifference. This notion, it may be said, somehow breathes from the pores of the act, although it seems to be contradicted in every way by the words in detail. And it has occurred to me that it might be that when a combination reached a certain size it might have attributed to it more of the character of a monopoly merely by virtue of its size than would be attributed to a smaller one. I am quite clear that it is only in connection with monopolies that size could play any part. But my answer has been indicated already. In the first place size in the case of railroads is an inevitable incident and if it were an objection under the act, the Great Northern and the Northern Pacific already were too great and encountered the law. In the next place in the case of railroads it is evident that the size of the combination is reached for other ends than those which would make them monopolies. The combinations are not formed for the purpose of excluding others from the field. Finally, even a small railroad will have the same tendency to exclude others from its narrow area that great ones have to exclude others from a greater one, and the statute attacks the small monopolies as well as the great. The very words of the act make such a distinction impossible in this case and it has not been attempted in express terms.

* * *

In view of my interpretation of the statute I do not go further into the question of the power of Congress. That has been dealt with by my brother White and I concur in the main with his views. I am happy to know that only a minority of my brethren adopt an interpretation of the law which in my opinion would make eternal the *bellum omnium contra omnes* and disintegrate society so far as it could into individual atoms. If that were its intent I should regard calling such a law a regulation of commerce as a mere pretense. It would be an attempt to reconstruct society. I am not concerned with the wisdom of such an attempt, but I believe that Congress was not entrusted by the Constitution with the power to make it and I am deeply persuaded that it has not tried.

Questions and Comments

Was the combination of these railroads likely to cause the price of freight shipments to rise? Would such a price rise be likely to encourage new entry by another railroad? Would it cause a shift by shippers to other forms of transportation? Did the Court know? Did it care?

What do you suppose Justice Harlan had in mind when he spoke of "the advantages [to the public] that flow from free competition"? Does every merger of competitors decrease these advantages to the public? Do only some mergers? Which ones?

Did this merger place enormous wealth in the control of a few? Did the merger's contribution to the concentration of wealth condemn it? Should it have condemned it? Does an increase in the wealth controlled by a few correlate with a lessening of competition?

Which is correct: Harlan's view that all combinations of competitors (or of large competitors) deprive the public of the advantages of free competition, or Holmes' view that the antitrust law is not about competition, and that in order to maintain a proper regard for liberty no combination should be illegal, regardless of its effect on competition, unless some act is done with the sinister intent to keep rivals out of the business or to ruin those already in it? Criticize both propositions. Do you agree with either one? If you were deciding the case, what would have been your guiding principle?

Is Justice Holmes correct that the natural result of the Court's holding is to atomize society? How about: The natural result of the Court's decision is to tend to preserve existing pluralism in society? Should antitrust preserve pluralism, or is that a perverse goal?

Holmes had been appointed to the Court by Roosevelt, who had made a large political investment in the *Northern Securities* case. Seldom reticent,

Roosevelt commented publicly on Holmes' dissent. He thought that Holmes showed "all the spirit of a banana." [51] That judgment is probably as unfair to Holmes as it is characteristic of Roosevelt. What Holmes sought to do in *Northern Securities* was consistent with his own libertarian philosophy. His view was that the antitrust laws were "humbug."[52] At the time, Holmes' position in *Northern Securities,* not Roosevelt's, was the more politically courageous. Yet, Holmes was a Supreme Court Justice, not an elected official. Was his legal reasoning in *Northern Securities* sound? Could he find support in American common law? Could he appropriately rely on English common law?

4. TRUST BUSTING IS INTENSIFIED: A "RULE OF REASON" IS BORN

a. The Taft Presidency

William Howard Taft, a former federal judge and future U.S. Chief Justice, was Roosevelt's hand-picked successor as President. Although Taft had supported Roosevelt's trust policy, he had reservations about both its wisdom and legality. Taft's legalistic world view led him to discard Roosevelt's moralistic distinctions among trusts. Taft outlined a functional distinction between combinations established specifically to eliminate competition, and those that happened to restrict trade en route to efficient production.[53]

Taft also rejected federal administration and regulation as the means to solve the trust problem. Rather, Taft favored more stringent enforcement of the Sherman Act. Hence he concentrated on filing antitrust suits—eighty-nine in four years. Taft also favored federal incorporation laws which would proscribe the corporate practices of issuing watered stock and purchasing the stock of other corporations.[54]

b. Reason and the Sherman Act

The courts still lacked a legal formula that would make interpretation of the Sherman Act consistent and effective. The early restraint of trade cases showed that the Supreme Court was divided between two views of the Sherman Act. By one view the act was a dramatically new law that prohibited combinations that produced power. Alternatively, the act was regarded as a federal codification of English common law, tolerant of combinations unless they deprived outsiders of the freedom to practice their trades. From 1888 to 1910, when Melville W. Fuller was Chief Justice, a majority of the Court had the first conception. Associate Justice Edward D. White was among the dissenters. Upon appointment of Oliver Wendell Holmes as Associate Justice in 1902, Holmes joined the dissenters. Fuller died in 1910, and President Taft elevated White to Chief Justice. As you will see, a new majority emerged. The case in which the new majority flexed its muscles involved the oil industry. To place the case in perspective, a little historical background may be helpful.

51. C.D. Bowen, Yankee from Olympus 370 (1944).

52. Holmes–Pollock Letters 163 (M.Howe ed., 1941).

53. See generally Power and Responsibility at 403–07; Law and Economic Policy at 252.

54. Regulation in Perspective at 68–69.

Oil was discovered in the northwestern corner of Pennsylvania in 1859. John D. Rockefeller, a young merchant in Cleveland, was at first skeptical of the oil rush, which was marked by the anarchy of drillers and diggers, by fires and disasters, and by the rise and fall of prices by several hundred percent.

But by 1862, prospects seemed more favorable. Rockefeller met and teamed up with a technologist, Andrews, who devised methods for obtaining a high yield of kerosene oil from crude oil. Rockefeller and Andrews established a refinery. They, and a new partner, Flagler, soon had the largest oil refinery in Cleveland.

Matthew Josephson, in The Robber Barons (1962), continues the story as follows (pp. 112–119, 161–163):

Rockefeller and Flagler approached the railroad which carried so many carloads of their oil toward the seaboard, and whose tariff figured heavily in the ultimate cost. They demanded from it concessions in freight rates that would enable them to meet the advantages of other refining centers such as Pittsburgh, Philadelphia and New York. Their company was now large enough to force the hand of the railroad, in this case, a branch of Vanderbilt's New York Central system; and they were granted their demands: a secret reduction or "rebate" on all their shipments of oil. "Such was the railroad's method," Rockefeller himself afterward admitted. He relates:

A public rate was made and collected by the railroad companies, but so far as my knowledge extends, was seldom retained in full; a portion of it was repaid to the shipper as a rebate. By this method the real rate of freight which any shipper paid was not known by his competitors, nor by other railroads, the amount being a matter of bargain with the carrying companies.

Once having gained an advantage Rockefeller pressed forward relentlessly. The volume of his business increased rapidly. Thanks to the collaboration of the railroad, he had placed his rivals in other cities and in Cleveland itself under a handicap, whose weight he endeavored to increase.

The railroads, as we see, possessed the strategic power, almost of life and death, to encourage one industrial group or cause another to languish. Their policy was based on the relative costs of handling small or large volume shipments. Thus as the Rockefeller company became the largest shipper of oil, its production rising in 1870 to 3,000 barrels a day, and offered to guarantee regular daily shipments of as much as sixty carloads, the railroads were impelled to accept further proposals for rebates. It was to their interest to do so in view of savings of several hundred thousand dollars a month in handling. On crude oil brought from the Oil Regions, Rockefeller paid perhaps 15 cents a barrel less than the open rate of 40 cents; on refined oil moving from Cleveland toward New York, he paid approximately 90 cents against the open rate of $1.30. These momentous agreements were maintained in utter secrecy, perhaps because of the persisting memory of their illegality, according to the common law ever since Queen Elizabeth's time, as a form of "conspiracy" in trade.

In January, 1870, Rockefeller, Flagler & Andrews were incorporated as a joint-stock company, a form increasingly popular, under the name of the Standard Oil Company of Ohio. At this time their worth was estimated at one million dollars; they employed over a thousand workers and were the largest refiners in the world. Despite deeply disturbed conditions in their trade during 1870, profits came to them in a mounting flood, while in the same year, it is noteworthy, four of their twenty-nine competitors in Cleveland gave up the ghost. The pious young man of thirty who feared only God, and thought of nothing but his business, gave not a sign of his greatly augmented wealth, which made him one of the leading personages of his city. His income was actually a fabulous one for the time. The Standard Oil Company from the beginning earned something like 100 per cent on its capital; and Rockefeller and his brother owned a full half-interest in it in 1870. But with an evangelistic fervor John Rockefeller was bent only upon further conquests, upon greater extensions of the power over industry which had come into the hands of the group he headed.

In the life of every conquering soul there is a "turning point," a moment when a deep understanding of the self coincides with an equally deep sense of one's immediate mission in the tangible world. For Rockefeller, brooding, secretive, uneasily scenting his fortune, this moment came but a few years after his entrance into the oil trade, and at the age of thirty. He had looked upon the disorganized conditions of the Pennsylvania oil fields, the only source then known, and found them not good: the guerilla fighting of drillers, of refining firms, of rival railroad lines, the mercurial changes in supply and market value—very alarming in 1870—offended his orderly and methodical spirit. But one could see that petroleum was to be the light of the world. From the source, from the chaotic oil fields where thousands of drillers toiled, the grimy stream of the precious commodity, petroleum, flowed along many diverse channels to narrow into the hands of several hundred refineries, then to issue once more in a continuous stream to consumers throughout the world. Owner with Flagler and Harkness of the largest refining company in the country, Rockefeller had a strongly entrenched position at the narrows of this stream. Now what if the Standard Oil Company should by further steps of organization possess itself wholly of the narrows? In this period of anarchic individual competition, the idea of such a movement of rationalization must have come to Rockefeller forcibly, as it had recently come to others.[1]

Even as early as 1868 the first plan of industrial combination in the shape of the pool had been originated in the Michigan Salt Association.

---

1. The English economist J.A. Hobson has written in this connection: "Each kind of commodity, as it passes through the many processes from the earth to the consumer, may be looked upon as a stream whose channel is broader at some points and narrow at others. Different streams of commodities narrow at different places. Some are narrowest and in fewest hands at the transport stage, others in one of the processes of manufacture, others in the hands of export merchants. . . ." In the case of petroleum the logical "narrows" was at the point of refinery; and inevitably, Rockefeller and Flagler set in motion their great plan to control the stream. "Just as a number of German barons planted their castles along the banks of the Rhine, in order to tax the commerce between East and West which was obliged to make use of this highway, so it is with these economic 'narrows.' Wherever they are found, monopolies plant themselves in the shape of 'rings,' 'corners,' 'pools,' 'syndicates,' or 'trusts.'" ("The Evolution of Modern Capitalism," p. 142.) [Footnote from original.]

Desiring to correct chaotic market conditions, declaring that "in union there is strength," the salt-producers of Saginaw Bay had banded together to control the output and sale of nearly all the salt in their region, a large part of the vital national supply. Secret agreements had been executed for each year, allotting the sales and fixing the price at almost twice what it had been immediately prior to the appearance of the pool. And though the inevitable greed and self-seeking of the individual salt-producers had tended to weaken the pool, the new economic invention was launched in its infantile form. Rockefeller's partners, Flagler and Harkness, had themselves participated in the historic Michigan Salt Association.

This grand idea of industrial rationalization owed its swift, ruthless, methodical execution no doubt to the firmness of character we sense in Rockefeller, who had the temper of a great, unconscionable military captain, combining audacity with thoroughness and shrewd judgment. His plan seemed to take account of no one's feelings in the matter. Indeed there was something revolutionary in it; it seemed to fly in the face of human liberties and deep-rooted custom and common law. The notorious "South Improvement Company," with its strange charter, ingeniously instrumenting the scheme of combination, was to be unraveled amid profound secrecy. By conspiring with the railroads (which also hungered for economic order), it would be terribly armed with the power of the freight rebate which garrotted all opposition systematically. . . .

I had our plan clearly in mind. It was right. I knew it as a matter of conscience. It was right between me and my God. If I had to do it tomorrow I would do it again in the same way—do it a hundred times.

The broad purpose was to control and direct the flow of crude petroleum into the hands of a narrowed group of refiners. The refiners would be supported by the combined railroad trunk lines which shipped the oil; while the producers' phase of the stream would be left unorganized—*but with power over their outlet to market* henceforth to be concentrated into the few hands of the refiners.

Saying nothing to others, bending over their maps of the industry, Rockefeller and Flagler first drew up a short list of the principal refining companies who were to be asked to combine with them. Then having banded together a sufficient number, they would persuade the railroads to give them special freight rates—on the ground of "evening" the traffic—guaranteeing equitable distribution of freight business; and this in turn would be a club to force other elements needed into union with them. They could control output, drive out competitors, and force all foreign countries throughout the world to buy their product from them at their own terms. They could finally dictate market prices on crude oil, stabilize the margin of profit at their own process, and do away at last with the dangerously speculative character of their business.

Their plans moved forward rapidly all through 1871. For a small sum of money the "conspirators" obtained the Pennsylvania charter of a defunct corporation, which had been authorized to engage in almost any kind of business under the sun. Those who were approached by the promoters, those whom they determined to use in their grand scheme, were compelled in a manner typical of all Rockefeller's projects to sign a written pledge of secrecy:

*I, ————, do solemnly promise upon my honor and faith as a
gentleman that I will keep secret all transactions which I may have with
the corporation known as the South Improvement Company; that should I
fail to complete any bargains with the said company, all the preliminary
conversations shall be kept strictly private; and finally that I will not
disclose the price for which I dispose of any products or any other facts
which may in any way bring to light the internal workings or organization
of the company. All this I do freely promise.*

At the same time, in confidential pourparlers with the officials of the
Erie, the Pennsylvania and the New York Central Railroads, the men of
the Standard Oil represented themselves as possessing secret control of
the bulk of the refining interest. Thus they obtained conditions more
advantageous than anything which had gone before; and this weapon in
turn of course ensured the triumph of their pool.

The refiners to be combined under the aegis of the South Improvement Company were to have a rebate of from 40 to 50 per cent on the
crude oil they ordered shipped to them and from 25 to 50 per cent on the
refined oil they shipped out. The refiners in the Oil Regions were to pay
twice as much by the new code (though nearer to New York) as the
Standard Oil Company at Cleveland. But besides the rebate the members
of the pool were to be given also a "drawback" consisting of part of the
increased tariff rate which "outsiders" were forced to pay. Half of the
freight payments of a rival refiner would in many cases be paid over to
the Rockefeller group. Their competitors were simply to be decimated;
and to make certain of this the railroads agreed—all being set down in
writing, in minutest detail—"to make manifests or way-bills of all petroleum or its product transported over any portion of its lines . . . which
manifests shall state the name of the consignee, the place of shipment
and the place of destination," this information to be furnished faithfully
to the officers of the South Improvement Company.

The railroad systems, supposedly public-spirited and impartial, were
to open all their knowledge of rival private business to the pool, thus
helping to concentrate all the oil trade into the few hands chosen. In
return for so much assistance, they were to have their freight "evened,"
and were enabled at last to enter into a momentous peace pact with each
other by which the oil traffic (over which they had quarreled bitterly) was
to be fairly allotted among themselves.

By January, 1872, after the first decade of the oil business, John
Rockefeller, with the aid of the railroad captains, was busily carrying out
a most "elaborate national plan" of his own for the control of his
industry—such planned control as the spokesman of the business system
asserted ever afterward was impossible. The first pooling of 1872, beauti-
ful as was its economic architecture and laudable its motive, had defects
which were soon plainly noticeable. All the political institutions, the
whole spirit of American law still favored the amiable, wasteful individualism of business, which in Rockefeller's mind had already become obsolete and must be supplanted by a centralized, one might say almost
collectivist—certainly cooperative rather than competitive—form of operation. Moreover, these "revolutionists" took little account of the social
dislocations their juggernaut would bring. Like the railroad baron,
Vanderbilt, working better than they knew, their eyes fixed solely upon

the immediate task rather than upon some millennium of the future, they desired simply, as they often said, to be "the biggest refiners in the world. . . ."

To the principal oil firms in Cleveland Rockefeller went one by one, explaining the plan of the South Improvement Company patiently, pointing out how important it was to oppose the crew refiners and save the Cleveland oil trade. . . .

Then if the men demurred, according to much of the testimony at the Senate Investigation of 1876, he would point out suavely that it was useless to resist; opposition would certainly be crushed. The offers of purchase usually made were for from a third to a half the actual cost of the property.

Now a sort of terror swept silently over the oil trade. In a vague panic, competitors saw the Standard Oil officers come to them and say (as Rockefeller's own brother and rival, Frank, testified in 1876): "if you don't sell your property to us it will be valueless, because we have got the advantage with the railroads."

The railroad rates indeed were suddenly doubled to the outsiders, and those refiners who resisted the pool came and expostulated; then they became frightened and disposed of their property. One of the largest competitors in Cleveland, the firm of Alexander, Scofield & Co., held out for a time, protesting before the railroad officials at the monstrous unfairness of the deal. But these officials when consulted said mysteriously: "*Better sell—better get clear*—better sell out—no help for it." Another powerful refiner, Robert Hanna, uncle of the famous Mark Alonzo, found that the railroads would give him no relief, and also was glad to sell out at 40 or 50 cents on the dollar for his property value. To one of these refiners, Isaac L. Hewitt, who had been his employer in boyhood, Rockefeller himself spoke with intense emotion. He urged Hewitt to take stock. Hewitt related: "He told me that it would be sufficient to take care of my family for all time . . . and asking for reasons, he made this expression, I remember: '*I have ways of making money that you know nothing of.*' ". . . .

During forty years the Standard Oil men marched from trial to trial like habitual felons, before the public was convinced that it was not dealing with the archcriminals of the age, but with destiny. The opposition was always on behalf of a laissez-faire individualism. Miss Tarbell, in her crusading days, before she turned official apologist for famous capitalists, was but championing (and in the name of her expropriated father) the wastefulness, the competitive anarchy of the independent Pennsylvania oil-producers. Rockefeller, on the other hand, was literally the instrument of economic determinism; he was the more or less conscious guiding genius of a process of concentration which held in view the national (and even international) rather than the local organization of oil exploiting. Under his example American capitalism advanced swiftly toward a new phase, transforming, as the most profound social prophet of the century was saying at this very time, "the pigmy property of the many into the titan property of the few, transforming the individual and scattered means of production into socially concentrated forms." This is the true character of the historic process which passes before our eyes in the American scene of the '70's and '80's.

It was an age which seemed "gilded" or "tarnished" or "dreadful" or "tragic" by turns; yet an immensely fruitful age, under whose surface movements of strife and confusion, of repulsion and attraction, one capitalist expropriated others, the strong steadily went on destroying the individual independence of the weak, and in systematic fashion "the large capitals got the better of the smaller ones." Thus all the scattered individual means of production were being brought together, as Marx wrote, into the "new centralization," hastening the development of society, breeding the new technical means for "those tremendous industrial undertakings which can only arise as the outcome of the centralization of capital." And the birth-throes of a new social order, but added to the turbulence of the age, with its sounds of ringing arms, its shouts of the conquerors, groans of the fallen. Under Rockefeller, a giant industrial machine was raising itself over the land.

Thenceforth, though persecuted and pilloried, himself the most hated man of the age, he would retain his lead, hang on like death to his great unifying idea, advancing anew after each momentary retreat, evading all attempts at regulation, until the Standard Oil, with its refineries, pipe lines, tank wagons, ships and foreign terminals, had become an industrial empire as far-spreading as the British Empire, until Babylon and Nineveh and Peiping were illuminated by Standard kerosene. Rockefeller's organizing genius would create the "mother of Trusts," soon to spawn a score of other great "Trusts" in whiskey, cattle, beef, sugar, coal, iron and copper. The Standard Oil "Trust," as a corporate device, as a capitalist construction, had the beauty of one of the new steel suspension bridges. A bridge between the past and the future.*

STANDARD OIL CO. OF NEW JERSEY v.
UNITED STATES
221 U.S. 1 (1911).

CHIEF JUSTICE WHITE: The Standard Oil Company of New Jersey and 33 other corporations, John D. Rockefeller, William Rockefeller and five other individual defendants prosecute this appeal to reverse a decree of the court below. . . .

The bill . . . was filed on November 15, 1906. . . . The detailed averments concerning the alleged conspiracy were arranged with reference to three periods, the first from 1870 to 1882, the second from 1882 to 1899, and the third from 1899 to the time of the filing of the bill.

* * *

. . . [O]n the one hand, with relentless pertinacity and minuteness of analysis, it is insisted that the facts establish that the assailed combination took its birth in a purpose to unlawfully acquire wealth by oppressing the public and destroying the just rights of others, and that its entire career exemplifies an inexorable carrying out of such wrongful intents, since, it is asserted, the pathway of the combination from the beginning to the time of the filing of the bill is marked with constant proofs of wrong inflicted upon the public and is strewn with the wrecks resulting from

---

*Copyright 1934 and renewed 1962 by
Matthew Josephson, reprinted by permission
of Harcourt Brace Jovanovich, Inc.

crushing out, without regard to law, the individual rights of others. Indeed, so conclusive, it is urged, is the proof on these subjects that it is asserted that the existence of the principal corporate defendant—the Standard Oil Company of New Jersey—with the vast accumulation of property which it owns or controls, because of its infinite potency for harm and the dangerous example which its continued existence affords, is an open and enduring menace to all freedom of trade and is a byword and reproach to modern economic methods. On the other hand, in a powerful analysis of the facts, it is insisted that they demonstrate that the origin and development of the vast business which the defendants control was but the result of lawful competitive methods, guided by economic genius of the highest order, sustained by courage, by a keen insight into commercial situations, resulting in the acquisition of great wealth, but at the same time serving to stimulate and increase production, to widely extend the distribution of the products of petroleum at a cost largely below that which would have otherwise prevailed, thus proving to be at one and the same time a benefaction to the general public as well as of enormous advantage to individuals. It is not denied that in the enormous volume of proof contained in the record in the period of almost a lifetime to which that proof is addressed, there may be found acts of wrongdoing, but the insistence is that they were rather the exception than the rule, and in most cases were either the result of too great individual zeal in the keen rivalries of business or of the methods and habits of dealing which, even if wrong, were commonly practised at the time. And to discover and state the truth concerning these contentions both arguments call for the analysis and weighing, as we have said at the outset, of a jungle of conflicting testimony covering a period of forty years, a duty difficult to rightly perform and, even if satisfactorily accomplished, almost impossible to state with any reasonable regard to brevity.

. . . [We] shall first come to consider the meaning of the first and second sections of the Anti-trust Act. . . .

* * *

The debates show that doubt as to whether there was a common law of the United States which governed the subject in the absence of legislation was among the influences leading to the passage of the act. They conclusively show, however, that the main cause which led to the legislation was the thought that it was required by the economic condition of the times, that is, the vast accumulation of wealth in the hands of corporations and individuals, the enormous development of corporate organization, the facility for combination which such organizations afforded, the fact that the facility was being used, and that combinations known as trusts were being multiplied, and the wide-spread impression that their power had been and would be exerted to oppress individuals and injure the public generally. Although debates may not be used as a means for interpreting a statute . . . that rule in the nature of things is not violated by resorting to debates as a means of ascertaining the environment at the time of the enactment of a particular law, that is, the history of the period when it was adopted.

There can be no doubt that the sole subject with which the first section deals is restraint of trade as therein contemplated, and that the attempt to monopolize and monopolization is the subject with which the second section is concerned. It is certain that those terms, at least in their rudimentary meaning, took their origin in the common law, and were also familiar in the law of this country prior to and at the time of the adoption of the act in question.

* * *

Generalizing these considerations, the situation is this: 1. That by the common law monopolies were unlawful because of their restriction upon individual freedom of contract and their injury to the public. 2. That as to necessaries of life the freedom of the individual to deal was restricted where the nature and character of the dealing was such as to engender the presumption of intent to bring about at least one of the injuries which it was deemed would result from monopoly, that is an undue enhancement of price. 3. That to protect the freedom of contract of the individual not only in his own interest, but principally in the interest of the common weal, a contract of an individual by which he put an unreasonable restraint upon himself as to carrying on his trade or business was void. . . .

. . . It is remarkable that nowhere at common law can there be found a prohibition against the creation of monopoly by an individual. This would seem to manifest, either consciously or intuitively, a profound conception as to the inevitable operation of economic forces and the equipoise or balance in favor of the protection of the rights of individuals which resulted. That is to say, as it was deemed that monopoly in the concrete could only arise from an act of sovereign power, and, such sovereign power being restrained, prohibitions as to individuals were directed, not against the creation of monopoly, but were only applied to such acts in relation to particular subjects as to which it was deemed, if not restrained, some of the consequences of monopoly might result. After all, this was but an instinctive recognition of the truisms that the course of trade could not be made free by obstructing it, and that an individual's right to trade could not be protected by destroying such right.

* * *

Without going into detail and but very briefly surveying the whole field, it may be with accuracy said that the dread of enhancement of prices and of other wrongs which it was thought would flow from the undue limitation on competitive conditions caused by contracts or other acts of individuals or corporations, led, as a matter of public policy, to the prohibition or treating as illegal all contracts or acts which were unreasonably restrictive of competitive conditions, either from the nature or character of the contract or act or where the surrounding circumstances were such as to justify the conclusion that they had not been entered into or performed with the legitimate purpose of reasonably forwarding personal interest and developing trade, but on the contrary were of such a character as to give rise to the inference or presumption that they had been entered into or done with the intent to do wrong to the general public and to limit the right of individuals, thus restraining the free flow of commerce and tending to bring about the evils, such as enhancement of prices, which were considered to be against public policy. . . .

Let us consider the language of the first and second sections, guided by the principle that where words are employed in a statute which had at the time a well-known meaning at common law or in the law of this country they are presumed to have been used in that sense unless the context compels to the contrary.

As to the first section, the words to be interpreted are: "Every contract, combination in the form of trust or otherwise, or conspiracy in restraint of trade or commerce . . . is hereby declared to be illegal." As there is no room for dispute that the statute was intended to formulate a rule for the regulation of interstate and foreign commerce, the question is what was the rule which it adopted?

In view of the common law and the law in this country as to restraint of trade, which we have reviewed, and the illuminating effect which that history must have under the rule to which we have referred, we think it results:

a. That the context manifests that the statute was drawn in the light of the existing practical conception of the law of restraint of trade, because it groups as within that class, not only contracts which were in restraint of trade in the subjective sense, but all contracts or acts which theoretically were attempts to monopolize, yet which in practice had come to be considered as in restraint of trade in a broad sense.

b. That in view of the many new forms of contracts and combinations which were being evolved from existing economic conditions, it was deemed essential by an all-embracing enumeration to make sure that no form of contract or combination by which an undue restraint of interstate or foreign commerce was brought about could save such restraint from condemnation. The statute under this view evidenced the intent not to restrain the right to make and enforce contracts, whether resulting from combination or otherwise, which did not unduly restrain interstate or foreign commerce, but to protect that commerce from being restrained by methods, whether old or new, which would constitute an interference that is an undue restraint.

c. And as the contracts or acts embraced in the provision were not expressly defined, since the enumeration addressed itself simply to classes of acts, those classes being broad enough to embrace every conceivable contract or combination which could be made concerning trade or commerce or the subjects of such commerce, and thus caused any act done by any of the enumerated methods anywhere in the whole field of human activity to be illegal if in restraint of trade, it inevitably follows that the provision necessarily called for the exercise of judgment which required that some standard should be resorted to for the purpose of determining whether the prohibitions contained in the statute had or had not in any given case been violated. Thus not specifying but indubitably contemplating and requiring a standard, it follows that it was intended that the standard of reason which had been applied at the common law and in this country in dealing with subjects of the character embraced by the statute, was intended to be the measure used for the purpose of determining whether in a given case a particular act had or had not brought about the wrong against which the statute provided.

* * *

Undoubtedly, the words "to monopolize" and "monopolize" as used in the [second] section reach every act bringing about the prohibited results. The ambiguity, if any, is involved in determining what is intended by monopolize. But this ambiguity is readily dispelled in the light of the previous history of the law of restraint of trade to which we have referred and the indication which it gives of the practical evolution by which monopoly and the acts which produce the same result as monopoly, that is, an undue restraint of the course of trade, all came to be spoken of as, and to be indeed synonymous with, restraint of trade. In other words, having by the first section forbidden all means of monopolizing trade, that is, unduly restraining it by means of every contract, combination, etc., the second section seeks, if possible, to make the prohibitions of the act all the more complete and perfect by embracing all attempts to reach the end prohibited by the first section, that is, restraints of trade, by any attempt to monopolize, or monopolization thereof, even although the acts by which such results are attempted to be brought about or are brought about be not embraced within the general enumeration of the first section. And, of course, when the second section is thus harmonized with and made as it was intended to be the complement of the first, it becomes obvious that the criteria to be resorted to in any given case for the purpose of ascertaining whether violations of the section have been committed, is the rule of reason guided by the established law and by the plain duty to enforce the prohibitions of the act and thus the public policy which its restrictions were obviously enacted to subserve. And it is worthy of observation, as we have previously remarked concerning the common law, that although the statute by the comprehensiveness of the enumerations embodied in both the first and second sections makes it certain that its purpose was to prevent undue restraints of every kind or nature, nevertheless by the omission of any direct prohibition against monopoly in the concrete it indicates a consciousness that the freedom of the individual right to contract when not unduly or improperly exercised was the most efficient means for the prevention of monopoly, since the operation of the centrifugal and centripetal forces resulting from the right to freely contract was the means by which monopoly would be inevitably prevented if no extraneous or sovereign power imposed it and no right to make unlawful contracts having a monopolistic tendency were permitted. In other words that freedom to contract was the essence of freedom from undue restraint on the right to contract. . . .

* * *

We see no cause to doubt the correctness of these conclusions [defendants violated Sections 1 and 2], . . . for the following reasons:

a. Because the unification of power and control over petroleum and its products which was the inevitable result of the combining in the New Jersey corporation by the increase of its stock and the transfer to it of the stocks of so many other corporations, aggregating so vast a capital, gives rise, in and of itself, in the absence of countervailing circumstances, to say the least, to the *prima facie* presumption of intent and purpose to maintain the dominancy over the oil industry, not as a result of normal methods of industrial development, but by new means of combination which were resorted to in order that greater power might be added than would otherwise have arisen had normal methods been followed, the whole with the purpose of excluding others from the trade and thus centralizing in the combination a perpetual control of the movements of petroleum and its products in the channels of interstate commerce.

b. Because the *prima facie* presumption of intent to restrain trade, to monopolize and to bring about monopolization resulting from the act of expanding the stock of the New Jersey corporation and vesting it with such vast control of the oil industry, is made conclusive by considering *1,* the conduct of the persons or corporations who were mainly instrumental in bringing about the extension of power in the New Jersey corporation before the consummation of that result and prior to the formation of the trust agreements of 1879 and 1882; *2,* by considering the proof as to what was done under those agreements and the acts which immediately preceded the vesting of power in the New Jersey corporation as well as by weighing the modes in which the power vested in that corporation has been exerted and the results which have arisen from it.

Recurring to the acts done by the individuals or corporations who were mainly instrumental in bringing about the expansion of the New Jersey corporation during the period prior to the formation of the trust agreements of 1879 and 1882, including those agreements, not for the purpose of weighing the substantial merit of the numerous charges of wrongdoing made during such period, but solely as an aid for discovering intent and purpose, we think no disinterested mind can survey the period in question without being irresistibly driven to the conclusion that the very genius for commercial development and organization which it would seem was manifested from the beginning soon begot an intent and purpose to exclude others which was frequently manifested by acts and dealings wholly inconsistent with the theory that they were made with the single conception of advancing the development of business power by usual methods, but which on the contrary necessarily involved the intent to drive others from the field and to exclude them from their right to trade and thus accomplish the mastery which was the end in view. And, considering the period from the date of the trust agreements of 1879 and 1882, up to the time of the expansion of the New Jersey corporation, the gradual extension of the power over the commerce in oil which ensued, the decision of the Supreme Court of Ohio, the tardiness or reluctance in conforming to the commands of that decision, the method first adopted and that which finally culminated in the plan of the New Jersey corporation, all additionally serve to make manifest the continued existence of the intent which we have previously indicated and which among other things impelled the expansion of the New Jersey corporation. The exercise of the power which resulted from that organization fortifies the foregoing conclusions, since the development which came, the acquisition here and there which ensued of every efficient means by which competition could have been asserted, the slow but resistless methods which followed by which means of transportation were absorbed and brought under control, the system of marketing which was adopted by which the country was divided into districts and the trade in each district in oil was turned over to a designated corporation within the combination and all others were excluded, all lead the mind up to a conviction of a purpose and intent which we think is so certain as practically to cause the subject not to be within the domain of reasonable contention.

The inference that no attempt to monopolize could have been intended, and that no monopolization resulted from the acts complained of, since it is established that a very small percentage of the crude oil produced was controlled by the combination, is unwarranted. As substantial power over the crude product was the inevitable result of the absolute control which existed over the refined product, the monopolization of the one carried with it the power to control the other, and if the inferences which this situation suggests were developed, which we deem it unnecessary to do, they might well serve to add additional cogency to the presumption of intent to monopolize which we have found arises from the unquestioned proof on other subjects.

We are thus brought to the last subject which we are called upon to consider, viz:

. . . *The remedy to be administered.*

It may be conceded that ordinarily where it was found that acts had been done in violation of the statute, adequate measure of relief would result from restraining the doing of such acts in the future. *Swift v. United States,* 196 U.S. 375. But in a case like this, where the condition which has been brought about in violation of the statute, in and of itself, is not only a continued attempt to monopolize, but also a monopolization, the duty to enforce the statute requires the application of broader and more controlling remedies. As penalties which are not authorized by law may not be inflicted by judicial authority, it follows that to meet the situation with which we are confronted the application of remedies twofold in character becomes essential: (1st.) To forbid the doing in the future of acts like those which we have found to have been done in the past which would be violative of the statute. (2d.) The exertion of such measure of relief as will effectually dissolve the combination found to exist in violation of the statute, and thus neutralize the extension and continually operating force which the possession of the power unlawfully obtained has brought and will continue to bring about.

*   *   *

Our conclusion is that the decree below [ordering dissolution of the combination] was right and should be affirmed, except as to . . . minor matters [identified]. . . .

And it is so ordered

JUSTICE HARLAN, concurring in part, and dissenting in part:

In order that my objections to certain parts of the court's opinion may distinctly appear, I must state the circumstances under which Congress passed the Anti-trust Act, and trace the course of judicial decisions as to its meaning and scope. This is the more necessary because the court by its decision, when interpreted by the language of its opinion, has not only upset the long-settled interpretation of the act, but has usurped the constitutional functions of the legislative branch of the Government. With all due respect for the opinions of others, I feel bound to say that what the court has said may well cause some alarm for the integrity of our institutions.   Let us see how the matter stands.

All who recall the condition of the country in 1890 will remember that there was everywhere, among the people generally, a deep feeling of unrest.   The Nation had been rid of human slavery—fortunately, as all now feel—but the conviction was universal that the country was in real danger from another kind of slavery sought to be fastened on the American people, namely, the slavery that would result from aggregations of capital in the hands of a few individuals and corporations controlling, for their own profit and advantage exclusively, the entire business of the country, including the production and sale of the necessaries of life.   Such a danger was thought to be then imminent, and all felt that it must be met firmly and by such statutory regulations as would adequately protect the people against oppression and wrong.   Congress therefore took up the matter and gave the whole subject the fullest consideration.   All agreed that the National Government could not, by legislation, regulate the domestic trade carried on wholly within the several States; for, power to regulate such trade remained with, because never surrendered by, the States.   But, under authority expressly granted to it by the Constitution, Congress could regulate commerce among the several States and with foreign states.   Its authority to regulate such commerce was and is paramount, due force being given to other provisions of the fundamental law devised by the fathers for the safety of the Government and for the protection and security of the essential rights inhering in life, liberty and property.

Guided by these considerations, and to the end that the people, *so far as interstate commerce* was concerned, might not be dominated by vast combinations and monopolies, having power to advance their own selfish ends, regardless of the general interests and welfare, Congress passed the Anti-trust Act of 1890. . . .

[M]y brethren, in their wisdom, have . . . now said to those who . . . object to all legislative prohibitions of contracts, combinations and trusts in restraint of interstate commerce, "You may *now* restrain such commerce, provided you are reasonable about it; only take care that the restraint in not undue."   The disposition of the case under consideration, according to the views of the defendants, will, it is claimed, quiet and give rest to "the business of the country."   On the contrary, I have a strong conviction that it will throw the business of the country into confusion and invite widely-extended and harassing litigation, the injurious effects of which will be felt for many years to come.   When Congress prohibited *every* contract, combination or monopoly, in restraint of commerce, it prescribed a simple, definite rule that all could understand, and which could be easily applied by everyone wishing to obey the law, and not to conduct their business in violation of law.   But now, it is to be feared, we are to have, in cases without number, the constantly recurring inquiry— difficult to solve by proof—whether the particular contract, combination, or trust involved in each case is or is not an "unreasonable" or "undue" restraint of trade. . . .

The Supreme Law of the Land—which is binding alike upon all—upon Presidents, Congresses, the Courts and the People—gives to Congress, and to Congress alone, authority to regulate interstate commerce, and when Congress forbids *any* restraint of such commerce, in any form, all must obey its mandate. . . .[55]

Questions and Comments

The Standard Oil case elicited strong responses. In announcing the "rule of reason," Chief Justice White broke the interpretational logjam that had characterized restraint of trade jurisprudence. But White's reasonableness standard differed from Taft's conception of the meaning of the Sherman Act. Although Taft clearly wanted judicial enforcement of the Sherman Act to be the cornerstone of his antitrust policy, he thought legality should turn on whether the defendants' restraint was an end in itself or was imposed in the service of other legitimate business goals. Taft believed that the new "rule of reason" gave the courts open-ended and arbitrary "power to say what was a reasonable restraint or a reasonable monopoly." Nevertheless, Taft reconciled himself to the opinion. It was the Democrats in Congress who contended that the Court had emasculated an already weak law by giving legal sanction to "reasonable" combinations.[56]

What, according to White, were the evils that gave rise to the Sherman Act? Do they include the vast accumulation of wealth in the hands of a few? The power to raise price? Who are the victims of the first evil? Who are the victims of the second? How does Justice Harlan view the evils that gave rise to the law? How do you?

The White opinion in *Standard Oil* seeks to trace the development of the concept, monopolization, from the Statute of Monopolies through the English and American common law. How convincing is this effort? Did the Standard Oil Company violate the law because it gained monopoly? Because it had a "bad" intent? Because it engaged in "bad acts"? Is there a clear enough common law tradition to give guidance as to which concept ought to dominate?

What is bad intent? What are bad acts? Does the end result, monopoly, make acts bad? Is an act bad if it hurts competitors? Can it be bad if it does not hurt consumers? How would most people have answered these questions in 1911? How would you answer them today?

If Standard Oil had obtained its monopoly power by buying out willing competitors at healthy prices, would the Court have characterized Standard Oil as a reasonable monopolist? Is the power of a monopolist to exploit the public a function of the reasonableness with which the monopolist got its power?

55. [Authors' Note:] Two weeks later the Court handed down its opinion in United States v. American Tobacco Co., 221 U.S. 106 (1911). Reiterating the rule of reason and stressing again the importance of freedom of contract, the Court, by Chief Justice White, held that the five major tobacco companies and American Tobacco Company, the firm into which they had merged, violated Sections 1 and 2 of the Sherman Act. The five majors merged after a period of fierce competition. They increased capital and spent "enormous" amounts of money to buy some 40 competitors. They exacted covenants not to compete from the sellers, and they closed down many of the purchased businesses. When competitors refused to sell to the tobacco combination, defendants started price wars, bankrupted the recalcitrants, and bought their remaining assets.

56. Law and Economic Policy at 252, 267.

If only "unreasonable" monopoly is illegal, and if all monopoly harms the public, is there a gap between public harm and legal proscriptions?

Note the Court's reference to sovereign power. If we preserve business freedom, ban only those contracts that unreasonably restrain trade, and keep government out, the market will work to protect the public. Is this assumption correct? Is it empirically verifiable? Does it reflect a philosophy that fits within the sphere of political economy? Compare O.W. Holmes, The Common Law 88–96 (1881); Demsetz, The Trust Behind Antitrust, in Industrial Concentration and the Market System: Legal, Economic, Social and Political Perspectives 45 (Fox and Halverson, eds. 1979); M. Friedman, Capitalism and Freedom (1962); A. Gilder, Wealth and Poverty (1981).

The government's political reasons for choosing Standard Oil as a target for antitrust enforcement seem clear enough. The ultimate result, if not the rationale, also seems justified if only because this trust was paradigmatic of those Congress was aiming at when it enacted the statute. But scholars continue to debate the economic wisdom of the decision. In an influential article that has become a cornerstone for "Chicago" antitrust theory,[57] John McGee contends that the Standard Oil Company never priced below its cost. He therefore concludes that its ability to engage in low pricing must have derived from its efficiencies. See also A. Nevins, John D. Rockefeller: The Heroic Age of American Enterprise (2 vols. 1940).

Rockefeller brought oil to the American people at a lower price than had ever before been achieved. May we assume that Standard Oil could price below the prices charged by its competitors because it had achieved economies of scale and they had not? That it was able to obtain a low rate from the railroads because it cost the railroads less to carry a unit of oil shipped by Standard Oil (given the assured large and continuous supply) than it cost the railroads to carry a unit of the oil shipped by its small competitors? Suppose that Standard Oil were able to get lower prices from railroads not because the railroads' cost to serve it was less, but because the railroads, needing Standard Oil's business, were afraid to offend it and were prepared to take a lower return on Standard Oil's traffic than on the traffic of smaller oil companies. Would you then say that the success of Standard Oil was merely a triumph of efficiencies? Would Standard Oil, because it persuaded railroads to price discriminate in its favor, become a "bad" trust?

If Standard Oil gained its market share largely by efficiencies, could its competitors have done the same thing? Could Standard Oil have attained or kept its dominant market share had it not operated more efficiently than anyone else and had it not sold oil at a price lower than anyone else? Could it force railroads or other suppliers to price discriminate in its favor if they were not motivated to do so independently of Standard Oil's threats or blandishments? Why might a particular railroad fall in with a price demand from Standard Oil? Might Standard Oil have played one railroad off against others?

Pursuant to the court's decree, the Standard Oil combination was dissolved. The assets of the parent company were distributed to its stockholders. The Rockefellers, the dominant holders of stock in the parent company, retained control of the oil business. They became the controlling sharehold-

57. McGee, Predatory Price Cutting: The Standard Oil (N.J.) Case, 1 J. of Law & Econ. 137 (1958).

ers in each of the subsidiaries after dissolution. Each subsidiary remained dominant in its region.[58] The *Standard Oil* decree did not greatly affect Standard Oil's powerful position within the oil industry, until, years later, the discovery of new oil fields brought new entry, and, over time, common control of subsidiary companies eroded through stock trading.[59]

c. Taft's Legislative Program

The Congress during Taft's administration was markedly different from the Congress during Roosevelt's administration. The conservatives' hold on Congress weakened after 1908, and the election of 1910 effected a more thorough erosion of the conservatives' power. The Democratic Party achieved a majority in the House and undercut the conservative bastion in the Senate. The Democrats elected reform-minded leaders and the Progressive Republicans began to dominate the more conservative members of their party.

As during Roosevelt's administration, Congress passed little antitrust legislation.[60] Taft's proposal for federal incorporation did not pass. Western Republicans feared that the proposed system would weaken the antitrust act while strengthening big business, a suspicion fueled by big business' support of federal incorporation.[61] Although Taft tried to reassure the Progressive Republicans (somewhat half-heartedly perhaps), his efforts failed. Some remembered an earlier address in which he had defended federal incorporation as a way of helping national corporations escape from state controls. Finally, some Democrats proposed amendments to the Sherman Act in response to the *Standard Oil* decision. They wanted to return to what they regarded as Justice Peckham's sounder interpretation. They would have explicitly prohibited *every* restraint of trade, presumably leaving the court free to characterize some arrangements such as partnerships as not being restraints at all. Congress did not act on the Democrats' proposal.

Like the oil industry, the steel industry consolidated; but the facts were different.

UNITED STATES v. UNITED STATES STEEL CORP.
251 U.S. 417 (1920).

JUSTICE McKENNA: The case was heard in the District Court by four judges. They agreed that the bill should be dismissed; they disagreed as to the reasons for it. 223 Fed.Rep. 55. One opinion (written by Judge Buffington and concurred in by Judge McPherson) expressed the view that the Steel Corporation was not formed with the intention or purpose to monopolize or restrain trade, and did not have the motive or effect "to prejudice the public interest by unduly restricting competition or unduly obstructing the course of trade." The corporation, in the view of the opinion, was an evolution, a natural consummation of the tendencies of the industry on account of changing conditions, practically a compulsion

58. See J. Blair, Economic Concentration: Structure, Behavior and Public Policy 563 (1972).

59. Power and Responsibility at 405.

60. E. Jones, The Trust Problem in the United States 330–331 (1921).

61. Era of Roosevelt at 286–287.

from "the metallurgical method of making steel and the physical method of handling it," this method, and the conditions consequent upon it, tending to combinations of capital and energies rather than diffusion in independent action. . . .

The other opinion (by Judge Woolley and concurred in by Judge Hunt, 223 Fed.Rep. 161) was in some particulars, in antithesis to Judge Buffington's. The view was expressed that neither the Steel Corporation nor the preceding combinations, which were in a sense its antetypes, had the justification of industrial conditions, nor were they or it impelled by the necessity for integration, or compelled to unite in comprehensive enterprise because such had become a condition of success under the new order of things. On the contrary, that the organizers of the corporation and the preceding companies had illegal purpose from the very beginning, and the corporation became "a combination of combinations, by which, directly or indirectly, approximately 180 independent concerns were brought under one business control," which, measured by the amount of production, extended to 80% or 90% of the entire output of the country, and that its purpose was to secure great profits which were thought possible in the light of the history of its constituent combinations, and to accomplish permanently what those combinations had demonstrated could be accomplished temporarily, and thereby monopolize and restrain trade.[1]

The organizers, however (we are still representing the opinion), underestimated the opposing conditions and at the very beginning the Corporation instead of relying upon its own power sought and obtained the assistance and the cooperation of its competitors (the independent companies). In other words the view was expressed that the testimony did "not show that the corporation in and of itself ever possessed or exerted sufficient power when acting alone to control prices of the products of the industry." Its power was efficient only when in cooperation with its competitors, and hence it concerted with them in the expedients of pools, associations, trade meetings, and finally in a system of dinners inaugurated in 1907 by the president of the company, E.H. Gary, and called "the Gary Dinners." The dinners were congregations of producers and "were nothing but trade meetings," successors of the other means of associated action and control through such action. They were instituted first in "stress of panic," but, their potency being demonstrated, they were after-

[Authors' note:] Footnotes within cases here and throughout are the footnotes of the court unless otherwise stated. The footnote numbers correspond with those in the opinion as originally reported.

1. As bearing upon the power obtained and what the Corporation did we give other citations from Judge Woolley's opinion as follows:

". . . As a last analysis of this testimony, it is sufficient to say it shows that, large as was the corporation, and substantial as was its proportion of the business of the industry, the corporation was not able in the first ten years of its history to maintain its position in the increase of trade. During that period, its proportion of the domestic business decreased from 50.1 per cent. to 40.9 per cent. and its increase of business during that period was but 40.6 per cent. of its original volume. Its increase of business, measured by percentage, was exceeded by eight of its competitors, whose increase of business, likewise measured by percentage, ranged from 63 to 3779. This disparity in the increase of production indicates that the power of the corporation is not commensurate with its size, and that the size and the consequent power of the corporation are not sufficient to retard prosperous growth of efficient competitors. . . ."

wards called to control prices "in periods of industrial calm." "They were pools without penalties" and more efficient in stabilizing prices. But it was the further declaration that "when joint action was either refused or withdrawn the Corporation's prices were controlled by competition."

The Corporation, it was said, did not at any time abuse the power or ascendency it possessed. It resorted to none of the brutalities or tyrannies that the cases illustrate of other combinations. It did not secure freight rebates; it did not increase its profits by reducing the wages of its employees—whatever it did was not at the expense of labor; it did not increase its profits by lowering the quality of its products, nor create an artificial scarcity of them; it did not oppress or coerce its competitors—its competition, though vigorous, was fair; it did not undersell its competitors in some localities by reducing its prices there below those maintained elsewhere, or require its customers to enter into contracts limiting their purchases or restricting them in resale prices; it did not obtain customers by secret rebates or departures from its published prices; there was no evidence that it attempted to crush its competitors or drive them out of the market, nor did it take customers from its competitors by unfair means, and in its competition it seemed to make no difference between large and small competitors. Indeed it is said in many ways and illustrated that "instead of relying upon its own power to fix and maintain prices, the corporation, at its very beginning sought and obtained the assistance of others." It combined its power with that of its competitors. It did not have power in and of itself, and the control it exerted was only in and by association with its competitors. Its offense, therefore, such as it was, was not different from theirs and was distinguished from theirs "only in the leadership it assumed in promulgating and perfecting the policy." This leadership it gave up, and it had ceased to offend against the law before this suit was brought. It was hence concluded that it should be distinguished from its organizers and that their intent and unsuccessful attempt should not be attributed to it, that it "in and of itself is not now and has never been a monopoly or a combination in restraint of trade," and a decree of dissolution should not be entered against it. . . .

It is the contention of the Corporation . . . (to quote the words of Judge Buffington, he quoting those of a witness,) . . . "that instead, as was then the practice, of having one mill to make 10 or 20 or 50 products, the greatest economy would result from having one mill make one product, and make that product continuously." In other words, that there was a necessity for integration, and rescue from the old conditions—from their improvidence and waste of effort; and that, in redress of the conditions, the Corporation was formed, its purpose and effect being "salvage not monopoly," to quote the words of counsel. It was, is the insistence, the conception of ability, "a vision of a great business which should embrace all lines of steel and all processes of manufacture from the ore to the finished product and which by reason of the economies thus to be effected and the diversity of products it would be able to offer, could successfully compete in all the markets of the world."

. . . We have seen that the judges of the District Court unanimously concurred in the view that the Corporation did not achieve monopoly, and such is our deduction, and it is against monopoly that the statute is directed, not against an expectation of it, but against its realization, and it is certain that it was not realized. . . . What then can now be urged against the Corporation? . . . It is greater in size and productive power than any of its competitors, equal or nearly equal to them all, but its power over prices was not and is not commensurate with its power to produce.

. . . The company's officers and, as well, its competitors and customers, testified that its competition was genuine, direct and vigorous, and was reflected in prices and production. No practical witness was produced by the Government in opposition. Its contention is based on the size and asserted dominance of the Corporation—alleged power for evil, not the exertion of the power in evil. Or as counsel put it, "a combination may be illegal because of its purpose; it may be illegal because it acquires a dominating power, not as a result of normal growth and development, but as a result of a combination of competitors." Such composition and its resulting power constitute, in the view of the Government, the offence against the law, and yet it is admitted "no competitor came forward and said he had to accept the Steel Corporation's prices." But this absence of complaint counsel urge against the Corporation. Competitors, it is said, followed the Corporation's prices because they made money by the imitation. Indeed the imitation is urged as an evidence of the Corporation's power. "Universal imitation," counsel assert, is "an evidence of power." In this concord of action, the contention is, there is the sinister dominance of the Corporation—"its extensive control of the industry is such that the others [independent companies] follow." Counsel, however, admit that there was "occasionally" some competition, but reject the suggestion that it extended practically to a war between the Corporation and the independents. Counsel say, "They [the Corporation is made a plural] called a few—they called 200 witnesses out of some forty thousand customers, and they expect with that customer evidence to overcome the whole train of price movement shown since the Corporation was formed." And "movement of prices" counsel explained "as shown by the published prices . . . they were the ones that the competitors were maintaining all during the interval."

It would seem that "200 witnesses" would be fairly representative. Besides the balance of the "forty thousand customers" was open to the Government to draw upon. Not having done so, is it not permissible to infer that none would testify to the existence of the influence that the Government asserts? At any rate, not one was called, but instead the opinion of an editor of a trade journal is adduced, and that of an author and teacher of economics whose philosophical deductions had, perhaps, fortification from experience as Deputy Commissioner of Corporations and as an employee in the Bureau of Corporations. His deduction was that when prices are constant through a definite period an artificial influence is indicated; if they vary during such a period it is a consequence of competitive conditions. It has become an aphorism that there is danger of deception in generalities, and in a case of this importance we should have something surer for judgment than speculation, something more than a deduction equivocal of itself even though the facts it rests on or asserts were not contradicted. . . .

But there are other paradoxes. The Government does not hesitate to present contradictions, though only one can be true, such being we were told in our school books the "principle of contradiction." In one competitors (the independents) are represented as oppressed by the superior power of the Corporation; in the other they are represented as ascending to opulence by imitating that power's prices which they could not do if at disadvantage from the other conditions of competition; and yet confederated action is not asserted. If it were this suit would take on another cast. The competitors would cease to be the victims of the Corporation and would become its accomplices. And there is no other alternative. The suggestion that lurks in the Government's contention that the acceptance of the Corporation's prices is the submission of impotence to irresistible power is, in view of the testimony of the competitors, untenable. They, as we have seen, deny restraint in any measure or illegal influence of any kind. The Government, therefore, is reduced to the assertion that the size of the Corporation, the power it may have, not the exertion of the power, is an abhorrence to the law, or as the Government says, "the combination embodied in the Corporation unduly restrains competition by its *necessary effect*, [the italics are the emphasis of the Government] and therefore is unlawful regardless of purpose." "A wrongful purpose," the Government adds, is "matter of aggravation." The illegality is statical, purpose or movement of any kind only its emphasis. To assent to that, to what extremes should we be led? Competition consists of business activities and ability—they make its life; but there may be fatalities in it. Are the activities to be encouraged when militant, and suppressed or regulated when triumphant because of the dominance attained? To such paternalism the Government's contention, which regards power rather than its use the determining consideration, seems to conduct. Certainly conducts we may say, for it is the inevitable logic of the Government's contention that competition must not only be free, but that it must not be pressed to the ascendency of a competitor, for in ascendency there is the menace of monopoly.

We have pointed out that there are several of the Government's contentions which are difficult to represent or measure, and, the one we are now considering, that is the power is "unlawful regardless of purpose," is another of them. It seems to us that it has for its ultimate principle and justification that strength in any producer or seller is a menace to the public interest and illegal because there is potency in it for mischief. The regression is extreme, but short of it the Government cannot stop. The fallacy it conveys is manifest.

The Corporation was formed in 1901, no act of aggression upon its competitors is charged against it, it confederated with them at times in offence against the law, but abandoned that before this suit was brought, and since 1911 no act in violation of law can be established against it except its existence be such an act. This is urged, as we have seen, and that the interest of the public is involved, and that such interest is paramount to corporation or competitors. Granted—though it is difficult to see how there can be restraint of trade when there is no restraint of competitors in the trade nor complaints by customers—how can it be worked out of the situation and through what proposition of law? Of course it calls for nothing other than a right application of the law and to repeat what we have said above, shall we declare the law to be that size is an offence even though it minds its own business because what it does is imitated? The Corporation is undoubtedly of impressive size and it takes an effort of resolution not to be affected by it or to exaggerate its influence. But we must adhere to the law and the law does not make mere size an offence or the existence of unexerted power an offence. It, we repeat, requires overt acts and trusts to its prohibition of them and its power to repress or punish them. It does not compel competition nor require all that is possible. . . .

In conclusion we are unable to see that the public interest will be served by yielding to the contention of the Government respecting the dissolution of the company or the separation from it of some of its subsidiaries; and we do see in a contrary conclusion a risk of injury to the public interest, including a material disturbance of, and, it may be serious detriment to, the foreign trade. And in submission to the policy of the law and its fortifying prohibitions the public interest is of paramount regard.

We think, therefore, that the decree of the District Court should be affirmed.

Justices McReynolds and Brandeis took no part in the consideration or decision of the case.

Justice Day dissented.

Questions and Comments

Does the Court's holding in *U.S. Steel* naturally follow from its opinion in *Standard Oil*? Does *U.S. Steel* effectively overrule *Northern Securities,* or are the cases fairly distinguishable?

Northern Securities was the first in a series of railroad cases that spanned a period of years ending in 1922. In each case, the Court held illegal the combination of great competing railroad lines even though the defendant companies had engaged in no brutalities or tyrannies. See, in addition to *Northern Securities,* United States v. Union Pacific R.R. Co., 226 U.S. 61 (1912), United States v. Reading Co., 253 U.S. 26 (1920) and United States v. Southern Pacific Co., 259 U.S. 214 (1922). Did the Court develop a separate rule for the railroads? If, in most industries, brutalities are required before a trust is unlawful, why might they be dispensed within railroad cases?

When the Court says that "mere size" and "the existence of unexerted power" are no offense, what does it mean? If in *U.S. Steel* the government had proved that the steel company gained power over price but had not proved that it brutalized its competitors, would the government have won or lost? If U.S. Steel held 80% to 90% of the market at the time the case came to court, would the government have won?

How does the Court's decision in *U.S. Steel* compare with the varying presidential views that had been expressed about trusts? Is it consistent with

Taft's view that there should be objective legal indicia? With Roosevelt's claim of administrative discretion to distinguish between good and bad trusts?

Does the Court suggest that U.S. Steel did have sufficient power over price to be a price leader, but not sufficient power to be a monopolist? Does price leadership restrain trade?

Consider the government's problems of proof. It introduced expert economic testimony regarding price movements (apparently the first time economic evidence was used). Prices appeared to be "administered," that is, set by steel companies in response to U.S. Steel's "price leadership." The steel companies do not appear to have been "price takers," forced by the market to price at cost. The court thought more persuasive than this testimony the fact that competitors and customers alike came forward to testify in favor of U.S. Steel, that none testified against it. Is there any reason why purchasers of steel might be indifferent to supra-competitive steel prices? If steel were an "input" into a further industrial process, might the buyer "pass on" the monopoly overcharge? Is there any reason why smaller competitors might be indifferent (or even favorably disposed) to supra-competitive pricing by U.S. Steel? Which body of evidence—the government's economic testimony or the reaction of competitors and customers—do you find more persuasive?

Consider the list of brutalities and tyrannies that (according to Judge Woolley) illustrate behavior of illegal combinations but not of U.S. Steel. As to each "brutality," consider: Does this conduct hurt competitors? Buyers? Both? Might some of the "brutalities" increase the intensity of competitive rivalry and lower prices to buyers and ultimate customers? Is it bad to take customers from competitors by low prices? By prices that are below a published price schedule? Do the brutalities listed by Judge Woolley and quoted by the Court refer predominantly to making life tough for competitors, or to exploiting buyers? Under what conditions might harm to consumers follow from harm to competitors? Might gain to consumers follow from harm to competitors? Under what circumstances? In the early 1900s economists were not writing about questions like these. They are today. In the early 1900s the Court did not make the distinctions suggested by these questions. It does today.

Were the Gary dinners, which concededly were abandoned before suit, properly invoked by U.S. Steel to disprove its power? Recall the Court's observations:

> [U.S. Steel] combined its power with that of its competitors. It did not have power in and of itself, and the control it exerted was only in and by association with its competitors. Its offense, therefore, such as it was, was . . . "only in the leadership it assumed in promulgating and perfecting the policy." This leadership it gave up [when it abandoned the Gary dinners].[62]

Remember the *U.S. Steel* opinion when we deal with cartels and cartel-like (oligopoly) behavior. Did the U.S. Steel mergers tend to induce oligopoly behavior, rather than lead to single-firm monopoly?

In later years the Court would focus more systematically on the effects of mergers in concentrated or concentrating markets, and would apply Section 1 of the Sherman Act [63] and Section 7 of the Clayton Act [64] when the mergers restrained competition, whether or not they threatened to produce monopoly.

62. 251 U.S. at 417, 441.   64. See id.

63. See infra, Appendix A.

5. TRUST BUSTING UNDER WILSON: LEGISLATIVE REFORMS ACHIEVED

The rule of reason had a mixed reception.[65] It displeased some because its stress on intent would make antitrust lawsuits even more difficult to win. It displeased others, even large firms, because it gave them no guidance as to what they could or could not legally do. Also, distrust of judicial discretion remained high. Moderates in both parties called for more explicit definition of illegal business conduct during the 1912 presidential campaign. The election of Woodrow Wilson seemed to express a national sentiment in favor of legislative amplification of antitrust.[66]

a. The 1912 Campaign and Antitrust Policy

The election of 1912 was a heated battle between three contestants: William Howard Taft, Theodore Roosevelt, and Woodrow Wilson. Taft, the Republican candidate, stood little chance of winning since his policies had alienated both the Progressives and business. Theodore Roosevelt, angered by Taft's actions (especially the antitrust suit against U.S. Steel), tried to recapture disaffected Progressive Republicans as well as Progressive Democrats as the leader of the new Progressive Party. The steel suit and Roosevelt's distinctive trust program catapulted him into the Presidential arena.[67] The Democratic Party nominated Woodrow Wilson.

Wilson was not well known. A lawyer and a political scientist, he gained administrative experience as the president of Princeton University and as the governor of New Jersey. Wilson occupied a middle ground between Roosevelt and Taft. He was fairly conservative and did not fully approve of the Progressives' social reforms. He did have political ambition and savvy, however, and he adopted a progressive stance out of political necessity.

Antitrust was an important campaign issue. Roosevelt drew heavily upon Herbert Croly's Promise of American Life (1909) to develop a more theoretical justification for his earlier antitrust policy. Harkening to Hamiltonian notions, Croly advocated the active participation of the federal government in the economic affairs of the nation. To Croly, opposition to a strong national government stemmed from an outdated Jeffersonian idea that central government is antidemocratic. Roosevelt used Croly's analysis to argue that the national government was now the only institution capable of securing democracy, and that government had to secure democracy through neo-Hamiltonian policies of direct intervention in the economy.[68] Roosevelt reiterated his proposal for a strong federal agency to directly supervise the large corporations. Roosevelt's beliefs clearly guided the Progressive Party platform. The platform papers stated that trusts were inevitable and essential even though they had abused their power. The platform called for a federal regulatory

65. See M. Watkins, Mergers and the Law 38–39 (1929).

66. Power and Responsibility at 448–50.

67. Id. at 418–21, 428.

68. Woodrow Wilson at 18–20.

commission to curb these abuses as well as to give business the certainty needed to conduct its affairs.[69]

The platform of the Republican Party was similar, but vaguer. It advocated the establishment of a federal trade commission to govern and administer federal laws dealing with interstate commerce and businesses, "thus placing in the hands of an administrative board many of the functions now necessarily exercised by the courts." The Republicans also argued for more detailed laws defining illegal activities "to the end that those who honestly intend to obey the law may have a guide for their action and those who aim to violate the law may the more surely be punished." [70]

With the help of Louis Brandeis, his chief economic advisor during the campaign, Wilson developed antitrust policies that contrasted sharply with Roosevelt's "new nationalism." [71] The Democratic Party joined the call for more detailed laws. But it called for a far-reaching law that would prohibit practices and structures such as holding companies, interlocking directorships, stock watering, and price discrimination. The Democratic Party condemned the Republicans for their historical acceptance of the notorious trusts such as the Standard Oil Company and the Tobacco Trust. Further, the Democrats criticized the Court's decision in the *Standard Oil* case, saying: "We regret that the Sherman Act has received a judicial construction depriving it of much of its efficiency and we favor the enactment of legislation which will restore to the statute the strength of which it has been deprived by such interpretation." [72]

Wilson's own program was called the "New Freedom." He wanted the federal government to ensure economic opportunity by enacting "a body of laws which will look after the men who are on the make rather than the men who are already made." [73] The government was to liberate business from the "shackles of monopoly and special privilege" and to enable the exercise of individual energy.[74] Wilson wanted to eliminate the influence of special interests groups, including labor, farm organizations, and the large corporations. He initially opposed federal regulatory commissions because of the likelihood that special interests would control them. He said: "If the government is to tell big business how to run their business, then don't you see that big businessmen have to get [even] closer to the government than they are now? Don't you see that they must capture the government, in order not to be restrained by it?" [75] Thus a strong, active government was dangerous; but massive corporate bureaucracies were dangerous, too.[76]

b. Government–Business Relations Under Wilson

While Wilson often espoused the virtues of competition and small businesses, he also recognized the virtues of size. Thus:

69. National Party Platforms at 178.

70. Id. at 184.

71. Regulation in Perspective at 28–36.

72. National Party Platforms at 169.

73. Wilson, The New Freedom in Progressive Movement at 171.

74. Woodrow Wilson at 21.

75. Progressive Movement at 176.

76. L. Hacker, The Course of American Economic Growth and Development 269 (1970).

The . . . time of individual competition is probably gone. . . . We will do business henceforth, when we do it, on a great and successful scale, by means of corporations . . . so that the thing we are after is not recognizing size in measuring capacity for damage, but measuring and comprehending the actual damage done.[77]

Like Roosevelt, Wilson maintained: "our objection to any given corporation must be, not that it is big, but that it behaves badly." [78] His object was not to shackle business but to ensure that it played by the rules of fair competition.[79]

c. Wilson's Legislative Record

The Wilson administration is much better known for its antitrust legislative program than for its prosecution record. Congress passed both the Clayton and the Federal Trade Commission (FTC) Acts during Wilson's tenure.

i. The Clayton Act

The House Committee on Banking and Currency established a subcommittee, the Pujo Committee, to investigate the "Money Trust" and to offer suggestions for banking reform. The Pujo Committee published its report in 1913. The report revealed that a financial oligarchy of a few banks directed numerous corporations. For example, four banks controlled 341 directorships in 112 corporations with an aggregate capitalization of $22 billion. A relatively small group of businessmen were the directors of almost all banks and all important industrial corporations. They met one another again and again on interlocking boards. The ultimate old-boy network controlled the country.[80]

The Pujo Report alarmed many Americans and prompted new efforts at reform. Banks had always been suspect institutions to some groups of Americans. The Jeffersonians, the Jacksonians, and the Populists all distrusted banks and suspected them of cheating people to make enormous profits.[81] The Pujo Report confirmed old suspicions. The immediate result was the Federal Reserve Act, which established a federal system of bank regulation.[82] The report also influenced the passage of the Federal Trade Commission and Clayton Acts.

The Clayton Act was the product of many aspirations, forces, and compromises. President Wilson wanted to prevent bad acts of powerful business and to give a clearer path to the entrepreneur. He wanted to proscribe the abusive practices revealed in the Pujo hearings. Some members of Congress wanted to make antitrust law more precise and more limited; other members of Congress wanted to maintain the law's

77. Quoted in Triumph of Conservatism at 206–207.

78. Quoted in id. at 69.

79. J.P. Miller, Woodrow Wilson's Contribution to Antitrust Policy, in The Philosophy and Policies of Woodrow Wilson 132, 134 (E. Latham ed. 1958).

80. Pujo Committee on the Money Trust, Sixty–Second Congress, 3d Sess., House Report No. 1593, v. III (1913), excerpted in Progressive Movement at 158.

81. For a history of banks and their political position in America, see B. Hammond, Banks and Politics: From the Revolution to the Civil War (1957).

82. Business did not necessarily oppose federal regulations of banks. See e.g., Triumph of Conservatism at 217–254.

generality, while specifying particular recurrent offenses. Responding to the call for specific prohibitions, the Clayton Bill singled out interlocking directorates, price discrimination, exclusive dealing arrangements, and stock acquisitions of competitors.

The Clayton Bill responded to other concerns as well. For example, it stated that labor was not commerce, and that the antitrust laws did not prohibit the formation of labor unions. It also forbade courts from issuing injunctions in labor cases. It declared peaceful boycotts and strikes legal. While these provisions were helpful to labor, their benefits were qualified (e.g., courts could issue anti-strike injunctions if " 'necessary to prevent irreparable injury to property' " [83]). The act did not give labor what it desired most—a complete exemption from the antitrust laws.[84]

Moreover, while proponents of antitrust won the battle to make the Clayton Act an addition to rather than a replacement for the Sherman Act, they lost the battle to outlaw the enumerated restraints per se. Progressive Republicans and others argued that a detailed listing of specific violations would lead to an inflexible law that would be quickly outdated. They succeeded in adding a qualifying clause; the specified conduct would be prohibited only if it substantially lessened competition or tended to create a monopoly. What was substantial or created the forbidden tendency would be left to the discretion of the agency.[85]

The Clayton Act drew a mixed response. Some, like La Follette, thought the law was much too weak.[86] Senator Reed complained, " 'When the Clayton bill was first written, it was a raging lion with a mouth full of teeth. It has degenerated to a tabby cat with soft gums, a plaintive mew, and an anaemic appearance. It is a sort of legislative apology to the trusts, delivered hat in hand and accompanied by assurances that no discourtesy is intended.' "[87] But while advocates of strong antitrust were somewhat disappointed, criticism by business was intense. Big industrialists passionately attacked the section of the act that prohibited interlocking directorates. Many business owners disliked the ban on price discrimination. Many business people were also displeased with the act's labor provisions. Wilson, meanwhile, took the role of statesman, and tried to reassure the business critics that the bill would aid the interests of sound business, not harm them.[88]

Kolko concludes that, overall, big business was pleased with the Clayton Act.[89]

ii. The Federal Trade Commission

Wilson initially proposed a federal trade commission with largely informational and reporting functions. Business, on the other hand, wanted a congenial, cooperative, government-business partnership in which the agency would act as a consultant to business, advising it on the legality of proposed conduct, while prohibiting unfair practices.[90] Wil-

83. See Appendix A.

84. Woodrow Wilson at 69–70.

85. Law and Economic Policy at 276.

86. Triumph of Conservatism at 263.

87. Quoted in Woodrow Wilson at 72–73.

88. Wilson to Morgan, Sept. 17, 1914, in The Papers of Woodrow Wilson 39–40 (A. Link ed. 1979) (hereinafter Wilson Papers).

89. Triumph of Conservatism at 268.

90. Woodrow Wilson at 66–68.

son's friend Louis Brandeis strongly supported the government-business partnership idea.[91] Wilson himself, who wanted to prevent bad behavior but to help and not hurt honest businessmen,[92] eventually was convinced.

The FTC Bill was supported, also, by progressive Republicans and others who believed that the agency would provide the expertise and flexibility to supervise corporations without endangering the economic health of business and the nation. On the other hand, some small business people, some Democrats, and more radical reformers opposed the agency because they feared that cooperation between big business and government would entrench the trusts.[93]

Given the constant complaint of businesses that they needed more certainty in the antitrust laws, it may seem puzzling that they would support an agency with broad discretion but oppose the Clayton Act with its more specific prohibitions; yet that is what they did. There was logic in their position. Big business anticipated that the new agency would be friendly to their interests; they expected to "capture" the agency, just as Wilson had at one time feared.[94] And they anticipated that the Clayton Act might be construed against them.

d. The New Freedom Begins and Legislative Reform Ends

Wilson publicly announced the arrival of the New Freedom in his annual address to Congress on December 8, 1914:

> Our program of legislation with regard to the regulation of business is now virtually complete. . . . The road at last lies clear and firm before business. It is a road which can be traveled without fear or embarrassment. [95]

Wilson's address signaled an end to legislative reform. Wilson had several reasons for his retreat. He and the Democrats believed that they had fulfilled their platform promises,[96] and that the new laws would curb bad tendencies. Perhaps Wilson thought he had succeeded in pleasing his political constituencies and had no further need to prove his dedication to popular reform. The most important incentive for abandoning further legislation, however, seems to have been the pressure Wilson received from business and from critics of the New Freedom during the nationwide depression in 1913–1914. Republicans blamed the nation's economic difficulties on the administration's policies and played on fears that regulation would hamper economic growth, arguing that the recent reforms had damaged business.[97]

In response to the criticism leveled against his administration, Wilson became more congenial to business interests. He invited business leaders to the White House to ask them for advice. He staffed the FTC with individuals who were sympathetic towards big business. He encouraged business managers who were in doubt about the legality of their practices

91. Id. at 71–72.

92. Id. at 70.

93. Businessmen and Reform at 139–140.

94. Id. at 140; Woodrow Wilson at 69.

95. Wilson Papers at 415.

96. Wilson Papers at 173.

97. Woodrow Wilson at 75; Businessmen and Reform at 143.

to consult, also, with the United States Department of Justice.[98] An era of government-business cooperation had arrived.

6. TRUST BUSTING ABATED: WORLD WAR I AND THE HAR-DING–COOLIDGE YEARS

Neither the Clayton Act nor the FTC Act seems to have had much immediate effect. World War I diverted national political attention from antitrust. Because of industry's devotion to the war effort and its demonstrated capacity to respond to national needs, many people began to respect and accept big business.[99] A period of prosperity and conservatism followed the end of the war. Neither the Presidency of Warren Harding (1921–1923) nor that of Calvin Coolidge (1923–1929) was noted for activism either in antitrust or other aspects of business regulation.

A few Sherman Act, Section 2 (monopoly) decisions reinforced the moral conception of good trusts and bad trusts. Standard Oil, a bad trust, and U.S. Steel, a good one, became models for the unreasonable and the reasonable trust. *International Harvester* reinforced the paradigm. A combination of the five major farm equipment companies, International Harvester Co. had been formed during the period of consolidations between 1900 to 1910, and had been one of the early targets of antitrust prosecution. In a 1914 consent decree the government required Harvester to spin off some assets, and as a consequence the company's share of the farm machinery market fell from 85 percent to 64 percent.

Nine years later the government asserted that competitive conditions had not been adequately restored, and the Justice Department petitioned to break the company into at least three separate parts. The Supreme Court found that International Harvester did not then have power to control or dictate price and that it had not priced below cost to drive out competitors. It affirmed dismissal of the petition. For the Court, Justice Sanford wrote:

> The most that can be said . . . is that many of its competitors have been accustomed, independently and as a matter of business expediency, to follow approximately the prices at which it has sold its harvesting machines; but one of its competitors has habitually sold its machines at somewhat higher prices. The law, however, does not make the mere size of a corporation, however impressive, or the existence of unexerted power on its part, an offense, when unaccompanied by unlawful conduct in the exercise of its power. *United States v. Steel Corporation*, 251 U.S. 417, 451. And the fact that competitors may see proper, in the exercise of their own judgment, to follow the prices of another manufacturer, does not establish any suppression of competition or show any sinister domination.[1]

Thus, by the late 1920s, judicial interpretation of the Sherman Antitrust Act stabilized. Cartels—at least naked, loose-knit agreements to fix prices—violated Section 1. Close-knit consolidation did not violate Section 1 or Section 2, absent a showing of fairly blatant efforts to drive out or discipline rivals or to force them into consolidation. As time passed,

---

98. Woodrow Wilson at 72–76.

99. Emergence of Oligopoly at 320.

1. United States v. International Harvester Co., 274 U.S. 693, 708–09 (1927).

changes in the law occurred. Those changes that began to evolve after the Great Depression of 1929 are better understood as chapters in modern law than as antecedents to it. At this point we abandon the largely historical perspective that has guided us, and adopt a functional organization in which monopoly, horizontal restraints, vertical restraints and mergers become our major categories.

Chapter 2

THE DEVELOPMENT OF THE MODERN LAW OF MONOPOLIZATION AND ATTEMPTS AND CONSPIRACIES TO MONOPOLIZE

A. THE 1920s AND EARLY 1930s AS TRANSITION YEARS: LETHARGIC GOVERNMENT AND ENERGETIC ECONOMISTS

In the 1920s business activity reached a high pitch. A wave of mergers, reminiscent of the turn of the century, went unchecked if not unnoticed. The business of government was, it seemed, to stay out of the way of business and to encourage technological development and the exchange of information. Calvin Coolidge, symbolic of business prosperity, did not seek reelection in 1928 and Herbert C. Hoover became President in 1929. Later that year the stock market crashed, precipitating massive, persistent economic hardship and unrelieved poverty, both urban and rural. In 1933 Franklin D. Roosevelt, elected with a mandate to lift the country out of depression, took office.

With the coming of the depression laissez faire fell into disrepute. The political and economic attitudes much in evidence in the twenties (which would become familiar again in the 1980s) nearly vanished from the mainstream of policy debate. The country began to look to government to solve its problems. Government's initial response was what is sometimes called corporatism. Under FDR's leadership Congress passed the National Recovery Act;[1] it contemplated a vast cartelization of industry under governmental aegis. Competitors and representatives of labor were brought together to write "Codes of Ethics" aimed at encouraging "fair" prices and wages and discouraging "chislers" who cut prices and paid poor wages. Cooperatively, business, government and organized labor would seek economic solutions. Through most of the 1920s, the government seemed indifferent to monopoly and cooperation, and in the

---

1. 48 Stat. 195 (1933).

early to mid–1930s it was actively fostering concerted action. At both stages, antitrust and the competitive ideal were held in abeyance.

B. NEOCLASSICAL THEORY ON THE ALLOCATIVE AND DISTRIBUTIVE EFFECTS OF MONOPOLY

What did economists have to say during this period when government seemed indifferent to monopoly? We noted in Chapter 1 that neo-classicism was well-developed by the turn of the century, largely through the influence of Marshall; it was the dominant mode of American economic thought during the first two decades of this century. This neoclassical mode of analysis provides a theoretical rationale for the idea of competition policy that is widely accepted today.

Since the time of Adam Smith, classical economists have recognized that a monopolistic producer not threatened by immediate invasion of its market is likely to produce less than consumers wish to buy because the producer can make more money by selling a restricted quantity at a higher price. Indeed, Chief Justice Popham suggested as much in the *Case of Monopolies* in 1603. But neo-classicism symbolized by the work of Marshall added significantly to the intellectual pallet. The earlier classical theory focused on production. The neoclassical theory gave equal attention to demand and supply and worked out geometric and mathematical models. What follows is a brief, simplified introduction that contrasts classical and neoclassical thought and presents the basic microeconomic models.

The classical economists developed their concepts within an economic environment that was characterized by private property and dominated by middle class merchants. Through the division of labor and accumulation of capital, self-interest yielded economic growth. A basic concept was the labor theory of value. It stated that the price of every product is determined by the amount of labor needed for its production. The so called "natural price" will be the amount needed to compensate the capitalist who forewent consumption to pay wages and rent. Given competition, the market price will cluster around this price. Market equilibrium is realized when the revenue of the producer equals its cost for production, including a fair return on investment.

There was a discernible similarity between this theoretical conception and the reality of eighteenth century commerce and industry. Smith and later classicists invigorated the liberal laissez faire politics of their day. But picture the American economic scene at the time of the Sherman Act. Due to increasing concentration, much of it achieved through consolidation, the American economy no longer looked like the static classical conception that presupposed a large number of small producers. Yet, American classicists clung to their conviction that, as long as the government followed laissez faire policies, including no tariff protection, competition would control prices.

It was at about this time that classical theory was significantly transformed by the "marginalists," also called mathematical economists or "neoclassicists." These followers of Marshall developed models from certain basic assumptions. The major assumptions were profit maximization as rational behavior for producers, maximization of utility as rational behavior for consumers and the freedom of all economic actors to decide whether or not to contract. Given scarcity, from these assumptions the "law of demand" was derived: As the price of a product increases demand for it diminishes. An example: Suppose you like oranges. If they are cheap enough you may buy them until you are sated. So may other buyers. But as the price goes up, you (and they) buy fewer. You want to maximize utility. To do so you must use for the purchase of other products some of the money that you would have had to spend to have all the oranges you could eat. Your orange purchases (and those of others) fall off because you (and they) would prefer things like coffee, eggs and bread for toast. Given these propensities among consumers we can imagine a market demand schedule for any specified product, indicating the number of units that will be purchased during a given segment of time at alternative prices.

In Graph 1 we have reproduced such a schedule. Market price is charted along the vertical, quantity along the horizontal, axis. The demand curve (for convenience, a straight line) represents the quantity that will be sold at different price levels. The demand curve for any product will be influenced by several factors: consumer taste; income levels; technology; size and structure of the market and relative prices of substitute products. It may be steep (close to the vertical) or shallow (close to the horizontal), or its steepness may vary over its length. Yet, given the "law of demand," the curve can be expected to have a negative slope.

Microtheory uses "static" models. Such a model is a "snap shot"; all relevant functions (e.g., consumer tastes) are assumed to be fixed and unchanging at the moment of analysis. Of course, theorists recognize that market conditions can change over time. Thus, the shape and location of the demand curve for any given product can be expected to alter over time, as changes occur among the factors that influence it. Consumer taste may change (either slowly as for washboards and buggy whips, or rapidly, as for hoola hoops and pet rocks); the relative price of substitutes may change (for example: changes in oil prices at the peak of power of the OPEC cartel influenced the price of coal, because both are to a certain extent exchangeable).

The above remarks concern the market demand for a product. Will the demand as perceived by an individual seller be the same? In reality even a monopolistic supplier may possess only limited information about the shape and location of its demand curve. It will know what quantity can be sold at current prices, and may have a good idea about how sales would decrease or increase with incremental changes in price. But a supplier will only be able to speculate on what effect on volume large changes in price would have. Nevertheless, as a rational market actor it will be aware that there is a direct relationship between the potential quantity that can be sold and the price charged.

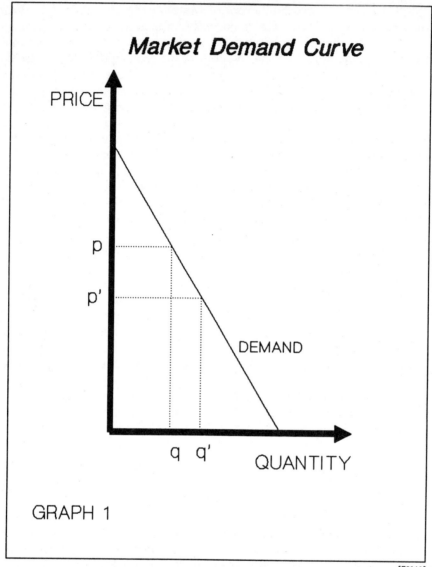

Market Demand Curve

PRICE

p

p'

DEMAND

q q'

QUANTITY

GRAPH 1

[E9161]

The basic theory of monopoly assumes away some of these information problems. It assumes that the monopolist knows its costs and the demand curve of this market in order to determine the price of its commodities.

The concepts of marginal revenue [MR in the graphs] and marginal cost are central to an understanding of the theory of monopoly. Marginal revenue is the increase of total revenue yielded by the sale of one additional unit of the product (the marginal or incremental unit). Knowing its own demand curve, a monopolist can derive its marginal revenue curve, as illustrated in Graph 2.

The MR curve reflects the fact that the monopolist receives less for each unit sold. If sales are to be increased prices have to be lowered.

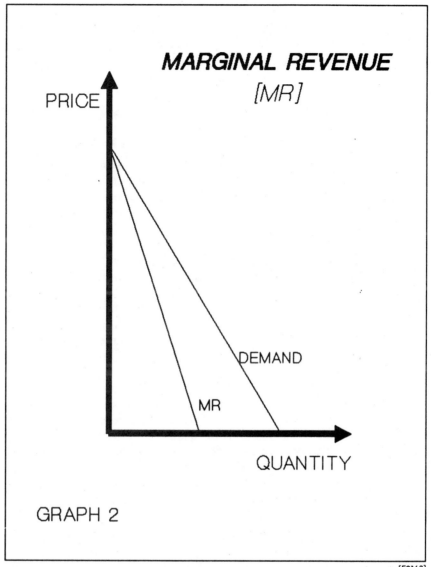

GRAPH 2

[E9162]

Thus both demand and the MR curve are downward sloping. MR,
however, decreases more rapidly than the demand curve because the
monopolist, to sell each additional unit, must reduce the price not only of
that marginal unit, but of all units. If the monopolist knew the maximum amount that each individual buyer would be willing to pay, the
monopolist could "perfectly discriminate" by selling to each buyer at that
buyer's maximum acceptable price. Each additional sale would then yield
its full price as its marginal revenue. The demand curve and the
marginal revenue curve would be equal. But the model assumes that the
monopolist cannot charge different prices to different buyers for an
identical product. Do you see why this assumption is made? Is it more
like the real world than the assumption of perfect discrimination would
be?

Marginal revenue will be significant to the profit maximizing monopolist, but so will marginal cost. Before completing the monopoly model we must understand the latter concept also.

The assumption of the model is that the total costs of production will vary according to the quantity produced. The cost of producing ten units will be less than the cost of producing 100. Since it is also assumed that producers know these relationships it is possible to draw up a schedule or curve showing the cost per unit of any given volume of production. What will the industry (or monopolist's) cost curve look like?

With increasing production the average cost per unit is usually assumed to fall rapidly, then to level out, and finally to rise. The reason for this is that total costs are made up of two components: fixed costs (costs such as rent for a plant, or interest on bonds sold to buy the plant, that do not vary with output) and variable costs (costs, such as the purchasing costs of raw materials, that rise or fall in direct correlation to the volume produced). The average cost per unit could be expected to have the characteristic shape above suggested when both fixed and variable costs are significant. At low levels of production the fixed costs must be divided among a few units of production. Per unit fixed costs fall rapidly as output goes up. As the plant reaches its efficient capacity these per unit costs tend to level off. At low and at efficient levels of production variable costs per unit, for material and labor, remain constant. Example: It might take 4 oranges and one can for each can of orange juice whether you make 100 or 1,000 cans. Thus, the fixed costs are most significant in affecting the shape of the average total costs curve. But as production exceeds the level of efficient capacity of the plant, variable costs start to rise rapidly, as a result of inefficient usage of workforce and machinery. Night shifts with labor cost differentials may be necessary. Additional space may have to be rented to store material or inventory. Defects and returns may become more common. These are the kinds of generalizations that the model builders try to take into account when they make their assumptions.

Having (or having assumed) an average cost curve which is built up by aggregating the fixed and the variable costs for each level of output, we can derive a marginal cost curve. Marginal cost is defined as the additional cost that must be incurred to produce one additional (the marginal) unit. (Because fixed costs do not increase or decrease with changes in output, marginal cost is a function only of variable costs.) When average cost is falling, marginal cost will be below average cost. When average cost starts to rise, marginal cost will exceed average cost. Given the average cost curve envisaged above, marginal cost would relate to the average cost as illustrated in Graph 3.

We now have a marginal revenue curve for a monopolist (derived from the industry demand curve) and a marginal cost curve (derived from the variable cost portion of an average cost curve). In Graph 4 we put the demand, marginal revenue and marginal cost curves on the same graph.

Recall, now, some of the assumptions of the model. The monopolist knows its demand and cost functions and behaves rationally in pursuing the only goal: maximizing immediate or short run profit. How much will

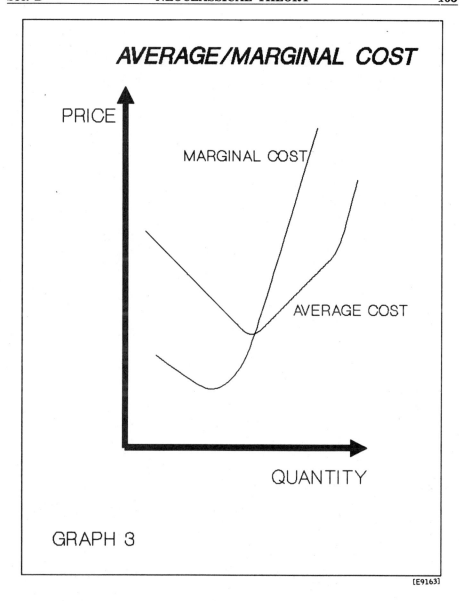

AVERAGE/MARGINAL COST

PRICE

MARGINAL COST

AVERAGE COST

QUANTITY

GRAPH 3

[E9163]

the monopolist produce, and at what price will it sell? Given the model's assumptions the answers are determinate; the problem is a tautology.

The monopolist will set its output at the point where marginal cost and marginal revenue are equal [q on the graph]. At any lower output (say, q′) marginal cost would be lower than marginal revenue; therefore, the monopolist could increase its profit by increasing output from q′ to q. Each additional unit would add a greater amount to revenue than to cost. At any higher output (say, q″) marginal cost would be higher than marginal revenue; therefore, the monopolist could increase its profit by decreasing output. Each unit reduction would reduce cost more than it would reduce revenue. Having thus determined the monopolist's output (q) we can, from the assumptions, immediately determine the monopolist's price. It will sell at the highest price that will clear the market, namely

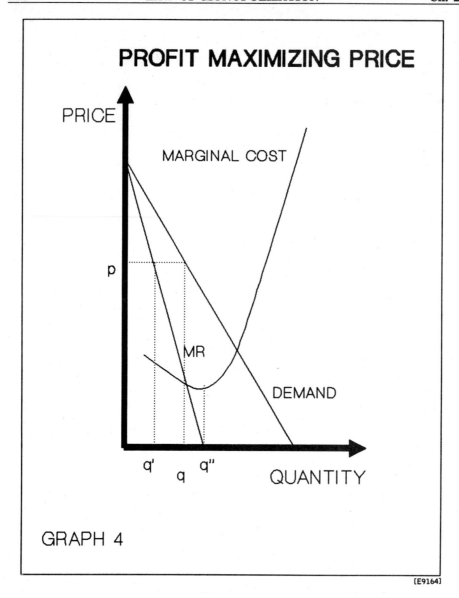

GRAPH 4

[E9164]

the price p, which is determined by the position of the demand curve. If it charged a higher price, it could not sell the total output, q, and inventory would build up; the resulting costs would reduce profits. If it set a lower price it would sell all units produced but would not reach maximum revenue.

In contrast to the monopolistic model the model of perfect competition assumes that the same industry, instead of being monopolized, is an industry of many competitive sellers, each with a share of total output so small that no individual seller's activity will have any significant influence on the market. Given this, each individual seller will take market price as a "given"; at that price it can sell its total production; at a higher price it can't sell anything. On those assumptions each seller will

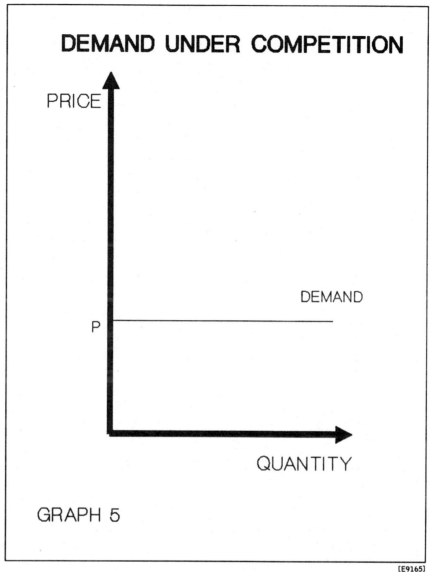

DEMAND UNDER COMPETITION

PRICE

P ———————————————— DEMAND

QUANTITY

GRAPH 5

[E9165]

regard its own demand curve not as downward sloping but as a horizontal line at the level of the current market price, as illustrated in Graph 5.

Each seller knows its own relevant cost functions, and to maximize profits is compelled to sell at the current market price and will produce such an amount that marginal costs will exactly equal marginal revenue. In all except the number of sellers the model of competition makes exactly the same assumptions as the model of monopolization. As a result, each seller sells the same (undifferentiated) product and industry-wide demand conditions remain constant. The monopolist gains no efficiencies (from its scale or otherwise) not accessible to the competitive firms. That is, the comparison assumes that at any given output for the market as a whole the aggregate costs experienced by individual firms would be the same as the costs of a single monopolist.

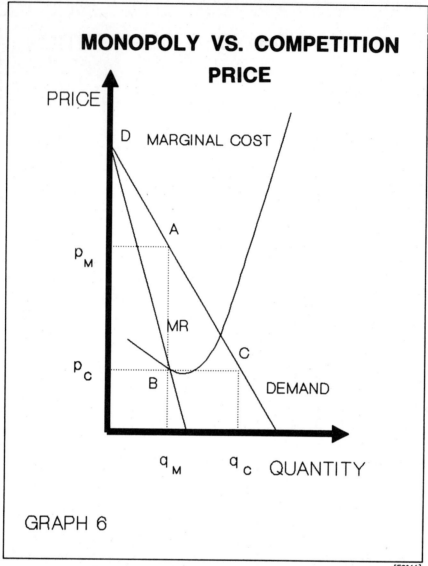

MONOPOLY VS. COMPETITION PRICE

GRAPH 6

[E9166]

Given these assumptions a comparison between the monopoly and the competitive model shows that output will always be higher and price always lower in a competitive environment. The relevant functions are plotted on Graph 6.

The monopolist will set price at q_m, the point where marginal costs and marginal revenue are equal, and will charge p_m. In competition, however, the individual seller, having a horizontal demand curve at the market price (Graph 5), will also have a horizontal marginal revenue at the market price. Perceiving no change in price with changes in its output, the competitive seller will experience an MR equal to the full price that it can obtain for each unit it produces and sells. Given this, the aggregate output for all firms in the competitive market will be at q_c, the point where marginal cost and demand (which signifies for each competitive firm its MR) are equal, and the price will be p_c. Like the monopoly result, the competitive result flows inexorably from the assumptions. Each competitive firm, which takes the market price as given, will always produce at an output where its marginal cost equals the market price. If it was producing either more or less it would be able to increase profits by decreasing or increasing output until that equality was attained. Neoclassical economic theory thus demonstrates, or exemplifies, the long accepted opinion that prices are higher and output is lower under monopoly conditions than under competitive conditions.

The same graphs, given the assumptions underlying them, also display other differences between competition and monopoly. Let us note some of these.

Assume that our model industry was first competitive and then monopolized. As price went up from p_c to p_m, and output fell from q_m to q_c. But note what happened to consumers and to the monopolist. The consumers now buying the q_m units pay a much higher per unit price than they paid under competition; there is an income transfer from these consumers to the monopolist equal to the rectangle p_c-p_m-A-B on Graph 6. Note also that there are many consumers who, under monopoly, do not get the product at all. This group is comprised of all those who, in the competitive situation, took the additional, higher output up to q_c, and who were willing to pay enough to cover the cost of producing this output, but who are not willing to pay p_m. Since the monopoly price exceeds the maximum price they are willing to pay, they must now turn to substitute products. These unsatisfied consumers in a monopolized market suffer the loss of the "consumer surplus" that they would have gained under competitive conditions—namely, the area measured by the triangle A–B–C on the graph. Given the downward slope of the demand curve, at any price there are some consumers who would have paid more for the product than its price if they were obliged to do so in order to get it. Thus, at any price, there will be a surplus for some consumers; but at a competitive price there will be a greater total consumer surplus than at the higher monopoly price. The total consumer surplus at the competitive price was $C-D-p_c$; at the monopoly price it is p_m-D-A. That portion of the consumer surplus lost by the change from competition to monopoly and measured by B–A–C is called a "dead weight loss" because everyone loses; it represents a surplus lost to consumers, and it represents profits producers might have taken but did not. By contrast, the area p_c-p_m-A-B, which also was part of the consumer surplus under competition and is not part of the consumer surplus under monopoly, is not viewed as a dead weight loss because the monopolist gets it; this rectangle represents the income transfer from the consumers to the monopolist.

How reliable are these models? Do they provide a compelling argument against monopoly and for competition? That depends, of course, on whether you believe that you can extrapolate confidently from these models to the real world. Are there real world markets that are like either the monopoly or competition model? Is the stock market or the market for wheat like the competitive model? Does anyone know? Are there ways to find out? Is, say, the sale and distribution of electric power in your area like the monopoly model? If you think it differs, in what ways? Assuming there may be markets that seem similar to the competitive model, and markets that seem similar to the monopoly model, do most markets look like one or the other, or like something quite different from either? What about automobiles? Air travel? Frozen food? Cereals? Steel?

One limit to the utility of these models is that few markets seem to be markets either of one or of many sellers. Most markets that have significance in the modern economy seem to be markets of several sellers, in many cases selling similar but differentiated products. We saw that for many staple products, such as oil, sugar and others, consolidation began to happen in existing markets at the end of the nineteenth century and early in the twentieth century. As new products developed—autos, airplanes, computers—producers either emerged full blown in concentrated patterns or also went through consolidation. Given the actual structure of many or most important markets many of the assumptions of the competition and monopoly models do not fit very well. Most industries today seem to be oligopolies of one kind or another. Some economists assume that markets of few sellers function much like competitive markets, but most economists do not. We will have occasion to discuss views about oligopoly as we go on. The only point that needs to be made now is that outcomes in oligopolistic markets are less predictable than those in either monopolized or competitive markets.

Is it realistic to assume that any specific market might be organized either competitively or monopolistically and that other things would remain the same? Is any movement from competitive to monopoly conditions going to change other relevant things, like cost, as well? If a consolidation increased both market power (so producers earned monopoly profits) and efficiency (because per unit costs fell) would the consolidation be favorable or unfavorable? Would you like to know whether prices to consumers went up or down?

The neoclassical models we have thus far presented do not deal specifically with cartelization, only with single-firm monopoly and competition. Until about the 1930s neoclassicists treated cartelization as a case of monopolization; there was little effort to deal with it through models unique to multifirm cooperation. In Chapter 3 we will consider how and when this attitude changed.

C. INDUSTRIAL ORGANIZATION ECONOMICS AND THE STUDY OF MODERN INDUSTRIAL STRUCTURE

Although neoclassical analysis was dominant during the early years of this century, by 1920 neoclassicism did not stand alone. A well-known economist provides this summary of other important theoretical developments:

By 1921 there were two strands of thought and research [about monopoly]. One was *neoclassical*. It took the theory of perfect competition to its austere extremes—as in Frank Knight's *Risk, Uncertainty and Profit.* It stressed the efficiency of the competitive system. It also relied on highly abstract analysis. The other approach was more *realistic.* It embraced the variety of conditions actually posed by monopoly and the mass of new information about its real-world roles. The neoclassical approach led to complacency, with the view that competition prevailed and that performance could not be improved. This stirred in the 1930s an overreaction, in which oligopoly came to be emphasized as being *the* problem. The 1920s had brought a second merger craze, fed by a stock-market boom. Many industries were converted into tight oligopolies. There was also a bizarre, frantic series of utility mergers and pyramiding. The stock-market collapse in 1929 accentuated the descent into the Depression of the 1930s.

The "realistic" approach now came to the fore, with new evidence and more detailed theories about the intermediate degrees of oligopoly. The importance of large corporations was explored by Adolf Berle and Gardiner Means. They argued that the largest firms were capturing an increasing share of the economy and that they were becoming units of unconstrained power. Edward Chamberlin and Joan Robinson staked out oligopoly and its price effects as the major new frontier for theory. The Depression, the rise of the Corporate State in Europe, and a seeming rise in American industrial monopoly lent the whole topic a stark urgency.

It is from this ferment of rethinking and rhetoric during the 1930s that the modern field of industrial organization emerged. The field has old roots, but it has taken form for only about . . . [now five] decades. It began to crystallize and grow in the 1930s as a major topic, with new theories, new measures of actual economic concentration, and a deep social concern about the nature of modern capitalism. In 1939 the first set of concentration ratios for industries (for the year 1935) were published. Data on prices, costs, output, and other industry features also began to be issued. All these fostered new statistical studies, with oligopoly concentration as the centerpiece.

From the 1930s, therefore, came a focus on industry conditions and on concentration. This differed from the earlier focus on individual firms and their market shares. In fact, the *industry* replaced the firm as the basis of thought and research. Meanwhile Edward S. Mason was leading a group of young specialists at Harvard toward intensive case studies of specific industries, as a different mode of research. And John M. Clark proposed in 1940 that "workable competition" was the reasonable criterion for good industry conditions. "Workable" might be far from "perfect" competition. Yet if a market seemed to have a reasonably competitive structure and pretty good performance, that could make it workable enough. Clark mentioned some eight elements of workability, and later students extended the list to more than twenty. Though the idea caught on, it was too unwieldy to be a basis for research.

W.G. Shepherd, The Economics of Industrial Organization 19–21 (1979).

Industrial organization economics (often called "I.O. economics") added the structure-conduct-performance paradigm to the well-developed neoclassical tradition. I.O. economists would first describe the structure of a particular industry. Structure includes all aspects of the industry that tended to be highly stable, especially numbers and market shares of firms, barriers to entry, extent of product differentiation and vertical relationships.   Next they would identify the determinants of the industry's structure; these might include such things as technology, the prices of inputs and established business practices and policies, whether predicated on costs or on analytical or strategic thinking.   They would also examine the conduct of firms, looking especially at pricing practices, styles of rivalry, and cooperation or collusion, if any.   Finally, the performance of the industry in terms of the public interest would be evaluated.   This drew attention to price-cost relationships (which directly effect allocative efficiency), innovativeness (or dynamic efficiency), and productive efficiency.   The basic I.O. ideas are, first, that industry details have to be understood before policymakers can gain useful insights (hence Shepherd's stress on "realism") and, second, that an industry's structure influences the conduct of firms within it.   This in turn, influences how well the public is served by the industry's performance—how allocatively, productively and dynamically efficient it will be.

As this mode of analysis became common there were interesting developments.   For one thing, the study of the details of particular industries and of the interaction between structure and conduct led to recognition that markets might fail to perform as envisaged by the neoclassical ideal and might do so for a wide variety of reasons.   Externalities are widespread.   These include costs, such as pollution from automobiles, and also benefits, such as the enhancement of the value of one owner's property due to development by a different owner.   Information is often inadequately and asymmetrically deployed.   Uncertainty is omnipresent.   Market power is widespread; it is caused by scale economies, product differentiation, and other factors.   Entry barriers may be inevitable.   Moreover, the relationship between structure and conduct is not one-directional.   It involves an interaction.   Firms attempt to exploit their environment and also to change it to their advantage.   For example, firms may not only take advantage of information failures and costs, but may contribute to them through either misleading or noninformational "image" advertising.   Another development, stimulated by the initial focus on the importance of structure, was cross-industry studies of the performance effects (most specifically, the profit effects) of concentration.

All of these ideas had considerable impact on antitrust after the mid–1930s.   Currently Chicago theorists, who have been particularly influential during the 1980s, have been challenging the value of I.O. economics.   They assert that antitrust should draw solely on the neoclassical tradition.   Nevertheless, the structure-conduct-performance paradigm, with refinements, continues to have relevance.   As we shall see in later parts of this chapter, the currently developing "new I.O." approach focuses on the dynamic and strategic elements of competitive interaction in concentrated markets.   It is, therefore, a potentially fruitful area for policy makers concerned about some of the most intractable problems of American industry.

D. THE "STRUCTURAL CONSENSUS" IS FORMED

1. THURMAN ARNOLD AND THE *ALCOA* LITIGATION

Both neoclassical and I.O. economists must have regarded the national policy to encourage cartelization that persisted during the NRA period as counterproductive. In all events, before Roosevelt's New Deal was very old, policy changed. Hitler rose to power in Germany, a profound and complex event and one many Americans perceived to have been facilitated by the cartels which dominated major German industries. Through them German industry was centralized and worked hand-in-hand with government in respect to external economic relations. German industry, already tightly organized, was readily brought to the service of the new fascist state. This German experience, along with the growth of communism and socialism in the western world, gave rise in America to a widespread concern that centralized control of the economy and the erosion of democratic institutions were closely related. Against that background, the new merger movement that was gaining energy in the United States looked ominous.

A related and more specific issue was the relationship between American and German industry. Some German-initiated cartels were transnational in scope. In some industries American firms participated. As the Nazi threat to peace and freedom grew there also developed among some in FDR's administration a conviction that to assure American security, U.S. corporations should break their connection with German cartels.

Responding to these views and also to increasing evidence that corporatism was not solving America's economic problems, President Roosevelt in 1938 called for the establishment of a Temporary National Economic Committee to study the causes and possible cures for industrial concentration. The Committee, subsequently authorized by Congress, held extensive hearings, lasting into the early 1940s. Its prodigious output testified to a heightened conviction that increasing industrial concentration was threatening virtually every aspect of American democratic life.

Also in 1938 FDR appointed a rather formidable Assistant Attorney General to head the Antitrust Division, Thurman Arnold. This marked a clear reversal of the administration's earlier course. Arnold was particularly aggressive in challenging cartels. He found them everywhere, a legacy of the indifferent twenties and the indulgent NRA period. He fought also against many other forms of trade restraints, often hidden behind transfers of technology and thus clothed with an aura of "progressiveness." See T. Arnold, The Bottlenecks of Business (1940).

Arnold also made his mark upon the law of monopoly. Even before his appointment, the United States brought suit against the sole producer of Aluminum in the United States, Aluminum Company of America (Alcoa), and its Canadian affiliate, Aluminum Limited. Arnold influenced the course of this case, which charged Alcoa with monopolizing the U.S.

market for aluminum, and also charged that Aluminum Limited, with foreign co-conspirators, operated an international cartel that restrained imports and kept all but a small amount of foreign aluminum out of the United States.

After a trial of two years and two months (which by 1940s' standards was astronomically long), the district court gave judgment for defendants. The government appealed to the Supreme Court.[2] Due to recusals the Court lacked the necessary quorum of six justices qualified to hear the case; it therefore referred the appeal to the Court of Appeals for the Second Circuit. The opinion there by Chief Judge Learned Hand is classic. It did much to shape the modern law of monopolization. We consider here only that part of the opinion that deals with the charge of monopolization against Alcoa.[3]

UNITED STATES v. ALUMINUM CO. OF AMERICA

148 F.2d 416 (2d Cir.1945).

CHIEF JUDGE LEARNED HAND: . . . Hall discovered a process by which [alumina could be isolated from bauxite and oxygen could be eliminated] and got a patent on April 2, 1889, which he assigned to "Alcoa," thus securing a legal monopoly of the manufacture of pure aluminum until April 2, 1906, when this patent expired. Meanwhile Bradley had invented a process by which the smelting could be carried on without the use of external heat, as had theretofore been thought necessary; and for this improvement he too got a patent on February 2, 1892. Bradley's improvement resulted in great economy in manufacture, so that, although after April 2, 1906, anyone could manufacture aluminum by the Hall process, for practical purposes no one could compete with Bradley or with his licensees until February 2, 1909, when Bradley's patent also expired. . . . Thus until February 2, 1909, "Alcoa" had either a monopoly of the manufacture of "virgin" aluminum ingot, or the monopoly of a process which eliminated all competition.

The extraction of aluminum from alumina requires a very large amount of electrical energy, which is ordinarily, though not always, most cheaply obtained from water power. Beginning at least as early as 1895, "Alcoa" secured such power from several companies by contracts, containing in at least three instances, covenants binding the power companies not to sell or let power to anyone else for the manufacture of aluminum. "Alcoa"—either itself or by a subsidiary—also entered into four successive "cartels" with foreign manufacturers of aluminum by which, in exchange for certain limitations upon its import into foreign countries, it secured covenants from the foreign producers, either not to import into the United

2. Until an amendment in 1974, the Expediting Act provided for direct appeal from the district court to the Supreme Court in antitrust cases brought by the United States. The 1974 amendment provides that appeal lies to a federal court of appeals unless a case is certified as one in which "immediate consideration of the appeal by the Supreme Court is of general public importance in the administration of justice," in which case appeal may proceed to the Supreme Court. Pub.L. 93–528, § 5, 88 Stat. 1708, 1709.

3. In another part of the opinion, the court held that there was an illegal international cartel to restrain imports into the United States and that Alcoa's Canadian affiliate (but not Alcoa) participated in that cartel.

States at all, or to do so under restrictions, which in some cases involved the fixing of prices. These "cartels" and restrictive covenants and certain other practices were the subject of a suit filed by the United States against "Alcoa" on May 16, 1912, in which a decree was entered by consent on June 7, 1912, declaring several of these covenants unlawful and enjoining their performance; and also declaring invalid other restrictive covenants obtained before 1903 relating to the sale of alumina. ("Alcoa" failed at this time to inform the United States of several restrictive covenants in water-power contracts; its justification—which the judge accepted—being that they had been forgotten.) "Alcoa" did not begin to manufacture alumina on its own behalf until the expiration of a dominant patent in 1903. In that year it built a very large alumina plant at East St. Louis, where all of its alumina was made until 1939, when it opened another plant in Mobile, Alabama.

None of the foregoing facts are in dispute, and the most important question in the case is whether the monopoly in "Alcoa's" production of "virgin" ingot, secured by the two patents until 1909, and in part perpetuated between 1909 and 1912 by the unlawful practices, forbidden by the decree of 1912, continued for the ensuing twenty-eight years; and whether, if it did, it was unlawful under § 2 of the Sherman Act. It is undisputed that throughout this period "Alcoa" continued to be the single producer of "virgin" ingot in the United States; and the plaintiff argues that this without more was enough to make it an unlawful monopoly. . . .

From 1902 onward until 1928 "Alcoa" was making ingot in Canada through a wholly owned subsidiary; so much of this as it imported into the United States it is proper to include with what it produced here. In the year 1912 the sum of these two items represented nearly ninety-one per cent of the total amount of "virgin" ingot available for sale in this country. This percentage varied year by year up to and including 1938. . .; with [three] exceptions it was always over eighty per cent of the total and for the last five years 1934–1938 inclusive it averaged over ninety per cent. The effect of such a proportion of the production upon the market we reserve for the time being, for it will be necessary first to consider the nature and uses of "secondary" ingot, the name by which the industry knows ingot made from aluminum scrap. This is of two sorts, though for our purposes it is not important to distinguish between them. One of these is the clippings and trimmings of "sheet" aluminum, when patterns are cut out of it, as a suit is cut from a bolt of cloth. The chemical composition of these is obviously the same as that of the "sheet" from which they come; and, although they are likely to accumulate dust or other dirt in the factory, this may be removed by well known processes. . . . Nevertheless, there is an appreciable "sales resistance" even to this kind of scrap, and for some uses (airplanes and cables among them), fabricators absolutely insist upon "virgin": just why is not altogether clear. The other source of scrap is aluminum which has once been fabricated and the article, after being used, is discarded and sent to the junk heap . . . as for example, cooking utensils, like kettles and pans, and the pistons or crank cases of motorcars. These are made with a substantial alloy and to restore the metal to its original purity costs more than it is worth. However, if the alloy is known both in quality and amount, scrap, when remelted, can be used again for the same purpose as before. In spite of this, as in the case of clippings and trimmings, the industry will ordinarily not accept ingot so salvaged upon the same terms as "virgin". . . .

There are various ways of computing "Alcoa's" control of the aluminum market—as distinct from its production—depending upon what one regards as competing in that market. The judge figured its share—during the years 1929–1938, inclusive—as only about thirty-three percent; to do so he included "secondary," and excluded that part of "Alcoa's own production which it fabricated and did not therefore sell as ingot. If, on the other hand, "Alcoa's" total production, fabricated and sold, be included, and balanced against the sum of imported "virgin" and "secondary," its share of the market was in the neighborhood of sixty-four per cent for that period. The percentage we have already mentioned—over ninety—results only if we both include all "Alcoa's" production and exclude "secondary". That percentage is enough to constitute a monopoly; it is doubtful whether sixty or sixty-four percent would be enough; and certainly thirty-three per cent is not. Hence it is necessary to settle what [w]e shall treat as competing in the ingot market. That part of its production which "Alcoa" itself fabricates, does not of course ever reach the market as ingot. . . . However, even though we were to assume that a monopoly is unlawful under § 2 only in case it controls prices, the ingot fabricated by "Alcoa," necessarily had a direct effect upon the ingot market. All ingot—with trifling exceptions—is used to fabricate intermediate, or end, products; and therefore all intermediate, or end, products which "Alcoa" fabricates and sells, pro tanto reduce the demand for ingot itself. . . . We cannot therefore agree that the computation of the percentage of "Alcoa's" control over the ingot market should not include the whole of its ingot production.

As to "secondary"[:] . . . At any given moment . . . "secondary" competes with "virgin" in the ingot market; further, it can, and probably does, set a limit or "ceiling" beyond which the price of "virgin" cannot go, for the cost of its production will in the end depend only upon the expense of scavenging and reconditioning. It might seem for this reason that in estimating "Alcoa's" control over the ingot market, we ought to include the supply of "secondary," as the judge did. Indeed, it may be thought a paradox to say that anyone has the monopoly of a market in which at all times he must meet a competition that limits his price. We shall show that it is not.

. . . "Alcoa" always knew that the future supply of ingot would be made up in part of what it produced at the time, and, if it was as far-sighted as it proclaims itself, that consideration must have had its share in determining how much to produce. How accurately it could forecast the effect of present production upon the future market is another matter. Experience, no doubt, would help; but it makes no difference that it had to guess; it is enough that it had an inducement to make the best guess it could, and that it would regulate that part of the future supply, so far as it should turn out to have guessed right. The competition of "secondary" must therefore be disregarded, as soon as we consider the position of

"Alcoa" over a period of years; it was as much within "Alcoa's" control as was the production of the "virgin" from which it had been derived. . . .

We conclude therefore that "Alcoa's" control over the ingot market must be reckoned at over ninety per cent; that being the proportion which its production bears to imported "virgin" ingot. If the fraction which it did not supply were the produce of domestic manufacture there could be no doubt that this percentage gave it a monopoly—lawful or unlawful, as the case might be. The producer of so large a proportion of the supply has complete control within certain limits. It is true that, if by raising the price he reduces the amount which can be marketed—as always, or almost always, happens—he may invite the expansion of the small producers who will try to fill the place left open; nevertheless, not only is there an inevitable lag in this, but the large producer is in a strong position to check such competition; and, indeed, if he has retained his old plant and personnel, he can inevitably do so. There are indeed limits to his power; substitutes are available for almost all commodities, and to raise the price enough is to evoke them. . . . Moreover, it is difficult and expensive to keep idle any part of a plant or of personnel; and any drastic contraction of the market will offer increasing temptation to the small producers to expand. But these limitations also exist when a single producer occupies the whole market; even then, his hold will depend upon his moderation in exerting his immediate power.

The case at bar is however different, because, for aught that appears there may well have been a practically unlimited supply of imports as the price of ingot rose. Assuming that there was no agreement between "Alcoa" and foreign producers not to import, they sold what could bear the handicap of the tariff and the cost of transportation. For the period of eighteen years—1920–1937—they sold at times a little above "Alcoa's" prices, at times a little under; but there was substantially no gross difference between what they received and what they would have received, had they sold uniformly at "Alcoa's" prices. While the record is silent, we may therefore assume—the plaintiff having the burden—that, had "Alcoa" raised its prices, more ingot would have been imported. Thus there is a distinction between domestic and foreign competition; the first is limited in quantity, and can increase only by an increase in plant and personnel; the second is of producers who, we must assume, produce much more than they import, and whom a rise in price will presumably induce immediately to divert to the American market what they have been selling elsewhere. It is entirely consistent with the evidence that it was the threat of greater foreign imports which kept "Alcoa's" prices where they were, and prevented it from exploiting its advantage as sole domestic producer; indeed, it is hard to resist the conclusion that potential imports did put a "ceiling" upon these prices. Nevertheless, within the limits afforded by the tariff and the cost of transportation, "Alcoa" was free to raise its prices as it chose, since it was free from domestic competition, save as it drew other metals into the market as substitutes. Was this a monopoly within the meaning of § 2? The judge found that, over the whole half century of its existence, "Alcoa's" profits upon capital invested, after payment of income taxes, had been only about ten per cent, and, although the plaintiff puts this figure a little higher, the difference is negligible. . . .   This assumed, it would be hard to say that "Alcoa" had made exorbitant profits on ingot, if it is proper to allocate the profit upon the whole business proportionately among all its products—ingot, and fabrications from ingot.   A profit of ten per cent in such an industry, dependent, in part at any rate, upon continued tariff protection, and subject to the vicissitudes of new demands, to the obsolescence of plant and process—which can never be accurately gauged in advance—to the chance that substitutes may at any moment be discovered which will reduce the demand, and to the other hazards which attend all industry; a profit of ten per cent, so conditioned, could hardly be considered extortionate.

There are however, two answers to any such excuse; and the first is that the profit on ingot was not necessarily the same as the profit of the business as a whole, and that we have no means of allocating its proper share to ingot.   It is true that the mill cost appears; but obviously it would be unfair to "Alcoa" to take, as the measure of its profit on ingot, the difference between selling price and mill cost; and yet we have nothing else.   It may be retorted that it was for the plaintiff to prove what was the profit upon ingot in accordance with the general burden of proof. We think not.   Having proved that "Alcoa" had a monopoly of the domestic ingot market, the plaintiff had gone far enough; if it was an excuse, that "Alcoa" had not abused its power, it lay upon "Alcoa" to prove that it had not.   But the whole issue is irrelevant anyway, for it is no excuse for "monopolizing" a market that the monopoly has not been used to extract from the consumer more than a "fair" profit.   The Act has wider purposes.   Indeed, even though we disregarded all but economic considerations, it would by no means follow that such concentration of producing power is to be desired, when it has not been used extortionately. Many people believe that possession of unchallenged economic power deadens initiative, discourages thrift and depresses energy; that immunity from competition is a narcotic, and rivalry is a stimulant, to industrial progress; that the spur of constant stress is necessary to counteract an inevitable disposition to let well enough alone.   Such people believe that competitors, versed in the craft as no consumer can be, will be quick to detect opportunities for saving and new shifts in production, and be eager to profit by them.   In any event the mere fact that a producer, having command of the domestic market, has not been able to make more than a "fair" profit, is no evidence that a "fair" profit could not have been made at lower prices. . . .   True, it might have been thought adequate to condemn only those monopolies which could not show that they had exercised the highest possible ingenuity, had adopted every possible economy, had anticipated every conceivable improvement, stimulated every possible demand.   No doubt, that would be one way of dealing with the matter, although it would imply constant scrutiny and constant supervision, such as courts are unable to provide.   Be that as it may, that was not the way that Congress chose; it did not condone "good trusts" and condemn "bad" ones; it forbad all.   Moreover, in so doing it was not necessarily actuated by economic motives alone.   It is possible, because of its indirect social or moral effect, to prefer a system of small producers, each dependent for his success upon his own skill and character, to one in which the great mass of those engaged must accept the direction of a few. These considerations, which we have suggested only as possible purposes of the Act, we think the decisions prove to have been in fact its purposes.

* * *

Starting . . . with the authoritative premise that all contracts fixing prices are unconditionally prohibited, the only possible difference between them and a monopoly is that while a monopoly necessarily involves an equal, or even greater, power to fix prices, its mere existence might be thought not to constitute an exercise of that power. That distinction is nevertheless purely formal; it would be valid only so long as the monopoly remained wholly inert; it would disappear as soon as the monopoly began to operate; for, when it did—that is, as soon as it began to sell at all—it must sell at some price and the only price at which it could sell is a price which it itself fixed. Thereafter the power and its exercise must needs coalesce. Indeed it would be absurd to condemn such contracts unconditionally, and not to extend the condemnation to monopolies; for the contracts are only steps toward that entire control which monopoly confers: they are really partial monopolies.

* * *

We have been speaking only of the economic reasons which forbid monopoly; but, as we have already implied, there are others, based upon the belief that great industrial consolidations are inherently undesirable, regardless of their economic results. In the debates in Congress Senator Sherman himself in the passage quoted in the margin showed that among the purposes of Congress in 1890 was a desire to put an end to great aggregations of capital because of the helplessness of the individual before them.[1] . . . That Congress is still of the same mind appears in the Surplus Property Act of 1944, 50 U.S.C.A. Appendix § 1611 et seq., and the Small Business Mobilization Act, 50 U.S.C.A. Appendix § 1101 et seq. Not only does § 2(d) of the first declare it to be one aim of that statute to "preserve the competitive position of small business concerns," but § 18 is given over to directions designed to "preserve and strengthen" their position. . . . Throughout the history of these statutes it has been constantly assumed that one of their purposes was to perpetuate and preserve, for its own sake and in spite of possible cost, an organization of industry in small units which can effectively compete with each other. We hold that "Alcoa's" monopoly of ingot was of the kind covered by § 2.

It does not follow because "Alcoa" had such a monopoly, that it "monopolized" the ingot market: it may not have achieved monopoly;

1. "If the concerted powers of this combination are intrusted to a single man, it is a kingly prerogative, inconsistent with our form of government, and should be subject to the strong resistance of the State and national authorities * * *." 21 Cong. Rec., 2457 (1890).

"The popular mind is agitated with problems that may disturb social order, and among them all none is more threatening than the inequality of condition, of wealth, and opportunity that has grown within a single generation out of the concentration of capital into vast combinations to control production and trade and to break down competition. These combinations already defy or control powerful transportation corporations and reach State authorities. They reach out their Briarean arms to every part of our country. They are imported from abroad. Congress alone can deal with them, and if we are unwilling or unable there will soon be a trust for every production and a master to fix the price for every necessity of life. * * *." 21 Cong. Rec. 2460 (1890). See also 21 Cong. Rec. 2598 (1890).

monopoly may have been thrust upon it. If it had been a combination of existing smelters which united the whole industry and controlled the production of all aluminum ingot, it would certainly have "monopolized" the market. In several decisions the Supreme Court has decreed the dissolution of such combinations, although they had engaged in no unlawful trade practices. . . .

* * *

[The Supreme Court has expressed compunctions against condemning size.] What engendered these compunctions is reasonably plain; persons may unwittingly find themselves in possession of a monopoly, automatically so to say: that is, without having intended either to put an end to existing competition, or to prevent competition from arising when none had existed; they may become monopolists by force of accident. Since the Act makes "monopolizing" a crime, as well as a civil wrong, it would be not only unfair, but presumably contrary to the intent of Congress, to include such instances. A market may, for example, be so limited that it is impossible to produce at all and meet the cost of production except by a plant large enough to supply the whole demand. Or there may be changes in taste or in cost which drive out all but one purveyor. A single producer may be the survivor out of a group of active competitors, merely by virtue of his superior skill, foresight and industry. In such cases a strong argument can be made that, although, the result may expose the public to the evils of monopoly, the Act does not mean to condemn the resultant of those very forces which it is its prime object to foster: finis opus coronat. The successful competitor, having been urged to compete, must not be turned upon when he wins. The most extreme expression of this view is in United States v. United States Steel Corporation, 251 U.S. 417, from which we quote in the margin; [2] and which Sanford, J., in part repeated in United States v. International Harvester Corporation, 274 U.S. 693, 708. It so chances that in both instances the corporation had less than two-thirds of the production in its hands, and the language quoted was not necessary to the decision; so that even if it had not later been modified, it has not the authority of an actual decision. But, whatever authority it does have was modified by the gloss of Cardozo, J., in United States v. Swift & Co., 286 U.S. 106, p. 116, when he said, "Mere size . . . is not an offense against the Sherman Act unless magnified to the point at which it amounts to a monopoly . . . but size carries with it an opportunity for abuse that is not to be ignored when the opportunity is proved to have been utilized in the past." "Alcoa's" size was "magnified" to make it a "monopoly"; indeed, it has never been anything else; and its size, not only offered it an "opportunity for abuse," but it "utilized" its size for "abuse," as can easily be shown.

It would completely misconstrue "Alcoa's" position in 1940 to hold that it was the passive beneficiary of a monopoly, following upon an involuntary elimination of competitors by automatically operative eco-

2. Justice McKenna for the majority said, 251 U.S. 417 at page 451: "The corporation is undoubtedly of impressive size, and it takes an effort of resolution not to be affected by it or to exaggerate its influence. But we must adhere to the law, and the law does not make mere size an offense, or the existence of unexerted power an offense. It, we repeat, requires overt acts and trusts to its prohibition of them and its power to repress or punish them. . . ."

nomic forces. Already in 1909, when its last lawful monopoly ended, it sought to strengthen its position by unlawful practices, and these concededly continued until 1912. In that year it had two plants in New York, at which it produced less than 42 million pounds of ingot; in 1934 it had five plants (the original two, enlarged; one in Tennessee; one in North Carolina; one in Washington), and its production had risen to about 327 million pounds, an increase of almost eight-fold. Meanwhile not a pound of ingot had been produced by anyone else in the United States. This increase and this continued and undisturbed control did not fall undesigned into "Alcoa's" lap; obviously it could not have done so. It could only have resulted, as it did result, from a persistent determination to maintain the control, with which it found itself vested in 1912. There were at least one or two abortive attempts to enter the industry, but "Alcoa" effectively anticipated and forestalled all competition, and succeeded in holding the field alone. True, it stimulated demand and opened new uses for the metal, but not without making sure that it could supply what it had evoked. There is no dispute as to this; "Alcoa" avows it as evidence of the skill, energy and initiative with which it has always conducted its business; as a reason why, having won its way by fair means, it should be commended, and not dismembered. We need charge it with no moral derelictions after 1912; we may assume that all it claims for itself is true. The only question is whether it falls within the exception established in favor of those who do not seek, but cannot avoid, the control of a market. It seems to us that that question scarcely survives its statement. It was not inevitable that it should always anticipate increases in the demand for ingot and be prepared to supply them. Nothing compelled it to keep doubling and redoubling its capacity before others entered the field. It insists that it never excluded competitors; but we can think of no more effective exclusion than progressively to embrace each new opportunity as it opened, and to face every newcomer with new capacity already geared into a great organization, having the advantage of experience, trade connections and the elite of personnel. Only in case we interpret "exclusion" as limited to manoeuvres not honestly industrial, but actuated solely by a desire to prevent competition, can such a course, indefatigably pursued, be deemed not "exclusionary." So to limit it would in our judgment emasculate the Act; would permit just such consolidations as it was designed to prevent.

* * *

We disregard any question of "intent." . . . In order to fall within § 2, the monopolist must have both the power to monopolize, and the intent to monopolize. To read [the language of Justice Holmes in the *Swift* case] as demanding any "specific," intent, makes nonsense of it, for no monopolist monopolizes unconscious of what he is doing. So here, "Alcoa" meant to keep, and did keep, that complete and exclusive hold upon the ingot market with which it started. That was to "monopolize" that market, however innocently it otherwise proceeded. So far as the judgment held that it was not within § 2, it must be reversed.

a. Alcoa and the Power Issue

By defining the market as a predicate to evaluating power, Judge Hand incorporated into law one of the analytical artifacts of I.O. economics: market definition. To aid in evaluating power, the market should be defined to include the putative monopolist and all other firms making products that significantly constrain its prices and push its prices down toward cost. If a defendant has a very high market share in a market so defined and if there are barriers to entry, one might infer that the defendant possesses monopoly power.

Is there an economic definition of monopoly power? Economists say that a firm has "market power" if by limiting output it can set its price at a point high enough above its costs to earn more on its investment than needed to attract and hold the investment. In the modern economy some degree of market power is not uncommon. Any firm selling a differentiated product in an oligopolistic market may have some market power; it may convince enough buyers of the unique values of its product so that its demand curve is downward sloping, not flat like that of the firm in the model competitive market. If that be so, all or most firms in such a market may have at least a small degree of market power. Think about the market for TVs. Do any firms in that market have market power? But monopoly power, with which the law is concerned, must be distinguished from trivial examples of what the economists call market power. Monopoly power can be seen as a large degree of market power held by the dominant firm in a market—power sufficient to enable the monopolist to set prices unreasonably in excess of efficient cost. Do you think any television manufacturer has such power?

Note that if a firm truly possesses monopoly power it will probably be pricing at a point that yields unreasonably high returns; it will be earning monopoly profits. The danger, typically, is not that such a monopolist will some day raise its price; its price on any monopolized product can be expected already to be either the short run "profit maximizing price" or some intuitive or calculated "limit price" well above cost, even though somewhere below the profit maximizing level. (A limit price would yield a supracompetitive return yet not encourage entry as rapidly as might the higher, short-run profit maximizing price.) A monopolist pricing at either the profit maximizing level or a limit price level will have no current incentive to raise price further. It will already have pushed prices to the point where some constraint would make the next higher level less attractive. If the current price is profit maximizing in the short run, an increase would not pay; too many buyers would switch to a now attractive alternative. And if the monopolist had selected a limit price, the constraint on an increase would be fear that taking even higher current profits would, by encouraging entry, shorten the time over which these returns would be available.

Suppose that Alcoa was already making monopoly profits. Would it then be appropriate to define the market to include the next closest constraint? A compelling argument can be made that it would not. Why?

Did the court in *Alcoa* include all alternative products that kept Alcoa's prices near its costs? On its own theory should it have included secondary aluminum? Should it have investigated the extent to which copper and other alternatives limited the price of aluminum?

Was there also an unexplored supply and supply substitutability issue in *Alcoa*? Might foreign firms have diverted more aluminum to the United States if prices went up? Might more domestic firms have started recycling secondary aluminum, for example, if Alcoa raised prices materially? Might some used fabrications that were uneconomic to recycle at their current prices have become economic to process into secondary ingot if prices went up? Should these be included in the market?

After defining the market, Judge Hand evaluated power by looking at the size of Alcoa's share. He thought a firm with one-third of the market would not be a monopolist, that two-thirds would be borderline, and that Alcoa's 90% was clearly enough to warrant characterizing the firm as a monopolist. Is this too great a simplification? For one thing, this approach assumes that the particular market definition chosen is, if not exactly right, at least close to being so. If you assume that the goal of market definition is to evaluate not pervasive presence in a particular industry, but power to raise prices to supracompetitive levels, getting the market definition close to right may be difficult. From this perspective, was it close enough to right in *Alcoa?* Is it often likely to be? In one view, market definition is a matter of drawing a series of concentric circles, each including additional but less sharp constraints on price as they move further from the center. In some cases, one particular circle might be no better a proxy for thinking about market power than another. Moreover, the height of barriers to entry and expansion can be as important as market definition. If entry barriers are high and smaller competitors cannot increase output at current costs while the dominant firm can, even one-third of a market might yield considerable power. By contrast, if barriers are low and competitors are currently operating well below capacity, even 90% would not yield much power.

Defining markets and assessing power often involve judgment and discretion. To what extent should evaluating power be a question of fact, to what extent a question of law? Are there ways of assigning burdens that might clarify the process of evaluation in particular cases? Are there ways of evaluating power which would leave less discretion to courts and juries, thus making outcomes in particular cases more predictable?

Judge Hand called Alcoa a monopolist but said that it was making no more than a reasonable return on investment. Is this an oxymoron? Does your answer depend on your view of the evils of monopoly?

Judge Hand referred to the evils of monopoly. Did he include power to raise prices significantly above cost? What else, according to Judge Hand, are among the evils of monopoly? Are his views consistent with those of Chief Justice White in *Standard Oil*? With those of Justice Harlan, concurring in *Standard Oil?* Was Alcoa's aluminum monopoly a good example of the evils that attend monopoly? What kept Alcoa's profits low if there were not effective competitors? How about laziness? Ineptness?

Some economists point out that a non-competitive market may lead not to high profits but to x-inefficiencies resulting in high costs. A firm under competitive pressure must perform competitively; it must find ways to cut costs. It must shop aggressively for inputs and bargain aggressively with labor. It cannot support excess capacity, nor are its managers likely to have posh offices or to drive company-owned luxury cars. But a monopolist may be able to slack off: pay too much for labor peace; pay the asking price for inputs and accept the sales rep's posh lunch and warm smile; build excess capacity so that scheduling will not be strained in high demand periods (and entry may be deterred); even install Picassos in the board room. If a monopolist's costs go up excessively because it was not forced by competition to control them, its profits (payments to stockholders) might be "normal." Are these the things Judge Hand had in mind when he referred to the "quiet life"?

b. Alcoa and the Conduct Issue

Assuming Alcoa had monopoly power, did it do anything wrong? Judge Hand found some norms about conduct in the early monopolization cases. What if anything, according to his opinion, must one prove in addition to power in order to prove monopolization in violation of Section 2? What, as he saw it, is the conduct test for monopolization in violation of Section 2? What are plaintiff's burdens and what are defendant's burdens?

Judge Hand alludes to becoming a monopolist "by force of accident," and to monopoly being "thrust upon" a firm. What do these concepts mean? Accident, as Judge Hand uses the term, does not include growth by aggressive competition, for Judge Hand says that specific intent to hurt competition or competitors is not a necessary ingredient of the offense; general intent is enough, and a firm is held to intend the expected consequences of its acts. Does that mean that a firm can violate Section 2 by competing vigorously? Suppose a firm aggressively cuts its own costs, maintains good quality, and drops price to the level of its costs, intending to drive out present competitors and to keep out new entrants. Could it gain monopoly this way? If it does thus gain and keep monopoly, has it monopolized? Can you imagine a firm's becoming the "passive beneficiary" of monopoly? Can you think of any business that has done so? Do you agree with Judge Hand's test for monopolization? Criticize the test. Defend it.

What did Alcoa do that lost it the "thrust upon" defense? Did it do anything more than compete vigorously? Of what relevance were the predatory acts before 1912 that demonstrated that Alcoa obtained or maintained its monopoly position by anticompetitive behavior? Of what relevance were the innuendos that Alcoa cooperated with foreign producers in their world-wide cartel? If Alcoa itself had invented basic processes, had developed and grown solely by reason of its own inventiveness and expansion to meet new needs, and was wholly unconnected with an international cartel, would the outcome have been same? What is the relevance of Alcoa's having expanded to meet all new opportunities? Would that alone have been a violation if it led to monopoly?

Suppose, shortly after *Alcoa* was decided, a firm with a major share of the magnesium market called upon you as its lawyer. It had heard rumblings of a new entrant and it wanted to reduce its very high price and also increase its capacity to dissuade entry. What do you advise your client? Can you articulate succinctly the principle developed by Judge Hand and its application to your client's proposed plan of action?

Does the law, as you have just explained it, help or hurt competition? Does it encourage efficiency? Does it encourage social welfare?

c. Alcoa and the Remedy Issue

In *Alcoa*, relief was deferred until after the end of the war. During the war, the government itself had developed and operated large aluminum facilities. When the war was over the government sold these to Reynolds and Kaiser. By 1948 Alcoa accounted for less than half of all aluminum sales in the United States. In the relief proceedings the government requested, among other things, that Alcoa be broken up into two parts.

An excerpt from the opinion of Chief Judge Knox on remedy follows.

UNITED STATES v. ALUMINUM CO. OF AMERICA
91 F.Supp. 333 (S.D.N.Y.1950).

JUDGE KNOX: . . . While I am firmly convinced that the Government is entitled to some relief, I am as strongly persuaded that, for the present at least, the organization of Alcoa's physical properties should not be disturbed. . . .

[A] strong and resourceful domestic aluminum industry is a vital necessity, not alone from the standpoint of national security, but also for the peacetime welfare of the general public. . . . [T]he future development of the industry depends upon its being composed of financially sound and well-integrated organizations. One must constantly remember that aluminum products are in fierce rivalry with articles composed of other materials, and which are manufactured and sold by concerns that, in size, are fully equal to Alcoa. . . .

If the aluminum industry is to develop fully, and be able to satisfy the tremendous demands to which, in the natural course of events, it will be subjected, it must not be reduced to a state of relative impotence. On the contrary, the industry, if its present stature is to be maintained, must carry on a continuous process of encroachment upon the preserves of other industries whose products are manufactured by corporations that will not abjectly surrender the trade positions they now hold. The success of any such effort to encroach upon fields of endeavor that are now occupied by strongly entrenched competitors can be achieved only by companies that are rich in resources, and which are capable of undertaking extensive scientific and market experimentations. At the present juncture, the weakening of any aluminum producer would lessen the buoyancy of the industry as a whole. Rightly or wrongly, from an economic and social standpoint, big business in many industries is an actuality, and if such enterprises are to be subjected to effective competition, their trade rivals must be of somewhat comparable strength.

This situation imposes a minimum effective size on any aluminum producer if it be a real contributor to the growth of the industry, and be, as well, a lively competitor with the producers of other metals. Unless fully persuaded—as I am not—that a divestiture of Alcoa's properties should take place, I am most reluctant to attempt to tamper unnecessarily with economic and industrial forces from which the public has reaped substantial benefits, and from which, also, it can continue to be served, and without detriment, in my opinion, to the national welfare.

The vertical divestiture of an integrated concern so as to create, at a minimum, another fully integrated and effective competitor would be, in its nature, a highly speculative—and even hazardous—venture. A corporation, designed to operate effectively as a single entity, cannot readily be dismembered of parts of its various operations without a marked loss of efficiency. And, to be sure that the segmented portions, when combined in a new organization, will be able to cohere successfully, it may be necessary that they be provided with compensatory advantages. . . . These inherent difficulties are considerably magnified in the present context.

To the extent that Alcoa possesses duplicate and comparable facilities, the problem of divestiture would be less troublesome. But, in an extremely important stage of production, a major impediment to a successful divestiture is to be found. Alcoa has two alumina plants. The one located at Mobile, Alabama, is its only facility economically comparable to the alumina plants of Reynolds and Kaiser. In order to produce alumina at East St. Louis (Alcoa's other plant), at costs that approach the competitive level, the use of domestic bauxite would be required. The diminution of these already scarce reserves, under readily imaginable circumstances, might possibly take on the proportions of a calamity. Similar unequal concentrations by Alcoa of particular productive operations, at a single plant, likewise exist in certain fields of fabrication.

The insurance of successful competition by any dissociated portion of Alcoa would depend upon the ability of the new corporation to supply itself with efficient and experienced management. Since Alcoa, for so long, was the only domestic producer of aluminum, there is but a limited number of persons outside of its staff, and the officialdom of Reynolds and Kaiser, of which a large part was trained in the Alcoa organization, who are able efficiently to function as executives and managers in this industry. Thus, although the independence of the new firm would be the purpose for its creation, it could not, in the first instance, completely sever its ties with Alcoa.

When account is taken of the personnel and equipment presently employed in research, an equally grave problem must be faced. It would be a singular disservice to the public if the skill and technique of Alcoa's research department were impaired. Any divestiture which would extend to this activity, almost surely, would have a baneful effect upon the future of the industry. Nor would independence be fostered by tying two firms to the same research department. Yet, to recruit, outfit and finance a research organization which would not be under a serious disadvantage to that of Alcoa would, indeed, be close to an impossible task.

* * *

Actually, any type of plan that would carry greater assurances for the success and independence of the new concern, and, at the same time, of necessity, be more crippling to Alcoa, is unnecessary in view of present competitive conditions, and the availability of other forms of relief. The Reynolds and Kaiser organizations are operating successfully and profitably, and there is little or no reason to think that either of them will be unable, under existing trade circumstances, to continue to thrive, and even to prosper. The Government disposal program has launched them with excellent properties, low investments, and safeguards for their future stability. The effective future competitive efforts of these two companies will be greatly enhanced if the shadow that now hangs over them in Alcoa's potential control of Aluminum Limited be removed.

* * *

My present conclusion is that, in addition to the relief . . . [prohibiting patent grant-backs and permitting the disposition of the Government's] St. Lawrence Plant, the shareholders of Alcoa be required to dispose of their stock interests either in Limited or in Alcoa. . . .

———

Again, as in *Standard Oil,* relief presented a dilemma. Monopoly may be evil because consumers lose the benefits of rivalry and progressiveness that competition stimulates, as well as the benefits of choice. But once monopoly exists, is court action dismembering the monopolist likely to achieve social gains? Would a two, three, or even four firm market be competitive? Would it lead to closer price-cost relationships? Would it encourage innovation? Would it foster more aggressive, cost-cutting management styles? Would the gains entail a sacrifice in efficiency? Is there any way to determine the answer to such questions?

Judge Knox had a relatively easy task. The government had created competition by establishing and then selling aluminum facilities and the court could readily create yet more competition by ending Alcoa's control of its Canadian subsidiary. What if these options were not available? What do you think Judge Knox would have done? What would you have done? What do you think Chief Judge Hand would have done?

While the *Alcoa* case was being prosecuted, the government was also proceeding against cartels (a subject we treat in Chapter 3). One case it brought was against the major firms in the tobacco industry. In this case the government alleged combinations and conspiracies to restrain trade and to monopolize. A year after the Court of Appeals for the Second Circuit decided *Alcoa,* the Supreme Court reviewed a conviction in this case, American Tobacco Co. v. United States, 328 U.S. 781 (1946). The Court affirmed the conviction and, in doing so, "welcome[d] the opportunity to endorse" the key passages in *Alcoa* describing the purposes of the statute and the elements of the offense of monopolization. 328 U.S. at 813–14.

Alcoa and *American Tobacco* began a new era in antitrust—the period of the "structural consensus." Structural analysis of the kind done by industrial organization economists such as Mason of Harvard and Bain of Berkeley became very influential. Policymakers and courts assumed that highly concentrated markets were likely to perform poorly.

We do not imply that courts saw the world just as did these I.O. economists. Indeed, even leading I.O. economists did not see the economic world in precisely the same terms as one another. For example, Mason believed that the basic paradigm that structure influences conduct and conduct determines performance implied the need for a deep and thorough examination of each particular market. Only from such a study could one understand the complex market interactions and devise antitrust rules or remedies that would improve performance. Bain, by contrast, did cross-industry studies aimed at showing economy-wide relationships between given levels of concentration and resulting price-cost-profit relationships. The work of Mason and his students was particularly influential in monopolization cases; Bain's work greatly influenced merger analysis (which we will study in Chapter 5). Do you see why?

In all events, *Alcoa* marked the beginning of a period when antitrust law was reasonably stable, a period that ran into the 1970s. The law developed by relatively modest accretions, all more or less in the same direction. I.O. economics with its recognition of the structure-conduct-performance relationship was infused not only into the law of monopolization but, as we shall see in later chapters, into the law of cartelization and mergers as well. A lengthy period of antitrust interventionism supported in Congress and by administrations of both political parties had begun. We shall now review the cases that (along with *Alcoa*) form the core source materials for the modern law of monopolization.

2. STRUCTURALISM AS THE APPROACH TO ISSUES OF POWER

Alcoa begins the modern law by demarcating the issue of power and the issue of conduct and specifying an approach to each. Most monopolization cases raise debatable issues in each category; sometimes emphasis is on power, sometimes on conduct. At this point we focus on cases dealing with power. Later we will look at post-*Alcoa* treatment of the conduct issue.

Ever since *Alcoa,* analysis of power has turned on an analysis of structure, primarily market definition and computation of market share. A most interesting case on market definition reached the Supreme Court in 1956.

UNITED STATES v. E.I. DU PONT DE NEMOURS & CO.
351 U.S. 377 (1956).

JUSTICE REED: . . .

The Government's direct appeal here . . . "attacks only the ruling that du Pont has not monopolized trade in cellophane." . . .

During the period that is relevant to this action, du Pont produced almost 75% of the cellophane sold in the United States, and cellophane constituted less than 20% of all "flexible packaging material" sales. . . .

. . . The court below found that the "relevant market for determining the extent of du Pont's market control is the market for flexible packaging materials," and that competition from those other materials prevented du Pont from possessing monopoly powers in its sales of cellophane.

. . . Every manufacturer is the sole producer of the particular commodity it makes but its control in the [monopoly] sense of the relevant market depends upon the availability of alternative commodities for buyers: i.e., whether there is a cross-elasticity of demand between cellophane and the other wrappings. This interchangeability is largely gauged by the purchase of competing products for similar uses considering the price, characteristics and adaptability of the competing commodities. The court below found that the flexible wrappings afforded such alternatives. This Court must determine whether the trial court erred in its estimate of the competition afforded cellophane by other materials. . . .

I. FACTUAL BACKGROUND . . .

In the early 1900's, Jacques Brandenberger, a Swiss chemist, attempted to make tablecloths impervious to dirt by spraying them with liquid viscose (a cellulose solution available in quantity from wood pulp) and by coagulating this coating. His idea failed, but he noted that the coating peeled off in a transparent film. This first "cellophane" was thick, hard, and not perfectly transparent, but Brandenberger apparently foresaw commercial possibilities in his discovery. By 1908 he developed the first machine for the manufacture of transparent sheets of regenerated cellulose. The 1908 product was not satisfactory, but by 1912 Brandenberger was making a saleable thin flexible film used in gas masks. He obtained patents to cover the machinery and the essential ideas of his process. . . .

In 1917 Brandenberger assigned his patents to La Cellophane Societe Anonyme and joined that organization. . . . Du Pont was an American leader in the field of synthetics and learned of cellophane's successes through an associate, Comptoir des Textiles Artificiel.

In 1923 du Pont organized with La Cellophane an American company for the manufacture of plain cellophane. The undisputed findings are that:

> ". . . La Cellophane licensed duPont Cellophane Company exclusively under its United States cellophane patents, and granted duPont Cellophane Company the exclusive right to make and sell in North and Central America under La Cellophane's secret processes for cellophane manufacture. DuPont Cellophane Company granted to La Cellophane exclusive rights for the rest of the world under any cellophane patents or processes duPont Cellophane Company might develop." . . .

Sylvania, an American affiliate of a Belgian producer of cellophane not covered by the license agreements above referred to, began the manufacture of cellophane in the United States in 1930. Litigation between the French and Belgian companies resulted in a settlement whereby La Cellophane came to have a stock interest in Sylvania, contrary to the La Cellophane-du Pont agreement. This resulted in adjustments as compensation for the intrusion into United States of La Cellophane that extended du Pont's limited territory. The details do not here seem important. Since 1934 Sylvania has produced about 25% of United States cellophane.

An important factor in the growth of cellophane production and sales was the perfection of moistureproof cellophane, a superior product of du Pont research and patented by that company through a 1927 application. Plain cellophane has little resistance to the passage of moisture vapor. Moistureproof cellophane has a composition added which keeps moisture in and out of the packed commodity. This patented type of cellophane has had a demand with much more rapid growth than the plain.

In 1931 Sylvania began the manufacture of moistureproof cellophane under its own patents. After negotiations over patent rights, du Pont in 1933 licensed Sylvania to manufacture and sell moistureproof cellophane produced under the du Pont patents at a royalty of 2% of sales. These licenses, with the plain cellophane licenses from the Belgian company, made Sylvania a full cellophane competitor, limited on moistureproof sales by the terms of the licenses to 20% of the combined sales of the two companies of that type by the payment of a prohibitive royalty on the excess. Finding 552. There was never an excess production. The limiting clause was dropped on January 1, 1945. . . .

Between 1928 and 1950, du Pont's sales of plain cellophane increased from $3,131,608 to $9,330,776. Moistureproof sales increased from $603,222 to $89,850,416, although prices were continuously reduced. It could not be said that this immense increase in use was solely or even largely attributable to the superior quality of cellophane or to the technique or business acumen of du Pont, though doubtless those factors were important. The growth was a part of the expansion of the commodity-packaging habits of business, a by-product of general efficient competitive merchandising to meet modern demands. The profits, which were large, apparently arose from this trend in marketing, the development of the industrial use of chemical research and production of synthetics, rather than from elimination of other producers from the relevant market. . . .

III. THE SHERMAN ACT, § 2—MONOPOLIZATION . . .

If cellophane is the "market" that du Pont is found to dominate, it may be assumed it does have monopoly power over that "market." Monopoly power is the power to control prices or exclude competition. It seems apparent that du Pont's power to set the price of cellophane has been limited only by the competition afforded by other flexible packaging materials. Moreover, it may be practically impossible for anyone to commence manufacturing cellophane without full access to du Pont's technique. However, du Pont has no power to prevent competition from other wrapping materials. The trial court consequently had to determine whether competition from the other wrappings prevented du Pont from possessing monopoly power in violation of § 2. Price and competition are so intimately entwined that any discussion of theory must treat them as one. It is inconceivable that price could be controlled without power over competition or vice versa. . . .

If a large number of buyers and sellers deal freely in a standardized product, such as salt or wheat, we have complete or pure competition. Patents, on the other hand, furnish the most familiar type of classic monopoly. As the producers of a standardized product bring about significant differentiations of quality, design, or packaging in the product that permit differences of use, competition becomes to a greater or less degree incomplete and the producer's power over price and competition greater over his article and its use, according to the differentiation he is able to create and maintain. A retail seller may have in one sense a monopoly on certain trade because of location, as an isolated country store or filling station, or because no one else makes a product of just the quality or attractiveness of his product, as for example in cigarettes. Thus one can theorize that we have monopolistic competition in every nonstandardized commodity with each manufacturer having power over the price and production of his own product. However, this power that, let us say, automobile or soft-drink manufacturers have over their trademarked products is not the power that makes an illegal monopoly. Illegal power must be appraised in terms of the competitive market for the product.

Determination of the competitive market for commodities depends on how different from one another are the offered commodities in character or use, how far buyers will go to substitute one commodity for another. For example, one can think of building materials as in commodity competition but one could hardly say that brick competed with steel or wood or cement or stone in the meaning of Sherman Act litigation; the products are too different. This is the interindustry competition emphasized by some economists. See Lilienthal, Big Business, c. 5. On the other hand, there are certain differences in the formulae for soft drinks but one can hardly say that each one is an illegal monopoly. Whatever the market may be, we hold that control of price or competition establishes the existence of monopoly power under § 2. . . .

IV. THE RELEVANT MARKET.—. . .

. . . [W]here there are market alternatives that buyers may readily use for their purposes, illegal monopoly does not exist merely because the product said to be monopolized differs from others. If it were not so, only physically identical products would be a part of the market. To accept the Government's argument [that substitutes must be substantially fungible to be included in the market], we would have to conclude that the manufacturers of plain as well as moistureproof cellophane were monopolists, and so with films such as Pliofilm, foil, glassine, polyethylene, and Saran, for each of these wrapping materials is distinguishable. These were all exhibits in the case. New wrappings appear, generally similar to cellophane: is each a monopoly? What is called for is an appraisal of the "cross-elasticity" of demand in the trade.

The varying circumstances of each case determine the result. In considering what is the relevant market for determining the control of price and competition, no more definite rule can be declared than that commodities reasonably interchangeable by consumers for the same purposes make up that "part of the trade or commerce," monopolization of which may be illegal. As respects flexible packaging materials, the market geographically is nationwide.

Industrial activities cannot be confined to trim categories. Illegal monopolies under § 2 may well exist over limited products in narrow fields where competition is eliminated. That does not settle the issue here. In determining the market under the Sherman Act, it is the use or uses to which the commodity is put that control. The selling price between commodities with similar uses and different characteristics may vary, so that the cheaper product can drive out the more expensive. Or, the superior quality of higher priced articles may make dominant the more desirable. Cellophane costs more than many competing products and less than a few. But whatever the price, there are various flexible wrapping materials that are bought by manufacturers for packaging their goods in their own plants or are sold to converters who shape and print them for use in the packaging of the commodities to be wrapped.

Cellophane differs from other flexible packaging materials. From some it differs more than from others. The basic materials from which the wrappings are made . . . are aluminum, cellulose acetate, chlorides, wood pulp, rubber hydrochloride, and ethylene gas. It will adequately illustrate the similarity in characteristics of the various products by noting here Finding 62 as to glassine [detailing the qualities of glassine]. Its use is almost as extensive as cellophane and many of its characteristics equally or more satisfactory to users.

It may be admitted that cellophane combines the desirable elements of transparency, strength and cheapness more definitely than any of the others. . . .

But, despite cellophane's advantages, it has to meet competition from other materials in every one of its uses. . . . Food products are the chief outlet, with cigarettes next. The Government makes no challenge to Finding 283 that cellophane furnishes less than 7% of wrappings for bakery products, 25% for candy, 32% for snacks, 35% for meats and poultry, 27% for crackers and biscuits, 47% for fresh produce, and 34% for frozen foods. Seventy-five to eighty percent of cigarettes are wrapped in cellophane. Finding 292. Thus, cellophane shares the packaging market with others. The over-all result is that cellophane accounts for 17.9% of flexible wrapping materials, measured by the wrapping surface. . . .

Moreover a very considerable degree of functional interchangeability exists between these products. . . . It will be noted, that except as to permeability to gases, cellophane has no qualities that are not possessed by a number of other materials. Meat will do as an example of interchangeability. Although du Pont's sales to the meat industry have reached 19,000,000 pounds annually, nearly 35%, this volume is attributed "to the rise of self-service retailing of fresh meat." In fact, since the popularity of self-service meats, du Pont has lost "a considerable proportion" of this packaging business to Pliofilm. Pliofilm is more expensive than cellophane, but its superior physical characteristics apparently offset cellophane's price advantage. While retailers shift continually between the two, the trial court found that Pliofilm is increasing its share of the business. . . .

An element for consideration as to cross-elasticity of demand between products is the responsiveness of the sales of one product to price changes of the other. If a slight decrease in the price of cellophane causes a considerable number of customers of other flexible wrappings to switch to cellophane, it would be an indication that a high cross-elasticity of demand exists between them; that the products compete in the same market. The court below held that the "[g]reat sensitivity of customers in the flexible packaging markets to price or quality changes" prevented du Pont from possessing monopoly control over price. The record sustains these findings.

We conclude that cellophane's interchangeability with the other materials mentioned suffices to make it a part of this flexible packaging material market.

The Government stresses the fact that the variation in price between cellophane and other materials demonstrates they are noncompetitive. As these products are all flexible wrapping materials, it seems reasonable to consider, as was done at the trial, their comparative cost to the consumer in terms of square area. Findings as to price competition are set out in the margin.[29] Cellophane costs two or three times as much, surface measure, as its chief competitors for the flexible wrapping market, glassine and greaseproof papers. Other forms of cellulose wrappings and those from other chemical or mineral substances, with the exception of aluminum foil, are more expensive. The uses of these materials are largely to wrap small packages for retail distribution. The wrapping is a relatively small proportion of the entire cost of the article. Different producers need different qualities in wrappings and their need may vary from time to time as their products undergo change. But the necessity for flexible wrappings is the central and unchanging demand. We cannot say that these differences in cost gave du Pont monopoly power over prices in view of the findings of fact on that subject.[31]

29. "132. The price of cellophane is today an obstacle to its sales in competition with other flexible packaging materials.

"133. Cellophane has always been higher priced than the two largest selling flexible packaging materials, wax paper and glassine, and this has represented a disadvantage to sales of cellophane.

"134. Du Pont considered as a factor in the determination of its prices, the prices of waxed paper, glassine, greaseproof, vegetable parchment, and other flexible packaging materials.

"135. Du Pont, in reducing its prices, intended to narrow price differential between cellophane and packaging papers, particularly glassine and waxed paper. The objective

of this effort has been to increase the use of cellophane. Each price reduction was intended to open up new uses for cellophane, and to attract new customers who had not used cellophane because of its price."

31. "140. Some users are sensitive to the cost of flexible packaging materials; others are not. Users to whom cost is important include substantial business: for example, General Foods, Armour, Curtiss Candy Co., and smaller users in the bread industry, cracker industry, and frozen food industry. These customers are unwilling to use more cellophane because of its relatively high price, would use more if the price were reduced, and have increased their use as the price of cellophane has been reduced.

It is the variable characteristics of the different flexible wrappings and the energy and ability with which the manufacturers push their wares that determine choice. A glance at "Modern Packaging," a trade journal, will give, by its various advertisements, examples of the competition among manufacturers for the flexible packaging market. The trial judge visited the 1952 Annual Packaging Show at Atlantic City, with the consent of counsel. He observed exhibits offered by "machinery manufacturers, converters and manufacturers of flexible packaging materials." He states that these personal observations confirmed his estimate of the competition between cellophane and other packaging materials.. . . .

The facts above considered dispose also of any contention that competitors have been excluded by du Pont from the packaging material market. That market has many producers and there is no proof du Pont ever has possessed power to exclude any of them from the rapidly expanding flexible packaging market. . . .

Nor can we say that du Pont's profits, while liberal (according to the Government 15.9% net after taxes on the 1937–1947 average), demonstrate the existence of a monopoly without proof of lack of comparable profits during those years in other prosperous industries. Cellophane was a leader, over 17%, in the flexible packaging materials market. There is no showing that du Pont's rate of return was greater or less than that of other producers of flexible packaging materials.

The "market" which one must study to determine when a producer has monopoly power will vary with the part of commerce under consideration. The tests are constant. That market is composed of products that have reasonable interchangeability for the purposes for which they are produced—price, use and qualities considered. While the application of the tests remains uncertain, it seems to us that du Pont should not be found to monopolize cellophane when that product has the competition and interchangeability with other wrappings that this record shows.

"141. The cost factor slips accounts away from cellophane. This hits at the precarious users, whose profit margins on their products are low, and has been put in motion by competitive developments in the user's trade. Examples include the losses of business to glassine in candy bar wraps in the 30's, frozen food business to waxed paper in the late 40's, and recent losses to glassine in cracker packaging.

"142. The price of cellophane was reduced to expand the market for cellophane. Du Pont did not reduce prices for cellophane with intent of monopolizing manufacture or with intent of suppressing competitors.

"143. Du Pont reduced cellophane prices to enable sales to be made for new uses from which higher prices had excluded cellophane, and to expand sales. Reductions were made as sales volume and market conditions warranted. In determining price reductions, du Pont considered relationship between its manufacturing costs and proposed prices, possible additional volume that might be gained by the price reduction, effect of price reduction upon the return du Pont would obtain on its investment. It considered the effect its lowered price might have on the manufacture by others, but this possible result of a price reduction was never a motive for the reduction.

"144. Du Pont never lowered cellophane prices below cost, and never dropped cellophane prices temporarily to gain a competitive advantage.

"145. As du Pont's manufacturing costs declined, 1924 to 1935, du Pont reduced prices for cellophane. When costs of raw materials increased subsequent to 1935, it postponed reductions until 1938 and 1939. Subsequent increases in cost of raw material and labor brought about price increases after 1947."

On the findings of the District Court, its judgment is

Affirmed.

CHIEF JUSTICE WARREN, joined by JUSTICES BLACK and DOUGLAS, dissenting: This case, like many under the Sherman Act, turns upon the proper definition of the market. In defining the market in which du Pont's economic power is to be measured, the majority virtually emasculate § 2 of the Sherman Act. They admit that "cellophane combines the desirable elements of transparency, strength and cheapness more definitely than any of" a host of other packaging materials. Yet they hold that all of those materials are so indistinguishable from cellophane as to warrant their inclusion in the market. . . .

* * *

[The Chief Justice described the different qualities possessed by each kind of flexible wrapping material.]

During the period covered by the complaint (1923–1947) cellophane enjoyed phenomenal growth. . . . Yet throughout this period the price of cellophane was far greater than that of glassine, waxed paper or sulphite paper. . . . [I]n 1929 cellophane's price was seven times that of glassine; in 1934, four times, and in 1949 still more than twice glassine's price. . . . [C]ellophane had a similar price relation to waxed paper and . . . sulphite paper sold at even less than glassine and waxed paper. We cannot believe that buyers, practical businessmen, would have bought cellophane in increasing amounts over a quarter of a century if close substitutes were available at from one-seventh to one-half cellophane's price. That they did so is testimony to cellophane's distinctiveness.

The inference yielded by the conduct of cellophane buyers is reinforced by the conduct of sellers other than du Pont. . . . Sylvania, the only other cellophane producer, absolutely and immediately followed every du Pont price change, even dating back its price list to the effective date of du Pont's change. Producers of glassine and waxed paper, on the other hand, displayed apparent indifference to du Pont's repeated and substantial price cuts. . . . [F]rom 1924 to 1932 du Pont dropped the price of plain cellophane 84%, while the price of glassine remained constant. And during the period 1933–1946 the prices for glassine and waxed paper actually increased in the face of a further 21% decline in the price of cellophane. If "shifts of business" due to "price sensitivity" had been substantial, glassine and waxed paper producers who wanted to stay in business would have been compelled by market forces to meet du Pont's price challenge just as Sylvania was. . . .

Du Pont's every action was directed toward maintaining dominance over cellophane. Its 1923 agreements with La Cellophane, the French concern which first produced commercial cellophane, gave du Pont exclusive North and Central American rights to cellophane's technology, manufacture and sale, and provided, without any limitation in time, that all existing and future information pertaining to the cellophane process be considered "secret and confidential," and be held in an exclusive common pool. In its subsequent agreements with foreign licensees, du Pont was careful to preserve its continental market inviolate. In 1929, while it was still the sole domestic producer of cellophane, du Pont won its long struggle to raise the tariff from 25% to 60%, ad valorem, on cellophane imports, substantially foreclosing foreign competition. When Sylvania became the second American cellophane producer the following year and du Pont filed suit claiming infringement of its moistureproof patents, they settled the suit by entering into a cross-licensing agreement. Under this agreement, du Pont obtained the right to exclude third persons from use of any patentable moistureproof invention made during the next 15 years by the sole other domestic cellophane producer, and, by a prohibitive royalty provision, it limited Sylvania's moistureproof production to approximately 20% of the industry's moistureproof sales. The record shows that du Pont and Sylvania were aware that, by settling the infringement suit, they avoided the possibility that the courts might hold the patent claims invalid and thereby open cellophane manufacture to additional competition. If close substitutes for cellophane had been commercially available, du Pont, an enlightened enterprise, would not have gone to such lengths to control cellophane.

As predicted by its 1923 market analysis, du Pont's dominance in cellophane proved enormously profitable from the outset. After only five years of production, when du Pont bought out the minority stock interests in its cellophane subsidiary, it had to pay more than fifteen times the original price of the stock. But such success was not limited to the period of innovation, limited sales and complete domestic monopoly. A confidential du Pont report shows that during the period 1937–1947, despite great expansion of sales, du Pont's "operative return" (before taxes) averaged 31%, while its average "net return" (after deduction of taxes, bonuses, and fundamental research expenditures) was 15.9%. Such profits provide a powerful incentive for the entry of competitors.[15] Yet from 1924 to 1951 only one new firm, Sylvania, was able to begin cellophane production. And Sylvania could not have entered if La Cellophane's secret process had not been stolen. It is significant that for 15 years Olin Industries, a substantial firm, was unsuccessful in its attempt to produce cellophane, finally abandoning the project in 1944 after having spent about $1,000,000. When the Government brought this suit, du Pont, "to reduce the hazard of being judged to have a monopoly of the U.S. cellophane business," decided to let Olin enter the industry. Despite this demonstration of the control achieved by du Pont through its exclusive dominion over the cellophane process, the District Court found that du Pont could not exclude competitors from the manufacture of cellophane. . . . This finding is "clearly erroneous."

. . . The trial judge thought that, if du Pont raised its price, the market would "penalize" it with smaller profits as well as lower sales.

15. See Stocking and Mueller, The Cellophane Case, XLV Amer. Economic Rev. 29, 60–63 (1955), where the authors compare the domestic economic history of rayon with that of cellophane. The first American rayon producer earned 64.2% on its investment in 1920, thereby attracting du Pont. After a loss in 1921, du Pont's average return for the next four years was roughly 32%. As more firms began rayon production, du Pont's and the industry's return on invest- ment began to drop. When 6 new firms entered the industry in 1930, bringing the number of producers to 20, average industry earnings for that year declined to 5% and du Pont suffered a net loss. "From the beginning of the depression in 1929 through the succeeding recovery and the 1938 recession du Pont averaged 29.6 per cent before taxes on its cellophane investment. On its rayon investment it averaged only 6.3 per cent." Id., at 62–63.

Du Pont proved him wrong. When 1947 operating earnings dropped below 26% for the first time in 10 years, it increased cellophane's price 7% and boosted its earnings in 1948. Du Pont's division manager then reported that "If an operative return of 31% is considered inadequate then an upward revision in prices will be necessary to improve the return." It is this latitude with respect to price, this broad power of choice, that the antitrust laws forbid. Du Pont's independent pricing policy and the great profits consistently yielded by that policy leave no room for doubt that it had power to control the price of cellophane. . . .

* * *

If competition is at the core of the Sherman Act, we cannot agree that it was consistent with that Act for the enormously lucrative cellophane industry to have no more than two sellers from 1924 to 1951. The conduct of du Pont and Sylvania illustrates that a few sellers tend to act like one and that an industry which does not have a competitive structure will not have competitive behavior. The public should not be left to rely upon the dispensations of management in order to obtain the benefits which normally accompany competition. Such beneficence is of uncertain tenure. Only actual competition can assure long-run enjoyment of the goals of a free economy. . . .

Questions and Comments

Using *du Pont's* interchangeability and cross-elasticity approach, comment on whether or not you would infer from each of the following statements whether flexible wrappings other than cellophane (or some of them) tend to push the price of cellophane towards its cost and therefore should be included in the relevant market. If the statement is not in itself sufficient to enable you to draw an inference, what more do you need to know?

1. Buyers had and used substitutes for every one of cellophane's uses.

2. With one exception (permeability to gases), cellophane had no qualities not possessed by one or more of a number of other materials.

3. No other product had the same combination of qualities and characteristics as cellophane.

4. As self-service meats became more popular, du Pont lost a considerable portion of its packaging business to pliofilm, a product more expensive than cellophane but with superior physical characteristics.

5. Cellophane was always priced higher than the other two largest selling flexible wrappings, wax paper and glassine, and if cellophane lowered its price somewhat it would have attracted more business from the buyers of these products.

6. When du Pont's costs declined between 1924 to 1935, it reduced its prices. When its costs increased after 1935, it made no further price reductions until 1938 and 1939.

7. During an eight-year period du Pont dropped the price of plain cellophane 84%; the price of glassine (which was far lower than the price of cellophane) remained constant.

8. Du Pont never priced below its costs.

9. As the trial judge observed on his visit to the Annual Packaging Show in Atlantic City, many flexible packaging materials were offered in competition with cellophane.

10. Sylvania, the only other producer of cellophane, followed every pricing move made by du Pont.

11. Du Pont made efforts to keep others from entering or expanding into the production and sale of cellophane.

12. From 1937 to 1947, du Pont's return before taxes was 31% ; its return after taxes, bonuses, and basic research expense was 15.9%. Production of rayon is an industry with similar capital requirements and risks. Du Pont entered the rayon market in 1921. By the end of 1930, the rayon industry was competitively structured, with 20 producers. From 1929 through 1938, du Pont averaged 29.6% before taxes on its investment in cellophane and 6.3% on its investment in rayon.

Now consider: How useful has the exercise been? Was the result of the effort inclusion of many or most flexible wrappings? Did this help you to understand whether du Pont did or did not have monopoly power?

The Court in *du Pont* (*Cellophane*) has been criticized for using interchangeability of use and cross-elasticity of demand at the *current* price as a criterion for market definition without regard to whether du Pont's prices were already significantly above its costs. See R.A. Posner, Antitrust Law: An Economic Perspective 125–134 (1976). See also D. Turner, Antitrust Policy and the Cellophane Case, 70 Harv.L.Rev. 281 (1956), suggesting that the test should "incorporate a consideration of costs, so that substitutes will be excluded where the government shows that at prices producing a high cross-elasticity the alleged monopolist has a substantial cost advantage." Id. at 308–09.

Do du Pont's challenged acts help you to determine whether the company had market power? Whether it thought it had market power? If a firm engages in acts or strategies that would not be profitable without power or the prospect of gaining it, should this point toward one rather than another market definition? In other words, should our inquiries about what the market is and what conduct is observed sometimes be organic and interrelated, rather than isolated and discreet?

Latent in the market definition problem are policy issues about how much power and what kind of power a firm must have before the law labels it a monopolist. Let us focus first on power over price. A firm selling cellophane faces an array of price constraints. If numerous other firms make and sell cellophane the firm is likely to have no choice but to sell at the cost of producing it. But suppose it is the only firm that can and does make cellophane. There will be a next most proximate competitive constraint. Let us assume it is pliofilm and that if the sole cellophane producer raises prices to more than 5% above costs its customers will switch in vast numbers to pliofilm. If the court identifies cellophane as the relevant market, the law is labelling as a monopolist a firm with a pricing discretion of 5%. But what are the implications of that conclusion? Does it matter that even in reasonably competitive markets many firms have at least that much pricing discretion due to product differentiation and advertising? Consider Mercedes Benz. It has a strong and quite secure niche in the automobile market and may well have power to price 5% above its efficient cost. If so, should it be called a monopolist? If not, is cellophane, in our hypothetical, not a market? Or can the law make practical judgments beyond measurements of pricing power; e.g., du Pont or Alcoa is a single seller of a discrete generic product and is therefore a monopolist; Mercedes Benz is not.

3. MARKET DEFINITION IN THE MODERN LAW OF MONOPO-LIZATION

The relevant market has a product/service dimension and a geographic dimension. Moreover, market definition involves looking at both the demand (buyer) side and the supply (seller) side.

We have treated some of these concepts above, in connection with *Alcoa* and *du Pont*. To that extent, this will provide a summary.

We have noted that current price—which is commonly used as the baseline—may already be a monopoly price. Accordingly, if we use current price as the baseline, definition of the market and estimation of a defendant's share within it can give us an idea of the limits of the defendant's power but cannot tell us what the market and market shares would look like if defendant were pricing at cost.

a. Demand Side

As a starting point, one takes the product (or service) of the alleged monopolist. One would include in the market all products (or services) that are either generically the same or regarded by buyers as reasonably good substitutes. If the defendant makes aluminum for cable and copper cable is a good substitute, buyers would shift among sellers of both. If the aluminum suppliers tried to exploit the buyers, the buyers would substitute copper. This is called demand substitutability.

Elasticity of demand is measured by the percent shift in quantity demanded caused by a 1% change in price. If a 1% price rise will cause more than a 1% shift of demand (and thus a reduction in total revenues), demand is said to be elastic. A firm with market power will price in the elastic portion of its demand curve. It will raise price up to the point where a further incremental rise would not be profitable.

Cross-elasticity of demand is measured by the percent shift in quantity demanded of one product caused by a 1% change in its price relative to the price of another product. Thus to determine whether aluminum wrap is cross-elastic with plastic wrap at the current price, one would observe whether, if the price of plastic wrap went up 1% while the price of aluminum wrap stayed constant, there would be more than a 1% shift from plastic to aluminum wrap. If so, aluminum wrap is cross-elastic with plastic wrap at its current price.

b. Supply Side

On the demand side we ask, where will the buyer turn if the seller raises the price of its product above cost? To consider supply side constraints we ask a different, but related, question. What existing or new sellers will start to supply the seller's customers if the existing seller should raise the price of its product above cost?

We start with the product and the service area of the alleged monopolist. We then include the product of all obvious close competitors, those who compete for the same business of the same customers. We then seek to identify additional price constraints that may come from *potential* suppliers. Such potential competition may come from any of three directions:

i. Supply Substitutability

A maker of plastic sheeting may be able to adjust its machinery to make plastic wrap very quickly. Indeed, if the price of plastic wrap should artificially rise and it appears that the price rise will be maintained for a reasonable period of time, these producers might find it profitable to shift the use of their machinery to share in the available extra profits to be made from plastic wrap. What factors in the plastic sheeting market might facilitate such shifting to the new product? What ones might inhibit it?

ii. Geographic Diversion

If the price of cars rises in the United States, European producer X, who has been selling only in Europe, may see the United States as a now lucrative market and may divert some of its product to the United States. What factors might facilitate or inhibit this?

iii. New Entry

The prospect of new entry can be a check on price if information about the market is widely defused, if barriers to entry are low, and if a new entrant would not have to make a large investment that it could not recoup upon exit. Can you think of a market where these conditions might be met?

Should markets be defined to include potential suppliers? Should the market include those who could or would shift from some other activity to make the relevant product? Should it include those who could or would divert portions of their output into the relevant geographic area from elsewhere? If so, at what level of price increase and within what time frame? If significant shifts would be likely to occur within one (or two) year(s) if, say, the apparent monopolist should raise price by 5% (or 10%) and hold price at that level even in the face of entry, should the incumbent escape classification as a monopolist?

Theoretically, if one assumes very easy entry on an efficient scale and completely mobile capital (which can be withdrawn without loss) one "proves" that incumbents cannot price at monopoly levels. See W. Baumol, J. Panzar and R. Willig, Contestable Markets and the Theory of Industrial Structure (1982). For that reason, if entry barriers are low, some economists may conclude that the firm does not have market power. They may label the market "contestable." Airline industry city-pair markets are usually used to provide the best examples of "contestable" markets. For example, if an airline serves New York–San Francisco and San Francisco–Los Angeles it might be able to enter New York–Los Angeles at relatively small sunk cost. If so, contestability theory asserts, firms serving New York–Los Angeles will price as though New York–San Francisco firms were already in the New York–Los Angeles market. There are, however, a priori reasons to doubt the assumed facts. Establishing recognition in a new city entails sunk costs; radar slots are scarce; entry cannot be immediate, nor only for a short term, and existing firms may successfully repel the new competitor by low pricing and increased capacity upon threats of entry. Thus far, empirical results are ambiguous. See G. Call and T. Keeler, Airline Deregulation, Fares and Market Behavior: Some Empirical Evidence in Analytical Studies in Transport Economics. (A.F. Daughety ed. 1985). Some economists doubt that real markets ever afford the requisite ease of entry and withdrawal. See Shepherd, Contestability vs. Competition, 74 Amer. Econ. Rev. 572 (1984).

c. The Submarket Concept

The modern legal tradition began with the *Alcoa* idea of defining "the" relevant market in each case. But every producer facing a series of constraints can be said to operate in several markets. Alcoa operated in the virgin aluminum ingot market, where it faced only foreign competition. It also operated in the aluminum ingot market where it competed with secondary ingot. It also faced the constraint of other metals; if aluminum prices went too high, buyers would begin to substitute. Recognizing this, courts have sometimes spoken of markets and submarkets. The concept (or at least the term, submarket) was first introduced in a merger case, Brown Shoe Co. v. United States, 370 U.S. 294 (1962). The concept and the term are sometimes used today in monopolization cases.

Where an industry provides heterogenous, highly differentiated products, rather than a homogeneous product like aluminum ingot, every differentiated brand (or at least every one with strong consumer loyalty) could conceivably be said to constitute a separate submarket. As the Court said in *du Pont (Cellophane)*, when products are differentiated competition becomes "to a greater or lesser degree incomplete. . . ." (351 U.S. at 392.) Normally, a single differentiated brand facing competition from other brands will not have substantial power over price, but there may be instances where it does. See Borden v. FTC, 674 F.2d 498 (6th Cir.1982), *vacated,* 461 U.S. 940 (1983). Even if not affording power over price, might a strong position in a single brand yield enough power to exclude rivals, perhaps by tying, or by predation? See generally, Campbell, Predation and Competition in Antitrust: The Case of Nonfungible Goods, 87 Colum.L.Rev. 1625 (1987).

Some commentators are critical of the submarket concept. They fear that the jury may find the monopolization of an unduly narrow submarket leading to relief that hurts rather than helps competition. See P. Areeda & H. Hovenkamp, Antitrust Law, 1987 Supplement, ¶ 518.1h (1987). Some speculate that this may have happened in the *Aspen Skiing* case, where the jury found a product market of destination ski resorts and a submarket of ski resorts in Aspen, Colorado. Id. See Aspen Highlands Skiing Corp. v. Aspen Skiing Co., 738 F.2d 1509 (10th Cir.1984) *aff'd on other grounds,* 472 U.S. 585 (1985).

In the *IBM* cases, manufacturers of "IBM-compatible peripherals" (input and output equipment that interface with IBM central processing units) sued IBM for monopolization; they alleged predatory pricing and excessively frequent and unnecessary design changes of interfaces. These cases, as you will later see, were very important to the development of the Section 2 law on monopolistic conduct; but market definition was also an important issue. If the relevant market or submarket was peripherals compatible with IBM, IBM had a very high share; but if the market was peripherals compatible with all central processing units, including Honeywell's, Univac's and Burroughs', IBM's share of the peripheral market was below 50%.

In Telex Corp. v. IBM, 367 F.Supp. 258 (N.D.Okl.1973), *rev'd,* 510 F.2d 894 (10th Cir.1975), *cert. dismissed,* 423 U.S. 802 (1975), the district court held that there was a separate IBM market because as a practical matter there was no competition between peripherals made for IBM systems and those made for other systems. Reversing, the court of appeals held that conclusion inconsistent with findings that non-IBM peripherals had at least indirectly constrained IBM's power over IBM peripherals. It would be feasible "in various instances" for suppliers of peripherals compatible with other systems to shift to produce IBM plug compatibles and vice versa, should the economic rewards become sufficiently attractive. Moreover, a senior vice president of Telex testified that "the engineering expense associated with the development of interfaces is a minimal expenditure" (510 F.2d at 916), and had urged Telex to modify its interfaces to be able to attach them to other systems.

Do you agree that peripherals for competing systems were necessarily in the same market? Would it matter whether:

1. IBM was purposely pricing selectively below its peripheral competitors' costs and/or changing interfaces frequently to impose costs on its peripheral competitors, all with a view towards chilling their competition in IBM-compatible peripherals and deterring them from making an investment in the next generation of IBM-compatible peripherals?

2. Honeywell, Univac and Burroughs were the only other major systems competitors and were also following the same strategy?

Can clusters of non-interchangeable products or services comprise markets? In United States v. Grinnell Corp., 384 U.S. 563 (1966), the Court found the insurance-accredited fire, burglary and waterflow central station protection service business to be a market. (But Justice Fortas said in dissent: "This Court now approves this strange red-haired, bearded, one-eyed man with a limp classification." *Id.* at 585, 591. In United States v. American Telephone & Telegraph Co., 524 F.Supp. 1336 (D.D.C.1981), the government alleged a telecommunications equipment market, including such diverse products as telephones and switching equipment. The firms involved in each of the aggregated submarkets were the same, the behavior being challenged was of the same sort, and the alleged structural conditions that made the behavior possible and profitable were the same. The court allowed the aggregation in the interests of avoiding duplicative evidence. It said, however, that if defendants could show that they had highly disparate market shares among the aggregated submarkets and that their alleged anticompetitive conduct related only to products "for which Bell's share was so low as to belie any claim of market power—then disaggregation may at that time become appropriate."

Can a single brand or company comprise a market? In *AT&T*, the government maintained that there was a separate Bell market for telecommunications equipment. The "Bell" companies, owned by AT&T, were the local telephone operating companies. Western Electric, also owned by AT&T, was the leading supplier of telecommunications equipment and virtually the sole supplier to the Bell companies.

To support its claim, the government asserted that the Bell companies were not sensitive to substantial price differences between Western Electric and its competitors; that the Bell companies were distinct customers; that Western Electric was a specialized vendor (it sold only to Bell companies); and that the industry recognized the existence of a Bell market. Do these allegations, if proven, support a separate Bell market? If you were the judge, how would you rule? Why? See id. at 1377–79. Is there a General Motors market for cars made up of GM dealers?

4. CONDUCT ISSUES IN THE CONTEXT OF STRUCTURAL ANALYSIS

After defining the market in a monopolization case the court must consider whether defendant has monopolized or attempted to monopolize that market. In *Alcoa* we had our first look both at power and conduct analysis. We now examine how the Section 2 conduct test developed and was applied during the consensus years that continued from the 1940s and into the 1970s. Although power issues will inevitably occur to you as you read cases in this section, our basic interest here is in tracing the development of the conduct test for monopolization.

UNITED STATES v. GRIFFITH
334 U.S. 100 (1948).

JUSTICE DOUGLAS: [The Griffiths owned four corporations which owned and operated motion picture theatres in Oklahoma, Texas and New Mexico. The corporations owned theatres in 53 towns in which there were no competing theatres, and in 32 towns in which there were competing theatres. Bargaining through two agents (each one representing a group of two of the corporate defendants), defendants negotiated a master agreement with each distributor covering an entire season. The agreements lumped together competitive and noncompetitive towns, generally gave defendants licenses for first-run exhibition in all of their theatres, and specified the rental in terms of a lump-sum for all theatres.]

* * *

. . . [T]he the use of monopoly power, however lawfully acquired, to foreclose competition, to gain a competitive advantage, or to destroy a competitor, is unlawful.

A man with a monopoly of theatres in any one town commands the entrance for all films into that area. If he uses that strategic position to acquire exclusive privileges in a city where he has competitors, he is employing his monopoly power as a trade weapon against his competitors. It may be a feeble, ineffective weapon where he has only one closed or monopoly town. But as those towns increase in number throughout a region, his monopoly power in them may be used with crushing effect on competitors in other places. . . .

The consequence of such a use of monopoly power is that films are licensed on a non-competitive basis in what would otherwise be competitive situations. That is the effect whether one exhibitor makes the bargain with the distributor or whether two or more exhibitors lump together their buying power, as appellees did here. It is in either case a misuse of monopoly power under the Sherman Act. If monopoly power can be used to beget monopoly, the Act becomes a feeble instrument indeed. Large-scale buying is not, of course, unlawful *per se*. It may yield price or other lawful advantages to the buyer. It may not, however, be used to monopolize or to attempt to monopolize interstate trade or commerce. Nor . . . may it be used to stifle competition by denying competitors less favorably situated access to the market.

* * *

What effect these practices actually had on the competitors of appellee exhibitors or on the growth of the Griffith circuit we do not know. The District Court, having started with the assumption that the use of circuit buying power was wholly lawful, naturally attributed no evil to it and thus treated the master agreements as legitimate weapons of competition. Since it found that no competitors were driven out of business, or acquired by appellees, or impeded in their business by threats or coercion, it concluded that appellees had not violated the Sherman Act in any of the ways charged in the complaint. These findings are plainly inadequate if we start, as we must, from the premise that the circuit buying power was unlawfully employed. On the record as we read it, it cannot be doubted that the monopoly power of appellees had some effect on their competitors and on the growth of the Griffith circuit. Its extent must be determined on a remand of the cause. We remit to the District Court not only that problem but also the fashioning of a decree which will undo as near as may be the wrongs that were done and prevent their recurrence in the future. . . .

Reversed.

Questions and Comments

What harm did the Court foresee from the master agreements? Did the Court view output limitation as a necessary ingredient of the violation? Was there any output limitation: fewer theaters and thus higher box office prices or downward pressure on prices paid to movie distributors, leading to reductions in the resources devoted to distribution? If not, what was the harm?

Was the Court saying that "fairness" to competing theaters requires that they be given an equal chance to bargain for first-runs, and that fairness outweighed the social gain from Griffith's and the distributors' cost savings? If so, would public benefits result from the decree?

Should the Court have honored the fairness claim of rival theaters—that they were deprived of the right to buy important inputs on the merits; that they were foreclosed from a significant competitive opportunity?

After the Court's decision, what was Griffith to do in order to realize the efficiencies of region-wide bargaining without violating the law?

5. FAIRNESS AS AN ANTITRUST VALUE

In this book, we will sometimes invoke "fairness." When we do, we are using the concept in a special way. There is a sense in which one might say that competition itself is unfair; the best endowed are more likely to win the race and endowments are given out arbitrarily. In this sense one could say that it is unfair for the "best" to compete too hard, for they will get too much of the business at the expense of the less well endowed. We do not use fairness this way; to give weight to fairness so conceived would be inconsistent with competition policy. It is an object of competition policy to facilitate production of the best products and services and an optimal product/service mix for consumers.

Also, some might say that competition is unfair when it takes away that which another member of the trade worked hard to get. A doctor or a lawyer may think it unfair—even unethical—to solicit the clients or patients of another. Even a sugar producer may think it unfair to undercut the prices of a fellow sugar maker. The doctors, the lawyers, the sugar makers may all have Codes of Ethics that say: It is unfair, undignified, unethical to hurt fellow members of the same trade, which is viewed as an extended family. When we speak of fairness as an antitrust value, we do not use it in this sense either. Such cooperation among people or firms poised to compete would totally undermine the rule of competition.

Also, some may think of fairness as achieving a generally satisfactory resolution of a particular dispute—perhaps by giving judgment to the party that behaved most honorably, perhaps by devising an outcome that "splits the difference." We do not use fairness in so personal or subjective a sense because we are discussing principles of law that must govern like behavior in the future.

Rather, fairness in the antitrust context has three different components, none of which is incompatible with consumer interests: (1) Is the defendant using power and position rather than merit to block the path of a less well-situated competitor? (2) Is the defendant using power to exploit a buyer or seller? (3) Does the defendant have such control over access to the process of competition itself that it can and does set arbitrary rules about who can participate and who is excluded? Each of these fairness factors has played a role in the evolution of the antitrust laws. One of them was at work in *Griffith*. Which one? Was fairness also involved in *Alcoa*?

Where conduct is unfair in one of these three senses it hurts either one or more competitors or one or more suppliers or customers. In many such situations the conduct will also hurt ultimate consumers. In sense (2), above, where an income transfer is involved, a fairness analysis may often replicate a resource allocation analysis.

(Fox & Sullivan) Antitrust ACB—7

For at least the last quarter of this century some jurists and scholars have been trying to excise fairness from the antitrust lexicon. They say that fairness and competition are like oil and water; they do not mix. These jurists and scholars define competition solely as a means to produce efficiency—primarily allocative efficiency—and contend that any competition policy that does not single-mindedly aim at efficiency will produce inefficiency and will therefore make all of us (counted by our aggregate wealth) worse off. Do you agree? Or do you think, to the contrary, that the fairness concern has a role in antitrust policy? Think about it as you meet new and different antitrust situations.

6. THE CONCEPT OF EXCLUSIONARY CONDUCT

The best known and most influential exclusionary conduct case during the years of the structural consensus was an opinion by a gifted district court judge, Charles Wyzanski.

UNITED STATES v. UNITED SHOE MACHINERY CORP.

110 F.Supp. 295 (D.Mass.1953), *aff'd per curiam*, 347 U.S. 521 (1954).

JUDGE WYZANSKI: December 15, 1947 the Government filed a complaint against United Shoe Machinery Corporation . . . [alleging] that since 1912 United had been "monopolizing interstate trade and commerce in the shoe machinery industry of the United States."

* * *

. . . United at the present time is supplying over 75%, and probably 85%, of the current demand in the American shoe machinery market, as heretofore defined. This is somewhat less than the share it was supplying in 1915. In the meantime, one important competitor, Compo Shoe Machinery Corporation, became the American innovator of the cement process of manufacture. In that sub-market Compo roughly equals United.

Machine types in all processes vary greatly in character. The more complex ones are the important revenue producers in the industry. They must be designed with great engineering skill, require large investments of time and money, and demand a knowledge of the art of shoemaking. Otherwise they cannot meet extraordinary elements of variability resulting from the variety of manufacturing processes and sub-processes, the preliminary preparatory stages of manufacture, the lasts, the sizes, the leather, and other aspects of the shoe-making business.

Once designed, a shoe machine can be copied, as German competitors have shown. But the copying is not easy, and an American machine manufacturer unfamiliar with the art of shoemaking would not ordinarily enter the field even if United gave him technical assistance, at least, unless he were assured that he would be encouraged to continue making similar machines for a long time.

* * *

Although at the turn of the century, United's patents covered the fundamentals of shoe machinery manufacture, those fundamental patents have expired. Current patents cover for the most part only minor developments, so that it is possible to "invent around" them, to use the words of United's chief competitor. However, the aggregation of patents does to some extent block potential competition. It furnishes a trading advantage. It leads inventors to offer their ideas to United, on the general principle that new complicated machines embody numerous patents. And it serves as a hedge or insurance for United against unforeseen competitive developments.

* * *

In supplying its complicated machines to shoe manufacturers, United, like its more important American competitors, has followed the practice of never selling, but only leasing. Leasing has been traditional in the shoe machinery field since the Civil War. So far as this record indicates, there is virtually no expressed dissatisfaction from consumers respecting that system; and Compo, United's principal competitor, endorses and uses it. Under the system, entry into shoe manufacture has been easy. The rates charged for all customers have been uniform. The machines supplied have performed excellently. United has, without separate charge, promptly and efficiently supplied repair service and many kinds of other service useful to shoe manufacturers. These services have been particularly important, because in the shoe manufacturing industry a whole line of production can be adversely affected, and valuable time lost, if some of the important machines go out of function, and because machine breakdowns have serious labor and consumer repercusions. The cost to the average shoe manufacturer of its machines and services supplied to him has been less than 2% of the wholesale price of his shoes.

However, United's leases, in the context of the present shoe machinery market, have created barriers to the entry by competitors into the shoe machinery field.

First, the complex of obligations and rights accruing under United's leasing system in operation deter a shoe manufacturer from disposing of a United machine and acquiring a competitor's machine. He is deterred more than if he owned that same United machine, or if he held it on a short lease carrying simple rental provisions and a reasonable charge for cancelation before the end of the term. The lessee is now held closely to United by the combined effect of the 10 year term, the requirement that if he has work available he must use the machine to full capacity, and by the return charge which can in practice, through the right of deduction fund, be reduced to insignificance if he keeps this and other United machines to the end of the periods for which he leased them.

Second, when a lessee desires to replace a United machine, United gives him more favorable terms if the replacement is by another United machine than if it is by a competitive machine.

Third, United's practice of offering to repair, without separate charges, its leased machines, has had the effect that there are no independent service organizations to repair complicated machines. In turn, this has had the effect that the manufacturer of a complicated machine must either offer repair service with his machine, or must face the obstacle of marketing his machine to customers who know that repair service will be difficult to provide.

Through its success with its principal and more complicated machines, United has been able to market more successfully its other machines, whether offered only for sale, or on optional sale or lease terms.

In ascending order of importance, the reasons for United's success with these simpler types are these. These other, usually more simple, machines are technologically related to the complex leased machines to which they are auxiliary or preparatory. Having business relations with, and a host of contacts with, shoe factories, United seems to many of them the most efficient, normal, and above all, convenient supplier. Finally, United has promoted the sale of these simple machine types by the sort of price discrimination between machine types, about to be stated.

Although maintaining the same nominal terms for each customer, United has followed, as between machine types, a discriminatory pricing policy. . . . Examples of this policy can be found in the wide, and relatively permanent, variations in the rates of return United secures upon its long line of machine types. United's own internal documents reveal that these sharp and relatively durable differentials are traceable, at least in large part, to United's policy of fixing a higher rate of return where competition is of minor significance, and a lower rate of return where competition is of major significance. Defendant has not borne the burden of showing that these variations in rates of return were motivated by, or correspond with, variations in the strength of the patent protection applicable to different machine types. Hence there is on this record no room for the argument that defendant's discriminatory pricing policy is entirely traceable to, and justified by, the patent laws of the United States.

* * *

Counsel appearing before this Court have spent much effort in analyzing the precise holdings in [the Section 2] cases. Though this analysis has been helpful, a District Judge knows that he cannot give any authoritative reconciliation of opinions rendered by appellate courts. And in connection with the Sherman Act, it is delusive to treat opinions written by different judges at different times as pieces of a jig-saw puzzle which can be, by effort, fitted correctly into a single pattern.

Yet, in these recent authorities there are discernible at least three different, but cognate, approaches.

The approach which has the least sweeping implications really antedates the decision in Aluminum. But it deserves restatement. An enterprise has monopolized in violation of § 2 of the Sherman Act if it has acquired or maintained a power to exclude others as a result of using an unreasonable "restraint of trade" in violation of § 1 of the Sherman Act. . . .

A more inclusive approach was adopted by Mr. Justice Douglas in United States v. Griffith, 334 U.S. 100. He stated that to prove a violation of § 2 it was not always necessary to show a violation of § 1. And he concluded that an enterprise has monopolized in violation of § 2 if it (a) has the power to exclude competition, and (b) has exercised it, or has the purpose to exercise it. The least that this conclusion means is that it is a violation of § 2 for one having effective control of the market to use, or plan to use, any exclusionary practice, even though it is not a technical restraint of trade. But the conclusion may go further.

Indeed the way in which Mr. Justice Douglas used the terms "monopoly power" and "effective market control" and cited Aluminum suggests that he endorses a third and broader approach, which originated with Judge Hand. It will be recalled that Judge Hand said that one who has acquired an overwhelming share of the market "monopolizes" whenever he does business, apparently even if there is no showing that his business involves any exclusionary practice. But, it will also be recalled that this doctrine is softened by Judge Hand's suggestion that the defendant may escape statutory liability if it bears the burden of proving that it owes its monopoly solely to superior skill, superior products, natural advantages, (including accessibility to raw materials or markets), economic or technological efficiency, (including scientific research), low margins of profit maintained permanently and without discrimination, or licenses conferred by, and used within, the limits of law, (including patents on one's own inventions, or franchises granted directly to the enterprise by a public authority).

In the case at bar, the Government contends that the evidence satisfies each of the three approaches to § 2 of the Sherman Act, so that it does not matter which one is taken.

If the matter were *res integra*, this Court would adopt the first approach, and, as a preliminary step to ruling upon § 2, would hold that it is a restraint of trade under § 1 for a company having an overwhelming share of the market, to distribute its more important products only by leases which have provisions that go beyond assuring prompt, periodic payments of rentals, which are not terminable cheaply, which involve discrimination against competition, and which combine in one contract the right to use the product and to have it serviced. But this inferior court feels precluded from so deciding because of the overhanging shadows of United States v. United Shoe Machinery Co. of N.J., 247 U.S. 32, and United Shoe Machinery Corp. v. United States, 258 U.S. 451, the Sherman and Clayton Act cases involving this company's predecessor and itself. Though these cases may ultimately be overruled by the Supreme Court, they have not yet lost all authority. . . .

This Court finds it unnecessary to choose between the second and third approaches. For, taken as a whole, the evidence satisfies the tests laid down in both Griffith and Aluminum. The facts show that (1) defendant has, and exercises, such overwhelming strength in the shoe machinery market that it controls that market, (2) this strength excludes some potential, and limits some actual, competition, and (3) this strength is not attributable solely to defendant's ability, economies of scale, research, natural advantages, and adaptation to inevitable economic laws.

In estimating defendant's strength, this Court gives some weight to the 75 plus percentage of the shoe machinery market which United serves.[1] But the Court considers other factors as well. In the relatively

1. This Court does not consider whether this high percentage, by itself, would warrant (but not compel) an inference that United has such overwhelming strength that it could exclude competition. Nor does this Court consider whether, drawing upon United ed States v. Griffith, 334 U.S. 100, 107, footnote 10, and United States v. Aluminum Co. of America, 2 Cir., 148 F.2d 416, 429, a bold, original court, mindful of what legal history teaches about the usual, if not invariable, relationship between overwhelming percent-

static shoe machinery market where there are no sudden changes in the style of machines or in the volume of demand, United has a network of long-term, complicated leases with over 90% of the shoe factories. These leases assure closer and more frequent contacts between United and its customers than would exist if United were a seller and its customers were buyers. Beyond this general quality, these leases are so drawn and so applied as to strengthen United's power to exclude competitors. Moreover, United offers a long line of machine types, while no competitor offers more than a short line. Since in some parts of its line United faces no important competition, United has the power to discriminate, by wide differentials and over long periods of time, in the rate of return it procures from different machine types. Furthermore, being by far the largest company in the field, with by far the largest resources in dollars, in patents, in facilities, and in knowledge, United has a marked capacity to attract offers of inventions, inventors' services, and shoe machinery businesses. And, finally, there is no substantial substitute competition from a vigorous secondhand market in shoe machinery.

To combat United's market control, a competitor must be prepared with knowledge of shoemaking, engineering skill, capacity to invent around patents, and financial resources sufficient to bear the expense of long developmental and experimental processes. The competitor must be prepared for consumers' resistance founded on their long-term, satisfactory relations with United, and on the cost to them of surrendering United's leases. Also, the competitor must be prepared to give, or point to the source of, repair and other services, and to the source of supplies for machine parts, expendable parts, and the like. Indeed, perhaps a competitor who aims at any large scale success must also be prepared to lease his machines. These considerations would all affect *potential* competition, and have not been without their effect on *actual* competition.

Not only does the evidence show United has control of the market, but also the evidence does not show that the control is due entirely to excusable causes. . . . [B]eyond criticism is the high quality of United's products, its understanding of the techniques of shoemaking and the needs of shoe manufacturers, its efficient design and improvement of machines, and its prompt and knowledgeable service. These have illustrated in manifold ways that "superior skill, foresight and industry" of which Judge Hand spoke in Aluminum.

But United's control does not rest solely on its original constitution, its ability, its research, or its economies of scale. There are other barriers to competition, and these barriers were erected by United's own business policies. Much of United's market power is traceable to the magnetic ties inherent in its system of leasing, and not selling, its more important

age of the market and control of the market, and desirous of enabling trial judges to escape the morass of economic data in which they are now plunged, might, on the basis of considerations of experience and judicial convenience, announce that an enterprise having an overwhelming percentage of the market was presumed to have monopoly power, that a plaintiff bore its burden of proof under § 2 of the Sherman Act if it satisfied the trier of fact that defendant had the prohibited percentage, and that defendant, to escape liability, must bear the burden of proving that its share of the market was attributable to its ability, natural advantage, legal license, or, perhaps, to others' lack of interest in entering the market.

machines. The lease-only system of distributing complicated machines has many "partnership" aspects, and it has exclusionary features such as the 10–year term, the full capacity clause, the return charges, and the failure to segregate service charges from machine charges. Moreover, the leasing system has aided United in maintaining a pricing system which discriminates between machine types.

* * *

In one sense, the leasing system and the miscellaneous activities just referred to (except United's purchases in the second-hand market) were natural and normal, for they were, in Judge Hand's words, "honestly industrial". They are the sort of activities which would be engaged in by other honorable firms. And, to a large extent, the leasing practices conform to long-standing traditions in the shoe machinery business. Yet, they are not practices which can be properly described as the inevitable consequences of ability, natural forces, or law. They represent something more than the use of accessible resources, the process of invention and innovation, and the employment of those techniques of employment, financing, production, and distribution, which a competitive society must foster. They are contracts, arrangements, and policies which, instead of encouraging competition based on pure merit, further the dominance of a particular firm. In this sense, they are unnatural barriers; they unnecessarily exclude actual and potential competition; they restrict a free market. While the law allows many enterprises to use such practices, the Sherman Act is now construed by superior courts to forbid the continuance of effective market control based in part upon such practices. Those courts hold that market control is inherently evil and constitutes a violation of § 2 unless economically inevitable, or specifically authorized and regulated by law.[2]

* * *

Defendant seems to suggest that even if its control of the market is not attributable exclusively to its superior performance, its research, and its economies of scale, nonetheless, United's market control should not be held unlawful, because only through the existence of some monopoly power can the thin shoe machinery market support fundamental research of the first order, and achieve maximum economies of production and distribution.

To this defense the shortest answer is that the law does not allow an enterprise that maintains control of a market through practices not economically inevitable, to justify that control because of its supposed

---

2. Underlying much of defendant's argument is the basic contention that Aluminum, Griffith, and related cases represent an unsound interpretation of the Sherman Act and an unwise public policy. A District Judge must leave this contention to the Supreme Court and to Congress. They are the only tribunals competent to consider whether appellate courts have unjustifiably gone beyond the 1890 legislative concern with force and fraud, with combination and conspiracy, and with the growth of trusts dwarfing ordinary men and ordinary governmental units; whether it is appropriate to read a statute having criminal and treble damage provisions as applying to the mere exercise of effective control of the market; and whether Congress contemplated the use of trial courts, moving within the traditional limits of judicial procedure and of legally admissible evidence, to solve subtle, complex, extensive economic controversies for which judges are not always well suited, and which hinder the prompt disposition of other meritorious cases.

social advantage. . . . It is for Congress, not for private interests, to determine whether a monopoly, not compelled by circumstances, is advantageous. And it is for Congress to decide on what conditions, and subject to what regulations, such a monopoly shall conduct its business.

Moreover, if the defense were available, United has not proved that monopoly is economically compelled by the thinness of the shoe machinery market. It has not shown that no company could undertake to develop, manufacture, and distribute certain types of machines, unless it alone met the total demand for those types of machines.

Nor has United affirmatively proved that it has achieved spectacular results at amazing rates of speed, nor has it proved that comparable research results and comparable economies of production, distribution, and service could not be achieved as well by, say, three important shoe machinery firms, as by one. Compo with a much smaller organization indicates how much research can be done on a smaller scale. Yet since Compo is limited to the simpler cement process machines, too much reliance should not be placed on this comparison. Nonetheless, one point is worth recalling. Compo's inventors first found practical ways to introduce the cement process which United had considered and rejected. This experience illustrates the familiar truth that one of the dangers of extraordinary experience is that those who have it may fall into grooves created by their own expertness. They refuse to believe that hurdles which they have learned from experience are insurmountable, can in fact be overcome by fresh, independent minds.

So far, nothing in this opinion has been said of defendant's *intent* in regard to its power and practices in the shoe machinery market. This point can be readily disposed of by reference once more to Aluminum. Defendant intended to engage in the leasing practices and pricing policies which maintained its market power. That is all the intent which the law requires when both the complaint and the judgment rest on a charge of "monopolizing", not merely "attempting to monopolize". Defendant having willed the means, has willed the end.

* * *

OPINION ON REMEDY

Where a defendant has monopolized commerce in violation of § 2, the principal objects of the decrees are to extirpate practices that have caused or may hereafter cause monopolization, and to restore workable competition in the market.

A trial judge, until he is otherwise directed by the Supreme Court or Congress, . . . must frame a decree upon the basis of the presuppositions underlying Aluminum and Griffith. He must accept these as the premises of the current interpretation of § 2 of the Sherman Act. Concentrations of power, no matter how beneficently they appear to have acted, nor what advantages they seem to possess, are inherently dangerous. Their good behavior in the past may not be continued; and if their strength were hereafter grasped by presumptuous hands, there would be no automatic check and balance from equal forces in the industrial market. And in the absence of this protective mechanism, the demand for public regulation, public ownership, or other drastic measures would become irresistible in time of crisis. Dispersal of private economic power is thus one of the ways to preserve the system of private enterprise. Moreover, well as a monopoly may have behaved in the moral sense, its economic performance is inevitably suspect. The very absence of strong competitors implies that there cannot be an objective measuring rod of the monopolist's excellence, and the test of its performance must, therefore, be largely theoretical. What appears to the outsider to be a sensible, prudent, nay even a progressive policy of the monopolist, may in fact reflect a lower scale of adventurousness and less intelligent risk-taking than would be the case if the enterprise were forced to respond to a stronger industrial challenge. Some truth lurks in the cynical remark that not high profits but a quiet life is the chief reward of monopoly power. And even if a particular enterprise seeks growth and not repose, an increased rate in the growth of ideas does not follow from an increased concentration of power. Industrial advance may indeed be in inverse proportion to economic power; for creativity in business as in other areas, is best nourished by multiple centers of activity, each following its unique pattern and developing its own esprit de corps to respond to the challenge of competition. The dominance of any one enterprise inevitably unduly accentuates that enterprise's experience and views as to what is possible, practical, and desirable with respect to technological development, research, relations with producers, employees, and customers. And the preservation of any unregulated monopoly is hostile to the industrial and political ideals of an open society founded on the faith that tomorrow will produce a better than the best.

Yet a trial judge's decree attempting to recreate a competitive market should be drafted in the spirit which has been attributed to Lord Acton— the most philosophical mind that has ever been directed to the evils of concentration of power. "No one can be sure what view Acton would have adopted on contemporary economic issues. What is certain is the principles and tests he would have employed. Of every proposal he would have asked, Is it just? Is it in accordance with the permanent will of the community? Is it practicable? Will it be efficient? Will it increase or diminish real freedom?". Fasnacht, Acton's Political Philosophy (1952), p. 124.

Judges in prescribing remedies have known their own limitations. They do not *ex officio* have economic or political training. Their prophecies as to the economic future are not guided by unusually subtle judgment. They are not so representative as other branches of the government. The recommendations they receive from government prosecutors do not always reflect the over-all approach of even the executive branch of the government, sometimes not indeed the seasoned and fairly informed judgment of the head of the Department of Justice. Hearings in court do not usually give the remote judge as sound a feeling for the realities of a situation as other procedures do. Judicial decrees must be fitted into the framework of what a busy, and none too expert, court can supervise. Above all, no matter with what authority he is invested, with what facts and opinion he is supplied, a trial judge is only one man, and should move with caution and humility.

That considerations of this type have always affected anti-trust courts is plain from the history of the Standard Oil, American Tobacco and Alcoa cases. To many champions of the anti-trust laws these cases indicate judicial timidity, economic innocence, lack of conviction, or paralysis of resolution. Yet there is another way of interpreting this judicial history. In the anti-trust field the courts have been accorded, by common consent, an authority they have in no other branch of enacted law. Indeed, the only comparable examples of the power of judges is the economic role they formerly exercised under the Fourteenth Amendment, and the role they now exercise in the area of civil liberties. They would not have been given, or allowed to keep, such authority in the anti-trust field, and they would not so freely have altered from time to time the interpretation of its substantive provisions, if courts were in the habit of proceeding with the surgical ruthlessness that might commend itself to those seeking absolute assurance that there will be workable competition, and to those aiming at immediate realization of the social, political, and economic advantages of dispersal of power.

Such self-restraining considerations have peculiar force in this case. Until Alcoa lost its case in 1945, there was no significant reason to suppose that United's conduct violated § 2 of the Sherman Act. The Supreme Court had three times . . . reviewed aspects of this company's, or its predecessor's, activities. What United is now doing is similar to what it was then doing, but the activities which were similar stood uncondemned,—indeed, one ought to go further and say they were in part endorsed. In the face of these decisions, it would be anomalous to charge the officers of United with any moral deficiency.

* * *

The Government's proposal that the Court dissolve United into three separate manufacturing companies is unrealistic. United conducts all machine manufacture at one plant in Beverly, with one set of jigs and tools, one foundry, one laboratory for machinery problems, one managerial staff, and one labor force. It takes no Solomon to see that this organism cannot be cut into three equal and viable parts.

Nor can the division of United's business be fairly accomplished by dividing the manufacture of machinery into three broad categories, and then issuing an injunction restraining the Beverly plant from manufacturing two broad categories of machine types, and vesting in each of two new companies the right to manufacture one of those categories. Such an order would create for the new companies the most serious type of problems respecting the acquisition of physical equipment, the raising of new capital, the allotment of managerial and labor forces, and so forth. The prospect of creating three factories where one grew before has not been thought through by its proponents.

A petition for dissolution should reflect greater attention to practical problems and should involve supporting economic data and prophesies such as are presented in corporate reorganization and public utility dissolution cases. Moreover, the petition should involve a more formal commitment by the Attorney General, than is involved in the divergent proposals that his assistants have made in briefs and in oral arguments addressed to the Court.

On the whole, therefore, the suggested remedy of dissolution is rejected.

From the opinion on defendant's violations it follows that some form of relief regarding defendant's leases and leasing practices is proper and necessary.

The Government does not propose that United should cease leasing machines. It does suggest that this Court order defendant to eliminate from the leases those provisions found to be restrictive, to offer for sale every type of machine which it offers for lease, and to make the sales terms somewhat more advantageous to customers, than the lease terms.

The Court agrees that it would be undesirable, at least until milder remedies have been tried, to direct United to abolish leasing forthwith. United is free to abolish leasing if it chooses to do so, but this Court hesitates to lay down any absolute ban for two reasons. First, if a ban were immediately applied, a substantial number of shoe factories would probably be put out of business, for they have not the assets, nor the capacity to borrow, requisite to purchase machines, even on conditional sales agreements. Second, if this Court forbade United to lease machines, it could not apply a similar ban to its competitors. This would constitute for United a major not a minor competitive handicap if one accepts the testimony of the large number of shoe manufacturers who have already expressed their preference for leasing rather than buying machines. . . .

Although leasing should not now be abolished by judicial decree, the Court agrees with the Government that the leases should be purged of their restrictive features. In the decree filed herewith, the term of the lease is shortened, the full capacity clause is eliminated, the discriminatory commutative charges are removed, and United is required to segregate its charges for machines from its charges for repair service. . . .

The Court also agrees with the Government that if United chooses to continue to lease any machine type, it must offer that type of machine also for sale. The principal merit of this proposal does not lie in its primary impact, that is, in its effect in widening the choices open to owners of shoe factories. For present purposes it may be assumed that the anti-trust laws are not designed, chiefly, if at all, to give a customer choice as to the selling methods by which his supplier offers that supplier's own products. The merit of the Government's proposal is in its secondary impact. Insofar as United's machines are sold rather than leased, they will ultimately, in many cases, reach a second-hand market. From that market, United will face a type of substitute competition which will gradually weaken the prohibited market power which it now exercises. Moreover, from that market, or from United itself, a competitor of United can acquire a United machine in order to study it, to copy its unpatented features, and to experiment with improvements in, or alterations of, the machine. Thus, in another and more direct way, United's market power will be diminished.

Furthermore, the creation of a sales market together with the purging of the restrictive features of the leases will, in combination, gradually diminish the magnetic hold now exercised by what United properly describes as the partnership features of the leasing system. As United's relationships with its customers grow feebler, competitors will have an enhanced opportunity to market their wares.

* * *

Questions and Comments

Judge Wyzanski's "law clerk" for the *United Shoe* case was Carl Kaysen, then a young economist who had studied with Mason. Kaysen later co-authored with Donald Turner of Harvard Law School a highly acclaimed book, Antitrust Policy: An Economic and Legal Analysis (1959).

After reading Judge Wyzanski's opinion in *United Shoe,* do you believe that United Shoe did anything "wrong"? Judge Wyzanski thought that United Shoe's conduct was unnecessarily exclusionary. What did he mean?

Suppose that a firm engages in conduct involving costs to it that could make economic sense only if the conduct imposed even greater costs on existing competitors or prevented the emergence of new competition. A rational, profit maximizing firm that expected to face competition just as strong after the conduct was implemented as it faced before would never engage in such conduct. Conduct of this kind—a practice that appeals to the firm using it only because it hurts competitors—is unambiguously anticompetitive. A firm using such a strategy would necessarily have specific intent to hurt competition (which, as Wyzanski affirms, is a higher level of intent than is necessary for a violation). A practice of this kind is often called "predatory." Judge Wyzanski's concept of illegal exclusionary conduct is a broader category. It includes predatory conduct but also conduct that is more restrictive of competition than necessary to achieve good business purposes.

During the period of the structural consensus it was generally assumed that identifying such conduct was an act of judgment—something of an art. One (a court? a jury?) looked at the full panoply of relevant market facts, thought about the pressures the monopolist was under, its options, the strategic decisions it made, and then decided: unreasonably exclusionary, or competition on the merits? Be mindful that things may be somewhat different today. Chicago theorists, regarding markets as potent engines for efficiency, would shrink the scope for violation and broaden the breathing space for business judgment. Even the "new" I.O. economists would move in the same direction.

Consider each of the exclusionary practices identified by the court. Were any of them predatory in the sense in which we have defined that term above? Consider how, if at all, the particular practice excluded competitors and potential competitors, and whether the practice harmed shoe manufacturers, consumers or both. Were some practices treated as illegally exclusionary only because small competitors could not offer customers as good a deal? If so, was United Shoe's advantageous position a result of its integration into related products and services? If so, could its competitors compete by similarly integrating? Should the court protect them against the need to do so? Suppose competitors could not feasibly integrate. Should United Shoe (and its customers) be denied the advantages of its integration? Does your answer depend upon whether the advantages are benefits of leverage (similar to those in *Griffith*) or of efficiencies? Did United Shoe's advantages stem from leverage or from efficiencies?

United Shoe's customers wanted to lease the defendant's machines rather than to buy them. They also wanted the "free" repair service. When they turned in one United Shoe machine for another they were happy to get the favorable replacement terms, too. In an action for monopolization, should it be a defense that the defendant pleased its customers? Putting it another way, is customer contentment conclusive or at least strong evidence that United Shoe was behaving competitively, not monopolistically? Is it relevant that many of United's customers were critical of the government for bringing this case?

How would Judge Wyzanski have answered these questions? Can we infer his answer from his assertion that the dominance of a market by one company unduly accentuates its "views as to what is possible, practical and desirable?" (110 F.Supp. at 347.) What do you think of his assertion that "preservation of any regulated monopoly is hostile to the industrial and political ideals of an open society founded on the faith that tomorrow will produce a better than the best"? Id. Is the first of these assertions an economic argument or a political policy argument? The second? Is an economic assertion more or less valid than a political policy assertion as a way to resolve an antitrust issue?

Unbundling in this case meant separating out the service charge from the charge for the machine. Over a period of years an unbundling might have led to a viable independent service market and, when the independent service market became established, shoe manufacturers would have been better off. In time unbundling might also have made entry into the shoe machinery market more attractive, since manufacturers too small to realize economies of scale in the service market would not have to bear the extra costs of providing repair service. New entry (and perhaps greater ease of entry without actual entry) promised to lead to increased competitive pressures. Similarly, a requirement that United Shoe sell machines to those who wanted to buy them promised to create a second-hand market, and that might even create more primary competition by facilitating copying. In these ways a government's suit such as *United Shoe* could make customers better off.

Is the converse possible: that judicial interference with producer decisions that coincide with buyer preferences is likely to make customers worse off? Who knows best about what is good for consumers? Is it appropriate or treacherous for an antitrust court to second-guess buyer preferences as expressed by their votes in the marketplace? Can a court in a particular case tell whether the risk is worth taking?

Is it possible, too, that shoe manufacturers would not be upset by monopoly returns to United Shoe because, as long as all shoe manufacturers paid them pro rata, and thus received no cost advantage over others, all would be able to pass them on to shoe purchasers in the form of higher shoe prices? In that case, amorphous "ultimate consumers" might be significantly benefited by a decree even if direct customers of *United Shoe* were indifferent to it.[5]

5. The possibility of passing on a monopoly overcharge gives rise to interesting damage and standing issues. If the customer of an unlawful monopolist sues to recover the monopoly overcharge should it be a defense that the customer passed the overcharge on to its own customers further downstream? The Court held that it was not. Hanover Shoe, Inc. v. United Shoe Machinery Corp., 392 U.S. 481 (1968). It also later held that a downstream consumer could not recover the portion of the overcharge it stood ready to

A company will not normally have great power to exploit consumers if entry barriers into its market are low; if it tries to raise prices significantly above cost, new competitors may enter. Some economists (following George Stigler) define barriers to entry to include only government-imposed barriers or absolute cost advantages enjoyed by the incumbent but not obtainable by the entrant. A strong trade name developed through years of advertising and promotion is thus not a barrier, because the new entrant can advertise, too. Others (following Joe Bain) define barriers more broadly to include anything that discourages entry, including customer loyalty to the incumbent's brand, high nonrecoverable costs (investment that must be made in order to enter but that cannot be recouped on exit), and an optimum efficient scale that is very large in relation to demand (say, more than 50% of demand at established prices). With which formulation would Judge Wyzanski agree? If the latter, what, in addition to absolute cost advantages would Judge Wyzanski regard as a barrier?

What is the relevance of Judge Wyzanski's finding that inventors will offer their ideas to United Shoe rather than to its competitors "on the general principle that new complicated machines embody numerous patents?" (110 F.Supp. at 339.) Does this imply that most shoe making inventions are more valuable to United Shoe than to its competitors? Would United Shoe be likely to pay the inventors more money for their inventions than its competitors would be willing to pay? Does an affirmative answer imply that persistent monopoly in high-technology markets is likely to be a natural result of efficiency (i.e., the dominant firm, which is perhaps already technologically superior, gets the new inventions as they come on the market because it is the most efficient exploiter of them)? Or will the dominant firm pay more money because it is buying an increment in market power? Should it matter to the legal outcome which explanation seems right?

Chicago school thinkers assert that consumer welfare (defined to mean the maximization of total wealth) should be the only concern. Is Judge Wyzanski concerned also with facilitating an impersonal competitive process? Is he concerned with fairness to excluded competitors? Do all of these objectives fit together in the worldview of Judge Wyzanski? Some antitrust commentators, the editors of this casebook among them, think that, given the legislative history of the law, antitrust analysis should focus not on a single specific economic goal, such as allocative efficiency, but should emphasize the goal of maintaining competitive process. These commentators say that maintaining competitive process will serve several more specific goals: the interest of consumers in reasonable prices and reasonable variety and choice, the interest of producers in access to the market and in not being coerced or otherwise treated unfairly and, in general, the broad economic, political and social goals of antitrust. Chicago school thinkers, by contrast, believe that allocative efficiency is the only defensible goal and that the view focusing on process indulges the fallacy of assuming that all good things are compatible.

prove had been passed on to it. Illinois Brick Co. v. Illinois, 431 U.S. 720 (1977). Subject to very limited exceptions, only the first purchaser from a monopolist has a cause of action to recover for a monopoly overcharge, and that purchaser has the cause of action regardless of whether it, in fact, passed on. For a criticism of this way of handling the problem see Harris & Sulli-van, Passing on the Monopoly Overcharge: A Comprehensive Analysis, 128 U.Pa.L.Rev. 269 (1979). For a defense of the Court's view see Lander & Posner, Should Indirect Purchases Have Standing to Sue Under the Antitrust Laws? An Economic Analysis of the Rule of Illinois Brick, 46 U.Chi.L.Rev. 602 (1979).

What do you think? Articles supporting the Chicago view are collected in footnote 2 and articles supporting the alternative view that prevailed during the structural consensus period collected in footnote 3 to the Appendix to Fox & Sullivan, Antitrust–Retrospective and Prospective: Where Are We Coming From? Where Are We Going? 62 N.Y.U.L.Rev. 936, at 969–70 (1987).

After long contemplation of the social harm emanating from dominant firm practices that entrenched its position, the *United Shoe* court ordered relief. Its decree was intended to help open up the market to more dynamic competition without interfering significantly with preferences of the existing customers. It ordered United Shoe to sell machines to those who wished to buy them, but allowed the company to continue leasing. It ordered United Shoe to unbundle service charges, but allowed them to continue servicing. The court denied the government's request that it break up United Shoe into three separate companies. Was the denial of that request wise or excessively cautious? If you were judge, what would you have done?

Ten years later, pursuant to a provision in the decree, the government reported to the district court on the decree's effectiveness. The government said that workable competition in the shoe machinery market had not come about, that United Shoe continued to dominate the market. The government petitioned for further relief. For its part, the company contended that the decree had done its job, that competition was restored, and that the decree should therefore be vacated. The district court denied the government's petition on grounds that the court lacked power to modify the decree except in the case of new and unforeseen circumstances. The Supreme Court reversed, stating that if a decree has not, within 10 years, restored workable competition, the district court must "prescribe other, and if necessary more definitive, means to achieve the result." United States v. United Shoe Machinery Corp., 391 U.S. 244 at 252 (1968).

When the case went back to the district court, the government and United Shoe negotiated a consent decree. The company agreed to divest itself of assets producing $8.5 million in revenues and thus to reduce its market share to 33 percent. It also agreed to license additional patents at reasonable royalties. 1969 Trade Cas. (CCH) ¶ 72,688 (D.Mass.1969).

Consider the background and training of a typical federal district court judge. Suppose such a judge is suddenly appointed Tzar of a large and important industry—say computers—and authorized to restructure the industry in the public interest. How is the judge likely to react? How will she go about the task? If you were the judge's law clerk, could you propose a sensible mode of proceeding?

Do you see any problems in allowing the government (represented by Department of Justice lawyers) and the defendant to work out a decree by negotiation? How is this likely to differ from a judge-crafted decree? What might the district court do to evaluate whether a proposed consent decree is in the public interest? The U.S. telephone industry was recently restructured by negotiation, as we discuss at part E. infra.

7. NOTE ON GRINNELL AND THE SECTION 2 CONDUCT TEST

We previously considered market definition aspects of the government's 1961 monopolization case against Grinnell Corporation and its subsidiaries. Grinnell was the leading manufacturer of plumbing supplies and fire sprinkler systems, the principal hardware needed by fire and burglar protection systems. Grinnell acquired American District Telegraph Company, Holmes Electric Protective Company, and Automatic Fire Alarm Company, which together had more than 87 percent of the nation's business in insurance-accredited central station protection service. The acquired service companies had previously fixed prices and allocated territories and customers among themselves; they had also acquired numerous competitors. After becoming part of the Grinnell family, some of the Grinnell protective service companies continued to operate offices at a loss in cities where there still were competitors.

The district court, by Judge Wyzanski, held that defendants had monopolized their markets. He ordered divestiture and other relief (including termination of the employment of the company's chief executive officer James Douglas Fleming, who, "for well over a decade and a half, [had been] vigorous captain of the defendants' conspiracy to monopolize." United States v. Grinnell Corp., 236 F.Supp. 244, 260 (D.R.I.1964)).

The Supreme Court affirmed the judgment of monopolization and remanded the case for further hearings on relief (United States v. Grinnell Corp., 384 U.S. 563 (1966)). It said that more divestiture was necessary but that termination of Mr. Fleming was inappropriate. As to the elements of monopolization, the Supreme Court said, by Justice Douglas:

> The offense of monopoly under § 2 of the Sherman Act has two elements: (1) the possession of monopoly power in the relevant market and (2) the willful acquisition or maintenance of that power as distinguished from growth or development as a consequence of a superior product, business acumen, or historic accident. We shall see that this second ingredient presents no major problem here, as what was done in building the empire was done plainly and explicitly for a single purpose. In *United States v. du Pont & Co.*, 351 U.S. 377, 391, we defined monopoly power as "the power to control prices or exclude competition." The existence of such power ordinarily may be inferred from the predominant share of the market. In *American Tobacco Co. v. United States*, 328 U.S. 781, 797, we said that "over two-thirds of the entire domestic field of cigarettes, and . . . over 80% of the field of comparable cigarettes" constituted "a substantial monopoly." In *United States v. Aluminum Co. of America*, 148 F.2d 416, 429, 90% of the market constituted monopoly power. In the present case, 87% of the accredited central station service business leaves no doubt that the congeries of these defendants have monopoly power which, as our discussion of the record indicates, they did not hesitate to wield—if that business is the relevant market. The only remaining question therefore is, what is the relevant market?

Id. at 570–71.

Is there any doubt that merger with or acquisition of competitors leading to monopoly power would alone be sufficient to violate Section 2? Would it matter whether the mergers also yielded efficiencies?

Can you now generalize about what kind of conduct violates Section 2? Can you give examples of conduct that might be defended but which is probably illegal and of conduct close to the line but probably on the legal side?

8. ATTEMPTS AND CONSPIRACIES TO MONOPOLIZE

We have seen above that monopolization requires two elements: possession of monopoly power (or being a "monopolist"), and the use of offensive conduct to obtain, protect, expand or exploit the monopoly. We have explored the question of market definition and analysis of the structure of the market—a process by which courts determine whether or not a firm is a monopolist. We have also considered how to identify the kind of conduct that amounts to "monopolization." As we go on we shall continue to explore the conduct question.

Here, we pause for a first look at two different, but related, problems: Section 2 of the Sherman Act bans not just monopolization but also attempts and combinations and conspiracies to monopolize. How do attempts and how do combinations and conspiracies to monopolize fit within the framework? What are the elements of these offenses and how do they differ from the elements needed to show monopolization? To address these questions, we turn to two older, leading cases: the *Swift* case, decided in 1905, still much cited as the touchstone for attempts to monopolize; and *American Tobacco (II)*,[6] a leading authority on combinations and conspiracies to monopolize.

a. Attempts to Monopolize

In the *Swift* case the government charged that a cartel of big meat companies occupying three-fifths of the market constituted a combination and conspiracy to monopolize. Defendants allegedly combined, first, to refrain from bidding against one another in the stockyards (and, at other times, to deliberately bid up prices for a few days to induce cattle raisers to ship more cattle, although they would often push prices down again before shipments arrived) and, second, to fix the prices at which they would sell to dealers. The government sought an injunction. The meat companies demurred, relying on the *Knight* case to argue that livestock was not a subject of interstate commerce; they also contended that the complaint was too vague, that no single act alleged was illegal, and that in any event the defendant companies did not have a monopoly. The lower court granted the government an injunction and the Supreme Court, by Justice Holmes, affirmed. Holding that the complaint was not too vague and that the various acts were part of a single plan that was illegal, the Court said:

Where acts are not sufficient in themselves to produce a result which the law seeks to prevent—for instance, the monopoly—but require further

6. American Tobacco was decided in 1911 two weeks after Standard Oil.

acts in addition to the mere forces of nature to bring that result to pass, an intent to bring it to pass is necessary in order to produce a dangerous probability that it will happen. . . .   But when that intent and the consequent dangerous probability exist, this statute, like many others and like the common law in some cases, directs itself against that dangerous probability as well as against the completed result.

Swift & Co. v. United States, 196 U.S. 375, 396 (1905).

Although *Swift* involved a combination and conspiracy, courts routinely cite it as stating the modern law on single-firm attempts to monopolize. Accordingly, the plaintiff in an attempt to monopolize case must prove: (1) that the defendant has specific intent to harm competition, and (2) that the offending acts create a dangerous probability of the success of the attempt to monopolize. See part F. infra.

There is a close relationship between the typical attempt case and the typical monopolization case. To prove dangerous probability of success in an attempt case, the plaintiff normally must prove that the defendant already has considerable power. To do so plaintiff usually must define the appropriate market, prove defendant's share, and prove any other structural elements that bear on power. To prove the specific intent required in attempt cases the plaintiff must show that defendants sought to destroy competitors or hurt competition. Plaintiff must also prove anticompetitive conduct which might, if unchecked, lead to monopoly. Thus, both power and conduct are crucial elements of the attempt offense, just as they are of monopolization. Because of this, and because the one additional element in attempt—the requisite specific intent—may be inferred from the bad conduct, the difference between attempt to monopolize and monopolization is shadowy. Often, it is mainly a matter of the degree of market power that must be shown.

b. Combinations and Conspiracies to Monopolize

Section 2 of the Sherman Act also prohibits combinations or conspiracies to monopolize. The Supreme Court summarized the elements of this offense in American Tobacco Company v. United States (American Tobacco II), 328 U.S. 781 (1946):

> [It is a] crime . . . ., under § 2 of the Sherman Act, for parties, as in these cases, to combine or conspire to acquire or maintain the power to exclude competitors from any part of the trade or commerce among the several states or with foreign nations, provided . . . they have the intent and purpose to exercise that power. . . .
>
>   . . . A combination may be one . . . to monopolize a part of such trade or commerce . . . in violation of the Sherman Act, although such restraint or monopoly may not have been actually attempted to any harmful extent.

Id. at 809, 811.

Thus, while the monopolization and the attempt violations require some monopolistic act or practice, a combination or conspiracy to monopolize does not. If all the cigarette makers in the country met in an auditorium and agreed to merge into a single firm they would have conspired to monopolize even though, as yet, they were still vigorously competing with each other. The offensive agreement itself is the violation. Even so, both structure and conduct are likely to play an evidentiary role. Can you see why?

This brief inquiry into attempt and conspiracy is intended, in part, to emphasize the significance of both power and conduct issues to all Section 2 litigation. As we return, shortly, to case law that focuses on whether market conduct is or is not anticompetitive, be mindful that such conduct must be proved in attempt cases, too; and that such conduct, if egregious enough, may be a basis for an inference about intent.

Should the conduct standard for attempt be identical with that for monopolization?

c. Relevant Market in Combinations, Conspiracies and Attempts to Monopolize

i. Combinations and Conspiracies

When defendants are charged with a combination or conspiracy to monopolize, the traditional view is that neither the scope of the relevant market nor the effect of the conspiracy is in issue; the agreement to commit the illegal act is the violation. Is there a counter argument, or at least a limiting case? Suppose all makers of lemon drops met together and agree to merge into a single firm. If they were charged with a conspiracy to monopolize, how would you defend them? Note that a combination or conspiracy to monopolize would also amount to a combination or conspiracy in restraint of trade (see Chapter 3 infra), and thus would constitute a Section 1 violation as well as a Section 2 violation. As you will later learn questions of power are attenuated in many Section 1 cases. See, e.g., United States v. Socony–Vacuum Oil Co., 310 U.S. 150, n. 59 (1940).

ii. Attempts to Monopolize

The traditional law is that in attempt to monopolize cases the plaintiff must prove the relevant market in order to show that the defendant is dangerously likely to achieve monopoly power. See, e.g., Pacific Engineering & Production Co. of Nevada v. Kerr McGee Corp., 551 F.2d 790 (10th Cir.), cert. denied, 434 U.S. 879 (1977). For many years the Ninth Circuit had a different rule, to the effect that specific intent to monopolize a part of trade and predatory conduct were sufficient to prove the attempt violation. Lessig v. Tidewater Oil Co., 327 F.2d 459, 474 (9th Cir.1964), cert. denied, 377 U.S. 993 (1964). Some panels in the Ninth Circuit have sometimes weakened the Lessig rule. See, e.g., Blair Foods, Inc. v. Ranchers Cotton Oil, 610 F.2d 665, 669 (9th Cir.1980). (While not indispensable, "evidence of market power is relevant.") Other panels, however, continue to apply Lessig apparently in its robust form. See Northrop Corp. v. McDonnell Douglas Corp., 705 F.2d 1030 (9th Cir.1983) (breach of contract by a dominant firm as an attempt to monopolize).

Even in circuits other than the Ninth, the plaintiff's burden in proving the relevant market in attempt cases may be lighter than its burden in a typical monopolization case because in attempt cases the conduct will often be unambiguously harmful to competition. See United States v. E. I. du Pont de Nemours & Co., 351 U.S. 377 (1956), n. 23.

The discussion thus far has supposed that attempt cases and monopolization cases are quite distinct categories, although with overlapping elements of proof. They are distinct, perhaps, in the sense that if single firm conduct is blatantly anticompetitive, its victim may charge an attempt to monopolize with at least some hope of success, even though the defendant's market share is clearly too low to yield any hope that monopolization might be found. On the other hand, a plaintiff in a position to make plausible allegations of monopolization usually includes a count alleging attempt. Do you see why?

E. MORE ON THE CONDUCT OF THE DOMINANT FIRM (OR THE FIRM THAT THREATENS DOMINATION)

1. THE DUTY TO DEAL

During the period of the structural consensus courts envisaged "anticompetitive conduct" largely in terms of strategies increasing the firm's dominance. Thus, in *Alcoa* and *United Shoe* conduct did not need to be excessively egregious to fall afoul of the law on monopolization. During the third quarter of the twentieth century there were cases in which conduct was likewise thought to be anticompetitive because it was abusive. Here, we examine two such cases where the dominant firm refused to deal. As you read *Lorain Journal* ask yourself these questions: Why did the defendant do what it did? Would a competitor trying to please customers ever engage in such conduct? When conduct is as blatant as this, should it matter to the Section 2 outcome whether the defendant *really* has power? Mightn't a court look at power and conduct interactively, so that when power is great enough only slightly anticompetitive conduct might constitute a violation, while if conduct is bad enough, even slight power will be enough?

LORAIN JOURNAL CO. v. UNITED STATES
342 U.S. 143 (1951).

JUSTICE BURTON: The principal question here is whether a newspaper publisher's conduct constituted an attempt to monopolize interstate commerce, justifying the injunction issued against it under §§ 2 and 4 of the Sherman Antitrust Act. For the reasons hereafter stated, we hold that the injunction was justified.

* * *

The appellant corporation, here called the publisher, has published the Journal in the City of Lorain since before 1932. In that year it, with others, purchased the Times–Herald which was the only competing daily paper published in that city. Later, without success, it sought a license to establish and operate a radio broadcasting station in Lorain.

The court below describes the position of the Journal, since 1933, as "a commanding and an overpowering one. It has a daily circulation in

Lorain of over 13,000 copies and it reaches ninety-nine per cent of the families in the city." 92 F.Supp. at 796. Lorain is an industrial city on Lake Erie with a population of about 52,000 occupying 11,325 dwelling units. The Sunday News, appearing only on Sundays, is the only other newspaper published there.

* * *

From 1933 to 1948 the publisher enjoyed a substantial monopoly in Lorain of the mass dissemination of news and advertising, both of a local and national character. However, in 1948 the Elyria–Lorain Broadcasting Company, a corporation independent of the publisher, was licensed by the Federal Communications Commission to establish and operate in Elyria, Ohio, eight miles south of Lorain, a radio station whose call letters, WEOL stand for Elyria, Oberlin and Lorain. Since then it has operated its principal studio in Elyria and a branch studio in Lorain. Lorain has about twice the population of Elyria and is by far the largest community in the station's immediate area. Oberlin is much smaller than Elyria and eight miles south of it.

* * *

The court below found that appellants knew that a substantial number of Journal advertisers wished to use the facilities of the radio station as well. For some of them it found that advertising in the Journal was essential for the promotion of their sales in Lorain County. It found that at all times since WEOL commenced broadcasting, appellants had executed a plan conceived to eliminate the threat of competition from the station. Under this plan the publisher refused to accept local advertisements in the Journal from any Lorain County advertiser who advertised or who appellants believed to be about to advertise over WEOL. The court found expressly that the purpose and intent of this procedure was to destroy the broadcasting company.

The court characterized all this as "bold, relentless, and predatory commercial behavior." 92 F.Supp. at 796. To carry out appellants' plan, the publisher monitored WEOL programs to determine the identity of the station's local Lorain advertisers. Those using the station's facilities had their contracts with the publisher terminated and were able to renew them only after ceasing to advertise through WEOL. The program was effective. Numerous Lorain County merchants testified that, as a result of the publisher's policy, they either ceased or abandoned their plans to advertise over WEOL.

"Having the plan and desire to injure the radio station, no more effective and more direct device to impede the operations and to restrain the commerce of WEOL could be found by the Journal than to cut off its bloodstream of existence—the advertising revenues which control its life or demise. . . .

". . . [T]he very existence of WEOL is imperiled by this attack upon one of its principal sources of business and income." *Id.*, at 798, 799. . . .

1. *The conduct complained of was an attempt to monopolize interstate commerce.* It consisted of the publisher's practice of refusing to accept local Lorain advertising from parties using WEOL for local adver-

tising. Because of the Journal's complete daily newspaper monopoly of local advertising in Lorain and its practically indispensable coverage of 99% of the Lorain families, this practice forced numerous advertisers to refrain from using WEOL for local advertising. That result not only reduced the number of customers available to WEOL in the field of local Lorain advertising and strengthened the Journal's monopoly in that field, but more significantly tended to destroy and eliminate WEOL altogether. Attainment of that sought-for elimination would automatically restore to the publisher of the Journal its substantial monopoly in Lorain of the mass dissemination of all news and advertising, interstate and national, as well as local. It would deprive not merely Lorain but Elyria and all surrounding communities of their only nearby radio station.

*   *   *

. . . [T]he publisher's conduct was aimed at *   *   * complete destruction and elimination of WEOL. The court found that the publisher, before 1948, enjoyed a substantial monopoly in Lorain of the mass dissemination not only of local news and advertising, but of news of out-of-state events transmitted to Lorain for immediate dissemination, and of advertising of out-of-state products for sale in Lorain. WEOL offered competition by radio in all these fields so that the publisher's attempt to destroy WEOL was in fact an attempt to end the invasion by radio of the Lorain newspaper's monopoly of interstate as well as local commerce.

*   *   *

2. *The publisher's attempt to regain its monopoly of interstate commerce by forcing advertisers to boycott a competing radio station violated § 2.* The findings and opinion of the trial court describe the conduct of the publisher upon which the Government relies. The surrounding circumstances are important. The most illuminating of these is the substantial monopoly which was enjoyed in Lorain by the publisher from 1933 to 1948, together with a 99% coverage of Lorain families. Those factors made the Journal an indispensable medium of advertising for many Lorain concerns. Accordingly, its publisher's refusals to print Lorain advertising for those using WEOL for like advertising often amounted to an effective prohibition of the use of WEOL for that purpose. Numerous Lorain advertisers wished to supplement their local newspaper advertising with local radio advertising but could not afford to discontinue their newspaper advertising in order to use the radio.

WEOL's greatest potential source of income was local Lorain advertising. Loss of that was a major threat to its existence. The court below found unequivocally that appellants' conduct amounted to an attempt by the publisher to destroy WEOL and, at the same time, to regain the publisher's pre–1948 substantial monopoly over the mass dissemination of all news and advertising.

To establish this violation of § 2 as charged, it was not necessary to show that success rewarded appellants' attempt to monopolize. The injunctive relief under § 4 sought to forestall that success. While appellants' attempt to monopolize did succeed insofar as it deprived WEOL of income, WEOL has not yet been eliminated. The injunction may save it.

"[W]hen that intent [to monopolize] and the consequent dangerous probability exist, this statute [the Sherman Act], like many others and like the common law in some cases, directs itself against that dangerous probability as well as against the completed result." *Swift & Co. v. United States,* 196 U.S. 375, 396.

. . . It seems clear that if all the newspapers in a city, in order to monopolize the dissemination of news and advertising by eliminating a competing radio station, conspired to accept no advertisements from anyone who advertised over that station, they would violate §§ 1 and 2 of the Sherman Act. [I]t is consistent with that result to hold here that a single newspaper, already enjoying a substantial monopoly in its area, violates the "attempt to monopolize" clause of § 2 when it uses its monopoly to destroy threatened competition.[8]

The publisher claims a right as a private business concern to select its customers and to refuse to accept advertisements from whomever it pleases. We do not dispute that general right. "But the word 'right' is one of the most deceptive of pitfalls; it is so easy to slip from a qualified meaning in the premise to an unqualified one in the conclusion. Most rights are qualified." *American Bank & Trust Co. v. Federal Bank,* 256 U.S. 350, 358. The right claimed by the publisher is neither absolute nor exempt from regulation. Its exercise as a purposeful means of monopolizing interstate commerce is prohibited by the Sherman Act. The operator of the radio station, equally with the publisher of the newspaper, is entitled to the protection of that Act. "*In the absence of any purpose to create or maintain a monopoly,* the act does not restrict the long recognized right of trader or manufacturer engaged in an entirely private business, freely to exercise his own independent discretion as to parties with whom he will deal." (Emphasis supplied.) *United States v. Colgate & Co.,* 250 U.S. 300, 307. . . .

. . . The judgment accordingly is

Affirmed.

Questions and Comments

There is a strong principle in U.S. law—unlike the law of many European countries—that a firm should be allowed to choose its customers; it should be free to deal or not, at its discretion. Should the Court have respected that principle in *Lorain Journal?*

8. Appellants have sought to justify their conduct on the ground that it was part of the publisher's program for the protection of the Lorain market from outside competition. The publisher claimed to have refused advertising from Elyria or other out-of-town advertisers for the reason that such advertisers might compete with Lorain concerns. The publisher then classified WEOL as the publisher's own competitor from Elyria and asked its Lorain advertisers to refuse to employ WEOL as an advertising medium in competition with the Journal. We find no principle of law which required Lorain advertisers thus to boycott an Elyria advertising medium merely because the publisher of a Lorain advertising medium had chosen to boycott some Elyria advertisers who might compete for business in the Lorain market. Nor do we find any principle of law which permitted this publisher to dictate to prospective advertisers that they might advertise either by newspaper or by radio but that they might not use both facilities.

Was this a simple refusal to deal case? Did Lorain Journal simply want nothing to do with advertisers who would advertise on WEOL or did it want (and expect) something else?

What market was Lorain Journal attempting to monopolize? Does this market make economic sense? Does it make sense not to trouble ourselves too much with market definition and probability of monopolizing the market in a case like *Lorain Journal?* Is there much doubt that defendant's intent was to injure or even destroy a competitor? Is there any doubt that its tactics lacked competitive merit and could be forbidden without any social cost? Of course, although the Court made no effort to check its metes and bounds, there was a plausible market in which Lorain Journal was dominant and would by its conduct probably retain dominance. Suppose there had not been; should the result be the same?

Let us turn now to another case involving refusal to deal.

OTTER TAIL POWER CO. v. UNITED STATES
410 U.S. 366 (1973).

JUSTICE DOUGLAS: In this civil antitrust suit brought by [the United States] against Otter Tail Power Co. (Otter Tail), an electric utility company, the District Court found that Otter Tail had attempted to monopolize and had monopolized the retail distribution of electric power in its service area in violation of § 2 of the Sherman Act. The District Court found that Otter Tail had attempted to prevent communities in which its retail distribution franchise had expired from replacing it with a municipal distribution system. The principal means employed were (1) refusals to sell power at wholesale to proposed municipal systems in the communities where it had been retailing power; (2) refusals to "wheel" power to such systems, that is to say, to transfer by direct transmission or displacement electric power from one utility to another over the facilities of an intermediate utility; (3) the institution and support of litigation designed to prevent or delay establishment of those systems; and (4) the invocation of provisions in its transmission contracts with several other power suppliers for the purpose of denying the municipal systems access to other suppliers by means of Otter Tail's transmission systems.

Otter Tail sells electric power at retail in 465 towns in Minnesota, North Dakota, and South Dakota. The District Court's decree enjoins it from refusing to sell electric power at wholesale to existing or proposed municipal electric power systems in the areas serviced by Otter Tail, from refusing to wheel electric power over the lines from the electric power suppliers to existing or proposed municipal systems in the area, from entering into or enforcing any contract which prohibits use of Otter Tail's lines to wheel electric power to municipal electric power systems, or from entering into or enforcing any contract which limits the customers to whom and areas in which Otter Tail or any other electric power company may sell electric power. . . .

In towns where Otter Tail distributes at retail, it operates under municipally granted franchises which are limited from 10 to 20 years. Each town in Otter Tail's service area generally can accommodate only one distribution system, making each town a natural monopoly market for the distribution and sale of electric power at retail. The aggregate of towns in Otter Tail's service area is the geographic market in which Otter Tail competes for the right to serve the towns at retail. That competition is generally for the right to serve the entire retail market within the composite limits of a town, and that competition is generally between Otter Tail and a prospective or existing municipal system. These towns number 510 and of those Otter Tail serves 91% or 465.

Otter Tail's policy is to acquire, when it can, existing municipal systems within its service areas. It has acquired six since 1947. Between 1945 and 1970, there were contests in 12 towns served by Otter Tail over proposals to replace it with municipal systems. In only three—Elbow Lake, Minnesota, Colman, South Dakota, and Aurora, South Dakota— were municipal systems actually established. Proposed municipal systems have great obstacles; they must purchase the electric power at wholesale. To do so they must have access to existing transmission lines. The only ones available belong to Otter Tail. While the Bureau of Reclamation has high-voltage bulk-power supply lines in the area, it does not operate a subtransmission network, but relies on wheeling contracts with Otter Tail and other utilities to deliver power for its bulk supply lines to its wholesale customers.

The antitrust charge against Otter Tail does not involve the lawfulness of its retail outlets, but only its methods of preventing the towns it served from establishing their own municipal systems when Otter Tail's franchises expired. The critical events centered largely in four towns— Elbow Lake, Minnesota, Hankinson, North Dakota, Colman, South Dakota, and Aurora, South Dakota. When Otter Tail's franchise in each of these towns terminated, the citizens voted to establish a municipal distribution system. Otter Tail refused to sell the new systems energy at wholesale and refused to agree to wheel power from other suppliers of wholesale energy.

Colman and Aurora had access to other transmission. Against them, Otter Tail used the weapon of litigation.

As respects Elbow Lake and Hankinson, Otter Tail simply refused to deal, although according to the findings it had the ability to do so. Elbow Lake, cut off from all sources of wholesale power, constructed its own generating plant. Both Elbow Lake and Hankinson requested the Bureau of Reclamation and various cooperatives to furnish them with wholesale power; they were willing to supply it if Otter Tail would wheel it. But Otter Tail refused, relying on provisions in its contracts which barred the use of its lines for wheeling power to towns which it had served at retail. Elbow Lake after completing its plant asked the Federal Power Commission, under § 202(b) of the Federal Power Act, to require Otter Tail to interconnect with the town and sell it power at wholesale. The Federal Power Commission ordered first a temporary and then a permanent connection. Hankinson tried unsuccessfully to get relief from the North Dakota Commission and then filed a complaint with the federal commission seeking an order to compel Otter Tail to wheel. While the application was pending, the town council voted to withdraw it and subsequently renewed Otter Tail's franchise.

It was found that Otter Tail instituted or sponsored litigation involving four towns in its service area which had the effect of halting or delaying efforts to establish municipal systems. Municipal power systems are financed by the sale of electric revenue bonds. Before such bonds can be sold, the town's attorney must submit an opinion which includes a statement that there is no pending or threatened litigation which might impair the value or legality of the bonds. The record amply bears out the District Court's holding that Otter Tail's use of litigation halted or appreciably slowed the efforts for municipal ownership. "The delay thus occasioned and the large financial burden imposed on the towns' limited treasury dampened local enthusiasm for public ownership." *

I

Otter Tail contends that by reason of the Federal Power Act it is not subject to antitrust regulation with respect to its refusal to deal. We disagree with that position.

"Repeals of the antitrust laws by implication from a regulatory statute are strongly disfavored, and have only been found in cases of plain repugnancy between the antitrust and regulatory provisions." *United States v. Philadelphia National Bank,* 374 U.S. 321, 350–351. Activities which come under the jurisdiction of a regulatory agency nevertheless may be subject to scrutiny under the antitrust laws.

* * *

III

The record makes abundantly clear that Otter Tail used its monopoly power in the towns in its service area to foreclose competition or gain a competitive advantage, or to destroy a competitor, all in violation of the antitrust laws. The District Court determined that Otter Tail has "a strategic dominance in the transmission of power in most of its service area" and that it used this dominance to foreclose potential entrants into the retail area from obtaining electric power from outside sources of supply. Use of monopoly power "to destroy threatened competition" is a violation of the "attempt to monopolize" clause of § 2 of the Sherman Act. *Lorain Journal v. United States,* 342 U.S. 143, 154. . . .

When a community serviced by Otter Tail decides not to renew Otter Tail's retail franchise when it expires, it may generate, transmit, and distribute its own electric power. We recently described the difficulties and problems of those isolated electric power systems. . . . There were no engineering factors that prevented Otter Tail from selling power at wholesale to those towns that wanted municipal plants or wheeling the power. The District Court found—and its findings are supported—that Otter Tail's refusals to sell at wholesale or to wheel were solely to prevent municipal power systems from eroding its monopolistic position.

* * *

---

* [Ed. Note: The Court vacated and remanded the district court's holding with respect to Otter Tail's litigation in light of *California Motor Transport Co. v. Trucking Unlimited,* 404 U.S. 508 (1972).]

V

Ruinous Comp. Otter Tail argues that, without the weapons which it used, more and more municipalities will turn to public power and Otter Tail will go downhill. The argument is a familiar one.

*   *   *

We do not suggest, however, that the District Court, concluding that Otter Tail violated the antitrust laws, should be impervious to Otter Tail's assertion that compulsory interconnection or wheeling will erode its integrated system and threaten its capacity to serve adequately the public. As the dissent properly notes, the Commission may not order interconnection if to do so "would impair [the utility's] ability to render adequate service to its customers." 16 U.S.C. § 824a(b). The District Court in this case found that the "pessimistic view" advanced in Otter Tail's "erosion study" "is not supported by the record." . . . Since the District Court has made future connections subject to Commission approval and in any event has retained jurisdiction to enable the parties to apply for "necessary or appropriate" relief and presumably will give effect to the policies embodied in the Federal Power Act, we cannot say under these circumstances that it has abused its discretion. . . .

Except for the provision of the order relating to Otter Tail's litigation activities [which we vacated and remanded], the judgment is

Affirmed.

Justice Stewart, with whom Chief Justice Burger and Justice Rehnquist joined, concurring in part and dissenting in part: . . . As the District Court found, Otter Tail is a vertically integrated power company. But the bulk of its business—some 90% of its income—derives from sales of power at retail. Left to its own judgment in dealing with its customers, it seems entirely predictable that Otter Tail would decline wholesale dealing with towns in which it had previously done business at retail. If the purpose of the congressional scheme is to leave such decisions to the power companies in the absence of a contrary requirement imposed by the Commission, it would appear that Otter Tail's course of conduct in refusing to deal with the municipal system at Elbow Lake and in refusing to promise to deal with the proposed system at Hankinson, was foreseeably within the zone of freedom specifically created by the statutory scheme. As a retailer of power, Otter Tail asserted a legitimate business interest in keeping its lines free for its own power sales and in refusing to lend a hand in its own demise by wheeling cheaper power from the Bureau of Reclamation to municipal consumers which might otherwise purchase power at retail from Otter Tail itself.

The opinion of the Court emphasizes that Otter Tail's actions were not simple refusals to deal—they resulted in Otter Tail's maintenance of monopoly control by hindering the emergence of municipal power companies. The Court cites *Lorain Journal v. United States,* 342 U.S. 143, for the proposition that "[u]se of monopoly power 'to destroy threatened competition' is a violation of the 'attempt to monopolize' clause of § 2 of the Sherman Act." . . . Here, by contrast [to competitive markets blocked by refusals to deal], a monopoly is sure to result either way. If the consumers of Elbow Lake receive their electric power from a municipally owned company or from Otter Tail, there will be a monopoly at the retail level, for there will in any event be only one supplier. The very reason for the regulation of private utility rates—by state bodies and by the Commission—is the inevitability of a monopoly that requires price control to take the place of price competition. Antitrust principles applicable to other industries cannot be blindly applied to a unilateral refusal to deal on the part of a power company, operating in a regime of rate regulation and licensed monopolies. . . .

Questions and Comments

Considered as a refusal-to-deal case, does *Otter Tail* follow from *Lorain Journal?* Did Otter Tail refuse to deal with municipalities for essentially the same reason that Lorain Journal refused to deal with "disloyal" advertisers? Which company had the stronger claim based on a right to choose its customers and to deal with whomever it wished? Which refusal to deal was more likely to raise price to consumers? To exclude a competitor from a market? In thinking about Otter Tail's conduct, consider separately its refusal to wheel the Bureau of Reclamation's power to the municipalities, and its refusal to sell its own power at wholesale to the municipalities. Which has greater consequences for competition?

Presumably, Otter Tail built its vertically integrated system by skill, foresight and industry. Should it have been free to use the advantages of its integration? To decide whether to be a wholesaler or retailer? Is it relevant that Otter Tail needed a government franchise to build its transmission lines? Notice that *either* Otter Tail *or* the municipality will serve any given local community, not both. Is it obvious which way the consumers will get a better deal? Is this case about output limitation and efficiency, or something else?

Suppose that Otter Tail had simply declined to sell at wholesale because it wished to continue to sell at retail, that the Bureau of Reclamation was not involved, and that Otter Tail had brought no disruptive litigation. Would the principle of the case still apply? Would the outcome be the same? Should it be?

Otter Tail is sometimes described as an "essential facility" case. The essential facility doctrine initially arose not under Section 2, but Section 1. In original form, the essence of the doctrine (which we will examine more fully in Chapter 3) was this: If a group of competitors act concertedly to create a facility that gives them a significant competitive advantage over excluded competitors, those competitors must afford access to the excluded competitors on reasonable terms. United States v. Terminal Railroad Association, 224 U.S. 383 (1912); Associated Press v. United States, 326 U.S. 1 (1945); Silver v. New York Stock Exchange, 373 U.S. 341 (1963).

Viewed against that background, can *Otter Tail* be taken to mean that whenever a monopolist invests in a facility that gives it a significant competitive advantage over competitors, they must be afforded access? Are there reasons why a monopolist ought not to be compelled to share its "better mouse trap" with competitors, even though a group of competitors who act jointly might not lawfully be able to exclude others? If monopolists, in general, ought not to have to share their inventions and facilities, is there anything in the *Otter Tail* facts to take the case out of the general rule? Is Otter Tail's public franchise a reasonable surrogate for the collective action that seemed critical to the original "essential facility" cases?

———

Before computerized airline reservation systems were devised, the "Official Airline Guide" was "the bible" of airline flight schedules and the standard reference for airline ticket offices, travel agents, businesses and business travelers. Reuben H. Donnelley Corp., itself not an air carrier, was the monopolist publisher. Donnelley carried a listing of connecting flights in the Guide, but refused to list the flight services of commuter airlines in this section. Rather, it listed the commuter flights separately, without giving information on connections. As a result, users of the Guide were steered to the major carriers for connecting flights. Because the relevant information about commuter airlines was not accessible, the commuter carriers were placed at a competitive disadvantage, and competition was injured. When asked to explain, Donnelley said that the commuter flights were less reliable and therefore travelers would be ill-served and dissatisfied if listings were integrated. The Commission found that the refusal was arbitrary and that a violation occurred.

OFFICIAL AIRLINE GUIDES, INC. v. FTC

630 F.2d 920 (2d Cir.1980).

JUDGE OAKES: * * *

Legal Duty of a Monopolist *vis-a-vis* its Customers

We turn then to the crucial issue in the case, whether Donnelley as a monopolist had some duty under section 5 of the FTC Act not to discriminate unjustifiably between the competing classes of carriers so as to place one class at a significant competitive disadvantage. In other words, does the FTC Act authorize the Commission to find unlawful the type of challenged activity engaged in by petitioner? . . .

The Commission's brief . . . refers us to two lines of cases with which it claims its decision is consistent. The first line recognizes limitations that may be placed upon a monopolist's rights to affect competition. Thus, in *Lorain Journal Co. v. United States*, 342 U.S. 143, . . . (1951), the Court held that a monopolist newspaper violated section 2 of the Sherman Act by refusing to sell advertising space to merchants who also purchased air advertising time from a local radio station. Though recognizing the general right of a private business to select its customers, the Court held that the exercise of this right for the purpose of monopolization violates the Sherman Act. . . . But *Lorain Journal*, unlike the present case, involved a monopolist seeking to preserve its *own* monopoly. The Commission similarly argues that its position is supported by *Otter Tail Power Co. v. United States*, 410 U.S. 366 . . . (1973), where the Court held that a monopolist may not abuse its monopoly power in one market to gain an improper advantage or to destroy threatened competition in an adjacent market in which it also operates. . . . But as the Commission itself pointed out, the instant case "differs from ordinary monopolization cases where challenged acts or practices were engaged in to benefit the monopolist competitively, either in the market in which the monopoly power existed or in some adjacent market into which the monopolist had extended its operations." Donnelley, though possibly a monopolist in the airline schedule publishing industry, admittedly had no anticompetitive motive or intent with respect to the airline industry and is engaged in a different line of commerce from that of the air carriers.

The second line of cases relied upon in the Commission's brief recognizes the duty that the joint owners of a scarce resource have to make the resource available to all potential users on nondiscriminatory terms.

* * *

Each of these cases, however, involved joint refusals to deal resulting in injury to the *defendants'* competitors, while the instant case involves only unilateral behavior by Donnelley which allegedly has affected competition among air carriers, a business in which Donnelley is not engaged.

* * *

. . . We note that the FTC with some justification states that the arbitrary refusal of a monopolist to deal leaves the disadvantaged competitor, even though in another field, with no recourse to overcome the disadvantage, and the Commission wants us to take the "small step" in terms of "the fundamental goals of antitrust."

But we think enforcement of the FTC's order here would give the FTC too much power to substitute its own business judgment for that of the monopolist in any decision that arguably affects competition in another industry. Such a decision would permit the FTC to delve into, as the Commission itself put the extreme case, "social, political, or personal reasons" for a monopolist's refusal to deal. Professors Areeda and Turner give examples of a monopolist theater which refuses to admit men with long hair or a monopolist newspaper which refuses to publish advertising from cigarette manufacturers. The Commission says that neither of these examples would trigger antitrust scrutiny because there is no competition among persons who attend movies, and refusing to publish advertisements for all cigarette companies would not place any of them at a disadvantage *vis-a-vis* a competitor. Nevertheless, the Commission's own example of its opinion of a monopolist newspaper refusing to take advertisements from a particular cigarette company because of the style of prior advertisements or the political views of its president shows just how far the Commission's opinion could lead us. What we are doing, as the Commission itself recognized, is weighing benefits to competition in the other field against the detrimental effect of allowing the Commission to pass judgment on many business decisions of the monopolist that arguably discriminate among customers in some way. Thus, if the only supermarket in town decides to stock Birdseye vegetables but not Green Giant vegetables, the FTC would be able to require it to stock Green Giant vegetables if it were to find Green Giant competitively disadvantaged.

. . . We think that even a monopolist, as long as he has no purpose to restrain competition or to enhance or expand his monopoly, and does not act coercively, retains this right. . . .

Questions and Comments

In what sense did Donnelly's refusal to deal on nondiscriminatory terms harm competition? Was there an output limitation? Unfairness? Would a duty to deal intrude unreasonably into the business judgment of the monopolist? Would undue judicial supervision be needed to assure non-discrimination?

Why do you think Donnelley discriminated against the commuter airlines? Do you believe its justification? If you were Donnelley and were concerned only about reliability of the commuter carriers, how would you have handled that problem? The Commission's counsel had first tried to prove that Donnelley was helping to carry out a conspiracy of the certificated carriers, but found insufficient evidence. Is there any basis for an inference that Donnelley's motivation was not to please users but to please the certificated carriers?

Questions about duty to deal continue to demand the attention of antitrust courts. Indeed, the Supreme Court's most recent monopolization case—*Aspen Skiing*—involves such a question. But before we consider that case, we continue with cases that illuminate the evolution of the law concerning dominant firm conduct, and the judicial response to the claim that antitrust handicaps competition.

2. NEW TECHNOLOGIES AND WORLD COMPETITION: THE 1970s AND 1980s

For about three decades following World War II, the American economy was strong and growing and American industry was generally regarded as number one in the world. Public concern often focused on providing better opportunity and access for individuals, especially the powerless. This "liberal" attitude affected not only civil rights law but competition law too. Also during this period, the traditional business ethic that competitors do not sue competitors broke down. Big companies sued even bigger dominant firms, alleging that the latter engaged in strategies that blocked their opportunities and in some cases threatened their demise. Berkey's suit against Kodak is an example, as are the several suits against IBM and AT & T. Also, the government brought two major monopolization cases. During the Johnson Administration the Justice Department sued IBM (the government case followed claims first asserted in a private suit by Control Data Corporation), and during the Ford Administration the government sued AT & T.

The modern monopolization suits could be distinguished from most monopolization cases that preceded them. None involved a homogenous product, as had *Alcoa,* nor were any in industries where only one firm was at all significant, as both United Shoe and Alcoa had been. Also, most of the modern cases involved technologically complex industries that were going through rapid technological and sometimes rapid structural change. Moreover, during the 1970s, while most of these private and governmental Section 2 cases were in the pretrial discovery process, economic and political conditions were changing. Foreign firms, particularly in Japan and West Germany, became strong challengers and began to make enormous inroads into U.S. markets. American firms that once had market power, such as U.S. Steel, found themselves with outmoded equipment and techniques, high costs and poor and eroding prospects. In policy making and even in judicial thinking, the pendulum began to swing from a bias towards protecting individual opportunity and access for nonestablished firms to a bias towards less government intervention and freedom for American firms to react to market changes in their own ways. The deregulation movement in airlines, trucking, telecommunications and other industries also developed during this period, bringing firms previously sheltered by regulation more directly under the constraint of markets and competition.

The argument was and is sometimes made that the antitrust laws harm American competition in international markets and therefore that the laws should be changed or not enforced. It is said, for example, that American firms suffer antitrust constraints that keep them from being efficient while Asian firms do not. It is sometimes argued that this is why Asian firms can outcompete American ones.

Others see the matter differently. They argue that when American firms prove ineffective against foreign competitors it is often because the American firms faced little competition until they encountered foreign competition. Occupying monopolistic or tightly oligopolistic markets, they did not have to be competitive. The status quo was good enough; they could live the quiet life. They could operate, for example, as the American auto industry seems to have done for several decades, settling labor demands by generous increases, buying inputs (such as steel) by splitting orders among the oligopolistic suppliers at going rates, and differentiating their products with frills and big advertising budgets. This argument asserts that if American firms had faced really aggressive antitrust enforcement that kept their markets competitive, the efficiencies Asian competition forced on American managements might have been achieved much earlier. Is this argument convincing? [7]

Might either of the above two positions about antitrust and foreign competition be validated empirically? What would it signify, for example, if there should be a positive correlation between industry concentration and hourly wage rates for manufacturing employees? See, e.g., Salinger, Tobin's q, Unionization, and the Concentration–Profits Relationship, 15 Rand J. of Econ. 159 (1984). What would you infer from a high correlation between concentration and excess capacity? See R. Hall, Chronic Excess Capacity in U.S. Industry (National Bureau of Economic Research, Working Paper No. 1973, 1986).

In the 1970s and early 1980s, a number of the "new wave" monopoly cases reached the courts. At the start of this period the *Alcoa* decision was still cited with respect and authority. Defendants, however, argued that aggressive application of the rule of *Alcoa* handicapped leading firms, required them to pull their punches, and slowed America down in the race for the top in world competition. Let us examine the impact of that argument on the developing case law.

7. Since the Asian challenge, GM, Ford, and Chrysler have: (1) controlled their labor costs better, (2) reduced their steel and other input costs by (a) design changes, (b) shopping more aggressively, and (c) scheduling input shipments to arrive when needed rather than warehousing them; and (3) sought to differentiate their product by striving for fuel efficiency, good quality control, and low price (rather than with bigger power plants, tail fins, and chrome displays). Is it likely that they would have done any of these things earlier if not "constrained" by the antitrust laws? Is it more likely that American firms would have become aggressive competitors earlier if antitrust had been applied more vigorously even before the foreign firms entered?

The first case we consider was decided by the court that, years earlier, had decided *Alcoa*.

BERKEY PHOTO, INC. v. EASTMAN KODAK CO.

603 F.2d 263 (2d Cir.1979).
cert. denied, 444 U.S. 1093 (1980).

JUDGE KAUFMAN: . . . To millions of Americans, the name Kodak is virtually synonymous with photography. Founded over a century ago by George Eastman, the Eastman Kodak Company has long been the preeminent firm in the amateur photographic industry. It provides products and services covering every step in the creation of an enduring photographic record from an evanescent image. Snapshots may be taken with a Kodak camera on Kodak film, developed by Kodak's Color Print and Processing Laboratories, and printed on Kodak photographic paper. The firm has rivals at each stage of this process, but in many of them it stands, and has long stood, dominant. It is one of the giants of American enterprise, with international sales of nearly $6 billion in 1977 and pre-tax profits in excess of $1.2 billion.

This action, one of the largest and most significant private antitrust suits in history, was brought by Berkey Photo, Inc., a far smaller but still prominent participant in the industry. Berkey competes with Kodak in providing photofinishing services—the conversion of exposed film into finished prints, slides, or movies. Until 1978, Berkey sold cameras as well. It does not manufacture film, but it does purchase Kodak film for resale to its customers, and it also buys photofinishing equipment and supplies, including color print paper, from Kodak.

The two firms thus stand in a complex, multifaceted relationship, for Kodak has been Berkey's competitor in some markets and its supplier in others. In this action, Berkey claims that every aspect of the association has been infected by Kodak's monopoly power in the film, color print paper, and camera markets, willfully acquired, maintained, and exercised in violation of § 2 of the Sherman Act. It also charges that Kodak conspired with flashlamp manufacturers in violation of § 1 of the Act. Berkey alleges that these violations caused it to lose sales in the camera and photofinishing markets and to pay excessive prices to Kodak for film, color print paper, and photofinishing equipment. A number of the charges arise from Kodak's 1972 introduction of the 110 photographic system, featuring a "Pocket Instamatic" camera and a new color print film, Kodacolor II, but the case is not limited to that episode. It embraces many of Kodak's activities for the last decade and, indeed, from preceding years as well.

After more than four years of pretrial maneuvering, the trial got under way in July 1977 before Judge Marvin E. Frankel of the Southern District of New York. Despite the daunting complexity of the case—the exhibits numbered in the thousands—Kodak demanded a jury. Accordingly, the trial was conducted in two parts, one to determine liability and the other to measure damages. It ran continuously, except for a one-month hiatus between the two segments, until the final verdict was rendered on March 22, 1978. The liability phase of the trial by itself consumed more than six months, and the damages aspect required approximately another month.   Except for a few specific questions relating primarily to market definitions, the jury was asked to render what was essentially a general verdict on each count.

After deliberating for eight days on liability and five on damages, the jury found for Berkey on virtually every point, awarding damages totalling $37,620,130.   Judge Frankel upheld verdicts aggregating $27,154,700 for lost camera and photofinishing sales and for excessive prices on film and photofinishing equipment, but he entered judgment n.o.v. for Kodak on the remainder.   Trebled and supplemented by attorneys' fees and costs pursuant to § 4 of the Clayton Act, Berkey's judgment reached a grand total of $87,091,309.47, with interest, of course, continuing to accrue.

Kodak now appeals this judgment. . . .

Resolution of the . . . competing claims requires us to settle a number of important and novel issues concerning § 2 of the Sherman Act. We believe that the district court committed several significant errors as it charted its course through the complexities of this case, and we are therefore compelled to reverse the judgment below in certain major respects.   But we cannot accept Kodak's contention that a properly charged jury could not find monopolization of any of the relevant markets and resulting damage to Berkey.   Accordingly, we remand for a new trial on several of the claims.

I.   THE AMATEUR PHOTOGRAPHIC INDUSTRY

* * *

A.   The Camera Market

The "amateur conventional still camera" market now consists almost entirely of the so-called 110 and 126 instant-loading cameras.   These are the direct descendants of the popular "box" cameras, the best-known of which was Kodak's so-called "Brownie."   Small, simple, and relatively inexpensive, cameras of this type are designed for the mass market rather than for the serious photographer.

Kodak has long been the dominant firm in the market thus defined. Between 1954 and 1973 it never enjoyed less than 61% of the annual unit sales, nor less than 64% of the dollar volume, and in the peak year of 1964, Kodak cameras accounted for 90% of market revenues.   Much of this success is no doubt due to the firm's history of innovation.   In 1963 Kodak first marketed the 126 "Instamatic" instant-loading camera, and in 1972 it came out with the much smaller 110 "Pocket Instamatic."   Not only are these cameras small and light, but they employ film packaged in cartridges that can simply be dropped in the back of the camera, thus obviating the need to load and position a roll manually.   Their introduction triggered successive revolutions in the industry.   Annual amateur still camera sales in the United States averaged 3.9 million units between 1954 and 1963, with little annual variation.   In the first full year after Kodak's introduction of the 126, industry sales leaped 22%, and they took an even larger quantum jump when the 110 came to market.   Other camera manufacturers, including Berkey, copied both these inventions but for several months after each introduction anyone desiring to purchase a camera in the new format was perforce remitted to Kodak.

Berkey has been a camera manufacturer since its 1966 acquisition of the Keystone Camera Company, a producer of movie cameras and equipment. In 1968 Berkey began to sell amateur still cameras made by other firms, and the following year the Keystone Division commenced manufacturing such cameras itself. From 1970 to 1977, Berkey accounted for 8.2% of the sales in the camera market in the United States, reaching a peak of 10.2% in 1976. In 1978, Berkey sold its camera division and thus abandoned this market.

B.   The Film Market

The relevant market for photographic film comprises color print, color slide, color movie, and black-and-white film. Kodak's grip on this market is even stronger than its hold on cameras. Since 1952, its annual sales have always exceeded 82% of the nationwide volume on a unit basis, and 88% in revenues. Foreign competition has recently made some inroads into Kodak's monopoly, but the Rochester firm concedes that it dominated film sales throughout the period relevant to this case. Indeed, in his summation, Kodak's trial counsel told the jury that "the film market . . . has been a market where there has not been price competition and where Kodak has been able to price its products pretty much without regard to the products of competitors."

Kodak's monopoly in the film market is particularly important to this case, because the jury accepted Berkey's contention, noted above, that it had been used to disadvantage rivals in cameras, photofinishing, photofinishing equipment, and other markets. Of special relevance to this finding is the color print film segment of the industry, which Kodak has dominated since it introduced "Kodacolor," the first amateur color print film, in 1942. In 1963, when Kodak announced the 126 Instamatic camera, it also brought out a new, faster color print film—Kodacolor X—which was initially available to amateur photographers only in the 126 format. Nine years later, Kodak repeated this pattern with the simultaneous introduction of the 110 Pocket Instamatic and Kodacolor II film. For more than a year, Kodacolor II was made only for 110 cameras, and Kodak has never made any other color print film in the 110 size.

C.   Photofinishing Services and Photofinishing Equipment

Before 1954, Kodak's Color Print and Processing Laboratories (CP & P) had a nearly absolute monopoly of color photofinishing maintained by a variety of practices. Accounting for over 95% of color film sales, Kodak sold every roll with an advance charge for processing included. Consumers had little choice but to purchase Kodak film, and in so doing they acquired the right to have that film developed and printed by CP & P at no further charge. Since few customers would duplicate their costs to procure the services of a non-Kodak photofinisher, Kodak was able to parlay its film monopoly to achieve equivalent market power in photofinishing.[9]

9. To be sure, Kodak could not in this fashion control the market for color re- prints—production of additional prints from slides or negatives. Here it resorted to other

This film/processing "tie-in" attracted the attention of the Justice Department, and in 1954 a consent decree changed the structure of the color photofinishing market drastically. Kodak was forbidden to link photofinishing to film sales, and it agreed to make its processing technology, chemicals, and paper available to rivals at reasonable rates. As a result, CP & P's share of the market plummeted from 96% in 1954 to 69% two years later, and it has declined sharply ever since. In 1970, CP & P accounted for but 17% of the market, and by 1976 its share reached a low of 10%. There are now approximately 600 independent photofinishers in the United States.

Berkey is one of the largest of these processors. . . .

A variety of equipment is used to process film, and the Kodak Apparatus Division (KAD) designs and produces most of the machinery used by CP & P. Kodak also sells some equipment to other photofinishers, but this is an insignificant portion of its business; indeed, until the introduction of the 110 system, Kodak made still film processing equipment for its own use only. Several other firms supply photofinishing equipment to the rival processors, and Berkey does not contend that Kodak monopolized or attempted to monopolize this market.

D.   The Color Paper Market

The market for color paper—that is, paper specially treated so that images from color film may be printed on it—effectively came into being after entry of the 1954 consent decree. Before then, Kodak was for all practical purposes the only color photofinisher, and its requirements for color paper were met entirely by the paper division of Kodak Park Works in Rochester. The remaining processors, who dealt with non-Kodak color film and used non-Kodak paper, occupied only four percent of the color photofinishing market. Consequently, the vertical foreclosure created by CP & P's lock on photofinishing and its exclusive use of Kodak color paper was virtually complete.

Although the 1954 decree steadily loosened Kodak's grip in photofinishing, it did not immediately affect the firm's control of color paper. For more than a decade, the independent photofinishers that sprang up after the decree was entered looked only to Kodak for their paper supplies. Indeed, although entry by both foreign and domestic paper manufacturers has reduced Kodak's share substantially, to a low of 60% in 1976, the firm's color paper operations have remained remarkably profitable. Between 1968 and 1975, while its market share was falling from 94% to 67%, Kodak's earnings from operations as a percentage of sales remained virtually constant, averaging 60% for the period. Moreover, the most recent telling event in the market has not been entry but exit: GAF Corporation announced in 1977 that it was abandoning its effort to sell color paper, leaving Kodak with only one domestic and two foreign competitors.

tactics. By refusing to sell the special paper or chemicals necessary to produce such reprints to rival photofinishers, it ensured— since there was no other adequate source for these supplies—that even this segment of the market did not escape its grip.

Kodak, then, is indeed a titan in its field, and accordingly has almost inevitably invited attack under § 2 of the Sherman Act. Few, if any, cases have presented so many diverse and difficult problems of § 2 analysis. It is appropriate, therefore, to elucidate some fundamental principles of law relating to that statutory provision.

II.   § 2 OF THE SHERMAN ACT

* * *

A.   Monopoly Power as the Essence of the § 2 Violation

* * *

Because, like all power, it is laden with the possibility of abuse; because it encourages sloth rather than the active quest for excellence; and because it tends to damage the very fabric of our economy and our society, monopoly power is "inherently evil." [United Shoe Machinery.] If a finding of monopoly power were all that were necessary to complete a violation of § 2, our task in this case would be considerably lightened. Kodak's control of the film and color paper markets clearly reached the level of a monopoly. And, while the issue is a much closer one, it appears that the evidence was sufficient for the jury to find that Kodak possessed such power in the camera market as well. But our inquiry into Kodak's liability cannot end there.

B.   The Requirement of Anticompetitive Conduct

Despite the generally recognized evils of monopoly power, it is "well settled" . . . that § 2 does not prohibit monopoly *simpliciter* . . . .

Thus, while proclaiming vigorously that monopoly power is the evil at which § 2 is aimed, courts have declined to take what would have appeared to be the next logical step—declaring monopolies unlawful *per se* unless specifically authorized by law. To understand the reason for this, one must comprehend the fundamental tension—one might almost say the paradox—that is near the heart of § 2. This tension creates much of the confusion surrounding § 2. It makes the cryptic *Alcoa* opinion a litigant's wishing well, into which, it sometimes seems, one may peer and find nearly anything he wishes.

The conundrum was indicated in characteristically striking prose by Judge Hand, who was not able to resolve it. Having stated that Congress "did not condone 'good trusts' and condemn 'bad' ones; it forbad all," *Alcoa*, 148 F.2d at 427, he declared with equal force, "The successful competitor, having been urged to compete, must not be turned upon when he wins," *id.* at 430. Hand, therefore, told us that it would be inherently unfair to condemn success when the Sherman Act itself mandates competition. Such a wooden rule, it was feared, might also deprive the leading firm in an industry of the incentive to exert its best efforts. Further success would yield not rewards but legal castigation. The antitrust laws would thus compel the very sloth they were intended to prevent. We must always be mindful lest the Sherman Act be invoked perversely in favor of those who seek protection against the rigors of competition.

* * *

C. Monopoly Power as a Lever in Other Markets

. . . Kodak, in the period relevant to this suit, was never close to gaining control of the markets for photofinishing equipment or services and could not be held to have attempted to monopolize them. Berkey nevertheless contends that Kodak illicitly gained an advantage in these areas by leveraging its power over film and cameras. Accordingly, we must determine whether a firm violates § 2 by using its monopoly power in one market to gain a competitive advantage in another, albeit without an attempt to monopolize the second market. We hold, as did the lower court, that it does.

This conclusion appears to be an inexorable interpretation of the antitrust laws. We tolerate the existence of monopoly power, we repeat, only insofar as necessary to preserve competitive incentives and to be fair to the firm that has attained its position innocently. There is no reason to allow the exercise of such power to the detriment of competition, in either the controlled market or any other. That the competition in the leveraged market may not be destroyed but merely distorted does not make it more palatable. Social and economic effects of an extension of monopoly power militate against such conduct.

* * *

Accordingly, the use of monopoly power attained in one market to gain a competitive advantage in another is a violation of § 2, even if there has not been an attempt to monopolize the second market. It is the use of economic power that creates the liability. But, as we have indicated, a large firm does not violate § 2 simply by reaping the competitive rewards attributable to its efficient size, nor does an integrated business offend the Sherman Act whenever one of its departments benefits from association with a division possessing a monopoly in its own market. So long as we allow a firm to compete in several fields, we must expect it to seek the competitive advantages of its broad-based activity—more efficient production, greater ability to develop complementary products, reduced transaction costs, and so forth. These are gains that accrue to any integrated firm, regardless of its market share, and they cannot by themselves be considered uses of monopoly power.

* * *

III. THE 110 SYSTEM

* * *

. . . Even before the 126 was introduced, . . . Kodak had set its sights on a new, smaller line of instamatic cameras. The aim of Kodak's Project 30, or P–30, as it was often called, was a camera barely one inch thick but capable of producing photographs as clear and large as its bulkier cousins.

Kodak's desire to produce large, high-quality snapshots from a small camera created successive ripples in a number of ponds. As camera size decreases, so does the area of film exposed when the shutter is opened. Thus the negative must be substantially enlarged to produce a print, and the P–30 group was concerned that the Kodak color print film then in use, Kodacolor X, might not be equal to the task. There was fear that it was too "grainy"—that full-size photographs printed from tiny Kodacolor X negatives would have an unacceptably speckled, pebbly appearance, reflecting the extreme magnification of the small light-sensitive grains constituting the film.

The early view at P–30 had been that despite this problem Kodacolor X would prove "quite adequate" for the new format. By 1966, however, the Kodacolor Future System Committee, considering Kodak's film sales in the 126 size as well as in the format being created by Project 30, began actively to consider the possibility of developing a new type of Kodacolor film. This engendered the second set of ripples, for the committee realized that basic changes in the film would require a new photofinishing process, conducted at temperatures higher than those used in the so-called C–22 method by which prints were made from Kodacolor X. Some committee members, therefore, expressed concern about the effect that a new process might have on independent photofinishers, who developed Kodak film and were purchasers of Kodak equipment and supplies. These concerns were shared by a number of Kodak scientists, such as D.M. Zwick, who feared an "unethical" attempt to create a "deliberate . . . incompatibility with systems other than Kodacolor." [16]

Nevertheless, on May 10, 1967, the committee recommended that Kodak proceed with the development of the new film and finishing process, tentatively labeled P–118. This recommendation was adopted at a meeting of the Kodak management on September 20. Although management believed that many of the film improvements were desirable "without regard to the P–30 program," it decided that Kodak should consider marketing the new film in the P–30 size for approximately one year before introducing it in the 126 format. A firm date was not set at that time for introduction of P–118, but by 1969 Kodak decided that P–118 should be used to help launch the P–30 camera system in March 1972. This decision appears to have been influenced by the views of those Kodak officers who believed that

> [w]ithout a new film, the [camera] program is not a new advertisable system. Without the film, our splicer and processors [for the new high-temperature photofinishing process] are not required.

To meet this self-imposed deadline for P–118, Kodak was required to act in great haste. Indeed, the minutes of a Film Process Subcommittee meeting of August 29, 1969, noted that the decision for a 1972 release date required a "crash program" by all participating divisions. Development schedules were altered and some tests eliminated altogether. Not surprisingly, then, as the target date approached, Kodak realized that its new film was plagued by a number of difficulties.

16. Writing on March 9, 1967, Zwick saw "no need" for a new film, which would require a higher-temperature process: "We can make *small* improvements in Kodacolor X grain and sharpness, in a film which could go through the C–22 process." On the same day, another Kodak scientist, N.H. Groet of the Color Photography Division, wrote that he was "convinced that Project 30 could go with the presently available Kodacolor X film." Like Zwick, Groet conceded that a finer-grained film "would be most welcome for P–30," but he did not believe that major changes in Kodacolor X would be necessary. Indeed, he believed that the new finishing process being considered by the Kodacolor Future System Committee would raise hell in the photofinishing business, would do little to decrease the cost of the operation, and that the ultimate customer would not benefit.

Shortly after initial production runs began in October 1971, Kodak recognized that "several product deficiencies" would exist in the film, now called Kodacolor II, at the time of introduction. Indeed, just eight days before the joint announcement of the new camera, film, and photofinishing process, a technical committee listed eleven "presently identified" problems that could affect "the customer's ultimate quality." Not only did Kodacolor II have a significantly shorter shelf life than had been anticipated, but it also proved grainier than Kodak had originally hoped. This problem was highly significant, of course, because low graininess was supposedly the quality that made Kodacolor II especially suitable for the Pocket Instamatic cameras.

Despite these deficiencies, Kodak proceeded with its plans for introduction of the 110 system, of which Kodacolor II had become an integral part. On March 16, 1972, amid great fanfare, the system was announced. Finally, said Kodak, there was a "little camera that takes big pictures." Kodacolor II was "a remarkable new film"—indeed, the best color negative film Kodak had ever manufactured. There had long been other small cameras, Kodak explained:

> But they weren't like these. Now there are films fine enough, and sharp enough, to give you big, sharp pictures from a very small negative.

In accord with Kodak's 1967 plan, Kodacolor II was sold only in the 110 format for eighteen months after introduction. It remains the only 110-size color print film Kodak has ever sold.

As Kodak had hoped, the 110 system proved to be a dramatic success. In 1972—the system's first year—the company sold 2,984,000 Pocket Instamatics, more than 50% of its sales in the amateur conventional still camera market. The new camera thus accounted in large part for a sharp increase in total market sales, from 6.2 million units in 1971 to 8.2 million in 1972. Rival manufacturers hastened to market their own 110 cameras, but Kodak stood alone until Argus made its first shipment of the "Carefree 110" around Christmas 1972. The next year, although Kodak's competitors sold over 800,000 110 cameras, Kodak retained a firm lead with 5.1 million. Its share of 110 sales did not fall below 50% until 1976. Meanwhile, by 1973 the 110 had taken over most of the amateur market from the 126, and three years later it accounted for nearly four-fifths of all sales.

* * *

Berkey contends that the introduction of the 110 system was both an attempt to monopolize and actual monopolization of the camera market. It also alleges that the marketing of the new camera constituted an impermissible leveraging of Kodak's film monopoly into the two photofinishing markets, services and equipment.

* * *

A. Attempt to Monopolize and Monopolization of the Camera Market

* * *

It will be useful at the outset to present the arguments on which Berkey asks us to uphold its verdict:

(1) Kodak, a film and camera monopolist, was in a position to set industry standards. Rivals could not compete effectively without offering products similar to Kodak's. Moreover, Kodak persistently refused to make film available for most formats other than those in which it made cameras. Since cameras are worthless without film, this policy effectively prevented other manufacturers from introducing cameras in new formats. Because of its dominant position astride two markets, and by use of its film monopoly to distort the camera market, Kodak forfeited its own right to reap profits from such innovations without providing its rivals with sufficient advance information to enable them to enter the market with copies of the new product on the day of Kodak's introduction. This is one of several "predisclosure" arguments Berkey has advanced in the course of this litigation.

(2) The simultaneous introduction of the 110 camera and Kodacolor II film, together with a campaign advertising the two jointly, enabled Kodak to garner more camera sales than if it had merely scaled down Kodacolor X to fit the new camera. The jury could conclude that Kodacolor II was an inferior product and not technologically necessary for the success of the 110. In any event, Kodak's film monopoly prevented any other camera manufacturer from marketing such a film-camera "system" and the joint introduction was therefore anticompetitive.

(3) For eighteen months after its introduction, Kodacolor II was available only in the 110 format. Thus it followed that any consumer wishing to use Kodak's "remarkable new film" had to buy a 110 camera. Since Kodak was the leading—and at first the only—manufacturer of such devices, its camera sales were boosted at the expense of its competitors.

For the reasons explained below, we do not believe any of these contentions is sufficient on the facts of this case to justify an award of damages to Berkey. We therefore reverse this portion of the judgment.

1. Predisclosure

* * *

Judge Frankel did not decide that Kodak should have disclosed the details of the 110 to other camera manufacturers prior to introduction. Instead, he left the matter to the jury, instructing them as follows:

> Standing alone, the fact that Kodak did not give advance warning of its new products to competitors would not entitle you to find that this conduct was exclusionary. Ordinarily a manufacturer has no duty to predisclose its new products in this fashion. It is an ordinary and acceptable business practice to keep one's new developments a secret. However, if you find that Kodak had monopoly power in cameras or in film, and if you find that this power was so great as to make it impossible for a competitor to compete with Kodak in the camera market unless it could offer products similar to Kodak's, you may decide whether in the light of other conduct you determine to be anticompetitive, Kodak's failure to predisclose was on balance an exclusionary course of conduct.

We hold that this instruction was error and that, as a matter of law, Kodak did not have a duty to predisclose information about the 110 system to competing camera manufacturers.

. . . It is the possibility of success in the marketplace, attributable to superior performance, that provides the incentives on which the proper functioning of our competitive economy rests. If a firm that has engaged in the risks and expenses of research and development were required in all circumstances to share with its rivals the benefits of those endeavors, this incentive would very likely be vitiated.

* * *

. . . [E]nforced predisclosure would cause undesirable consequences beyond merely encouraging the sluggishness the Sherman Act was designed to prevent. A significant vice of the theory propounded by Berkey lies in the uncertainty of its application. Berkey does not contend, in the colorful phrase of Judge Frankel, that "Kodak has to live in a goldfish bowl," disclosing every innovation to the world at large. However predictable in its application, such an extreme rule would be insupportable. Rather, Berkey postulates that Kodak had a duty to disclose limited types of information to certain competitors under specific circumstances. But it is difficult to comprehend how a major corporation, accustomed though it is to making business decisions with antitrust considerations in mind, could possess the omniscience to anticipate all the instances in which a jury might one day in the future retrospectively conclude that predisclosure was warranted. And it is equally difficult to discern workable guidelines that a court might set forth to aid the firm's decision. For example, how detailed must the information conveyed be? And how far must research have progressed before it is "ripe" for disclosure? These inherent uncertainties would have an inevitable chilling effect on innovation. They go far, we believe, towards explaining why no court has ever imposed the duty Berkey seeks to create here.

* * *

 . . . [T]he ability to introduce the new format without predisclosure was solely a benefit of integration and not, without more, a use of Kodak's power in the film market to gain a competitive advantage in cameras.

* * *

Our analysis, however, must proceed beyond the conclusion that introduction of film to meet Kodak's new camera format was not in itself an exercise of the company's monopoly power in film. Berkey contends that Kodak in the past used its film monopoly to stifle format innovations by any other camera manufacturer. Accordingly, it argues that Kodak was barred from reaping the benefits of such developments without making predisclosure to allow its rivals to share from the beginning in the rewards.

There is, indeed, little doubt that the jury could have found that Kodak, by refusing to make film available on economical terms, obstructed sales of cameras in competing formats. Thus, Kodak has never supplied film to fit the Minox, a small camera that uses a cartridge similar to that of the Instamatics and that has been on the market since the 1930s, or similar cameras by Minolta and Mamiya that were also introduced before the Kodak 126. Merchants of these cameras, including Berkey, made numerous requests that Kodak sell film packaged in their formats, with or without the Kodak name. As an alternative, they asked Kodak to sell bulk film rolls large enough to permit the camera manufacturers economically to cut the film down to the appropriate size and spool it. Kodak denied all such appeals. Some of the miniature cameras did survive but, as even Kodak's own economic expert testified, its policy drastically reduced the ability of rival manufacturers to compete by introducing new camera formats.

* * *

. . . . It may be that Kodak violated the Sherman Act when it refused to sell Berkey bulk film for use in the Minolta camera, and Berkey might well have recovered for its loss of Minolta sales and for any additional expenses incurred because of Kodak's conduct.

But Berkey did not sue Kodak then for its refusal to sell film, and it concedes that it is not now claiming a right to damages on this basis.

* * *

2. Systems Selling

Berkey's claims regarding the introduction of the 110 camera are not limited to its asserted right to predisclosure. The Pocket Instamatic not only initiated a new camera format, it was also promoted together with a new film. As we noted earlier, the view was expressed at Kodak that "[w]ithout a new film, the [camera] program is not a new advertisable system." Responding in large measure to this perception, Kodak hastened research and development of Kodacolor II so that it could be brought to market at the same time as the 110 system. Based on such evidence, and the earlier joint introduction of Kodacolor X and the 126 camera, the jury could readily have found that the simultaneous release of Kodacolor II and the Pocket Instamatic was part of a plan by which Kodak sought to use its combined film and camera capabilities to bolster faltering camera sales. Berkey contends that this program of selling was anticompetitive and therefore violated § 2. We disagree.

It is important to identify the precise harm Berkey claims to have suffered from this conduct. It cannot complain of a product introduction *simpliciter* for the same reason it could not demand predisclosure of the new format: any firm, even a monopolist, may generally bring its products to market whenever and however it chooses. Rather, Berkey's argument is more subtle. It claims that by marketing the Pocket Instamatics in a system with a widely advertised new film, Kodak gained camera sales at Berkey's expense. And, because Kodacolor II was not necessary to produce satisfactory 110 photographs and in fact suffered from several deficiencies, these gains were unlawful.

It may be conceded that, by advertising Kodacolor II as a "remarkable new film" capable of yielding "big, sharp pictures from a very small negative," Kodak sold more 110 cameras than it would have done had it merely marketed Kodacolor X in 110–size cartridges. The quality of the end product—a developed snapshot—is at least as dependent upon the characteristics of the film as upon those of the camera. It is perfectly plausible that some customers bought the Kodak 110 camera who would have purchased a competitor's camera in another format had Kodacolor II not been available and widely advertised as capable of producing "big, sharp pictures" from the tiny Pocket Instamatic. Moreover, there was also sufficient evidence for the jury to conclude that a new film was not necessary to bring the new cameras to market. . . .

But necessity is a slippery concept. Indeed, the two scientists, Zwick and Groet, conceded that improvements in the quality of Kodacolor X would be "most welcome." Even if the 110 camera would produce adequate snapshots with Kodacolor X, it would be difficult to fault Kodak for attempting to design a film that could provide better results. The attempt to develop superior products is, as we have explained, an essential element of lawful competition. Kodak could not have violated § 2 merely by introducing the 110 camera with an improved film.

Accordingly, much of the evidence at trial concerned the dispute over the relative merits of Kodacolor II and Kodacolor X.

* * *

. . . [N]o one can determine with any reasonable assurance whether one product is "superior" to another. Preference is a matter of individual taste. The only question that can be answered is whether there is sufficient demand for a particular product to make its production worthwhile, and the response, so long as the free choice of consumers is preserved, can only be inferred from the reaction of the market.

When a market is dominated by a monopolist, of course, the ordinary competitive forces of supply may not be fully effective. Even a monopolist, however, must generally be responsive to the demands of customers, for if it persistently markets unappealing goods it will invite a loss of sales and an increase of competition. If a monopolist's products gain acceptance in the market, therefore, it is of no importance that a judge or jury may later regard them as inferior, so long as that success was not based on any form of coercion. Certainly the mere introduction of Kodacolor II along with the Pocket Instamatics did not coerce camera purchasers. Unless consumers desired to use the 110 camera for its own attractive qualities, they were not compelled to purchase Kodacolor II—especially since Kodak did not remove any other films from the market when it introduced the new one. If the availability of Kodacolor II spurred sales of the 110 camera, it did so because some consumers regarded it as superior, at least for the smaller format.[39]

* * *

We conclude, therefore, that Kodak did not contravene the Sherman Act merely by introducing Kodacolor II simultaneously with the Pocket Instamatic and advertising the advantages of the new film for taking pictures with a small camera.

3. Restriction of Kodacolor II to the 110 Format

There is another aspect to Berkey's claim that introduction of Kodacolor II simultaneously with the Pocket Instamatic camera was anticompetitive. For eighteen months after the 110 system introduction,

---

39. Thus, the situation might be completely different if, upon the introduction of the 110 system, Kodak had ceased producing film in the 126 size, thereby compelling camera purchasers to buy a Kodak 110 camera. Or had Kodak shifted production in all formats from Kodacolor X to Kodacolor II be- fore other photofinishers could process the new film, it would force photographers to procure their photofinishing services from CP & P. In such a case the technological desirability of the product change might bear on the question of monopolistic intent.

Kodacolor II was available only in the 110 format. Since Kodak was the first to have the 110s on the market, Berkey asserts it lost camera sales because consumers who wished to use the "remarkable new film" would be compelled to buy a Kodak camera. This facet of the claim, of course, is not dependent on a showing that Kodacolor II was inferior in any respect to Kodacolor X. Quite the opposite is true. The argument is that, since consumers were led to believe that Kodacolor II was superior to Kodacolor X, they were more likely to buy a Kodak 110, rather than a Berkey camera, so that the new film could be used.

* * *

. . . [T]o prevail, Berkey must . . . demonstrate that some consumers who would have bought a Berkey camera were dissuaded from doing so because Kodacolor II was available only in the 110 format. This it has failed to establish. The record is totally devoid of evidence that Kodak or its retailers actually attempted to persuade customers to purchase the Pocket Instamatic because it was the only camera that could use Kodacolor II, or that, in fact, any consumers did choose the 110 in order to utilize the finer-grained film.

* * *

. . . We conclude, therefore, that the jury could not find Berkey suffered more than *de minimis* injury, if any, because Kodacolor II was limited to the 110 format.

* * *

We, therefore, reverse so much of the judgment as awarded Berkey damages based on the introduction of the 110 camera.

B. *Photofinishing and Photofinishing Equipment Markets*

* * *

1. *Damages*

Berkey's damages claims here are based on the fact that Kodacolor II, introduced along with the 110 camera, required the new, high-temperature C–41 finishing process instead of the C–22 process used for Kodacolor X and similar films. Thus independent photofinishers could not offer processing service for Kodacolor II—the only color print film Kodak ever offered in the 110 size—until they bought new equipment and received instruction in and supplies for C–41 processing. Moreover, Kodak did not give advance warning to the independents that the new film would be introduced, nor did it predisclose the C–41 process to other makers of photofinishing equipment. Accordingly, CP & P was able to begin processing Kodacolor II several weeks before its competitors.

Furthermore, it is urged that Berkey faced greater expense in finishing Kodacolor II than did CP & P, because Kodak refused to divulge the formulae for chemicals used in the C–41 process. Large photofinishers like Berkey preferred to buy these compounds from chemical suppliers in bulk, both to save money and to gain flexibility. But to be able to process Kodacolor II, they were forced to buy pre-mixed "kits" from Kodak at twice the price. Kodak, meanwhile, provided all but one of the CP & P plants with bulk chemicals. And, because for some time Kodak was the only manufacturer of machinery capable of processing the new film, the independent photofinishers were required to purchase this equipment in order to proceed at all. The jury found that Kodak's prices were excessive and almost certainly found also that the equipment Kodak sold to the independents was vastly inferior to its product for CP & P.

Because of its early jump and greater efficiency in the C–41 process, CP & P gained a disproportionately high share of 110 finishing, an effect Berkey contends lasted through the end of 1973. There was clear evidence that Kodak was aware of the impact its conduct would have on the business of its photofinishing rivals. One Kodak marketing officer urged introduction of Kodacolor II along with the 110 cameras in part to compel the independent photofinishers to buy Kodak C–41 equipment, and Kodak engineers realized that the machinery their firm planned to sell would not allow independents to do more than "limp through the C–22 to P–118 transition stage." Not surprisingly, one Kodak scientist noted early in the development of the 110 system that the new process would "raise hell in the photofinishing business" without benefit to the consumer. And, shortly after Kodacolor II came to market, a worried Kodak employee predicted that CP & P's announcement of its early readiness to process the new film would "cause some photofinishing reaction due to the fact that we are using 110 to gain business over their operations."

Kodak's conduct with respect to the independent photofinishers perhaps may be criticized as shoddy treatment of firms providing an essential service for Kodak products. Indeed, largely for that reason a number of Kodak employees urged that photofinishers and equipment manufacturers be given advance warning of the C–41 process. The purpose of the Sherman Act, however, is not to maintain friendly business relations among firms in the same industry nor was it designed to keep these firms happy and gleeful. Moreover, it is clear that Kodak did not monopolize or attempt to monopolize the photofinishing or equipment markets. Thus, it is not liable under § 2 for the actions described above unless it gained a competitive advantage in these markets by use of the monopoly power it possessed in other segments of the industry.

It bears emphasis that only the wielding of power will support recovery in this context; advantages inuring to Kodak's photofinishing and equipment arms by virtue of membership in an integrated firm will not.

* * *

It is not clear, however, whether in bringing forth the 110 system Kodak did anything that a smaller firm with integrated capabilities but no market control might not have done. Kodak did not use its power to shift the entire photofinishing market from C–22 to the C–41 process, for Kodacolor II was introduced only in the 110 size and at first represented a minuscule percentage of all color print photofinishing. Indeed, the film was not marketed in other formats until eighteen months later, long after the original surprise had worn off. In sum, Kodak's ability to gain a rapidly diminishing competitive advantage with the introduction of the 110 system may have been attributable to its innovation of a new system of photography, and not to its monopoly power. On the other hand, we cannot dismiss the possibility that Kodak's monopoly power in other markets was at least a partial root of its ability to gain an advantage over its photofinishing competitors and to sell them overpriced equipment.

For example, it may be that, had Kodak possessed only a small portion of the film market, other manufacturers would have found it more feasible to bring out their C–22 films in the 110 size. CP & P would then have had no competitive advantage for a large percentage of 110 photofinishing. Moreover, absent a Kodak film monopoly, the independent photofinishers might not have felt an urgent need to buy expensive equipment for the C–41 process.

We cannot resolve this ambiguity. The instructions to the jury did not draw with sufficient sharpness the distinction between exercises of power and the natural benefits of size and integration. Nor is the record so clear that we can say with certainty on which side of this demarcation the facts fall. The parties quite naturally gave relatively little attention to this aspect of the case, in light of the comparatively small sums involved. If the parties wish to pursue these claims to a final determination, therefore, a new trial will be necessary.

2. *Equitable Relief*

Although Berkey's claim for damages in the photofinishing market was limited to the events surrounding the 110 introduction, the plaintiff also made extensive allegations that Kodak had used its control over other markets to disadvantage photo-finishing competitors. For example, Berkey complained about Kodak's policy, evidently discontinued after the commencement of this suit, in the sale of color paper. The emulsions on each production run of paper are slightly different, yielding a variance of color characteristics. Because tests and machinery adjustments are necessary each time a roll of paper from a new "emulsion run" is used, large photofinishers like Berkey naturally wish to buy as many rolls as possible from a single run. Kodak, however, refused to sell more than 400 rolls from any one run to each photofinisher. Given Kodak's monopoly power in color paper, this refusal to deal would, unless justified by a valid business reason, appear to violate § 2 and form the basis for a grant of equitable relief.

* * *

IV. FILM AND COLOR PAPER CLAIMS

* * *

Excessive prices, maintained through exercise of a monopolist's control of the market, constituted one of the primary evils that the Sherman Act was intended to correct. . . . But unless the monopoly has bolstered its power by wrongful actions, it will not be required to pay damages merely because its prices may later be found excessive. Setting a high price may be a use of monopoly power, but it is not in itself anti-competitive. Indeed, although a monopolist may be expected to charge a somewhat higher price than would prevail in a competitive market, there is probably no better way for it to guarantee that its dominance will be challenged than by greedily extracting the highest price it can. If a firm has taken no action to destroy competition it may be unfair to deprive it of the ordinary opportunity to set prices at a profit-maximizing level. Thus, no court has required a lawful monopolist to forfeit to a purchaser three times the increment of its price over that which would prevail in a competitive market. Indeed, as one commentator who might favor such a rule concedes, such judicial oversight of pricing policies would place the courts in a role akin to that of a public regulatory commission. We would be wise to decline that function unless Congress clearly bestows it upon us. . . .

Questions and Comments

Consider the language of *Berkey* and of *Alcoa* and the attitude about competition policy that each reflects. Is *Berkey* consistent in spirit with *Alcoa?* Did Judge Hand think that high concentration tends to deaden initiative—and thus reduce innovativeness? Does Judge Kaufman? Does Judge Kaufman think that constraining the conduct of a dominant firm may lead to a less efficient industry? Did Judge Hand? Are industries led by dominant firms inevitable in modern America? If so, and if antitrust constraints threaten to reduce efficiency without significantly reducing their dominance, antitrust may be socially costly. But if monopoly (or dominance) is a remediable evil, not an inevitable one, then antitrust constraints on dominant firm conduct may be more sensible. They may make dominance a less attractive goal and thus may reduce the likelihood that dominance will emerge or increase. Between *Alcoa* and *Berkey* did the Second Circuit change its collective mind on the inevitability of dominance? Did national experience between the 1940s and the 1980s warrant a change of mind?

What does the *Berkey* opinion do to Judge Hand's holding that the offense of monopolization does not require specific intent to harm competition? Consider each one of the acts that Judge Kaufman said would or might be illegal under a proper application of Section 2. In each case, does the offense presuppose that Kodak had a specific intent to harm competition? Can you give an example of anything that Kodak might do without specific intent to harm competition that would nonetheless be illegal under Judge Kaufman's conception of Section 2?

In view of Kodak's monopoly position in film, cameras, and color print paper, did Kodak monopolize by:

1. Introducing a smaller-sized camera without disclosing to camera competitors the size of film that the new camera would accept?

    a. Would a duty to disclose the dimensions of the new film be more likely to help or hurt: (1) inventiveness; (2) rivalry in the camera marketplace?

2. Selling the new camera as a single system with the widely advertised slogan, "remarkable new film," although (as the jury might have found) the new film was not so remarkable and the old film would have given a good (if somewhat grainier) image if cut down to the smaller size?

    a. Would it matter if Kodak purposely rushed the new film to market to be able to advertise and sell a new system with the goal of selling some new cameras simply because buyers wanted the film?

    b. If 2. is a violation, what was Kodak's duty? That is, what should Kodak have done to fulfill the requirements of the law? How would recognition of this duty affect inventiveness? rivalry?

3. Restricting the new film to the small format for one-and-one-half years although (as the jury might have found) most of the qualities of the

new film could have been captured in the larger size that fit the standard 126 camera?

4. Giving its own photofinishing arm (CP & P) the necessary equipment to process the new film and providing it with the chemicals and formula for mixing the solution required for processing the new film, while giving the independent photofinishers inferior equipment and selling them the processing solution only as premixed, for twice the price of its elements?

5. Refusing to supply any one photofinisher with more than 400 rolls of color print paper at a time, although a larger quantity was needed for efficient adjustments of each run?

Are your answers influenced by Kodak's purpose or intent? What was its purpose or intent? How can purpose or intent help you figure out whether conduct is procompetitive or anticompetitive? In each case, would condemnation of the conduct hurt or help consumers? Would it promote or retard inventiveness? Would it be unfair, in the antitrust sense, to competitors? Some commentators argue that intent is not a reliable benchmark because effective firms always intend to beat out their competitors and because stress on intent gives too much influence to hyperbolic statement intended to whip up enthusiasm among salespeople. How significant are these concerns? Is it significant that many large firms have strategic planning staffs that may leave paper trails of plans, one or more of which may ultimately be adopted at the highest executive levels?

a. Note on Corporate Strategy, "Satisficing," and the Significance of Structure

If there is a difference between the Hand (*Alcoa*) and Kaufman (*Berkey–Kodak*) view of the probable social effects of market dominance, which of them is nearer to the truth? You have had a brief introduction to neo-classical thinking, and an even briefer one into industrial organization as an economic discipline. A neoclassicist who normally assumes strong profit-maximizing drives might well find much of value in the Kaufman approach. An I.O. economist, by contrast, might suppose that a dominant firm not faced by significant competition is not pushed very strongly toward efficiency. Yet a third tradition in recent economic thought is that of Nobel prize winner Herbert A. Simon and his followers, R.M. Cyert and J.G. March.

These behaviorists think that economic actors often do not maximize profits; they think they "satisfice" instead. They stress the inertial force in economic activity. By and large goods are made today the way they were made yesterday. Goods are priced through simple, repetitive formulas, such as cost plus X%. Prices are lowered (or raised) only when inventories build up excessively (or diminish very rapidly). Goods are distributed through the usual, established channels. If a firm enters a business and has no habits of its own, it borrows some. It emulates what others in the industry (or, if none, in another like and adjacent, and thus readily visible industry) do. Things tend simply to run along—inertia leads to continuities. Of course, changes do occur. For example, a firm may do research trying to improve its product and reduce costs. (If so, the reason it has a research activity, the way it researches, and the frequency and manner in which R & D outputs come "on line" can also all be explained in satisficing terms). The generalization is that firms fall into patterns of behavior and that these patterns continue so long as they seem to be working reasonably well—so long as there is no perturbation that pushes too hard against the status quo.

Of course, significant perturbations do occur—say, a prolonged period when profits are so low that the stockholders' dividend must be cut or passed, thus forcing stock prices down and making stockholders restive, or a trend toward declining market share which the chief executive officer finds galling. When perturbations like these are experienced some strategic response will follow. Personnel may be shaken up; product may be redesigned or some parts of the line cut back or suspended and others newly emphasized; advertising patterns (and agencies) may be changed; distribution patterns may be altered; internal structure—lines of authority, or line-staff relationships—may be repatterned; prices may be lowered, or increased, overall or selectively. But even where such reactive change is generated, the range of alternatives considered and evaluated will be limited. People in the sales department will propose sales oriented responses. There may be champions for different particular solutions, but the sales department head, largely by intuition, and out of a sense for the quality of the people proposing each, will probably choose among them and pass on only one solution. People in manufacturing will have other ideas, as will research people, financial people, and so on. In the end a limited number of ideas will receive serious consideration. Ultimately a strategic decision will be made at higher executive levels. It is likely to be made without a great deal of relevant data. It will be made out of what might be called "an experienced judgment," or "intuition"; for, given the limits of knowledge, time, and data collection, we must operate in a world of bounded rationality. The new policies will then be implemented. There will, by this time, be a considerable emotive investment by significant people in the organization in making them work. A new inertial stage will have been reached. This is satisficing. See Simon, Rational Decision Making in Business Organization, 69 Am.Econ.Rev. 493 (1979); Simon, A Behavioral Model of Rational Choice, 69 Q.J.Econ. 99 (1955); R.M. Cyert & J.G. March, A Behavioral Theory of the Firm (1963). For a review of the extensive literature at odds with the invisible hand theorum, see Morris & Mueller, The Corporation, Competition and the Invisible Hand, 118 J.Econ.Lit. 32, especially, 58–59 (1980).

To the extent satisficing within bounded rationality actually describes industrial and commercial behavior, neoclassical assumptions about market pressure toward efficiency are, at the least, an exaggeration. They are, moreover, likely to be wider of the mark when an industry is tightly structured (a monopoly or tight oligopoly) than when it is loosely structured (a competitive or loosely oligopolistic market). If Simon is right one might want to discount the fear that legal constraints placed on dominant firms in the interest of discouraging dominance will impose too high a social cost by blocking efficient options. If Simon is right the conduct of such firms might be improved if they felt under legal compulsion to justify their conduct on efficiency grounds when it caused injury to rivals.

Is Simon right? Certainly, there is value in his insights. However, the planning of competitive strategies may have become more analytical in recent years. More firms are setting up strategic planning staffs that survey operations and then develop well documented plans based on theory and data. See, e.g., M. Porter, Competitive Strategy (1980) and M. Porter, Competitive Advantage (1985). Such planning may limit the scope for satisficing and may increase the scope for informed rationality.

After *Berkey–Kodak* was decided another new wave monopolization case came before the FTC. It raised questions about conduct by E.I. du Pont in the titanium-dioxide industry. Titanium dioxide is a chemical pigment used as a whitener. It is made by one of two basic manufacturing processes, the sulphate process, which requires rutile ore, and the chloride process, which is made with ilmenite ore. The sulphate process was old. The chloride process was developed shortly after World War II by du Pont through "notable technological achievement." However, for many years, rutile ore deposits were abundant and the chloride process had no cost advantage over the sulphate process.

In about 1970, two changes occurred: rutile fell into short supply throughout the world and anti-pollution regulations imposed costly requirements on sulphate producers. As a result, the chloride process gained a distinct cost advantage. Du Pont developed a strategy to expand and increase its market share. From 1972 to 1975 it increased its share from approximately 30% to 42%. Given its cost advantage, it proposed to capture virtually all of the growth in domestic demand, and expected to achieve a 55% share by 1985.

The Federal Trade Commission sued, alleging an attempt to monopolize.

E.I. Du PONT DE NEMOURS & CO.
(Titanium Dioxide)
96 FTC 650 (1980).

COMMISSIONER CLANTON: . . . [I]t is useful to restate complaint counsel's fundamental objection to DuPont's growth plan. In essence, complaint counsel contend that it was logical for DuPont to do what it did only if monopoly power could be attained in the future. It is argued that DuPont's construction/pricing/nonlicensing policy involved a current foregoing of available profits, that DuPont recognized that it could recoup those profits down the road through high volume and higher prices, and that DuPont's policy only made sense if those excess profits would become available at a later date.

Put differently, DuPont presumably would not have tried to capture all future demand growth, and thereby risked the costs of operating a plant the size of DeLisle at less than capacity, unless it was reasonably assured that other competitors could not expand. DuPont obtained this assurance, it is claimed, not through normal market forces, but rather through its own efforts, as evidenced by the combination of expansion, announcement, pricing and licensing policies. As further proof of the overall strategy, complaint counsel cite to DuPont's pricing forecasts, which it is argued clearly reveal respondent's plan to sacrifice short-term profits for long-term monopoly gains.

We simply cannot accept this analysis. The rationality of DuPont's program hardly seems dependent on its ability to extract monopoly profits in the future. DuPont had a highly efficient process, indeed the most efficient in the industry, and it anticipated expanding market demand. To serve that demand, DuPont enlarged its existing facilities to optimal levels and built a new plant of efficient scale (but not above efficient levels and no larger than necessary to satisfy predicted demand) to serve the market it expected would develop. Given respondent's level of efficiency, expansion of the magnitude undertaken would make sense, regardless of whether the firm would eventually be able to raise prices above competitive levels. Moreover, DuPont's pricing policies were entirely consistent with its cost advantage and apparently (for there is no suggestion that it engaged in predatory pricing) were profitable, even during the '70s when respondent was arguably foregoing additional profits.

Even if DuPont could earn future profits equal to those it was passing up in the mid–1970s only if existing competitors were dissuaded from expanding, it does not necessarily follow that actions leading to that result should constitute an illegal attempt to monopolize. As we have observed, DuPont's ability to pursue its strategy derived from substantial economic efficiencies; it did not stem from below cost pricing, false plant announcements, construction of excess capacity or other plainly anticompetitive conduct. Complaint counsel contend, however, that notwithstanding these efficiencies and DuPont's conceded right to expand, there were less restrictive alternatives available that would have less adverse competitive consequences. In particular, they cite DuPont's own more moderate expansion program—a program discarded in favor of the more aggressive growth plan in 1972—which contemplated only expansion of existing plants. More generally, complaint counsel and their expert witness, Professor Shepherd, urged that DuPont should have pursued *any* less aggressive strategy than the one it did. In other words, respondent should not have attempted to capture all the growth in the market, thereby making it more difficult for competitors to expand to the scale justified by DuPont's technology.

While it is proper and desirable to consider alternative courses of conduct open to DuPont, we firmly believe the course chosen was not unreasonable. When DuPont conceived its strategy in 1972, its estimates of demand growth and supply shortfall seemed reasonable, and there has been no suggestion to the contrary. In competing for this growth, DuPont realized that even expansion of its existing plants to their practical limits could not satisfy all of the additional demand expected through the early 1980s. A new plant would be required. To build such a plant at efficient scale, afforded by DuPont's developed technology, meant that there would be little, if any, room left for expansion by competitors. Yet, to deny DuPont the opportunity to compete for all of the projected demand growth unduly penalizes its technological success. To require respondent to build a smaller, less efficient plant, or no plant, under these circumstances would be an unjustified restraint on competitive incentives and an unjustified denial of the benefits of competition to consumers.

To be sure, DuPont had another alternative. It could have licensed its technology to competitors, as suggested by complaint counsel, thereby enabling respondent's rivals to close the technological gap more quickly. But, in the context of this case, we can find no basis for concluding that DuPont's refusal to license its technology, whether taken separately or together with the other conduct, was unjustified. There is no evidence, for example, that respondent used unreasonable means to acquire its know-how, or that it joined with others in preventing access by competitors. Complaint counsel cite no authority for the proposition that DuPont should have licensed its technology, and we are aware of none.[40] Whatever may be the proper result in other factual settings, we are not persuaded that the refusal to license in this situation provides a basis for liability; in fact, imposition of a duty to license might serve to chill the very kind of innovative process that led to DuPont's cost advantage.

Turning to the pricing options available to respondent, there is, of course, no evidence that DuPont priced below its costs, since the case was not tried on such a theory. As for the issue of limit pricing,* the literature discussed previously suggests that predation may occur even in circumstances where prices are above the dominant firm's costs (whether measured by average variable or average total cost). In this respect, it seems clear that respondent sought to price in a fashion that took account of the propensities and abilities of competitors to expand, although the firm's pricing decisions were affected at least in part by independent economic forces, such as demand conditions. Given this situation, it can be argued that these pricing policies went too far, that they transformed an otherwise legitimate method of expansion into an unlawful course of conduct.

We do not agree. DuPont's pricing strategy stemmed from its clear cost advantage over competitors and occurred in conjunction with its long-term plan to capture future market growth, a plan which we have pointed out before was consistent with foreseeable demand and scale economies. Thus, this is not a case where DuPont was attempting solely to preserve its market power through selective, temporary price cuts to deter new entry or expansion by existing competitors. Even complaint counsel do not attack respondent's pricing as an independent violation; rather they

40. To the contrary, the recent *Berkey* and *IBM* cases suggest that firms (monopolists and non-monopolists) that have achieved success through superior products and business acumen, and not unlawful anticompetitive conduct, are under no duty to license or disclose their technology to their rivals. *Berkey Photo, Inc. v. Eastman Kodak Co.* 603 F.2d 263 (2d Cir.1979); *California Computer Products, Inc. v. IBM Corp.*, 613 F.2d 727 (9th Cir.1979); *Transamerica Computer Co. v. IBM Corp.*, 481 F.Supp. 965 (N.D. Cal.1979); *ILC Peripherals Leasing Corp. v. IBM Corp.*, 458 F.Supp. 423 (N.D.Cal.1978). Here, DuPont's refusal to license its technol-

ogy is not a factor that would make otherwise reasonable behavior unreasonably anticompetitive. And, if the other conduct were itself unreasonable, the refusal to license would add little to the case, except, of course, as a possible basis for remedial action. See also *SCM Corp. v. Xerox Corp.*, 463 F.Supp. 983 (D.Conn.1978) [, *rev'd on other grounds*, 645 F.2d 1195 (2d Cir.1981), *cert. denied*, 455 U.S. 1016 (1982)].

* Authors' note: Limit pricing is pricing above costs but below the short run profit-maximizing price at a point low enough to deter entry or expansion by competitors.

argue that it is unlawful as part of a broader pattern of behavior. For our part, even if DuPont's pricing can be characterized as a form of limit pricing, we do not find it to be unreasonable, absent at least some evidence of below-cost pricing, in view of the firm's cost advantage, its market position and its legitimate expansion efforts. While there may be circumstances where above cost pricing is unjustifiably exclusionary, those circumstances clearly are not present here.

We also do not find that DuPont's announcements of its early plans to build an unidentified additional facility or its later announcements identifying the DeLisle plant were unfairly exaggerated or misleading threats or signals in the strategic sense suggested by the commentators. Because of the lead time required for obtaining environmental permits and for completing construction, DuPont's early disclosure of its plans appears logical. The documents also reflect DuPont's strong belief that unfavorable customer reaction could be expected if it cancelled or postponed DeLisle for any significant length of time, so that there were disincentives to making false or exaggerated announcements. Had these announcements been false or grossly disproportionate, under circumstances suggesting they served little purpose except to mislead and discourage competition, there might have been a basis for liability. But that is not the case before us. Moreover, DuPont's decisions to scale back the size of DeLisle and delay its start-up are attributable, in large measure, to unforeseen changes in supply and demand and therefore do not render the otherwise justified announcements unreasonable.

As an additional argument, complaint counsel contend that DuPont's cost advantage is largely fortuitous, owing to technology developed many years before. Without expressly suggesting that the result should be different had DuPont developed the ilmenite process in 1972, complaint counsel nevertheless argue that DuPont's allegedly superior skills and business acumen should be given little weight. More specifically, they contend that DuPont had demonstrated no contemporaneous technological superiority because it has not "*recently* distinguished itself as an organizational innovator," citing Williamson, *Dominant Firms and the Monopoly Problem: Market Failure Considerations,* 85 Harv.L.Rev. 1512, 1527 (1972) (emphasis in original). But the point of Williamson's discussion is whether an established monopolist should be able to defend against a charge of monopolization on traditional grounds of business acumen or historic accident, where such causes bear little relationship to the reasons for the firm's continuing dominance. The issues here are considerably different.

We believe it would be anomalous to downgrade the significance of DuPont's technological superiority simply because the fruits were not reaped simultaneously with the discovery of the process. It may well be that DuPont anticipated possible future shortages of rutile and other ores back in the '40s and '50s, even though it could not have anticipated precisely the events that occurred in the late '60s. In any event, DuPont's development of an alternative supply source reflects the kind of skill and foresight that should be encouraged, whether the benefits materialize immediately or at some later date.

With the possible exception of *Alcoa,* which involved repeated increases in output by a monopolist, there is nothing in the case precedents to suggest that DuPont's expansion program unnecessarily heightened entry barriers or otherwise unreasonably excluded competition. Nor does the conduct appear to be sufficiently similar to the preemptive kinds of expansion described by Professors Scherer and Williamson to warrant condemnation. To the extent that the effects of DuPont's expansion bear any resemblance to those models, a review of factors such as those suggested by Scherer's rule-of-reason approach would still call for a finding of reasonableness.

It may be that DuPont ultimately will achieve a monopoly share of the market. As its share increases, other firms may find it harder to capture the efficiencies enjoyed by DuPont due to the scale economies associated with the ilmenite process. Those effects should be weighed carefully, and we have done so. Antitrust policy wisely disfavors monopoly, but it also seeks to promote vigorous competitive behavior. Indeed, the essence of the competitive process is to induce firms to become more efficient and to pass the benefits of the efficiency along to consumers. That process would be ill-served by using antitrust to block hard, aggressive competition that is solidly based on efficiencies and growth opportunities, even if monopoly is a possible result. Such a view, we believe, is entirely consistent with the "superior skill, foresight and industry" exception in *Alcoa* and subsequent cases, for those decisions clearly indicate that monopolies may be lawfully created by superior competitive ability.[42]

As we have previously indicated, DuPont engaged in conduct consistent with its own technological capacity and market opportunities. It did not attempt to build excess capacity or to expand temporarily as a means of deterring entry. Nor did respondent engage in other conduct that might tip the scales in the direction of liability, such as pricing below cost, making false announcements about future expansion plans, or attempting to lock up customers in requirements contracts to assure the success of its growth plans. In short, we find DuPont's conduct to be reasonable. Accordingly, we affirm the [administrative law judge's] dismissal of the complaint.

Questions and Comments

Is *du Pont (Titanium Dioxide)* consistent with *Alcoa?* With *United Shoe Machinery?* If one takes *Berkey–Kodak* as authoritative is the *du Pont (Titanium Dioxide)* outcome compelled? Is it a harder or easier case than *Berkey?* Based on this decision could you fashion a rule indicating when capital investment in an industry is predatory or exclusionary?

Should the chloride technology have been treated as a scarce resource or essential facility to which competitors should have access? Does *du Pont*

---

42. If a monopoly proves impervious to competitive inroads and is unjustified by scale economies or other efficiencies, antitrust action in this or some other forum may be warranted, even in the absence of abusive conduct. See [P. Areeda & D. Turner, Antitrust Law ¶ 6236]; see also Statement of the Federal Trade Commission to the National Commission for the Review of Antitrust Laws and Procedures (Nov. 17, 1978). Report to the President and the Attorney General 407 (Jan. 22, 1979). That, however, is an issue entirely different from the one before us.

(Titanium Dioxide) undercut *Otter Tail* at all? If after ten years du Pont achieves 100% of the titanium dioxide market as a result of its expansion, pricing policy and refusal to license, should the technology then be treated as a scarce resource or essential facility to which competitors should have reasonable access? What terms for access would be "reasonable"? The marginal cost of granting access? Cost plus a competitive profit? Cost plus a return adequate to reward du Pont for being innovative? Cost plus a monopoly profit? Who should decide what is reasonable? What data should be considered?

The availability of relief both manageable for a court and likely to improve competitive conditions may be a key factor in formulating the substantive law. If you had been complaint counsel for the FTC, what relief would you have sought in the *du Pont (Titanium Dioxide)* case? What effect would an FTC victory, accompanied by this relief, have had on competition in the whitener market?

b. Fraud on the Patent Office

By procuring a patent, the patentee obtains the legal right to exclude all others from practicing the patent. If the patent (or the patented product) is a market unto itself—i.e., there are no good substitutes, the patentee has procured a legal monopoly. But if the patent is obtained by fraud on the Patent Office, the fraudulent procurement can amount to monopolization or attempt to monopolize. Walker Process Equipment Inc. v. Food Machinery & Chemical Corp., 382 U.S. 172 (1965).

Normally, private parties have a privilege to petition government, even for anticompetitive advantage. See Eastern R.R. Presidents Conference v. Noerr Motor Freight, Inc., 365 U.S. 127 (1961), which we treat in Chapter 3. Where the parties petition by fraud or bribery, is the *Noerr* immunity lost? Should it be?

c. The Computer Reservation System Problem

Today, most airline bookings are made through travel agents who use computer reservation systems (CRS) that display flight information on the screen. (Donnelley's publication is now obsolete). There are four or five CRS systems. The two most successful are owned and operated by two large airlines, United and American. Each charges airlines for listing information and charges travel agents for access to the information. Travel agents need only one system and the five CRS operators compete for placement in travel agencies. They compete, for example, by offering special "deals" to travel agents who switch to them. There is probably little competition in the price charged to airlines, however. Because each travel agent uses only one system all air carriers feel compelled to list with every existing system in order to reach all travelers.

If a traveler wants to fly from New York to San Francisco on a given day and wants to leave New York at 5 p.m., the travel agent calls up on her display screen New York–San Francisco flights leaving at about that time. Four or five flights will normally show up on the first display. If none is satisfactory (or all are filled) the agent can call up another display. Suppose American were to bias its system so that any non-stop flight of its own leaving within two hours of the proposed departure time always shows up first, followed, on the first display, only by flights of others that make intervening stops. Would that conduct violate the antitrust laws? Would it disadvantage competitors? Would it tend to raise airline fares? Would it impair consumer choice in a significant way? Is it unfair? Suppose both American or United used "subtle bias"—that is, listed all flights on the basis of seemingly objective criteria like starting time, arrival time, meal service, movie service, wide body, etc., but that each gave preference to those objective factors which would give it the best display position. Would that be a violation? Should it be? See Report to Congress on Airline Computer Reservations System [CRS] Prepared by the CAB in Consultation with the DOJ (1984).

In thinking about this hypothesized airline conduct, you may have wondered whether certain technical requirements of Section 2 are satisfied. Consider the following hypothetical situations: [9]

1. Airline A is the only air carrier or has 80% to 90% of the traffic on specified city pair routes. It also has 30% of the CRS market. Its operation in reservation systems is likely to steer to its airline an additional 5% of the traffic on those routes where it does not now have the bulk of the traffic and an additional 0.5% on the routes where it does. Similar facts apply to Airline B, although it and Airline U are dominant or near dominant on different routes. Has A monopolized or attempted to monopolize the national air travel market? Specified city-pair markets or submarkets? The national CRS market? The market or submarket for its own proprietary CRS (or for access to the travel agents listing on it)?

2. The facts are the same as in 1 except that A and U are major factors on the same airline routes and only by combining their shares could one argue that they have a monopoly or near monopoly position on certain airline routes. Has A or U monopolized or attempted to monopolize any relevant market or submarket? Compare *United States v. National Broadcasting Co.,* 449 F.Supp. 1127 (1978).

3. Neither A nor U, acting alone or together, occupies a monopoly position on any airline route, but Airline A operates the only airline reservation system in the country and expects to steer to its airline approximately 10% to 15% more passengers, increasing its share to as much as 50% on key routes. Since Airline A's system is the established reservation system throughout the country and it makes its system available to the travel agents at cost, new entry into the reservation systems market is not expected.

4. A builds its share of the CRS market up to 20% by providing CRS listings to travel agents at prices well below A's cost. It then charges monopoly prices to competing airlines that must list on its CRS. Has A monopolized or attempted to monopolize any relevant market or submarket? (Could the facts here asserted

9. One of the editors is a consultant to attorneys involved in CRS related antitrust litigation. Some of these hypotheticals are suggested by some of the issues arising in that litigation.

ever be proved? Providing CRS service to travel agents and listings to airlines entail costs many, perhaps most, of which are joint. How will you decide what portion of joint costs to attribute to service to travel agents and what portion to attribute to listing airlines?)

5. The facts are the same as in 1 except that there is no basis for concluding that A built its CRS share to 20% by charging travel agents less than cost. Given that competing airlines are commercially compelled to list on A's CRS, is CRS an essential facility even though there are other CRSs (to which competing airlines also need access)? If so, must A provide access for competing airlines on reasonable, non-discriminatory terms? Would an obligation to do so depend on a finding that by denial of such access A threatened to monopolize the national air travel market or specified city pair markets or submarkets, or would it be enough that through its conduct A gained a competitive advantage in the downstream air travel market? (If A does have such a duty does the joint cost problem mentioned in 4 present any difficulty?)

Does Section 2 of the Sherman Act cover these problems? If not, does any other antitrust law apply? Does Section 5 of the FTC Act? (Is there a contract or combination in restraint of trade? See Chapter 3 infra.) Should *some* antitrust (or regulatory) law prohibit (or regulate) this activity? See In re Air Passenger Computer Reservations Systems Antitrust Litigation, 694 F.Supp. 1443 (C.D.Cal.1988).

d. The Telephone Monopoly Cases

At midcentury, the government brought monopoly suits against both AT & T and IBM. It settled both suits by consent decrees in January 1956. United States v. Western Electric Co., 1956 Trade Cas. ¶ 68,246 (D.N.J.1956); United States v. IBM Corp., 1956 Trade Cas. ¶ 68,245 (S.D.N.Y.1956).

Nearly 25 years after the first suits were brought, the government again sued both companies (IBM in 1969, AT & T in 1974). (See discussion of *United States v. IBM* at page 214 et seq. below.) As the AT & T suit alleged, AT & T had (lawful) monopolies of local telephone service through the Bell Operating Companies ("BOCs"). It also provided long distance (intercity) service which connected BOCs into a nationwide network, and, through Western Electric, provided telephone equipment to consumers, to AT & T and to the BOCs for intercity and local service. Local telephone service was clearly a natural monopoly. Although intercity service may once have been a natural monopoly, by 1974 new technologies made competition feasible for long distance communication. The sale and installation of telephone hardware was never a natural monopoly. The government's complaint alleged that the defendants, AT & T and its subsidiaries, monopolized the telecommunications market in the United States by restricting and eliminating competition from other long distance telecommunications companies and from other manufacturers of telecommunications equipment.

The trial began and the government put in its case in chief. The government introduced evidence showing, among other things, that AT & T had engaged in a series of strategies designed to keep out of the market equally good or better telephone equipment and long distance service. For many years it succeeded in repressing competing telephone equipment by requiring competitors to lease expensive and unnecessary protective connecting arrangements (PCAs) and by making PCAs unavailable. It put up barriers to prevent General Electric and MCI (microwave long distance service) from making the necessary interconnections into the intercity markets. It caused the Bell Operating Companies to purchase from Western Electric virtually all equipment of the sort made by Western Electric, and not to purchase the equipment of competitors even if no Bell equipment was available of equal quality, cost or sophistication. As to this portion of the case, the court said:

> Th[e] evidence tended to show that the general trade manufacturers encountered a considerable number of obstacles in trying to design equipment for, and to sell this equipment to, the Bell Operating Companies, and that these obstacles perpetuated a buy-Western bias. For example, the competitors had difficulty in locating the employee in Western or the Operating Companies authorized to negotiate a sale; in obtaining from Bell compatibility specifications (without which general trade products could not be designed for interconnection with the Bell network); and in persuading Bell Labs to complete objective evaluations (which were usually required before sales could be effected). The government's evidence further indicated that Bell did not authorize the purchase of the general trade equipment even if no Bell product of equivalent quality, cost, or technical sophistication was available; instead, crash programs were initiated to develop competing Western products (to the extent that, in one instance, Western literally copied the general trade product so that it did not need to wait for the design and development of its own model). Operating Company employees were under pressure from AT & T officials to buy from Western (even when a general trade product was cheaper or of better quality) or to wait until a Western product comparable to the desired general trade equipment was available, and they were required to provide detailed justifications for general trade purchases which were not necessary for the purchase of Western equipment.

* * *

The government's evidence has depicted defendants as sole arbiters of what equipment is suitable for use in the Bell System—a role that carries with it a power of subjective judgment that can be and has been used to advance the sale of Western Electric's products at the expense of the general trade. First, AT & T, in conjunction with Bell Labs and Western Electric, sets the technical standards under which the telephone network operates and the compatibility specifications which equipment must meet. Second, Western Electric and Bell Labs . . . serve as counselors to the Operating Companies in their procurement decisions, ostensibly helping them to purchase equipment that meets network standards. Third, Western also produces equipment for sale to the Operating Companies in competition with general trade manufacturers.

The upshot of this "wearing of three hats" is, according to the government's evidence, a rather obviously anticompetitive situation. By setting technical or compatibility standards and by either not communicating these standards to the general trade or changing them in mid-stream, AT & T has the capacity to remove, and has in fact removed, general trade products from serious consideration by the Operating Companies on "network integrity" grounds. By either refusing to evaluate general trade products for the Operating Companies or producing biased or speculative evaluations, AT & T has been able to influence the Operating Companies, which lack independent means to evaluate general trade products, to buy Western. And the in-house production and sale of Western equipment provides AT & T with a powerful incentive to exercise its "approval" power to discriminate against Western's competitors.

United States v. American Telephone & Telegraph Co., 524 F.Supp. 1336, 1371–72 (D.D.C.1981).

The government also introduced evidence of anticompetitive pricing strategies, which we present along with the IBM price predation cases, p. 214 et seq. infra.

Defendants moved to dismiss at the close of plaintiff's evidence. They argued that they merely sought to protect the integrity of their system and to take advantage of their efficiencies, and that the government should not second-guess their decisions.

The court, by Judge Greene, denied the motion to dismiss. *Id.* With respect to long distance competitors' right of access to intercity connections, Judge Greene invoked the essential facility doctrine and relied on *Terminal Railroad* and *Otter Tail.* With respect to equipment competitors' foreclosure from sales to the BOCs, and the government's contention that the BOCs had the duty to release technical information and compatability specifications, the court said:

. . . Defendants argue that their alleged failure to release technical information or compatibility specifications to the general trade cannot serve as a basis for antitrust liability, relying primarily upon *Berkey Photo, Inc. v. Eastman Kodak Co.* Berkey competed with Kodak in processing film (photofinishing). Its claim was that Kodak's introduction, without advance notice to the industry, of a new film, requiring a new photofinishing process which could be done only with equipment purchased from Kodak, allowed Kodak to begin processing the new film several weeks before its competitors and thus gave Kodak a competitive advantage. Berkey also claimed that Kodak's failure to disclose the chemicals used in the new process caused Berkey greater expense and competitive injury. The court held that the advantages in information flow possessed by an integrated firm do not constitute antitrust violations, unless they provide a means for the firm to gain a competitive advantage in one market through monopoly power in another.

There are two fundamental differences between *Berkey* and the instant case. First, in *Berkey* the entity failing to disclose information to the industry was different from the buyers of the service to whom the information was useful; in the present case, it is the Bell System which both has failed to release the information and has purchased the equipment which cannot be properly designed without the information. Second, Berkey was still able to process the new film despite Kodak's failure to disclose the chemicals used in the new process, albeit at greater expense; but no piece of equipment can be interconnected with the country-wide public switched network unless it conforms to the compatibility standards set by Bell. An inability to obtain Bell technical information/compatibility standards thus constitutes an insuperable barrier to entry to the market (and the record does not show a reasonable basis for defendants' having withheld this type of information).

Id. at 1374–75.

Questions and Comments

In each of three areas, among others, the court held that the government had introduced sufficient evidence for a fact-finder to find a violation:

1. Interconnection of customer-provided terminal equipment.

2. Interconnection of intercity competitors to local facilities.

3. Procurement of equipment by the Bell companies.

Suppose that you are a staff attorney for the government. As to each area, what is your theory of violation? What must you prove to prevail? Must you prove anticompetitive intent? If so, what evidence will suffice? Must you prove output limitation?

Now suppose you represent AT & T. What facts would you attempt to prove at trial regarding each of the three alleged violations? What explanations, justifications, or market conditions would or should entitle you to prevail? Do you have an efficiency, integrity-of-the-system, or business judgment defense? A public good defense?

Suppose now that you are the trial judge and at the close of trial you find a violation in each of the three areas. What relief do you order? Are you satisfied that the relief is in the public interest?

In addition to the Justice Department suit (which was settled and therefore not fully litigated), several of AT & T's competitors also sued AT & T. Some won large judgments and some lost on substantially similar facts. See Litton Systems, Inc. v. AT & T, 700 F.2d 785 (2d Cir.1983), *cert. denied,* 464 U.S. 811 (1984) (judgment for plaintiff), Southern Pacific Communications Co. v. AT & T, 556 F.Supp. 825 (D.D.C.1982), amended, 1983–1 CCH Trade Cas. ¶ 65,373 (D.D.C.1983) (judgment for defendant). See also MCI Communications Corp. v. AT & T, 708 F.2d 1081 (7th Cir.1983), *cert. denied,* 464 U.S. 891 (1983).

More than ten years after the Justice Department filed its suit against AT & T, and while the case was still pending, William Baxter became Assistant Attorney General in charge of the Antitrust Division. Mr. Baxter, who took a theoretical, economic approach to antitrust and regulation, was concerned that AT & T's ownership of both regulated monopolies (the BOCs) and nonregulated business tended to distort allocative efficiency. For example, since the regulated BOCs bought hardware from nonregulated Western Electric, AT & T would have the incentive to cause the BOCs to pay Western Electric a hidden premium for the hardware, and to pass on the overcharge through the rate base for local telephone service. It would also have the incentive to get monopoly prices in markets where it faced little competition (this was true of long lines for many years until the development of new technology such as microwave) and to subsidize markets in which there was intense political pressure for lower prices (local telephone service). As a result of these distortions, users would get the wrong price signals. If people are offered local telephone service at below its cost, they will use an inefficiently large amount of it. If people can make long distance calls only at a price above their cost, they will make too few of them. (The "efficient" amount of usage is by definition the amount of usage people will choose if the good or service is priced at cost.)

To correct these distortions, Mr. Baxter strongly supported a plan for the break-up of AT & T; the local monopolies would be separate from Long Lines (which were subject to regulation that, Baxter urged, should be eliminated) and Western Electric. Baxter thought Long Lines could appropriately remain with Western Electric. The plan recommended itself to AT & T: the litigation was risky and expensive, and continuation of it might damage the company; also, under the settlement proposed the company could rid itself of the least profitable and most politically pressured part of its enterprise, the local telephone monopolies. Thus, AT & T agreed to the settlement. See *Competitive Impact Statement on Settlement with AT & T* [Jan.–June], Antitrust & Trade Reg. Rep. (BNA) No. 1052, at 401 (Feb. 18, 1982).

Many telephone users reacted to the case much as United Shoe's customers had reacted to the government case against it. Was the suit in the public interest? Was the relief granted desirable? Was it adequate? Is there anything wrong or incomplete about relief based on the assumption that allocative efficiency is the sole antitrust goal *and* that any settlement that eliminates "perverse incentives" is desirable?

Assume that after the breakup Western Electric still has a monopoly share of the market for the supply of telecommunications hardware, that AT & T's Long Lines Division still has the major share of long distance business, and that AT & T still buys most of the hardware for long distance service from Western Electric. Do these facts indicate that further relief may be appropriate? Do they, on the contrary, indicate that AT & T is the best supplier? What additional facts do you want to know?

3. PREDATION AND MODERN LAW OF MONOPOLIZATION

Much of the monopoly law of the last quarter of the twentieth century involves alleged predatory strategies of dominant firms. A predatory strategy is any course of conduct by a dominant firm designed to drive out, discipline or set back competitors by acts that, but for their anticompetitive impact, would not be economically sensible for the dominant firm. Such conduct will not benefit consumers (or, if it does in the short run, will hurt them soon after; its net competitive effect is predictably harmful). In theory there could be a wide range of possible predatory strategies. Strategies could include investing in excess capacity which will overhang the market and discourage entry, bribing suppliers not to supply competitors, filling all of the niches in the market, or responding selectively by entering the same niche the entrant is considering or has attempted, redesigning product to make entry with interfacing peripheral equipment more difficult, excessive advertising, harrassing through lawsuits, inducing key employees to leave en mass, and drastically cutting price. In essence, any tactic or set of tactics that will add more to the rival's costs than to the costs of the monopolist, or will diminish the rival's revenues more than those of the monopolist could be an effective predatory device. Antitrust analysts must consider, however, whether condemning any such strategies may hold more costs for competition than would condoning them, since some of the activity caught up in the prohibited category might be competitively responsive behavior that we want firms to be free to take.

Some neoclassical microeconomics literature, especially that associated with the Chicago school, defines predation narrowly and assumes that predation occurs very rarely or not at all because it would almost never pay off (barriers to entry are presumed to be low and reentry easy). By this narrow definition, predatory pricing is pricing below marginal cost by a dominant firm when intended and likely to destroy all significant competitors, where the predator retains power to raise price and recoup more than its losses before attracting reentry or expansion that would force price down again. Writers in the Chicago vein urge that all other low pricing puts greater pressure on the predator than on the victim and would not be profitable even if the victim were driven out. When the predator tried to recoup its losses through monopoly profits, new entry would occur. Chicagoans are convinced that, since such a strategy could rarely be successful, it is not a problem and should not be a concern of antitrust. See Easterbrook, Predatory Strategies and Counter-strategies, 48 U.Chi.L.Rev. 263 (1981). The literature is reviewed from a different prospective in Brodley & Hay, Predatory Pricing: Competing Economic Theories and Evolution of Legal Standards, 66 Cornell L.Rev. 738 (1981).

Other scholars regard predation as a real problem that antitrust should monitor. They would include in a possibly suspect category predatory pricing, product change and many of the other strategies mentioned above. They would include competition chilling, as well as competition killing activity under the definition of predation. They are more likely to regard recoupment by a predator as feasible because structural barriers to entry or reentry may be high and because a reputation for predation may have lasting, entry discouraging value. Would-be entrants and those that finance them often shy away from markets dominated by predation-prone firms. See Williamson, Kreps & Wilson, Reputation and Imperfect Information, 27 J.Econ.Theory 253 (1982); Williamson, Delimiting Antitrust, 76 Geo.L.J. 271 (1988); Krattenmaker, Lande & Salop, Monopoly Power and Market Power in Antitrust Law, 76 Geo.L.J. 241 (1988); Campbell, Predation and Competition In Antitrust: The Case of Non–Fungible Goods, 87 Colum.L.Rev. 1625 (1987); F. Scherer, Industrial Market Structure and Economic Performance 335 (2d ed. 1980); Schmalensee, Entry Deterrence in the Ready-to-Eat Breakfast Cereal Industry, 9 Bell J.Econ. 305 (1978).

Approaches taken by Williamson, Scherer, Salop and others go beyond the original I.O. conception, which emphasized the effect of structure (often taken as a given) on conduct more than the effect of conduct on structure. The "new industrial organization" scholars are primarily concerned with strategies by which firms either exploit market imperfections or create or enhance imperfections so that they can exploit them. Some of them blend the traditions of I.O. economics and neoclassical theory. See, e.g., A. Jacquemin, The New Industrial Organization (MIT Press 1987).

Of all predation problems, predatory pricing has received the most judicial and scholarly attention; predatory product change has also received notable attention. In this section we present some background on predatory pricing, and then discuss the *IBM* cases (the earliest of which were brought in the late 1960s) and some related cases on pricing and product change.

a. Predatory Pricing and the Robinson–Patman Act

Conventional business history teaches that price discrimination and price predation were used as tools to build up the trusts and monopolies that appeared at the end of the nineteenth and the beginning of the twentieth century. In 1887 Congress passed the Interstate Commerce Act, prohibiting price discrimination in railroad traffic. 24 Stat. 379 (1887). In 1890, Congress passed the Sherman Act. The *Standard Oil* case, dealing with the Rockefeller Oil Trust, documents a prominent example of monopoly by price predation. The enormous buying power of that trust was used to force the railroads to give the trust low rates while charging its competitors high rates. As a seller, the Oil Trust charged high prices to customers in monopoly areas, while engaging in local price cutting designed to force recalcitrant competitors to sell out to the trust or be destroyed. In Predatory Price Cutting: The Standard Oil (N.J.) Case, 1 J. Law & Econ. 137 (1958), one of the earliest expressions of the view that selling below cost is unlikely to yield monopoly profits, John S. McGee argues that the record in *Standard Oil* warrants the conclusion that the trust's low prices never fell below its costs.

In 1914 Congress passed the Clayton Act to shore up the Sherman Act and to specifically target certain offensive practices, including price discrimination. Section 2 of the Clayton Act, as enacted in 1914, prohibited sellers from discriminating in price between different purchasers of goods of like grade and quality "where the effect of such discrimination may be to substantially lessen competition or tend to create a monopoly in any line of commerce," unless the discrimination was cost justified. 38 Stat. 730. A purpose of Section 2 of the Clayton Act was to protect small sellers from selective low pricing by dominant competitors designed to hurt or eliminate them. See H.R.Rep. No. 2287, 74th Cong., 2d Sess. 3–6 (1936).

In 1936 Congress passed the Robinson–Patman Act which amends Section 2 of the Clayton Act. Pursuant to the amendment, old Section 2 became Section 2(a). This section deals with what has come to be called "primary line" discrimination—harm to competition at the seller's level.

As amended it also prohibits discrimination causing "secondary line" competitive injury—discrimination which disadvantages a disfavored buyer in its competition with a favored buyer. 15 U.S.C. § 13. We deal with this subject in Chapter 4.

The Robinson–Patman Act prohibits price discrimination only where it may substantially lessen competition or lead to monopoly. Until the 1970s there was very little law examining the circumstances under which this condition would be met at the primary line. One important case, however, was *Utah Pie Company v. Continental Baking Company.* In 1957 Utah Pie pioneered frozen dessert pies in Salt Lake City; within a year, just before the alleged predations, it accounted for two-thirds of the frozen dessert pie sales in Salt Lake City. Beginning in 1958, its position was challenged by Continental Baking Company, Carnation Company and Pet Milk Company. These firms, all of which sold frozen dessert pies in other areas, charged selective low prices in the area newly dominated by Utah Pie. This price competition reduced Utah Pie's share to almost 45%, although Utah Pie constantly increased its sales volume and continued to make a profit. Utah Pie sued for treble damages and injunctive relief for violations of Section 2(a) of the Clayton Act. It proved that each of the defendants contributed to a "deteriorating price structure," and that each sold frozen pies in the Salt Lake area at lower prices than those it charged in places closer to its plants. There was evidence that the discriminatory sales were unprofitable to Continental, that its price "was less than its direct cost plus an allocation for overhead . . . ." Id. at 698.

The jury found for Utah Pie and the district court entered judgment on the verdict. The court of appeals reversed on the ground that the evidence did not support a finding of injury to competition. The Supreme Court reversed the appellate court. It stressed defendants' "predatory intent" to injure Utah Pie, gleaned from documents such as one by Pet's management which "identified Utah Pie as an 'unfavorable factor,' one which 'd[u]g holes in our operation' and posed a constant 'check' on Pet's performance in the Salt Lake City market." Id. at 697. The Court also noted that Continental made a price cut to a big buyer, Safeway, immediately after which Utah Pie made a deeper price cut. We include below the Court's discussion of competitive injury.

UTAH PIE CO. v. CONTINENTAL BAKING CO.
386 U.S. 685 (1967).

JUSTICE WHITE: . . . The jury could rationally have concluded that had Utah not lowered its price, Continental, which repeated its offer once, would have continued it, that Safeway would have continued to buy from Continental and that other buyers, large as well as small, would have followed suit. It could also have reasonably concluded that a competitor who is forced to reduce his price to a new all-time low in a market of declining prices will in time feel the financial pinch and will be a less effective competitive force.

. . . It is true that many of the primary line cases that have reached the courts have involved blatant predatory price discriminations employed with the hope of immediate destruction of a particular competitor. On

(Fox & Sullivan) Antitrust ACB—9

the question of injury to competition such cases present courts with no difficulty, for such pricing is clearly within the heart of the proscription of the Act. Courts and commentators alike have noted that the existence of predatory intent might bear on the likelihood of injury to competition. In this case there was some evidence of predatory intent with respect to each of these respondents.[14] There was also other evidence upon which the jury could rationally find the requisite injury to competition. The frozen pie market in Salt Lake City was highly competitive. At times Utah Pie was a leader in moving the general level of prices down, and at other times each of the respondents also bore responsibility for the downward pressure on the price structure. We believe that the Act reaches price discrimination that erodes competition as much as it does price discrimination that is intended to have immediate destructive impact. In this case, the evidence shows a drastically declining price structure which the jury could rationally attribute to continued or sporadic price discrimination. The jury was entitled to conclude that "the effect of such discrimination," by each of these respondents, "may be substantially to lessen competition . . . or to injure, destroy, or prevent competition with any person who either grants or knowingly receives the benefit of such discrimination. . . ." The statutory test is one that necessarily looks forward on the basis of proven conduct in the past. Proper application of that standard here requires reversal of the judgment of the Court of Appeals.

Questions and Comments

Suppose that Continental's pricing conduct is to be challenged as monopolization or an attempt to monopolize in violation of Section 2. Could geographically selective price reductions, allegedly aimed at doing (or threatening to do) injury to a smaller competitor, be evaluated under any of the formulations courts have used as norms for dominant firm conduct? Do you get adequate guidance from the rule of *Alcoa? United Shoe? Berkey–Kodak?* Is selective price-cutting different from other dominant firm conduct? Do we need a special rule focused solely on selective price cutting?

What is a "predatory intent"? Did Pet and Continental have a such an intent? How does a predatory intent differ from a competitive intent? Should intent matter? In evaluating predation should a court focus solely, or in part, on effect? Is there a difference between the effect caused by predatory pricing and that caused by aggressive, competitive pricing? Could a court, without considering either intent or effect, evaluate allegedly predatory pricing against objective norms that relate price to cost? Would you, as a consumer of frozen dessert pies, have preferred a different result in *Utah Pie?*

14. It might be argued that the respondents' conduct displayed only fierce competitive instincts. Actual intent to injure another competitor does not, however, fall into that category, and neither, when viewed in the context of the Robinson–Patman Act, do persistent sales below cost and radical price cuts themselves discriminatory. Nor does the fact that a local competitor has a major share of the market make him fair game for discriminatory price cutting free of Robinson–Patman Act proscriptions. "The Clayton Act proscription as to discrimination in price is not nullified merely because of a showing that the existing competition in a particular market had a major share of the sales of the product involved." . . .

The holding in *Utah Pie* caused some scholars and policy makers concern. They feared that the decision might dampen price competition. Eventually, as the predatory pricing cases of the 1970s began to emerge and to reach appellate courts, the law of predatory pricing began to change. The first changes were apparent in Section 2 cases. But these changes also affected construction of the Robinson–Patman Act. Although there is not complete synchronization between the legal tests imposed by the two acts, several appellate courts have now indicated that the standards for judging primary line Robinson–Patman offenses and Section 2 predatory pricing offenses require essentially the same analysis. In the one case the court determines whether competition is being lessened, in the other whether monopoly is being attempted or protected. See *O. Hommel Co. v. Ferro Corp.*, 659 F.2d 340 (3d Cir.1981), *cert. denied*, 455 U.S. 1017 (1982); cf. William Inglis & Sons Baking Co. v. ITT Continental Baking Co., Inc., 668 F.2d 1014, 1039–42 (9th Cir.1981), *cert. denied*, 459 U.S. 825 (1982); Henry v. Chloride, 809 F.2d 1334 (8th Cir. 1987).

b. *Recent Predatory Pricing and Predatory Design-Change Cases*

Changes in the law about predatory pricing were triggered mainly by private cases against IBM. The first case to be tried was brought by Telex, which, on the basis of IBM's allegedly predatory price cuts (never shown to have gone below IBM's costs) obtained a large judgment in 1975. About that time, Professors Philip Areeda and Donald Turner published an influential article, Predatory Pricing and Related Practices Under Section 2 of the Sherman Act, 88 Harv.L.Rev. 697 (1975). In that article (as amended in minor respects in Chapter 7C, Volume III, of the same authors' treatise, Antitrust Law (1978)), Areeda and Turner express the view that a firm, even a dominant one, is not likely to be able to outcompete an equally efficient rival by predatory pricing because the predator must itself take a lower return on every unit of the product that it sells during the predatory campaign. Indeed, because the dominant firm has a much larger market share than its victim, it will have to give up a great deal of revenue to force the rival to give up even a small amount. On this basis, the authors conclude that predatory pricing is not likely to be a rational profit maximizing strategy; therefore, it will rarely if ever actually be used. If it is used, the predator will probably learn rather quickly from the market that its conduct costs too much for what it yields, and will thus back off. Moreover, low pricing induces price competition and is normally good for consumers. Accordingly, the authors would err on the side of letting some predatory pricing slip through the net.

Areeda and Turner propose a legal rule based on these observations: (1) a short run profit-maximizing or loss-minimizing price is non-predatory, even though below short run average cost; (2) a price at or above reasonably anticipated short run marginal cost is non-predatory, even though below short run average cost and below the short run profit maximizing or loss minimizing level; (3) a price below reasonably anticipated short run marginal cost is predatory, unless (because the firm is producing at a level in excess of that which minimizes short run average cost) the price exceeds short run average cost; (4) where accounting records are not adequate to compute short run marginal cost, reasonably anticipated short run average variable cost may serve as a surrogate for short run marginal cost, unless (because of overcapacity) short run average variable cost is discernibly below short run marginal cost.[8] In such instances (since short run average variable cost can never be less than short run average (full) cost), the qualification in (3) falls out and the norm becomes: prices at or above reasonably anticipated short run average variable cost are non-predatory; those below that level are predatory.

This proposal has generated much discussion among legal scholars and economists, much of it emphasizing the limits of the proposed rule.[9]

Scherer, one of the first commentators, suggests that short run welfare maximization is the wrong baseline when the strategic goal of a pricing policy is to give up some immediate, short run profits in order to gain future monopoly returns. Scherer would look to long term welfare maximization. Scherer would seek to minimize the sum of current period losses and discounted future period losses. His analysis would take into account factors such as the relative cost positions of the monopolist and the fringe firms, the scale of entry needed for minimum cost, whether fringe firms are being driven out or merely suppressed, whether or not the monopolist expands its output to replace that of rivals driven out, and whether expansion by the monopolist yields investment in more efficient plant.

Posner is critical of the Areeda-Turner rule on generally similar grounds but proposes alternatively a two-pronged rule focused mainly on cost: (1) any price below short run marginal cost is predatory; (2) any price below long run marginal cost is predatory if done with the intent to exclude a competitor. Posner recognizes the measurement problems, as well as difficulties with intent analysis, but does not try to work them through, except to suggest "average balance sheet costs" as a substitute for long run marginal costs.

Williamson points out that the short run time frame of Areeda–Turner does not meet the temporal, strategic problem of predatory pricing. He stresses the insignificance of welfare gains from prices temporari-

8. Marginal cost is very difficult to ascertain. Average variable cost is much easier to ascertain and the authors claim that it is a relatively good proxy for marginal cost. Variable costs are costs that are not fixed. Average variable cost equals variable costs divided by all units made. The average variable cost curve is below marginal cost when marginal cost is falling; it intersects the marginal cost curve at its lowest point, and it is above marginal cost when marginal cost is rising.

9. See, e.g., Joskow & Klevorick, A Framework for Analyzing Predatory Policy, 89 Yale L.J. 213 (1979); Posner, Antitrust Law: An Economic Perspective 191–93 (1976); Baumol, Quasi–Permanence of Price Reductions: A Policy for Prevention of Predatory Pricing, 89 Yale L.J. 1, 8–10 (1979); Schmalensee, On the Use of Economic Models in Antitrust: The ReaLemon Case, 127 U.Pa.L.Rev. 994, 1018 (1979); Scherer, Predatory Pricing and Some Last Words on Predatory Pricing and the Sherman Act: A Comment, 89 Harv.L.Rev. 901 (1976) [hereinafter cited as Scherer, Some Last Words]; Williamson, Predatory Pricing: A Strategic Welfare Analysis, 87 Yale L.J. 284, 286–306 (1977) [hereinafter cited as Williamson, Predatory Pricing]; Brodley & Hay, Predatory Pricing: Competing Economic Theories and the Evolution of Legal Standards, 66 Cornell L.Rev. 738 (1981).

ly dropped to short run marginal cost to deter entry. He stresses that firms will make pre- and post-threat of entry responses to the governing rule, and that adoption of the Areeda–Turner rule would leave monopolists free to take supracompetitive returns both before and after entry is threatened. He designs a rule—concededly rather complex—that constrains post entry output decisions by the monopolist and that in his view has demonstrably better welfare effects than Areeda–Turner.

Despite the criticism, the Areeda–Turner rule has had a remarkable allure for courts,[10] presumably because of its seemingly self-executing simplicity. It had an effect on the *Telex* outcome on appeal and on several other IBM and non-IBM cases. The Supreme Court has not yet considered the Areeda–Turner test. It has twice in dicta indicated that a judgment about predation may be made, at least in part, on the basis of a comparison between price and cost. In Matsushita Electric Industrial Co. v. Zenith Radio Corp., 475 U.S. 574, 585 n. 8 (1986), the Court suggested that predatory pricing may require either "(i) pricing below the level necessary to sell their products, or (ii) pricing below some appropriate measure of cost." See page 468, infra. In Cargill v. Monfort of Colorado, 479 U.S. 104 (1986), the Court observed that "[m]ost commentators reserve the term predatory pricing for pricing below some measure of cost, although they differ on the appropriate measures." *Id.* at 117 n. 12. Despite this caution and disarray, institutional pressure for a simple test for predatory pricing has been intense. Indeed, some courts have converted the Areeda–Turner test into a legal rule.

Is predatory pricing a problem that compels courts to choose between one theoretical economic approach or another, and announce as law either a simple formula or a complex analysis that would be difficult for courts to apply? Could a court announce the law's norms in broader, more general terms, and let the economic debate work its way through the judicial system much as would any other debate among experts? How would you phrase such a legal test? Do you get guidance from Judge Hand in *Alcoa?* Judge Wyzanski in *United Shoe?* Judge Kaufman in *Berkey-Kodak?* Would intent have a role in your test? How about language like that we have used to describe predatory conduct in general, e.g.: Predatory conduct is conduct that a rational, profit maximizing firm would not undertake except to discourage entry, drive out competitors, force competitors to compete less aggressively, or otherwise reduce or inhibit competition.

Consider the relationship between price and non-price predation. Recently, Thomas Campbell published an article dealing with a particular kind of non-price predation in markets for differentiated products (specifically, a tactic whereby the dominant firm responds to entry by redesigning its product, or moving its geographic location, to be closer to the product or location of the entrant). Campbell, Predation and Competition in Antitrust: The Case of Nonfungible Goods, 87 Colum.L.Rev. 1625 (1987). Campbell shows that predation of this kind will not cost the

---

10. The judicial reactions to the Areeda–Turner approach are discussed in detail and with precision in Hurwitz & Kovacic, Judicial Analysis of Predation: The Emerging Trends, 35 Vand.L.Rev. 63 (1982). E.g., commentaries cited supra at note 9.

dominant firm as much as it costs the victim. Campbell observes that the reason the dominant firm engaging in price predation may incur greater costs than its rival is because it rarely will be able to price discriminate. To force the rival to reduce its prices the predator will normally have to reduce its own price on all the units it sells. A predator "which can identify precisely the customers of [its] . . . target and cut price only to them" would not face the market deterrent from predatory pricing upon which Areeda and Turner rely.

In the 1960s, IBM devised a tightly knit series of price and non-price strategies. In 1968, a competitor, Control Data, sued IBM for monopolization. In 1969, the United States sued IBM for monopolization. Thereafter, several other competitors brought suit. The background of the IBM cases has been summarized by one of the authors.

SULLIVAN, MONOPOLIZATION: CORPORATE STRATEGY, THE IBM CASES, AND THE TRANSFORMATION OF THE LAW
60 Texas L.Rev. 587, 599–604 (1982).

IBM is the world's largest computer company. In 1971, its sales totaled $8.273 billion and its after-tax earnings came to $1.079 billion. But while total sales and earnings were up, its share of the computer market—about 70%—was lower than in earlier years; in 1964, it had sold about 75% of all computer equipment.

Marketing was an important element in IBM's success. The company perceived its business not as selling equipment, but as providing "data-processing systems." It attempted to become the prime source of such equipment for most of its customers, and encouraged them to lease rather than to buy in an attempt to satisfy their capital requirements while offering them protection against obsolescence. This strategy facilitated trade-ins as bigger, better, and more costly systems were introduced. The new systems were appealing because they provided a better price-performance ratio, and they were profitable for IBM because customers used them more extensively as performance and quality improved and prices fell.

Initially, IBM rented hardware and provided software, service, and advice without additional charge. In the 1960s, under threat of antitrust prosecution, IBM began to charge separately for these items. It introduced a standard rental agreement that contained a basic monthly rental that covered use for a specified number of hours per week and an additional rental, which could run as high as 40% more, to cover additional time. IBM provided service on the rented equipment under a separate contract, the price of which also varied with use.

In 1964, IBM introduced its 360 Series, a new line of computer systems; by 1967, over fifty percent of the total value of IBM machines installed in the United States were 360 Series. The new Series provided major advantages over past systems. A computer system includes a central processing unit, where calculations and comparisons are made, information is stored, and such peripheral devices as printers, terminals, tape drives, and disk drives are kept.

A significant feature of the 360 Series was a "standard interface" and a wide range of peripheral devices that could be connected and used with (or were "plug-compatible" with) all 360 Series models.   Although the peripherals themselves were virtually unchanged from the equipment previously available, the standard interface allowed wider choice and greater flexibility because users could change from one central processing unit to another without a change in peripherals. As a customer's requirements changed, additional marketing opportunities were available for IBM.

As the number and value of 360 Series systems in the hands of customers (IBM's "installed base") grew, an increasingly large market for plug-compatible peripheral equipment developed.   IBM was originally the only supplier of this equipment, but in 1967 it began to encounter competition.   The original competitors were Management Assistance, Inc. (MAI) and Telex Corporation (Telex), which offered tape drives for use with IBM's 360 Series.   The MAI and Telex devices performed as well as or better than the IBM devices, yet could be rented at much lower prices.   IBM initially regarded its own strategy as sound, and in August 1968 it responded to the entry of MAI and Telex with only a small price reduction for tape drives.

When additional companies making devices plug-compatible with IBM computers (plug-compatible manufacturers or PCMs) entered the market and new product announcements accelerated, however, customer resistance to the use of non-IBM peripherals declined and PCM sales increased.   IBM had hardly altered its tape drive technology in over fifteen years, and the new entrants succeeded in mastering the technology and making improvements.   Although their costs were probably higher than IBM's, they nevertheless succeeded in earning satisfactory profits while renting at rates well below IBM's.   Before long, PCMs began introducing disk drives and were able to match or exceed IBM's performance at substantially lower prices.

Some time thereafter, IBM surveyed its lease installations and discovered that Telex and MAI had installed almost three thousand tape drives to IBM's more than fifty thousand, and that Telex, Memorex Corporation (Memorex), and one other firm had installed close to one thousand disk drives as compared to IBM's nearly sixty-five thousand.[71]   In February 1970 IBM designated this intrusion a "Key Corporate Strategic Issue" and directed the vice-president of IBM's Systems' Development Division to set up a task force to study the problem and recommend action.   IBM gathered and analyzed data about both the competitive posture of PCMs and IBM's own potential and designed competitive strategies calculated to alter the situation to IBM's advantage.   By engaging in strategic planning, IBM thus implemented management techniques (new at that time,

71.   D. Abell, Defining the Business: The Starting Point of Strategic Planning 35–36 (1980).   In October 1969, a study by the General Accounting Office of the federal government showed that comparable tape drives could be purchased from PCMs at 58% below IBM's prices and rented at 25% below IBM's prices; in addition, PCMs offered savings of 29% on all sales of disk drives and savings of 24% on rented disk drives. . . .

but common today) designed to influence the business environment in which antitrust norms must apply.

IBM's task force estimated that by 1973, PCMs would control 22.2% of the IBM tape drive market and 10.1% of the IBM disk drive market, and that by 1976 the corresponding figures would be 38% and 30%. The task force studied the structure, resources, and capacities of the PCMs and concluded that they were "viable enterprises" that could "achieve 25%–30% profit margins." Though the PCMs might encounter some difficulty raising needed capital, "financial barriers [would] not be significant enough to prevent the PCMs from growing." The task force also found that the PCMs had good marketing organizations and provided reliable on-site service, attractive delivery schedules, and "equal or better functional performance" at lower cost.

The task force recommended several steps to protect IBM's market. One was to transfer most data storage functions on the 370 Series (then in development) from tapes to disks, which would be harder for PCMs to duplicate; another was to cut prices on tape drives; a third was to place disk control units inside the central processing unit, repackage the unit, and sell this package at 30% below the aggregate cost of the individual units that the repackaged unit would replace. IBM's Management Review Committee, its highest policymaking body, rejected any straight price cut, but it accepted the repackaging proposal.

The PCMs reacted to IBM by introducing their own price cuts. Although the difference between the PCMs' prices for disk drives and IBM's remained much narrower than it had been before, and a similar series of moves in late 1970 reduced the price differential on tape drives, the PCMs continued to place tape drives and disk drives successfully. And these were not the only peripherals on which PCMs were making headway; PCMs offered printers and core memory with increasing success. Telex, for example, made a printer for use on 360 and 370 Series computers that was both faster and cheaper than IBM's unit.

IBM's strategic planning continued apace. In 1971, the Management Review Committee rejected a task force proposal for deep price cuts and, instead, called for a plan based on long-term leases. In June 1971 IBM announced the Fixed Term Plan (FTP), in which customers who forewent the thirty-day cancellation privilege on tape drives, disk drives, or printers were entitled to an 8% discount on one-year leases and a 16% discount on two-year leases. The FTP leases eliminated additional use charges as well. For the average customer, the effective discount on a two-year lease was 25% to 30%; for some, it was as high as 35%. IBM thus cut prices selectively and simultaneously reduced the time during which its products were vulnerable to competition from the PCMs. Consequently, as IBM introduced the new 370 Series computers, it frequently foreclosed PCMs from the opportunity for orders on peripherals for up to two years.

IBM's revenue reduction from FTP leases was projected to reach $31.5 million in 1971 and $44.1 million in 1972, but a month after announcing these reductions, IBM increased its prices on products not covered by the FTP and also raised its charges for service and maintenance. The net effect was that most customers paid IBM about the same amount as before implementation of the FTP; they paid less for products in areas in which PCMs competed, but more for products not subject to competition. Indeed, IBM analysts believed that there would be no net decrease in system costs and that the change in its volume would not be significant. IBM estimated, however, that the impact on PCMs would be adverse and substantial. Not surprisingly, concern developed in the capital markets about the viability of the PCMs in light of IBM's effective action, and the PCMs responded with their own long-term plans, which kept their prices below IBM's. Yet, despite their efforts to maintain at least a modest price differential, PCM tape drive sales fell 62% and disk drive sales fell 48%.

Notwithstanding declines in sales, the PCMs did not withdraw. They introduced technical improvements, such as automatic threading on tape drives and increases in the storage capacity of disk drives without expansion of their physical dimensions. Shortly after IBM announced the impending manufacture of its high-speed disk drive for the 370 Series in 1971, the PCMs announced competing products; indeed, a 1972 IBM study showed IBM to be deficient in quality when compared with the competition with respect to seven products, equal to the competition in four, and superior in only two. In light of the PCMs' technological superiority, IBM concluded that the FTP was not an adequate long-range strategy and that further changes were in order.

IBM effected a final series of moves, designated as its "SMASH program," in 1972. It cut prices on disk drives in order to "price below competitor costs" and shifted controllers into the central processing unit in order to "shield [these units] from competition" and force the PCMs to redesign their disk drives to interface with the inboard controller. Following in the wake of the steps already described, these new measures might have been successful and PCM competition countered at last, but Telex responded to SMASH by bringing suit. Subsequent developments would be determined by the courts.

At first the lawsuits did not go well for IBM. Control Data—a systems competitor who was a principal target of IBM and whose case was rumored to be a strong one—embarked upon large scale discovery against IBM. It developed an elaborate data base—a computerized index of 200,000 documents selected out of millions of documents produced by IBM and collected from numerous depositions and exhibits. The Control Data lawyers worked closely with the Department of Justice lawyers, regularly supplying them with information. Also putting IBM on the defensive, Telex, a principal target of IBM's blue-ribbon SMASH program, sued and proceeded to trial.

1973 was a year of victory and defeat for IBM. In January, IBM settled with Control Data and did so in a way that yielded a strategic advantage over the government. As part of the settlement Control Data destroyed the indices of its documents.[11] This greatly set back the work of the government attorneys, who had relied on Control Data's efforts. After the destruction was discovered, Control Data's attorneys defended their action on grounds that the data base was attorneys' work product and thus privileged. If you were attorney for Control Data and if IBM offered you an especially lucrative settlement in return for destruction of the data base, would you agree to do so? (You may assume that the law provides a work product privilege for attorneys' work). Suppose you were the judge and Control Data and IBM came before you with a settlement and a proposed order of dismissal. The settlement agreement contained Control Data's promise to destroy the data base.[12] Would you sign the order of dismissal?

There was a second major event in 1973; Telex won a $259.5 million judgment against IBM in the district court. 367 F.Supp. 258 (N.D.Okl. 1973). (IBM won a $22 million off-set against Telex on its counterclaim for copyright infringement.) The court held, among other things, that IBM's selective, targeted price cuts to levels below Telex's costs constituted predatory pricing even though the prices never went below IBM's own costs, because the strategy was specifically intended to ruin Telex (whose product had become better and—when IBM was pricing at its normal levels—cheaper than IBM's), and because the strategy was likely to ruin Telex.

Thereafter, however, the tide turned rather decidedly for IBM. Areeda and Turner published their predatory pricing article. The Tenth Circuit Court of Appeals reversed the *Telex* judgment on grounds, among others, that IBM was merely "engaging in the type of competition prevalent throughout the industry." 510 F.2d 894 (10th Cir.1975) (per curiam), *cert. dismissed,* 423 U.S. 802 (1975). Relying on concepts urged by Areeda and Turner, the appellate court held that IBM's prices could not have been predatory because they never went below IBM's costs. Id. at 926. Following this initial victory IBM won a series of cases. See Memorex Corp. v. IBM, 636 F.2d 1188 (9th Cir.1980) (per curiam), *cert. denied,* 452 U.S. 972 (1981); California Computer Products, Inc. v. IBM, 613 F.2d 727 (9th Cir.1979); Transamerica Computer Co. v. IBM, 698 F.2d 1377 (9th Cir. 1983), *cert. denied,* 464 U.S. 955 (1983). And when, in one case, IBM lost on a motion to dismiss, it settled. See Greyhound Computer Corp. v. IBM, 559 F.2d 488 (9th Cir.1977) *cert. denied,* 434 U.S. 1040 (1978).

Most of these IBM cases were based primarily on charges of predatory pricing and predatory product redesign. We first present here excerpts regarding product change from the district court opinion in *Transamerica* and on predatory pricing from the appellate court opinion in *Calcomp.* These are followed by excerpts—presenting a different approach—from the appellate court opinion in *Transamerica* and from the opinion in the government case against AT & T.

11. See Control Data Corp. v. IBM Corp., 1973–1 Trade Cas. (CCH) ¶ 74,363 (D.Minn. 1973).

12. In fact, this part of the agreement was not in writing. The judge signed the dismissal order on Saturday, January 13, 1973, and some time that weekend the attorneys destroyed the data base. If you assume that the judge was not told of the oral agreement to destroy the data base, does that alter your assessment of the ethical question?

In re IBM PERIPHERAL EDP DEVICES ANTITRUST LITIGATION

TRANSAMERICA COMPUTER CO. v. INTERNATIONAL BUSINESS MACHINES CORP.

481 F.Supp. 965 (N.D.Cal.1979), *aff'd,* 698 F.2d 1377 (9th Cir.)
cert. denied, 464 U.S. 955 (1983).

JUDGE SCHNACKE: . . .

DESIGN CONDUCT

It is not difficult to imagine situations where a monopolist could utilize the design of its own product to maintain market control or to gain a competitive advantage. For instance, the PCMs were only able to offer IBM's customers an alternative because they had duplicated the interface, the electrical connection between the IBM System/360 CPU and the IBM peripheral (or peripheral subsystem). Had IBM responded to the PCMs' inroads on its assumed monopoly by changing the System/360 interfaces with such frequency that PCMs would have been unable to attach and unable to economically adapt their peripherals to the ever-changing interface designs, and, if those interface changes had no purpose and effect other than the preclusion of PCM competition, this Court would not hesitate to find that such conduct was predatory. Or, if a monopolist frequently changed the teleprocessing interface by which its computers communicate with remote terminals in such a way that its terminals would continue to function while others would fail, and, if the only purpose and effect of the change was to gain a competitive advantage in the terminal market (where the monopolist lacked monopoly power), that use of monopoly power would be condemned.

It is more difficult to formulate a legal standard for design conduct than it is to imagine clearly illegal situations. Any such standard must properly balance a concern for the preservation of desirable incentives with the need to prevent monopolization by technology. Like pricing, equipment design can have pro-competitive as well as anti-competitive aspects. Truly new and innovative products are to be encouraged, and are an important part of the competitive process. For this reason, the acquisition or maintenance of monopoly power as a result of a superior product does not violate the Sherman Act. One court has even suggested that where there is a valid engineering dispute over a product's superiority the inquiry should end; the product is innovative and the design is legal. That view, probably the result of a concern for the creativity that has characterized the history of computers, is overprotective. It ignores the possibility that a superior product might be used as a vehicle for tying sales of other products, and would pronounce products superior even where the predominant evidence indicated they were not.

Another approach would be to examine the designers' intent. If a technological design were chosen for an illegal purpose (such as to effectuate a tie) and if that purpose was fulfilled, it would be illegal. If that standard were to apply only where the intent was solely an illegal one, creativity would not be stifled. But usually many results are intended, and if only one, even the predominating, intent is illegal, and thus punished, legitimate incentives will be imperiled. Discerning corporate intent is seldom easy, and, in any event, the law against monopolization is much more concerned with the effect of conduct rather than with its purpose.

A more generalized standard, one applicable to all types of otherwise legal conduct by a monopolist, and one recently adopted by the Ninth Circuit, must be applied to the technological design activity at issue here. If the design choice is unreasonably restrictive of competition, the monopolist's conduct violates the Sherman Act. This standard will allow the factfinder to consider the effects of the design on competitors; the effects of the design on consumers; the degree to which the design was the product of desirable technological creativity; and the monopolist's intent, since a contemporaneous evaluation by the actor should be helpful to the factfinder in determining the effects of a technological change.

A. *Interface Changes.*

The PCMs were engaged primarily in replacing only peripherals attached to IBM systems. To the extent that IBM could prevent (or make inordinately expensive) the physical attachment of such gear, it had the power to eliminate competition. Transamerica complains that this was what was done by interface changes made when the new products at issue here were designed.

The interface between the Aspen tape drives (3420 Models 3, 5 and 7) and the Aspen control unit (3803) differed significantly from the interface utilized by the immediate predecessor tapes (2420s) and control units (2803s). PCMs wishing to attach their 2420 copies to the new and improved control unit were effectively precluded from doing so. The cost of adapting a 2420 to the new interface format were prohibitive. Transamerica charges that the interface change was unnecessary, and that its only purpose and effect was to preclude PCM competition for tapes attachable to the 3803.

The evidence is to the contrary. Not only was the 3803 a superior product (as Transamerica concedes), the interface itself was a superior product. It had fewer wires and connectors. This meant switching between tapes and control units could be done more simply (fewer switch points), enabling IBM to integrate the switching mechanism into the control unit and thereby eliminate the need for a costly and bulky separate switching device. The pulses on the wires were multiplexed. That meant more sense information could be transmitted and diagnostics and maintenance were improved. Signals were converted from analog to digital at the tape head (rather than in the control unit), meaning information could be transmitted more reliably (with less noise interference). And, tape drives were attached to the 3803 radially (rather than serially), making maintenance and computer room layout easier. All of these changes required interface changes, and all were undeniably improvements.

Transamerica (which never owned any 2420s anyway) will not be heard to complain that it was somehow injured by an improved product.

The Aspen interface was just that. It was adopted by IBM because it was a product improvement, and even if its effect was to injure competitors, the antitrust laws do not contemplate relief in such situations.

* * *

A more complex problem is presented by the interface between the 2319A and the IFA. The IFA represented a different mode of peripheral attachment than had been utilized on most System/360 CPUs. Instead of a CPU to channel to control unit to peripheral attachment, the IFA resided in the CPU itself and attached directly to the peripheral device. That eliminated the need for control units and channels, saving the user space and money. The IFA, unquestionably a superior product, was an optional feature for sale or lease on the 145 and 135 System/370 CPUs.

From approximately 1969 until mid–1970, IBM's Endicott laboratory, responsible for the design of the 145, planned to design the IFA so that IBM 2314–type disks would attach with minor modifications. This was known as the Apricot plan. IBM's Hursley laboratory in England, responsible for the development of the 135, the sister to the 145 CPU, opposed this plan and, as early as 1968, and again in 1969, had proposed specifications for disk drives that were ultimately adopted by IBM in the summer of 1970 and announced as the 2319, code named Mallard. Under Apricot, a user could have attached IBM 2312s (one spindle), IBM 2318s (two spindles), or IBM 2313s (four spindles) in any combination. IBM 2314–type spindles would attach because the planned Apricot interface duplicated the interface between the 2314 control unit and the drives. PCM 2314–type drives would not have attached without modification to the Apricot IFA, but because the 2314 interface was well known, the PCMs could have quickly and easily duplicated that interface and made their drives available for attachment to the IFA. Primarily because of this exposure to PCM competition, IBM dropped Apricot and adopted the Mallard (2319A) plan.

With Mallard, one of the spindles was removed from the frame of a 2313. Into that vacant space IBM moved some of the control electronics that would have resided in the CPU under Apricot. The result was that the interface into the IFA was different under Mallard than under Apricot. And because it was different, and unknown to the PCMs, their efforts at copying the interface had to be delayed until they could examine the device IBM had produced.

With Mallard IBM bought itself some time. The interface change meant that PCM copies would not be available as quickly as if a known interface had been used. In a lease oriented market, where product obsolescence limits rental lives, time is money. If the PCMs could be sufficiently delayed, their market might even be limited to the point that the expense and trouble of duplicating the 2319A interface would no longer be worth it.

IBM's predominant intent in adopting the Mallard design was undoubtedly to preclude or delay PCM competition and gain a competitive advantage. However, other considerations also played a role. Mallard alleviated some difficult technical problems. It saved some space in the space-critical 135 CPU; it resulted in the location of a diagnostic device (the CE panel) near the drives where it was easier to use; it reduced cable lengths and electrical noise interference problems; and it simplified engineering control and record keeping for IBM by assuring that the engineers and the laboratories that were most familiar with the disk-related electronics would be responsible for them. On this record, the Mallard concept was a superior design.

Mallard's effect should also be considered. It appears the market segment affected by the 2319A was not something that held a great attraction for PCMs. The 2319A was expected to be an interim disk file for the 135 and the 145. Once IBM's 3330 became available, 2314–type devices would no longer be very attractive because the 3330's offered better performance at lower price. And during that interim, PCMs had their hands full supplying System/360 users with 2314–type disk drives and control units. These subsystems were more profitable for the PCMs (and therefore more attractive) than supplying only disk drives for attachment to the once-contemplated Apricot would have been. For instance, Telex had a backlog of orders for 2314–type subsystems that lasted until November of 1973, and thus, had little capacity or motivation to copy either the Apricot or Mallard interface in order to supply the less profitable drives. And, in any event, PCMs were not effectively precluded from competing for disk placements on the 135 and 145. Selector channels were available on the machines, and PCM subsystems attached without modification to those channels.

Mallard was a design adopted primarily to preclude PCM competition, but it was a superior design, and its effect on competition was negligible. A finding adverse to IBM on this aspect of its conduct would amount to a punishment for intent alone. This Court concludes that Mallard interface did not unreasonably restrict competition, and did not violate the Sherman Act.

B. *Price Differences Justified by Design Changes.*

Transamerica alleges that the Aspen and Mandan tapes, and the 2319s were in reality simply repackaged old devices, that the design changes that differentiated them from their predecessors were meaningless except insofar as they permitted IBM to continue to enjoy monopoly profits on its on-lease older equipment while meeting PCM competition with lower priced "new" machines. This price discrimination between users is, they say, entry barrier raising conduct of the type condemned in *United Shoe.*

The premise for this argument, the identity of products, is inapplicable to the Aspen tape drives. The Aspen 3420s were partly built from parts salvaged from 2420s, but over half of the 3420 parts were new. Conversion of a 2420 drive to the 3420 drive was impossible. And the changes made resulted in an improved product. Newer technology was used for the circuitry. A data format not available on the 2420 could be used on the 3420 (NRZI). And changes were made to enhance the reliability, availability and serviceability of the newer tapes. The Aspen tapes were different and better products than the 2420s, available to all customers, not price discrimination.

The differences between the 2314s and the 2319s were not as great. The functional characteristics (including reliability, availability, and serviceability) were identical. Packaging was different. The 2319s came only in three-spindle versions; prior to the 2319 announcements, no 2314s were available in three-spindle packages. Even if that is insufficient to conclude that different products are involved, the manner in which the 2319s were marketed refutes any allegations that they represented price discrimination. The 2319As were widely publicized and available to all customers whether or not PCM competition threatened. The same is true with the 2319Bs. Within one year of the announcement, IBM had placed over 20,000 2319B spindles, more than they predicted they would place. Users knew that the 2319B was a 2314–type device with a lower pre-spindle price, and they chose it in great numbers. No price discrimination was involved with the 2319s.

The 2319B price discrimination claim surfaced early in the trial, and IBM convincingly refuted it. Mandan was different. Both parties essentially ignored the alleged price discrimination aspect of Mandan. That was probably because Mandan was a relatively insignificant program; only 550 Mandan units were ever sold by IBM.

The Mandan 2401 Model 2 was a slow (75 inches per second) tape drive introduced by IBM in 1964. By 1970 IBM had a warehouse full of these older drives and 2803 controllers. To make them more competitive, IBM made the minimal interface changes already described, changed the name plates, and offered a seven-track only, Mandan subsystem (the 2401 Model 2 came in either seven or nine-track versions) at reduced prices. There is some evidence that IBM did not put its greatest marketing efforts into the Mandan program. But to conclude it was discriminatorily priced would require an inference from its poor market reception that it was only offered to customers if PCM competition threatened. That is an inference this Court will not make on the skimpy record before it. And, in any event, this Court previously endorsed a conclusive presumption that price manipulations resulting in prices greater than average cost were legal. Mandan's prices were above average cost and would have eliminated only less efficient competitors. Mandan did not unreasonably restrict competition, and did not violate the Sherman Act.

C. *Design Changes on the System/370 Models 115 and 125.*

The 115 and 125 were the smallest of IBM's fourth generation System/370 CPUs. Initially it was planned that an improved product, the 3340 disk drive, would attach natively to these machines through an IFA-type device. When it became apparent that the 3340 would not be ready at the time of the announcement of the 115 and 125, IBM planned to natively attach third generation disk drives (2314 types) as an interim disk solution. That plan did not last long. IBM realized that permitting third generation IBM equipment also meant permitting third generation PCM equipment, and that once users had third generation disk equipment installed, they would resist efforts to persuade them to migrate to IBM's fourth generation disks. The plans to natively attach third generation disk equipment on these machines were dropped in favor of fourth generation equipment.

Transamerica claims the failure to introduce a new CPU with native attachment capabilities for old disk equipment violates the Sherman Act. There is no doubt that the 115 and the 125 were superior products. Nor is there any doubt that the disks ultimately selected were superior products. Their data rates, access times, and capacity exceeded the performance available in third generation disks. This performance improvement was critical if the machines were to operate efficiently in a virtual mode, and a virtual operating system later became standard on both the 115 and the 125. Even if, as Transamerica suggests, the switch to newer and better disks was done to impact competition and occasioned some delay in the program, this Court would find that the introduction of an improved CPU with a superior disk natively attached did not violate the law.

At one time, the 115/125 plans called for a selector channel to be made available on these machines. A selector channel would have permitted attachment of all the higher speed devices that were attachable to selector channels on the older System/360 CPUs. But that meant IBM would be exposed to PCM competition from channel attached third generation tapes and disks, while trying to sell the natively attached fourth generation equipment. Primarily to preclude this competitive threat, IBM investigated the possibility of dropping the plans for a selector channel.

At that point it was determined that the selector channel had become superfluous. A different plan had already emerged to attach IBM's System 7 process control computers, and the IBM disks and tapes that would have attached to the selector, could be natively attached instead. The number of potential users of these systems that were already using systems with channel attached peripherals was insignificant. By far the greatest number of "migrator systems" were ones that did not have selector channels or peripherals that would attach to selectors. In short, IBM had no further need for the selector; its only function would have been to provide a means of PCM attachment. Eliminating it saved IBM time and development expense. The selector channel elimination did not unreasonably restrict competition.

The 115 and 125 also included a byte multiplexor channel for attaching slower speed devices. A byte multiplexor channel can operate in either byte mode or burst mode. If a multiplexor can operate in burst mode at the same speed at which a tape or disk peripheral can operate, it is possible to attach some relatively slow devices to it.

The byte multiplexor on the 115 and the 125 was initially planned to be able to transfer data at a rate of 50,000 characters per second (50KB). That would have permitted attachment of PCM copies of IBM's 2401 Model 1 and 2415 Model 6 tape drives which operated at 30,000 characters per second (30KB). When the head of the IBM's Computer Division called upon the engineer in charge of the 115 and 125 project to investigate the possibility of removing the selector channel, he also inquired about removing the multiplexor. The engineer's response was that while selector channel removal was feasible, multiplexor channel removal was not, but he would like "to investigate further the possibility of reducing the speed of the multiplexor channel and eliminating the possibility of attaching higher speed devices, e.g., 30KB magnetic tape."

When they were announced, the byte multiplexor on the 115 and the 125 were capable of operating at 29 thousand characters per second (29KB), just short of the speed that would have enabled the PCMs to attach. IBM's explanation is that an engineering problem caused by virtual storage operation caused the degradation. But there is no contemporaneous evidence of any such problem.

IBM degraded system performance, making its product less attractive to users. The only purpose served and the only effect of the degradation was the preclusion of competition. The law tolerates the perpetuation of a monopoly only where necessary to preserve competitive incentives and to avoid being unfair to the innocent monopolist. The law need not tolerate deliberate acts where the only purpose and effect is to use monopoly power to gain a competitive advantage. Slowing down the multiplexor on the 115 and 125 was unreasonably restrictive of competition and would have violated Section 2 of the Sherman Act if IBM had monopoly power.[109]

* * *

IBM did not lie dead in the water when faced with competition. It took action. And the action it took may have caused some competitors to suffer more than other actions would have. But the action IBM took, under the circumstances in which it acted, did not unreasonably restrict competition, and thus, did not violate the law.

———

The Court of Appeals for the Ninth Circuit affirmed Judge Schnacke's dismissal of the design change charges on grounds that the court's finding that Transamerica suffered no damages was not clearly erroneous. We include excerpts from the price predation portion of the appellate court's opinion below. But before we do, we present Judge Choy's approach to design predation.

CALIFORNIA COMPUTER PRODUCTS, INC. v. IBM CORP.

613 F.2d 727 (9th Cir.1979).

Judge Choy: . . .b. Design changes

As noted above, when IBM introduced its System 370 Model 145 in September, 1970, it announced the 2319A as the standard disk product for

---

109. It should be noted here that any finding this Court might make that the multiplexor degradation violated the Sherman Act would be accompanied by a finding that Transamerica suffered no injury as a result of that conduct. The market for the tapes excluded by this conduct was insignificant. Only tape drives with data rates between 30 and 50KB were affected. Those were older, low performance technology devices that would only have been competitive at prices far below those contemplated in Transamerica's damage claim. Transamerica probably owned some of them, but its President didn't know how many, and any Transamerica owned were purchased in the second Telex tape contract. Because that contract was not an arms-length transaction, this Court would be reluctant to award Transamerica any damages on the equipment purchased thereunder. Also, there is no evidence that Transamerica in the past supplied peripherals for the 115/125 migrator systems, or that it intended to, or took any steps to supply peripherals for the 115 and 125 systems.

use with the 145. The control function for the 2319A disk drive was integrated into the Model 145 CPU, and thus the interface between the disk drive and its control function was different from earlier models.[28] CalComp claimed that it was competitively disadvantaged as a result of these design changes, because it could not legally begin to copy the 2319A until IBM shipped the first of these disk drives, thereby disclosing the design requirements.

In February, 1971, IBM introduced its optional Integrated Storage Controller for use with its System 370 Models 158 and 168 which integrated the disk control function into the CPU. CalComp claimed it was injured by the introduction of ISC and the similar IFA, described above, because it was thereby precluded from replacing the control functions on CPUs with these options.[29]

CalComp characterized these design changes as "technological manipulation" which did not improve performance. It also complained of the fact that the newly integrated functions were priced below their non-integrated counterparts. But as we have stated, price and performance are inseparable parts of any competitive offering; and equivalent function at lower cost certainly represents a superior product from the buyer's point of view. The evidence at trial was uncontroverted that integration was a cost-saving step, consistent with industry trends, which enabled IBM effectively to reduce prices for equivalent functions. Moreover, there was substantial evidence as well that in the case of Models 145, 158 and 168 the integration of control and memory functions also represented a performance improvement.

One of CalComp's witnesses stated: "I think in general the manufacturer will try and minimize his costs and where he integrates the control unit the assumption must be that he is achieving a lower cost solution." [30] Other of CalComp's evidence showed that among the reasons a separate control unit is more expensive than integrated control circuitry are that the former requires its own cabinet, frames, power supply, additional cabling and electronics. According to an IBM witness, the monolithic systems technology that preceded the 145–2319A system required a large standalone controller, whereas the new generation technology represented by the 145–2319A system produced a comparable control function "which was in the area of ten times smaller. . . . [Y]ou could now put that into the 145 system, utilizing its frames and its covers and then passing on the advantages of that to the customer in a price reduction." CalComp's

---

28. Unlike the 2319A, the 2319B—introduced for use with all System 360 models—attached to IBM's 2314 stand-alone controller.

29. The System 370 Models 158 and 168 also featured substantial minimum memory integrated within the CPU. CalComp claimed that this redesign injured add-on memory manufacturers by making it impossible for them to compete for the integrated portion of these models' memories.

30. This same witness reported that the inclusion of a minimum memory capacity within the CPU was made possible by the reduction in memory size, "reflecting the product evolution from relatively large magnetic cores to high density semi-conductor packaging." He continued:

As the basic cycle speed of the memory increases, it becomes important to minimize the distance between components. It may well be impractical to keep the new memories external to the processor. . . .

Chairman stated that as a result of integration, the customer uses less floor space which "tends to be relatively expensive in a computer room."

IBM, assuming it was a monopolist, had the right to redesign its products to make them more attractive to buyers—whether by reason of lower manufacturing cost and price or improved performance. It was under no duty to help CalComp or other peripheral equipment manufacturers survive or expand. IBM need not have provided its rivals with disk products to examine and copy, nor have constricted its product development so as to facilitate sales of rival products. The reasonableness of IBM's conduct in this regard did not present a jury issue.

* * *

Compare Judge Schnacke's formulation of the law on predatory product change with that of Judge Choy. Compare both with Judge Kaufman's approach in *Berkey/Kodak,* supra at page 177. Which formulation is most likely to induce progressiveness and help consumers? Do you need more facts or empirical evidence to answer this question? If so, what would you like to know? If the progressiveness question is indeterminate (and perhaps even if it is not), what other values or goals would influence your formulation if you were judge? Is there any wise and workable role for fairness?

Let us now return to price.

TRANSAMERICA COMPUTER CO. v. IBM CORP.

698 F.2d 1377 (9th Cir.), cert. denied, 464 U.S. 955 (1983).

JUDGE PREGERSON: Appellant Transamerica Computer Company (Transamerica), a wholly owned subsidiary of Transamerica Corporation, alleges that Appellee International Business Machines (IBM) violated Section 2 of the Sherman Act when it took various actions to combat emerging competition in the "plug-compatible" peripherals market. The district court held that IBM's actions did not violate the antitrust laws.

On appeal, Transamerica challenges the district court's ruling that IBM's acts did not "unreasonably restrict" competition and, in particular, challenges the court's test for predatory pricing. We affirm the district court's decision but modify its test for predatory pricing.

* * *

PREDATORY PRICING

A. *The District Court's Findings*

In response to the challenge from the PCMs, IBM introduced several "new" products which actually were repackaged versions of existing products. The "new" products were priced below the older versions. Transamerica asserts that these lower prices were predatory.

The district court carefully examined these price cuts. It concluded that IBM expected the new products to "return substantial profits"; that, in fact, the products were profitable; and that the prices at issue exceeded the average total cost of producing the products. After an extensive analysis, the court concluded that IBM's pricing policy was legal.

The district court's finding that the challenged prices exceeded IBM's average cost is not clearly erroneous. The district court, however, applied an incorrect test in deciding whether such prices are predatory. We set out the correct test below, apply that test to this case, and conclude that IBM's pricing policy was legal.

B. The Economic and Legal Background

We differ with the district court on the proper analysis of situations where a defendant's prices are alleged to be predatory even though they exceed the defendant's average total cost. To analyze such situations, a preliminary discussion of economic terminology and legal precedents is helpful.

Predatory pricing occurs when a company that controls a substantial market share lowers its prices to drive out competition so that it can charge monopoly prices, and reap monopoly profits, at a later time. It can be difficult, however, to distinguish predatory price cuts intended to eliminate competition from legitimate price cuts designed to meet or beat competition. An influential attempt to clarify the distinction was made by Professors Phillip Areeda and Donald Turner, who proposed a "cost-based" test for predation.[4] Under such a test, the relation between the cost of producing a product and the price charged for it is the criterion for determining whether the price is predatory.

Economists, however, measure a firm's costs in a number of ways, and these measures are relevant in understanding the Areeda–Turner proposal and this court's reaction to it. Costs are divided into *fixed costs* (those that do not vary with changes in output) and *variable costs* (which do so vary). *Total cost* is the sum of fixed and variable costs. *Marginal cost* is the increment to total cost that results from producing an additional unit of output. *Average cost,* or *average total cost,* is obtained by dividing total cost by output. Likewise, *average variable cost* is the sum of all variable costs divided by output. Average cost is thus higher than average variable cost for all output levels.

Areeda and Turner suggest that prices be considered *per se* lawful (i.e., non-predatory) if they exceed the defendant's marginal cost or average variable cost,[6] and that prices be considered *per se* illegal (predatory) if they are below marginal or average variable cost.[7] The rationale for this cost-based *per se* test is the belief that a company that makes a profit, however small, on each additional product does so because it is efficient, and should not face antitrust challenges, whereas a company that loses money on the sale of an additional product is doing so presumably for anti-competitive reasons.

4. Areeda & Turner, *Predatory Pricing and Related Practices Under Section 2 of the Sherman Act,* 88 Harv.L.Rev. 697 (1975).

6. Areeda and Turner favor using marginal cost as "the economically sound division between acceptable, competitive behavior and 'below-cost' predation." Areeda & Turner, *supra,* note 4, at 716. They recognized, however, that marginal cost is usually difficult or impossible to compute and suggested using average variable cost—which is likely to approximate marginal cost—as a surrogate. *Id.* at 716–18.

7. Areeda and Turner make an exception where marginal cost exceeds average total cost. In this rare case, the price "floor" for permissible pricing is average total cost. Areeda & Turner, *supra,* note 4, at 713.

The Areeda–Turner test has provoked much judicial and academic comment.[8] This court has been influenced by the Areeda–Turner test without unqualifiedly embracing it. In a series of opinions during the three years preceding the district court's decision reviewed here, we approved the use of marginal or average variable cost in establishing predation without making that mode of proof exclusive, as Areeda and Turner advocate. Indeed, we adopted neither the Areeda–Turner test's conclusive presumption that prices above marginal or average variable cost are legal, nor its conclusive presumption that prices below that cut-off point are predatory.

The closest we were willing to move to the Areeda–Turner approach was to acknowledge that a "price set at or above marginal cost should not *ordinarily* form the basis for an antitrust violation." *Janich Bros., Inc. v. American Distilling Co.,* 570 F.2d [848,] 857 (9th Cir.1977) cert. denied, 439 U.S. 829 (1978) (footnote omitted) (emphasis added).

Any doubt that this circuit rejects the *per se* aspects of the Areeda–Turner test was dispelled in *William Inglis & Sons Baking Co. v. ITT Continental Baking Co., Inc.,* 668 F.2d 1014 (9th Cir.1981), *cert. denied,* 495 U.S. 825, (1982), decided after the district court's decision in the instant case. In *Inglis* we explained that prices are predatory when their justification rests, "not on their effectiveness in minimizing losses, but on their tendency to eliminate rivals and create a market structure enabling the seller to recoup his losses." *Id.* at 1035. We emphasized that this standard, "and not rigid adherence to a particular cost-based rule . . . must govern our analysis of alleged predatory pricing." *Id.* Yet *Inglis* did not, as Transamerica contends here, repudiate all cost-based tests. Rather, it laid down a cost-based test for allocating the burden of proof on the predation issue in place of one designed (like the Areeda–Turner test) to resolve that issue conclusively:

> [T]o establish predatory pricing a plaintiff must prove that the anticipated benefits of defendant's price depended on its tendency to discipline or eliminate competition and thereby enhance the firm's long-term ability to reap the benefits of monopoly power. If the defendant's prices were below average total cost but above average variable cost, the plaintiff bears the burden of showing defendant's pricing was predatory. If, however, the plaintiff proves that the defendant's prices were below average variable cost, the plaintiff has established a prima facie case of predatory pricing and the burden shifts to the defendant to prove that the

8. While no courts have explicitly adopted the Areeda–Turner test in its entirety for all cases, a number of courts have adopted elements of the Areeda–Turner test. . . . The Areeda–Turner test also generated a number of counter proposals for evaluating predatory pricing. Sullivan, for example, suggests that courts look to "human animus" in market conduct. He would focus on the "traces" a predator leaves behind, such as documents containing information about competitors. Sullivan, *Economics and More Humanistic Disciplines: What are the Sources of Wisdom for Antitrust?,* 127 U.Pa. L.Rev. 1214, 1229–30, 1232 (1977). . . . Williamson considers output a more important factor than cost or price. He would prohibit a monopolist confronted with a new competitor from increasing its output for twelve to eighteen months. This restraint would diminish as the entrant gained experience and economies of scale. Williamson, *Predatory Pricing,* 87 Yale L.J. 284 (1977).

prices were justified without regard to any anticipated destructive effect they might have on competitors.

Id. at 1035–36.

C.   The Treatment of Prices Above Average Total Cost

The *Inglis* test, quoted above, addresses only two categories of prices— those below average variable cost (which, under burden shifting, the defendant must prove are nonpredatory) and those above average variable cost but below average total cost (which the plaintiff has the burden of proving are predatory).   The *Inglis* test says nothing about how to evaluate prices for antitrust purposes that exceed average total cost. Indeed, *Inglis* explicitly left this question open.   668 F.2d at 1035 n. 30.

In the instant case, the district court, which did not have the benefit of *Inglis* and its clarification of our previous discussions of the Areeda– Turner test, held that prices above average total cost "should be conclusively presumed legal."   We disagree for several reasons.

First, this court has already recognized that prices exceeding average total cost might nevertheless be predatory in some circumstances.   The specific example we discussed was "limit pricing," in which a monopolist sets prices above average total cost but below the short-term profit- maximizing level so as to discourage new entrants and thereby maximize profits over the long run.   We explained that "limit pricing by a monopolist might, on a record which presented the issue, be held an impermissible predatory practice."   *CalComp,* 613 F.2d at 743.   A similar pricing strategy would be for a monopolist to make *temporary* reductions to a level above average total cost but below the profit-maximizing price whenever a new entrant appears ready to enter the market.   One or two such reductions could discourage potential entrants in a market that requires sizable initial investments, leaving the monopolist free to raise his prices to monopoly levels.   Such a pricing strategy, like limit pricing, could well be found predatory.[13]

Second, the district court's *per se* test rests on the notion that price reductions to average total cost result from efficient production and harm only less efficient competitors.   But companies may lower their prices for temporary strategic reasons as well.   One critic of the Areeda–Turner test points out that a monopolist can employ price strategies that jeopardize consumers' long-run welfare without lowering prices below average total cost and concludes that "it is unrealistic and even analytically wrong to apply a simple short-run price-cost rule for determining whether exclusionary pricing by a monopolist is socially undesirable and therefore predatory."   Scherer, *Predatory Pricing and the Sherman Act: A Comment,* 89 Harv.L.Rev. 869, 890 (1976).   It may be difficult in many or most instances to assess the long-run consequences of challenged pricing policies.   But where those difficulties can be overcome, the law should not prevent plaintiffs from proving antitrust violations.

---

13.   We do not mean to suggest that all pricing that is not profit maximizing in the short run is illegal.   As we stated in *Inglis,* prices below the level at which profit is maximized "may legitimately be justified on long-term considerations, as long as those do not include the anticipation of enhanced market power as a result of predation." *Inglis,* 668 F.2d at 1034 n. 29.

Third, the uncertainty and imprecision inherent in determining "costs" counsel against basing conclusive presumptions on the relation between prices and costs. Assessing those relations for the products of a multi-product firm requires allocating known and estimated costs and revenues among various products. While accounting problems do not warrant ignoring cost figures completely, they do make it unwise to rely *exclusively* on such figures.

Finally, we should hesitate to create a "free zone" in which monopolists can exploit their power without fear of scrutiny by the law. A rule based exclusively on cost forecloses consideration of other important factors, such as intent, market power, market structure, and long-run behavior in evaluating the predatory impact of a pricing decision.[15]

For these reasons, we disagree with the district court's conclusion that prices above average total cost should be legal *per se*. Rather, we believe that *Inglis* adopted the proper approach to the use of cost figures in determining whether prices are predatory: cost categories should be used to allocate the burden of proof on the issue of predation. By this approach, we give due weight to the economic considerations which suggest that prices are presumptively lawful if they exceed marginal or average variable cost and presumptively predatory if they do not. And, of course, this approach does not preclude a litigant from introducing evidence sufficient to overcome these presumptions. *Inglis* followed this approach in evaluating prices below average variable cost and prices between average variable cost and average total cost. The logic of the *Inglis* approach applies with equal force in evaluating prices above average total cost.

The test for determining the antitrust legality of prices that exceed average total cost should be consistent with the *Inglis* approach and with our view that cost-price relations should not be the exclusive method of proving predation. In addition, the test should be consistent with the economic analysis of Areeda and Turner. Their analysis indicates that prices above average total cost will rarely be predatory.[16] Therefore, it is appropriate to impose on the plaintiff a greater burden of proving that prices above average total cost are predatory than the burden imposed by *Inglis* to prove that prices between average variable and average total cost are predatory. We therefore hold that if the challenged prices exceed

15. The Seventh Circuit also recognizes the importance of considering non-price factors in evaluating whether a pricing policy is predatory. *Chillicothe Sand & Gravel Co. v. Martin Marietta Corp.,* 615 F.2d 427, 432 (7th Cir.1980); *see also MCI Communications Corp. v. American Tel. & Tel. Co.,* [ed. note: 708 F.2d 1081 (7th Cir.1983), *cert. denied,* 464 U.S. 891 (1983)]. *Cf. Pacific Eng'g & Prod. Co. v. Kerr–McGee Corp.,* 551 F.2d 790, 797 (10th Cir.), *cert. denied,* 434 U.S. 879 (1977).

This is also the position of the National Commission for the Review of Antitrust Laws and Procedures, Report to the President and the Attorney General (Jan. 22, 1979). The report recommends that the Sherman Act should be amended to provide that, although marginal cost should be considered in determining whether prices are predatory, a showing of pricing below marginal cost should not be a prerequisite to make out an attempt to monopolize based on pricing practices. Report to the President at 40.

16. Predatory pricing should not be countenanced merely because it would be difficult to detect in situations where price exceeds average total cost. *See Chillicothe Sand & Gravel Co. v. Martin Marietta Corp.,* 615 F.2d 427, 432 (9th [sic, 7th] Cir.1980) ("Section 2 of the Sherman Act makes no exceptions for cases involving administrative difficulty.").

average total cost, the plaintiff must prove by clear and convincing evidence—i.e., that it is highly probably true—that the defendant's pricing policy was predatory.

D.   The Proper Test Applied to This Case.

While we modify the test applied by the district court, we affirm the court's decision that IBM's pricing policy did not violate the antitrust laws.

The district court found that IBM's prices were above its average total cost. This finding was not clearly erroneous. Thus, to prevail on its claim of predatory pricing, Transamerica must prove by clear and convincing evidence that IBM's pricing policy unreasonably restricted competition. The exhaustive trial record, containing a plethora of evidence on pricing behavior, market structure, production costs, marketing strategies, and other related information, fails to provide any clear and convincing evidence of predatory pricing. Transamerica did not, for example, introduce evidence that IBM's prices rose once competition had left the market. The only price increases cited by Transamerica were modest increases in the mid–1970s. During that inflationary period, however, IBM increased prices on all its products, not just those involved in this case. Transamerica did not prove that IBM engaged in limit pricing. Transamerica simply introduced evidence of an initial price cut, hardly an unusual act in the computer industry or unusual in the face of competition. Transamerica's evidence of predatory pricing falls far short of the type of clear and convincing evidence that would permit the trier of fact to find predatory pricing when prices are above average total cost.

Judge Lucas concurred. He "disagree[d] with the court's modification of the trial court's test for predatory pricing" on grounds that pricing above total cost will rarely be anticompetitive; the court's rule could inhibit procompetitive low pricing; and it "may well increase the number of meritless antitrust actions."

Judge Lucas' approach is mirrored in Barry Wright Corp. v. ITT Grinnell Corp., 724 F.2d 227 (1st Cir.1983), wherein the court, by Judge Breyer, rejected the *Transamerica* rule and declared that a price that is above both incremental and total cost is per se lawful. Thus:

> In sum, we believe that such above-cost price cuts are typically sustainable; that they are normally desirable (particularly in concentrated industries); that the "disciplinary cut" is difficult to distinguish in practice; that it, in any event, primarily injures only higher cost competitors; that its presence may well be "wrongly" asserted in a host of cases involving legitimate competition; and that to allow its assertion threatens to "chill" highly desirable procompetitive price cutting. For these reasons, we believe that a precedent allowing this type of attack on prices that exceed both incremental and average costs would more likely interfere with the procompetitive aims of the antitrust laws than further them. Hence, we conclude that the Sherman Act does not make unlawful prices that exceed both incremental and average costs. 724 F.2d at 235–36.

Which court has the better of the argument, the Ninth Circuit or the First Circuit?

As the *IBM* cases progressed through the courts, so, too, did litigation against another putative monopolist, AT & T. You have already read other parts of the opinion by Judge Greene denying AT&T's motion to dismiss the government's monopolization case, supra, page 202. Here are excerpts from the part of that opinion dealing with the government's charge that AT & T engaged in predatory pricing in the private line service field when it began to encounter competition in that field.

UNITED STATES v. AMERICAN TELEPHONE & TELEGRAPH CO.

524 F.Supp. 1336 (S.D.N.Y.1981).

JUDGE GREENE: . . .

Intercity Pricing

The government has charged that defendants have priced their intercity services without regard to the cost of these services, on the following basis.[118]

Subsequent to the time the *Above 890,* the *MCI,* and the *Specialized Common Carriers* decisions were issued the Bell System has had to contend with competition in the intercity private line services field, but prior to 1978 no such competition was allowed in the provision of MTS- or WATS-type service. Under these circumstances, the government claims,

---

118. The evidence adduced on intercity pricing concerns various AT & T private line tariffs, as follows:

The Telpack tariff was implemented in 1961, at the same time that private microwave systems began developing after the FCC's *Above 890* decision. Telpak . . . provided discounted rates for customers using multiple channels. According to the government, the Telpak rates were based not on cost but on what AT & T believed to be the cost of building and operating a private microwave system. Although theoretically the tariff was designed to provide customers with multiple circuits between two given points, in reality such customers did not have to route even one private line circuit between those two endpoints. Telpak was thus entirely a "paper" network which allowed the Telpak customers to lower the costs of their private line needs. Moreover, because the incremental cost of additional circuits was minimal, customers had substantial incentives to satisfy all of their private line requirements through AT & T. The tariff expired by its own terms in May, 1981, after the Court of Appeals for this Circuit refused to review the objections raised by Telpak users who opposed the tariff's termination.

In 1969, while Telpak was the subject of an FCC inquiry, AT & T filed the Series 11,000 experimental tariff which permitted customers to lease specific networks within a seven-state area. The tariff was eliminated in 1972 after AT & T permitted the three-year experimental period to expire.

Another tariff in issue is AT & T's digital data service (DDS). In 1969, Datran applied to the FCC to develop a digital communications network through the use of a microwave system. In response to this competitive threat, AT & T began developing its own digital data transmission service. The DDS tariff rates were 40 percent below those proposed by Datran.

In 1974, the FCC approved AT & T's Hi/Lo tariff which replaced the nationwide averaged private line rates with a two-level rate structure. Under Hi/Lo, rates were lowered in areas with high density use and raised in areas with low density use. According to the government, Hi/Lo was a preemptive rate cut, to be put in place before the specialized carriers became entrenched, and it was not based on reliable cost studies. In 1976, the FCC declared the Hi/Lo tariff unlawful. As a result, AT & T filed the Multi–Schedule Private Line Tariff (MPL), but the FCC ultimately found that tariff, too, to be unlawful.

Bell had an incentive to set its prices high in the MTS and WATS areas (where it enjoyed a monopoly) and low in private line areas (where it was faced with competition) so as to exclude the existing competition and to deter further entry into the intercity services market.[119]

Bell accomplished its objective, according to the government, by deliberately pricing its intercity services without regard to their costs, with the objective of maintaining maximum flexibility for such cross-subsidization. Specifically, it is contended that Bell failed to calculate accurately the costs of providing intercity private line services or, to the extent that costs were calculated, to consider these costs in setting prices. From these failures, it is said, the Court may infer that Bell deliberately intended to exclude competition on the basis indicated.

Defendants' principal responses to the government's pricing claim are (1) that the government's pricing-without-regard-to-cost theory fails to meet the standards established for violations of the antitrust laws, is unsupported by legal precedent, and is meaningless under economic analysis, and (2) that, even if the charge is valid in principle, it is unsupported by evidence in the record. For ease of analysis, it is convenient to discuss these two defenses in inverse order.

A. [The evidence supports the government's charge.] . . .

B. With respect to the legal and economic underpinnings of the government's pricing case, defendants argue that the "only accepted test for predatory pricing is whether rates were intentionally set at a level below marginal costs" and that the government's failure to allege below-cost pricing therefore completely bars all of its pricing contentions. The Court will not sustain this argument at this juncture, for the following reasons.

In the first place, defendants overstate the extent to which the marginal cost test (or its surrogate, the average variable cost test), advanced by Areeda and Turner, in *Predatory Pricing and Related Practices Under Section 2 of the Sherman Act,* 88 Harv.L.Rev. 697 (1975), has become the sole legal standard for identifying non-compensatory pricing. Although courts have frequently incorporated these cost tests into their pricing analysis, they have done so with the clear understanding that the relationship between prices and marginal (or average variable) costs is not the sole criterion appropriately considered to distinguish predatory from competitive pricing. . . . Recent professional literature has likewise pointed to the fallacy of a mechanical application of a marginal or average variable cost test. See Williamson, *Predatory Pricing: A Strategic and Welfare Analysis,* 87 Yale L.J. 284 (1977); Scherer, *Predatory Pricing and the Sherman Act: A Comment,* 89 Harv.L.Rev. 869 (1976); Baumol, *Quasi-Permanence of Price Reductions: A Policy for Prevention of Predatory Pricing,* 89 Yale L.J. 1 (1979); Joskow & Klevorick, *A Framework for Analyzing Predatory Pricing Policy,* 89 Yale L.J. 213 (1979).

---

119. This opportunity to subsidize competitive services with revenues from monopoly profits in the markets in which competition was foreclosed was and is particularly tempting, it is said, because defendants are regulated primarily with respect to their overall rate of return (as distinguished from regulation of the individual return for each of the services they provide).

C. Furthermore, and perhaps more significantly, although economists disagree on the frequency with which the phenomenon of predatory pricing occurs, the conditions under which it is likely to exist, and the indicia by which it may be detected, there is consensus that the term refers to "the deliberate sacrifice of present revenues for the purpose of driving rivals out of the market and then recouping the losses through higher profits earned in the absence of competition." 3 Areeda & Turner, [Antitrust Law] ¶ 771b, at p. 151.

Whatever may be the appropriateness of the marginal (or the average variable) cost test in such a context, the pricing phenomenon that is challenged in this action is quite different. The government does not allege an intertemporal shift in profits—a sacrifice of profits in the short-run in return for more than their recoupment in the long-run—but an inter-service shift. Specifically, it is claimed that the Bell System has engaged in pricing practices which allow it to sacrifice profits from one service and to recoup the lost profits during the same period in another service. In such circumstances, a pricing-without-regard-to-cost approach is not necessarily inappropriate, for the opportunity which a multiproduct firm subject to rate of return regulation has to cross-subsidize low prices for one product across other products (rather than across time) renders it far more likely to engage in anticompetitive pricing than the firm that must wait to hope to recoup its losses. See Posner, *Natural Monopoly and its Regulation,* 21 Stan.L.Rev. 548, 615–16 (1969). Because the likelihood that anticompetitive pricing will occur in a particular context is a salient—and perhaps the critical—factor affecting the choice of a standard for the legality *vel non* of the pricing, this increased probability of anticompetitive pricing may alone be a sufficient reason to relax a standard such as the marginal cost test, whose use is predicated upon the assumption that such pricing is unlikely. See Joskow & Klevorick, *supra,* at 215; Easterbrook, *Predatory Strategies and Counterstrategies,* 48 U.Chi.L.Rev. 263, 265–318.

D. Defendants object that a pricing-without-regard-to-cost approach reverses normal procedure by imposing upon them the burden of proving that their pricing was reasonable. But such a conclusion would not necessarily be fatal to the government's theory, for a shifting of the burden of production of evidence may well be legitimate under certain circumstances.[135]

It is not necessary to decide that question, however, for the government's evidence is probative, at a minimum, on the issue of defendants' intent, and that is the purpose for which it is apparently being offered.

---

135. See Joskow & Klevorick, *supra* at 261. That burden might appropriately be placed upon defendants in this context because (1) the Bell System probably sustains a higher proportion of common costs than any other business entity and the proper allocation of such costs may be more intractable than any other firm's, (2) the Bell System's costs appear to have proved impervious to ascertainment and hence to analysis by outsiders including the FCC, and (3) Bell possesses the rare opportunity to exploit these factors because of the regulatory scheme and the coexistence of competitive and entry-restricted services. Where those unusual—possibly unique—circumstances prevail, it may not be unreasonable to require the party being accused of anticompetitive pricing to produce evidence which demonstrates that its pricing practices were not designed either to drive out its competitors (in areas where there was competition) or to prevent or discourage entry (in areas where such entry was legally feasible).

To consider pricing-without-regard-to-cost evidence on this basis would not shift the burden of persuasion to defendants; it would merely be a recognition that, given the circumstances of this case, the evidence is adequate to meet the government's initial burden of proving that defendants possessed anticompetitive intent. . . .

E. The government has presented, by its own admission, a novel approach. In response to the objection that its theory is unknown to either law or economics, it states in effect that the mapping of virgin territory is warranted by the uniqueness of the American Telephone & Telegraph Company, which is able to shift profits almost at will between monopoly and competitive services, and whose cost data are apparently impenetrable even to its own regulators. Although the government may not be able to rely upon direct legal precedent, it has presented persuasive theoretical underpinnings for its claim, and it has documented its allegations with extensive (if in places overly conclusory) testimonial and documentary evidence.

The Court may eventually conclude that only proof of predatory pricing in the sense in which that concept is employed in the *Northeastern Telephone Co.* [651 F.2d 76 (2d Cir.1981), *cert. denied,* 455 U.S. 943 (1982)] line of cases will suffice to support a charge of violation of the Sherman Act [137] (or even the intent element of such a charge). However, in an area as fraught with uncertainty as the complex intercity service pricing question at issue in this proceeding, it would be unwise to truncate the hearing of these issues at this point. . . .

_____

The government, having won round one in its case against AT & T,[13] proceeded to negotiate a settlement that would be heralded as the biggest break-up in American industrial history.

137. A principal purpose of the antitrust laws is to promote price competition. Any rule which restricts anyone (including a monopolist) from engaging in vigorous competition would deter the very action that is intended to be encouraged (see *Berkey Photo v. Eastman Kodak Co.,* 603 F.2d 263, 273 (2d Cir.1979), *cert. denied,* 444 U.S. 1093 (1980): *Schine Chain Theaters v. United States,* 334 U.S. 110, 120 (1948). For that reason, the courts must exercise great care in differentiating between legitimate price competition and predatory pricing. See *Janich Brothers, Inc. v. American Distilling Co., supra,* 570 F.2d at 856.

13. Of recent cases alleging monopolization or attempt by predatorily low prices, Judge Greene's district court opinion in *AT & T* and the ninth circuit opinion in *Transamerica* are among the ones most favorable to plaintiffs. Several cases stay closer to the Areeda–Turner line. For example, in Henry v. Chloride, Inc., 809 F.2d 1334, 1346 (8th Cir.1987), it was held that prices above average variable cost are pre-sumptively lawful, even if below full cost, and that prices below average variable cost are presumptively unlawful. Similarly, in D.E. Rogers Associates v. Gardner–Denver Co., 718 F.2d 1431 (6th Cir.1983), the court held that prices above average variable cost were presumptively non-predatory. The same court later implied that prices above full cost would be conclusively so. See Arthur S. Langenderfer, Inc. v. S.E. Johnson Co., 729 F.2d 1050, 1056 (6th Cir.1984), *cert. denied,* 469 U.S. 1036 (1984). There are, nevertheless, cases, that treat the literal, short run Areeda–Turner test critically when conditions seem particularly inapt for its use. For example, in MCI Communications Corp. v. AT & T, 708 F.2d 1081 (7th Cir.1983), *cert. denied,* 464 U.S. 891 (1983), the court rejected the Areeda–Turner rule in a situation where fixed costs were a relatively high percentage of total costs and variable (and marginal) costs were a relatively low percentage. The court recognized that in such a situation a price covering only variable (or marginal) cost could be predatory and

In its conduct of the *IBM* case, the government never achieved an efficient pace. Administrations changed, antitrust chiefs changed, the government litigation team changed, but IBM held constant. It had mustered its troups—solidly organized and hundreds strong [14]—and kept them effectively engaged. Discovery took six years and four months. Trial on liability took four years. Despite the uneven litigation strength, as discovery material accumulated, many observers thought that the government was "winning"; that the court would give judgment for the government. Then administrations changed once again and William Baxter became Assistant Attorney General in charge of Antitrust.

Baxter had never been enamoured of the government case against IBM. Indeed, he generally opposed monopolization suits against dominant firms (apart from the special situation of regulated monopolies like AT & T that engage also in nonregulated business, where he saw risks of cross-subsidization and resulting inefficiency). Baxter believed that monopoly suits induced successful firms to pull their punches rather than to compete aggressively and thereby tended to protect inefficient rivals from competition.[15]

On January 8, 1982 (the same day on which it announced the AT & T settlement), the Justice Department withdrew the government suit against IBM. A memo signed by the Acting Assistant Attorney General "at the direction of Assistant Attorney General Baxter in his absence" explained the stipulation to dismiss the action, as follows:

U.S. Department of Justice
Antitrust Division

Office of the Assistant Attorney General
Washington, D.C. 20530

January 6, 1982

Memorandum for the Attorney General
(Information Memorandum)

Re: *U.S. v. International Business Machines Corp.*

As you may be aware from my previous public comments, I have been devoting a substantial amount of time to reviewing our antitrust case against IBM, with a view toward becoming informed on the issues to a degree sufficient to allow me to supervise the case adequately. After numerous meetings and the review of voluminous materials prepared by

therefore adopted average long-run incremental (or marginal) cost as the proper standard. In U.S. Philips Corp. v. Windmere Corp., 861 F.2d 695 (Fed.Cir.1988), the court held that evidence "that a firm with 90 percent of a market that has substantial entry barriers drastically slashes its prices in response" to new entry is sufficient to show monopolization. See also McGahee v. Northern Propane Gas Co., 858 F.2d 1487, 1495–96 (11th Cir.1988), accepting full cost as an appropriate standard and describing the Areeda–Turner rule as being, like Venus de Milo, "much admired . . . but rarely embraced."

14. For an informative look at the IBM litigation from the point of view of IBM's attorneys, see J. Stewart, The Partners: Inside America's Most Powerful Law Firms 53–113 (1983).

15. See Baxter, How Government Cases Get Selected—Comments from Academe, 46 Antitrust L.J. 586 (1977); Report from Official Washington—Interview with William F. Baxter, 52 Antitrust L.J. 23, 27 (1983).

our trial staff, counsel for IBM, and others, I am convinced that the only responsible course open to the government is to seek IBM's agreement to a stipulation of dismissal of this action. I expect IBM to agree to that proposal and that I will file a stipulation of dismissal on Friday, January 8. Because you and the Deputy Attorney General are recused on this matter, this memorandum is for purposes of information only, to enable you to respond to such inquiries as may result from our actions. As I am sure you will understand, I request that you hold this information in confidence pending public disclosure, anticipated to occur sometime Friday morning.

The *IBM* case was filed on January 17, 1969. Now, 13 years later, the trial, which began in early 1975, is finally in its closing stages. Proposed findings of fact are scheduled to be filed on February 1, 1982. A decision cannot be expected from the district court until at least 1983 and possibly 1984. That decision will not even consider relief issues; they have been deferred pending submission of the liability case. If the government prevails with respect to liability, substantial additional litigation regarding relief would be necessary. Finally, if the court's decision on relief, as well as its decision on liability, is favorable to the government, IBM will certainly appeal, with unknown result. Thus, unless the government loses the case at some earlier point, it will be many years before the litigation ends.

My review of the case has involved numerous meetings and discussions and the consideration of voluminous written materials. In a series of seven meetings starting in September and concluding in December, Division staff attorneys and counsel for IBM met with me to explain their respective views of the evidence. Prior to each meeting in this series, the trial staff and IBM counsel submitted, and I have carefully reviewed, written materials supporting their positions. I have also reviewed written materials submitted by the trial staff as follow-up to those meetings. In addition, I have studied several extensive reports prepared by an internal Division task force, aided by several distinguished outside consultants. That task force was assigned to study the case during the Carter Administration for purposes very similar to those of my own review. I have also considered a response to the task force reports written by the trial staff.

In addition to the series of meetings referred to above, I have met with the trial staff, without IBM counsel present, to hear their views and to share with them my reactions to the various materials and presentations. I have also met to discuss various issues in the case with the members of the internal Division task force mentioned above, and with several senior Division officials who attended the meetings and who reviewed the same written materials as I.

Before explaining the basis for my decision in greater detail, I would emphasize two related aspects of the review process itself. First, the work of all involved has been of very high quality. The members of the trial staff, in particular, distinguished themselves by producing a vast amount of highly informative material under substantial time pressures. Second, and primarily as the result of the high quality of the work just described, I believe that I have fulfilled my original goal—to acquire familiarity with the case sufficient to supervise it adequately. While no decision of this nature is ever completely free of doubt, I am thoroughly convinced that I have considered all available courses of action, and that I have heard the most compelling arguments for and against each.

In reaching my conclusions concerning this case, I weighed the financial and social costs of continuing the litigation, the government's likelihood of success, and the potential benefits to be obtained if the government should win. Viewed in this way, these considerations lead almost inexorably to the conclusion that we must dismiss the case. There are many factors that compel this decision, but prominent among them are the following:

1. It may well be that IBM is a monopolist and controls some segment of the computer market. However, even if that were so, the government's case does not allege that IBM achieved that position illegally. Rather, the complaint alleges that IBM maintained a monopoly position lawfully achieved through a series of illegal actions ("bad acts") against its competitors. I have examined the merits of the government's case concerning IBM's "bad acts" and have concluded that, while several may have occurred in the manner and with the intent alleged, the most persuasive episodes concern computer systems that are not included within the market IBM is alleged to have monopolized. The company that was the target of IBM's actions in the most convincing episode, Control Data Corporation, received a substantial payment in settlement of its own lawsuit against IBM. Other allegations concern IBM's actions against manufacturers of peripheral equipment designed to operate with IBM systems. Most of these manufacturers sued on their own behalf, and all of them lost either at trial or at the appellate level.

2. Whatever the chances that the government will prevail at trial, the likelihood of success on appeal is small. The case would be appealed to the Second Circuit, which recently decided *Berkey.* In that opinion, the court defined the offense of monopolization in a manner which indicates it may be unreceptive to the theory of this case. As in *Berkey,* some of the allegations in this case involve efforts by a monopolist to make life difficult for its competitors through changes in its products. Also, the sheer length of the trial and the large number of pre-trial and trial rulings involved make it possible that there were errors at trial which may in themselves warrant reversal.

3. Finally, even assuming that the government could prove IBM's liability, there is no assurance that appropriate relief could be obtained. Where illegal acts have been proven, the purpose of relief is to remove the defendant's ability and incentive to engage in similar acts in the future. This can be done by injunction or divestiture, with courts expressing a preference to avoid structural relief where possible. *See, e.g., United States v. United Shoe Machinery Corp.,* 110 F.Supp. 295 (D.Mass.1953), *aff'd per curiam,* 374 U.S. 521 (1954); *United States v. General Electric Co.,* 115 F.Supp. 835 (D.N.J.1953). It could also be done by punitive sanctions in a criminal case. In addition, the United States could attempt

to recover any damages it may have suffered as a result of illegal behavior.

In this case, injunctions are likely to be ineffective. The conduct episodes that appear most promising as potential bases for liability are time-bound and highly specific to the immediate context in which they occurred. It is impossible to fashion injunctions to prevent similar future violations that are neither so specific that they would be meaningless outside those now-extinct circumstances, nor so general that they would simply echo the language of the antitrust laws themselves, which continue to be applicable to IBM in any event. Other conduct concerning manufacturers of IBM-compatible products might theoretically be ameliorated by injunctions. However, it is likely that such injunctions would be either so general as to be easily circumvented, or so stringent as to retard innovation in this technologically dynamic industry.

On the other hand, structural relief in this case would be totally disproportionate to the nature and scope of the violations that we might be able to prove. Moreover, despite years of effort, no structural relief proposal has been identified that would inject new competition into the industry while retaining the efficiencies necessary to create viable successor companies.

In my view, the most appropriate relief in cases of this nature may be to impose fines or other penalties commensurate with the gravity of any illegal behavior. Such relief could deter illegal conduct by punishing responsible individuals, and by depriving the perpetrator of some or all of the benefits from that behavior. However, the government here precluded the possibility of obtaining fines or incarceration of responsible individuals by pursuing a civil rather than a criminal action in 1969. Today the allegations would be time-barred.

Finally, while the United States could, as a theoretical matter, now seek to recover damages from IBM for any injury that it may have suffered as a result of illegal conduct, certain factors make this an unrealistic option at present. First, the difficulties already described in attaining a favorable adjudication of liability would also be encountered in establishing IBM's liability for damages. Second, insofar as the government alleges that IBM charged unlawfully low prices for its products, the government, as a purchaser of those products, may have benefitted. Finally, considering the length of time that has passed, the possibility of estimating any damage to the government with the requisite degree of accuracy is so remote, and the cost of doing so would be so great, that pursuit of damage claims would almost certainly result in no net benefit to the government.

For all the foregoing reasons, I have decided to dismiss the case. I have also considered two other options. First, I considered instructing the trial staff to pursue the case as they have been, or with some modifications suggested by me. Second, I considered approaching IBM counsel about settlement.

Pursuing this litigation would be the easiest and, in some respects, the least controversial course of action. I am convinced, however, that this is the least appropriate option. In my view, continuing the case would commit the government to years of additional litigation with little prospect of victory or meaningful remedy. The cost to the government of further litigation is expected to be between $1 million and $2 million per year for the foreseeable future. One cannot ignore the significance of these costs in the current fiscal climate.

Rather than continue the case, I could attempt instead to negotiate a settlement with IBM. While this option has many advantages over continued litigation, it presents some of the same problems. For the reasons discussed above, no appropriate injunctive or structural relief can be specified. Accordingly, it is difficult to identify the goals that we would seek in a settlement. Moreover, I am pessimistic that IBM would agree at this point to more than token measures. In negotiations conducted at the end of the Carter Administration, IBM demonstrated its reluctance to settle for structural and injunctive relief measures far short of those proposed in the course of this litigation by the government. While it might have been possible to negotiate a purely cosmetic settlement, to do so would not have been in the best interests of the public.

In sum, the government is not likely to win this case. Even if it did, there is no relief I could recommend in good conscience. I am convinced that continuing the case would be an expensive and ultimately futile endeavor. I cannot and would not wish to speak for those of my predecessors whose decisions to continue this litigation have brought us to this point. I am certain that they acted in the public interest based upon the best information then available. Based upon the information available to me, I can see only one responsible course of action: to terminate this litigation as rapidly as possible.

Abbott B. Lipsky, Jr.
Acting Assistant Attorney General Antitrust Division
at the direction of Assistant Attorney General Baxter in his absence.

———

Even as IBM was convincing the U.S. Antitrust Division that its strategies were procompetitive and that any government intervention against it would chill its inventiveness and kill the goose that laid the golden egg, authorities from the Commission for the European Economic Community (EEC) began expressing concern that IBM was abusing its dominant position in the Common Market, an offense prohibited by Article 86 of the Treaty of Rome. Baxter, America's antitrust enforcement official, tried to dissuade the EEC officials from commencing proceedings on grounds that IBM's conduct was procompetitive and that relief would have major extraterritorial effects, handicapping a successful U.S. firm in its world competition. These efforts failed and the EEC Commission commenced proceedings.[16]

The European Commission was concerned that IBM unreasonably excluded competitors from the market for peripheral equipment compatible with the IBM mainframe by bundling memory and mainframe and by announcing new equipment sometimes a year before shipment while

16. See EEC Commission Will Continue with Antitrust Case Against IBM, [Jan.– June] Antitrust & Trade Reg. Rep. (BNA) No. 1064, at 1030 (May 13, 1982).

failing to make the new interface configuration available to PCM competitors; the competitors had to wait until the new IBM equipment was on the market before they could examine the new interface and design compatible peripherals. Accordingly, the Commission proposed the following relief: (1) that IBM unbundle memory and mainframe, and (2) that, after IBM announces a design change on equipment to be sold in the Common Market, IBM must disclose the new configuration of the interface on request by users or competitors in the common market.

After several years of discovery, negotiation, and a brief hearing, the Commission entered into a settlement agreement with IBM. IBM agreed to unbundle (a practice it had discontinued when proceedings were brought), and it agreed to provide PCM makers and users with interface information (but not trade secrets) for a reasonable fee for all new products that are part of IBM System 370 and that are announced but not shipped within four months of the announcement. See IBM, EEC Settle, Both Claim Victory, Electronic News, Aug. 6, 1984.

Questions and Comments

The twin problems of predatory pricing and predatory product change are two of the most difficult problems in the current law of monopolization. On predatory pricing, consider the differences between Judge Schnacke, Judge Greene, Judge Choy, and Judge Breyer. Whose formulation is best for consumers and healthy competition in the middle to long run? What assumptions about markets influence your judgment? Would your choice of rule for predatory product change be more, less or equally permissive to defendant? Explain.

Suppose that a peripheral firm such as Telex makes a disk attachment that outperforms the similar attachment supplied by IBM. IBM decides to design a new interface that will make the competitor's disk incompatible with the IBM system for which it is designed.

Assume that IBM has monopoly power in the market for computer systems. Has IBM violated the law? What is its duty? To what extent does and should the violation depend on IBM's intent? On the effect of its conduct in the market place? On whether it would have been economically rational for IBM to plan and release the new design even if it did not set back competitors? On whether relief can be devised that will not chill incentives to invent?

Should it matter whether the competitors are only temporarily disadvantaged, and in a small way; or if competitors are forced from the market? IBM's strategy has made competitors' prospects so risky that potential entrants will choose not to enter? Note that credible threats of frequent interface changes by the dominant systems firm will tend to increase the costs of capital needed by new entrants into plug-compatible markets. Does that matter? Would it matter if there were convincing proof that the defendant carefully and methodically designed its product strategies to achieve these results?

What if IBM's intent was primarily to drive out competitors but that in the course of designing the new interface, IBM greatly improves the system by eliminating a problem that it had previously not solved. Does this justify IBM's conduct even though all competing manufacturers of compatible disks are seriously set back?

What if IBM's *only* intent was to improve its system; exclusion of competitors was a "mere" by-product. In retrospect, however, the improvement achieved is minor but the effect in excluding or setting back virtually all peripheral compatible competitors is great. Is there a violation? Should there be?

Suppose you were Deputy to the newly appointed Assistant Attorney General in Charge of Antitrust in 1981–1982. The IBM case, brought by a prior administration, was still pending. Your boss has said to you: I think IBM is a model progressive firm. I am afraid that continuation of our case against it will undermine the company's inventiveness and competitiveness. If we should win (and with Judge Edelstein as the judge we might well win), the Court of Appeals for the Second Circuit will reverse. This case cannot survive *Berkey–Kodak*. If the Court of Appeals does not reverse, the Supreme Court will reverse. And if I am wrong on all of those counts and Judge Edelstein grants relief to the government, that relief will set back IBM and the precedent will chill the competitiveness of all other progressive American firms. In other words, I believe that we should consent to a dismissal of this case. But before I state this view to the Attorney General or to IBM, I want you to be devil's advocate. Convince me that I am wrong.

Write a memorandum to the Assistant Attorney General. State the best plaintiff's position for (1) market power of IBM, (2) predatory pricing, predatory product change and other predatory strategies, and (3) relief that promises to be procompetitive. Be sure to state the legal standard you assert to be appropriate for predatory pricing and for predatory product change. Are you guided by efficiency only? By fairness?

After this exercise your boss asks you: Now, what do you recommend? What *do* you recommend?

Many books and articles have been written about the *IBM* cases and the legal problems involved in them. For a book supportive of IBM, see F. Fisher, Folded, Spindled and Mutilated: Economic Analysis and U.S. v. IBM (1983). For a book supportive of the case against IBM, see R.T. DeLamarter, Big Blue: IBM's Use and Abuse of Power (1986). For articles presenting theories about product change predation, see Ordover & Willig, An Economic Definition of Predation: Pricing and Product Innovation, 91 Yale L.J. 8 (1981) (authors concerned about product change predation); Sidak, Debunking Predatory Innovation, 83 Colum.L.Rev. 1121 (1983) (arguing that product change is virtually always good and should not be scrutinized), Ordover, Sykes & Willing, Predatory Systems Rivalry: A Reply, 83 Colum.L. Rev. 1150 (1983). See Campbell, Predation and Competition in Antitrust: The Case of Nonfungible Goods, 87 Colum.L.Rev. 1625 (1987), proposing a theory of predation where the dominant firm, through pricing, product change, disparagement, development of systems, brand proliferation, sham litigation and related strategies, diminishes the area of profitable return for competitors, squeezes out competitors, and makes entry unattractive. Campbell observes that several of the product innovation cases against IBM "*appear* to involve the symptoms described." Id. at 1657. (Emphasis in original).

The Campbell article invites one more observation. Most allegedly predatory strategies actually identified in the market place are not of a single kind. Firms do not attempt predation by product one year, and by price cuts the next. Competitive strategies tend to deal in a unified way with planning, design, production and marketing. When a broad antitrust norm is used, and especially when intent is identified as a relevant factor, the full range of defendant's conduct may be brought to bear in evaluating the purpose and probable effect of each part of defendant's strategy. See generally Sullivan, Monopolization: Corporate Strategy, the IBM Cases, and the Transformation of the Law, 60 Tex.L.Rev. 587 (1982), parts of which are quoted above.

4. DUTIES TO CONTINUE DEALING: VERTICAL INTEGRATION AND OTHER STRATEGIES THAT CHANGE THE PATTERN OF DISTRIBUTION

The *AT & T* cases, *Lorain Journal* and *Otter Tail* involved duty to deal issues. A set of related cases involves an asserted duty-to-continue dealing. We will deal with two situations: (1) a producer wishes to integrate forward, eliminating its independent distributors; the producer asserts that efficiencies will be achieved; and (2) a dominant seller, making no claim that the change will yield efficiencies, terminates a well-established pattern of cooperation with a competitor. We start with the case of vertical integration.

A firm that has a monopoly in the manufacture of a product and that sells at wholesale to independent distributors might decide to integrate forward to distribute its own product. As a by-product of doing so, it might terminate its former distributors and refuse to deal further with them. There are at least three Section 2 theories that might be used to challenge this conduct. (1) The integration or the refusal to deal is an attempt to monopolize the downstream market and thus a violation of Section 2. (2) The action does or may constitute monopolization in the upstream market through abuse of monopoly power in that market. (3) The action constitutes monopolizing the downstream market by leveraging power from the upstream market into the downstream market. (If the terminated distributors are the plaintiffs, does their standing depend on the choice of theory?)

Early cases seemed to hold that one or more of these theories for Section 2 liability were available. In Eastman Kodak Company v. Southern Photo Materials Company, 273 U.S. 359 (1927), Kodak acquired various independent film dealers in the Atlanta area. It tried to buy Southern Photo, but Southern Photo refused to sell its business to Kodak. Thereupon, Kodak ceased selling film to Southern Photo. Southern Photo sued. A jury found that Kodak's refusal to deal was in furtherance of its purpose to monopolize the distribution of film and was not undertaken for a legitimate business reason. The Supreme Court affirmed the judgment for Southern Photo.

The government's recent case against AT & T (settled by a consent decree that required separation of the local telephone monopolies and several private suits against AT & T (some won, some lost), all alleged that AT & T's obstructionism regarding long line competitors' requests to interconnect with BOCs violated Section 2. Also, remember *Otter Tail*, page 168 supra, dealing with a monopolist in the power generating and distribution field. Otter Tail controlled a scarce good. It refused to sell power at wholesale or to wheel power to municipalities whose residents it served at retail. It wanted to reserve the downstream market for itself. This was a violation.

All such cases could be explained in restrictive terms. Kodak may have raised the costs of its film competitors by depriving them of independent distributors; Otter Tail refused to sell or wheel power of the Bureau of Reclamation, preventing the competitor from reaching its would-be customers; and AT & T, not just a local market monopolist but a local market public utility, refused access to its long distance lines competitors. But the opinions in *Kodak* and *Otter Tail* both stress the problem of using power at the production level to monopolize the distribution level.

Recent lower court cases, however, are sympathetic towards forward-integrating monopolists. Some are newspaper cases: the publisher wants to terminate independents and do its own distributing. In these cases the outcome has been influenced by welfare economics based on neo-classical price theory and by a presumption that firms act efficiently, a style of analysis and an assumption that the DOJ has advanced in recent years. This mode of analysis (which would apply also, you should note, to newspaper distributor termination and to facts like those in *Otter Tail* or *Eastman Kodak*) focuses solely on effects on consumers. It proceeds like this:

If the upstream firm has a monopoly, it cannot increase its monopoly return by integrating forward into the distribution of its own (monopolized) product, unless (1) the integration raises barriers to entry or imposes costs on competitors in the market for the manufacture of the already monopolized good; [17] or (2) the integration helps the firm evade a government ceiling on prices in a regulated market; [18] or (3) the integration facilitates price discrimination, which may allow the monopoly firm to extract more consumer surplus even without lessening output. See F.M. Scherer, Industrial Market Structure and Economic Performance 302–06 (2d ed. 1980).

In other situations the downstream price to consumer after forward integration would not be expected to increase. Before integration, the profit maximizing monopolist would compute the profit maximizing monopoly price at the downstream level and then sell to the reseller at that price less the estimated cost to the reseller of efficient distribution. It would rely on competition or the constraint of limited demand at the distribution level to assure that distributors resold at their aggregate costs, which (added to the price the monopolist charged the distributor) would equal the profit maximizing price identified and aimed at by the monopolist. Integrating forward would not alter that price. After inte-

17. Southern Photo may have been such a case. If Kodak film is available only through Kodak dealers, if 90% of all film sold is Kodak brand film, and if independent dealers cannot afford to carry competitors' film without also carrying Kodak film, Kodak's film competitors would lose the only efficient distribution system for bringing their film to market.

18. For example, state government regulates the price of local telephone service.

When AT & T, parent of Western Electric, also owned the local telephone monopolies, the system could maximize profits by Western Electric's charging the local monopolies more than a competitive price for telecommunications hardware. The local monopoly could incorporate the overcharge as a cost in its rate base and pass it on to users of local service. The increment would have been disguised for the regulators as a cost of an input.

gration the monopolist would directly set the profit maximizing monopoly price at the downstream level; the full price would go to the monopolist which would now bear the cost of distribution. Assuming it could distribute as efficiently as the displaced downstream firms, its net, or monopoly return, would remain the same. Its return would increase only if it could distribute at lower cost than could the independents (and would go down if it incurred greater distribution costs than the independents).

If entry barriers were raised (the theory assumes that to be rare) the monopoly return would go up. If the integration enables the monopolist to evade price controls (as in the government's theory of the AT & T case), the monopoly return would go up. As to price discrimination, an integration might enable a monopolist to charge a higher price to buyers who value the product more highly.[19] This would also increase the monopoly return. However, the theory teaches that price discrimination does not usually cause a loss in "social welfare" (which is defined by the theory as the sum of consumer surplus and producer profits). It usually causes a gain in social welfare by leading to increased output which yields an increase in producer profits. As to consumer surplus there are a variety of effects: a stand-off for those consumers that buy the product but pay the same for it as if no discrimination took place; a gain for those consumers who obtain the product and who would have done without or paid more absent discrimination; and a loss for those who pay more for the product and who would have obtained it for less under a single price system. The net effect is, at least in general and probably in most specific cases, indeterminate.

We have thus far assumed that the upstream monopolist is displacing a competitive market of distributors by integrating forward. Suppose there is a downstream monopolist that is being displaced by the upstream firm's refusal to deal. Does that change the analysis? If there were two successive monopolies, one at each of two vertically adjacent stages (e.g., a monopolist for the generation of electric energy and a separate monopolist for its distribution) and if all relevant functions (the shape of the demand curve, the cost of efficient distribution, etc.) were known, then the joint profit maximizing monopoly downstream price would be determinable;

---

19. See United States v. Aluminum Co. of America, 148 F.2d 416, 437–38 (2d Cir.1945). Alcoa sold ingot and also fabricated rolled sheet and aluminum cable. It offered ingot at a price so high and rolled sheet and cable at a price so low that, the government charged, it squeezed out independents and monopolized the fabrication markets. The court found a violation with respect to rolled aluminum sheet since Alcoa could have returned a profit on sales of ingot to independent fabricators without setting the price of ingot so high. It found no violation with respect to cable because copper cable put such pressure on the price of aluminum cable that Alcoa could not have priced ingot low enough to allow a sufficient spread for cable fabricators to operate profitably.

In fact, Alcoa's integration into fabrication was probably a way to price discriminate. If the price of rolled sheet was not constrained by a near substitute, Alcoa could make a supracompetitive profit either on sales of rolled sheet or on sales of ingot for use in making rolled sheet, but only if it could avoid arbitrage. Since the price of aluminum cable was closely constrained by copper cable, Alcoa could make only a reasonable profit on sales of aluminum cable and, if it sold aluminum to other, competing cable fabricators, it would have to sell to them at cost. This was the rub. One would expect arbitrage. Buyers of aluminum for cable would buy more than they needed and resell it to sheet fabricators at a low price, undermining Alcoa's higher price to sheet fabricators. Alcoa therefore could make a higher profit overall by selling aluminum to sheet manufacturers at monopoly prices and fabricating the cable itself.

but there would be a bargaining game between the upstream and downstream firms to see how those profits were to be shared. If either firm miscalculated about the intentions of the other, stalemate might occur. Even without miscalculation, either one might profit by charging a little more than its bilateral monopolist's share, for its gain from the higher price might be more than its share of the loss. In other respects the analysis doesn't change. Vertical integration between the two monopolists, therefore, might increase social welfare by eliminating the bargaining uncertainties and strategic games between them.

In the end, welfare theorists generally conclude that except in the two rather rare situations (raising of barriers, as may have occurred in *Eastman Kodak,* and evasion of rate regulation, as may have occurred in *AT & T*), vertical integration by an upstream monopolist does not lessen social welfare and may increase it.

PASCHALL v. KANSAS CITY STAR CO.

727 F.2d 692 (8th Cir.), *cert. denied,* 469 U.S. 872 (1984).

JUDGE MCMILLIAN: . . .

I. FACTUAL BACKGROUND

. . . Star Co. owns the two major daily newspapers in Kansas City, Missouri—*The Kansas City Star* and *The Kansas City Times.* Star Co.'s road to dominance in the Kansas City market, however, was marred by a conviction for attempted and actual monopolization in violation of § 2 of the Sherman Act. Both newspapers historically were distributed by independent contract carriers who bought the newspapers at wholesale from Star Co. and then resold them to the public at varying retail prices. The retail prices for the newspapers are set by these contract carriers. . . . The wholesale price is set by Star Co. Originally the wholesale price was a set sum per delivered copy. . . .

Each contract carrier held a contract from the Star Co. which gave it the exclusive right to sell Star Co.'s newspapers along established routes. No contract carrier competed against any other contract carrier for retail business in any significant way. Instead, each contract carrier sold its newspapers only within its own territory or along its own route. Star Co., however, did reserve by contract the right to sell directly to subscribers if it felt that the contract carrier was not providing proper service. This right was exercised on at least one occasion and all of the contract carriers were acutely aware of the existence of Star Co.'s contractual right to compete at the retail level. . . .

In 1974, Star Co. informed the contract carriers by letter that in the future Star Co. might have to alter the way it distributed its two newspapers. This announcement so upset the contract carriers, all of whom had invested substantial sums in their routes, that it led one of them to bring this anti-trust lawsuit. Then, in 1977, Capital Cities Communications, Inc. (Capital Cities) acquired control over Star Co. through a stock tender offer. Shortly thereafter, Capital Cities announced that it would terminate all contract carriers and replace them with Star Co.'s own delivery agents, thereby enabling Star Co. to sell its two newspapers directly to readers. It was also announced that once the delivery agent system was in place, Star Co. would no longer sell its two newspapers at wholesale to anyone. According to Star Co., the delivery agent system would be a significant improvement over the contract carrier system because Star Co. could set an area-wide uniform price for its newspapers and provide readers with better, more responsive service. . . .

In response to these announcements, plaintiff-appellee Gweldon Paschall, along with approximately 250 other contract carriers, moved for and obtained a preliminary injunction against Star Co. barring it from implementing the delivery agent system. After a non-jury trial on the merits, the district court found that Star Co.'s planned vertical integration into delivery, coupled with its refusal to deal with the contract carriers, would violate § 2 of the Sherman Act because it would permit Star Co. to extend its monopoly in newspaper publishing into the retail newspaper market. The district court, therefore, permanently enjoined Star Co. from refusing to deal with the contract carriers or dealing with them in a discriminatory or predatory manner. On appeal a divided panel of this court affirmed the permanent injunction but reduced the district court's award of attorney fees to appellees to $2.5 million. On Star Co.'s petition, this court agreed to reconsider the case *en banc.*

II. § 2 OF THE SHERMAN ACT—MONOPOLIZATION

. . . We adopt the district court's finding of monopoly power because it is not clearly erroneous.

* * *

. . . [T]he central issue of this case is whether the combination of Star Co.'s vertical integration and refusal to deal has resulted in any *unreasonable* anticompetitive effects in the market. . . .

Two contrasting theories have been advanced in this case to provide a conceptual framework for ascertaining and analyzing the impact of Star Co.'s proposed change in its method of distribution. One theory, the potential competitor theory, has been relied upon to impose liability on Star Co. The other, the optimum monopoly price theory, has been used in defense.

1. Potential Competitor Theory

. . . It is said that a potential competitor, merely by its presence at the edge of the market, will have a retardant effect on price and will provide an incentive for better service among those already in the market. This is so because if the existing market competitors practice price gouging or provide inferior service, the potential competitor will enter the competitive fray with lower prices and better service, thereby capturing a substantial share of the market. . . .

The district court grafted this potential competitor theory onto § 2 of the Sherman Act and applied it to the facts of this case. . . . [A]lthough Star Co. had not competed in the retail newspaper market to any significant degree in the past, Star Co. nonetheless existed as a powerful competitive force in the retail newspaper market because it was a potential competitor. Star Co. reserved by contract the right to sell directly to subscribers if it felt that the contract carrier was not providing proper service. As an example . . . [i]n April of 1970, a contract carrier "arbitrarily" raised its retail subscription price for *The Star* to readers in an apartment complex. . . .   Many residents . . . complained. . . . Eventually, Star Co. delivered its newspapers at a lower price directly to . . . residents who requested direct delivery. . . .   Thus, according to the district court, the mere presence of Star Co. as a potential competitor in the retail market produced a substantial retardant effect on the contract carriers' prices and gave the contract carriers a significant incentive to provide the best service possible. . . .

The panel majority accepted the district court's potential competitor theory, but subjected the theory to a more rigorous and searching antitrust analysis. . . .   After a careful review of the record evidence, the panel majority concluded that

> the anticompetitive consequences of the Star's proposed refusal to deal . . . will likely outweigh any competitive benefits. The refusal will eliminate the Star as a potential competitor in the retail market, will likely result in higher prices and poorer services to readers, and will not lead to a more efficient delivery system. . . .

2. *Optimum Monopoly Price Theory*

The panel dissent championed the optimum monopoly price theory advanced by Star Co., the *amicus* [the Justice Department], and several leading antitrust economics scholars of the "Chicago school."   . . .

Under any given set of cost and demand curves for a product, there is one price at which a monopolist can maximize its profits. This price is determined by computing the quantity of product that is produced at the point where the monopolist's cost in making one more item (marginal cost) equals the revenue received from selling that additional item (marginal revenue). The price at which the public will buy all of that quantity, but no more (demand curve), will be the optimum monopoly price. If the monopolist charges more than this price, its profits will decline because the lost revenues from the reduced number of sales would more than offset the added revenue from the higher price. If the monopolist charges less, the added revenue from increased sales will not compensate for the reduced revenue per sale and the added marginal costs in producing that quantity. Thus, the monopolist's profit will be less than at the optimum monopoly price.

If the demand for the product is at all elastic, forward vertical integration may have substantial procompetitive effects in the form of lower prices and more efficient use of resources. Further, Star Co. points out that a large portion of its revenue comes from advertising. For that revenue Star Co. must compete with many other media and, quite significantly here, advertising revenues, in turn, are dependent upon circulation. The result is that Star Co. has a greater incentive than the contract carriers have to keep the retail price as low as possible in order to increase circulation. Star Co. contends that this need to increase circulation provides a greater retardant effect on prices than any influence it exerted in the market by its mere presence as a potential competitor. . . .

III. Evaluation of Anticompetitive Effects

Each of the above theories contains a certain amount of truth about the effect Star Co.'s proposed change in distribution will have on the retail newspaper market in the Kansas City area. . . .

It may well be true, as the panel majority opinion pointed out, that in certain circumstances a first level monopolist will desire to integrate forward even if it is less efficient than the second level entity. These situations include (1) price or service discrimination, (2) increased barriers to entry at the first level, and (3) evasion of government regulation of first level monopoly profits. . . . In the present case, these circumstances do not exist.

We are not unaware of certain record evidence of two possible anticompetitive effects of the delivery agent system: increased prices and reduced services. There is testimony which tends to show that Star Co. believed at the time of trial that it could not deliver newspapers more efficiently than the contract carriers and that any additional profits would have to come from increased revenues. Indeed, according to the panel majority, most Star Co. readers would pay more for their subscriptions under the announced delivery agent retail prices. While it may be true that many readers initially will have to pay more for their subscriptions, it is also true that many readers will pay less.

* * *

On balance, we agree with the panel dissent that appellees have not borne their burden as plaintiffs of proving that the procompetitive effects generated by optimum monopoly pricing and the unique nature of a newspaper's revenues are outweighed by the minimal anticompetitive effect of eliminating potential competition from the retail market. Moreover, we find it hard to ignore the fact that every other antitrust case brought against a newspaper publisher challenging the newspaper's decision to forwardly integrate into distribution has been resolved in favor of the newspaper. . . . Each case must be resolved on its own particular facts. In this case appellees have failed to prove that any anticompetitive effects that might result from Star Co.'s vertical integration and refusal to deal are unreasonable. Accordingly, we reverse the judgment of the district court, dissolve the permanent injunction, and vacate the award of attorney fees.

Questions and Comments

Paschall applied for certiorari. One of the authors of this casebook in an amicus brief in support of the petition argued, among other things, that the instructions were not in error, that the evidence warranted the finding for plaintiffs, but that the court of appeals had improperly replaced the district court findings with deductive generalizations drawn from Chicago school economics. It was also argued that, properly applied, economics showed that the integration resulted in inefficiencies because it removed the potential competition of the Kansas City Star; the potential competition had kept the independent distributors' rates down, whereas the integration enabled the Star, as distributor, to charge a single, often higher monopoly price, thus discriminating against the customers in densely-populated areas where per unit distribution costs were lower. The other author of this casebook is critical of this statement, arguing that if the Star had monopoly power it would take its monopoly profits one place or another; it did not gain power by deciding to distribute. What do you think of the argument? With three Justices noting that they would have granted it, the petition for certiorari was denied.

What factors or interests should determine the legality of vertical integration of a monopolist that replaces competing distributors? Freedom to deal of the downstream firms? Freedom to deal unless output is limited? Consumer interests (raising the economic questions posed in the petition for certiorari)? Fairness to the excluded distributors? To what extent is the issue one of law, to what extent fact? If the monopolization question goes to the jury, how should the district court formulate its instructions on the elements of monopolization? Is there a special rule for vertical integration by a monopolist or should we apply general norms, such as those expressed in *United Shoe Machinery,* or *Berkey–Kodak,* or one or another *IBM* case? If adequate instructions are given, should the court enter judgment not withstanding a verdict for plaintiffs if the judge is convinced, as a matter of deductive economic theory, that the integration did not reduce efficiency? Does it matter whether (as was the case in *Paschall*), the monopolist had originally attained its power by means that violated Section 2?

Is a jury competent to decide which distribution system is more efficient, that run by the Star, or that run by the independent distributors? Is a district judge? An appellate court? Should there be a presumption one way or the other? Based on what?

Variations are possible in cases of integration downstream by an upstream monopolist. Suppose the upstream monopolist first encourages the distributors to invest in distribution and then, shortly after they make the investment, eliminates them and takes over the downstream function causing capital losses to distributors. Has the monopolist acted unfairly? In the antitrust sense? Or did the distributors simply make a bad bargain when they failed to get contract protection? Would it be unfair to leave the distributors to state law remedies based on contract, misrepresentation or other common law concepts that might be relevant? See Photovest Corp. v. Fotomat Corp., 606 F.2d 704 (7th Cir.1979), *cert. denied,* 445 U.S. 917 (1980), in which defendant was held to have violated Section 2 by opening its own retail units in a market in which it had previously franchised plaintiff to operate. Suppose defendant does not terminate its distributors but makes its own retail investment in the same area. If the defendant's added retail capacity clearly exceeds what the market could profitably absorb, is its investment then "predatory"? Is it unfair? Is it anticompetitive?

Refusal to deal may also arise in the following form: a dominant firm may refuse to cooperate with a competitor. Remember *FTC v. du Pont,* supra p 195. That case implies that a monopolist need not aid its competitors; if it builds a better mouse trap it need not share the boon. Are there limits to that generalization? Is a single firm monopolist ever obliged to enter into joint marketing arrangements with a competitor? Not long ago, most commentators would have answered that question with an unqualified, "No." Then the Supreme Court decided *Aspen Skiing.*

ASPEN SKIING CO. v. ASPEN HIGHLANDS SKIING CORP.

472 U.S. 585 (1985).

JUSTICE STEVENS: In a private treble damages action, the jury found that petitioner Aspen Skiing Company (Ski Co.) had monopolized the market for downhill skiing services in Aspen, Colorado. The question presented is whether that finding is erroneous as a matter of law because it rests on an assumption that a firm with monopoly power has a duty to cooperate with its smaller rivals in a marketing arrangement in order to avoid violating § 2 of the Sherman Act.

I

Aspen is a destination ski resort with a reputation for "super powder," "a wide range of runs," and an "active night life," including "some of the best restaurants in North America." Between 1945 and 1960, private investors independently developed three major facilities for downhill skiing: Aspen Mountain (Ajax), Aspen Highlands (Highlands), and Buttermilk. A fourth mountain, Snowmass, opened in 1967.

The development of any major additional facilities is hindered by practical considerations and regulatory obstacles. The identification of appropriate topographical conditions for a new site and substantial financing are both essential. Most of the terrain in the vicinity of Aspen that is suitable for downhill skiing cannot be used for that purpose without the approval of the United States Forest Service. That approval is contingent, in part, on environmental concerns. Moreover, the county government must also approve the project, and in recent years it has followed a policy of limiting growth.

Between 1958 and 1964, three independent companies operated Ajax, Highlands, and Buttermilk. In the early years, each company offered its own day or half-day tickets for use of its mountain. In 1962, however, the three competitors also introduced an interchangeable ticket. The 6–day, all-Aspen ticket provided convenience to the vast majority of skiers who visited the resort for weekly periods, but preferred to remain flexible about what mountain they might ski each day during the visit. It also emphasized the unusual variety in ski mountains available in Aspen.

* * *

In 1964, Buttermilk was purchased by Ski Co., but the interchangeable ticket program continued. . . .

In the 1971–1972 season, the coupon booklets were discontinued and an "around the neck" all-Aspen ticket was developed. This refinement on the interchangeable ticket was advantageous to the skier, who no longer found it necessary to visit the ticket window every morning before gaining access to the slopes. Lift operators at Highlands monitored usage of the ticket in the 1971–1972 season by recording the ticket numbers of persons going onto the slopes of that mountain. Highlands officials periodically met with Ski Co. officials to review the figures recorded at Highlands, and to distribute revenues based on that count.

There was some concern that usage of the all-Aspen ticket should be monitored by a more scientific method than the one used in the 1971–1972 season. After a one-season absence, the 4–area ticket returned in the 1973–1974 season with a new method of allocating revenues based on usage. Like the 1971–1972 ticket, the 1973–1974 4–area ticket consisted of a badge worn around the skier's neck. Lift operators punched the ticket when the skier first sought access to the mountain each day. A random-sample survey was commissioned to determine how many skiers with the 4–area ticket used each mountain, and the parties allocated revenues from the ticket sales in accordance with the survey's results.

In the next four seasons, Ski Co. and Highlands used such surveys to allocate the revenues from the 4–area, 6–day ticket. Highlands' share of the revenues from the ticket was 17.5% in 1973–1974, 18.5% in 1974–1975, 16.8% in 1975–1976, and 13.2% in 1976–1977. During these four seasons, Ski Co. did not offer its own 3–area, multi-day ticket in competition with the all-Aspen ticket. By 1977, multi-area tickets accounted for nearly 35% the total market. Holders of multi-area passes also accounted for additional daily ticket sales to persons skiing with them.

. . . [F]or the 1977–1978 season, Ski Co. offered to continue the all-Aspen ticket only if Highlands would accept a 13.2% fixed share of the ticket's revenues.

* * *

In the 1970's the management of Ski Co. increasingly expressed their dislike for the all-Aspen ticket. They complained that a coupon method of monitoring usage was administratively cumbersome. They doubted the accuracy of the survey and decried the "appearance, deportment, [and] attitude" of the college students who were conducting it. In addition, Ski Co.'s President had expressed the view that the 4–area ticket was siphoning off revenues that could be recaptured by Ski Co. if the ticket was discontinued. In fact, Ski Co. had reinstated its 3–area, 6–day ticket during the 1977–1978 season, but that ticket had been outsold by the 4–area, 6–day ticket nearly two to one.

In March 1978, the Ski Co. management recommended to the Board of Directors that the 4–area ticket be discontinued for the 1978–1979 season. The Board decided to offer Highlands a 4–area ticket provided that Highlands would agree to receive a 12.5% fixed percentage of the revenue—considerably below Highland's historical average based on usage. Later in the 1978–1979 season, a member of Ski Co.'s Board of Directors candidly informed a Highland's official that he had advocated making Highlands "an offer that [it] could not accept."

Finding the proposal unacceptable, Highlands suggested a distribution of the revenues based on usage to be monitored by coupons, electronic counting or random sample surveys. If Ski Co. was concerned about who was to conduct the survey, Highlands proposed to hire disinterested ticket counters at its own expense—"somebody like Price Waterhouse"—to count or survey usage of the 4–area ticket at Highlands. Ski Co. refused to consider any counterproposals, and Highlands finally rejected the offer of the fixed percentage.

As far as Ski Co. was concerned, the all-Aspen ticket was dead. In its place Ski Co. offered the 3–area, 6–day ticket featuring only its mountains. In an effort to promote this ticket, Ski Co. embarked on a national advertising campaign that strongly implied to people who were unfamiliar with Aspen that Ajax, Buttermilk, and Snowmass were the only ski mountains in the area. For example, Ski Co. had a sign changed in the Aspen Airways waiting room at Stapleton Airport in Denver. The old sign had a picture of the four mountains in Aspen touting "Four Big Mountains" whereas the new sign retained the picture but referred only to three.

Ski Co. took additional actions that made it extremely difficult for Highlands to market its own multi-area package to replace the joint offering. Ski Co. discontinued the 3–day, 3–area pass for the 1978–1979 season,[13] and also refused to sell Highlands any lift tickets, either at the tour operator's discount or at retail.[14] Highlands finally developed an alternative product, the "Adventure Pack," which consisted of a 3–day pass at Highlands and three vouchers, each equal to the price of a daily lift ticket at a Ski Co. mountain. The vouchers were guaranteed by funds on deposit in an Aspen bank, and were redeemed by Aspen merchants at full value. Ski Co., however, refused to accept them.

Later, Highlands redesigned the Adventure Pack to contain American Express Traveler's Checks or money orders instead of vouchers. Ski Co. eventually accepted these negotiable instruments in exchange for daily lift tickets.[15] Despite some strengths of the product, the Adventure Pack met considerable resistance from tour operators and consumers who had grown accustomed to the convenience and flexibility provided by the all-Aspen ticket.

Without a convenient all-Aspen ticket, Highlands basically "becomes a day ski area in a destination resort." Highlands' share of the market for downhill skiing services in Aspen declined steadily after the 4–area ticket based on usage was abolished in 1977: from 20.5% in 1976–1977, to 15.7% in 1977–1978, to 13.1% in 1978–1979, to 12.5% in 1979–1980, to 11% in 1980–1981. Highlands' revenues from associated skiing services

13. Highlands' owner explained that there was a key difference between the 3–day, 3–area ticket and the 6–day, 3–area ticket: "with the three day ticket, a person could ski on the . . . Aspen Skiing Corporation mountains for three days and then there would be three days in which he could ski on our mountain; but with the six-day ticket, we are absolutely locked out of those people." As a result of "tremendous consumer demand" for a 3–day ticket, Ski Co. reinstated it late in the 1978–1979 season, but without publicity or a discount off the daily rate.

14. In the 1977–1978 negotiations, Ski Co. previously had refused to consider the sale of any tickets to Highlands noting that it was "obviously not interested in helping sell" a package competitive with the 3–area ticket. Later, in the 1978–1979 negotiations,

Ski Co.'s Vice President of Finance told a Highlands official that "We will not have anything to do with a four-area ticket sponsored by the Aspen Highlands Skiing Corporation." When the Highlands official inquired why Ski Co. was taking this position considering that Highlands was willing to pay full retail value for the daily lift tickets, the Ski Co. official answered tersely: "we will not support our competition."

15. Of course, there was nothing to identify Highlands as the source of these instruments, unless someone saw the skier "taking it out of an Adventure Pack envelope." For the 1981–1982 season, Ski Co. set its single ticket price at $22 and discounted the 3–area, 6–day ticket to $114. According to Highlands, this price structure made the Adventure Pack unprofitable.

like the ski school, ski rentals, amateur racing events, and restaurant facilities declined sharply as well.

II

In 1979, Highlands filed a complaint in the United States District Court for the District of Colorado naming Ski Co. as a defendant. Among various claims, the complaint alleged that Ski Co. had monopolized the market for downhill skiing services at Aspen in violation of § 2 of the Sherman Act, and prayed for treble damages. The case was tried to a jury which rendered a verdict finding Ski Co. guilty of the § 2 violation and calculating Highlands' actual damages at $2.5 million.

In her instructions to the jury, the District Judge explained that the offense of monopolization under § 2 of the Sherman Act has two elements: (1) the possession of monopoly power in a relevant market, and (2) the willful acquisition, maintenance, or use of that power by anticompetitive or exclusionary means or for anticompetitive or exclusionary purposes. . . . Ski Co. does not challenge the jury's special verdict finding that it possessed monopoly power.[20] Nor does Ski Co. criticize the trial court's instructions to the jury concerning the second element of the § 2 offense.

On this element, the jury was instructed that it had to consider whether "Aspen Skiing Corporation willfully acquired, maintained, or used that power by anti-competitive or exclusionary means or for anti-competitive or exclusionary purposes." The instructions elaborated:

"In considering whether the means or purposes were anti-competitive or exclusionary, you must draw a distinction here between practices which tend to exclude or restrict competition on the one hand and the success of a business which reflects only a superior product, a well-run business, or luck, on the other. The line between legitimately gained monopoly, its proper use and maintenance, and improper conduct has been described in various ways. It has been said that obtaining or maintaining monopoly power cannot represent monopolization if the power was gained and maintained by conduct that was honestly industrial. Or it is said that monopoly power which is thrust upon a firm due to its superior business ability and efficiency does not constitute monopolization.

"For example, a firm that has lawfully acquired a monopoly position is not barred from taking advantage of scale economies by constructing a large and efficient factory. These benefits are a consequence of size and not an exercise of monopoly power. Nor is a corporation which possesses monopoly power under a duty to cooperate with its business rivals. Also a company which possesses monopoly power and which refuses to enter into a joint operating agreement with a competitor or otherwise refuses to deal with a competitor in some manner does not violate Section 2 if valid business reasons exist for that refusal.

20. The jury found that the relevant product market was "[d]ownhill skiing at destination ski resorts," that the "Aspen area" was a relevant geographic submarket, and that during the years 1977–1981, Ski Co. possessed monopoly power, defined as the power to control prices in the relevant market or to exclude competitors.

"In other words, if there were legitimate business reasons for the refusal, then the defendant, even if he is found to possess monopoly power in a relevant market, has not violated the law. We are concerned with conduct which unnecessarily excludes or handicaps competitors. This is conduct which does not benefit consumers by making a better product or service available—or in other ways—and instead has the effect of impairing competition. . . ."

The jury answered a specific interrogatory finding the second element of the offense as defined in these instructions.

Ski Co. filed a motion for judgment notwithstanding the verdict, contending that the evidence was insufficient to support a § 2 violation as a matter of law. In support of that motion, Ski Co. incorporated the arguments that it had advanced in support of its motion for a directed verdict, at which time it had primarily contested the sufficiency of the evidence on the issue of monopoly power. Counsel had, however, in the course of the argument at that time, stated: "Now, we also think, Judge, that there clearly cannot be a requirement of cooperation between competitors." The District Court denied Ski Co.'s motion and entered a judgment awarding Highlands treble damages of $7,500,000, costs and attorney's fees.

The Court of Appeals affirmed in all respects. . . .

* * *

III

* * *

. . . Ski Co. . . . is surely correct in submitting that even a firm with monopoly power has no general duty to engage in a joint marketing program with a competitor. Ski Co. is quite wrong, however, in suggesting that the judgment in this case rests on any such proposition of law. For the trial court unambiguously instructed the jury that a firm possessing monopoly power has no duty to cooperate with its business rivals.

The absence of an unqualified duty to cooperate does not mean that every time a firm declines to participate in a particular cooperative venture, that decision may not have evidentiary significance, or that it may not give rise to liability in certain circumstances. The absence of a duty to transact business with another firm is, in some respects, merely the counterpart of the independent businessman's cherished right to select his customers and his associates. The high value that we have placed on the right to refuse to deal with other firms does not mean that the right is unqualified.

In *Lorain Journal v. United States,* 342 U.S. 143 (1951), we squarely held that this right was not unqualified. Between 1933 and 1948 the publisher of the Lorain Journal, a newspaper, was the only local business disseminating news and advertising in that Ohio town. In 1948, a small radio station was established in a nearby community. In an effort to destroy its small competitor, and thereby regain its "pre–1948 substantial monopoly over the mass dissemination of all news and advertising," the Journal refused to sell advertising to persons that patronized the radio station.

. . . The Court [held that the refusal to sell violated Section 2 and] approved the entry of an injunction ordering the Journal to print the advertisements of the customers of its small competitor.

In *Lorain Journal,* the violation of § 2 was an "attempt to monopolize," rather than monopolization, but the question of intent is relevant to both offenses. In the former case it is necessary to prove a "specific intent" to accomplish the forbidden objective—as Judge Hand explained, "an intent which goes beyond the mere intent to do the act." *United States v. Aluminum Co. of America,* 148 F.2d 416, 432 (CA2 1945). In the latter case evidence of intent is merely relevant to the question whether the challenged conduct is fairly characterized as "exclusionary" or "anticompetitive"—to use the words in the trial court's instructions—or "predatory," to use a word that scholars seem to favor. Whichever label is used, there is agreement on the proposition that "no monopolist monopolizes unconscious of what he is doing." As Judge Bork stated more recently: "Improper exclusion (exclusion not the result of superior efficiency) is always deliberately intended." [29]

The qualification on the right of a monopolist to deal with whom he pleases is not so narrow that it encompasses no more than the circumstances of *Lorain Journal.* In the actual case that we must decide, the monopolist did not merely reject a novel offer to participate in a cooperative venture that had been proposed by a competitor. Rather, the monopolist elected to make an important change in a pattern of distribution that had originated in a competitive market and had persisted for several years. The all-Aspen, 6–day ticket with revenues allocated on the basis of usage was first developed when three independent companies operated three different ski mountains in the Aspen area. It continued to provide a desirable option for skiers when the market was enlarged to include four mountains, and when the character of the market was changed by Ski Co.'s acquisition of monopoly power. Moreover, since the record discloses that interchangeable tickets are used in other multi-mountain areas which apparently are competitive, it seems appropriate to infer that such tickets satisfy consumer demand in free competitive markets.

Ski Co.'s decision to terminate the all-Aspen ticket was thus a decision by a monopolist to make an important change in the character of the market.[31] Such a decision is not necessarily anticompetitive, and Ski Co. contends that neither its decision, nor the conduct in which it engaged to implement that decision, can fairly be characterized as exclusionary in this case. . . .

. . . Since the jury was unambiguously instructed that Ski Co.'s refusal to deal with Highlands "does not violate § 2 if valid business reasons exist for that refusal," we must assume that the jury concluded that there were no valid business reasons for the refusal. The question then is whether that conclusion finds support in the record.

29. R. Bork, The Antitrust Paradox 160 (1978) (hereinafter Bork).

31. "In any business, patterns of distribution develop over time; these may reasonably be thought to be more efficient than alternative patterns of distribution that do not develop. The patterns that do develop and persist we may call the optimal patterns. By disturbing optimal distribution patterns one rival can impose costs upon another, that is, force the other to accept higher costs." Bork 156. . . .

IV

The question whether Ski Co.'s conduct may properly be characterized as exclusionary cannot be answered by simply considering its effect on Highlands. In addition, it is relevant to consider its impact on consumers and whether it has impaired competition in an unnecessarily unrestrictive way.[32] If a firm has been "attempting to exclude rivals on some basis other than efficiency," [33] it is fair to characterize its behavior as predatory. It is, accordingly, appropriate to examine the effect of the challenged pattern of conduct on consumers, on Ski Co.'s smaller rival, and on Ski Co. itself.

Superior Quality of the All–Aspen Ticket

* * *

. . . [T]he evidence supports a conclusion that consumers were adversely affected by the elimination of the 4–area ticket. In the first place, the actual record of competition between a 3–area ticket and the all-Aspen ticket in the years after 1967 indicated that skiers demonstrably preferred four mountains to three. Highlands' expert marketing witness testified that many of the skiers who come to Aspen want to ski the four mountains, and the abolition of the 4–area pass made it more difficult to satisfy that ambition. A consumer survey undertaken in the 1979–1980 season indicated that 53.7% of the respondents wanted to ski Highlands, but would not; 39.9% said that they would not be skiing at the mountain of their choice because their ticket would not permit it.

Expert testimony and anecdotal evidence supported these statistical measures of consumer preference. A major wholesale tour operator asserted that he would not even consider marketing a 3–area ticket if a 4–area ticket were available. During the 1977–1978 and 1978–1979 seasons, people with Ski Co.'s 3–area ticket came to Highlands "on a very regular basis" and attempted to board the lifts or join the ski school. Highlands officials were left to explain to angry skiers that they could only ski at Highlands or join its ski school by paying for a 1–day lift ticket. Even for the affluent, this was an irritating situation because it left the skier the option of either wasting one day of the 6–day, 3–area pass or obtaining a refund which could take all morning and entailed the forfeit of the 6–day discount. An active officer in the Atlanta Ski Club testified that the elimination of the 4–area pass "infuriated" him.

Highlands' Ability to Compete

The adverse impact of Ski Co.'s pattern of conduct on Highlands is not disputed in this Court. Expert testimony described the extent of its pecuniary injury. The evidence concerning its attempt to develop a substitute product either by buying Ski Co.'s daily tickets in bulk, or by marketing its own Adventure Pack, demonstrates that it tried to protect itself from the loss of its share of the patrons of the all–Aspen ticket. The development of a new distribution system for providing the experience

32. "Thus, 'exclusionary' comprehends at the most behavior that not only (1) tends to impair the opportunities of rivals, but also (2) either does not further competition on the merits or does so in an unnecessarily restrictive way." 3 P. Areeda & D. Turner, Antitrust Law 78 (1978).

33. Bork 138.

that skiers had learned to expect in Aspen proved to be prohibitively expensive. As a result, Highlands' share of the relevant market steadily declined after the 4–area ticket was terminated. The size of the damages award also confirms the substantial character of the effect of Ski Co.'s conduct upon Highlands.

Ski Co.'s Business Justification

Perhaps most significant, however, is the evidence relating to Ski Co. itself, for Ski Co. did not persuade the jury that its conduct was justified by any normal business purpose. Ski Co. was apparently willing to forgo daily ticket sales both to skiers who sought to exchange the coupons contained in Highlands' Adventure Pack, and to those who would have purchased Ski Co. daily lift tickets from Highlands if Highlands had been permitted to purchase them in bulk. The jury may well have concluded that Ski Co. elected to forgo these short run benefits because it was more interested in reducing competition in the Aspen market over the long run by harming its smaller competitor.

That conclusion is strongly supported by Ski Co.'s failure to offer any efficiency justification whatever for its pattern of conduct.[39] In defending the decision to terminate the jointly offered ticket, Ski Co. claimed that usage could not be properly monitored. The evidence, however, established that Ski Co. itself monitored the use of the 3–area passes based on a count taken by lift operators, and distributed the revenues among its mountains on that basis. Ski Co. contended that coupons were administratively cumbersome, and that the survey takers had been disruptive and their work inaccurate. Coupons, however, were no more burdensome than the credit cards accepted at Ski Co. ticket windows. Moreover, in other markets Ski Co. itself participated in interchangeable lift tickets using coupons. As for the survey, its own manager testified that the problems were much overemphasized by Ski Co. officials, and were mostly resolved as they arose. Ski Co.'s explanation for the rejection of Highlands' offer to hire—at its own expense—a reputable national accounting firm to audit usage of the 4–area tickets at Highlands' mountain, was that there was no way to "control" the audit.

In the end, Ski Co. was pressed to justify its pattern of conduct on a desire to disassociate itself from—what it considered—the inferior skiing services offered at Highlands. The all-Aspen ticket based on usage, however, allowed consumers to make their own choice on these matters of quality. Ski Co.'s purported concern for the relative quality of Highlands' product was supported in the record by little more than vague insinuations, and was sharply contested by numerous witnesses. Moreover, Ski Co. admitted that it was willing to associate with what it considered to be inferior products in other markets.

39. "The law can usefully attack this form of predation only when there is evidence of specific intent to drive others from the market by means other than superior efficiency and when the predator has overwhelming market size, perhaps 80 or 90 percent. Proof of specific intent to engage in predation may be in the form of statements made by the officers or agents of the company, evidence that the conduct was used threateningly and did not continue when a rival capitulated, or *evidence that the conduct was not related to any apparent efficiency.* These matters are not so difficult of proof as to render the test overly hard to meet." Bork 157 (emphasis added).

Although Ski Co.'s pattern of conduct may not have been as " 'bold, relentless, and predatory' " as the publisher's actions in *Lorain Journal,*[41] the record in this case comfortably supports an inference that the monopolist made a deliberate effort to discourage its customers from doing business with its smaller rival. The sale of its 3–area, 6–day ticket, particularly when it was discounted below the daily ticket price, deterred the ticket holders from skiing at Highlands. The refusal to accept the Adventure Pack coupons in exchange for daily tickets was apparently motivated entirely by a decision to avoid providing any benefit to Highlands even though accepting the coupons would have entailed no cost to Ski Co. itself, would have provided it with immediate benefits, and would have satisfied its potential customers. Thus the evidence supports an inference that Ski Co. was not motivated by efficiency concerns and that it was willing to sacrifice short run benefits and consumer good will in exchange for a perceived long-run impact on its smaller rival.

Because we are satisfied that the evidence in the record,[44] construed most favorably in support of Highlands' position, is adequate to support the verdict under the instructions given by the trial court, the judgment of the Court of Appeals is

Affirmed.

Questions and Comments

Aspen Skiing, decided unanimously for the plaintiff (8–0), is the latest Supreme Court case on monopolization. Why did the conduct of Aspen Skiing violate the law? In answering this question be mindful of the instruction given by the district court on the conduct issue, an instruction with which the Supreme Court found no fault. If you represented a plaintiff in a Section 2 case, would you like such an instruction? Can a plaintiff now expect to be able to obtain such an instruction in a refusal to deal case? A case involving refusal to license a patent? A case involving predatory product manipulation?

Did Aspen Skiing use its monopoly power to lessen output? Do you suspect that fewer people went skiing and that prices went up (in Aspen) as a result of Aspen Skiing's strategy? If defendant had disproved this hypothesis, would it have won? Would you say that the Court focused on a consumer interest other than output? What interest? Does the Court consider the excluded competitor's interest? Does it consider whether Aspen Skiing's refusal to deal was unfair?

Note that the Court purports to rely on the writings of Professor Bork. Would Bork agree with the Court?

41. *Lorain Journal Co. v. United States,* 342 U.S., at 149 (quoting opinion below 92 F.Supp. 794, 796 (ND Ohio 1950)).

44. Given our conclusion that the evidence amply supports the verdict under the instructions as given by the trial court, we find it unnecessary to consider the possible relevance of the "essential facilities" doctrine, or the somewhat hypothetical question whether nonexclusionary conduct could ever constitute an abuse of monopoly power if motivated by an anticompetitive purpose. If, as we have assumed, no monopolist monopolizes unconscious of what he is doing, that case is unlikely to arise.

The Court declines to engage in an essential facilities analysis, although the court of appeals did so. Why? Is the essential facilities doctrine helpful here?

Suppose Aspen Skiing had never previously cooperated with Highlands. Would the result be the same or different?

Aspen Skiing offered several justifications for its conduct. The Court seemed to regard these as unconvincing, post-dispute rationalizations. Apparently the Court thought Aspen Skiing acted for the deliberate purpose of getting for itself as much of the revenue as it could, regardless of the impact on Highland. Suppose that had been its frankly stated and sole motive; suppose it had said to Highland: "We've got a competitive advantage over you—three mountains to your one. If we stop joining with you in a multi-mountain ticket, total skiing revenues in Aspen may go down slightly; people like to go to resorts where there are multi-mountain tickets, and a four mountain joint ticket destination is more appealing than a three mountain joint ticket destination. But surely Aspen won't lose much of its aggregate business, and because we'll be the only Aspen ski operator to offer a multi-mountain ticket we'll get most of the business that is here. In our judgment, we'll make more money by that course than by continuing to cooperate with you. Therefore, effective the end of the current season, no more joint tickets." Would that have been a violation? Would such a course of conduct have reduced allocative efficiency in any market?

Suppose Aspen Skiing proved that Aspen had recently been losing ground to other destination ski resorts, and that Aspen Skiing wanted to use its three mountain appeal to raise its own revenues by getting as large a share of skiers already in Aspen as possible, enabling it to increase its promotion of Aspen in major cities from which skiing trips originate. Aspen's only conduct was to refuse to continue dealing. Did it violate Section 2?

Suppose that all Aspen Skiing had done was to make the following offer: "We will continue to participate in a four-mountain ticket if you accept 13.2% of the revenues, which we estimate to be your share of the runs in the coming year, minus an access fee equivalent to 4% of total revenues. The access fee is a modest payment for the extensive advertising and promotion we do that draws skiers to this area." Highland refuses because it cannot afford to accept. What result?

What must Aspen Skiing do as a result of the opinion? On what terms must it now deal with Highlands? To what extent can and should the district court supervise the terms? Can Aspen Skiing, in bargaining with plaintiff, exact a monopoly share of the joint ticket revenues (can it, for example, now make an offer like the one in the paragraph above)?

When the case reached the Supreme Court, the relevant sub-market had already been defined as skiing in Aspen; in the Supreme Court the market definition issue was no longer open. Was that a satisfactory definition? Is it sensible to evaluate the effect of defendant's conduct on competition in Aspen alone? Assume that a jury is waived and you are the trial judge. Aspen Skiing has proved convincingly that ninety-five percent of the skiers in Aspen come from afar and that the price for skiing in Aspen is tightly constrained by the price for skiing at other destination ski resorts. Aspen Skiing argues that you are compelled to take destination ski resorts as the appropriate market and find that there is no monopoly. Plaintiff, however, has proved convincingly that Aspen Skiing has the power to drive it out of the market by refusing to join in multi-mountain tickets, or by demanding a more than proportionate share of joint revenues. Plaintiff cites *du Pont (Cellophane)* for the proposition that monopoly power is the power to raise price *or* exclude competition. It points out that there are also local skiers and that, even if they are protected by competition from other destination ski resorts against defendant's charging monopoly prices, they will, if plaintiff is driven out, be deprived of a significant market option—a choice. In order to protect this choice, and to protect plaintiff from being arbitrarily and unfairly driven out, plaintiff argues that you must find that skiing in Aspen is a relevant submarket and that Aspen Skiing has monopoly power (power to exclude competition) in that submarket. What should you do? Suppose the case is tried to a jury. Does market definition go to the jury? If so, with what instructions?

In *Olympia Equipment,* a recent "duty to continue to deal" case, Judge Posner expressed his view about the scope of *Aspen Skiing:*

OLYMPIA EQUIPMENT LEASING CO. v. WESTERN UNION TELEGRAPH CO.
797 F.2d 370 (7th Cir.1986).

JUDGE POSNER: The plaintiffs, affiliated companies (now defunct) and their assignee—we shall refer to the plaintiffs collectively as "Olympia"—brought this suit in 1977 against Western Union Telegraph Company, seeking damages for monopolization and attempted monopolization under section 2 of the Sherman Act, and for breach of contract under state law. . . .

Trial was to a jury, which awarded (after remittitur) $12 million in antitrust damages and alternatively $12 million for breach of contract. The antitrust damages were trebled as required by law, making the total judgment $36 million plus a reasonable attorney's fee. Western Union appeals. . . .

Although the trial lasted more than six weeks and produced the usual mountain of testimony and exhibits, the facts relevant to this appeal are simple. We state them as favorably to Olympia as the record permits, in view of the jury's verdict. As a natural evolution from its historic telegraph service, Western Union created "Telex," a switched message transmission service provided over communications lines owned or leased by Western Union and routed through exchanges owned by it. Western Union runs an access line from its local exchange to the subscriber's premises, where the line is hooked up to a terminal. The subscriber to the service can dial any other subscriber and, when connection is made, can transmit messages from his terminal to the other subscriber's terminal. Thus telex service is like telephone service except that the communications transmitted are messages rather than voice communications. Until the 1970s Western Union required its subscribers to lease their telex terminals from it. It bought these terminals from the Teletype Corporation; indeed the earliest and still a common type of telex terminal is the familiar teletypewriter. The price of telex service—a price regulated by the Federal Communications Commission—was a "bundled" price, meaning that it covered both telex service and the telex terminal. In 1971 Western Union bought from AT & T a service similar to and competitive

with telex—TWX. We shall refer to the two services jointly as "telex."
. . .

Beginning with the *Carterfone* decision in 1968, the Federal Communications Commission opened the telephone terminal equipment market, historically dominated by AT & T (which like Western Union required its subscribers to lease their terminal equipment from it), to competition from independent providers of such equipment. Required to do the same in the telex terminal equipment market as a condition of being allowed to acquire TWX, and in any event wanting to sell its terminals in order to raise capital to buy communications satellites for the transmission leg of its telex and other services, Western Union in 1973 announced that it was opening the telex terminal market to competition. It unbundled its pricing of service and equipment, told its subscribers they could cancel their existing leases of terminal equipment on 30 days notice and lease or buy such equipment from anyone they pleased, and told prospective vendors of such equipment that it would put them on a list which its salesmen would give new subscribers to telex service who were seeking terminals. Western Union even held a seminar for prospective vendors to encourage entry into the equipment market. Finally, it told its salesmen to try to sell its "installed base" of terminals—the 90,000 odd terminals that it owned and had leased to subscribers—to the lessees.

Since Western Union did not plan to buy additional telex terminals, the effect of this series of steps was to put Western Union on the road to withdrawing from the telex terminal market, the withdrawal to be completed when its last terminal was sold to the lessee of the terminal. . . .

Olympia, formed in 1975 to take advantage of the opportunity that Western Union had opened up for independent providers of telex terminals, bought terminals from Teletype Corporation just as Western Union had done. To obtain customers for its terminals Olympia relied on referrals from Western Union's salesmen—for Olympia had no sales force of its own, being a skeletal enterprise created largely for tax reasons. And yet for a period of several months in 1975, when Western Union's schedule of sales commissions encouraged its salesmen to push independently supplied terminals and when these salesmen were routinely showing the list of independent vendors to new telex subscribers, Olympia throve, installing 1,800 terminals—20 percent of all the telex terminals installed during this period.

Then the roof caved in. Western Union decided that it was liquidating its own inventory of telex terminals too slowly. It changed the schedule of commissions to encourage its salesmen to sell more Western Union terminals, and there is evidence that it also told the salesmen to stop showing the list of vendors to its subscribers. Between August and October 1975, sales and leases of terminals by Western Union to new customers rose from about 500 a month to 1,300 while Olympia's new leases fell from 425 to zero and sales and leases by other vendors fell from 1,300 to 500. Vendors who had their own sales forces were able to hang on, as these figures show. Olympia, which previously had depended entirely on referrals by Western Union's salesmen, tried to survive by hiring its own salesmen to solicit lessees of Western Union terminals. It hoped to persuade some of the lessees to cancel their leases. This effort to compete against Western Union's installed base enraged Western Union, which in the most dramatic document in the case announced that "these turkeys . . . ought to be flushed." But nothing was done, or had to be done. Olympia's effort failed without any additional measures by Western Union, and Olympia went out of business in 1976.

On these facts, could a rational trier of fact find that Olympia was a victim of monopolization? . . . .

[I]f Western Union had monopoly power over telex service, it could use that power to curtail competition in the complementary equipment market. . . . [T]he record compiled in this case, which included evidence that even a steep increase in the price of telex service would not have caused many subscribers to switch to substitute services (thus implying a low elasticity of demand for telex service, and therefore monopoly power for the firm that controlled the service—Western Union), a rational jury could have found that Western Union had monopoly power in the market for telex service; so we must repress our skepticism.

But the bare fact that a firm has monopoly power in Market X does not imply that it will have an incentive to obtain monopoly power over Y, an input into X. In general a monopolist like any other firm wants to minimize its input costs; the lower those costs are, the greater the monopoly profits it will be able to make. Therefore the rational monopolist will usually want his input markets to be competitive, for competition usually will minimize the costs that he has to pay for his inputs. There are, however, special circumstances in which a rational monopolist may want to restrict competition in an input market; as it happens, one of those circumstances is where the monopolist's rates are regulated. Western Union's monopoly of telex service was a regulated monopoly, and a regulated monopolist may have an incentive to project its monopoly into related but unregulated markets.

* * *

. . . Not the possession, but the abuse, of monopoly power violates section 2. And far from abusing any monopoly power it may have had, by excluding independent providers of terminal equipment from selling to its telex customers, Western Union encouraged the entry of independent providers. It did this by unbundling its telex prices, by shortening its lease terms, by ceasing to buy additional terminals, by creating a sales commission structure that encouraged its salesmen to push equipment supplied by independent providers, and by putting the names of those providers on a list for its salesmen to show new telex subscribers. Obviously none of this conduct violated the antitrust laws. The alleged violation came when, having created and nurtured new competition, Western Union stopped helping the new competitors because it found it could not liquidate its terminal inventory as rapidly as it had hoped to be able to do.

* * *

Today it is clear that a firm with lawful monopoly power has no general duty to help its competitors, whether by holding a price umbrella over their heads or by otherwise pulling its competitive punches. . . . .

If a monopolist does extend a helping hand, though not required to do so, and later withdraws it as happened in this case, does he incur antitrust liability? We think not. Conceivably he may be liable in tort or contract law, under theories of equitable or promissory estoppel or implied contract (of which more shortly), or by analogy to the common law tort rule that though there is no duty to help a bystander in distress, once help is extended it may not be withdrawn, at least if the effect is to make the bystander's rescue by someone else less likely. But the controlling consideration in an antitrust case is antitrust policy rather than common law analogies. Since Western Union had no duty to encourage the entry of new firms into the equipment market, the law would be perverse if it made Western Union's encouraging gestures the fulcrum of an antitrust violation. Then no firm would dare to attempt a graceful exit from a market in which it was a major seller. . . .

Some cases hold, however, that a firm which controls a facility essential to its competitors may be guilty of monopolization if it refuses to allow them access to the facility. We accept the authority of these cases absolutely. They are well illustrated by *Otter Tail Power Co. v. United States,* 410 U.S. 366 (1973), where a wholesale supplier of electricity refused to supply electric power to a power system that competed with it in the retail electrical power market and had no other source of supply. It might seem that if a monopolist's refusal to sell his products or services to a competitor can thus be actionable under antitrust law, it must mean that monopolists sometimes do have a duty to help their competitors and that the cases which deny this proposition are wrong. But the monopolistic-refusal-to-deal cases qualify rather than refute the no-duty-to-help-competitors cases. If a competitor is also a customer his relationship to the monopolist is not only a competitive one. The monopoly supplier who retaliates against customers who have the temerity to compete with him, by cutting such customers off, is severing a collateral relationship in order to discourage competition.

The present case would be an essential-facility case if Western Union had refused to supply telex service to a customer who got his terminal equipment from Olympia rather than from it, or if Olympia were a competing supplier of telex service who, like the specialized common carriers in the long-distance telephone market, depended on the owner of the local exchanges (here Western Union) to complete its service. Neither condition is satisfied. The essential feature of the refusal-to-deal cases—a monopoly supplier's discriminating against a customer because the customer has decided to compete with it—is missing here. Western Union did not withhold from one member of the public a service offered to the rest; nor was it in the habit of supplying vendor lists free of charge, and balked only when the recipient turned out to be a competitor. From the outset the vendor list was a form of special assistance rendered gratis to competitors, and there is no more duty to give or continue such assistance than there is to lend money to a competitor. Conceivably a firm in the business of making loans may not be allowed to withhold a loan from a competitor (if the lender has monopoly power), but clearly a firm that is not in that business is not required to lend money to a competitor merely because the loan would increase competition.

Aspen Skiing Co. v. Aspen Highlands Skiing Corp. goes the furthest of any case we know toward imposing (more precisely, allowing a jury to impose) a duty under antitrust law to help a competitor; and as a recent decision by the Supreme Court it requires our most careful and respectful consideration. The Aspen Skiing Company owned three of the four mountains that make up the Aspen skiing complex. Aspen Highlands Skiing Corporation owned the fourth. The two companies had offered their customers a joint ticket, usable on all four mountains, and the suit arose because Aspen Skiing Company terminated this cooperative arrangement. The Supreme Court found that for the convenience of customers an owner of a ski mountain in a multi-mountain skiing area normally would want to offer a ski ticket usable on any of the mountains. The joint ticket had originated at a time when there was competition among the different ski mountains at Aspen, and similar tickets were offered at other multi-mountain ski areas. In other words, competition required some cooperation among competitors. *Aspen Highlands* is not a conventional monopoly refusal-to-deal case like *Otter Tail* because Aspen Highlands was never a customer of Aspen Skiing Company; the skiers are the customers. But it is like the essential-facility cases in that the plaintiff could not compete with the defendant without being able to offer its customers access to the defendant's larger facilities.

Olympia analogizes access to all the major mountains at Aspen to Western Union's vendor list, and argues that just as Aspen Highlands could not survive without access to the mountains so Olympia could not survive without the list. The analogy lacks not only plausibility but also evidentiary support. There is no evidence that suppliers of telecommunications equipment customarily provide their customers with lists containing the names of competing suppliers or that without such lists a new entrant cannot compete with established firms. Although some customers of Western Union may not have known about alternative vendors, nothing prevented those vendors from acquainting the customers with their existence. Virtually by definition, a consumer will not know of the existence of a brand-new firm; but this point is not usually understood to imply a duty in existing firms to tell their customers about the new firm, even if the existing firms have monopoly power. Brand-new firms are expected to make their own way in the market, by advertising or other means of promotion. Particularly where, as in this case, the consumers are business firms rather than individuals, a new competitor should have no difficulty informing consumers of its existence.

Aspen Highlands could not acquire three more mountains in the Aspen area in order to be able to compete more effectively with the Aspen Skiing Company but Olympia could and did hire salesmen to substitute for the Western Union sales force that had been helping it. If Western Union had tried to prevent Olympia from making the substitution it would have been guilty of exclusionary conduct. But Olympia had no right under antitrust law to take a free ride on its competitor's sales force. You cannot conscript your competitor's salesmen to sell your product even if the competitor has monopoly power and you are a struggling new entrant. Advertising a competitor's products free of charge is not a form of cooperation commonly found in competitive markets; it is the antithesis of competition. . . .

Olympia cites *Aspen Highlands* for the proposition that if a firm with monopoly power cannot give a good business justification for not cooperating with a competitor, its refusal to cooperate violates antitrust law. Conjoined with other evidence, lack of business justification may indicate probable anticompetitive effect. But there is a clear business justification in this case: Western Union wanted to liquidate its supply of telex terminals faster, so it stopped promoting a competitor's supply. The main economic objection to monopoly is that the monopolist restricts output compared to what it would be under competition. The monopolist cannot be faulted for wanting to sell *more* output unless he is engaged in some predatory or exclusionary scheme the long-run effect of which may be to restrict output (perhaps in a different market, as in a case where the regulated monopolist takes over a related market in an effort to evade profit regulation and thus keep profits up, and output down, in the monopoly market). There is no such scheme here; Western Union's long-run design is to get out of the telex terminal market. The defendant in *Aspen Highlands* discontinued a service that its customers valued, thus forgoing normal competitive benefits in the hope (so the jury found at any rate) of reaping long-term anticompetitive gains; there is no prospect of such gains in the unusual case—which is the present case—of a monopolist who is voluntarily relinquishing his monopoly position.

* * *

The *Aspen Highlands* decision, on which Olympia naturally rests the main weight of its argument, is narrowly written. If it stands for any principle that goes beyond its unusual facts, it is that a monopolist may be guilty of monopolization if it refuses to cooperate with a competitor in circumstances where some cooperation is indispensable to effective competition. No reasonable finder of fact could have found this factual premise satisfied in this case. The experience of the other independent vendors, competitors of Olympia and Western Electric, shows—what is anyway obvious—that Olympia did not have to use Western Union's sales force (gratis) in order to compete with Western Union.

We add, what has become an antitrust commonplace, that if conduct is not objectively anticompetitive the fact that it was motivated by hostility to competitors ("these turkeys") is irrelevant. The importance of intent in such fields as tort and criminal law makes it natural to suppose that it should play an important role in antitrust law as well, for an antitrust violation is a statutory tort. But there is an insoluble ambiguity about anticompetitive intent that is not encountered in the ordinary tort case. If A strikes B deliberately, we are entitled to infer, first, that A's act was more dangerous than if the blow had been accidental (you are more likely to hurt someone if you are trying to hurt him than if you are trying, however ineptly, to avoid hurting him, as in the typical accident case), and, second, that the cost of avoidance to the injurer would have been less than if the blow had been accidental; indeed, the cost of forebearing to commit an act of deliberate aggression is negative, because the act requires effort. Similar inferences would be possible in antitrust cases if the purpose of antitrust law were to protect the prosperity or solvency (corresponding to the bodily integrity of potential tort victims) of competitors, but it is not. Competition, which is always deliberate, has never been a tort, intentional or otherwise. See *Keeble v. Hickeringill,* 11 East. 574 (K.B. 1706 or 1707). If firm A through lower prices or a better or more dependable product succeeds in driving competitor B out of business, society is better off, unlike the case where A and B are individuals and A kills B for B's money. In both cases the "aggressor" seeks to transfer his victim's wealth to himself, but in the first case we applaud the result because society as a whole benefits from the competitive process. That Western Union wanted to "flush these turkeys" tells us nothing about the lawfulness of its conduct.

Most businessmen don't like their competitors, or for that matter competition. They want to make as much money as possible and getting a monopoly is one way of making a lot of money. That is fine, however, so long as they do not use methods calculated to make consumers worse off in the long run. Consumers would be worse off if a firm with monopoly power had a duty to extend positive assistance to new entrants, or having extended it voluntarily a duty to continue it indefinitely. The imposition of such a duty would make firms that possessed or might be thought to possess monopoly power, however laudably obtained, timid about relinquishing that power or, having done so, timid about competing with new entrants. The question therefore is not whether Western Union withdrew the vendor list in order to make money at the expense of Olympia, which of course it did, but whether such withdrawal was an objectively anticompetitive act. It was not, once the basic premise that monopolists are not required to help their competitors, but need only refrain from anticompetitive acts such as denial of access to essential facilities, is granted.

We turn now to Olympia's contract claim . . . . [The court found the evidence insufficient as a matter of law to make out a contract.]

* * *

. . . . The judgment of the district court is reversed with directions to enter judgment for Western Union.

Problems

1. Mead Data produces and sells the Lexis computer-assisted legal research and reporting service. Mead has most of this market. Its only competitor is West Publishing Company which offers the Westlaw system. Using official and other public domain sources, Mead has built its database from state and federal case reports from about 1900. As Mead builds its database further back in time, it incurs greater and greater per case expense, for it must search out old, inaccessible, official copies of judicial opinions not otherwise reported except in West Publishing Company's National Reporter System. West Publishing is the dominant supplier of printed texts of federal and state case reports and the only easily accessible source for many reports, including most reports older than 1900. Mead wants to copy from the readily accessible West reports. This method would reduce the cost of creating a complete data bank. Mead also wants to insert into the Lexis database an indication of every page break, volume and page number from every extant volume in West's National Reporter System (a practice Mead calls "star

pagination.") Mead asserts that star pagination would increase the useful-ness of Lexis by enabling Lexis users to cite to internal portions of cases in the way that has become most common.

West not only adds headnotes, key numbers and parallel citations to the case it reports, but also corrects grammatical errors and miscitations. West asserts that copyright law and tort law on misappropriation (e.g. International News Service v. Associated Press, 248 U.S. 215 (1918)) preclude Mead both from copying West's old reports (even if Mead deletes from its data bank the material that it can tell was added by West) and from adopting star pagina-tion. If Mead copies from West reports to expand its data bank or if Mead star paginates, West threatens to sue.

Assume that Mead copies, then star paginates, old West reports. West sues for copyright infringement and tort, and Mead counterclaims alleging monopolization. Does Mead have a good claim? [20]

2. During the pendancy of the suit Mead proposes to settle on the following basis: (1) Mead will acknowledge that West has valid copyright and common law interests which Mead's copying and star pagination infringe; (2) West will give Mead a long term, renewable license to copy from West reports and to star paginate, in return for which Mead will pay to West a percentage of Mead's gross revenues from Lexis. West asks its lawyer whether this settlement would raise any antitrust problems. Does it? West settles on this basis, Newco enters the market, and Newco seeks the same licensing arrange-ment that West gave Mead. Can West say no? [21]

F. THE CONDUCT REQUIREMENT: DIFFERENTIATING MONOPOLIZATION AND ATTEMPTS TO MONOPOLIZE

We have already explored the "black letter" elements of the attempt offense: specific intent to monopolize, dangerous probability of success, and anticompetitive conduct that produces that dangerous probability. We have also explored the varied dimensions of anticompetitive conduct, and some of the cases we have studied—e.g., *Lorain Journal, du Pont (Titanium Dioxide),* and *Telex–IBM*—have arisen as attempt cases rather than as (or as well as) monopolization cases. You should recognize by now that most conduct issues that have arisen in monopolization cases could also arise in cases where defendant's power was modest or marginal—that is, in cases in which the only, or the more serious, charge would be attempt to monopolize. One should not infer, however, that the conduct standard in attempt and monopoly cases is precisely the same. The conduct standard for the monopolist must be stricter. A firm charged only with attempt is still engaged in a competitive contest; the law ought to be particularly sensitive so as not to foreclose such a firm from strategies that might yield efficiencies or, indeed, from strategies that could cause significant social risks only if dominating power had already been attained. For example, it might be appropriate to forbid a monopo-

20. This problem is based on allegations in litigation between Mead Data Central, Inc. and West Publishing Company, in con-nection with which one of the authors served as a consultant to attorneys for West.

21. This problem is not based on facts involved in the actual Mead–West relation-ship.

list from adopting a lease only policy (as did the court in *United Shoe*), yet be inappropriate to forbid a non-dominant firm to follow such a policy. Of course, the legal issue is never likely to come up in such a pure form. If a firm finds itself defending against a monopolization or attempt charge because of its competitive strategies, the attack is not likely to focus only on single aspects of that strategy; the firm will (again as in *United Shoe*) find the entire interactive pattern of its production, product development and marketing strategies under scrutiny. Thus, although lease only, considered alone, might be unlawful to a monopolist, but not for a firm with less power charged with attempt, nevertheless the full panoply of United Shoe's conduct might have made that defendant vulnerable to an attempt charge even if its market share was still marginal—say fifty percent or so.

As the above remarks suggest, many attempt cases, perhaps most, are embryonic monopolization cases. Whether defendant has sufficient power to be called a monopolist may be debatable or doubtful, but at least as plaintiff sees the facts, defendant is well on its way to a dominant position. In that context, the defendant's conduct may be subject to scrutiny even if the competitive effects of the conduct are ambiguous. But there are other instances where (as in *Lorain Journal*) defendant's conduct is unambiguously noncompetitive but where (unlike *Lorain Journal*) it is not credible to assert that defendant possesses or will soon possess dominant power. We examine two such cases where, despite conduct not on the competitive merits, there remained a question whether the law was violated.

UNITED STATES v. EMPIRE GAS CORP.

537 F.2d 296 (8th Cir.1976),
cert. denied, 429 U.S. 1122 (1977).

JUDGE ROSS: This civil antitrust action against Empire Gas Corporation was brought by the United States under sections 1 and 2 of the Sherman Act. The case was tried to the court, judgment was for Empire and the government now appeals. We affirm the district court.

Empire is a retailer and to a lesser extent a wholesaler of liquefied petroleum (LP). LP is a generic term for any of various gaseous fuels such as propane and butane, which are compressed into their liquid states for marketing. Retailers generally store their LP inventories at bulk plants, from which it is distributed by tank truck to consumers for heating, cooking and other uses. Because of the high cost of this method of transportation, a retailer's sales are usually limited in area to approximately a 30 mile radius around his bulk plant. Frequently LP retailers are small, local, family-run businesses.

Empire was founded in Missouri in 1963 and still maintains its home office in Wheaton. During the first 10 years of its life it greatly expanded its business in Missouri and added bulk plants in 24 other states. This expansion was largely through acquisition of 81 other LP gas retail companies with close to 400 bulk plants.

The complaint alleged several violations of the antitrust laws, but on appeal the United States has concentrated on their contentions that

Empire violated section 2 of the Sherman Act by attempting to monopolize the retail sale of LP in areas surrounding Lebanon and Wheaton, Missouri, and that Empire restrained commerce in violation of section 1 by obtaining covenants not to compete from its employees and others.

* * *

The relevant geographic areas here are the Lebanon and Wheaton market areas; however, at oral argument the United States contended that Empire's actions in other areas could support an inference of monopolistic intent in the relevant geographic areas. With this we agree. We have stressed the importance of viewing the evidence as a whole to give the antitrust plaintiff the full benefit of his proof, rather than tightly compartmentalizing the case and wiping the slate clean after considering each piece of evidence. . . .

To show specific intent plaintiff introduced evidence of market allocation agreements, acquisitions of competitors and covenants not to compete, among other things. However, the greatest part of the evidence of specific intent, and that which we find persuasive, relates to pricing practices of the defendant.

The evidence establishes a pattern followed by Empire in which it attempted to use price cuts or threats thereof to influence competitors' prices or methods of competition. Empire's Vice President of Finance from 1969 to 1972 testified that around 1970 he was present at staff meetings when the company president, Robert W. Plaster, indicated that Empire's competition should be encouraged to pass increased costs of LP supplies to the retailer on to the ultimate consumer, and sales department employees thereafter contacted Empire's competitors for this purpose.

Several of these competitors testified at trial. Exemplary of their testimony is that of W.L. Arthur, the owner of Arthur Gas and Appliances of Marshfield, Missouri. Arthur competed with Empire in the overlapping Niangua and Lebanon market areas. Mr. Rex Shaddox, one of the top officials of Empire Gas, frequently stopped in to visit with the witness or his father. During these conversations, Shaddox invariably tried to convince the Arthurs to sell their business to Empire and to set their LP prices higher. At the time, Arthur was selling gas in the Lebanon area at a lower price than Empire. In late 1965, during one of these discussions of price, Shaddox told the Arthurs that Empire was too large to compete with, and could put Arthur out of business. The following day Mr. Plaster, Empire's president, called and asked that Arthur raise his LP prices. Arthur testified that when he refused Plaster said that he was going to put him out of business. A few days later Empire began doing business in Arthur's home area of Niangua. Empire's route salesman solicited door to door with an offer of LP gas at one and a half or two cents less than Arthur was selling for. Arthur testified he could not make a sufficient profit at this price. The Empire salesman also told those he solicited that Arthur Gas was going out of business, according to the witness.

Arthur's testimony concerning Empire's retaliatory price cut was corroborated by Raymond E. Dore, Empire's treasurer from June, 1963, to September, 1967. He testified that Shaddox and Plaster were upset about the competition that Arthur was giving Empire in the Lebanon area and therefore they planned to retaliate by selling low priced LP in the Niangua area where Arthur was located. Dore was instructed by Mr. Plaster to form Niangua Gas Company for this purpose, and he did so.

Arthur testified that he and other companies in the Niangua area were affected by Empire's price cut. Finally an intermediary worked out an agreement between Empire and the other gas companies which apparently included a temporary hike in the retail price of LP.

In 1967 Empire acquired Arthur's supplier. Because of the problems which Arthur had experienced with Empire, Arthur and his son met with Shaddox to see if there was a way out of the supply contract that Arthur had with Empire's predecessor, the rights to which had been assigned to Empire. Arthur also offered to sell his company to Empire at this time. According to Arthur, Shaddox refused to cancel the contract or buy Arthur out, and told him that "we have you right where we want you." Thereafter Empire raised the price at which it sold LP to Arthur so that he could not retail the product at a competitive price and still make a profit. Arthur also testified that Empire limited his credit to two loads of gas. This would not have been objectionable except that Empire would not mail Arthur invoices so he could pay his bills, and on this pretense they frequently refused to sell him the propane he needed. Finally, in the spring of 1967, Arthur broke his supply contract with the defendant.

Other competitors testified to similar experiences with the defendant.

Charles O. Bridges operated a company in Adrian, Missouri, beginning in 1969. In the summer of 1970 an Empire district manager and plant manager called on him and said the price of LP gas in the area was going to be either 9.5 or 15.9. At the time Bridges was buying gas wholesale at 8.7 cents a gallon, and shortly thereafter his wholesale price rose to 9.7. When Bridges pointed out that a profit could not be made at a retail price of 9.5 cents the manager told him that Empire was large enough that some subsidiaries could carry others, and that Empire was selling at 9 or 9.5 in Springfield. Shortly thereafter Empire lowered its price. Bridges testified he came as close as he could to 9.5, but eventually set his price at 15.9 cents per gallon. Gary Jennings competed with Empire in the same area as Bridges, and was also contacted by the Empire district manager and plant manager in 1970. When he refused to raise his prices he was given the impression that Empire would cut their prices. At the time Jennings bought his gas from Empire at 8 or 9 cents. Shortly thereafter Empire dropped the price to its retail customers to 9 or 9.5 cents, according to Jennings' testimony. A few weeks later he raised his price.

Testimony was offered by Lloyd Geiger, who ran Gygrgas of Boonville, Missouri. In January, 1967, Mr. Shaddox called to express displeasure because Geiger was selling gas at two cents per gallon less than Empire in Jefferson City. Shaddox demanded that he come up two cents or Empire was going to play "burnout" with him. Geiger did not raise his price and two months later Empire set up a subsidiary in Boonville. The Empire company hired one of Gygrgas' employees and solicited Geiger's customers at a price of five cents per gallon.

Raymond Dore, Empire's former treasurer, testified that Mr. Plaster, Empire's president, had him incorporate the Boonville subsidiary to retaliate against Gygrgas for selling at a lower price in Jefferson City, just as the Niangua company had been organized to hurt Arthur Gas and Appliances.

* * *

Several other dealers testified to threats and price cuts of the defendant which were designed to make them raise prices or stop soliciting Empire customers.

The district court found that the United States had failed to show that Empire had ever threatened to reduce prices with the intent of inducing competitors to increase prices or refrain from soliciting Empire's customers, or that it ever reduced its prices for this purpose. The court also found that Empire never attempted to enter into any price fixing arrangement. The trial judge concluded that the government had not established Empire's specific intent by the evidence of pricing actions or otherwise.

We find the district court's conclusion in this regard to be clearly erroneous.

* * *

The specific intent which makes price cutting a monopolistic tool may take various forms. The record before us establishes that the defendant attempted to use price cuts or threats of price cuts to prevent competitors from soliciting Empire customers. Actions such as these, designed to prevent competitors from increasing their share of the market at the expense of the antitrust defendant, clearly show intent to monopolize. . . .

In addition to the above actions designed to reduce competition from other retailers, the evidence establishes that many of the defendant's price cuts were designed to give Empire *control* over the retail *price* of LP gas. The defendant, through its agents, represented to competitors that because of its size other subsidiaries could carry those which had to resort to price cuts for some time in order to discipline uncooperative competitors. . . . Whether this representation was true or not, it seems obvious that the defendant wished to intimidate its competitors into raising their retail prices to the level that Empire thought would insure it a sufficient profit. Liberal price cuts reenforced the message.

These actions taken with the object of manipulating the price of LP gas to the consumer show specific intent to monopolize, as do Empire's attempts to control competitors' solicitation of its customers.

* * *

B. Dangerous Probability of Success.

* * *

The record shows that the LP gas business is highly competitive in the Lebanon and Wheaton markets as elsewhere. The defendant has many competitors wherever it does business, and new ones spring up frequently. The barriers to entry in this industry are minimal; all that are needed are a supply of LP, a truck, and perhaps a storage tank.

The United States conducted a survey which purported to show that Empire had about 50% of the market in dollars' sales in the Lebanon area and 47% in Wheaton. We agree with the district court that the survey's reliability was extremely doubtful. . . . But even if we accept the government's survey as proof that Empire had 50% of the Lebanon market and 47% of the Wheaton market, that alone is not sufficient to show a dangerous probability of success.

. . . It is the theory of the United States, however, that Empire's large market shares in conjunction with its anticompetitive conduct gave rise to a dangerous probability that it would be able to control prices in the Lebanon and Wheaton markets. The record, however, reveals no instance in which competitors *in these areas* were susceptible to Empire's intimidation. There is insufficient proof that the competitors of Empire: (a) raised or fixed prices because of Empire's threats; (b) stopped soliciting Empire customers, or (c) decided not to enter the LP business or decided to leave the business on account of defendant's actions.

The government relies heavily on the testimony of its expert economist to show dangerous probability. The economist testified that a greater likelihood of monopoly power existed because of Empire's size and anticompetitive practices. He also felt that the price trends in the Lebanon and Wheaton markets were indicative of monopolistic power. In the former area he found prices to be steadily rising and at a high level and in the latter area prices were extremely stable: both patterns characteristic of monopoly, according to the economist. Finally, he found Empire's profitability to be significantly higher than other LP businesses or American industry as a whole, which indicated monopoly power. The expert testified that by looking at industry structure, industry conduct and industry performance he could conclude that there was a dangerous probability that Empire would attain or had attained monopoly power, but he would not attempt to reach a conclusion without looking at all three factors.

We have several problems with the expert's testimony, as did the district court. [The court believed that the expert testimony and the studies on which it was based were not reliable for various reasons, and the testimony was discredited.]

Taking the evidence of dangerous probability of success as a whole, as is proper in an antitrust case . . . we cannot find the requisite proof. The government established that: (a) Empire had a large share of the market in Lebanon and Wheaton in 1972: about 50%; (b) it has engaged in anticompetitive conduct in various areas, which has not been shown to have been effective in the Lebanon or Wheaton areas; (c) the price of LP in Lebanon may be slightly higher than in some other areas, but the reasons for this are a matter of speculation; (d) the defendant has had a fairly high rate of profit for the past ten years. We cannot conclude from this inconclusive evidence that there is a dangerous probability that the defendant will be able to monopolize the LP gas business, or exert control over prices or competition in the Lebanon or the Wheaton market areas. Therefore, we hold that the district court was not clearly erroneous when it found that the government failed to prove dangerous probability of success in its attempt to control competition or its attempt to raise prices by price intimidation. . . .

*   *   *

Questions and Comments

Empire's strategy was to make life difficult (and destruction imminent) for its competitors, until they stopped their price competition and stopped competing for Empire's customers. The strategy worked in Springfield, Niangua, and elsewhere. The government did not press violations in those markets, however, because Empire's market share was well below 50%. If you were the lawyer for the government, would you have pressed your case in those areas? On what theory? Would you (should you) have won? Would you have worried that your law suit would suppress low-price competition?

Empire Gas was a predator. It was "investing" money in keeping or increasing its market share by harassing its competitors. It must have anticipated a pay-back at least equal to its costs. Thus, it must have expected sufficient time to recoup its expenses and make elevated profits. If entry was as easy as the court thought, the strategy was mistaken, even dumb; no pay-back was possible because entry barriers were and would remain low. But Empire Gas must have taken a different view of the likelihood of entry than did the court; otherwise it wouldn't have bothered to carry out its strategy. Does the use of the strategy serve, of itself, to raise entry barriers? Given the possibility that Empire Gas might have been right and the court wrong about the market effect, who should run the risk that the strategy would work?

Perhaps Empire was not aiming at market dominance, but at market leadership, a kind of invited or even forced interdependence in pricing, an arrangement yielding outcomes like a cartel. It might have thought that it could be a successful "price leader." It had a market share of 17% or so, gained in part by predation. It might have thought that if it set a supracompetitive price, other firms would follow, recognizing that doing so was advantageous to them as well as to Empire, and that if they did not do so they might face predation. If for reasons like these Empire's strategy threatened supracompetitive prices and profits, should it matter under a Section 2 attempt theory whether the profits were to come from single-firm dominance or from cooperative behavior among competitors initiated by one firm and achieved through threatened or actual coercion? The legal standard for attempt to monopolize is usually stated as requiring that plaintiff prove a "dangerous probability of success." Success at what? Attaining monopoly? Achieving oligopolistic interdependence? Cartelizing? Chilling competitors' incentives to compete by price or otherwise? What should the concept "dangerous probability of success" comprehend?

The court thought Empire Gas' conduct "merely" an unfair trade practice (properly condemned, perhaps, under state unfair trade practice laws) but not a proper subject for antitrust constraint. Where should the line be drawn between a mere unfair trade practice and an antitrust violation?

Section 5 of the Federal Trade Commission catches some anticompetitive conduct that is not vulnerable under the Sherman Act. If the FTC found conduct like Empire's to violate that act, would the court that decided *Empire Gas* have affirmed?

UNITED STATES v. AMERICAN AIRLINES, INC.

743 F.2d 1114 (5th Cir.1984),
cert. dismissed, 474 U.S. 1001 (1985).

JUDGE DAVIS: The question presented in this antitrust case is whether the government's complaint states a claim of attempted monopolization under section 2 of the Sherman Act against the defendants, American Airlines, and its president Robert L. Crandall, for Crandall's proposal to the president of Braniff Airlines that the two airlines control the market and set prices. The district court dismissed the complaint for failure to state a claim under Federal Rule of Civil Procedure 12(b)(6) on the grounds that the failure to allege an agreement to monopolize was a fatal defect in the complaint and that more than an allegation of solicitation to monopolize was required to state a claim for attempted monopolization. We disagree and reverse.

I.

In February 1982, American Airlines (American) and Braniff Airlines (Braniff) each had a major passenger airline complex, or "hub" at the Dallas–Fort Worth International Airport (DFW). These hubs enabled American and Braniff to gather passengers from many cities, concentrate them at DFW, and then arrange connections for them on American and Braniff flights to other cities. The hub systems gave American and Braniff a marked competitive advantage over other airlines that served or might wish to serve DFW. In addition, the limitations on arrivals imposed by the Federal Aviation Administration (FAA) after the 1981 air traffic controllers' strike impeded any significant expansion or new entry by airlines into service at DFW. These limitations helped enable American and Braniff to maintain their high market shares in relation to other competitors.

In February 1982, American and Braniff together enjoyed a market share of more than ninety percent of the passengers on non-stop flights between DFW and eight major cities, and more than sixty percent of the passengers on flights between DFW and seven other cities. The two airlines had more than ninety percent of the passengers on many flights connecting at DFW, when no non-stop service was available between the cities in question. Overall, American and Braniff accounted for seventy-six percent of monthly enplanements at DFW.

For some time before February 1982, American and Braniff were competing fiercely for passengers flying to, from and through DFW, by offering lower fares and better service. During a telephone conversation between Robert Crandall, American's president, and Howard Putnam, Braniff's president, the following exchange occurred:

> Crandall: I think it's dumb as hell for Christ's sake, all right, to sit here and pound the ＊　＊　＊　＊ out of each other and neither one of us making a ＊ ＊ dime.
>
> Putnam: Well—

Crandall: I mean, you know, goddamn, what the * * * * is the point of it?

Putnam: Nobody asked American to serve Harlingen. Nobody asked American to serve Kansas City, and there were low fares in there, you know, before. So—

Crandall: You better believe it, Howard. But, you, you, you know, the complex is here—ain't gonna change a goddamn thing, all right. We can, we can both live here and there ain't no room for Delta. But there's, ah, no reason that I can see, all right, to put both companies out of business.

Putnam: But if you're going to overlay every route of American's on top of over, on top of every route that Braniff has—I can't just sit here and allow you to bury us without giving our best effort.

Crandall: Oh sure, but Eastern and Delta do the same thing in Atlanta and have for years.

Putnam: Do you have a suggestion for me?

Crandall: Yes. I have a suggestion for you. Raise your goddamn fares twenty percent. I'll raise mine the next morning.

Putnam: Robert, we—

Crandall: You'll make more money and I will too.

Putnam: We can't talk about pricing.

Crandall: Oh bull * * * *, Howard. We can talk about any goddamn thing we want to talk about.

Putnam did not raise Braniff's fares in response to Crandall's proposal; instead he presented the government with a tape recording of the conversation.

The United States subsequently sought an injunction under section 4 of the Sherman Act against American Airlines and Crandall based on an alleged violation of section 2 of the act which forbids an attempted monopolization. On a motion by the defendants, the district court dismissed the government's complaint for failure to state a claim under Fed. R.Civ.P. 12(b)(6).

The government asserts that the district court erred in holding that (1) an agreement is required for the offense of attempted monopolization; and (2) an attempt must amount to more than a solicitation to commit a crime.

II.

The language of the Sherman Act, its legislative history, the general criminal law relating to attempt and the jurisprudence relating to attempt specifically under the Sherman Act, lead us to the same conclusion: the government need not allege or prove an agreement to monopolize in order to establish an attempted joint monopolization under section 2 of the Sherman Act.

* * *

The Sherman Act "is designed to sweep away all appreciable obstructions so that the statutory policy of free trade might be effectively achieved." *United States v. Yellow Cab Co.,* 332 U.S. 218, 226

(1947). . . . In creating the Sherman Act, Congress deliberately chose not to define all of the activities which might contravene the Act, in order to avoid creating loopholes. *Appalachian Coals, Inc. v. United States,* 288 U.S. 344, 359–60 (1933). Instead it gave the Sherman Act "a generality and adaptability comparable to that found to be desirable in constitutional provisions." *Id.*

* * *

. . . In *American Tobacco,* the Court explained:

[I]t is undoubtedly true . . . that trade and commerce are "monopolized" within the meaning of the federal statute, when, as a result of efforts to that end, such power is obtained that a few persons acting together can control the prices of a commodity moving in interstate commerce. It is not necessary that the power thus obtained should be exercised. Its existence is sufficient.

328 U.S. at 811.

Applying these principles to the case at hand, we conclude that if Putnam had accepted Crandall's offer, the two airlines, at the moment of acceptance, would have acquired monopoly power. At that same moment, the offense of joint monopolization would have been complete.

* * *

. . . The offense of attempted monopolization . . . has two elements: (1) specific intent to accomplish the illegal result; and (2) a dangerous probability that the attempt to monopolize will be successful. When evaluating the element of dangerous probability of success, we do not rely on hindsight but examine the probability of success at the time the acts occur.

The government unequivocally alleged that Crandall proposed to enlist his chief competitor in a cartel so that American and Braniff, acting together, could control prices and exclude competition at DFW; as Crandall explained to Putnam, "we can both live here and there ain't no room for Delta." As a result of the monopolization, Braniff would "make more money and I will too."

Both Crandall and Putnam were the chief executive officers of their airlines; each arguably had the power to implement Crandall's plan. The airlines jointly had a high market share in a market with high barriers to entry. American and Braniff, at the moment of Putnam's acceptance, would have monopolized the market. Under the facts alleged, it follows that Crandall's proposal was an act that was the most proximate to the commission of the completed offense that Crandall was capable of committing. Considering the alleged market share of American and Braniff, the barriers to entry by other airlines, and the authority of Crandall and Putnam, the complaint sufficiently alleged that Crandall's proposal had a dangerous probability of success.

* * *

The district court . . . concluded that an agreement was a necessary element of an attempt to monopolize. We disagree. . . .

III.

Our decision that the government's complaint states a claim of attempted monopolization is consistent with the Act's language and purpose. The application of section 2 principles to defendants' conduct will deter the formation of monopolies at their outset when the unlawful schemes are proposed, and thus, will strengthen the Act.

Under appellees' construction of the Act, an individual is given a strong incentive to propose the formation of cartels. If the proposal is accepted, monopoly power is achieved; if the proposal is declined, no antitrust liability attaches. If section 2 liability attaches to conduct such as that alleged against Crandall, naked proposals for the formation of cartels are discouraged and competition is promoted.

Appellees argue that price fixing is an offense under section 1 of the Sherman Act and since the government charges that Crandall sought to have American and Braniff fix prices, the government's complaint in reality seeks to have us write an attempt provision into section 1. This argument is meritless. Appellees confuse the section 1 offense of price fixing with the power to control price following acquisition of monopoly power under section 2. Under the facts alleged in the complaint, Crandall wanted both to obtain joint monopoly power and to engage in price fixing. That he was not able to price fix and thus, has no liability under section 1, has no effect on whether his unsuccessful efforts to monopolize constitute attempted monopolization.

Nor do we agree with appellees' suggestion that firms or executives will be subject to liability for ambiguous or "intemperate words". We first note that under the allegations of the complaint Crandall's statements are not ambiguous. Second, a person must specifically intend to monopolize for his conduct to violate section 2; without the requisite intent, no liability attaches.

CONCLUSION

We hold that an agreement is not an absolute prerequisite for the offense of attempted joint monopolization and that the government's complaint sufficiently alleged facts that if proved would permit a finding of attempted monopolization by defendants. We therefore vacate the dismissal of the complaint and remand for further proceedings consistent with this opinion.

Questions and Comments

Why isn't *American Airlines* merely a case of unsuccessful solicitation of an agreement to monopolize? An unsuccessful solicitation of a conspiracy is not a violation of Section 1 of the Sherman Act, because no contract, combination or conspiracy has yet been formed. Should the same rule apply in Section 2 cases? Assume that American Airlines had one third of a relevant market for air travel and solicited Braniff (with one third) and Eastern (with one third) to join in a price-raising conspiracy. What policy reasons suggest holding this to be a violation by American? What are the policy reasons against it?

Can you reconcile *American Airlines* and *Empire Gas*?

How broad is the holding in *American Airlines?* If A proposes an agreement to B and B says no, is A always violating Section 2 if, had B said yes, the agreement would have violated Section 2?

G. END NOTE ON CONDUCT NOT ON THE COMPETITIVE MERITS

The dominant firm may run afoul of Section 2 of the Sherman Act in at least five ways. First, it may actively suppress competition, acting in ways that are against its customers' interests and that impose costs on itself in order to force greater costs on its competitors, with the expectation of ruining, disabling, containing or intimidating the competitors and then recouping its losses and entrenching its market power. *Lorain Journal* is such a case. Aspects of AT & T's strategies and several of the allegations against IBM also fit this mold.

Second, the dominant firm may use its leverage to exclude its competitors from significant inputs or important outlets, foreclosing competitors and preserving or increasing its market share. The conduct may amount to unreasonably exclusionary conduct (conduct that excludes competitors from opportunities to compete on the merits and is usually not explainable as an attempt to respond to customers' wishes).[22] Leveraging by Griffith Theatres and by United Shoe fits this pattern. Unreasonably broad requirements or exclusive dealing contracts are also examples. See Hoffmann La Roche Co. v. Commission of the European Communities [1979] E.C.R. 461 for similar Common Market law.

Third, the offense may be to create or increase market power by merger or acquisition, which may be the case if a near monopoly firm acquires an important actual or potential competitor or acquires significant patents. *Grinnell* and the early *Eastman Kodak* cases are examples.

Fourth are the exploitative conduct offenses. The monopolist may set a profit maximizing monopoly price; but this is not unlawful.[23] But it might use tie ins, price discrimination, and resale price maintenance to exploit its customers, and such strategies may be illegal, as we shall see in Chapter 4.

Fifth, the dominant firm may withhold needed access or benefit from less well situated competitors. The essential facilities aspects of *Terminal Railroad, Otter Tail,* and *AT & T* are in this category. While this is a narrow category and contemporary jurists have expressed reluctance to

---

22. In some cases the conduct may have some short-term consumers' benefits, but the long-term anticompetitive effect arguably outweighs these benefits. This was the case in United Shoe Machinery, where United Shoe bundled "free" service with its machines and thereby made it virtually impossible for the smaller competitors—who could not sustain an efficient servicing unit—to wage effective competition.

23. Pricing for a monopoly profit, though not a violation of U.S. law, for reasons which we have explored—principally, difficulties of identification and supervision—can run afoul of competition law in the Common Market and some European and other nations. See United Brands Co.: United Brands Continental B.V. v. Commission of the European Communities [1978] E.C.R. 207 (company can abuse dominant position by charging prices 'excessive in relation to the economic value of the product supplied'); General Motors Continental N.V. v. Commission of the European Communities [1975] E.C.R. 1367; Siragusa, The Application of Article 86 to the Pricing Policy of Dominant Companies: Discriminatory and Unfair Prices, 16 Common Mkt.L.Rev. 179 (1979).

expand it, developments in technology may create more and more situations—such as unique data banks and networks—for which access may be essential for reasons both of efficiency and fairness.

Are all of these strategies illegal under contemporary law? Does illegality turn on output limitation? Which strategies are most vulnerable? Which are most likely to be sustained as efficient or as reasonable exercises of business judgment?

We turn, now, from Section 2 of the Sherman Act and problems of single firm anticompetitive conduct to Section 1 of the Sherman Act and concerted conduct by two or more firms. You will find parallels between the ways in which Sections 1 and 2 developed over time, yet some anomalies. The analytical techniques you have learned in dealing with Section 2 will aid your understanding of both the legal issues and the policy questions that lie behind them.

Chapter 3

THE MODERN LAW: HORIZONTAL ARRANGEMENTS RESTRAINING COMPETITION

We saw in Chapter 1 that during its first two or three decades the Sherman Act was quite effective against the blatant price-fixing cartel—the kind of arrangement encountered in *Trans–Missouri* and *Addyston Pipe and Steel*. In this chapter we examine the law of horizontal restraints as it developed from the turn of the century to the current period. In order to approach subjects conceptually we do not present all of the cases chronologically, but we do suggest ways in which some of the cases may have been affected by the attitudes of the time in which they were decided.

A. ALTERNATIVE MODES OF ANALYSIS: PER SE RULES AND THE RULE OF REASON

The early debate about Section 1 is reflected in *Standard Oil, Addyston Pipe and Steel,* and *Trans–Missouri*. Justice White championed a rule of reason; he would condemn only unreasonable restraints, Justices Peckham and Harlan would outlaw "every" restraint. Broadly conceived, this was a debate about the proper role of courts. Justice Peckham thought judicial rules about industrial structure and conduct had to be explicit for business people to follow them and courts to apply them. Justice White thought explicit rules would condemn too much or too little. He thought that courts could examine the details of particular industrial situations and come to sensible results. Early on, a compromise seems to have been reached. We have examined *Standard Oil,* which applied a "rule of reason" in the context of an industry-wide consolidation. We've also examined *Trans–Missouri* and *Addyston Pipe and Steel,* which imply that at least one practice—naked price-fixing among ostensibly competing firms—was always unreasonable and thus unlawful. How broadly was this per se approach to apply? How were arrangements among competitors to be treated if they did not expressly fix but might nevertheless affect prices? Suppose competitors tried to fix market prices, but lacked power to do so? What of arrangements reducing aspects of non-price competition, such as agreements standardizing products?

Between 1918 and 1940 the Court rendered decisions suggesting that some loose-knit arrangements were subject to the rule of reason and others to the per se rule. The Court seemed to assume that trial court judges and lawyers ought to be able to tell the difference between per se situations and rule of reason situations and, when the latter rule applied, ought to be able to tell what kind of an analysis was called for. See whether you can make such discriminations.

BOARD OF TRADE OF THE CITY OF CHICAGO v. UNITED STATES

246 U.S. 231 (1918).

JUSTICE BRANDEIS: Chicago is the leading grain market in the world. Its Board of Trade is the commercial center through which most of the trading in grain is done. . . . Its 1600 members include brokers, commission merchants, dealers, millers, maltsters, manufacturers of corn products and proprietors of elevators. Grains there dealt in are graded . . . and . . . sold. . . . The standard forms of trading are: (a) Spot sales; that is, sales of grain already in Chicago . . . for immediate delivery. . . . (b) Future sales; that is, agreements for delivery later in the current or in some future month. (c) Sales "to arrive"; that is, agreements to deliver on arrival grain which is already in transit to Chicago or is to be shipped there within a time specified. On every business day sessions of the Board are held at which all bids and sales are publicly made. Spot sales and future sales are made at the regular sessions of the Board from 9:30 A.M. to 1:15 P.M., except on Saturdays, when the session closes at 12 M. Special sessions, termed the "Call," are held immediately after the close of the regular session, at which sales "to arrive" are made. . . . At all these sessions transactions are between members only; but they may trade either for themselves or on behalf of others. Members may also trade privately with one another at any place, either during the sessions or after, and they may trade with non-members at any time except on the premises occupied by the Board.

Purchases of grain "to arrive" are made largely from country dealers and farmers throughout the whole [agricultural] territory tributary to Chicago. . . . The purchases are sometimes the result of bids to individual country dealers made by telegraph or telephone either during the sessions or after; but most purchases are made by the sending out from Chicago by the afternoon mails to hundreds of country dealers offers to buy, at the prices named, any number of carloads, subject to acceptance before 9:30 A.M. on the next business day.

In 1906 the Board adopted what is known as the "Call" rule. By it members were prohibited from purchasing or offering to purchase, during the period between the close of the Call and the opening of the session on the next business day, any wheat, corn, oats or rye "to arrive" at a price other than the closing bid at the Call. The Call was over, with rare exceptions, by two o'clock. The change effected was this: Before the adoption of the rule, members fixed their bids throughout the day at such prices as they respectively saw fit; after the adoption of the rule, the bids had to be fixed at the day's closing bid on the Call until the opening of the next session.

In 1913 the United States filed in the District Court for the Northern District of Illinois this suit against the Board and its executive officers and directors, to enjoin the enforcement of the Call rule, alleging it to be in violation of the Anti-Trust Law. The defendants admitted the adoption and enforcement of the Call rule, and averred that its purpose was not to prevent competition or to control prices, but to promote the convenience of members by restricting their hours of business and to break up a monopoly in that branch of the grain trade acquired by four or five warehousemen in Chicago. On motion of the Government the allegations concerning the purpose of establishing the regulation were stricken from the record. The case was then heard upon evidence; and a decree was entered which declared that defendants became parties to a combination or conspiracy to restrain interstate and foreign trade and commerce "by adopting, acting upon and enforcing" the "Call" rule; and enjoined them from acting upon the same or from adopting or acting upon any similar rule.

No opinion was delivered by the District Judge. The Government proved the existence of the rule and described its application and the change in business practice involved. It made no attempt to show that the rule was designed to or that it had the effect of limiting the amount of grain shipped to Chicago; or of retarding or accelerating shipment; or of raising or depressing prices; or of discriminating against any part of the public; or that it resulted in hardship to anyone. The case was rested upon the bald proposition, that a rule or agreement by which men occupying positions of strength in any branch of trade, fixed prices at which they would buy or sell during an important part of the business day, is an illegal restraint of trade under the Anti-Trust Law. But the legality of an agreement or regulation cannot be determined by so simple a test, as whether it restrains competition. Every agreement concerning trade, every regulation of trade, restrains. To bind, to restrain, is of their very essence. The true test of legality is whether the restraint imposed is such as merely regulates and perhaps thereby promotes competition or whether it is such as may suppress or even destroy competition. To determine that question the court must ordinarily consider the facts peculiar to the business to which the restraint is applied; its condition before and after the restraint was imposed; the nature of the restraint and its effect, actual or probable. The history of the restraint, the evil believed to exist, the reason for adopting the particular remedy, the purpose or end sought to be attained, are all relevant facts. This is not because a good intention will save an otherwise objectionable regulation or the reverse; but because knowledge of intent may help the court to interpret facts and to predict consequences. The District Court erred, therefore, in striking from the answer allegations concerning the history and purpose of the Call rule and in later excluding evidence on that subject. But the evidence admitted makes it clear that the rule was a reasonable regulation of business consistent with the provisions of the Anti-Trust Law.

First: The nature of the rule: The restriction was upon the period of price-making. It required members . . . who desired to buy grain "to arrive" to make up their minds before the close of the Call how much they were willing to pay during the interval before the next session of the Board. The rule made it to their interest to attend the Call; and if they did not fill their wants by purchases there, to make the final bid high enough to enable them to purchase from country dealers.

Second: The scope of the rule: It is restricted in operation to grain "to arrive." It applies only to a small part of the grain shipped from day to day to Chicago, and to an even smaller part of the day's sales: members were left free to purchase grain already in Chicago from anyone at any price throughout the day. It applies only during a small part of the business day; members were left free to purchase during the sessions of the Board grain "to arrive," at any price, from members anywhere and from non-members anywhere except on the premises of the Board. It applied only to grain shipped to Chicago: members were left free to purchase at any price throughout the day from either members or non-members, grain "to arrive" at any other market. . . .

Third: The effects of the rule: . . . [T]he rule had no appreciable effect on general market prices; nor did it materially affect the total volume of grain coming to Chicago. But within the narrow limits of its operation the rule helped to improve market conditions thus:

(*a*) It created a public market for grain "to arrive." Before its adoption, bids were made privately. . . .

(*b*) It brought into the regular market hours of the Board sessions more of the trading in grain "to arrive."

(*c*) It brought buyers and sellers into more direct relations; because on the Call they gathered together for a free and open interchange of bids and offers.

(*d*) It distributed the business in grain "to arrive" among a far larger number of Chicago receivers and commission merchants than had been the case there before.

(*e*) It increased the number of country dealers engaging in this branch of the business; supplied them more regularly with bids from Chicago; and also increased the number of bids received by them from competing markets.

(*f*) It eliminated risks necessarily incident to a private market, and thus enabled country dealers to do business on a smaller margin. In that way the rule made it possible for them to pay more to farmers without raising the price to consumers.

(*g*) It enabled country dealers to sell some grain to arrive which they would otherwise have been obliged either to ship to Chicago commission merchants or to sell for "future delivery."

(*h*) It enabled those grain merchants of Chicago who sell to millers and exporters to trade on a smaller margin and, by paying more for grain or selling it for less, to make the Chicago market more attractive for both shippers and buyers of grain.

(*i*) Incidentally it facilitated trading "to arrive" by enabling those engaged in these transactions to fulfil their contracts by tendering grain arriving at Chicago on any railroad, whereas formerly shipments had to be made over the particular railroad designated by the buyer.

. . . . Every board of trade and nearly every trade organization imposes some restraint upon the conduct of business by its members. Those relating to the hours in which business may be done are common; and they make a special appeal where, as here, they tend to shorten the working day or, at least, limit the period of most exacting activity. The decree of the District Court is reversed with directions to dismiss the bill.

Questions and Comments

A board of trade provides a marketplace in which offers to buy and to sell are matched up. Participants get information on current market price almost instantaneously. Trading on a board of trade approximates trading in a perfectly competitive market. Would the information available during trading hours be available to farmers choosing to sell at night? To night buyers? If the information available at night was relatively limited—and, perhaps, asymmetrically deployed—would that be a good reason to deny exchange members freedom to deal at night? Is there a less restrictive way of dealing with such an "information problem"?

Obviously, there are situations where the deployment of information can be improved by the establishment of an organized market and when, in consequence, such a market will improve competition. Will there be times when, in order to organize such a market, it will be necessary to impose restrictions on participants? If so, and given the approach taken in *Addyston Pipe and Steel,* should such restrictions—ancillary and reasonably necessary to the development of the market—be lawful?

During evening hours broker-members were deprived of the freedom to decide at what price they would offer to buy. Under the principles set out in *Trans–Missouri, Joint–Traffic* and *Standard Oil* was it proper for the Court to inquire further into purpose and effect?

The Court identified as a problem the "monopoly" of the few members of the exchange who were not solely brokers but who also owned grain warehouses in Chicago; they bought for their warehouses on their own accounts. A theory sometimes used to explain the Call Rule suggests that broker-warehouse owners, by operating at night, freed themselves from the bidding pressure of brokers buying for others, and thus facilitated cartelization or interdependent bidding at night. Does this seem likely?

Another theory notes that at the time of the case brokerage commissions for transactions on the exchange were fixed by rule. On night transactions brokers could negotiate for fees. The theory infers that brokers dealing at night were seeking to undercut the cartel fee and thus do extra business. Does this seem likely?

The Court seemed to justify the Call Rule in part by its various social benefits—such as helping the farmers and the small country dealers, reducing the work day, etc. Does one need such extra-competitive bases to justify the Call Rule? Can you justify the outcome of *Chicago Board of Trade* solely on the basis of competition principles?

In *Chicago Board of Trade,* while the competitors imposed a restraint, the market set the market price. In an important subsequent case, the competitors set the price. Nonetheless, they attempted to justify their activity on the ground of reasonableness.

UNITED STATES v. TRENTON POTTERIES CO.

273 U.S. 392 (1927).

JUSTICE STONE: Respondents, twenty individuals and twenty-three corporations, were convicted in the district court for southern New York of violating the Sherman Anti-trust Law. . . .

The indictment was in two counts. The first charged a combination to fix and maintain uniform prices for the sale of sanitary pottery, in restraint of interstate commerce; the second, a combination to restrain interstate commerce by limiting sales of pottery to a special group known to respondents as "legitimate jobbers." On appeal, the court of appeals for the second circuit reversed the judgment of conviction on both counts. . . .   This Court granted certiorari.

* * *

There is no contention here that the verdict was not supported by sufficient evidence that respondents, controlling some 82 per cent. of the business of manufacturing and distributing in the United States vitreous pottery of the type described, combined to fix prices and to limit sales in interstate commerce to jobbers.

The issues raised here by the government's specification of errors relate only to the decision of the court of appeals upon its review of certain rulings of the district court made in the course of the trial. It is urged that the court below erred in holding in effect . . . that the trial court should have submitted to the jury the question whether the price agreement complained of constituted an unreasonable restraint of trade;
. . . .

REASONABLENESS OF RESTRAINT.

The trial court charged, in submitting the case to the jury, that if it found the agreements or combination complained of, it might return a verdict of guilty without regard to the reasonableness of the prices fixed, or the good intentions of the combining units, whether prices were actually lowered or raised or whether sales were restricted to the special jobbers, since both agreements of themselves were unreasonable restraints. . . .

* * *

The question therefore to be considered here is whether the trial judge correctly withdrew from the jury the consideration of the reasonableness of the particular [price] restraints charged.

. . . [O]nly those restraints upon interstate commerce which are unreasonable are prohibited by the Sherman Law. . . .   But it does not follow that agreements to fix or maintain prices are reasonable restraints and therefore permitted by the statute, merely because the prices themselves are reasonable. Reasonableness is not a concept of definite and unchanging content. Its meaning necessarily varies in the different fields of the law, because it is used as a convenient summary of the dominant considerations which control in the application of legal doctrines. Our view of what is a reasonable restraint of commerce is controlled by the recognized purpose of the Sherman Law itself. Whether this type of restraint is reasonable or not must be judged in part at least in the light of its effect on competition, for whatever difference of opinion there may be among economists as to the social and economic desirability of an unrestrained competitive system, it cannot be doubted that the Sherman Law and the judicial decisions interpreting it are based upon the assumption that the public interest is best protected from the evils of monopoly and price control by the maintenance of competition.

The aim and result of every price-fixing agreement, if effective, is the elimination of one form of competition. The power to fix prices, whether reasonably exercised or not, involves power to control the market and to fix arbitrary and unreasonable prices. The reasonable price fixed today may through economic and business changes become the unreasonable price of tomorrow. Once established, it may be maintained unchanged because of the absence of competition secured by the agreement for a price reasonable when fixed. Agreements which create such potential power may well be held to be in themselves unreasonable or unlawful restraints, without the necessity of minute inquiry whether a particular price is reasonable or unreasonable as fixed and without placing on the government in enforcing the Sherman Law the burden of ascertaining from day to day whether it has become unreasonable through the mere variation of economic conditions. Moreover, in the absence of express legislation requiring it, we should hesitate to adopt a construction making the difference between legal and illegal conduct in the field of business relations depend upon so uncertain a test as whether prices are reasonable—a determination which can be satisfactorily made only after a complete survey of our economic organization and a choice between rival philosophies. . . .

* * *

Respondents rely upon *Chicago Board of Trade v. United States* [246 U.S. 231], in which an agreement by members of the Chicago Board of Trade controlling prices during certain hours of the day in a special class of grain contracts and affecting only a small proportion of the commerce in question was upheld. The purpose and effect of the agreement there was to maintain for a part of each business day the price which had been that day determined by open competition on the floor of the Exchange. That decision, dealing as it did with a regulation of a board of trade, does not sanction a price agreement among competitors in an open market such as is presented here.

* * *

It follows that the judgment of the circuit court of appeals must be reversed and the judgment of the district court reinstated.

Reversed.

Purk puck

Questions and Comments

Why shouldn't the reasonableness of the prices fixed be a good defense? Who could be harmed by reasonable prices? How did Judge Taft treat this issue in *Addyston Pipe*?

A per se rule means merely that certain conduct is illegal in and of itself, without inquiry as to its purpose or effect. What is the per se rule of *Trenton Potteries*? Does it make sense as a matter of policy? What are its benefits? Its drawbacks? Should the rule apply even when the combining firms do not have market power? Even where there is enormous overcapacity and free market forces are ruining the industry by pushing competing sellers to cut prices down to variable costs? We look at these issues in *Appalachian Coals*, and then *Socony–Vacuum*.

APPALACHIAN COALS, INC. v. UNITED STATES
288 U.S. 344 (1933).

CHIEF JUSTICE HUGHES: This suit was brought to enjoin a combination alleged to be in restraint of interstate commerce in bituminous coal and in attempted monopolization of part of that commerce, in violation of §§ 1 and 2 of the Sherman Anti–Trust Act. . . .

Defendants, other than Appalachian Coals, Inc., are 137 producers of bituminous coal in eight districts (called for convenience Appalachian territory) lying in Virginia, West Virginia, Kentucky and Tennessee. . . . In 1929 (the last year for which complete statistics were available) the total production of bituminous coal east of the Mississippi river was 484,786,000 tons, of which defendants mined . . . 11.96 per cent. In the so-called Appalachian territory and the immediately surrounding area, the total production was 107,008,209 tons, of which defendants' production was 54.21 per cent, or 64 per cent if the output of "captive" mines (16,455,001 tons) be deducted. . . .

The challenged combination lies in the creation by the defendant producers of an exclusive selling agency. This agency is the defendant Appalachian Coals, Inc., which may be designated as the Company. Defendant producers own all its capital stock, their holdings being in proportion to their production. The majority of the common stock, which has exclusive voting right, is held by seventeen defendants. By uniform contracts, separately made, each defendant producer constitutes the Company an exclusive agent for the sale of all coal (with certain exceptions) which the producer mines in Appalachian territory. The Company agrees to establish standard classifications, to sell all of the coal of all its principals at the best prices obtainable and, if all cannot be sold, to apportion orders upon a stated basis. . . .

The Government's contention, which the District Court sustained, is that the plan violates the Sherman Anti–Trust Act,—in the view that it eliminates competition among the defendants themselves and also gives the selling agency power substantially to affect and control the price of bituminous coal in many interstate markets. . . .

* * *

First. There is no question as to the test to be applied in determining the legality of the defendants' conduct. The purpose of the Sherman Anti–Trust Act is to prevent undue restraints of interstate commerce, to maintain its appropriate freedom in the public interest, to afford protection from the subversive or coercive influences of monopolistic endeavor. As a charter of freedom, the Act has a generality and adaptability comparable to that found to be desirable in constitutional provisions. It does not go into detailed definitions which might either work injury to legitimate enterprise or through particularization defeat its purpose by providing loopholes for escape. The restrictions the Act imposes are not mechanical or artificial. Its general phrases, interpreted to attain its fundamental objects, set up the essential standard of reasonableness. They call for vigilance in the detection and frustration of all efforts unduly to restrain the free course of interstate commerce, but they do not seek to establish a mere delusive liberty either by making impossible the normal and fair expansion of that commerce or the adoption of reasonable measures to protect it from injurious and destructive practices and to promote competition upon a sound basis. The decisions establish, said this Court in Nash v. United States, 229 U.S. 373, 376, "that only such contracts and combinations are within the act as, by reason of intent or the inherent nature of the contemplated acts, prejudice the public interests by unduly restricting competition or unduly obstructing the course of trade."

In applying this test, a close and objective scrutiny of particular conditions and purposes is necessary in each case. Realities must dominate the judgment. The mere fact that the parties to an agreement eliminate competition between themselves is not enough to condemn it. "The legality of an agreement or regulation cannot be determined by so simple a test, as whether it restrains competition. Every agreement concerning trade, every regulation of trade, restrains." Chicago Board of Trade v. United States, 246 U.S. 231.

Second. The findings of the District Court, upon abundant evidence, leave no room for doubt as to the economic condition of the coal industry. That condition, as the District Court states, "for many years has been indeed deplorable." Due largely to the expansion under the stimulus of the Great War, "the bituminous mines of the country have a developed capacity exceeding 700,000,000 tons" to meet a demand "of less than 500,000,000 tons." In connection with this increase in surplus production, the consumption of coal in all the industries which are its largest users has shown a substantial relative decline. The actual decrease is partly due to the industrial condition but the relative decrease is progressing, due entirely to other causes. Coal has been losing markets to oil, natural gas and water power and has also been losing ground due to greater efficiency in the use of coal. The change has been more rapid during the last few years by reason of the developments of both oil and gas fields. The court below found that "Based upon the assumption that bituminous coal would have maintained the upward trend prevailing between 1900 and 1915 in percentage of total energy supply in the United States, the total substitution between 1915 and 1930 has been equal to more than 200,000,000 tons per year." . . . [T]he adverse influence upon the coal industry, including the branch of it under review, of the use of substitute fuels and of improved methods is apparent.

This unfavorable condition has been aggravated by particular practices. One of these relates to what is called "distress coal." The greater part of the demand is for particular sizes of coal such as nut and slack, stove coal, egg coal, and lump coal. Any one size cannot be prepared without making several sizes. According to the finding of the court below, one of the chief problems of the industry is thus involved in the practice "of producing different sizes of coal even though orders are on hand for only one size, and the necessity of marketing all sizes." Usually there are no storage facilities at the mines and the different sizes produced are placed in cars on the producer's tracks, which may become so congested that either production must be stopped or the cars must be moved regardless of demand. This leads to the practice of shipping unsold coal to billing points or on consignment to the producer or his agent in the consuming territory. If the coal is not sold by the time it reaches its destination, and is not unloaded promptly, it becomes subject to demurrage charges which may exceed the amount obtainable for the coal unless it is sold quickly. The court found that this type of "distress coal" presses on the market at all times, includes all sizes and grades, and the total amount from all causes is of substantial quantity.

"Pyramiding" of coal is another "destructive practice." It occurs when a producer authorizes several persons to sell the same coal, and they may in turn offer it for sale to other dealers. In consequence "the coal competes with itself, thereby resulting in abnormal and destructive competition which depresses the price for all coals in the market." Again, there is misrepresentation by some producers in selling one size of coal and shipping another size which they happen to have on hand. "The lack of standardization of sizes and the misrepresentation as to sizes" are found to have been injurious to the coal industry as a whole. The court added, however, that the evidence did not show the existence of any trade war or widespread fraudulent conduct. The industry also suffers through "credit losses," which are due to the lack of agencies for the collection of comprehensive data with respect to the credits that can safely be extended.

In addition to these factors, the District Court found that organized buying agencies, and large consumers purchasing substantial tonnages, "constitute unfavorable forces." "The highly organized and concentrated buying power which they control and the great abundance of coal available have contributed to make the market for coal a buyers' market for many years past."

It also appears that the "unprofitable condition" of the industry has existed particularly in the Appalachian territory where there is little local consumption, as the region is not industrialized. "The great bulk of the coal there produced is sold in the highly competitive region east of the Mississippi river and north of the Ohio river under an adverse freight rate which imposes an unfavorable differential from 35 cents to 50 cents per ton." And in a graphic summary of the economic situation, the court found that "numerous producing companies have gone into bankruptcy or into the hands of receivers, many mines have been shut down, the number of days of operation per week have [sic] been greatly curtailed, wages to labor have been substantially lessened, and the States in which coal producing companies are located have found it increasingly difficult to collect taxes."

Third. The findings also fully disclose the proceedings of the defendants in formulating their plan and the reasons for its adoption. The serious economic conditions had led to discussions among coal operators and state and national officials, seeking improvement of the industry. Governors of States had held meetings with coal producers. The limits of official authority were apparent. A general meeting of producers, sales agents and attorneys was held in New York in October, 1931, a committee was appointed and various suggestions were considered. At a second general meeting in December, 1931, there was further discussion and a report which recommended the organization of regional sales agencies, and was supported by the opinion of counsel as to the legality of proposed forms of contract, was approved. Committees to present the plan to producers were constituted for eighteen producing districts including the eight districts in Appalachian territory. Meetings of the representatives of the latter districts resulted in the organization of defendant Appalachian Coals, Inc. It was agreed that a minimum of 70 per cent and a maximum of 80 per cent of the commercial tonnage of the territory should be secured before the plan should become effective. Approximately 73 per cent was obtained. A resolution to fix the maximum at 90 per cent was defeated. The maximum of 80 per cent was adopted because a majority of the producers felt that an organization with a greater degree of control might unduly restrict competition in local markets. The minimum of 70 per cent was fixed because it was agreed that the organization would not be effective without this degree of control. The court below also found that it was the expectation that similar agencies would be organized in other producing districts including those which were competitive with Appalachian coal, and that it was "the particular purpose of the defendants in the Appalachian territory to secure such degree of control therein as would eliminate competition among the 73 per cent of the commercial production." . . .

When, in January, 1932, the Department of Justice announced its adverse opinion, the producers outside Appalachian territory decided to hold their plans in abeyance pending the determination of the question by the courts. The District Court found that "the evidence tended to show that other selling agencies with a control of at least 70 per cent of the production in their respective districts will be organized if the petition in this case is dismissed;" that in that event "there will result an organization in most of the districts whose coal is or may be competitive with Appalachian coal; but the testimony tends to show that there will still be substantial, active competition in the sale of coal in all markets in which Appalachian coal is sold."

* * *

Fourth. Voluminous evidence was received with respect to the effect of defendants' plan upon market prices. As the plan has not gone into operation, there are no actual results upon which to base conclusions.

The question is necessarily one of prediction. The court below found that, as between defendants themselves, competition would be eliminated. . . .

The more serious question relates to the effect of the plan upon competition between defendants and other producers. As already noted, the District Court found that "the great bulk" of the coal produced in Appalachian territory is sold "in the highly competitive region east of the Mississippi river and north of the Ohio river under an adverse freight rate." . . . [T]he bituminous coal industry under normal conditions affords most exceptional competitive opportunities. . . . "[Enormous] excess capacity over actual production," the [lower] court said, "could be brought into production at moderate expense and with reasonable promptness." . . .

* * *

Fifth. We think that the evidence requires the following conclusions:

(1). With respect to defendant's purposes, we find no warrant for determining that they were other than those they declared. Good intentions will not save a plan otherwise objectionable, but knowledge of actual intent is an aid in the interpretation of facts and prediction of consequences. Chicago Board of Trade v. United States [246 U.S. 231]. The evidence leaves no doubt of the existence of the evils at which defendants' plan was aimed. The industry was in distress. It suffered from over-expansion and from a serious relative decline through the growing use of substitute fuels. It was afflicted by injurious practices within itself,— practices which demanded correction. If evil conditions could not be entirely cured, they at least might be alleviated. The unfortunate state of the industry would not justify any attempt unduly to restrain competition or to monopolize, but the existing situation prompted defendants to make, and the statute did not preclude them from making, an honest effort to remove abuses, to make competition fairer, and thus to promote the essential interests of commerce. The interests of producers and consumers are interlinked. When industry is grievously hurt, when producing concerns fail, when unemployment mounts and communities dependent upon profitable production are prostrated, the wells of commerce go dry. So far as actual purposes are concerned, the conclusion of the court below was amply supported that defendants were engaged in a fair and open endeavor to aid the industry in a measurable recovery from its plight. The inquiry then, must be whether despite this objective the inherent nature of their plan was such as to create an undue restraint upon interstate commerce.

(2). The question thus presented chiefly concerns the effect upon prices. The evidence as to the conditions of the production and distribution of bituminous coal, the available facilities for its transportation, the extent of developed mining capacity, and the vast potential undeveloped capacity, makes it impossible to conclude that defendants through the operation of their plan will be able to fix the price of coal in the consuming markets. The ultimate finding of the District Court is that the defendants "will not have monopoly control of any market, nor the power to fix monopoly prices;" and in its opinion the court stated that "the selling agency will not be able, we think, to fix the market price of coal."

Defendants' coal will continue to be subject to active competition. In addition to the coal actually produced and seeking markets in competition with defendants' coal, enormous additional quantities will be within reach and can readily be turned into the channels of trade if an advance of price invites that course. . . .

* * *

. . . We agree that there is no ground for holding defendants' plan illegal merely because they have not integrated their properties and have chosen to maintain their independent plants, seeking not to limit but rather to facilitate production. We know of no public policy, and none is suggested by the terms of the Sherman Act, that in order to comply with the law those engaged in industry should be driven to unify their properties and businesses in order to correct abuses which may be corrected by less drastic measures. . . .

. . . We think that the Government has failed to show adequate grounds for an injunction in this case. We recognize, however, that the case has been tried in advance of the operation of defendants' plan, and that it has been necessary to test that plan with reference to purposes and anticipated consequences without the advantage of the demonstrations of experience. If in actual operation it should prove to be an undue restraint upon interstate commerce, if it should appear that the plan is used to the impairment of fair competitive opportunities, the decision upon the present record should not preclude the Government from seeking the remedy which would be suited to such a state of facts. . . .

* * *

Reversed and remanded.

Questions and Comments

What was the purpose of the Appalachian coal producers' joint selling agency? Would it be fair to say that they planned, through the selling agent, to coordinate the price of their coal, and that they expected their agent to set a reasonable price? If so, why isn't this case controlled by *Trenton Potteries*? If the vitreous pottery producers had called their arrangement a joint selling agency and had proved that they would reduce their costs by eliminating the need for a duplicative sales network, would they have prevailed? On such facts, should the cooperating firms prevail?

The Court found that defendants' intent was to remove abuses and evils of overproduction. How did the Court in *Trans–Missouri* and *Joint–Traffic* deal with the similar argument of destructive competition? Should the railroad cases have controlled the outcome of *Appalachian Coals*? Is there a relevant factual difference?

The Court assumed that defendants, even combined, did not have power to exact a monopoly price because there were so many other sellers of coal who were not participating. Is this assumption correct? Would it be if producers in other districts also combined? Analyze the probable effect of the coal producers' collaboration in *Appalachian Coals*. Consider supply, demand, size characteristics of buyers and sellers, location of customers, the number of producers (many or few) competing for the business of the Appalachian coal producers' customers, and conditions of entry. What do you think would have happened if the Appalachian coal producers did not form a joint selling agency?

If the Appalachian producers when combined did not have power to increase price by withholding supply, then their arrangement would not hurt consumers. But who should run the risk? Suppose that you were arguing the case for the government and Chief Justice Hughes said to you: "These small Appalachian coal producers cannot command supracompetitive prices. What is the public interest in enjoining their selling agency?" What is your answer?

Assume that the participants had power; their combination kept prices from falling more steeply. Nonetheless, the coal companies argue, given the shockingly depressed conditions in the market—companies going bankrupt, workers on bread lines, whole communities facing catastrophe—a crisis cartel is socially essential. Cooperative action, they argue, is the only way for the industry to reduce overproduction, withdraw excess capacity, and return the industry to a viable state. Is there anything wrong with this argument as a matter of fact or policy? Would a holding that the Sherman Act condoned a cartel in such circumstances have been a defensible interpretation of the statute?

Defendants argued that they could have integrated their operations by merger without violating the antitrust laws; a joint sales agency is less restrictive than a merger; therefore the joint sales agency cannot be an unreasonable restraint. Assume that such a merger would have been lawful. Is the argument then compelling? Argue, to the contrary, that there is good basis for distinction between permissible mergers and permissible loose-knit agreements. In framing your argument think about the significance of integration. Can it be socially beneficial? In what ways? Could a consolidation among these coal companies yield more integration benefits than could the joint sales agency they actually formed? We saw in Chapter 1 that during the early years of the Sherman Act the Court was hostile to price fixing, yet soft on consolidation. Was there an underlying (even if then unintended) wisdom in that distinction?

This is the first set of facts we have studied in which the collaboration of the competitors takes a form that might be called a "joint venture." A joint venture, as we use the term, involves some degree of integration of facilities and activities of the participants, but a degree falling short of the complete integration that might be achieved through merger. In *Trenton Potteries* and *Addyston Pipe & Steel*, the defendants jointly set prices. They did not integrate any other activities or any facilities at all. Mere joint price setting would not be called a joint venture, but a cartel. In *Trans–Missouri* and *Joint–Traffic*, the railroads combined to "self regulate." There was an integration, though of very modest degree; defendants did not merely agree on the prices each would charge; they also appointed a single agent to set prices and to make sales for all participants.

Appalachian Coals gave rise to the notion that the rule of reason was broad and the per se rule narrow. At a minimum *Appalachian Coals* gave hope to industry members that crisis cartels might be justified as reasonable. That hope was soon tested in the famous *Socony–Vacuum* case.

UNITED STATES v. SOCONY–VACUUM OIL CO.

310 U.S. 150 (1940).

JUSTICE DOUGLAS: Respondents were convicted by a jury under an indictment charging violations of § 1 of the Sherman Anti-trust Act. The Circuit Court of Appeals reversed and remanded for a new trial. . . .

I. THE INDICTMENT.

The indictment was returned in December 1936 in the United States District Court for the Western District of Wisconsin. It charges that certain major oil companies, selling gasoline in the Mid–Western area . . . (1) "combined and conspired together for the purpose of artificially raising and fixing the tank car prices of gasoline" in the "spot markets" in the East Texas and Mid–Continent fields; (2) "have artificially raised and fixed said spot market tank car prices of gasoline and have maintained said prices at artificially high and non-competitive levels, and at levels agreed upon among them and have thereby intentionally increased and fixed the tank car prices of gasoline contracted to be sold and sold in interstate commerce as aforesaid in the Mid–Western area"; (3) "have arbitrarily," by reason of the provisions of the prevailing form of jobber contracts which made the price to the jobber dependent on the average spot market price, "exacted large sums of money from thousands of jobbers with whom they have had such contracts in said Mid–Western area"; and (4) "in turn have intentionally raised the general level of retail prices prevailing in said Mid–Western area."

* * *

. . . Each defendant major oil company owns, operates or leases retail service stations in this area. It supplies those stations, as well as independent retail stations, with gasoline from its bulk storage plants. All but one sell large quantities of gasoline to jobbers in tank car lots under term contracts. In this area these jobbers exceed 4,000 in number and distribute about 50% of all gasoline distributed to retail service stations therein, the bulk of the jobbers' purchases being made from the defendant companies. The price to the jobbers under those contracts with defendant companies is made dependent on the spot market price, pursuant to a formula hereinafter discussed. And the spot market tank car prices of gasoline directly and substantially influence the retail prices in the area. In sum, it is alleged that defendants by raising and fixing the tank car prices of gasoline in these spot markets could and did increase the tank car prices and the retail prices of gasoline sold in the Mid–Western area. The vulnerability of these spot markets to that type of manipulation or stabilization is emphasized by the allegation that spot market prices published in the journals were the result of spot sales made chiefly by independent refiners of a relatively small amount of the gasoline sold in that area—virtually all gasoline sold in tank car quantities in spot market transactions in the Mid–Western area being sold by independent refiners, such sales amounting to less than 5% of all gasoline marketed therein.

* * *

II. BACKGROUND OF THE ALLEGED CONSPIRACY.

Evidence was introduced (or respondents made offers of proof) showing or tending to show the following conditions preceding the commencement of the alleged conspiracy in February 1935. As we shall develop later, these facts were in the main relevant to certain defenses which respondents at the trial unsuccessfully sought to interpose to the indictment.

Beginning about 1926 there commenced a period of production of crude oil in such quantities as seriously to affect crude oil and gasoline markets throughout the United States. Overproduction was wasteful, reduced the productive capacity of the oil fields and drove the price of oil down to levels below the cost of production from pumping and stripper wells. When the price falls below such cost, those wells must be abandoned. Once abandoned, subsurface changes make it difficult or impossible to bring those wells back into production. Since such wells constitute about 40% of the country's known oil reserves, conservation requires that the price of crude oil be maintained at a level which will permit such wells to be operated. As Oklahoma and Kansas were attempting to remedy the situation through their proration laws, the largest oil field in history was discovered in East Texas. That was in 1930. The supply of oil from this field was so great that at one time crude oil sank to 10 or 15 cents a barrel, and gasoline was sold in the East Texas field for $2\frac{1}{8}$¢ a gallon. Enforcement by Texas of its proration law was extremely difficult. Orders restricting production were violated, the oil unlawfully produced being known as "hot oil" and the gasoline manufactured therefrom, "hot gasoline." Hot oil sold for substantially lower prices than those posted for legal oil. Hot gasoline therefore cost less and at times could be sold for less than it cost to manufacture legal gasoline. The latter, deprived of its normal outlets, had to be sold at distress prices. The condition of many independent refiners using legal crude oil was precarious. In spite of their unprofitable operations they could not afford to shut down, for if they did so they would be apt to lose their oil connections in the field and their regular customers. Having little storage capacity they had to sell their gasoline as fast as they made it. As a result their gasoline became "distress" gasoline—gasoline which the refiner could not store, for which he had no regular sales outlets and which therefore he had to sell for whatever price it would bring. Such sales drove the market down.

In the spring of 1933 conditions were acute. The wholesale market was below the cost of manufacture. As the market became flooded with cheap gasoline, gasoline was dumped at whatever price it would bring. On June 1, 1933, the price of crude oil was 25¢ a barrel; the tank car price of regular gasoline was $2\frac{5}{8}$¢ a gallon. In June 1933 Congress passed the National Industrial Recovery Act (48 Stat. 195). Sec. 9(c) of that Act authorized the President to forbid the interstate and foreign shipment of petroleum and its products produced or withdrawn from storage in violation of state laws. By Executive Order the President on July 11, 1933, forbade such shipments. On August 19, 1933, a code of fair competition for the petroleum industry was approved. The Secretary of the Interior was designated as Administrator of that Code. He established a Petroleum Administrative Board to "advise with and make recommendations" to him. A Planning and Coordination Committee was appointed, of which respondent Charles E. Arnott, a vice-president of Socony–Vacuum, was a member, to aid in the administration of the Code. In addressing that Committee in the fall of 1933 the Administrator said: "Our task is to stabilize the oil industry upon a profitable basis." Considerable progress was made. The price of crude oil was a dollar a barrel near the end of September 1933, as a result of the voluntary action of the industry, but, according to respondents, in accordance with the Administrator's policy and desire. In April 1934 an amendment to the Code was adopted under which an attempt was made to balance the supply of gasoline with the demand by allocating the amount of crude oil which each refiner could process with the view of creating a firmer condition in the market and thus increasing the price of gasoline. This amendment also authorized the Planning and Coordination Committee, with the approval of the President, to make suitable arrangements for the purchase of gasoline from non-integrated or semi-integrated refiners and the resale of the same through orderly channels. Thereafter four buying programs were approved by the Administrator. These permitted the major companies to purchase distress gasoline from the independent refiners. Standard forms of contract were provided. The evil aimed at was, in part at least, the production of hot oil and hot gasoline. The contracts (to at least one of which the Administrator was a party) were made pursuant to the provisions of the National Industrial Recovery Act and the Code and bound the purchasing company to buy fixed amounts of gasoline at designated prices on condition that the seller should abide by the provisions of the Code. According to the 1935 Annual Report of the Secretary of the Interior, these buying programs were not successful as "the production of gasoline from 'hot oil' continued, stocks of gasoline mounted, wholesale prices for gasoline remained below parity with crude-oil prices, and in the early fall of 1934 the industry approached a serious collapse of the wholesale market."   . . .

The flow of hot oil out of East Texas continued. Refiners in the field could procure such oil for 35¢ or less a barrel and manufacture gasoline from it for 2 or 2½¢ a gallon. This competition of the cheap hot gasoline drove the price of legal gasoline down below the cost of production. The problem of distress gasoline also persisted. The disparity between the price of gasoline and the cost of crude oil which had been at $1 per barrel since September 1933 caused losses to many independent refiners, no matter how efficient they were. In October 1934 the Administrator set up a Federal Tender Board and issued an order making it illegal to ship crude oil or gasoline out of East Texas in interstate or foreign commerce unless it were accompanied by a tender issued by that Board certifying that it had been legally produced or manufactured. Prices rose sharply. But the improvement was only temporary as the enforcement of § 9(c) of the Act was enjoined in a number of suits. On January 7, 1935, this Court held § 9(c) to be unconstitutional. *Panama Refining Co. v. Ryan*, 293 U.S. 388. Following that decision there was a renewed influx of hot gasoline into the Mid–Western area and the tank car market fell.

Meanwhile the retail markets had been swept by a series of price wars. These price wars affected all markets—service station, tank wagon, and tank car. Early in 1934 the Petroleum Administrative Board tried to deal with them—by negotiating agreements between marketing companies and persuading individual companies to raise the price level for a period. On July 9, 1934, that Board asked respondent Arnott, chairman of the Planning and Coordination Committee's Marketing Committee, if he would head up a voluntary, cooperative movement to deal with price wars. According to Arnott, he pointed out that in order to stabilize the retail market it was necessary to stabilize the tank car market through elimination of hot oil and distress gasoline. . . .

. . . After receiving [a] letter [of authorization from the Administrator,] Arnott appointed a General Stabilization Committee with headquarters in Washington and a regional chairman in each region. Over fifty state and local committees were set up. The Petroleum Administrative Board worked closely with Arnott and the committees until the end of the Code near the middle of 1935. The effort was to eliminate price wars by negotiation and by persuading suppliers to see to it that those who bought from them sold at a fair price. In the first week of December 1934, Arnott held a meeting of the General Stabilization Committee in Chicago and a series of meetings on the next four or five days attended by hundreds of members of the industry from the middle west. These meetings were said to have been highly successful in elimination of many price wars. Arnott reported the results to members of the Petroleum Administrative Board on December 18, 1934, and stated that he was going to have a follow-up meeting in the near future. It was at that next meeting that the groundwork for the alleged conspiracy was laid.

III. THE ALLEGED CONSPIRACY.

The alleged conspiracy is not to be found in any formal contract or agreement. It is to be pieced together from the testimony of many witnesses and the contents of over 1,000 exhibits, extending through the 3,900 printed pages of the record. What follows is based almost entirely on unequivocal testimony or undisputed contents of exhibits, only occasionally on the irresistible inferences from those facts.

A. *Formation of the Mid-continent Buying Program.*

The next meeting of the General Stabilization Committee was held in Chicago on January 4, 1935, and was attended by all of the individual respondents, by representatives of the corporate respondents, and by others. Representatives of independent refiners, present at the meeting, complained of the failure of the price of refined gasoline to reach a parity with the crude oil price of $1 a barrel. And complaints by the independents of the depressing effect on the market of hot and distress gasoline were reported. Views were expressed to the effect that "if we were going to have general stabilization in retail markets, we must have some sort of a firm market in the tank car market." As a result of the discussion Arnott appointed a Tank Car Stabilization Committee to study the situation and make a report, or, to use the language of one of those present, "to consider ways and means of establishing and maintaining an active and strong tank car market on gasoline." Three days after this committee was appointed, this Court decided *Panama Refining Co. v. Ryan, supra.* As we have said, there was evidence that following that decision there was a renewed influx of hot gasoline into the Mid–Western area with a consequent falling off of the tank car market prices.

The first meeting of the Tank Car Committee was held February 5, 1935, and the second on February 11, 1935. At these meetings the alleged conspiracy was formed, the substance of which, so far as it pertained to the Mid–Continent phase, was as follows:

It was estimated that there would be between 600 and 700 tank cars of distress gasoline produced in the Mid–Continent oil field every month by about 17 independent refiners. These refiners, not having regular outlets for the gasoline, would be unable to dispose of it except at distress prices. Accordingly, it was proposed and decided that certain major companies (including the corporate respondents) would purchase gasoline from these refiners. The Committee would assemble each month information as to the quantity and location of this distress gasoline. Each of the major companies was to select one (or more) of the independent refiners having distress gasoline as its "dancing partner," [20] and would assume responsibility for purchasing its distress supply. . . . Purchases were to be made at the "fair going market prices."

* * *

. . . [T]he final details of the Mid–Continent buying program were worked out, including an assignment of the "dancing partners" among the major companies. . . . Before the month was out all companies alleged to have participated in the program (except one or two) made purchases; 757 tank cars were bought from all but three of the independent refiners who were named in the indictment as sellers.

B. The Mid–Continent Buying Program in Operation.

No specific term for the buying program was decided upon, beyond the first month. But it was started with the hope of its continuance from month to month. And in fact it did go on for over a year.

* * *

20. Respondent R.W. McDowell, a vice president of Mid–Continent, testified as follows respecting the origin and meaning of this term:

"The phrase 'dancing partners' came up right there after Mr. Ashton had gone around the room. There were these 7 or 8 small refiners whom no one had mentioned. He said this situation reminded him of the dances that he used to go to when he was a young fellow. He said, 'Here we are at a great economic ball.' He said, 'We have these major companies who have to buy gasoline and are buying gasoline, and they are the strong dancers.' And he said, 'They have asked certain people to dance with them. They are the better known independent refiners.' He said, 'Here are 7 or 8 that no one seems to know.' He said, 'They remind me of the wallflowers that always used to be present at those old country dances.' He said, 'I think it is going to be one of the jobs of this Committee to introduce some of these wallflowers to some of the strong dancers, so that everybody can dance.' And from that simile, or whatever you want to call it, the term 'dancing partner' arose."

V. APPLICATION OF THE SHERMAN ACT.

Charge to the Jury.

The court charged the jury that it was a violation of the Sherman Act for a group of individuals or corporations to act together to raise the prices to be charged for the commodity which they manufactured where they controlled a substantial part of the interstate trade and commerce in that commodity. The court stated that where the members of a combination had the power to raise prices and acted together for that purpose, the combination was illegal; and that it was immaterial how reasonable or unreasonable those prices were or to what extent they had been affected by the combination. It further charged that if such illegal combination existed, it did not matter that there may also have been other factors which contributed to the raising of the prices. In that connection, it referred specifically to the economic factors which we have previously discussed and which respondents contended were primarily responsible for the price rise and the spot markets' stability in 1935 and 1936, viz., control of production, the Connally Act, the price of crude oil, an increase in consumptive demand, control of inventories and manufacturing quotas, and improved business conditions. The court then charged that, unless the jury found beyond a reasonable doubt that the price rise and its continuance were "caused" by the combination and not caused by those other factors, verdicts of "not guilty" should be returned. It also charged that there was no evidence of governmental approval which would exempt the buying programs from the prohibitions of the Sherman Act; and that knowledge or acquiescence of officers of the government or the good intentions of the members of the combination would not give immunity from prosecution under that Act.

The Circuit Court of Appeals held this charge to be reversible error, since it was based upon the theory that such a combination was illegal *per se*. In its view respondents' activities were not unlawful unless they constituted an unreasonable restraint of trade. Hence, since that issue had not been submitted to the jury and since evidence bearing on it had been excluded, that court reversed and remanded for a new trial so that the character of those activities and their effect on competition could be determined. In answer to the government's petition respondents here contend that the judgment of the Circuit Court of Appeals was correct, since there was evidence that they had affected prices only in the sense that the removal of the competitive evil of distress gasoline by the buying programs had permitted prices to rise to a normal competitive level; that their activities promoted rather than impaired fair competitive opportunities; and therefore that their activities had not unduly or unreasonably restrained trade. . . .

In United States v. Trenton Potteries Co., 273 U.S. 392, this Court sustained a conviction under the Sherman Act where the jury was charged that an agreement on the part of the members of a combination, controlling a substantial part of an industry, upon the prices which the members are to charge for their commodity is in itself an unreasonable restraint of trade without regard to the reasonableness of the prices or the good intentions of the combining units. . . . This Court reviewed the various price-fixing cases under the Sherman Act . . . and said ". . . it has since often been decided and always assumed that uniform price-fixing by those controlling in any substantial manner a trade or business in interstate commerce is prohibited by the Sherman Law, despite the reasonableness of the particular prices agreed upon." (273 U.S. 398). . . .

* * *

But respondents claim that other decisions of this Court afford them adequate defenses to the indictment. Among those on which they place reliance [is] Appalachian Coals v. United States, 288 U.S. 344. . . .

. . . [W]e are of the opinion that *Appalachian Coals* is not in point. . . . [T]he plan did not either contemplate or involve "the fixing of market prices;" defendants would not be able to fix the price of coal in the consuming markets; their coal would continue to be subject to "active competition." . . .

. . . [I]n reality the only essential thing in common between the instant case and the *Appalachian Coals* case is the presence in each of so-called demoralizing or injurious practices. The methods of dealing with them were quite divergent. . . . Unlike the plan in the instant case, the plan in the *Appalachian Coals* case was not designed to operate vis à vis the general consuming market and to fix the prices on that market. Furthermore, the effect, if any, of that plan on prices was not only wholly incidental but also highly conjectural. For the plan had not then been put into operation. Hence this Court expressly reserved jurisdiction in the District Court to take further proceedings if, inter alia, in "actual operation" the plan proved to be "an undue restraint upon interstate commerce." And as we have seen it would per se constitute such a restraint if price-fixing were involved.

* * *

. . . [F]or over forty years this Court has consistently and without deviation adhered to the principle that price-fixing agreements are unlawful per se under the Sherman Act and that no showing of so-called competitive abuses or evils which those agreements were designed to eliminate or alleviate may be interposed as a defense. . . .

Therefore the sole remaining question on this phase of the case is the applicability of the rule of the *Trenton Potteries* case to these facts.

Respondents seek to distinguish the *Trenton Potteries* case from the instant one. They assert that in that case the parties substituted an agreed-on price for one determined by competition; that the defendants there had the power and purpose to suppress the play of competition in the determination of the market price; and therefore that the controlling factor in that decision was the destruction of market competition, not whether prices were higher or lower, reasonable or unreasonable. Respondents contend that in the instant case there was no elimination in the spot tank car market of competition which prevented the prices in that market from being made by the play of competition in sales between independent refiners and their jobber and consumer customers; that during the buying programs those prices were in fact determined by such competition; that the purchases under those programs were closely related to or dependent on the spot market prices; that there was no evidence that the purchases of distress gasoline under those programs had any effect on the competitive market price beyond that flowing from the removal of a competitive evil; and that if respondents had tried to do more than free competition from the effect of distress gasoline and to set an arbitrary non-competitive price through their purchases, they would have been without power to do so.

But we do not deem those distinctions material.

In the first place, there was abundant evidence that the combination had the purpose to raise prices. And likewise, there was ample evidence that the buying programs at least contributed to the price rise and the stability of the spot markets, and to increases in the price of gasoline sold in the Mid–Western area during the indictment period. That other factors also may have contributed to that rise and stability of the markets is immaterial. So far as cause and effect are concerned it is sufficient in this type of case if the buying programs of the combination resulted in a price rise and market stability which but for them would not have happened. For this reason the charge to the jury that the buying programs must have "caused" the price rise and its continuance was more favorable to respondents than they could have required. Proof that there was a conspiracy, that its purpose was to raise prices, and that it caused or contributed to a price rise is proof of the actual consummation or execution of a conspiracy under § 1 of the Sherman Act.

Secondly, the fact that sales on the spot markets were still governed by some competition is of no consequence. For it is indisputable that that competition was restricted through the removal by respondents of a part of the supply which but for the buying programs would have been a factor in determining the going prices on those markets. But the vice of the conspiracy was not merely the restriction of supply of gasoline by removal of a surplus. As we have said, this was a well organized program. The timing and strategic placement of the buying orders for distress gasoline played an important and significant role. Buying orders were carefully placed so as to remove the distress gasoline from weak hands. Purchases were timed. Sellers were assigned to the buyers so that regular outlets for distress gasoline would be available. The whole scheme was carefully planned and executed to the end that distress gasoline would not overhang the markets and depress them at any time. And as a result of the payment of fair going market prices a floor was placed and kept under the spot markets. Prices rose and jobbers and consumers in the Mid–Western area paid more for their gasoline than they would have paid but for the conspiracy. Competition was not eliminated from the markets; but it was clearly curtailed, since restriction of the supply of gasoline, the timing and placement of the purchases under the buying programs and the placing of a floor under the spot markets obviously reduced the play of the forces of supply and demand.

The elimination of so-called competitive evils is no legal justification for such buying programs. The elimination of such conditions was sought primarily for its effect on the price structures. Fairer competitive prices, it is claimed, resulted when distress gasoline was removed from the market. But such defense is typical of the protestations usually made in price-fixing cases. Ruinous competition, financial disaster, evils of price cutting and the like appear throughout our history as ostensible justifications for price-fixing. If the so-called competitive abuses were to be appraised here, the reasonableness of prices would necessarily become an issue in every price-fixing case. In that event the Sherman Act would soon be emasculated; its philosophy would be supplanted by one which is wholly alien to a system of free competition; it would not be the charter of freedom which its framers intended.

The reasonableness of prices has no constancy due to the dynamic quality of business facts under lying price structures. Those who fixed reasonable prices today would perpetuate unreasonable prices tomorrow, since those prices would not be subject to continuous administrative supervision and readjustment in light of changed conditions. Those who controlled the prices would control or effectively dominate the market. And those who were in that strategic position would have it in their power to destroy or drastically impair the competitive system. But the thrust of the rule is deeper and reaches more than monopoly power. Any combination which tampers with price structures is engaged in an unlawful activity. Even though the members of the price-fixing group were in no position to control the market, to the extent that they raised, lowered, or stabilized prices they would be directly interfering with the free play of market forces. The Act places all such schemes beyond the pale and protects that vital part of our economy against any degree of interference. Congress has not left with us the determination of whether or not particular price-fixing schemes are wise or unwise, healthy or destructive. It has not permitted the age-old cry of ruinous competition and competitive evils to be a defense to price-fixing conspiracies. It has no more allowed genuine or fancied competitive abuses as a legal justification for such schemes than it has the good intentions of the members of the combination. If such a shift is to be made, it must be done by the Congress. Certainly Congress has not left us with any such choice. Nor has the Act created or authorized the creation of any special exception in favor of the oil industry. Whatever may be its peculiar problems and characteristics, the Sherman Act, so far as price-fixing agreements are concerned, establishes one uniform rule applicable to all industries alike. . . .

Nor is it important that the prices paid by the combination were not fixed in the sense that they were uniform and inflexible. . . . [P]rices are fixed within the meaning of the *Trenton Potteries* case if the range within which purchases or sales will be made is agreed upon, if the prices paid or charged are to be at a certain level or on ascending or descending scales, if they are to be uniform, or if by various formula they are related to the market prices. They are fixed because they are agreed upon. And the fact that, as here, they are fixed at the fair going market price is immaterial. For purchases at or under the market are one species of price-fixing.   In this case, the result was to place a floor under the market—a floor which served the function of increasing the stability and firmness of market prices.   That was repeatedly characterized in this case as stabilization.   But in terms of market operations stabilization is but one form of manipulation.   And market manipulation in its various manifestations is implicitly an artificial stimulus applied to (or at times a brake on) market prices, a force which distorts those prices, a factor which prevents the determination of those prices by free competition alone. . . .

* * *

Under the Sherman Act a combination formed for the purpose and with the effect of raising, depressing, fixing, pegging, or stabilizing the price of a commodity in interstate or foreign commerce is illegal per se. Where the machinery for price-fixing is an agreement on the prices to be charged or paid for the commodity in the interstate or foreign channels of trade, the power to fix prices exists if the combination has control of a substantial part of the commerce in that commodity.   Where the means for price-fixing are purchases or sales of the commodity in a market operation or, as here, purchases of a part of the supply of the commodity for the purpose of keeping it from having a depressive effect on the markets, such power may be found to exist though the combination does not control a substantial part of the commodity.   In such a case that power may be established if as a result of market conditions, the resources available to the combinations, the timing and the strategic placement of orders and the like, effective means are at hand to accomplish the desired objective.   But there may be effective influence over the market though the group in question does not control it.   Price-fixing agreements may have utility to members of the group though the power possessed or exerted falls far short of domination and control.   Monopoly power is not the only power which the Act strikes down. . . .   Proof that a combination was formed for the purpose of fixing prices and that it caused them to be fixed or contributed to that result is proof of the completion of a price-fixing conspiracy under § 1 of the Act.[59]   The indictment in this case

⊀ **59.** Under this indictment proof that prices in the Mid–Western area were raised as a result of the activities of the combination was essential, since sales of gasoline by respondents at the increased prices in that area were necessary in order to establish jurisdiction in the Western District of Wisconsin.   Hence we have necessarily treated the case as one where exertion of the power to fix prices (i.e., the actual fixing of prices) was an ingredient of the offense.   But that does not mean that both a purpose and a power to fix prices are necessary for the establishment of a conspiracy under § 1 of the Sherman Act.   That would be true if power or ability to commit an offense was necessary in order to convict a person of conspiring to commit it.   But it is well established that a person "may be guilty of conspiring although incapable of committing the objective offense."   United States v. Rabinowich, 238 U.S. 78, 86.   And it is like-

wise well-settled that conspiracies under the Sherman Act are not dependent on any overt act other than the act of conspiring. Nash v. United States, 229 U.S. 373, 378.   It is the "contract, combination . . . or conspiracy in restraint of trade or commerce" which § 1 of the Act strikes down, whether the concerted activity be wholly nascent or abortive on the one hand, or successful on the other.   See United States v. Trenton Potteries Co., 273 US 392, 402.   And the amount of interstate or foreign trade involved is not material, since § 1 of the Act brands illegal the character of the restraint not the amount of commerce affected.   In view of these considerations a conspiracy to fix prices violates § 1 of the Act though no overt act is shown, though it is not established that the conspirators had the means available for accomplishment of their objective, and though the conspiracy embraced but a part of the interstate or foreign com-

charged that this combination had that purpose and effect. And there was abundant evidence to support it. Hence the existence of power on the part of members of the combination to fix prices was but a conclusion from the finding that the buying programs caused or contributed to the rise and stability of prices.

As to knowledge or acquiescence of officers of the Federal government little need be said. The fact that Congress through utilization of the precise methods here employed could seek to reach the same objectives sought by respondents does not mean that respondents or any other group may do so without specific congressional authority. Admittedly no approval of the buying programs was obtained under the National Industrial Recovery Act prior to its termination on June 16, 1935, (§ 2(c)) which would give immunity to respondents from prosecution under the Sherman Act. Though employees of the government may have known of those programs and winked at them or tacitly approved them, no immunity would have thereby been obtained. For Congress had specified the precise manner and method of securing immunity. None other would suffice. Otherwise national policy on such grave and important issues as this would be determined not by Congress nor by those to whom Congress had delegated authority but by virtual volunteers. The method adopted by Congress for alleviating the penalties of the Sherman Act through approval by designated public representatives would be supplanted by a foreign system. But even had approval been obtained for the buying programs, that approval would not have survived the expiration in June 1935 of the Act which was the source of that approval. As we have seen the buying program continued unabated during the balance of 1935 and far into 1936. . . .

Accordingly we conclude that the Circuit Court of Appeals erred in reversing the judgments on this ground. . . .

Questions and Comments

What was the purpose and effect of the oil producers' agreement? Was it socially beneficial to phase out the evils of overproduction in an orderly way? Was it reasonable to do so, especially where government officials were involved and encouraged the arrangement?

merce in the commodity. . . . Price-fixing agreements may or may not be aimed at complete elimination of price competition. The group making those agreements may or may not have power to control the market. But the fact that the group cannot control the market prices does not necessarily mean that the agreement as to prices has no utility to the members of the combination. The effectiveness of price-fixing agreements is dependent on many factors, such as competitive tactics, position in the industry, the formula underlying price policies. Whatever economic justification particular price-fixing agreements may be thought to have, the law does not permit an inquiry into their reasonableness. They are all banned because of their actual or potential threat to the central nervous system of the economy.

The existence or exertion of power to accomplish the desired objective becomes important only in cases where the offense charged is the actual monopolizing of any part of trade or commerce in violation of § 2 of the Act. An intent and a power to produce the result which the law condemns are then necessary. As stated in Swift & Co. v. United States, 196 US 375, 396, ". . . when that intent and the consequent dangerous probability exist, this statute, like many others and like the common law in some cases, directs itself against that dangerous probability as well as against the completed result." . . .

The jury found that the defendants had market power. Did they have power to charge more than cost plus a reasonable profit? Did they have power to moderate the decline in price? Was market power a necessary ingredient of the offense?

State the holding of the Court. Frame the holding in terms of a per se rule. Note that *Socony–Vacuum* is the first antitrust case to use the language of per se illegality. Despite the disclaimer, does *Socony–Vacuum* overrule *Appalachian Coals?*

Socony–Vacuum answers two questions left open by *Trenton Potteries* and reexamines a central question of *Appalachian Coals:* (1) Is market power a necessary ingredient of a price-fixing violation? (2) Is there a crisis-cartel defense to a price-fixing violation? What are the answers?

Under certain other systems of law, including the law of the European Economic Community and of Japan, a crisis cartel is or may be permissible. Argue in favor of permitting crisis cartels. Which is the better rule of law?

On the issue of power, consider this case: Three small grocery chains of three stores each in a large metropolitan market agree that they will set the same prices on oranges and corn flakes. When asked why they did this they stand mute. Have they violated the Sherman Act? Does it make sense to conclude that they have? What if they prove that the reason for their agreement is that they want to place a joint ad in a local newspaper circulating throughout the area where all three have stores—a promotional activity each thought too expensive to undertake on its own. Could a court properly hold the unexplained agreement per se unlawful and the explained agreement reasonable and lawful? Can you restate the per se rule in a way that distinguishes between these two situations?

Socony–Vacuum was a criminal case. Was it unfair for the Court to sustain convictions of corporations and business leaders for doing what government officials encouraged them to do, and what *Appalachian Coals* seemed to condone?

In contrasting *Appalachian Coals* with *Socony–Vacuum* one should be mindful of history. Perhaps each case is a product of convictions dominant at the time it was decided. During the early New Deal period the national administration was committed to the idea that industry-wide cooperation among businesses and unions was essential to promote recovery. By 1940, when *Socony–Vacuum* was decided, the country was recovering from the economic trauma of the 1930s. The enemy was not depression, but Nazi Germany. Attorney General Thurman Arnold was aggressively attacking national and international cartels, many of which had created scarcities in goods and materials critical to the war effort. We shall continue to examine the strict rule of *Socony–Vacuum,* which makes no concessions to claims by competitors that competition will harm the public interest.

B. PRICE RESTRAINTS TODAY

Throughout the 1940s, '50s and '60s the unyielding per se rule of *Socony–Vacuum* was generally perceived as the governing law. Lawyers counselling on antitrust matters drew a vivid distinction between per se cases and rule of reason cases. They labored to keep their clients from committing per se offenses; they labored to find all the possible justifications for conduct that was subject to the rule of reason. They assumed a client credibly charged with a per se offense would lose; they assumed a client charged with a rule of reason offense would probably win. That apparent doctrinal stability did not last forever.

Between 1978 and the time we go to press, the Supreme Court handed down seven major decisions that have helped to map the terrains of the rule of reason and the per se rule as they apply to competitors' agreements. These cases suggest a relationship between the two modes of analysis somewhat more complex than that which lawyers in the early post war decades perceived. We present five of these seven cases at this juncture. The two others are reserved for our study of group boycotts.[1]

In the earliest Sherman Act cases, the courts spoke more about restraint of trade than restraint of competition; indeed, while the antitrust bill originally introduced in 1888 was aimed at combinations threatening "competition" (S. 3440, 19 Cong.Rec. 7512), the Sherman Act speaks only in terms of restraint of trade.

Today courts speak more commonly of restraints on competition or restraints that lessen competition. What is a restraint on competition? Is any interference with the competitive process a restraint on competition? Would you classify as a restraint on competition a covenant not to make a competitive bid, or a covenant not to advertise the price of one's services? Or, to constitute a restraint on competition, must the restraint cause a reduction in output, thus increasing price and distorting allocation of resources?

As you might expect, those from the neoclassical tradition, who would limit the scope of Section 2 because they regard markets as robust, show the same reliance on the invisible hand theorem when discussing Section 1; they are likely to say the competition is not restrained unless output is limited and resource allocation distorted, and that concerted action among market participants should never violate Section 1 unless it is shown to have this consequence. By contrast, commentators (and judges) who are keenly aware of the myriad imperfections found in markets and of efforts by market actors to reinforce and exploit market imperfections are likely to stress the importance of maintaining competitive process.

As you study each case in the following group, think about what the individual Justices mean by "competition" and "restraint on competition." In general, as you study antitrust law, think about whether the challenged restraint produces or is likely to produce output restriction. There is a widespread consensus that any such restraint has seriously anticompetitive properties even though there is no consensus that this is the only harm worth worrying about. If a challenged restraint seems not to restrict output, think about whether it restrains competitive process. If it seems to do so, identify how and consider whether or not the social interest would be served by forbidding the restraint. If you think the restraint should be forbidden, try to explain precisely the way in which you think doing so would serve the public interest.

1. See page 401 infra, discussing Northwest Wholesale Stationers, Inc. v. Pacific Stationery and Printing Co., 472 U.S. 284 (1985); FTC v. Indiana Federation of Dentists, 476 U.S. 447 (1986).

National Society of Professional Engineers, the first of the modern price restraint cases, begins an important development affecting the relationship between rule of reason and per se analysis. The case is one of a series of cases concerning restraints imposed by members of a profession in the name of professional self-regulation. For many years, the traditional professions (doctors, lawyers, accountants) asserted with some success that their activities were not business in the commercial sense and that Congress could not have intended the antitrust laws to apply to them. Although the Supreme Court had never adopted this view, the contention that the professions were immune from the antitrust laws had some currency at least until 1975, when the Court decided *Goldfarb v. Virginia State Bar,* 421 U.S. 773 (1975). In *Goldfarb,* the Supreme Court dealt with price fixing that resulted from the use of minimum fee schedules for lawyers. The Court held that professionals (like others) could not fix prices. The appropriate treatment of a variety of other restraints by professionals, however, remained open to question, as we shall see in the *Professional Engineers* case.

NATIONAL SOCIETY OF PROFESSIONAL ENGINEERS v. UNITED STATES

435 U.S. 679 (1978).

JUSTICE STEVENS: This is a civil antitrust case brought by the United States to nullify an association's canon of ethics prohibiting competitive bidding by its members. The question is whether the canon may be justified under the Sherman Act because it was adopted by members of a learned profession for the purpose of minimizing the risk that competition would produce inferior engineering work endangering the public safety. The District Court rejected this justification without making any findings on the likelihood that competition would produce the dire consequences foreseen by the association. The Court of Appeals affirmed. We granted certiorari to decide whether the District Court should have considered the factual basis for the proffered justification before rejecting it. Because we are satisfied that the asserted defense rests on a fundamental misunderstanding of the Rule of Reason frequently applied in antitrust litigation, we affirm.

I

Engineering is an important and learned profession. There are over 750,000 graduate engineers in the United States, of whom about 325,000 are registered as professional engineers. Registration requirements vary from State to State. . . . About half of those who are registered engage in consulting engineering on a fee basis. . . . Engineering fees, amounting to well over $2 billion each year, constitute about 5% of total construction costs. . . .

The National Society of Professional Engineers (Society) was organized in 1935 to deal with . . . the promotion of the professional, social, and economic interests of its members. . . .

The charges of a consulting engineer may be computed in different ways. . . . Suggested fee schedules for particular types of services in certain areas have been promulgated from time to time by various local societies. This case does not, however, involve any claim that the National Society has tried to fix specific fees, or even a specific method of calculating fees. It involves a charge that the members of the Society have unlawfully agreed to refuse to negotiate or even to discuss the question of fees until after a prospective client has selected the engineer for a particular project. Evidence of this agreement is found in § 11(c) of the Society's Code of Ethics, adopted in July 1964.[3]

The District Court found that the Society's Board of Ethical Review has uniformly interpreted the "ethical rules against competitive bidding for engineering services as prohibiting the submission of any form of price information to a prospective customer which would enable that customer to make a price comparison on engineering services." If the client requires that such information be provided, then § 11(c) imposes an obligation upon the engineering firm to withdraw from consideration for that job. . . .[6]

In 1972 the Government filed its complaint against the Society alleging that members had agreed to abide by canons of ethics prohibiting the submission of competitive bids for engineering services and that, in consequence, price competition among the members had been suppressed and customers had been deprived of the benefits of free and open competition. The complaint prayed for an injunction terminating the unlawful agreement.

In its answer the Society admitted the essential facts alleged by the Government and pleaded a series of affirmative defenses, only one of which remains in issue. In that defense, the Society averred that the standard set out in the Code of Ethics was reasonable because competition among professional engineers was contrary to the public interest. It was averred that it would be cheaper and easier for an engineer "to design and specify inefficient and unnecessarily expensive structures and methods of construction." Accordingly, competitive pressure to offer engineering services at the lowest possible price would adversely affect the quality of engineering. Moreover, the practice of awarding engineering contracts to

---

3. That section, which remained in effect at the time of trial, provided:

"Section 11—The Engineer will not compete unfairly with another engineer by attempting to obtain employment or advancement or professional engagements by competitive bidding. . . .

"c. He shall not solicit or submit engineering proposals on the basis of competitive bidding. Competitive bidding for professional engineering services is defined as the formal or informal submission, or receipt, of verbal or written estimates of cost or proposals in terms of dollars, man days of work required, percentage of construction cost, or any other measure of compensation whereby the prospective client may compare engineering services on a price basis prior to the time that one engineer, or one engineering organization, has been selected for negotia-

tions. The disclosure of recommended fee schedules prepared by various engineering societies is not considered to constitute competitive bidding. As Engineer requested to submit a fee proposal or bid prior to the selection of an engineer or firm subject to the negotiation of a satisfactory contract, shall attempt to have the procedure changed to conform to ethical practices, but if not successful he shall withdraw from consideration for the proposed work. These principles shall be applied by the Engineer in obtaining the services of other professions."

6. Having been selected, the engineer may then, in accordance with the Society's canons of ethics, negotiate a satisfactory fee arrangement with the client. If the negotiations are unsuccessful, then the client may withdraw his selection and approach a new engineer.

the lowest bidder, regardless of quality, would be dangerous to the public health, safety, and welfare. For these reasons, the Society claimed that its Code of Ethics was not an "unreasonable restraint of interstate trade or commerce."

. . . The District Court did not, however, make any finding on the question whether, or to what extent, competition had led to inferior engineering work which, in turn, had adversely affected the public health, safety, or welfare. That inquiry was considered unnecessary because the court was convinced that the ethical prohibition against competitive bidding was "on its face a tampering with the price structure of engineering fees in violation of § 1 of the Sherman Act."

. . . [T]he Court of Appeals affirmed its conclusion that the agreement was unlawful on its face and therefore "illegal without regard to claimed or possible benefits."

II

In *Goldfarb v. Virginia State Bar*, 421 U.S. 773, the Court held that a bar association's rule prescribing minimum fees for legal services violated § 1 of the Sherman Act. In that opinion the Court noted that certain practices by members of a learned profession might survive scrutiny under the Rule of Reason even though they would be viewed as a violation of the Sherman Act in another context. The Court said:

> "The fact that a restraint operates upon a profession as distinguished from a business is, of course, relevant in determining whether that particular restraint violates the Sherman Act. It would be unrealistic to view the practice of professions as interchangeable with other business activities, and automatically to apply to the professions antitrust concepts which originated in other areas. The public service aspect, and other features of the professions may require that a particular practice, which could properly be viewed as a violation of the Sherman Act in another context, be treated differently. We intimate no view on any other situation than the one with which we are confronted today." 421 U.S., at 788–789, n. 17.

Relying heavily on this footnote, and on some of the major cases applying a Rule of Reason—principally *Mitchel v. Reynolds*, 1 P.Wms. 181 (1711); *Standard Oil Co. v. United States*, 221 U.S. 1; *Chicago Board of Trade v. United States*, 246 U.S. 231; and *Continental T.V., Inc. v. GTE Sylvania Inc.*, 433 U.S. 36—petitioner argues that its attempt to preserve the profession's traditional method of setting fees for engineering services is a reasonable method of forestalling the public harm which might be produced by unrestrained competitive bidding. To evaluate this argument it is necessary to identify the contours of the Rule of Reason and to discuss its application to the kind of justification asserted by petitioner.

A. The Rule of Reason.

One problem presented by the language of § 1 of the Sherman Act is that it cannot mean what it says. The statute says that "every" contract that restrains trade is unlawful. But, as Mr. Justice Brandeis perceptively noted [in *Chicago Board of Trade*], restraint is the very essence of every contract; read literally, § 1 would outlaw the entire body of private contract law. Yet it is that body of law that establishes the enforceability of commercial agreements and enables competitive markets—indeed, a competitive economy—to function effectively.

. . . The legislative history [of the Sherman Act] makes it perfectly clear that courts [are] to give shape to the statute's broad mandate by drawing on common-law tradition. The Rule of Reason, with its origins in common-law precedents long antedating the Sherman Act, has served that purpose. . . . [T]he Rule . . . focuses directly on the challenged restraint's impact on competitive conditions.

This principle is apparent in even the earliest of cases applying the Rule of Reason, *Mitchel v. Reynolds, supra. Mitchel* involved the enforceability of a promise by the seller of a bakery that he would not compete with the purchaser of his business. The covenant was for a limited time and applied only to the area in which the bakery had operated. It was therefore upheld as reasonable, even though it deprived the public of the benefit of potential competition. The long-run benefit of enhancing the marketability of the business itself—and thereby providing incentives to develop such an enterprise—outweighed the temporary and limited loss of competition.

The Rule of Reason suggested by *Mitchel v. Reynolds* has been regarded as a standard for testing the enforceability of covenants in restraint of trade which are ancillary to a legitimate transaction, such as an employment contract or the sale of a going business. Judge (later Mr. Chief Justice) Taft so interpreted the Rule in his classic rejection of the argument that competitors may lawfully agree to sell their goods at the same price as long as the agreed-upon price is reasonable. *United States v. Addyston Pipe & Steel Co.,* 85 F. 271, 282–283 (CA6 1898), aff'd, 175 U.S. 211. That case, and subsequent decisions by this Court, unequivocally foreclose an interpretation of the Rule as permitting an inquiry into the reasonableness of the prices set by private agreement.

The early cases also foreclose the argument that because of the special characteristics of a particular industry, monopolistic arrangements will better promote trade and commerce than competition. . . .

* * *

There are, thus, two complementary categories of antitrust analysis. In the first category are agreements whose nature and necessary effect are so plainly anticompetitive that no elaborate study of the industry is needed to establish their illegality—they are "illegal *per se.*" In the second category are agreements whose competitive effect can only be evaluated by analyzing the facts peculiar to the business, the history of the restraint, and the reasons why it was imposed. In either event, the purpose of the analysis is to form a judgment about the competitive significance of the restraint; it is not to decide whether a policy favoring competition is in the public interest, or in the interest of the members of an industry. Subject to exceptions defined by statute, that policy decision has been made by the Congress.

B. *The Ban on Competitive Bidding.*

Price is the "central nervous system of the economy," *United States v. Socony–Vacuum Oil Co.,* 310 U.S. 150, 226 n. 59, and an agreement that "interfere[s] with the setting of price by free market forces" is illegal on its face. In this case we are presented with an agreement among competitors to refuse to discuss prices with potential customers until after negotiations have resulted in the initial selection of an engineer. While this is not price fixing as such, no elaborate industry analysis is required to demonstrate the anticompetitive character of such an agreement. It operates as an absolute ban on competitive bidding, applying with equal force to both complicated and simple projects and to both inexperienced and sophisticated customers. . . .

The Society's affirmative defense confirms rather than refutes the anticompetitive purpose and effect of its agreement. The Society argues that the restraint is justified because bidding on engineering services is inherently imprecise, would lead to deceptively low bids, and would thereby tempt individual engineers to do inferior work with consequent risk to public safety and health. The logic of this argument rests on the assumption that the agreement will tend to maintain the price level; if it had no such effect, it would not serve its intended purpose. . . .

It may be, as petitioner argues, that competition tends to force prices down and that an inexpensive item may be inferior to one that is more costly. There is some risk, therefore, that competition will cause some suppliers to market a defective product. Similarly, competitive bidding for engineering projects may be inherently imprecise and incapable of taking into account all the variables which will be involved in the actual performance of the project. Based on these considerations, a purchaser might conclude that his interest in quality—which may embrace the safety of the end product—outweighs the advantages of achieving cost savings by pitting one competitor against another. . . .

The Sherman Act does not require competitive bidding; it prohibits unreasonable restraints on competition. Petitioner's ban on competitive bidding prevents all customers from making price comparisons in the initial selection of an engineer, and imposes the Society's views of the costs and benefits of competition on the entire marketplace. It is this restraint that must be justified under the Rule of Reason, and petitioner's attempt to do so on the basis of the potential threat that competition poses to the public safety and the ethics of its profession is nothing less than a frontal assault on the basic policy of the Sherman Act.

* * *

. . . . [T]he cautionary footnote in *Goldfarb,* 421 U.S., at 788–789, n. 17, quoted *supra,* cannot be read as fashioning a broad exemption under the Rule of Reason for learned professions. We adhere to the view expressed in *Goldfarb* that, by their nature, professional services may differ significantly from other business services, and, accordingly, the nature of the competition in such services may vary. Ethical norms may serve to regulate and promote this competition, and thus fall within the Rule of Reason. But the Society's argument in this case is a far cry from such a position. We are faced with a contention that a total ban on competitive bidding is necessary because otherwise engineers will be tempted to submit deceptively low bids. Certainly, the problem of professional deception is a proper subject of an ethical canon. But, once again, the equation of competition with deception, like the similar equation with safety hazards, is simply too broad; we may assume that competition is not entirely conducive to ethical behavior, but that is not a reason, cognizable under the Sherman Act, for doing away with competition.

In sum, the Rule of Reason does not support a defense based on the assumption that competition itself is unreasonable. Such a view of the Rule would create the "sea of doubt" on which Judge Taft refused to embark in *Addyston* and which this Court has firmly avoided ever since.

III

The judgment entered by the District Court, as modified by the Court of Appeals, prohibits the Society from adopting any official opinion, policy statement, or guideline stating or implying that competitive bidding is unethical. Petitioner argues that this judgment abridges its First Amendment rights. We find no merit in this contention.

Having found the Society guilty of a violation of the Sherman Act, the District Court was empowered to fashion appropriate restraints on the Society's future activities both to avoid a recurrence of the violation and to eliminate its consequences. . . .

* * *

The judgment of the Court of Appeals is

Affirmed.

Justice Brennan took no part in the consideration or decision of this case.

Justice Blackmun, with whom Justice Rehnquist joined, concurred in part and concurred in the judgment. He said:

My skepticism about . . . shaping the Rule of Reason to such a narrow last as does the majority, arises from the fact that there may be ethical rules which have a more than *de minimis* anticompetitive effect and yet are important in a profession's proper ordering. A medical association's prescription of standards of minimum competence for licensing or certification may lessen the number of entrants. A bar association's regulation of the permissible forms of price advertising for nonroutine legal services or limitation of in-person solicitation, see *Bates v. State Bar of Arizona,* 433 U.S. 350 (1977), may also have the effect of reducing price competition. In acknowledging that "professional services may differ significantly from other business services" and that the "nature of the competition in such services may vary," but then holding that ethical norms can pass muster under the Rule of Reason only if they promote competition, I am not at all certain that the Court leaves enough elbowroom for realistic application of the Sherman Act to professional services.

Chief Justice Burger, concurred in part and dissented in part stating:

I concur in the Court's judgment to the extent it sustains the finding of a violation of the Sherman Act but dissent from that portion of the judgment prohibiting petitioner from stating in its published standards of ethics the view that competitive bidding is unethical. The First Amendment guarantees the right to express such a position and that right cannot be impaired under the cloak of remedial judicial action.

Questions and Comments

The challenged agreement assured that no engineer would engage in competitive bidding before being selected by a client for negotiations. Did the Court treat this as per se illegal? As subject to the rule of reason? Something in between? Was the decision mandated by prior Supreme Court holdings?

Suppose that the Engineers proved that a regime of intense price competition would lead to vigorous efforts by engineers to cut their costs and thus would consistently produce inferior engineering work. If the ethical rule was a good faith response to this problem, what result? What should be the result? What would Justices Blackmun and Rehnquist decide? If it really were the case that intense price competition tends to produce inferior engineering work and thus impairs safety, how should society deal with this problem? How has society dealt with similar contentions about the effect of competition in the airline industry?

Does *Professional Engineers* hold that competitors may not interfere with price competition in order to achieve some "non-economic" social good, like safer bridges (or, more generally, better public health and safety)? Does it go further? Does it hold that, even in full blown rule-of-reason analysis, such social benefits may not be weighed in the scale against competitive harms? If so, is it consistent with *Chicago Board of Trade?*

Analyze the restraint in terms of purpose and intent, power, and effect on competition, assuming that at least most of the engineers devised, approved of, and implemented their Code of Ethics as public-spirited citizens and not as predators.

These three inquiries—purpose, power and effect—outline the conventional paradigm for antitrust analysis. Effect analysis usually begins with an inquiry about the effect on price and output. Should it stop there? What about the effect on the range of choice open both to consumers and producers. Under a conventional Chicago school view, antitrust intervention should be evaluated solely on the basis of whether it will improve allocative or allocative and productive efficiency. But others are concerned, also, with the character and quality of the process by which allocation is achieved, not only because of the effect of process on outcome, but because of the intrinsic value of a process that maximizes the room for voluntary action—that maximizes the range of choice open to participants. They "value . . . the act of choosing as such. . . ." Lindbeck, Individual Freedom and Welfare State Policy, 32 Eur.Econ.Rev. 221 (1988).

The Engineers' Code of Ethics was a loose-knit agreement. Shortly thereafter a tighter-knit agreement came before the Court—one that involves some integration of functions but that may affect price or influence other outcomes of competitive process.

BROADCAST MUSIC, INC. v. COLUMBIA BROADCASTING SYSTEM, INC.

441 U.S. 1 (1979).

JUSTICE WHITE: This case involves an action under the antitrust and copyright laws brought by respondent Columbia Broadcasting System, Inc. (CBS), against petitioners, American Society of Composers, Authors and Publishers (ASCAP) and Broadcast Music, Inc. (BMI), and their members and affiliates. The basic question presented is whether the issuance by ASCAP and BMI to CBS of blanket licenses to copyrighted musical compositions at fees negotiated by them is price fixing *per se* unlawful under the antitrust laws.

I

CBS operates one of three national commercial television networks, supplying programs to approximately 200 affiliated stations and telecasting approximately 7,500 network programs per year. Many, but not all, of these programs make use of copyrighted music recorded on the soundtrack. CBS also owns television and radio stations in various cities. It is " 'the giant of the world in the use of music rights,' " the " 'No. 1 outlet in the history of entertainment.' "

Since 1897, the copyright laws have vested in the owner of a copyrighted musical composition the exclusive right to perform the work publicly for profit, but the legal right is not self-enforcing. In 1914, Victor Herbert and a handful of other composers organized ASCAP because those who performed copyrighted music for profit were so numerous and widespread, and most performances so fleeting, that as a practical matter it was impossible for the many individual copyright owners to negotiate with and license the users and to detect unauthorized uses. "ASCAP was organized as a 'clearing-house' for copyright owners and users to solve these problems" associated with the licensing of music. As ASCAP operates today, its 22,000 members grant it nonexclusive rights to license nondramatic performances of their works, and ASCAP issues licenses and distributes royalties to copyright owners in accordance with a schedule reflecting the nature and amount of the use of their music and other factors.

BMI, a nonprofit corporation owned by members of the broadcasting industry, was organized in 1939, is affiliated with or represents some 10,000 publishing companies and 20,000 authors and composers, and operates in much the same manner as ASCAP. Almost every domestic copyrighted composition is in the repertory either of ASCAP, with a total of three million compositions, or of BMI, with one million.

Both organizations operate primarily through blanket licenses, which give the licensees the right to perform any and all of the compositions owned by the members or affiliates as often as the licensees desire for a stated term. Fees for blanket licenses are ordinarily a percentage of total revenues or a flat dollar amount, and do not directly depend on the amount or type of music used. Radio and television broadcasters are the largest users of music, and almost all of them hold blanket licenses from both ASCAP and BMI. Until this litigation, CBS held blanket licenses from both organizations for its television network on a continuous basis since the late 1940's and had never attempted to secure any other form of license from either ASCAP or any of its members.

The complaint filed by CBS charged various violations of the Sherman Act and the copyright laws. . . . After an 8–week trial, limited to the issue of liability, the court dismissed the complaint. . . .

. . . [T]he Court of Appeals [reversed, holding] that the blanket license issued to television networks was a form of price fixing illegal per se under the Sherman Act. . . .

Because we disagree with the Court of Appeals' conclusions with respect to the per se illegality of the blanket license, we reverse its judgment and remand the cause for further appropriate proceedings.

II

In construing and applying the Sherman Act's ban against contracts, conspiracies, and combinations in restraint of trade, the Court has held that certain agreements or practices are so "plainly anticompetitive," and so often "lack . . . any redeeming virtue," that they are conclusively presumed illegal . . . This per se rule is a valid and useful tool of antitrust policy and enforcement. . . . But easy labels do not always supply ready answers.

A

. . . As generally used in the antitrust field, "price fixing" is a shorthand way of describing certain categories of business behavior to which the per se rule has been held applicable. The Court of Appeals' literal approach does not alone establish that this particular practice is one of those types or that it is "plainly anticompetitive" and very likely without "redeeming virtue." . . . When two partners set the price of their goods or services they are literally "price fixing," but they are not per se in violation of the Sherman Act. . . . Thus, it is necessary to characterize the challenged conduct as falling within or without that category of behavior to which we apply the label "per se price fixing." That will often, but not always, be a simple matter.

* * *

B

* * *

The Department of Justice first investigated allegations of anticompetitive conduct by ASCAP over 50 years ago. A criminal complaint was filed in 1934, but the Government was granted a midtrial continuance and never returned to the courtroom. In separate complaints in 1941, the United States charged that the blanket license, which was then the only license offered by ASCAP and BMI, was an illegal restraint of trade and that arbitrary prices were being charged as the result of an illegal copyright pool. The Government sought to enjoin ASCAP's exclusive licensing powers and to require a different form of licensing by that organization. The case was settled by a consent decree that imposed tight restrictions on ASCAP's operations. . . .

Under the [decree as amended in 1950] which still substantially controls the activities of ASCAP, members may grant ASCAP only nonexclusive rights to license their works for public performance. Members, therefore, retain the rights individually to license public performances, along with the rights to license the use of their compositions for other purposes. . . . ASCAP is required to grant to any user making written application a nonexclusive license to perform all ASCAP compositions, either for a period of time or on a per-program basis. ASCAP may not insist on the blanket license, and the fee for the per-program license, which is to be based on the revenues for the program on which ASCAP music is played, must offer the applicant a genuine economic choice between the per-program license and the more common blanket license. . . .

* * *

. . . [I]t cannot be ignored that the Federal Executive and Judiciary have carefully scrutinized ASCAP and the challenged conduct, have imposed restrictions on various of ASCAP's practices, and, by the terms of the decree, stand ready to provide further consideration, supervision, and perhaps invalidation of asserted anticompetitive practices. In these circumstances, we have a unique indicator that the challenged practice may have redeeming competitive virtues and that the search for those values is not almost sure to be in vain. Thus, although CBS is not bound by the Antitrust Division's actions, the decree is a fact of economic and legal life in this industry, and the Court of Appeals should not have ignored it completely in analyzing the practice. That fact alone might not remove a naked price-fixing scheme from the ambit of the per se rule, but, as discussed infra, Part III, here we are uncertain whether the practice on its face has the effect, or could have been spurred by the purpose, of restraining competition among the individual composers.

* * *

Finally, we note that Congress, itself in the new Copyright Act, has chosen to employ the blanket license and similar practices. . . .

. . . [T]here is no nearly universal view that either the blanket or the per-program licenses issued by ASCAP at prices negotiated by it are a form of price fixing subject to automatic condemnation under the Sherman Act, rather than to a careful assessment under the rule of reason.

III

* * *

A

As a preliminary matter, we are mindful that the Court of Appeals' holding would appear to be quite difficult to contain. If, as the court held, there is a per se antitrust violation whenever ASCAP issues a blanket license to a television network for a single fee, why would it not also be automatically illegal for ASCAP to negotiate and issue blanket licenses to individual radio or television stations or to other users who perform copyrighted music for profit? Likewise, if the present network licenses issued through ASCAP on behalf of its members are per se violations, why would it not be equally illegal for the members to authorize ASCAP to issue licenses establishing various categories of uses that a network might have for copyrighted music and setting a standard fee for each described use?

Although the Court of Appeals apparently thought the blanket license could be saved in some or even many applications, it seems to us that the per se rule does not accommodate itself to such flexibility and that the observations of the Court of Appeals with respect to remedy tend to impeach the per se basis for the holding of liability.

CBS would prefer that ASCAP be authorized, indeed directed, to make all its compositions available at standard per-use rates within negotiated categories of use. But if this in itself or in conjunction with blanket licensing constitutes illegal price fixing by copyright owners, CBS urges that an injunction issue forbidding ASCAP to issue any blanket license or to negotiate any fee except on behalf of an individual member for the use of his own copyrighted work or works.[29] Thus, we are called upon to determine that blanket licensing is unlawful across the board. We are quite sure, however, that the per se rule does not require any such holding.

B

. . . Those who would use copyrighted music in public performances must secure consent from the copyright owner or be liable at least for . . . infringement. . . . Furthermore, nothing in the Copyright Act of 1976 indicates in the slightest that Congress intended to weaken the rights of copyright owners to control the public performance of musical compositions. Quite the contrary is true. Although the copyright laws confer no rights on copyright owners to fix prices among themselves or otherwise to violate the antitrust laws, we would not expect that any market arrangements reasonably necessary to effectuate the rights that are granted would be deemed a per se violation of the Sherman Act. . . .

C

More generally, in characterizing this conduct under the per se rule,[33] our inquiry must focus on whether the effect and, here because it tends to show effect, . . . the purpose of the practice are to threaten the proper operation of our predominantly free-market economy—that is, whether the practice facially appears to be one that would always or almost always tend to restrict competition and decrease output, and in what portion of the market, or instead one designed to "increase economic efficiency and render markets more, rather than less, competitive." . . .

29. In its complaint, CBS alleged that it would be "wholly impracticable" for it to obtain individual licenses directly from the composers and publishing houses, but it now says that it would be willing to do exactly that if ASCAP were enjoined from granting blanket licenses to CBS or its competitors in the network television business.

33. The scrutiny occasionally required must not merely subsume the burdensome analysis required under the rule of reason, see National Society of Professional Engineers v. United States, 435 U.S. 679, 690–692 (1978), or else we should apply the rule of reason from the start. That is why the per se rule is not employed until after considerable experience with the type of challenged restraint.

The blanket license, as we see it, is not a "naked restrain[t] of trade with no purpose except stifling of competition," but rather accompanies the integration of sales, monitoring, and enforcement against unauthorized copyright use. See L. Sullivan, Handbook of the Law of Antitrust § 59, p 154 (1977). As we have already indicated, ASCAP and the blanket license developed together out of the practical situation in the marketplace: thousands of users, thousands of copyright owners, and millions of compositions. Most users want unplanned, rapid, and indemnified access to any and all of the repertory of compositions, and the owners want a reliable method of collecting for the use of their copyrights. Individual sales transactions in this industry are quite expensive, as would be individual monitoring and enforcement, especially in light of the resources of single composers. Indeed, as both the Court of Appeals and CBS recognize, the costs are prohibitive for licenses with individual radio stations, nightclubs, and restaurants, and it was in that milieu that the blanket license arose.

A middleman with a blanket license was an obvious necessity if the thousands of individual negotiations, a virtual impossibility, were to be avoided. Also, individual fees for the use of individual compositions would presuppose an intricate schedule of fees and uses, as well as a difficult and expensive reporting problem for the user and policing task for the copyright owner. Historically, the market for public-performance rights organized itself largely around the single-fee blanket license, which gave unlimited access to the repertory and reliable protection against infringement. When ASCAP's major and user-created competitor, BMI, came on the scene, it also turned to the blanket license.

* * *

D

This substantial lowering of costs . . . differentiates the blanket license from individual use licenses. The blanket license is composed of the individual compositions plus the aggregating service. Here, the whole is truly greater than the sum of its parts; it is, to some extent, a different product. The blanket license has certain unique characteristics: It allows the licensee immediate use of covered compositions, without the delay of prior individual negotiations, and great flexibility in the choice of musical material. Many consumers clearly prefer the characteristics and cost advantages of this marketable package, and even small performing-rights societies that have occasionally arisen to compete with ASCAP and BMI have offered blanket licenses. . . .

E

Finally, we have some doubt—enough to counsel against application of the per se rule—about the extent to which this practice threatens the "central nervous system of the economy," that is, competitive pricing as the free market's means of allocating resources. Not all arrangements among actual or potential competitors that have an impact on price are per se violations of the Sherman Act or even unreasonable restraints. Mergers among competitors eliminate competition, including price competition, but they are not per se illegal, and many of them withstand attack under any existing antitrust standard. Joint ventures and other cooperative arrangements are also not usually unlawful, at least not as price-fixing schemes, where the agreement on price is necessary to market the product at all.

Here, the blanket-license fee is not set by competition among individual copyright owners, and it is a fee for the use of any of the compositions covered by the license. But the blanket license cannot be wholly equated with a simple horizontal arrangement among competitors. ASCAP does set the price for its blanket license, but that license is quite different from anything any individual owner could issue. The individual composers and authors have not agreed either to sell individually in any other market or to use the blanket license to mask price fixing in such other markets. Moreover, the substantial restraints placed on ASCAP and its members by the consent decree must not be ignored. The District Court found that there was no legal, practical, or conspiratorial impediment to CBS's obtaining individual licenses; CBS, in short, had a real choice.

* * *

IV

. . . We reverse [the] judgment [of the Court of Appeals], and the copyright misuse judgment dependent upon it, and remand for further proceedings to consider any unresolved issues that CBS may have properly brought to the Court of Appeals. Of course, this will include an assessment under the rule of reason of the blanket license as employed in the television industry, if that issue was preserved by CBS in the Court of Appeals.

* * *

JUSTICE STEVENS, dissenting: The Court holds that ASCAP's blanket license is not a species of price fixing categorically forbidden by the Sherman Act. I agree with that holding. The Court remands the case to the Court of Appeals, leaving open the question whether the blanket license as employed by ASCAP and BMI is unlawful under a rule-of-reason inquiry. I think that question is properly before us now and should be answered affirmatively.

* * *

. . . In my judgment, a remand is not necessary. The record before this Court is a full one, reflecting extensive discovery and eight weeks of trial. The District Court's findings of fact are thorough and well supported. They clearly reveal that the challenged policy does have a significant adverse impact on competition. I would therefore affirm the judgment of the Court of Appeals.

II

Under our prior cases, there would be no question about the illegality of the blanket-only licensing policy if ASCAP and BMI were the exclusive sources of all licenses. A copyright, like a patent, is a statutory grant of monopoly privileges. The rules which prohibit a patentee from enlarging his statutory monopoly by conditioning a license on the purchase of unpatented goods, or by refusing to grant a license under one patent unless the licensee also takes a license under another, are equally applicable to copyrights.

* * *

. . . ASCAP does not have exclusive control of the copyrights in its portfolio, and it is perfectly possible—at least as a legal matter—for a user of music to negotiate directly with composers and publishers for whatever rights he may desire. The availability of a practical alternative alters the competitive effect of a blockbooking or blanket-licensing policy. ASCAP is therefore quite correct in its insistence that its blanket license cannot be categorically condemned on the authority of the blockbooking and package-licensing cases. While these cases are instructive, they do not directly answer the question whether the ASCAP practice is unlawful.

The answer to that question depends on an evaluation of the effect of the practice on competition in the relevant market. And, of course, it is well settled that a sales practice that is permissible for a small vendor, at least when no coercion is present, may be unreasonable when employed by a company that dominates the market. We therefore must consider what the record tells us about the competitive character of this market.

III

The market for music at issue here is wholly dominated by ASCAP-issued blanket licenses. Virtually every domestic copyrighted composition is in the repertoire of either ASCAP or BMI. And again, virtually without exception, the only means that has been used to secure authority to perform such compositions is the blanket license.

The blanket all-or-nothing license is patently discriminatory. The user purchases full access to ASCAP's entire repertoire, even though his needs could be satisfied by a far more limited selection. The price he pays for this access is unrelated either to the quantity or the quality of the music he actually uses, or, indeed, to what he would probably use in a competitive system. Rather, in this unique all-or-nothing system, the price is based on a percentage of the user's advertising revenues, a measure that reflects the customer's ability to pay but is totally unrelated to factors—such as the cost, quality, or quantity of the product—that normally affect price in a competitive market. The ASCAP system requires users to buy more music than they want at a price which, while not beyond their ability to pay and perhaps not even beyond what is "reasonable" for the access they are getting, may well be far higher than what they would choose to spend for music in a competitive system. It is a classic example of economic discrimination.

The record plainly establishes that there is no price competition between separate musical compositions. Under a blanket license, it is no more expensive for a network to play the most popular current hit in prime time than it is to use an unknown composition as background music in a soap opera. Because the cost to the user is unaffected by the amount used on any program or on all programs, the user has no incentive to economize by, for example, substituting what would otherwise be less expensive songs for established favorites or by reducing the quantity of music used on a program. The blanket license thereby tends to encourage the use of more music, and also of a larger share of what is really more valuable music, than would be expected in a competitive system characterized by separate licenses. And since revenues are passed on to composers on a basis reflecting the character and frequency of the use of their music, the tendency is to increase the rewards of the established composers at the expense of those less well known. Perhaps the prospect is in any event unlikely, but the blanket license does not present a new songwriter with any opportunity to try to break into the market by offering his product for sale at an unusually low price. The absence of that opportunity, however unlikely it may be, is characteristic of a cartelized rather than a competitive market.

* * *

IV

Since the record describes a market that could be competitive and is not, and since that market is dominated by two firms engaged in a single, blanket method of dealing, it surely seems logical to conclude that trade has been restrained unreasonably. ASCAP argues, however, that at least as to CBS, there has been no restraint at all since the network is free to deal directly with copyright holders.

The District Court found that CBS had failed to establish that it was compelled to take a blanket license from ASCAP. While CBS introduced evidence suggesting that a significant number of composers and publishers, satisfied as they are with the ASCAP system, would be "disinclined" to deal directly with the network, the court found such evidence unpersuasive in light of CBS's substantial market power in the music industry and the importance to copyright holders of network television exposure. Moreover, it is arguable that CBS could go further and, along with the other television networks, use its economic resources to exploit destructive competition among purveyors of music by driving the price of performance rights down to a far lower level. But none of this demonstrates that ASCAP's practices are lawful, or that ASCAP cannot be held liable for injunctive relief at CBS's request.

The fact that CBS has substantial market power does not deprive it of the right to complain when trade is restrained. Large buyers, as well as small, are protected by the antitrust laws. Indeed, even if the victim of a conspiracy is himself a wrongdoer, he has not forfeited the protection of the law. . . .

* * *

Questions and Comments

CBS had also alleged that ASCAP and BMI had unlawfully tied together wanted and unwanted musical compositions, but this claim was dismissed on grounds that CBS was not coerced to accept unwanted compositions, since it had the option of dealing with the composers. The Court of Appeals affirmed the dismissal of the tying claim and CBS did not appeal on this count. In its appeal to the Supreme Court, CBS pressed the argument that the blanket license was price fixing, illegal per se.

Assume that you represent CBS. Why is blanket licensing price fixing? Who is price fixing?

How critical to the result was the fact that the individual copyright owners remained free to license particular songs (or groups of songs) individually, since they did not (and could not) make ASCAP or BMI exclusive agents to license?

Suppose individual copyright owners got together and pooled their copyrights, and then granted to either ASCAP or BMI exclusive authority to grant blanket licenses. Suppose they did so because:

1. Vast numbers of musical compositions competed against one another; overproduction was driving the prices to levels so low that (it was feared) incentives to compose were impaired and creativity was significantly reduced.

2. The buyers market was comprised principally of three big buyers, the television networks. The thousands of copyright owners felt the need to organize lest the networks, acting concertedly or interdependently, insist upon unreasonably low prices.

3. Individual copyright owners could not feasibly engage in price negotiations. Two sales agencies were in place, each had great expertise developed over many years, and the agencies incurred far lower aggregate transaction costs than the individual copyright owners could have done on their own.

In each case, is the pooling of the product price fixing and illegal per se? Or should analysis proceed under the rule of reason?

If either purpose (1) or (2) was one purpose of the arrangement and (3) was another, would the arrangement be lawful? Suppose (3) were the sole purpose but the arrangement also resulted in higher prices to networks?

In some cases it is not immediately apparent whether a restraint is under the per se rule or is subject to the rule of reason. In those cases, the court must take a brief look at the restraint in order to characterize it. The brief look is actually a short rule-of-reason analysis; it involves at least a cursory examination of purpose, power and effect. For example our earlier hypothetical about the three small grocery chains that agreed on some prices to facilitate a joint newspaper ad might be thought to suggest a "characterization defense" to a price fixing charge. If all one knows is that three ostensibly competing firms agreed on prices, the per se rule is invoked. But suppose that on the basis of a truncated analysis one also knows (1) that the firms apparently lack power, and (2) that they did not intend to affect market prices, but rather to facilitate an integration of their advertising so that they could compete more effectively with larger firms. Could one then conclude: they were not engaged in price fixing at all; therefore, the per se rule does not apply. What would be the benefits of such a refinement? Its dangers?

Try, now, a truncated analysis of the facts at hand in *BMI*. What are the apparent purpose and probable effect of:

(1) The composers' decisions to use a common sales agent?

(2) ASCAP's decision and practice to license musical compositions on a blanket (overall or per program) basis?

(3) ASCAP's refusal to license on a per use basis?

Which is the appropriate point of inquiry—(1), (2) or (3)? Could (3) be a Section 1 violation? (Is it or does it reflect a contract, combination, or conspiracy?)

Compare the Court's opinion by Justice White with the dissenting opinion of Justice Stevens. Note that the touchstone for Justice White is output restriction. Does Justice Stevens' opinion revolve also around output considerations; e.g., if ASCAP gave licenses on a per use basis, would output tend to be more nearly optimal?

After the Supreme Court handed down its opinion in *BMI*, some claimed that the per se rule was dead. In the *Catalano* case, decided a year later, beer wholesalers argued that they could legally agree to stop granting credit to retailers to require retailers to pay for beer on delivery. They contended that given the specific facts in their market, their agreement did not lessen competition but increased it.

CATALANO, INC. v. TARGET SALES, INC.
446 U.S. 643 (1980).

PER CURIAM: Petitioners, . . . beer retailers . . ., brought suit against respondent wholesalers alleging that they had conspired to eliminate short-term trade credit formerly granted on beer purchases in violation of § 1 of the Sherman Act. The District Court entered an interlocutory order, which . . . denied petitioners' "motion to declare this a case of *per se* illegality," and then certified to the United States Court of Appeals for the Ninth Circuit the question whether the alleged agreement among competitors fixing credit terms, if proved, was unlawful on its face. The Court of Appeals granted permission to appeal, and, with one judge dissenting, agreed with the District Court that a horizontal agreement among competitors to fix credit terms does not necessarily contravene the antitrust laws. We . . . reverse. . . .

[Petitioners allege and we assume:] . . . [B]eginning in early 1967, respondent wholesalers secretly agreed, in order to eliminate competition among themselves, that as of December 1967 they would sell to retailers only if payment were made in advance or upon delivery. Prior to the agreement, the wholesalers had extended credit without interest up to the 30– and 42–day limits permitted by state law. According to the petition, prior to the agreement wholesalers had competed with each other with respect to trade credit, and the credit terms for individual retailers had varied substantially. After entering into the agreement, respondents uniformly refused to extend any credit at all.

The Court of Appeals decided that the credit-fixing agreement . . . might actually enhance competition (1) "by removing a barrier perceived by some sellers to market entry," and (2) "by the increased visibility of price. . . ."

In dissent, Judge Blumenfeld expressed the opinion that an agreement to eliminate credit was a form of price fixing. . . .

Our cases fully support Judge Blumenfeld's analysis and foreclose both of the possible justifications on which the majority relied. . . .

It is virtually self-evident that extending interest-free credit for a period of time is equivalent to giving a discount equal to the value of the use of the purchase price for that period of time. Thus, credit terms must be characterized as an inseparable part of the price. An agreement to terminate the practice of giving credit is thus tantamount to an agreement to eliminate discounts, and thus falls squarely within the traditional *per se* rule against price fixing. While it may be that the elimination of a practice of giving variable discounts will ultimately lead in a competitive market to corresponding decreases in the invoice price, that is surely not necessarily to be anticipated. It is more realistic to view an agreement to eliminate credit sales as extinguishing one form of competition among the sellers. In any event, when a particular concerted activity entails an obvious risk of anticompetitive impact with no apparent potentially redeeming value, the fact that a practice may turn out to be harmless in a particular set of circumstances will not prevent its being declared unlawful *per se.*

The majority of the panel of the Court of Appeals suggested, however, that a horizontal agreement to eliminate credit sales may remove a barrier to other sellers who may wish to enter the market. But in any case in which competitors are able to increase the price level or to curtail production by agreement, it could be argued that the agreement has the effect of making the market more attractive to potential new entrants. If that potential justifies horizontal agreements among competitors imposing one kind of voluntary restraint or another on their competitive freedom, it would seem to follow that the more successful an agreement is in raising the price level, the safer it is from antitrust attack. Nothing could be more inconsistent with our cases.

Nor can the informing function of the agreement, the increased price visibility, justify its restraint on the individual wholesaler's freedom to select his own prices and terms of sale. For, again, it is obvious that any industrywide agreement on prices will result in a more accurate understanding of the terms offered by all parties to the agreement. As the *Sugar Institute* case demonstrates, however, there is a plain distinction between the lawful right to publish prices and terms of sale, on the one hand, and an agreement among competitors limiting action with respect to the published prices, on the other.

*   *   *

Accordingly, the judgment of the Court of Appeals is reversed, and the case is remanded for further proceedings consistent with this opinion.

Questions and Comments

The majority applied the traditional per se rule against raising, lowering or stablizing price. Did the wholesalers fix or lessen competition in the price of beer? If competitors who had been giving credit on beer agreed to stop doing so, might they continue to compete on price? If so, what would you expect to happen to the price of beer? Might your answer be influenced by market structure and demand and supply elasticity?

The wholesalers claimed that they made prices more transparent. Is this claim plausible? Does its plausibility depend on market structure?

Some economists argue that sellers cannot effectively fix the price of a product by fixing the price of only one component. For example, suppose plywood were sold and delivered on an invoice that specifies the price for the wood and the price for delivery. If the competitors tried to fix price by fixing the delivery charge alone, the claim is made that the attempt would be abortive; if the "fixed" delivery component exceeded the cost of delivery the market would force down the unfixed price for the wood to correct for the delivery overcharge. Is this analysis relevant to *Catalano?* Does the analysis make sense? If so would plywood sellers bother to fix the price of delivery?[2] If beer sellers could not reduce pressure on price by agreeing to deny credit, would they bother to do so?

Meanwhile, for more than 30 years the Court had not decided a case involving maximum price-fixing by competitors. In *Kiefer–Stewart Co. v. Joseph E. Seagram & Sons,* 340 U.S. 211 (1951), the Court held that maximum price-fixing by competitors is illegal per se despite the fact it may put a lid on prices. But in more recent times the Court has focused concern on consumers' interests. See *Reiter v. Sonotone Corp.,* 442 U.S. 330 (1979). Some Justices have identified output restraint as the appropriate touchstone for antitrust prohibitions. See *BMI, supra.* Some scholars have shown that maximum price-fixing can improve economic welfare and thus one must carefully analyze power and probable market effect before concluding that maximum price fixing by competitors lowers output and decreases welfare. See Easterbrook, Maximum Price Fixing, 48 U.Chi.L.Rev. 886 (1981).

In view of these developments and arguments, some questioned whether *Kiefer–Stewart* survived *BMI* and other precedents of the eighties. Against this background, the *Maricopa County* case came to the Supreme Court.

ARIZONA v. MARICOPA COUNTY MEDICAL SOCIETY

457 U.S. 332 (1982).

JUSTICE STEVENS: The question presented is whether § 1 of the Sherman Act has been violated by an agreement among competing physicians setting, by majority vote, the maximum fees that they may claim in full payment for health services provided to policyholders of specified insurance plans. The United States Court of Appeals for the Ninth Circuit held that the question could not be answered without evaluating the actual purpose and effect of the agreement at a full trial. Because the undisputed facts disclose a violation of the statute, we granted certiorari, and now reverse.

* * *

II

The Maricopa Foundation for Medical Care is a non-profit Arizona corporation composed of licensed doctors of medicine, osteopathy, and podiatry engaged in private practice. Approximately 1,750 doctors, representing about 70% of the practitioners in Maricopa County, are members.

The Maricopa foundation . . . performs three primary activities. It establishes the schedule of maximum fees that participating doctors agree to accept as payment in full for services performed for patients insured under plans approved by the foundation. It reviews the medical necessity and appropriateness of treatment provided by its members to such insured

2. See In re Plywood Antitrust Litigation, 655 F.2d 627 (5th Cir.1981), *cert. dismissed,* 462 U.S. 1125 (1983).

persons. It is authorized to draw checks on insurance company accounts to pay doctors for services performed for covered patients. . . .

The Pima Foundation for Medical Care, which includes about 400 member doctors, performs similar functions. For the purposes of this litigation, the parties seem to regard the activities of the two foundations as essentially the same. . . .

* * *

The fee schedules limit the amount that the member doctors may recover for services performed for patients insured under plans approved by the foundations. To obtain this approval the insurers—including self-insured employers as well as insurance companies [11]—agree to pay the doctors' charges up to the scheduled amounts, and in exchange the doctors agree to accept those amounts as payment in full for their services. The doctors are free to charge higher fees to uninsured patients and they also may charge any patient less than the scheduled maxima. A patient who is insured by a foundation-endorsed plan is guaranteed complete coverage for the full amount of his medical bills only if he is treated by a foundation member. He is free to go to a nonmember physician and is still covered for charges that do not exceed the maximum fee schedule, but he must pay any excess. . . .

The impact . . . is a matter of dispute. The State of Arizona contends that the periodic upward revisions of the maximum fee schedules have the effect of stabilizing and enhancing the level of actual charges by physicians, and that the increasing level of their fees in turn increases insurance premiums. The foundations, on the other hand, argue that the schedules impose a meaningful limit on physicians' charges, and that the advance agreement by the doctors to accept the maxima enables the insurance carriers to limit and to calculate more efficiently the risks they underwrite and therefore serves as an effective cost containment mechanism that has saved patients and insurers millions of dollars. . . . [We] must assume that the respondents' view of the genuine issues of fact is correct.

This assumption presents, but does not answer, the question whether the Sherman Act prohibits the competing doctors from adopting, revising, and agreeing to use a maximum fee schedule in implementation of the insurance plans.

III

The respondents recognize that our decisions establish that price fixing agreements are unlawful on their face. But they argue that the *per se* rule does not govern this case because the agreements at issue are

11. Seven different insurance companies underwrite health insurance plans that have been approved by the Maricopa foundation, and three companies underwrite the plans approved by the Pima foundation. The record contains no firm data on the portion of the health care market that is covered by these plans. The State relies upon a 1974 analysis indicating that the insurance plans endorsed by the Maricopa foundation had about 63% of the prepaid health care market, but the respondents contest the accuracy of this analysis.

horizontal and fix maximum prices, are among members of a profession, are in an industry with which the judiciary has little antitrust experience, and are alleged to have procompetitive justifications. . . .

A

* * *

The application of the *per se* rule to maximum price fixing agreements in *Kiefer–Stewart Co. v. Seagram & Sons,* 340 U.S. 211 (1951), followed ineluctably from *Socony–Vacuum:*

> "For such agreements, no less than those to fix minimum prices, cripple the freedom of traders and thereby restrain their ability to sell in accordance with their own judgment. We reaffirm what we said in *United States v. Socony–Vacuum Oil Co.,* 310 U.S. 150, 223: 'Under the Sherman Act a combination formed for the purpose and with the effect of raising, depressing, fixing, pegging, or stabilizing the price of a commodity in interstate or foreign commerce is illegal *per se.*' " *Id.,* at 213.

Over the objection that maximum price fixing agreements were not the "economic equivalent" of minimum price fixing agreements, *Keifer–Stewart* was reaffirmed in *Albrecht v. Herald Co.,* 390 U.S. 145 (1968). . . .

We have not wavered in our enforcement of the *per se* rule against price fixing. . . .

B

Our decisions foreclose the argument that the agreements at issue escape *per se* condemnation because they are horizontal and fix maximum prices. . . .

Nor does the fact that doctors—rather than nonprofessionals—are the parties to the price fixing agreements support the respondents' position. . . . The price fixing agreements in this case . . . are not premised on public service or ethical norms. The respondents do not argue . . . that the quality of the professional service that their members provide is enhanced by the price restraint. . . . [T]he claim that the price restraint will make it easier for customers to pay does not distinguish the medical profession from any other provider of goods or services.

We are equally unpersuaded by the argument that we should not apply the *per se* rule in this case because the judiciary has little antitrust experience in the health care industry. . . . [T]he result of this reasoning was the adoption by the Court of Appeals of a legal standard based on the reasonableness of the fixed prices, an inquiry we have so often condemned. . . .

The respondents' principal argument is that the *per se* rule is inapplicable because their agreements are alleged to have procompetitive justifications. . . . The anticompetitive potential inherent in all price fixing agreements justifies their facial invalidation even if procompetitive justifications are offered for some. Those claims of enhanced competition are so unlikely to prove significant in any particular case that we adhere to the rule of law that is justified in its general application. Even when the respondents are given every benefit of the doubt, the limited record in this case is not inconsistent with the presumption that the respondents' agreements will not significantly enhance competition.

The respondents contend that their fee schedules are pro-competitive because they make it possible to provide consumers of health care with a uniquely desirable form of insurance coverage that could not otherwise exist. The features of the foundation-endorsed insurance plans that they stress are a choice of doctors, complete insurance coverage, and lower premiums. The first two characteristics, however, are hardly unique to these plans. Since only about 70% of the doctors in the relevant market are members of either foundation, the guarantee of complete coverage only applies when an insured chooses a physician in that 70%. If he elects to go to a non-foundation doctor, he may be required to pay a portion of the doctor's fee. It is fair to presume, however, that at least 70% of the doctors in other markets charge no more than the "usual, customary, and reasonable" fee that typical insurers are willing to reimburse in full. . . .

. . . Even if a fee schedule is . . . desirable, it is not necessary that the doctors do the price fixing. The record indicates that the Arizona Comprehensive Medical/Dental Program for Foster Children is administered by the Maricopa foundation pursuant to a contract under which the maximum fee schedule is prescribed by a state agency rather than by the doctors. . . . [I]nsurers are capable not only of fixing maximum reimbursable prices but also of obtaining binding agreements with providers guaranteeing the insured full reimbursement of a participating provider's fee. . . .

The most that can be said for having doctors fix the maximum prices is that doctors may be able to do it more efficiently than insurers. The validity of that assumption is far from obvious,[28] but in any event there is no reason to believe that any savings that might accrue from this arrangement would be sufficiently great to affect the competitiveness of these kinds of insurance plans. . . .

C

Our adherence to the *per se* rule is grounded not only on economic prediction, judicial convenience, and business certainty, but also on a recognition of the respective roles of the Judiciary and the Congress in regulating the economy. Given its generality, our enforcement of the Sherman Act has required the Court to provide much of its substantive content. By articulating the rules of law with some clarity and by adhering to rules that are justified in their general application, however, we enhance the legislative prerogative to amend the law. . . .

28. In order to create an insurance plan under which the doctor would agree to accept as full payment a fee prescribed in a fixed schedule, someone must canvass the doctors to determine what maximum prices would be high enough to attract sufficient numbers of individual doctors to sign up but low enough to make the insurance plan competitive. In this case that canvassing function is performed by the foundation; the foundation then deals with the insurer. It would seem that an insurer could simply bypass the foundation by performing the canvassing function and dealing with the doctors itself. . . .

IV

Having declined the respondents' invitation to cut back on the *per se* rule against price fixing, we are left with the respondents' argument that their fee schedules involve price fixing in only a literal sense. For this argument, the respondents rely upon *Broadcast Music, Inc. v. Columbia Broadcasting System, Inc.,* 441 U.S. 1 (1979).

* * *

This case is fundamentally different. Each of the foundations is composed of individual practitioners who compete with one another for patients. Neither the foundations nor the doctors sell insurance, and they derive no profits from the sale of health insurance policies. The members of the foundations sell medical services. Their combination in the form of the foundation does not permit them to sell any different product. Their combination has merely permitted them to sell their services to certain customers at fixed prices and arguably to affect the prevailing market price of medical care.

The foundations are not analogous to partnerships or other joint arrangements in which persons who would otherwise be competitors pool their capital and share the risks of loss as well as the opportunities for profit. In such joint ventures, the partnership is regarded as a single firm competing with other sellers in the market. The agreement under attack is an agreement among hundreds of competing doctors concerning the price at which each will offer his own services to a substantial number of consumers. It is true that some are surgeons, some anesthesiologists, and some psychiatrists, but the doctors do not sell a package of three kinds of services. If a clinic offered complete medical coverage for a flat fee, the cooperating doctors would have the type of partnership arrangement in which a price fixing agreement among the doctors would be perfectly proper. But the fee agreements disclosed by the record in this case are among independent competing entrepreneurs. They fit squarely into the horizontal price fixing mold.

The judgment of the Court of Appeals is reversed.

JUSTICE POWELL, with whom CHIEF JUSTICE BURGER and JUSTICE REHNQUIST join, dissenting: The medical care plan condemned by the Court today is a comparatively new method of providing insured medical services at predetermined maximum costs. It involves no coercion. Medical insurance companies, physicians, and patients alike are free to participate or not as they choose. On its face, the plan seems to be in the public interest.

. . . [R]ather than identifying clearly the controlling principles and remanding for decision on a completed record, this Court makes its own *per se* judgment of invalidity. The respondents' contention that the "consumers" of medical services are benefitted substantially by the plan is given short shrift. The Court concedes that "the parties conducted [only] a limited amount of pretrial discovery", leaving undeveloped facts critical to an informed decision of this case. I do not think today's decision on an incomplete record is consistent with proper judicial resolution of an issue of this complexity, novelty, and importance to the public. I therefore dissent.

* * *

II

* * *

Several . . . aspects of the record are of key significance. . . . First, the foundation arrangement forecloses *no* competition. Unlike the classic cartel agreement, the foundation plan does not instruct potential competitors: "Deal with consumers on the following terms and no others." Rather, physicians who participate in the foundation plan are free both to associate with other medical insurance plans—at any fee level, high or low—and directly to serve uninsured patients—at any fee level, high or low. Similarly, insurers that participate in the foundation plan also remain at liberty to do business outside the plan with any physician— foundation member or not—at any fee level. Nor are physicians locked into a plan for more than one year's membership. Thus freedom to compete, as well as freedom to withdraw, is preserved.

Second, on this record . . . insurers represent consumer inter- ests. . . . [O]nce a consumer . . . has chosen a medical insurance plan . . . he is largely indifferent to the amount that his physician charges. . . . The insurer, however, is *not* indifferent. To keep insur- ance premiums at a competitive level and to remain profitable, insurers— including those who have contracts with the foundations—step into the consumer's shoes with his incentive to contain medical costs. . . .

III

It is settled law that once an arrangement has been labeled as "price fixing" it is to be condemned *per se*. But it is equally well settled that this characterization is not to be applied as a talisman to every arrangement that involves a literal fixing of prices. Many lawful contracts, mergers, and partnerships fix prices. But our cases require a more discerning approach Before characterizing an arrangement as a *per se* price fixing agreement meriting condemnation, a court should determine whether it is a "naked restrain[t] of trade with no purpose except stifling of competi- tion." . . .

As part of this inquiry, a court must determine whether the procom- petitive economies that the arrangement purportedly makes possible are substantial and realizable in the absence of such an agreement.

* * *

. . . And, as our cases demonstrate, the *per se* label should not be assigned without carefully considering substantial benefits and procompe- titive justifications. This is especially true when the agreement under attack is novel, as in this case. . . .

Questions and Comments

The majority opinion contains no adverse implications regarding insur- ance plans that specify maximum fees, as long as the maximum is not set concertedly by doctors paid under the plan. The central problem is who determines the maximum fee? Would you expect a maximum fee set concertedly by doctors to differ from one set by an insurance company? Suppose the schedule of maximum medical fees was prepared not by one insurance company, but by several acting concertedly. Would that be lawful?

In *Maricopa*, whose idea was it that the doctors set the fee? Is there any reason why an insurance company might, in its own interest, want doctors to do it? If an insurance company were to set the maximum fee itself, how would it be likely to go about the process? Would the resulting schedule differ from a schedule produced by doctors?

Suppose the rule of reason applied. If you represented the medical societies what facts would you use to show that the arrangement tended to decrease costs of the insurance company? Of insured patients? Of uninsured patients? If you represented the State of Arizona what facts would you want to prove to show that the arrangement tended to increase costs or at least would not contain them?

Suppose that, for inclusion in an insurance plan, doctors conspired to fix maximum fees that were higher than competitive prices. What might constrain them from doing so? Would competitiveness in the market for the sale of insurance policies affect the degree of constraint? Would competitiveness in the market for doctors' services have an effect?

If the insurance market operates competitively, which the dissent assumes (since all inferences must be drawn against the moving party), how strong is the argument that the doctors' arrangement facilitates the provision of a new product in the most efficient way? Is there a strong analogy to *BMI*?

Are the pro-efficiency justifications for this challenged practice also pro-competition justifications? For example, if the arrangement permits an insurance company to save the costs of assembling the information necessary to determine the lowest fee that will be acceptable to a sufficient number of doctors, will this cost-savings improve competition among insurance companies?

On the other hand, the arrangement does provide a forum for the doctors to compare costs and fees. Does the process by which the doctors agree to the maximum fees hold dangers to competition in the medical service market?

If this arrangement holds possibilities for lowering costs in the insurance market, but dangers of raising fees in the medical service market, what is the appropriate response?

The majority respected the established per se rule against price fixing, with little reexamination. It did so not because all price fixing tends to raise price and lessen output, but because pricing freedom is at the heart of the competitive process and pricing restraints threaten to distort the natural flow of trade. Even so, the majority took a quick look at the credibility of defendants' contention that their price fixing was different because it would increase competition. Even assuming that insurance price ceilings are good, the Court saw no reason why the doctors had to do the price fixing.

The dissent started from a fundamentally different point. It narrowly defined the per se rule as one that prohibits only restraints that have no purpose except to stifle competition (meaning, to raise price). To the dissenting Justices only such restraints should be called naked; they would not summarily invalidate an arrangement if its tendency to elevate price is not manifest and if it might benefit consumers. One can envision a factual setting wherein doctors' fixing of maximum fees to insureds would not raise the price of medical services and could benefit buyers of insurance policies. For example, if only a small percentage of all doctors participated and consumers of medical services were well informed price shoppers, then the participating doctors would not be able to increase price or reduce output. Given this possibility, the dissenting Justices endorsed a full rule of reason inquiry.

Does one approach imply a robust market ideology, while the other implies an interventionist ideology, or at least a skepticism about the power of laissez faire policies to protect the public? Is one approach more consistent with the preexisting law?

We turn now to the final case in our series, and move from health care to college sports. As you read the *National Collegiate Athletic Association* case, compare it with *BMI, Professional Engineers* and *Maricopa County*.

NATIONAL COLLEGIATE ATHLETIC ASSOCIATION v. UNIVERSITY OF OKLAHOMA
468 U.S. 85 (1984).

JUSTICE STEVENS: The University of Oklahoma and the University of Georgia contend that the National Collegiate Athletic Association has unreasonably restrained trade in the televising of college football games. . . . [T]he District Court . . . granted injunctive relief. The Court of Appeals agreed that the statute had been violated but modified the remedy in some respects. We granted certiorari, and now affirm.

I

The NCAA

. . . [T]he NCAA . . . [regulates] amateur collegiate sports. It has adopted and promulgated playing rules, standards of amateurism, standards for academic eligibility, regulations concerning recruitment of athletes, and rules governing the size of athletic squads and coaching staffs. . . .

The NCAA has approximately 850 voting members. . . . Division I includes 276 colleges with major athletic programs. . . .

Some years ago, five major conferences together with major football-playing independent institutions organized the College Football Association (CFA). The original purpose of the CFA was to promote the interests of major football-playing schools within the NCAA structure. The Universities of Oklahoma and Georgia, respondents in this Court, are members of the CFA.

History of the NCAA Television Plan

* * *

The Current Plan

The plan adopted in 1981 for the 1982–1985 seasons . . ., like each of its predecessors, recites that it is intended to reduce, insofar as possible, the adverse effects of live television upon football game attendance. . . .

In separate agreements with each of the carrying networks, ABC and the Columbia Broadcasting System (CBS), the NCAA granted each the right to telecast the 14 live "exposures" described in the plan, in accordance with the "ground rules" set forth therein. Each of the networks agreed to pay a specified "minimum aggregate compensation to the participating NCAA member institutions" during the 4-year period in an amount that totaled $131,750,000. In essence the agreement authorized each network to negotiate directly with member schools for the right to televise their games. The agreement itself does not describe the method of computing the compensation for each game, but the practice that has developed over the years and that the District Court found would be followed under the current agreement involved the setting of a recommended fee by a representative of the NCAA for different types of telecasts, with national telecasts being the most valuable, regional telecasts being less valuable, and Division II or Division III games commanding a still lower price. The aggregate of all these payments presumably equals the total minimum aggregate compensation set forth in the basic agreement. Except for differences in payment between national and regional telecasts, and with respect to Division II and Division III games, the amount that any team receives does not change with the size of the viewing audience, the number of markets in which the game is telecast, or the particular characteristic of the game or the participating teams. Instead, the "ground rules" provide that the carrying networks make alternate selections of those games they wish to televise, and thereby obtain the exclusive right to submit a bid at an essentially fixed price to the institutions involved.

The plan also contains "appearance requirements" and "appearance limitations" which pertain to each of the 2-year periods that the plan is in effect. The basic requirement imposed on each of the two networks is that it must schedule appearances for at least 82 different member institutions during each 2-year period. Under the appearance limitations no member institution is eligible to appear on television more than a total of six times and more than four times nationally, with the appearances to be divided equally between the two carrying networks. The number of exposures specified in the contracts also sets an absolute maximum on the number of games that can be broadcast.

Thus, . . . the current plan . . . limits the total amount of televised intercollegiate football and the number of games that any one team may televise. . . .

Background of this Controversy

Beginning in 1979 CFA members began to advocate that colleges with major football programs should have a greater voice in the formulation of football television policy than they had in the NCAA. CFA therefore investigated the possibility of negotiating a television agreement of its own, developed an independent plan, and obtained a contract offer from the National Broadcasting Co. (NBC). This contract, which it signed in August 1981, would have allowed a more liberal number of appearances for each institution, and would have increased the overall revenues realized by CFA members.

In response the NCAA publicly announced that it would take disciplinary action against any CFA member that complied with the CFA–NBC contract. The NCAA made it clear that sanctions would not be limited to the football programs of CFA members, but would apply to other sports as well. On September 8, 1981, respondents commenced this action. . . .

Decision of the District Court

After a full trial, the District Court held that the controls exercised by the NCAA over the televising of college football games violated the Sherman Act. The District Court defined the relevant market as "live college football television" because it found that alternative programming has a significantly different and lesser audience appeal. The District Court then concluded that the NCAA controls over college football are those of a "classic cartel". . . .

Decision of the Court of Appeals

The Court of Appeals . . . rejected . . . the argument that the television plan promoted live attendance, noting that since the plan involved a concomitant reduction in viewership the plan did not result in a net increase in output and hence was not procompetitive. Second, the Court of Appeals rejected as illegitimate the NCAA's purpose of promoting athletically balanced competition. It held that such a consideration amounted to an argument that "competition will destroy the market"—a position inconsistent with the policy of the Sherman Act. Moreover, assuming *arguendo* that the justification was legitimate, the court agreed with the District Court's finding "that any contribution the plan made to athletic balance could be achieved by less restrictive means." Third, the Court of Appeals refused to view the NCAA plan as competitively justified by the need to compete effectively with other types of television programming, since it entirely eliminated competition between producers of football and hence was illegal *per se*.

Finally, the Court of Appeals concluded that even if the television plan were not *per se* illegal, its anticompetitive limitation on price and output was not offset by any procompetitive justification sufficient to save the plan even when the totality of the circumstances was examined. The case was remanded to the District Court for an appropriate modification in its injunctive decree.

II

* * *

. . . [T]hese practices share characteristics of restraints we have previously held unreasonable. . . . By participating in an association which prevents member institutions from competing against each other on the basis of price or kind of television rights that can be offered to broadcasters, the NCAA member institutions have created a horizontal restraint—an agreement among competitors on the way in which they will compete with one another. . . . Because it places a ceiling on the number of games member institutions may televise, the horizontal agreement places an artificial limit on the quantity of televised football that is available to broadcasters and consumers. By restraining the quantity of television rights available for sale, the challenged practices create a limitation on output. . . . Moreover, . . . the minimum aggregate price . . . preclude[s] any price negotiation. . . .

Horizontal price fixing and output limitation are ordinarily . . . "illegal *per se* " . . . without inquiry into the particular market context. . . . Nevertheless, we have decided that it would be inappropriate to apply a *per se* rule . . . [because] this case involves an industry in which horizontal restraints on competition are essential if the product is to be available at all.

. . . [T]he NCAA seeks to market a particular brand of football— college football. The identification of this "product" with an academic tradition differentiates college football from and makes it more popular than professional sports to which it might otherwise be comparable, such as, for example, minor league baseball. In order to preserve the character and quality of the "product," athletes must not be paid, must be required to attend class, and the like. And the integrity of the "product" cannot be preserved except by mutual agreement. . . .

Broadcast Music squarely holds that a joint selling arrangement may be so efficient that it will increase sellers' aggregate output and thus be procompetitive. Similarly, . . . a restraint in a limited aspect of a market may actually enhance marketwide competition. . . . Thus, despite the fact that this case involves restraints on the ability of member institutions to compete in terms of price and output, a fair evaluation of their competitive character requires consideration of the NCAA's justifications for the restraints.

Our analysis of this case under the Rule of Reason, of course, does not change the ultimate focus of our inquiry. Both *per se* rules and the Rules of Reason are employed "to form a judgment about the competitive significance of the restraint." *National Society of Professional Engineers v. United States,* 435 U.S. 679, 692 (1978). . . .

Per se rules are invoked when surrounding circumstances make the likelihood of anticompetitive conduct so great as to render unjustified further examination of the challenged conduct. But whether the ultimate finding is the product of a presumption or actual market analysis, the essential inquiry remains the same—whether or not the challenged restraint enhances competition.[26] . . .

III

Because it restrains price and output, the NCAA's television plan has a significant potential for anticompetitive effects. The findings of the District Court indicate that this potential has been realized. . . .

. . . Individual competitors lose their freedom to compete. Price is higher and output lower than they would otherwise be, and both are unresponsive to consumer preference. This latter point is perhaps the most significant, since "Congress designed the Sherman Act as a 'consumer welfare prescription.' " *Reiter v. Sonotone Corp.,* 442 U.S. 330, 343. A restraint that has the effect of reducing the importance of consumer

26. Indeed, there is often no bright line separating *per se* from Rule of Reason analysis. *Per se* rules may require considerable inquiry into market conditions before the evidence justifies a presumption of anticompetitive conduct. . . .

preference in setting price and output is not consistent with this fundamental goal of antitrust law. . . . At the same time [as restraining price and output], the television plan eliminates competitors from the market, since only those broadcasters able to bid on television rights covering the entire NCAA can compete. . . .

Petitioner argues, however, that its television plan can have no significant anticompetitive effect since the record indicates that it has no market power—no ability to alter the interaction of supply and demand in the market. We must reject this argument for two reasons, one legal, one factual.

As a matter of law, the absence of proof of market power does not justify a naked restriction on price or output. To the contrary, when there is an agreement not to compete in terms of price or output, "no elaborate industry analysis is required to demonstrate the anticompetitive character of such an agreement." *Professional Engineers,* 435 U.S., at 692. . . .

As a factual matter, it is evident that petitioner does possess market power. The District Court employed the correct test for determining whether college football broadcasts constitute a separate market—whether there are other products that are reasonably substitutable for televised NCAA football games. Petitioner's argument that it cannot obtain supracompetitive prices from broadcasters since advertisers, and hence broadcasters, can switch from college football to other types of programming simply ignores the findings of the District Court. . . . Indeed, the District Court's subsidiary finding that advertisers will pay a premium price per viewer to reach audiences watching college football because of their demographic characteristics is vivid evidence of the uniqueness of this product. . . .

We turn now to the NCAA's proffered justifications.

IV

Relying on *Broadcast Music,* petitioner argues that its television plan constitutes a cooperative "joint venture" which assists in the marketing of broadcast rights and hence is procompetitive. While joint ventures have no immunity from the antitrust laws, as *Broadcast Music* indicates, a joint selling arrangement may "mak[e] possible a new product by reaping otherwise unattainable efficiencies." *Arizona v. Maricopa County Medical Society,* 457 U.S. 332, 365. The essential contribution made by the NCAA's arrangement is to define the number of games that may be televised, to establish the price for each exposure, and to define the basic terms of each contract between the network and a home team. The NCAA does not, however, act as a selling agent for any school or for any conference of schools. The selection of individual games, and the negotiation of particular agreements, are matters left to the networks and the individual schools. Thus, the effect of the network plan is not to eliminate individual sales of broadcasts, since these still occur, albeit subject to fixed prices and output limitations. Unlike *Broadcast Music*'s blanket license covering broadcast rights to a large number of individual compositions, here the same rights are still sold on an individual basis, only in a non-competitive market.

The District Court did not find that the NCAA's television plan produced any procompetitive efficiencies which enhanced the competitiveness of college football television rights; to the contrary it concluded that NCAA football could be marketed just as effectively without the television plan. There is therefore no predicate in the findings for petitioner's efficiency justification. . . .

* * *

V

Throughout the history of its regulation of intercollegiate football telecasts, the NCAA has indicated its concern . . . that fan interest in a televised game may adversely affect ticket sales for games that will not appear on television.

. . . Under the current plan, games are shown on television during all hours that college football games are played. The plan simply does not protect live attendance. . . .

There is, however, a more fundamental reason for rejecting this defense. The NCAA's argument that its television plan is necessary to protect live attendance is not based on a desire to maintain the integrity of college football as a distinct and attractive product, but rather on a fear that the product will not prove sufficiently attractive to draw live attendance when faced with competition from televised games. At bottom the NCAA's position is that ticket sales for most college games are unable to compete in a free market. The television plan protects ticket sales by limiting output—just as any monopolist increases revenues by reducing output. . . . [P]etitioner forwards a justification that is inconsistent with the basic policy of the Sherman Act. . . .

VI

* * *

. . . It is reasonable to assume that most of the regulatory controls of the NCAA are justifiable means of fostering competition among amateur athletic teams and therefore procompetitive because they enhance public interest in intercollegiate athletics. The specific restraints on football telecasts that are challenged in this case do not, however, fit into the same mold as do rules defining the conditions of the contest, the eligibility of participants, or the manner in which members of a joint enterprise shall share the responsibilities and the benefits of the total venture.

The NCAA does not claim that its television plan has equalized or is intended to equalize competition within any one league. The plan is nationwide in scope and there is no single league or tournament in which all college football teams complete. There is no evidence of any intent to equalize the strength of teams in [different divisions]. . . .

* * *

VII

The NCAA plays a critical role in the maintenance of a revered tradition of amateurism in college sports. There can be no question but that it needs ample latitude to play that role, or that the preservation of the student-athlete in higher education adds richness and diversity to intercollegiate athletics and is entirely consistent with the goals of the Sherman Act. But consistent with the Sherman Act, the role of the NCAA must be to *preserve* a tradition that might otherwise die; rules that restrict output are hardly consistent with this role. . . . Accordingly, the judgment of the Court of Appeals is

Affirmed.

JUSTICE WHITE, with whom JUSTICE REHNQUIST joins, dissenting:

* * *

I

. . . The NCAA's member institutions have designed their competitive athletic programs "to be a vital part of the educational system." Deviations from this goal, produced by a persistent and perhaps inevitable desire to "win at all costs," have in the past led, and continue to lead, to a wide range of competitive excesses that prove harmful to students and institutions alike. The fundamental policy underlying the NCAA's regulatory program, therefore, is to minimize such deviations and "to maintain intercollegiate athletics as an integral part of the educational program and the athlete as an integral part of the student body and, by so doing, retain a clear line of demarcation between college athletics and professional sports."

* * *

In pursuit of its fundamental goal and others related to it, the NCAA imposes numerous controls on intercollegiate athletic competition among its members. . . . One clear effect of most, if not all, of these regulations is to prevent institutions with competitively and economically successful programs from taking advantage of their success by expanding their programs, improving the quality of the product they offer, and increasing their sports revenues. Yet each of these regulations represents a desirable and legitimate attempt "to keep university athletics from becoming professionalized to the extent that profit making objectives would overshadow educational objectives."

* * *

II

. . . Because some schools' games contribute disproportionately to the total value of the package, the manner in which the minimum aggregate compensation is distributed among schools whose games are televised has given rise to a situation under which less prominent schools receive more in rights fees than they would receive in a competitive market and football powers like respondents receive less.

. . . [T]he Court does not hold, nor did the Court of Appeals hold, that this redistributive effect alone would be sufficient to subject the television plan to condemnation under § 1 of the Sherman Act. Nor should it, for an agreement to share football revenues to a certain extent is an essential aspect of maintaining some balance of strength among competing colleges and of minimizing the tendency to professionalism in the dominant schools. Sharing with the NCAA itself is also a price legitimately exacted in exchange for the numerous benefits of membership in the NCAA, including its many-faceted efforts to maintain a system of competitive, amateur athletics. . . .

The Court relies instead primarily on the District Court's findings that (1) the television plan restricts output; and (2) the plan creates a noncompetitive price structure that is unresponsive to viewer demand. . . .

. . . To the extent that output is measured solely in terms of the number of televised games, I need not deny that it is reduced by the NCAA's television plan. But this measure of output is not the proper one. The District Court . . . made no finding concerning the effect of the plan on total viewership, which is the more appropriate measure of output or, at least, of the claimed anticompetitive effects of the NCAA plan. The NCAA would surely be an irrational "profit maximizer" if this were not the case. In the absence of a contrary finding by the District Court, I cannot conclude that respondents carried their burden of showing that the television plan has an adverse effect on output and is therefore anticompetitive.

Second, and even more important, I am unconvinced that respondents have proved that any reduction in the number of televised college football games brought about by the NCAA's television plan has resulted in an anticompetitive increase in the price of television rights. . . . [T]he market for television rights to college football competitions should not be equated to the markets for wheat or widgets. Reductions in output by monopolists in most product markets enable producers to exact a higher price for *the same product.* By restricting the number of games that can be televised, however, the NCAA creates *a new product* —exclusive television rights—that are more valuable to networks than the products that its individual members could market independently.

* * *

III

Even if I were convinced that the District Court did not err in failing to look to total viewership, as opposed to the number of televised games, when measuring output and anticompetitive effect and in failing fully to consider whether the NCAA possesses power to fix the package price, as opposed to the distribution of that package price among participating teams, I would nevertheless hold that the television plan passes muster under the Rule of Reason. . . .

It is one thing to say that "NCAA football is a unique product," that "intercollegiate football telecasts generate an audience uniquely attractive to advertisers and that competitors are unable to offer programming that can attract a similar audience." It is quite another, in my view, to say that maintenance or enhancement of the quality of NCAA football telecasts is unnecessary to enable those telecasts to compete effectively against other forms of entertainment. The NCAA has no monopoly power when competing against other types of entertainment. . . .

* * *

IV

Finally, I return to the point with which I began—the essentially noneconomic nature of the NCAA's program of self-regulation. . . . Although the NCAA does not enjoy blanket immunity from the antitrust laws, it is important to remember that the Sherman Act "is aimed primarily at combinations having commercial objectives and is applied only to a very limited extent to organizations . . . which normally have other objectives." . . .

* * *

When [legitimate noneconomic] values are factored into the balance, the NCAA's television plan seems eminently reasonable. . . .

* * *

Questions and Comments

In the past, to assert that a joint arrangement was a "naked restraint" was a rhetorical device for asserting that the arrangement should be per se unlawful. What did the Court mean here by a "naked restraint"? What were the reasons for not treating this restraint as a per se violation? Were the reasons similar to those that avoided a per se response in *BMI?* In *Appalachian Coals?*

Was *NCAA* a rule of reason case? If so, why did the majority reject the relevance of market power? This is the first rule of reason case in which defendants were held liable without a showing that they had the power to affect price or had the purpose to do so.

If one believes, as did the dissenters in *Maricopa County,* that output reduction is a necessary characteristic of a restraint on competition, should one ever countenance a rule of reason analysis that foregoes a consideration of market power (or the surrogates, purpose or effect)?

By one alternative approach, no market power analysis is needed where the restraint is naked. Why? Is this the view taken by the majority?

The Court apparently would allow some justification even for output-limiting restraints. What possible justification?

After *Catalano* and *Maricopa County* one cannot say that the per se rule is dead. After *Professional Engineers, BMI* and *NCAA* one must say that the area for analysis is widened, but that analysis need not be wider than necessary to reach a confident result. When analysis is needed the major foci will be output limitation and efficiency. Their validity is universally recognized. Minor foci will be coercion, market access and fairness. Their validity is denied by some commentators, but not by others and they still play a role in some court decisions.

Consider output limitation and efficiency. Is one of greater concern than the other? Can an analysis be truncated, or at least facilitated by focusing first on one, with the expectation that its consideration may terminate the analysis?

The analysis of power is something antitrust courts and commentators have experience with—more experience, at any rate, than they have in analyzing claims of efficiency. Analysis usually looks first at power. For example, in The Antitrust Paradox 278–79 (1978) Robert Bork suggests a mode of analysis for arrangements that examines productive activity and ancillary restraints fixing prices or dividing markets. He first asks whether collective market shares make output limitation likely and whether participants have demonstrated a primary purpose to limit output. If neither is true he says that the arrangement should be lawful. Only if power or a primary purpose to restrict output has been shown, must a court consider whether efficiencies are achieved and whether the restraint is essential in order for the arrangement to be carried out.

A recent FTC opinion, Massachusetts Board of Registration in Optometry Trade Cas. (CCH) (Docket No. 9195, June 13, 1988), make an interesting contrast. Commissioner Calvani suggests that the first question is whether there is an inherently suspect restraint, one that, absent efficiency enhancement, would reduce output. Horizontal price fixing is an example. If not, the arrangement is lawful unless vulnerable under the full blown rule of reason. If there is a suspect restraint, the next question is whether there is a plausible efficiency defense for the practice—an efficiency justification that cannot be rejected without an extensive factual inquiry. If not, the restraint is unlawful. If there is a plausible efficiency claim the next step is a factual inquiry to determine whether it is valid. If not, the practice is unlawful. If there is a valid efficiency claim, it must be balanced against any output limitation.

Which approach seems best, to focus first, as Bork does, on market power, or on efficiency, as Commissioner Calvani does? What result would you reach if you used Bork's approach in *Professional Engineers? BMI? NCAA?* If you used the Commissioner's approach? Which of the two approaches would courts be best able to handle? Would one require a less extensive inquiry as applied to one or more of those cases? Do one or both miss any considerations that the Court considered salient in one or more of the cases?

* * *

In this chapter you have studied four major cases of alleged cartels decided during the formative years of antitrust—*Chicago Board of Trade, Trenton Potteries, Appalachian Coals* and *Socony–Vacuum;* you have also studied five such cases of recent vintage—*National Society of Professional Engineers, BMI, Catalano, Maricopa County,* and *NCAA.* You will recall that in Chapter 2 we noted three categories of conduct: exploitative of buyers or sellers, responsive to buyers needs and interests, and unreasonably exclusionary of competitors who could otherwise respond to buyers needs and interests. The same three categories are relevant to competitor collaboration. Unlike the monopoly law, for monopoly pricing is not illegal, the core Section 1 offense, cartelization, is exploitative. By combining, the cartellists override the market and extract more from suppliers or buyers than an unrigged market would allow. We have no trouble condemning exploitation by cartels, but we do not condemn the comparable exploitation by monopolists. Why?

In the next section we will study horizontal market division and we will see that market division is one more way, like price fixing, to achieve classic cartelization. As we proceed to study other subjects, such as boycotts and the use of standards to exclude, we will see how cartellists, like monopolists, may use exclusionary devices to keep out or to hold back competitors who might otherwise break the cartel by suppling the unmet demand.

C. HORIZONTAL MARKET DIVISION

We have just studied cartelization through price agreements. Cartelization can also be achieved in other ways. A full blown European cartel of the inter-war period might have assigned production quotas to all participants, and may have policed participants to see that the quotas as well as prices were maintained. Alternatively, cartel members might divide markets, effectively making each a monopolist within its area. Markets may be divided in various ways. For example, cartelists might agree that Abe will make luxury cars, Baker mid-size cars, Carla compacts; or that Abe will make cars that sell for more than $20,000, Baker, $10,000 to $20,000, Carla, below $10,000; or that Abe will bid on federal contracts, Baker on state contracts, Carla on private work; or that Abe will sell west of the Rockies, Baker in the East, Carla in Europe. If each cartelist has its own segment of the market and does not encounter competition from outsiders, each has a monopoly. If it should produce more than the cartel recommends, its production increases would affect only its own ability to sell all of its production at supracompetitive prices. Consider each of the market division techniques here suggested. As to each, can you imagine circumstances in which it would work? In which it would fail?

Particularly in the 1920s and 1930s, American firms joined international cartels which carved up the world. The titanium cartel is an example. See *United States v. National Lead Co.*, 63 F.Supp. 513 (S.D. N.Y.1945), *aff'd*, 332 U.S. 319 (1947). Commonly, market division schemes are associated with price fixing. For example, the members of the iron pipe cartel in *United States v. Addyston Pipe and Steel Company* divided territories in aid of their larger price-fixing conspiracy (see page 45 *supra*).

In *Timken Roller Bearing Co. v. United States*, 341 U.S. 593 (1951), and later in *United States v. Sealy, Inc.*, 388 U.S. 350 (1967), territorial divisions were part of an aggregation of trade restraints including price fixing, and the Supreme Court held the aggregation illegal. Generally not only was market division accompanied by price fixing, but the defendants had market power and their combination caused prices to rise to supracompetitive levels.

Before 1972, although commentators often asserted that agreements by competitors' to divide markets were, without more, per se unlawful, there was as yet no case explicitly so holding.

UNITED STATES v. TOPCO ASSOCIATES
405 U.S. 596 (1972).

JUSTICE MARSHALL: . . .

* * *

I

Topco is a cooperative association of approximately 25 small and medium-sized regional supermarket chains that operate stores in some 33 States. Each of the member chains operates independently; there is no pooling of earnings, profits, capital, management, or advertising resources. No grocery business is conducted under the Topco name. Its basic function is to serve as a purchasing agent for its members. In this capacity, it procures and distributes to the members more than 1,000 different food and related nonfood items, most of which are distributed under brand names owned by Topco. . . .

All of the stock in Topco is owned by the members, with the common stock, the only stock having voting rights, being equally distributed. . . .

. . . By 1964, Topco's members had combined retail sales of more than $2 billion; by 1967, their sales totaled more than $2.3 billion, a figure exceeded by only three national grocery chains.[4]

Members of the association vary in the degree of market share that they possess in their respective areas. The range is from 1.5% to 16%, with the average being approximately 6%. . . .

II

. . . [T]he Government alleged that there existed: "a continuing agreement, understanding and concert of action among the co-conspirator member firms acting through Topco, the substantial terms of which have been and are that each co-conspirator or member firm will sell Topco-controlled brands only within the marketing territory allocated to it, and will refrain from selling Topco-controlled brands outside such marketing territory."

The division of marketing territories to which the complaint refers consists of a number of practices by the association.

Article IX, § 2, of the Topco bylaws establishes three categories of territorial licenses that members may secure from the association:

"(a) *Exclusive* —An exclusive territory is one in which the member is licensed to sell all products bearing specified trademarks of the Association, to the exclusion of all other persons.

"(b) *Non-exclusive* —A non-exclusive territory is one in which a member is licensed to sell all products bearing specified trademarks of the Association, but not to the exclusion of others who may also be licensed to sell products bearing the same trademarks of the Association in the same territory.

"(c) *Coextensive* —A coextensive territory is one in which two (2) or more members are licensed to sell all products bearing specified trademarks of the Association to the exclusion of all other persons. . . ."

When applying for membership, a chain must designate the type of license that it desires. Membership must first be approved by the board of directors, and thereafter by an affirmative vote of 75% of the association's members. If, however, the member whose operations are closest to those of the applicant, or any member whose operations are located within 100 miles of the applicant, votes against approval, an affirmative vote of 85% of the members is required for approval. Because, as indicated by

4. The three largest chains are A & P, Safeway, and Kroger.

the record, members cooperate in accommodating each other's wishes, the procedure for approval provides, in essence, that members have a veto of sorts over actual or potential competition in the territorial areas in which they are concerned.

Following approval, each new member signs an agreement with Topco designating the territory in which that member may sell Topco-brand products. No member may sell these products outside the territory in which it is licensed. Most licenses are exclusive, and even those denominated "coextensive" or "non-exclusive" prove to be de facto exclusive. Exclusive territorial areas are often allocated to members who do no actual business in those areas on the theory that they may wish to expand at some indefinite future time and that expansion would likely be in the direction of the allocated territory. . . .

The Government maintains that this scheme of dividing markets violates the Sherman Act because it operates to prohibit competition in Topco-brand products among grocery chains engaged in retail operations. . . .

. . . Topco essentially maintains that it needs territorial divisions to compete with larger chains; that the association could not exist if the territorial divisions were anything but exclusive; and that by restricting competition in the sale of Topco-brand goods, the association actually increases competition by enabling its members to compete successfully with larger regional and national chains.

The District Court, considering all these things relevant to its decision, agreed with Topco. It recognized that the panoply of restraints that Topco imposed on its members worked to prevent competition in Topco-brand products, but concluded that "[w]hatever anti-competitive effect these practices may have on competition in the sale of Topco private label brands is far outweighed by the increased ability of Topco members to compete both with the national chains and other supermarkets operating in their respective territories." The court held that Topco's practices were procompetitive and, therefore, consistent with the purposes of the antitrust laws. But we conclude that the District Court used an improper analysis in reaching its result.

III

* * *

While the Court has utilized the "rule of reason" in evaluating the legality of most restraints alleged to be violative of the Sherman Act, it has also developed the doctrine that certain business relationships are per se violations of the Act without regard to a consideration of their reasonableness. . . .

. . . One of the classic examples of a *per se* violation of § 1 is an agreement between competitors at the same level of the market structure to allocate territories in order to minimize competition. Such concerted action is usually termed a "horizontal" restraint, in contradistinction to combinations of persons at different levels of the market structure, e.g., manufacturers and distributors, which are termed "vertical" restraints. This Court has reiterated time and time again that "horizontal territorial limitations . . . are naked restraints of trade with no purpose except stifling of competition." Such limitations are per se violations of the Sherman Act.

We think that it is clear that the restraint in this case is a horizontal one, and, therefore, a *per se* violation of § 1. The District Court failed to make any determination as to whether there were *per se* horizontal territorial restraints in this case simply and applied a rule of reason in reaching its conclusions that the restraints were not illegal. In so doing, the District Court erred.

* * *

Whether or not we would decide this case the same way under the rule of reason used by the District Court is irrelevant to the issue before us. The fact is that courts are of limited utility in examining difficult economic problems. Our inability to weigh, in any meaningful sense, destruction of competition in one sector of the economy against promotion of competition in another sector is one important reason we have formulated *per se* rules.

In applying these rigid rules, the Court has consistently rejected the notion that naked restraints of trade are to be tolerated because they are well intended or because they are allegedly developed to increase competition.

Antitrust laws in general, and the Sherman Act in particular, are the Magna Carta of free enterprise. They are as important to the preservation of economic freedom and our free-enterprise system as the Bill of Rights is to the protection of our fundamental personal freedoms. And the freedom guaranteed each and every business, no matter how small, is the freedom to compete—to assert with vigor, imagination, devotion, and ingenuity whatever economic muscle it can muster. Implicit in such freedom is the notion that it cannot be foreclosed with respect to one sector of the economy because certain private citizens or groups believe that such foreclosure might promote greater competition in a more important sector of the economy.

The District Court determined that by limiting the freedom of its individual members to compete with each other, Topco was doing a greater good by fostering competition between members and other large supermarket chains. But, the fallacy in this is that Topco has no authority under the Sherman Act to determine the respective values of competition in various sectors of the economy. . . .

. . . If a decision is to be made to sacrifice competition in one portion of the economy for greater competition in another portion, this . . . is a decision that must be made by Congress and not by private forces or by the courts. Private forces are too keenly aware of their own interests in making such decisions and courts are ill-equipped and ill-situated for such decisionmaking. To analyze, interpret, and evaluate the myriad of competing interests and the endless data that would surely be brought to bear on such decisions, and to make the delicate judgment on the relative values to society of competitive areas of the economy, the judgment of the elected representatives of the people is required.

* * *

We reverse the judgment of the District Court and remand the case for entry of an appropriate decree.

JUSTICE BLACKMUN, concurring in the result: The conclusion the Court reaches has its anomalous aspects, for surely, as the District Court's findings make clear, today's decision in the Government's favor will tend to stultify Topco members' competition with the great and larger chains. The bigs, therefore, should find it easier to get bigger and, as a consequence, reality seems at odds with the public interest. The *per se* rule, however, now appears to be so firmly established by the Court that, at this late date, I could not oppose it. Relief, if any is to be forthcoming, apparently must be by way of legislation.

CHIEF JUSTICE BURGER, dissenting: This case does not involve restraints on interbrand competition or an allocation of markets by an association with monopoly or near-monopoly control of the sources of supply of one or more varieties of staple goods. Rather, we have here an agreement among several small grocery chains to join in a cooperative endeavor that, in my view, has an unquestionably lawful principal purpose; in pursuit of that purpose they have mutually agreed to certain minimal ancillary restraints that are fully reasonable in view of the principal purpose and that have never before today been held by this Court to be *per se* violations of the Sherman Act.

* * *

With all respect, I believe that there are two basic fallacies in the Court's approach here. First, while I would not characterize our role under the Sherman Act as one of "rambl[ing] through the wilds," it is indeed one that requires our "examin[ation of] difficult economic problems." We can undoubtedly ease our task, but we should not abdicate that role by formulation of *per se* rules with no justification other than the enhancement of predictability and the reduction of judicial investigation. Second, from the general proposition that *per se* rules play a necessary role in antitrust law, it does not follow that the particular *per se* rule promulgated today is an appropriate one. Although it might well be desirable in a proper case for this Court to formulate a *per se* rule dealing with horizontal territorial limitations, it would not necessarily be appropriate for such a rule to amount to a blanket prohibition against all such limitations. More specifically, it is far from clear to me why such a rule should cover those division-of-market agreements that involve no price fixing and which are concerned only with trademarked products that are not in a monopoly or near-monopoly position with respect to competing brands. . . .

Questions and Comments

Suppose several sellers of the same product, without any degree of integration whatsoever, agree to divide territories. Is *Topco* an authority for the proposition that the agreement is per se unlawful? Do the *Topco* facts themselves present an equally "naked" division of markets?

Why did the supermarket chains form Topco Associates? Why did they agree to assign territories? Are these territorial restraints similar to or different from those in *Addyston Pipe & Steel* or the international titanium cartel? Are they ancillary restraints? If so, ancillary to what? Are they essential to the achievement of a legitimate main purpose of the agreement? Do they help significantly in achieving it?

The Court refers to two sectors of the economy, intrabrand competition among sellers of Topco brand, and interbrand competition, which includes competition of Topco members with other supermarket chains and other sellers of groceries. Topco argued that the intrabrand restraints made its members more effective competitors against other sellers of groceries. How might it have done that?

In a consent judgment entered in *Topco* after the Supreme Court decision, the government agreed to let the Topco members contract for territories of "prime responsibility" (an area assigned to each wherein it would be primarily responsible for promoting and selling the *Topco* brand). Members were also permitted to agree that if a member sold outside of its primary area it would pay the incumbent a percentage of revenues, to compensate for the seller's use of the incumbent's investment in advertising and promotion. 1983 Trade Cas. (CCH) ¶ 74,391 (E.D.Ill.1972). Does this solution provide a less restrictive way of doing what the original Topco restraint was trying to accomplish? Will the alternative achieve the venturers' goal as well, or nearly as well, as the original restraint? Which are higher—the costs or the benefits of the consent judgment?

Competition can yield differentiation, but it can also yield convergence. Have you noticed that, when you see a McDonald's outlet, a Wendy's or Burger King is likely to be close at hand? There is more than one reason for competitive convergence. An important one is simple imitation. But the McDonald's–Burger King phenomenon involves a perception shared by competing suppliers that buyer demand is concentrated within a "bell curve" distribution, with the consequence that a competing supplier, to maximize market share, will each want to make an offering that places it near the center of the bell curve. When this occurs, might an improved social result arise from a concerted decision among competitors about the configuration of product or service that each will offer?

Consider the following fable based on the observations of an economist named Hotelling.[4] There is a bathing beach running north to south. It is two miles long. Bathers are deployed evenly along its full length. Seller 1, building a hot dog stand on the beach, will place it precisely in the middle; this maximizes the convenience of access of all her customers. Seller 2, the second to enter, sets his stand right next to the first. If he moved further north or south he would gain preferred access to customers between his stand and the end of the beach toward which he moved. But by such a move he would not only give the other seller preferred access to all customers on the other half of the beach, but would also give her equal access to some of the customers on the half toward which he moved. Thus, such a move would assure Seller 2 of preferred access to something less than half of all customers, but only at the expense of granting Seller 1 preferred access to a greater

4. The fable is drawn from Hotelling's basic work on competition through differentiating location, Stability in Competition, 39 Econ.J. 41 (1929), reprinted in Am.Econ. Ass'n, Readings in Price Theory 467 (G. Stigler & K. Boulding, eds., 1952).

number of customers. Seller 2's best non-collusive strategy, then, is to join Seller 1 in the middle where both sellers have equal access to all buyers wherever located.

But is this the socially optimal choice? Would not things be improved if, on Seller 2's decision to enter, Seller 1 moved to the mid point of the north half of the beach and Seller 2 located at the mid point of the south half? This would reduce the distance that many customers would need to travel for a hot dog. True, many customers would have to contend with one access being considerably more convenient than the other; these customers might forego the kind of comparison shopping they would do if the two stands were side by side. But the new configuration leaves significant numbers of buyers who are as close or almost as close to one stand as the other. As long as these buyers cannot be discriminated against, social welfare could be improved by an agreement between the two sellers under which each moved half way toward a different end of the beach from that selected by the other. Is excessive convergence, then, an identifiable market failure in some situations? If so, should antitrust law countenance concerted efforts to mitigate the failure and improve the social performance of the market? Why or why not?

Are there other situations in which market division might enhance social welfare? Picture three firms all making machine tools for a given industry. Each makes a full line with the dual consequence that none ever has a very long production run on any tool or size and each must maintain a large inventory covering the full line. The firms agree to specialize and agree that each, hereafter, will make a cohesive group of the tools representing about one-third of the types and styles that previously all had made. Through longer production runs and lower inventory costs, all three firms experience lower per unit costs. Because the firms encounter actual and potential competition from German and Japanese firms, the greater part of these cost savings are passed on to buyers.

The competition law of the European Economic Community authorizes "specialization agreements" like that described above when resulting cost savings are adequately reflected in price reductions. Commission Regulation (EEC) No. 417/85 of 19 December 1984 on the Application of Article 85(3) of the Treaty to Categories of Specialization Agreements, OJ No. L53, 22.2, p. 1 (1985). Would that be a sound policy for America? In *BMI* and *NCAA* we saw "characterization" exercises—conduct that might have been labelled price fixing and brought under the per se rule was called something else and thus brought under the rule of reason. Could the law differentiate between a market division (a per se offense) and a specialization agreement, and subject the latter to full rule of reason inquiry? To do so, would *Topco* have to be overruled?

D. HORIZONTAL RESTRAINTS AND PATENTS

1. PRICE RESTRICTED LICENSES

United States v. General Electric Co., 272 U.S. 476 (1926), raised a basic question about the relationship between patents and antitrust. General Electric had a very strong patent for incandescent light bulbs, a patent that probably gave it monopoly power. General Electric made and sold light bulbs itself. It also licensed Westinghouse to do so, but Westinghouse agreed not only to pay a royalty but also to sell only at the prices and other terms specified by General Electric, from time to time, on its own sales. This explicit horizontal price fixing contract seemed vulnerable; *Addyston Pipe* and *Trans–Missouri* had been decided over two decades earlier. Deferring to the policies of the patent law, the Court sanctioned the price restricted license.

The Court said that a patentee that licenses another to make and sell may limit the method of sale and the price,

> provided the conditions of sale are normally and reasonably adapted to secure pecuniary reward for the patentee's monopoly. One of the valuable elements of the exclusive right of a patentee is to acquire profit by the price at which the article is sold. . . . When the patentee licenses another to make and vend, and retains the right to continue to make and vend on his own account, the price at which his licensee will sell will necessarily affect the price at which he can sell his own patented goods. 272 U.S. at 490.

Is the Court's response sound? The Court assumes a price restricted license will be used when the patentee fears that the license will undercut the patentee's own prices. Will this often be a realistic fear? In what kinds of circumstances? If a patentee has such a fear could it protect itself without a price term in the license? If so, how?

The Court's language implies that a restraint in a patent license does not automatically escape antitrust prohibition on a showing that it may increase the patentee's reward; to escape, the restraint must be "normally and reasonably adapted" to that purpose. Price fixing passes that test, at least in the *General Electric* context. What other restraints might the court think pass? What restraints might it think fail?

If writing on a clean slate one might say that a license restriction should be allowed when it tends to advance the purposes of the patent law significantly. One of those purposes is to encourage investment in innovation. Will the level of such investment be sensitive to fine tuning of the patent-antitrust intersection? Might American technology fall behind that of other countries if America does not allow patent holders to give price restrictive licenses while other countries do?

Perhaps price fixing licenses should be allowed in order to encourage licensing. Just as there is a social interest in the level of innovation, there is a social interest in the wide deployment of new technology once it is invented. Does allowing price fixing in licenses have a tendency to advance that social interest? Does licensing have any other advantage? Does it have any social disadvantages that might off-set its advantages?

How significant is allowing price fixing as a spur to licensing? For what reasons might a patentee consider licensing? Given the reasons for which a patentee might wish to license and given its alternatives to price fixing as a way to avoid license price cutting, would a rule forbidding patentees to restrict the prices at which licensees sell be likely to discourage licensing significantly?

What are the limits to the application of *General Electric?* Consider *United States v. New Wrinkle,* 342 U.S. 371 (1952). A patent, though valid, might provide merely one more technology not significantly more efficient than several already in the public domain. Would we want the patent used to organize the industry and to set prices substantially above cost?

General Electric may not be a very robust authority, as United States v. Line Material Co., 333 U.S. 287 (1948) illustrates. In that case one Justice distinguished *General Electric* on the ground that the price restriction in the case at hand, unlike that in *General Electric,* covered both a basic patent and an improvement patent. Four other Justices voted for the same outcome, a holding that the price fixing license violated Section 1, but expressed readiness to overrule *General Electric.* The four remaining Justices voted to apply *General Electric* and uphold the price fix. In *United States v. Huck Manufacturing Co.,* 382 U.S. 197 (1965), the government urged the Court to reverse *General Electric.* Although four Justices appeared ready to do so, the Court affirmed by a four to four vote the district court decision which, in reliance on *General Electric,* had held that a price fixing license was lawful.

General Electric has also been held inapplicable when the patent holder and licensees account for a substantial share of the market (*United States v. United States Gypsum Co.,* 333 U.S. 364 (1948)). Lower courts, moreover, have distinguished it in a variety of situations—for example when the patent covers a process and the price restriction applies to the resulting product (*American Equipment Co. v. Tuthill Bldg. Material Co.,* 69 F.2d 406 (7th Cir.1934)). See generally L. Sullivan, The Law of Antitrust § 185 (1977).

2. TERRITORY AND FIELD OF USE RESTRICTED LICENSES

The purposes for and the effects of territorial restrictions may be similar to the purposes that motivate and the effects that result from price restrictions. This is true when patents are involved just as it is in other instances. In most areas of law, territorial and price restraints are treated similarly, but in the case of patent restrictions the law differs because of Section 261 of the Patent Code, 66 Stat. 810, 35 U.S.C. Sec. 261. That section provides that "patents, or interests therein, shall be assignable" and that a patentee may "grant and convey an exclusive right . . . to the whole or any specified part of the United States." Perhaps that language need not have been read as authorizing territorial restrictions in licenses (see Baxter, Legal Restrictions on Exploitation of the Patent Monopoly: An Economic Analysis, 76 Yale L.J. 267, 349–51 (1966)), but the case law has consistently upheld such license restrictions. See L. Sullivan, The Law of Antitrust § 184 (1977).

The use of territorial assignments is not the only way to divide markets. They may also be divided between the patentee and licensees by restricting the field of use open to each licensee. These arrangements are seldom challenged and have been held, quite consistently, to be "normally and reasonably adapted" to increasing the patentee's return, and thus lawful. See L. Sullivan, The Law of Antitrust § 186 (1977).

Suppose IBM were to obtain a patent on a uniquely powerful memory chip, adaptable to use in computer and in telecommunication technology, and capable, in both fields, of making equipment not utilizing the chip obsolete.   If IBM licensed the chip to AT & T for use only in the telecommunications field, and retained for itself the exclusive use of the chip in the computer field, would competition be adversely affected? Should such a license be lawful?

3. PATENT POOLS AND SETTLEMENTS

The issues that were raised in *Standard Oil Co. (Indiana) v. United States*, 283 U.S. 163 (1931) can be suggested by the following problem: IBM, AT & T, Control Data and Hewlett–Packard have all been doing R & D work on memory chips.   Each has produced a new, powerful, chip and has obtained a patent on it.   Each patentee claims: (1) that its own invention is nonobvious and was not anticipated by any prior art and that its patent is thus valid; (2) that the patent held by each of the other three firms is invalid for lack of invention; and (3) that the technology embodied in the chips made by each of the other three firms infringes its own, valid patent.   Infringement suits brought by each of the four firms against the other three are consolidated.   After extensive discovery, a settlement is reached.   The four firms organize a jointly owned subsidiary, Chip Co.   Each of the four assigns its patent to Chip Co.   Chip Co. gives royalty-free licenses on all four of the patents to each of the four parent companies and will engage in the business of licensing the four patents to others.

The decision in *Standard Oil (Indiana)* can be read as implying that settlement of a patent dispute by aggregating several competing patents into a pool is reasonable, and therefore lawful under Section 1 of the Sherman Act, unless the technology in the pool is sufficiently crucial to end product production costs that the pool, by fixing the price for access to the technology, effectively fixes end product prices.   *Standard Oil (Indiana)* was decided before *Socony–Vacuum*.   Would the Court that decided *Professional Engineers, BMI, Maricopa County* and *NCAA* be open to the argument that the crucial question is not the effect of the pool on end product prices but the effect of the pool on the cost of access to the technology?

How would you analyze the competitive effect of the Chip Co. pool? Suppose that there is no alternative even remotely comparable to the technology controlled by Chip Co.   On that assumption, the pool would lead to higher technology prices than would most of the possible outcomes to which the litigation might have led, would it not?   There is one possible outcome from continued litigation that would lead to technology prices comparably high; do you see what it is?   In evaluating the "reasonableness" of the Chip Co. pool as a settlement, should you try to assess the likelihood of the various alternative outcomes that might have resulted from continued litigation?   Do you give any weight to the social interest in settling the patent dispute amicably?   Does *Professional Engineers* bear, at all, on these questions?

In the Chip Co. hypothetical we assumed that the patent dispute concerned whether the inventions claimed were anticipated or made obvious by prior technology.   Suppose validity of one or more of the patents was challenged on the ground that the patent had been obtained by fraud on the patent office. Would that change the analysis? Compare *American Cyanamid Co. v. Federal Trade Commission*, 363 F.2d 757 (6th Cir.1966).

E. DATA DISSEMINATION

1. EVALUATING THE LEGALITY OF PROGRAMS TO EXCHANGE INFORMATION

Sometimes competitors exchange competitive data. They might do so to shore up a price-fixing agreement. In part 2 of this section we ask: When and under what circumstances may an inference of price fixing be based on evidence that competitors have been exchanging price data? In this part our questions are related but different. Suppose the competitors have not agreed on price; nevertheless, their exchange of price and related information affects the prices that each decides to charge. Is the effect of their information exchange "anticompetitive"? Should such exchanges violate Section 1?

Historically, exchanges of price and related data took place under the aegis of trade associations. Accordingly, we start our inquiry and analysis with a historical note on the American trade association movement.

"Associationalism," as it is sometimes called, had its roots prior to World War I. Hawley discusses this development in Antitrust and the Association Movement, 1920–1940, in National Competition Policy: Historians' Perspectives on Antitrust and Government–Business Relationship in the United States 98–142 (Office of Special Projects—Bureau of Competition, Federal Trade Commission, August 1981) (hereafter, Historians' Perspective). The movement stemmed in part from American idealism. Teddy Roosevelt once expressed the prayer that no man should be so mean spirited as to refuse to devote some time to the uplift of his trade.

The movement stemmed also from profit-conscious traders; prominently, Jerome Eddy. Eddy had observed that businesses in the same industry often announced prices at levels that would yield "fair" profits (i.e., price comfortably above costs), but that a major hindrance to such profitable cooperation was secret price shading. A firm might follow the industry rate on most sales, but secretly cut prices to get additional business. Once the process started, firm after firm would cut and, doing so, increase output. Prices would erode all along the line. Eddy had a solution. If every sale was immediately publicized no one would cut prices. Each seller would know that if it did, retaliation would be swift.

Eddy's 1912 book, The New Competition, became classic. It proposed "open price associations," trade associations that would supply members with complete information on industry production, inventories and sales. Eddy preached this message to responsive audiences. Soon, open price associations became significant features of American industrial structure. There was some antitrust resistance to Eddy's views, but his supporters regarded antitrust uncertainty about open price associations as a reason to reform or modernize the antitrust laws. These laws were, indeed, largely suspended during World War I, as a new bureaucratic structure, part private, part public, emerged to deal with the production needs of a nation at war. See R.D. Cuff, Antitrust Adjourned: Mobilizations and the Rise of the National Security State in Historians' Perspectives, *supra,* 208–260.

During the 1920s, the association movement gained new champions, the most notable being Herbert Hoover. Hoover, a war time production bureaucrat, became Secretary of Commerce under Harding and Coolidge. He found associations useful.

Hoover disliked old time cartels. But he was an engineer by training, and a thorough-going technocrat. He saw the new associations as expressive of the dynamic elements in industrial society. They were, he thought, a way to assure greater efficiency, more orderly growth, better social integration, and a higher degree of American competitiveness in world markets. The small town foundry and backwoods mill would remain moribund, unless they could be brought into the modern industrial age. By disseminating technical information about both production and management, the industry association might save them. In Hoover's vision, trade associations should be encouraged by government and would maintain links both to the Department of Commerce and the Chamber of Commerce. The Department would give them status and would help disseminate information they generated, and the Chamber would serve as a kind of Congress of Associations. Such a system would assure that industrial policy was made by the enlightened.

In this environment, the American Hardwood Manufacturers' Association apparently flourished. It became, however, the target of an antitrust attack that threatened the whole association movement.

AMERICAN COLUMN & LUMBER CO. v. UNITED STATES
257 U.S. 377 (1921).

JUSTICE CLARKE:

* * *

The unincorporated "American Hardwood Manufacturers' Association" was formed in December, 1918, by the consolidation of two similar associations, from one of which it took over a department of activity designated the "Open Competition Plan," and hereinafter referred to as the "Plan."

Participation in the "Plan" was optional with the members of the Association, but, at the time this suit was commenced, of its 400 members, 365, operating 465 mills, were members of the "Plan." The importance and strength of the Association are shown by the admission in the joint answer that while the defendants operated only five per cent. of the number of mills engaged in hardwood manufacture in the country, they produced one-third of the total production of the United States. . . .

* * *

The record shows that the "Plan" was evolved by a committee, which, in recommending its adoption, said:

"The purpose of this plan is to disseminate among members accurate knowledge of production and market conditions so that each member may gauge the market intelligently instead of guessing at it; to make competition open and above board instead of secret and concealed; to substitute, in estimating market conditions, frank and full statements of our competitors for the frequently misleading and colored statements of the buyer."

* * *

"The chief concern of the buyer, as we all know, is to see that the price he pays is no higher than that of his competitors, against whom he must sell his product in the market. The chief concern of the seller is to get as much as anybody else for his lumber; in other words to get what is termed the top of the market for the quality he offers. By making prices known to each other they will gradually tend toward a standard *in harmony with market conditions,* a situation advantageous to both buyer and seller."

. . . [A] further explanation of . . . the "Plan" was made in an appeal to members to join it . . .:

"The theoretical proposition at the basis of the Open Competition plan is that,

"*Knowledge regarding prices actually made is all that is necessary to keep prices at reasonably stable and normal levels.*

"The Open Competition plan is a central clearing house for information on prices, trade statistics and practices. By keeping all members fully and quickly informed of what the others have done, the work of the plan results in *a certain uniformity of trade practice.* There is no agreement to follow the practice of others, *although members do naturally follow their most intelligent competitors,* if they know what these competitors have been actually doing.

"The monthly meetings held in various sections of the country each month have improved *the human relations* existing between the members before the organization of this plan."

And in another later, and somewhat similar, appeal sent to all the members, this is found:

"Competition, blind, vicious, unreasoning, may stimulate trade to abnormal activity but such condition is no more sound than that mediæval spirit some still cling to of taking a club and going out and knocking the other fellow and taking away his bone.

"The keynote to modern business success is mutual confidence and co-operation. *Co-operative Competition, not Cut-throat Competition.* Co-operation is a matter of business because it pays, because it enables you to get the best price for your product, because you come into closer *personal contact with the market.*

"Co-operation will only replace *undesirable competition* as you develop a co-operative spirit. For the first time in the history of the industry, the hardwood manufacturers are organized into one compact, comprehensive body, equipped to serve the whole trade in a thorough and efficient manner. . . . More members mean more power to do more good for the industry. With co-operation of this kind we will very soon have enlisted in our efforts practically every producing interest, *and you know what that means.*"

* * *

. . . [T]he fully worked out paper plan as adopted . . . required each member to make six reports to the Secretary, viz:

1. A *daily* report of all sales actually made, with the name and address of the purchaser, the kind, grade and quality of lumber sold and all special agreements of every kind, verbal or written with respect thereto. "These reports are to be exact copies of orders taken."

2. A *daily* shipping report, with exact copies of the invoices, all special agreements as to terms, grade, etc. The classification shall be the same as with sales.

3. A *monthly* production report, showing the production of the member reporting during the previous month, with the grades and thickness classified as prescribed in the "Plan."

4. A *monthly* stock report by each member, showing the stock on hand on the first day of the month, sold and unsold, green and dry, with the total of each kind, grade and thickness.

5. Price-lists. Members must file at the beginning of each month price-lists showing prices f.o.b. shipping point, which shall be stated. New prices must be filed with the association as soon as made.

6. Inspection reports. These reports are to be made to the association by a service of its own, established for the purpose of checking up grades of the various members and the "Plan" provides for a chief inspector and sufficient assistants to inspect the stocks of all members from time to time.

The declared purpose of the inspection service is not to change any member's grading except with his consent, but to furnish each member a basis on which he can compare his prices with those of other members, thereby making all members' reports more intelligible and accurate.

All of these reports by members are subject to complete audit by representatives of the association. . . .

* * *

The secretary is required to send to each member:

1. A *monthly* summary showing the production of each member for the previous month, "subdivided as to grade, kind, thickness," etc.

2. A *weekly* report, not later than Saturday, of all sales, to and including the preceding Tuesday, giving each sale and the price, and the name of the purchaser.

3. On Tuesday of each week . . . a report of each shipment by each member, complete up to the evening of the preceding Thursday.

4. . . . [A] *monthly* report, showing the individual stock on hand of each member and a summary of all stocks, green and dry, sold and unsold. . . .

* * *

This extensive interchange of reports, supplemented as it was by monthly meetings at which an opportunity was afforded for discussion "of all subjects of interest to the members," very certainly constituted an organization through which agreements, actual or implied, could readily be arrived at and maintained, if the members desired to make them.

Such, in outline, was the paper plan adopted by the association, but elaborate though it was, in practice three important additions were made to it.

First of all, . . . forty-nine of these meetings were held between January 31, 1919, and February 19, 1920,—approximately one for each week, in some part of the territory.

Second. Before each of these meetings a questionnaire was sent out to the members, and from the replies received, supplementing the other reports, the statistician compiled an estimate of the condition of the market, actual and prospective, which was distributed to the members attending each meeting, and was mailed to those not present. There were eleven questions on this list of which the most important were:

"4th. What was your total production of hardwoods during the last month? What do you estimate your production will probably be for the next two months?"

"10th. Do you expect to shut down within the next few months on account of shortage of logs or for any other reason? If so, please state how long mill will be idle?"

"11th. What is your view of market conditions for the next few months? What is the general outlook for business? State all reasons for your conclusions."

The "Plan" on paper provided only for reports of past transactions and much is made of this in the record and in argument—that reporting to one another past transactions cannot fix prices for the future. But each of these three questions plainly invited an estimate and discussion of future market conditions by each member, and a coordination of them by an expert analyst could readily evolve an attractive basis for cooperative, even if unexpressed, "harmony" with respect to future prices.

Third. The "Plan" provided for a monthly "market report letter" to go to all members of the association. . . . [These] were discussed at all but one or two of the forty-nine meetings which were held. . . .

This elaborate plan . . . not only furnishes . . . information, with respect to stock, sales and prices, but also reports, giving the views of each member as to "market conditions for the next few months"; what the production of each will be for the next "two months"; frequent analyses of the reports by an expert, with, we shall see, significant suggestions as to both future prices and production; and opportunities for future meetings for the interchange of views, which the record shows were very important. It is plain that the only element lacking in this scheme to make it a familiar type of the competition suppressing organization is a definite agreement as to production and prices. But this is supplied: by the disposition of men "to follow their most intelligent competitors," especially when powerful; by the inherent disposition to make all the money possible, joined with the steady cultivation of the value of "harmony" of action; and by the system of reports, which makes the discovery of price reductions inevitable and immediate. The sanctions of the plan obviously are, financial interest, intimate personal contact, and business honor, all operating under the restraint of exposure of what would be deemed bad faith and of trade punishment by powerful rivals.

* * *

Thus, at the meeting held at Cincinnati, on January 21, 1919, in the discussion of business conditions, the chairman said:

"If there is *no increase in production,* particularly in oak, there is going to be good business." "*No man is safe in increasing his production.* If he does, he will be in bad shape, as the demand won't come."

Again, at the meeting held on May 9th, at Memphis, in the discussion of market conditions, appears this paragraph:

"Reference was made to members who contemplate running day and night, and it was stated that the lumber industry had seen these unusual market conditions before and that we ought to be very sure that the market is capable of taking care of night and day lumber."

This warning of May 9th against producing too much lumber was followed, on May 17th, by a sales report sent out by the Manager of Statistics to all members, which was headed, "Stop, Look and Listen." After saying that the hardwood market had assumed a decidedly better tone, with a tendency in quotations upward, with the demand on the increase and with stocks below normal, the writer continues:

"The lumbermen have gone through several lean years, but we are confronted with the possibility of killing the goose that laid the golden egg. *Overproduction will spell disaster,* as it should always be borne in mind that the maximum productive capacity of the sawmills of the country is much in excess of any demand the country has ever known."

* * *

Again, a week later, . . ., one of the members declared: that in his opinion it was "*suicidal to run mills night and day;* that the pine mills had done it, but he hoped they [we] would profit by their past experience and not do it this year."

Much more of like purport appears in the minutes of the meetings throughout the year. . . .

* * *

The "Plan" is, essentially, simply an expansion of the gentlemen's agreement of former days, skilfully devised to evade the law. To call it open competition because the meetings were nominally open to the public, or because some voluminous reports were transmitted to the Department of Justice, or because no specific agreement to restrict trade or fix prices is proved, cannot conceal the fact that the fundamental purpose of the "Plan" was to procure "harmonious" individual action among a large number of naturally competing dealers with respect to the volume of production and prices, without having any specific agreement with respect to them, and to rely for maintenance of concerted action in both respects, not upon fines and forfeitures as in earlier days, but upon what experience has shown to be the more potent and dependable restraints, of business honor and social penalties,—cautiously reinforced by many and elaborate reports, which would promptly expose to his associates any disposition in any member to deviate from the tacit understanding that all were to act together under the subtle direction of a single interpreter of their common purposes, as evidenced in the minute reports of what they had done and in their expressed purposes as to what they intended to do.

. . . Affirmed. Violation

JUSTICE HOLMES, dissenting: . . . I should have supposed that the Sherman Act did not set itself against knowledge—did not aim at a transitory cheapness unprofitable to the community as a whole because not corresponding to the actual conditions of the country. I should have thought that the ideal of commerce was an intelligent interchange made with full knowledge of the facts as a basis for a forecast of the future on both sides. A combination to get and distribute such knowledge, notwith- standing its tendency to equalize, not necessarily to raise, prices, is very far from a combination in unreasonable restraint of trade. It is true that it is a combination of sellers only, but the knowledge acquired is not secret, it is public, and the buyers, I think I may assume, are not less active in their efforts to know the facts. . . .

JUSTICE BRANDEIS, dissenting, with whom JUSTICE McKENNA concurs: . . . In the case before us there was clearly no coercion. There is no claim that a monopoly was sought or created. There is no claim that a division of territory was planned or secured. There is no claim that uniform prices were established or desired. There is no claim that by agreement, force, or fraud, any producer, dealer or consumer was to be or has in fact been controlled or coerced. The Plan is a voluntary system for collecting from these independent concerns detailed information concern- ing the business operations of each, and its opinions as to trade conditions, prospects and policy; and of collating, interpreting, and distributing the data so received among the members of the association and others. No information gathered under the Plan was kept secret from any producer, any buyer or the public. Ever since its inception in 1917, a copy of every report made and of every market letter published has been filed with the Department of Justice, and with the Federal Trade Commission. The district meetings were open to the public. Dealers and consumers were invited to participate in the discussions and to some extent have done so.

* * *

It is insisted that there was a purpose to curtail production. No evidence of any such purpose was introduced. There was at no time uniformity in the percentage of production to capacity. . . . There were, it is true, from time to time, warnings in the "Market Letters" and otherwise, against overproduction—warnings which seem not to have been heeded. But surely Congress did not intend by the Sherman Act to prohibit self-restraint—and it was for self-restraint that the only appeal was made. . . .

It is urged that this was a concerted effort to enhance prices. There was at no time uniformity in prices. So far as appears every mill charged for its product as much as it could get. There is evidence that the hardwood mills expected, by adopting the Plan, to earn more in profits; and to do so, at least in part, by getting higher prices for their product. It may be that the distribution of the trade data, the editorial comment and the conferences enabled the producers to obtain, on the average, higher prices than would otherwise have been possible. But there is nothing in the Sherman Law to indicate that Congress intended to condemn cooperative action in the exchange of information, merely because prophecy resulting from comment on the data collected may lead, for a period, to higher market prices. . . .

The cooperation which is incident to this Plan does not suppress competition. On the contrary it tends to promote all in competition which is desirable. By substituting knowledge for ignorance, rumor, guess and suspicion, it tends also to substitute research and reasoning for gambling and piracy, without closing the door to adventure or lessening the value of prophetic wisdom.

* * *

Questions and Comments

Was Eddy right about data dissemination? Was Hoover? Could both have been right?

Does economic theory help you to decide? Perfect market information is a necessary condition to perfect competition. Incomplete information is a market imperfection. Complete information facilitates rational, self-interested conduct by each firm acting on the information. Each of these propositions is consistent with theory. Nevertheless, more complete information is not unambiguously procompetitive because rational, self-interested market activity is not always competitive. In highly concentrated markets rational self-interest might be served by collusion or interdependence pricing. In such situations, information sharing may facilitate or underlie either an explicit cartel or cartel-like cooperative behavior.

Does *American Column & Lumber* condemn the mere exchange of information, or only that plus something more? Does it condemn exchange of information only under certain circumstances? Precisely what does the case hold? Is it a rule of reason case? A per se case?

Was the exchanged information itself—e.g., past prices, and current supply and demand data—good for competition in this industry? Suppose the information tended to "stabilize" price by bringing all prices closer to the average price without causing any change in the average price. Would that impact be anticompetitive? If the information tended to raise prices because small, scattered sellers learned more accurately what the market would bear, would that impact be anticompetitive?

Perhaps the plan should be called anticompetitive if it tended to raise prices by developing a camaraderie among producers and a shared attitude that producers should hold production down and refrain from undercutting one another. Could 365 producers who represented less than one-third of production count on one another to cooperate? If they did cooperate, could they achieve a supracompetitive price?

Justice Brandeis was not a technocrat like President Hoover. His support of trade associations is probably explained by their benefits to small business and by his fear of the consolidation movement, which he saw as bureaucratizing industry. He was not particularly interested in the economic goals of antitrust, but he was very interested in the social and political goals. He thought a healthy polity required a wide dispersion of economic power and a large number of people with their own investments in the economy and their own independent, decisionmaking roles. He thought the pressures to rationalize production—to avoid boom and bust and to assure efficiency and growth—were strong. In the inevitable effort to achieve these goals, Brandeis hoped that cooperation among small firms would prove a viable alternative to consolidation leading to large, bureaucratic firms. T. McCraw, the Prophets of Regulation 133–35 (1984).

A few years later, another trade association case came before the Court. Many viewed it as a new test case, an effort to salvage something of the association movement despite the blow resulting from *American Column & Lumber.*

MAPLE FLOORING MANUFACTURERS ASS'N v. UNITED STATES

268 U.S. 563 (1925).

JUSTICE STONE:

* * *

The defendants are the Maple Flooring Manufacturers Association, an unincorporated "trade association"; twenty-two corporate defendants, members of the Association, engaged in the business of selling and shipping maple, beech and birch flooring in interstate commerce.

. . . The activities of the present Association of which the Government complains may be summarized as follows:

(1) The computation and distribution among the members of the association of the average cost to association members of all dimensions and grades of flooring.

(2) The compilation and distribution among members of a booklet showing freight rates on flooring from Cadillac, Michigan, to between five and six thousand points of shipment in the United States.

(3) The gathering of statistics which at frequent intervals are supplied by each member of the Association to the Secretary of the Association giving complete information as to the quantity and kind of flooring sold and prices received by the reporting members, and the amount of stock on hand, which information is summarized by the Secretary and transmitted to members without, however, revealing the identity of the members in connection with any specific information thus transmitted.

(4) Meetings at which the representatives of members congregate and discuss the industry and exchange views as to its problems.

. . . [I]t is neither alleged nor proved that there was any agreement among the members of the Association either affecting production, fixing prices or for price maintenance. . . . Nor was there any direct proof that the activities of the Association had affected prices adversely to consumers. On the contrary, the defendants offered a great volume of evidence tending to show that the trend of prices of the product of the defendants corresponded to the law of supply and demand. . . .

[The district court gave judgment to the Government and ordered dissolution of the defendants' association.]

The contention of the Government is that there is a combination among the defendants, which is admitted; that the effect of the activities of the defendants carried on under the plan of the Association must necessarily be to bring about a concerted effort on the part of members of the Association to maintain prices at levels having a close relation to the average cost of flooring reported to members and that consequently there is a necessary and inevitable restraint of interstate commerce. . . .

* * *

The Government [criticized] the use of [a] freight-rate book. . . .

It cannot, we think, be questioned that data as to the average cost of flooring circulated among the members of the Association when combined with a calculated freight rate which is either exactly or approximately the freight rate from the point of shipment, plus an arbitrary percentage of profit, could be made the basis for fixing prices. . . . But, . . . the record is barren of evidence that the published list of costs and the freight-rate book have been so used. . . .

It is contended by the Government that an analysis of the reporting system adopted by the defendants shows that there is no information withheld by one member from another, and that every member is perfectly familiar not only with the summaries which show the exact market condition generally, but also with the exact condition of the business of each of his fellow members. An examination of the record discloses that this is not an accurate statement of the statistical information distributed. . . . At the time of the filing of the bill, members reported weekly to the Secretary of the Association on forms showing dates of sales made by the reporting member, the quantity, the thickness and face, the grade, the kind of wood, the delivery, the prices at which sold, the average freight rate to destination and the rate of commission paid, if any. Members also reported monthly the amount of flooring on hand of each dimension and grade and the amount of unfilled orders. Monthly reports were also required showing the amount of production for each period and the new orders booked for each variety of flooring. The Association promptly reported back to the members statistics compiled from the reports of members including the identifying numbers of the mills making the reports, and information as to quantities, grades, prices, freight rates, etc., with respect to each sale. The names of purchasers were not reported and from and after July 19, 1923, the identifying number of the mill making the report was omitted. . . .

. . . During the year in which the bill of complaint was filed meetings appear to have been held monthly. . . . Trade conditions generally, as reflected by the statistical information disseminated among members, were discussed. . . . [T]here was no discussion of prices in meetings. There was no occasion to discuss past prices, as those were fully detailed in the statistical reports, and the Association was advised by counsel that future prices were not a proper subject of discussion. It was admitted by several witnesses, however, that upon occasion the trend of prices and future prices became the subject of discussion outside the meeting among individual representatives of the defendants attending the meeting. The Government, however, does not charge, nor is it contended, that there was any understanding or agreement, either express or implied, at the meetings or elsewhere, with respect to prices.

* * *

It is not, we think, open to question that the dissemination of pertinent information concerning any trade or business tends to stabilize that trade or business and to produce uniformity of price and trade practice. Exchange of price quotations of market commodities tends to produce uniformity of prices in the markets of the world. Knowledge of the supplies of available merchandise tends to prevent over-production and to avoid the economic disturbances produced by business crises resulting from over-production. But the natural effect of the acquisition of wider and more scientific knowledge of business conditions, on the minds of the individuals engaged in commerce, and its consequent effect in stabilizing production and price, can hardly be deemed a restraint of commerce or if so it cannot, we think, be said to be an unreasonable restraint, or in any respect unlawful.

It is the consensus of opinion of economists and of many of the most important agencies of Government that the public interest is served by the gathering and dissemination, in the widest possible manner, of information with respect to the production and distribution, cost and prices in actual sales, of market commodities, because the making available of such information tends to stabilize trade and industry, to produce fairer price levels and to avoid the waste which inevitably attends the unintelligent conduct of economic enterprise. Free competition means a free and open market among both buyers and sellers for the sale and distribution of commodities. Competition does not become less free merely because the conduct of commercial operations becomes more intelligent through the free distribution of knowledge of all the essential factors entering into the commercial transaction.[1] General knowledge that there is an accumulation of surplus of any market commodity would undoubtedly tend to diminish production, but the dissemination of that information cannot in itself be said to be restraint upon commerce in any legal sense. The manufacturer is free to produce, but prudence and business foresight based on that knowledge influence free choice in favor of more limited production. Restraint upon free competition begins when improper use is made of that information through any concerted action which operates to restrain the freedom of action of those who buy and sell.

* * *

We do not . . . think that the proper application of the principles of decision of *Eastern States Retail Lumber Association v. United States* or *American Column & Lumber Co. v. United States* or *United States v. American Linseed Oil Company* leads to . . . [a different] result. The

---

1. See a suggestive analysis of the Competitive System by various Economists collected and commented on in Marshall's Readings on Industrial Society, 294, 419, 479, 498, 935. See Hobson The Evolution of Modern Capitalism, 403, 5; Elementary Principles of Economics, Irving Fisher, 427, et seq.

court held that the defendants in those cases were engaged in conspiracies against interstate trade and commerce because it was found that the character of the information which had been gathered and the use which was made of it led irresistibly to the conclusion that they had resulted, or would necessarily result, in a concerted effort of the defendants to curtail production. . . .

The decree of the District Court is reversed. No VIOLATION

Chief Justice Taft and Justices McReynolds and Sanford dissented.

———

On the day its decision in *Maple Flooring* was handed down the Supreme Court also announced its decision in *Cement Manufacturers Protective Association v. United States,* 268 U.S. 588 (1925). Manufacturers of Portland cement, a standardized, perishable product, had a widespread practice of selling a portion of their cement through "specific job contracts." These obligated the manufacturer to deliver to the buyer the cement necessary to complete a specified construction job, and to do so at the price stated in the contract or the market price, whichever was lower at the time of delivery. The buyer, however, was not obligated to accept the cement. Why would cement manufacturers develop and follow this practice? Under what circumstances would such contracts be advantageous to manufacturers? Would they help manufacturers if the industry was atomized and price competition keen? Would they help manufacturers if the industry was a loose oligopoly that had been cartelized? If it was a tight oligopoly in which participants priced interdependently?

"Fraudulent" buyers tried to make these contracts work to their advantage. They would contract with more than one manufacturer for the full amount of cement required for a job and, if the market price rose, they would exercise their call on all of this cement at the low contract price. To identify and root out such frauds, the manufacturers, through their trade association, collected and exchanged the fullest details of their specific job contracts.

The cement manufacturers engaged in some additional exchanges of data. Their prices were uniform, but since no agreement to fix price was shown, the Court assumed that the uniformity resulted from competition. Justice Stone said, for the Court (268 U.S. at 604):

> . . . [I]n our view, the gathering and dissemination of information which will enable sellers to prevent the perpetration of fraud upon them, which information they are free to act upon or not as they choose, cannot be held to be an unlawful restraint upon commerce, even though in the ordinary course of business most sellers would act on the information and refuse to make deliveries for which they were not legally bound.

Questions and Comments

Does *Maple Flooring* overrule *American Column & Lumber?* What are the factual differences? How significant were they for antitrust analysis, circa 1925? How significant would they be today? Is there any reason to think that the association in *Maple Flooring* had less power than that in

American Column & Lumber? Was its purpose more benign? Did one association behave more offensively than the other?

Depending upon the structure of the cement market and the elasticity of demand facing the market (factors that the Court did not explore), is it possible that these Eddy-like exchanges of information facilitated a rise in price by facilitating cooperative behavior? If this were the case, how would the Court today treat facts like those in *Cement Manufacturers?* Does *National Society of Professional Engineers* have a bearing? *BMI? NCAA?*

A few years later the Great Depression began. The country sought economic stability with the aid of the National Industrial Recovery Act of 1933. Industries were encouraged to develop codes of ethics; "fair competition" rather than hard competition was encouraged. "Chislers" who cut prices below fair levels (and those who paid low wages) became objects of public disdain. You will recall that in 1933 the Supreme Court decided *Appalachian Coals,* which gave considerable scope for cooperative activity to an industry plagued with overproduction. But by 1940, the Court limited that scope and held, in *Socony–Vacuum,* that a cooperative effort to stabilize an unruly market was illegal.

Changing political and economic conditions during the twenties and thirties also affected attitudes toward the trade association movement. In the depth of the depression the Court decided *Sugar Institute v. United States,* 297 U.S. 553 (1936). Following the philosophy of *Appalachian Coals,* the Court ruled that an industry "plagued" by secret price concessions granted by "unethical" refiners in a market of declining demand for a standardized product could lawfully agree to open, advance announcement of price changes, along with exchanges of statistical information. Defendants were enjoined only from one phase of their activity: agreeing with each other to adhere to their announced prices. As long as the producers each maintained ultimate freedom of pricing action, they were allowed to act cooperatively "to end abuses and to foster fair competitive opportunities. . . ." 297 U.S. at 598.

> Nor does the fact that the correction of abuses may tend to stabilize a business, or to produce fairer price levels, require that abuses should go uncorrected or that an effort to correct them should for that reason alone be stamped as an unreasonable restraint of trade. Id.

The *Sugar Institute* defendants admitted that they wanted to end abuses, including secret price shading. What does this goal imply about the probable competitive effect of their agreement?

In the 1920s (the time of the sugar refiners' pact), the sugar industry had just been relieved of wartime price controls. Under the wartime regime prices had been fixed and all price concessions forbidden. Fifteen companies—all defendants—refined practically all of the imported raw sugar processed in the United States. They supplied 70% to 80% of the sugar consumed in the United States, and they competed with sellers of beet sugar and imported refined sugar. A public "slimmers" campaign was discouraging the use of sugar.

Trade associations continued to flourish but by midcentury they became more cautious, lest they run afoul of the antitrust laws. The next case, although significant for trade association operations, is not itself a trade association case, but rather a competitor-to-competitor "loose" exchange of certain data.

UNITED STATES v. CONTAINER CORPORATION OF AMERICA

393 U.S. 333 (1969).

JUSTICE DOUGLAS: This is a civil antitrust action charging a price-fixing agreement in violation of § 1 of the Sherman Act as amended, 15 U.S.C. § 1. The District Court dismissed the complaint. . . .

The case as proved is unlike any other price decisions we have rendered. There was here an exchange of price information but no agreement to adhere to a price schedule as in *Sugar Institute v. United States,* 297 U.S. 553, or *United States v. Socony–Vacuum Oil Co.,* 310 U.S. 150. There was here an exchange of information concerning specific sales to identified customers, not a statistical report on the average cost to all members, without identifying the parties to specific transactions, as in *Maple Flooring Mfrs. Assn. v. United States,* 268 U.S. 563. While there was present here, as in *Cement Mfrs. Protective Assn. v. United States,* 268 U.S. 588, an exchange of prices to specific customers, there was absent the controlling circumstance, *viz.,* that cement manufacturers, to protect themselves from delivering to contractors more cement than was needed for a specific job and thus receiving a lower price, exchanged price information as a means of protecting their legal rights from fraudulent inducements to deliver more cement than needed for a specific job.

Here all that was present was a request by each defendant of its competitor for information as to the most recent price charged or quoted, whenever it needed such information and whenever it was not available from another source. Each defendant on receiving that request usually furnished the data with the expectation that it would be furnished reciprocal information when it wanted it. That concerted action is of course sufficient to establish the combination or conspiracy, the initial ingredient of a violation of § 1 of the Sherman Act.

There was of course freedom to withdraw from the agreement. But the fact remains that when a defendant requested and received price information it was affirming its willingness to furnish such information in return.

There was to be sure an infrequency and irregularity of price exchanges between the defendants; and often the data were available from the records of the defendants or from the the customers themselves. Yet the essence of the agreement was to furnish price information whenever requested.

* * *

The defendants account for about 90% of the shipment of corrugated containers from plants in the Southeastern United States. While containers vary as to dimensions, weight, color, and so on, they are substantially identical, no matter who produces them, when made to particular specifications. . . . Suppliers . . . do not exceed a competitor's price. It is common for purchasers to buy from two or more suppliers concurrently.

A defendant supplying a customer with containers would usually quote the same price on additional orders, unless costs had changed. Yet where a competitor was charging a particular price, a defendant would normally quote the same price or even a lower price.

. . . Capacity has exceeded the demand from 1955 to 1963, the period covered by the complaint, and the trend of corrugated container prices has been downward. Yet despite this excess capacity and the downward trend of prices, the industry has expanded in the Southeast from 30 manufacturers with 49 plants to 51 manufacturers with 98 plants. An abundance of raw materials and machinery makes entry into the industry easy with an investment of $50,000 to $75,000.

The result of this reciprocal exchange of prices was to stabilize prices though at a downward level. Knowledge of a competitor's price usually meant matching that price. The continuation of some price competition is not fatal to the Government's case. The limitation or reduction of price competition brings the case within the ban, for as we held in *United States v. Socony–Vacuum Oil Co., supra*, at 224, n. 59, interference with the setting of price by free market forces is unlawful *per se*. Price information exchanged in some markets may have no effect on a truly competitive price. But the corrugated container industry is dominated by relatively few sellers. The product is fungible and the competition for sales is price. The demand is inelastic, as buyers place orders only for immediate, short-run needs. The exchange of price data tends toward price uniformity. For a lower price does not mean a larger share of the available business but a sharing of the existing business at a lower return. Stabilizing prices as well as raising them is within the ban of § 1 of the Sherman Act. . . .

Price is too critical, too sensitive a control to allow it to be used even in an informal manner to restrain competition.

Reversed.

JUSTICE FORTAS, concurring: I join in the judgment and opinion of the Court. I do not understand the Court's opinion to hold that the exchange of specific information among sellers as to prices charged to individual customers, pursuant to mutual arrangement, is a *per se* violation of the Sherman Act.

* * *

In summary, the record shows that the defendants sought and obtained from competitors who were part of the arrangement information about the competitors' prices to specific customers. "[I]n the majority of instances," the District Court found that once a defendant had this information he quoted substantially the same price as the competitor, although a higher or lower price would "occasionally" be quoted. Thus the exchange of prices made it possible for individual defendants confidently to name a price equal to that which their competitors were asking. The obvious effect was to "stabilize" prices by joint arrangement—at least to limit any price cuts to the minimum necessary to meet competition. . . .

* * *

JUSTICE MARSHALL, with whom JUSTICES HARLAN, and STEWART, join, dissenting: I agree with the Court's holding that there existed an agreement among the defendants to exchange price information whenever requested. However, I cannot agree that that agreement should be condemned, either as illegal *per se,* or as having had the purpose or effect of restricting price competition in the corrugated container industry in the Southeastern United States.

* * *

Complete market knowledge is certainly not an evil in perfectly competitive markets. This is not, however, such a market, and there is admittedly some danger that price information will be used for anticompetitive purposes, particularly the maintenance of prices at a high level. If the danger that price information will be so used is particularly high in a given situation, then perhaps exchange of information should be condemned.

* * *

In a competitive situation, each seller will cut his price in order to increase his share of the market, and prices will ultimately stabilize at a competitive level—*i.e.,* price will equal cost, including a reasonable return on capital. Obviously, it would be to a seller's benefit to avoid such price competition and maintain prices at a higher level, with a corresponding increase in profit. In a market with very few sellers, and detailed knowledge of each other's price, such action is possible. However, I do not think it can be concluded that this particular market is sufficiently oligopolistic, especially in light of the ease of entry, to justify the inference that price information will necessarily be used to stabilize prices. Nor do I think that the danger of such a result is sufficiently high to justify imposing a *per se* rule without actual proof.

In this market, we have a few sellers presently controlling a substantial share of the market. We have a large number competing for the remainder of the market, also quite substantial. And total demand is increasing. In such a case, I think it just as logical to assume that the sellers, especially the smaller and newer ones, will desire to capture a larger market share by cutting prices as it is that they will acquiesce in oligopolistic behavior. The likelihood that prices will be cut and that those lower prices will have to be met acts as a deterrent to setting prices at an artificially high level in the first place. Given the uncertainty about the probable effect of an exchange of price information in this context, I would require that the Government prove that the exchange was entered into for the purpose of, or that it had the effect of, restraining price competition.

* * *

Questions and Comments

Did the government prove the existence of an agreement? (Could the fact finder have gone either way on the evidence?) Did the government prove facts from which the fact-finder could infer an anticompetitive effect?

Does Justice Douglas lay down a qualified per se rule—a rule invalidating any agreement among competitors to exchange price information under specified structural circumstances? What circumstances? How important is the mode of exchange? The structure of the market? The characteristics of the product? Purpose?

Suppose that you are a salesperson for a container manufacturer. A competitor calls you and says, "I was just trying to sell my cartons to Joe Jones at Procter and Gamble for $10 a dozen. He tells me he can get cartons from you at $9.50 a dozen. Is that true?" If it is true, will you say so? Suppose you actually quoted Jones $10.50. Will you tell your counterpart?

In his dissent, Justice Marshall takes issue less with the Court's legal norm than with its characterization of the structure of the market. Do you agree with Justice Douglas or Justice Marshall about whether the structure of this market facilitates collaborative price behavior? If the hardwood companies in *American Column & Lumber* (in place of their Open Competition Plan) had exchanged price information in the *Container* manner, would their exchange have pushed price upward? What about the flooring companies in *Maple Flooring?* The *Sugar Institute* members?

After *Container,* is there a structural test for the legality of direct exchanges of price information among competing sellers? If so, does the *Container* test modify, replace, or complement the test in *American Column & Lumber?*

Note Justice Douglas's reference to a "controlling circumstance." Is there a "controlling circumstance defense" to price information exchanges? Would sellers' need to protect themselves from buyer fraud constitute a controlling circumstance and justify an interseller price exchange that is likely to have a price-raising effect? The next case, *United States v. United States Gypsum Company,* 438 U.S. 422 (1978), will help you to answer these questions.

In the 1970s the major manufacturers of gypsum board were indicted for a criminal price-fixing conspiracy. The government alleged that the companies agreed to fix prices and that one way in which they carried out their conspiracy was by telephoning their competitors to find out what the competition was currently charging a specific customer. The defendants denied that they fixed prices. They admitted that they telephoned competitors to get information about prices to specific customers, but asserted that they did so because of the "lying buyer" problem. Allegedly, a buyer of gypsum board, negotiating with a major manufacturer, would tell the manufacturer that it had a lower-price offer from another manufacturer. Subject as it was to the Robinson–Patman Act, the manufacturer could not generally offer a discriminatorily low price to one buyer and not to that buyer's competitors. If, however, the lower price was necessary to meet competition from another manufacturer, the selling company would have a Robinson–Patman defense: the good faith meeting of competition. (Robinson–Patman Act, § 2(b).) The gypsum manufacturers asserted that their telephone conversations were necessary to verify whether the buyer had really been offered a lower price by a competitor and thus to establish a meeting-competition defense to the Robinson–Patman Act.

At the trial the judge charged the jury as follows: To return a verdict of guilty, the jury must find that the defendants had a purpose to fix prices; that information exchanges made in good faith to comply with the Robinson–Patman Act was not sufficient by itself to establish an agreement to fix prices. If the jury found that the effect of the exchanges was to raise, fix, or stabilize price, they could presume the forbidden purpose from that effect, because people are presumed to intend the necessary consequences of their acts.

The gypsum board industry had the following characteristics:

Gypsum board is a laminated type of wallboard composed of paper, vinyl, or other specially treated coverings over a gypsum core. The product is essentially fungible; differences in price, credit terms, and delivery services largely dictate the purchasers' choice between competing suppliers. Overall demand, however, is governed by the level of construction activity and is only marginally affected by price fluctuations.

The gypsum board industry is highly concentrated, with the number of producers ranging from 9 to 15 in the period 1960–1973. The eight largest companies accounted for some 94% of the national sales with the seven "single-plant producers" accounting for the remaining 6%. Most of the major producers and a large number of the single-plant producers are members of the Gypsum Association which since 1930 has served as a trade association of gypsum board manufacturers.

The jury, in *Gypsum,* returned a verdict of guilty. The court of appeals reversed, and the Supreme Court affirmed the appellate court. The Supreme Court held, first, that the trial judge's charge was reversible error. The charge allowed, and may have required, the jury to find criminal liability if it found that defendants' activity had an effect on prices, regardless of whether defendants intended or even were aware of the price effect. Though reversing on *mens rea* grounds, the Court rejected defendants' "controlling circumstance" defense on the facts.

Here are excerpts.

UNITED STATES v. UNITED STATES GYPSUM CO.
438 U.S. 422 (1978).

JUSTICE BURGER: . . . We are unwilling to construe the Sherman Act as mandating a regime of strict-liability criminal offenses.[13]

* * *

Close attention to the type of conduct regulated by the Sherman Act buttresses [the] conclusion [that *mens rea* is an element of the criminal violation]. With certain exceptions for conduct regarded as *per se* illegal because of its unquestionably anticompetitive effects, see, *e.g., United States v. Socony–Vacuum Oil Co.,* 310 U.S. 150 (1940), the behavior proscribed by the Act is often difficult to distinguish from the gray zone of socially acceptable and economically justifiable business conduct. Indeed, the type of conduct charged in the indictment in this case—the exchange of price information among competitors—is illustrative in this regard.[16]

13. Our analysis focuses solely on the elements of a criminal offense under the antitrust laws, and leaves unchanged the general rule that a civil violation can be established by proof of either an unlawful purpose or an anticompetitive effect. See *United States v. Container Corp.,* 393 U.S. 333, 337 (1969); *id.,* at 341 (Marshall, J., dissenting). . . .

16. The exchange of price data and other information among competitors does not in-variably have anticompetitive effects; indeed such practices can in certain circumstances increase economic efficiency and render markets more, rather than less, competitive. For this reason, we have held that such exchanges of information do not constitute a *per se* violation of the Sherman Act. See, *e.g., United States v. Citizens & Southern Nat. Bank,* 422 U.S. 86, 113 (1975); *United States v. Container Corp.,* 393 U.S., at 338 (Fortas, J., concurring). A number of factors

The imposition of criminal liability on a corporate official, or for that matter on a corporation directly, for engaging in such conduct which only after the fact is determined to violate the statute because of anticompetitive effects, without inquiring into the intent with which it was undertaken, holds out the distinct possibility of overdeterrence; salutary and procompetitive conduct lying close to the borderline of impermissible conduct might be shunned by businessmen who chose to be excessively cautious in the face of uncertainty regarding possible exposure to criminal punishment for even a good-faith error of judgment.[17] . . .

* * *

. . . Although an effect on prices may well support an inference that the defendant had knowledge of the probability of such a consequence at the time he acted, the jury must remain free to consider additional evidence before accepting or rejecting the inference. . . .[22]

[In civil cases, however, the government need not prove *mens rea;* proof of the effect on price of conduct deliberately entered into is enough to prove the violation.]

* * *

including most prominently the structure of the industry involved and the nature of the information exchanged are generally considered in divining the procompetitive or anticompetitive effects of this type of interseller communication. See *United States v. Container Corp., supra.* See generally L. Sullivan, Law of Antitrust 265–274 (1977). Exchanges of current price information, of course, have the greatest potential for generating anticompetitive effects and although not *per se* unlawful have consistently been held to violate the Sherman Act. See *American Column & Lumber Co. v. United States,* 257 U.S. 377 (1921); *United States v. American Linseed Oil Co.,* 262 U.S. 371 (1923); *United States v. Container Corp., supra.*

17. The possibility that those subjected to strict liability will take extraordinary care in their dealings is frequently regarded as one advantage of a rule of strict liability. However, where the conduct proscribed is difficult to distinguish from conduct permitted and indeed encouraged, as in the antitrust context, the excessive caution spawned by a regime of strict liability will not necessarily redound to the public's benefit. The antitrust laws differ in this regard from, for example, laws designed to insure that adulterated food will not be sold to consumers. In the latter situation, excessive caution on the part of producers is entirely consistent with the legislative purpose.

21. [Editors' Note: Text accompanying this footnote has been deleted.] . . . [P]roof that the defendant's conduct was undertaken with knowledge of its probable consequences will satisfy the Government's burden [to prove criminal intent].

22. Certainly our decision in *United States v. Container Corp.,* 393 U.S. 333 (1969), is fairly read as indicating that proof of an anticompetitive effect is a sufficient predicate for liability. In that case, liability followed from proof that "the exchange of price information has had an anticompetitive effect in the industry," *id.,* at 337, and no suggestion was made that proof of a purpose to restrain trade or competition was also required.

. . . Nor are the prior cases treating exchanges of information among competitors more favorable to respondents' position. See *American Column & Lumber Co. v. United States,* 257 U.S., at 400 ("[A]ny concerted action . . . to cause, or which in fact does cause, . . . restraint of competition . . . is unlawful"); *United States v. American Linseed Oil Co.,* 262 U.S. 371, 389 (1923) ("[A] necessary tendency . . . to suppress competition . . . [is] unlawful"); *Maple Flooring Mfrs. Assn. v. United States,* 268 U.S. 563, 585 (1925) (purpose to restrain trade or conduct which "had resulted, or would necessarily result, in tending arbitrarily to lessen production or increase prices" sufficient for liability). While in *Cement Mfrs. Protective Assn. v. United States,* 268 U.S. 588 (1925), an exception from Sherman Act liability was recognized for conduct intended to prevent fraud, we do not read that case as repudiating the rule set out in prior cases; instead *Cement* highlighted a narrow limitation on the application of the general rule that either purpose or effect will support liability.

There remains the possibility that in a limited number of situations a seller may have substantial reasons to doubt the accuracy of reports of a competing offer and may be unable to corroborate such reports in any of the generally accepted ways. . . .

[Price verification for the purpose of taking advantage of the Robinson–Patman meeting-competition defense is not a "controlling circumstance" within the meaning of *Container Corporation*. The Robinson–Patman requirement can usually "be satisfied by efforts falling short of interseller verification."]

* * *

. . . As an abstract proposition, resort to interseller verification as a means of checking the buyer's reliability seems a possible solution to the seller's plight, but careful examination reveals serious problems with the practice.

Both economic theory and common human experience suggest that interseller verification—if undertaken on an isolated and infrequent basis with no provision for reciprocity or cooperation—will not serve its putative function of corroborating the representations of unreliable buyers regarding the existence of competing offers. Price concessions by oligopolists generally yield competitive advantages only if secrecy can be maintained; when the terms of the concession are made publicly known, other competitors are likely to follow and any advantage to the initiator is lost in the process. Thus, if one seller offers a price concession for the purpose of winning over one of his competitor's customers, it is unlikely that the same seller will freely inform its competitor of the details of the concession so that it can be promptly matched and diffused. Instead, such a seller would appear to have at least as great an incentive to misrepresent the existence or size of the discount as would the buyer who received it. Thus verification, if undertaken on a one-shot basis for the sole purpose of complying with the § 2(b) defense, does not hold out much promise as a means of shoring up buyers' representations.

The other variety of interseller verification is, like the conduct charged in the instant case, undertaken pursuant to an agreement, either tacit or express, providing for reciprocity among competitors in the exchange of price information. Such an agreement would make little economic sense, in our view, if its sole purpose were to guarantee all participants the opportunity to match the secret price concessions of other participants under § 2(b). For in such circumstances, each seller would know that his price concession could not be kept from his competitors and no seller participating in the information exchange arrangement would, therefore, have any incentive for deviating from the prevailing price level in the industry. Regardless of its putative purpose, the most likely consequence of any such agreement to exchange price information would be the stabilization of industry prices. Instead of facilitating use of the § 2(b) defense, such an agreement would have the effect of eliminating the very price concessions which provide the main element of competition in oligopolistic industries and the primary occasion for resort to the meeting-competition defense.

Especially in oligopolistic industries such as the gypsum board industry, the exchange of price information among competitors carries with it the added potential for the development of concerted price-fixing arrangements which lie at the core of the Sherman Act's prohibitions. . . .

We are left, therefore, on the one hand, with doubts about both the need for and the efficacy of interseller verification as a means of facilitating compliance with § 2(b), and, on the other, with recognition of the tendency for price discussions between competitors to contribute to the stability of oligopolistic prices and open the way for the growth of prohibited anticompetitive activity. To recognize even a limited "controlling circumstance" exception for interseller verification in such circumstances would be to remove from scrutiny under the Sherman Act conduct falling near its core with no assurance, and indeed with serious doubts, that competing antitrust policies would be served thereby. In *Automatic Canteen Co. v. FTC,* 346 U.S. 61, 74 (1953), the Court suggested that as a general rule the Robinson–Patman Act should be construed so as to insure its coherence with "the broader antitrust policies that have been laid down by Congress"; that observation buttresses our conclusion that exchanges of price information—even when putatively for purposes of Robinson–Patman Act compliance—must remain subject to close scrutiny under the Sherman Act.[32]

* * *

Questions and Comments

Gypsum was decided in 1978, after Chief Justice Warren had retired, Burger had been appointed Chief Justice, and a new antitrust majority was visible. Prior to *Gypsum,* the Court had usually assumed that there is a broad margin between anticompetitive and procompetitive behavior and had not expressed concern about over-deterrence. In *Gypsum,* for the first time, we see a strong statement of concern that overly restrictive rules will deter procompetitive conduct.

The Court in *Gypsum* cited Justice Fortas' concurring opinion in *Container* for the proposition that information exchanges are not illegal per se. Yet at the end of its opinion the Court stated its economic theory that, under certain market conditions, interseller verification is likely (1) to stabilize oligopolistic prices, and (2) to lead to a full-fledged price-fixing agreement.

Suppose that interseller verification of the sort found in *Container* occurred in the gypsum board industry and the United States sued to enjoin it. What, in light of *Gypsum,* would the government have to prove to make out a prima facie case? Would the government have to prove anticompetitive effect by means other than inferences from economic theory? Given *Container* and *Gypsum,* do we have a structural test for the legality of interseller information exchanges in civil litigation?

When exchange involves certain kinds of data and certain modes of exchange the dangers of oligopolistic price coordination and ultimately a real price-fixing conspiracy are highest. Risky data include: current prices, costs

---

32. * * * § 2(b) affords only a defense to liability and not an affirmative right under the Act. While sellers are, of course, entitled to take advantage of the defense when they can satisfy its requirements, efforts to increase its availability at the expense of broader, affirmative antitrust policies must be rejected.

and output, plans for future prices and output, and predictions or advice for future prices and output for one's own firm or for the industry. The riskiest mode of exchange is direct personal contact among competitors.

Because of the anticompetitive dangers, antitrust lawyers frequently advise that competitors should never exchange facts or predictions about current or prospective price, cost and output and, further, that they should never exchange industry information by direct, personal contact with competitors. A limited exception is made for discussion of common economic problems and trends. Discussion of economic problems common to the industry frequently takes place at trade association meetings. Are there important benefits of such discussions? How great are the anticompetitive dangers? What would you advise your client before she or he participates in such discussions? Would a well advised association have a lawyer present at such meetings? Would it keep an accurate and reasonably complete record of the proceeding?

Trade associations frequently compile industry data, including price and production information, and distribute it to their members. Antitrust precautions include the following:

1. Gather information as to past transactions only.

2. Use an independent person (not an employee of any of the members) to receive and compile the data, so that no member sees the raw data of its competitor.

3. Disseminate the information in aggregate form only, so that members cannot attribute information to individual firms.

If the industry is highly concentrated, would you suggest other precautions? Would providing the information to all interested persons, including buyers and non-members, help your client's antitrust posture? Is there a degree of concentration at which you would advise against any exchange of price and production data (e.g., three firms in a high-barrier market with a standardized product)?

Suppose the firms in a highly concentrated market want to exchange information regarding credit reliability of the buyers in the industry. What would you advise? Why? See *L.C.L. Theatres v. Columbia Pictures Industries,* 421 F.Supp. 1090 (N.D.Tex.1976).

Because bona fide information exchanges generally have procompetitive benefits but may also pose antitrust risks, groups wishing to implement plans for the exchange of data often ask the Justice Department for a business review letter passing upon such a plan. The Justice Department has issued a number of such letters responding favorably to data exchange plans.[5]

2. INFERRING PRICE FIXING FROM INFORMATION EXCHANGES

In the above cases, defendants had collaborated to exchange information and the question was whether that collaboration lessened competition. In other cases the question is whether defendants had a price-fixing agreement. We want to know: can the fact finder infer from the information exchange (or from it and other evidence) that defendants

---

5. A "favorable" business review letter generally states that the government does not plan to challenge the proposed transaction.

have agreed to fix prices? If so, is such an inference merely permissible, or is it compelled? Data exchanges may facilitate actual price-fixing agreements. Exchanges of cost and sales data can provide competitors with the information they need to arrive at a jointly profit-maximizing price, publicize a consensus price, and (if transactions are visible) help participants to monitor a cartel. Thus, data exchange are sometimes a clue to an underlying cartel.

In the following case plaintiffs, the Goldfarbs, needed a title opinion by a lawyer in order to purchase a home. Although the house that they wanted to buy was part of a development and the title to all of the parcels in the development had just been searched in connection with the development, the Goldfarbs could find no lawyer to do the title search at less than 1% of the value of the property. As it happened, one percent of the sales prices of a house was the fee "suggested" in the minimum fee schedule published by the Fairfax County Bar Association. The State Bar had a disciplinary rule stating that it was unethical for lawyers to charge unreasonably low prices and lawyers were subject to discipline if they did so more than occasionally.

How does publication of a suggested fee schedule relate to the concept of data exchange? What was the purpose and effect of the schedule in *Goldfarb?* Note how a series of cartel-facilitating devices may work together.

GOLDFARB v. VIRGINIA STATE BAR
421 U.S. 773 (1975)

CHIEF JUSTICE BURGER: * * * The fee schedule the lawyers referred to is a list of recommended minimum prices for common legal services. Respondent Fairfax County Bar Association published the fee schedule although, as a purely voluntary association of attorneys, the County Bar has no formal power to enforce it. Enforcement has been provided by respondent Virginia State Bar which is the administrative agency through which the Virginia Supreme Court regulates the practice of law in that State; membership in the State Bar is required in order to practice in Virginia. Although the State Bar has never taken formal disciplinary action to compel adherence to any fee schedule, it has published reports [4]

4. In 1962 the State Bar published a minimum-fee-schedule report that listed a series of fees and stated that they "represent the considered judgment of the Committee [on Economics of Law Practice] as to [a] fair minimum fee in each instance." The report stated, however, that the fees were not mandatory, and it recommended only that the State Bar *consider* adopting such a schedule. Nevertheless, shortly thereafter the County Bar adopted its own minimum-fee schedule that purported to be "a conscientious effort to show lawyers in their true perspective of dignity, training and integrity." The suggested fees for title examination were virtually identical to those in the State Bar report. In accord with Opinion 98 of the State Bar Committee on Legal Ethics the schedule stated that, although there is an ethical duty to charge a lower fee in a deserving case, if a lawyer

"'purely for his own advancement, intentionally and regularly bills less than the customary charges of the bar for similar services . . . [in order to] increase his business with resulting personal gain, it becomes a form of solicitation contrary to Canon 27 and also a violation of Canon 7, which forbids the efforts of one lawyer to encroach upon the employment of another.'" App. 30.

In 1969 the State Bar published a second fee-schedule report that, as it candidly stated, "reflect[ed] a general scaling up of fees for legal services." The report again stated

condoning fee schedules, and has issued two ethical opinions indicating that fee schedules cannot be ignored. The most recent opinion states that "evidence that an attorney *habitually* charges less than the suggested minimum fee schedule adopted by his local bar Association, raises a presumption that such lawyer is guilty of misconduct. . . ." [6]

Because petitioners could not find a lawyer willing to charge a fee lower than the schedule dictated, they had their title examined by the lawyer they had first contacted. They then brought this class action against the State Bar and the County Bar alleging that the operation of the minimum-fee schedule, as applied to fees for legal services relating to residential real estate transactions, constitutes price fixing in violation of § 1 of the Sherman Act. Petitioners sought both injunctive relief and damages.

* * *

The County Bar argues that because the fee schedule is merely advisory, the schedule and its enforcement mechanism do not constitute price fixing. Its purpose, the argument continues, is only to provide legitimate information to aid member lawyers in complying with Virginia professional regulations. Moreover, the County Bar contends that in practice the schedule has not had the effect of producing fixed fees. The facts found by the trier belie these contentions, and nothing in the record suggests these findings lack support.

A purely advisory fee schedule issued to provide guidelines, or an exchange of price information without a showing of an actual restraint on trade, would present us with a different question. The record here, however, reveals a situation quite different from what would occur under a purely advisory fee schedule. Here a fixed, rigid price floor arose from respondents' activities: every lawyer who responded to petitioners' inquiries adhered to the fee schedule, and no lawyer asked for additional information in order to set an individualized fee. The price information disseminated did not concern past standards, but rather minimum fees to be charged in future transactions, and those minimum rates were increased over time. The fee schedule was enforced through the prospect of professional discipline from the State Bar, and the desire of attorneys to comply with announced professional norms, * * * the motivation to conform was reinforced by the assurance that other lawyers would not compete by underbidding. This is not merely a case of an agreement that

that no local bar association was bound by its recommendations; however, respondent County Bar again quickly moved to publish an updated minimum-fee schedule, and generally to raise fees. The new schedule stated that the fees were not mandatory, but tempered that by referring again to Opinion 98. This time the schedule also stated that lawyers should feel free to charge *more* than the recommended fees; and to avoid condemnation of higher fees charged by some lawyers, it cautioned County Bar members that "to . . . publicly criticize lawyers who charge more than the suggested fees herein might in itself be evidence of solicitation. . . ."

6. The parties stipulated that these opinions are a substantial influencing factor in lawyers' adherence to the fee schedules. One reason for this may be because the State Bar is required by statute to "investigat[e] and report . . . the violation of . . . rules and regulations as are adopted by the [Virginia Supreme Court] to a court of competent jurisdiction for such proceedings as may be necessary. . . ." Va.Code Ann. § 54–49 (1972). Therefore any lawyer who contemplated ignoring the fee schedule must have been aware that professional sanctions were possible, and that an enforcement mechanism existed to administer them.

may be inferred from an exchange of price information, *United States v. Container Corp.*, 393 U.S. 333, 337 (1969); for here a naked agreement was clearly shown, and the effect on prices is plain.[9] *Id.*, at 339 (Fortas, J., concurring).

* * *

Questions and Comments

In *Goldfarb* the market was highly fragmented, but nonetheless collusion was feasible. It was made possible by state regulation of entry and conduct (licensing and disciplinary rules) and by pervasive industry self-regulation. Codes of ethics instilled and reinforced the notion that competition was unprofessional and unethical. The risk of discovery and the threat of discipline brought about adherence. Moreover, buyers could not shift to any substitute product; they had to get a title examination by a lawyer in order to get financing; suppliers not "bound" by the Code of Ethics could not offer the service because "only an attorney licensed to practice in Virginia may legally examine a title. . . ."

Is there a case to be made that the legal profession (or any other profession) will serve the public interest better if it is protected from rigorous competition?

The next case involves the same question that *Goldfarb* raised—does the data exchange indicate price fixing—but the business context is very different.

UNITED STATES v. CITIZENS & SOUTHERN NATIONAL BANK
422 U.S. 86 (1975).

JUSTICE STEWART: [Georgia legislation prohibited city banks from opening branches in suburban areas. Citizens & Southern National Bank ("C & S") desired to open its own branches, but being unable to do so lawfully, it embarked upon a program of sponsoring suburban banks, taking a 5% ownership interest in each and forming a correspondent bank relationship with each. When Georgia repealed the prohibition against branch banking, C & S sought to acquire the remainder of the stock of its 5% banks. The government sued, principally to enjoin the acquisitions. The government's complaint also included a charge of price-fixing.] * * * Each of these banks was founded *ab initio* through the sponsorship of C & S. Except for that sponsorship, they would very probably not exist. The record shows that other banking organizations had been unsuccessful in attempting to launch new banks in the area, and C & S affiliation and financial backing were instrumental in convincing state and federal banking authorities to charter these new banks. In short,

---

9. The Court of Appeals accurately depicted the situation:

"[I]t is clear from the record that all or nearly all of the [County Bar] members charged fees equal to or exceeding the fees set forth in the schedule for title examinations and other services involving real estate." 497 F.2d 1, 12 (CA4 1974).

" 'A significant reason for the inability of [petitioners] to obtain legal services . . .

for less than the fee set forth in the Minimum Fee Schedule . . . was the operation of the minimum fee schedule system.' " *Id.*, at 4.

"It is abundantly clear from the record before us that the fee schedule and the enforcement mechanism supporting it act as a substantial restraint upon competition among attorneys practicing in Fairfax County." *Id.*, at 13.

these banks represented a policy by C & S of *de facto* branching through the formation of new banking units, rather than through the acquisition, and consequent elimination, of pre-existing, independent banks.

. . . Had the new banks been *de jure* branches of C & S, the whole process would have been beyond reproach. Branching allows established banks to extend their services to new markets, thereby broadening the choices available to consumers in those markets. Having access to parent-bank financial support, expert advice, and proved banking services, branches of several city banks can often enter a market not yet large or developed enough to support a variety of independent, unit banks. Branching thus offers competitive choice to markets where monopoly or oligopoly might otherwise prevail. . . .

It is, of course, conceded that C & S's *de facto* branches have not behaved as active competitors with respect either to each other or to C & S National and its majority-owned affiliates. But the Government goes further and contends that the correspondent associate programs have actually encompassed at least a tacit agreement to fix interest rates and service charges, so as to make the interrelationships—to that extent at least—illegal *"per se."* . . .

C & S did regularly notify the 5–percent banks—as it did its *de jure* branches—of the interest rates and service charges in force at C & S National and its affiliates. But the dissemination of price information is not itself a *per se* violation of the Sherman Act. A few of the memoranda distributed by C & S could be construed as advocating price uniformity; on the other hand, the memoranda were almost without exception stamped "for information only," and the 5–percent banks were admonished by C & S, several times and very clearly, to use their own judgment in setting prices; indeed, the banks were warned that the antitrust laws required no less. . . .

Were we dealing with independent competitors having no permissible reason for intimate and continuous cooperation and consultation as to almost every facet of doing business, the evidence adduced here might well preclude a finding that the parties were not engaged in a conspiracy to affect prices. But, as we indicate below, the correspondent associate programs, as such, were permissible under the Sherman Act. In this unusual light, we cannot hold clearly erroneous the District Court's finding that the lack of significant price competition did not flow from a tacit agreement but instead was an indirect, unintentional, and formally discouraged result of the sharing of expertise and information which was at the heart of the correspondent associate programs.

* * *   *No violation*

Questions and Comments

As we have seen, an agreement to exchange competitive information may be illegal even in the absence of an agreement to fix prices. Yet, if plaintiff can prove that defendants agreed to fix prices, liability is clear; if plaintiff proves merely that defendants agreed to exchange data, hurdles remain. *Goldfarb* and *C & S* illustrate the fact-specific nature of inferring that defendants agreed to fix prices. In *Goldfarb*, would an adverse finding by the trial court also have been sustained?

What if data is exchanged through the press? Consider the case of the airlines. The airline industry was deregulated in 1978. Deregulation led to new entry, some failures and exits, intense fare competition for a time and, eventually, to a series of consolidations. On March 15, 1983, when price competition still seemed intense, American Airlines, the second largest domestic airline, announced through the press a new simplified fare structure based on mileage that would eliminate "thousands of unneeded fares" and would go into effect April 15.

SALPUKAS, AMERICAN TO BASE FARES ON MILEAGE

New York Times, March 15, 1983 at D1, col. 3.

American Airlines, in a sweeping attempt to simplify fares, announced a plan yesterday to replace thousands of different fares with four basic ones tied to the distance traveled.

Expressing the hope that the rest of the industry would follow suit, Thomas G. Plaskett, senior vice president for marketing, said: "The new streamlined fare structure will help reduce fare confusion and make airline ticket prices more equitable for everyone."

Two major carriers, Trans World and United, reacted favorably to the plan. But other airlines were doubtful that the new system would be supported in highly competitive markets.

Al Becker, manager of corporate communications for American, acknowledged that American would have to match fares lower than its own in order to remain competitive.

How New Fares Would Work

Under American's proposal, the lowest rate, 15 cents a mile, would be for trips of over 2,500 miles; the highest, 53 cents a mile, would apply to trips of under 250 miles. American said the new system would be phased in starting April 2 and would be completely in place by April 15.

* * *

"At first glance it's a good move," said Jerry Cosley, vice president of public affairs at T.W.A. "It's very businesslike.

* * *

Chuck Novak, manager of corporate communications for United, said, "We'll certainly look at it, but it's going to be tough to sell to the industry." . . .

* * *

SALPUKAS, CARRIERS BACK AMERICAN ON SIMPLIFIED FARE PLAN

New York Times, March 19, 1983 at B1, col. 3

Most of the nation's major airlines yesterday came out in support of a plan by American Airlines to tie fares to the distance traveled.

Trans World Airlines and Continental Air Lines said that they would apply the new fare structure to their entire route systems. This extends the markets that would be affected, because the two carriers fly some routes not served by American.

Neil Effman, senior vice president of airline planning for T.W.A., said that the proposal could be a "major break in the deep discounting that has led to airline losses in the past year or so. It represents an excellent attempt to rationalize a pricing system that has gotten totally out of hand."

Yesterday's moves strengthened the outlook for the new fare system, which needs the backing of most of the industry to be effective.

Spokesmen for Eastern Airlines and Western Airlines said that while those carriers had not made a final decision, they supported the basic concept of the plan.

The president of Delta Air Lines, David C. Garrett Jr., said that the idea of tying fares to the distance traveled was a good one and that Delta would decide today whether to go along.

United Airlines, the nation's largest carrier, had said on Tuesday that it would adopt the proposal on the routes where it competes with American, 60 percent of its system.

United estimated yesterday that the new fare structure could eliminate up to 600,000 of the 2 million domestic fares that are now stored in its reservations system.

Andrew Kim, an airline analyst at F. Eberstadt & Company, a securities firm, cautioned that, as the major carriers came on board, it would become more attractive for the regional carriers and some of the newer airlines to undercut fares in some markets in a bid to gain market share.

While the airlines could benefit from the end of deep discounts under the plan, consumers would end up paying higher fares in some major markets.*

* * *

Suppose that it is spring of 1983 and you are Assistant Attorney General in charge of the Antitrust Division. You read these articles and your staff investigates. You are convinced that the airlines did not communicate with one another except through their press releases. American Airlines put its plan into effect; each airline that then announced it would probably adopt the proposal did so shortly thereafter. Have the airlines hurt competition? Do you sue? On what theory? For what relief?

F. PRODUCT STANDARDIZATION AND RELATED PROGRAMS

Throughout industrial history, examples can be found of rivals agreeing on product standardization—for utility, safety, or cartelization. Contract terms in complex transactions (e.g., mortgage loans) are sometimes standardized also (although leaving room for variation on critical terms

such as price, points, and prepayment penalties.) Often the standardization programs are adopted under the aegis of a trade association. In the
rare case, as in standardization of railroad track dimensions, standardization is virtually essential. Standardization will almost always have some
advantage for consumers. Standard sizes of candy bars, cans of soup, or
other consumer goods make it easier for consumers to compare prices of
competing brands. So, too, standardization of non-price terms of a mortgage may facilitate price comparison. Safety and efficiency may also be
served by standardization. If the configuration of the dashboard and
control levers on automobiles were to be standardized, a driver might
more easily adjust when driving a rented car. Also, safety features that
meet industry standards can protect users. On the other hand, agreements to standardize products chill the competition to provide variety
(thus, standardization may lessen the chances the producers will make a
less safe but cheaper chain saw or that they will devise a new and better
method of constructing plywood). Moreover, by making the relevant
product more homogeneous, standardization agreements can facilitate
cartelization or interdependence and thus produce higher prices. Also,
standardization agreements are sometimes accompanied by mechanisms
to suppress and exclude rivals who do not meet the standards; and while
such exclusion may sometimes have benefits such as safety, exclusion
eliminates competition.

Standardization programs with exclusionary features—e.g. "you cannot sell this product unless you follow these standards"—are normally
addressed under the law of boycotts which we treat in section G below.
Exploitative standardization—e.g., "we movie distributors will not deal
with you theatre operators unless you accept our standard forms and
agree to arbitration"—is also sometimes treated as a boycott since it
constitutes a concerted refusal to deal except on undesired terms. In
theory, however, the exploitative qualities of such refusals to deal are
more akin to price-fixing agreements than to exclusionary boycotts.

In any standardization case, as in many other cases under Section 1 of
the Sherman Act, you will want to ask three main questions: (1) Is this
program or agreement a cover or a facilitating device for a cartel? (Can
price fixing be inferred from it?) (2) Does it, given its particulars and the
structural circumstances, lead to interdependent, supracompetitive pricing? (Is it, all things considered, an unreasonable restraint because of its
probable competitive effects?) (3) Does the program so significantly eliminate competition in product variety by reducing competitors' freedom to
provide "deviant" size, shape, or composition of the product as to seriously
reduce consumer options and so hurt competition?

If the answer to (1), above is affirmative the price fixing per se rule is
invoked and the inquiry ends. However, affirmative answers to (2) or (3)
above, do not trigger a traditional per se rule. In these instances one
must go on to ask: Does the program yield competitive benefits, such as
efficiencies? If so, do the efficiencies outweigh the competitive harms?
Others might ask the question differently: Is this program intended for a
good business purpose? How much weight do we give to good business
purpose? In respect to question 3, the competitive harm does not attack

the "central nervous system" of competition. Would a court be more open to claims about offsetting benefits? Would a health benefit be cognizable, despite *Professional Engineers?* Suppose, for example, that major food packagers agreed not to use MSG, which added materially to shelf life, because of its apparent adverse health consequences. Is this agreement unlawful?

Problem

The highest quality wheat for making pasta is durum wheat. Durum becomes scarce. The members of the pasta producers association (who account for 50% of all U.S. purchases of durum) agree as follows: No more than 50% of the wheat component of all pasta products will be satisfied by durum for the duration of the shortage. They are concerned that purchases of durum for pasta will drive up the price of durum. If so, these purchases would also drive up the price of bread and other staples. To allay this problem, the members of the association argue that their agreement is in the public interest. Is the agreement legal? Is it governed by a per se rule or a rule of reason? See *National Macaroni Manufacturers Association v. FTC,* 345 F.2d 421 (7th Cir.1965). In analyzing the problem try to be consistent with *BMI,* and *National Society of Professional Engineers.* When you review this material also consider *Indiana Federation of Dentists* which you will meet in the next section.

As you study the materials below on boycotts and their effects, we will analyze additional problems posed by standardization.

G. BOYCOTTS

A boycott is a concerted refusal to deal with others or to deal only on unfavorable terms in order directly or indirectly to discipline or exclude a target. Often the boycotters' ultimate purpose is to insulate their business from the targets' competition.

The earliest boycott case to reach the United States Supreme Court was *Montague & Company v. Lowry.*

MONTAGUE & CO. v. LOWRY
193 U.S. 38 (1904).

[Plaintiffs were partners doing business in San Francisco. The Tile, Mantel & Grate Association of California was composed of wholesale dealers and manufacturers of the named products. The members of the Association did not have manufacturing facilities in California.]

* * * The objects of the association, as stated in the constitution thereof, were to unite all acceptable dealers in tiles, fireplace fixtures and mantels in San Francisco and vicinity, (within a radius of 200 miles,) and all American manufacturers of tiles, and by frequent interchange of ideas advance the interests and promote the mutual welfare of its members.

By its constitution, it was provided that any individual, corporation or firm engaged in or contemplating engaging in the tile, mantel or grate business in San Francisco, or within a radius of 200 miles thereof, (not manufacturers,) having an established business and carrying not less than

$3,000 worth of stock, and having been proposed by a member in good standing and elected, should, after having signed the constitution and by-laws governing the association, and upon the payment of an entrance fee as provided, enjoy all the privileges of membership. It was provided . . . that all associated and individual manufacturers of tiles and fireplace fixtures throughout the United States might become non-resident members of the association upon the payment of an entrance fee as provided. . . . The initiation fee was, for active members, $25, and for non-resident members $10, and each active member of the association was to pay $10 per year as dues, but no dues were charged against non-residents.

An executive committee was to be appointed, whose duty it was to examine all applications for membership in the association and report on the same to the association. It does not appear what vote was necessary to elect a member, but it is alleged in the complaint that it required the unanimous consent of the association to become a member thereof, and it was further alleged that by reason of certain business difficulties there were members of the association who were antagonistic to plaintiffs, and who would not have permitted them to join, if they had applied, and that plaintiffs were not eligible to join the association for the further reason that they did not carry at all times stock of the value of $3,000.

The by-laws enacted as follows:

"SEC. 7. No dealer and active member of this association shall purchase, directly or indirectly, any tile or fireplace fixtures from any manufacturer or resident or traveling agent of any manufacturer not a member of this association, neither shall they sell or dispose of, directly or indirectly, any unset tile for less than list prices to any person or persons not a member of this association, under penalty of expulsion from the association.

"SEC. 8. Manufacturers of tile or fireplace fixtures or resident or traveling agents or manufacturers selling or disposing, directly or indirectly, their products or wares to any person or persons not members of the Tile, Mantel and Grate Association of California, shall forfeit their membership in the association."

The term "list prices," referred to in the seventh section, was a list of prices adopted by the association, and when what are called "unset" tiles were sold by a member to any one not a member, they were sold at the list prices so adopted, which were more than fifty per cent higher than when sold to a member of the association.

The plaintiffs had established a profitable business and were competing with all the defendants, who were dealers and engaged in the business of purchasing and selling tiles, grates and mantels in San Francisco prior to the formation of this association. The plaintiffs had also before that time been accustomed to purchase all their tiles from tile manufacturers in Eastern States, (who were also named as parties defendants in this action,) and all of those manufacturers subsequently joined the association. The plaintiffs were not members of the association and had never been, and had never applied for membership therein and had never been invited to join the same.

The proof shows that by reason of the formation of this association the plaintiffs have been injured in their business, because they were unable to procure tiles from the manufacturers at any price, or from the dealers in San Francisco, at less than the price set forth in the price list mentioned in the seventh section of the by-laws, *supra,* which was more than fifty per cent over the price at which members of the association could purchase the same. . . .

* * *

JUSTICE PECKHAM: The question raised by the plaintiffs in error in this case is, whether this association, described in the foregoing statement of facts, constituted or amounted to an agreement or combination in restraint of trade within the meaning of the so-called Anti–Trust Act of July 2, 1890?

The result of the agreement when carried out was to prevent the dealer in tiles in San Francisco, who was not a member of the association, from purchasing or procuring the same upon any terms from any of the manufacturers who were such members, and all of those manufacturers who had been accustomed to sell to the plaintiffs were members. The non-member dealer was also prevented by the agreement from buying tiles of a dealer in San Francisco who was a member, excepting at a greatly enhanced price over what he would have paid to the manufacturers or to any San Francisco dealer who was a member, if he, the purchaser, were also a member of the association. The agreement, therefore, restrained trade, for it narrowed the market for the sale of tiles in California from the manufacturers and dealers therein in other States, so that they could only be sold to the members of the association, and it enhanced prices to the non-member as already stated.

* * *

 . . . [I]t is contended the sale of unset tiles is so small in San Francisco as to be a negligible quantity; that it does not amount to one per cent of the business of the dealers in tiles in that city. The amount of trade in the commodity is not very material, but even though such dealing heretofore has been small, it would probably largely increase when those who formerly purchased tiles from the manufacturers are shut out by reason of the association and their non-membership therein from purchasing their tiles from those manufacturers, and are compelled to purchase them from the San Francisco dealers. Either the extent of the trade in unset tiles would increase between the members of the association and outsiders, or else the latter would have to go out of business, because unable to longer compete with their rivals who were members. In either event, the combination, if carried out, directly effects a restraint of interstate commerce.

It is also contended that, as the expressed object of the association was to unite therein all the dealers in San Francisco and vicinity, the plaintiffs had nothing more to do than join the association, pay their fees and dues and become like one of the other members. It was not, however, a matter of course to permit any dealer to join. The constitution only provided for "all acceptable dealers" joining the association. As plaintiffs were not invited to be among its founders, it would look as if they were not regarded as acceptable. However that may be, they never subsequently to its formation applied for admission. It is plain that the question of their admission, if they had so applied, was one to be arbitrarily determined by the association. . . .

The judgment is *affirmed.*

Questions and Comments

We asserted earlier that Justice Peckham preferred clear norms that were understandable to business people and reduced the discretion of courts and juries. Does he fashion such a rule here? Restate his rule.

What was the effect of the manufacturers' agreement not to sell tiles to non-member dealers? Do we know whether plaintiffs had other sources of supply? Do we know what percent of tiles was manufactured by members of the association? Do we know how easy it would be for new entrants to manufacture tiles? Do any of these things matter? Were there any efficiencies achieved for either manufacturers or dealers?

Does the fact of the suit give us any clues to the purpose and effect of the arrangement (i.e., whether it was important to non-member dealers to have access to the member-manufacturers' tiles)? Does the mere fact of an agreement give us any clues? Might they have had a purpose other than to limit competition?

If plaintiffs had been clearly eligible to join the association but chose not to, would they still have had a good cause of action?

Note that this was a private action and the private harm was allegedly caused by exclusion or refusal to deal. If you were Assistant Attorney General, would you have sued?

In the next case the government sued. Defendants raised a different question: Was there a boycott at all?

EASTERN STATES LUMBER DEALERS' ASSOCIATION v. UNITED STATES

234 U.S. 600 (1914).

JUSTICE DAY: . . . This is an action brought by the United States for an injunction against certain alleged combinations of retail lumber dealers, which, it was averred, had entered into a conspiracy to prevent wholesale dealers from selling directly to consumers of lumber. . . .

The . . . defendant associations are constituted largely of retail lumber dealers. . . .

The record discloses a systematic circulation among the members of the defendant associations of [reports.] The method of operation as stated by the learned counsel for the appellants is thus summarized in his brief:

"The names [of wholesalers] on this list are obtained and placed thereon as the result of complaints made by individual retailers. When an individual member of a retail association learns of a sale by a wholesaler to one of the customers of the retailer he may complain in writing to the secretary of his association, whose duty it is thereupon to ascertain the facts by correspondence with the wholesaler in question and such other means as may seem proper. . . . Should any wholesaler desire to have his name removed from the list he can have it done upon satisfactory assurance to the local secretary that he is no longer selling in competition with the retailers. . . ."

. . . [T]here can be but one purpose in giving the information . . . to the members . . .. These lists were quite commonly spoken of as blacklists, and when the attention of a retailer was brought to the name of a wholesaler who had acted in this wise it was with the evident purpose that he should know of such conduct and act accordingly. True it is that there is no agreement among the retailers to refrain from dealing with listed wholesalers, nor is there any penalty annexed for the failure so to do, but he is blind indeed who does not see the purpose . . ..

In other words, the circulation of such information among the hundreds of retailers as to the alleged delinquency of a wholesaler with one of their number had and was intended to have the natural effect of causing such retailers to withhold their patronage from the concern listed.

* * *

But it is said that in order to show a combination or conspiracy within the Sherman Act some agreement must be shown under which the concerted action is taken. It is elementary, however, that conspiracies are seldom capable of proof by direct testimony and may be inferred from the things actually done, and when in this case by concerted action the names of wholesalers who were reported as having made sales to consumers were periodically reported to the other members of the associations, the conspiracy to accomplish that which was the natural consequence of such action may be readily inferred.

* * *

A retail dealer has the unquestioned right to stop dealing with a wholesaler for reasons sufficient to himself, and may do so because he thinks such dealer is acting unfairly in trying to undermine his trade. "But," as was said by Mr. Justice Lurton, speaking for the court in *Grenada Lumber Co. v. Mississippi*, 217 U.S. 433, 440, "when the plaintiffs in error combine and agree that no one of them will trade with any producer or wholesaler who shall sell to a consumer within the trade range of any of them, quite another case is presented. An act harmless when done by one may become a public wrong when done by many acting in concert, for it then takes on the form of a conspiracy, and may be prohibited or punished, if the result be hurtful to the public or to the individual against whom the concerted action is directed."

* * *

Questions and Comments

Did these retailers agree with each other not to buy from dual distributors (wholesalers who also sell at retail), or is this case only about collaboration to deploy information that is then used to make individual choices?

The Court observed that the "blacklist" successfully discouraged retailers from dealing with dual distributors. From what does this tendency flow? Did each retailer who cut off offending wholesalers act on its own? Would each have cut off offending wholesalers even if it were the only one to do so? If, by contrast, all or most acted in the confident expectation that all or most others would act the same way did the retailers "agree" with one another not to deal with blacklisted firms?

Consider the purpose of the participating retailers. Can we infer that their purpose was to drive dual distributors out of retailing? Could they possibly have accomplished this purpose by a black list? If so, would output fall and price rise? Could the court tell on the facts before it? Did it care?

If output reduction is not an essential element of the boycott offense, what is?

PARAMOUNT FAMOUS LASKY CORP. v. UNITED STATES

282 U.S. 30 (1930).

JUSTICE McREYNOLDS: By this proceeding the United States seek to prevent further violation of Section 1 (Sherman Act) through an alleged combination and conspiracy to restrain interstate commerce in motion picture films.

Appellants are the Paramount Famous Lasky Corporation and nine other Corporations (Distributors), producers and distributors throughout the Union of sixty per cent of the films used for displaying motion pictures by some 25,000 theatre owners (Exhibitors); the Motion Picture Producers and Distributors of America, a corporation * * * composed of the above-mentioned Distributors; and thirty-two Film Boards of Trade, which severally function within certain defined Regions.

* * *

Under an agreement amongst themselves Appellant Distributors will only contract with Exhibitors according to the terms of the Standard Exhibition Contract, dated May 1, 1928. . . .

This Standard Contract is an elaborate document, covering eight pages of the record. Under it the Distributor licenses the Exhibitor to display specified photo plays at a designated theatre on definite dates. . . . Section 18 provides in substance that each party shall submit any controversy that may arise to a Board of Arbitration, in the city where the Distributor's Exchange is located, established under and controlled by written rules adopted May 1, 1928; accept as conclusive the findings of this Board; and forego the right to trial by jury. . . .

* * *

. . . [T]en competitors in interstate commerce, controlling sixty per cent of the entire film business, have agreed to restrict their liberty of action by refusing to contract for display of pictures except upon a Standard Form which provides for compulsory joint action by them in respect of dealings with one who fails to observe such a contract with any Distributor, all with the manifest purpose to coerce the Exhibitor and limit the freedom of trade.

The United States maintains that the necessary and inevitable tendency of the outlined agreement and combination . . . is to produce material and unreasonable restraint of interstate commerce in violation of the Sherman Act. The court below accepted this view and directed an appropriate injunction against future action under the unlawful plan. We agree with its conclusion and the challenged decree must be affirmed.

The Appellants claim: (1) The Standard Exhibition Contract and Rules of Arbitration dated May 1, 1928, having been evolved after six years of discussion and experimentation, are reasonable and normal regulations; so that whatever restraint follows falls short of unlawful coercion. (2) Arbitration is well adapted to the needs of the motion picture industry. (3) The manner in which the Contract and Rules have worked out in practice, and the significant absence of complaints, reflect their reasonable character. . . .

. . . "The purpose of the Sherman Act is to prohibit monopolies, contracts and combinations which probably would unduly interfere with the free exercise of their rights by those engaged, or who wish to engage, in trade and commerce—in a word to preserve the right of freedom to trade." *United States v. Colgate & Co.*, 250 U.S. 300, 307. "The fundamental purpose of the Sherman Act was to secure equality of opportunity and to protect the public against evils commonly incident to destruction of competition through monopolies and combinations in restraint of trade." *Ramsay Co. v. Bill Posters Assn.*, 260 U.S. 501, 512. "The Sherman Act was intended to secure equality of opportunity and to protect the public against evils commonly incident to monopolies and those abnormal contracts and combinations which tend directly to suppress the conflict for advantage called competition—the play of the contending forces ordinarily engendered by an honest desire for gain." *United States v. American Oil Co.*, 262 U.S. 371, 388.

The fact that the Standard Exhibition Contract and Rules of Arbitration were evolved after six years of discussion and experimentation does not show that they were either normal or reasonable regulations. . . . Certainly [the arrangement] is unusual and we think it necessarily and directly tends to destroy "the kind of competition to which the public has long looked for protection." *United States v. American Oil Co., supra*, 390.

* * *

It may be that arbitration is well adapted to the needs of the motion picture industry; but when under the guise of arbitration parties enter into unusual arrangements which unreasonably suppress normal competition their action becomes illegal.

In order to establish violation of the Sherman Act it is not necessary to show that the challenged arrangement suppresses all competition between the parties or that the parties themselves are discontented with the arrangement. The interest of the public in the preservation of competition is the primary consideration. The prohibitions of the statute cannot ". . . be evaded by good motives. The law is its own measure of right and wrong, of what it permits, or forbids, and the judgment of the courts cannot be set up against it in a supposed accommodation of its policy with the good intention of parties, and it may be, of some good results." *Standard Sanitary Mfg. Co. v. United States*, 226 U.S. 20, 49.

* * *

The challenged decree must be *affirmed*.

Questions and Comments

Unlike the defendants in *Montague* and perhaps *Eastern States Lumber*, the defendants in *Paramount Famous Lasky* were not trying to exclude their competitors; they were trying to exploit or impose conditions on their customers. Does this make the matter more like a cartel than a boycott?

In *Montague* and *Eastern States Lumber* the major social concern seems to be to assure unencumbered market access to potential competitors, rather than to protect consumers from being exploited. If the concerted action here is more like a cartel than a boycott should attention shift again to consumers? Was output limitation a probable result of this concerted action? If not, or if one cannot tell, why was the Court concerned?

Should the Court have remanded for a determination whether arbitration was reasonable? Should it have asked the trial court to determine whether arbitration in one of a few large cities was a more efficient method of dispute resolution than court actions in localities scattered around the country? On facts like these would *National Society of Professional Engineers* require a factual determination of reasonableness? If arbitration was efficient, was the agreement reasonable?

Exhibitors probably believed they were more likely to win before juries than before arbitrators. Moreover, the standard form imposed burdens on them. They would have to travel to a big city, such as New York, where the distributors could always appear in person and would be guided by their New York counsel. Are these facts relevant? Might they have influenced the Court? Is it material that the concerted action of the distributors would tend to shift wealth from exhibitors to distributors?

In the late 1920s the movie business was in deep trouble. Exhibitors were failing and many were making fraudulent transfers of theatres in efforts to escape debts to distributors. To alleviate the widespread losses resulting from these transfers, the movie distributors agreed to procedures for obtaining credit information and for circulating and acting upon it. The distributors caused their Film Boards of Trade to adopt written rules. Under the rules, all new theatre owners were required to answer a series of questions including whether the new owner would assume outstanding contracts between the prior owner and any of the distributors. If a new theatre owner would not assume the outstanding contracts, the new owner was required to furnish cash security to the distributor in a "reasonable" amount set by the Film Board. The distributors agreed that if a new owner would neither assume nor furnish security no distributors would deal with that owner (except for "spot" or immediate bookings, which, alone, would not sustain a theatre). In *United States v. First National Pictures*, 282 U.S. 44 (1930), a companion case to *Paramount Famous Lasky* the Government challenged this arrangement. What should be the result? What result would follow from *National Society of Professional Engineers?*

The Court said in *First National Pictures:*

The obvious purpose of the arrangement is to restrict the liberty of those who have representatives on the Film Boards and secure their concerted action for the purpose of coercing certain purchasers of theatres by excluding them from the opportunity to deal in a free and untrammeled market. *Id.* at 54.

In examining trade association activities, you encountered the associationist movement, which thrived in some quarters during the early part of this century. Cases such as *American Column and Lumber* displayed judiciary hostility towards that movement; cases such as *Maple Flooring,* on the other hand, reflected receptivity to the movement. Are *Paramount Famous Lasky* and *First National Pictures* of a piece with *American Column and Lumber,* valuing both the independence of individual business people and the privacy of judicial regulation over private regulation? Does the next case fit into the same pattern?

FASHION ORIGINATORS' GUILD OF AMERICA, INC. v. FEDERAL TRADE COMMISSION
312 U.S. 457 (1941).

JUSTICE BLACK:

* * *

Some of the members of the combination design, manufacture, sell and distribute women's garments—chiefly dresses. Others are manufacturers, converters or dyers of textiles from which these garments are made. Fashion Originators' Guild of America (FOGA), an organization controlled by these groups, is the instrument through which petitioners work to accomplish the purposes condemned by the Commission. The garment manufacturers claim to be creators of original and distinctive designs of fashionable clothes for women, and the textile manufacturers claim to be creators of similar original fabric designs. After these designs enter the channels of trade, other manufacturers systematically make and sell copies of them, the copies usually selling at prices lower than the garments copied. Petitioners call this practice of copying unethical and immoral, and give it the name of "style piracy." And although they admit that their "original creations" are neither copy-righted nor patented . . ., they nevertheless urge that sale of copied designs constitutes an unfair trade practice and a tortious invasion of their rights. Because of these alleged wrongs, petitioners, while continuing to compete with one another in many respects, combined among themselves to combat and, if possible, destroy all competition from the sale of garments which are copies of their "original creations." They admit that to destroy such competition they have in combination purposely boycotted and declined to sell their products to retailers who follow a policy of selling garments copied by other manufacturers from designs put out by Guild members. As a result of their efforts, approximately 12,000 retailers throughout the country have signed agreements to "cooperate" with the Guild's boycott program, but more than half of these signed the agreements only because constrained by threats that Guild members would not sell to retailers who failed to yield to their demands—threats that have been carried out by the Guild practice of placing on red cards the names of non-cooperators (to whom no sales are to be made), placing on white cards the names of cooperators (to whom sales are to be made), and then distributing both sets of cards to the manufacturers.

The one hundred and seventy-six manufacturers of women's garments who are members of the Guild occupy a commanding position in their line of business. In 1936, they sold in the United States more than 38% of all women's garments wholesaling at $6.75 and up, and more than 60% of those at $10.75 and above. The power of the combination is great; competition and the demand of the consuming public make it necessary for most retail dealers to stock some of the products of these manufacturers. . . .

The Guild maintains a Design Registration Bureau for garments, and the Textile Federation maintains a similar Bureau for textiles. The Guild employs "shoppers" to visit the stores of both cooperating and non-cooperating retailers, "for the purpose of examining their stocks, to determine and report as to whether they contain . . . copies of registered designs . . ." An elaborate system of trial and appellate tribunals exists, for the determination of whether a given garment is in fact a copy of a Guild member's design. In order to assure the success of its plan of registration and restraint, and to ascertain whether Guild regulations are being violated, the Guild audits its members' books. And if violations of Guild requirements are discovered, as, for example, sales to red-carded retailers, the violators are subject to heavy fines.

In addition to the elements of the agreement set out above, all of which relate more or less closely to competition by so-called style copyists, the Guild has undertaken to do many things apparently independent of and distinct from the fight against copying. Among them are the following: the combination prohibits its members from participating in retail advertising; regulates the discount they may allow; prohibits their selling at retail; cooperates with local guilds in regulating days upon which special sales shall be held; prohibits its members from selling women's garments to persons who conduct businesses in residences, residential quarters, hotels or apartment houses; and denies the benefits of membership to retailers who participate with dress manufacturers in promoting fashion shows unless the merchandise used is actually purchased and delivered.

If the purpose and practice of the combination of garment manufacturers and their affiliates runs counter to the public policy declared in the Sherman and Clayton Acts, the Federal Trade Commission has the power to suppress it as an unfair method of competition. . . .

. . . [T]he findings of the Commission bring petitioners' combination in its entirety well within the inhibition of the policies declared by the Sherman Act itself. . . . Among the many respects in which the Guild's plan runs contrary to the policy of the Sherman Act are these: it narrows the outlets to which garment and textile manufacturers can sell and the sources from which retailers can buy (*Montague & Co. v. Lowry*, 193 U.S. 38, 45); subjects all retailers and manufacturers who decline to comply with the Guild's program to an organized boycott (*Eastern States Retail Lumber Dealers' Assn. v. United States*, 234 U.S. 600, 609–611); takes away the freedom of action of members by requiring each to reveal to the Guild the intimate details of their individual affairs; and has both as its necessary tendency and as its purpose and effect the direct suppression of competition from the sale of unregistered textiles and copied designs. In addition to all this, the combination is in reality an extra-governmental agency, which prescribes rules for the regulation and restraint of interstate commerce, and provides extra-judicial tribunals for determination and punishment of violations, and thus "trenches upon the power of the national legislature and violates the statute." *Addyston Pipe & Steel Co. v. United States,* 175 U.S. 211, 242.

Petitioners, however, argue that the combination cannot be contrary to the policy of the Sherman and Clayton Acts, since the Federal Trade Commission did not find that the combination fixed or regulated prices, parcelled out or limited production, or brought about a deterioration in quality. But action falling into these three categories does not exhaust the types of conduct banned by the Sherman and Clayton Acts. And as previously pointed out, it was the object of the Federal Trade Commission Act to reach not merely in their fruition but also in their incipiency combinations which could lead to these and other trade restraints and practices deemed undesirable. In this case, the Commission found that the combination exercised sufficient control and power in the women's garments and textile businesses "to exclude from the industry those manufacturers and distributors who do not conform to the rules and regulations of said respondents, and thus tend to create in themselves a monopoly in the said industries." While a conspiracy to fix prices is illegal, an intent to increase prices is not an ever-present essential of conduct amounting to a violation of the policy of the Sherman and Clayton Acts; a monopoly contrary to their policies can exist even though a combination may temporarily or even permanently reduce the price of the articles manufactured or sold. For as this Court has said, "Trade or commerce under those circumstances may nevertheless be badly and unfortunately restrained by driving out of business the small dealers and worthy men whose lives have been spent therein, and who might be unable to readjust themselves to their altered surroundings. Mere reduction in the price of the commodity dealt in might be dearly paid for by the ruin of such a class, and the absorption of control over one commodity by an all-powerful combination of capital."[7] . . .

The decision below is accordingly *affirmed.*   ~~violation~~

Questions and Comments

Consider the nature and purpose of the plan in *Fashion Originators Guild of America* (hereafter *FOGA*). Was there a boycott? If so was it horizontal or vertical? Was it primary or secondary?

In obvious respects *FOGA* can be analogized to *Montague* and *Eastern States Lumber,* but there are differences. In neither of those previous cases did the defendants offer credible justification for their conduct, which similarly tended to limit or foreclose competitors. Did the petitioners in *FOGA* have a "good" reason for their plan? Why did their justification fail? Would it fail today? By what authority?

What was the probable effect of the *FOGA* plan on the price of women's garments? On the style? Would the boycott have wiped out copiers of textile

7. *United States v. Trans–Missouri Freight Assn.,* 166 U.S. 290, 323.

designs if it had not been enjoined? Would it have made inroads into the copier's market share? Does illegality depend upon these effects?

The Court implies that the question is whether the practice tends toward monopoly (which, perhaps, can be read in context as meaning supracompetitive pricing by Guild members). But the Court states also that fixing price, limiting production, or impairing quality are not the only types of conduct banned by the antitrust laws. Is the Court confused about whether illegality requires a price rise? What harms does the Court identify that are independent of a tendency toward monopoly? Suppose defendants proved that the concerted effort could not have produced monopoly because, for example, imitators of designs could efficiently sell to independent manufacturers, wholesalers and retailers that carried only copies. Suppose defendants proved also that only by concerted action could the designers effectively prevent free-riding by the pirates. How would the Court then have decided the case? How would it decide the case today? What are your authorities?

Consider this hypothetical: One of the problems of the packaged airline tour business is that some unscrupulous operators publish misleading ads. For example, they advertise the availability of a 747 airplane to fly to and from Puerto Rico on specified dates, and they accept reservations only upon advance payments. If they have enough reservations, they provide a 747. If not, passengers may find a DC7 when they arrive at the airport. Legitimate tour packagers are concerned because these practices give the whole industry a bad name and hurt their business. They have founded an association and published a code of ethics. A committee of the association has identified five non-complying packagers. It has provided their names to the companies that rent planes to packagers and have informed these companies that, if any company thereafter rents a plane to any of the five non-complying packagers, the committee will notify all association members of that fact. Is the combination lawful under *FOGA*? Is it lawful today?

When a boycott is sponsored by competing firms in order to drive out or discipline competitors at the same level, some courts have labelled the conduct a "classic group boycott." *E.g., Smith v. Pro–Football, Inc.,* 593 F.2d. 1173, 1178 (D.C.Cir.1978). Is this type of boycott likely to be so harmful to competition and so unlikely to have procompetitive value that it can safely be treated as unlawful per se?

The next case is more ambiguous than the classic horizontal boycott.

KLOR'S v. BROADWAY–HALE STORES
359 U.S. 207 (1959).

JUSTICE BLACK: Klor's, Inc., operates a retail store on Mission Street, San Francisco, California; Broadway–Hale Stores, Inc., a chain of department stores, operates one of its stores next door. The two stores compete in the sale of radios, television sets, refrigerators and other household appliances. Claiming that Broadway–Hale and 10 national manufacturers and their distributors have conspired to restrain and monopolize commerce in violation of §§ 1 and 2 of the Sherman Act, Klor's brought this action for treble damages and injunction in the United States District Court.

In support of its claim Klor's made the following allegations: George Klor started an appliance store some years before 1952 and has operated

it ever since either individually or as Klor's, Inc. Klor's is as well
equipped as Broadway–Hale to handle all brands of appliances. Nevertheless, manufacturers and distributors of such well-known brands as
General Electric, RCA, Admiral, Zenith, Emerson and others have conspired among themselves and with Broadway–Hale either not to sell to
Klor's or to sell to it only at discriminatory prices and highly unfavorable
terms. Broadway–Hale has used its "monopolistic" buying power to bring
about this situation. . . . The concerted refusal to deal with Klor's has
seriously handicapped its ability to compete and has already caused it a
great loss of profits, goodwill, reputation and prestige.

The defendants did not dispute these allegations, but sought summary
judgment and dismissal of the complaint for failure to state a cause of
action. They submitted unchallenged affidavits which showed that there
were hundreds of other household appliance retailers, some within a few
blocks of Klor's who sold many competing brands of appliances, including
those the defendants refused to sell to Klor's. From the allegations of the
complaint, and from the affidavits supporting the motion for summary
judgment, the District Court concluded that the controversy was a "purely
private quarrel" between Klor's and Broadway–Hale, which did not
amount to a "public wrong proscribed by the [Sherman] Act." On this
ground the complaint was dismissed and summary judgment was entered
for the defendants. The Court of Appeals for the Ninth Circuit affirmed
the summary judgment. It stated that "a violation of the Sherman Act
requires conduct of defendants by which the public is or conceivably may
be ultimately injured." It held that here the required public injury was
missing since "there was no charge or proof that by any act of defendants
the price, quantity, or quality offered the public was affected, nor that
there was any intent or purpose to effect a change in, or an influence on,
prices, quantity, or quality. . . . " The holding, if correct, means that
unless the opportunities for customers to buy in a competitive market are
reduced, a group of powerful businessmen may act in concert to deprive a
single merchant, like Klor, of the goods he needs to compete effectively.
We granted certiorari to consider this important question in the administration of the Sherman Act.

We think Klor's allegations clearly show one type of trade restraint
and public harm the Sherman Act forbids, and that defendants' affidavits
provide no defense to the charges. Section 1 of the Sherman Act makes
illegal any contract, combination or conspiracy in restraint of trade, and
§ 2 forbids any person or combination from monopolizing or attempting to
monopolize any part of interstate commerce. In the landmark case of
Standard Oil Co. v. United States, 221 U.S. 1, this Court read § 1 to
prohibit those classes of contracts or acts which the common law had
deemed to be undue restraints of trade and those which new times and
economic conditions would make unreasonable. *Id.,* at 59–60. The Court
construed § 2 as making "the prohibitions of the act all the more complete and perfect by embracing all attempts to reach the end prohibited by
the first section, that is, restraints of trade, by any attempt to monopolize,
or monopolization thereof. . . . " *Id.,* at 61. The effect of both sections,
the Court said, was to adopt the common-law proscription of all "contracts
or acts which it was considered had a monopolistic tendency . . . " and

which interfered with the "natural flow" of an appreciable amount of interstate commerce. *Id.*, at 57, 61; *Eastern States Lumber Assn. v. United States*, 234 U.S. 600, 609. The Court recognized that there were some agreements whose validity depended on the surrounding circumstances. It emphasized, however, that there were classes of restraints which from their "nature or character" were unduly restrictive, and hence forbidden by both the common law and the statute. 221 U.S., at 58, 65. As to these classes of restraints, the Court noted, Congress had determined its own criteria of public harm and it was not for the courts to decide whether in an individual case injury had actually occurred. *Id.*, at 63–68.

Group boycotts, or concerted refusals by traders to deal with other traders, have long been held to be in the forbidden category. They have not been saved by allegations that they were reasonable in the specific circumstances, nor by a failure to show that they "fixed or regulated prices, parcelled out or limited production, or brought about a deterioration in quality." *Fashion Originators' Guild v. Federal Trade Comm'n*, 312 U.S. 457, 466, 467–468. Even when they operated to lower prices or temporarily to stimulate competition they were banned. For, as this Court said in *Kiefer–Stewart Co. v. Seagram & Sons*, 340 U.S. 211, 213, "such agreements, no less than those to fix minimum prices, cripple the freedom of traders and thereby restrain their ability to sell in accordance with their own judgment."

Plainly the allegations of this complaint disclose such a boycott. This is not a case of a single trader refusing to deal with another, nor even of a manufacturer and a dealer agreeing to an exclusive distributorship. Alleged in this complaint is a wide combination consisting of manufacturers, distributors and a retailer. This combination takes from Klor's its freedom to buy appliances in an open competitive market and drives it out of business as a dealer in the defendants' products. It deprives the manufacturers and distributors of their freedom to sell to Klor's at the same prices and conditions made available to Broadway–Hale, and in some instances forbids them from selling to it on any terms whatsoever. It interferes with the natural flow of interstate commerce. It clearly has, by its "nature" and "character," a "monopolistic tendency." As such it is not to be tolerated merely because the victim is just one merchant whose business is so small that his destruction makes little difference to the economy.[7] Monopoly can as surely thrive by the elimination of such small businessmen, one at a time, as it can by driving them out in large groups. In recognition of this fact the Sherman Act has consistently been read to forbid all contracts and combinations "which 'tend to create a

---

7. The court below relied heavily on *Apex Hosiery Co. v. Leader*, 310 U.S. 469, in reaching its conclusion. While some language in that case can be read as supporting the position that no restraint on trade is prohibited by § 1 of the Sherman Act unless it has or is intended to have an effect on market prices, such statements must be considered in the light of the fact that the defendant in that case was a labor union. The Court in *Apex* recognized that the Act is aimed primarily at combinations having commercial objectives and is applied only to a very limited extent to organizations, like labor unions, which normally have other objectives. Moreover, cases subsequent to *Apex* have made clear that an effect on prices is not essential to a Sherman Act violation. See, *e.g., Fashion Originators' Guild v. Federal Trade Comm'n*, 312 U.S. 457, 466.

monopoly,'" whether "the tendency is a creeping one" or "one that proceeds at full gallop." *International Salt Co. v. United States*, 332 U.S. 392, 396.

The judgment of the Court of Appeals is reversed and the cause is remanded to the District Court for trial. *Violation*

Questions and Comments

In *Klor's*, the Court assumed that the alleged conspiracy was a purely private dispute between two retailers, Klor's and a big, nearby competitor, Broadway–Hale. It also assumed that Broadway–Hale used its buying power to persuade its suppliers (ten important national manufacturers) to boycott Klor's. How would you characterize the conspiracy? Was it horizontal or vertical? Does it matter? Do you have any reason to believe or disbelieve that the manufacturers conspired among themselves? Why would the manufacturers agree with each other not to supply Klor's? What would they get from this bargain? On the other hand, if Broadway–Hale was a big, important customer, might each, individually, have been persuaded by Broadway–Hale to "ignore" Klor's? If Broadway–Hale went to each manufacturer with such a request, might they have had any reason to check with others before responding? Would any one manufacturer hestitate to do what Broadway–Hale asked unless assured that its competitors would also stop selling to Klor's?

Suppose that GE was the most important manufacturer of electrical appliances and the alleged boycott was limited to the following circumstance: Broadway–Hale sought and got GE's agreement not to supply Klor's. Would the result be the same? Would the case be any different if Broadway–Hale could return a reasonable profit on GE's goods because near by, Klor's was siphoning off its customers? Would the result be different if Klor's siphoned off sales by discounting? (Remember this problem, for we will meet it again in Chapter 4, on vertical restraints.) Would it matter if Klor's siphoned off customers by "bait and switch" tactics?

The Court in *Klor's*, as in *FOGA*, seemed to believe that the boycott tended towards monopoly, even though it also recognized that there were hundreds of retailers in the vicinity and that the boycott might not affect price, output or quality. Are these perceptions inconsistent? If so, which is correct?

The following year the court decided *Radiant Burners, Inc. v. Peoples Gas Light & Coke Co.*, 364 U.S. 656 (1961), and in doing so it relied heavily on *Klor's*. A trade association comprising pipeline companies, gas distributors and manufacturers of gas burners tested burners for safety and granted seals of approval to products that passed the test. The gas distributor members agreed that they would not supply gas for unapproved burners. Meanwhile, Radiant Burners developed a new burner, submitted it for approval, and was turned down. It sued, alleging that the association applied its standards arbitrarily and discriminatorily. Defendants moved to dismiss and won in the trial court and Court of Appeals on the ground that the mere exclusion of one manufacturer did not amount to harm to competition. The Court of Appeals noted that unlike the situation in *Klor's*, defendants had no buyer-seller relationship with plaintiff. The Supreme Court reversed, saying:

It is obvious that petitioner cannot sell its gas burners, whatever may be their virtues, if, because of the alleged conspiracy, the purchasers cannot buy gas for use in those burners. The conspiratorial refusal "to provide gas for use in the plaintiff's Radiant Burner[s] [because they] are not approved by AGA" therefore falls within one of the "class of restraints which from their 'nature or character' [are] unduly restrictive, and hence forbidden by both the common law and the statute. . . . As to these classes of restraints . . . Congress [has] determined its own criteria of public harm and it [is] not for the courts to decide whether in an individual case injury [has] actually occurred." [*Klor's,* 356 U.S. at 211]. The alleged conspiratorial refusal to provide gas for use in plaintiff's Radiant Burners "interferes with the natural flow of interstate commerce [and] clearly has, by its 'nature' and 'character,' a 'monopolistic tendency.' As such it is not to be tolerated merely because the victim is just one [manufacturer] whose business is so small that his destruction makes little difference to the economy." [*Klor's* at 213].

Radiant Burners Inc. v. Peoples Gas Light & Coke Co., 364 U.S. 656, 659–60 (1961).

The tradition of *Klor's* was continued and expanded in *Silver v. New York Stock Exchange,* 373 U.S. 341 (1963). The New York Stock Exchange is a private, self-regulating exchange. The Securities Exchange Act of 1934 gives it the duty and power to regulate members of the Exchange and to approve and cancel private wire connections between member firms and others. Only member firms may deal on the Exchange; nonmember dealers and brokers must execute transactions through members. Plaintiff was a non-member broker-dealer who had obtained direct private telephone wire connections with trading departments of member firms and the trading desks of nonmember firms. Silver depended upon those lines, which gave him "important business advantages." Without giving Silver notice, explanation, a statement of the charges against him, or an opportunity for a hearing, the Exchange's Department of Member Firms disapproved the connections, so notified the member firms, and instructed them to discontinue their wire connections with Silver. The members did so. Silver sued the Exchange and its members and sought an injunction and treble damages.

The Court stated that the collective removal of wires in the manner described was a boycott, and that it would be illegal per se unless the statutory scheme provided the necessary justification. The court held that the statutory scheme offered no justification for disconnection of the wires without notice and hearing, and that, adequate notice and hearing not having been given, the collective disconnection could not be justified; hence it was illegal under Section 1 of the Sherman Act. The Court, through Justice Goldberg, said:

* * *

Unlike listed securities, there is no central trading place for securities traded over the counter. The market is established by traders in the numerous firms all over the country through a process of constant communication to one another of the latest offers to buy and sell. The private wire connection, which allows communication to occur with a flip of a switch, is an essential part of this process. Without the instantaneously available market information provided by private wire connections, an over-the-counter dealer is hampered substantially in his crucial endeavor—to buy, whether it be for customers or on his own account, at the lowest quoted price and sell at the highest quoted price. Without membership in the network of simultaneous communication, the over-the-counter dealer loses a significant volume of trading with other members of the network which would come to him as a result of his easy accessibility. These important business advantages were taken away from petitioners by the group action of the Exchange and its members. Such "concerted refusals by traders to deal with other traders . . . have long been held to be in the forbidden category," *Klor's, Inc., v. Broadway–Hale Stores, Inc.,* 359 U.S., at 212, of restraints which "because of their inherent nature or effect . . . injuriously restrained trade," *United States v. American Tobacco Co.,* 221 U.S. 106, 179.[5] Hence, absent any justification derived from the policy of another statute or otherwise, the Exchange acted in violation of the Sherman Act. In this case, however, the presence of another statutory scheme, that of the Securities Exchange Act of 1934, means that such a conclusion is only the beginning, not the end, of inquiry.

* * *

Our decision today recognizes that the action here taken by the Exchange would clearly be in violation of the Sherman Act unless justified by reference to the purposes of the Securities Exchange Act, and holds that that statute affords no justification for anticompetitive collective action taken without according fair procedures.[16] Congress in effecting a scheme of self-regulation designed to insure fair dealing cannot be thought to have sanctioned and protected self-regulative activity when carried out in a fundamentally unfair manner.[17] The point is not that

5. The fact that the consensus underlying the collective action was arrived at when the members bound themselves to comply with Exchange directives upon being admitted to membership rather than when the specific issue of Silver's qualifications arose does not diminish the collective nature of the action. A blanket subscription to possible future restraints does not excuse the restraints when they occur. *Associated Press v. United States,* 326 U.S. 1. Nor does any excuse derive from the fact that the collective refusal to deal was only with reference to the private wires, the member firms remaining willing to deal with petitioners for the purchase and sale of securities. See *Bigelow v. RKO Radio Pictures, Inc.,* 327 U.S. 251; *United States v. Paramount Pictures, Inc.,* 334 U.S. 131, 167. A valuable service germane to petitioners' business and important to their effective competition with others was withheld from them by collective action. That is enough to create a violation of the Sherman Act. *United States v. Terminal R. Assn. of St. Louis,* 224 U.S. 383; *United States v. First National Pictures, Inc.,* 282 U.S. 44; *Associated Press v. United States, supra;* cf. *Anderson v. United States,* 171 U.S. 604, 618–619.

16. It may be assumed that the Securities and Exchange Commission would have had the power, under § 19(b) of the Exchange Act, 15 U.S.C. § 78s(b), pp. 352–353, 357 & note 7, *supra,* to direct the Exchange to adopt a general rule providing a hearing and attendant procedures to nonmembers. However, any rule that might be adopted by the Commission would, to be consonant with the antitrust laws, have to provide as a minimum the procedural safeguards which those laws make imperative in cases like this. Absent Commission adoption of a rule requiring fair procedure, and in light of both the utility of such a rule as an antitrust matter and its compatibility with securities-regulation principles, see p. 361, *supra,* no incompatibility with the Commission's power inheres in announcement by an antitrust court of the rule. Compare *Colorado Anti-Discrimination Comm'n v. Continental Air Lines, Inc.,* 372 U.S. 714, 723–724.

17. The basic nature of the rights which we hold to be required under the antitrust laws in the circumstances of today's decision is indicated by the fact that public agencies, labor unions, clubs, and other associations have, under various legal principles, all been required to afford notice, a hearing, and an opportunity to answer charges to one who is about to be denied a valuable right. *Goldsmith v. United States Board of Tax Appeals,* 270 U.S. 117; *Russell v. Duke of Norfolk,* [1949] 1 All E.R. 109 (C.A.); Fellman, Constitutional Rights of Association, in The Suthe antitrust laws impose the requirement of notice and a hearing here, but rather that, in acting without according petitioners these safeguards in response to their request, the Exchange has plainly exceeded the scope of its authority under the Securities Exchange Act to engage in self-regulation and therefore has not even reached the threshold of justification under that statute for what would otherwise be an antitrust violation. . . .

Klor's and its progeny have been much criticized by Chicago School theorists on grounds that in each of these cases "only" a trader and not competition (in the price theory sense) was hurt. The defenders of *Klor's*, on the other hand, say that the antitrust laws protect traders against coercive refusals to deal which are calculated to exclude or to harm them and not to bring better products to consumers. *Silver* has been criticized further for using the antitrust laws to serve non-market ends—the ends of fair procedure rather than those of vigorous competition. It has been defended on grounds that antitrust properly protects process, especially where one group or one competitor has the power to write the rules of the game. Compare *Allied Tube & Conduit Corp. v. Indian Head, Inc.,* ___ U.S. ___, 108 S.Ct. 1931, 1937 (1988). In *Indian Head* a private standard setting association published the National Electric Code, which it revised every three years. Many state and local governmental bodies routinely adopted the current version of the code into law (raising the petitioning-government [*Noerr*] defense, which we treat infra at page 416). A manufacturer of plastic conduit sought to have the code changed to approve its conduit. When the question came up before the association's annual meeting the nation's largest producer of steel conduit agreed with others to pack the meeting with friends who would vote against the proposal. Referring to cases in which *Noerr* is not a shield, the Court said that the rule of reason applies to product standard-setting by private associations because such standards have significant procompetitive effects when "based on the merits of objective expert judgment and [adopted] through procedures that prevent . . . bias." (Id. at 1937). Although "rounding up supporters is an acceptable . . . method of influencing elections [it] does not mean that rounding up economically interested persons to set private standards must also be protected." (Id. at 1939).

The Supreme Court continues to cite *Klor's* with approval, as it did in *Associated General Contractors of California v. California State Council of Carpenters,* 459 U.S. 519, 528 (1983):

> Coercive activity that prevents its victims from making free choices between market alternatives is inherently destructive of competitive conditions and may be condemned even without proof of its actual market effect. Cf. *Klor's, Inc. v. Broadway–Hale Stores, Inc.,* 359 U.S. 207, 210–14 (1959).

Consider, now, whether the Supreme Court has limited *Silver* or *Klor's* in the *Stationers* case, which follows.

preme Court Review, 1961 (Kurland ed.), 74, 104, 112–113; Developments in the Law—Judicial Control of Actions of Private Associations, 76 Harv.L.Rev. 983, 1026–1037 (1963); see authorities cited note 18, *infra;* cf. *Vitarelli v. Seaton,* 359 U.S. 535; *Cafeteria & Restaurant Workers Union, Local 478, AFL–CIO v. McElroy,* 367 U.S. 886, 894–895; *Willner v. Committee on Character and Fitness, ante,* p. 96.

NORTHWEST WHOLESALE STATIONERS, INC. v.
PACIFIC STATIONERY & PRINTING CO.
472 U.S. 284 (1985).

JUSTICE BRENNAN: This case requires that we decide whether a *per se* violation of § 1 of the Sherman Act occurs when a cooperative buying agency comprising various retailers expels a member without providing any procedural means for challenging the expulsion. The case also raises broader questions as to when *per se* antitrust analysis is appropriately applied to joint activity that is susceptible of being characterized as a concerted refusal to deal.

I

Because the District Court ruled on cross-motions for summary judgment after only limited discovery, this case comes to us on a sparse record. Certain background facts are undisputed. Petitioner Northwest Wholesale Stationers is a purchasing cooperative made up of approximately 100 office supply retailers in the Pacific Northwest States. The cooperative acts as the primary wholesaler for the retailers. Retailers that are not members of the cooperative can purchase wholesale supplies from Northwest at the same price as members. At the end of each year, however, Northwest distributes its profits to members in the form of a percentage rebate on purchases. Members therefore effectively purchase supplies at a price significantly lower than do nonmembers. Northwest also provides certain warehousing facilities. The cooperative arrangement thus permits the participating retailers to achieve economies of scale in purchasing and warehousing that would otherwise be unavailable to them. . . .

Respondent Pacific Stationery, Inc., sells office supplies at both the retail and wholesale levels. . . . Pacific became a member of Northwest in 1958. In 1974 Northwest amended its bylaws to prohibit members from engaging in both retail and wholesale operations. A grandfather clause preserved Pacific's membership rights . . . [until] . . . 1977 [when] ownership of a controlling share of the stock of Pacific changed hands. . . .

In 1978 the membership of Northwest voted to expel Pacific. Most factual matters relevant to the expulsion are in dispute. . . . Pacific argues that the expulsion resulted from Pacific's decision to maintain a wholesale operation. . . . Northwest contends that the expulsion resulted from Pacific's failure to notify the cooperative members of the change in stock ownership. . . . It is undisputed that Pacific received approximately $10,000 in rebates from Northwest in 1978, Pacific's last year of membership. Beyond a possible inference of loss from this fact, however, the record is devoid of allegations indicating the nature and extent of competitive injury the expulsion caused Pacific to suffer.

Pacific brought suit in 1980 in the United States District Court for the District of Oregon alleging a violation of § 1 of the Sherman Act. . . . Finding no anticompetitive effect on the basis of the record as presented, the court granted summary judgment for Northwest.

(Fox & Sullivan) Antitrust ACB—15

The Court of Appeals for the Ninth Circuit reversed, holding "that the uncontroverted facts of this case support a finding of *per se* liability."
. . .

* * *

II

. . . Whether [expulsion of Pacific] . . . violates § 1 of the Sherman Act depends on whether it is adjudged an *unreasonable* restraint. . . . Rule-of-reason analysis guides the inquiry, unless the challenged action falls into the category of "agreements or practices which because of their pernicious effect on competition and lack of any redeeming virtue are conclusively presumed to be unreasonable and therefore illegal without elaborate inquiry as to the precise harm they have caused or the business excuse for their use."

* * *

A

The Court of Appeals drew from *Silver v. New York Stock Exchange* a broad rule that the conduct of a cooperative venture—including a concerted refusal to deal—undertaken pursuant to a legislative mandate for self-regulation is immune from *per se* scrutiny and subject to rule of reason analysis only if adequate procedural safeguards accompany self-regulation. We disagree and conclude that the approach of the Court in *Silver* has no proper application to the present controversy.

. . . Because the New York Stock Exchange occupied such a dominant position in the securities trading markets that the boycott would devastate the nonmember, the Court concluded that the refusal to deal with the nonmember would amount to a *per se* violation of § 1 unless the Securities Exchange Act provided an immunity. . . . The question for the Court thus was whether effectuation of the policies of the Securities Exchange Act required partial repeal of the Sherman Act insofar as it proscribed this aspect of exchange self-regulation.

Finding exchange self-regulation—including the power to expel members and limit dealings with nonmembers—to be an essential policy of the Securities Exchange Act, the Court held that the Sherman Act should be construed as having been partially repealed to permit the type of exchange activity at issue. But the interpretive maxim disfavoring repeals by implication led the Court to narrow permissible self-policing to situations in which adequate procedural safeguards had been provided. . . .

* * *

. . . [T]here can be no argument that § 4 of the Robinson–Patman Act should be viewed as a broad mandate for industry self-regulation. No need exists, therefore, to narrow the Sherman Act in order to accommodate any competing congressional policy requiring discretionary self-policing. Indeed, Congress would appear to have taken some care to make clear that no constriction of the Sherman Act was intended. In any event, the absence of procedural safeguards can in no sense determine the antitrust analysis. If the challenged concerted activity of Northwest's members would amount to a *per se* violation of § 1 of the Sherman Act, no amount of procedural protection would save it. If the challenged action would not amount to a violation of § 1, no lack of procedural protections would convert it into a *per se* violation because the antitrust laws do not themselves impose on joint ventures a requirement of process.

B

This case therefore turns not on the lack of procedural protections but on whether the decision to expel Pacific is properly viewed as a group boycott or concerted refusal to deal mandating *per se* invalidation. "Group boycotts" are often listed among the classes of economic activity that merit *per se* invalidation under § 1. . . . Exactly what types of activity fall within the forbidden category is, however, far from certain. "[T]here is more confusion about the scope and operation of the *per se* rule against group boycotts than in reference to any other aspect of the *per se* doctrine." L. Sullivan, Law of Antitrust 229–230 (1977). Some care is therefore necessary in defining the category of concerted refusals to deal that mandate *per se* condemnation. . . .

Cases to which this Court has applied the *per se* approach have generally involved joint efforts by a firm or firms to disadvantage competitors by "either directly denying or persuading or coercing suppliers or customers to deny relationships the competitors need in the competitive struggle." In these cases, the boycott often cut off access to a supply, facility, or market necessary to enable the boycotted firm to compete, and frequently the boycotting firms possessed a dominant position in the relevant market. In addition, the practices were generally not justified by plausible arguments that they were intended to enhance overall efficiency and make markets more competitive. Under such circumstances the likelihood of anticompetitive effects is clear and the possibility of counter-vailing procompetitive effects is remote.

Although a concerted refusal to deal need not necessarily possess all of these traits to merit *per se* treatment, not every cooperative activity involving a restraint or exclusion will share with the *per se* forbidden boycotts the likelihood of predominantly anticompetitive consequences. . . .

Wholesale purchasing cooperatives such as Northwest are not a form of concerted activity characteristically likely to result in predominantly anticompetitive effects. . . .

* * *

The District Court appears to have followed the correct path of analysis—recognizing that not all concerted refusals to deal should be accorded *per se* treatment and deciding this one should not. The foregoing discussion suggests, however, that a satisfactory threshold determination whether anticompetitive effects would be likely might require a more detailed factual picture of market structure than the District Court had before it. Nonetheless, in our judgment the District Court rejection of *per se* analysis in this case was correct. A plaintiff seeking application of the *per se* rule must present a threshold case that the challenged activity falls into a category likely to have predominantly anticompetitive effects. The mere allegation of a concerted refusal to deal does not suffice because not all concerted refusals to deal are predominantly anticompetitive. When the plaintiff challenges expulsion from a joint buying cooperative, some showing must be made that the cooperative possesses market power or unique access to a business element necessary for effective competition. Focusing on the argument that the lack of procedural safeguards required *per se* liability, Pacific did not allege any such facts. Because the Court of Appeals applied an erroneous *per se* analysis in this case, the court never evaluated the District Court's rule-of-reason analysis rejecting Pacific's claim. A remand is therefore appropriate for the limited purpose of permitting appellate review of that determination.

III

. . . The judgment of the Court of Appeals is therefore reversed, and the case is remanded for further proceedings consistent with this opinion.

It is so ordered.

Questions and Comments

Restate the *Silver* doctrine in light of the *Northwest Wholesale Stationers* case. Is *Silver* limited to instances in which Congress has partially repealed the Sherman Act? Is it limited to cases in which defendants have a dominant share of the market? Where *Silver* applies, is a concerted refusal to deal illegal per se if it effectively excludes a competitor and is carried out without due process? Or is it illegal only if it harms competition, perhaps because it raises prices? If concerted exclusion of a single competitor violates the law, regardless of output reduction or price enhancement, from what must the competitor be excluded? A well-defined market? An essential facility?

How would you state the *Klor's* doctrine in light of the *Northwest Wholesale Stationers* case? Consider these three propositions: (1) Joint refusal by competitors to supply a would-be customer is always illegal per se. (2) Such conduit is illegal only when the suppliers have market power. (3) It is illegal only when exclusion of the boycotted buyer will hurt competition by raising prices. Which proposition best states the law?

Does *Northwest Wholesale Stationers* overrule *Klor's* or would it be fair to regard case as simply limiting *Klor's*, for *Klor's* concerned an alleged naked agreement to boycott, while *Northwest Wholesale Stationers* concerned cooperative arrangements justified by efficiency. Is the case easier for defendants if we think of it not as a boycott problem but as a duty-to-deal problem?

Does the Court in *Northwest Wholesale Stationers* give sufficient guidance on how to analyze the case under a rule of reason? Suppose the case goes to trial. Pacific does not prove that defendants together have market power, but does prove that the only motive for expulsion was to penalize Pacific because the co-op members feared the aggressive competition posed by the dual distributor. Plaintiff cites *Eastern States*. Who wins? Suppose on the other hand that defendants do have market power, but that the only motive for expulsion was to penalize a breach of the association's by-laws? Does it matter in either case whether Pacific alone or with other available partners could realize all available economies of scale in purchasing and warehousing? Does it matter whether Pacific's membership creates or increases the association's buying power? Can there be a violation even if the expulsion of Pacific will have no negative effect on consumers? One explanation for *Northwest Wholesale Stationers* is that, properly conceived, it is not a boycott case at all, but a failed essential facilities case. Defendants concertedly put together a new facility and excluded plaintiff. They are as free to do that as would be two lawyers forming a partnership and excluding a third unless plaintiff could prove that access to the facility was essential to enable plaintiff effectively to compete.

After *Northwest Wholesale Stationers,* how would you state the per se rule against boycotts? Remember the fallacy of the "boycott pigeonhole". As the Supreme Court reminded us in *Northwest Wholesale Stationers,* not all concerted refusals to deal are a "unitary phenomenon." Perhaps we should be searching for qualified per se rules or structured rules of reason. The Supreme Court will remind us of the pigeonhole fallacy in the case below— which is not an exclusionary boycott but a concerted refusal to deal on certain terms. The Federal Trade Commission brought suit under Section 5 of the Federal Trade Commission Act.

FTC v. INDIANA FEDERATION OF DENTISTS
476 U.S. 447 (1986).

JUSTICE WHITE: This case concerns commercial relations among certain Indiana dentists, their patients, and the patients' dental health care insurers. The question presented is whether the Federal Trade Commission correctly concluded that a conspiracy among dentists to refuse to submit x rays to dental insurers for use in benefits determinations constituted an "unfair method of competition" in violation of § 5 of the Federal Trade Commission Act.

I

Since the 1970's, dental health insurers, responding to the demands of their policyholders, have attempted to contain the cost of dental treatment by, among other devices, limiting payment of benefits to the cost of the "least expensive yet adequate treatment" suitable to the needs of individual patients. Implementation of such cost-containment measures, known as "alternative benefits" plans, requires evaluation by the insurer of the diagnosis and recommendation of the treating dentist, either in advance of or following the provision of care. In order to carry out such evaluation, insurers frequently request dentists to submit, along with insurance claim forms requesting payment of benefits, any dental x rays that have been used by the dentist in examining the patient as well as other information concerning their diagnoses and treatment recommendations. Typically, claim forms and accompanying x rays are reviewed by lay claims examiners, who either approve payment of claims or, if the materials submitted raise a question whether the recommended course of treatment is in fact necessary, refer claims to dental consultants, who are licensed dentists, for further review. On the basis of the materials available, supplemented where appropriate by further diagnostic aids, the dental consultant may recommend that the insurer approve a claim, deny it, or pay only for a less expensive course of treatment.

Such review of diagnostic and treatment decisions has been viewed by some dentists as a threat to their professional independence and economic well-being. In the early 1970's, the Indiana Dental Association, a professional organization comprising some 85% of practicing dentists in the

State of Indiana, initiated an aggressive effort to hinder insurers' efforts to implement alternative benefits plans by enlisting member dentists to pledge not to submit x rays in conjunction with claim forms.[1] The Association's efforts met considerable success: large numbers of dentists signed the pledge, and insurers operating in Indiana found it difficult to obtain compliance with their requests for x rays and accordingly had to choose either to employ more expensive means of making alternative benefits determinations (for example, visiting the office of the treating dentist or conducting an independent oral examination) or to abandon such efforts altogether.

By the mid–1970's, fears of possible antitrust liability had dampened the Association's enthusiasm for opposing the submission of x rays to insurers. In 1979, the Association and a number of its constituent societies consented to a Federal Trade Commission order requiring them to cease and desist from further efforts to prevent member dentists from submitting x rays. *In re Indiana Dental Assn.,* 93 F.T.C. 392 (1979). Not all Indiana dentists were content to leave the matter of submitting x rays to the individual dentist. In 1976, a group of such dentists formed the Indiana Federation of Dentists, respondent in this case, in order to continue to pursue the Association's policy of resisting insurers' requests for x rays. The Federation, which styled itself a "union" in the belief that this label would stave off antitrust liability,[2] immediately promulgated a "work rule" forbidding its members to submit x rays to dental insurers in conjunction with claim forms. Although the Federation's membership was small, numbering less than 100, its members were highly concentrated in and around three Indiana communities: Anderson, Lafayette, and Fort Wayne. The Federation succeeded in enlisting nearly 100% of the dental specialists in the Anderson area, and approximately 67% of the dentists in and around Lafayette. In the areas of its strength, the Federation was successful in continuing to enforce the Association's prior policy of refusal to submit x rays to dental insurers.

In 1978, the Federal Trade Commission issued a complaint against the Federation, alleging in substance that its efforts to prevent its members

---

1. A presentation made in 1974 by Dr. David McClure, an Association official and later one of the founders of respondent Indiana Federation of Dentists, is revealing as to the motives underlying the dentists' resistance to the provision of x rays for use by insurers in making alternative benefits determinations:

"The problems associated with third party programs are many, but I believe the 'Indiana Plan' [*i.e.,* the policy of refusing to submit x rays] to be sound and if we work together, we can win this battle. We are fighting an economic war where the very survival of our profession is at stake.

"How long can some of the leaders of dentistry in other states be so complacent and willing to fall into the trap that is being set for us. If only they would take the time, to see from whence come the arrows that are heading in our direction.

The Delta Dental Plans have bedded down with the unions and have been a party to setting up the greatest controls that any profession has ever known in a free society. . . .

"The name of the game is money. The government and labor are determined to reduce the cost of the dental health dollar at the expense of the dentist. There is no way a dental service can be rendered cheaper when the third party has to have its share of the dollar.

"Already we are locked into a fee freeze that could completely control the quality of dental care, if left on long enough." FTC Complaint Counsel's Trial Exhibit CX 372A, F, App. 104.

2. Respondent no longer makes any pretense of arguing that it is immune from antitrust liability as a labor organization.

from complying with insurers' requests for x rays constituted an unfair method of competition in violation of § 5 of the Federal Trade Commission Act. Following lengthy proceedings including a full evidentiary hearing before an Administrative Law Judge, the Commission ruled that the Federation's policy constituted a violation of § 5 and issued an order requiring the Federation to cease and desist from further efforts to organize dentists to refuse to submit x rays to insurers. *In re Indiana Federation of Dentists,* 101 F.T.C. 57 (1983). The Commission based its ruling on the conclusion that the Federation's policy of requiring its members to withhold x rays amounted to a conspiracy in restraint of trade that was unreasonable and hence unlawful under the standards for judging such restraints developed in this Court's precedents interpreting § 1 of the Sherman Act. *E.g., Chicago Board of Trade v. United States,* 246 U.S. 231, 38 S.Ct. 242, 62 L.Ed. 683 (1918); *National Society of Professional Engineers v. United States,* 435 U.S. 679, 98 S.Ct. 1355, 55 L.Ed.2d 637 (1978). The Commission found that the Federation had conspired both with the Indiana Dental Association and with its own members to withhold cooperation with dental insurers' requests for x rays; that absent such a restraint, competition among dentists for patients would have tended to lead dentists to compete with respect to their policies in dealing with patients' insurers; and that in those areas where the Federation's membership was strong, the Federation's policy had had the actual effect of eliminating such competition among dentists and preventing insurers from obtaining access to x rays in the desired manner. These findings of anticompetitive effect, the Commission concluded, were sufficient to establish that the restraint was unreasonable even absent proof that the Federation's policy had resulted in higher costs to the insurers and patients than would have occurred had the x rays been provided. Further, the Commission rejected the Federation's argument that its policy of withholding x rays was reasonable because the provision of x rays might lead the insurers to make inaccurate determinations of the proper level of care and thus injure the health of the insured patients: the Commission found no evidence that use of x rays by insurance companies in evaluating claims would result in inadequate dental care. Finally, the Commission rejected the Federation's contention that its actions were exempt from antitrust scrutiny because the withholding of x rays was consistent with the law and policy of the State of Indiana against the use of x rays in benefit determination by insurance companies. The Commission concluded that no such policy existed, and that in any event the existence of such a policy would not have justified the dentists' private and unsupervised conspiracy in restraint of trade.

. . . [T]he United States Court of Appeals for the Seventh Circuit . . . vacated the order. . . . 745 F.2d 1124 (1984). Accepting the Federation's characterization of its rule against submission of x rays as merely an ethical and moral policy designed to enhance the welfare of dental patients, the majority concluded that the Commission's findings that the policy was anticompetitive were erroneous. According to the majority, the evidence did not support the finding that in the absence of restraint dentists would compete for patients by offering cooperation with the requests of the patients' insurers, nor, even accepting that finding, was there evidence that the Federation's efforts had prevented such competition. Further, the court held that the Commission's findings were inadequate because of its failure both to offer a precise definition of the market in which the Federation was alleged to have restrained competition and to establish that the Federation had the power to restrain competition in that market. Finally, the majority faulted the Commission for not finding that the alleged restraint on competition among dentists had actually resulted in higher dental costs to patients and insurers. The third member of the Court of Appeals panel concurred in the judgment solely on the ground that there was insufficient proof that cooperation with insurers was an element of dental services as to which dentists would tend to compete. . . .

. . . We now reverse.

* * *

. . . [T]he sole basis of the FTC's finding of an unfair method of competition was the Commission's conclusion that the Federation's collective decision to withhold x rays from insurers was an unreasonable and conspiratorial restraint of trade in violation of § 1 of the Sherman Act. Accordingly, the legal question before us is whether the Commission's factual findings, if supported by evidence, make out a violation of Sherman Act § 1.

III

The relevant factual findings are that the members of the Federation conspired among themselves to withhold x rays requested by dental insurers for use in evaluating claims for benefits, and that this conspiracy had the effect of suppressing competition among dentists with respect to cooperation with the requests of the insurance companies. As to the first of these findings there can be no serious dispute: abundant evidence in the record reveals that one of the primary reasons—if not *the* primary reason—for the Federation's existence was the promulgation and enforcement of the so-called "work rule" against submission of x rays in conjunction with insurance claim forms.

As for the second crucial finding—that competition was actually suppressed—the Seventh Circuit held it to be unsupported by the evidence, on two theories. First, the court stated that the evidence did not establish that cooperation with requests for information by patients' insurance companies was an aspect of the provision of dental services with respect to which dentists would, in the absence of some restraint, compete. Second, the court found that even assuming that dentists would otherwise compete with respect to policies of cooperating or not cooperating with insurance companies, the Federation's policy did not impair that competition, for the member dentists continued to allow insurance companies to use other means of evaluating their diagnoses when reviewing claims for benefits: specifically, "the IFD member dentists allowed insurers to visit the dental office to review and examine the patient's x rays along with all of the other diagnostic and clinical aids used in formulating a proper course of dental treatment." 745 F.2d, at 1143.

Neither of these criticisms of the Commission's findings is well founded. The Commission's finding that "[i]n the absence of . . . concerted behavior, individual dentists would have been subject to market forces of competition, creating incentives for them to . . . comply with the requests of patients' third-party insurers," 101 F.T.C., at 173, finds support not only in common sense and economic theory, upon both of which the FTC may reasonably rely, but also in record documents, including newsletters circulated among Indiana dentists, revealing that Indiana dentists themselves perceived that unrestrained competition tended to lead their colleagues to comply with insurers' requests for x rays. See App. to Pet. for Cert. 289a, 306a–308a. Moreover, there was evidence that outside of Indiana, in States where dentists had not collectively refused to submit x rays, insurance companies found little difficulty in obtaining compliance by dentists with their requests. 101 F.T.C., at 172. A "reasonable mind" could conclude on the basis of this evidence that competition for patients, who have obvious incentives for seeking dentists who will cooperate with their insurers, would tend to lead dentists in Indiana (and elsewhere) to cooperate with requests for information by their patients' insurers.

The Commission's finding that such competition was actually diminished where the Federation held sway also finds adequate support in the record. The Commission found that in the areas where Federation membership among dentists was most significant (that is, in the vicinity of Anderson and Lafayette) insurance companies were unable to obtain compliance with their requests for submission of x rays in conjunction with claim forms and were forced to resort to other, more costly, means of reviewing diagnoses for the purpose of benefit determination. Neither the opinion of the Court of Appeals nor the brief of respondent identifies any evidence suggesting that the Commission's finding that the Federation's policy had an actual impact on the ability of insurers to obtain the x rays they requested was incorrect. The lower court's conclusion that this evidence is to be discounted because Federation members continued to cooperate with insurers by allowing them to use more costly—indeed, prohibitively costly—methods of reviewing treatment decisions is unpersuasive. The fact remains that the dentists' customers (that is, the patients and their insurers) sought a particular service: cooperation with the insurers' pretreatment review through the forwarding of x rays in conjunction with claim forms. The Federation's collective activities resulted in the denial of the information the customers requested in the form that they requested it, and forced them to choose between acquiring that information in a more costly manner or forgoing it altogether. To this extent, at least, competition among dentists with respect to cooperation with the requests of insurers was restrained.

IV

The question remains whether these findings are legally sufficient to establish a violation of § 1 of the Sherman Act—that is, whether the Federation's collective refusal to cooperate with insurers' requests for x rays constitutes an "unreasonable" restraint of trade. Under our precedents, a restraint may be adjudged unreasonable either because it fits within a class of restraints that has been held to be "*per se*" unreasonable, or because it violates what has come to be known as the "Rule of Reason," under which the "test of legality is whether the restraint imposed is such as merely regulates and perhaps thereby promotes competition or whether it is such as may suppress or even destroy competition." *Chicago Board of Trade v. United States,* 246 U.S., at 238.

The policy of the Federation with respect to its members' dealings with third-party insurers resembles practices that have been labeled "group boycotts": the policy constitutes a concerted refusal to deal on particular terms with patients covered by group dental insurance. Although this Court has in the past stated that group boycotts are unlawful *per se,* we decline to resolve this case by forcing the Federation's policy into the "boycott" pigeonhole and invoking the *per se* rule. As we observed last Term in *Northwest Wholesale Stationers, Inc. v. Pacific Stationery and Printing Co.,* 472 U.S. 284 (1985), the category of restraints classed as group boycotts is not to be expanded indiscriminately, and the *per se* approach has generally been limited to cases in which firms with market power boycott suppliers or customers in order to discourage them from doing business with a competitor—a situation obviously not present here. Moreover, we have been slow to condemn rules adopted by professional associations as unreasonable *per se,* see *National Society of Professional Engineers v. United States,* 435 U.S. 679 (1978), and, in general, to extend *per se* analysis to restraints imposed in the context of business relationships where the economic impact of certain practices is not immediately obvious, see *Broadcast Music, Inc. v. CBS,* 441 U.S. 1 (1979). Thus, as did the FTC, we evaluate the restraint at issue in this case under the Rule of Reason rather than a rule of *per se* illegality.

Application of the Rule of Reason to these facts is not a matter of any great difficulty. The Federation's policy takes the form of a horizontal agreement among the participating dentists to withhold from their customers a particular service that they desire—the forwarding of x rays to insurance companies along with claim forms. "While this is not price fixing as such, no elaborate industry analysis is required to demonstrate the anticompetitive character of such an agreement." *Society of Professional Engineers, supra,* 435 U.S. at 692. A refusal to compete with respect to the package of services offered to customers, no less than a refusal to compete with respect to the price term of an agreement, impairs the ability of the market to advance social welfare by ensuring the provision of desired goods and services to consumers at a price approximating the marginal cost of providing them. Absent some countervailing procompetitive virtue—such as, for example, the creation of efficiencies in the operation of a market or the provision of goods and services, see *Broadcast Music, Inc. v. CBS, supra; Chicago Board of Trade, supra;* cf. *NCAA v. Board of Regents of Univ. of Okla.,* 468 U.S. 85 (1984)—such an agreement limiting consumer choice by impeding the "ordinary give and take of the market place," *Society of Professional Engineers, supra,* 435 U.S. at 692, cannot be sustained under the Rule of Reason. No credible argument has been advanced for the proposition that making it more costly for the insurers and patients who are the dentists' customers to obtain information needed for evaluating the dentists' diagnoses has any such procompetitive effect.

The Federation advances three principal arguments for the proposition that, notwithstanding its lack of competitive virtue, the Federation's policy of withholding x rays should not be deemed an unreasonable restraint of trade. First, as did the Court of Appeals, the Federation suggests that in the absence of specific findings by the Commission concerning the definition of the market in which the Federation allegedly restrained trade and the power of the Federation's members in that market, the conclusion that the Federation unreasonably restrained trade is erroneous as a matter of law, regardless of whether the challenged practices might be impermissibly anticompetitive if engaged in by persons who together possessed power in a specifically defined market. This contention, however, runs counter to the Court's holding in *NCAA v. Board of Regents, supra,* that "[a]s a matter of law, the absence of proof of market power does not justify a naked restriction on price or output," and that such a restriction "requires some competitive justification even in the absence of a detailed market analysis." 468 U.S., at 109–110. Moreover, even if the restriction imposed by the Federation is not sufficiently "naked" to call this principle into play, the Commission's failure to engage in detailed market analysis is not fatal to its finding of a violation of the Rule of Reason. The Commission found that in two localities in the State of Indiana (the Anderson and Lafayette areas), Federation dentists constituted heavy majorities of the practicing dentists and that as a result of the efforts of the Federation, insurers in those areas were, over a period of years, actually unable to obtain compliance with their requests for submission of x rays. Since the purpose of the inquiries into market definition and market power is to determine whether an arrangement has the potential for genuine adverse effects on competition, "proof of actual detrimental effects, such as a reduction of output" can obviate the need for an inquiry into market power, which is but a "surrogate for detrimental effects." 7 P. Areeda, Antitrust Law ¶ 1511, p. 429 (1986). In this case, we conclude that the finding of actual, sustained adverse effects on competition in those areas where IFD dentists predominated, viewed in light of the reality that markets for dental services tend to be relatively localized, is legally sufficient to support a finding that the challenged restraint was unreasonable even in the absence of elaborate market analysis.

Second, the Federation, again following the lead of the Court of Appeals, argues that a holding that its policy of withholding x rays constituted an unreasonable restraint of trade is precluded by the Commission's failure to make any finding that the policy resulted in the provision of dental services that were more costly than those that the patients and their insurers would have chosen were they able to evaluate x rays in conjunction with claim forms. This argument, too, is unpersuasive. Although it is true that the goal of the insurers in seeking submission of x rays for use in their review of benefits claims was to minimize costs by choosing the least expensive adequate course of dental treatment, a showing that this goal was actually achieved through the means chosen is not an essential step in establishing that the dentists' attempt to thwart its achievement by collectively refusing to supply the requested information was an unreasonable restraint of trade. A concerted and effective effort to withhold (or make more costly) information desired by consumers for the purpose of determining whether a particular purchase is cost-justified is likely enough to disrupt the proper functioning of the price-setting mechanism of the market that it may be condemned even absent proof that it resulted in higher prices or, as here, the purchase of higher-priced services, than would occur in its absence. *Society of Professional Engineers, supra.* Moreover, even if the desired information were in fact completely useless to the insurers and their patients in making an informed choice regarding the least costly adequate course of treatment—or, to put it another way, if the costs of evaluating the information were far greater than the cost savings resulting from its use—the Federation would still not be justified in deciding on behalf of its members' customers that they did not need the information: presumably, if that were the case, the discipline of the market would itself soon result in the insurers' abandoning their requests for x rays. The Federation is not entitled to pre-empt the working of the market by deciding for itself that its customers do not need that which they demand.

Third, the Federation complains that the Commission erred in failing to consider, as relevant to its Rule of Reason analysis, noncompetitive "quality of care" justifications for the prohibition on provision of x rays to insurers in conjunction with claim forms. This claim reflects the Court of Appeals' repeated characterization of the Federation's policy as a "legal, moral, and ethical policy of quality dental care, requiring that insurers examine and review all diagnostic and clinical aids before formulating a proper course of dental treatment." 745 F.2d, at 1144. The gist of the claim is that x rays, standing alone, are not adequate bases for diagnosis of dental problems or for the formulation of an acceptable course of treatment. Accordingly, if insurance companies are permitted to determine whether they will pay a claim for dental treatment on the basis of x rays as opposed to a full examination of all the diagnostic aids available to the examining dentist, there is a danger that they will erroneously decline to pay for treatment that is in fact in the interest of the patient, and that the patient will as a result be deprived of fully adequate care.

The Federation's argument is flawed both legally and factually. The premise of the argument is that, far from having no effect on the cost of dental services chosen by patients and their insurers, the provision of x rays will have too great an impact: it will lead to the reduction of costs through the selection of inadequate treatment. Precisely such a justification for withholding information from customers was rejected as illegitimate in the *Society of Professional Engineers* case. The argument is, in essence, that an unrestrained market in which consumers are given access to the information they believe to be relevant to their choices will lead them to make unwise and even dangerous choices. Such an argument amounts to "nothing less than a frontal assault on the basic policy of the Sherman Act." *Society of Professional Engineers, supra,* 435 U.S. at 695, 98 S.Ct. at 1367. Moreover, there is no particular reason to believe that the provision of information will be more harmful to consumers in the market for dental services than in other markets. Insurers deciding what level of care to pay for are not themselves the recipients of those services, but it is by no means clear that they lack incentives to consider the welfare of the patient as well as the minimization of costs. They are themselves in competition for the patronage of the patients—or, in most cases, the unions or businesses that contract on their behalf for group insurance coverage—and must satisfy their potential customers not only that they will provide coverage at a reasonable cost, but also that that coverage will be adequate to meet their customers' dental needs. There is thus no more reason to expect dental insurance companies to sacrifice quality in return for cost savings than to believe this of consumers in, say, the market for engineering services. Accordingly, if noncompetitive quality-of-service justifications are inadmissible to justify the denial of information to consumers in the latter market, there is little reason to credit such justifications here.

In any event, the Commission did not, as the Federation suggests, refuse even to consider the quality of care justification for the withholding of x rays. Rather, the Commission held that the Federation had failed to introduce sufficient evidence to establish such a justification. . . . The Commission was amply justified in concluding on the basis of this conflicting evidence that even if concern for the quality of patient care could under some circumstances serve as a justification for a restraint of the sort imposed here, the evidence did not support a finding that the careful use of x rays as a basis for evaluating insurance claims is in fact destructive of proper standards of dental care.

* * *

V

The factual findings of the Commission regarding the effect of the Federation's policy of withholding x rays are supported by substantial evidence, and those findings are sufficient as a matter of law to establish a violation of § 1 of the Sherman Act, and, hence, § 5 of the Federal Trade Commission Act. Since there has been no suggestion that the cease-and-desist order entered by the Commission to remedy this violation is itself improper for any reason distinct from the claimed impropriety of the finding of a violation, the Commission's order must be sustained. The judgment of the Court of Appeals is accordingly

Reversed.

Questions and Comments

By concertedly denying x-rays to the insurers whom did the dentists wrong? What was the nature of that wrong?

Is it always an antitrust violation for sellers concertedly to refuse to supply a product that some consumers want? What language in the opinion answers that question?

Can you imagine a situation in which an agreement among competitors limiting consumer choice will yield efficiencies? Are there any "procompetitive virtues" besides efficiencies? If so, can you think of a situation where concerted action would yield such a benefit? Suppose defendants prove that a product concertedly withdrawn can not do what consumers think it will do?

Suppose defendants prove that it will harm consumers economically? Suppose defendants prove that the product (for example, DES) threatens to harm health. In any of these instances would an agreement among sellers to take the product off the market be legal? Might one conclude that an agreement among competitors limiting consumer choice benefits competition if the agreement rectifies in whole or in part, a market failure resulting from limited consumer information? For example, could toy makers agree not to use anything toxic in the paints used on toys?

The Court speaks of "some countervailing procompetitive benefit" that might offset "an agreement limiting consumer choice." Does this imply that when such a benefit is identified it must still be weighed against the limitation on choice? How is that weighing to be done? Does the market power of defendants become relevant? Does the search for a "less restrictive alternative" come into play? Who has the burden of proving what? Suppose plaintiff proves an agreement limiting consumer choice but does not prove market power, defendants then prove a countervailing benefit, and plaintiff proves in response that the benefit could have been achieved without lessening consumer choice? Does plaintiff win? Could defendants have prevailed if their proof went further and established that they had no market power? Would proof of lack of market power counter plaintiff's initial showing that consumer choice was limited?

Individuals associated with the Chicago School, including those on the bench, often describe current antitrust law in the language of output limitation. They would condemn only output-limiting restraints, and extol restraints that prevent inefficiencies. E.g., *Olympia Equipment Leasing Co. v. Western Union Telegraph Co.*, 797 F.2d 370, 378 (7th Cir.1986) (Judge Posner), *cert. denied*, 480 U.S. 934 (1987); *Rothery Storage & Van Co. v. Atlas Van Lines, Inc.*, 792 F.2d 210, 211 (D.C.Cir.1986) (Judge Bork), *cert. denied*, 479 U.S. 1033 (1987); *Polk Bros., Inc. v. Forest City Enterprises, Inc.*, 776 F.2d 185, 188–91 (7th Cir.1985) (Judge Easterbrook). Is *Indiana Federation of Dentists* consistent with claims that antitrust abhors only output limitation, even if offset by efficiencies?

The legislative history of the Sherman Act identifies many other goals in addition to avoiding output limitation and price enhancement. See H. Thorelli, The Federal Antitrust Policy: Origination of the All American Tradition (1954) (presenting a detailed history of American antitrust). See also 21 Cong. Rec. 457–60, 4098, 4100 (1890). The argument for confining antitrust analysis to output limitation and price enhancement is that this alone assures efficiency and also that courts are not competent to balance such vague objectives as the legislative history may identify. Critics of this view, the editors among them, answer that the legislative goals will tend to be advanced if courts focus on protecting the competitive process in the market place, and that protecting the competitive process is a task courts are competent to perform. Does the language in *Indiana Federation of Dentists,* quoted in part from *National Society of Professional Engineers,* about "impeding the 'ordinary give and take of the market place'" tend to support the latter view? Are courts competent to reliably decide whether a practice will reduce output? Are they competent to decide whether it impedes the ordinary working of the competitive market place? If you had to select one or the other as the more conventional type of task for judges and juries, which would you choose?

In the *Dentists* case, the Court characterizes its analysis as rule of reason analysis. Might its rule of decision be characterized more accurately either as a qualified per se rule or as a modified rule of reason? Does the Court view as anticompetitive on its face the dentists' concerted withholding from insurers (who are equated with consumers) information that the insurers think they need? In *National Society of Professional Engineers* and *NCAA* the Court indicated that in a rule of reason case it would search for procompetitive offsets to any harm. Did it make such a search here?

Suppose defendants had proved that they had no market power and that their conduct had no effect on price or output. Would they have won? Could defendants have won by proof that their refusal minimized costs? Could they have won by proof that supplying the x-rays would have undermined quality care? By such proof plus proof of a lack of market power?

Problem

Doctors Triester and Marrese were certified orthopedic surgeons with staff privileges at several hospitals. They were known for their willingness to treat surgical out-patients on a high-volume, low-price basis. Both applied to become members of the prestigious American Academy of Orthopedic Surgeons. Both were refused membership without a hearing or explanation.

The Academy has 10,000 members. The vast majority of orthopedic surgeons in the United States are members of the Academy. The Academy's meetings are important professional events. The meetings are open to all, although members and nonmembers wear distinguishing badges. Members of the Academy refer numerous matters to one another, and seldom refer to nonmembers.

Marrese and Triester sue the Academy. Do they have a good cause of action if they prove only that their applications were not objectively evaluated? If they prove that the Academy failed to evaluate their applications objectively and that they, the plaintiffs engage in a high-volume, low-price practice? What if plaintiffs prove that they were denied admission because they were feared competitors and (to substantiate this point) that other doctors with the same style of high-volume, low-price practice were and are also denied admission? Must they prove that, in consequence of such systematic exclusion, entry into high-volume, low-price practice is discouraged and that the general level of prices for orthopedic surgery is higher than it would be if all technically qualified physicians were admitted to the Academy? At what point would Marrese and Triester have made out a prima facie case? At what point would they have prevailed? See *Marrese v. American Academy of Orthopaedic Surgeons*, 470 U.S. 373 (1985).

For a recent and unsuccessful effort by defendant doctors and other medical industry defendants to shelter a peer review activity from boycott scrutiny by asserting the state action defense, see *Patrick v. Burget*, ___ U.S. ___, 108 S.Ct. 1658 (1988). Plaintiff, a surgeon, declined an invitation to join respondents as a partner and instead entered practice in competition with them. Defendants then initiated and participated in peer review proceedings to terminate plaintiff's privileges in the community's only hospital. Plaintiff obtained a treble damage judgment for violation of Section 1 of the Sherman Act on evidence that defendants had used the peer review process in bad faith to disadvantage a competitor rather than to improve patient care. The Court of Appeals reversed holding the state action doctrine applicable, given a state policy to encourage peer review by doctors. The Supreme Court reversed, holding that active state supervision was lacking in the absence of adequate review of peer decisions by any state agency, official or court.

The Health Care Quality Improvements Act of 1986, 42 U.S.C. §§ 11101–11152, provides in substance that, subject to opt-out provisions available to states, persons engaged in professional peer review activities meeting standards specified in the statute shall not, on account of such action, be liable in damages under any law of the United States or any state. The standards require that adequate notice and hearing be given and that the peer review action be taken with reasonable belief that it is in the furtherance of health care and that it is warranted by facts known after reasonable effort to obtain the facts. Professional review actions shall be presumed to meet the standards unless the presumption is rebutted by a preponderance of the evidence. If this statute had been applicable could the result in *Patrick v. Burget* have been the same?

H. A NOTE ON POLITICAL ACTION

We pause here to introduce a new concept—activity that may harm competition might nonetheless be beyond the reach of the antitrust laws. It may be private political activity of a sort that the law was not meant to condemn. This political action doctrine is not intrinsic to boycotts; it is relevant to other conspiratorial restraints as well and also to monopolization and attempts to monopolize, and we briefly referred to the concept in that connection. Perhaps most frequently, however, the doctrine protecting political action is invoked in the boycott context.

In the 1950s eastern railroads were threatened by competition from truckers in the long-distance freight hauling market. The railroads met under the aegis of their trade association, the Eastern Railroad Presidents Conference, and banded together to encourage the passage of state laws that would limit the weight of trucks on the roads and that would tax heavy trucks. They persuaded the Governor of Pennsylvania to veto a bill which would have allowed truckers in Pennsylvania to carry heavier loads. The conference also enlisted a public relations firm to conduct a campaign meant to foster public distrust of truckers.

The truckers sued the railroads for an antitrust conspiracy. The truckers won in the district court, and the railroads appealed.

EASTERN RAILROAD PRESIDENT'S CONFERENCE v. NOERR MOTOR FREIGHT
365 U.S. 127 (1961).

JUSTICE BLACK: . . . [T]he Sherman Act does not prohibit two or more persons from associating together in an attempt to persuade the legislature or the executive to take particular action with respect to a law that would produce a restraint or a monopoly. Although such associations could perhaps, through a process of expansive construction, be brought within the general proscription of "combination[s] . . . in restraint of trade," they bear very little if any resemblance to the combinations normally held violative of the Sherman Act, combinations ordinarily characterized by an express or implied agreement or understanding that the participants will jointly give up their trade freedom, or help one another to take away the trade freedom of others through the use of such devices as price-fixing agreements, boycotts, market-division agreements, and other similar arrangements. This essential dissimilarity between an agreement jointly to seek legislation or law enforcement and the agreements traditionally condemned by § 1 of the Act, even if not itself conclusive on the question of the applicability of the Act, does constitute a warning against treating the defendants' conduct as though it amounted to a common-law trade restraint. And we do think that the question is conclusively settled, against the application of the Act, when this factor of essential dissimilarity is considered along with the other difficulties that would be presented by a holding that the Sherman Act forbids associations for the purpose of influencing the passage or enforcement of laws.

In the first place, such a holding would substantially impair the power of government to take actions through its legislature and executive that operate to restrain trade. In a representative democracy such as this, these branches of government act on behalf of the people and, to a very large extent, the whole concept of representation depends upon the ability of the people to make their wishes known to their representatives. To hold that the government retains the power to act in this representative capacity and yet hold, at the same time, that the people cannot freely inform the government of their wishes would impute to the Sherman Act a purpose to regulate, not business activity, but political activity, a purpose which would have no basis whatever in the legislative history of that Act.[17] Secondly, and of at least equal significance, such a construction of the Sherman Act would raise important constitutional questions. The right of petition is one of the freedoms protected by the Bill of Rights, and we cannot, of course, lightly impute to Congress an intent to invade these freedoms. Indeed, such an imputation would be particularly unjustified in this case in view of all the countervailing considerations enumerated above. For these reasons, we think it clear that the Sherman Act does not apply to the activities of the railroads at least insofar as those activities comprised mere solicitation of governmental action with respect to the passage and enforcement of laws. We are thus called upon to

17. In *Parker v. Brown*, [317 U.S. 341 (1943)], this Court was unanimous in the conclusion that the language and legislative history of the Sherman Act would not warrant the invalidation of a state regulatory program as an unlawful restraint upon trade. In so holding, we rejected the contention that the program's validity under the Sherman Act was affected by the nature of the political support necessary for its implementation—a contention not unlike that rejected here. The reasoning underlying that conclusion was stated succinctly by Mr. Chief Justice Stone: "Here the state command to the Commission and to the program committee of the California Prorate Act is not rendered unlawful by the Sherman Act since, in view of the latter's words and history, it must be taken to be a prohibition of individual and not state action. It is the state which has created the machinery for establishing the prorate program. Although the organization of a prorate zone is proposed by producers, and a prorate program, approved by the Commission, must also be approved by referendum of producers, it is the state, acting through the Commission, which adopts the program and which enforces it with penal sanctions, in the execution of a governmental policy. The prerequisite approval of the program upon referendum by a prescribed number of producers is not the imposition by them of their will upon the minority by force of agreement or combination which the Sherman Act prohibits. The state itself exercises its legislative authority in making the regulation and in prescribing the conditions of its application." 317 U.S., at 352.

consider whether the courts below were correct in holding that, notwithstanding this principle, the Act was violated here because of the presence in the railroads' publicity campaign of additional factors sufficient to take the case out of the area in which the principle is controlling.

The first such factor relied upon was the fact, established by the finding of the District Court, that the railroads' sole purpose in seeking to influence the passage and enforcement of laws was to destroy the truckers as competitors for the long-distance freight business. But we do not see how this fact, even if adequately supported in the record,[18] could transform conduct otherwise lawful into a violation of the Sherman Act. All of the considerations that have led us to the conclusion that the Act does not apply to mere group solicitation of governmental action are equally applicable in spite of the addition of this factor. The right of the people to inform their representatives in government of their desires with respect to the passage or enforcement of laws cannot properly be made to depend upon their intent in doing so. It is neither unusual nor illegal for people to seek action on laws in the hope that they may bring about an advantage to themselves and a disadvantage to their competitors. . . . Indeed, it is quite probably people with just such a hope of personal advantage who provide much of the information upon which governments must act. A construction of the Sherman Act that would disqualify people from taking a public position on matters in which they are financially interested would thus deprive the government of a valuable source of information and, at the same time, deprive the people of their right to petition in the very instances in which that right may be of the most importance to them. We reject such a construction of the Act. . . .

Questions and Comments

In *United Mine Workers of America v. Pennington,* 381 U.S. 657 (1965), large coal mine owners and union officials were sued by small coal producers for having combined to persuade the Secretary of Labor to raise the minimum wage for coal miners, thus injuring the small coal producers, whose mining practices were labor intensive. The Supreme Court extended *Noerr* to attempts to influence the executive branch. The now widely known *Noerr–Pennington* doctrine emerged.

Sometimes competitors *seem* to be petitioning government, but they are actually using a petition to government as a cloak to stymie competition, without regard to a favorable government response. Such was the case in *California Motor Transport Company v. Trucking Unlimited,* 404 U.S. 508 (1972). The defendant, California Motor Transport, automatically opposed every competitor's application for a license, knowing and intending that the mere opposition would impose costs on the competitors that would chill the application process. The court denied immunity to California Motor Trans-

18. A study of the record reveals that the only evidence or subsidiary findings upon which this conclusory finding could be based is the undisputed fact that the railroads did seek laws by arguments and propaganda that could have had the effect of damaging the competitive position of the truckers. There is thus an absence of evidence of intent independent of the efforts that were made to influence legislation and law enforcement. We nonetheless accept the finding of the District Court on this issue for, in our view, the disposition of this case must be the same regardless of that fact.

port, and thereby established the "sham" exception to the *Noerr–Pennington* doctrine.

The *Noerr-Pennington* doctrine dovetails with the state action doctrine, alluded to by the Court in its citation to *Parker* v. *Brown* in footnote 17. The railroads had a privilege to combine to get state action. Once they procured state action, that is, once the state acted to limit truckers' carriage of heavy loads on the roads, the competition between truckers and railroads was injured by the state, not by private restraint. See *Southern Motor Carriers Rate Conference v. United States*, 471 U.S. 48 (1985): The Sherman Act does not proscribe state action; where the state has a clearly articulated and affirmatively expressed policy, and actively supervises private conduct pursuant to that policy, the private party has a state action defense. Compare *Patrick v. Burget*, __ U.S. __, 108 S.Ct. 1658 (1988): Physicians' hospital peer review activities culminating in the termination of a doctor's hospital privileges were not immune from antitrust challenge; although the state required hospitals to establish and regularly review peer review procedures, it did not actively supervise their decisions.

Local government action is not per se immune, but it does get the benefit of the state action immunity when it is the foreseeable result of clearly articulated state policy to replace competition with regulation. See *Town of Hallie v. City of Eau Claire*, 471 U.S. 34 (1985). Moreover, the Local Government Antitrust Act of 1984, 15 U.S.C.A. §§ 34–36 (1987), eliminated damage liability for any antitrust violations by local governments and their officials and employees acting in an official capacity.

Let us return now to the *Noerr-Pennington* doctrine and its recent invocation in the case of trade association standard-setting where the standards were routinely adopted by states.

ALLIED TUBE & CONDUIT CORP. v. INDIAN HEAD, INC.
__ U.S. __, 108 S.Ct. 1931 (1988).

JUSTICE BRENNAN: Petitioner contends that its efforts to affect the product standard-setting process of a private association are immune from antitrust liability under the *Noerr* doctrine primarily because the association's standards are widely adopted into law by state and local governments. The United States Court of Appeals for the Second Circuit held that *Noerr* immunity did not apply. We affirm.

I

The National Fire Protection Association (Association) is a private, voluntary organization with more than 31,500 individual and group members representing industry, labor, academia, insurers, organized medicine, firefighters, and government. The Association, among other things, publishes product standards and codes related to fire protection through a process known as "consensus standard making." One of the codes it publishes is the National Electrical Code, which establishes product and performance requirements for the design and installation of electrical wiring systems. Revised every three years, the National Electric Code (Code) is the most influential electrical code in the nation. A substantial number of state and local governments routinely adopt the Code into law with little or no change; private certification laboratories, such as Underwriters Laboratories, normally will not list and label an electrical product that does not meet Code standards; many underwriters will refuse to insure structures that are not built in conformity with the Code; and many electrical inspectors, contractors, and distributors will not use a product that falls outside the Code.

Among the electrical products covered by the Code is electrical conduit, the hollow tubing used as a raceway to carry electrical wires through the walls and floors of buildings. Throughout the relevant period, the Code permitted using electrical conduit made of steel, and almost all conduit sold was in fact steel conduit. Starting in 1980, respondent began to offer plastic conduit made of polyvinyl chloride. Respondent claims its plastic conduit offers significant competitive advantages over steel conduit, including pliability, lower installed cost, and lower susceptibility to short circuiting. In 1980, however, there was also a scientific basis for concern that, during fires in high-rise buildings, polyvinyl chloride conduit might burn and emit toxic fumes.

Respondent initiated a proposal to include polyvinyl chloride conduit as an approved type of electrical conduit in the 1981 edition of the Code. Following approval by one of the Association's professional panels, this proposal was scheduled for consideration at the 1980 annual meeting, where it could be adopted or rejected by a simple majority of the members present. Alarmed that, if approved, respondent's product might pose a competitive threat to steel conduit, petitioner, the nation's largest producer of steel conduit, met to plan strategy with, among others, members of the steel industry, other steel conduit manufacturers, and its independent sales agents. They collectively agreed to exclude respondent's product from the 1981 Code by packing the upcoming annual meeting with new Association members whose only function would be to vote against the polyvinyl chloride proposal.

Combined, the steel interests recruited 230 persons to join the Association and to attend the annual meeting to vote against the proposal. Petitioner alone recruited 155 persons—including employees, executives, sales agents, the agents' employees, employees from two divisions that did not sell electrical products, and the wife of a national sales director. Petitioner and the other steel interests also paid over $100,000 for the membership, registration, and attendance expenses of these voters. At the annual meeting, the steel group voters were instructed where to sit and how and when to vote by group leaders who used walkie-talkies and hand signals to facilitate communication. Few of the steel group voters had any of the technical documentation necessary to follow the meeting. None of them spoke at the meeting to give their reasons for opposing the proposal to approve polyvinyl chloride conduit. Nonetheless, with their solid vote in opposition, the proposal was rejected and returned to committee by a vote of 394 to 390. Respondent appealed the membership's vote to the Association's Board of Directors, but the Board denied the appeal on the ground that, although the Association's rules had been circumvented, they had not been violated.

In October 1981, respondent brought this suit in Federal District Court, alleging that petitioner and others had unreasonably restrained trade in the electrical conduit market in violation of § 1 of the Sherman Act. A bifurcated jury trial began in March 1985. Petitioner conceded that it had conspired with the other steel interests to exclude respondent's product from the Code and that it had a pecuniary interest to do so. The jury, instructed under the rule of reason that respondent carried the burden of showing that the anticompetitive effects of petitioner's actions outweighed any procompetitive benefits of standard setting, found petitioner liable. In answers to special interrogatories, the jury found that petitioner did not violate any rules of the Association and acted, at least in part, based on a genuine belief that plastic conduit was unsafe, but that petitioner nonetheless did "subvert" the consensus standard making process of the Association. The jury also made special findings that petitioner's actions had an adverse impact on competition, were not the least restrictive means of expressing petitioner's opposition to the use of polyvinyl chloride conduit in the marketplace, and unreasonably restrained trade in violation of the antitrust laws. The jury then awarded respondent damages, to be trebled, of $3.8 million for lost profits resulting from the effect that excluding polyvinyl chloride conduit from the 1981 Code had of its own force in the marketplace. No damages were awarded for injuries stemming from the adoption of the 1981 Code by governmental entities.

The District Court then granted a judgment n.o.v. for petitioner, reasoning that *Noerr* immunity applied because the Association was "akin to a legislature" and because petitioner, "by the use of methods consistent with acceptable standards of political action, genuinely intended to influence the [Association] with respect to the National Electrical Code, and to thereby influence the various state and local legislative bodies which adopt the [Code]." The Court of Appeals reversed, rejecting both the argument that the Association should be treated as a "quasi-legislative" body because legislatures routinely adopt the Code and the argument that efforts to influence the Code were immune under *Noerr* as indirect attempts to influence state and local governments. We granted certiorari to address important issues regarding the application of *Noerr* immunity to private standard-setting associations.

II

Concerted efforts to restrain or monopolize trade by petitioning government officials are protected from antitrust liability under the doctrine established by *Noerr*. The scope of this protection depends, however, on the source, context, and nature of the anticompetitive restraint at issue. "[W]here a restraint upon trade or monopolization is the result of valid governmental action, as opposed to private action," those urging the governmental action enjoy absolute immunity from antitrust liability for the anticompetitive restraint. *Noerr*, 365 U.S., at 136. In addition, where, independent of any government action, the anticompetitive restraint results directly from private action, the restraint cannot form the basis for antitrust liability if it is "incidental" to a valid effort to influence governmental action. The validity of such efforts, and thus the applicability of *Noerr* immunity, varies with the context and nature of the activity. A publicity campaign directed at the general public, seeking legislation or executive action, enjoys antitrust immunity even when the campaign employs unethical and deceptive methods. But in less political arenas, unethical and deceptive practices can constitute abuses of administrative or judicial processes that may result in antitrust violations.

In this case, the restraint of trade on which liability was predicated was the Association's exclusion of respondent's product from the Code, and no damages were imposed for the incorporation of that Code by any government. The relevant context is thus the standard-setting process of a private association. Typically, private standard-setting associations, like the Association in this case, include members having horizontal and vertical business relations. There is no doubt that the members of such associations often have economic incentives to restrain competition and that the product standards set by such associations have a serious potential for anticompetitive harm. Agreement on a product standard is, after all, implicitly an agreement not to manufacture, distribute, or purchase certain types of products. Accordingly, private standard-setting associations have traditionally been objects of antitrust scrutiny. When, however, private associations promulgate safety standards based on the merits of objective expert judgments and through procedures that prevent the standard-setting process from being biased by members with economic interests in stifling product competition, those private standards can have significant procompetitive advantages. It is this potential for procompetitive benefits that has led most lower courts to apply rule of reason analysis to product standard-setting by private associations.

Given this context, petitioner does not enjoy the immunity accorded those who merely urge the government to restrain trade. We agree with the Court of Appeals that the Association cannot be treated as a "quasi-legislative" body simply because legislatures routinely adopt the Code the Association publishes. Whatever *de facto* authority the Association enjoys, no official authority has been conferred on it by any government, and the decisionmaking body of the Association is composed, at least in part, of persons with economic incentives to restrain trade. "We may presume, absent a showing to the contrary, that [a government] acts in the public interest. A private party, on the other hand, may be presumed to be acting primarily on his or its own behalf." *Hallie v. Eau Claire,* 471 U.S. 34, 45. The dividing line between restraints resulting from governmental action and those resulting from private action may not always be obvious. But where, as here, the restraint is imposed by persons unaccountable to the public and without official authority, many of whom have personal financial interests in restraining competition, we have no difficulty concluding that the restraint has resulted from private action.

Noerr immunity might still apply, however, if, as petitioner argues, the exclusion of polyvinyl chloride conduit from the Code, and the effect that exclusion had of its own force in the marketplace, were incidental to a valid effort to influence governmental action. Petitioner notes that the lion's share of the anticompetitive effect in this case came from the predictable adoption of the Code into law by a large number of state and local governments. Indeed, petitioner argues that, because state and local governments rely so heavily on the Code and lack the resources or technical expertise to second-guess it, efforts to influence the Association's standard-setting process are the most effective means of influencing legislation regulating electrical conduit. This claim to *Noerr* immunity has some force. The effort to influence governmental action in this case certainly cannot be characterized as a sham given the actual adoption of the 1981 Code into a number of statutes and local ordinances. Nor can we quarrel with petitioner's contention that, given the widespread adoption of the Code into law, any effect the 1981 Code had in the marketplace of its own force was, in the main, incidental to petitioner's genuine effort to influence governmental action. And, as petitioner persuasively argues, the claim of *Noerr* immunity cannot be dismissed on the ground that the conduct at issue involved no "direct" petitioning of government officials, for *Noerr* itself immunized a form of "indirect" petitioning. See *Noerr*, 365 U.S. 127 (1961) (immunizing a publicity campaign directed at the general public on the ground that it was part of an effort to influence legislative and executive action).

Nonetheless, the validity of petitioner's actions remains an issue. We cannot agree with petitioner's absolutist position that the *Noerr* doctrine immunizes every concerted effort that is genuinely intended to influence governmental action. If all such conduct were immunized then, for example, competitors would be free to enter into horizontal price agreements as long as they wished to propose that price as an appropriate level for governmental ratemaking or price supports. Horizontal conspiracies or boycotts designed to exact higher prices or other economic advantages from the government would be immunized on the ground that they are genuinely intended to influence the government to agree to the conspirators' terms. Firms could claim immunity for boycotts or horizontal output restrictions on the ground that the are intended to dramatize the plight of their industry and spur legislative action. Immunity might even be claimed for anticompetitive mergers on the theory that they give the merging corporations added political clout. Nor is it necessarily dispositive that packing the Association's meeting may have been the most effective means of securing government action, for one could imagine situations where the most effective means of influencing government officials is bribery, and we have never suggested that that kind of attempt to influence the government merits protection. We thus conclude that the *Noerr* immunity of anticompetitive activity intended to influence the government depends not only on its impact, but also on the context and nature of the activity.

* * *

What distinguishes this case from *Noerr* and its progeny is that the context and nature of petitioner's activity make it the type of commercial activity that has traditionally had its validity determined by the antitrust laws themselves. . . .

———

Justice White, joined by Justice O'Connor, dissented. They believed that *Noerr* immunity applied because petitioners' actions were a genuine attempt to influence governmental action; indeed it was a much more direct and focused attempt than in *Noerr*.

Questions and Comments

While in *Noerr, Pennington* and *Indian Head* defendants sought government action in order to hurt competitors, in *State of Missouri v. National Organization for Women*, 620 F.2d 1301 (8th Cir.), *cert. denied*, 449 U.S. 842 (1980), defendants took concerted action that would hurt a state's economy to get government action. The National Organization For Women (NOW) invited would-be convention goers to boycott states which had not ratified the Equal Rights Amendment. NOW hoped the resulting economic pressure on those states would convince their legislatures to ratify the ERA. Is such a political boycott covered by the antitrust laws? Should it be? The court held for NOW, asserting that resort to "a boycott in a non-competitive political arena for the purpose of influencing legislation is not proscribed by the Sherman Act." 620 F.2d 1301 at 1315.

The court added in a footnote:

The Sherman Act may apply in some situations to noncommercial and non-economic boycotts. However, we do not rest our decision in this case upon the basis that the boycott was noncommercial and non-economic. Our decision is based upon the right to use political activities to petition the government, as was the underlying factor in *Noerr*. Id. at n. 16.

Judge Gibson dissented. As he noted, the court did not establish that NOW was exercising a protected constitutional right; the court found only that constitutionally protected interests were implicated. Also, Gibson invoked the presumption against implied exclusions from the antitrust laws. Further, he said:

NOW may not have economic interests at stake in this controversy, but the boycott severely affects the competitive posture of Missouri convention interests and the overall economic welfare of Missouri residents. Thus, the technical characterization of the boycott as noncommercial and noneconomic is misleading and actually erroneous in important respects. The anticompetitive economic and commercial effects of the boycott on Missouri's legitimate business interests and welfare are identical, regardless of whether the motivation for the boycott is political or economic. The majority thus places the court's imprimatur upon a boycott with potentially severe economic and commercial consequences simply on the basis of the boycott's motivation. The precedential support for drawing this distinction is tenuous at best. Id. at 1322–23.

Who is right? Does *Indian Head* provide an answer?

At what point, if any, does economic activity for political purposes become constitutionally protected, rather than merely implicating constitutional interests? In March 1966, black citizens of Claiborne County, Mississippi, submitted to white elected officials a list of demands aimed at achieving racial equality. The white officials' response was unsatisfactory. At a meeting of the local NAACP, several hundred black citizens voted to boycott the white merchants of the area.

In April 1969 when the boycott was still in effect, Charles Evers, Field Secretary for the NAACP, gave a speech in which he said: "If we catch any of you going in any . . . racist stores, we're going to break your damn neck."

Generally, however, the boycott was peaceful and orderly. Names of boycott violators were read aloud at church meetings and were published in a black newspaper. Violators were demeaned and ostracized. Four incidents of violence were reported, including shots fired at a house and a brick thrown through a windshield. The boycott caused substantial business to be diverted from the area's white merchants to its black merchants and to merchants outside of the area. The white merchants sued the NAACP for tortious conduct and a violation of Mississippi's antitrust law.

The lower courts found liability for violation of a Mississippi statute outlawing threats of bodily harm and coercion. They held that since force and violence were involved, the First Amendment afforded no protection. Reversing, the Supreme Court said:

> We hold that the nonviolent elements of petitioners' activities are entitled to the protection of the First Amendment.

> * * *

> The First Amendment does not protect violence. . . . No federal rule of law restricts a State from imposing tort liability for business losses that are caused by violence and by threats of violence. When such conduct occurs in the context of constitutionally protected activity, however, "precision of regulation" is demanded.

> * * *

> . . . Petitioners withheld their patronage from the white establishment of Claiborne County to challenge a political and economic system that had denied them the basic rights of dignity and equality that this country had fought a Civil War to secure. While the State legitimately may impose damages for the consequences of violent conduct, it may not award damages for the consequences of nonviolent protected activity. Only those losses proximately caused by unlawful conduct may be recovered.

> The First Amendment similarly restricts the ability of the state to impose liability on an individual solely because of his association with another.[9]

Does *Claiborne* answer the questions the NOW court thought were still open? Is *Indian Head* consistent with *Claiborne?* Is it possible to reconcile these cases by asking whether the boycotters had a constitutional right to engage in the joint action they undertook? Did NOW have a constitutional right to boycott states not ratifying the ERA? Did steel conduit makers have a constitutional right to pack the meeting of the standard setting association?

Problems

1. In the 1970s Bechtel Corporation, along with other U.S. construction firms, sought to preserve their important business relationships with the Arab League countries by agreeing with the Arab League countries to boycott (e.g., as subcontractors) all friends of Israel. Was this boycott illegal if it lessened competition? (How do we decide whether it lessened competition?) See *United States v. Bechtel Corp.,* 1979–1 Trade Cas. (CCH) ¶ 62,429 (N.D.Cal. 1979).

9. NAACP v. Claiborne Hardware Co.,
458 U.S. 886, 915–919 (1982).

Also in the 1970s, the OPEC nations conspired to dramatically increase the price of oil. A group of gas station owners convened and allegedly agreed to close their stations on Sundays as a means to coerce federal energy officials to permit greater profit margins for the stations. The oil companies sued. Did they have a good cause of action? See *Crown Central Petroleum Corp. v. Waldman*, 486 F.Supp. 759 (M.D.Pa.1980), *reversed on other grounds*, 634 F.2d 127 (3rd Cir.1980).

2. A city ordinance governs court appointment of lawyers to represent indigent defendants charged with crimes. The ordinance provides for an hourly rate substantially below the going market rate for legal services of comparable worth. As a result, there is a shortage of lawyers for indigent criminal defendants. The city bar association lobbies the city council to adopt an ordinance increasing the rates for court-appointed lawyers. The council does nothing and the bar association adopts a resolution encouraging lawyers to withhold their services until the city council acts. Has the bar association violated the Sherman Act?

The court-appointed lawyers, many of whom make their living by serving in this capacity, go on strike. They refuse to accept new appointments until fees are increased, and they mobilize other attorneys on the assignment list to do the same, creating an emergency. When interviewed, the striking lawyers state that they are vitally concerned about the minimal and insufficient representation of indigent defendants, whose Sixth Amendment rights are being violated. City officials are likewise concerned about the representation of the poor, and give moral support to the strikers. As a result of the strike, almost no lawyers can be found to accept court appointment to represent criminal defendants. Three weeks after the strike begins, the city council votes an increase in court-appointed lawyers' fees. Did the lawyers violate the antitrust laws? See *Superior Court Trial Lawyers' Association Case*, 856 F.2d 226 (D.C. Cir. 1988), cert. granted. Who would sue? Why?

I. JOINT ACTIVITIES THAT INVOLVE SIGNIFICANT INTEGRATION

We have dealt at various points with some joint activities that involved a degree of integration. *BMI, NCAA* and *Northwest Wholesale Stationers* are examples. In *Appalachian Coals*, the Court treated the arrangement as a legitimate joint sales agency (although it might well have seen the joint sales arrangement as a cover for a cartel). In *Maricopa County*, the Court considered whether the doctors' maximum price fixing was akin to price setting by an integrated partnership, but decided it was not. As we learned from these examples, courts are often faced with a threshold problem of characterizing collaboration: is it merely cartel-like, or is there bona fide integration? If the former, a court is likely to hold the arrangement unlawful, either citing the per se rule or performing a very truncated rule of reason analysis. If the latter, the court is likely to characterize the arrangement as a joint venture. In joint venture analysis, three questions may be asked: (1) Is the integration achieved through the venture unreasonably anticompetitive? (2) If the integration is accompanied by related contractual restraints that have anticompetitive properties, are they, on balance, anticompetitive? (3) Will the venture confer such advantages on participants that they must grant access to the venture to outsiders in order to protect competition? We explore these problems in this section. We start with older cases which focused upon access. Hence, our first subsection deals primarily with the third of the three questions. Next, we present contemporary cases involving covenants not to compete and other contractual restraints that sometimes accompany significant integration, thus dealing with the second question above. Finally, we consider the analysis necessary to determine whether the joint venture is anticompetitive in its essence. We note in this regard that some joint ventures, those in formal, enduring form, are akin to mergers and acquisitions. We will treat problems arising from joint ventures of this sort in Chapter 5 below, the chapter on mergers.

1. ACCESS TO AND EXCLUSION FROM VENTURES (INCLUDING "ESSENTIAL FACILITIES")

UNITED STATES v. TERMINAL RAILROAD ASSOCIATION OF ST. LOUIS

224 U.S. 383 (1912).

JUSTICE LURTON: [The Terminal Company—a joint venture—was organized in 1889 by six railroad companies. At first it controlled only one of three independent lines connecting railroads terminating on either side of the Mississippi River at St. Louis. At great expense it acquired the other two lines. Because of the topography of St. Louis and its environs, including the river, great hills, and already occupied valleys, and because of the prohibitive expense of building another system, no railroad could enter the City of St. Louis and give access to its industries and commerce or provide means of connection to lines on the opposite side of the river except by using the terminal facilities controlled by the Terminal Company.

The railroads which organized the Terminal Company allowed others to join the joint venture provided there was unanimous consent to their admission and their admission price. By the time the complaint alleging monopolization and combination was filed, 14 companies were joint owners. Nonproprietors were permitted to use the facilities for the same fee paid by the proprietors. The Terminal Company asserted that no company would be excluded from joint use or ownership.]

. . . The fact that the Terminal Company is not an independent corporation at all is of the utmost significance. There are twenty-four railroads converging at St. Louis. The relation of the Terminal Company is not one of impartiality to each of them.

* * *

That through their ownership and exclusive control they are in possession of advantages in respect to the enormous traffic which must use the St. Louis gateway, is undeniable. That the proprietary companies have not availed themselves of the full measure of their power to impede free competition of outside companies, may be true. Aside from their power under all of the conditions to exclude independent entrance to the city by any outside company, their control has resulted in certain methods which are not consistent with freedom of competition. To these acts we shall refer later.

We are not unmindful of the essential difference between terminal systems . . . and railroad transportation companies. The first are but instrumentalities which assist the latter in the transfer of traffic between different lines, and in the collection and distribution of traffic. They are a modern evolution in the doing of railroad business, and are of the greatest public utility. They, under proper conditions, do not restrain, but promote commerce.

. . . Referring to the legitimate use of terminal companies, [a] Missouri court said: . . .

"St. Louis is a city of great magnitude in the extent of its area, its population, and its manufacturing and other business. A very large number of trunk line railroads converge in this city. In the brief of one of the well-informed counsel in this case it is said that St. Louis is one of the largest railroad centers in the world. Suppose it were required of every railroad company to effect its entrance to this city as best it could and establish its own terminal facilities, we would have a large number of passenger stations, freight depots and switch yards scattered all over the vast area and innumerable vehicles employed in hauling passengers and freight to and from those stations and depots. Or suppose it became necessary in the exigency of commerce that all incoming trains should reach a common focus, but every railroad company provide its own track; then not only would the expense of obtaining the necessary rights of way be so enormous as to amount to the exclusion of all but a few of the strongest roads, but, if it could be accomplished, the city would be cut to pieces with the many lines of railroad intersecting it in every direction, and thus the greatest agency of commerce would become the greatest burden."

182 Missouri, 284, 299.

. . . [C]ounsel say that the issue presented by this record is, "whether the common control or ownership of all the terminal facilities (mechanical devices for the exchange, receipt and distribution of traffic) of a large commercial and manufacturing center by all of the railroad companies, and for the benefit of all upon equal terms and facilities, without discrimination, is condemned by the Sherman act."

Let us analyze the proposition included in the issue, as stated by counsel, quoted above: Counsel assume that the combined terminals have come under a "common control or ownership." But this is not the case. That the instrumentalities so combined are not jointly owned or managed by all of the companies compelled to use them is a significant fact which must be taken into account for the purpose of determining whether there has been a violation of the Anti-trust Act. The control and ownership is that of the fourteen roads which are defendants. The railroad systems and the coal roads converging at St. Louis, which are not associated with the proprietary companies are under compulsion to use the terminal system, and yet have no voice in its control.

It cannot be controverted that, in ordinary circumstances, a number of independent companies might combine for the purpose of controlling or acquiring terminals for their common but exclusive use. In such cases other companies might be admitted upon terms or excluded altogether. If such terms were too onerous, there would ordinarily remain the right and power to construct their own terminals. But the situation at St. Louis is most extraordinary, and we base our conclusion in this case, in a large measure, upon that fact. The "physical or topographical condition peculiar to the locality," which is advanced as a prime justification for a unified system of terminals, constitutes a most obvious reason why such a unified system is an obstacle, a hindrance and a restriction upon interstate commerce, unless it is the impartial agent of all who, owing to conditions, are under such compulsion, as here exists, to use its facilities. . . .

The terminal properties in question are not so controlled and managed, in view of the inherent local conditions, as to escape condemnation as a restraint upon commerce. They are not under a common control and ownership. Nor can this be brought about unless the prohibition against the admission of other companies to such control is stricken out and provision made for the admission of any company to an equal control and management upon an equal basis with the present proprietary companies.

There are certain practices of this Terminal Company which operate to the disadvantage of the commerce which must cross the river at St. Louis, and of non-proprietary railroad lines compelled to use its facilities. One of them grows out of the fact that the Terminal Company is a terminal company and something more. It does not confine itself to supplying and operating mere facilities for the interchange of traffic between railroads and to assistance in the collecting and distributing of traffic for the carrier companies. It, as well as several of the absorbed terminal companies, were organized under ordinary railroad charters. If the combination which has occurred is to escape condemnation as a combination of parallel and competing railroad companies, it is because of the essential difference between railroad and terminal companies proper—differences pointed out by the Missouri Supreme Court in the case heretofore referred to. Indeed, the defense to this proceeding is based upon the insistence that the Terminal Company is solely engaged in operating terminal facilities, defined in the briefs, "as mechanical devices for the exchange, receipt and distribution of traffic." This Terminal Company, in addition to its schedule for terminal charges proper, such as switching, warehousing, etc., files its rate-sheets for the transportation of every class of merchandise from the termini of the railroads on the Illinois side of the river to destinations across the river over its lines. [Arbitrary rates] . . . cast a burden upon short hauls, which has led to much complaint, as being both discriminatory and extortionate.

*   *   *

We come now to the remedy. . . . If, as we have already said, the combination of two or more mere terminal companies into a single system does not violate the prohibition of the statute against contracts and combinations in restraint of interstate commerce, it is because such a combination may be of the greatest public utility. But when, as here, the inherent conditions are such as to prohibit any other reasonable means of entering the city, the combination of every such facility under the exclusive ownership and control of less than all of the companies under compulsion to use them violates both the first and second sections of the act, in that it constitutes a contract or combination in restraint of commerce among the States and an attempt to monopolize commerce among the States which must pass through the gateway at St. Louis.

* * *

Plainly the combination which has occurred would not be an illegal restraint under the terms of the statute if it were what is claimed for it, a proper terminal association acting as the impartial agent of every line which is under compulsion to use its instrumentalities. If, as we have pointed out, the violation of the statute, in view of the inherent physical conditions, grows out of administrative conditions which may be eliminated and the obvious advantages of unification preserved, such a modification of the agreement between the Terminal Company and the proprietary companies as shall constitute the former the *bona fide* agent and servant of every railroad line which shall use its facilities, and an inhibition of certain methods of administration to which we have referred, will amply vindicate the wise purpose of the statute, and will preserve to the public a system of great public advantage.

These considerations lead to a reversal of the decree dismissing the bill. This is accordingly adjudged and the case is remanded to the District Court, with directions that a decree be there entered directing the parties to submit to the court, within ninety days after receipt of mandate, a plan for the reorganization of the contract between the fourteen defendant railroad companies and the Terminal Company, which we have pointed out as bringing the combination within the inhibition of the statute.

First. By providing for the admission of any existing or future railroad to joint ownership and control of the combined terminal properties, upon such just and reasonable terms as shall place such applying company upon a plane of equality in respect of benefits and burdens with the present proprietary companies.

Second. Such plan of reorganization must also provide definitely for the use of the terminal facilities by any other railroad not electing to become a joint owner, upon such just and reasonable terms and regulations as will, in respect of use, character and cost of service, place every such company upon as nearly an equal plane as may be with respect to expenses and charges as that occupied by the proprietary companies.

Third. By eliminating from the present agreement between the Terminal Company and the proprietary companies any provision which restricts any such company to the use of the facilities of the Terminal Company.

[Fourth and Fifth. By abolishing discriminatory charges.] . . *Violation*

Questions and Comments

In *Terminal Railroads*, the Court assumed that the public interest was served by combining three terminal systems into one; thus, it assumed that the combination itself was lawful. If there was a violation, it lay not in combining separate systems, but in failing to operate the combined one as a public utility. The access aspect of *Terminal Railroads* has contemporary relevance, and indeed the case is often cited as a model for the bottleneck or essential facilities doctrine. You should not assume, however, that contemporary courts would allow a "public interest" justification for a consolidation that might well have produced monopoly. Today, facts like these might be thought to raise the question whether the combination itself injured competition.

In *Terminal Railroads,* the proprietary railroads had control of a "bottleneck facility." Competitors needed access in order to pass from one side of the river to the other. The facility was capable of serving all comers. There was no claim that private parties had invested in a facility of limited capacity and needed the capacity for their own use. This is the classic example in which the Supreme Court imposed a public utility obligation on a joint venture; the proprietors were required to give access to all and to do so on reasonable, nondiscriminatory terms.

Is leverage involved in *Terminal Railroads?* Are defendants using power in the upstream terminal market to gain an advantage in the downstream rail transportation market? Are they threatening monopoly in the downstream market? Are they injuring competition there?

How important is concert of action to the result in *Terminal Railroad?* Suppose the terminal company had always been a single firm; it first owned a railroad and then constructed the terminal facilities. Would the result be the same? Does *Otter Tail* help you decide? What would be the result if Terminal Railroads for a time granted but later refused to grant access? Does *Aspen Skiing* help you decide?

In *Terminal Railroad* the Supreme Court remanded the case for entry of the decree. The district court would have to exercise continuing surveillance over a decree ordering reasonable, nondiscriminating access. Consider the difficulties of judicial oversight. Was there any better alternative?

What norm ought to govern the terms of access? Are the proprietary railroads entitled to charge a price that yields a monopoly return? Should they be limited to a price just covering average total cost? Should they be limited to their incremental (or marginal) costs? Must the proprietors allow other railroads to become proprietors if applicant railroads want that status? Could the proprietors *require* applicant railroads to become proprietors and to make the necessary capital investment as a condition to access?

Suppose that after airline deregulation Airlines A and U jointly set up a computerized reservation system. Because a large number of travel agents use this system and agents have the incentive to use only one system, all other airlines are convinced that their flights must be listed on it. A and U stand ready to list the schedules of competing airlines, but only for a supracompetitive price. The latter airlines sue, asserting that the charge is unreasonable because it raises their costs substantially above those of A and U, thus enabling A and U to cut air travel prices, advertise more extensively, provide frills, or otherwise gain significant competitive advantages in the air carriage market. A and U assert that the charge is a reasonable reward for their innovative initiative. The case is tried to you as judge. What legal norm do you apply? Alternatively, the case is tried to a jury and you must instruct the jury. What will you tell the jurors? Does the issue of "reasonableness" present a problem of balancing ex ante and ex post concerns similar to that we raised in connection with *Aspen Skiing* and other Section 2 cases? Is there a legal norm that gives guidance as to how the balance must be struck? Or is this a factual issue to be sorted out in each case under the general rubric of reasonableness?

Some years after *Terminal Railroad* the Supreme Court tested the limits of the duty to give access. If a facility is jointly developed in order to gain access must an excluded firm prove that the facility is essential, or merely important to effective competition?

ASSOCIATED PRESS v. UNITED STATES
326 U.S. 1 (1945).

JUSTICE BLACK: The publishers of more than 1,200 newspapers are members of the Associated Press (AP), a cooperative association incorporated under the Membership Corporation Law of the State of New York. Its business is the collection, assembly and distribution of news. The news it distributes is originally obtained by direct employees of the Association, employees of the member newspapers, and the employees of foreign independent news agencies with which AP has contractual relations, such as the Canadian Press. Distribution of the news is made through interstate channels of communication to the various newspaper members of the Association, who pay for it under an assessment plan which contemplates no profit to AP.

* * *

The heart of the government's charge was that appellants had by concerted action set up a system of By–Laws which prohibited all AP members from selling news to non-members, and which granted each member powers to block its non-member competitors from membership. . . . [The government sought an injunction and moved for summary judgment.] The District Court, composed of three judges, held that the By–Laws unlawfully restricted admission to AP membership, and violated the Sherman Act insofar as the By–Laws' provisions clothed a member with powers to impose or dispense with conditions upon the admission of his business competitor. Continued observance of these By–Laws was enjoined.

* * *

These By–Laws, for a violation of which members may be thus fined, suspended, or expelled, require that each newspaper member publish the AP news regularly in whole or in part, and that each shall "promptly furnish to the corporation, through its agents or employees, all the news of such member's district, the area of which shall be determined by the Board of Directors." All members are prohibited from selling or furnishing their spontaneous news to any agency or publisher except to AP. Other By–Laws require each newspaper member to conduct his or its business in such manner that the news furnished by the corporation shall not be made available to any non-member in advance of publication. The joint effect of these By–Laws is to block all newspaper non-members from any opportunity to buy news from AP or any of its publisher members. Admission to membership in AP thereby becomes a prerequisite to obtaining AP news or buying news from any one of its more than twelve hundred publishers. The erection of obstacles to the acquisition of membership consequently can make it difficult, if not impossible, for non-members to get any of the news furnished by AP or any of the individual members of this combination of American newspaper publishers.[4]

The By–Laws provide a very simple and non-burdensome road for admission of a non-competing applicant. The Board of Directors in such case can elect the applicant without payment of money or the imposition of any other onerous terms. In striking contrast are the By–Laws which govern admission of new members who do compete. Historically, as well as presently, applicants who would offer competition to old members have a hard road to travel. This appears from the following facts found by the District Court.

* * *

. . . These By–Laws, presently involved, leave the Board of Directors free to elect new members unless the applicant would compete with old members, and in that event the Board cannot act at all in the absence of consent by the applicant's member competitor. Should the old member object to admission of his competitor, the application must be referred to a regular or special meeting of the Association. As a prerequisite to election, he must (a) pay to the Association 10% of the total amount of the regular assessments received by it from old members in the same competitive field during the entire period from October 1, 1900 to the first day of the month preceding the date of the election of the applicant,[5] (b) relinquish any exclusive rights the applicant may have to any news or news picture services and, when requested to do so by his member competitor in that field, must "require the said news or news picture services, or any of them, to be furnished to such member or members, upon the same terms as they are made available to the applicant," and (c) receive a majority vote of the regular members who vote in person or by proxy. These obstacles to membership, and to the purchase of AP news, only existed where there was a competing old member in the same field.

The District Court found that the By–Laws in and of themselves were contracts in restraint of commerce in that they contained provisions designed to stifle competition in the newspaper publishing field. The court also found that AP's restrictive By–Laws had hindered and impeded the growth of competing newspapers. This latter finding, as to the *past* effect of the restrictions, is challenged. We are inclined to think that it is supported by undisputed evidence, but we do not stop to labor the point. For the court below found, and we think correctly, that the By–Laws on their face, and without regard to their past effect, constitute restraints of trade. Combinations are no less unlawful because they have not as yet resulted in restraint. An agreement or combination to follow a course of conduct which will necessarily restrain or monopolize a part of trade or

4. The court found that out of the 1,803 daily English language newspapers published in the United States, with a total circulation of 42,080,391, 1,179 of them, with a circulation of 34,762,120, were under joint contractual obligations not to supply either AP or their own "spontaneous" news to any non-member of AP.

5. Under these terms, a new applicant could not have entered the morning field in New York without paying $1,432,142.73, and in Chicago, $416,631.90. For entering the evening field in the same cities it would have cost $1,095,003.21, and $595,772.31, respectively.

commerce may violate the Sherman Act, whether it be "wholly nascent or abortive on the one hand, or successful on the other." [Socony-Vacuum Oil Co., 310 U.S. at 225.] For these reasons the argument, repeated here in various forms, that AP had not yet achieved a complete monopoly is wholly irrelevant. Undisputed evidence did show, however, that its By–Laws had tied the hands of all of its numerous publishers, to the extent that they could not and did not sell any part of their news so that it could reach any of their non-member competitors. In this respect the court did find, and that finding cannot possibly be challenged, that AP's By–Laws had hindered and restrained the sale of interstate news to non-members who competed with members.

Inability to buy news from the largest news agency, or any one of its multitude of members, can have most serious effects on the publication of competitive newspapers, both those presently published and those which, but for these restrictions, might be published in the future.[10] This is illustrated by the District Court's finding that, in 26 cities of the United States, existing newspapers already have contracts for AP news and the same newspapers have contracts with United Press and International News Service under which new newspapers would be required to pay the contract holders large sums to enter the field. The net effect is seriously to limit the opportunity of any new paper to enter these cities. Trade restraints of this character, aimed at the destruction of competition, tend to block the initiative which brings newcomers into a field of business and to frustrate the free enterprise system which it was the purpose of the Sherman Act to protect.

*   *   *

It has been argued that the restrictive By–Laws should be treated as beyond the prohibitions of the Sherman Act, since the owner of the property can choose his associates and can, as to that which he has produced by his own enterprise and sagacity, efforts or ingenuity, decide for himself whether and to whom to sell or not to sell. While it is true in a very general sense that one can dispose of his property as he pleases, he cannot "go beyond the exercise of this right, and by contracts or combinations, express or implied, unduly hinder or obstruct the free and natural flow of commerce in the channels of interstate trade." *United States v. Bausch & Lomb Co.*, 321 U.S. 707, 722. The Sherman Act was specifically intended to prohibit independent businesses from becoming "associates" in a common plan which is bound to reduce their competitor's opportunity to buy or sell the things in which the groups compete. Victory of a member of such a combination over its business rivals achieved by such collective means cannot consistently with the Sherman Act or with practical, everyday knowledge be attributed to *individual* "enterprise and sagacity"; such hampering of business rivals can only be attributed to that which really makes it possible—the collective power of an unlawful combination. . . . [T]hese publishers have, by concerted arrangements,

---

10. The District Court found as a fact that "It is practically impossible for any one newspaper alone to establish or maintain the organization requisite for collecting all of the news of the world, or any substantial part thereof; aside from the administrative and organization difficulties thereof, the financial cost is so great that no single newspaper acting alone could sustain it."

pooled their power to acquire, to purchase, and to dispose of news reports through the channels of commerce. They have also pooled their economic and news control power and, in exerting that power, have entered into agreements which the District Court found to be "plainly designed in the interest of preventing competition." [15]

It is further contended that since there are other news agencies which sell news, it is not a violation of the Act for an overwhelming majority of American publishers to combine to decline to sell their news to the minority. But the fact that an agreement to restrain trade does not inhibit competition in all of the objects of that trade cannot save it from the condemnation of the Sherman Act. It is apparent that the exclusive right to publish news in a given field, furnished by AP and all of its members, gives many newspapers a competitive advantage over their rivals.[17] Conversely, a newspaper without AP service is more than likely to be at a competitive disadvantage. The District Court stated that it was to secure this advantage over rivals that the By–Laws existed. It is true that the record shows that some competing papers have gotten along without AP news, but morning newspapers, which control 96% of the total circulation in the United States, have AP news service. And the District Court's unchallenged finding was that "AP is a vast, intricately reticulated organization, the largest of its kind, gathering news from all over the world, the chief single source of news for the American press, universally agreed to be of great consequence."

Nevertheless, we are asked to reverse these judgments on the ground that the evidence failed to show that AP reports, which might be attributable to their own "enterprise and sagacity," are clothed "in the robes of indispensability." The absence of "indispensability" is said to have been established under the following chain of reasoning: AP has made its news generally available to the people by supplying it to a limited and select group of publishers in the various cities; therefore, it is said, AP and its member publishers have not deprived the reading public of AP news; all local readers have an "adequate access" to AP news, since all they need do in any city to get it is to buy, on whatever terms they can in a protected market, the particular newspaper selected for the public by AP and its members. We reject these contentions. The proposed "indispensability" test would fly in the face of the language of the Sherman Act and all of our previous interpretations of it. . . .

. . . [It is] said that we reach our conclusion by application of the "public utility" concept to the newspaper business. This is not correct.

15. Even if additional purposes were involved, it would not justify the combination, since the Sherman Act cannot "be evaded by good motives. The law is its own measure of right and wrong, of what it permits, or forbids, and the judgment of the courts cannot be set up against it in a supposed accommodation of its policy with the good intention of parties, and it may be, of some good results." *Standard Sanitary Mfg. Co. v. United States,* 226 U.S. 20, 49.

17. The District Court pointed out that, "monopoly is a relative word. If one means by it the possession of something absolutely necessary to the conduct of an activity, there are few except the exclusive possession of some natural resource without which the activity is impossible. Most monopolies, like most patents, give control over only some means of production for which there is a substitute; the possessor enjoys an advantage over his competitors, but he can seldom shut them out altogether; his monopoly is measured by the handicap he can impose. . . . And yet that advantage alone may make a monopoly unlawful. . . .

We merely hold that arrangements or combinations designed to stifle competition cannot be immunized by adopting a membership device accomplishing that purpose.

Finally, the argument is made that to apply the Sherman Act to this association of publishers constitutes an abridgment of the freedom of the press guaranteed by the First Amendment. . . . The First Amendment, far from providing an argument against application of the Sherman Act, here provides powerful reasons to the contrary. That Amendment rests on the assumption that the widest possible dissemination of information from diverse and antagonistic sources is essential to the welfare of the public, that a free press is a condition of a free society. Surely a command that the government itself shall not impede the free flow of ideas does not afford non-governmental combinations a refuge if they impose restraints upon that constitutionally guaranteed freedom. . . . Freedom to publish is guaranteed by the Constitution, but freedom to combine to keep others from publishing is not. . . .

We now turn to the decree. Having adjudged the By-Laws imposing restrictions on applications for membership to be illegal, the court enjoined the defendants from observing them, or agreeing to observe any new or amended By-Law having a like purpose or effect. It further provided that nothing in the decree should prevent the adoption by the Associated Press of new or amended By-Laws "which will restrict admission, provided that members in the same city and in the same 'field' (morning, evening or Sunday), as an applicant publishing a newspaper in the United States of America or its Territories, shall not have power to impose, or dispense with, any conditions upon his admission and that the By-Laws shall affirmatively declare that the effect of admission upon the ability of such applicant to compete with members in the same city and 'field' shall not be taken into consideration in passing upon his application." Some of appellants argue that this decree is vague and indefinite. They argue that it will be impossible for the Association to know whether or not its members took into consideration the competitive situation in passing upon applications for membership. We cannot agree that the decree is ambiguous. We assume, with the court below, that AP will faithfully carry out its purpose. Interpreting the decree to mean that AP news is to be furnished to competitors of old members without discrimination through By-Laws controlling membership, or otherwise, we approve it. . . .

———

Justice Roberts dissented from the Court's opinion in *Associated Press* on the grounds that AP did not in any way restrain the gathering of news, which remained open to all persons; the organization was merely a vehicle for efficiently collecting and sharing a literary product produced through the thought and research of its members. Moreover, excluded newspapers could have become affiliated with one of the other two news services. Justice Murphy dissented on grounds that the law does not require an organization that has achieved a competitive advantage by sagacity and foresight to share that advantage with competitors, and that the record did not show that AP had a purpose or effect of hampering competition. Both dissenters were concerned about governmental restraints on the press.

Questions and Comments

For what purpose was Associated Press organized? What was the purpose of the by-law that gave members a veto over participation by their local competitors? What was the purpose of the by-law that prohibited members from selling their news to nonmembers? Was the main thrust of these by-law restraints to keep the competitors out of the market and preserve the members' monopoly? Or was the purpose and probable effect to protect a member's exclusive right to a product that it had worked so hard to create (i.e., to protect it against free riders)? Was it, perhaps, a little of both? In view of *Professional Engineers, BMI, NCAA,* and *Northwest Wholesale Stationers* would the Justice Department today obtain summary judgment on the legality of the by-law?

Consider other sources of current law on the duty to share the work product or creation of a collaborative effort. Do you get guidance from the contemporary law of monopolization? In *du Pont-titanium dioxide,* was du Pont required to share its superior, but individual, technology? Even at a price? In *Berkey–Kodak,* was Kodak required to predisclose its camera and film inventions to Berkey?

Is access to collaborative work product different from access to that of a single firm? Suppose IBM and AT&T collaborated in an effort to develop breakthrough technology in data systems. They justify their joint venture on grounds that neither could hope to achieve alone the goal that they hope to achieve together. Their joint effort is successful and yields a remarkably advanced twenty-first century product which, by agreement, the joint venture sells only to IBM and AT&T. IBM greatly strengthens its position in computers and AT&T greatly strengthens its position in long-distance telephone service. Is there a violation? What violation? What remedy?

Suppose that at the start of the venture IBM agreed not to use the output of the venture in long lines telephone applications and that AT&T agreed to use the output only in such applications. Could such an arrangement be defended if (a) the venture, as a practical matter, required the participation of both firms, and (b) neither was willing to invest in the venture if the other remained free to license or supply competitors of its venture partner? Suppose, now, that the partners did not agree in advance about use of the output of the venture. After a successful collaboration, each participant exploits the output only in its own field. When asked to explain why, each answers: "Pure self interest; if we entered our partner's field or supplied or licensed our partner's competitors, it would enter our field." Is there a violation?

The *Berkey–Kodak* case, while largely a monopoly case, included a charge that Kodak had entered into two joint development agreements for flash cube attachments, one with Sylvania, and one with GE. In each agreement Kodak and its partner agreed not to disclose the invention to any other camera manufacturer. In both instances the Kodak partner developed an important new invention—the magicube by Sylvania and the flipflash by GE—and Kodak (which contributed very little to the innovation) insisted that the invention be withheld from its own competitors. The trial judge instructed the jury that it should determine whether the joint development agreements were unreasonable restraints of trade and should consider whether the legitimate ends of the agreement might have been accomplished by less restrictive alternatives. The jury found the agreement unreasonable. The court of appeals affirmed the charge (although it would have preferred a charge that asked the jury whether the restraints exceeded reasonably necessary limits). In response to Kodak's observation that a judgment for plaintiff would in effect require disclosure of innovation and thereby chill innovation, the court said: "There is a vast difference . . . between actions legal when taken by a single firm and those permitted for two or more companies acting in concert." 603 F.2d 263 (2d Cir.1979), *cert. denied,* 444 U.S. 1093 (1980). Is the court correct? The dissent from denial of certiorari, written by Justice Rehnquist, found facets of the Appeals Court decision "little less than bizarre." Justice Rehnquist rejected the idea that the Sherman Act, "designed to foster competition, requires one competitor to disclose to another, in advance of marketing a product to the general public, its plan to introduce the new product . . . ." *Id.* at 1094.

2. CONTRACTUAL RESTRAINTS SUCH AS COVENANTS NOT TO COMPETE

The parties to a joint arrangement may agree to forego their own freedom in various respects. For example, they might agree not to compete with the venture, or with other participants in the venture. We saw earlier in *Topco* that even a progressive joint venture does not necessarily legitimate competitor-partners' covenants not to compete. But what if the partners, together, do not have market power and the covenant is reasonably necessary to make the joint venture work? What if it just helps to make the joint venture more efficient? *Topco* seemed to say: That doesn't matter. Judge Bork disagrees.

ROTHERY STORAGE & VAN CO. v. ATLAS VAN LINES, INC.

792 F.2d 210 (D.C.Cir.1986), cert. denied, 479 U.S. 1033 (1987).

JUDGE BORK: Appellants, plaintiffs below, seek review of the district court's decision dismissing their antitrust action against Atlas Van Lines, Inc. ("Atlas"). Appellants are five present and three former agents of Atlas. For convenience, we will frequently refer to them by the name of the first-named appellant, Rothery Storage & Van Co. ("Rothery"). Rothery claims that Atlas and several of the carrier agents affiliated with Atlas adopted a policy constituting a "group boycott" in violation of section 1 of the Sherman Act. . . . The trial court granted Atlas' motion for summary judgment on several alternative grounds. Because we find that Atlas' policy is designed to make the van line more efficient rather than to decrease the output of its services and raise rates, we affirm.

I.

Atlas operates as a nationwide common carrier of used household goods under authority granted by the Interstate Commerce Commission. It contracts to provide moving services to individuals and to businesses transferring employees. Like most national moving companies, Atlas exercises its interstate authority by employing independent moving companies throughout the country as its agents. . . .

* * *

The deregulation of the moving industry, beginning in 1979, produced changes that had a profound impact on the relationship between van lines and their agents. Prior to the regulatory changes, independent moving companies had little ability to obtain their own interstate transportation authority. The ICC's Policy Statement on Motor Carrier Regulation (1979), and the Motor Carrier Act of 1980, greatly increased the ability of common carriers to obtain interstate moving authority. In 1981, moreover, the ICC repealed its requirement that carrier agents [agents with their own interstate authority] charge the same rate for agency shipments and shipments carried on their own accounts. Thus, agents could obtain interstate authority and could cut prices to attract business for their own accounts that otherwise might have constituted agency shipments for the van line's account.

This increased potential for the diversion of interstate business to its carrier agents posed free-rider problems for Atlas. . . .

To meet these problems . . . Atlas announced that it would terminate the agency contract of any affiliated company that persisted in handling interstate carriage on its own account as well as for Atlas. Under the new policy, any carrier agent already affiliated with Atlas could continue to exercise independent interstate authority only by transferring its independent interstate authority to a separate corporation with a new name. These new entities could not use the facilities or services of Atlas or any of its affiliates.

II.

Because Atlas and its affiliates refuse to deal with any carrier agent that does not comply, several Atlas carrier agents, appellants here, charged that Atlas' new policy constitutes a "group boycott." They filed this action, and after the completion of discovery on the issue of liability, both sides filed cross motions for summary judgment.

The district court granted summary judgment to Atlas.

* * *

While we do not agree that the challenged arrangement lacks the elements of a horizontal agreement, we uphold the trial judge's conclusion that Atlas' new policy does not offend the antitrust laws. The challenged restraint is ancillary to the economic integration of Atlas and its agents so that the rule of per se illegality does not apply. Neither are the other tests of the rule of reason offended since Atlas' market share is far too small for the restraint to threaten competition or to have been intended to do so. . . .

III.

* * *

Since the restraint on competition within the Atlas system involves an agreement not to deal with those who do not comply with Atlas' policy, and so may be characterized as a boycott, or a concerted refusal to deal, Rothery contends that Supreme Court decisions require a holding of per se illegality. It cannot be denied that the Court has often enunciated that broad proposition. . . .

Despite the seeming inflexibility of the rule as enunciated by the Court, it has always been clear that boycotts are not, and cannot ever be, per se illegal. To apply so rigid and simplistic an approach would be to destroy many common and entirely beneficial business arrangements. . . .[1]

The Supreme Court has now made explicit what had always been understood. In *Northwest Wholesale Stationers, Inc. v. Pacific Stationery & Printing Co.*, 472 U.S. 284 (1985), the plaintiff, a stationer, challenged as per se illegal its expulsion from a wholesale purchasing cooperative for violating the group's bylaws. The Court said that "not all concerted refusals to deal should be accorded *per se* treatment." . . . It is sufficient for present purposes to note that appellants' contention about the per se illegality of all boycotts has now been squarely rejected by the Supreme Court.

IV.

Appellants contend, however, that Atlas' restraints include horizontal price maintenance since the agents must ship on rates established by Atlas. We take this to be a claim that the horizontal elimination of competition within the system is illegal per se or, failing that, is nevertheless unlawful under a rule-of-reason analysis.

Before turning to the case law, we analyze the economic nature and effects of the system Atlas has created. It will be seen to be a system of a very familiar type, one commonly used in many fields of commercial endeavor.

Atlas has required that any moving company doing business as its agent must not conduct independent interstate carrier operations. Thus, a carrier agent, in order to continue as an Atlas agent, must either abandon its independent interstate authority and operate only under Atlas' authority or create a new corporation (a "carrier affiliate") to conduct interstate carriage separate from its operation as an Atlas agent. Atlas' agents may deal only with Atlas or other Atlas agents.

The result of this is an interstate system for the carriage of household goods in which legally separate companies integrate their activities by contract. In this way the participants achieve many of the same benefits

---

1. The truth of this may be easily demonstrated. When a law firm refuses to hire an applicant there is a concerted refusal to deal since the lawyers in the firm are separate legal entities and capable of practicing law independently. It is also a boycott if the Ivy League refuses to admit a new college to membership or the American League refuses to admit a baseball team. It is no less a boycott if any of these groups refuses to deal because the applicant's grades are too low, or its football program has standards unacceptable to the Ivy League, or the would-be baseball franchise is currently a slowpitch softball team in an industrial league. A ruling that concerted refusals to deal are per se illegal would mean that Atlas not only must retain carrier agents that compete with it but must admit as an agent any trucker who applied regardless of the need for an additional agent, the trucker's financial condition, its safety record, or its ability to serve customers. That is what a per se rule means: no group may impose a standard of any kind as a condition of dealing. That nonsensical requirement would destroy all of the groups concerned or force them into one ownership in order to claim the immunity of the *Copperweld* rule [467 U.S. 725 (1984)].

or efficiencies that would be available if they were integrated through ownership by Atlas. At the outset of this opinion, we set out the functions performed by Atlas and by the agents and stated that the system is a contract integration, one identical, in economic terms, to a partnership formed by agreement. Analysis might begin and end with the observation that Atlas and its agents command between 5.1 and 6% of the relevant market, which is the interstate carriage of used household goods. It is impossible to believe that an agreement to eliminate competition within a group of that size can produce any of the evils of monopoly. A monopolist (or those acting together to achieve monopoly results) enhances its revenues by raising the market price. It can do that only if its share of the market is so large that by reducing its output of goods or services the amount offered by the industry is substantially reduced so that the price is bid up. If a group of Atlas' size reduced its output of services, there would be no effect upon market price because firms making up the other 94% of the market would simply take over the abandoned business. The only effect would be a loss of revenues to Atlas. Indeed, so impotent to raise prices is a firm with a market share of 5 or 6% that any attempt by it to engage in a monopolistic restriction of output would be little short of suicidal.

Appellants argue that Atlas' 6% national market share understates the market power of Atlas and its agents to impose an anticompetitive result because appellants introduced evidence of the existence of distinct product geographic submarkets and because of evidence that the national market "approximates a tight oligopoly." Each of these propositions is wrong. With respect to the existence of submarkets, plaintiffs conceded the existence of a nationwide market and did not offer the district court any evidence that created a genuine issue of material fact as to the existence of submarkets. The district judge, therefore, had only the national market before him. Indeed, so clear is the state of the evidence that we would affirm on this basis even if we thought it was not the rationale of the district court's decision.

The criteria for defining markets are well-known. Because the ability of consumers to turn to other suppliers restrains a firm from raising prices above the competitive level, the definition of the "relevant market" rests on a determination of available substitutes. As Professor Sullivan has stated:

> To define a market in product and geographic terms is to say that if prices were appreciably raised or volume appreciably curtailed for the product within a given area, while demand held constant, supply from other sources could not be expected to enter promptly enough and in large enough amounts to restore the old price and volume.

L. Sullivan, *Antitrust* § 12, at 41 (1977). The degree to which a similar product will be substituted for the product in question is said to measure the cross-elasticity of demand, while the capability of other production facilities to be converted to produce a substitutable product is referred to as the cross-elasticity of supply. The higher these cross-elasticities, the more likely it is that similar products or the capacity of production facilities now used for other purposes are to be counted in the relevant market.

* * *

All that was before the district court, and all that is before us, therefore, is a nationwide market. Atlas, it is agreed, did 6% of the business in that market. And the relevance of this figure as a measure of market power is in no way diminished by appellants' fanciful claims of "tight oligopoly" in the national market.

Given the fact that this industry consists of 1100 to 1300 interstate carriers, employing about 8000 agents, it would seem to be impossible to entertain any notion of market power. What plaintiffs offered to support their theory of "tight oligopoly" was a list of van lines and market shares that affirmatively proved their market power contention to be chimerical.

* * *

We might well rest, therefore, upon the absence of market power as demonstrated both by Atlas' 6% national market share and by the structure of the market. If it is clear that Atlas and its agents by eliminating competition among themselves are not attempting to restrict industry output, then their agreement must be designed to make the conduct of their business more effective. No third possibility suggests itself. But we need not rely entirely upon that inference because the record made in the district court demonstrates that the challenged agreement enhances the efficiency of the van line. The chief efficiency, as already noted, is the elimination of the problem of the free ride.

A carrier agent can attract customers because of Atlas' "national image" and can use Atlas' equipment and order forms when undertaking carriage for its own account. The carrier agents "benefit from use of the services of moving and storage firms affiliated with Atlas, for origin or destination work at remote locations, when operating independently of Atlas." This benefit involves not only the availability of a reliable network of firms providing such services, but also includes the benefit of Atlas' "mediating collection matters" among its affiliates. To the degree that a carrier agent uses Atlas' reputation, equipment, facilities, and services in conducting business for its own profit, the agent enjoys a free ride at Atlas' expense. The problem is that the van line's incentive to spend for reputation, equipment, facilities, and services declines as it receives less of the benefit from them. That produces a deterioration of the system's efficiency because the things consumers desire are not provided in the amounts they are willing to pay for. In the extreme case, the system as a whole could collapse.

By their own assertions, appellants establish that the carrier agents in the Atlas organization have benefited from Atlas' business infrastructure in carrying shipments made for their own accounts. . . . We find the district court's conclusion that free riding existed to be amply supported and by no means clearly erroneous.

A few examples will suffice. Plaintiff-appellants conceded below that the carrier agents "benefited" from their association with Atlas' "national image." We cannot rationally infer that this consumer identification advantage did not benefit the carrier agents in operating on their own accounts while using Atlas equipment and personnel trained by Atlas. Rothery also allowed that, while the carrier agents bore the bulk of costs associated with their operations, Atlas did make "some small contributions" to the group advertising programs and "some contributions" to the painting of trucks on which the Atlas logo appeared.

Rothery also credited Atlas with providing a dispatching service, a clearinghouse service for the settlement of accounts among its affiliates, assistance in settling claims among affiliates, certain written forms, sales meetings to provide exposure to national customers, driver and employee training programs, and the screening of the quality and reliability of affiliated firms that provided origin and destination services for the carrier agents.

Rothery did not assert in its Statement of Material Undisputed Facts, nor may we infer, that the carrier agents could not avail themselves of the benefits derived from these services when operating for their own accounts. Many of these services confer intangible advantages that redound to the benefit of the carrier agent as a whole, and do not admit of easy segregation as between shipments on Atlas' interstate authority and shipments on the carrier agent's authority. For example, if Atlas provides superior training to the employees of its carrier agents, that training improves the quality of work not only on shipments undertaken for Atlas but also on shipments made on the carrier agent's own interstate authority. And because carrier agents may elect to use their own or Atlas' interstate authority for a given shipment, exposure to national clients at Atlas' sales meetings can provide them with interstate customers for their own, as well as for Atlas', accounts.

These examples are not exhaustive, but they illustrate the point. Even though entitled to every favorable inference, Rothery, in light of the facts it deemed undisputed below, could not seriously contend that the carrier agents' association with Atlas did not provide them with benefits that aided them in conducting business in competition with Atlas. Thus, because the plaintiff-appellants asserted that the carrier agents paid Atlas only for its clearinghouse service and for the provision of written forms, we agree with the district court's finding that many of the services supplied as part of Atlas' arrangement with the carrier agents' arrangement resulted in Atlas subsidizing its competitors.

If the carrier agents could persist in competing with Atlas while deriving the advantages of their Atlas affiliation, Atlas might well have found it desirable, or even essential, to decrease or abandon many such services. . . . Of that tendency there can be no doubt. When a person or business providing goods or services begins to receive declining revenues, then, other things being equal, that person or firm will provide fewer goods or services. As marginal revenue drops, so does output. Thus, when Atlas' centralized services, equipment, and national image amount to a subsidy of competing carrier agents, this cuts down the marginal revenue derived from the provision of such things so that less will be offered than the market would reward.

On the other side, the firm receiving a subsidized good or service will take more of it. As cost declines, then, other things being equal, demand increases. Carrier agents, that is, will increase the use of Atlas' services, etc., on interstate carriage for their own accounts, over-consuming that which they can obtain at less than its true cost. In this way, free riding distorts the economic signals within the system so that the van line loses effectiveness in serving consumers. The restraint at issue in this case, therefore, is a classic attempt to counter the perceived menace that free riding poses. By compelling carrier agents to transfer their interstate authority to a separate entity, Atlas can continue providing services at optimal levels, confident that it will be paid for those services.

The Atlas agreements thus produce none of the evils of monopoly but enhance consumer welfare by creating efficiency. There seems no reason in the rationale of the Sherman Act, or in any comprehensible policy, to invalidate such agreements. Nevertheless, at one, intermediate, point in the history of antitrust, Supreme Court decisions seemed to require just that result. It seems clear, however, that the law has returned to the original understanding so that the agreements before us are plainly lawful. . . .

[A lengthy analysis of the case law follows.]

At one time, as we have seen, the Supreme Court stated in *Topco* and *Sealy* that the rule for all horizontal restraints was one of per se illegality. The difficulty was that such a rule could not be enforced consistently because it would have meant the outlawing of very normal agreements (such as that of law partners not to practice law outside the firm) that obviously contributed to economic efficiency. The alternative formulation was that of Judge Taft in *Addyston Pipe & Steel:* a naked horizontal restraint, one that does not accompany a contract integration, can have no purpose other than restricting output and raising prices, and so is illegal per se; an ancillary horizontal restraint, one that is part of an integration of the economic activities of the parties and appears capable of enhancing the group's efficiency, is to be judged according to its purpose and effect. In *BMI, NCAA,* and *Pacific Stationery,* the Supreme Court returned the law to the formulation of *Addyston Pipe & Steel* and thus effectively overruled *Topco* and *Sealy* as to the per se illegality of all horizontal restraints.

The application of these principles to Atlas' restraints is obvious because, as we have seen, these restraints are ancillary to the contract integration or joint venture that constitutes the Atlas van line. The restraints preserve the efficiencies of the nationwide van line by eliminating the problem of the free ride. There is, on the other hand, no possibility that the restraints can suppress market competition and so decrease output. Atlas has 6% or less of the relevant market, far too little to make even conceivable an adverse effect upon output. If Atlas should reduce its output, it would merely shrink in size without having any impact upon market price. Under the rule of *Addyston Pipe & Steel, BMI, NCAA,* and *Pacific Stationery,* therefore, it follows that the Atlas agreements do not violate section 1 of the Sherman Act.[11]

11. Two additional points should be made. First, we do not think it significant to the outcome that Atlas' policy allowed agents to exercise their own interstate authority through separate corporations. Once it is clear that restraints can only be intended to enhance efficiency rather than to restrict output, the degree of restraint is a matter of business rather than legal judgment. Second, though it is sometimes said

A joint venture made more efficient by ancillary restraints, is a fusion of the productive capacities of the members of the venture. That, in economic terms, is the same thing as a corporate merger. Merger policy has always proceeded by drawing lines about allowable market shares and these lines are based on rough estimates of effects because that is all the nature of the problem allows. If Atlas bought the stock of all its carrier agents, the merger would not even be challenged under the Department of Justice Merger Guidelines because of inferences drawn from Atlas' market share and the structure of the market. We can think of no good reason not to apply the same inferences to Atlas' ancillary restraints.

JUDGE WALD, concurring: I concur in the result and in much of the reasoning of the panel's opinion. I write separately, however, to point out several concerns that I have about the panel's analysis once it establishes that no *per se* violation existed and the restraint should be looked at under the rule of reason. I believe that the District Court correctly undertook, in the traditional way, to "carefully balance" the "anticompetitive evils of the challenged practice . . . against its procompetitive virtues." *Smith v. Pro Football, Inc.*, 593 F.2d 1173, 1183 (D.C.Cir.1978). In fact, at one point the panel concedes that the record made in the District Court demonstrates, even without reliance on inferences drawn from market power, "that the challenged agreement enhances the efficiency of the van lines." I am uncomfortable, therefore, with the panel's suggestions that the District Court's balancing was unnecessary, and indeed a useless exercise.

The panel concludes that no balancing was required here since a defendant lacking significant market power cannot act anticompetitively by reducing output and increasing prices. If, as the panel assumes, the *only* legitimate purpose of the antitrust laws is this concern with the potential for decrease in output and rise in prices, reliance on market power alone might be appropriate.[1] But, I do not believe that the debate over the purposes of antitrust laws has been settled yet.[2] Until the

that, in the case of restraints like these, it is necessary to weigh procompetitive effects against anticompetitive effects, we do not think that a useable formula if it implies an ability to quantify the two effects and compare the values found. Here, there are no anticompetitive effects and so there is nothing to place on that side of the scale. If the underlying contract integration is lawful, *i.e.*, not of such size as to violate the Sherman Act, restraints ancillary to the integration, in the sense we have described, should be lawful. Weighing effects in any direct sense will usually be beyond judicial capabilities but predictions about effects may be reflected in rules about allowable size. The concurrence appears to suggest that the district court conducted a balancing of effects in some fashion other than by drawing inferences from market share and structure. If so, the district court did not explain its alternative method and made no findings on the subject. Nor does the concurrence articu-

late an alternative means of weighing procompetitive and anticompetitive effects.

1. In *Northwest Wholesale Stationers, Inc. v. Pacific Stationery & Printing Co.*, 472 U.S. 284 (1985), the Court held that the *per se* rule of illegality did not apply absent an allegation that the "cooperative possesses market power or unique access to a business element necessary for effective competition." Since the plaintiffs had not alleged any such market advantage, the Court remanded for rule of reason analysis. According to the panel's analysis, plaintiff's failure to allege market power should have been determinative of the rule of reason inquiry as well. Nothing in *BMI*, *NCAA*, or *Pacific Stationery* supports the panel's new *per se* rule of legality.

2. *Compare* Bork, *The Antitrust Paradox* (1978) (only goal is to increase economic efficiency); R. Posner, *Antitrust Law: An Economic Perspective* (1976) (efficiency is not

Supreme Court provides more definitive instruction in this regard,[3] I think it premature to construct an antitrust test that ignores all other potential concerns of the antitrust laws except for restriction of output and price raising.

The panel also suggests that even if some kind of balancing[4] were appropriate, the only feasible way of doing it would be to use market share as a surrogate for anticompetitive effects. ("Though it is sometimes said that in cases of restrictions like these, it is necessary to weigh procompetitive effects against anticompetitive effects, we do not think that a usable formula. . . . Weighing effects in any direct sense will usually be beyond judicial capabilities but predictions about effects may be reflected in rules about allowable size."). I acknowledge that traditional rule of reason balancing does not lend itself to neat equations, or percentages, or even Herfindahl–Hirschman indices providing a definitive answer. Nonetheless, to my knowledge, the Supreme Court has so far not decided rule of reason cases solely by looking at market shares. Instead, it has looked to the totality of circumstances surrounding a restraint to determine whether, on balance, it constitutes an unreasonable restraint of trade. *See, e.g., N.C.A.A. v. Board of Regents of the University of Oklahoma,* 468 U.S. 85, (1984) (looking at asserted procompetitive virtues even after determining that defendant had monopoly power); *Broadcast Music Industries v. CBS,* 441 U.S. 1 (1979) (instructing lower court to take procompetitive virtues of blanket licensing into account even though defendants had huge market shares).[5]

Until the Supreme Court indicates that the *only* goal of antitrust law is to promote efficiency, as the panel uses that term, I think it more prudent to proceed with a pragmatic, albeit nonarithmetic and even untidy rule of reason analysis, than to adopt a market power test as the

only important goal, it is the only goal of antitrust law) *with* Pitofsky, *The Political Content of Antitrust,* 127 U.Pa.L.Rev. 1051 (1979) (antitrust laws promote political values including fear of excessive concentration of economic power and a desire to enhance individual and business freedom); Schwartz, *"Justice" and Other Non–Economic Goals of Antitrust,* 127 U.Pa.L.Rev. 1076, 1076 (1979) ("putative economic gains should not be the exclusive or decisive factors in resolving antitrust controversies"); Lande, *Wealth Transfers as the Original and Primary Concern of Antitrust: The Efficiency Interpretation Challenged,* 32 Hastings L.J. 65, 68 (1983) ("Congress passed the antitrust laws to further economic objectives, but primarily objectives of a distributive rather than of an efficiency nature"); *see generally Symposium: The Goals of Antitrust: A Dialogue on Policy,* 65 Colum.L.Rev. 33 (1965).

3. I do not think that *Reiter v. Sonotone,* 442 U.S. 330, 343 (1979), answers the question. There, the Court was asked to decide whether consumers who purchase goods for their own use have standing to sue under section 4 of the Clayton Act. It is thus hardly surprising that the Court answered

the question by saying that the floor debates suggest that Congress designed the Sherman Act as a "consumer welfare prescription." *Id.* Moreover, even if one thinks that the Court intended to exclude all other considerations, the phrase "consumer welfare" surely includes far more than simple economic efficiency.

4. I am also somewhat troubled by the panel's statement that "[o]nce it is clear that restraints can only be intended to enhance efficiency rather than to restrict output, the degree of restraint is a matter of business rather than legal judgment." I understand the panel's position to be that the breadth of the restraint is a matter to be analyzed in determining whether the restraint is ancillary in the first place. If the restraint is not ancillary, it is a naked restraint, subject to the *per se* rule of illegality.

5. Although both of these examples involve the Court's balancing of potential procompetitive virtues against a market power presumption of anticompetitiveness, the panel's argument that genuine balancing is technically impossible would seem to apply there as well.

exclusive filtering-out device for all potential violaters who do not command a significant market share. Under any analysis, market power is an important consideration; I am not yet willing to say it is the only one.[6]

Questions and Comments

Is Judge Bork correct that, after *BMI, NCAA* and *Northwest Wholesale Stationers,* horizontal restraints accompanied by some integration are legal unless they limit output? Has *Topco* been overruled?

Is Judge Bork correct that weighing anticompetitive against procompetitive effects is beyond judicial competence? Is Judge Bork correct that only by adopting his model (restraints that do not limit output are legal per se) can judges work within the area of their competence? Can this view be reconciled with the existence of the antitrust laws?

While extolling restraints that protect against free riding, does Bork ignore inefficiency properties of the restraint? Are there efficiency properties inherent in preserving the carriers' freedom to compete against Atlas? Are there net efficiencies or inefficiencies? Properly approached, does the efficiency inquiry require balancing?

Rothery is representative of Chicago School logic but is not necessarily a bellwether for the law. For a contemporary boycott case with a different style and approach, see *Koefoot v. American College of Surgeons,* 692 F.Supp. 843 (N.D.Ill.1988); 610 F.Supp. 1298 (N.D.Ill.1985); 1987–1 Trade Cas. (CCH) ¶ 67,508–511 (N.D.Ill.1987).

Indiana Federation of Dentists was decided after *Rothery.* Is Judge Bork's approach consistent with the analysis in the *Dentists* case? In *NCAA?* Note that the Bork opinion draws heavily on the style of analysis in *Addyston Pipe.* Even if the extremes of the Bork view are undermined by recent Supreme Court cases, could you draw from *Rothery* a model for analysis that would be consistent with cases such as *BMI, NCAA* and *Indiana Federation of Dentists?*

Problems

1. Brunswick and Yamaha form a joint venture to produce outboard motors in Japan. Brunswick is number two in the very highly concentrated U.S. market. Yamaha is a potential entrant into the U.S. market. The joint venture will sell its motors half to Brunswick and half to Yamaha. Yamaha agrees not to sell these or any other outboard motors in the United States.

6. In addition to my doctrinal difficulties with the panel's approach, I am also concerned about its heavy reliance on the 6% figure representing Atlas' share of the national market for intercity transport of used household goods. Although the panel concludes that the national market was not *sufficiently* contested as the only relevant market to establish a genuine issue of fact, the fact remains that the exclusivity of that market was indeed contested before the District Court and the District Court made no findings on the issue. Conceding that the national market was *a* relevant market, plaintiffs went on to explain that within the national market, there are product submarkets of new and used household goods shipments and submarkets divided according to the type of shipment, including national account, government and c.o.d. shipments, and including long-haul and short-haul shipments. Geographically, markets are national, regional and local.

Plaintiffs produced *affidavits and other evidence* for the proposition that these were separate markets, and that in some of the geographic markets, Atlas' market shares were 30% and 40%, and in one large geographic market, 60%. . . .

Assume for the moment that the joint venture is not in essence anticompetitive. This might be the case if, for example, there were several other more likely potential entrants, and the joint venture enabled Brunswick to develop a new line of outboard motors that it could not otherwise make. Is the covenant not to compete legal or illegal? How would Judge Bork look at the covenant? How does this covenant differ from the covenants in *Rothery?* Would the covenant protect against free rider effects? Could a plaintiff prove that it probably restricts output? Is it possible to condemn the covenant without such a showing? See *Brunswick Corp. v. FTC,* 657 F.2d 971 (8th Cir. 1981), *cert. denied,* 456 U.S. 915 (1982). (We discuss this case further in Chapter 5).

2. Worthen Bank and Trust Company is a member of an issuing bank for National Bankamericard, Inc. (NBI) and Interbank/Master Charge (MC). NBI and MC are the only national bank credit card systems in the country. Issuing banks for NBI issue cards, extend credit, perform various functions necessary to maintain the system, pay fees to defray expenses, and earn dividends. NBI's by-laws prohibit its issuing banks from being an issuing bank in any other national credit card organization. Worthen sues to enjoin enforcement of the by-law. Asserting that the by law is illegal per se, it moves for summary judgment. NBI defends the restriction as necessary to preserve competition between the two national bank card systems. You are the judge. Do you grant summary judgment? See *Worthen Bank & Trust Co. v. National Bank-Americard Inc.,* 485 F.2d 119 (8th Cir.1973), *cert. denied,* 415 U.S. 918 (1974).

3. IS THE JOINT VENTURE ANTICOMPETITIVE IN ESSENCE?

When we analyze a joint ventures we ask these questions: (1) Is it anticompetitive in essence (that is, at its core)? (2) Does it contain unreasonably anticompetitive covenants or restrictions? (3) Must it grant access to competitors who want to join? We started this section with analysis of the duty to grant access. We proceeded to examine ancillary restraints that might be anticompetitive while assuming that the combination itself was essentially reasonable. Now we turn to whether the venture is anticompetitive—do the participants, through their integration in the venture, aggregate so much power that the integration itself is anticompetitive. We will treat this question briefly here; it is treated more fully in the merger chapter, Chapter 5. As you will note, sometimes questions of essential reasonableness and of reasonableness of restraints become intertwined.

Can we assume that a joint venture is not in essence anticompetitive if the partners together do not have market power and their purpose is to combine talents, skills and other resources in order to invent or produce or market more cheaply than they could do otherwise? Have you seen any cases that would so suggest? Does *Northwest Wholesale Stationers* have implications here? Is a venture essentially procompetitive (even if the participants have market power) if it yields significant advantages to consumers in the form of otherwise unavailable "new products" or services, significant efficiencies, or other competitive advantages, and if competitive harms are adequately protected against? What do you learn from *Terminal Railroads? Associated Press? BMI?* Can we assume that a venture is in essence anticompetitive if the participants have substantial market power and the venture does not yield significant competitive advantages or does not adequately protect against anticompetitive tendencies?

Problems

1. Producer-distributors A, B, C and D distribute their films to movie theatres, then to network television, and then to cable television. They account for approximately one third of the movies available for cable television, and they receive about one half of all revenues paid by cable television companies for movies that have been exhibited first in theatres. Movies, especially the successful films of the big movie companies, are the mainstay of cable television, and successful movies—box office hits—are scarce.

Home Box Office (HBO) is the dominant cable television network. (It licenses programming from the producer/distributors, packages it, and provides it to the cable operators). It also produces some films itself which it distributes to cable operators and to other outlets by licensing others. HBO accounts for more than 80% of the cable network market. As a result of its buying power, it is able to bargain for low prices in dealing with the movie companies.

Movie production companies are dissatisfied with the revenues they derive from cable television. Several of the larger ones decide to form their own cable television network, Premiere, to compete with HBO. In order to facilitate Premier's entry into the cable market, the movie companies wish to assure Premiere sufficient product as well as a distinctive package of films. Therefore they agree to make all of their films available to Premiere for the first cable run of these films, and to make those films available to no other cable network for the first nine months of cable release.

Does the Premiere joint venture lessen competition? Or does it increase competition in cable distribution and by doing so increase incentives of movie makers to produce films? Is the intent of the joint venturers relevant? Does it matter if one joint venturer said that his goal was to eliminate HBO? If he said that his goal was to pressure HBO into paying more for licenses? See *United States v. Columbia Pictures Industries, Inc.,* 507 F.Supp. 412 (S.D.N.Y. 1980).

2. There are three minority-owned architectural firms in the Nashville area. The state airport authority is letting contracts for reconstruction of the airport in Nashville and must satisfy a minority set-aside provision (approximately 10% of the project) in order to get federal funding. The three firms, each of which feels that it has been discriminated against in the past and that standing alone it will never get more than a token 10% project, form a joint venture called COMPACT. By aggregating their individual capabilities they hope that they will have a shot at a major participation in the project. The joint venturers agree that they will not bid individually on any project targeted by COMPACT. COMPACT bids for a major participation in the Nashville airport project and loses. In a token attempt to satisfy the set-aside requirements the airport authority awards an access-road project to a minority architect in Atlanta who happens to be licensed in Tennessee. COMPACT sues, alleging a civil rights violation, and it is met with an antitrust defense. Is COMPACT anticompetitive and therefore illegal? Is the agreement not to

compete on targeted projects illegal per se? Does the set-aside statute create a market of minority architects? In *Compact v. Metropolitan Government of Nashville,* 594 F.Supp. 1567 (M.D.Tenn.1984), *remanded,* 786 F.2d 227 (1986), the court held that COMPACT was illegal. Argue its case.

J. CONTRACT, COMBINATION AND CONSPIRACY

1. CIRCUMSTANTIAL EVIDENCE OF CONCERT

Look again at the language of Section 1 of the Sherman Act. As a condition to the finding of a violation, it requires collaboration by two or more parties or actors. It prohibits restraints of trade only if they are achieved by contract, combination or conspiracy. When dealing with joint ventures, or with other modes of joint action that are concededly subject to the rule of reason, there is usually no serious issue about whether concerted action is involved. Separate and otherwise competitive firms have openly combined forces to attain a joint end; legality turns on power, purpose and effect. But joint conduct fairly characterized as cartelization is blatantly anticompetitive and clearly unlawful. When it occurs, those participating can be expected to proceed in clandestine ways. In such instances determining whether joint action occurred may be the major or even the only issue presented.

Thus far in this chapter concert of action has usually been clear or presumed. In this section it is not. Here we ask: (1) What does Section 1 of the Sherman Act mean by "contract, combination, or conspiracy"? (2) What constitutes sufficient evidence from which the fact-finder may find that defendants' conduct occurred pursuant to contract, combination or conspiracy?

The first question is a one of law. Does the law require an explicit agreement? If not, what will suffice? Must there be at least a nod or wink which might be read as accepting a proposed course of action? What if all competitors simply follow a common course of action because each knows that all will be better off if they follow the same path?

Explicit agreement is not necessary; an understanding is enough. But what suffices for an "understanding" and where is the borderline between consciously parallel but unconcerted conduct and "combination"?

In this section we treat three important cases. Two of them, *Interstate Circuit* and *Theatre Enterprises,* date from early in the period of structural consensus; the third, *Matsushita,* is a recent decision. We also examine several cases between these poles. We start with *Interstate Circuit.*

INTERSTATE CIRCUIT, INC. v. UNITED STATES
306 U.S. 208 (1939).

JUSTICE STONE: . . . The case is now before us on findings of the District Court specifically stating that appellants did in fact agree with each other to enter into and carry out the contracts, which the court found to result in unreasonable and therefore unlawful restraints of interstate commerce.

Appellants comprise the two groups of defendants in the District Court. The members of one group of eight corporations which are distributors of motion picture films, and the Texas agents of two of them. The other group, corporations and individuals engaged in exhibiting motion pictures in Texas, and some of them in New Mexico, appeals in [Case] No. 269. The distributor appellants are engaged in the business of distributing in interstate commerce motion picture films, copyrights on which they own or control, for exhibition in theatres throughout the United States. They distribute about 75 per cent. of all first-class feature films exhibited in the United States. . . .

The exhibitor group of appellants consists of Interstate Circuit, Inc., and Texas Consolidated Theatres, Inc., and Hoblitzelle and O'Donnell, who are respectively president and general manager of both and in active charge of their business operations. The two corporations are affiliated with each other and with Paramount Pictures Distributing Co., Inc., one of the distributor appellants.

Interstate operates forty-three first-run and second-run motion picture theatres, located in six Texas cities.[1] It has a complete monopoly of first-run theatres in these cities, except for one in Houston operated by one distributor's Texas agent. In most of these theatres the admission price for adults for the better seats at night is 40 cents or more. Interstate also operates several subsequent-run theatres in each of these cities, twenty-two in all, but in all but Galveston there are other subsequent-run theatres which compete with both its first- and subsequent-run theatres in those cities.

Texas Consolidated operates sixty-six theatres, some first- and some subsequent-run houses, in various cities and towns in the Rio Grande Valley and elsewhere in Texas and in New Mexico. In some of these cities there are no competing theatres, and in six leading cities there are no competing first-run theatres. It has no theatres in the six Texas cities in which Interstate operates. That Interstate and Texas Consolidated dominate the motion picture business in the cities where their theatres are located is indicated by the fact that at the time of the contracts in question Interstate and Consolidated each contributed more than 74 per cent, of all the license fees paid by the motion picture theatres in their respective territories to the distributor appellants.

On July 11, 1934, following a previous communication on the subject to the eight branch managers of the distributor appellants, O'Donnell, the manager of Interstate and Consolidated, sent to each of them a letter [3] on

---

1. A first-run theatre is one in which a picture is first exhibited in any given locality. A subsequent-run theatre is one in which there is a subsequent exhibition of the same picture in the same locality.

3. The letter follows:

INTERSTATE CIRCUIT, INC.,

Majestic Theatre Building,

Dallas, Texas,

July 11, 1934.

Messrs.: J.B. Dugger, Herbert MacIntyre, Sol Sachs, C.E. Hilgers, Leroy Bickel, J.B. Underwood, E.S. Olsmyth, Doak Roberts.

GENTLEMEN: On April 25th, the writer notified you that in purchasing product for the coming season 34–35, it would be necessary

the letterhead of Interstate, each letter naming all of them as addressees, in which he asked compliance with two demands as a condition of Interstate's continued exhibition of the distributors' films in its 'A' or first-run theatres at a night admission of 40 cents or more.[4] One demand was that the distributors "agree that in selling their product to subsequent runs, that this 'A' product will never be exhibited at any time or in any theatre at a smaller admission price than 25¢ for adults in the evening." The other was that "on 'A' pictures which are exhibited at a night admission of 40¢ or more—they shall never be exhibited in conjunction with another feature picture under the so-called policy of double features." The letter added that with respect to the "Rio Grande Valley situation," with which Consolidated alone was concerned, "We must insist that all pictures exhibited in our 'A' theatres at a maximum night admission price of 35¢ must also be restricted to subsequent runs in the Valley at 25¢."

The admission price customarily charged for preferred seats at night in independently operated subsequent-run theatres in Texas at the time of these letters was less than 25 cents. In seventeen of the eighteen independent theatres of this kind whose operations were described by witnesses the admission price was less than 25 cents. In one only was it 25 cents. In most of them the admission was 15 cents or less. It was also the general practice in those theatres to provide double bills either on certain days of the week or with any feature picture which was weak in drawing power. The distributor appellants had generally provided in their license contracts for a minimum admission price of 10 or 15 cents,

for all distributors to take into consideration in the sale of subsequent runs that Interstate Circuit, Inc., will not agree to purchase product to be exhibited in its 'A' theatres at a price of 40¢ or more for night admission, unless distributors agree that in selling their product to subsequent runs, that this 'A' product will never be exhibited at any time or in any theatre at a smaller admission price than 25¢ for adults in the evening.

In addition to this price restriction, we also request that on 'A' pictures which are exhibited at a night admission price of 40¢ or more—they shall never be exhibited in conjunction with another feature picture under the so-called policy of double-features.

At this time the writer desires to again remind you of these restrictions due to the fact that there may be some delay in consummating all our feature film deals for the coming season, and it is imperative that in your negotiations that you afford us this clearance.

In the event that a distributor sees fit to sell his product to subsequent runs in violation of this request, it definitely means that we cannot negotiate for his product to be exhibited in our 'A' theatres at top admission prices.

We naturally, in purchasing subsequent runs from the distributors in certain of our cities, must necessarily eliminate double featuring and maintain the maximum 25¢ admission price, which we are willing to do.

Right at this time the writer wishes to call your attention to the Rio Grande Valley situation. We must insist that all pictures exhibited in our 'A' theatres at a maximum night admission price of 35¢ must also be restricted to subsequent runs in the Valley at 25¢. Regardless of the number of days which may intervene, we feel that in exploiting and selling the distributors' product, that subsequent runs should be restricted to at least a 25¢ admission scale.

The writer will appreciate your acknowledging your complete understanding of this letter.

Sincerely,

(Signed) R.J. O'DONNELL,

4. A Class 'A' picture is a "feature picture" having five reels or more of film each approximately 1,000 feet in length, shown in theatres of the specified Texas cities charging 40 cents or more for adult admission at night. Approximately fifty per cent. of the pictures released by the distributor defendants in Texas cities in 1934–1935 were Class 'A' pictures.

and three of them had included provisions restricting double-billing. But none was at any time previously subject to contractual compulsion to continue the restrictions. The trial court found that the proposed restrictions constituted an important departure from prior practice.

The local representatives of the distributors, having no authority to enter into the proposed agreements, communicated the proposal to their home offices. Conferences followed between Hoblitzelle and O'Donnell, acting for Interstate and Consolidated, and the representatives of the various distributors. In these conferences each distributor was represented by its local branch manager and by one or more superior officials from outside the state of Texas. In the course of them each distributor agreed with Interstate for the 1934–35 season to impose both the demanded restrictions upon their subsequent-run licensees in the six Texas cities served by Interstate, except Austin and Galveston. While only two of the distributors incorporated the agreement to impose the restrictions in their license contracts with Interstate, the evidence establishes, and it is not denied, that all joined in the agreement, four of them after some delay in negotiating terms other than the restrictions and not now material. These agreements for the restrictions—with the immaterial exceptions noted—were carried into effect by each of the distributors' imposing them on their subsequent-run licensees in the four Texas cities during the 1934–35 season. One agreement, that of Metro–Goldwyn–Mayer Distributing Corporation, was for three years. The others were renewed in the two following seasons and all were in force when the present suit was begun.

* * *

The trial court found that the distributor appellants agreed and conspired among themselves to take uniform action upon the proposals made by Interstate, and that they agreed and conspired with each other and with Interstate to impose the demanded restrictions upon all subsequent-run exhibitors in Dallas, Fort Worth, Houston and San Antonio; that they carried out the agreement by imposing the restrictions upon their subsequent-run licensees in those cities, causing some of them to increase their admission price to 25 cents, either generally or when restricted pictures were shown, and to abandon double-billing of all such pictures, and causing the other subsequent-run exhibitors, who were either unable or unwilling to accept the restrictions, to be deprived of any opportunity to exhibit the restricted pictures, which were the best and most popular of all new feature pictures; that the effect of the restrictions upon "low-income members of the community" patronizing the theatres of these exhibitors was to withhold from them altogether the "best entertainment furnished by the motion picture industry"; and that the restrictions operated to increase the income of the distributors and of Interstate and to deflect attendance from later-run exhibitors who yielded to the restrictions to the first-run theatres of Interstate.

* * *

The trial court drew the inference of agreement from the nature of the proposals made on behalf of Interstate and Consolidated; from the manner in which they were made; from the substantial unanimity of action taken upon them by the distributors; and from the fact that appellants did not call as witnesses any of the superior officials who negotiated the contracts with Interstate or any official who, in the normal course of business, would have had knowledge of the existence or non-existence of such an agreement among the distributors. This conclusion is challenged by appellants because not supported by subsidiary findings or by the evidence. We think this inference of the trial court was rightly drawn from the evidence. In the view we take of the legal effect of the cooperative action of the distributor appellants in carrying into effect the restrictions imposed upon subsequent-run theatres in the four Texas cities and of the legal effect of the separate agreements for the imposition of those restrictions entered into between Interstate and each of the distributors, it is unnecessary to discuss in great detail the evidence concerning this aspect of the case.

The O'Donnell letter named on its face as addressees the eight local representatives of the distributors, and so from the beginning each of the distributors knew that the proposals were under consideration by the others. Each was aware that all were in active competition and that without substantially unanimous action with respect to the restrictions for any given territory there was risk of a substantial loss of the business and good will of the subsequent-run and independent exhibitors, but that with it there was the prospect of increased profits. There was, therefore, strong motive for concerted action, full advantage of which was taken by Interstate and Consolidated in presenting their demands to all in a single document.

There was risk, too, that without agreement diversity of action would follow. Compliance with the proposals involved a radical departure from the previous business practices of the industry and a drastic increase in admission prices of most of the subsequent-run theatres. Acceptance of the proposals was discouraged by at least three of the distributors' local managers. Independent exhibitors met and organized a futile protest which they presented to the representatives of Interstate and Consolidated. While as a result of independent negotiations either of the two restrictions without the other could have been put into effect by any one or more of the distributors and in any one or more of the Texas cities served by Interstate, the negotiations which ensued and which in fact did result in modifications of the proposals resulted in substantially unanimous action of the distributors, both as to the terms of the restrictions and in the selection of the four cities where they were to operate.

One distributor, it is true, did not agree to impose the restrictions in Houston, but this was evidently because it did not grant licenses to any subsequent-run exhibitor in that city, where its own affiliate operated a first-run theatre. The proposal was unanimously rejected as to Galveston and Austin, as was the request that the restrictions should be extended to the cities of the Rio Grande Valley served by Consolidated. We may infer that Galveston was omitted because in that city there were no subsequent-run theatres in competition with Interstate. But we are unable to find in the record any persuasive explanation, other than agreed concert of action, of the singular unanimity of action on the part of the distributors by which the proposals were carried into effect as written in four Texas cities but not in a fifth or in the Rio Grande Valley. Numerous variations in the form of the provisions in the distributors' license agreements and the fact that in later years two of them extended the restrictions into all six cities, do not weaken the significance or force of the nature of the response to the proposals made by all the distributor appellants. It taxes credulity to believe that the several distributors would, in the circumstances, have accepted and put into operation with substantial unanimity such far-reaching changes in their business methods without some understanding that all were to join, and we reject as beyond the range of probability that it was the result of mere chance.

* * *

[The inference of agreement] was supported and strengthened when the distributors, with like unanimity, failed to tender the testimony, at their command, of any officer or agent of a distributor who knew, or was in a position to know, whether in fact an agreement had been reached among them for concerted action. When the proof supported, as we think it did, the inference of such concert, the burden rested on appellants of going forward with the evidence to explain away or contradict it. They undertook to carry that burden by calling upon local managers of the distributors to testify that they had acted independently of the other distributors, and that they did not have conferences with or reach agreements with the other distributors or their representatives. The failure under the circumstances to call as witnesses those officers who did have authority to act for the distributors and who were in a position to know whether they had acted in pursuance of agreement is itself persuasive that their testimony, if given, would have been unfavorable to appellants. The production of weak evidence when strong is available can lead only to the conclusion that the strong would have been adverse. Silence then becomes evidence of the most convincing character.

While the District Court's finding of an agreement of the distributors among themselves is supported by the evidence, we think that in the circumstances of this case such agreement for the imposition of the restrictions upon subsequent-run exhibitors was not a prerequisite to an unlawful conspiracy. It was enough that, knowing that concerted action was contemplated and invited, the distributors gave their adherence to the scheme and participated in it. Each distributor was advised that the others were asked to participate; each knew that coöperation was essential to successful operation of the plan. They knew that the plan, if carried out, would result in a restraint of commerce, which, we will presently point out, was unreasonable within the meaning of the Sherman Act, and knowing it, all participated in the plan. The evidence is persuasive that each distributor early became aware that the others had joined. With that knowledge they renewed the arrangement and carried it into effect for the two successive years.

It is elementary that an unlawful conspiracy may be and often is formed without simultaneous action or agreement on the part of the conspirators. Acceptance by competitors, without previous agreement, of an invitation to participate in a plan, the necessary consequence of which, if carried out, is restraint of interstate commerce, is sufficient to establish an unlawful conspiracy under the Sherman Act. . . .

Questions and Comments

Interstate Circuit is called the "rimless wheel" case. O'Donnell is the hub. Each of the "big eight" distributors—Columbia, Fox, Loews, Paramount, RKO, United Artists, Universal and Warner—stands on a point along the imaginary rim, and each is joined to the hub by its own spoke. The question is whether the fact-finder can link the big eight, the points on the rim.[8] As you see, the fact-finder did "discover" the rim, and the Supreme Court agreed that it was there.

From what does the Court infer that the distributors agreed to impose common terms on the theatres? Did the Court infer that the distributors must have expressly agreed to do so? Suppose that *Interstate Circuit* had been tried to a jury; the jury found no agreement among the distributors and the government moved for judgment notwithstanding verdict. What result?

In *Interstate Circuit* the Court assumed—and stressed—that the parallel conduct of the movie distributors would have been profitable only if all acted the same way. This is the essence of interdependence. It gives firms a strong motive to consult with each other to coordinate their conduct. If interdependence is present, does plaintiff need other evidence before an inference of agreement is warranted? If it is missing should plaintiff lose? Was the Court correct in finding interdependence in *Interstate Circuit?* Could any one of the producers profitably have said yes to Interstate if all others had said no?

What does Justice Stone mean by the dictum that agreement is "not a prerequisite to an unlawful conspiracy"? Does he mean only that an express agreement is not essential and that an implied agreement would be enough? Could he mean that interdependent adoption of a new market strategy should be treated the same way as an actual agreement to implement the strategy? Suppose in a tight oligopoly one firm acted as price leader, others followed, and supracompetitive pricing was maintained. Would such conduct fall within Justice Stone's condemnation? How could such conduct be remedied?

We have raised two quite distinguishable issues: When can a conventional agreement be inferred? And is a conventional agreement essential when interdependent action has been shown? Let us leave the second question for now and concentrate on the first. To the extent that the Court was concerned with inferences of conventional agreement to be drawn from circumstantial evidence, the problem is one of experience and logic. The trier of fact must ask, what facts does plaintiff rely upon? Precisely what inferences does plaintiff urge should be drawn from these facts? To find concerted action from circumstantial evidence alone, the fact-finder must be able to conclude that the inference of concerted action is more compelling than the inference of independent action. Consider the following three cases:

1. A, B, C and D each submits a sealed bid to build a state highway. When a state official opens the bids, she finds that those of A, C, and D are exactly the same, down to five decimal points, and all contain

---

8. At the time of Interstate Circuit, it was an open question whether the licensor of a copyrighted film could lawfully agree with the licensee/theatre on the price of admission to be charged for the film at the box office. Do not get sidetracked here with the validity of the vertical restraint. (See Chapter 5.) Simply consider, was there a horizontal combination; that is, one among the distributors?

the same subsidiary terms. B's bid differs only in that it is three percent lower than the others on one significant item.

2. A, a maker of small computers, announces to the press a significant change in its method of business, including a new plan to rent computers on the basis of short term leases. Two days after the announcement is printed, B, A's major competitor, announces exactly the same plan. (Alternatively, suppose the second announcement was two weeks later; two minutes later.)

3. Reconsider case 1 with this added fact: On an evening about ten days after the state invited bids, an executive from A, from B and from D checked into the same airport motel.

4. Reconsider case 1 with this added fact: Over the last few years the state has let contracts on several highway projects. The bidding pattern has been essentially the same, but each of the four firms has been low bidder on about one fourth of the contracts.

Can you draw an inference of concerted action in any of these cases? If so, how strong is the inference?

Competition drives prices to uniformity, especially if the product is standardized. Moreover, in oligopolistic markets where demand is inelastic, firms may maximize profits by interdependent behavior, such as following the price leader, without conversations with competitors. Further, for a variety of benign reasons, firms are often aware that their conduct is uniform with that of their rivals.

Because mere conscious uniformity of price or much other consciously uniform conduct (sometimes called conscious parallelism) can often be explained by factors other than collusion, a plaintiff relying on conscious parallelism must introduce some "plus" factor to raise a jury question of collusion. The plus factor can be any fact that makes the inference of collusion stronger than the inference of independent choice. For example: (1) The day before they all raised their prices, the defendant competitors held a secret meeting to discuss prices. (This provided an opportunity for collusion under circumstances that cast suspicion). (2) The defendants' identical bids were sealed, and there was no apparent non-collusive way they could have known the bids of one another. (This was conformity under circumstances making it unlikely to be mere coincidence). (3) If any one competitor had pursued the course of conduct alone, it would have been unprofitable or economically not feasible, but if all or most followed the same course, each would gain. (Interdependence provided a motive for common action).

When plaintiff's evidence raises an inference of collusion defendant may introduce evidence that tends to rebut that inference. If plaintiff's inferential evidence goes to motive, defendant will try to convince the fact-finder that it had an independent reason for its behavior and would have so behaved regardless of what its rivals did; if defendant succeeds it rebuts the inference suggested by plaintiff. If plaintiff's evidence warrants an inference of communication, defendant's evidence will be aimed at showing that no communication occurred. Does the defendant rebut the inference that may arise from evidence of interdependence as a motive for agreement (as in (3) above) by showing that the market structure and product characteristics were so conducive to oligopolistic interdependence that defendants did not *have* to agree in order to embark upon a price-raising course of behavior—that each would be aware (and would be aware that all others would be aware) that a rise in price would be in their common interest?

We turn now to a case that concerns a basing point system with delivered pricing. The mechanics of this system are described in the opinion. Basing point systems may appeal to collusion-prone rivals. If competitors wish to avoid price competition, they must establish a consensus price. If the price to each customer is significantly different, because, for example, customers are dispersed and shipping costs are high, it might be very complicated for competitors to reach a consensus price, especially without conversations about prices; it might also be difficult to police a price-fixing agreement. A basing point delivered price system could greatly simplify that task by making the prices charged more apparent to competitors.

FEDERAL TRADE COMMISSION v. CEMENT INSTITUTE
333 U.S. 683 (1948).

JUSTICE BLACK: We granted certiorari to review the decree of the Circuit Court of Appeals which, with one judge dissenting, vacated and set aside a cease and desist order issued by the Federal Trade Commission against the respondents. Those respondents are: The Cement Institute, an unincorporated trade association composed of 74 corporations which manufacture, sell and distribute cement; the 74 corporate members of the Institute; and 21 individuals who are associated with the Institute. . . . The core of the charge was that the respondents had restrained and hindered competition in the sale and distribution of cement by means of a combination among themselves made effective through mutual understanding or agreement to employ a multiple basing point system of pricing[, and that this conduct amounted to an unfair method of competition in violation of Section 5 of the Federal Trade Commission Act]. It was alleged that this system resulted in the quotation of identical terms of sale and identical prices for cement by the respondents at any given point in the United States. This system had worked so successfully, it was further charged, that for many years prior to the filing of the complaint, all cement buyers throughout the nation, with rare exceptions, had been unable to purchase cement for delivery in any given locality from any one of the respondents at a lower price or on more favorable terms than from any of the other respondents.

*   *   *

Resting upon its findings, the Commission ordered that respondents cease and desist from "carrying out any planned common course of action, understanding, agreement, combination, or conspiracy" to do a number of things, all of which things, the Commission argues, had to be restrained in order effectively to restore individual freedom of action among the separate units in the cement industry. . . . [I]f the order stands, its terms are broad enough to bar respondents from acting in concert to sell cement on a basing point delivered price plan which so eliminates competition that respondents' prices are always identical at any given point in the United States.

*   *   *

The Multiple Basing Point Delivered Price System.—Since the multiple basing point delivered price system of fixing prices and terms of cement sales is the nub of this controversy, it will be helpful at this preliminary stage to point out in general what it is and how it works. A brief reference to the distinctive characteristics of "factory" or "mill prices" and "delivered prices" is of importance to an understanding of the basing point delivered price system here involved.

Goods may be sold and delivered to customers at the seller's mill or warehouse door or may be sold free on board (f.o.b.) trucks or railroad cars immediately adjacent to the seller's mill or warehouse. In either event the actual cost of the goods to the purchaser is, broadly speaking, the seller's "mill price" plus the purchaser's cost of transportation. However, if the seller fixes a price at which he undertakes to deliver goods to the purchaser where they are to be used, the cost to the purchaser is the "delivered price." A seller who makes the "mill price" identical for all purchasers of like amount and quality simply delivers his goods at the same place (his mill) and for the same price (price at the mill). He thus receives for all f.o.b. mill sales an identical net amount of money for like goods from all customers. But a "delivered price" system creates complications which may result in a seller's receiving different net returns from the sale of like goods. The cost of transporting 500 miles is almost always more than the cost of transporting 100 miles. Consequently if customers 100 and 500 miles away pay the same "delivered price," the seller's net return is less from the more distant customer. . . .

The best known early example of a basing point price system was called "Pittsburgh plus." It related to the price of steel. The Pittsburgh price was the base price, Pittsburgh being therefore called a price basing point. In order for the system to work, sales had to be made only at delivered prices. Under this system the delivered price of steel from anywhere in the United States to a point of delivery anywhere in the United States was in general the Pittsburgh price plus the railroad freight rate from Pittsburgh to the point of delivery. Take Chicago, Illinois, as an illustration of the operation and consequences of the system. A Chicago steel producer was not free to sell his steel at cost plus a reasonable profit. He must sell it at the Pittsburgh price plus the railroad freight rate from Pittsburgh to the point of delivery. Chicago steel customers were by this pricing plan thus arbitrarily required to pay for Chicago produced steel the Pittsburgh base price plus what it would have cost to ship the steel by rail from Pittsburgh to Chicago had it been shipped. The theoretical cost of this fictitious shipment became known as "phantom freight." But had it been economically possible under this plan for a Chicago producer to ship his steel to Pittsburgh, his "delivered price" would have been merely the Pittsburgh price, although he actually would have been required to pay the freight from Chicago to Pittsburgh. Thus the "delivered price" under these latter circumstances required a Chicago (non-basing point) producer to "absorb" freight costs. That is, such a seller's net returns became smaller and smaller as his deliveries approached closer and closer to the basing point.

Several results obviously flow from use of a single basing point system such as "Pittsburgh plus" originally was. One is that the "delivered prices" of all producers in every locality where deliveries are made are always the same regardless of the producers' different freight costs. Another is that sales made by a non-base mill for delivery at different localities result in net receipts to the seller which vary in amounts equivalent to the "phantom freight" included in, or the "freight absorption" taken from the "delivered price."

As commonly employed by respondents, the basing point system is not single but multiple. That is, instead of one basing point, like that in "Pittsburgh plus," a number of basing point localities are used. In the multiple basing point system, just as in the single basing point system, freight absorption or phantom freight is an element of the delivered price on all sales not governed by a basing point actually located at the seller's mill. And all sellers quote identical delivered prices in any given locality regardless of their different costs of production and their different freight expenses. Thus the multiple and single systems function in the same general manner and produce the same consequences—identity of prices and diversity of net returns.

* * *

Findings and Evidence.—It is strongly urged that the Commission failed to find that the respondents had by combination, agreements, or understandings among themselves utilized the multiple basing point delivered price system as a restraint to accomplish uniform prices and terms of sale. A subsidiary contention is that assuming the Commission did so find, there is no substantial evidence to support such a finding. We think that adequate findings of combination were made and that the findings have support in the evidence.

The Commission's findings of fact set out at great length and with painstaking detail numerous concerted activities carried on in order to make the multiple basing point system work in such way that competition in quality, price and terms of sale of cement would be nonexistent, and that uniform prices, job contracts, discounts, and terms of sale would be continuously maintained. The Commission found that many of these activities were carried on by the Cement Institute, the industry's unincorporated trade association, and that in other instances the activities were under the immediate control of groups of respondents. Among the collective methods used to accomplish these purposes, according to the findings, were boycotts; discharge of uncooperative employees; organized opposition to the erection of new cement plants; selling cement in a recalcitrant price cutter's sales territory at a price so low that the recalcitrant was forced to adhere to the established basing point prices; discouraging the shipment of cement by truck or barge; and preparing and distributing freight rate books which provided respondents with similar figures to use as actual or "phantom" freight factors, thus guaranteeing that their delivered prices (base prices plus freight factors) would be identical on all sales whether made to individual purchasers under open bids or to governmental agencies under sealed bids. These are but a few of the many activities of respondents which the Commission found to have been done in combination to reduce or destroy price competition in cement. After having made these detailed findings of concerted action, the Commission followed them by a general finding that "the capacity, tendency, and effect of the combination maintained by the respondents herein in the manner aforesaid . . . is to . . . promote and maintain their multiple basing-point delivered-price system and obstruct and defeat any form of competition which threatens or tends to threaten the continued use and maintenance of said system and the uniformity of prices created and maintained by its use.". . .

. . . The findings are sufficient. The contention that they are not is without substance.

Disposition of this question brings us to the related contention that there was no substantial evidence to support the findings. . . .

Although there is much more evidence to which reference could be made, we think that the following facts shown by evidence in the record, some of which are in dispute, are sufficient to warrant the Commission's finding of concerted action.

When the Commission rendered its decision there were about 80 cement manufacturing companies in the United States operating about 150 mills. Ten companies controlled more than half of the mills and there were substantial corporate affiliations among many of the others. This concentration of productive capacity made concerted action far less difficult than it would otherwise have been. The belief is prevalent in the industry that because of the standardized nature of cement, among other reasons, price competition is wholly unsuited to it. That belief is historic. It has resulted in concerted activities to devise means and measures to do away with competition in the industry. Out of those activities came the multiple basing point delivered price system. Evidence shows it to be a handy instrument to bring about elimination of any kind of price competition. The use of the multiple basing point delivered price system by the cement producers has been coincident with a situation whereby for many years, with rare exceptions, cement has been offered for sale in every given locality at identical prices and terms by all producers. Thousands of secret sealed bids have been received by public agencies which corresponded in prices of cement down to a fractional part of a penny.[15]

Occasionally foreign cement has been imported, and cement dealers have sold it below the delivered price of the domestic product. Dealers who persisted in selling foreign cement were boycotted by the domestic producers. Officers of the Institute took the lead in securing pledges by

15. The following is one among many of the Commission's findings as to the identity of sealed bids:

An abstract of the bids for 6,000 barrels of cement to the United States Engineer Office at Tucumcari, New Mexico, opened April 23, 1936, shows the following:

Name of Bidder	Price per Bbl.
Monarch	$3.286854
Ash Grove	3.286854
Lehigh	3.286854
Southwestern	3.286854

U.S. Portland Cement Co.	$3.286854
Oklahoma	3.286854
Consolidated	3.286854
Trinity	3.286854
Lone Star	3.286854
Universal	3.286854
Colorado	3.286854

All bids subject to 10¢ per barrel discount for payment in 15 days.

producers not to permit sales f.o.b. mill to purchasers who furnished their own trucks, a practice regarded as seriously disruptive of the entire delivered price structure of the industry.

During the depression in the 1930's, slow business prompted some producers to deviate from the prices fixed by the delivered price system. Meetings were held by other producers; an effective plan was devised to punish the recalcitrants and bring them into line. The plan was simple but successful. Other producers made the recalcitrant's plant an involuntary base point. The base price was driven down with relatively insignificant losses to the producers who imposed the punitive basing point, but with heavy losses to the recalcitrant who had to make all its sales on this basis. In one instance, where a producer had made a low public bid, a punitive base point price was put on its plant and cement was reduced 10¢ per barrel; further reductions quickly followed until the base price at which this recalcitrant had to sell its cement dropped to 75¢ per barrel, scarcely one-half of its former base price of $1.45. Within six weeks after the base price hit 75¢, capitulation occurred and the recalcitrant joined a portland cement association. Cement in that locality then bounced back to $1.15, later to $1.35, and finally to $1.75.

The foregoing are but illustrations of the practices shown to have been utilized to maintain the basing point price system. Respondents offered testimony that cement is a standardized product, that "cement is cement," that no differences existed in quality or usefulness, and that purchasers demanded delivered price quotations because of the high cost of transportation from mill to dealer. There was evidence, however, that the Institute and its members had, in the interest of eliminating competition, suppressed information as to the variations in quality that sometimes exist in different cements. Respondents introduced the testimony of economists to the effect that competition alone could lead to the evolution of a multiple basing point system of uniform delivered prices and terms of sale for an industry with a standardized product and with relatively high freight costs. These economists testified that for the above reasons no inferences of collusion, agreement, or understanding could be drawn from the admitted fact that cement prices of all United States producers had for many years almost invariably been the same in every given locality in the country. There was also considerable testimony by other economic experts that the multiple basing point system of delivered prices as employed by respondents contravened accepted economic principles and could only have been maintained through collusion.

The Commission did not adopt the views of the economists produced by the respondents. It decided that even though competition might tend to drive the price of standardized products to a uniform level, such a tendency alone could not account for the almost perfect identity in prices, discounts, and cement containers which had prevailed for so long a time in the cement industry. The Commission held that the uniformity and absence of competition in the industry were the results of understandings or agreements entered into or carried out by concert of the Institute and the other respondents. It may possibly be true, as respondents' economists testified, that cement producers will, without agreement express or implied and without understanding explicit or tacit, always and at all times (for such has been substantially the case here) charge for their cement precisely, to the fractional part of a penny, the price their competitors charge. Certainly it runs counter to what many people have believed, namely, that without agreement, prices will vary—that the desire to sell will sometimes be so strong that a seller will be willing to lower his prices and take his chances. We therefore hold that the Commission was not compelled to accept the views of respondents' economist-witnesses that active competition was bound to produce uniform cement prices. The Commission was authorized to find understanding, express or implied, from evidence that the industry's Institute actively worked, in cooperation with various of its members, to maintain the multiple basing point delivered price system; that this pricing system is calculated to produce, and has produced, uniform prices and terms of sale throughout the country; and that all of the respondents have sold their cement substantially in accord with the pattern required by the multiple basing point system.

Some of the respondents contend that particularly as to them crucial findings of participation by them in collective action to eliminate price competition and to bring about uniformity of cement prices are without testimonial support. . . .

These companies support their separate contentions for particularized consideration by pointing out among other things that there was record evidence which showed differences between many of their sales methods and those practiced by other respondents. Each says that there was no direct evidence to connect it with all of the practices found to have been used by the Institute and other respondents to achieve delivered price uniformity.

The record does show such differences as those suggested. It is correct to say, therefore, that the sales practices of these particular respondents, and perhaps of other respondents as well, were not at all times precisely like the sales practices of all or any of the others. . . . Northwestern and Superior assert that among other distinctive practices of theirs, they were willing to and did bid for government contracts on a mill price rather than a delivered price basis. Huron points out that it permitted the use of trucks to deliver cement, which practice, far from being consistent with the plan of others to maintain the basing point delivered price formulas, was frowned on by the Institute and others as endangering the success of the plan. Marquette emphasizes that it did not follow all the practices used to carry out the anti-competition plan, and urges that although the Commission rightly found that it had upon occasion undercut its competitors, it erroneously found that its admitted abandonment of price cutting was due to the combined pressure of other respondents, including the Institute.

What these particular respondents emphasize does serve to underscore certain findings which show that some respondents were more active and influential in the combination than were others, and that some companies probably unwillingly abandoned competitive practices and entered into the combination. But none of the distinctions mentioned, or any other differences relied on by these particular respondents, justifies a holding that there was no substantial evidence to support the Commission's findings that they cooperated with all the others to achieve the ultimate objective of all—the elimination of price competition in the sale of cement. . . .

The evidence commonly applicable to these and the other respondents showed that all were members of the Institute and that the officers of some of these particular respondents were or had been officers of the Institute. We have already sustained findings that the Institute was organized to maintain the multiple basing point system as one of the "customs and usages" of the industry and that it participated in numerous activities intended to eliminate price competition through the collective efforts of the respondents. Evidence before the Commission also showed that the delivered prices of these respondents, like those of all the other respondents, were, with rare exceptions, identical with the delivered prices of all their competitors. Furthermore, there was evidence that all of these respondents . . . employed the multiple basing point delivered price system on a portion of their sales.

* * *

Unfair Methods of Competition.—We sustain the Commission's holding that concerted maintenance of the basing point delivered price system is an unfair method of competition prohibited by the Federal Trade Commission Act.. . . .

. . . We uphold the Commission's conclusion that the basing point delivered price system employed by respondents is an unfair trade practice which the Trade Commission may suppress.[19] . . .

JUSTICE BURTON, dissenting: [The opinion of the court below] reviewed the evidence and pointed out many weaknesses in the inferences upon which the Commission had based its finding of the existence of the alleged unlawful combination.[8]

* * *

On the view of the evidence taken by the court below and by me, that evidence does not support the Commission's finding of the combination as charged. Unlike the Commission and the majority of this Court, the lower court and I, therefore, have faced the further issue presented by the Commission's charges unsupported by a finding of the

------

19. While we hold that the Commission's findings of combination were supported by evidence, that does not mean that existence of a "combination" is an indispensable ingredient of an "unfair method of competition" under the Trade Commission Act. See *Federal Trade Comm'n v. Beech–Nut Packing Co.,* 257 U.S. 441, 455.

------

8. A further review of the insufficiently supported inferences would be of little value here. By way of illustration, however, it may be noted that the Commission and this Court, in its note 15, have emphasized the fact that secret sealed bids for 6,000 barrels of cement were received by a public agency from ten or more of the respondent companies and that the bid of each company was precisely $3.286854 a barrel. Such a fractional identity of price would, on its face, create an inference of collusion. However, the Commission failed to explain, as has the court below, that the highly fractional figure merely reflected the freight charge. The bid, apart from the freight charge, was $2.10 per barrel while "the land grant freight rate to which the government was entitled from the nearest mill of the eleven bidders was $1.1865854 [$1.186854] per barrel."

alleged combination. This has led us to consider an issue quite different from that decided by this Court today. That issue lies within the long-established and widespread practice by individuals of bona fide competition by freight absorption with which practice Congress has declined to interfere, although asked to do so.[11] This is the field where a producer, for his own purposes and without collusion, often ships his product to a customer who, in terms of freight charges, is located nearer to one or more of the producer's competitors than to the producer himself. In selling to such a customer, this producer is at an obvious freight disadvantage. To meet the lower delivered-price of his competitor, the producer, therefore, reduces his delivered-price in that area by a sum sufficient to absorb his freight disadvantage. He might do this for many reasons. For example, this customer might be such a large customer that the volume of his orders would yield such a return to the producer that the producer, by distributing his fixed charges over the resultingly increased volume of business, could absorb the freight differential without loss of profit to his business as a whole and without raising any charges to his other customers. The securing of this particular business might even enable the producer to reduce his own basic factory price to all his customers. It might make the difference between a profitable and a losing business, resulting in the producer's solvency or bankruptcy. If the advantage to be derived from this customer's business were not sufficient, in itself, thus completely to absorb the freight differential, the producer might absorb all or part of such differential by a reduction in his net earnings without affecting his other customers. . . .

I conclude, therefore, that the judgment of the Court of Appeals setting aside the order of the Federal Trade Commission should have been affirmed. . . .

Questions and Answers

Is Justice Burton correct that evidence in the record rebuts the inference of agreement that arises from the fact that the sealed bids were identical? If so, is there sufficient other evidence to support the inference of collusion? Would it be possible for the putative basing point practice to work without collusion? Is "mere" interdependent adoption of a basing point system illegal?

The Court documents a case in which meetings were held about an "offending" company, and as a result "the offending company agreed that it would 'play the game 100%'; that it would not countenance 'chiseling'; that it would not knowingly invade territory of its competitors, or 'tear down the price structure.'" 333 U.S. 718–19 at n. 18. Suppose that, at trial, each of the individuals who attended the meeting introduced evidence of an independent business reason for embracing the terms of "the game," and testified that

---

11. "Furthermore, the basing point price system has been in use by industry for almost a half century. There has been and is a marked diversity of opinion among economists, lawmakers and people generally as to whether it is good or bad. Numerous bills have been introduced in Congress seeking to outlaw its use. Countless time has been spent in hearings by Congressional committees, before whom it has been assailed and defended. The pages of the Congressional Record bear mute but indisputable proof of the fact that Congress has repeatedly refused to declare its use illegal. . . ." *Aetna Portland Cement Co. v. Federal Trade Comm'n* [157 F.2d 533,] 573. . . .

the company would have taken the same action regardless of what its competitors did. Would such testimony, if believed, rebut an inference of agreement? If A, B and C are competitors can they get together to tell one another what they plan to do about price and why? Does the legality of such a meeting turn on whether an inference of agreement on price is warranted? Does it even turn on whether the meeting results in a common price?

THEATRE ENTERPRISES, INC. v. PARAMOUNT FILM DISTRIBUTING CORP.

346 U.S. 537 (1954).

JUSTICE CLARK: Petitioner brought this suit for treble damages and an injunction under §§ 4 and 16 of the Clayton Act, alleging that respondent motion picture producers and distributors had violated the antitrust laws by conspiring to restrict "first-run" pictures to downtown Baltimore theatres, thus confining its suburban theatre to subsequent runs and unreasonable "clearances." [5] [The trial judge entered judgment on a verdict for respondents, denying petitioner's motion for a directed verdict. The court of appeals affirmed.]

* * *

. . . Petitioner now urges, as it did in the Court of Appeals, that the trial judge should have directed a verdict in its favor and submitted to the jury only the question of the amount of damages. . . .

. . . [P]etitioner owns and operates the Crest Theatre, located in a neighborhood shopping district some six miles from the downtown shopping center in Baltimore, Maryland. The Crest, possessing the most modern improvements and appointments, opened on February 26, 1949. Before and after the opening, petitioner, through its president, repeatedly sought to obtain first-run features for the theatre. Petitioner approached each respondent separately, initially requesting exclusive first-runs, later asking for first-runs on a "day and date" basis.[7] But respondents uniformly rebuffed petitioner's efforts and adhered to an established policy of restricting first-runs in Baltimore to the eight downtown theatres. Admittedly there is no direct evidence of illegal agreement between the respondents and no conspiracy is charged as to the independent exhibitors in Baltimore, who account for 63% of first-run exhibitions. The various respondents advanced much the same reasons for denying petitioner's offers. Among other reasons, they asserted that day-and-date first-runs are normally granted only to noncompeting theatres. Since the Crest is in "substantial competition" with the downtown theatres, a day-and-date arrangement would be economically unfeasible. And even if respondents wished to grant petitioner such a license, no downtown exhibitor would waive his clearance rights over the Crest and agree to a simultaneous showing. As a result, if petitioner were to receive first-runs, the license would have to be an exclusive one. However, an exclusive license would

5. "A clearance is the period of time, usually stipulated in license contracts, which must elapse between runs of the same feature within a particular area or in specified theatres." *United States v. Paramount Pictures, Inc.*, 334 U.S. 131, 144, n. 6 (1948).

7. A first-run "day and date" means that two theatres exhibit a first-run at the same time. Had petitioner's request for a day-and-date first-run been granted, the Crest and a downtown theatre would have exhibited the same features simultaneously.

be economically unsound because the Crest is a suburban theatre, located in a small shopping center, and served by limited public transportation facilities; and, with a drawing area of less than one-tenth that of a downtown theatre, it cannot compare with those easily accessible theatres in the power to draw patrons. Hence the downtown theatres offer far greater opportunities for the widespread advertisement and exploitation of newly released features, which is thought necessary to maximize the over-all return from subsequent runs as well as first-runs. The respondents, in the light of these conditions, attacked the guaranteed offers of petitioner, one of which occurred during the trial, as not being made in good faith. Respondents Loew's and Warner refused petitioner an exclusive license because they owned the three downtown theatres receiving their first-run product.

The crucial question is whether respondents' conduct toward petitioner stemmed from independent decision or from an agreement, tacit or express. To be sure, business behavior is admissible circumstantial evidence from which the fact finder may infer agreement. But this Court has never held that proof of parallel business behavior conclusively establishes agreement or, phrased differently, that such behavior itself constitutes a Sherman Act offense. Circumstantial evidence of consciously parallel behavior may have made heavy inroads into the traditional judicial attitude toward conspiracy; but "conscious parallelism" has not yet read conspiracy out of the Sherman Act entirely. Realizing this, petitioner attempts to bolster its argument for a directed verdict by urging that the conscious unanimity of action by respondents should be "measured against the background and findings in the *Paramount* case." In other words, since the same respondents had conspired in the *Paramount* case to impose a uniform system of runs and clearances without adequate explanation to sustain them as reasonable restraints of trade, use of the same device in the present case should be legally equated to conspiracy. But the *Paramount* decrees, even if admissible, were only prima facie evidence of a conspiracy covering the area and existing during the period there involved. Alone or in conjunction with the other proof of the petitioner, they would form no basis for a directed verdict. Here each of the respondents had denied the existence of any collaboration and in addition had introduced evidence of the local conditions surrounding the Crest operation which, they contended, precluded it from being a successful first-run house. They also attacked the good faith of the guaranteed offers of the petitioner for first-run pictures and attributed uniform action to individual business judgment motivated by the desire for maximum revenue. This evidence, together with other testimony of an explanatory nature, raised fact issues requiring the trial judge to submit the issue of conspiracy to the jury. . . .

Questions and Comments

Suppose that, at the close of the evidence, defendants moved to dismiss for insufficiency of the evidence. Plaintiff opposed, on the strength of *Interstate Circuit*. Should the trial judge have granted the motion?

During the 1950s, 60s and early 70's, following the holding and spirit of *Interstate Circuit,* judges liberally sent to the jury cases in which plaintiffs showed suspicious circumstances of commonality. Indeed, when judges in treble damage cases substituted their view for that of the jury and gave summary judgment to defendants, the courts of appeal were quick to reverse. Even the Supreme Court declared that questions of combination or conspiracy are questions for the jury, and that summary judgment should not be lightly given. One important such case was *First National Bank of Arizona v. Cities Service Company,* 391 U.S. 253 (1968). As time went on, pressures began moving in the other direction. Complex litigation imposed new burdens on the judicial system. Most antitrust cases are not more complex than other federal court litigation. See K.G. Elzinga & W.C. Wood, The Costs of the Legal System in Private Antitrust Enforcement, in Private Antitrust Litigation: New Evidence, New Learning 107 (L.J. White (ed.) (1988)). However, a significant number of antitrust cases are complex, long and expensive. Moreover antitrust cases may, at times, entail vexatious use of the treble damage remedy to force a settlement. If a defendant's chance of losing a given case is, say, one in forty, one would not expect the defendant to feel at risk. But suppose the case is a treble damage price-fixing class action. Then, each individual defendant is potentially liable for three times the aggregate amount of the overcharges found to have been imposed by all members of the industry over a period of many years, and a losing defendant cannot seek contribution from its co-conspirators. In such a case, the worst case risk for every defendant may reach billions of dollars. True, the likelihood that such a judgment will be executed against any particular defendant may be small— certainly far less than the forty to one chance that plaintiffs will win at all. Nevertheless, a defendant, even if possessing a high sense of rectitude about its own conduct, may pay more than a "nuisance" sum to avoid such high exposure. For reasons like these, by the mid 1970s courts were beginning to be selective about application of the Supreme Court language that discouraged the use of summary judgment in antitrust cases. Then, in the mid 1980s, the *Matsushita* case came before the Supreme Court.

The Japanese television manufacturers had been "invading" the U.S. market, and, with prices below or nearly below what the U.S. manufacturers could bear, the Japanese firms were seriously injuring the American industry. The American manufacturers sued, alleging a low-price conspiracy. On the basis of a voluminous factual record, Judge Becker of the Eastern District of Pennsylvania granted summary judgment for defendants, finding that plaintiffs had not raised a genuine issue of material fact as to the existence of a conspiracy that could have harmed them. The Court of Appeals for the Third Circuit reversed. The Supreme Court granted certiorari.

MATSUSHITA ELECTRIC INDUSTRIAL CO. v. ZENITH RADIO CORP.
475 U.S. 574 (1986).

JUSTICE POWELL: This case requires that we again consider the standard district courts must apply when deciding whether to grant summary judgment in an antitrust conspiracy case.

I

* * *

A

Petitioners, defendants below, are 21 corporations that manufacture or sell "consumer electronic products" (CEPs)—for the most part, television sets. Petitioners include both Japanese manufacturers of CEPs and American firms, controlled by Japanese parents, that sell the Japanese-manufactured products. Respondents, plaintiffs below, are Zenith Radio Corporation (Zenith) and National Union Electric Corporation (NUE). Zenith is an American firm that manufactures and sells television sets. NUE is the corporate successor to Emerson Radio Company, an American firm that manufactured and sold television sets until 1970, when it withdrew from the market after sustaining substantial losses. Zenith and NUE began this lawsuit in 1974, claiming that petitioners had illegally conspired to drive American firms from the American CEP market. According to respondents, the gist of this conspiracy was a " 'scheme to raise, fix and maintain artificially *high* prices for television receivers sold by [petitioners] in Japan and, at the same time, to fix and maintain *low* prices for television receivers exported to and sold in the United States.' " These "low prices" were allegedly at levels that produced substantial losses for petitioners. The conspiracy allegedly began as early as 1953, and . . . was in full operation by sometime in the late 1960's. . . .

* * *

The District Court [decided] petitioners' motions for summary judgment. In an opinion spanning 217 pages, the court found that the admissible evidence did not raise a genuine issue of material fact as to the existence of the alleged conspiracy. At bottom, the court found, respondents' claims rested on the inferences that could be drawn from petitioners' parallel conduct in the Japanese and American markets, and from the effects of that conduct on petitioners' American competitors. After reviewing the evidence both by category and *in toto*, the court found that any inference of conspiracy was unreasonable, because (i) some portions of the evidence suggested that petitioners conspired in ways that did not injure respondents, and (ii) the evidence that bore directly on the alleged price-cutting conspiracy did not rebut the more plausible inference that petitioners were cutting prices to compete in the American market and not to monopolize it. Summary judgment therefore was granted. . . .

B

The Court of Appeals for the Third Circuit reversed. The court began by examining the District Court's evidentiary rulings, and determined that much of the evidence excluded by the District Court was in fact admissible. These evidentiary rulings are not before us.

On the merits, and based on the newly enlarged record, the court found that the District Court's summary judgment decision was improper. The court acknowledged that "there are legal limitations upon the inferences which may be drawn from circumstantial evidence," but it found that "the legal problem . . . is different" when "there is direct evidence of concert of action." Here, the court concluded, "there is both direct evidence of certain kinds of concert of action and circumstantial evidence having some tendency to suggest that other kinds of concert of action may have occurred." Thus, the court reasoned, cases concerning the limitations on inferring conspiracy from ambiguous evidence were not dispositive. Turning to the evidence, the court determined that a factfinder reasonably could draw the following conclusions:

1. The Japanese market for CEPs was characterized by oligopolistic behavior, with a small number of producers meeting regularly and exchanging information on price and other matters. This created the opportunity for a stable combination to raise both prices and profits in Japan. American firms could not attack such a combination because the Japanese Government imposed significant barriers to entry.

2. Petitioners had relatively higher fixed costs than their American counterparts, and therefore needed to operate at something approaching full capacity in order to make a profit.

3. Petitioners' plant capacity exceeded the needs of the Japanese market.

4. By formal agreements arranged in cooperation with Japan's Ministry of International Trade and Industry (MITI), petitioners fixed minimum prices for CEPs exported to the American market. The parties refer to these prices as the "check prices," and to the agreements that require them as the "check price agreements."

5. Petitioners agreed to distribute their products in the United States according to a "five company rule": each Japanese producer was permitted to sell only to five American distributors.

6. Petitioners undercut their own check prices by a variety of rebate schemes. Petitioners sought to conceal these rebate schemes both from the United States Customs Service and from MITI, the former to avoid various customs regulations as well as action under the antidumping laws, and the latter to cover up petitioners' violations of the check-price agreements.

Based on inferences from the foregoing conclusions, the Court of Appeals concluded that a reasonable factfinder could find a conspiracy to depress prices in the American market in order to drive out American competitors, which conspiracy was funded by excess profits obtained in the Japanese market. . . .

. . . We reverse. . . .

II

We begin by emphasizing what respondents' claim is *not*. Respondents cannot recover antitrust damages based solely on an alleged cartelization of the Japanese market, because American antitrust laws do not regulate the competitive conditions of other nations' economies. Nor can respondents recover damages for any conspiracy by petitioners to charge higher than competitive prices in the American market. Such conduct would indeed violate the Sherman Act, but it could not injure respondents: as petitioners' competitors, respondents stand to gain from any conspiracy to raise the market price in CEPs. Finally, for the same reason, respondents cannot recover for a conspiracy to impose nonprice restraints that have the effect of either raising market price or limiting output. Such restrictions, though harmful to competition, actually *benefit* competitors by making supracompetitive pricing more attractive. Thus, neither petitioners' alleged supracompetitive pricing in Japan, nor the five company rule that limited distribution in this country, nor the check prices insofar as they established minimum prices in this country, can by themselves give respondents a cognizable claim against petitioners for antitrust damages. The Court of Appeals therefore erred to the extent that it found evidence of these alleged conspiracies to be "direct evidence" of a conspiracy that injured respondents.

Respondents nevertheless argue that these supposed conspiracies, if not themselves grounds for recovery of antitrust damages, are circumstantial evidence of another conspiracy that *is* cognizable: a conspiracy to monopolize the American market by means of pricing below the market level. The thrust of respondents' argument is that petitioners used their monopoly profits from the Japanese market to fund a concerted campaign to price predatorily and thereby drive respondents and other American manufacturers of CEPs out of business. Once successful, according to respondents, petitioners would cartelize the American CEP market, restricting output and raising prices above the level that fair competition would produce. The resulting monopoly profits, respondents contend, would more than compensate petitioners for the losses they incurred through years of pricing below market level.

The Court of Appeals found that respondents' allegation of a horizontal conspiracy to engage in predatory pricing,[8] if proved,[9] would be a *per se* violation of § 1 of the Sherman Act. Petitioners did not appeal from that conclusion. The issue in this case thus becomes whether respondents adduced sufficient evidence in support of their theory to survive summary judgment. We therefore examine the principles that govern the summary judgment determination.

8. Throughout this opinion, we refer to the asserted conspiracy as one to price "predatorily." This term has been used chiefly in cases in which a single firm, having a dominant share of the relevant market, cuts its prices in order to force competitors out of the market, or perhaps to deter potential entrants from coming in. In such cases, "predatory pricing" means pricing below some appropriate measure of cost.

There is a good deal of debate, both in the cases and in the law reviews, about what "cost" is relevant in such cases. We need not resolve this debate here [for] this is a Sherman Act § 1 case. For purposes of this case, it is enough to note that respondents have not suffered an antitrust injury unless petitioners conspired to drive respondents out of the relevant markets by (i) pricing below the level necessary to sell their prod-

ucts, or (ii) pricing below some appropriate measure of cost. An agreement without these features would either leave respondents in the same position as would market forces or would actually benefit respondents by raising market prices. Respondents therefore may not complain of conspiracies that, for example, set maximum prices above market levels, or that set minimum prices at *any* level.

9. We do not consider whether recovery should *ever* be available on a theory such as respondents' when the pricing in question is above some measure of incremental cost. As a practical matter, it may be that only direct evidence of below-cost pricing is sufficient to overcome the strong inference that rational businesses would not enter into conspiracies such as this one.

III

To survive petitioners' motion for summary judgment, respondents must establish that there is a genuine issue of material fact as to whether petitioners entered into an illegal conspiracy that caused respondents to suffer a cognizable injury. This showing has two components. First, respondents must show more than a conspiracy in violation of the antitrust laws; they must show an injury to them resulting from the illegal conduct. Respondents charge petitioners with a whole host of conspiracies in restraint of trade. Except for the alleged conspiracy to monopolize the American market through predatory pricing, these alleged conspiracies could not have caused respondents to suffer an "antitrust injury," because they actually tended to benefit respondents. Therefore, unless, in context, evidence of these "other" conspiracies raises a genuine issue concerning the existence of a predatory pricing conspiracy, that evidence cannot defeat petitioners' summary judgment motion.

Second, the issue of fact must be "genuine." When the moving party has carried its burden under Rule 56(c), its opponent must do more than simply show that there is some metaphysical doubt as to the material facts. In the language of the Rule, the nonmoving party must come forward with "specific facts showing that there is a *genuine issue for trial.*" Fed.Rule Civ.Proc. 56(e) (emphasis added). Where the record taken as a whole could not lead a rational trier of fact to find for the nonmoving party, there is no "genuine issue for trial."

It follows from these settled principles that if the factual context renders respondents' claim implausible—if the claim is one that simply makes no economic sense—respondents must come forward with more persuasive evidence to support their claim than would otherwise be necessary. [*First National Bank of Arizona v. Cities Service Co.*, 391 U.S. 253 (1968)] is instructive. The issue in that case was whether proof of the defendant's refusal to deal with the plaintiff supported an inference that the defendant willingly had joined an illegal boycott. Economic factors strongly suggested that the defendant had no motive to join the alleged conspiracy. . . . Since the defendant lacked any rational motive to join the alleged boycott, and since its refusal to deal was consistent with the defendant's independent interest, the refusal to deal could not by itself support a finding of antitrust liability.

. . . [The] antitrust law limits the range of permissible inferences from ambiguous evidence in a § 1 case. Thus, in *Monsanto Co. v. Spray-Rite Service Corp.*, 465 U.S. 752 (1984), we held that conduct as consistent with permissible competition as with illegal conspiracy does not, standing alone, support an inference of antitrust conspiracy. To survive a motion for summary judgment or for a directed verdict, a plaintiff seeking damages for a violation of § 1 must present evidence "that tends to exclude the possibility" that the alleged conspirators acted independently. Respondents in this case, in other words, must show that the inference of conspiracy is reasonable in light of the competing inferences of independent action or collusive action that could not have harmed respondents.

Petitioners argue that these principles apply fully to this case. According to petitioners, the alleged conspiracy is one that is economically irrational and practically infeasible. Consequently, petitioners contend, they had no motive to engage in the alleged predatory pricing conspiracy; indeed, they had a strong motive *not* to conspire in the manner respondents allege. Petitioners argue that, in light of the absence of any apparent motive and the ambiguous nature of the evidence of conspiracy, no trier of fact reasonably could find that the conspiracy with which petitioners are charged actually existed. This argument requires us to consider the nature of the alleged conspiracy and the practical obstacles to its implementation.

IV

A

A predatory pricing conspiracy is by nature speculative. Any agreement to price below the competitive level requires the conspirators to forgo profits that free competition would offer them. The forgone profits may be considered an investment in the future. For the investment to be rational, the conspirators must have a reasonable expectation of recovering, in the form of later monopoly profits, more than the losses suffered. As then-Professor Bork, discussing predatory pricing by a single firm, explained:

> "Any realistic theory of predation recognizes that the predator as well as his victims will incur losses during the fighting, but such a theory supposes it may be a rational calculation for the predator to view the losses as an investment in future monopoly profits (where rivals are to be killed) or in future undisturbed profits (where rivals are to be disciplined). The future flow of profits, appropriately discounted, must then exceed the present size of the losses." R. Bork, The Antitrust Paradox 145 (1978).

See also McGee, Predatory Pricing Revisited, 23 J.Law & Econ. 289, 295–297 (1980). As this explanation shows, the success of such schemes is inherently uncertain: the short-run loss is definite, but the long-run gain depends on successfully neutralizing the competition. Moreover, it is not enough simply to achieve monopoly power, as monopoly pricing may breed quick entry by new competitors eager to share in the excess profits. The success of any predatory scheme depends on *maintaining* monopoly power for long enough both to recoup the predator's losses and to harvest some additional gain. Absent some assurance that the hoped-for monopoly will materialize, *and* that it can be sustained for a significant period of time, "[t]he predator must make a substantial investment with no assurance that it will pay off." Easterbrook, Predatory Strategies and Counterstrategies, 48 U.Chi.L.Rev. 263, 268 (1981). For this reason, there is a consensus among commentators that predatory pricing schemes are rarely tried, and even more rarely successful. See, *e.g.*, Bork, *supra*, at 149–155; Areeda & Turner, Predatory Pricing and Related Practices Under Section 2 of the Sherman Act, 88 Harv.L.Rev. 697, 699 (1975); Easterbrook, *supra*; Koller, The Myth of Predatory Pricing—An Empirical Study, 4 Antitrust Law & Econ.Rev. 105 (1971); McGee, Predatory Price Cutting: The *Standard Oil (N.J.) Case*, 1 J.Law & Econ. 137 (1958); McGee, Predatory Pricing Revisited, 23 J.Law & Econ., at 292–294.

These observations apply even to predatory pricing by a *single firm* seeking monopoly power. In this case, respondents allege that a large number of firms have conspired over a period of many years to charge below-market prices in order to stifle competition. Such a conspiracy is incalculably more difficult to execute than an analogous plan undertaken by a single predator. The conspirators must allocate the losses to be sustained during the conspiracy's operation, and must also allocate any gains to be realized from its success. Precisely because success is speculative and depends on a willingness to endure losses for an indefinite period, each conspirator has a strong incentive to cheat, letting its partners suffer the losses necessary to destroy the competition while sharing in any gains if the conspiracy succeeds. The necessary allocation is therefore difficult to accomplish. Yet if conspirators cheat to any substantial extent, the conspiracy must fail, because its success depends on depressing the market price for *all* buyers of CEPs. If there are too few goods at the artificially low price to satisfy demand, the would-be victims of the conspiracy can continue to sell at the "real" market price, and the conspirators suffer losses to little purpose.

Finally, if predatory pricing conspiracies are generally unlikely to occur, they are especially so where, as here, the prospects of attaining monopoly power seem slight. In order to recoup their losses, petitioners must obtain enough market power to set higher than competitive prices, and then must sustain those prices long enough to earn in excess profits what they earlier gave up in below-cost prices. Two decades after their conspiracy is alleged to have commenced, petitioners appear to be far from achieving this goal: the two largest shares of the retail market in television sets are held by RCA and respondent Zenith, not by any of the petitioners. Moreover, those shares, which together approximate 40% of sales, did not decline appreciably during the 1970's. Petitioners' collective share rose rapidly during this period, from one-fifth or less of the relevant markets to close to 50%. Neither the District Court nor the Court of Appeals found, however, that petitioners' share presently allows them to charge monopoly prices; to the contrary, respondents contend that the conspiracy is ongoing—that petitioners are still artificially *depressing* the market price in order to drive Zenith out of the market. The data in the record strongly suggest that that goal is yet far distant.[15]

15. Respondents offer no reason to suppose that entry into the relevant market is especially difficult, yet without barriers to entry it would presumably be impossible to maintain supracompetitive prices for an extended time. Judge Easterbrook, commenting on this case in a law review article, offers the following sensible assessment:

"The plaintiffs [in this case] maintain that for the last fifteen years or more at least ten Japanese manufacturers have sold TV sets at less than cost in order to drive United States firms out of business. Such conduct cannot possibly produce profits by harming competition, however. If the Japanese firms drive some United States firms out of business, they could not recoup. Fifteen years of losses could be made up only by very high prices for the indefinite future. (The losses are like investments, which must be recovered with compound interest.) If the defendants should try to raise prices to such a level, they would attract new competition. There are no barriers to entry into electronics, as the proliferation of computer and audio firms shows. The competition would come from resurgent United States firms, from other foreign firms (Korea and many other nations make TV sets), and from defendants themselves. In order to recoup, the Japanese firms would need to suppress competition among themselves. On plaintiffs' theory, the cartel would need to last at least thirty years, far longer than any in history,

The alleged conspiracy's failure to achieve its ends in the two decades of its asserted operation is strong evidence that the conspiracy does not in fact exist. Since the losses in such a conspiracy accrue before the gains, they must be "repaid" with interest. And because the alleged losses have accrued over the course of two decades, the conspirators could well require a correspondingly long time to recoup. Maintaining supracompetitive prices in turn depends on the continued cooperation of the conspirators, on the inability of other would-be competitors to enter the market, and (not incidentally) on the conspirators' ability to escape antitrust liability for their *minimum* price-fixing cartel.[16] Each of these factors weighs more heavily as the time needed to recoup losses grows. If the losses have been substantial—as would likely be necessary in order to drive out the competition [17]—petitioners would most likely have to sustain their cartel for years simply to break even.

Nor does the possibility that petitioners have obtained supracompetitive profits in the Japanese market change this calculation. Whether or not petitioners have the *means* to sustain substantial losses in this country over a long period of time, they have no *motive* to sustain such losses absent some strong likelihood that the alleged conspiracy in this country will eventually pay off. The courts below found no evidence of any such success, and—as indicated above—the facts actually are to the contrary: RCA and Zenith, not any of the petitioners, continue to hold the largest share of the American retail market in color television sets. More important, there is nothing to suggest any relationship between petitioners' profits in Japan and the amount petitioners could expect to gain from a conspiracy to monopolize the American market. In the absence of any such evidence, the possible existence of supracompetitive profits in Japan simply cannot overcome the economic obstacles to the ultimate success of this alleged predatory conspiracy.[18]

B

In *Monsanto*, we emphasized that courts should not permit factfinders to infer conspiracies when such inferences are implausible, because the

even when cartels were not illegal. None should be sanguine about the prospects of such a cartel, given each firm's incentive to shave price and expand its share of sales. The predation recoupment story therefore does not make sense, and we are left with the more plausible inference that the Japanese firms did not sell below cost in the first place. They were just engaged in hard competition." Easterbrook, The Limits of Antitrust, 63 Texas L.Rev. 1, 26–27 (1984) (footnotes omitted).

16. The alleged predatory scheme makes sense only if petitioners can recoup their losses. In light of the large number of firms involved here, petitioners can achieve this only by engaging in some form of price fixing *after* they have succeeded in driving competitors from the market. Such price fixing would, of course, be an independent violation of § 1 of the Sherman Act.

17. The predators' losses must actually *increase* as the conspiracy nears its objective: the greater the predators' market share, the more products the predators sell; but since every sale brings with it a loss, an increase in market share also means an increase in predatory losses.

18. The same is true of any supposed excess production capacity that petitioners may have possessed. The existence of plant capacity that exceeds domestic demand does tend to establish the ability to sell products abroad. It does not, however, provide a motive for selling at prices lower than necessary to obtain sales; nor does it explain why petitioners would be willing to *lose* money in the United States market without some reasonable prospect of recouping their investment.

effect of such practices is often to deter procompetitive conduct. Respondents, petitioners' competitors, seek to hold petitioners liable for damages caused by the alleged conspiracy to cut prices. Moreover, they seek to establish this conspiracy indirectly, through evidence of other combinations (such as the check-price agreements and the five company rule) whose natural tendency is to raise prices, and through evidence of rebates and other price-cutting activities that respondents argue tend to prove a combination to suppress prices.[19] But cutting prices in order to increase business often is the very essence of competition. Thus, mistaken inferences in cases such as this one are especially costly, because they chill the very conduct the antitrust laws are designed to protect.

In most cases, this concern must be balanced against the desire that illegal conspiracies be identified and punished. That balance is, however, unusually one-sided in cases such as this one. As we earlier explained, predatory pricing schemes require conspirators to suffer losses in order eventually to realize their illegal gains; moreover, the gains depend on a host of uncertainties, making such schemes more likely to fail than to succeed. These economic realities tend to make predatory pricing conspiracies self-deterring: unlike most other conduct that violates the antitrust laws, failed predatory pricing schemes are costly to the conspirators. Finally, unlike predatory pricing by a single firm, *successful* predatory pricing conspiracies involving a large number of firms can be identified and punished once they succeed, since some form of minimum price-fixing agreement would be necessary in order to reap the benefits of predation. Thus, there is little reason to be concerned that by granting summary judgment in cases where the evidence of conspiracy is speculative or ambiguous, courts will encourage such conspiracies.

V

As our discussion in Part IV–A shows, petitioners had no motive to enter into the alleged conspiracy. To the contrary, as presumably rational businesses, petitioners had every incentive *not* to engage in the conduct with which they are charged, for its likely effect would be to generate losses for petitioners with no corresponding gains. The Court of Appeals did not take account of the absence of a plausible motive to enter into the alleged predatory pricing conspiracy. It focused instead on whether there was "direct evidence of concert of action." The Court of Appeals erred in two respects: (i) the "direct evidence" on which the court relied had little, if any, relevance to the alleged predatory pricing conspiracy; and (ii) the

19. Respondents also rely on an expert study suggesting that petitioners have sold their products in the American market at substantial losses. The relevant study is not based on actual cost data; rather, it consists of expert opinion based on a mathematical construction that in turn rests on assumptions about petitioners' costs. The District Court analyzed those assumptions in some detail and found them both implausible and inconsistent with record evidence. Although the Court of Appeals reversed the District Court's finding that the expert report was inadmissible, the court did not disturb the District Court's analysis of the factors that substantially undermine the probative value of that evidence. We find the District Court's analysis persuasive. Accordingly, in our view the expert opinion evidence of below-cost pricing has little probative value in comparison with the economic factors, discussed in Part IV–A, *supra*, that suggest that such conduct is irrational.

court failed to consider the absence of a plausible motive to engage in predatory pricing.

The "direct evidence" on which the court relied was evidence of *other* combinations, not of a predatory pricing conspiracy. Evidence that petitioners conspired to raise prices in Japan provides little, if any, support for respondents' claims: a conspiracy to increase profits in one market does not tend to show a conspiracy to sustain losses in another. Evidence that petitioners agreed to fix *minimum* prices (through the "check price" agreements) for the American market actually works in petitioners' favor, because it suggests that petitioners were seeking to place a floor under prices rather than to lower them. The same is true of evidence that petitioners agreed to limit the number of distributors of their products in the American market—the so-called five company rule. That practice may have facilitated a horizontal territorial allocation, see *United States v. Topco Associates, Inc.*, 405 U.S. 596 (1972), but its natural effect would be to raise market prices rather than reduce them. Evidence that tends to support any of these collateral conspiracies thus says little, if anything, about the existence of a conspiracy to charge below-market prices in the American market over a period of two decades.

. . .[I]n light of the absence of any rational motive to conspire, neither petitioners' pricing practices, nor their conduct in the Japanese market, nor their agreements respecting prices and distribution in the American market, suffice to create a "genuine issue for trial." Fed.Rule Civ.Proc. 56(e).[21]

On remand, the Court of Appeals is free to consider whether there is other evidence that is sufficiently unambiguous to permit a trier of fact to find that petitioners conspired to price predatorily for two decades despite the absence of any apparent motive to do so. The evidence must "ten[d] to exclude the possibility" that petitioners underpriced respondents to compete for business rather than to implement an economically senseless conspiracy. *Monsanto*, 465 U.S., at 764. In the absence of such evidence, there is no "genuine issue for trial" under Rule 56(e), and petitioners are entitled to have summary judgment reinstated.

* * *

The decision of the Court of Appeals is reversed, and the case is remanded for further proceedings consistent with this opinion.

JUSTICE WHITE, with whom JUSTICES BRENNAN, BLACKMUN, and STEVENS join, dissenting:

It is indeed remarkable that the Court, in the face of the long and careful opinion of the Court of Appeals, reaches the result it does. The Court of Appeals faithfully followed the relevant precedents . . . After surveying the massive record, including very significant evidence that the District Court erroneously had excluded, the Court of Appeals concluded that the evidence taken as a whole creates a genuine issue of fact whether

---

21. We do not imply that, if petitioners had had a plausible reason to conspire, ambiguous conduct could suffice to create a triable issue of conspiracy. Our decision in *Monsanto Co. v. Spray–Rite Service Corp.*, 465 U.S. 752 (1984), establishes that conduct that is as consistent with permissible competition as with illegal conspiracy does not, without more, support even an inference of conspiracy.

petitioners engaged in a conspiracy in violation of §§ 1 and 2 of the Sherman Act and § 2(a) of the Robinson–Patman Act. . . .

* * *

I

. . . [Language of the Court] suggests that a judge hearing a defendant's motion for summary judgment in an antitrust case should go beyond the traditional summary judgment inquiry and decide for himself whether the weight of the evidence favors the plaintiff. *Cities Service* and *Monsanto* do not stand for any such proposition. Each of those cases simply held that a particular piece of evidence standing alone was insufficiently probative to justify sending a case to the jury. These holdings in no way undermine the doctrine that all evidence must be construed in the light most favorable to the party opposing summary judgment.

If the Court intends to give every judge hearing a motion for summary judgment in an antitrust case the job of determining if the evidence makes the inference of conspiracy more probable than not, it is overturning settled law. If the Court does not intend such a pronouncement, it should refrain from using unnecessarily broad and confusing language.

II

* * *

The Court, in discussing the unlikelihood of a predatory conspiracy, also consistently assumes that petitioners valued profit-maximization over growth. In light of the evidence that petitioners sold their goods in this country at substantial losses over a long period of time, I believe that this is an assumption that should be argued to the factfinder, not decided by the Court.

III

In reversing the Third Circuit's judgment, the Court identifies two alleged errors: "(i) [T]he 'direct evidence on which the [Court of Appeals] relied had little, if any, relevance to the alleged predatory pricing conspiracy; and (ii) the court failed to consider the absence of a plausible motive to engage in predatory pricing." The Court's position is without substance.

A

The first claim of error is that the Third Circuit treated evidence regarding price fixing in Japan and the so-called five-company rule and check prices as " 'direct evidence' of a conspiracy that injured respondents." The passage from the Third Circuit's opinion in which the Court locates this alleged error makes what I consider to be a quite simple and correct observation, namely, that this case is distinguishable from traditional "conscious parallelism" cases, in that there is direct evidence of concert of action among petitioners. The Third Circuit did not, as the Court implies, jump unthinkingly from this observation to the conclusion that evidence regarding the five-company rule could support a finding of antitrust injury to respondents. The Third Circuit twice specifically noted that horizontal agreements allocating customers, though illegal, do not ordinarily injure competitors of the agreeing parties. However, after reviewing evidence of cartel activity in Japan, collusive establishment of dumping prices in this country, and long-term, below-cost sales, the Third Circuit held that a factfinder could reasonably conclude that the five-company rule was not a simple price-raising device:

> "[A] factfinder might reasonably infer that the allocation of customers in the United States, combined with price-fixing in Japan, was intended to permit concentration of the effects of dumping upon American competitors while eliminating competition among the Japanese manufacturers in either market."

I see nothing erroneous in this reasoning.

B

The Court's second charge of error is that the Third Circuit was not sufficiently skeptical of respondents' allegation that petitioners engaged in predatory pricing conspiracy. But the Third Circuit is not required to engage in academic discussions about predation; it is required to decide whether respondents' evidence creates a genuine issue of material fact. The Third Circuit did its job, and remanding the case so that it can do the same job again is simply pointless.

The Third Circuit indicated that it considers respondents' evidence sufficient to create a genuine factual issue regarding long-term, below-cost sales by petitioners. The Court tries to whittle away at this conclusion by suggesting that the "expert opinion evidence of below-cost pricing has little probative value in comparison with the economic factors . . . that suggest that such conduct is irrational." But the question is not whether the Court finds respondents' experts persuasive, or prefers the District Court's analysis; it is whether, viewing the evidence in the light most favorable to respondents, a jury or other factfinder could reasonably conclude that petitioners engaged in long-term, below-cost sales. I agree with the Third Circuit that the answer to this question is "yes."

It is misleading for the Court to state that the Court of Appeals "did not disturb the District Court's analysis of the factors that substantially undermine the probative value of [evidence in the DePodwin Report respecting below-cost sales]." The Third Circuit held that the exclusion of the portion of the DePodwin Report regarding below-cost pricing was erroneous because "the trial court ignored DePodwin's uncontradicted affidavit that all data relied on in his report were of the type on which experts in his field would reasonably rely." In short, the Third Circuit found DePodwin's affidavit sufficient to create a genuine factual issue regarding the correctness of his conclusion that petitioners sold below cost over a long period of time. Having made this determination, the court saw no need—nor do I—to address the District Court's analysis point by point. The District Court's criticisms of DePodwin's methods are arguments that a factfinder should consider. . . .

———

Questions and Comments

Was *Matsushita* correctly decided? Was there evidence from which a jury could infer that the Japanese producers agreed to a price that was lower than the price competition would have produced? If so, what was that evidence?

Suppose that the cost of the American producers (including a sufficient return to survive) was $100; cost to the Japanese was $90; competition among the Japanese producers would have driven price to $90; by collaboration the Japanese producers held price at $98. Were the American producers injured by the Japanese producers' conspiracy?

Did the Court legitimately use the neoclassical competition model to predict behavior of Japanese producers? Is it implausible to suppose that Japanese producers would *not* behave like American short-term profit maximizers?

Suppose that the *Matsushita* plaintiffs proved: Japanese often pursue an increased market share even at the expense of low or no profits, especially in foreign markets (see Kristoff, Japan Winning Race in China, N.Y. Times, April 29, 1987, at D1, col. 3: "For now it's hara-kiri. Later we will recover a profit."); Japanese tend to act by consensus and would strongly resist "cheating" once committed to an international conspiracy (cf. C. Johnson, MITI, and The Japanese Miracle 8 (1982)); Japanese, once having decided to build market share, would take a very long run, not a short run, perspective in evaluating the enterprise (see E. Vogel, Japan as Number One: Lessons for America 134–35 (1979). Could such evidence have trumped defendants' implausibility card?

Assume that there is a rational basis for the fact-finder to infer a low-price conspiracy. The Japanese firms then argue (as does the Justice Department) that the plaintiffs should nevertheless be out of court: there is no way that a low-price conspiracy in a low-barrier market can cause "antitrust injury." Even if the Japanese will provide the product at a low price (ousting the Americans who are less efficient or less well subsidized), no redressable harm is done. If the Japanese raise price, the Americans will come back in; thus, there is an absolute check on supracompetitive pricing. Because consumers benefit, there is no loss to competition. Is this standing argument convincing? Should the American producers have a legal right to freedom from price-fixing that harms them? Would relief for the American producers harm consumers?

What would the Court that decided *Interstate Circuit* have done in *Matsushita?*

2. OLIGOPOLISTIC INTERDEPENDENCE AS CONCERT OF ACTION OR UNFAIR METHOD OF COMPETITION

In some circumstances where firms do the same thing at the same time (e.g., change a pattern of distribution, as in *Interstate Circuit,* or use the same pricing system, as in *Cement Institute*), the existence of interdependence may support an inference that they acted by agreement. But in such situations there may also be evidence that no agreement took place and a trier of fact might well so conclude. Moreover there may also be circumstances of tight oligopoly where strong interdependence, far from supporting the inference of agreement, may negate that inference because it convincingly indicates that consciously parallel, non-competitive behavior would be achieved without agreement. What should the law do when firms do not behave like rivals because oligopolistic forces facilitate or even lead them into collaborative patterns? Should clearly interdependent conduct having anticompetitive consequences be treated as a violation of Section 1 not only when a fact finder infers agreement, but always, on the legal theory that such interdependent coordination is, itself, a contract, combination or conspiracy?

BOGOSIAN v. GULF OIL CORP.

561 F.2d 434 (3rd Cir.1977), cert. denied, 434 U.S. 1086 (1978).

CHIEF JUDGE SEITZ: In separate lawsuits, two independent service station dealers, Bogosian and Parisi, sued their respective lessors, Gulf and Exxon, alleging that the lease contracts imposed a tie-in in violation of § 1 of the Sherman Act. Each plaintiff also joined as party defendants fourteen other major oil companies whom they alleged, together with Gulf and Exxon, engaged in what they now argue was concerted action to unlawfully tie the leasing and subleasing of gas station sites to the purchase of gasoline supplied by each dealer's lessor. More specifically, plaintiffs alleged that, at least since 1957, and continuing to the present, "defendants, through a course of interdependent consciously parallel action, have required all dealers who lease, sublease, or renew such leases or subleases for one or more of defendants' service stations to:

(a) license the use of the lessor's trademark;

(b) sell only the lessor's gasoline; and

(c) not sell gasoline purchased from any other source under the licensed trademark."

Plaintiffs alleged that these restrictions forced them to buy gasoline at whatever price their lessor offered and prevented them from selling other brands of gasoline. . . .

* * *

The district court held that the complaint failed to allege either a "contract or conspiracy," and that the allegation of "interdependent consciously parallel action" did not plead the concerted action required to state a claim under § 1. Although the court recognized that, together with other evidence, consciously parallel business behavior may support an inference of conspiracy, it thought that an allegation of contract, conspiracy or combination is essential to state a claim. The court regarded the omission of the word "conspiracy" for the complaint to be a "deliberately employed strategy" by "experienced and learned attorneys in the field of antitrust litigation." Thus, it reasoned that although it terminated plaintiffs' actions for failure to plead the word "conspiracy" it was not resurrecting the requirement of pleading "magic words" which characterized common law pleading.

Plaintiffs argue that the complaint fairly read as a whole alleges a "combination," and that such an allegation combined with a statement of the specific course of conduct alleged to be unlawful clearly states a claim. We agree.

Paragraphs 16, 17, and 19 of the second amended complaint [hereinafter complaint] expressly refer to an unlawful combination. It is unnecessary to restate defendants' linguistic arguments to the effect that the word "combination" was not used to refer to an actual combination. Suffice it to say that their acceptance would hardly be consistent with the precept that the complaint be liberally construed.

Even if we had no doubt that plaintiffs' substitution of "combination" for "conspiracy" was deliberate and purposeful, we would be unwilling to speculate at this stage as to plaintiffs' theory. Plaintiffs' complaint alleges an unlawful combination and their briefs have not sought to explain that allegation in terms other than that of a classic combination or conspiracy. We perceive no distinction between the terms combination and conspiracy which would distinguish the two complaints. Our reading of § 1 cases indicates that the two terms are used interchangeably. As one commentator has noted, the cases have interpreted the statute as "present[ing] a single concept about common action, not three separate ones: 'contract . . . combination or conspiracy' becomes an alliterative compound noun, roughly translated to mean 'concerted action.' There is little need to grapple with issues about the meanings of the particular words of the statute nor to mark nice distinctions among them." L. Sullivan, *Law of Antitrust* 312 (1977). We therefore consider the sufficiency of a complaint which fairly read alleges a combination or conspiracy based upon interdependent consciously parallel action among defendants to impose allegedly unlawful tie-in agreements upon defendants' respective lessees.

The law is settled that proof of consciously parallel business behavior is circumstantial evidence from which an agreement, tacit or express, can be inferred but that such evidence, without more, is insufficient unless the circumstances under which it occurred make the inference of rational, independent choice less attractive than that of concerted action. We recently articulated those circumstances in *Venzie Corp. v. United States Mineral Products, Co.*, 521 F.2d 1309[, 1314] (3d Cir.1975):

"(1) a showing of acts by defendants in contradiction of their own economic interests . . .; and

"(2) satisfactory demonstration of a motivation to enter an agreement . . . ."

Plaintiffs argue that, given an opportunity to conduct discovery, they will prove that both of these circumstances are present. They contend that independent self interest would indicate that each oil company seek to market gasoline to their competitors' lessees, and that the failure to so compete can be explained only by a mutual understanding, tacit or expressed, that gasoline be marketed to lessee-dealers on an exclusive basis. The motivation to participate in such an agreement, of course, is the elimination of price competition among oil companies at the wholesale level. We need not, at this time, consider whether this theory would necessarily carry the day, for we are satisfied that, at the least, it does not appear to a certainty that plaintiffs can prove no set of facts which under *Venzie* would entitle them to reach the jury.

* * *

Plaintiffs also contend that even if their complaints are construed not to allege a combination, that an allegation of interdependent consciously parallel action states a § 1 claim. Neither plaintiffs nor defendants offer a definition of interdependence, however. A situation of interdependence has been said to exist when, in a highly concentrated market, there is an awareness that, because of the limited number of sellers, any variation in price or price-related structures will necessarily have a demonstrable effect on the sales of others such that each firm bases its decisions, at least in part, on the anticipated reactions of the others to its initiative. *See Sullivan, supra,* § 116.

There is a lively debate, however, concerning the relationship of interdependence to collusion. On the one hand, Professor Posner, for example, has said that interdependence cannot occur without, and hence is a product of, collusion. *See* Posner, *Oligopoly and the Antitrust Laws: A Suggested Approach,* 21 Stan.L.Rev. 1562–76; 1591–92 (1969). On the other hand, Professor Sullivan has said that interdependence can exist apart from collusion, but that noncollusive interdependent activity can, under certain circumstances, amount to an unlawful combination. *Sullivan, supra* § 122; *See* Turner, *The Definition of Agreement Under the Sherman Act: Conscious Parallelism and Refusals to Deal,* 75 Harv.L.Rev. 655, 660–81 (1962).

If these theories are to be tested, it should be done on a fully developed factual record which probes the conflicting economic facts on which they are premised. The complaint is much too blunt an instrument with which to forge fundamental policies regarding the meaning of competition in concentrated industries. We conclude that the ruling that the specific allegation of interdependent consciously parallel action made here fails to state a claim should be vacated so that the issue can be decided, if necessary, after the relevant facts are fully developed. . . .

———

Judge Aldisert dissented on grounds that "an allegation of consciously parallel behavior, without more, would not state a Sherman Act claim."

Questions and Comments

In *Interstate Circuit,* you will recall, the Court said that "agreement . . . was not a prerequisite" to a violation; that "[i]t was enough that, knowing that concerted action was contemplated and invited, the distributors gave their adherence to the scheme and participated in it" (supra, pp. 450, 455. Does that dictum support a construction of Section 1 that sweeps up all strongly interdependent and anticompetitive conduct? Does the legislative history of the Sherman Act support that broad construction? Does the statutory language and its key concepts?

Note again the remedial problems: if interdependent, supracompetitive pricing in a three firm industry were an unlawful "contract, combination or conspiracy" would enjoining that contract, combination or conspiracy be meaningful? Could the injunction be more specific—e.g., do not price above marginal cost (or cost plus a fair return, or cost plus a specified percentage return)? Do you see any administrative problems with such an approach? If interdependent pricing was found unlawful under Section 1, could a court order a structural remedy—e.g., break up the oligopoly?

Note the anomalies in holding non-collusive, interdependent pricing by oligopolists to be a violation while holding that monopoly pricing by a monopolist is lawful.

The remedial problems may not be so severe in instances of interdependence other than mere supracompetitive prices. For example, even though a court might hesitate to order marginal cost pricing it might not hesitate to enjoin the use of a delivered pricing system. Could the existence of a violation be made to turn on the availability of a feasible remedy?

Are there some forms of interdependence (e.g., price leadership) that are or should be beyond the reach of Section 1 as a matter of law, while other forms (e.g., restrictive clauses) should be within the reach of the law?

In the 1950s the government sued General Electric, Westinghouse and Allis Chalmers for a conspiracy to fix the price of large turbine generators. The litigations were concluded in 1962 by entry of consent decrees, which enjoined the companies from communicating price information to one another until after the information had been released to the trade. Shortly thereafter, Allis Chalmers withdrew from the market, leaving only General Electric and Westinghouse as suppliers. Despite the 1962 decree, General Electric and Westinghouse did not compete on price. They priced in tandem. This was accomplished by a series of practices that the government called "price signalling." The government's claims of price fixing by signalling were settled in 1977 with the modification of the 1962 decree. Below is the court's description of the practices and the agreed-upon remedy.

UNITED STATES v. GENERAL ELECTRIC CO.
1977–2 Trade Cas. (CCH) ¶ 61,659–660 (E.D.Pa.1977).

JUDGE McGLYNN: The matter before this court concerns the proposed modification of the 1962 consent decrees entered into between the United States and General Electric and Westinghouse Corporation. . . .

In December of 1976, the parties to the 1962 consent decrees jointly filed with this court proposals to modify that final judgment. After reviewing the competitive impact statement filed by the government, the memoranda of the parties and amici curiae, the numerous comments of interested parties, and after hearing oral argument on the various issues presented, this court finds that entry of the modifications as proposed by the government and the defendants is in the public interest and accordingly, the proposed modifications by consent will be approved.

The 1962 consent decrees grew out of a civil action filed by the government charging General Electric, Westinghouse, and Allis–Chalmers Manufacturing Corporation with fixing the price of large turbine generators and seeking injunctive relief against further violations of section 1 of the Sherman Act. That action ended with the entry of consent decrees against the corporations, enjoining them from, *inter alia*, communicating pricing information to one another until after the information had been released generally to the trade.

In 1972, the government undertook an investigation of the competitive condition in the turbine generator industry. The investigation revealed that beginning in 1963 there had been an elimination of price competition between G.E. and Westinghouse. By December, 1962, Allis-Chalmers had withdrawn from the market for turbine generators and, therefore, is not a party to this proceeding, nor was it a target of the government's investigation. The government does not contend that the elimination of price competition was the result of any direct covert communication between the parties, but rather that it was the result of the conscious adoption and publication of identical pricing policies in 1963–64 and the strict adherence to those policies since that time.

In 1963 both General Electric and Westinghouse published similar and unusually extensive price books enabling each to predict not only the exact price that the other would bid in a particular situation, but also the precise type and size of the machine. Both companies also adopted a price protection plan which provided that if the price was lowered by a manufacturer for a particular customer, any buyer within the previous six month period would be given an identical discount retroactively. Thus, each manufacturer was assured that the other would not engage in discounting because of the substantial self-imposed penalty involved. Also, both companies published a list of outstanding bids whenever there was a price change so that there would be no confusion as to which customers were being charged the old rate and thus no suspicions of discounting would be aroused. These practices resulted in a pattern of equal pricing in the sale of large turbine generators and the government contends that contemporaneous internal documents indicate that this result was the deliberate intent of the defendants.

The government concluded that it would be appropriate to file suit against G.E. and Westinghouse and informed them of its intention to do so. In the course of subsequent negotiations, the defendants, while vigorously denying any liability, agreed to a modification of the 1962 agreement whereby they would be precluded from publicly disseminating price information and enjoined from entering into price protection agreements with their customers. This modification would grant the government all the relief it would have sought in a Sherman Act suit, while avoiding the considerable delay and expense and the uncertainty of a trial.

* * *

[The court modified the 1962 consent judgment by adding the following prohibitions:]

* * *

Now, Therefore, before any testimony has been taken, the Court being advised and having considered the matter it is hereby Ordered, Adjudged and Decreed that the Final Judgment entered herein on October 1, 1962, is hereby modified as follows:

1. ["Large turbine-generator" defined.]

2. That the defendant, its successors, assignees, transferees, and respective officers, agents, and employees, be enjoined and restrained from:

(a) publishing or distributing any information intended to communicate directly or indirectly an invitation to agree, or willingness to agree, with any manufacturer of large turbine-generators (i) to raise, fix, maintain, stabilize, or otherwise affect the price or other terms and conditions for the sale of large turbine-generators, or (ii) to reduce or eliminate competition in the guaranteed or actual performance of large turbine-generators;

(b) hereafter offering a price protection policy or entering into any agreement whereby the price of a large turbine-generator to any customer would be retroactively reduced or the defendant would be subject to any penalty or disadvantage as the direct result of offering or providing a lower price or more favorable terms and conditions of sale to any subsequent customer or potential customer;

(c) beginning three months from the effective date of this modification, using any price book, price list, or compilation of prices for the sale of large turbine-generators other than a price book, price list, or compilation of prices

    (i) compiled by the defendant after the effective date of this modification;

    (ii) based on the defendant's own individually determined criteria and costs; and

    (iii) not based on the prices in any price book, price list, or compilation of prices in effect during the period beginning May 20, 1963 and extending up to and including the effective date of this modification;

provided, however, that this subsection 2(c) shall not be construed to prohibit the defendant from selling a large turbine-generator to a specific customer at any price it sees fit consistent with the provisions of this modification; and provided further, that defendant shall be allowed to use its price books issued prior to the date this provision takes effect solely for the purpose of calculating prices for turbine-generators ordered before that date;

(d) preparing or using any price book or price list for large turbine-generators after the effective date of this modification that is related to any previous price book or price list by a uniform multiplier or percentage, or computing the price of a large turbine-generator by applying a uniform multiplier or percentage to any previous price book or price list, except where necessary to compute the price of a turbine-generator ordered prior to the effective date of this modification;

(e) distributing or revealing to any person not employed by the defendant a price book or price list relating to large turbine-generators;

(f) communicating to any person not employed by the defendant

    (i) a policy regarding negotiation or bargaining involving the price or terms and conditions of sale for large turbine-generators;

    (ii) a policy regarding performance guarantees for large turbine-generators;

(iii) a policy regarding negotiation or bargaining involving the price of spare parts for large turbine-generators;

(iv) a policy regarding the use of a formula or system for pricing large turbine-generators;

(v) a formula or system for pricing large turbine-generators, provided that nothing in this subsection 2(f)(v) shall be construed to prohibit the defendant from using price escalation clauses to adjust prices to reflect changes in costs or other economic indices between the date of order and the date of delivery or from selling large turbine-generators under a cost-reimbursement contract; and

(vi) any change in the price of large turbine-generators, provided that the defendant shall not be prohibited from communicating to a specific customer, potential customer, or his agent, a change in a price previously furnished to such customer or agent for a particular large turbine-generator;

(g) distributing or revealing to any person not employed by the defendant (i) prices and terms and conditions for the sale of large turbine-generators; (ii) the exhaust end load limits for large turbine-generators; and (iii) performance guarantees, including but not limited to heat rates for large turbine-generators.

Nothing in section 2(g) shall be construed to prohibit the defendant (1) from conveying to a specific customer or potential customer, or his agent, the information necessary to respond, in good faith, to a request from such customer or agent for the defendant to bid on, or to engage in negotiations regarding the purchase of, one or more large turbine-generators, or (2) from conveying information necessary to respond in good faith to a request from a customer or his agent for information in connection with discussions regarding the purchase of one or more large turbine-generators by that customer;

(h)(i) expressing to any person not employed by the defendant the price of a large turbine-generator in terms of a multiple or percentage of a book or list price or a separately stated price or (ii) expressing to any person not employed by the defendant a relation of the price of a large turbine generator to a separately stated price or to a price furnished to a different customer;

(i) publishing, or communicating directly or indirectly to any person not employed by the defendant, any compilation of (a) outstanding bids or quotations for the sale of large turbine-generators for a period of five years from the date such bids or quotations are made; or (b) prices and terms and conditions of sale quoted on transactions involving the sale of large turbine-generators for a period of thirty months from the date of such quotations;

(j)(i) using or retaining a price book, price list, or compilation of list or book prices or standard terms and conditions, for the sale of large turbine-generators, prepared by Westinghouse after May 1, 1963, or a copy thereof;

(ii) using or retaining a price book, price list, or compilation of list or book prices or standard terms and conditions, for the sale of large turbine-generators prepared after the effective date of this modification by a manufacturer other than Westinghouse, or a copy thereof;

(k) receiving or examining any part of any document, prepared or distributed by Westinghouse, or copy thereof, and including prices, terms and conditions of sale, or performance guarantees regarding the sale of a large turbine-generator; provided, however, that a representative of the defendant may be permitted to view a bid prepared by Westinghouse, at the option of the customer and prior to the award of the order, solely for the purpose of verifying, in good faith, representations made by the customer or its agent concerning the content of such Westinghouse bid; and provided further that independent counsel, acting on behalf of General Electric, may be employed to verify that an award of a public sealed bid is legal; such lawyer may employ independent technical advisers, so long as neither the lawyer nor technical advisers communicate to any General Electric employee the contents of such Westinghouse bid.

3. Nothing contained herein shall be construed to prohibit the defendant (a) from conveying information in compliance with any order, or in connection with participation in any proceeding, of a court, legislative body, or administrative agency; (b) from conveying information to any person retained by the defendant for a legitimate purpose, provided that, with regard to any such information that refers or relates to price, terms and conditions of sale, exhaust end load limits, and performance guarantees, the defendant shall secure from such person a legally binding commitment not to publish or re-use said information; (c) from using or conveying information in connection with the rendering of legal advice or participating in a legal proceeding; (d) from responding to competition by changing price or terms and conditions of sale furnished to a customer in a manner otherwise consistent with the provisions of this decree; or (e) from complying with contractual commitments to any customer undertaken prior to the effective date of this modification by:

(i) expressing the price of a large turbine-generator in terms of (a) a price book or price list issued prior to the effective date of this modification or (b) a multiplier or percentage established prior to the effective date of this modification applied to any such price book or price list;

(ii) expressing the price or any performance guarantee for a large turbine-generator in terms of a formula included or incorporated by reference in a contract entered into prior to the effective date of this modification.

4. The defendant is ordered to retain in its files records of calculations and determinations involved in the computation of a price for any large turbine-generator, or in the preparation of any price book or price list for such machines, for a period of five years after such computation or preparation.

5. The defendant, its successors, assignees and transferees, and its officers, agents and employees are ordered:

(a) to print conspicuously on each of its price books or price lists for the sale of large turbine-generators prepared after the effective date of this modification a notice that distribution of the price book or price list to persons not employed by the defendant will constitute a violation of this modification and that said violation may be punishable as contempt of court; and

(b) to number each of its price books or price lists for the sale of large turbine-generators prepared after the effective date of this modification, and maintain a log which shall indicate: (i) the name and position of every person to whom a price book or price list is distributed and (ii) the date of such distribution. . . .

Questions and Comments

Neither *General Electric* nor *Bogosian* answers the central question: Does anticompetitive interdependence violate Section 1? Should it? Or is the cure for interdependence not feasible, or worse than the disease?

One scholar has suggested that analysis should focus on "avoidable acts." See Hay, Oligopoly, Shared Monopoly, and Antitrust Law, 67 Cornell L.Rev. 439 (1982). Oligopolists might naturally reach a consensus price by pure interdependence. But they might also engage in additional practices that would be economically irrational if each acted alone. The additional practices might be intended to simplify the process of reaching a consensus price or to increase the chances that all competitors will be good citizens of the oligopoly. Such practices are called facilitating mechanisms or facilitating devices.

Why would General Electric offer to give all present and future customers price protection clauses? (For example, General Electric says to its customer: If in the future I give any customer a better price, I will give the benefit of the same lower price to you, retroactively.) Price protection clauses are expensive to General Electric *if* General Electric should lower its prices. General Electric will have more to lose than to gain by discounting to capture a new customer. Therefore General Electric is likely to adhere to the consensus price. Can we regard price protection clauses as a means used by General Electric to assure its rivals that General Electric will not be cutting prices below its announced prices?

Identify each facilitating practice in *General Electric*. If each practice was adopted interdependently rather than conspiratorially, should or could the practice be enjoined? Are treble (or even single) damages appropriate? If so, how should they be measured? Is plaintiff given the benefit of an assumption that, but for the facilitating mechanism, prices would be at a competitive level? If plaintiff must prove what the price would have been but for use of the mechanism, how might it go about that task?

Can and should the problem of oligopolistic interdependence be addressed through Section 5 of the Federal Trade Commission Act, which prohibits unfair methods of competition and does not require joint action? Or should it be addressed through Section 1 of the Sherman Act, which requires joint action?

The Federal Trade Commission attempted to deal with interdependence under Section 5 in the market for lead antiknock additives to gasoline. The FTC sued the four producers for using four facilitating practices to lessen competition. The Commission found a violation, after finding the market highly concentrated, sluggish and unresponsive, and entry unlikely. Chairman Miller dissented. Miller saw the market as highly competitive. He thought entry was easy, and that each challenged practice was employed for a good business purpose that was responsive to consumers. The case was appealed to the Court of Appeals for the Second Circuit. The appellate court adopted the Miller version of the facts.

E.I. DU PONT DE NEMOURS & CO. v. FEDERAL TRADE COMMISSION
729 F.2d 128 (2d Cir.1984).

JUDGE MANSFIELD: E.I. Du Pont De Nemours and Company ("Du Pont") and Ethyl Corporation ("Ethyl"), the nation's two largest manufacturers of lead antiknock gasoline additives, petition this court to review and set aside a final order of the Federal Trade Commission ("FTC") entered with an accompanying opinion on April 1, 1983. The FTC held that Du Pont, Ethyl and two other antiknock compound manufacturers, PPG Industries, Inc. ("PPG") and Nalco Chemical Company ("Nalco"), had engaged in unfair methods of competition in violation of § 5(a)(1) of the Federal Trade Commission Act when each firm independently and unilaterally adopted at different times some or all of three business practices that were neither restrictive, predatory, nor adopted for the purpose of restraining competition. These challenged practices were: (1) the sale of the product by all four firms at a delivered price which included transportation costs, (2) the giving by Du Pont and Ethyl of extra advance notice of price increases, over and above the 30 days provided by contract, and (3) the use by Du Pont and Ethyl (and infrequently by PPG) of a "most favored nation" clause under which the seller promised that no customer would be charged a higher price than other customers. The Commission reasoned that, although the petitioners' adoption of these practices was non-collusive, they collectively had the effect, by removing some of the uncertainties about price determination, of substantially lessening competition by facilitating price parallelism at non-competitive levels higher than might have otherwise existed. The order is set aside.

Lead-based antiknock compounds have been used in the refining of gasoline since the 1920s. The compounds are essentially homogeneous, consisting in part of tetraethyl lead (TEL), originally produced in the 1920s, and tetramethyl lead (TML), first produced in 1960. They are now usually sold as mixtures, sometimes with additives. The compounds are added to gasoline to prevent "knock," i.e., premature detonation in a gasoline engine's cylinders. Resistance to knock is measured by octane ratings; for a gasoline refiner use of lead-based antiknock mixtures is the most economical way to raise the octane rating of gasoline for vehicles that take leaded gas. Since the compounds are highly toxic and volatile, great care must be taken in transporting and storing them. Refiners therefore maintain only limited inventories. Since an uninterrupted supply is important, the refiner usually purchases the compounds periodically from at least two antiknock producers pursuant to one-year contracts.

From the 1920s until 1948, Ethyl was the sole domestic producer of antiknock compounds. Demand for the compounds increased with the increase in gasoline use, however, and in 1948 Du Pont entered the industry and captured a substantial market share. In 1961 PPG (then known as Houston Chemical Company) began to manufacture and sell the compounds; and in 1964 Nalco followed suit. By 1974, Du Pont had 38.4% of the market; Ethyl 33.5%; PPG 16.2%; and Nalco 11.8%. During 1974–1979, the period of the alleged violations, these were the only four domestic producers and sellers of the compounds. No other firm has ever made or sold the compounds in this country. Thus the industry has always been highly concentrated. However, there are no technological or financial barriers to new entries.

The only purchasers of lead antiknocks are the gasoline refining companies which are large, aggressive and sophisticated buyers. Indeed, several are among the largest industrial corporations in the world. If prospective profits from the sale of antiknock compounds were sufficiently attractive, nothing would prevent them from integrating backwards into the antiknock industry. Of the 154 refiners who purchase the product, the ten largest buy about 30% of the total amount produced in this country.

* * *

Following extensive hearings before the ALJ, the ALJ [found] . . . that the alleged practices, which were not disputed, constituted both "unfair methods of competition" and "unfair acts and practices" in violation of § 5. He entered an order prohibiting advance notice of price increases, uniform delivered prices, use of "most favored nation" clauses by Du Pont and Ethyl, and limiting announcements of price increases to the press and others.

Upon appeal the FTC, by a 3–1 margin with Chairman Miller dissenting, on March 22, 1983, issued a 119–page Final Order and Opinion finding that Du Pont and Ethyl had engaged in "unfair methods of competition" through the combined use of the "most favored nation" contractual clauses, uniform delivered pricing, and extra advance notice to customers of price increases beyond the 30–day contractual period. PPG and Nalco were found to have violated § 5 only with regard to the use of uniform delivered pricing. The Commission acknowledged that § 5 of the Act does not prohibit independent pricing by individual firms, even at high levels, in an oligopolistic industry. Yet, the Commission took the view that because § 5 is not confined to the strictures of the Sherman and Clayton Acts but prohibits a broader range of conduct, it can be violated even in the absence of agreement if the firms engage in interdependent conduct that, because of the market structure and conditions, facilitates price coordination in a way that substantially lessens competition in the industry.

As support for its theory the Commission relied upon the legislative history of § 5, certain prior decisions dealing with its challenges to basing point pricing schemes, and general statements of the Supreme Court and commentators regarding the reach of § 5. Rejecting petitioners' contention that § 5 liability requires a showing of at least a tacit agreement, the

Commission articulated what it called a "rule of reason" test whereby unilateral business practices could violate the Act if the structure of the industry rendered it susceptible to anticompetitive price coordination, if there was substantial evidence of actual noncompetitive performance, and if there was no "pro-competitive" justification offsetting the harmful effect of the practices.

The Commission concluded from its examination of the record that the structure of the antiknock industry—high concentration, high barriers to entry, a homogeneous product, and inelastic demand—rendered it susceptible to unilateral but interdependent conduct which lessened competition. The Commission further decided that the record contained substantial evidence of noncompetitive performance in the industry: highly uniform prices and price changes, limited price discounting, stable market shares, relatively high profits, prices in excess of marginal cost, and rising prices despite excess capacity and sluggish demand. On such a record, the FTC held that unilateral but interdependent practices engaged in by the petitioners constituted an unfair method of competition in violation of § 5. Conceding that the challenged practices each had a legitimate business purpose, the Commission concluded nevertheless that the anticompetitive effect of those practices rendered them unlawful. Specifically rejected by the majority were the ALJ's findings that the practices also constituted "unfair acts and practices" under § 5 and that the contractual requirement of 30 days advance notice to buyers of price increases and the press announcements of such price increases were unlawful. Thus, the Commission found that giving buyers 30 days advance notice of price increases was not unlawful but giving buyers a few more days advance notice of price increases was an unfair method of competition. Furthermore, even though none of the practices by itself was an unfair method of competition, and none of the practices was undertaken in agreement with the other manufacturers, the FTC concluded that their cumulative effect was to reduce competition and that the practices thus constituted unfair methods of competition in violation of the Act.

The FTC issued a cease and desist order only against Ethyl and Du Pont, prohibiting them from announcing price changes prior to the 30–day contractual period and from using "most favored nation" clauses in their sales contracts. The order also required Ethyl and Du Pont to afford their customers the option of purchasing antiknock additives at a "point of origin" price. The Commission did not prohibit the use of press releases or the 30–day advance notice of price increases. No order was entered against PPG because that company has withdrawn from the industry and no order was entered against Nalco because of the Commission's conclusion that Nalco was unlikely to be an initiator of price increases.

DISCUSSION

The essential question is whether, given the characteristics of the antiknock industry, the Commission erred in holding that the challenged business practices constitute "unfair methods of competition" in violation of § 5 simply because they "facilitate" consciously parallel pricing at identical levels. The question goes to the scope of the Commission's power. Although its interpretation of § 5 is entitled to great weight, and its power to declare trade practices unfair is broad, it is the function of the court ultimately to determine the scope of the statute upon which the Commission's jurisdiction depends.

Congress' use of the vague general term "unfair methods of competition" in § 5 without defining what is "unfair" was deliberate. The statute's legislative history reveals that, in reaction to the relatively narrow terms of the Sherman Act as limited by the Supreme Court's adoption of the Rule of Reason in *Standard Oil Co. v. United States,* 221 U.S. 1 (1911), Congress sought to provide broad and flexible authority to the Commission as an administrative body of presumably practical men with broad business and economic expertise in order that they might preserve business' freedom to compete from restraints. Congress' aim was to protect society against oppressive anti-competitive conduct and thus assure that the conduct prohibited by the Sherman and Clayton Acts would be supplemented as necessary and any interstices filled. Indeed, Congress, in the process of drafting § 5, gave up efforts to define specifically which methods of competition and practices are competitively harmful and abandoned a proposed laundry list of prohibited practices for the reason that there were too many practices to define and many more unforeseeable ones were yet to be created by ingenious business minds. The specific practices that might be barred were left to be defined by the Commission, applying its expertise, subject to judicial review. Congress did not, however, authorize the Commission under § 5 to bar any business practice found to have an adverse effect on competition. Instead, the Commission could proscribe only "unfair" practices or methods of competition. Review by the courts was essential to assure that the Commission would not act arbitrarily or without explication but according to definable standards that would be properly applied.

During the period since the enactment of the Federal Trade Commission Act the courts have established certain principles bearing on the scope of the Commission's powers. Although the Commission may under § 5 enforce the antitrust laws, including the Sherman and Clayton Acts, it is not confined to their letter. It may bar incipient violations of those statutes, and conduct which, although not a violation of the letter of the antitrust laws, is close to a violation or is contrary to their spirit. In prosecuting violations of the spirit of the antitrust laws, the Commission has, with one or two exceptions, confined itself to attacking collusive, predatory, restrictive or deceitful conduct that substantially lessens competition.

The Commission here asks us to go further and to hold that the "unfair methods of competition" provision of § 5 can be violated by non-collusive, non-predatory and independent conduct of a non-artificial nature, at least when it results in a substantial lessening of competition. We recognize that § 5 invests the Commission with broad powers designed to enable it to cope with new threats to competition as they arise. . . . However, appropriate standards must be adopted and applied to protect a respondent against abuse of power. As the Commission moves away from attacking conduct that is either a violation of the antitrust laws or collusive, coercive, predatory, restrictive or deceitful, and seeks to break new ground by enjoining otherwise legitimate practices, the closer must be our scrutiny upon judicial review. A test based solely upon restraint of competition, even if qualified by the requirement that the conduct be "analogous" to an antitrust violation, is so vague as to permit arbitrary or undue government interference with the reasonable freedom of action that has marked our country's competitive system. . . .

The term "unfair" is an elusive concept, often dependent upon the eye of the beholder. A line must therefore be drawn between conduct that is anticompetitive and legitimate conduct that has an impact on competition. Lessening of competition is not the substantial equivalent of "unfair methods" of competition. Section 5 is aimed at conduct, not at the result of such conduct, even though the latter is usually a relevant factor in determining whether the challenged conduct is "unfair." Nor does the statute obligate a business to engage in competition; if that were the case, many acceptable pricing and market decisions would be barred. A manufacturer, for instance, would be prevented from making a concededly lawful change in its distribution system, designed to increase sales efficiency, by unilaterally reducing the number of its wholesalers, since the effect would be to diminish substantial competition at the wholesaler level. Similarly, if anticompetitive impact were the sole test, the admittedly lawful unilateral closing of a plant or refusal to expand capacity could be found to be "unfair." The holder of a valid product patent could be prevented from exercising its lawful monopoly to charge whatever the traffic would bear, even though "a monopolist, as long as he has no purpose to restrain competition or to enhance or expand his monopoly, and does not act coercively, retains [the right to trade with whom he wishes]." *Official Airline Guides, Inc. v. FTC,* 630 F.2d 920, 927–28 (2d Cir.1980), *cert. denied,* 450 U.S. 917 (1981).

When a business practice is challenged by the Commission, even though, as here, it does not violate the antitrust or other laws and is not collusive, coercive, predatory or exclusionary in character, standards for determining whether it is "unfair" within the meaning of § 5 must be formulated to discriminate between normally acceptable business behavior and conduct that is unreasonable or unacceptable. Otherwise the door would be open to arbitrary or capricious administration of § 5; the FTC could, whenever it believed that an industry was not achieving its maximum competitive potential, ban certain practices in the hope that its action would increase competition. The mere existence of an oligopolistic market structure in which a small group of manufacturers engage in consciously parallel pricing of an identical product does not violate the antitrust laws. It represents a condition, not a "method;" indeed it could be consistent with intense competition. Labelling one producer's price change in such a market as a "signal," parallel price changes as "lockstep," or prices as "supracompetitive," hardly converts its pricing into an "unfair" method of competition. To so hold would be to condemn any such price increase or moves, however independent; yet the FTC has not suggested that § 5 authorizes it to ban all price increases in an oligopolistic market. On the contrary, it states that "Section 5 should not prohibit oligopolistic pricing *alone,* even supracompetitive parallel prices, in the absence of specific conduct which promotes such a result." (Emphasis in original). This fine distinction creates doubt as to the types of otherwise legitimate conduct that are lawful and those that are not. The doubt is increased by the Commission's concession that price uniformity is normal in a market with few sellers and homogeneous products, such as that in the antiknock compound industry.

* * *

In our view, before business conduct in an oligopolistic industry may be labelled "unfair" within the meaning of § 5 a minimum standard demands that, absent a tacit agreement, at least some indicia of oppressiveness must exist such as (1) evidence of anticompetitive intent or purpose on the part of the producer charged, or (2) the absence of an independent legitimate business reason for its conduct. If, for instance, a seller's conduct, even absent identical behavior on the part of its competitors, is contrary to its independent self-interest, that circumstance would indicate that the business practice is "unfair" within the meaning of § 5. In short, in the absence of proof of a violation of the antitrust laws or evidence of collusive, coercive, predatory, or exclusionary conduct, business practices are not "unfair" in violation of § 5 unless those practices either have an anticompetitive purpose or cannot be supported by an independent legitimate reason. To suggest, as does the Commission in its opinion, that the defendant can escape violating § 5 only by showing that there are "countervailing procompetitive justifications" for the challenged business practices goes too far.

In the present case the FTC concedes that the petitioners did not engage in the challenged practices by agreement or collusively. Each acted independently and unilaterally. There is no evidence of coercive or predatory conduct. If the petitioners nevertheless were unable to come forward with some independent legitimate reason for their adoption of these practices, the Commission's argument that they must be barred as "unfair" when they have the effect of facilitating conscious price parallelism and interdependence might have some merit. But the evidence is overwhelming and undisputed, as the ALJ found, that each petitioner independently adopted its practices for legitimate business reasons which we have described.

* * *

The Commission contends that although the business practices at issue here might not be unfair under other market conditions, they assume that unlawful character when adopted in a concentrated or oligopolistic market in which a few producers sell a homogenous product, demand is inelastic, prices are "supracompetitive," and barriers to entry are high. It is argued that in such a milieu the practices assist the producers in independently maintaining prices at higher levels than would otherwise be the case. Perhaps this argument would be acceptable if the market were clearly as so described and a causal connection could be shown between the practices and the level of prices. Indeed the Commission majority concedes that "facilitating practices will be found to violate § 5 as unfair methods of competition only if the weight of the evidence shows that competition has been substantially lessened" and that it was required to "establish a *clear nexus* between the challenged conduct and adverse competitive effects before invoking our authority in this regard." But the record does not contain substantial evidence supporting many of the Commission's conclusions or showing a causal connection between the challenged practices and market prices. Indeed, it appears to be riddled with deficiencies and inconsistencies, many of which are noted by Chairman Miller in his dissent.

In the first place, price uniformity and parallelism was much more limited than the FTC would have it. During the relevant period (1974–1979) Nalco extended price discounts on more than 80% of its sales and PPG on more than one-third of its sales, the latter increasing to 58% of its sales in 1979 as the sellers competed for fewer buyers in a diminishing market. Although there was for the most part price parallelism on the part of Du Pont and Ethyl, they effectively met the price discounts of the other two producers by providing competition in the form of extensive services which had the effect of retaining old customers or luring away new ones. Thus the total package, including free valuable services and discounts, presents a picture of a competitive market in which large, sophisticated and aggressive buyers were making demands and were satisfied with the results. To the extent that there was price uniformity, that condition is as consistent with competitive as with anticompetitive behavior.

The problems faced by anyone thinking of entering the market were not "barriers" in the usual sense used by economists, such as requirements for high capital investment or advanced technological know-how. The main problem has been that market demand, due to factors uncontrolled by petitioners, is sharply declining. A dying market, which will soon dry up altogether, does not attract new entries. Absent some reasonable prospect that a price reduction would increase demand—and there is none—it is not surprising that existing producers have not engaged in as much price competition as might exist under other conditions. To suggest that industry-wide use of delivered instead of f.o.b. pricing restrained price competition in such a market ignores the de minimis part freight charges played in the price paid by customers. It also overlooks the fact that f.o.b. pricing is not necessarily more competitive than delivered pricing.

In short, we do not find substantial evidence in this record as a whole that the challenged practices significantly lessened competition in the antiknock industry or that the elimination of those practices would improve competition. The Commission's expert, Dr. George Hay, stated merely that "the market would have operated differently absent these practices"; he could not estimate the extent of that difference. All four of the petitioners' experts, however, who had impressive credentials and experience, stated conclusively that the lack of perfect competition in the antiknock industry was due to the structure of the industry and that the challenged practices had little if any effect on competition. The Commission contends that the practices reduced uncertainty about prices in the industry; the petitioners' experts convincingly argued, on the other hand, that regardless of the practices, competitors learned of each other's prices anyway within hours and that most of the significant competition within the industry occurred on non-price terms. Thus, even if the Commission has authority under § 5 to forbid legitimate, non-collusive business practices which substantially lessen competition, there has not been a sufficient showing of lessening of competition in the instant case to permit the exercise of that power.

The Federal Trade Commission's order is vacated.

JUDGE LUMBARD, concurring and dissenting: In propounding a more flexible standard for § 5 violations, the FTC has imposed on itself the heightened requirement of showing that challenged practices have had a substantial adverse effect on competition. As I agree with Judge Mansfield that the record does not support the FTC's finding of substantial effect here, I concur in denying enforcement of the FTC's proposed order.

As this failure alone requires us to deny enforcement, it is unnecessary for us to reach the broader question raised by the FTC's order: whether, as my colleagues hold, the FTC's authority under § 5 is limited to conduct that is either *per se* pernicious (i.e., collusive, coercive, predatory or exclusionary) or could not have been adopted for other than pernicious reasons; or whether, as the FTC now argues, it extends also to conduct that may be acceptable in some situations but not in others, in light of poor industry structure and performance, substantial anticompetitive effects, and lack of offsetting procompetitive justification. I would prefer to leave that question to another day, when the FTC has developed a record that more strongly supports the power it now seeks, and has better defined the standards for its exercise. . . .

Questions and Comments

If the FTC's factual conclusions were correct, would the antiknock makers have violated the law? Would there have been a violation under Judge Lumbard's standard? Under Judge Mansfield's? Should there be a violation? Assuming that we do not want to enjoin practices that are procompetitive or at least are in good faith responsive to consumers' needs or wishes, and that we do want to enjoin practices that are anticompetitive as long as the injunction does not work perversely to harm consumers, what test would you adopt for condemning facilitating practices?

3. NOTE ON INTRA-ENTERPRISE CONSPIRACY

Sometimes Section 1 actions have been brought against members of the same corporate family, and there are no other co-conspirators. The question arises: Can a corporation combine with its parent or subsidiaries, or with its affiliates or divisions, or with its officers or employees? Does a collaborative effort among or between such actors qualify as a combination for purposes of Section 1?

For many years, where the alleged co-conspirators were separate corporate entities, the answer seemed to be affirmative. Thus, in *United States v. Yellow Cab Company*, 332 U.S. 218 (1947), the Court said:

> The test of illegality under the Act is the presence or absence of unreasonable restraint on interstate commerce. . . . [T]he common ownership and control of the various corporate appellees are impotent to liberate the

alleged combination and conspiracy from the impact of the Act. Id. at 227.

The Supreme Court repeated this message in *Timken Roller Bearing Co. v. United States*, 341 U.S. 593 (1951) and in *Kiefer–Stewart Co. v. Joseph E. Seagram & Sons*, 340 U.S. 211 (1951), where defendants held themselves out as competitors.

The question came back to the Supreme Court in 1984, after Copperweld bought Regal, a steel tubing manufacturer; Regal's former vice president formed his own steel tubing company, Independence; and Independence sued Copperweld and Regal for a conspiracy to put it out of business under cover of protecting its trade secrets. The district court found liability, and the appellate court affirmed.

COPPERWELD CORP. v. INDEPENDENCE TUBE CORP.

467 U.S. 752 (1984).

CHIEF JUSTICE BURGER: . . . We granted certiorari to determine whether a parent corporation and its wholly owned subsidiary are legally capable of conspiring each other under § 1 of the Sherman Act.

I

A

The predecessor to petitioner Regal Tube Co. was established in Chicago in 1955 to manufacture structural steel tubing used in heavy equipment, cargo vehicles, and construction. From 1955 to 1968 it remained a wholly owned subsidiary of C.E. Robinson Co. In 1968 Lear Siegler, Inc., purchased Regal Tube Co. and operated it as an unincorporated division. David Grohne, who had previously served as vice president and general manager of Regal, became president of the division after the acquisition.

In 1972 petitioner Copperweld Corp. purchased the Regal division from Lear Siegler; the sale agreement bound Lear Siegler and its subsidiaries not to compete with Regal in the United States for five years. Copperweld then transferred Regal's assets to a newly formed, wholly owned Pennsylvania corporation, petitioner Regal Tube Co. The new subsidiary continued to conduct its manufacturing operations in Chicago but shared Copperweld's corporate headquarters in Pittsburgh.

Shortly before Copperweld acquired Regal, David Grohne accepted a job as a corporate officer of Lear Siegler. After the acquisition, while continuing to work for Lear Siegler, Grohne set out to establish his own steel tubing business to compete in the same market as Regal. In May 1972 he formed respondent Independence Tube Corp., which soon secured an offer from the Yoder Co. to supply a tubing mill. In December 1972 respondent gave Yoder a purchase order to have a mill ready by the end of December 1973.

When executives at Regal and Copperweld learned of Grohne's plans, they initially hoped that Lear Siegler's noncompetition agreement would thwart the new competitor. Although their lawyer advised them that

Grohne was not bound by the agreement, he did suggest that petitioners might obtain an injunction against Grohne's activities if he made use of any technical information or trade secrets belonging to Regal. The legal opinion was given to Regal and Copperweld along with a letter to be sent to anyone with whom Grohne attempted to deal. The letter warned that Copperweld would be "greatly concerned if [Grohne] contemplates entering the structural tube market . . . in competition with Regal Tube" and promised to take "any and all steps which are necessary to protect our rights under the terms of our purchase agreement and to protect the know-how, trade secrets, etc., which we purchased from Lear Siegler." Petitioners later asserted that the letter was intended only to prevent third parties from developing reliance interests that might later make a court reluctant to enjoin Grohne's operations.

When Yoder accepted respondent's order for a tubing mill on February 19, 1973, Copperweld sent Yoder one of these letters; two days later Yoder voided its acceptance. After respondent's efforts to resurrect the deal failed, respondent arranged to have a mill supplied by another company, which performed its agreement even though it too received a warning letter from Copperweld. Respondent began operations on September 13, 1974, nine months later than it could have if Yoder had supplied the mill when originally agreed.

Although the letter to Yoder was petitioners' most successful effort to discourage those contemplating doing business with respondent, it was not their only one. Copperweld repeatedly contacted banks that were considering financing respondent's operations. One or both petitioners also approached real estate firms that were considering providing plant space to respondent and contacted prospective suppliers and customers of the new company.

B

In 1976 respondent filed this action in the District Court against petitioners and Yoder. The jury found that Copperweld and Regal had conspired to violate § 1 of the Sherman Act but that Yoder was not part of the conspiracy. It also found that Copperweld, but not Regal, had interfered with respondent's contractual relationship with Yoder; that Regal, but not Copperweld, had interfered with respondent's contractual relationship with a potential customer of respondent, Deere Plow & Planter Works, and had slandered respondent to Deere; and that Yoder had breached its contract to supply a tubing mill.

* * *

C

The United States Court of Appeals for the Seventh Circuit affirmed. . . .

We granted certiorari to reexamine the intra-enterprise conspiracy doctrine and we reverse.

II

Review of this case calls directly into question whether the coordinated acts of a parent and its wholly owned subsidiary can, in the legal sense contemplated by § 1 of the Sherman Act, constitute a combination or conspiracy. The so-called "intra-enterprise conspiracy" doctrine provides that § 1 liability is not foreclosed merely because a parent and its subsidiary are subject to common ownership. The doctrine derives from declarations in several of this Court's opinions.

* * *

The problem began with *United States v. Yellow Cab Co.,* 332 U.S. 218 (1947). The controlling shareholder of the Checker Cab Manufacturing Corp., Morris Markin, also controlled numerous companies operating taxicabs in four cities. With few exceptions, the operating companies had once been independent and had come under Markin's control by acquisition or merger. The complaint alleged conspiracies under §§ 1 and 2 of the Sherman Act among Markin, Checker, and five corporations in the operating system. The Court stated that even restraints in a vertically integrated enterprise were not "necessarily" outside of the Sherman Act, observing that an unreasonable restraint

> "*may result as readily from a conspiracy among those who are affiliated or integrated under common ownership as from a conspiracy among those who are otherwise independent.* Similarly, any affiliation or integration flowing from an illegal conspiracy cannot insulate the conspirators from the sanctions which Congress has imposed. *The corporate interrelationships of the conspirators, in other words, are not determinative of the applicability of the Sherman Act. . . .*
>
> "*And so in this case, the common ownership and control of the various corporate appellees are impotent to liberate the alleged combination and conspiracy from the impact of the Act.* The complaint charges that the restraint of interstate trade was not only effected by the combination of the appellees but was the primary object of the combination. The theory of the complaint . . . is that 'dominating power' over the cab operating companies 'was not obtained by normal expansion . . . but by deliberate, calculated purchase for control.' " [*Appalachian Coals, Inc. v. United States,* 288 U.S. 344] at 227–228 (emphasis added) (quoting *United States v. Reading Co.,* 253 U.S. 26, 57 (1920)).

It is the underscored language that later breathed life into the intra-enterprise conspiracy doctrine. The passage as a whole, however, more accurately stands for a quite different proposition. It has long been clear that a pattern of acquisitions may itself create a combination illegal under § 1, especially when an original anticompetitive purpose is evident from the affiliated corporations' subsequent conduct.

* * *

The ambiguity of the *Yellow Cab* holding yielded the one case giving support to the intra-enterprise conspiracy doctrine. In *Kiefer–Stewart Co. v. Joseph E. Seagram & Sons, Inc.,* 340 U.S. 211 (1951), the Court held that two wholly owned subsidiaries of a liquor distiller were guilty under § 1 of the Sherman Act for jointly refusing to supply a wholesaler who declined to abide by a maximum resale pricing scheme. The Court offhandedly dismissed the defendants' argument that "their status as 'mere instrumentalities of a single manufacturing-merchandizing unit' makes it impossible for them to have conspired in a manner forbidden by the Sherman Act." With only a citation to *Yellow Cab* and no further analysis, the Court stated that the

> "suggestion runs counter to our past decisions that common ownership and control does not liberate corporations from the impact of the antitrust laws"

and stated that this rule was "especially applicable" when defendants "hold themselves out as competitors." 340 U.S., at 215.

Unlike the *Yellow Cab* passage, this language does not pertain to corporations whose initial affiliation was itself unlawful. In straying beyond *Yellow Cab,* the *Kiefer–Stewart* Court failed to confront the anomalies an intra-enterprise doctrine entails. It is relevant nonetheless that, were the case decided today, the same result probably could be justified on the ground that the subsidiaries conspired with wholesalers other than the plaintiff. An intra-enterprise conspiracy doctrine thus would no longer be necessary to a finding of liability on the facts of *Kiefer–Stewart.*

Later cases invoking the intra-enterprise conspiracy doctrine do little more than cite *Yellow Cab* or *Kiefer–Stewart,* and in none of the cases was the doctrine necessary to the result reached. *Timken Roller Bearing Co. v. United States,* 341 U.S. 593 (1951), involved restrictive horizontal agreements between an American corporation and two foreign corporations in which it owned 30 and 50 percent interests respectively. The *Timken* Court cited *Kiefer–Stewart* to show that "[t]he fact that there is common ownership or control of the contracting corporations does not liberate them from the impact of the antitrust laws." But the relevance of this statement is unclear. The American defendant in *Timken* did not own a majority interest in either of the foreign corporate conspirators and, as the District Court found, it did not control them. Moreover, as in *Yellow Cab,* there was evidence that the stock acquisitions were themselves designed to effectuate restrictive practices. The Court's reliance on the intra-enterprise conspiracy doctrine was in no way necessary to the result.

* * *

III

Petitioners, joined by the United States as *amicus curiae,* urge us to repudiate the intra-enterprise conspiracy doctrine. The central criticism is that the doctrine gives undue significance to the fact that a subsidiary is separately incorporated and thereby treats as the concerted activity of two entities what is really unilateral behavior flowing from decisions of a single enterprise.

We limit our inquiry to the narrow issue squarely presented: whether a parent and its wholly owned subsidiary are capable of conspiring in violation of § 1 of the Sherman Act. We do not consider under what circumstances, if any, a parent may be liable for conspiring with an affiliated corporation it does not completely own.

A

The Sherman Act contains a "basic distinction between concerted and independent action." *Monsanto Co. v. Spray–Rite Service Corp.,* 465 U.S.

752, 761 (1984). The conduct of a single firm is governed by § 2 alone and is unlawful only when it threatens actual monopolization. It is not enough that a single firm appears to "restrain trade" unreasonably, for even a vigorous competitor may leave that impression. For instance, an efficient firm may capture unsatisfied customers from an inefficient rival, whose own ability to compete may suffer as a result. This is the rule of the marketplace and is precisely the sort of competition that promotes the consumer interests that the Sherman Act aims to foster. In part because it is sometimes difficult to distinguish robust competition from conduct with long-run anticompetitive effects, Congress authorized Sherman Act scrutiny of single firms only when they pose a danger of monopolization. Judging unilateral conduct in this manner reduces the risk that the antitrust laws will dampen the competitive zeal of a single aggressive entrepreneur.

Section 1 of the Sherman Act, in contrast, reaches unreasonable restraints of trade effected by a "contract, combination . . . or conspiracy" between *separate* entities. It does not reach conduct that is "wholly unilateral." *Albrecht v. Herald Co.*, 390 U.S. 145, 149 (1968). Concerted activity subject to § 1 is judged more sternly than unilateral activity under § 2. Certain agreements, such as horizontal price fixing and market allocation, are thought so inherently anticompetitive that each is illegal *per se* without inquiry into the harm it has actually caused. Other combinations, such as mergers, joint ventures, and various vertical agreements, hold the promise of increasing a firm's efficiency and enabling it to compete more effectively. Accordingly, such combinations are judged under a rule of reason, an inquiry into market power and market structure designed to assess the combination's actual effect. Whatever form the inquiry takes, however, it is not necessary to prove that concerted activity threatens monopolization.

The reason Congress treated concerted behavior more strictly than unilateral behavior is readily appreciated. Concerted activity inherently is fraught with anticompetitive risk. It deprives the marketplace of the independent centers of decisionmaking that competition assumes and demands. . . .

B

The distinction between unilateral and concerted conduct is necessary for a proper understanding of the terms "contract, combination . . . or conspiracy" in § 1. Nothing in the literal meaning of those terms excludes coordinated conduct among officers or employees of the *same* company. But it is perfectly plain that an internal "agreement" to implement a single, unitary firm's policies does not raise the antitrust dangers that § 1 was designed to police. The officers of a single firm are not separate economic actors pursuing separate economic interests, so agreements among them do not suddenly bring together economic power that was previously pursuing divergent goals. Coordination within a firm is as likely to result from an effort to compete as from an effort to stifle competition. In the marketplace, such coordination may be necessary if a business enterprise is to compete effectively. For these reasons, officers or employees of the same firm do not provide the plurality of actors imperative for a § 1 conspiracy.

There is also general agreement that § 1 is not violated by the internally coordinated conduct of a corporation and one of its unincorporated divisions. Although this Court has not previously addressed the question, there can be little doubt that the operations of a corporate enterprise organized into divisions must be judged as the conduct of a single actor. The existence of an unincorporated division reflects no more than a firm's decision to adopt an organizational division of labor. A division within a corporate structure pursues the common interests of the whole rather than interests separate from those of the corporation itself; a business enterprise establishes divisions to further its own interests in the most efficient manner. Because coordination between a corporation and its division does not represent a sudden joining of two independent sources of economic power previously pursuing separate interests, it is not an activity that warrants § 1 scrutiny.

Indeed, a rule that punished coordinated conduct simply because a corporation delegated certain responsibilities to autonomous units might well discourage corporations from creating divisions with their presumed benefits. This would serve no useful antitrust purpose but could well deprive consumers of the efficiencies that decentralized management may bring.

C

For similar reasons, the coordinated activity of a parent and its wholly owned subsidiary must be viewed as that of a single enterprise for purposes of § 1 of the Sherman Act. A parent and its wholly owned subsidiary have a complete unity of interest. Their objectives are common, not disparate; their general corporate actions are guided or determined not by two separate corporate consciousnesses, but one. They are not unlike a multiple team of horses drawing a vehicle under the control of a single driver. With or without a formal "agreement," the subsidiary acts for the benefit of the parent, its sole shareholder. If a parent and a wholly owned subsidiary do "agree" to a course of action, there is no sudden joining of economic resources that had previously served different interests, and there is no justification for § 1 scrutiny. . . .

IV

We hold that Copperweld and its wholly owned subsidiary Regal are incapable of conspiring with each other for purposes of § 1 of the Sherman Act. To the extent that prior decisions of this Court are to the contrary, they are disapproved and overruled. Accordingly, the judgment of the Court of Appeals is reversed.

JUSTICE STEVENS, with whom JUSTICES BRENNAN and MARSHALL join, dissenting: . . . Today the Court announces a new *per se* rule: a wholly owned subsidiary is incapable of conspiring with its parent under § 1 of the Sherman Act. Instead of redefining the word "conspiracy," the Court would be better advised to continue to rely on the Rule of Reason. Precisely because they do not eliminate competition that would otherwise exist but rather enhance the ability to compete, restraints which enable effective integration between a corporate parent and its subsidiary—the type of arrangement the Court is properly concerned with protecting—are not prohibited by § 1. Thus, the Court's desire to shield such arrangements from antitrust liability provides no justification for the Court's new rule.

In contrast, the case before us today presents the type of restraint that has precious little to do with effective integration between parent and subsidiary corporations. Rather, the purpose of the challenged conduct was to exclude a potential competitor of the subsidiary from the market. The jury apparently concluded that the two defendant corporations—Copperweld and its subsidiary Regal—had successfully delayed Independence's entry into the steel tubing business by applying a form of economic coercion to potential suppliers of financing and capital equipment, as well as to potential customers. Everyone seems to agree that this conduct was tortious as a matter of state law. This type of exclusionary conduct is plainly distinguishable from vertical integration designed to achieve competitive efficiencies. If, as seems to be the case, the challenged conduct was manifestly anti-competitive, it should not be immunized from scrutiny under § 1 of the Sherman Act.

I

* * *

. . . .[W]e are not writing on a clean slate. "[W]e must bear in mind that considerations of *stare decisis* weigh heavily in the area of statutory construction, where Congress is free to change this Court's interpretation of its legislation." *Illinois Brick Co. v. Illinois*, 431 U.S. 720, 736 (1977). There can be no doubt that the Court today changes what has been taken to be the long-settled rule: a rule that Congress did not revise at any point in the last four decades. At a minimum there should be a strong presumption against the approach taken today by the Court. It is to the merits of that approach that I now turn.

II

* * *

Holding that affiliated corporations cannot constitute a plurality of actors is . . . inconsistent with the objectives of the Sherman Act. Congress was particularly concerned with "trusts," hence it named them in § 1 as a specific form of "combination" at which the statute was directed. Yet "trusts" consisted of affiliated corporations. As Senator Sherman explained:

* * *

The sole object of such a combination is to make competition impossible. It can control the market, raise or lower prices, as will best promote its selfish interests, reduce prices in a particular locality and break down competition and advance prices at will where competition does not exist. Its governing motive is to increase the profits of the parties composing it. The law of selfishness, uncontrolled by competition, compels it to disregard the interest of the consumer. It dictates terms to transportation companies, it commands the price of labor without fear of strikes, for in its field it allows no competitors. . . . It is this kind of a combination we have to deal with now. 21 Cong.Rec. 2457 (1890).

Thus, the corporate subsidiary, when used as a device to eliminate competition, was one of the chief evils to which the Sherman Act was addressed.[18] The anomaly in today's holding is that the corporate devices most similar to the original "trusts" are now those which free an enterprise from antitrust scrutiny.

III

. . . [T]he problem with the Court's new rule is that it leaves a significant gap in the enforcement of § 1 with respect to anticompetitive conduct that is entirely unrelated to the efficiencies associated with integration.

Since at least *United States v. Colgate & Co.,* 250 U.S. 300 (1919), § 1 has been construed to require a plurality of actors. This requirement, however, is a consequence of the plain statutory language, not of any economic principle. As an economic matter, what is critical is the presence of market power, rather than a plurality of actors. From a competitive standpoint, a decision of a single firm possessing power to reduce output and raise prices above competitive levels has the same consequence as a decision by two firms acting together who have acquired an equivalent amount of market power through an agreement not to compete.

* * *

. . . The Court does not even try to explain why [the] common ownership [of Copperweld and Regal] meant that [they] were merely obtaining benefits associated with the efficiencies of integration. Both the District Court and the Court of Appeals thought that their agreement had a very different result—that it raised barriers to entry and imposed an appreciable marketwide restraint. The Court's discussion of the justifications for corporate affiliation is therefore entirely abstract—while it dutifully lists the procompetitive justifications for corporate affiliation, it fails to explain how any of them relate to the conduct at issue in this case. What is challenged here is not the fact of integration between Regal and Copperweld, but their specific agreement with respect to Independence. That agreement concerned the exclusion of Independence from the market, and not any efficiency resulting from integration. The facts of this very case belie the conclusion that affiliated corporations are incapable of engaging in the kind of conduct that threatens marketwide competition. The Court does not even attempt to assess the competitive significance of the conduct under challenge here—it never tests its economic assumptions against the concrete facts before it. Use of economic theory without reference to the competitive impact of the particular economic arrangement at issue is properly criticized when it produces overly broad *per se* rules of antitrust liability; criticism is no less warranted when a *per se* rule of antitrust immunity is adopted in the same way.

In sum, the question that the Court should ask is not why a wholly owned subsidiary should be treated differently from a corporate division,

---

18. This legislative history thus demonstrates the error in the majority's conclusion that only acquisitions of corporate affiliates fall within § 1. The conduct of the trusts that Senator Sherman and others objected to went much further than mere acquisitions. Indeed, the irony of the Court's approach is that, had it been adopted in 1890, it would have meant that § 1 would have no application to trust combinations which had already been formed—the very trusts to which Senator Sherman was referring. . . .

since the immunity accorded that type of arrangement is a necessary consequence of *Colgate.* Rather the question should be why two corporations that engage in a predatory course of conduct which produces a marketwide restraint on competition and which, as separate legal entities, can be easily fit within the language of § 1, should be immunized from liability because they are controlled by the same godfather. That is a question the Court simply fails to confront. I respectfully dissent.

Questions and Comments

Does *Copperweld* virtually abolish the doctrine of intra-enterprise conspiracy? Does part of the doctrine survive? Is *Copperweld* correct? Is it consistent with current trends to narrow antitrust doctrine?

Consider the following situations. As to each, is there a combination for purposes of Section 1?

1. McDonald's does business by selling franchises to independent companies (the franchisees) and providing uniform facilities for each of the franchisees.

    a. McDonald's directs all of its franchisees to sell hamburgers at a stated price, and each agrees by contract to do so.

    b. McDonald's does not suggest a price, but all of its franchisees get together and decide what price they will charge.

2. ICI and each of its foreign rivals cross-license patents and in connection with the patent licenses each agrees to sell only in its own territory. Thereafter, ICI acquires its foreign rivals and forms a new parent corporation, and the parent directs each of the new subsidiaries to stay in its own territory.

3. IBM wishes to form a subsidiary in a developing country. As required by the home country's laws IBM gives up a 51% interest to nationals; however, it retains de facto working control. IBM assigns to this subsidiary, just as it does to its fully owned subsidiaries, a territory for which it is responsible; at IBM's request each subsidiary (including the 49%–owned firm) agrees not to ship into the territory of any other subsidiary.

4. Showman is the moving force in creating six corporations, each of which owns a movie theatre. Showman buys 40% of the shares of each corporation; silent investors (none of whom invest in more than one corporation) buy the rest. Showman operates the chain as a single integrated business. In each of three small towns, the corporation owns the only theatre in town. "Showman" buys film licenses for the entire chain at once. He also sets the admission prices for each theatre.

5. The *Copperweld* case.

K. THE OLIGOPOLY PROBLEM

We have looked at the possibility of gaining better performance in oligopolistic markets by using Section 1 of the Sherman Act to challenge interdependent behavior. Is there a broader case to be made for improving performance and preventing anticompetitive behavior in such markets? Is there a serious and inadequately addressed oligopoly problem?

Some of the economic observations that follow will be familiar to you; we reflect on them now in a different context.

In markets of few sellers, the sellers may have market power. This is more likely to be the case where barriers to entry and to expansion by fringe firms are high, the product is homogeneous and simple, buyers are numerous and have no acceptable substitutes, and there are many, continuous and open sales. Where most of these circumstances are present, the few sellers may be able to avoid price competition and to achieve a higher than competitive price without entering into an "agreement" proscribed by Section 1 of the Sherman Act. Indeed it may be easier for firms in an oligopoly to achieve a supracompetitive price without any agreement than it is for firms in more fragmented markets to achieve a supracompetitive price through an explicit cartel.

In oligopoly markets, the same phenomena that facilitate cooperative pricing may also produce less aggressive technological competition. Research and development initiatives may be directed more towards style changes than break-throughs that could make obsolete existing stocks, plants, and modes of doing business. Moreover, in such markets x-inefficiencies may abound. Firms may not work as hard at cutting costs as they would under competitive pressure. Advertising expenditures may be high and may emphasize image or trivial product differences, and may not provide price or other information of significant value to consumers. Firms in these markets may earn only normal profits for stockholders, yet they may buy peace with unions at the cost of excessive wage rates; split orders for inputs among oligopolistic sellers and buy at going prices rather than shopping aggressively; provide executives with costly amenities (plush offices, health clubs, cars, jets, Picassos in the board room); pay $300 and more per hour for lawyers to look over the shoulders of executives and managers. In short, they may funnel potential "monopoly returns" into a great many pockets other than their stockholders' pockets. See Harris and Sullivan, Horizontal Merger Policy: Promoting Competition and American Competitiveness, 31 Antitrust Bull. 871 (1986).

While some observers detect these phenomena, others believe that there is no oligopoly problem. They believe that firms in markets of few sellers will not implicitly collude because the market forces will punish them if they do so. They observe or postulate that buyers almost always have alternatives, and that new sellers can and will almost always move quickly into the market if the incumbents allow themselves to be distracted from their central task of giving consumers what they want. See, e.g., R. Bork, The Antitrust Paradox: A Policy at War With Itself (1978), and D. Armentano, Antitrust and Monopoly: Anatomy of a Policy Failure (1982). The latter perspective is not new. It has been a counterpoint to concerns about concentrated markets for virtually as long as the United States has had a federal antitrust law. See McGee, In Defense of Industrial Concentration (1971).

Through the years, however, a number of people, including policy makers, scholars and jurists, have been sufficiently concerned about the competitive evils of undue concentration to lead to the following initiatives:

(1) Congress passed and later amended a statute specifically addressed to mergers and specifically intended to prevent undue concentration through merger. We analyze this statute when we deal with mergers in Chapter 5.

(2) Congress has seriously considered (but has not passed) legislation designed to break up into several parts the leading firms in concentrated markets. Senator Phillip Hart was a major proponent of such legislation in the late 1960s. His and other proposals are discussed in L. Sullivan, Antitrust Law, Sections 128 and 129 (1977).

(3) Courts have ordered relief involving break up, spin off and divestiture. Such relief is commonly granted in merger cases. See Chapter 5, *infra.* It has been granted in a few, notable monopoly cases. See, e.g., *Standard Oil Co. v. United States,* 221 U.S. 1 (1911); *Eastman Kodak Co. of New York v. Southern Photo Materials Co.*, 273 U.S. 359 (1927); *United States v. United Shoe Machinery Corp.,* 110 F.Supp. 295 (D.Mass 1953), *aff'd,* 347 U.S. 521 (1954). However, where markets have evolved into oligopolies by internal growth or by mergers that went unchallenged or survived challenge in earlier days of laissez faire (e.g., mergers in the steel and automobile industries), no traditional antitrust challenge has been available.

(4) Enforcers have sought to extend the law to deal with the oligopoly problem. These initiatives have taken two forms. First, the Department of Justice and the Federal Trade Commission have targeted "facilitating practices"—practices that foster oligopolistic coordination, as we saw above. Second, the Federal Trade Commission issued a complaint to break up a tight oligopoly under Section 5 of the Federal Trade Commission Act, which we deal with below.

In the 1960s the staff of the FTC attempted to identify a test oligopoly case. That endeavor is described in the following headnote, printed in The Antitrust Law and Economics Review, along with a 1969 memorandum by FTC Bureau Chief Rufus E. Wilson asking the Commission to open an investigation of the cereals industry.

THE FTC'S DECONCENTRATION CASE AGAINST THE BREAKFAST–CEREAL INDUSTRY: A NEW 'BALLGAME' IN ANTITRUST?

Knowledgeable antitrust-watchers in Washington have known for some time now that a policy debate of fairly heroic proportions was in progress at the FTC and that the breakfast-cereal industry was very much in the eye of this particular storm. Unimpressed by the progress antitrust had made in reducing industrial concentration during the eight decades since the passage of the Sherman Act in 1890, a number of attorneys in FTC's then Bureau of Restraint of Trade (now called the Bureau of Competition) reportedly began "lobbying" their superiors for permission to bring a series of lawsuits aimed at deconcentrating a number of the country's major oligopolies in the mid–1960s. Finally, on June 4, 1969, one of the Bureau's division chiefs, Rufus E. Wilson, signed and forwarded to the five FTC commissioners one of these proposals, a request by his staff attorneys for permission to investigate the breakfast-cereal industry with an eye toward requiring its larger firms—Kellogg, General Mills, and General Foods—to separate themselves (by "spin-off") into several cereal firms each. Various newspaper accounts of this proposed "investigation" have appeared since that time but few knowledgeable students of the FTC, and certainly not the country's antitrust lawyers, have suspected that anything significant was going to come of the matter. The members of that agency, as we have emphasized in these pages a number of times during the past four years, are for the most part constrained by political and intellectual limitations to much shallower waters than these.

Now, however, we are being assured that the FTC's new reform Chairman might well be for real; that his new head of the agency's Bureau of Economics is seriously studying a number of major American oligopolies with an eye toward deconcentrating them; that the heads of his two legal bureaus are serious about reducing concentration and product differentiation in the more important oligopoly industries; that his new policy-planning chief is actually attempting to introduce the FTC to structural economic analysis and cost-benefit concepts; and that, as proof of all this, the agency has completed its investigation of the breakfast-cereal industry and is on the very eve of filing the first case in antitrust history that seeks to (1) declare high concentration (oligopoly) and its accompanying super-competitive prices illegal and (2) actually do something about the structure of such an industry, namely, deconcentrate it.

If such a case is in fact filed by the FTC, it would easily be the most important antitrust action in the nation's history, one that, by its mere filing, would amount to nothing less than a challenge to the legality of perhaps a third of the country's manufacturing sector, the third that, in Professor Galbraith's phrase, constitutes the country's "industrial heartland." The notion that America is about to seriously address itself to its long festering monopoly problem—and, what is more, that it is about to do so through so unlikely an instrument as the "little old lady of Pennsylvania Avenue" (as the droller members of the antitrust bar have always referred to the FTC)—is not, to put it conservatively, one that enjoys wide currency among the more cynical students of such matters. If a complaint should actually issue against the cereal producers, this group maintains, it will either be (a) focused on some economically insignificant aspects of the industry's "conduct"—e.g., false advertising, price discrimination, or the like—or (b) accompanied by a meaningless consent-order "settlement" under which the cereal producers will agree, as the quid pro quo for being allowed to retain their concentrated industry structure and thus their power to charge super-competitive prices, to "cease and desist" doing something that has nothing to do with their monopoly power anyway, the economic equivalent of an order to stop spitting on the sidewalks in Battle Creek.*

-----

* 4 Antitrust Law & Econ.Rev. 57 (1971), reprinted by permission.

In 1972 the complaint issued. The Federal Trade Commission sued the four largest manufacturers of ready-to-eat (RTE) cereals, alleging that their actions and non-actions for at least the past 30 years resulted in maintenance of a highly concentrated, noncompetitive market structure in violation of Section 5 of the Federal Trade Commission Act. The four firms and their approximate market shares prior to suit were:

Kellogg Co.	—	45%
General Mills, Inc	—	21%
General Foods Corp.	—	16%
Quaker Oats Co.[10]	—	9%

The complaint alleged, among other things, that respondents proliferated brands; artificially differentiated products through promotion of trademarks and intensive advertising; made numerous acquisitions during the prior 70 years, eliminating sources of private label RTE cereals; refused to make private label products, although they had unused capacity; and, through Kellogg's services in providing shelf space in supermarkets and placing cereals on it, perpetuated their market shares and limited the exposure of other producers' product. Complaint counsel's brand proliferation theory was highly developed: RTE cereal can be differentiated in several ways: grain used; shape; texture; sweetness. Some buyers may like sweet, soggy wheat, others bland, crunchy oats. Although in some segments (e.g., those filled by corn flakes, wheaties, shredded wheat) the popularity of particular products was stable, in other segments products introduced tended to have relatively short life cycles. The essence of the FTC's brand proliferation theory was that possible grain, texture, shape and sweetness variations were finite and that the cumulative result of the strategies of the RTE companies was to keep every plausible product nitch filled by repeatedly and promptly introducing and promoting new brands in each nitch where the popularity of an existing brand was falling and its producer could be expected to let it lapse. Thus, as predicted, the complaint did not attack structure alone; but on the other hand, it did not rest either on collusion or on conduct that, if engaged in by one firm only, would have been subject to challenge.

Respondents and critics of the FTC's theory used the phrase "shared monopoly" in an effort to discredit the theory of the case; the term suggested something radical and untested. Meanwhile, government lawyers and others tried to make a virtue of the terminology. They used it descriptively to identify a structural condition involving oligopoly so tight that the participating sellers are able to approximate the monopoly result by interdependent behavior.

Perhaps because of the ambiguities of the phrase, some who criticized prosecution of the case as well as some who approved it shied away from the shared monopoly label. Many who did so emphasized the similarity of tight oligopoly with collusion, not monopoly. This partly semantic controversy was not adequately resolved.

The case was tried before an administrative law judge, who stressed the FTC staff's failure of proof and decided in favor of the cereal compa-

---

10. Quaker Oats was dropped from the case before trial.

nies. The then director of the Bureau of Competition filed a notice of intent to appeal. At about that time, administrations changed from that of President Carter to that of President Reagan. Reagan appointed James C. Miller III as head of the Federal Trade Commission. Miller was hostile to the case. Miller's newly appointed head of the FTC's Bureau of Competition, Thomas Campbell, withdrew the earlier notice of intent to appeal. The pre-Reagan Commissioners expressed some concern, and the Commission took the unusual step of reviewing the record to determine whether the case should continue.

IN THE MATTER OF KELLOGG CO.
99 F.T.C. 8 (1982).

STATEMENT OF COMMISSIONER CLANTON: This case raises important issues concerning the application of Section 5 of the FTC Act to oligopolistic conduct. Because of these issues and the present posture of this case—Administrative Law Judge Berman's decision in favor of respondents coupled with the Bureau Director's decision not to appeal—it seems highly desirable for the Commission to determine now whether a full briefing on the merits is warranted.

Of course, even in the absence of an appeal, the Commission has the right . . . to undertake a thorough review of the record. However, I believe the circumstances of this case justify an exception to that practice. Given the theories of liability and proposed relief under consideration, it is entirely proper for us to see if there is a likely basis for issuing an order, even if the facts conform closely to what complaint counsel contend.

. . . I cannot find a basis for continuing the case. In its most succinct form, complaint counsel urge that liability be premised on the basis of two related but distinct theories. The first is a traditional conspiracy to monopolize based upon principles contained in Section 2 of the Sherman Act; the second is a shared monopoly theory under Section 5 of the FTC Act, a theory which does not depend upon a showing of collusion. Under either of these theories, complaint counsel argue that the only effective form of relief would be a divestiture order, including royalty-free licensing of respondents' cereal trademarks.

As to the first theory, I agree with ALJ Berman that a conspiracy to monopolize was not properly pled. As for the separate shared monopoly theory, I do not believe such a theory, however characterized, can serve as a predicate for the Commission to restructure an industry, at least in the absence of clear predatory behavior, which is not claimed here.

I do want to emphasize, however, that Section 5 may well provide the Commission with sufficient authority to attack noncollusive behavior that contributes to or enhances anticompetitive conduct, and which is without compelling business justification. In such circumstances, the principal remedial tool for dealing with this kind of behavior would be a conduct order.

Before elaborating further on these points, I would offer a comment about the characterizations, or mischaracterizations, that have been advanced in the past by critics of this case. An awful lot of rhetoric has been spilled on this subject, with some critics claiming that the case is just the first step in a broad-based attack on concentrated industries. Others have accused the agency of attacking competitive forms of behavior, such as product differentiation and brand proliferation; while still others have derided the "shared monopoly" concept, suggesting that this is evidence alone of the Commission's confused thinking since the description itself is a contradiction in terms.

Suffice it to say, I do not share all of the views of the critics of this case. In issuing the complaint, I think the Commission sought to address a legitimate concern, not about oligopolies per se, but rather about oligopolistic behavior that is uniquely anticompetitive. Respected antitrust commentators of different persuasions—such as Professor Posner and Professors Areeda and Turner have advocated different approaches for dealing with collusive-type behavior among oligopolists.[1] Whether the theories of relief proposed by complaint counsel are proper is one thing, but it is clear to me that the Commission was not attempting through this case to challenge structure or bigness *per se*.

Conspiracy to Monopolize

As one of their principal prongs of liability, complaint counsel now contend that an implied conspiracy to monopolize can be inferred from respondents' course of dealing over the past twenty years. It is contended that respondents have consistently eschewed various forms of price competition and channelled their energies instead into promotional activities and brand diversification.[2] Whether this conduct gives rise to a conspiracy to monopolize can be addressed only if a conspiracy in fact was properly tried.

* * *

. . . The pleadings might have been adequate to encompass a conspiracy to monopolize theory had it not been for complaint counsel's insistent denials that a conspiracy was at issue in the case.

* * *

Section 5 Shared Monopoly

Even if a conspiracy count is not present, that does not end the matter. Complaint counsel alternatively argue that even absent a con-

---

1. See P. Areeda & D. Turner, III *Antitrust Law*, Ch. 8E (1978); R. Posner, *Antitrust Law: An Economic Perspective*, 39–77 (1976).

2. Complaint counsel's conspiracy case depends primarily upon a showing that respondents' roughly parallel behavior on several fronts—instituting price changes, stopping trade deals, eliminating in-pack premiums, refusing to sell to private labelers, fortification—over a twenty year period cannot be explained away as a coincidence of independent judgments. While it is unnecessary to delve into this issue at any great length, since the conspiracy theory, as discussed hereinafter, is not properly before us, I would observe that this kind of evidentiary approach to proving collusion is not unprece-

dented. Cases such as *American Tobacco v. United States*, 328 U.S. 781 (1946) and *Wall Products Co. v. National Gypsum Co.*, 326 F.Supp. 295 (N.D.Cal.1971), indicate quite clearly that conspiracy can be inferred from proof of parallel actions coupled with economic conditions that appear to negate an inference of innocent, independent business conduct. This point is not to suggest that the case before us unquestionably involves a conspiracy, for, among other things, the evidence of simultaneity of behavior, (e.g., price leadership) here is perhaps not as strong as it was in the aforementioned cases. What it does suggest is that a conspiracy theory is not impotent to deal with oligopolistic behavior that exhibits more than a casual trend toward interdependent conduct. . . .

spiracy the conduct is sufficiently like one to justify a finding of liability under Section 5 of the FTC Act. It is quite clear, of course, that Section 5 can reach anticompetitive behavior that is not covered by the Clayton or Sherman Acts. And, I believe such authority extends to non-collusive, marketwide behavior that may not involve traditional forms of predation. Presumably, this could include behavior that would not be illegal for a single firm to engage in but, due to the industrywide nature of the practice, could lead to significant anticompetitive effects.

Various commentators have also urged that the antitrust laws are flexible enough to deal with shared monopolies or oligopolistic behavior outside the context of a traditional conspiracy.[5] In highly concentrated industries competitors may learn to react to each others' moves in a fashion that is closely analogous to the workings of a cartel. Firms will recognize that it is not in their self-interest to chart an independent course because other competitors will be able to quickly detect and match their moves, thereby leading to lower profits for the industry as a whole. The degree to which this phenomena occurs, and its success, are obviously subjects of great debate and the identification of markets in which firms are operating in a closely interdependent fashion is admittedly complex.

Because of the difficulties in proving collusion, Professors Areeda and Turner have advocated a different approach to the problem of single firm monopolization and shared monopolies. In their recent treatise, they suggest that evidence of persistent monopoly performance in a market, whether exhibited by a single firm or a small group of firms, should be sufficient to justify sweeping relief in the form of divestiture or other like remedies. Of course, they would require fairly strong evidence that the market is performing badly and that structural remedies would not lead to inefficiencies. They also believe that such actions should be limited to government initiatives and not allowed in private suits. In essence, their proposal does not depend on improper conduct for establishing liability and is akin to various no-fault monopoly proposals that have been advanced in the past.

But even Areeda and Turner recognize that the kinds of markets that might warrant intervention under such an approach are limited, even more so in the shared monopoly area than for single firm monopolies.

Complaint counsel, of course, are not advocating a no-fault approach in this case. Instead, they have attempted to develop their case in a way that focuses on the extent to which respondents' interrelated behavior has exacerbated competitive problems in the RTE cereal industry. Their theory depends less on the unreasonableness of specific forms of behavior than it does on the totality of the conduct.

Nevertheless, even under complaint counsel's theory, one must recognize the implications of using such an approach to restructure an entire industry. As complaint counsel acknowledge, the kind of theory and relief they are seeking require extensive proof of industry structure, performance and conduct. While that kind of analysis is highly com-

---

5. E.g., P. Areeda & D. Turner, *supra,* note 1; L. Sullivan, *Handbook of the Law of Antitrust,* § 125 (1977).

mendable, it provides a less than certain guide as to what kinds of conduct or market conditions would be subjected to antitrust attack. In addition, such an approach, of necessity, dramatically limits the number of instances where market intervention is warranted and, even then, it does not fully remove the risks associated with developing a structural remedy for an industry.

Thus, absent collusion or clear evidence of predatory behavior, I believe it would be unwise for the Commission to seek dissolution of an industry on the basis of the cumulative effects of multi-firm behavior. That does not mean, however, that such behavior would go unaddressed. Rather, it means that the kind of relief sought—namely, conduct remedies—would reflect two realities about the oligopolistic market context: (1) the lower probability that serious anticompetitive problems will exist for long, and (2) the potentially greater costs of attempting to restructure an industry. Because of the complexity involved, it may take many years to recover the costs of obtaining and implementing a successful dissolution order. Those costs may be worth incurring where we can be fairly confident that the market behavior under attack cannot be justified. The rigor of conspiracy analysis can help to provide that assurance, and strong evidence of predatory behavior may also provide the necessary predicate for divestiture.

But to pursue structural relief in less compelling circumstances carries with it too great a risk of wrong or imperfect judgments. The alternative, conduct relief, obviously has its limitations. Such a focus, however, enables more precise judgments to be made about the reasonableness of particular behavior without the risk of overkill.[7] To be sure, conduct relief may not be feasible in all oligopolistic market settings, but neither is divestiture. After all, antitrust deals primarily with probabilities. Where the probable benefits of improving competition are very high, as they are in breaking up a horizontal price-fixing conspiracy, there is little risk that the imposition of harsh sanctions will chill desirable competitive behavior. But, as the difficulty of distinguishing between harmful and beneficial conduct increases, so does the danger of imposing maximum remedies. Therefore, in my view, remedial restraint is called for, even in the kind of tightly concentrated market presented to us here, where profitability is good, market shares are stable and new entry has been minimal.

Although I am opposed to structural remedies, I reiterate my belief that the Commission can reach non-collusive, industrywide behavior under Section 5 of the FTC Act. An example of such an approach is the Commission's decision in *Boise Cascade*, 91 F.T.C. 1 (1978), rev'd, *Boise Cascade Corp. v. FTC* [1980–2 Trade Cases ¶ 63,323], 637 F.2d 573 (9th Cir.

---

7. Apart from their suggested approach for dealing with persistent shared monopoly, Areeda and Turner also have expressed the view that the antitrust laws even more clearly can reach exclusionary behavior engaged in by shared monopolists. Such a theory would, they believe, amount to a logical extension of attempted monopolization, since the primary missing ingredient would be the absence of a dangerous probability of a single firm monopoly. P. Areeda & Turner, *supra*, note 1, ¶ 856–61. Whether the courts would be willing to extend Section 2 of the Sherman Act this far is not clear, but, in any event, such an approach would appear to be within the scope of ¶ 5 of the FTC Act.

1980). There, the Commission found that the industrywide use of an artificial freight factor contributed to price stability and could not be justified by market exigencies. Although the Ninth Circuit Court of Appeals felt that the Commission did not make a satisfactory showing of anticompetitive effect, the appellate decision did not foreclose the possibility that the Commission could employ Section 5 to reach unjustified forms of noncollusive behavior which are practiced on a marketwide basis. It should also be emphasized that the Commission in *Boise Cascade* believed that it could fashion an effective conduct order that would not be highly regulatory in nature.

*   *   *

In this instance, assuming complaint counsel's case were to be established, several practices might be singled out for possible action. For example, a central issue in the case is brand proliferation. Complaint counsel argue that respondents have engaged in excessive product differentiation as a less disruptive form of competition than price competition. It is claimed that by carving up the market into smaller and smaller product segments, respondents have made it extremely difficult for new firms to enter, since an entrant would have to offer several brands to achieve minimal scale economies. . . .

Without getting into an extended discussion of these allegations, there does seem to be considerable evidence that brand proliferation has made entry more difficult. But that is not the end of the analysis. Whatever the social value of these products, we are not dealing with the kind of product design or change that is introduced primarily as a blocking device to discipline competitors. In other words, we are not talking about predatory conduct that serves little, if any, legitimate competitive ends. For the most part, the myriad cereal brands on the market are self-sustaining and they appear to generate significant consumer demand. Even if we would prefer to see fewer brands and more price competition, it would be extremely difficult to distinguish between legitimate and illegitimate brand proliferation. Certainly, it would be quite inadvisable and impractical to attempt to limit advertising expenditures or new brand offerings. Thus, an order provision directed to this practice does not seem very promising.

A second practice that might be susceptible to correction concerns respondents' shelf space recommendations to grocery retailers. These plans rely largely on past market shares as the benchmark for allocating space. Complaint counsel contend that these recommendations, which many retailers have adhered to in principle, tend to stabilize competition among existing competitors and make it more difficult for new entrants to get shelf space. Indeed, this is the only practice from which complaint counsel have sought conduct relief.

It could be argued that an order restricting or preventing respondents from making shelf space recommendations would help to inject more competitive pressures into an important area of non-price competition, without intruding unnecessarily into respondents' day-to-day business judgments. On the other hand, this type of activity is undoubtedly normal commercial behavior that is engaged in by many other food manufacturers, although it is not clear whether the nature and pattern of recommendations in the cereal industry are followed in other markets.

However, regardless of whether a workable remedy could be crafted on this subject, it is questionable whether the issue is all that important from a remedial standpoint. Dr. Schmalensee, one of the complaint counsel's expert witnesses in the case, expressed the view in a separate article that shelf space plans were probably not powerful deterrent devices. Schmalensee, "Entry Deterrence in the Ready–to–Eat Breakfast Cereal Industry," 9 Bell J.Econ. 305, 307, n. 4 (1978).

A third area for possible relief involves the exchange of recent advertising expenditure data among respondents through the vehicle of a third party reporting service. It is not entirely clear whether this particular practice, specifically with respect to the accuracy and currency of the data exchanged, is unique to the cereal industry or occurs frequently in other industries. While this exchange makes it easier to monitor the actions of competitors it may be less sensitive than an exchange of price information, since the quantity of advertising expenditures does not necessarily reveal the effectiveness of those expenditures. Of course, the effectiveness of restricting this practice depends on how easily and quickly respondents could obtain similar data through other means. But, even if an order restriction would make that task substantially more difficult, it is not at all clear that it would inject a very significant destabilizing force into the market. To be sure, advertising is a major factor in respondents' non-price competition, but inducing more rivalry in this area is not necessarily calculated to produce similar spin-off effects in the pricing of RTE cereals.

Another candidate for reform is respondents' fairly consistent refusal to supply private brand cereals to retailers. While increased private brand competition could bring about more price competition, an order requiring respondents to supply such product is fraught with all kinds of problems, and could easily lead to a highly intrusive regulatory-type order.

Finally, with respect to other allegedly anticompetitive conduct, such as respondents' refusal to offer trade deals or other off-list discounts, it is quite clear that the Commission cannot mandate respondents to compete. Such behavior, if it does not involve collusion, represents the kind of passive noncompetitive behavior for which there is probably no practical enforcement remedy.

Thus, a review of possible avenues for conduct relief suggests that, assuming a Section 5 case can be made out, the available remedial alternatives are either intrinsically undesirable or hold little promise for producing beneficial results. . . . While we might desire a better mix of price and nonprice competition in the RTE cereal industry, the potential costs associated with a divestiture order, not to mention the difficulty in getting a court to approve such an exercise of our remedial discretion, lead me to reject this approach. I am also simply not persuaded that the class of cases reflected here is sufficiently large to warrant pursuing this kind of complicated, time-consuming remedial avenue. Even if this is the one case in a thousand that might justify such an approach, I do not feel that we ought to apply our Section 5 powers in this way, for what would be an essentially one-time, ad hoc law enforcement initiative.

Accordingly, it is my belief that the Commission should not pursue this case further.

COMMISSIONER PERTSCHUK, dissenting: . . . The Commission today takes an unprecedented step in refusing to hear the appeal of this matter. This decision raises serious implications for the integrity and propriety of Commission adjudicatory procedures.

[Commissioner Pertschuk notes respondents' "aggressive legal and political maneuver," intensive lobbying, and Congressional intervention.]

* * *

The shared monopoly theory, as reflected in the Commission's complaint in this matter, was predicated upon an allegation of high concentration, as evidenced by a three-firm concentration exceeding 80%; poor competitive performance, as measured, for example, by sustained high profits and the absence of price competition; and high barriers to entry caused by exclusionary conduct of industry members, as evidenced, for example, by the absence of significant new entry since 1950. Thus, the theory of the case does not "condemn the [industry] structure itself" as the Bureau Director's statement of December 11 supposes.

Such a theory is supported by scholarly commentary, including that of Professors Areeda and Turner, Professor Sullivan and others. Thus, it is not the case that "the theory has . . . utterly failed to enter the mainstream of economic thought," as the respondents claim. Rather, this case represents a serious, carefully thought out attempt by a no-nonsense Republican-led Commission in 1972 to deal with the problem of a tight oligopoly and a poorly performing industry.

Today, the Commission turns its back on this attempt, not wishing to deal with the difficult but necessary task of spelling out whether and under what circumstances the antitrust laws reach this problem. Such a step by the Commission is a significant one, with major ramifications for government antitrust policy. We should make no mistake about it: the problem of high concentration—industries operated by a few giant companies with poor competitive performance, as indicated by the absence of meaningful price competition and the absence of significant entry of new competitors over a long period—is not going to disappear from our economy in the coming decades. Our economy is now made up of a number of highly concentrated industries without meaningful price competition and, if the merger laws are not to be enforced vigorously, this situation will become more frequent, not less.

I for one believe that § 5 of the Federal Trade Commission Act does reach a situation where an industry is highly concentrated; the performance of the industry as measured by profit levels, lack of price competition or other factors, is poor; effective barriers to entry are created by exclusionary conduct on the part of the firms; and a government-ordered remedy can be shown to be likely to improve competition. I also believe that it is possible for this Commission and for the courts to identify, after careful study, which industries are appropriate for restructuring in order to deal with this problem, and which industries are not. But I also conclude that the prospect for some future Commission effectively to apply this theory is highly unlikely. It is not that there will not be farsighted and courageous Commissions in the future, nor certainly that there will be an absence of careful economic analysis capable of identifying industries which should be addressed; nor do I view this decision by the Commission today in any way as a legal precedent which deserves to be followed by a future Commission or by the courts. Rather, I view today's decision as confirmation of the political inability of a Commission to see such a case through to the end.

As our political system provides, the Commission reflects, to a large extent, the prevailing political attitudes and the economic philosophy of the current administration. And, quite properly, future Commissions will reflect the then prevailing political philosophy. Unfortunately, an attempt by the inherently lengthy process of litigation to deal with the oligopolistic problem I have described requires a political consensus that an independent commission is legitimate and competent to carry out the task, and a political environment which gives it the room and time to carry it out. Today's decision seems to me to tell us that such a consensus is unlikely. Therefore, I believe strongly that Congress, not this one perhaps, but some future one, should brace itself for the task of spelling out in careful, responsible legislation what [the] government's role is in dealing with the problem of oligopoly. And I emphasize again that it is a problem which is destined to become more, rather than less, significant for our society.

STATEMENT OF COMMISSIONER BAILEY: . . . [T]he paramount difficulty with [the shared monopoly] case has always been the question of remedy. For whatever it is that Kellogg and the other respondents may have done, the proposed solution—to carve new cereal companies from the hides of existing ones and to force the licensing of successful trade names to the newly created competitors—is both draconian and manifestly uncertain to achieve the relief complaint counsel postulates that it will.

Areeda and Turner have stated:

> Quite apart from statutory limitations, even a czar would consider restructuring only where it is likely to improve net economic performance substantially; and we say "substantially" to take account of the costs of the process, including the risk of erroneous judgments.

Thus, assuming that the appropriate substantial and noncompetitive market structure required for a shared monopoly is present, the key issue becomes whether relief is available significantly to improve economic performance without sacrificing such economically worthy goals as substantial economies of scale.

The difficulties possibly attendant to divestiture relief make it less than clear that improved industry performance is the inevitable consequence. Respondents and intervenors (the grain millers union) view the industry restructuring proposal as "an unprecedented and unworkable experiment in industry reorganization." Dismantling of existing cereal plants, including those that now make other non-cereal products as well, may cause substantial interruptions or reductions in production. Existing labor-management harmony may be disrupted. Trademark licensing may result in excess capacity and stifle product development, and disrupt economies of scale in production, distribution and sales. Of course, all of this may be the conjecture of self-serving private interests, but the complex dismantling of a long-existing industry is sufficiently clouded with doubts to give one pause. Indeed, even complaint counsel's own expert has stated that the remedy proposed may "for reasons unforeseen bring about the opposite result or may impose debilitating losses upon the big three."

* * *

I come ultimately to the view that industry restructuring, such as is proposed here, is essentially a legislative concern, and as an agency that fairly can be characterized as an arm of the Congress, we should not undertake to restructure an industry under Section 5 of the FTC Act without a clear supportive signal from the Congress. In this case, the signals are, for the present, quite to the contrary—as they were not so apparently in 1972 when this complaint issued. The Federal Trade Commission has from time to time commented favorably on various legislative proposals amounting to industrial restructuring. None of these proposals has taken root as a preferred route for industrial market reorganization. I do believe that if the Congress were to endorse a shared monopoly approach to restructuring an oligopoly, this agency has the power to effect this sort of change under a viable and respectable theory. But the use of the power of divestiture or divorcement under Section 5 of the FTC Act is the ultimate exercise in administrative authority. It should be used only to achieve a Congressionally endorsed result, or at least not to defy a clearly expressed congressional animus, as exists here. I note, too, that even candidates of both major political parties in the last national election denounced this case as ill-advised and contrary to the public interest.

Why all this concern has risen to the level that it has is difficult to explain, in light of the fact that the Commission is only mid-stream in this case, and both Commission and court review—not to mention potential congressional action—lie ahead to safeguard against any precipitous or unwarranted action in this matter. The issue here is larger than the *Kellogg* case, to be sure. Professor Joseph Brodley reflected in some depth on the practical, as well as the philosophical, problem of exercising prosecutorial discretion to its ultimate end in cases of this sort:

> In law, as in politics, public policy must often be the art of the possible. For this, as well as for other reasons, I put to one side the proposal that existing concentrated oligopoly firms be broken up . . . (A)ny large or even moderate scale attack on existing industrial concentration would run into congressional stormwaters of imposing magnitude.

> In part, this may simply reflect an ambivalence of attitude in United States antitrust laws. The British writer, Neale, has noted the tendency of Americans "to take a romantic view of the achievements and efficiency of large industrial organizations even while they take a suspicious view of their power." Such an attitude has made the remedy of divestiture rare even in Sherman Act cases.

Perhaps, more basically, in a nation so throughly pragmatic as this one, there is an understandable reluctance to push an economic theory, however well founded, to the extreme conclusion of causing drastic rearrangements of large sections of American industry. . . . [16]

The paradox we are left with is that while there may be a legitimate concern about the anticompetitive effects of the exercise of oligopoly power, it is rarely true that these concerns will mandate an administrative agency decision to restructure an industry, short of a legislative warrant to that effect. Therefore, I will vote that this appeal be terminated, not for the reasons relied upon by the Administrative Law Judge, but because the promulgation of relief by this agency will not, in any eventuality conceivably lead to a restructuring of the cereal firms. . . .

Questions and Comments

In order to test the wisdom of the FTC's action, let us suppose the following, much of which complaint counsel sought to prove:

1. Prices of RTE cereal were significantly higher than necessary to cover costs including the cost of capital.

2. If the respondent cereal companies had not introduced a plethora of new brands (they introduced more than 75 brands from 1960 to 1970), other companies producing RTE cereal would have made inroads into the market.

3. The respondent cereal companies had a significant amount of unused capacity for a substantial period of time. Nonetheless, they refused to make private label brands for others. They would have made a profit by doing so, but calculated that this profit would be less than the increment in prices from lessened output.

4. Kellogg's shelf space program resulted in a space allocation favoring Kellogg's cereals. General Mills', General Foods' and Quaker Oats' cereals were given positions and quantity of space relative to their market shares, and cereals of lesser known manufacturers were usually kept out of the eye of the shopper. The storekeeper might have chosen the same allocation, in view of consumers' past choices, and therefore the shopkeeper found it efficient to let Kellogg provide the shelf space services. If, however, all of the thousands of shopkeepers performed the shelf-space function, results would have varied and many lesser known manufacturers would have achieved better and more space.

Assume also that the FTC has the power to order a break up or any other relief it deems appropriate. Under the above circumstances, should the FTC have found a violation? If so, how would you express the rule of law that was violated? How would you summarize the structure, conduct or performance that constituted the violation? Did the cereal companies do anything wrong? Does that matter? What are the benefits and costs of finding a violation? Consider, as always, not just the target industry, but also firms in other industries and firms in the future that might run up against the rule of law you articulate.

16. Brodley, "Oligopoly Power Under the Sherman and Clayton Acts—From Oligopoly Theory to Legal Policy," 19 Stan.L.Rev. 285, 344–45 (1967).

If the FTC did find a violation, what relief could it and should it have ordered? If break up were ordered, what should this consist of? What are the beneficial and the negative aspects of a break-up order?

Assume that the break-up option is rejected. What other relief is available? Consider, in particular, means by which barriers to entry and expansion could be lowered. Can you frame relief that you would be relatively confident would make consumers better off?

Suppose the Commission decided that break up was the best relief and that this could be accomplished without great difficulty because each of the three big cereal companies had two or three separate plants that produced separate brands of cereals. Should the Commission order the break up? Is the wisdom of a break up a legislative or a judicial question?

In the late 1970s, while the cereal case was being tried before the administrative law judge, the FTC came under intensive fire from Congress. In addition to its concentrated-industry initiatives, the Commission was seeking to regulate television advertising aimed at children, abuses by funeral directors and used car dealers, and restraints by medical professionals. Detractors accused the Commission of being the "national nanny"; of interfering with the "normal" business and professional affairs of providers of goods and services that people wanted. Congress threatened to disapprove the FTC's budget reauthorization for the coming year unless the FTC came to heel; in fact the FTC was closed down briefly while Congress held up and finally passed an authorization bill that revoked some of the FTC's authority, notably regarding its consumer protection function. See M. Pertschuk, Revolt Against Regulation: The Rise and Pause of the Consumer Movement (1982).

If the FTC had ordered a break up of the cereal industry, would there have been political consequences? Does congressional inaction on Senator Hart's Concentrated Industries Bill give some clue as to whether prosecutorial discretion should be used to pursue a structural remedy for oligopolistic interdependence?

Chapter 4

VERTICAL RESTRAINTS: COLLABORATION AND PRACTICES IN THE COURSE OF DISTRIBUTION AND LICENSING

Introduction

Verticality, in industry organization and in antitrust, refers to the imaginary vertical line from extraction of raw materials through the stages of production and marketing to the ultimate consumer. Thus, vertical restraints are those imposed by one participant along the vertical chain on another participant. An example is a resale price-fixing agreement; e.g., the manufacturer extracts from the retailer a promise to resell widgets at no less than $10. Other examples are requirements contracts, exclusive dealing contracts, tying, and customer and territorial restraints imposed by manufacturers on wholesalers and retailers. The most nearly permanent vertical arrangement is structural integration, so that one firm performs the successive functions.

For many years vertical contractual restraints were seriously suspect and often condemned outright under the antitrust laws. Analyzed most commonly under Section 1 of the Sherman Act and Section 3 of the Clayton Act, and occasionally, if monopolistic, under Section 2 of the Sherman Act, vertical restraints were condemned as instruments for limiting entrepreneurial freedom, exploiting customers, and excluding small sellers from free and open access to markets. More recently, the intellectual tide has turned. As we near the end of the twentieth century and as Chicago School economics permeates discourse, a new and simple conception of vertical restraints has taken hold in many quarters, namely: If the restraint is vertical it must be efficient and it must be good for consumers. As society has become more solicitous of the needs of established business, the law has changed to be more hospitable to vertical restraints.

We start our analysis of vertical restraints with a study of restraints imposed by sellers that limit the activity of the intermediaries to whom they resell. This category includes price, customer and territorial restraints. The restraints imposed are often referred to as distribution

522

restraints, for they are restraints in the course of distribution of a product.

A. RESTRAINTS IMPOSED BY SELLERS THAT LIMIT THE COMPETITIVE OPTIONS OF BUYERS

1. RESALE PRICE MAINTENANCE (RPM)

a. *The Basic Rule*

RPM is vertical price fixing. It refers to the situation in which the manufacturer dictates the price at which its buyers, who are intermediaries in the vertical chain, may resell.

When a manufacturer states a fixed resale price, as by price-tagging a pair of running shoes, often obliging the retailer to charge that price, is the price a maximum or a minimum? Such a practice may be intended to establish a price floor; that is, to keep the price above what it might otherwise have been. Yet in another sense the price is a maximum, for retailers ordinarily could not convince consumers to pay more than the tagged price. When a fixed resale price is intended to hold prices up rather than to push them down, it is treated as minimum resale price fixing.

The earliest RPM case decided by the Supreme Court is *Dr. Miles*.

DR. MILES MEDICAL CO. v. JOHN D. PARK & SONS CO.
220 U.S. 373 (1911).

JUSTICE HUGHES: This is a writ of certiorari to review a judgment of the Circuit Court of Appeals for the Sixth Circuit which affirmed a judgment of the Circuit Court dismissing, on demurrer, the bill of complaint for want of equity.

The complainant Dr. Miles Medical Company, an Indiana corporation, is engaged in the manufacture and sale of proprietary medicines, prepared by means of secret methods and formulas and identified by distinctive packages, labels and trade-marks. It has established an extensive trade throughout the United States and in certain foreign countries. It has been its practice to sell its medicines to jobbers and wholesale druggists who in turn sell to retail druggists for sale to the consumer. In the case of each remedy, it has fixed not only the price of its own sales to jobbers and wholesale dealers, but also the wholesale and retail prices. The bill alleged that most of its sales were made through retail druggists and that the demand for its remedies largely depended upon their good will and commendation, and their ability to realize a fair profit; that certain retail establishments, particularly those known as department stores, had inaugurated a "cut-rate" or "cut-price" system which had caused "much confusion, trouble and damage" to the complainant's business and "injuriously affected the reputation" and "depleted the sales" of its remedies; that this injury resulted "from the fact that the majority of retail druggists as a rule cannot, or believe that they cannot realize sufficient profits" by the sale of the medicines "at the cut-prices announced by the cut-rate and department stores," and therefore are "unwilling to, and do not keep" the medicines "in stock" or "if kept in stock, do not urge or favor sales thereof, but endeavor to foist off some similar remedy or substitute, and from the fact that in the public mind an article advertised or announced at 'cut' or 'reduced' price from the established price suffers loss of reputation and becomes of inferior value and demand." . . .

[The wholesale and retail prices of the medicines were fixed as follows:]

"Medicines, of which the retail price is $1.00; $8.00 per dozen.

"Medicines (if any) of which the retail price is 50 cents; $4.00 per dozen.

"Medicines, of which the retail price is 25 cents; $2.00 per dozen.

* * *

[The wholesaler received a commission of 10 percent of its gross sales, plus a further 5 percent on net receipts for early payment.]

It was alleged that all wholesale and retail druggists, "and all dealers in proprietary medicines," had been given full opportunity, without discrimination, to sign contracts in the form stated, and that such contracts were in force between the complainant "and over four hundred jobbers and wholesalers and twenty-five thousand retail dealers in proprietary medicines in the United States."

The defendant is a Kentucky corporation conducting a wholesale drug business. The bill alleged that the defendant had formerly dealt with the complainant and had full knowledge of all the facts relating to the trade in its medicines; that it had been requested, and refused, to enter into the wholesale contract required by the complainant; that in the city of Cincinnati, Ohio, where the defendant conducted a wholesale drug store, there were a large number of wholesale and retail druggists who had made contracts, of the sort described, with the complainant, and kept its medicines on sale pursuant to the agreed terms and conditions. It was charged that the defendant, "in combination and conspiracy with a number of wholesale and retail dealers in drugs and proprietary medicines, who have not entered into said wholesale and retail contracts" required by the complainant's system and solely for the purpose of selling the remedies to dealers "to be advertised, sold and marketed at cut-rates," and "to thus attract and secure custom and patronage for other merchandise, and not for the purpose of making or receiving a direct money profit" from the sales of the remedies, had unlawfully and fraudulently procured them from the complainant's "wholesale and retail agents" by means "of false and fraudulent representations and statements, and by surreptitious and dishonest methods, and by persuading and inducing, directly and indirectly," a violation of their contracts.

It is further charged that the defendant, having procured the remedies in this manner, had advertised and sold them at less than the jobbing and retail prices established by the complainant. . . .

The bill prayed for an injunction restraining the defendant from inducing or attempting to induce any party to any of the said "wholesale or retail agency contracts" to "violate or break the same, or to sell or deliver to the defendant, or to any person for it" the complainant's remedies; from procuring or attempting to procure in any way any of these remedies from wholesale or retail dealers who had executed the contracts; from advertising, selling or offering for sale the remedies obtained by any of the described means at less "than the established retail price thereof" or to dealers who had not entered into contract with the complainant. . . .

* * *

The bill asserts complainant's "right to maintain and preserve the aforesaid system and method of contracts and sales adopted and established by it." It is, as we have seen, a system of interlocking restrictions by which the complainant seeks to control not merely the prices at which its agents may sell its products, but the prices for all sales by all dealers at wholesale or retail, whether purchasers or subpurchasers, and thus to fix the amount which the consumer shall pay, eliminating all competition. The essential features of such a system are thus described by Mr. Justice Lurton (then Circuit Judge), in [a related] opinion . . .: "The contracting wholesalers or jobbers covenant that they will sell to no one who does not come with complainant's license to buy, and that they will not sell below a minimum price dictated by complainant. Next, all competition between retailers is destroyed, for each such retailer can obtain his supply only by signing one of the uniform contracts prepared for retailers, whereby he covenants not to sell to anyone who proposes to sell again unless the buyer is authorized in writing by the complainant, and not to sell at less than a standard price named in the agreement. Thus all room for competition between retailers, who supply the public, is made impossible. If these contracts leave any room at any point of the line for the usual play of competition between the dealers in the product marketed by complainant, it is not discoverable. Thus a combination between the manufacturer, the wholesalers and the retailers to maintain prices and stifle competition has been brought about."

That these agreements restrain trade is obvious. That, having been made, as the bill alleges, with "most of the jobbers and wholesale druggists and a majority of the retail druggists of the country" and having for their purpose the control of the entire trade, they relate directly to interstate as well as intrastate trade, and operate to restrain trade or commerce among the several States, is also clear.

But it is insisted that the restrictions are not invalid either at common law or under the act of Congress of July 2, 1890, c. 647, 26 Stat. 209, upon the following grounds, which may be taken to embrace the fundamental contentions for the complainant: (1) That the restrictions are valid because they relate to proprietary medicines manufactured under a secret process; and (2) that, apart from this, a manufacturer is entitled to control the prices on all sales of his own products.

First. [The use of trade secrets in the process of manufacture does not confer the right to restrain trade in the sale of the product.]

Second. We come, then, to the second question, whether the complainant, irrespective of the secrecy of its process, is entitled to maintain the restrictions by virtue of the fact that they relate to products of its own manufacture.

The basis of the argument appears to be that, as the manufacturer may make and sell, or not, as he chooses, he may affix conditions as to the use of the article or as to the prices at which purchasers may dispose of it. The propriety of the restraint is sought to be derived from the liberty of the producer.

But because a manufacturer is not bound to make or sell, it does not follow that in case of sales actually made he may impose upon purchasers every sort of restriction. Thus a general restraint upon alienation is ordinarily invalid. "The right of alienation is one of the essential incidents of a right of general property in movables, and restraints upon alienation have been generally regarded as obnoxious to public policy, which is best subserved by great freedom of traffic in such things as pass from hand to hand. General restraint in the alienation of articles, things, chattels, except when a very special kind of property is involved, such as a slave or an heirloom, have been generally held void. 'If a man,' says Lord Coke, in Coke on Littleton, section 360, 'be possessed of a horse or any other chattel, real or personal, and give his whole interest or property therein, upon condition that the donee or vendee shall not alien the same, the same is void, because his whole interest and property is out of him, so as he hath no possibility of reverter; and it is against trade and traffic and bargaining and contracting between man and man.'" *Park v. Hartman,* [153 Fed.Rep. 24]. . . .

* * *

With respect to contracts in restraint of trade, the earlier doctrine of the common law has been substantially modified in adaptation to modern conditions. But the public interest is still the first consideration. To sustain the restraint, it must be found to be reasonable both with respect to the public and to the parties and that it is limited to what is fairly necessary, in the circumstances of the particular case, for the protection of the covenantee. Otherwise restraints of trade are void as against public policy. As was said by this court in *Gibbs v. Baltimore Gas Co.,* 130 U.S. p. 409, "The decision in *Mitchel v. Reynolds,* 1 P.Wms. 181, is the foundation of the rule in relation to the invalidity of contracts in restraint of trade; but as it was made under a condition of things, and a state of society, different from those which now prevail, the rule laid down is not regarded as inflexible, and has been considerably modified. Public welfare is first considered, and if it be not involved, and the restraint upon one party is not greater than protection to the other party requires, the contract may be sustained. The question is, whether, under the particular circumstances of the case and the nature of the particular contract involved in it, the contract is, or is not, unreasonable.

"The true view at the present time," said Lord Macnaghten in *Nordenfelt v. Maxim–Nordenfelt &c. Co.,* 1904, A.C. p. 565, "I think, is this: The public have an interest in every person's carrying on his trade freely: so has the individual. All interference with individual liberty of action in trading, and all restraints of trade of themselves, if there is nothing more, are contrary to public policy, and therefore void. That is the general rule. But there are exceptions: restraints of trade and interference with individual liberty of action may be justified by the special circumstances of a particular case. It is a sufficient justification, and indeed it is the only justification, if the restriction is reasonable— reasonable, that is, in reference to the interests of the parties concerned and reasonable in reference to the interests of the public, so framed and so guarded as to afford adequate protection to the party in whose favor it is imposed, while at the same time it is in no way injurious to the public."

The present case is not analogous to that of a sale of good will, or of an interest in a business, or of the grant of a right to use a process of manufacture. The complainant has not parted with any interest in its business or instrumentalities of production. It has conferred no right by virtue of which purchasers of its products may compete with it. It retains complete control over the business in which it is engaged, manufacturing what it pleases and fixing such prices for its own sales as it may desire. Nor are we dealing with a single transaction, conceivably unrelated to the public interest. The agreements are designed to maintain prices, after the complainant has parted with the title to the articles, and to prevent competition among those who trade in them.

The bill asserts the importance of a standard retail price and alleges generally that confusion and damage have resulted from sales at less than the prices fixed. But the advantage of established retail prices primarily concerns the dealers. The enlarged profits which would result from adherence to the established rates would go to them and not to the complainant. It is through the inability of the favored dealers to realize these profits, on account of the described competition, that the complainant works out its alleged injury. If there be an advantage to a manufacturer in the maintenance of fixed retail prices, the question remains whether it is one which he is entitled to secure by agreements restricting the freedom of trade on the part of dealers who own what they sell. As to this, the complainant can fare no better with its plan of identical contracts than could the dealers themselves if they formed a combination and endeavored to establish the same restrictions, and thus to achieve the same result, by agreement with each other. If the immediate advantage they would thus obtain would not be sufficient to sustain such a direct agreement, the asserted ulterior benefit to the complainant cannot be regarded as sufficient to support its system.

But agreements or combinations between dealers, having for their sole purpose the destruction of competition and the fixing of prices, are injurious to the public interest and void. They are not saved by the advantages which the participants expect to derive from the enhanced price to the consumer.

The complainant's plan falls within the principle which condemns contracts of this class. It, in effect, creates a combination for the prohibited purposes. No distinction can properly be made by reason of the particular character of the commodity in question. It is not entitled to special privilege or immunity. It is an article of commerce and the rules concerning the freedom of trade must be held to apply to it. Nor does the fact that the margin of freedom is reduced by the control of production make the protection of what remains, in such a case, a negligible matter. And where commodities have passed into the channels of trade and are owned by dealers, the validity of agreements to prevent competition and to maintain prices is not to be determined by the circumstance whether they were produced by several manufacturers or by one, or whether they were previously owned by one or by many. The complainant having sold its product at prices satisfactory to itself, the public is entitled to whatever advantage may be derived from competition in the subsequent traffic.

Judgment affirmed.

JUSTICE HOLMES, dissenting: . . . [T]he only question is whether the law forbids a purchaser to contract with his vendor that he will not sell below a certain price. . . .

* * *

But I go farther. There is no statute covering the case; there is no body of precedent that by ineluctable logic requires the conclusion to which the court has come. The conclusion is reached by extending a certain conception of public policy to a new sphere. On such matters we are in perilous country. I think that, at least, it is safe to say that the most enlightened judicial policy is to let people manage their own business in their own way, unless the ground for interference is very clear. What then is the ground upon which we interfere in the present case? Of course, it is not the interest of the producer. No one, I judge, cares for that. It hardly can be the interest of subordinate vendors, as there seems to be no particular reason for preferring them to the originator and first vendor of the product. Perhaps it may be assumed to be the interest of the consumers and the public. On that point I confess that I am in a minority as to larger issues than are concerned here. I think that we greatly exaggerate the value and importance to the public of competition in the production or distribution of an article (here it is only distribution), as fixing a fair price. What really fixes that is the competition of conflicting desires. We, none of us, can have as much as we want of all the things that we want. Therefore, we have to choose. As soon as the price of something that we want goes above the point at which we are willing to give up other things to have that, we cease to buy it and buy something else. Of course, I am speaking of things that we can get along without. There may be necessaries that sooner or later must be dealt with like short rations in a shipwreck, but they are not Dr. Miles's medicines. With regard to things like the latter it seems to me that the point of most profitable returns marks the equilibrium of social desires and determines the fair price in the only sense in which I can find meaning in those words. The Dr. Miles Medical Company knows better than we do what will enable it to do the best business. We must assume its retail price to be reasonable, for it is so alleged and the case is here on demurrer; so I see nothing to warrant my assuming that the public will not be served best by the company being allowed to carry out its plan. I cannot believe that in the long run the public will profit by this court permitting knaves to cut reasonable prices for some ulterior purpose of their own and thus to impair, if not to destroy, the production and sale of articles which it is assumed to be desirable that the public should be able to get. . . .

Questions and Comments

Why would Dr. Miles want to prevent discounting? He could have simply decided what price he wished to extract from his customers, the wholesalers, and let competition among resellers of his and all competing remedies determine the consumer price. Either Dr. Miles had no market power and would be obliged to live with the price set by the marketplace, or he had market power and would want to keep the extra profits for himself—which he could do by a high price on the first sale. How, then, can we explain the facts? Surely Dr. Miles did not want to give away extra profits to wholesalers and retailers.

Perhaps Dr. Miles feared that without assured margins wholesalers would not sufficiently promote his medicines, retailers would not stock enough of his medicines, and retailers would offer Dr. Miles' pills cheap and then induce customers to switch to competing medicines that promised more profit. Is this a plausible explanation?

Perhaps Dr. Miles had only a few competitors and they calculated that they would all be better off if they behaved cooperatively. Each would fix the resale prices of its own medicine with an eye on the resale prices imposed by its competitors. RPM across the board would assure orderly marketing; it would keep price competition from breaking out. Is this plausible?

Perhaps Dr. Miles faced powerful dealers. They wanted to extract or at least to share in the extra profits that Dr. Miles' pills commanded and they had the power to force this result. Does this scenario make sense? Is this what Justice Hughes meant when he said that "the enlarged profits would go to [the wholesalers and retailers]"?

Several years before this case, Dr. Miles and its competitors agreed to settle a government price-fixing case in which they and an association of retailers were charged with cooperating to stifle competition in patent medicines. United States v. National Ass'n of Retail Druggists (U.S.Dist.Ct., D.Ind. May term 1907, No. 10593). Does this information tend to confirm one of your hypotheses?

Can courts as a practical matter distinguish between vertical restraints deriving from dealer pressure (dealers' cartels), vertical restraints reflecting and supporting a manufacturers' cartel, vertical restraints designed to exploit a single manufacturer's market power, and unilateral restraints designed solely to enhance resellers' incentives to promote and sell?

The questions we ask are "modern" questions. The Hughes opinion, however, fits nicely within the early twentieth century tradition. Pricing freedom was seen as a necessary condition for a free and competitive society. Justice Hughes added a more sophisticated economic insight: If dealers have the right to bargain with the manufacturer for RPM, dealers with power are likely to do so, to the detriment of the rest of society. Justice Holmes, dissenting, saw the world from the other end of the telescope: Producers should be free to manage their businesses the way they choose; the way they choose to behave is bound to be best for consumers. Does the Hughes–Holmes tension remind you of the contemporary debate? Does each side start with a presumption about how well markets work? Does each have an instinct about whether firms can and do obtain and use market power?

b. Legislative Responses: Fair Trade

The *Dr. Miles* rule was not entirely popular. Opposition heightened during the depression of 1929. Small retailers and their trade associations complained that large "monopolistic" dealers engaged in "loss-leader" selling and price cutting to crush small business. State legislators came to their aid. In 1931 California passed the first "fair trade" law. 1931 Cal.Stat. 583. The California law permitted producers or owners of trademarked goods to enter into contracts with buyers that forbade resale "except at the price stipulated by the vendor," as long as the goods were in "fair and open competition with commodities of the same general class" produced by others. The statute, however, proved ineffective. As long as retailers did not have to sign contracts agreeing to the trade price, it was impossible for vendors to maintain the minimum price. California, therefore, amended its statute to provide that all nonsigners having notice of a fair trade contract for goods of a certain manufacturer would be bound by it. 1933 Cal.Stat. 793. By 1937, more than half of the states had passed fair trade laws with such nonsigner clauses, and by 1945 all but three states had done so. Justice Frankfurter details this history in his dissenting opinion in *Schwegmann Bros. v. Calvert Distillers Corp.*, 341 U.S. 384, 397–98 (1951).

One problem remained. In view of *Dr. Miles*, resale price maintenance was illegal *per se*. Could a state, by authorizing RPM contracts, grant immunity from federal law to private price fixers? The dilemma produced the 1937 Miller–Tydings Amendment to Section 1 of the Sherman Act. Miller–Tydings declared that nothing in Section 1 of the Sherman Act shall render illegal "contracts or agreements prescribing minimum prices for the resale" of trademarked goods that are in free and open competition with goods of the same general class produced by others when under state law "contracts or agreements of that description are lawful as applied to intrastate transactions."

We print below portions of the senate report that describe the purposes of the Miller–Tydings Amendment, in view of state fair trade policies.

SENATE REPORT NO. 2053
74th Cong., 2d Sess. (1937).

* * *

The purpose of the California act, as expressed in its title, was to protect trade-mark owners, distributors, and the general public against injurious and uneconomic practices in the distribution of articles of standard quality under a trade mark, brand, or name, and the particular practice against which it was directed was the so-called "loss-leader selling."

Since the passage of the California act similar legislation has been enacted in 12 other States, namely, New York, Illinois, Pennsylvania, New Jersey, Oregon, Washington, Wisconsin, Iowa, Maryland, Ohio, Virginia, and Rhode Island (the last three since the introduction of the proposed bill).

In still other States contracts stipulating minimum resale prices are valid at common law.

In the States where such contracts are lawful it has been found that loss-leader selling of identified merchandise sold under competitive conditions operates as a fraud on the consumer, destroys the producer's goodwill in his trade mark, and is used by the large merchant to eliminate his small independent competitor.

In recommending the passage of S. 3822 the committee, while fully recognizing the evils of loss-leader selling, is not required to determine the effectiveness of the device adopted by the States to eliminate the same.

It is sufficient that this type of selling unquestionably has had a disastrous effect upon the small independent retailer, thereby tending to create monopoly, and that a large number of States have found that its evil effects can be mitigated, if not eliminated, by legalizing contracts stipulating minimum resale prices.

* * *

S. 3822 removes the doubt as to the applicability of the Sherman Act by expressly legalizing such contracts where legal under the laws of the State where made or where they are to be performed. . . .

The State acts are in no sense general price-fixing acts. They merely authorize a manufacturer or producer to enter into contracts for the maintenance of his price, but they do not compel him to do so. In other words, they are merely permissive. . . .

They apply only to commodities which are in free and open competition with commodities of the same general class produced by others, and they therefore do not in any sense restrain trade or competition. In fact, they legalize a device which is intended to increase competition and prevent monopoly.

But most important, from the standpoint of the Congress, the proposed bill merely permits the individual States to function, without Federal restraint, within their proper sphere, and does not commit the Congress to a national policy on the subject matter of the State laws. . . .[1]

But Miller–Tydings was silent as to nonsigners. As the Supreme Court would soon hold, private maintenance of RPM systems through the aid of state nonsigners statutes was not immune from the Sherman Act.

SCHWEGMANN BROS. v. CALVERT DISTILLERS CORP.

341 U.S. 384 (1951).

JUSTICE DOUGLAS: Respondents, Maryland and Delaware corporations, are distributors of gin and whiskey. They sell their products to wholesalers in Louisiana, who in turn sell to retailers. Respondents have a price-

---

1. Reproduced in Appendix to dissenting opinion of Justice Frankfurter in Schweg- mann Bros. v. Calvert Corp., *supra,* 341 U.S. at 402, 406–11.

fixing scheme whereby they try to maintain uniform retail prices for their products. They endeavor to make retailers sign price-fixing contracts under which the buyers promise to sell at not less than the prices stated in respondents' schedules. They have indeed succeeded in getting over one hundred Louisiana retailers to sign these agreements. Petitioner, a retailer in New Orleans, refused to agree to the price-fixing scheme and sold respondents' products at a cut-rate price. Respondents thereupon brought this suit . . . to enjoin petitioner from selling the products at less than the minimum prices fixed by their schedules.

It is clear from our decisions under the Sherman Act that this interstate marketing arrangement would be illegal, that it would be enjoined, that it would draw civil and criminal penalties, and that no court would enforce it. Fixing minimum prices, like other types of price fixing, is illegal *per se*. *United States v. Socony–Vacuum Oil Co.*, 310 U.S. 150; *Kiefer–Stewart Co. v. Seagram & Sons*, 340 U.S. 211. Resale price maintenance was indeed struck down in *Dr. Miles Medical Co. v. Park & Sons Co.*, 220 U.S. 373. The fact that a state authorizes the price fixing does not, of course, give immunity to the scheme, absent approval by Congress.

* * *

Louisiana has a . . . [fair trade] law. . . . It not only allows a distributor and retailer to make a "contract" fixing the resale price; but once there is a price-fixing "contract," known to a seller, with any retailer in the state, it also condemns as unfair competition a sale at less than the price stipulated even though the seller is not a party to the "contract." In other words, the Louisiana statute enforces price fixing not only against parties to a "contract" but also against nonsigners. So far as Louisiana law is concerned, price fixing can be enforced against all retailers once any single retailer agrees with a distributor on the resale price. And the argument is that the Miller–Tydings Act permits the same range of price fixing.

* * *

. . . The [Miller–Tydings] Act sanctions only "contracts or agreements." If a distributor and one or more retailers want to agree, combine, or conspire to fix a minimum price, they can do so if state law permits. Their contract, combination, or conspiracy—hitherto illegal—is made lawful. They can fix minimum prices pursuant to their contract or agreement with impunity. When they seek, however, to impose price fixing on persons who have not contracted or agreed to the scheme, the situation is vastly different. That is not price fixing by contract or agreement; that is price fixing by compulsion. That is not following the path of consensual agreement; that is resort to coercion.

* * *

It should be noted in this connection that the Miller–Tydings Act expressly continues the prohibitions of the Sherman Act against "horizontal" price fixing by those in competition with each other at the same functional level. Therefore, when a state compels retailers to follow a parallel price policy, it demands private conduct which the Sherman Act forbids. See *Parker v. Brown*, 317 U.S. 341, 350. Elimination of price competition at the retail level may, of course, lawfully result if a distributor successfully negotiates individual "vertical" agreements with all his retailers. But when retailers are *forced* to abandon price competition, they are driven into a compact in violation of the spirit of the proviso which forbids "horizontal" price fixing. . . .

The contrary conclusion would have a vast and devastating effect on Sherman Act policies. If it were adopted, once a distributor executed a contract with a single retailer setting the minimum resale price for a commodity in the state, all other retailers could be forced into line. Had Congress desired to eliminate the consensual element from the arrangement and to permit blanketing a state with resale price fixing if only one retailer wanted it, we feel that different measures would have been adopted—either a nonsigner provision would have been included or resale price fixing would have been authorized without more. Certainly the words used connote a voluntary scheme. Contracts or agreements convey the idea of a cooperative arrangement, not a program whereby recalcitrants are dragged in by the heels and compelled to submit to price fixing. . . .

* * *

Retailers responded to *Schwegmann* with vigorous lobbying, and in 1952 Congress passed the McGuire Act. The McGuire Act amended Miller–Tydings to extend Sherman Act immunity to RPM systems embracing nonsigners in cases in which state law endorsed nonsigner clauses.

Within the next decade, the costs of RPM became visible and organized opposition ensued. Opposition increased as inflation fueled price rises. Studies showed that prices of fair traded goods were about 19 percent higher than prices of goods of the same brand in states that did not authorize fair trade contracts. (Survey conducted by the Department of Justice in 1956, reported in F.M. Scherer, Industrial Market Structure and Economic Performance 593 (2d ed. 1980)). Several states responded to consumer lobbying by withdrawing their statutory exemptions, thus reinstating the rule of *Dr. Miles*. Some state courts held their statutory nonsigner clauses invalid under their state constitutions.

The early 1970s was a period of severe inflation, a flourishing consumer movement, and growing support for rigorous competition. In 1975, despite claims by small retailers that they would be forced out of business, the pro-consumer and pro-competition forces coalesced to secure passage of the Consumer Goods Pricing Act, Pub.L. 94–145, 89 Stat. 801 (1975), which repealed the Miller–Tydings and McGuire Acts.[2]

2. Congressional committees considering repeal of Miller–Tydings and McGuire in 1975 heard and rejected the argument that RPM was necessary to ensure the manufacturer that discounting dealers would not free ride on promotion, information and service offered by non-discounters. See Fair Trade: Hearings on S. 5408 Before the Subcommittee on Antitrust and Monopoly of the Senate Comm. on the Judiciary, 94th Cong., 1st Sess. 13 (1975) at 94–95, 97–99, 108–14, 126–33 (hereafter "1975 Senate Hearings"); Fair Trade: Hearings on H.R. 2384 Before the Subcommittee on Monopolies and Commer- cial Law of the House Committee on the Judiciary, 94th Cong., 1st Sess. 32, 105, 179–81 (hereafter 1975 House Hearings). Congressional committees also heard and found not compelling the following justifications for RPM: RPM protects new entrants (1975 House Hearings at 51, 55, 61–64; 1975 Senate Hearings 76–77, 86–92); it lessens the dangers of "cut-throat" competition (1975 House Hearings 29; it maintains quality (1975 House Hearings 33, 36; 1975 Senate Hearings (71, 78, 109); it prevents predatory pricing (1975 House Hearings 40–41; 1975 Senate Hearings 113–16); it prevents "loss

c. Fair Trade and State Action: The Preemption Issue

The repeal of the federal authorization for state fair trade laws still left open questions of federalism and preemption. If a state had a policy in favor of fair trade (price floors) and state legislation implemented that policy, did the state law oust the federal law even without a specific federal exemption? The applicable law began to develop during the fair trade era. In *Parker v. Brown*, 317 U.S. 341 (1943), California had adopted a system for the orderly marketing of raisins. It did so by statute designed to alleviate severe problems of overproduction. The system was tantamount to a state-sponsored cartel of raisin growers. Parker, a "dissident" California farmer who wanted to grow more raisins than the cartel allowed, sued California state officials (Brown and others) to enjoin them from implementing the state law. The case reached the United States Supreme Court and the Court dismissed the antitrust claim. The Court observed that the program "derived its authority and its efficacy from the legislative command of the state," 317 U.S. at 350, and it held that "nothing in the language of the Sherman Act or its history" suggested that the act was intended "to nullify a state's control over its . . . agents" or "to restrain state action." 317 U.S. at 350–51. Thus was born the *Parker v. Brown* state action doctrine. When *Schwegmann, supra*, 341 U.S. 384 (1951), arose several years later, the Court put a gloss on *Parker*. *Schwegmann* involved enforcement of the Sherman Act against nonsigner retailers who, before enactment of the McGuire Act, were forced by state law to comply with an RPM system. The Court declared, in effect, that a state cannot sanction horizontal conspiracies that coerce individuals to join a private cartel. Federal law applied, and the state nonsigner clauses were invalidated.

Much later, a California statute required all producers and wholesalers of wine to file fair trade contracts with the state or to post a resale price schedule, and it prohibited wholesalers from selling below the posted prices. Violations were punishable by fine and by suspension or revocation of the violator's license. A California statute required all producers and wholesalers of wine to file fair trade contracts with the state or to post a resale price schedule, and it prohibited wholesalers from selling below the posted prices. Violations were punishable by fine and by suspension or revocation of the violator's license. A California wholesaler sold 27 cases of Gallo wine below the posted prices. Charged with violating the statute, the wholesaler took the initiative and sued the State Department of Alcoholic Beverage Control in the California courts for an injunction against enforcement of the system. The California Court of Appeals granted the injunction, holding that the state's scheme violated the Sherman Act, was not immune under the state action doctrine of *Parker v. Brown*, and was not protected by the Twenty–First Amendment to the Constitution, which gives states control over the transportation and importation of liquor into their territory. The Department of Alcoholic

leaders" from destroying brand reputation (1975 Senate Hearings 85, 136); it prevents big, low-overhead merchandisers from driving out small dealers (1975 Senate Hearings at 76, 78, 84, 11, 118, 128); it benefits "store brands" (1975 House Hearings 32, 49, 73, 76; 1975 Senate Hearings 82, 115); it helps promote interbrand competition (1975 House Hearings 24–25, 73–75; 1975 Senate Hearings 83, 118).

Beverage Control did not appeal. The retailers, however, had an interest they wished to pursue, and the California Retail Liquor Dealers Association intervened. It unsuccessfully sought to appeal to the California Supreme Court. When its appeal was denied, it filed for and was granted a writ of certiorari.

CALIFORNIA RETAIL LIQUOR DEALERS ASS'N v. MIDCAL ALUMINUM, INC.

445 U.S. 97 (1980).

JUSTICE POWELL: . . .

II

The threshold question is whether California's plan for wine pricing violates the Sherman Act. This Court has ruled consistently that resale price maintenance illegally restrains trade. In *Dr. Miles Medical Co. v. John D. Park & Sons Co.*, 220 U.S. 373, 407 (1911), the Court observed that such arrangements are "designed to maintain prices . . ., and to prevent competition among those who trade in [competing goods]." See *Albrecht v. Herald Co.*, 390 U.S. 145 (1968); *United States v. Parke, Davis & Co.*, 362 U.S. 29 (1960); *United States v. A. Schrader's Son, Inc.*, 252 U.S. 85 (1920). For many years, however, the Miller–Tydings Act of 1937 permitted the States to authorize resale price maintenance. 50 Stat. 693. The goal of that statute was to allow the States to protect small retail establishments that Congress thought might otherwise be driven from the marketplace by large-volume discounters. But in 1975 that congressional permission was rescinded. The Consumer Goods Pricing Act of 1975, 89 Stat. 801, repealed the Miller–Tydings Act and related legislation. Consequently, the Sherman Act's ban on resale price maintenance now applies to fair trade contracts unless an industry or program enjoys a special antitrust immunity.

California's system for wine pricing plainly constitutes resale price maintenance in violation of the Sherman Act. *Schwegmann Bros. v. Calvert Corp.*, 341 U.S. 384 (1951); see *Albrecht v. Herald Co., supra; Kiefer–Stewart Co. v. Joseph E. Seagram & Sons*, 340 U.S. 211 (1951); *Dr. Miles Medical Co. v. John D. Park & Sons Co., supra.* The wine producer holds the power to prevent price competition by dictating the prices charged by wholesalers. As Mr. Justice Hughes pointed out in *Dr. Miles*, such vertical control destroys horizontal competition as effectively as if wholesalers "formed a combination and endeavored to establish the same restrictions . . . by agreement with each other." 220 U.S., at 408.[7] . . .

Thus, we must consider whether the State's involvement in the price-setting program is sufficient to establish antitrust immunity under *Parker v. Brown*, 317 U.S. 341 (1943). That immunity for state regulatory

---

7. In *Rice*, the California Supreme Court found direct evidence that resale price maintenance resulted in horizontal price fixing. See *supra*, at n. 3 [citing evidence "that in July 1976 five leading brands of gin each sold in California for $4.89 for a fifth of a gallon, and that five leading brands of Scotch whiskey sold for either $8.39 or $8.40 a fifth."] Although the Court of Appeal made no such specific finding in this case, the court noted that the wine pricing system "cannot be upheld for the same reasons the retail price maintenance provisions were declared invalid in *Rice.*" *Midcal Aluminum, Inc. v. Rice*, 90 Cal.App.3d 979, 983, 153 Cal. Rptr. 757, 760 (1979).

programs is grounded in our federal structure. "In a dual system of government in which, under the Constitution, the states are sovereign, save only as Congress may constitutionally subtract from their authority, an unexpressed purpose to nullify a state's control over its officers and agents is not lightly to be attributed to Congress." *Id.*, at 351. In *Parker v. Brown*, this Court found in the Sherman Act no purpose to nullify state powers. Because the Act is directed against "individual and not state action," the Court concluded that state regulatory programs could not violate it. *Id.*, at 352.

Under the program challenged in *Parker*, the State Agricultural Prorate Advisory Commission authorized the organization of local cooperatives to develop marketing policies for the raisin crop. The Court emphasized that the Advisory Commission, which was appointed by the Governor, had to approve cooperative policies following public hearings: "It is the state which has created the machinery for establishing the prorate program. . . . [I]t is the state, acting through the Commission, which adopts the program and enforces it. . . ." *Ibid.* In view of this extensive official oversight, the Court wrote, the Sherman Act did not apply. Without such oversight, the result could have been different. The Court expressly noted that "a state does not give immunity to those who violate the Sherman Act by authorizing them to violate it, or by declaring that their action is lawful. . . ." *Id.*, at 351.

Several recent decisions have applied *Parker's* analysis. In *Goldfarb v. Virginia State Bar*, 421 U.S. 773 (1975), the Court concluded that fee schedules enforced by a state bar association were not mandated by ethical standards established by the State Supreme Court. The fee schedules therefore were not immune from antitrust attack. "It is not enough that . . . anticompetitive conduct is 'prompted' by state action; rather, anticompetitive activities must be compelled by direction of the State acting as a sovereign." *Id.*, at 791. Similarly, in *Cantor v. Detroit Edison Co.*, 428 U.S. 579 (1976), a majority of the Court found that no antitrust immunity was conferred when a state agency passively accepted a public utility's tariff [that required it to "give" light bulbs to its electricity customers]. In contrast, Arizona rules against lawyer advertising were held immune from Sherman Act challenge because they "reflect[ed] a clear articulation of the State's policy with regard to professional behavior" and were "subject to pointed re-examination by the policymaker—the Arizona Supreme Court—in enforcement proceedings." *Bates v. State Bar of Arizona*, 433 U.S. 350, 362 (1977).

Only last Term, this Court found antitrust immunity for a California program requiring state approval of the location of new automobile dealerships. *New Motor Vehicle Bd. of Cal. v. Orrin W. Fox Co.*, 439 U.S. 96 (1978). That program provided that the State would hold a hearing if an automobile franchisee protested the establishment or relocation of a competing dealership. *Id.*, at 103. In view of the State's active role, the Court held, the program was not subject to the Sherman Act. The "clearly articulated and affirmatively expressed" goal of the state policy was to "displace unfettered business freedom in the matter of the establishment and relocation of automobile dealerships." *Id.*, at 109.

These decisions establish two standards for antitrust immunity under *Parker v. Brown*. First, the challenged restraint must be "one clearly articulated and affirmatively expressed as state policy"; second, the policy must be "actively supervised" by the State itself. *City of Lafayette v. Louisiana Power & Light Co.*, 435 U.S. 389, 410 (1978) (opinion of BRENNAN, J.). The California system for wine pricing satisfies the first standard. The legislative policy is forthrightly stated and clear in its purpose to permit resale price maintenance. The program, however, does not meet the second requirement for *Parker* immunity. The State simply authorizes price setting and enforces the prices established by private parties. The State neither establishes prices nor reviews the reasonableness of the price schedules; nor does it regulate the terms of fair trade contracts. The State does not monitor market conditions or engage in any "pointed reexamination" of the program.[9] The national policy in favor of competition cannot be thwarted by casting such a gauzy cloak of state involvement over what is essentially a private price-fixing arrangement. As *Parker* teaches, "a state does not give immunity to those who violate the Sherman Act by authorizing them to violate it, or by declaring that their action is lawful. . . ." 317 U.S., at 351.

III

Petitioner contends that even if California's system of wine pricing is not protected state action, the Twenty-first Amendment bars application of the Sherman Act in this case. . . .

A

* * *

. . . The Twenty-first Amendment grants the States virtually complete control over whether to permit importation or sale of liquor and how to structure the liquor distribution system. Although States retain substantial discretion to establish other liquor regulations, those controls may be subject to the federal commerce power in appropriate situations. The competing state and federal interests can be reconciled only after careful scrutiny of those concerns in a "concrete case."

B

The federal interest in enforcing the national policy in favor of competition is both familiar and substantial.

> "Antitrust laws in general, and the Sherman Act in particular, are the Magna Carta of free enterprise. They are as important to the preservation of economic freedom and our free-enterprise system as the Bill of Rights is to the protection of our fundamental personal freedoms." *United States v. Topco Associates, Inc.*, 405 U.S. 596, 610 (1972).

See *Northern Pacific R. Co. v. United States*, 356 U.S. 1, 4 (1958). Although this federal interest is expressed through a statute rather than a constitutional provision, Congress "exercis[ed] all the power it possessed" under the Commerce Clause when it approved the Sherman Act.

---

9. The California program contrasts with the approach of those States that completely control the distribution of liquor within their boundaries. Such comprehensive regulation would be immune from the Sherman Act under *Parker v. Brown*, since the State would "displace unfettered business freedom" with its own power.

Atlantic Cleaners & Dyers v. United States, 286 U.S. 427, 435 (1932); see *City of Lafayette v. Louisiana Power & Light Co.,* 435 U.S., at 398. We must acknowledge the importance of the Act's procompetition policy.

* * *

In *Rice,* the State Supreme Court found two purposes behind liquor resale price maintenance: "to promote temperance and orderly market conditions." 21 Cal.3d, at 451, 579 P.2d, at 490. The court found little correlation between resale price maintenance and temperance. It cited a state study showing a 42% increase in per capita liquor consumption in California from 1950 to 1972, while resale price maintenance was in effect. . . .

The *Rice* opinion identified the primary state interest in orderly market conditions as "protect[ing] small licensees from predatory pricing policies of large retailers." *Id.,* at 456, 579 P.2d, at 493. In gauging this interest, the court adopted the views of the Appeals Board of the Alcoholic Beverages Control Department, which first ruled on the claim in *Rice.* The state agency "rejected the argument that fair trade laws were necessary to the economic survival of small retailers. . . ." *Ibid.* The agency relied on a congressional study of the impact on small retailers of fair trade laws enacted under the Miller–Tydings Act. The study revealed that "states with fair trade laws had a 55 percent higher rate of firm failures than free trade states, and the rate of growth of small retail stores in free trade states between 1956 and 1972 was 32 per cent higher than in states with fair trade laws." *Ibid.,* citing S.Rep. No. 94–466, p. 3 (1975). Pointing to the congressional abandonment of fair trade in the 1975 Consumer Goods Pricing Act, the State Supreme Court found no persuasive justification to continue "fair trade laws which eliminate price competition among retailers." The Court of Appeal came to the same conclusion with respect to the wholesale wine trade.

We have no basis for disagreeing with the view of the California courts that the asserted state interests are less substantial than the national policy in favor of competition. That evaluation of the resale price maintenance system for wine is reasonable, and is supported by the evidence cited by the State Supreme Court in *Rice.* Nothing in the record in this case suggests that the wine pricing system helps sustain small retail establishments. Neither the petitioner nor the State Attorney General in his *amicus* brief has demonstrated that the program inhibits the consumption of alcohol by Californians. We need not consider whether the legitimate state interests in temperance and the protection of small retailers ever could prevail against the undoubted federal interest in a competitive economy. The unsubstantiated state concerns put forward in this case simply are not of the same stature as the goals of the Sherman Act.

We conclude that the California Court of Appeal correctly decided that the Twenty-first Amendment provides no shelter for the violation of the Sherman Act caused by the State's wine pricing program. The judgment of the California Court of Appeal, Third Appellate District, is *affirmed.*

———

After the Supreme Court handed down its decision in *Midcal,* numerous states were obliged to recognize that their wine and liquor resale price laws were void and should be repealed or revised. As repeal or revision occurred, prices fell by approximately 20%. See Waldon, Foes Map Liquor War Tactics, New York Times, Sun. Jan. 14, 1979, § XI, 1, col. 1; Sullivan, Jersey Will Remove Liquor Price Rules, New York Times, Jan. 3, 1979, p. 1, col. 1.[3]

d. Consignment and Agency Arrangements—Avoiding the Rule of Dr. Miles

We return to the aftermath of *Dr. Miles.* The facts of *Dr. Miles* raised a possible consignment issue. (We deleted the discussion of the consignment problem from the Court's opinion because the parties did not stress it and the Court did not address it.) In essence the issue is this: While Dr. Miles could not legally control resale prices on goods he *sold,* could he control those prices if he retained title and merely consigned the merchandise to retailers for sale?

Some years after *Dr. Miles,* an RPM case arose that involved consignment; namely, *United States v. General Electric Company,* 272 U.S. 476 (1926). GE owned the patents for electric lamps with tungsten filaments. It manufactured lamps embodying its patents and sold these through hundreds of wholesale "agents" and thousands of retail "agents" under contracts whereby it retained the business risks and retained title until the retail sale. The Court upheld the contracts as bona fide consignment contracts. The agents were not purchasers but consignees, and therefore, the Court held, GE had the right to set the wholesale and retail price.

After *GE* and at least into the 1950s, antitrust specialists generally assumed that consignment contracts provided a way to avoid the rule of *Dr. Miles.* This assumption was put to a serious test before the Warren Court in the 1960s.

SIMPSON v. UNION OIL CO. OF CALIFORNIA
377 U.S. 13 (1964).

JUSTICE DOUGLAS: This is a suit for damages under § 4 of the Clayton Act. . . . The complaint grows out of a so-called retail dealer "consignment" agreement which, it is alleged, Union Oil requires lessees of its retail outlets to sign, of which Simpson was one. The "consignment" agreement is for one year and thereafter until canceled, is terminable by either party at the end of any year and, by its terms, ceases upon any termination of the lease. The lease is also for one year; and it is alleged that it is used to police the retail prices charged by the consignees, renewals not being made if the conditions prescribed by the company are not met. The company, pursuant to the "consignment" agreement, sets the prices at which the retailer sells the gasoline. While "title" to the consigned gasoline "shall remain in Consignor until sold by Consignee," and while the company pays all property taxes on all gasoline in posses-

3. For further development of the state action doctrine, *see* Chapter 3 *supra* at p. 419.

sion of Simpson, he must carry personal liability and property damage insurance by reason of the "consigned" gasoline and is responsible for all losses of the "consigned" gasoline in his possession, save for specified acts of God. Simpson is compensated by a minimum commission and pays all the costs of operation in the familiar manner.

The retail price fixed by the company for the gasoline during the period in question was 29.9 cents per gallon; and Simpson, despite the company's demand that he adhere to the authorized price, sold it at 27.9 cents, allegedly to meet a competitive price. Solely because Simpson sold gasoline below the fixed price, Union Oil refused to renew the lease; termination of the "consignment" agreement ensued; and this suit was filed.. . .[1]

After two pretrial hearings, the company moved for a summary judgment. Simpson moved for a partial summary judgment—that the consignment lease program is in violation of §§ 1 and 2 of the Sherman Act. The District Court, concluding that "all the factual disputes" had been eliminated from the case, entertained the motions. The District Court granted the company's motion and denied Simpson's, holding as to the latter that he had not established a violation of the Sherman Act and, even assuming such a violation, that he had not suffered any actionable damage. The Court of Appeals affirmed. While it assumed that there were triable issues of law, it concluded that Simpson suffered no actionable wrong or damage. . . .

We disagree with the Court of Appeals that there is no actionable wrong or damage if a Sherman Act violation is assumed. If the "consignment" agreement achieves resale price maintenance in violation of the Sherman Act, it and the lease are being used to injure interstate commerce by depriving independent dealers of the exercise of free judgment whether to become consignees at all, or remain consignees, and, in any event, to sell at competitive prices. The fact that a retailer can refuse to deal does not give the supplier immunity if the arrangement is one of those schemes condemned by the antitrust laws.

There is actionable wrong whenever the restraint of trade or monopolistic practice has an impact on the market; and it matters not that the complainant may be only one merchant. . . . The fact that, on failure to renew a lease, another dealer takes Simpson's place and renders the same service to the public is no[t] an answer. . . . For Congress, not the oil distributor, is the arbiter of the public interest; and Congress has closely patrolled price fixing whether effected through resale price maintenance agreements or otherwise. The exclusive requirements contracts struck down in *Standard Oil Co. v. United States*, 337 U.S. 293, were not saved because dealers need not have agreed to them, but could have gone elsewhere. If that were a defense, a supplier could regiment thousands of

---

1. As of December 31, 1957, Union Oil supplied gasoline to 4,133 retail stations in the eight western States of California, Washington, Oregon, Nevada, Arizona, Montana, Utah and Idaho. Of that figure, 2,003 stations were owned or leased by Union Oil and, in turn, leased or subleased to an independent retailer; 14 were company-operated training stations; and the remaining 2,116 stations were owned by the retailer or leased by him from third persons. Union Oil had "consignment" agreements as of that date with 1,978 (99%) of the lessee-retailers and with 1,327 (63%) of the nonlessee-retailers.

otherwise competitive dealers in resale price maintenance programs merely by fear of nonrenewal of short-term leases.

We made clear in *United States v. Parke Davis & Co.*, 362 U.S. 29, that a supplier may not use coercion on its retail outlets to achieve resale price maintenance. We reiterate that view, adding that it matters not what the coercive device is. . . . Here we have . . . an agreement; it is used coercively, and, it promises to be equally if not more effective in maintaining gasoline prices than were the *Parke, Davis* techniques in fixing monopoly prices on drugs.

Consignments perform an important function in trade and commerce, and their integrity has been recognized by many courts, including this one. Yet consignments, though useful in allocating risks between the parties and determining their rights *inter se*, do not necessarily control the rights of others. . . .

* * *

. . . Here we have an antitrust policy expressed in Acts of Congress. Accordingly, a consignment, no matter how lawful it might be as a matter of private contract law, must give way before the federal antitrust policy. . . . [Section] 1 of the Sherman Act [does not] tolerate agreements for retail price maintenance.

We are enlightened on present-day marketing methods by recent congressional investigations. In the automobile field the price is "the manufacturer's suggested retail price," not a price coercively exacted; nor do automobiles go on consignment; they are sold. Resale price maintenance of gasoline through the "consignment" device is increasing. The "consignment" device in the gasoline field is used for resale price maintenance. The theory and practice of gasoline price fixing in vogue under the "consignment" agreement has been well exposed by Congress. A Union Oil official in recent testimony before a House Committee on Small Business explained the price mechanism:

"Mr. ROOSEVELT. Who sets the price in your consignment station, dealer consignment station?

"Mr. RATH. We do.

"Mr. ROOSEVELT. You do?

"Mr. RATH. Yes. We do it on this basis: You see, he is paid a commission to sell these products for us. Now, we go out into the market area and find out what the competitive major price is, what that level is, and we set our house-brand price at that."[6]

6. See Hearings, House Select Committee on Small Business, 85th Cong., 1st Sess., H.R.Res. 56, Pt. III, pp. 79–80. The same official gave this justification for the consignment program—a justification similar to that traditionally advanced for resale price maintenance:

"Consignment is our method of protecting our dealers' profit margins during disturbed retail price conditions, at the same time maintaining our dealers' positions as people handling a premium quality product. We have not used consignment as a means of unfair competition, nor has it been used to price any dealer out of any station. It has instead been used by us to maintain a competitive relationship between our dealers' prices and those of our competitors.

"We are proud of our retail consignment program which has accomplished the ends outlined above. We have been able to make these accomplishments without taking away any of the independence of our dealers. Through our consignment program we have established and maintained under all conditions the minimum guaranteed margins for

Dealers, like Simpson, are independent businessmen; and they have all or most of the indicia of entrepreneurs, except for price fixing. The risk of loss of the gasoline is on them, apart from acts of God. Their return is affected by the rise and fall in the market price, their commissions declining as retail prices drop. Practically the only power they have to be wholly independent businessmen, whose service depends on their own initiative and enterprise, is taken from them by the proviso that they must sell their gasoline at prices fixed by Union Oil. By reason of the lease and "consignment" agreement dealers are coercively laced into an arrangement under which their supplier is able to impose noncompetitive prices on thousands of persons whose prices otherwise might be competitive. The evil of this resale price maintenance program . . . is its inexorable potentiality for and even certainty in destroying competition in retail sales of gasoline by these nominal "consignees" who are in reality small struggling competitors seeking retail gas customers.

As we have said, an owner of an article may send it to a dealer who may in turn undertake to sell it only at a price determined by the owner. There is nothing illegal about that arrangement. When, however, a "consignment" device is used to cover a vast gasoline distribution system, fixing prices through many retail outlets, the antitrust laws prevent calling the "consignment" an agency, for then the end result of *United States v. Socony–Vacuum Oil Co., supra,* would be avoided merely by clever manipulation of words, not by differences in substance. The present, coercive "consignment" device, if successful against challenge under the antitrust laws, furnishes a wooden formula for administering prices on a vast scale.[9]

our dealers that are the best in the industry. It has brought our dealers one other substantial benefit also—and I would like to point this out strongly—they have available for other uses the investment which otherwise would be in gasoline inventories. This amounts to an average of $2,500 per dealer.

"If there is any suspicion or resentment by any dealers or dealer groups, it certainly appears that Union Oil Co.'s retail consignment program is a greatly misunderstood one. It does not remove any aspect of a dealer's independence other than giving us the right to name the dealer's selling prices. It has not been used to create or disturb any retail price situations and instead has, as a matter of fact, contributed materially to the economic welfare of our dealers.

"If we were today to withdraw the consignment program as it is now set up, we know that such action would be bitterly opposed by our dealers. Any problems that are laid at its doorstep—and there were some problems as there are in any new program—have been corrected to the point that a survey of our dealers today would reveal that the great majority of them are heartily in favor of consignment. We are able to offer the names of hundreds of our

dealers who are in favor of the program." *Id.,* at 86–87.

9. A.A. Berle recently described the critical importance of price control to money making by the large oligarchies of business, or the "behemoths" as he calls them:

"Are these behemoths good at making goods—or merely good at making money? Do they come out better because they manufacture more efficiently—or because they 'control the market' and collect unduly high prices from the long-suffering American consumer?

"Again, no one quite knows. It is pretty clear that most prices are established only partly by competition, and partly by administration. Economists are just beginning to wrestle with the problem of 'administered' prices. The three or four 'bigs' in any particular line are happy to stay with a good price level for their product. If the price gets too high, some smart vice president in charge of sales may see a chance to take a fat slice of business away from his competitors.

"But while any one of the two or three bigs knows he can reduce prices and start taking all the business there is, he knows,

Reliance is placed on *United States v. General Electric Co.*, 272 U.S. 476, where a consignment arrangement was utilized to market patented articles. Union Oil correctly argues that the consignment in that case somewhat parallels the one in the instant case. The Court in the *General Electric* case did not restrict its ruling to patented articles; it, indeed, said that the use of the consignment device was available to the owners of articles "patented or otherwise." *Id.*, at 488. But whatever may be said of the *General Electric* case on its special facts, involving patents, it is not apposite to the special facts here.

* * *

The patent laws which give a 17–year monopoly on "making, using, or selling the invention" are *in pari materia* with the antitrust laws and modify them *pro tanto*. That was the *ratio decidendi* of the *General Electric* case. See 272 U.S., at 485. We decline the invitation to extend it.

To allow Union Oil to achieve price fixing in this vast distribution system through this "consignment" device would be to make legality for antitrust purposes turn on clever draftsmanship. We refuse to let a matter so vital to a competitive system rest on such easy manipulation. . . .

* * *

. . . [W]e hold only that resale price maintenance through the present, coercive type of "consignment" agreement is illegal under the antitrust laws, and that petitioner suffered actionable wrong or damage. We reserve the question whether, when all the facts are known, there may be any equities that would warrant only prospective application in damage suits of the rule governing price fixing by the "consignment" device which we announce today.

Reversed and remanded.

JUSTICE STEWART, dissenting:

* * *

. . . [T]he root error in this case, it seems to me, was the District Court's decision to terminate the controversy by way of a summary judgment. I therefore agree with the Court that the judgment of the Court of Appeals should be set aside and the case remanded to the District Court for a trial on the merits. But I think that upon remand there should be a full trial of all the issues in this litigation, because I completely disagree with the Court that whenever a bona fide consignor, employing numerous agents, sets the price at which *his* property is to be sold, "the antitrust laws prevent calling the 'consignment' an agency," and transform the consignment into a sale. In the present posture of this case, such a determination, overruling as it does a doctrine which has

too, that one or all of his associates will soon drop the price below that. In the ensuing price war, nobody will make money for quite a while.

"So, an uneasy balance is struck, and everyone's price remains about the same. Shop around for an automobile and you will see how this works. Economists call it 'imperfect competition'—a tacitly accepted price that is not necessarily the price a stiff competitive free market would create. Only big concerns can swing this sort of competition effectively.

"We do not really know whether bigs make more money because they are efficient or because, through their size, they can 'administer' prices." Bigness: Curse or Opportunity? New York Times Magazine, Feb. 18, 1962, pp. 18, 55, 58.

stood unquestioned for almost 40 years, is unwarranted, unnecessary and premature.

*   *   *

Questions and Comments

Simpson apparently wanted to charge a low price rather than a high one. Does the *Simpson* case undercut the *Dr. Miles'* hypothesis that the dealers are the beneficiaries of resale price fixing? Or are both the nondiscounting dealers and the producers likely to benefit? See the opinion in *Simpson,* footnote 6.

Take special note of the Court's footnote 9. The Court believed that RPM was a device that facilitated "administered pricing." The contemporary term for administered pricing is tacit collusion. The Court thought Simpson's low pricing threatened to destabilize a producers' cartel. One concern of the Court, then, was the interest of the consumer.

However, much of the Court's attention lay elsewhere. Why was the Court concerned about Simpson and similar entrepreneurs? Did the Court want to protect independence of entrepreneurs? Did it merely want to do what was fair? Do the entrepreneurial interests and the consumer interests seem to coincide? Does there seem to be a free rider problem here?

Does the principle of *Simpson* intrude unduly on consignment-agency relationships? Is it good or bad policy to "pierce" consignment relationships where there are thousands of consignees and the manufacturer dictates resale price? Does it matter if the use of RPM facilitates oligopolistic interdependence in pricing by manufacturers? Should we ask, also, whether illegality of such a distribution system will induce the manufacturers to integrate forward and whether full integration would be more or less desirable than separate firms "linked" by RPM?

Is Justice Stewart right that *Simpson* overrules *General Electric?* Or are there still consignment arrangements under which the consignor can set her own price?[4] College textbooks (including law casebooks) are often sold under price-fixed consignment arrangements. Are there special business considerations in this market that make consignments particularly apt? Would such arrangements be lawful if they covered thousands of college bookstores, all with many indicia of independent businesses? What if they covered only a few hundred campus law bookstores?

Justice Douglas distinguished *General Electric* on the ground that GE's product was patented. Is this a principled distinction?

In the early 1970s, after General Electric's basic patents expired, the Department of Justice again challenged the company's consignment distribution system—the same system that was declared lawful in 1926. Citing *Simpson* and the expiration of the patents, the district court held that the system constituted resale price fixing and was illegal *per se. United States v. General Electric Co.,* 358 F.Supp. 731, 733, 737–38 (S.D.N.Y.1973).

4. Cf. Ryko Manufacturing Co. v. Eden Services, 823 F.2d 1215 (8th Cir.1987) with Greene v. General Foods Corp., 517 F.2d 635 (5th Cir.1975), *cert. denied,* 424 U.S. 942 (1976).

e. *Refusal to Deal and Resale Prices: Can You Imply an Agreement?*

The cases you have seen thus far involved or presupposed a contractual arrangement giving the upstream firm control over the prices charged downstream. Suppose the upstream supplier has no explicit contract, but it refuses to deal with price cutters. When is there a contract, combination or conspiracy to set resale prices? When it exists, who are the parties to it (thus, who are subject to civil or criminal sanctions)?

In 1919 the Court retreated somewhat from its 1911 *Dr. Miles* opinion, at least to the extent that it generously characterized action as unilateral rather than concerted. Then, for a long time, the Court seemed to dissociate itself from that 1919 retreat; it liberally found combinations. More recently, however, the Court has again redrawn the line between unilateral and concerted vertical activity. It has also distinguished concerted vertical activity "merely" to cut off discounters from concert to fix resale prices. Consider, first, the 1919 case.

UNITED STATES v. COLGATE & CO.
250 U.S. 300 (1919).

JUSTICE MCREYNOLDS: [Upon writ of error from a district court quashing an indictment,] "[w]e must accept that court's interpretation of the indictments and confine our review to the question of the construction of the statute involved in its decision." *United States v. Carter,* 231 U.S. 492, 493; *United States v. Miller,* 223 U.S. 599, 602.

Being of opinion that "the indictment should set forth such a state of facts as to make it clear that a manufacturer, engaged in what was believed to be the lawful conduct of its business, has violated some known law, before it is haled into court to answer the charge of the commission of a crime" and holding that it "fails to charge any offense under the Sherman Act or any other law of the United States, that is to say, as to the substance of the indictment and the conduct and acts charged therein" the trial court sustained a demurrer to the one before us. Its reasoning and conclusions are set out in a written opinion. 253 Fed.Rep. 522.

We are confronted by an uncertain interpretation of an indictment itself couched in rather vague and general language. Counsel differ radically concerning the meaning of the opinion below and there is much room for the controversy between them.

The indictment runs only against Colgate & Company, a corporation engaged in manufacturing soap and toilet articles and selling them throughout the Union. It makes no reference to monopoly, and proceeds solely upon the theory of an unlawful combination. After setting out defendant's organization, place and character of business and general methods of selling and distributing products through wholesale and retail merchants, it alleges—

". . . the defendant knowingly and unlawfully created and engaged in a combination with said wholesale and retail dealers, in the eastern district of Virginia and throughout the United States, for the purpose and with the effect of procuring adherence on the part of such dealers (in reselling such products sold to them as aforesaid) to resale prices fixed by the defendant, and of preventing such dealers from reselling such products at lower prices, thus suppressing competition amongst such wholesale dealers, and amongst such retail dealers, ..."

Following this is a summary of things done to carry out the purposes of the combination: Distribution among dealers of letters, telegrams, circulars and lists showing uniform prices to be charged; urging them to adhere to such prices and notices, stating that no sales would be made to those who did not; requests, often complied with, for information concerning dealers who had departed from specified prices; investigation and discovery of those not adhering thereto and placing their names upon "suspended lists"; requests to offending dealers for assurances and promises of future adherence to prices, which were often given; uniform refusals to sell to any who failed to give the same; sales to those who did; similar assurances and promises required of, and given by, other dealers followed by sales to them; unrestricted sales to dealers with established accounts who had observed specified prices, etc.

Immediately thereafter comes this paragraph:

"By reason of the foregoing, wholesale dealers in the aforesaid products of the defendant in the eastern district of Virginia and throughout the United States, with few exceptions, resold, at uniform prices fixed by the defendant, the aforesaid products, sold to them by the defendant, and refused to resell such products at lower prices to retail dealers in the States where the respective wholesale dealers did business and in other States. For the same reason retail dealers in the aforesaid products of the defendant in the eastern district of Virginia and throughout the United States resold, at uniform prices fixed by the defendant, the aforesaid products, sold to them by the defendant and by the aforesaid wholesale dealers, and refused to sell such products at lower prices to the consuming public. . . .

In the course of its opinion the trial court said:

* * *

"In the view taken by the court, the indictment here fairly presents the question of whether a manufacturer of products shipped in interstate trade, is subject to criminal prosecution under the Sherman Act, for entering into a combination in restraint of such trade and commerce, because he agrees with his wholesale and retail customers, upon prices claimed by them to be fair and reasonable, at which the same may be resold, and declines to sell his products to those who will not thus stipulate as to prices. This, at the threshold, presents for the determination of the court how far one may control and dispose of his own property; that is to say, whether there is any limitation thereon, if he proceeds in respect thereto in a lawful and bona fide manner. That he may not do so fraudulently, collusively, and in unlawful combination with others, may be conceded. But it by no means follows that, being a manufacturer of a given article, he may not, without incurring any criminal liability, refuse absolutely to sell the same at any price, or to sell at a named sum to a customer, with the understanding that such customer will resell only at an agreed price between them, and, should the customer not observe the understanding as to retail prices, exercise his undoubted right to decline further to deal with such person."

* * *

"The pregnant fact should never be lost sight of that no averment is made of any contract or agreement having been entered into whereby the defendant, the manufacturer, and his customers, bound themselves to enhance and maintain prices . . . ."

Our problem is to ascertain, as accurately as may be, what interpretation the trial court placed upon the indictment—not to interpret it ourselves; and then to determine whether, so construed, it fairly charges violation of the Sherman Act. Counsel for the Government maintain, in effect, that, as so interpreted, the indictment adequately charges an unlawful combination (within the doctrine of *Dr. Miles Medical Co. v. Park & Sons Co.,* 220 U.S. 373) resulting from restrictive agreements between defendant and sundry dealers whereby the latter obligated themselves not to resell except at agreed prices; and to support this position they specifically rely upon the above-quoted sentence in the opinion which begins "In the view taken by the court," etc. On the other hand, defendant maintains that looking at the whole opinion it plainly construes the indictment as alleging only recognition of the manufacturer's undoubted right to specify resale prices and refuse to deal with anyone who failed to maintain the same.

Considering all said in the opinion (notwithstanding some serious doubts) we are unable to accept the construction placed upon it by the Government. We cannot, *e.g.*, wholly disregard the statement [also made by the district court] that "The retailer, after buying, could, if he chose, give away his purchase, or sell it at any price he saw fit, or not sell it at all; his course in these respects being affected only by the fact that he might by his action incur the displeasure of the manufacturer, who could refuse to make further sales to him, as he had the undoubted right to do." And we must conclude that, as interpreted below, the indictment does not charge Colgate & Company with selling its products to dealers under agreements which obligated the latter not to resell except at prices fixed by the company.

* * *

The judgment of the District Court must be *affirmed.*

Questions and Comments

Did *Colgate* gut *Dr. Miles*? In view of *Colgate,* could any well informed manufacturer effectively control downstream prices?

But how can a manufacturer execute a unilateral policy to fix downstream prices and assure that it is not crossing over the line to "agreement"? In the 1960s, not very easily.

UNITED STATES v. PARKE, DAVIS & CO.
362 U.S. 29 (1960).

JUSTICE BRENNAN: The Government sought an injunction under § 4 of the Sherman Act against the appellee, Parke, Davis & Company, on a complaint alleging that Parke Davis conspired and combined, in violation of §§ 1 and 3 of the Act, with retail and wholesale druggists in Washington, D.C., and Richmond, Virginia, to maintain the wholesale and retail prices of Parke Davis pharmaceutical products. The violation was alleged to have occurred during the summer of 1956 when there was no Fair Trade Law in the District of Columbia or the State of Virginia. After the Government completed the presentation of its evidence at the trial, and without hearing Parke Davis in defense, the District Court for the District of Columbia dismissed the complaint [for failure to introduce sufficient evidence of concerted action] . . .

Parke Davis makes some 600 pharmaceutical products which it markets nationally through drug wholesalers and drug retailers. The retailers buy these products from the drug wholesalers or make large quantity purchases directly from Parke Davis. Sometime before 1956 Parke Davis announced a resale price maintenance policy in its wholesalers' and retailers' catalogues. The wholesalers' catalogue contained a Net Price Selling Schedule listing suggested minimum resale prices on Parke Davis products sold by wholesalers to retailers. The catalogue stated that it was Parke Davis' continuing policy to deal only with drug wholesalers who observed that schedule and who sold only to drug retailers authorized by law to fill prescriptions. Parke Davis, when selling directly to retailers, quoted the same prices listed in the wholesalers' Net Price Selling Schedule but granted retailers discounts for volume purchases. Wholesalers were not authorized to grant similar discounts. The retailers' catalogue contained a schedule of minimum retail prices applicable in States with Fair Trade Laws and stated that this schedule was suggested for use also in States not having such laws. These suggested minimum retail prices usually provided a 50% markup over cost on Parke Davis products purchased by retailers from wholesalers but, because of the volume discount, often in excess of 100% markup over cost on products purchased in large quantities directly from Parke Davis.

There are some 260 drugstores in Washington, D.C., and some 100 in Richmond, Virginia. Many of the stores are units of Peoples Drug Stores, a large retail drug chain. There are five drug wholesalers handling Parke Davis products in the locality who do business with the drug retailers. The wholesalers observed the resale prices suggested by Parke Davis. However, during the spring and early summer of 1956 drug retailers in the two cities advertised and sold several Parke Davis vitamin products at prices substantially below the suggested minimum retail prices; in some instances the prices apparently reflected the volume discounts on direct purchases from Parke Davis since the products were sold below the prices listed in the wholesalers' Net Price Selling Schedule. The Baltimore office manager of Parke Davis in charge of the sales district which included the two cities sought advice from his head office on how to handle this situation. The Parke Davis attorney advised that the company could legally "enforce an adopted policy arrived at unilaterally" to sell only to customers who observed the suggested minimum resale prices. He further advised that this meant that "we can lawfully say 'we will sell you only so long as you observe such minimum retail prices' but cannot say 'we will sell you only if you agree to observe such minimum retail prices,' since except as permitted by Fair Trade legislations [sic] agreements as to resale price maintenance are invalid." Thereafter in July the branch manager put into effect a program for promoting observance of the suggested minimum retail prices by the retailers involved. The program contemplated the participation of the five drug wholesalers. In order to insure that retailers who did not comply would be cut off from sources of supply, representatives of Parke Davis visited the wholesalers and told them, in effect, that not only would Parke Davis refuse to sell to wholesalers who did not adhere to the policy announced in its catalogue, but also that it would refuse to sell to wholesalers who sold Parke Davis products to retailers who did not observe the suggested minimum retail prices. Each wholesaler was interviewed individually but each was informed that his competitors were also being apprised of this. The wholesalers without exception indicated a willingness to go along.

Representatives called contemporaneously upon the retailers involved, individually, and told each that if he did not observe the suggested minimum retail prices, Parke Davis would refuse to deal with him, and that furthermore he would be unable to purchase any Parke Davis products from the wholesalers. Each of the retailers was also told that his competitors were being similarly informed.

Several retailers refused to give any assurances of compliance and continued after these July interviews to advertise and sell Parke Davis products at prices below the suggested minimum retail prices. Their names were furnished by Parke Davis to the wholesalers. Thereafter Parke Davis refused to fill direct orders from such retailers and the wholesalers likewise refused to fill their orders. This ban was not limited to the Parke Davis products being sold below the suggested minimum prices but included all the company's products, even those necessary to fill prescriptions.

The president of Dart Drug Company, one of the retailers cut off, protested to the assistant branch manager of Parke Davis that Parke Davis was discriminating against him because a drugstore across the street, one of the Peoples Drug chain, had a sign in its window advertising Parke Davis products at cut prices. The retailer was told that if this were so the branch manager "would see Peoples and try to get them in line." The branch manager testified at the trial that thereafter he talked to a vice-president of Peoples and that the following occurred:

"Q. Well, now, you told Mr. Downey [the vice-president of Peoples] at this meeting, did you not, Mr. Powers, [the assistant branch manager of Parke Davis] that you noticed that Peoples were cutting prices?

"A. Yes.

"Q. And you told him, did you not, that it had been the Parke Davis policy for many years to do business only with individuals that maintained the scheduled prices?

"A. I told Mr. Downey that we had a policy in our catalog, and that anyone that did not go along with our policy, we were not interested in doing business with them.

. . .

"Q. . . . Now, Mr. Downey told you on the occasion of this visit, did he not, that Peoples would stop cutting prices and would abide by the Parke Davis policy, is that right?

"A. That is correct.

. . .

"Q. When you went to call on Mr. Downey, you solicited his support of Parke Davis policies, is not that right?

"A. That is right.

"Q. And he said, I will abide by your policy?

"A. That is right."

The District Court found, apparently on the basis of this testimony, that "The Peoples' representative stated that Peoples would stop cutting prices on Parke Davis' products and Parke Davis continued to sell to Peoples."

But five retailers continued selling Parke Davis products at less than the suggested minimum prices from stocks on hand. Within a few weeks Parke Davis modified its program. Its officials believed that the selling at discount prices would be deterred, and the effects minimized of any isolated instances of discount selling which might continue, if all advertising of such prices were discontinued. In August the Parke Davis representatives again called on the retailers individually. When interviewed, the president of Dart Drug Company indicated that he might be willing to stop advertising, although continuing to sell at discount prices, if shipments to him were resumed. Each of the other retailers was then told individually by Parke Davis representatives that Dart was ready to discontinue advertising. Each thereupon said that if Dart stopped advertising he would also. On August 28 Parke Davis reported this reaction to Dart. Thereafter all of the retailers discontinued advertising of Parke Davis vitamins at less than suggested minimum retail prices and Parke Davis and the wholesalers resumed sales of Parke Davis products to them. However, the suspension of advertising lasted only a month. One of the retailers again started newspaper advertising in September and, despite efforts of Parke Davis to prevent it, the others quickly followed suit. Parke Davis then stopped trying to promote the retailers' adherence to its suggested resale prices, and neither it nor the wholesalers have since declined further dealings with them. A reason for this was that the Department of Justice, on complaint of Dart Drug Company, had begun an investigation of possible violation of the antitrust laws.

The District Court held that the Government's proofs did not establish a violation of the Sherman Act because "the actions of [Parke Davis] were properly unilateral and sanctioned by law under the doctrine laid down in the case of United States v. Colgate & Co., 250 U.S. 300. . . ." 164 F.Supp. at 829. . . .

* * *

The Government concedes for the purposes of this case that under the *Colgate* doctrine a manufacturer, having announced a price maintenance policy, may bring about adherence to it by refusing to deal with customers who do not observe that policy. The Government contends, however, that subsequent decisions of this Court compel the holding that what Parke Davis did here by entwining the wholesalers and retailers in a program to promote general compliance with its price maintenance policy went beyond mere customer selection and created combinations or conspiracies to enforce resale price maintenance in violation of §§ 1 and 3 of the Sherman Act.

The history of the *Colgate* doctrine is best understood by reference to a case which preceded the *Colgate* decision, *Dr. Miles Medical Co. v. Park & Sons Co.,* 220 U.S. 373. Dr. Miles entered into written contracts with its customers obligating them to sell its medicine at prices fixed by it. The Court held that the contracts were void because they violated both the common law and the Sherman Act. The *Colgate* decision distinguished *Dr. Miles* on the ground that the *Colgate* indictment did not charge that company with selling its products to dealers *under agreements* which obligated the latter not to resell except at prices fixed by the seller. The *Colgate* decision created some confusion and doubt as to the continuing vitality of the principles announced in *Dr. Miles.* . . .

* * *

. . . [W]hatever uncertainty previously existed as to the scope of the *Colgate* doctrine, *Bausch & Lomb* [321 U.S. 707 (1944)] and *Beech–Nut* [257 U.S. 441 (1922)] plainly fashioned its dimensions as meaning no more than that a simple refusal to sell to customers who will not resell at prices suggested by the seller is permissible under the Sherman Act. In other words, an unlawful combination is not just such as arises from a price maintenance *agreement,* express or implied; such a combination is also organized if the producer secures adherence to his suggested prices by means which go beyond his mere declination to sell to a customer who will not observe his announced policy.

In the cases decided before *Beech–Nut* the Court's inquiry was directed to whether the manufacturer had entered into illicit contracts, express or implied. The District Court in this case apparently assumed that the Government could prevail only by establishing a contractual arrangement, albeit implied, between Parke Davis and its customers. . . . The District Court premised its ultimate finding that Parke Davis did not violate the Sherman Act on an erroneous interpretation of the standard to be applied. The *Bausch & Lomb* and *Beech–Nut* decisions cannot be read as merely limited to particular fact complexes justifying the inference of an agreement in violation of the Sherman Act. Both cases teach that judicial inquiry is not to stop with a search of the record for evidence of purely contractual arrangements. The Sherman Act forbids combinations of traders to suppress competition. True, there results the same economic effect as is accomplished by a prohibited combination to suppress price competition if each customer, although induced to do so solely by a manufacturer's announced policy, independently decides to observe specified resale prices. So long as *Colgate* is not overruled, this result is tolerated but only when it is the consequence of a mere refusal to sell in the exercise of the manufacturer's right "freely to exercise his own independent discretion as to parties with whom he will deal." When the manufacturer's actions, as here, go beyond mere announcement of his policy and the simple refusal to deal, and he employs other means which effect adherence to his resale prices, this countervailing consideration is not present and therefore he has put together a combination in violation of the Sherman Act. Thus, whether an unlawful combination or conspiracy is proved is to be judged by what the parties actually did rather than by the words they used. . . .

The program upon which Parke Davis embarked to promote general compliance with its suggested resale prices plainly exceeded the limitations of the *Colgate* doctrine and under *Beech–Nut* and *Bausch & Lomb* effected arrangements which violated the Sherman Act. Parke Davis did not content itself with announcing its policy regarding retail prices and following this with a simple refusal to have business relations with any retailers who disregarded that policy. Instead Parke Davis used the refusal to deal with the wholesalers in order to elicit their willingness to deny Parke Davis products to retailers and thereby help gain the retailers' adherence to its suggested minimum retail prices. The retailers who disregarded the price policy were promptly cut off when Parke Davis supplied the wholesalers with their names. The large retailer who said he would "abide" by the price policy, the multi-unit Peoples Drug chain, was not cut off.[6] In thus involving the wholesalers to stop the flow of Parke Davis products to the retailers, thereby inducing retailers' adherence to its suggested retail prices, Parke Davis created a combination with the retailers and the wholesalers to maintain retail prices and violated the Sherman Act. . . .

Moreover, Parke Davis also exceeded the "limited dispensation which [*Colgate*] confers." *Times–Picayune Pub. Co. v. United States,* 345 U.S. 594, 626, in another way, which demonstrates how far Parke Davis went beyond the limits of the *Colgate* doctrine. With regard to the retailers' suspension of advertising, Parke Davis did not rest with the simple announcement to the trade of its policy in that regard followed by a refusal to sell to the retailers who would not observe it. First it discussed the subject with Dart Drug. When Dart indicated willingness to go along the other retailers were approached and Dart's apparent willingness to cooperate was used as the lever to gain their acquiescence in the program. Having secured those acquiescences Parke Davis returned to Dart Drug with the report of that accomplishment. Not until all this was done was the advertising suspended and sales to all the retailers resumed. In this manner Parke Davis sought assurances of compliance and got them, as well as the compliance itself. It was only by actively bringing about substantial unanimity among the competitors that Parke Davis was able to gain adherence to its policy. . . . [I]f a manufacturer is unwilling to rely on individual self-interest to bring about general voluntary acquiescence which has the collateral effect of eliminating price competition, and takes affirmative action to achieve uniform adherence by inducing each customer to adhere to avoid such price competition, the customers' acquiescence is not then a matter of individual free choice prompted alone by the desirability of the product. The product then comes packaged in a competition-free wrapping—a valuable feature in itself—by virtue of concerted action induced by the manufacturer. The manufacturer is thus the

6. Indeed, if Peoples resumed adherence to the Parke Davis price scale after the interview between its vice-president and Parke Davis' assistant branch manager, p. 34, *supra*, shows [*sic*, showing] that Parke Davis and Peoples entered into a price maintenance agreement, express, tacit or implied, such agreement violated the Sherman Act without regard to any wholesalers' participation.

organizer of a price-maintenance combination or conspiracy in violation of the Sherman Act. Under that Act "competition not combination, should be the law of trade." *National Cotton Oil Co. v. Texas,* 197 U.S. 115, 129, and "a combination formed for the purpose and with the effect of raising, depressing, fixing, pegging, or stabilizing the price of a commodity in interstate or foreign commerce is illegal *per se.*" *United States v. Socony–Vacuum Oil Co.,* 310 U.S. 150, 223. . . .

* * *

The judgment is reversed and the case remanded to the District Court with directions to enter an appropriate judgment enjoining Parke Davis from further violations of the Sherman Act unless the company elects to submit evidence in defense and refutes the Government's right to injunctive relief established by the present record.

JUSTICE STEWART, concurring: I concur in the judgment. The Court's opinion amply demonstrates that the present record shows an illegal combination to maintain retail prices. I therefore find no occasion to question, even by innuendo, the continuing validity of the *Colgate* decision. . . .

JUSTICE HARLAN, whom JUSTICE FRANKFURTER and JUSTICE WHITTAKER join, dissenting.

The Court's opinion reaches much further than at once may meet the eye, and justifies fuller discussion than otherwise might appear warranted. Scrutiny of the opinion will reveal that the Court has done no less than send to its demise the *Colgate* doctrine which has been a basic part of antitrust law concepts since it was first announced in 1919 in *United States v. Colgate,* 250 U.S. 300.

* * *

. . . The Court now says that the seller runs afoul of the Sherman Act when he goes beyond mere announcement of his policy and refusal to sell, not because the bare announcement and refusal fall outside the statutory phrase, but because any additional step removes a "countervailing consideration" in favor of permitting a seller to choose his customers. But we are left wholly in the dark as to what the purported new standard is for establishing a "contract, combination . . . or conspiracy."
. . .

* * *

. . . [T]he Court finds that Parke Davis' conduct exceeded the permissible limits of *Colgate* in two respects. The first is that Parke Davis announced that it would, and did, cut off wholesalers who continued to sell to price-cutting retailers. The second is that the Company in at least one instance reported its talks with one or more retailers to other retailers; that in "this manner Parke Davis sought assurances of compliance and got them"; and that it "was only by actively bringing about substantial unanimity among the competitors that Parke Davis was able to gain adherence to its policy."

There are two difficulties with the Court's analysis on these scores. The first is the findings of the District Court. As to refusals to sell to wholesalers, the lower court found that such conduct did not involve any concert of action, but was wholly unilateral on Parke Davis' part. And I cannot see how such unilateral action, permissible in itself, becomes any less unilateral because it is taken simultaneously with similar unilateral action at the retail level. As to the other respect in which the Court holds Parke Davis' conduct was illegal, the District Court found that the Company did not make "the enforcement of its policies as to any one wholesaler or retailer dependent upon the action of any other wholesaler or retailer." And it further stated that the "evidence is clear that both wholesalers and retailers valued defendant's business so highly that they acceded to its policy," and that such acquiescence was not brought about by "coercion" or "agreement." Even if this were not true, so that concerted action among the retailers at the "horizontal" level might be inferred, as the Court indicates, under the principles of *Interstate Circuit, Inc., v. United States*, 306 U.S. 208, I do not see how that itself would justify an inference that concerted action at the "vertical" level existed between Parke Davis and the retailers or wholesalers.

The second difficulty with the Court's analysis is that even reviewing the District Court's findings only as a matter of law, as the Court purports to do, the cases do not justify overturning the lower court's resulting conclusions. . . .

In light of the whole history of the *Colgate* doctrine, it is surely this Court, and not the District Court, that has proceeded on erroneous premises in deciding this case. Unless there is to be attributed to the Court a purpose to overturn the findings of fact of the District Court— something which its opinion not only expressly disclaims doing, but which would also be in plain defiance of the Federal Rules of Civil Procedure, Rule 52(a), and principles announced in past cases * * *—I think that what the Court has really done here is to throw the *Colgate* doctrine into discard. . . .

*   *   *

After *Parke Davis*, the Supreme Court decided *Albrecht v. Herald Company*, 390 U.S. 145 (1968). In *Albrecht* it held that actions by a newspaper to place a *ceiling* on prices charged by its distributors violated Section 1 of the Sherman Act. The Court found a "combination" between (1) the Herald Company, the defendant newspaper, (2) a company it hired to telephone the customers of Albrecht to advise them that the Herald Company itself would sell its paper for a price less than Albrecht charged, and (3) a new delivery person, to whom the Herald turned over former customers of Albrecht who wanted to switch. Dissenting in *Albrecht*, Justice Harlan distinguished maximum from minimum resale price-fixing, and he referred as follows to his earlier dissent in *Parke Davis*:

    *   *   * It would often be proper to infer, in situations in which a manufacturer dictates a minimum price to a retailer, that the manufacturer is the mechanism for enforcing a very real combinatorial restraint among retailers who should be competing horizontally.[5] Instead of under-

---

5. See Turner, The Definition of Agreement Under the Sherman Act: Conscious Parallelism and Refusals to Deal, 75 Harv.L. Rev. 655. Professor Turner (as he then was) suggested the overruling of *United States v. Colgate & Co.*, 250 U.S. 300, arguing, *inter alia*, that *Colgate* behavior by a manufacturer tends to produce tacit or implied mini-

taking to analyze when this inference would be proper, the Court has in the past followed the rough approximation adopted in *Parke Davis:* there is no "combination" when a manufacturer simply states a resale price and announces that he will not deal with those who depart from it; there is a combination when the manufacturer goes one inch further. The magical quality in this transformation is more apparent than real, for the underlying horizontal combination may frequently be there and the Court has simply failed to state what it is.[7]   . . .

Questions and Comments

Parke Davis involved an elaborate scheme for RPM. The manufacturer enlisted the efforts of wholesalers and induced the compliance of retailers by personal visits and by representations to them that other discounters had submitted to the "common effort." Does Justice Harlan imply that, in a minimum price situation, these facts give rise to an inference of agreements— both horizontal and vertical? Does he imply that there also may be other minimum price plans that go beyond simple announcement of policy and refusal to deal with violators but are nonetheless within *Colgate* protection? Shift, now, to maximum price-fixing. Does Justice Harlan imply that circumstantial evidence sufficient to justify an inference of concerted action is difficult to imagine in a maximum price fixing situation? Do you agree?

After *Parke Davis,* antitrust lawyers generally advised their clients that (at least absent a monopoly situation) *Colgate* was still alive. In theory manufacturers could lawfully announce their price policy and refuse to deal with violators, as long as they did nothing more to induce conformance. Nevertheless, as many lawyers told their clients, *Colgate* was not reliable as a basis for business planning; it would be too difficult to assure oneself that all personnel would stay on the safe side of the line. A unilateral refusal to deal would quickly spill over into a real conspiracy; nondiscounters would complain and manufacturers would accede to their wishes to enforce conformance. Shortly after *Colgate* was limited by *Parke Davis,* the Court of Appeals for the Second Circuit described the remnants of the *Colgate* doctrine as follows:

> The Supreme Court has left a narrow channel through which a manufacturer may pass even though the facts would have to be of such Doric simplicity as to be somewhat rare in this day of complex business enterprise.

George W. Warner & Co. v. Black & Decker Mfg. Co., 277 F.2d 787, 790 (2d Cir. 1960).

mum price agreements among otherwise competitive retailers. He suggested that "it should be perfectly clear to any manufacturer that a policy of refusing to deal with *price cutters* is no more nor less than an invitation [to retailers] to agree [with each other as well as with the manufacturer] on . . . a *minimum* price. . . ." *Id.,* at 689. (Emphasis added.)

7. I thought at the time *Parke Davis* was decided (see my dissenting opinion in that case, 362 U.S., at 49) and continue to believe, that the result reached could not be sup-

ported on the majority's reasoning. I am frank to say, however, that I now consider that the *Parke Davis* result can be supported on Professor Turner's rationale. See Turner, *supra,* n. 5, at 684–691. Further reflection on the matter also leads me to say that my statement in dissent to the effect that *Parke Davis* had overruled the *Colgate* case was overdrawn, and further that I am not yet prepared to say that Professor Turner's rationale necessarily carries the total discard of *Colgate.*

For a number of years, the FTC aspired to test the viability of *Colgate*. Its chance came in *Russell Stover Candies Inc.* The facts were as follows: (1) Stover distributed candy through retail dealers, designated the resale prices it wanted retailers to use through price lists and pre-ticketing, and told retailers that it would not deal with any retailer that did not sell at the prices Stover proposed. (2) The numerous retailers that sold Stover candies at locations across the country overwhelmingly complied with these suggested prices.

The FTC sued under Section 5 of the Federal Trade Commission Act, designedly alleging a contract, combination or conspiracy in restraint of trade (although concerted action is not a necessary condition of Section 5). The administrative law judge dismissed the complaint, relying on *Colgate*. On appeal, the Commission vacated the order of dismissal and entered a cease and desist order. It found that the candy retailers' widespread compliance with the system over a substantial period of time in a national market warranted a factual inference that some retailers had complied, not voluntarily, but out of fear of termination if they cut prices. The Commission ruled that "the *Colgate* doctrine . . . does not preclude . . . a finding of agreement when a buyer unwillingly complies . . . in order to avoid termination." 100 F.T.C. 1, 45–46 (1982). Stover appealed, and won. While the appellate court saw the concept of unilateral action as a narrow one, it found that Stover's actions steered within *Colgate*'s gateway. The Commission observed that the mission of overturning *Colgate* (i.e., expanding the common and judicial understanding of when RPM is maintained by concert) is one for the Supreme Court, not the Commission or lower courts.

Russell Stover merely acknowledged that *Colgate* breathes; but *Colgate* has continued to live uneasily with *Dr. Miles*. In the mid 1980s the Reagan Justice Department sought to expand *Colgate* and overturn *Dr. Miles*, because it believed that, if a producer desires RPM, RPM is efficient and good for consumers. The Justice Department sought a vehicle to argue its case to the Supreme Court. It found this vehicle in *Monsanto v. Spray–Rite*, wherein it participated as friend of the court. However, when the Justice Department advocated in its brief that the Supreme Court overrule *Dr. Miles* and abolish the per se rule against RPM agreements, Congress was angered, and it refused to allow the Department of Justice to spend a penny of its authorized budget on repeal of the rule. Pub.L. No. 98–166 § 510, 97 Stat. 1102 (1983).

MONSANTO CO. v. SPRAY–RITE SERVICE CORP.
465 U.S. 752 (1984).

JUSTICE POWELL: This case presents a question as to the standard of proof required to find a vertical price-fixing conspiracy in violation of § 1 of the Sherman Act.

I

Petitioner Monsanto Co. manufactures chemical products, including agricultural herbicides. By the late 1960's, the time at issue in this case, its sales accounted for approximately 15% of the corn herbicide market and 3% of the soybean herbicide market. In the corn herbicide market, the market leader commanded a 70% share. In the soybean herbicide market, two other competitors each had between 30% and 40% of the market. Respondent Spray–Rite Service Corp. was engaged in the wholesale distribution of agricultural chemicals from 1955 to 1972. Spray–Rite was essentially a family business, whose owner and president, Donald Yapp, was also its sole salaried salesman. Spray–Rite was a discount operation, buying in large quantities and selling at a low margin.

Spray–Rite was an authorized distributor of Monsanto herbicides from 1957 to 1968. In October 1967, Monsanto announced that it would appoint distributors for 1–year terms, and that it would renew distributorships according to several new criteria. Among the criteria were: (i) whether the distributor's primary activity was soliciting sales to retail dealers; (ii) whether the distributor employed trained salesmen capable of educating its customers on the technical aspects of Monsanto's herbicides; and (iii) whether the distributor could be expected "to exploit fully" the market in its geographical area of primary responsibility. Shortly thereafter, Monsanto also introduced a number of incentive programs, such as making cash payments to distributors that sent salesmen to training classes, and providing free deliveries of products to customers within a distributor's area of primary responsibility.[1]

In October 1968, Monsanto declined to renew Spray–Rite's distributorship. At that time, Spray–Rite was the 10th largest out of approximately 100 distributors of Monsanto's primary corn herbicide. Ninety percent of Spray–Rite's sales volume was devoted to herbicide sales, and 16% of its sales were of Monsanto products. After Monsanto's termination, Spray–Rite continued as a herbicide dealer until 1972. It was able to purchase some of Monsanto's products from other distributors, but not as much as it desired or as early in the season as it needed. Monsanto introduced a new corn herbicide in 1969. By 1972, its share of the corn herbicide market had increased to approximately 28%. Its share of the soybean herbicide market had grown to approximately 19%.

Spray–Rite brought this action under § 1 of the Sherman Act. It alleged that Monsanto and some of its distributors conspired to fix the resale prices of Monsanto herbicides. Its complaint further alleged that Monsanto terminated Spray–Rite's distributorship, adopted compensation programs and shipping policies, and encouraged distributors to boycott Spray–Rite in furtherance of this conspiracy. Monsanto denied the allegations of conspiracy, and asserted that Spray–Rite's distributorship had been terminated because of its failure to hire trained salesmen and promote sales to dealers adequately.

The case was tried to a jury. The District Court instructed the jury that Monsanto's conduct was *per se* unlawful if it was in furtherance of a conspiracy to fix prices. In answers to special interrogatories, the jury found that (i) the termination of Spray–Rite was pursuant to a conspiracy between Monsanto and one or more of its distributors to set resale prices, (ii) the compensation programs, areas of primary responsibility, and/or shipping policies were created by Monsanto pursuant to such a conspiracy, and (iii) Monsanto conspired with one or more distributors to limit Spray–Rite's access to Monsanto herbicides after 1968.[2] The jury awarded $3.5

---

1. These areas of primary responsibility were not exclusive territorial restrictions. Approximately 10 to 20 distributors were assigned to each area, and distributors were permitted to sell outside their assigned area.

2. The three special interrogatories were as follows:

"1. Was the decision by Monsanto not to offer a new contract to plaintiff for 1969

million in damages, which was trebled to $10.5 million. Only the first of the jury's findings is before us today.

The Court of Appeals for the Seventh Circuit affirmed. 684 F.2d 1226 (1982). It held that there was sufficient evidence to satisfy Spray–Rite's burden of proving a conspiracy to set resale prices. The court stated that "proof of termination following competitor complaints is sufficient to support an inference of concerted action." *Id.,* at 1238.[4] Canvassing the testimony and exhibits that were before the jury, the court found evidence of numerous complaints from competing Monsanto distributors about Spray–Rite's price-cutting practices. It also noted that there was testimony that a Monsanto official had said that Spray–Rite was terminated because of the price complaints.

In substance, the Court of Appeals held that an antitrust plaintiff can survive a motion for a directed verdict if it shows that a manufacturer terminated a price-cutting distributor in response to or following complaints by other distributors. This view brought the Seventh Circuit into direct conflict with a number of other Courts of Appeals. We granted certiorari to resolve the conflict. 460 U.S. 1010 (1983). We reject the statement by the Court of Appeals for the Seventh Circuit of the standard of proof required to submit a case to the jury in distributor-termination litigation, but affirm the judgment under the standard we announce today.

II

This Court has drawn two important distinctions that are at the center of this and any other distributor-termination case. First, there is the basic distinction between concerted and independent action—a distinction not always clearly drawn by parties and courts. Section 1 of the Sherman Act requires that there be a "contract, combination . . . or conspiracy" between the manufacturer and other distributors in order to establish a violation. Independent action is not proscribed. A manufacturer of course generally has a right to deal, or refuse to deal, with whomever it likes, as long as it does so independently. *United States v. Colgate & Co.,* 250 U.S. 300, 307 (1919); cf. *United States v. Parke, Davis & Co.,* 362 U.S. 29 (1960). Under *Colgate,* the manufacturer can announce its resale prices in advance and refuse to deal with those who fail to

made by Monsanto pursuant to a conspiracy or combination with one or more of its distributors to fix, maintain or stabilize resale prices of Monsanto herbicides?

"2. Were the compensation programs and/or areas of primary responsibility, and/or shipping policy created by Monsanto pursuant to a conspiracy to fix, maintain or stabilize resale prices on Monsanto herbicides?

"3. Did Monsanto conspire or combine with one or more of its distributors so that one or more of those distributors would limit plaintiff's access to Monsanto herbicides after 1968?"

The jury answered "Yes" to each of the interrogatories.

4. The court later in the same paragraph restated the standard of sufficiency as follows: "Proof of distributorship termination *in response to* competing distributors' complaints about the terminated distributor's pricing policies is sufficient to raise an inference of concerted action." 684 F.2d, at 1239 (emphasis added). It may be argued that this standard is different from the one quoted in text in that this one requires a showing of a minimal causal connection between the complaints and the termination of the plaintiff, while the textual standard requires only that the one "follow" the other. As we explain *infra,* the difference is not ultimately significant in our analysis.

comply. And a distributor is free to acquiesce in the manufacturer's demand in order to avoid termination.

The second important distinction in distributor-termination cases is that between concerted action to set prices and concerted action on nonprice restrictions. The former have been *per se* illegal since the early years of national antitrust enforcement. See *Dr. Miles Medical Co. v. John D. Park & Sons Co.*, 220 U.S. 373, 404–409 (1911). The latter are judged under the rule of reason, which requires a weighing of the relevant circumstances of a case to decide whether a restrictive practice constitutes an unreasonable restraint on competition. See *Continental T.V., Inc. v. GTE Sylvania Inc.*, 433 U.S. 36 (1977).[7]

While these distinctions in theory are reasonably clear, often they are difficult to apply in practice. In *Sylvania* we emphasized that the legality of arguably anticompetitive conduct should be judged primarily by its "market impact." But the economic effect of all of the conduct described above—unilateral and concerted vertical price setting, agreements on price and nonprice restrictions—is in many, but not all, cases similar or identical. And judged from a distance, the conduct of the parties in the various situations can be indistinguishable. For example, the fact that a manufacturer and its distributors are in constant communication about prices and marketing strategy does not alone show that the distributors are not making independent pricing decisions. A manufacturer and its distributors have legitimate reasons to exchange information about the prices and the reception of their products in the market. Moreover, it is precisely in cases in which the manufacturer attempts to further a particular marketing strategy by means of agreements on often costly nonprice restrictions that it will have the most interest in the distributors' resale prices. The manufacturer often will want to ensure that its distributors earn sufficient profit to pay for programs such as hiring and training additional salesmen or demonstrating the technical features of the product, and will want to see that "freeriders" do not interfere. Thus, the manufacturer's strongly felt concern about resale prices does not necessarily mean that it has done more than the *Colgate* doctrine allows.

Nevertheless, it is of considerable importance that independent action by the manufacturer, and concerted action on nonprice restrictions, be distinguished from price-fixing agreements, since under present law the

7. The Solicitor General (by brief only) and several other *amici* suggest that we take this opportunity to reconsider whether "contract[s], combination[s] . . . or conspirac[ies]" to fix resale prices should always be unlawful. They argue that the economic effect of resale price maintenance is little different from agreements on nonprice restrictions. See generally *Continental T.V., Inc. v. GTE Sylvania Inc.*, 433 U.S., at 69–70 (White, J., concurring in judgment) (citing sources); Baker, Interconnected Problems of Doctrine and Economics in the Section One Labyrinth: Is *Sylvania* a Way Out?, 67 Va.L. Rev. 1457, 1465–1466 (1981). They say that the economic objections to resale price maintenance that we discussed in *Sylvania, su-* pra, at 51, n. 18—such as that it facilitates horizontal cartels—can be met easily in the context of rule-of-reason analysis.

Certainly in this case we have no occasion to consider the merits of this argument. This case was tried on *per se* instructions to the jury. Neither party argued in the District Court that the rule of reason should apply to a vertical price-fixing conspiracy, nor raised the point on appeal. In fact, neither party before this Court presses the argument advanced by *amici*. We therefore decline to reach the question, and we decide the case in the context in which it was decided below and argued here.

latter are subject to *per se* treatment and treble damages. On a claim of concerted price fixing, the antitrust plaintiff must present evidence sufficient to carry its burden of proving that there was such an agreement. If an inference of such an agreement may be drawn from highly ambiguous evidence, there is a considerable danger that the doctrines enunciated in *Sylvania* and *Colgate* will be seriously eroded.

The flaw in the evidentiary standard adopted by the Court of Appeals in this case is that it disregards this danger. Permitting an agreement to be inferred merely from the existence of complaints, or even from the fact that termination came about "in response to" complaints, could deter or penalize perfectly legitimate conduct. As Monsanto points out, complaints about price cutters "are natural—and from the manufacturer's perspective, unavoidable—reactions by distributors to the activities of their rivals." Such complaints, particularly where the manufacturer has imposed a costly set of nonprice restrictions, "arise in the normal course of business and do not indicate illegal concerted action." *Roesch, Inc. v. Star Cooler Corp.,* 671 F.2d 1168, 1172 (CA8 1982), on rehearing en banc, 712 F.2d 1235 (CA8 1983) (affirming District Court judgment by an equally divided court). Moreover, distributors are an important source of information for manufacturers. In order to assure an efficient distribution system, manufacturers and distributors constantly must coordinate their activities to assure that their product will reach the consumer persuasively and efficiently. To bar a manufacturer from acting solely because the information upon which it acts originated as a price complaint would create an irrational dislocation in the market. See F. Warren–Boulton, Vertical Control of Markets 13, 164 (1978). In sum, "[t]o permit the inference of concerted action on the basis of receiving complaints alone and thus to expose the defendant to treble damage liability would both inhibit management's exercise of its independent business judgment and emasculate the terms of the statute." *Edward J. Sweeney & Sons, Inc. v. Texaco, Inc.,* 637 F.2d 105, 111, n. 2 (CA3 1980), cert. denied, 451 U.S. 911 (1981).[8]

Thus, something more than evidence of complaints is needed. There must be evidence that tends to exclude the possibility that the manufacturer and nonterminated distributors were acting independently. As Judge Aldisert has written, the antitrust plaintiff should present direct or circumstantial evidence that reasonably tends to prove that the manufacturer and others "had a conscious commitment to a common scheme designed to achieve an unlawful objective." *Edward J. Sweeney & Sons, supra,* at 111; cf. *American Tobacco Co. v. United States,* 328 U.S. 781, 810 (1946) (Circumstances must reveal "a unity of purpose or a common design and understanding, or a meeting of minds in an unlawful arrangement").[9]

8. We do not suggest that evidence of complaints has no probative value at all, but only that the burden remains on the antitrust plaintiff to introduce additional evidence sufficient to support a finding of an unlawful contract, combination, or conspiracy.

9. The concept of "a meeting of the minds" or "a common scheme" in a distributor-termination case includes more than a showing that the distributor conformed to the suggested price. It means as well that evidence must be presented both that the distributor communicated its acquiescence or agreement, and that this was sought by the manufacturer.

III

A

Applying this standard to the facts of this case, we believe there was sufficient evidence for the jury reasonably to have concluded that Monsanto and some of its distributors were parties to an "agreement" or "conspiracy" to maintain resale prices and terminate price cutters. In fact there was substantial *direct* evidence of agreements to maintain prices. There was testimony from a Monsanto district manager, for example, that Monsanto on at least two occasions in early 1969, about five months after Spray–Rite was terminated, approached price-cutting distributors and advised that if they did not maintain the suggested resale price, they would not receive adequate supplies of Monsanto's new corn herbicide. When one of the distributors did not assent, this information was referred to the Monsanto regional office, and it complained to the distributor's parent company. There was evidence that the parent instructed its subsidiary to comply, and the distributor informed Monsanto that it would charge the suggested price. Evidence of this kind plainly is relevant and persuasive as to a meeting of minds.[10]

An arguably more ambiguous example is a newsletter from one of the distributors to his dealer-customers. The newsletter is dated October 1, 1968, just four weeks before Spray–Rite was terminated. It was written after a meeting between the author and several Monsanto officials, and discusses Monsanto's efforts to "ge[t] the 'market place in order.'" The newsletter reviews some of Monsanto's incentive and shipping policies, and then states that in addition "every effort will be made to maintain a minimum market price level." The newsletter relates these efforts as follows:

> "In other words, we are assured that Monsanto's company-owned outlets will not retail at less than their suggested retail price to the trade as a whole. Furthermore, those of us on the distributor level are not likely to deviate downward on price to anyone as the idea is implied that doing this possibly could discolor the outlook for continuity as one of the approved distributors during the future upcoming seasons. So, none interested in the retention of this arrangement is likely to risk being deleted from this customer service opportunity. Also, as far as the national accounts are concerned, they are sure to recognize the desirability of retaining Monsanto's favor on a continuing basis by respecting the wisdom of participating in the suggested program in a manner assuring order on the retail level 'playground' throughout the entire country. It is elementary that harmony can only come from following the rules of the game and that in case of dispute, the decision of the umpire is final."

It is reasonable to interpret this newsletter as referring to an agreement or understanding that distributors and retailers would maintain prices, and Monsanto would not undercut those prices on the retail level and

---

10. In addition, there was circumstantial evidence that Monsanto sought agreement from the distributor to conform to the resale price. The threat to cut off the distributor's supply came during Monsanto's "shipping season" when herbicide was in short supply. The jury could have concluded that Monsanto sought this agreement at a time when it was able to use supply as a lever to force compliance.

would terminate competitors who sold at prices below those of complying distributors; these were "the rules of the game."[11]

B

If, as the courts below reasonably could have found, there was evidence of an agreement with one or more distributors to maintain prices, the remaining question is whether the termination of Spray–Rite was part of or pursuant to that agreement. It would be reasonable to find that it was, since it is necessary for competing distributors contemplating compliance with suggested prices to know that those who do not comply will be terminated. Moreover, there is some circumstantial evidence of such a link. Following the termination, there was a meeting between Spray–Rite's president and a Monsanto official. There was testimony that the first thing the official mentioned was the many complaints Monsanto had received about Spray–Rite's prices.[12] In addition, there was reliable testimony that Monsanto never discussed with Spray–Rite prior to the termination the distributorship criteria that were the alleged basis for the action. By contrast, a former Monsanto salesman for Spray–Rite's area testified that Monsanto representatives on several occasions in 1965–1966 approached Spray–Rite, informed the distributor of complaints from other distributors—including one major and influential one—and requested that prices be maintained. Later that same year, Spray–Rite's president testified, Monsanto officials made explicit threats to terminate Spray–Rite unless it raised its prices.[13]

IV

We conclude that the Court of Appeals applied an incorrect standard to the evidence in this case. The correct standard is that there must be evidence that tends to exclude the possibility of independent action by the manufacturer and distributor. That is, there must be direct or circumstantial evidence that reasonably tends to prove that the manufacturer and others had a conscious commitment to a common scheme designed to achieve an unlawful objective. Under this standard, the evidence in this case created a jury issue as to whether Spray–Rite was terminated

11. The newsletter also is subject to the interpretation that the distributor was merely describing the likely reaction to unilateral Monsanto pronouncements. But Monsanto itself appears to have construed the flyer as reporting a price-fixing understanding. Six weeks after the newsletter was written, a Monsanto official wrote its author a letter urging him to "correct immediately any misconceptions about Monsanto's marketing policies." The letter disavowed any intent to enter into an agreement on resale prices. The interpretation of these documents and the testimony surrounding them properly was left to the jury.

12. Monsanto argues that the reference could have been to complaints by Monsanto employees rather than distributors, sug-

gesting that the price controls were merely unilateral action, rather than accession to the demands of the distributors. The choice between two reasonable interpretations of the testimony properly was left for the jury. See also Tr. 1298 (identifying source of one complaint as a distributor).

13. The existence of the illegal joint boycott after Spray–Rite's termination, a finding that the Court of Appeals affirmed and that is not before us, is further evidence that Monsanto and its distributors had an understanding that prices would be maintained, and that price cutters would be terminated. This last, however, is also consistent with termination for other reasons, and is probative only of the ability of Monsanto and its distributors to act in concert.

pursuant to a price-fixing conspiracy between Monsanto and its distributors.[14]   The judgment of the court below is affirmed.

Questions and Comments

What evidence is needed to prove concerted action? Why did the Court take pains not to make proof of concerted action too easy? Why did the Court fear that nondiscounters' complaints about the low prices of a discounter might be misconstrued?

If Monsanto agreed with one or more distributors to eliminate Spray–Rite, did it automatically violate the law? Is there a credible economic argument that the case should not turn on the existence or nonexistence of an agreement, but on something else? What else?

Look hard at the evidence on which the Court unanimously affirmed the plaintiff's verdict: (1) Up to and through the time Monsanto terminated Spray–Rite, it never expressed any unhappiness with its performance. (2) After Spray–Rite's termination, Monsanto approached other price cutters and told them that if they did not maintain prices they would not receive supplies of a new product. (3) Monsanto made the same statement of its intention to the parent of a price cutter. The parent then told its subsidiary to "comply" (i.e., to follow Monsanto's suggested prices). (4) A distributor informed dealers through an "ambiguous" newsletter about what steps Monsanto was taking in order to maintain an orderly market. How does each set of facts tend to prove Spray–Rite's case? Which sets of facts are at least equally consistent with Monsanto's claim of independent action as with Spray–Rite's claim of concert?

After *Monsanto,* must the plaintiff show that the manufacturer agreed with a dealer to get rid of a discounter and that the agreement fixed a price that would prevail thereafter? Is it enough that the manufacturer agreed with one dealer, or must it have agreed with more than one dealer?

Suppose that Monsanto independently determined that dismissal of discounting Spray–Rite was in its best interests, but then agreed with the nondiscounters to cut off Spray–Rite. Would "good business purpose" be a defense to a termination pursuant to an RPM agreement?

Was *Monsanto* a victory or a setback for the government?

---

14. Monsanto's contrary evidence has force, but we agree with the courts below that it was insufficient to take the issue from the jury. It is true that there was no testimony of any complaints about Spray–Rite's pricing for the 15 months prior to termination. But it was permissible for the jury to conclude that there were complaints during that period from the evidence that they continued after 1968 and from the testimony that they were mentioned at Spray–Rite's post-termination meeting with Monsanto. There is also evidence that resale prices in fact did not stabilize after 1968. On the other hand, the former Monsanto salesman testified that prices were more stable in 1969–1970 than in his earlier stint in 1965–1966. *Id.,* at 217. And, given the evidence that Monsanto took active measures to stabilize prices, it may be that distributors did not assent in sufficient numbers, or broke their promises. . . .

f. Agreement to Terminate a Discounter as a Nonprice Restraint

BUSINESS ELECTRONICS CORP. v. SHARP ELECTRONICS CORP.

485 U.S. 717.

JUSTICE SCALIA: Petitioner Business Electronics Corporation seeks review of a decision of the United States Court of Appeals for the Fifth Circuit holding that a vertical restraint is *per se* illegal under § 1 of the Sherman Act only if there is an express or implied agreement to set resale prices at some level. We granted certiorari to resolve a conflict in the Courts of Appeals regarding the proper dividing line between the rule that vertical price restraints are illegal *per se* and the rule that vertical nonprice restraints are to be judged under the rule of reason.

I

In 1968, petitioner became the exclusive retailer in the Houston, Texas area of electronic calculators manufactured by respondent Sharp Electronics Corporation. In 1972, respondent appointed Gilbert Hartwell as a second retailer in the Houston area. During the relevant period, electronic calculators were primarily sold to business customers for prices up to $1000. While much of the evidence in this case was conflicting—in particular, concerning whether petitioner was "free riding" on Hartwell's provision of presale educational and promotional services by providing inadequate services itself—a few facts are undisputed. Respondent published a list of suggested minimum retail prices, but its written dealership agreements with petitioner and Hartwell did not obligate either to observe them, or to charge any other specific price. Petitioner's retail prices were often below respondent's suggested retail prices and generally below Hartwell's retail prices, even though Hartwell too sometimes priced below respondent's suggested retail prices. Hartwell complained to respondent on a number of occasions about petitioner's prices. In June 1973, Hartwell gave respondent the ultimatum that Hartwell would terminate his dealership unless respondent ended its relationship with petitioner within 30 days. Respondent terminated petitioner's dealership in July 1973.

Petitioner brought suit in the United States District Court for the Southern District of Texas, alleging that respondent and Hartwell had conspired to terminate petitioner and that such conspiracy was illegal *per se* under § 1 of the Sherman Act. The case was tried to a jury. The District Court submitted a liability interrogatory to the jury that asked whether "there was an agreement or understanding between Sharp Electronics Corporation and Hartwell to terminate Business Electronics as a Sharp dealer because of Business Electronics' price cutting." The District Court instructed the jury at length about this question.

> "The Sherman Act is violated when a seller enters into an agreement or understanding with one of its dealers to terminate another dealer because of the other dealer's price cutting. Plaintiff contends that Sharp terminated Business Electronics in furtherance of Hartwell's desire to eliminate Business Electronics as a price-cutting rival.

"If you find that there was an agreement between Sharp and Hartwell to terminate Business Electronics because of Business Electronics' price cutting, you should answer yes to Question Number 1.

. . .

"A combination, agreement or understanding to terminate a dealer because of his price cutting unreasonably restrains trade and cannot be justified for any reason. Therefore, even though the combination, agreement or understanding may have been formed or engaged in . . . to eliminate any alleged evils of price cutting, it is still unlawful. . . .

"If a dealer demands that a manufacturer terminate a price cutting dealer, and the manufacturer agrees to do so, the agreement is illegal if the manufacturer's purpose is to eliminate the price cutting." App. 18–19.

The jury answered Question 1 affirmatively and awarded $600,000 in damages. The District Court rejected respondent's motion for judgment notwithstanding the verdict or a new trial, holding that the jury interrogatory and instructions had properly stated the law. It entered judgment for petitioner for treble damages plus attorney's fees.

The Fifth Circuit reversed, holding that the jury interrogatory and instructions were erroneous, and remanded for a new trial. It held that, to render illegal *per se* a vertical agreement between a manufacturer and a dealer to terminate a second dealer, the first dealer "must expressly or impliedly agree to set its prices at some level, though not a specific one. The distributor cannot retain complete freedom to set whatever price it chooses." 780 F.2d, at 1218.

II

A

* * *

Although vertical agreements on resale prices have been illegal *per se* since *Dr. Miles Medical Co. v. John D. Park & Sons Co.*, 220 U.S. 373 (1911), we have recognized that the scope of *per se* illegality should be narrow in the context of vertical restraints. In *Continental T.V., Inc. v. GTE Sylvania Inc.*, [433 U.S. 36 (1977)] we refused to extend *per se* illegality to vertical nonprice restraints, specifically to a manufacturer's termination of one dealer pursuant to an exclusive territory agreement with another. We noted that especially in the vertical restraint context "departure from the rule-of-reason standard must be based on demonstrable economic effect rather than . . . upon formalistic line drawing." *Id.*, 433 U.S., at 58–59. We concluded that vertical nonprice restraints had not been shown to have such a " 'pernicious effect on competition' " and to be so " 'lack[ing] [in] . . . redeeming value' " as to justify *per se* illegality. *Id.*, at 58. Rather, we found, they had real potential to stimulate interbrand competition, "the primary concern of antitrust law", 433 U.S., at 52, n. 19:

"[N]ew manufacturers and manufacturers entering new markets can use the restrictions in order to induce competent and aggressive retailers to make the kind of investment of capital and labor that is often required in the distribution of products unknown to the consumer. Established manufacturers can use them to induce retailers to engage in promotional activities or to provide service and repair facilities necessary to the efficient marketing of their products. Service and repair are vital for many products. . . . The availability and quality of such services affect a manufacturer's goodwill and the competitiveness of his product. Because of market imperfections such as the so-called 'free-rider' effect, these services might not be provided by retailers in a purely competitive situation, despite the fact that each retailer's benefit would be greater if all provided the services than if none did." *Id.,* at 55.

Moreover, we observed that a rule of *per se* illegality for vertical nonprice restraints was not needed or effective to protect *intra* brand competition. First, so long as interbrand competition existed, that would provide a "significant check" on any attempt to exploit intrabrand market power. In fact, in order to meet that interbrand competition, a manufacturer's dominant incentive is to lower resale prices. Second, the *per se* illegality of vertical restraints would create a perverse incentive for manufacturers to integrate vertically into distribution, an outcome hardly conducive to fostering the creation and maintenance of small businesses.

Finally, our opinion in *GTE Sylvania* noted a significant distinction between vertical nonprice and vertical price restraints. That is, there was support for the proposition that vertical price restraints reduce *inter* brand price competition because they " 'facilitate cartelizing.' " *Id.,* at 51, n. 18. The authorities cited by the Court suggested how vertical price agreements might assist horizontal price fixing at the manufacturer level (by reducing the manufacturer's incentive to cheat on a cartel, since its retailers could not pass on lower prices to consumers) or might be used to organize cartels at the retailer level. See R. Posner, Antitrust: Cases, Economic Notes and Other Materials 134 (1974); E. Gellhorn, Antitrust Law and Economics 252, 256 (1976); Note, Vertical Territorial and Customer Restrictions in the Franchising Industry, 10 Colum.J.L. & Soc.Prob. 497, 498, n. 12 (1974). Similar support for the cartel-facilitating effect of vertical non-price restraints was and remains lacking.

We have been solicitous to assure that the market-freeing effect of our decision in *GTE Sylvania* is not frustrated by related legal rules. In *Monsanto Co. v. Spray–Rite Service Corp.,* 465 U.S. 752, 763 (1984), which addressed the evidentiary showing necessary to establish vertical concerted action, we expressed concern that "[i]f an inference of such an agreement may be drawn from highly ambiguous evidence, there is considerable danger that the doctrin[e] enunciated in *Sylvania* . . . will be seriously eroded." We eschewed adoption of an evidentiary standard that "could deter or penalize perfectly legitimate conduct" or "would create an irrational dislocation in the market" by preventing legitimate communication between a manufacturer and its distributors. *Id.,* at 763.

Our approach to the question presented in the present case is guided by the premises of *GTE Sylvania* and *Monsanto:* that there is a presumption in favor of a rule-of-reason standard; that departure from that standard must be justified by demonstrable economic effect, such as the facilitation of cartelizing, rather than formalistic distinctions; that interbrand competition is the primary concern of the antitrust laws; and that rules in this area should be formulated with a view towards protecting the doctrine of *GTE Sylvania*. These premises lead us to conclude that the line drawn by the Fifth Circuit is the most appropriate one.

There has been no showing here that an agreement between a manufacturer and a dealer to terminate a "price cutter," without a further agreement on the price or price levels to be charged by the remaining dealer, almost always tends to restrict competition and reduce output. Any assistance to cartelizing that such an agreement might provide cannot be distinguished from the sort of minimal assistance that might be provided by vertical nonprice agreements like the exclusive territory agreement in *GTE Sylvania*, and is insufficient to justify a *per se* rule. Cartels are neither easy to form nor easy to maintain. Uncertainty over the terms of the cartel, particularly the prices to be charged in the future, obstructs both formation and adherence by making cheating easier. Without an agreement with the remaining dealer on price, the manufacturer both retains its incentive to cheat on any manufacturer-level cartel (since lower prices can still be passed on to consumers) and cannot as easily be used to organize and hold together a retailer-level cartel.[2]

The District Court's rule on the scope of *per se* illegality for vertical restraints would threaten to dismantle the doctrine of *GTE Sylvania*. Any agreement between a manufacturer and a dealer to terminate another dealer who happens to have charged lower prices can be alleged to have been directed against the terminated dealer's "price cutting." In the vast majority of cases, it will be extremely difficult for the manufacturer to convince a jury that its motivation was to ensure adequate services, since price cutting and some measure of service cutting usually go hand in hand. Accordingly, a manufacturer that agrees to give one dealer an exclusive territory and terminates another dealer pursuant to that agreement, or even a manufacturer that agrees with one dealer to terminate another for failure to provide contractually-obligated services, exposes itself to the highly plausible claim that its real motivation was to terminate a price cutter. Moreover, even vertical restraints that do not result in dealer termination, such as the initial granting of an exclusive territory or the requirement that certain services be provided, can be attacked as designed to allow existing dealers to charge higher prices. Manufacturers would be likely to forgo legitimate and competitively useful conduct rather than risk treble damages and perhaps even criminal penalties.

We cannot avoid this difficulty by invalidating as illegal *per se* only those agreements imposing vertical restraints that contain the word "price," or that affect the "prices" charged by dealers. Such formalism was explicitly rejected in *GTE Sylvania*. As the above discussion indicates, all vertical restraints, including the exclusive territory agreement

---

2. The dissent's principal fear appears to be not cartelization at either level, but Hartwell's assertion of dominant retail power. This fear does not possibly justify adopting a rule of *per se* illegality. Retail market power is rare, because of the usual presence of interbrand competition and other dealers, and it should therefore not be assumed but rather must be proved. Cf. Baxter, The Viability of Vertical Restraints Doctrine, 75 Calif.L.Rev. 933, 948–949 (1987). Of course this case was not prosecuted on the theory, and therefore the jury was not asked to find, that Hartwell possessed such market power.

held not to be *per se* illegal in *GTE Sylvania,* have the potential to allow dealers to increase "prices" and can be characterized as intended to achieve just that. In fact, vertical nonprice restraints only accomplish the benefits identified in *GTE Sylvania* because they reduce intrabrand price competition to the point where the dealer's profit margin permits provision of the desired services. As we described it in *Monsanto:* "The manufacturer often will want to ensure that its distributors earn sufficient profit to pay for programs such as hiring and training additional salesmen or demonstrating the technical features of the product, and will want to see that 'free-riders' do not interfere." 465 U.S., at 762–763.

The dissent erects a much more complex analytic structure, which ultimately rests, however, upon the same discredited premise that the only function this nonprice vertical restriction can serve is restraint of dealer-level competition. Specifically, the dissent's reasoning hinges upon its perception that the agreement between Sharp and Hartwell was a "naked" restraint—that is, it was not "ancillary" to any other agreement between Sharp and Hartwell. But that is not true, unless one assumes, contrary to *GTE Sylvania* and *Monsanto,* and contrary to our earlier discussion, that it is not a quite plausible purpose of the restriction to enable Hartwell to provide better services under the sales franchise agreement.[3] From its faulty conclusion that what we have before us is a "naked" restraint, the dissent proceeds, by reasoning we do not entirely follow, to the further conclusion that it is therefore a horizontal rather than a vertical restraint. We pause over this only to note that in addition to producing what we think the wrong result in the present case, it

---

3. The conclusion of "naked" restraint could also be sustained on another assumption, namely that an agreement is not "ancillary" unless it is designed to enforce a contractual obligation of one of the parties to the contract. The dissent appears to accept this assumption. It is plainly wrong. The classic "ancillary" restraint is an agreement by the seller of a business not to compete within the market. See *Mitchel v. Reynolds,* 1 P. Wms. 181 (1711); Restatement (Second) of Contracts § 188(2)(a) (1981). That is not ancillary to any other contractual obligation, but, like the restraint here, merely enhances the value of the contract, or permits the "enjoyment of [its] fruits." *United States v. Addyston Pipe & Steel Co.,* 85 F. 271, 282 (CA6 1898), aff'd, 175 U.S. 211, 20 S.Ct. 96, 44 L.Ed. 136 (1899); cf. Restatement (Second) of Contracts §§ 187, 188 (1981) (restraint may be ancillary to a "transaction *or relationship*") (emphasis added); R. Bork, The Antitrust Paradox 29 (1978) (hereinafter Bork) (vertical arrangements are ancillary to the "transaction of supplying and purchasing").

More important than the erroneousness of the dissent's common-law analysis of "naked" and "ancillary" restraints are the perverse enconomic consequences of permitting nonprice vertical restraints to avoid *per se* invalidity only through attachment to an express contractual obligation. Such an approach is contrary to the express views of the principal scholar on whom the dissent relies. See 7 P. Areeda, Antitrust Law § 1457c, p. 170 (1986) (hereinafter Areeda) (legality of terminating price cutter should not depend upon formal adoption of service obligations that termination is assertedly designed to protect). In the precise case of a vertical agreement to terminate other dealers, for example, there is no conceivable reason why the existence of an exclusivity commitment by the manufacturer to the one remaining dealer would render anticompetitive effects less likely, or the procompetitive effects on services more likely—so that the dissent's line for *per se* illegality fails to meet the requirement of *Continental T.V., Inc. v. GTE Sylvania Inc., supra,* 433 U.S., at 59, that it be based on "demonstrable economic effect." If anything, the economic effect of the dissent's approach is perverse, encouraging manufacturers to agree to otherwise inefficient contractual provisions for the sole purpose of attaching to them efficient nonprice vertical restraints which, only by reason of such attachment, can avoid *per se* invalidity as "naked" restraints. The dissent's approach would therefore create precisely the kind of "irrational dislocation in the market" that legal rules in this area should be designed to avoid.

introduces needless confusion into antitrust terminology. Restraints imposed by agreement between competitors have traditionally been denominated as horizontal restraints, and those imposed by agreement between firms at different levels of distribution as vertical restraints.[4]

Finally, we do not agree with petitioner's contention that an agreement on the remaining dealer's price or price levels will so often follow from terminating another dealer "because of [its] price cutting" that prophylaxis against resale price maintenance warrants the District Court's *per se* rule. Petitioner has provided no support for the proposition that vertical price agreements generally underlie agreements to terminate a price cutter. That proposition is simply incompatible with the conclusion of *GTE Sylvania* and *Monsanto* that manufacturers are often motivated by a legitimate desire to have dealers provide services, combined with the reality that price cutting is frequently made possible by "free riding" on the services provided by other dealers. The District Court's *per se* rule would therefore discourage conduct recognized by *GTE Sylvania* and *Monsanto* as beneficial to consumers.

B

In resting our decision upon the foregoing economic analysis, we do not ignore common-law precedent concerning what constituted "restraint of trade" at the time the Sherman Act was adopted. But neither do we give that pre–1890 precedent the dispositive effect some would. The term "restraint of trade" in the statute, like the term at common law, refers not to a particular list of agreements, but to a particular economic consequence, which may be produced by quite different sorts of agreements in varying times and circumstances.

Petitioner's principal contention has been that the District Court's rule on *per se* illegality is compelled not by the old common law, but by our more recent Sherman Act precedents. First, petitioner contends that since certain horizontal agreements have been held to constitute price fixing (and thus to be *per se* illegal) though they did not set prices or price levels, see, *e.g., Catalano, Inc. v. Target Sales, Inc.,* 446 U.S. 643, 647–650 (1980) (*per curiam*), it is improper to require that a vertical agreement set prices or price levels before it can suffer the same fate. This notion of equivalence between the scope of horizontal *per se* illegality and that of

---

4. The dissent apparently believes that whether a restraint is horizontal depends upon whether its anticompetitive *effects* are horizontal, and not upon whether it is the product of a horizontal agreement. That is of course a conceivable way of talking, but if it were the language of antitrust analysis there would be no such thing as an unlawful vertical restraint, since all anticompetitive effects are by definition horizontal effects. The dissent quotes a statement of Prof. Areeda as supposed adoption of its definition of horizontal restraint. That statement seems to us to be, to the contrary, Prof. Areeda's attempt to explain a peculiar usage of the term "horizontal" in *Cernuto, Inc. v. United Cabinet Corp.,* 595 F.2d 164, 168 (CA3 1979), noting that (even though *Cernuto* did not involve a horizontal restraint) the use of the term "horizontal" was "appropriate to capture the fact that dealer interests opposed to those of the manufacturer were being served." Areeda § 1457d, p. 174. The dissent also seeks to associate Judge Bork with its terminological confusion. Quoting Bork 288. What the quoted passage says, however, is that a facially vertical restraint imposed by a manufacturer only because it has been coerced by a "horizontal carte[l]" agreement among his distributors is in reality a horizontal restraint. That says precisely what we say: that a restraint is horizontal not because it has horizontal effects, but because it is the product of a horizontal agreement.

vertical *per se* illegality was explicitly rejected in *GTE Sylvania* as it had to be, since a horizontal agreement to divide territories is *per se* illegal, see *United States v. Topco Assocs., Inc.,* 405 U.S. 596, 608 (1972), while *GTE Sylvania* held that a vertical agreement to do so is not.

Second, petitioner contends that *per se* illegality here follows from our two cases holding *per se* illegal a group boycott of a dealer because of its price cutting. See *United States v. General Motors Corp.,* 384 U.S. 127 (1966); *Klor's, Inc. v. Broadway–Hale Stores, Inc.,* 359 U.S. 207 (1959). This second contention is merely a restatement of the first, since both cases involved horizontal combinations.

Third, petitioner contends, relying on *Albrecht v. Herald Co.,* 390 U.S. 145 (1968), and *United States v. Parke Davis & Co.,* 362 U.S. 29, 80 S.Ct. 503 (1960), that our vertical price-fixing cases have already rejected the proposition that *per se* illegality requires setting a price or a price level. We disagree. In *Albrecht,* the maker of the product formed a combination to force a retailer to charge the maker's advertised retail price. This combination had two aspects. Initially, the maker hired a third party to solicit customers away from the noncomplying retailer. This solicitor "was aware that the aim of the solicitation campaign was to force [the noncomplying retailer] to lower his price" to the suggested retail price. Next, the maker engaged another retailer who "undertook to deliver [products] at the suggested price" to the noncomplying retailer's customers obtained by the solicitor. This combination of maker, solicitor, and new retailer was held to be *per se* illegal. It is plain that the combination involved both an explicit agreement on resale price and an agreement to force another to adhere to the specified price.

In *Parke Davis,* a manufacturer combined first with wholesalers and then with retailers in order to gain "the retailers' adherence to its suggested minimum retail prices." 362 U.S., at 45–46, and n. 6. The manufacturer also brokered an agreement among its retailers not to advertise prices below its suggested retail prices, which agreement was held to be part of the *per se* illegal combination. This holding also does not support a rule that an agreement on price or price level is not required for a vertical restraint to be *per se* illegal—first, because the agreement not to advertise prices was part and parcel of the combination that contained the price agreement, and second because the agreement among retailers that the manufacturer organized was a *horizontal* conspiracy among competitors.

* * *

In sum, economic analysis supports the view, and no precedent opposes it, that a vertical restraint is not illegal *per se* unless it includes some agreement on price or price levels. Accordingly, the judgment of the Fifth Circuit is *affirmed.*

JUSTICE STEVENS, with whom JUSTICE WHITE joins, dissenting: In its opinion the majority assumes, without analysis, that the question presented by this case concerns the legality of a "vertical nonprice restraint." As I shall demonstrate, the restraint that results when one or more dealers threatens to boycott a manufacturer unless it terminates its relationship with a price-cutting retailer is more properly viewed as a "horizontal restraint." Moreover, an agreement to terminate a dealer because of its price cutting is most certainly not a "nonprice restraint." The distinction between "vertical nonprice restraints" and "vertical price restraints," on which the majority focuses its attention, is therefore quite irrelevant to the outcome of this case. Of much greater importance is the distinction between "naked restraints" and "ancillary restraints" that has been a part of our law since the landmark opinion written by Judge (later Chief Justice) Taft in *United States v. Addyston Pipe & Steel Co.*, 85 F. 271 (CA6 1898), aff'd, 175 U.S. 211 (1899).

I

The plain language of § 1 of the Sherman Act prohibits "every" contract that restrains trade. Because such a literal reading of the statute would outlaw the entire body of private contract law, and because Congress plainly intended the Act to be interpreted in the light of its common-law background, the Court has long held that certain "ancillary" restraints of trade may be defended as reasonable. As we recently explained without dissent:

> "The Rule of Reason suggested by *Mitchel v. Reynolds* [1 P. Wms. 181 (1711)] has been regarded as a standard for testing the enforceability of covenants in restraint of trade which are ancillary to a legitimate transaction, such as an employment contract or the sale of a going business. Judge (later Mr. Chief Justice) Taft so interpreted the Rule in his classic rejection of the argument that competitors may lawfully agree to sell their goods at the same price as long as the agreed-upon price is reasonable. *United States v. Addyston Pipe & Steel Co.* . . . ." *National Society of Professional Engineers v. United States,* 435 U.S. 679, 689 (1978).

Judge Taft's rejection of an argument that a price-fixing agreement could be defended as reasonable was based on a detailed examination of common-law precedents. He explained that in England there had been two types of objection to voluntary restraints on one's ability to transact business. "One was that by such contracts a man disabled himself from earning a livelihood with the risk of becoming a public charge, and deprived the community of the benefit of his labor. The other was that such restraints tended to give to the covenantee, the beneficiary of such restraints, a monopoly of the trade, from which he had thus excluded one competitor, and by the same means might exclude others." 85 F., at 279. Certain contracts, however, such as covenants not to compete in a particular business, for a certain period of time, within a defined geographical area, had always been considered reasonable when necessary to carry out otherwise procompetitive contracts, such as the sale of a business. The difference between ancillary covenants that may be justified as reasonable and those that are "void" because there is "nothing to justify or excuse the restraint," *id.*, at 282–283, was described in the opinion's seminal discussion:

> "[T]he contract must be one in which there is a main purpose, to which the covenant in restraint of trade is merely ancillary. The covenant is inserted only to protect one of the parties from the injury which, in the execution of the contract or enjoyment of its fruits, he may suffer from

the unrestrained competition of the other. The main purpose of the contract suggests the measure of protection needed, and furnishes a sufficiently uniform standard by which the validity of such restraints may be judicially determined. In such a case, if the restraint exceeds the necessity presented by the main purpose of the contract, it is void for two reasons: First, because it oppresses the covenantor, without any corresponding benefit to the covenantee; and, second, because it tends to a monopoly. But where the sole object of both parties in making the contract as expressed therein is merely to restrain competition, and enhance or maintain prices, it would seem that there was nothing to justify or excuse the restraint, that it would necessarily have a tendency to monopoly, and therefore would be void. In such a case there is no measure of what is necessary to the protection of either party, except the vague and varying opinion of judges as to how much, on principles of political economy, men ought to be allowed to restrain competition. There is in such contracts no main lawful purpose, to subserve which partial restraint is permitted, and by which its reasonableness is measured, but the sole object is to restrain trade in order to avoid the competition which it has always been the policy of the common law to foster." *Id.,* at 282–283.

Although Judge Taft was writing as a Circuit judge, his opinion is universally accepted as authoritative. We affirmed his decision without dissent, we have repeatedly cited it with approval, and it is praised by a respected scholar as "one of the greatest, if not the greatest, antitrust opinions in the history of the law." R. Bork, The Antitrust Paradox 26 (1978). In accordance with the teaching in that opinion, it is therefore appropriate to look more closely at the character of the restraint of trade found by the jury in this case.

II

It may be helpful to begin by explaining why the agreement in this case does not fit into certain categories of agreement that are frequently found in antitrust litigation. First, despite the contrary implications in the majority opinion, this is not a case in which the manufacturer is alleged to have imposed any vertical nonprice restraints on any of its dealers. The term "vertical nonprice restraint," as used in *Continental T.V., Inc. v. GTE Sylvania Inc.,* 433 U.S. 36 (1977), and similar cases, refers to a contractual term that a dealer must accept in order to qualify for a franchise. Typically, the dealer must agree to meet certain standards in its advertising, promotion, product display, and provision of repair and maintenance services in order to protect the goodwill of the manufacturer's product. Sometimes a dealer must agree to sell only to certain classes of customers—for example, wholesalers generally may only sell to retailers and may be required not to sell directly to consumers. In *Sylvania,* to take another example, we examined agreements between a manufacturer and its dealers that included "provisions barring the retailers from selling franchised products from locations other than those specified in agreements." *Id.,* 433 U.S., at 37. Restrictions of that kind, which are a part of, or ancillary to, the basic franchise agreement, are perfectly lawful unless the "rule of reason" is violated. Although vertical nonprice restraints may have some adverse effect on competition, as long as they serve the main purpose of a procompetitive distribution agreement, the ancillary restraints may be defended under the rule of reason. And, of course, a dealer who violates such a restraint may properly be terminated by the manufacturer.

In this case, it does not appear that respondent imposed any vertical nonprice restraints upon either petitioner or Hartwell.

Second, this case does not involve a typical vertical price restraint. As the Court of Appeals noted, there is some evidence in the record that may support the conclusion that respondent and Hartwell implicitly agreed that Hartwell's prices would be maintained at a level somewhat higher than petitioner had been charging before petitioner was terminated. The illegality of the agreement found by the jury does not, however, depend on such evidence. For purposes of analysis, we should assume that no such agreement existed and that respondent was perfectly willing to allow its dealers to set prices at levels that would maximize their profits.

Third, this is not a case in which the manufacturer acted independently. Indeed, given the jury's verdict, it is not even a case in which the termination can be explained as having been based on the violation of any distribution policy adopted by respondent. The termination was motivated by the ultimatum that respondent received from Hartwell and that ultimatum, in turn, was the culmination of Hartwell's complaints about petitioner's competitive price cutting. The termination was plainly the product of coercion by the stronger of two dealers rather than an attempt to maintain an orderly and efficient system of distribution.

In sum, this case does not involve the reasonableness of any vertical restraint imposed on one or more dealers by a manufacturer in its basic franchise agreement. What the jury found was a simple and naked " 'agreement between Sharp and Hartwell to terminate Business Electronics because of Business Electronics' price cutting.' "

III

Because naked agreements to restrain the trade of third parties are seldom identified with such stark clarity as in this case, there appears to be no exact precedent that determines the outcome here. There are, however, perfectly clear rules that would be decisive if the facts were changed only slightly.

Thus, on the one hand, if it were clear that respondent had acted independently and decided to terminate petitioner because respondent, for reasons of its own, objected to petitioner's pricing policies, the termination would be lawful. See *United States v. Parke, Davis & Co.*, 362 U.S. 29, 43–45 (1960). On the other hand, it is equally clear that if respondent had been represented by three dealers in the Houston market instead of only two, and if two of them had threatened to terminate their dealerships "unless respondent ended its relationship with petitioner within 30 days," an agreement to comply with the ultimatum would be an obvious violation of the Sherman Act. See, *e.g., United States v. General Motors Corp.*, 384 U.S. 127 (1966); *Klor's, Inc. v. Broadway–Hale Stores, Inc.*, 359 U.S.

207 (1959).[5] The question then is whether the two-party agreement involved in this case is more like an illegal three-party agreement or a legal independent decision. For me, the answer is plain.

The distinction between independent action and joint action is fundamental in antitrust jurisprudence.[6] Any attempt to define the boundaries of *per se* illegality by the number of parties to different agreements with the same anticompetitive consequences can only breed uncertainty in the law and confusion for the businessman.

More importantly, if instead of speculating about irrelevant vertical nonprice restraints, we focus on the precise character of the agreement before us, we can readily identify its anticompetitive nature. Before the agreement was made, there was price competition in the Houston retail market for respondent's products. The stronger of the two competitors was unhappy about that competition; it wanted to have the power to set the price level in the market and therefore it "complained to respondent on a number of occasions about petitioner's prices." Quite obviously, if petitioner had agreed with either Hartwell or respondent to discontinue its competitive pricing, there would have been no ultimatum from Hartwell and no termination by respondent. It is equally obvious that either

---

5. Thus, a boycott "is not to be tolerated merely because the victim is just one merchant whose business is so small that his destruction makes little difference to the economy. Monopoly can as surely thrive by the elimination of such small businessmen, one at a time, as it can be driving them out in large groups." *Klor's, Inc. v. Broadway–Hale Stores, Inc.,* 359 U.S. 207, 213, 79 S.Ct. 705, 710, 3 L.Ed.2d 741 (1959) (footnote omitted). Again, Judge Adams' analysis in the *Cernuto* opinion, n. 4, *supra,* is relevant:

"The importance of the horizontal nature of this arrangement is illustrated by *United States v. General Motors Corp.,* 384 U.S. 127, 86 S.Ct. 1321, 16 L.Ed.2d 415 . . . (1966). Although General Motors, the manufacturer, was seemingly imposing vertical restraints when it pressured recalcitrant automobile dealers not to deal with discounters, the Supreme Court noted that in fact these restraints were induced by the dealers seeking to choke off aggressive competitors at their level, and found a *per se* violation, rejecting the suggestion that only unilateral restraints were at issue. So here, if [the manufacturer and the sales representative acted at the nonterminated dealer's] direction, both the purpose and effect of the termination was to eliminate competition at the retail level, and not, as in *GTE Sylvania,* to promote competition at the manufacturer level. Accordingly, the pro-competitive redeeming virtues so critical in *GTE Sylvania* may not be present here." 595 F.2d, at 168 (footnote omitted).

As we said in *General Motors:*

"The protection of price competition from conspiratorial restraint is an object of special solicitude under the antitrust laws. We cannot respect that solicitude by closing our eyes to the effect upon price competition of the removal from the market, by combination or conspiracy, of a class of traders. Nor do we propose to construe the Sherman Act to prohibit conspiracies to fix prices at which competitors may sell, but to allow conspiracies or combinations to put competitors out of business entirely." 384 U.S. at 148, 86 S.Ct., at 1332.

6. See *United States v. Colgate & Co.,* 250 U.S. 300, 307–308, 39 S.Ct. 465, 468, 63 L.Ed. 992 (1919). In *Monsanto Co. v. Spray–Rite Service Corp.,* 465 U.S. 752, 761, 104 S.Ct. 1464, 1469, 79 L.Ed.2d 775 (1984), we noted that "the basic distinction between concerted and independent action" was "not always clearly drawn by parties and courts." In its opinion today the majority virtually ignores that basic distinction. Thus, *ante,* at 1521, the majority discusses the manufacturer's risks arising out of its agreement "with one dealer to terminate another for failure to provide contractually obligated services." But if such a breach of contract has occurred, the manufacturer should have an independent motivation for acting and need not enter into any agreement with a dealer to do so. As we held in *Monsanto,* the mere fact that the breach of contract may have been called to the manufacturer's attention by another dealer does not make the manufacturer's independent decision to terminate a price-cutting dealer unlawful.

of those agreements would have been illegal *per se*.[7] Moreover, it is also reasonable to assume that if respondent were to replace petitioner with another price-cutting dealer, there would soon be more complaints and another ultimatum from Hartwell. Although respondent has not granted Hartwell an exclusive dealership—it retains the right to appoint multiple dealers—its agreement has protected Hartwell from price competition. Indeed, given the jury's finding and the evidence in the record, that is the *sole function* of the agreement found by the jury in this case. It therefore fits squarely within the category of "naked restraints of trade with no purpose except stifling of competition." *White Motor Co. v. United States*, 372 U.S. 253, 263 (1963).

This is the sort of agreement that scholars readily characterize as "inherently suspect."[8] When a manufacturer responds to coercion from a dealer, instead of making an independent decision to enforce a predetermined distribution policy, the anticompetitive character of the response is evident.[9] As Professor Areeda has correctly noted, the fact that the agreement is between only one complaining dealer and the manufacturer does not prevent it from imposing a "horizontal" restraint.[10] If two critical facts are present—a naked purpose to eliminate price competition

---

7. "We have not wavered in our enforcement of the *per se* rule against price fixing." *Arizona v. Maricopa County Medical Society*, 457 U.S. 332, 347, 102 S.Ct. 2466, 2475, 73 L.Ed.2d 48 (1982). Thus, in *Dr. Miles Medical Co. v. John D. Park & Sons Co.*, 220 U.S. 373, 31 S.Ct. 376, 55 L.Ed. 502 (1911), the Court determined that vertical price fixing is *per se* invalid because resale price maintenance plans serve the profit motives of the dealers, not the manufacturers, and are thereby similar to plans pursuant to which the dealers themselves conspire to fix prices. *Id.*, at 407–408, 31 S.Ct. at 384. There is no doubt that horizontal intrabrand price fixing is *per se* illegal, even if the conspirators lack the market power to affect interbrand competition in a manner that would violate the rule of reason.

8. "[S]cenarios that involve a firm or firms at one level of activity using vertical restraints deliberately to confer market power on firms at an adjacent level are inherently suspect. To do so is, typically, to inflict self-injury, just as it would be for consumers to confer market power on the retailers from whom they buy." Baxter, The Viability of Vertical Restraints Doctrine, 75 Calif.L.Rev. 933, 938 (1987).

9. "Termination responses reflecting the manufacturer's own distribution policy differ greatly from those imposed upon him by a complaining dealer. In the latter case, the manufacturer's compliance with the complainer's demand is more likely to be anticompetitive. There is a superficial resemblance to *Parke Davis* in that three parties are involved, but my earlier analysis suggested that the key to that case was 'complex enforcement,' which is absent where a complaining dealer simply threatens to abandon the manufacturer who continues selling to discounting dealers." 7 P. Areeda, Antitrust Law § 1457, p. 166 (1986).

10. Commenting on Judge Adams' opinion in *Cernuto*, see nn. 4 and 5, *supra*, Professor Areeda wrote:

"That the complainer was a single firm did not weaken the 'horizontal' characterization. Because the elimination of price competition was the purpose of the complaint and the termination, the court declared that per se illegality would be appropriate. However, the court made clear that no illegal agreement would be found if United was implementing its own unilaterally chosen distribution policy. Thus, the court's implicit theory was that an agreement arose when the manufacturer bowed to the complainer's will. In that situation, the 'horizontal' characterization is appropriate to capture the fact that dealer interests opposed to those of the manufacturer were being served." Areeda, *supra*, at 174 (footnotes omitted).

See also R. Bork, The Antitrust Paradox 288 (1978):

"A restraint—whether on price, territory, or any other term—is vertical, according to the usage employed here, when a firm operating at one level of an industry places restraints upon rivalry at another level for its own benefit. (This definition excludes restraints, vertical in form only, that are actually imposed by horizontal cartels at any level of the industry, e.g., resale price maintenance that is compelled not by the manufacturer but by the pressure of organized retailers.)"

as such and coercion of the manufacturer [11]—the conflict with antitrust policy is manifest.[12]

Indeed, since the economic consequences of Hartwell's ultimatum to respondent are identical to those that would result from a comparable ultimatum by two of three dealers in a market—and since a two-party price-fixing agreement is just as unlawful as a three-party price-fixing agreement—it is appropriate to employ the term "boycott" to characterize this agreement. In my judgment the case is therefore controlled by our decision in *United States v. General Motors Corp.*, 384 U.S. 127 (1966).

The majority disposes quickly of both *General Motors* and *Klor's, Inc. v. Broadway–Hale Stores, Inc.*, 359 U.S. 207 (1959), by concluding that "both cases involved horizontal combinations." But this distinction plainly will not suffice. In *General Motors*, a group of Chevrolet dealers

---

11. The two critical facts that had not yet been determined by a jury in the *Cernuto* case are perfectly plain in this case. As Professor Areeda explained:

"The *Cernuto* case was decided on summary judgment which accepted the plaintiff's view of the facts. But two facts critical for the court will often be obscure. *First,* was it the manufacturer's purpose to eliminate price competition as such? Let us assume that termination was not based on such completely independent grounds as non-payment of bills. Even so, the existence of an inevitable price effect does not establish a purpose to control prices in a forbidden way. A purpose to facilitate point-of-sale services or to protect minimum economies of scale could induce a manufacturer to limit intrabrand competition. Notwithstanding price effects, such limitations are lawful when reasonable and not subject to automatic condemnation. Indeed, termination of one dealer in order to grant another exclusive distribution rights in an area is generally lawful. Nevertheless, so long as the manufacturer is not implementing his own interest but that of the complainer, the vice of eliminating 'horizontal' competition with the complainer's rivals seems equally present when the complainer thereby succeeds in eliminating horizontal competition with respect to customers or territories. *Second,* was the manufacturer coerced or was he indulging his own preferences? As we have seen, this question cannot be answered in the abstract. The court correctly acknowledged that the manufacturer might also be implementing his own unilateral vision of optimal distribution without regard to the complainer's desires and held that no illegal agreement would arise if that were the case." Areeda, *supra,* at 174–175 (footnotes omitted).

12. "Let us defer for the moment problems of proof and assume that a manufacturer does not wish to terminate the plaintiff dealer but does so to placate the complaining dealer, who would otherwise cease handling the product. This manufacturer would rather keep both dealers but, when forced to choose between them, concludes that terminating the plaintiff hurts him less (considering sales lost, transaction costs in finding and perhaps training a replacement, and any spillover effects upon his relations with other dealers) than losing the complainer's patronage.

"The present situation is *Colgate* in reverse. In *Colgate,* it was the supplier who was controlling the dealer's behavior. Here a dealer is conditioning his patronage in a way that controls the manufacturer's behavior. The agreement concept seems parallel. But the economic effects can be very different. From the policy viewpoint, it can matter greatly whether manufacturer or dealer interests are being served. The former is more likely to seek efficient distribution, which stimulates interbrand competition; the latter is more likely to seek excess profits, which dampen interbrand competition. Accordingly, antitrust policy can be more hospitable toward manufacturer efforts to control dealer prices, customers, or territories than toward the efforts of dealers to control *their* competitors through the manufacturer.

"Of course, manufacturer and dealer interests are not necessarily antagonistic. Like the manufacturer, dealers might also believe that restricted distribution increases dealer services and sales and thus strengthens interbrand competition. However, this objective seems unlikely when the manufacturer is forced to violate the distribution policy he thinks best. Although he might be mistaken about what his optimal distribution policy ought to be, he should be presumed a better judge of that than coercing dealers who always desire excess profits unnecessary for efficient distribution." Areeda, *supra,* at 167–168 (footnotes omitted).

conspired with General Motors to eliminate sales from the manufacturer to discounting dealers. We held that "[e]limination, by joint collaborative action, of discounters from access to the market is a *per se* violation of the Act," 384 U.S., at 145, and explained that "inherent in the success of the combination in this case was a substantial restraint upon price competition—a goal unlawful *per se* when sought to be effected by combination or conspiracy." *Id.*, at 147. Precisely the same goal was sought and effected in this case—the elimination of price competition at the dealer level. Moreover, the method of achieving that goal was precisely the same in both cases—the manufacturer's refusal to sell to discounting dealers. The difference between the two cases is not a difference between horizontal and vertical agreements—in both cases the critical agreement was between market actors at the retail level on the one hand and the manufacturer level on the other. Rather, the difference is simply a difference in the number of conspirators. Hartwell's coercion of respondent in order to eliminate petitioner because of its same-level price competition is not different in kind from the Chevrolet dealers' coercion of General Motors in order to eliminate other, price-cutting dealers; the only difference between the two cases—one dealer seeking a naked price-based restraint in today's case, many dealers seeking the same end in *General Motors*—is merely a difference in degree. Both boycotts lack any efficiency justification—they are simply naked restraints on price competition, rather than integral, or ancillary, parts of the manufacturers' predetermined distribution policies.

IV

What is most troubling about the majority's opinion is its failure to attach any weight to the value of intrabrand competition. In *Continental T.V., Inc. v. GTE Sylvania Inc.*, 433 U.S. 36 (1977), we correctly held that a demonstrable benefit to interbrand competition will outweigh the harm to intrabrand competition that is caused by the imposition of vertical nonprice restrictions on dealers. But we also expressly reaffirmed earlier cases in which the illegal conspiracy affected only intrabrand competition. Not a word in the *Sylvania* opinion implied that the elimination of intrabrand competition could be justified as reasonable without any evidence of a purpose to improve interbrand competition.

In the case before us today, the relevant economic market was the sale at retail in the Houston area of calculators manufactured by respondent.[14] There is no dispute that an agreement to fix prices in that

---

14. It might be helpful to note at this point that although the majority mentions only the reduction of interbrand competition as a justification for a *per se* rule against vertical price restraints, our opinion in *Sylvania* was quite different. As we stated then:

"The market impact of vertical restrictions is complex because of their potential for a simultaneous reduction of intrabrand competition and stimulation of interbrand competition. Significantly, the Court in *Schwinn* did not distinguish among the challenged restrictions on the basis of their individual potential for intrabrand harm or interbrand benefit. Restrictions that completely eliminated intrabrand competition among Schwinn distributors were analyzed no differently from those that merely moderated intrabrand competition among retailers." 433 U.S., at 51–52 (footnotes omitted).

In the following pages, we pointed out that because vertical nonprice restrictions imposed by manufacturers may serve to advance interbrand competition, the restriction on intrabrand competition should be subject only to a rule of reason analysis.

market, either horizontally between petitioner and Hartwell or vertically between respondent and either or both of the two dealers, would violate the Sherman Act. The "quite plausible" assumption that such an agreement might enable the retailers to provide better services to their customers would not have avoided the strict rule against price fixing that this Court has consistently enforced in the past.

Under petitioner's theory of the case, an agreement between respondent and Hartwell to terminate petitioner because of its price cutting was just as indefensible as any of those price-fixing agreements. At trial the jury found the existence of such an agreement to eliminate petitioner's price competition. Respondent had denied that any agreement had been made and asked the jury to find that it had independently decided to terminate petitioner because of its poor sales performance,[15] but after hearing several days of testimony, the jury concluded that this defense was pretextual.

Neither the Court of Appeals nor the majority questions the accuracy of the jury's resolution of the factual issues in this case. Nevertheless, the rule the majority fashions today is based largely on its concern that in

Along these same lines, we explained that "[e]conomists also have argued that manufacturers have an economic interest in maintaining as much intrabrand competition as is consistent with the efficient distribution of their products." *Id.,* at 56, 97 S.Ct., at 2560. Thus, although the majority neglects to mention it, fostering intrabrand competition has been recognized as an important goal of antitrust law, and although a manufacturer's efficiency-enhancing vertical nonprice restraints may subject a reduction of intrabrand competition only to a rule of reason analysis, a similar reduction without the procompetitive "redeeming virtues" of manufacturer-imposed vertical nonprice restraints, *id.,* 433 U.S., at 54, 97 S.Ct., at 2560, causes nothing but economic harm. As one commentator has recently stated:

> "Intrabrand competition can benefit the consumer, and it is therefore important to insure that a manufacturer's motive for a vertical restriction is not simply to acquiesce in his distributors' desires to limit competition among themselves. The Supreme Court has recognized that restrictions on intrabrand competition can only be tolerated because of the countervailing positive impact on interbrand competition." Piraino, The Case for Presuming the Legality of Quality Motivated Restrictions on Distribution, 63 Notre Dame L.Rev. 1, 17 (1988) (footnotes omitted).

See also H.R.Rep. No. 100–421, pp. 23, 38 (1987) (accompanying bill H.R. 585, the Freedom from Vertical Price Fixing Act of 1987, passed by the House and currently pending before the Senate; criticizing the Fifth Circuit's decision in this case, and restating "plainly and unequivocally that *all forms* of resale price maintenance are illegal per se under the antitrust laws," including "where a conspiracy exists between a supplier and distributor to terminate or cut off supply to a second distributor because of the second distributor's pricing policies") (emphasis in original); Departments of Commerce, Justice, and State, the Judiciary and Related Agencies Appropriation Act, 1986, Pub.L. 99–180, 99 Stat. 1169–1170 (congressional resolution that Department of Justice Vertical Restraints Guidelines "are inconsistent with established antitrust law, . . . in maintaining that such policy guidelines do not treat vertical price fixing when, in fact, some provisions of such policy guidelines suggest that certain price fixing conspiracies are legal if such conspiracies are 'limited' to restricting intrabrand competition; . . . in stating that vertical restraints that have an impact upon prices are subject to the per se rule of illegality only if there is an 'explicit agreement' as to the specific prices' "); Report of Attorney General's National Committee to Study the Antitrust Laws 149–155 (1955) (criticizing laws that permit resale price maintenance as a "throttling of price competition in the process of distribution").

15. The court instructed the jury:

"Sharp, on the other hand, contends that it terminated Business Electronics unilaterally, not as a result of any agreement or understanding with Hartwell, but because of Business Electronics' sales performance. If you find that Sharp did not terminate Business Electronics pursuant to an agreement or understanding with Hartwell to eliminate price cutting by Business Electronics, then you should answer 'no' to question number 1."

other cases juries will be unable to tell the difference between truthful and pretextual defenses. Thus, it opines that "even a manufacturer that agrees with one dealer to terminate another for failure to provide contractually obligated services, exposes itself to the highly plausible claim that its real motivation was to terminate a price cutter." But such a "plausible" concern in a hypothetical case that is so different from this one should not be given greater weight than facts that can be established by hard evidence. If a dealer has, in fact, failed to provide contractually obligated services, and if the manufacturer has, in fact, terminated the dealer for that reason, both of those objective facts should be provable by admissible evidence. Both in its disposition of this case and in its attempt to justify a new approach to agreements to eliminate price competition, the majority exhibits little confidence in the judicial process as a means of ascertaining the truth.[17]

The majority fails to consider that manufacturers such as respondent will only be held liable in the rare case in which the following can be proved: First, the terminated dealer must overcome the high hurdle of *Monsanto Co. v. Spray–Rite Service Corp.*, 465 U.S. 752 (1984). A terminated dealer must introduce "evidence that tends to exclude the possibility that the manufacturer and nonterminated distributors were acting independently." *Id.*, at 764. Requiring judges to adhere to the strict test for agreement laid down in *Monsanto*, in their jury instructions or own findings of fact, goes a long way toward ensuring that many legitimate dealer termination decisions do not succumb improperly to antitrust liability.

Second, the terminated dealer must prove that the agreement was based on a purpose to terminate it because of its price cutting. Proof of motivation is another commonplace in antitrust litigation of which the majority appears apprehensive, but as we have explained or demonstrated many times, see, *e.g., Aspen Skiing Co. v. Aspen Highlands Skiing Corp.*, 472 U.S. 585, 610–611 (1985); in antitrust, as in many other areas of the law, motivation matters and factfinders are able to distinguish bad from good intent.

Third, the manufacturer may rebut the evidence tending to prove that the sole purpose of the agreement was to eliminate a price cutter by offering evidence that it entered the agreement for legitimate, nonprice-related reasons.

Although in this case the jury found a naked agreement to terminate a dealer because of its price cutting, the majority boldly characterizes the same agreement as "this nonprice vertical restriction." That characterization is surely an oxymoron when applied to the agreement the jury actually found. Nevertheless, the majority proceeds to justify it as "ancillary" to a "quite plausible purpose . . . to enable Hartwell to provide better services under the sales franchise agreement." There are two significant reasons why that justification is unacceptable.

17. See L. Sullivan, Law of Antitrust 202 (1977) ("A shorthand method which may help to identify a restraint affecting price as naked is to examine the arguments which are being pressed in justification of the practice").

First, it is not supported by the jury's verdict. Although it did not do so with precision, the District Court did instruct the jury that in order to hold respondent liable it had to find that the agreement's purpose was to eliminate petitioner because of its price cutting and that no valid vertical nonprice restriction existed to which the motivation to eliminate price competition at the dealership level was merely ancillary.

Second, the "quite plausible purpose" the majority hypothesizes as salvation for the otherwise anticompetitive elimination of price competition—"to enable Hartwell to provide better services under the sales franchise agreement,"—is simply not the type of concern we sought to protect in *Continental T.V., Inc. v. GTE Sylvania Inc.* I have emphasized in this dissent the difference between restrictions imposed in pursuit of a manufacturer's structuring of its product distribution, and those imposed at the behest of retailers who care less about the general efficiency of a product's promotion than their own profit margins. *Sylvania* stressed the importance of the former, not the latter; we referred to the use that *manufacturers* can make of vertical nonprice restraints, and nowhere did we discuss the benefits of permitting dealers to structure intrabrand competition at the retail level by coercing manufacturers into essentially anticompetitive agreements. Thus, while Hartwell may indeed be able to provide better services under the sales franchise agreement with petitioner out of the way, one would not have thought, until today, that the mere possibility of such a result—at the expense of the elimination of price competition and absent the salutary overlay of a manufacturer's distribution decision with the entire product line in mind—would be sufficient to legitimate an otherwise purely anticompetitive restraint. In fact, given the majority's total reliance on "economic analysis," it is hard to understand why, if such a purpose were sufficient to avoid the application of a *per se* rule in this context, the same purpose should not also be sufficient to trump the *per se* rule in all other price-fixing cases that arguably permit cartel members to "provide better services."

* * *

The "plausible purpose" posited by the majority as its sole justification for this mischaracterized "nonprice vertical restriction" is inconsistent with the legislative judgment that underlies the Sherman Act itself. Under the facts as found by the jury in this case, the agreement before us is one whose "sole object is to restrain trade in order to avoid the competition which it has always been the policy of the common law to foster." *United States v. Addyston Pipe & Steel Co.,* 85 F., at 283, aff'd, 175 U.S. 211 (1899).

V

In sum, this simply is not a case in which procompetitive vertical nonprice restraints have been imposed; in fact, it is not a case in which *any* procompetitive agreement is at issue. The sole purpose of the agreement between respondent and Hartwell was to eliminate price competition at Hartwell's level. As Judge Bork has aptly explained:

> "Since the naked boycott is a form of predatory behavior, there is little doubt that it should be a per se violation of the Sherman Act."

Bork, The Antitrust Paradox, at 334.

I respectfully dissent.

Questions and Comments

In view of *Sharp*, how would you now state the scope of the per se rule against vertical price fixing? How would you formulate the rule of reason for nonprice vertical restraints? What is the difference between price and nonprice vertical restraints?

Justice Scalia approached his task by applying "economics" and then looking to see whether "law" required a different outcome. Suppose that you are a Justice judging the *Sharp* case; you are skeptical that economics can solve the problem, and in any event you believe that your task is to derive the appropriate principle of law from legal precedent; that is, the Sherman Act as interpreted by Supreme Court opinions. In deriving the appropriate principle of law from precedent-setting cases, you believe that you should look at the whole case; its spirit and holding as well. The principal cases before you are *Dr. Miles, Parke Davis, Klor's, General Motors* (discounter termination case), *Albrecht, GTE Sylvania,* and *Monsanto.* What principle (determinative of *Sharp*) do you derive from the body of law? *Can* you derive a determinative principle from the law? If not, how should you reason out the result? Did Justice Scalia treat the precedents disinterestedly? Did Justice Stevens, in his dissent?

Would you regard Justice Scalia's economic analysis as scientific? Intuitive? Impressionistic? Is the answer he "derives" from economics the one true answer? Is it, at least, strongly suggested by "right economics"?

As we noted earlier, economics helps us to ask illuminating questions and it provides some tools for answering them, but the analysis must be based on assumptions including assumptions about how businesses and markets behave. (Economic analysis can also be based on other assumptions; in *Sharp*, it is based on assumptions about the competency of jurors to make certain distinctions). The assumptions that underlie the economic analysis often drive the outcome.

Justice Scalia's opinion contains various assumptions in the second half of Part II. A. Identify these assumptions. What is their source? Would a different outcome follow from different but equally plausible assumptions or perspectives; e.g.: Discounting has dynamic qualities that serve consumers; free riding that degrades service levels desired by the manufacturer is rare; retailers' power is not rare; brand differentiation can produce not insignificant market power; cartels are not so hard to form and maintain; juries can be trusted to distinguish between cut-offs of discounters to serve an efficiency interest of the manufacturer and cut-offs of well-performing discounters solely to give powerful retailers freedom from aggressive competition?

According to the fact-finder in *Sharp*, the *Sharp* case was not about free riding; it was about retailer power to squelch a pesky low-price competitor. (See dissenting opinion at note 15). Formulate a possible per se rule or modified per se rule that would cover this situation but would not unduly cabin manufacturers' freedom to dismiss inefficient dealers. Now consider the limitations of your proposed rule. On balance, is your rule more likely to promote or to undercut competition and efficiency interests?

After *Sharp,* would you advise your clients that they may freely cut off discounters, even at the request of other dealers, as long as they themselves have not cartelized with their competitors? (Is *Dr. Miles* an obstacle to this broad advice? Would you argue that the philosophy of *Sharp* requires the overruling of *Dr. Miles?*)

g. Note on the Economics of RPM

Let us pause for a moment to reflect on the policy debate that is swirling around RPM. Led by members of the Chicago School, an articulate group of scholars and policy makers contend that resale price maintenance, where used vertically only and not to advance a cartel, is either procompetitive or benign. Normally, they assert use of RPM reflects a manufacturer's awareness of a free rider problem and the manufacturer's attempt to cure the market failure by making sure that under-investing dealers do not reap the benefits of the "good" dealers who made the appropriate investment in (e.g.) service, training, displays, information, and promotion. If the under-investing (usually discounting) dealers continue to reap the good dealers' crops, the latter will not continue to sow the seeds with appropriate attention and care and the manufacturer's sales and profits will suffer. RPM can assure the good dealers of a sufficient margin to continue investing in the crop. Moreover, use of RPM and putting dealers into competition with one another will induce the dealers to compete on service provision, since they cannot compete on price.[5]

These scenarios are possible. RPM can in theory be used to increase efficiencies, and if sufficient competitive marketplace pressures exist, efficiencies are procompetitive. But RPM can also be used (1) to police a cartel or, more subtly, to facilitate collaborative behavior even when there is not sufficient evidence to warrant inferring an agreement, (2) to facilitate exploitation of the consumer by the manufacturer or by a manufacturer/dealer collaboration, and (3) to facilitate exploitation of the consumer and perhaps of the manufacturer by a powerful dealer or by a group of dealers.

We bring together here several prospectives on how and why RPM is used and the dominant effects of its usage, in addition to the Chicago view noted above and in addition to the cartel explanation. Note that much of the relatively contemporary thinking about RPM stemmed from consideration of the wisdom of fair trade laws rather than from consideration of the *Dr. Miles* rule. The fair trade laws as applied virtually legalized RPM per se, without consideration of anticompetitive effects. *Dr. Miles* invalidated RPM per se, without consideration of procompetitive effects. You might consider whether in view of the contemporary burdens on plaintiffs under a rule of reason, the gap between the two is as large as it may seem.

The bilateral monopoly hypothesis: Professor Ward S. Bowman, Jr. (with credentials as a rigorous microtheorist of Chicago School persuasion)

5. See generally R. Bork, The Antitrust Paradox: A Policy at War With Itself 32 (1978) (hereinafter The Antitrust Paradox); Posner, The Next Step in the Antitrust Treatment of Restricted Distribution: *Per Se* Legality, 48 U.Chi.L.Rev. 6 (1981); Easterbrook, Vertical Arrangements and the Rule of Reason, 53 Antitrust L.J. 135, 171 (1984).

developed the bilateral monopoly hypothesis.[6] Professor Bowman showed that RPM cannot normally be maintained unless the product enjoys some degree of market power.[7] Moreover, using Chicago School's rationality, perfect information and profit-maximizing assumptions to argue against legalizing RPM, he concluded that resale price probably cannot be maintained without horizontal cooperation [8] and that RPM is a rational and effective device for a supplier "where there is a substantial departure from competitive standards both on the producing or manufacturing level *and* on the reselling level. . . ."[9] In sum, RPM is likely to signify the existence and exploitation of bilateral market power, shared by the supplier and dealers.[10]

Product differentiation: RPM may be used to differentiate a manufacturer's product more effectively, and thus to obtain brand preference. Differentiation has mixed effects. While it may, in one sense, increase consumers' happiness (consumers now "know" whose product they want), it also tends to increase market power. Differentiation, usually obtained through intensive noninformational advertising, disaggregates markets, making the demand curve steeper and allowing the supplier to price above the competitive level. Differentiation can give a brand the economic characteristics of a separate market.

Welfare analysis not confined to the margin: Chicago School analysis looks only at the margin and asks whether a strategy increases or decreases sales; if it increases sales it is assumed to be procompetitive and good. RPM could in theory induce more advertising, promotion and service by assuring significant profit margins, and more advertising promotion or service can mean more sales. For Chicago School this would be the end of the inquiry. Professor Comanor focuses also on infra-marginal consumers (those who would buy the good anyway—with or without the new advertising or service). Many of these individuals prefer the no-frills product; they know about the product and would prefer to pay the lower price but can no longer get the product at the lower price; therefore they lose consumer surplus. Professor Comanor shows that, because of this effect, RPM can decrease consumer welfare (depending upon the relationship between the losses and gains in consumer welfare).[11]

Others (normally not economists) add that the right to get a product at a lower price is more valuable than the right to get a product with a service. Economists often answer that this is a value judgment a "neutral" person cannot make. Is this value judgment appropriate or relevant in construing the antitrust laws? Is it a value judgment that the law allows us (commands us?) to make? (Note that this last paragraph is not about traditional economic "welfare" analysis, because welfare analysis

6. Bowman, Resale Price Maintenance—A Monopoly Problem, 25 J. of Bus. 141 (1952).

7. Id. at 145.

8. Id. at 145 n. 15.

9. Id. at 148.

10. Note that, despite rhetoric to the contrary, RPM does not eliminate free riding. A dealer who prefers to rely on her competing dealer's advertising or services can do so whether or not RPM is used as a strategy. Under RPM, however, she must choose a method other than lower price to entice the customer. That method might be her own tailored advertising or services.

11. See Comanor, Vertical Arrangements and Antitrust Analysis, in The Fall and Rise of Antitrust: Law and Policy in the Second Century (First, Fox and Pitofsky, eds. 1989).

deals in dollar aggregates; economists normally conceive of welfare in terms of net dollar benefits (or losses) to all consumers and producers, aggregated. Do the antitrust laws deal in such aggregates?)

Taking account of retailer differentiation: Support for RPM would be most convincingly justified if every retailer were just like every other and there was one "right" resale price for all. The theory would be strongest if either all value were added at the manufacturing level and retailers did nothing but deliver the product, or all retailers added the same value. In that homogeneous world all "efficient" retailers would have the same costs. It is the sum of these costs (including efficient point-of-sale promotion costs) that must be covered by the manufacturer-imposed price. But retailing is actually vastly more varied and complex.[12] Manufacturers please buyers (an economist would say add value) in a variety of ways, including differentiating their product to make it more attractive to some consumers. Retailers, to please buyers, add value in a variety of ways: through maintaining an inventory, through location, through amenity, through showing the product with complementary, comparable or related products, through providing information, through service, and through lower price.

Different retailers can vary their offerings in all of these respects and often their offerings vary considerably, one from another. There are significant differences in the amounts of value different retailers add, and, in consequence, large differences in the costs they experience. One retailer is close at hand, another well stocked, stylish and informed, the third cheap. Each is obliged by competition to set prices commensurate with its own rent, inventory, personnel, promotion and other costs. Each attracts consumers that prefer its particular mix. Not only are products differentiated by manufacturers, but retail services are differentiated, thus widening consumer choice.

Taking account of dynamic factors: Just as retailers differ—and experiment, develop and change over time—so, too, consumer demand changes with time. One of the most sensitive aspects of retailing is the task of responding to and seeking to anticipate changes through price and inventory adjustments.[13] These changes occur at different times and rates for different retailers. A centralized response, dictated by the supplier for all retailers, is likely to be a less sensitive response than the reactions generated by countless individual traders who read and take action on ever changing market factors with which they individually interact.

---

12. Note also that retail establishments are almost always multi-product outlets and that this may have consequences for RPM analysis. Rent, salaries and overhead costs are common to all products they sell. Thus, retailers must spread common costs over all products sold, and the efficient course is to do so inversely to the elasticity of demand for the products. Baumol and Bradford, Optimal Departures from Marginal Cost Pricing, 60 Am.Econ.Rev. 265 (1970). This being so, the efficient price of any product for any retailer will vary with the particular mix of products that the retailer sells.

13. See Irvine, An Optimal Middleman Firm Price Adjustment Policy: The "Short-Run Inventory-Based Policy," 19 Econ.Inquiry 245 (1981); Irvine, Econometric Tests of the Hypothesis that Market-Market Firms Follow a "Short-Run Inventory-Based Pricing Policy," 53 J. of Bus. 1 (1980).

Distortion of the price-service mix: When the supplier makes the price-service mix decision for all dealers, an over-investment in service by dealers may occur. All dealers will not be of the same size, nor experience the same population density, nor be equally efficient. Thus, the price the supplier sets will have to be high enough to cover the costs of the highest cost dealer that the supplier wants to keep in the market. Others, initially earning a supracompetitive return, may want to bid against each other for more customers. If they are not able to bid by lowering their price, they may by increasing outlays for advertising and service. They may act just like the airlines acted before deregulation—more to eat, more to drink, more advertising to tell you they serve more to eat, but never lower price.[14]

Inefficient results: Empirical evidence, although episodic and impressionistic,[15] shows that RPM leads to higher consumer prices and often lower output.[16] Professor Steiner, who reviewed theoretical and empirical material and marketing literature, rejects the notion that unless RPM reflects a dealer cartel it is welfare increasing.[17] Steiner concludes that RPM occurs mostly in industries (especially distributive trades) in which consumers are poorly informed. In such industries restraints on intrabrand competition evolve whether or not any free-rider problem exists.[18] Consumer welfare is injured and supplier welfare may be injured also, since suppliers tend to continue such restraints long after they serve their interests.[19]

14. If low cost outlets are encouraged to spend on promotion rather than to exploit their low cost by price reductions, they may be forced into the same inflationary, amenities-increasing spiral that affected the airline industry before deregulation. See 2 A. Kahn, The Economics of Regulation 208–220 (1966); CAB Practices and Procedures, Report, Subcomm. on Adm.Prac. and Proc., Comm. on the Judiciary, U.S. Senate, 94th Cong., 1st Sess. 6 (1975).

15. See Frankel, The Effects of Fair Trade: Fact and Fiction in the Statistical Findings, 29 J. of Bus. 182 (1955).

16. H.R.Rep. No. 341, 94th Cong., 1st Sess. 3 (1975); 121 Cong. Rec. Senate–20872 (daily ed. December 2, 1975); 1975 Senate Hearings 3–4, 11, 26–27, 51–52, 150–151, 174, 176, 216 and authorities there cited at 174 n. 5. per store sales are lower (perhaps because there are more small stores) where fair trade is in effect than when it is not. See ABA Antitrust Section, Monograph No. 2, Vertical Restrictions Limiting Intrabrand Competition 80 (1977). There are confirming studies of particular segments. E.g., W.A. Sandridge, The Effects of Fair Trade on Retail Prices of Electrical Housewares in Washington, Baltimore and Richmond, (Ph. D. Dissertation, Univ. of Va., 1960), cited in S.C. Hollander, United States of America, in Yamey (ed.), Resale Price Maintenance, *supra* at 85 n. 48 (1966); Bowman, The Prereq-

uisites and Effects of Resale Price Maintenance, supra at 852–73 (one-half of tooth paste sales in non-fair trade states and one-third in fair trade states below suggested price); Hourihan and Markham, The Effects of Fair Trade Repeal: The Case of Rhode Island (1974); Pickering, The Abolition of Resale Price Maintenance in Great Britain, 26 Oxford Econ. Papers 120 (1975); Keoch, The Abolition of Resale Price Maintenance: Some Notes on Canadian Experience, 31 Economica 260 (1964). Most recently, after state liquor RPM laws were repealed following this Court's *Midcal* decision, retail prices fell about 20%. See New York Times, Sun., Jan. 14, 1979, § XI, p. 1, col. 1; New York Times Jan. 3, 1979, p. 1, col. 1.

17. Steiner, Vertical Restraints and Economic Efficiency, supra at 2. See also Buchanan, Resale Price Maintenance: An Historic Perspective in Sixteenth New England Antitrust Conference 356 (ALI–ABA 1982).

18. Id. at 8–11.

19. Id. at 12–13. See also Oster, The FTC v. Levi Strauss: An Analysis of the Economic Issues (Consultant's Report to FTC, Rev. March 1982); McEachern and Romeo, Audio Components Industry: An Economic Analysis of FTC Intervention (Consultant's Report to FTC, 1981).

The need to tame competition on product variety: Some consumer advocates assert that competing on brand-differentiated goods by means of increased promotional expenditures that tilt the demand curve more steeply and increase prices is not socially desirable even if it leads to greater sales of the particular brand. There is already too much competition based on product variety and product image and too little based on price, it is said. If forbidding RPM yields more of the latter and less of the former, that is all to the good. See The Closed Enterprise System: the Nader Study Group Report On Antitrust Enforcement 23–30 (M. Green ed. 1971).

Do discounting options undermine consumer choice and welfare?—empirical questions: A premise of free-rider theory is that outlets providing little or no service tend to drive out those providing significant service, making it difficult for manufacturers to generate point of sale promotion and the delivery of information and other services. Does the marketplace tell a different story? Small, local stores with relatively high per-unit overhead remain in business beside larger, more centrally located stores with lower per-unit costs that sell for lower prices. The small, local stores provide convenience, service and amenity that the larger, centrally deployed units cannot match. Some consumers (having the choice) pay more to get what they value more. Even within limited areas of central cities, high amenity, high-rent, full service department stores with large inventories, displays, informed sales help, and service facilities thrive within blocks of discount houses offering less amenity, less information, less service and lower prices. Some consumers prefer the amenity and reliability of Macy's to Dottie's Discount or even Crazy Eddie's. Some will pay even more for an "exclusive" or "boutique" atmosphere. Yet others will frequent the deep-discount shops located in warehouse districts. If observation seems to belie the theory, one may wish to see empirical evidence supporting or disproving the underlying hypothesis. For example:

1. Do discounters significantly free ride—i.e., are a significant portion of their sales attributable to expenditures by their non-discounting competitors?

2. Does RPM significantly lower the level of free riding?

3. Does the RPM–linked free riding induce the non-discounting dealers to make significant cut-backs in investment in services or advertising that the manufacturer wishes its dealers to offer?

4. If so, can the manufacturer efficiently ensure the level of service it chooses by means other than RPM? E.g., it might pay for advertising; it might require and police provision of services; it might require after-sale service only for a store's own customers or for a cost-covering price; it might give bonuses for pre-sale service levels.

How should these mixed social and economic theories, perpectives, predictions and concerns influence the law?

h. Note on the Recent Politics of RPM

In *Maricopa*, supra, p. 327, the Court said that adherence to the per se rule against price fixing, horizontal or vertical, was based not only on "economic prediction, judicial convenience and business certainty," but also on a recognition of the "respective roles" of Congress and the courts. Has modern economic thinking demolished the conclusion that opposition to RPM is based on economic prediction? Should the Court overrule *Dr. Miles?* (Congress will not.)

Congress has amended the antitrust laws six times in ten years without changing the *Dr. Miles* rule.[20] The last Congressional response to RPM was repeal of the Miller–Tydings and McGuire Acts,[21] which had authorized states to legalize RPM. Is this legislative action, and the underlying legislative record of hostility to RPM, relevant? The Reagan administration's Justice Department did not think so. Convinced that RPM is efficiency yielding unless it is used in aid of upstream cartelization or multibrand downstream cartelization, the Reagan administration challenged the *Dr. Miles* rule in a variety of ways. We noted its failed attempt to do so in *Monsanto.*

In 1985, the Department of Justice published Vertical Restraints Guidelines aimed, in part, at weakening *Dr. Miles.* The guidelines characterize as unilateral much of the conduct likely to be caught under *Parke Davis.* They also characterize conduct conventionally viewed as price restraints as nonprice restraints. Relatedly, they characterize horizontal arrangements between downstream firms as vertical as long as no more than one brand is affected.

In response, the House Judiciary Committee criticized the guidelines as an "attempt to dilute or trivialize the generality of the *per se* rule against price fixing, both horizontal and vertical." [22] Moreover, Congress itself resolved:

"Whereas . . . [the] guidelines are inconsistent with established antitrust law . . . in stating that vertical restraints that have an impact upon prices are subject to the per se rule of legality only if there is an 'explicit agreement as to the specific prices' . . .

Now, therefore, be it

Resolved, that it is the sense of the Congress that the antitrust enforcement policy [stated in the guidelines] . . . [is] not an accurate expression of the Federal antitrust laws or Congressional intent with regard to the application of such laws to resale price maintenance. . . ." [23]

20. Antitrust Procedures and Penalties Act of 1984, Pub.L. No. 93–528, 88 Stat. 1706; National Cooperative Research Act of 1984, Pub.L. No. 98–462, 98 Stat. 1815; Foreign Trade Antitrust Improvement Act of 1982, Pub.L. No. 97–290, 96 Stat. 1233; Antitrust Procedural Improvements Act of 1980, Pub.L. No. 96–349; FTC Improvements Act of 1980, Pub.L. No. 96–252, 93 Stat. 374; Hart–Scott–Rodino Antitrust Improvements Act of 1976, Pub.L. No. 94–435, 90 Stat. 1390.

21. Consumer Goods Pricing Act of 1975, Pub.L. No. 94–145, 89 Stat. 801.

22. House Judiciary Committee Report on Vertical Restraints Guidelines Resolution, H.R.Rep. No. 99–399, 99th Cong., 1st Sess. 6 (1985).

23. Pub.L. No. 99–180, 99 Stat. 1136, 1169–70 (1985).

Sharp was decided after Congress passed the foregoing resolution. Is *Sharp* in tension with Congress's notion of the line between price and nonprice restraints?

A bill pending at the time of this writing, S. 430 (100th Cong., 1st Sess.1987), would reaffirm the per se rule of *Dr. Miles* and, as well, make it easier for terminated dealers alleging RPM to get to a jury on the question of concert.

2. MAXIMUM RESALE PRICES

KIEFER–STEWART CO. v. JOSEPH E. SEAGRAM & SONS, INC.

340 U.S. 211 (1951).

JUSTICE BLACK: The petitioner, Kiefer–Stewart Company, is an Indiana drug concern which does a wholesale liquor business. Respondents, Seagram and Calvert corporations, are affiliated companies that sell liquor in interstate commerce to Indiana wholesalers. Petitioner brought this action in a federal district court for treble damages under the Sherman Act. 15 U.S.C. §§ 1, 15. The complaint charged that respondents had agreed or conspired to sell liquor only to those Indiana wholesalers who would resell at prices fixed by Seagram and Calvert, and that this agreement deprived petitioner of a continuing supply of liquor to its great damage. On the trial, evidence was introduced tending to show that respondents had fixed maximum prices above which the wholesalers could not resell. The jury returned a verdict for petitioner and damages were awarded. The Court of Appeals for the Seventh Circuit reversed. 182 F.2d 228. It held that an agreement among respondents to fix maximum resale prices did not violate the Sherman Act because such prices promoted rather than restrained competition. It also held the evidence insufficient to show that respondents had acted in concert. Doubt as to the correctness of the decision on questions important in antitrust litigation prompted us to grant certiorari. 340 U.S. 863.

The Court of Appeals erred in holding that an agreement among competitors to fix maximum resale prices of their products does not violate the Sherman Act. For such agreements, no less than those to fix minimum prices, cripple the freedom of traders and thereby restrain their ability to sell in accordance with their own judgment. We reaffirm what we said in *United States v. Socony–Vacuum Oil Co.*, 310 U.S. 150, 223: "Under the Sherman Act a combination formed for the purpose and with the effect of raising, depressing, fixing, pegging, or stabilizing the price of a commodity in interstate or foreign commerce is illegal *per se*."

The Court of Appeals also erred in holding the evidence insufficient to support a finding by the jury that respondents had conspired to fix maximum resale prices. The jury was authorized by the evidence to accept the following as facts: Seagram refused to sell to petitioner and others unless the purchasers agreed to the maximum resale price fixed by Seagram. Calvert was at first willing to sell without this restrictive condition and arrangements were made for petitioner to buy large quantities of Calvert liquor. Petitioner subsequently was informed by Calvert, however, that the arrangements would not be carried out because Calvert had "to go along with Seagram." Moreover, about this time conferences were held by officials of the respondents concerning sales of liquor to petitioner. Thereafter, on identical terms as to the fixing of retail prices, both Seagram and Calvert resumed sales to other Indiana wholesalers who agreed to abide by such conditions, but no shipments have been made to petitioner.

The foregoing is sufficient to justify the challenged jury finding that respondents had a unity of purpose or a common design and understanding when they forbade their purchasers to exceed the fixed ceilings. . . .

Respondents introduced evidence in the District Court designed to show that petitioner had agreed with other Indiana wholesalers to set minimum prices for the sale of liquor in violation of the antitrust laws. It is now contended that the trial court erred in charging the jury that petitioner's part in such a conspiracy, even if proved, was no defense to the present cause of action. We hold that the instruction was correct. Seagram and Calvert acting individually perhaps might have refused to deal with petitioner or with any or all of the Indiana wholesalers. But the Sherman Act makes it an offense for respondents to agree among themselves to stop selling to particular customers. If petitioner and others were guilty of infractions of the antitrust laws, they could be held responsible in appropriate proceedings brought against them by the Government or by injured private persons. The alleged illegal conduct of petitioner, however, could not legalize the unlawful combination by respondents nor immunize them against liability to those they injured. Cf. *Fashion Originators' Guild v. Trade Comm'n,* 312 U.S. 457. * * **

Questions and Comments

Did the Court in *Kiefer–Stewart* reach the question of vertical maximum resale price fixing?

The Court supplied almost no factual background. Some additional facts appear in the following excerpt from a law review comment.

THE PER SE ILLEGALITY OF PRICE–FIXING—SANS POWER, PURPOSE, OR EFFECT
19 U.Chi.L.Rev. 837, 838–39 (1952).

* * * Shortly after termination of OPA ceilings in October 1946 and following a meeting of the Indiana Wholesale Liquor Dealers Association, Kiefer–Stewart and every other liquor wholesaler in Indiana filed identical schedules of increased prices with state authorities. The new schedules were arrived at by computing the customary fifteen per cent wholesaler's mark-up on the basis of costs plus taxes, whereas OPA regulations had required the computation to be made exclusive of taxes added during the period of OPA control. Subsequently (November 6, 1946), Seagram, which had spent some $500,000 advertising against inflated whisky prices, notified Indiana wholesalers that wholesale prices were

---

* We have deleted the paragraph on intra-enterprise conspiracy, which is treated at p. 497, *supra.*

to be kept at OPA levels. Upon the wholesalers' concerted refusal to comply, Seagram suspended all shipments to Indiana distributors. Immediately prior to this action Kiefer–Stewart and Calvert Distilling Company, a wholly owned subsidiary of Seagram, had concluded negotiations giving Kiefer–Stewart a Calvert distributorship; and even after Seagram had severed relations, Calvert representatives had assured Kiefer–Stewart that their relationship would be unaffected by the parent company's defection and that cases of liquor would be delivered as promised. Within a week the deal was called off, and the jury found that Calvert's reversal of position was the result of an agreement with Seagram and not independent action. By February of the next year all Indiana wholesalers except Kiefer–Stewart had filed notification of a return to the OPA method of calculating mark-ups and by July 1, 1947, had entered into fair trade contracts with both distillers which stipulated similar minimum wholesale prices.[14]

Taking into account these additional facts, and the *Copperweld* decision as well, *supra* p. 498, how do you analyze the *Kiefer–Stewart* problem? Is this principally a horizontal or a vertical problem? Is it principally a private action or a state action problem? If Seagram and Calvert are treated as one entity, did Kiefer–Stewart have standing to bring this case—i.e., to challenge Seagram's RPM (minimum or maximum?) agreements with all other wholesalers? Can Kiefer–Stewart challenge Seagram's refusal to deal with it unless it agrees to resell at "too low" a price? Is *Colgate* relevant?

ALBRECHT v. HERALD CO.

390 U.S. 145 (1968).

JUSTICE WHITE: * * * Respondent publishes the Globe–Democrat, a morning newspaper distributed in the St. Louis metropolitan area by independent carriers who buy papers at wholesale and sell them at retail. There are 172 home delivery routes. Respondent advertises a suggested retail price in its newspaper. Carriers have exclusive territories which are subject to termination if prices exceed the suggested maximum. Petitioner, who had Route 99, adhered to the advertised price for some time but in 1961 raised the price to customers.[2] After more than once objecting to this practice, respondent wrote petitioner on May 20, 1964, that because he was overcharging and because respondent had reserved the right to compete should that happen, subscribers on Route 99 were being informed by letter that respondent would itself deliver the paper to those who wanted it at the lower price. In addition to sending these letters to petitioner's customers, respondent hired Milne Circulation Sales, Inc., which solicited readers for newspapers, to engage in telephone and

---

14. Despite allegations in the Kiefer–Stewart briefs, these contracts were a logical extension of the original policy since competition for retail business is sufficiently strong among Indiana wholesalers to make minimum prices maximum prices. Besides, a regulation of the Indiana Alcoholic Beverage Commission, effective July 1, 1947, made fair trade contracts a prerequisite to "price and brand" advertising by distillers. . . .

2. The record indicates that petitioner raised his price by 10 cents a month. [The suggested retail rate for delivery by carrier was $1.60 per month for the daily paper plus 20 cents for each issue of the weekend paper. 367 F.2d 517, 519.]

LIMITING BUYERS' OPTIONS **591**

house-to-house solicitation of all residents on Route 99. As a result, about 300 of petitioner's 1,200 customers switched to direct delivery by respondent. Meanwhile, respondent continued to sell papers to petitioner but warned him that should he continue to overcharge, respondent would not have to do business with him. Since respondent did not itself want to engage in home delivery, it advertised a new route of 314 customers as available without cost. Another carrier, George Kroner, took over the route knowing that respondent would not tolerate overcharging and understanding that he might have to return the route if petitioner discontinued his pricing practice.[3] On July 27 respondent told petitioner that it was not interested in being in the carrier business and that petitioner could have his customers back as long as he charged the suggested price. Petitioner brought this lawsuit on August 12. In response, petitioner's appointment as a carrier was terminated and petitioner was given 60 days to arrange the sale of his route to a satisfactory replacement. Petitioner sold his route for $12,000, $1,000 more than he had paid for it but less than he could have gotten had he been able to turn over 1,200 customers instead of 900.

Petitioner's complaint charged a combination or conspiracy in restraint of trade under § 1 of the Sherman Act. At the close of the evidence the complaint was amended to charge only a combination between respondent and "plaintiff's customers and/or Milne Circulation Sales, Inc. and/or George Kroner." The case went to the jury on this theory, the jury found for respondent, and judgment in its favor was entered on the verdict. The court denied petitioner's motion for judgment notwithstanding the verdict, which asserted that the undisputed facts showed as a matter of law a combination to fix resale prices of newspapers which was per se illegal under the Sherman Act. The Court of Appeals affirmed. In its view "the undisputed evidence fail[ed] to show a Sherman Act violation," because respondent's conduct was wholly unilateral and there was no restraint of trade. The previous decisions of this Court were deemed inapposite to a situation in which a seller establishes maximum prices to be charged by a retailer enjoying an exclusive territory and in which the seller, who would be entitled to refuse to deal, simply engages in competition with the offending retailer.

On the undisputed facts recited by the Court of Appeals respondent's conduct cannot be deemed wholly unilateral and beyond the reach of § 1 of the Sherman Act. That section covers combinations in addition to contracts and conspiracies, express or implied. . . .

. . . [T]here can be no doubt that a combination arose between respondent, Milne, and Kroner to force petitioner to conform to the advertised retail price. When respondent learned that petitioner was overcharging, it hired Milne to solicit customers away from petitioner in order to get petitioner to reduce his price. It was through the efforts of Milne, as well as because of respondent's letter to petitioner's customers, that about 300 customers were obtained for Kroner. Milne's purpose was

3. The record shows that at about this time petitioner lowered his price to respondent's advertised price. Although petitioner notified all his customers of this change, respondent apparently remained unaware of it.

undoubtedly to earn its fee, but it was aware that the aim of the solicitation campaign was to force petitioner to lower his price. Kroner knew that respondent was giving him the customer list as part of a program to get petitioner to conform to the advertised price, and he knew that he might have to return the customers if petitioner ultimately complied with respondent's demands. He undertook to deliver papers at the suggested price and materially aided in the accomplishment of respondent's plan. Given the uncontradicted facts recited by the Court of Appeals, there was a combination within the meaning of § 1 between respondent, Milne, and Kroner, and the Court of Appeals erred in holding to the contrary.[6]

The Court of Appeals also held there was no restraint of trade, despite the long-accepted rule in § 1 cases that resale price fixing is a per se violation of the law whether done by agreement or combination.[7]

In *Kiefer–Stewart*, [340 U.S. 211 (1951)], liquor distributors combined to set maximum resale prices. The Court of Appeals held the combination legal under the Sherman Act because in its view setting maximum prices ". . . constituted no restraint on trade and no interference with plaintiff's right to engage in all the competition it desired." 182 F.2d 228, 235 (C.A.7th Cir.1950). This Court rejected that view and reversed the Court of Appeals, holding that agreements to fix maximum prices "no less than those to fix minimum prices, cripple the freedom of traders and thereby restrain their ability to sell in accordance with their own judgment."[8] 340 U.S. 211, 213.

6. Petitioner's original complaint broadly asserted an illegal combination under § 1 of the Sherman Act. [P]etitioner could have claimed a combination between respondent and himself, at least as of the day he unwillingly complied with respondent's advertised price. Likewise, he might successfully have claimed that respondent had combined with other carriers because the firmly enforced price policy applied to all carriers, most of whom acquiesced in it. These additional claims, however, appear to have been abandoned by petitioner when he amended his complaint in the trial court.

Petitioner's amended complaint did allege a combination between respondent and petitioner's customers. Because of our disposition of this case it is unnecessary to pass on this claim. It was not, however, a frivolous contention.

7. Our Brother Harlan seems to state that suppliers have no interest in programs of minimum resale price maintenance, and hence that such programs are "essentially" horizontal agreements between dealers even when they appear to be imposed unilaterally and individually by a supplier on each of his dealers. Although the empirical basis for determining whether or not manufacturers benefit from minimum resale price programs appears to be inconclusive, it seems beyond dispute that a substantial number of manufacturers formulate and enforce com-

plicated plans to maintain resale prices because they deem them advantageous. As a theoretical matter, it is not difficult to conceive of situations in which manufacturers would rightly regard minimum resale price maintenance to be in their interest. Maintaining minimum resale prices would benefit manufacturers when the total demand for their product would not be increased as much by the lower prices brought about by dealer competition as by some other nonprice, demand-creating activity. In particular, when total consumer demand (at least within that price range marked at the bottom by the minimum cost of manufacture and distribution and at the top by the highest price at which a price maintenance scheme can operate effectively) is affected less by price than by the number of retail outlets for the product, the availability of dealer services, or the impact of advertising and promotion, it will be in the interest of manufacturers to squelch price competition through a scheme of resale price maintenance in order to concentrate on nonprice competition. Finally, if the retail price of each of a group of competing products is stabilized through manufacturer-imposed price maintenance schemes, the danger to all the manufacturers of severe interbrand price competition is apt to be alleviated.

8. Our Brother Harlan appears to read *Kiefer–Stewart* as prohibiting only combina-

We think *Kiefer–Stewart* was correctly decided and we adhere to it. Maximum and minimum price fixing may have different consequences in many situations. But schemes to fix maximum prices, by substituting the perhaps erroneous judgment of a seller for the forces of the competitive market, may severely intrude upon the ability of buyers to compete and survive in that market. Competition, even in a single product, is not cast in a single mold. Maximum prices may be fixed too low for the dealer to furnish services essential to the value which goods have for the consumer or to furnish services and conveniences which consumers desire and for which they are willing to pay. Maximum price fixing may channel distribution through a few large or specifically advantaged dealers who otherwise would be subject to significant nonprice competition. Moreover, if the actual price charged under a maximum price scheme is nearly always the fixed maximum price, which is increasingly likely as the maximum price approaches the actual cost of the dealer, the scheme tends to acquire all the attributes of an arrangement fixing minimum prices.[9] It is our view, therefore, that the combination formed by the respondent in this case to force petitioner to maintain a specified price for the resale of the newspapers which he had purchased from respondent constituted, without more, an illegal restraint of trade under § 1 of the Sherman Act.

We also reject the suggestion of the Court of Appeals that *Kiefer–Stewart* is inapposite and that maximum price fixing is permissible in this case. The Court of Appeals reasoned that since respondent granted exclusive territories, a price ceiling was necessary to protect the public from price gouging by dealers who had monopoly power in their own territories. But neither the existence of exclusive territories nor the economic power they might place in the hands of the dealers was at issue before the jury. Likewise, the evidence taken was not directed to the question of whether exclusive territories had been granted or imposed as the result of an illegal combination in violation of the antitrust laws. Certainly on the record before us the Court of Appeals was not entitled to assume, as its reasoning necessarily did, that the exclusive rights granted by respondent were valid under § 1 of the Sherman Act, either alone or in conjunction with a price-fixing scheme. See *United States v. Arnold, Schwinn & Co.*, 388 U.S. 365, 373, 379 (1967).* The assertion that illegal price fixing is justified because it blunts the pernicious consequences of another distribution practice is unpersuasive. If, as the Court of Appeals said, the economic impact of territorial exclusivity was such that the public could be protected only by otherwise illegal price fixing itself

---

tions of suppliers to squeeze retailers from the top. Under this view, scarcely derivable from the opinion in that case, signed contracts between a single supplier and his many dealers to fix maximum resale prices would not violate the Sherman Act. With all deference, we reject this view, which seems to stem from the notion that there can be no agreement violative of § 1 unless that agreement accrues to the benefit of both parties, as determined in accordance with some *a prior* economic model.

9. In *Kiefer–Stewart* after the manufacturer established the maximum price at which its product could be sold, it fair-traded the product so as to fix that price as the legally permissible minimum.

* *Schwinn* held a system of vertically-imposed exclusive territories illegal *per se*. *Schwinn* was later overruled. Continental T.V., Inc. v. GTE Sylvania Inc., 433 U.S. 36 (1977); treated *infra* at p. 606.

injurious to the public, the entire scheme must fall under § 1 of the Sherman Act.

In sum, the evidence cited by the Court of Appeals makes it clear that a combination in restraint of trade existed. Accordingly, it was error to affirm the judgment of the District Court which denied petitioner's motion for judgment notwithstanding the verdict. The judgment of the Court of Appeals is reversed and the case is remanded to that court for further proceedings consistent with this opinion.

Reversed and remanded.

JUSTICE DOUGLAS, concurring.

While I join the opinion of the Court, there is a word I would add. This is a "rule of reason" case stemming from *Standard Oil Co.* v. *United States*, 221 U.S. 1, 62. Whether an exclusive territorial franchise in a vertical arrangement is *per se* unreasonable under the antitrust laws is a much mooted question. A fixing of prices for resale is conspicuously unreasonable, because of the great leverage that price has over the market. *United States* v. *Socony-Vacuum Oil Co.*, 310 U.S. 150, 221. The Court quite properly refuses to say whether in the newspaper distribution business an exclusive territorial franchise is illegal. . . .

JUSTICE HARLAN, dissenting.

While I entirely agree with the views expressed by my Brother Stewart and have joined his dissenting opinion, the Court's disregard of certain economic considerations underlying the Sherman Act warrants additional comment.

I.

The practice of setting genuine price "ceilings," that is maximum prices, differs from the practice of fixing minimum prices, and no accumulation of pronouncements from the opinions of this Court can render the two economically equivalent.

The allegation of a combination of persons to fix maximum prices undoubtedly states a Sherman Act cause of action. In order for a plaintiff to win such a § 1 case, however, he must be able to prove the existence of the alleged combination, and the defendant must be unable, either by virtue of a *per se* rule or by failure of proof at trial, to show an adequate justification. It is on these two points that price ceilings differ from price floors: to hold that a combination may be inferred from the vertical dictation of a maximum price simply because it may be permissible to infer a combination from the vertical dictation of a minimum price ignores economic reality; to conclude that no acceptable justification for fixing maximum prices can be found simply because there is no acceptable justification for fixing minimum prices is to substitute blindness for analysis.

Resale price maintenance, a practice not involved here, lessens horizontal intrabrand competition. The effects, higher prices, less efficient use of resources, and an easier life for the resellers, are the same whether the price maintenance policy takes the form of a horizontal conspiracy among resellers or of vertical dictation by a manufacturer plus reseller acquiescence. This means two things. First, it is frequently possible to infer a combination of resellers behind what is presented to the world as a vertical and unilateral price policy, because it is the resellers and not the manufacturer who reap the direct benefits of the policy. Second, price floors are properly considered *per se* restraints, in the sense that once a combination to create them has been demonstrated, no proffered justification is an acceptable defense. Following the rule of reason, combinations to fix price floors are invariably unreasonable: to the extent that they achieve their objective, they act to the direct detriment of the public interest as viewed in the Sherman Act. In the absence of countervailing fair trade laws, all asserted justifications are, upon examination, found wanting, either because they are too trivial or elusive to warrant the expense of a trial (as is the case, for example, with a defense that price floors maintain the prestige of a product) or because they run counter to Sherman Act premises (as is the case with the defense that price maintenance enables inefficient sellers to stay in business).

Vertically imposed price ceilings are, as a matter of economic fact that this Court's words cannot change, an altogether different matter. Other things being equal, a manufacturer would like to restrict those distributing his product to the lowest feasible profit margin, for in this way he achieves the lowest overall price to the public and the largest volume. When a manufacturer dictates a minimum resale price he is responding to the interest of his customers, who may treat his product better if they have a secure high margin of profits. When the same manufacturer dictates a price ceiling, however, he is acting directly in his own interest, and there is no room for the inference that he is merely a mechanism for accomplishing anticompetitive purposes of his customers.

Furthermore, the restraint imposed by price ceilings is of a different order from that imposed by price floors. In the present case the Court uses again the fallacious argument that price ceilings and price floors must be equally unreasonable because both "cripple the freedom of traders and thereby restrain their ability to sell in accordance with their own judgment." The fact of the matter is that this statement does not in itself justify a *per se* rule in either the maximum or minimum price case, and that the real justification for a *per se* rule in the case of minimums has not been shown to exist in the case of maximums.

It has long been recognized that one of the objectives of the Sherman Act was to preserve, for social rather than economic reasons, a high degree of independence, multiplicity, and variety in the economic system. Recognition of this objective does not, however, require this Court to hold that every commercial act that fetters the freedom of some trader is a proper subject for a *per se* rule in the sense that it has no adequate provable justification. The *per se* treatment of price maintenance is justified because analysis alone, without the burden of a trial in each individual case, demonstrates that price floors are invariably harmful on balance. Price ceilings are a different matter: they do not lessen horizontal competition; they drive prices toward the level that would be set by intense competition, and they cannot go below this level unless the manufacturer who dictates them and the customer who accepts them have both miscalculated. Since price ceilings reflect the manufacturer's view that there is insufficient competition to drive prices down to a competitive level, they have the arguable justification that they prevent retailers or wholesalers from reaping monopoly or supercompetitive profits.

When price floors and price ceilings are placed side by side, then, and the question is asked of each, "Does analysis justify a no-trial rule?" the answers must be quite different. Both practices share the negative attribute that they restrict individual discretion in the pricing area, but only the former imposes upon the public the much more significant evil of lessened competition, and, as just seen, the latter has an important arguable justification that the former does not possess. . . .[4]

II.

The Court's discovery in this case of (a) a combination and (b) a restraint that is *per se* unreasonable is beset with pitfalls. The Court relies directly on combinations with Milne and Kroner, two third parties who were simply hired and paid to do telephoning and distributing jobs that respondent could as effectively have done itself. Neither had any special interest in respondent's objective of setting a price ceiling. If the critical question is whether a company pays one of its own employees to perform a routine task, or hires an outsider to do the same thing, the requirement of a "combination" in restraint of trade has lost all significant meaning. The point is more than that the words in a statute ought to be taken to mean something of substance. The premise of § 1 adjudication has always been that it is quite proper for a firm to set its own prices and determine its own territories, but that it may not do so in conjunction with another firm with which, in combination, it can generate market power that neither would otherwise have. A firm is not "combining" to fix its own prices or territory simply because it hires outside accountants, market analysts, advertisers by telephone or otherwise, or delivery boys. Once it is recognized that Kroner had no interest whatever in forcing his competitor to lower his price, and was merely being paid to perform a delivery job that respondent could have done itself, it is clear respondent's activity was in its essence unilateral.

* * *

. . . [Respondent] simply advertised the maximum home delivery price and created competition with any distributor not observing it.

---

4. The same points may be made from the perspective of the retailers or wholesalers subject to the price dictation. When the issue is minimum resale prices, those sellers who are more efficient and ambitious are likely to object to price restrictions, while the lazier and less efficient sellers will welcome their protection. When the issue is price ceilings, the matter is different. Assuming the ceilings are high enough to permit a return that will enable the seller to stay in business, a seller will object to price ceilings only because they deny him the supercompetitive return that the imperfections of competition would otherwise permit. At the same time, in stark contrast to the situation involved in resale price maintenance, no seller has any interest in insisting that price ceilings be imposed on his competitors; he is not worried that they may sell at a higher price than his own. Thus while resale price maintenance establishes what is the equivalent of a single horizontal restraint on otherwise competitive sellers, price ceilings establish merely a series of distinct vertical relationships between manufacturer and seller, with no one seller economically interested in the maintenance of the vertical relationship with any other seller.

Today's decision leaves respondent with no alternative but to use its own trucks.

*   *   *

JUSTICE STEWART also dissented.

Questions and Comments

Newspapers have an industry-specific reason for maximum resale price fixing. The distributor that purchases a newspaper for resale represents only one source of revenue to the publisher. A publisher receives most of its revenues from advertising. The advertiser buys "circulation"; it pays more per inch if readership is greater, because its goal is to reach the greatest number of potential customers. The publisher therefore has an interest in keeping price down to the point at which circulation is optimal. If competition does not squeeze the distributor and put downward pressure on price, then the publisher has the incentive to do this job itself.

When Dr. Miles distributed his drugs he could have relied on distributor and dealer competition to squeeze distribution profits out of consumer prices. Could a newspaper publisher do that? Or does efficient newspaper distribution counsel single-person routes?

One might doubt that *Albrecht* survived *GTE Sylvania* (which we discuss below, infra at 606, and *BMI,* supra at 316. Yet, *Albrecht* was cited by the Supreme Court with approval in *Midcal* in 1980, and with explicit confirmation in *Maricopa* in 1982 (see 329 supra), and Justice Scalia took pains to distinguish *Albrecht* in *Sharp.* See 570 supra.

What do you make of all this? What is the theory on which fixing maximum resale prices is an antitrust violation? Is there an appropriate analogy to the theory on which horizontal maximums are faulted? Who suffers from maximum resale price fixing (assuming that we are sure that the maximum *is* a maximum)? How important is the downstream firm's loss of freedom to make its own decisions about important matters?

If you were writing the rule for vertical maximum resale price fixing, what would it be? A rule of reason? What considerations would drive your rule of reason?

Alternatively, should vertical maximum resale price fixing be subject to a modified per se rule, or a presumption of illegality subject to justification? What circumstances should qualify as justification? Should Seagram & Sons have been permitted to defend the suit against it on grounds of a wholesaler cartel? Should the Herald Company have been permitted to defend the suit against it on grounds that the maximum was a true maximum intended to induce more sales at a lower price, that there was no danger that the price would become a minimum because the Herald Company had the incentive to hold price down, and that the maximum was needed to prevent dealers from taking monopoly profits?

Do you agree with the Court in *Albrecht* that there was a contract, combination or conspiracy? Or was Herald's act in creating competition against Albrecht, and then terminating Albrecht, unilateral? Does *Monsanto* undercut the finding of a combination by the Court in *Albrecht?* Does the theory of the Court in *Sharp* undercut this finding?

Would Albrecht have made a better case by alleging that the Herald Company attempted to coerce him to conform to an illegal contract, but that he, Albrecht, refused to succumb and was therefore dismissed?

Problem 1

In California, Blue Shield and the three other insurers offer prepaid prescription drug plans. In each case, the insurer has two sets of agreements, one with each of its insureds and one with each pharmacy that participates in its plan. The contract with the pharmacy sets the total price to be paid to the pharmacy for various drugs (an amount intended to cover cost plus a reasonable profit), designates the portion of the price that the insurer will pay, and provides that the pharmacy will collect from the insured no more than the balance of the agreed price (called the "deductible"). The contract with the insured provides that, when the insured buys prescription drugs from a participating pharmacy, the insured will pay the pharmacy a specified deductible on the cost of the drugs and the insurer will pay the rest. For example, the insured might have to pay $2 (the deductible) to the pharmacy towards the cost of an $8 drug, the insurer paying $6. The agreements with the participating pharmacies are prepared by the insurance company and are presented to pharmacies on a take-it-or-leave-it basis. Any pharmacy can participate or not, as it elects.

A group of pharmacies, some of whom have signed such agreements and some of whom have not, sue Blue Shield and the other insurers who have similar plans, alleging violations of the Sherman Act. There is no evidence that any of the insurers conferred or spoke with one another regarding any of the matters complained of. Plaintiffs do not contest the assertion by each insurance company that its purpose was to maximize its profits by paying as little as possible to the insured and to the pharmacy. Blue Shield and the other insurers move to dismiss. You are the judge. Do you grant the motion?

See *Sausalito Pharmacy, Inc. v. Blue Shield of California*, 544 F.Supp. 230 (N.D.Cal.1981), *aff'd per curiam*, 677 F.2d 47 (9th Cir.), *cert. denied*, 459 U.S. 1016 (1982).

Problem 2

Most gasoline sold at retail is refined by one of the major integrated oil companies and sold either through its own retail outlets or to its franchised dealers, who sell only the franchisor's gasoline. In any geographic market at any particular time retail prices for the gasoline of the various majors are approximately the same. In urban markets, gas is also sold to the consumer by unintegrated "independent" retailers. The independents buy gas from various refiners and generally sell it at prices lower than the majors. Their gas is of quality equal to that of the majors; indeed, it is derived from the same source.

One of the majors wishes to organize a maximum resale price plan aimed at reducing the differential between its gas and that sold by independents. It hopes to cut into the independents' market share. Can it do so legally? Would it matter if the major gas company is likely to drive all or most independents out of the urban markets in which it implements its plan? Do you need to know the structure of the market before and after the maximum price campaign? Is it significant that there would still be other vertically integrated refiners retailing gas?

See *USA Petroleum Co. v. Atlantic Richfield Co.*, 859 F.2d 687 (9th Cir. 1988).

3. ANTITRUST INJURY AND STANDING TO CHALLENGE RPM AND MAXIMUM RESALE PRICES

At the government level, both the Department of Justice and the FTC can sue sellers who fix resale prices. As recently as 1980 both were doing so—indeed, the Justice Department had brought a criminal proceeding for an RPM violation. But political swings affect enforcement. For the eight years beginning in 1981, the Justice Department stopped RPM enforcement. Given their assumptions, officials thought RPM was solitary or benign.

If government is out of the business of enforcing the law against RPM, who is left to enforce it (if it should be enforced at all)? Would a buyer of Monsanto chemicals have had standing to challenge Monsanto's cut-off of a discounter if she bought from the discounter? Would the buyer have standing if she bought from the nondiscounting co-conspirator? To show impact and antitrust injury, would she have to prove that the cut-off and underlying agreement not only eliminated discounters but raised the prices of nondiscounters?

Suppose a distributor maintained prices at Monsanto's urging, only because price maintenance was the sole way to get the brand. Would this distributor, who wanted to sell for less but was afraid to do so out of fear, have standing?

Does the discounting distributor have standing to challenge its own cut-off? Does it suffer antitrust injury? Does it suffer antitrust injury if resale prices were elevated simply to reflect the costs of providing information and service that, the manufacturer determined, were important to the reputation of the product? Must the discounting distributor prove, to show standing and antitrust injury, that the cut-off was carried out pursuant to an RPM scheme that lessened output? Should Monsanto, in *Monsanto v. Spray–Rite,* have moved to dismiss the case for lack of standing of Spray–Rite?

The standing question is raised even more starkly in the case of a franchised dealer whose franchisor insisted on low prices in order to make good on the special deals it advertised. Consider the analysis offered by Judge Posner in this maximum resale price case.

JACK WALTERS & SONS CORP. v. MORTON BUILDING, INC.

737 F.2d 698 (7th Cir.1984).

JUDGE POSNER: * * * The next question is whether Morton violated the per se rule against resale price maintenance. Several times each year Morton would advertise special deals for its buildings. The advertising was directed to the consuming public and mentioned special prices at which consumers could buy the buildings from dealers such as Walters, listing them by name. Morton gave dealers a discount from the wholesale price to make it easier for the dealers to offer consumers the special retail price that Morton had advertised. It was important to Morton that dealers not charge a higher price than the advertised price, because if they did Morton's advertising would lack credibility—indeed, would be deceptive and create ill will. So, according to Walters' affidavits, Morton took various steps to see that its dealers sold its buildings at no more than the advertised price. These steps included threatening the dealers with termination if they went above that price, offering if they did to sell directly to the public at the advertised price, and checking up on the dealers to see whether they were charging more. . . .

* * *

. . . If it is lawful to advertise a retail price, it should be lawful to take at least the minimum steps necessary to make that advertising beneficial. It would be pretty embarrassing for a manufacturer who had advertised a special retail price to be bombarded by complaints from consumers that dealers were refusing to sell to them at that price. Such refusals would make the advertising misleading and might even expose the manufacturer to legal sanctions under the Federal Trade Commission Act or counterpart state regulations. So if retail price advertising by manufacturers is to be feasible the manufacturer must be allowed to take reasonable measures to make sure the advertised price is not exceeded. These measures include trying to persuade dealers to adhere to the advertised price and checking around to make sure they are adhering. These are the respects in which Morton is alleged to have gone beyond the simple announcement of policy and refusal to deal with noncompliers that would be permissible even if it were trying to get its dealers to adhere to its suggested retail prices across the board. See *Monsanto Co. v. Spray-Rite Service Corp.*, 104 S.Ct. at 1469. They are the minimum steps that Morton had to take if its advertised price was to have any value at all, and they are therefore lawful. . . .

* * *

Even if what Morton did was price fixing, Walters could not challenge it. A private plaintiff can complain only of an antitrust injury. *Brunswick Corp. v. Pueblo Bowl-O-Mat, Inc.*, 429 U.S. 477, 489 (1977). It is not enough that the plaintiff would not have been injured but for the defendant's alleged violation of the antitrust laws; the injury must be the sort of thing that the antitrust laws are intended to forbid. The plaintiff in *Brunswick* was complaining that the defendant's acquisition of a rival would enable the rival to become a more efficient company, and therefore a more effective competitor of the plaintiff. The Supreme Court held that the plaintiff could not complain about the injury. It would have been different if the complaint was that the acquisition would lead to the rival's engaging in predatory pricing or some other method of competition with the plaintiff that the antitrust laws are intended to prevent.

There is nothing esoteric about the *Brunswick* rule. It is the application to antitrust law of venerable principles of tort causation. . . . Walters will not be heard to complain about having to meet lawful price competition, which antitrust law seeks to encourage, merely because the competition may have been enabled by an antitrust violation. . . .

* * *

After *Brunswick* (as interpreted by Judge Posner), is there either no maximum price fixing violation or no private remedy for the wrong? Consider *Matsushita*, supra p. 468, in light of the standing concepts we have been discussing. If the Japanese producers of electronics products were engaged in a low-price conspiracy, did the Americans have standing to complain? Is there any merit in the argument that if Congress made particular conduct illegal it must have meant for those most directly and predictably harmed to sue? With the *Jack Walters* excerpt, compare *USA Petroleum Co.* v. *Atlantic Richfield Co., supra,* p. 599 in which the court was very critical of the *Jack Walters* opinion.

4. TERRITORIAL, CUSTOMER AND LIKE RESTRICTIONS

Thus far we have focused on efforts by upstream firms to control downstream pricing. Suppose the upstream firm, instead, restricts the territories in which or customers to whom its distributors or dealers may sell. Despite *Dr. Miles,* the McGuire Act and state fair trade legislation facilitated RPM during the 1930s and 1940s. When state legislatures began to repeal these laws and state courts began to invalidate them, manufacturers began to think of other ways to moderate intrabrand competition. Territorial and customer restrictions were possible substitutes. If a manufacturer authorized one dealer to resell only in New York, another only in Connecticut, another only in Pennsylvania, and so forth, the impact on downstream competition would be much the same as if the manufacturer had used RPM. Indeed it could be more severe. Except to the extent that buyers were mobile, all resale competition in the manufacturer's brand could be ended.

As territorial, customer, and related restraints became more common their legality became the subject of speculation. Most antitrust lawyers saw grave antitrust risks in their use. Case analysis pointed that way. If the per se rule prohibited horizontal price fixing, horizontal territorial divisions, and vertical price restraints, it was hard to see why it would not also govern vertical territorial restraints. See, e.g., Rifkind, Division of Territories, in Van Cise & Dunn, eds., How to Comply with the Antitrust Laws (1954). Moreover, territorial restraints threatened to bring about many of the same economic and social harms as did RPM. To the extent that the concern underlying the ban on RPM was dealer independence, a value stressed in *Dr. Miles,* certainly the effects of territorial and customer restraints were as serious as those of price restraints. To the extent that the concern was competitive price, quality and service, freeing downstream firms from all intrabrand competition would surely be at least as baneful as freeing them from price competition only.

Moreover, territorial and customer restraints could arise from dealer pressure just as RPM could, thus inviting dealer cartels. And if used by most competing manufacturers, these restraints, like RPM, might facilitate producer cartelization (sometimes reflected by soft, administered or cooperative price setting).

For all of these reasons it was no surprise when in 1949 the Department of Justice took the position that vertical territorial and customer restraints were per se unlawful. Indeed, when the Department brought a series of enforcement proceedings under Section 1 of the Sherman Act seeking to enjoin such restraints, it initially faced little resistance. Several cases were settled by consent decrees which forbade territorial or customer restraints but allowed manufacturers to designate areas for which each dealer would be primarily responsible. That was the state of things when White Motor Company, one of the targets in the Department's enforcement program, decided to resist. Its case reached the Supreme Court.

WHITE MOTOR CO. v. UNITED STATES
372 U.S. 253 (1963).

JUSTICE DOUGLAS: [White Motor Company manufactured trucks and sold them to distributors, dealers, and certain large users. It limited the territories within which and the customers to whom its distributors and dealers could sell, and it restricted certain resale prices. The government sued to enjoin the restrictions, and it moved for summary judgment, which the district court granted. White Motor appealed from the ruling regarding customer and territorial restraints.]

* * *

Appellant, in arguing for a trial of the case on the merits, made the following representations to the District Court: the territorial clauses are necessary in order for appellant to compete with those who make other competitory kinds of trucks; appellant could theoretically have its own retail outlets throughout the country and sell to users directly; that method, however, is not feasible as it entails a costly and extensive sales organization; the only feasible method is the distributor or dealer system; for that system to be effective against the existing competition of the larger companies, a distributor or dealer must make vigorous and intensive efforts in a restricted territory, and if he is to be held responsible for energetic performance, it is fair, reasonable, and necessary that appellant protect him against invasions of his territory by other distributors or dealers of appellant; that appellant in order to obtain maximum sales in a given area must insist that its distributors and dealers concentrate on trying to take sales away from other competing truck manufacturers rather than from each other. Appellant went on to say:

> "The plain fact is, as we expect to be able to show to the satisfaction of the Court at a trial of this case on the merits, that the outlawing of exclusive distributorships and dealerships in specified territories would reduce competition in the sale of motor trucks and not foster such competition."

As to the customer clauses, appellant represented to the District Court that one of their purposes was to assure appellant "that 'national accounts,' 'fleet accounts' and Federal and State governments and departments and political subdivisions thereof, which are classes of customers with respect to which the defendant is in especially severe competition with the manufacturers of other makes of trucks and which are likely to have a continuing volume of orders to place, shall not be deprived of their appropriate discounts on their purchases of repair parts and accessories from any distributor or dealer, with the result of becoming discontented with The White Motor Company and the treatment they receive with reference to the prices of repair parts and accessories for White trucks."

The agreements fixing prices of parts and accessories to these customers were, according to appellant, only an adjunct to the customer restriction clauses and amounted merely to an agreement to give these classes of customers their proper discounts. ". . . The provisions are necessary if the defendant's future sales to 'National Accounts,' 'Fleet Accounts' and Federal and State governments and departments and political subdivisions thereof, in competition with other truck manufacturers, are not to be seriously jeopardized."

* * *

In this Court appellant defends the customer clauses on the ground that "the only sure way to make certain that something really important is done right, is to do it for oneself. The size of the orders, the technicalities of bidding and delivery, and other factors all play a part in this decision."

* * *

As already stated, there was price fixing here and that part of the injunction issued by the District Court is not now challenged. In any price-fixing case restrictive practices ancillary to the price-fixing scheme are also quite properly restrained. . . . No such finding was made in this case; and whether or not the facts would permit one we do not stop to inquire.

* * *

We are asked to extend the holding in *Timken Roller Bearing Co. v. United States* (which banned *horizontal* arrangements among competitors to divide territory), to a *vertical* arrangement by one manufacturer restricting the territory of his distributors or dealers. We intimate no view one way or the other on the legality of such an arrangement, for we believe that the applicable rule of law should be designed after a trial.

This is the first case involving a territorial restriction in a *vertical* arrangement; and we know too little of the actual impact of both that restriction and the one respecting customers to reach a conclusion on the bare bones of the documentary evidence before us.

* * *

Horizontal territorial limitations, like "[g]roup boycotts, or concerted refusals by traders to deal with other traders" (*Klor's v. Broadway–Hale Stores [supra* p. 394]), are naked restraints of trade with no purpose except stifling of competition. A vertical territorial limitation may or may not have that purpose or effect. We do not know enough of the economic and business stuff out of which these arrangements emerge to be certain. They may be too dangerous to sanction or they may be allowable protections against aggressive competitors or the only practicable means a small company has for breaking into or staying in business and within the "rule of reason." We need to know more than we do about the actual impact of these arrangements on competition to decide whether they have such a "pernicious effect on competition and lack . . . any redeeming virtue" and therefore should be classified as *per se* violations of the Sherman Act.

* * *

Justice White took no part in the decision. Justice Brennan concurred, distinguishing territorial restraints from resale price maintenance. He believed that White Motor's territorial restraints could have a procompetitive justification, but would want to be sure that even justifiable restraints were not "more restrictive than necessary, or excessively anticompetitive, when viewed in the light of the [manufacturer's] extenuating interests." Id. at 264, 270. Justice Brennan viewed the customer restraints as inherently anticompetitive and saw no countervailing benefits.

Justice Clark, with whom Chief Justice Warren and Justice Black joined, dissented. The restraints, he said, had no purpose except to eliminate competition and should be illegal per se.

Upon remand, White Motor's resistance collapsed. It signed a consent decree in the form that had become standard. Four years later the Court had another opportunity to consider the issue, this time after trial.

Arnold, Schwinn and Company was a major manufacturer of bicycles. In 1951 it was the largest seller in the United States bicycle market, accounting for 22.5% of sales. In the next 10 years, its market share fell to 12.8%. Importers, and mass marketers carrying private label brands, had eroded its share and were powerful competitors.

Schwinn sold about 75% of its bicycles directly to retailers under an agency or consignment plan. It sold the rest to distributors. Each of its 22 distributors was the exclusive wholesaler within an assigned territory. Each was forbidden to sell outside of its territory, and within its territory could sell only to retailers franchised by Schwinn. These franchised retailers could sell only at designated locations. They could sell only to consumers, not to nonfranchised retailers, and thus not to discounters.

The Department of Justice brought suit. After trial, the district court held illegal and enjoined only the territorial limitations imposed on distributors to whom Schwinn sold the bicycles. On appeal to the Supreme Court the government abandoned its previously asserted per se theory. It asked the Court to hold that the territorial restrictions on distributors were unreasonable under the circumstances of the case, whether incident to consignment or sale; that confinement of distributors to franchised retailers was unreasonable; and that provisions preventing franchised retailers from supplying nonfranchised retailers were also unreasonable.

The Supreme Court reversed in material part. Regarding territorial restraints, the Court drew a line between sale and consignment. Restraints regarding *consigned* bicycles were judged under the rule of reason; these restraints were deemed reasonable in view of intense competition from mass merchandisers. By contrast, all post-sale restraints on distributors and retailers were held illegal per se. The Court said:

As the District Court held, where a manufacturer *sells* products to his distributor subject to territorial restrictions upon resale, a per se violation of the Sherman Act results. And, as we have held, the same principle applies to restrictions of outlets with which the distributors may deal and to restraints upon retailers to whom the goods are sold. Under the Sherman Act, it is unreasonable without more for a manufacturer to seek to restrict and confine areas or persons with whom an article may be traded after the manufacturer has parted with dominion over it. *White Motor,* supra; *Dr. Miles,* supra. Such restraints are so obviously destructive of competition that their mere existence is enough. If the manufacturer parts with dominion over his product or transfers risk of loss to another, he may not reserve control over its destiny or the conditions of its resale. To permit this would sanction franchising and confinement of distribution as the ordinary instead of the unusual method which may be permissible in an appropriate and impelling competitive setting, since most merchandise is distributed by means of purchase and sale. On the other hand, as indicated in *White Motor,* we are not prepared to introduce the inflexibility which a per se rule might bring if it were applied to prohibit all vertical restrictions of territory and all franchising, in the sense of designating specified distributors and retailers as the chosen instruments through which the manufacturer, retaining ownership of the goods, will distribute them to the public. Such a rule might severely hamper smaller enterprises resorting to reasonable methods of meeting the competition of giants and of merchandising through independent dealers, and it might sharply accelerate the trend towards vertical integration of the distribution process. But to allow this freedom where the manufacturer has parted with dominion over the goods—the usual marketing situation—would violate the ancient rule against restraints on alienation and open the door to exclusivity of outlets and limitation of territory further than prudence permits.

388 U.S. at 379–80.

For the next 10 years there was much debate about the merits and demerits of the per se rule of *Schwinn.* On the one hand, the rule was clear and easy to apply; it was an effective deterrent; it facilitated compliance and it eased the litigation process. Substantively, it protected the freedom of the reseller to sell where and to whom it chose, thus facilitating intrabrand competition, producing a variety of price/service packages, and derivatively putting pressure on interbrand competition by adding intrabrand competitive activity to the field.

But another possible effect cut in the other direction—the effect of the free rider. By protecting Schwinn dealers from the competition of other Schwinn dealers, Schwinn could encourage promotion and service at the point of sale. But without intrabrand restraints, "shoe string" dealers might free ride on their fellow dealers' investments, filling the demand primed by the loyal service providers. Having lower costs, the no-frills operations could discount their product, capturing market share at the expense of the service providers. The service providers would soon understand that they do not reap the benefits of their investment in service and promotion; they will cut back their investment, and the manufacturer will lose image, reputation and sales. As we noted in connection with RPM, there are ways in which manufacturers can minimize the free rider problem. For example, the manufacturer could pay for promotion and the retailer could charge for post-sale service. Moreover, there is much dispute as to whether the possibility of a free rider effect seriously impairs incentives of nondiscounters to make optimal investments in service. But Chicagoans and others assume the free riding effect is both dominant and serious. Accordingly they argue that when a manufacturer unilaterally imposes a vertical restraint, the manufacturer's interest is the consumers' interest (since the manufacturer has no interest in giving extra profits to the dealer and can unilaterally exact on a first sale whatever price its power confers); therefore if a manufacturer imposes a customer or territorial restraint, its purpose must be to distribute its product more efficiently by protecting against the free rider effect.

As time went on, the free rider argument became more familiar and criticism of *Schwinn* became more widespread. This argument seemed increasingly plausible as—in the 1970s—U.S. firms lost market power and market share to foreign competitors. If firms using vertical restraints had no market power, they must have been using the restraints to be more efficient rather than to exploit, or so it was said. This was the context of debate and discussion when the *Schwinn* issue came before the Supreme Court once again in *Continental T.V., Inc. v. GTE Sylvania Inc.*

CONTINENTAL T.V., INC. v. GTE SYLVANIA INC.

433 U.S. 36 (1977).

JUSTICE POWELL: * * * Respondent GTE Sylvania, Inc. (Sylvania) manufactures and sells television sets through its Home Entertainment Products Division. Prior to 1962, like most other television manufacturers, Sylvania sold its televisions to independent or company-owned distributors who in turn resold to a large and diverse group of retailers. Prompted by a decline in its market share to a relatively insignificant 1% to 2% of national television sales,[1] Sylvania conducted an intensive reassessment of its marketing strategy, and in 1962 adopted the franchise plan challenged here. Sylvania phased out its wholesale distributors and began to sell its televisions directly to a smaller and more select group of franchised retailers. An acknowledged purpose of the change was to decrease the number of competing Sylvania retailers in the hope of attracting the more aggressive and competent retailers thought necessary to the improvement of the company's market position. To this end, Sylvania limited the number of franchises granted for any given area and required each franchisee to sell his Sylvania products only from the location or locations at which he was franchised.[3] A franchise did not constitute an exclusive territory, and Sylvania retained sole discretion to increase the number of retailers in an area in light of the success or failure of existing retailers in developing their market. The revised marketing strategy appears to have been successful during the period at issue here, for by 1965 Sylvania's share of national television sales had

---

1. RCA at that time was the dominant firm with as much as 60% to 70% of national television sales in an industry with more than 100 manufacturers.

3. Sylvania imposed no restrictions on the right of the franchisee to sell the products of competing manufacturers.

increased to approximately 5%, and the company ranked as the Nation's eighth largest manufacturer of color television sets.

This suit is the result of the rupture of a franchiser-franchisee relationship that had previously prospered under the revised Sylvania plan. Dissatisfied with its sales in the city of San Francisco,[4] Sylvania decided in the spring of 1965 to franchise Young Brothers, an established San Francisco retailer of televisions, as an additional San Francisco retailer. The proposed location of the new franchise was approximately a mile from a retail outlet operated by petitioner Continental T.V., Inc. (Continental), one of the most successful Sylvania franchisees. Continental protested that the location of the new franchise violated Sylvania's marketing policy, but Sylvania persisted in its plans. Continental then canceled a large Sylvania order and placed a large order with Phillips, one of Sylvania's competitors.

During this same period, Continental expressed a desire to open a store in Sacramento, Cal., a desire Sylvania attributed at least in part to Continental's displeasure over the Young Brothers decision. Sylvania believed that the Sacramento market was adequately served by the existing Sylvania retailers and denied the request.[6] In the face of this denial, Continental advised Sylvania in early September 1965, that it was in the process of moving Sylvania merchandise from its San Jose, Cal., warehouse to a new retail location that it had leased in Sacramento. Two weeks later, allegedly for unrelated reasons, Sylvania's credit department reduced Continental's credit line from $300,000 to $50,000. In response to the reduction in credit and the generally deteriorating relations with Sylvania, Continental withheld all payments owed to John P. Maguire & Co., Inc. (Maguire), the finance company that handled the credit arrangements between Sylvania and its retailers. Shortly thereafter, Sylvania terminated Continental's franchises, and Maguire filed this diversity action in the United States District Court for the Northern District of California seeking recovery of money owed and of secured merchandise held by Continental.

The antitrust issues before us originated in cross-claims brought by Continental against Sylvania and Maguire. Most important for our purposes was the claim that Sylvania had violated § 1 of the Sherman Act by entering into and enforcing franchise agreements that prohibited the sale of Sylvania products other than from specified locations. At the close of evidence in the jury trial of Continental's claims, Sylvania requested the District Court to instruct the jury that its location restriction was illegal only if it unreasonably restrained or suppressed competition. Relying on this Court's decision in *United States v. Arnold, Schwinn & Co.,* [388 U.S. 365 (1967)] the District Court rejected the proffered instruction in favor of the following one:

> "Therefore, if you find by a preponderance of the evidence that Sylvania entered into a contract, combination or conspiracy with one or more of its dealers pursuant to which Sylvania exercised dominion or control over

---

4. Sylvania's market share in San Francisco was approximately 2.5%—half its national and northern California average.

6. Sylvania had achieved exceptional results in Sacramento, where its market share exceeded 15% in 1965.

the products sold to the dealer, after having parted with title and risk to the products, you must find any effort thereafter to restrict outlets or store locations from which its dealers resold the merchandise which they had purchased from Sylvania to be a violation of Section 1 of the Sherman Act, regardless of the reasonableness of the location restrictions."

In answers to special interrogatories, the jury found that Sylvania had engaged "in a contract, combination or conspiracy in restraint of trade in violation of the antitrust laws with respect to location restrictions alone," and assessed Continental's damages at $591,506, which was trebled pursuant to 15 U.S.C. § 15 to produce an award of $1,774,515.

On appeal, the Court of Appeals for the Ninth Circuit, sitting en banc, reversed by a divided vote. 537 F.2d 980 (1976). The court acknowledged that there is language in *Schwinn* that could be read to support the District Court's instruction but concluded that *Schwinn* was distinguishable on several grounds. Contrasting the nature of the restrictions, their competitive impact, and the market shares of the franchisers in the two cases, the court concluded that Sylvania's location restriction had less potential for competitive harm than the restrictions invalidated in *Schwinn* and thus should be judged under the "rule of reason" rather than the *per se* rule stated in *Schwinn*. The court found support for its position in the policies of the Sherman Act and in the decisions of other federal courts involving nonprice vertical restrictions.[10]

We granted Continental's petition for certiorari to resolve this important question of antitrust law. 429 U.S. 893 (1976).

II

A

We turn first to Continental's contention that Sylvania's restriction on retail locations is a *per se* violation of § 1 of the Sherman Act as interpreted in *Schwinn*. . . .

[The Court in *Schwinn*] articulate[d] the following "bright line" *per se* rule of illegality for vertical restrictions: "Under the Sherman Act, it is unreasonable without more for a manufacturer to seek to restrict and confine areas or persons with whom an article may be traded after the manufacturer has parted with dominion over it." [388 U.S.] at 379. * * * The Court apparently perceived no material distinction between the restrictions on distributors and retailers, for it held:

"The principle is, of course, equally applicable to sales to retailers, and the decree should similarly enjoin the making of any sales to retailers upon any condition, agreement or understanding limiting the retailer's freedom as to where and to whom it will resell the products." *Id.*, at 378.

Applying the rule of reason to the restrictions that were not imposed in conjunction with the sale of bicycles, the Court had little difficulty finding

---

10. There were two major dissenting opinions. Judge Kilkenny argued that the present case is indistinguishable from *Schwinn* and that the jury had been correctly instructed. Agreeing with Judge Kilkenny's interpretation of *Schwinn*, Judge Browning stated that he found the interpretation responsive to and justified by the need to protect " 'individual traders from unnecessary restrictions upon their freedom of action.' "

them all reasonable in light of the competitive situation in "the product market as a whole." *Id.*, at 382.

B

In the present case, it is undisputed that title to the television sets passed from Sylvania to Continental. Thus, the *Schwinn per se* rule applies unless Sylvania's restriction on locations falls outside *Schwinn's* prohibition against a manufacturer's attempting to restrict a "retailer's freedom as to where and to whom it will resell the products." *Id.*, at 378. As the Court of Appeals conceded, the language of *Schwinn* is clearly broad enough to apply to the present case. Unlike the Court of Appeals, however, we are unable to find a principled basis for distinguishing *Schwinn* from the case now before us.

Both Schwinn and Sylvania sought to reduce but not to eliminate competition among their respective retailers through the adoption of a franchise system. Although it was not one of the issues addressed by the District Court or presented on appeal by the Government, the Schwinn franchise plan included a location restriction similar to the one challenged here. These restrictions allowed Schwinn and Sylvania to regulate the amount of competition among their retailers by preventing a franchisee from selling franchised products from outlets other than the one covered by the franchise agreement. To exactly the same end, the Schwinn franchise plan included a companion restriction, apparently not found in the Sylvania plan, that prohibited franchised retailers from selling Schwinn products to nonfranchised retailers. In *Schwinn* the Court expressly held that this restriction was impermissible under the broad principle stated there. In intent and competitive impact, the retail-customer restriction in *Schwinn* is indistinguishable from the location restriction in the present case. In both cases the restrictions limited the freedom of the retailer to dispose of the purchased products as he desired. The fact that one restriction was addressed to territory and the other to customers is irrelevant to functional antitrust analysis and, indeed, to the language and broad thrust of the opinion in *Schwinn.* As Mr. Chief Justice Hughes stated in *Appalachian Coals, Inc. v. United States*, 288 U.S. 344, 360, 377 (1933): "Realities must dominate the judgment. . . . The Anti–Trust Act aims at substance."

III

Sylvania argues that if *Schwinn* cannot be distinguished, it should be reconsidered. Although *Schwinn* is supported by the principle of *stare decisis, Illinois Brick Co. v. Illinois*, 431 U.S. 720, 736 (1977), we are convinced that the need for clarification of the law in this area justifies reconsideration. *Schwinn* itself was an abrupt and largely unexplained departure from *White Motor Co. v. United States*, 372 U.S. 253 (1963), where only four years earlier the Court had refused to endorse a *per se* rule for vertical restrictions. Since its announcement, *Schwinn* has been the subject of continuing controversy and confusion, both in the scholarly journals and in the federal courts. The great weight of scholarly opinion has been critical of the decision, and a number of the federal courts confronted with analogous vertical restrictions have sought to limit its reach. . . .

The traditional framework of analysis under § 1 of the Sherman Act is familiar and does not require extended discussion. Section 1 prohibits "[e]very contract, combination . . ., or conspiracy, in restraint of trade or commerce." Since the early years of this century a judicial gloss on this statutory language has established the "rule of reason" as the prevailing standard of analysis. *Standard Oil Co. v. United States*, 221 U.S. 1 (1911). Under this rule, the factfinder weighs all of the circumstances of a case in deciding whether a restrictive practice should be prohibited as imposing an unreasonable restraint on competition. *Per se* rules of illegality are appropriate only when they relate to conduct that is manifestly anticompetitive. As the Court explained in *Northern Pac. R. Co. v. United States*, 356 U.S. 1, 5 (1958), "there are certain agreements or practices which because of their pernicious effect on competition and lack of any redeeming virtue are conclusively presumed to be unreasonable and therefore illegal without elaborate inquiry as to the precise harm they have caused or the business excuse for their use."[16]

In essence, the issue before us is whether *Schwinn's per se* rule can be justified under the demanding standards of *Northern Pac. R. Co.* The Court's refusal to endorse a *per se* rule in *White Motor Co.* was based on its uncertainty as to whether vertical restrictions satisfied those standards. Addressing this question for the first time, the Court stated:

> "We need to know more than we do about the actual impact of these arrangements on competition to decide whether they have such a 'pernicious effect on competition and lack . . . any redeeming virtue' (*Northern Pac. R. Co. v. United States*, [*infra*, p. 664]) and therefore should be classified as *per se* violations of the Sherman Act." 372 U.S., at 263.

Only four years later the Court in *Schwinn* announced its sweeping *per se* rule without even a reference to *Northern Pac. R. Co.* and with no explanation of its sudden change in position. We turn now to consider *Schwinn* in light of *Northern Pac. R. Co.*

The market impact of vertical restrictions [18] is complex because of their potential for a simultaneous reduction of intrabrand competition

---

16. *Per se* rules thus require the Court to make broad generalizations about the social utility of particular commercial practices. The probability that anticompetitive consequences will result from a practice and the severity of those consequences must be balanced against its pro-competitive consequences. Cases that do not fit the generalization may arise, but a *per se* rule reflects the judgment that such cases are not sufficiently common or important to justify the time and expense necessary to identify them. Once established, *per se* rules tend to provide guidance to the business community and to minimize the burdens on litigants and the judicial system of the more complex rule-of-reason trials, see *Northern Pac. R. Co. v. United States*, 356 U.S., at 5; *United States v. Topco Associates, Inc.*, 405 U.S. 596, 609–

610 (1972), but those advantages are not sufficient in themselves to justify the creation of *per se* rules. If it were otherwise, all of antitrust law would be reduced to *per se* rules, thus introducing an unintended and undesirable rigidity in the law.

18. As in *Schwinn*, we are concerned here only with nonprice vertical restrictions. The *per se* illegality of price restrictions has been established firmly for many years and involves significantly different questions of analysis and policy. As Mr. Justice White notes, *post*, some commentators have argued that the manufacturer's motivation for imposing vertical price restrictions may be the same as for nonprice restrictions. There are, however, significant differences that could easily justify different treatment. In

and stimulation of interbrand competition.[19] Significantly, the Court in *Schwinn* did not distinguish among the challenged restrictions on the basis of their individual potential for intrabrand harm or interbrand benefit. Restrictions that completely eliminated intrabrand competition among Schwinn distributors were analyzed no differently from those that merely moderated intrabrand competition among retailers. The pivotal factor was the passage of title: All restrictions were held to be *per se* illegal where title had passed, and all were evaluated and sustained under the rule of reason where it had not. The location restriction at issue here would be subject to the same pattern of analysis under *Schwinn*.

It appears that this distinction between sale and nonsale transactions resulted from the Court's effort to accommodate the perceived intrabrand harm and interbrand benefit of vertical restrictions. The *per se* rule for sale transactions reflected the view that vertical restrictions are "so obviously destructive" of intrabrand competition that their use would "open the door to exclusivity of outlets and limitation of territory further than prudence permits." 388 U.S., at 379–380.[21] Conversely, the contin-

his concurring opinion in *White Motor Co. v. United States*, Mr. Justice Brennan noted that, unlike nonprice restrictions, "[r]esale price maintenance is not only designed to, but almost invariably does in fact, reduce price competition not only *among* sellers of the affected product, but quite as much *between* that product and competing brands." 372 U.S., at 268. Professor Posner also recognized that "industry-wide resale price maintenance might facilitate cartelizing." Posner [Antitrust Policy and the Supreme Court: An Analysis of the Restricted Distribution, Horizontal Merger and Potential Competition Decisions, 75 Colum.L.Rev. 282, 294 (1975)] (footnote omitted). . . . Furthermore, Congress recently has expressed its approval of a *per se* analysis of vertical price restrictions by repealing those provisions of the Miller–Tydings and McGuire Acts allowing fair-trade pricing at the option of the individual States. Consumer Goods Pricing Act of 1975, 89 Stat. 801, amending 15 U.S.C. §§ 1, 45(a). No similar expression of congressional intent exists for nonprice restrictions.

19. Interbrand competition is the competition among the manufacturers of the same generic product—television sets in this case—and is the primary concern of antitrust law. The extreme example of a deficiency of interbrand competition is monopoly, where there is only one manufacturer. In contrast, intrabrand competition is the competition between the distributors— wholesale or retail—of the product of a particular manufacturer.

The degree of intrabrand competition is wholly independent of the level of interbrand competition confronting the manufacturer. Thus, there may be fierce intrabrand competition among the distributors of a product produced by a monopolist and no intrabrand competition among the distributors of a product produced by a firm in a highly competitive industry. But when interbrand competition exists, as it does among television manufacturers, it provides a significant check on the exploitation of intrabrand market power because of the ability of consumers to substitute a different brand of the same product.

21. The Court also stated that to impose vertical restrictions in sale transactions would "violate the ancient rule against restraints on alienation." 388 U.S., at 380. This isolated reference has provoked sharp criticism from virtually all of the commentators on the decision, most of whom have regarded the Court's apparent reliance on the "ancient rule" as both a misreading of legal history and a perversion of antitrust analysis. We quite agree with Mr. Justice Stewart's dissenting comment in *Schwinn* that "the state of the common law 400 or even 100 years ago is irrelevant to the issue before us: the effect of the antitrust laws upon vertical distributional restraints in the American economy today." 388 U.S., at 392.

We are similarly unable to accept Judge Browning's interpretation of *Schwinn*. In his dissent below he argued that the decision reflects the view that the Sherman Act was intended to prohibit restrictions on the autonomy of independent businessmen even though they have no impact on "price, quality, and quantity of goods and services," 537 F.2d, at 1019. This view is certainly not explicit in *Schwinn*, which purports to be based on an examination of the "impact [of the restrictions] upon the marketplace." 388 U.S., at 374. Competitive economies have social and political as well as economic advantages, see *e.g.*, *Northern Pac. R. Co. v.*

ued adherence to the traditional rule of reason for nonsale transactions reflected the view that the restrictions have too great a potential for the promotion of interbrand competition to justify complete prohibition. The Court's opinion provides no analytical support for these contrasting positions. . . .

Vertical restrictions reduce intrabrand competition by limiting the number of sellers of a particular product competing for the business of a given group of buyers. Location restrictions have this effect because of practical constraints on the effective marketing area of retail outlets. Although intrabrand competition may be reduced, the ability of retailers to exploit the resulting market may be limited both by the ability of consumers to travel to other franchised locations and, perhaps more importantly, to purchase the competing products of other manufacturers. None of these key variables, however, is affected by the form of the transaction by which a manufacturer conveys his products to the retailers.

Vertical restrictions promote interbrand competition by allowing the manufacturer to achieve certain efficiencies in the distribution of his products. These "redeeming virtues" are implicit in every decision sustaining vertical restrictions under the rule of reason. Economists have identified a number of ways in which manufacturers can use such restrictions to compete more effectively against other manufacturers. . . .[23] For example, new manufacturers and manufacturers entering new markets can use the restrictions in order to induce competent and aggressive retailers to make the kind of investment of capital and labor that is often required in the distribution of products unknown to the consumer. Established manufacturers can use them to induce retailers to engage in promotional activities or to provide service and repair facilities necessary to the efficient marketing of their products. Service and repair are vital for many products, such as automobiles and major household appliances. The availability and quality of such services affect a manufacturer's goodwill and the competitiveness of his product. Because of market imperfections such as the so-called "free rider" effect, these services might not be provided by retailers in a purely competitive situation, despite the fact that each retailer's benefit would be greater if all provided the services than if none did.

United States, 356 U.S., at 4, but an antitrust policy divorced from market considerations would lack any objective benchmarks. As Mr. Justice Brandeis reminded us: "Every agreement concerning trade, every regulation of trade, restrains. To bind, to restrain, is of their very essence." *Chicago Bd. of Trade v. United States,* 246 U.S., at 238. Although Mr. Justice White's opinion endorses Judge Browning's interpretation, *post,* it purports to distinguish *Schwinn* on grounds inconsistent with that interpretation. . . .

23. Marketing efficiency is not the only legitimate reason for a manufacturer's desire to exert control over the manner in which his products are sold and serviced. As a result of statutory and common-law developments, society increasingly demands that manufacturers assume direct responsibility for the safety and quality of their products. For example, at the federal level, apart from more specialized requirements, manufacturers of consumer products have safety responsibilities under the Consumer Product Safety Act, 15 U.S.C. § 2051 *et seq.* (1970 ed., Supp. V), and obligations for warranties under the Consumer Product Warranties Act, 15 U.S.C. § 2301 *et seq.* (1970 ed., Supp. V). Similar obligations are imposed by state law. *See, e.g.,* Cal.Civ.Code Ann. § 1790 *et seq.* (West 1973). The legitimacy of these concerns has been recognized in cases involving vertical restrictions. *See, e.g., Tripoli Co. v. Wella Corp.,* 425 F.2d 932 (CA3 1970).

Economists also have argued that manufacturers have an economic interest in maintaining as much intrabrand competition as is consistent with the efficient distribution of their products. Bork, The Rule of Reason and the Per Se Concept: Price Fixing and Market Division [II], 75 Yale L.J. 373, 403 (1966); Posner, *supra*, n. [18], at 283, 287–288.[24] Although the view that the manufacturer's interest necessarily corresponds with that of the public is not universally shared, even the leading critic of vertical restrictions concedes that *Schwinn*'s distinction between sale and nonsale transactions is essentially unrelated to any relevant economic impact. Comanor, Vertical Territorial and Customer Restrictions: White Motor and Its Aftermath, 81 Harv.L.Rev. 1419, 1422 (1968).[25] Indeed, to the extent that the form of the transaction is related to interbrand benefits, the Court's distinction is inconsistent with its articulated concern for the ability of smaller firms to compete effectively with larger ones. Capital requirements and administrative expenses may prevent smaller firms from using the exception for nonsale transactions.

We conclude that the distinction drawn in *Schwinn* between sale and nonsale transactions is not sufficient to justify the application of a *per se* rule in one situation and a rule of reason in the other. The question remains whether the *per se* rule stated in *Schwinn* should be expanded to include nonsale transactions or abandoned in favor of a return to the rule of reason. We have found no persuasive support for expanding the *per se* rule. . . .

We revert to the standard articulated in *Northern Pac. R. Co.*, and reiterated in *White Motor,* for determining whether vertical restrictions must be "conclusively presumed to be unreasonable and therefore illegal without elaborate inquiry as to the precise harm they have caused or the business excuse for their use." 356 U.S., at 5. Such restrictions, in varying forms, are widely used in our free market economy. As indicated above, there is substantial scholarly and judicial authority supporting their economic utility. There is relatively little authority to the contrary.[28] Certainly, there has been no showing in this case, either generally or with respect to Sylvania's agreements, that vertical restrictions have or are likely to have a "pernicious effect on competition" or that they "lack

24. "Generally a manufacturer would prefer the lowest retail price possible, once its price to dealers has been set, because a lower retail price means increased sales and higher manufacturer revenues." Note, 88 Harv.L.Rev. 636, 641 (1975). In this context, a manufacturer is likely to view the difference between the price at which it sells to its retailers and their price to the consumer as its "cost of distribution," which it would prefer to minimize. Posner, *supra*, n. [18], at 283.

25. Professor Comanor argues that the promotional activities encouraged by vertical restrictions result in product differentiation and, therefore, a decrease in interbrand competition. This argument is flawed by its necessary assumption that a large part of

the promotional efforts resulting from vertical restrictions will not convey socially desirable information about product availability, price, quality, and services. Nor is it clear that a *per se* rule would result in anything more than a shift to less efficient methods of obtaining the same promotional effects.

28. There may be occasional problems in differentiating vertical restrictions from horizontal restrictions originating in agreements among the retailers. There is no doubt that restrictions in the latter category would be illegal *per se, see, e.g., United States v. General Motors Corp.,* 384 U.S. 127 (1966); *United States v. Topco Associates, Inc.,* [405 U.S. 596 (1972)], but we do not regard the problems of proof as sufficiently great to justify a *per se* rule.

. . . any redeeming virtue." *Ibid.*[29] Accordingly, we conclude that the *per se* rule stated in *Schwinn* must be overruled. In so holding we do not foreclose the possibility that particular applications of vertical restrictions might justify *per se* prohibition under *Northern Pac. R. Co.* But we do make clear that departure from the rule-of-reason standard must be based upon demonstrable economic effect rather than—as in *Schwinn*—upon formalistic line drawing.

In sum, we conclude that the appropriate decision is to return to the rule of reason that governed vertical restrictions prior to *Schwinn*. When anticompetitive effects are shown to result from particular vertical restrictions they can be adequately policed under the rule of reason, the standard traditionally applied for the majority of anticompetitive practices challenged under § 1 of the Act. Accordingly, the decision of the Court of Appeals is *affirmed*.

JUSTICE REHNQUIST took no part in the decision of this case.

JUSTICE WHITE, concurring in the judgment.

Although I agree with the majority that the location clause at issue in this case is not a *per se* violation of the Sherman Act and should be judged under the rule of reason, I cannot agree that this result requires the overruling of *United States v. Arnold, Schwinn & Co.*, 388 U.S. 365 (1967). In my view this case is distinguishable from *Schwinn* because there is less potential for restraint of intrabrand competition and more potential for stimulating interbrand competition. As to intrabrand competition, Sylvania, unlike Schwinn, did not restrict the customers to whom or the territories where its purchasers could sell. As to interbrand competition, Sylvania, unlike Schwinn, had an insignificant market share at the time it adopted its challenged distribution practice and enjoyed no consumer preference that would allow its retailers to charge a premium over other brands. In two short paragraphs, the majority disposes of the view, adopted after careful analysis by the Ninth Circuit en banc below, that these differences provide a "principled basis for distinguishing *Schwinn*," despite holdings by three Courts of Appeals and the District Court on remand in *Schwinn* that the *per se* rule established in that case does not apply to location clauses such as Sylvania's. To reach out to overrule one of this Court's recent interpretations of the Sherman Act, after such a cursory examination of the necessity for doing so, is surely an affront to the principle that considerations of *stare decisis* are to be given particularly strong weight in the area of statutory construction. *Illinois Brick Co. v. Illinois*, 431 U.S. 720, 736–737 (1977). . . .

One element of the system of interrelated vertical restraints invalidated in *Schwinn* was a retail-customer restriction prohibiting franchised

---

29. The location restriction used by Sylvania was neither the least nor the most restrictive provision that it could have used. But we agree with the implicit judgment in *Schwinn* that a *per se* rule based on the nature of the restriction is, in general, undesirable. Although distinctions can be drawn among the frequently used restrictions, we are inclined to view them as differences of degree and form. We are unable to perceive significant social gain from channeling transactions into one form or another. Finally, we agree with the Court in *Schwinn* that the advantages of vertical restrictions should not be limited to the categories of new entrants and failing firms. Sylvania was faltering, if not failing, and we think it would be unduly artificial to deny it the use of valuable competitive tools.

retailers from selling Schwinn products to nonfranchised retailers. The Court rests its inability to distinguish *Schwinn* entirely on this retail-customer restriction, finding it "[i]n intent and competitive impact . . . indistinguishable from the location restriction in the present case," because "[i]n both cases the restrictions limited the freedom of the retailer to dispose of the purchased products as he desired." The customer restriction may well have, however, a very different "intent and competitive impact" than the location restriction: It prevents discount stores from getting the manufacturer's product and thus prevents intrabrand price competition. Suppose, for example, that interbrand competition is sufficiently weak that the franchised retailers are able to charge a price substantially above wholesale. Under a location restriction, these franchisers are free to sell to discount stores seeking to exploit the potential for sales at prices below the prevailing retail level. One of the franchised retailers may be tempted to lower its price and act in effect as a wholesaler for the discount house in order to share in the profits to be had from lowering prices and expanding volume.

Under a retail customer restriction, on the other hand, the franchised dealers cannot sell to discounters, who are cut off altogether from the manufacturer's product and the opportunity for intrabrand price competition. This was precisely the theory on which the Government successfully challenged Schwinn's customer restrictions in this Court. The District Court in that case found that "[e]ach one of [Schwinn's franchised retailers] knows also that he is not a wholesaler and that he cannot sell as a wholesaler or act as an agent for some other unfranchised dealer, such as a discount house retailer who has not been franchised as a dealer by Schwinn." 237 F.Supp. 323, 333 (ND Ill.1965). The Government argued on appeal, with extensive citations to the record, that the effect of this restriction was "to keep Schwinn products out of the hands of discount houses and other price cutters so as to discourage price competition in retailing. . . ."[2]

It is true that, as the majority states, Sylvania's location restriction inhibited to some degree "the freedom of the retailer to dispose of the purchased products" by requiring the retailer to sell from one particular place of business. But the retailer is still free to sell to any type of customer—including discounters and other unfranchised dealers—from any area. I think this freedom implies a significant difference for the effect of a location clause on intrabrand competition. . . .

An additional basis for finding less restraint of intrabrand competition in this case, emphasized by the Ninth Circuit en banc, is that *Schwinn* involved restrictions on competition among distributors at the wholesale level. . . .

2. Given the Government's emphasis on the inhibiting effect of the Schwinn restrictions on discounting activities, the Court may well have been referring to this effect when it condemned the restrictions as "obviously destructive of competition." 388 U.S., at 379. But the Court was also heavily influenced by its concern for the freedom of dealers to control the disposition of products they purchased from Schwinn. In any event the record in *Schwinn* illustrates the potentially greater threat to intrabrand competition posed by customer as opposed to location restrictions.

Moreover, like its franchised retailers, Schwinn's distributors were absolutely barred from selling to nonfranchised retailers, further limiting the possibilities of intrabrand price competition.

*   *   *

Just as there are significant differences between *Schwinn* and this case with respect to intrabrand competition, there are also significant differences with respect to interbrand competition. Unlike Schwinn, Sylvania clearly had no economic power in the generic product market. At the time they instituted their respective distribution policies, Schwinn was "the leading bicycle producer in the Nation," with a national market share of 22.5%, whereas Sylvania was a "faltering, if not failing" producer of television sets, with "a relatively insignificant 1% to 2%" share of the national market in which the dominant manufacturer had a 60% to 70% share. Moreover, the Schwinn brand name enjoyed superior consumer acceptance and commanded a premium price as, in the District Court's words, "the Cadillac of the bicycle industry." This premium gave Schwinn dealers a margin of protection from interbrand competition and created the possibilities for price cutting by discounters that the Government argued were forestalled by Schwinn's customer restrictions. Thus, judged by the criteria economists use to measure market power—product differentiation and market share—Schwinn enjoyed a substantially stronger position in the bicycle market than did Sylvania in the television market. This Court relied on Schwinn's market position as one reason not to apply the rule of reason to the vertical restraints challenged there. "Schwinn was not a newcomer, seeking to break into or stay in the bicycle business. It was not a 'failing company.' On the contrary, at the initiation of these practices, it was the leading bicycle producer in the Nation." 388 U.S., at 374. And the Court of Appeals below found "another significant distinction between our case and *Schwinn*" in Sylvania's "precarious market share," which "was so small when it adopted its location practice that it was threatened with expulsion from the television market."

In my view there are at least two considerations, both relied upon by the majority to justify overruling *Schwinn,* that would provide a "principled basis" for instead refusing to extend *Schwinn* to a vertical restraint that is imposed by a "faltering" manufacturer with a "precarious" position in a generic product market dominated by another firm. The first is that, as the majority puts it, "when interbrand competition exists, as it does among television manufacturers, it provides a significant check on the exploitation of intrabrand market power because of the ability of consumers to substitute a different brand of the same product." Second is the view, argued forcefully in the economic literature cited by the majority, that the potential benefits of vertical restraints in promoting interbrand competition are particularly strong where the manufacturer imposing the restraints is seeking to enter a new market or to expand a small market share. The majority even recognizes that *Schwinn* "hinted" at an exception for new entrants and failing firms from its *per se* rule.

In other areas of antitrust law, this Court has not hesitated to base its rules of *per se* illegality in part on the defendant's market power. . . . I see no doctrinal obstacle to excluding firms with such minimal market power as Sylvania's from the reach of the *Schwinn* rule.

I have, moreover, substantial misgivings about the approach the majority takes to overruling *Schwinn*. The reason for the distinction in *Schwinn* between sale and nonsale transactions was not, as the majority would have it, "the Court's effort to accommodate the perceived intrabrand harm and interbrand benefit of vertical restrictions"; the reason was rather, as Judge Browning argued in dissent below, the notion in many of our cases involving vertical restraints that independent businessmen should have the freedom to dispose of the goods they own as they see fit. Thus the first case cited by the Court in *Schwinn* for the proposition that "restraints upon alienation . . . are beyond the power of the manufacturer to impose upon its vendees and . . . are violations of § 1 of the Sherman Act," was this Court's seminal decision holding a series of resale-price-maintenance agreements *per se* illegal, *Dr. Miles Medical Co. v. John D. Park & Sons Co.,* 220 U.S. 373 (1911). In *Dr. Miles* the Court stated that "a general restraint upon alienation is ordinarily invalid," citing Coke on Littleton, and emphasized that the case involved "agreements restricting the freedom of trade on the part of dealers who own what they sell." . . .

This concern for the freedom of the businessman to dispose of his own goods as he sees fit is most probably the explanation for two subsequent cases in which the Court allowed manufacturers to achieve economic results similar to that in *Dr. Miles* where they did not impose restrictions on dealers who had purchased their products. [United States v. Colgate & Co., 250 U.S. 300 (1919); United States v. General Electric Co., 272 U.S. 476 (1926).] Although these two cases have been called into question by subsequent decisions, see *United States v. Parke, Davis & Co.,* 362 U.S. 29 (1960), and *Simpson v. Union Oil Co.,* 377 U.S. 13 (1964), their rationale runs through our case law in the area of distributional restraints. In *Kiefer–Stewart Co. v. Joseph E. Seagram & Sons,* 340 U.S. 211, 213 (1951), the Court held that an agreement to fix resale prices was *per se* illegal under § 1 because "such agreements, no less than those to fix minimum prices, cripple the freedom of traders and thereby restrain their ability to sell in accordance with their own judgment." Accord, *Albrecht v. Herald Co.,* 390 U.S. 145, 152 (1968).

After summarily rejecting this concern, reflected in our interpretations of the Sherman Act, for "the autonomy of independent businessmen," the majority not surprisingly finds "no justification" for *Schwinn* 's distinction between sale and nonsale transactions because the distinction is "essentially unrelated to any relevant economic impact." But while according some weight to the businessman's interest in controlling the terms on which he trades in his own goods may be anathema to those who view the Sherman Act as directed solely to economic efficiency,[9] this principle is without question more deeply embedded in our cases than the notions of "free rider" effects and distributional efficiencies borrowed by

9. *E.g.,* Bork, Legislative Intent and the Policy of the Sherman Act, 9 J. Law & Econ. 7 (1966); Bork, The Rule of Reason and the Per Se Concept: Price Fixing and Market Division [I], 74 Yale L.J. 775 (1965).

the majority from the "new economics of vertical relationships." Perhaps the Court is right in partially abandoning this principle and in judging the instant nonprice vertical restraints solely by their "relevant economic impact"; but the precedents which reflect this principle should not be so lightly rejected by the Court. The rationale of *Schwinn* is no doubt difficult to discern from the opinion, and it may be wrong; it is not, however, the aberration the majority makes it out to be here.

I have a further reservation about the majority's reliance on "relevant economic impact" as the test for retaining *per se* rules regarding vertical restraints. It is common ground among the leading advocates of a purely economic approach to the question of distribution restraints that the economic arguments in favor of allowing vertical nonprice restraints generally apply to vertical price restraints as well. Although the majority asserts that "the *per se* illegality of price restrictions . . . involves significantly different questions of analysis and policy," I suspect this purported distinction may be as difficult to justify as that of *Schwinn* under the terms of the majority's analysis. Thus Professor Posner, in an article cited five times by the majority, concludes: "I believe that the law should treat price and nonprice restrictions the same and that it should make no distinction between the imposition of restrictions in a sale contract and their imposition in an agency contract." Posner, *supra*, [Opinion of Court, n. 18], at 298. Indeed, the Court has already recognized that resale price maintenance may increase output by inducing "demand-creating activity" by dealers (such as additional retail outlets, advertising and promotion, and product servicing) that outweighs the additional sales that would result from lower prices brought about by dealer price competition. *Albrecht v. Herald Co., supra*, at 151 n. 7. These same output-enhancing possibilities of nonprice vertical restraints are relied upon by the majority as evidence of their social utility and economic soundness, and as a justification for judging them under the rule of reason. The effect, if not the intention, of the Court's opinion is necessarily to call into question the firmly established *per se* rule against price restraints.

* * *

In order to decide this case, the Court need only hold that a location clause imposed by a manufacturer with negligible economic power in the product market has a competitive impact sufficiently less restrictive than the *Schwinn* restraints to justify a rule-of-reason standard, even if the same weight is given here as in *Schwinn* to dealer autonomy. I therefore concur in the judgment.

Justice Brennan, with whom Justice Marshall joins, dissenting.

I would not overrule the *per se* rule stated in *United States v. Arnold, Schwinn & Co.*, 388 U.S. 365 (1967), and would therefore reverse the decision of the Court of Appeals for the Ninth Circuit.

Questions and Comments

Was the Court correct to uphold the location clauses? Should it have done so by overruling *Schwinn* or distinguishing *Schwinn?* If you were a Justice and wished to distinguish *Schwinn,* by what formulation would you do so? In deciding whether to follow, overrule or distinguish *Schwinn,* would you give any weight to stare decisis? Would you give play to your own notions of political economy? To your view of the best mix of competition, efficiency and the freedom of firms to pursue their own strategies? To what extent should your obligations as jurist constrain you?

Is there a tension, as Justice White suggests, between *Dr. Miles* and *Sylvania?* If the interest in facilitating efficient marketing strategies drives *Sylvania,* does the same interest undermine *Dr. Miles?* Can you reconcile retention of the per se ban on vertical price fixing with elimination of the per se ban on customer and territory restraints? Is Justice Powell's distinction the correct one? Did Justice Powell's distinction augur a narrowing of the circumstances in which conduct would be identified as concerted vertical price fixing? Was it a harbinger of the Court's opinion in *Monsanto?* In *Sharp?* (pp. 556 and 564, supra.)

Does the Court's opinion in *Sylvania* give any content or structure to the rule of reason that will henceforth be applicable? Do customer and territorial restraints, including location clauses, automatically count as restraints on competition that have to be offset by benefits to interbrand competition? What does the Court imply? What would Judge Posner argue? Is the question settled after *Sharp?*

On remand in *Sylvania,* the district court found that Sylvania's location clauses were reasonable as a matter of law. The Court of Appeals affirmed, holding that the plaintiff has the burden of proving that a non-price vertical restraint is unreasonable, given its overall effect on intrabrand and interbrand competition; proving an adverse intrabrand effect does not shift the burden of justification to defendant. Continental T.V., Inc. v. GTE Sylvania Inc., 694 F.2d 1132 (9th Cir.1982).

Questions and Comments

Do you agree that the procompetitive aspects of the restraint in *Sylvania* outbalanced the anticompetitive aspects? How would you strike the balance if Sylvania had used a tight territorial restraint? How would you strike the balance if the restraint was imposed in response to demands of competing dealers? If there was no free rider effect? If the market was highly concentrated?

Do you see the need for structure for the rule of reason? How would you structure a rule of reason: (1) If your only concern is to prevent output-limiting restraints in the interbrand market? (2) If you worry also about exploitation of consumers by producers and distributors of distinctive brands, and you believe that dealers' freedom of trade tends to produce a better deal for consumers?

To successfully challenge a nonprice vertical restriction, must plaintiff at least show that defendant has market power? Compare *Valley Liquors, Inc. v. Renfield Importers, Ltd.,* infra p. 622, 678 F.2d 742 (7th Cir.1982) (elimination of price discounting is not equivalent to harm to intrabrand competition) and *Oreck Corp. v. Whirlpool Corp.,* 579 F.2d 126 (2d Cir.1978), *cert. denied,* 439 U.S. 946 (1978) (plaintiff must prove an anticompetitive effect in market as a whole), with *Eiberger v. Sony Corp. of America,* 622 F.2d 1068 (2d Cir. 1980) (anticompetitive impact on intrabrand competition alone can support a finding of a violation; Sony's imposition of warranty fees for sales outside the territory was illegal where the fees bore no relationship to the provision of warranty services and their sole purpose was to enforce territorial and customer restrictions). Reason from *Sharp Electronics,* supra p. 564, *Indiana Federation of Dentists,* supra p. 405 and *Northwest Wholesale Stationers,* supra p. 401 as to whether proof of market power is a necessary element of plaintiff's case, and as to whether plaintiff must show an anticompetitive effect on interbrand competition.

When is a restraint a price restraint, and when is it merely a territorial restraint? When is a restraint horizontal, and when is it only vertical? If a restraint is intrabrand, it it necessarily vertical? If Mercedes Benz dealers get together and agree to stop making sales below the manufacturer's suggested price, is their agreement horizontal or vertical? What if one powerful dealer uses the manufacturer as "cat's paw" to prevent the other dealers from selling below list? See *United States v. General Motors Corp.,* 384 U.S. 127 (1966); *Klor's, Inc. v. Broadway–Hale Stores, Inc.,* 359 U.S. 207 (1959). Justice Scalia and Justice Stevens joined issue on these questions in *Sharp Electronics* (supra p. 564). Who had the better side of the argument?

Problem 1

In a new effort to improve a declining position in a market beset by Japanese competition, Zeno TV wishes to assign exclusive distributors to stated regions and to confine their sales to authorized retailers within each territory. Zeno's general counsel asks for your advice. Zeno is the leading American producer. Its share of U.S. sales is 8%. Is its plan lawful?

Zeno puts this plan into operation, pursuant to (or in spite of) your advice. Some of its exclusive distributors make slow and incomplete deliveries of Zeno TV sets to the retailers. To create competition, Zeno wants to allow Distributor A to sell in the territory of Distributor B, but only if A does so at a price no lower than that which appears on a circulated price list. Zeno consults you. What is your advice? If a territorial restraint is lawful, is an ancillary price restraint lawful? The price restraint relaxes a lawful territorial restraint. See *Eastern Scientific Co. v. Wild Heerbrugg Instruments, Inc.,* 572 F.2d 883 (1st Cir.1978); *Jack Walters & Sons Corp. v. Morton Building, Inc.,* 737 F.2d 698 (7th Cir.1984) (see p. 599 supra).

Problem 2

Twenty small, independent, supermarkets form a private label association. They jointly buy canned goods and frozen foods under their label and all contribute to advertising the new brand. They also agree to honor exclusive territories. Does the prosecution have a sure winner on a per se theory under *Topco?* (See p. 344 supra.) Or do the supermarkets have a sure dismissal under a contemporary combination of *Sylvania, Sharp Electronics, BMI* and *NCAA?*

Note on Collateral Issues

In dealing with vertical price restraints you were introduced to a number of collateral issues: consignment and agency; contract, combination and conspiracy; antitrust injury and standing. These issues come into play also in the context of nonprice vertical restraints. Quickly review the *Colgate–Monsanto* issue and the *General Electric–Simpson* issue and apply the learning to territorial restraints. Next, drawing on the Posner opinion in *Jack*

Walters, consider how you might argue that a dealer terminated for selling in violation of a territorial restraint suffered no antitrust injury.

After *Sylvania* and through most of the 1980s, there has been virtually no governmental enforcement against vertical restraints. On the other side of the coin, a private plaintiff—for example, a terminated dealer—must face the complexities and uncertainties not only of the *Sylvania* rule of reason but also those that derive from *Monsanto, Sharp,* the consignment-agency cases, and the antitrust injury argument. As a practical matter, does the combination of principles move us towards a rule of de facto legality for all nonprice vertical restraints? Can you fashion a rule based on manageable and sensible presumptions and burdens that would facilitate challenges to anticompetitive nonprice vertical restraints?

B. EXCLUSIVE SELLING

In part A we examined a panoply of price and nonprice restraints by which a manufacturer dictated to its distributors or dealers where, to whom, and at what prices to resell. Now we focus not on the restraint imposed on the downstream firm but on the restraint the manufacturer imposes on itself not to create intrabrand competition. The paradigm problem is this: A firm wants to become or remain a manufacturer's distributor, but it is denied that opportunity because the manufacturer has promised a different distributor that it will appoint no one else to do that job.

Manufacturers often agree to restrict their own freedom. A manufacturer might appoint a single dealer as its only dealer in a given territory. The manufacturer might add: "Having appointed only you to serve this territory, I promise not to appoint anyone else, and I promise that I myself will not sell in your territory." Such arrangements are variously called sole outlets, exclusive selling, exclusive franchise, or exclusive dealerships. Alternatively, a manufacturer might agree to appoint two but not three distributors in a territory; or it might agree to appoint qualifying service-oriented dealers but not non-qualifying, no-frill dealers. This section deals with cases wherein the manufacturer, expressly or impliedly, binds its own hands and as a result eliminates or limits intrabrand competition.

Restrictions might arise after an incumbent dealer complains about the agressive or "unfair" competition of another and requests that the latter be terminated. (We dealt above with the question when these interactions result in resale price agreements.) Alternatively, a manufacturer, in recruiting a distributor, might commit itself to protect the distributor from specified types of competition.

Standing alone, an agreement by the manufacturer that a particular distributor or distributors will be the only one(s) appointed in a specified area is less restrictive than arrangements, studied above, that also bind the distributor not to sell outside of its territory. Nonetheless, disappointed distributors sometimes challenge the simpler agreement. We present excerpts from a contemporary case.

VALLEY LIQUORS, INC. v. RENFIELD IMPORTERS, LTD.

678 F.2d 742 (7th Cir.1982).

JUDGE POSNER: Valley Liquors, Inc., is a wholesale wine and liquor distributor in northern Illinois, and Renfield Importers, Ltd., is one of its suppliers. Effective November 1, 1981, Renfield terminated Valley as a distributor of Renfield products (which include such popular brands as Gordon's and Martini & Rossi) in two counties, McHenry and Du Page . . . Valley sued, charging that Renfield had violated section 1 of the Sherman Act, 15 U.S.C. § 1, which forbids conspiracies or other agreements in restraint of trade. The case is before us on Valley's appeal under 28 U.S.C. § 1292(a)(1) from the denial by the district court of a motion for a preliminary injunction under section 16 of the Clayton Act. 15 U.S.C. § 26.

Until November 1, Renfield generally sold its products to several wholesalers in the same county. But its sales had not been growing as rapidly in Illinois as in the rest of the country, and it decided to adopt a system of restricted distribution whereby it would sell to one, or at most two, wholesalers in each county. (In some instances, however, the plan resulted in an increase in the number of wholesalers from one to two.) Although Valley was Renfield's largest wholesaler in McHenry and Du Page Counties, accounting for some 50 percent of Renfield's total sales there, the new plan terminated Valley and all of Renfield's other distributors in the two counties except Continental and Romano; they were, however, terminated in some other areas. There is unrebutted evidence that Valley had been selling Renfield products at prices five percent below those charged by Renfield's other distributors in McHenry and Du Page Counties and that Valley's termination followed discussions between Renfield and Continental and between Renfield and Romano in which Continental and Romano had expressed unhappiness at Renfield's terminating them in other areas. There is virtually no evidence concerning Renfield's motivation for the adoption of a more restricted distribution system and the concomitant realignment of wholesaler territories, except that it was a reaction to Renfield's disappointing sales in Illinois.

Valley contends that two distinct restraints of trade can be inferred from these facts. The first is a conspiracy among Renfield, Continental, and Romano to increase the wholesale prices of Renfield products in McHenry and Du Page Counties by cutting off Valley—Valley's termination being a concession demanded by Continental and Romano in exchange for consenting to the proposed realignment, under which they lost some of their territories. This is alleged to be a "horizontal" conspiracy, unlawful without more ("per se") under section 1 of the Sherman Act. The second alleged restraint of trade is the exclusion of Valley, pursuant to its distribution agreement with Renfield, from McHenry and Du Page Counties. Valley argues that this "vertical" restriction is unreasonable and hence unlawful under section 1's "Rule of Reason."

The district judge denied a preliminary injunction against Renfield's termination of Valley because he did not think that Valley had demonstrated that it was likely to win the case if tried in full. . . .

* * *

Questions and Comments

As in RPM cases, litigation challenging exclusive selling normally arises upon termination. The unhappy terminated dealer sues, and usually alleges concerted action that hurt competition. A jury might be instructed that concerted dealer termination is unreasonable and thus unlawful (1) if the termination was not justified by good business reasons of the manufacturer (see *Eiberger v. Sony Corp. of America,* 622 F.2d 1068 (2d Cir.1980); or (2) if the agreement caused a lessening of intrabrand competition not outweighed by benefits to interbrand competition (see *Continental T.V., Inc. v. GTE Sylvania Inc.,* supra and *Eiberger v. Sony Corp. of America,* 622 F.2d 1068 (2d Cir.1980); or (3) only if the agreement and termination increased the market power of the manufacturer. See *Valley Liquors,* supra. Which standard seems to you to be the proper one? Is the appropriate standard now dictated by *Monsanto* or *Sharp?*

Dealer termination cases always involve factual issues. The terminated dealer asserts that her aggressive competitive behavior led to an agreement between the manufacturer and other dealers to terminate her dealership. The manufacturer normally replies that it, unilaterally, terminated the dealer and it did so because the dealer did not meet one or another of its standards, such as maintenance of inventory, volume of sales, cleanliness, training of personnel, or prompt payment of invoices. Some observers assert that juries are likely to favor the terminated distributor, especially if there is any evidence of her aggressive competition. Some also assert that a manufacturer is unlikely to terminate distributors who are doing a good job in getting its product to the customers. Putting these two observations together, some argue that terminated distributor plaintiffs should face a very high burden of proof. Do you agree?

The prior cases involved products in markets with considerable interbrand competition. Consider the following case, which does not. Is exclusive selling more problematic in a monopoly situation?

OMEGA SATELLITE PRODUCTS CO. v. CITY OF INDIANAPOLIS
694 F.2d 119 (7th Cir.1982).

JUDGE POSNER: * * * [The] ordinance provides that any cable television system using any of the public ways of the City of Indianapolis must obtain a franchise from the City. . . .

[The city awarded a franchise to an applicant for unincorporated suburban areas outside of the city limits, and the applicant assigned this franchise to Indianapolis Cablevision. The city awarded a franchise to American Cablevision for the city and incorporated towns outside the city limits. Omega Satellite Products Company began to do business by installing earth stations on roofs of apartment complexes, and tried, through perfunctory correspondence, to persuade the City Council to offer additional cable franchises and to award such a franchise to it. After it failed to elicit a favorable response, Omega ran a cable through a drainage culvert to connect two buildings that it was servicing with an earth station. It then sued for an injunction to prevent the city from removing the cable. Omega alleged, among other things, that the city had granted de facto exclusive franchises, in violation of Section 1 of the Sherman Act. Omega was denied a preliminary injunction by the district court, and appealed.]

* * *

Omega does not have an overwhelming probability of winning on the Sherman Act count in the complaint. This is not because the City of Indianapolis surely is immune from the Sherman Act, as the City argues. *Community Communications Co. v. City of Boulder*, ___ U.S. ___, 102 S.Ct. 835, 70 L.Ed.2d 810 (1982), holds that the acts of a municipality are not immune from attack under the federal antitrust laws merely because the state has given its municipalities "the full right of self-government in both local and municipal matters," 102 S.Ct. at 836–37 n. 1; their acts are immune only if "undertaken pursuant to a clearly articulated and affirmatively expressed state policy," 102 S.Ct. at 842. Omega alleges a tacit agreement between the City and its two franchisees to exclude competing cable television systems from their areas, and nothing in any Indiana statute or other source of state policy suggests that the state actively desires local monopolies in the cable television industry.

* * *

. . . [The state authorization] comes pretty close to saying that municipalities in Indiana are authorized to grant exclusive franchises. But it may fall short of the Supreme Court's requirement of "a clearly articulated and affirmatively expressed state policy" in favor of the specific restriction that is challenged. This issue will require further exploration in the district court.

Even if the City of Indianapolis is not immune from the Sherman Act, and even if it has as alleged tacitly agreed to give its franchises exclusive territories[,] . . . this would not necessarily prove a violation of the Sherman Act . . . Competitors who agree to keep out of each other's sales territories commit a per se violation of the Sherman Act, but "vertically" imposed exclusive territories are illegal under the Sherman Act only if unreasonable, *Valley Liquors, Inc. v. Renfield Importers, Ltd.*, 678 F.2d 742 (7th Cir.1982), and if there was such an agreement here it was vertical. The City of Indianapolis is not a competitor of Indianapolis Cablevision or American Cablevision but a representative of the potential customers of these companies. It has an interest in getting for its residents, the prospective consumers of cable television, the best service at the lowest price, though maybe not an undivided interest—some cities see cable television as a source of tax revenues as well as consumer benefits. But we cannot, on the facts before us, assume that the City of Indianapolis is indifferent to consumer welfare, or dismiss the hypothesis that one way to promote that welfare might be—we do not say it would be—to give each franchisee an exclusive territory.

The cost of the cable grid appears to be the biggest cost of a cable television system and to be largely invariant to the number of subscribers the system has. We said earlier that once the grid is in place—once every major street has a cable running above or below it that can be hooked up to the individual residences along the street—the cost of adding another subscriber probably is small. If so, the average cost of cable television would be minimized by having a single company in any given geographical area; for if there is more than one company and therefore more than one grid, the cost of each grid will be spread over a smaller number of subscribers, and the average cost per subscriber, and hence price, will be higher.

If the foregoing accurately describes conditions in Indianapolis[,] . . . it describes what economists call a "natural monopoly," wherein the benefits, and indeed the very possibility, of competition are limited. You can start with a competitive free-for-all—different cable television systems frantically building out their grids and signing up subscribers in an effort to bring down their average costs faster than their rivals—but eventually there will be only a single company, because until a company serves the whole market it will have an incentive to keep expanding in order to lower its average costs. In the interim there may be wasteful duplication of facilities. This duplication may lead not only to higher prices to cable television subscribers, at least in the short run, but also to higher costs to other users of the public ways, who must compete with the cable television companies for access to them. An alternative procedure is to pick the most efficient competitor at the outset, give him a monopoly, and extract from him in exchange a commitment to provide reasonable service at reasonable rates. In essence Omega's antitrust allegations accuse the City of Indianapolis of having taken this alternative route to the monopoly that may be the inevitable destination to which all routes converge.

Although there is language in some Supreme Court opinions, notably *National Society of Professional Engineers v. United States*, 435 U.S. 679, 688, 690 (1978), to the effect that the only thing to consider in deciding whether a practice violates the Sherman Act is the effect on competition, it is unlikely that the Court meant to overturn the established proposition that the antitrust laws do not require the impossible—a competitive market under conditions of natural monopoly. If a market has room for only one firm, it would be an effort worthy of King Canute to keep two firms in it. True, a cartel among the competing firms in such a market would be illegal per se, even if the alternative was the destruction, through unbridled competition, of all but one. See *United States v. Trans–Missouri Freight Ass'n*, 166 U.S. 290, 330–32, 338–40 (1897). But that is because the cartel, by holding a price umbrella over the least efficient firms, would retard the evolution of the market toward its optimal state, which would be to have only one firm.

It is also true that the antitrust laws protect competition not only in, but for, the market—that is, competition to be the firm to enjoy a natural monopoly, and by a modest extension competition to replace the existing natural monopolist. If the most efficient method of determining which firm should have the natural monopoly is a competitive process that will inevitably destroy the other firms, the antitrust laws presumably would forbid interference with that process. If, therefore, Omega were challenging an agreement between Indianapolis Cablevision and American Cablevision not to invade each other's territories, or to cooperate in repelling an invasion of either territory by a third party such as Omega, the antitrust laws would condemn the agreement as an artificial interference with a natural, if in a sense destructive, competitive process. The case would be little different from the cartel agreement struck down in the *Trans–Missouri* case, *supra*.

But that is not Omega's complaint. It is rather that officials of the City of Indianapolis—the representatives of the consumers of cable television—have granted the existing franchisees de facto exclusive franchises. If consumers *want* to be spared a competitive free-for-all, though, and to this end, through their elected representatives, grant an exclusive franchise to a natural monopolist, it may be that no greater objection can be made in the name of the antitrust laws than was made to the full-requirements contract in *Tampa Elec. Co. v. Nashville Coal Co.*, 365 U.S. 320 (1961), and rejected by the Supreme Court—especially now that the Court has told us that consumer welfare is to be the lodestar in interpreting and applying those laws, see e.g., *Reiter v. Sonotone Corp.*, 442 U.S. 330, 343 (1979). There is no precedent for condemning an exclusive franchise in these circumstances, at least out of hand, and it would be perilous to assume that this or any other court will soon create one. But that is not to say that Omega will not prevail on its Sherman Act count at trial. It may be able to prove that the City officials were not acting in the consumer interest, that cable television in Indianapolis is not a natural monopoly, that exclusive franchising is a needlessly restrictive way of dealing with natural monopoly, or other propositions that separately or together might establish a violation of the Sherman Act under the Rule of Reason. All we hold is that on this record Omega has not established a sufficient probability of prevailing to persuade us that it is entitled to a preliminary injunction on the basis of its Sherman Act claim.

* * *

Questions and Comments

Omega is an example of an exclusive distributorship that has the effect of airtight territorial confinement. The entity imposing the restriction is, however, not a manufacturer but rather a city, presumably acting in the interest of its citizens as consumers. Before any award is made, cable operators compete to *be* the monopolist; the competition process includes presentations to the city. Does this process adequately protect consumer interests? Might the degree of consumer protection be a function of the length of the monopoly franchise and the proportion of franchise costs that are sunk costs? Should we assume that the city acts to protect its citizens as consumers? Or should the courts inquire whether the market has room for more than one firm without loss of efficiency and disallow exclusivity if room is apparent? Is there another alternative?

Consider the undecided question in *Albrecht:* Should a court second-guess a decision to appoint an exclusive distributor? In a monopoly market, such as in *Omega* or *Albrecht*, entity *A* makes the decision to appoint an exclusive distributor and to insulate the distributor's territory from incursions by any other distributor. In which case would you be more confident that *A*'s decision coincides with consumer interests: where *A* is a municipality, or where *A* is a manufacturer? Is it more important to know the identity of A, or to know the strength of the competition to be the monopoly franchisee?

C. FORECLOSING RESTRAINTS

1. EXCLUSIVE DEALING AND REQUIREMENTS CONTRACTS

In Part B we looked at restraints imposed on or accepted by the seller; typically: "I will appoint you, alone." Now we look at restraints imposed on the buyer; e.g., "You must deal with me (the seller), alone; you must not deal with my competitors." Such restraints are often referred to as foreclosing restraints, for they foreclose the competitors of the seller from competing for the business of the locked-in buyer.

There are various kinds of foreclosing restraints. An exclusive dealing contract commits a buyer to buy exclusively from a certain seller. A requirements contract commits a buyer to buy all of its requirements from a certain seller, which amounts to the same thing. Pursuant to tying arrangements, the seller offers a product with high market acceptance (the "tying product") only on condition that the buyer also purchase from it a different "tied" product. All three types of arrangements can be challenged under Section 3 of the Clayton Act, Section 1 of the Sherman Act, or Section 5 of the Federal Trade Commission Act. We address exclusive dealing and requirements contracts in this section, and the somewhat more complex tying issues in the next section.

In the early 1900s, large and powerful sellers often required their customers to deal exclusively with them, blocking opportunities for sales by their rivals and limiting the freedom of their customers to choose alternative sources of supply. Such requirements were widely perceived as oppressive. By the time of the election of 1912 reformers were calling for a law against them. Representative Henry D. Clayton, Chairman of the House Judicial Committee, proposed a bill to declare illegal all sales or leases of goods on condition that the buyer not use the goods of a competitor. Section 3 of the Clayton Bill was at first designed to flatly prohibit these and related practices, but (as a result of legislative compromise) the Act prohibits the enumerated practices not outright but where the "effect . . . may be to substantially lessen competition or tend to create a monopoly in any line of commerce."

STANDARD FASHION CO. v. MAGRANE–HOUSTON CO.

258 U.S. 346 (1922).

JUSTICE DAY: * * *

Petitioner is a New York corporation engaged in the manufacture and distribution of patterns. Respondent conducted a retail dry goods business . . . in Boston. . . . [T]he parties entered into a contract by which the petitioner granted to the respondent an agency for the sale of Standard Patterns at respondent's store, for a term of two years from the date of the contract, and from term to term thereafter until the agreement should be terminated as thereinafter provided. Petitioner agreed to sell to respondent Standard Patterns at a discount of 50% from retail prices, with advertising matter and publications upon terms stated. . . . Respondent agreed to purchase a substantial number of standard fashion sheets, to purchase and keep on hand at all times, except during the period of exchange, $1,000 value in Standard Patterns at net invoice prices, and to pay petitioner for the pattern stock to be selected by it on terms of payment which are stated. Respondent agreed . . . not to sell or permit to be sold on its premises during the term of the contract any other make of patterns, and not to sell Standard Patterns except at label prices. . . .

* * *

The principal question in the case and the one upon which the writ of certiorari was granted involves the construction of § 3 of the Clayton Act. . . .

* * *

The contract required the purchaser not to deal in goods of competitors of the seller. It is idle to say that the covenant was limited to the premises of the purchaser, and that sales might be made by it elsewhere. The contract should have a reasonable construction. The purchaser kept a retail store in Boston. It was not contemplated that it would make sales elsewhere. The covenant, read in the light of the circumstances in which it was made, is one by which the purchaser agreed not to sell any other make of patterns while the contract was in force. The real question is: Does the contract of sale come within the third section of the Clayton Act because the covenant not to sell the patterns of others "may be to substantially lessen competition or tend to create a monopoly."

The Clayton Act, as its title and the history of its enactment disclose, was intended to supplement the purpose and effect of other anti-trust legislation, principally the Sherman Act of 1890. . . .

* * *

The Clayton Act sought to reach the agreements embraced within . . . [the Sherman Act's] sphere in their incipiency, and in the section under consideration to determine their legality by specific tests of its own which declared illegal contracts of sale made upon the agreement or understanding that the purchaser shall not deal in the goods of a competitor or competitors of the seller, which may "substantially lessen competition or tend to create a monopoly."

* * *

Section 3 condemns sales or agreements where the effect of such sale or contract of sale "may" be to substantially lessen competition or tend to create monopoly. It thus deals with consequences to follow the making of the restrictive covenant limiting the right of the purchaser to deal in the goods of the seller only. But we do not think that the purpose in using the word "may" was to prohibit the mere possibility of the consequences described. It was intended to prevent such agreements as would under the circumstances disclosed probably lessen competition, or create an actual tendency to monopoly. That it was not intended to reach every remote lessening of competition is shown in the requirement that such lessening must be substantial.

Both courts below found that the contract interpreted in the light of the circumstances surrounding the making of it was within the provisions of the Clayton Act as one which substantially lessened competition and tended to create monopoly. These courts put special stress upon the fact found that, of 52,000 so-called pattern agencies in the entire country, the petitioner, or a holding company controlling it and two other pattern companies, approximately controlled two-fifths of such agencies. . . .

We agree with these conclusions, and have no doubt that the contract, properly interpreted, with its restrictive covenant, brings it fairly within the section of the Clayton Act under consideration.

Affirmed.

Questions and Comments

The Clayton Act is an "incipiency" statute. Violation requires only that a lessening of competition be threatened, not that it have occurred. Nonetheless, to determine whether a violation may result, one must ask questions similar to those that are relevant to Sherman Act problems.

The *Standard Fashion* case was decided in 1922. It was preceded by a few years by *Chicago Board of Trade, U.S. Steel,* and *Colgate.* See pp. 283, 85, and 545 supra. While this was not a period of vigorous commitment to antitrust, the unanimous Court that decided *Standard Fashion* seemed sympathetic to the spirit of the Clayton Act. In any event, the Court had little doubt about its judicial duty to enforce the Act.

How sound is Justice Day's economics? (In this case, as in many early cases, the Court used "monopoly" to include "oligopoly".) Is the Court correct that the exclusive dealing clauses tended to enhance monopoly or oligopoly power, leading to "evils, such as enhancement of prices"?

Assume these to be the facts: Standard and two other pattern companies that used similar contracts had, in the aggregate, contracted with two-fifths of all fabric retailers in the country. The contracts committed each of these retailers to carry only one brand. Many small towns had only one such retailer. Most members of the public who wanted patterns bought them from fabric retailers. What are the competitive implications? In the small towns is it likely that the arrangement would produce monopoly? If so, who got the monopoly return? Would the single fabric retailer in a small town have power to resist a pattern company's demand for exclusive dealing? If Standard sold only at a monopoly price to the single fabric retailer, and this dealer was bound to Standard by an exclusive dealing clause, what response would you expect from other actual or potential retailers in town? From other pattern makers? Is the Court correct that in larger cities, where there were several pattern outlets, exclusive dealing clauses might facilitate combination?

In the context of the facts of *Standard Fashion,* are the clauses so harmful that they should be banned outright? Should they be presumptively unlawful, subject to a procompetition justification? Or are they benign? Might they increase consumers' benefits? With what degree of enthusiasm or suspicion should we approach exclusive dealing?

STANDARD OIL CO. OF CALIFORNIA v. UNITED STATES

337 U.S. 293 (1949).

JUSTICE FRANKFURTER: This is an appeal to review a decree enjoining the Standard Oil Company of California and its wholly-owned subsidiary, Standard Stations, Inc., from enforcing or entering into exclusive supply contracts with any independent dealer in petroleum products and automobile accessories. 78 F.Supp. 850. The use of such contracts was successfully assailed by the United States as violative of § 1 of the Sherman Act and § 3 of the Clayton Act.

The Standard Oil Company of California, a Delaware corporation, owns petroleum-producing resources and refining plants in California and sells petroleum products in what has been termed in these proceedings the "Western area"—Arizona, California, Idaho, Nevada, Oregon, Utah and Washington. It sells through its own service stations, to the operators of independent service stations, and to industrial users. It is the largest seller of gasoline in the area. In 1946 its combined sales amounted to 23% of the total taxable gallonage sold there in that year: sales by company-owned service stations constituted 6.8% of the total, sales under exclusive dealing contracts with independent service stations, 6.7% of the total; the remainder were sales to industrial users. Retail service-station sales by Standard's six leading competitors absorbed 42.5% of the total taxable gallonage; the remaining retail sales were divided between more than seventy small companies. It is undisputed that Standard's major competitors employ similar exclusive dealing arrangements. In 1948 only 1.6% of retail outlets were what is known as "split-pump" stations, that is, sold the gasoline of more than one supplier.

Exclusive supply contracts with Standard had been entered into, as of March 12, 1947, by the operators of 5,937 independent stations, or 16% of the retail gasoline outlets in the Western area, which purchased from Standard in 1947, $57,646,233 worth of gasoline and $8,200,089.21 worth of other products. Some outlets are covered by more than one contract so that in all about 8,000 exclusive supply contracts are here in issue. These are of several types, but a feature common to each is the dealer's undertaking to purchase from Standard all his requirements of one or more products. . . .

Between 1936 and 1946 Standard's sales of gasoline through independent dealers remained at a practically constant proportion of the area's total sales. . . .

Since § 3 of the Clayton Act was directed to prohibiting specific practices even though not covered by the broad terms of the Sherman Act, it is appropriate to consider first whether the enjoined contracts fall within the prohibition of the narrower Act. . . .

Obviously the contracts here at issue would be proscribed if § 3 stopped short of the qualifying clause beginning, "where the effect of such lease, sale, or contract for sale. . . ." If effect is to be given that clause, however, it is by no means obvious, in view of Standard's minority share of the "line of commerce" involved, of the fact that that share has not recently increased, and of the claims of these contracts to economic utility, that the effect of the contracts may be to lessen competition or tend to create a monopoly. It is the qualifying clause, therefore, which must be construed.

The District Court held that the requirement of showing an actual or potential lessening of competition or a tendency to establish monopoly was adequately met by proof that the contracts covered "a substantial number of outlets and a substantial amount of products, whether considered comparatively or not." 78 F.Supp. at 875. Given such quantitative substantiality, the substantial lessening of competition—so the court reasoned—is an automatic result, for the very existence of such contracts denies dealers opportunity to deal in the products of competing suppliers and excludes suppliers from access to the outlets controlled by those dealers. Having adopted this standard of proof, the court excluded as immaterial testimony bearing on "the economic merits or demerits of the present system as contrasted with a system which prevailed prior to its establishment and which would prevail if the court declared the present arrangement [invalid]." The court likewise deemed it unnecessary to make findings, on the basis of evidence that was admitted, whether the number of Standard's competitors had increased or decreased since the inauguration of the requirements-contract system, whether the number of their dealers had increased or decreased, and as to other matters which would have shed light on the comparative status of Standard and its competitors before and after the adoption of that system. . . .

The issue before us, therefore, is whether the requirement of showing that the effect of the agreements "may be to substantially lessen competition" may be met simply by proof that a substantial portion of commerce is affected or whether it must also be demonstrated that competitive activity has actually diminished or probably will diminish.

Since the Clayton Act became effective, this Court has passed on the applicability of § 3 in eight cases, in five of which it upheld determinations that the challenged agreement was violative of that Section. . . .

* * *

. . . [Four involved patents or other evidence of a dominant position and] regarded domination of the market as sufficient in itself to support the inference that competition had been or probably would be lessened. . . .

It is thus apparent that none of these cases controls the disposition of the present appeal, for Standard's share of the retail market for gasoline, even including sales through company-owned stations, is hardly large enough to conclude as a matter of law that it occupies a dominant position, nor did the trial court so find. The cases do indicate, however, that some sort of showing as to the actual or probable economic consequences of the agreements, if only the inferences to be drawn from the fact of dominant power, is important, and to that extent they tend to support appellant's position.

* * *

But then came *International Salt Co. v. United States,* 332 U.S. 392. That decision, at least as to contracts tying the sale of a nonpatented to a patented product, rejected the necessity of demonstrating economic consequences once it has been established that "the volume of business affected" is not "insignificant or insubstantial" and that the effect of the contracts is to "foreclose competitors from [a] substantial market." *Id.* at 396. Upon that basis we affirmed a summary judgment granting an injunction against the leasing of machines for the utilization of salt products on the condition that the lessee use in them only salt supplied by defendant. . . .

In favor of confining the standard laid down by the *International Salt* case to tying agreements, important economic differences may be noted. Tying agreements serve hardly any purpose beyond the suppression of competition. . . .

Requirements contracts, on the other hand, may well be of economic advantage to buyers as well as to sellers, and thus indirectly of advantage to the consuming public. In the case of the buyer, they may assure supply, afford protection against rises in price, enable long-term planning on the basis of known costs,[9] and obviate the expense and risk of storage in the quantity necessary for a commodity having a fluctuating demand. From the seller's point of view, requirements contracts may make possible the substantial reduction of selling expenses, give protection against price fluctuations, and—of particular advantage to a newcomer to the field to whom it is important to know what capital expenditures are justified—offer the possibility of a predictable market. They may be useful, moreover, to a seller trying to establish a foothold against the counter-attacks of entrenched competitors. . . .

Thus, even though the qualifying clause of § 3 is appended without distinction of terms equally to the prohibition of tying clauses and of requirements contracts, pertinent considerations support, certainly as a matter of economic reasoning, varying standards as to each for the proof necessary to fulfill the conditions of that clause. . . .

Yet serious difficulties would attend the attempt to apply . . . [economic tests to evaluate the effect of requirements contracts]. We may assume, as did the court below, that no improvement of Standard's competitive position has coincided with the period during which the requirements-contract system of distribution has been in effect. We may assume further that the duration of the contracts is not excessive and that Standard does not by itself dominate the market. But Standard was a major competitor when the present system was adopted, and it is possible that its position would have deteriorated but for the adoption of that system. When it is remembered that all the other major suppliers have also been using requirements contracts, and when it is noted that the relative share of the business which fell to each has remained about the same during the period of their use, it would not be farfetched to infer that their effect has been to enable the established suppliers individually

9. This advantage is not conferred by Standard's contracts, each of which provides that the price to be paid by the dealer is to be the "Company's posted price to its dealers generally at time and place of delivery."

to maintain their own standing and at the same time collectively, even though not collusively, to prevent a late arrival from wresting away more than an insignificant portion of the market. If, indeed, this were a result of the system, it would seem unimportant that a short-run by-product of stability may have been greater efficiency and lower costs, for it is the theory of the antitrust laws that the long-run advantage of the community depends upon the removal of restraints upon competition. . . .

Moreover, to demand that bare inference be supported by evidence as to what would have happened but for the adoption of the practice that was in fact adopted or to require firm prediction of an increase of competition as a probable result of ordering the abandonment of the practice, would be a standard of proof, if not virtually impossible to meet, at least most ill-suited for ascertainment by courts.[13] . . .

We are dealing here with a particular form of agreement specified by § 3 and not with different arrangements, by way of integration or otherwise, that may tend to lessen competition. To interpret that section as requiring proof that competition has actually diminished would make its very explicitness a means of conferring immunity upon the practices which it singles out. Congress has authoritatively determined that those practices are detrimental where their effect may be to lessen competition. It has not left at large for determination in each case the ultimate demands of the "public interest. . . ." Though it may be that such an alternative to the present system as buying out independent dealers and making them dependent employees of Standard Stations, Inc., would be a greater detriment to the public interest than perpetuation of the system, this is an issue, like the choice between greater efficiency and freer competition, that has not been submitted to our decision. . . .

* * *

We conclude, therefore, that the qualifying clause of § 3 is satisfied by proof that competition has been foreclosed in a substantial share of the line of commerce affected. It cannot be gainsaid that observance by a dealer of his requirements contract with Standard does effectively foreclose whatever opportunity there might be for competing suppliers to attract his patronage, and it is clear that the affected proportion of retail sales of petroleum products is substantial. In view of the widespread adoption of such contracts by Standard's competitors and the availability of alternative ways of obtaining an assured market, evidence that competitive activity has not actually declined is inconclusive. Standard's use of the contracts creates just such a potential clog on competition as it was the purpose of § 3 to remove wherever, were it to become actual, it would impede a substantial amount of competitive activity.

Since the decree below is sustained by our interpretation of § 3 of the Clayton Act, we need not go on to consider whether it might also be sustained by § 1 of the Sherman Act. . . .

13. The dual system of enforcement provided for by the Clayton Act must have contemplated standards of proof capable of administration by the courts as well as by the Federal Trade Commission and other designated agencies. Our interpretation of the Act, therefore, should recognize that an appraisal of economic data which might be practicable if only the latter were faced with the task may be quite otherwise for judges unequipped for it either by experience or by the availability of skilled assistance.

*   *   *

The judgment below is *affirmed.*

JUSTICE DOUGLAS: *   *   *

It is common knowledge that a host of filling stations in the country are locally owned and operated. Others are owned and operated by the big oil companies. This case involves directly only the former. It pertains to requirements contracts that the oil companies make with these independents. It is plain that a filling-station owner who is tied to an oil company for his supply of products is not an available customer for the products of other suppliers. The same is true of a filling-station owner who purchases his inventory a year in advance. His demand is withdrawn from the market for the duration of the contract in the one case and for a year in the other. The result in each case is to lessen competition if the standard is day-to-day purchases. Whether it is a substantial lessening of competition within the meaning of the Anti–Trust Laws is a question of degree and may vary from industry to industry.

The Court answers the question for the oil industry by a formula which under our decisions promises to wipe out large segments of independent filling-station operators. The method of doing business under requirements contracts at least keeps the independents alive. They survive as small business units. The situation is not ideal from either their point of view or that of the nation. But the alternative which the Court offers is far worse from the point of view of both.

*   *   *

Justice Jackson, with whom Chief Justice Vinson and Justice Burton join, dissenting: *   *   * I cannot agree that the requirements contract is *per se* an illegal one under the antitrust law, and that is the substance of what the Court seems to hold. I am not convinced that the requirements contract as here used is a device for suppressing competition instead of a device for waging competition. If we look only at its effect in relation to particular retailers who become parties to it, it does restrain their freedom to purchase their requirements elsewhere and prevents other companies from selling to them. Many contracts have the effect of taking a purchaser out of the market for goods he already has bought or contracted to take. But the retailer in this industry is only a conduit from the oil fields to the driver's tank, a means by which the oil companies compete to get the business of the ultimate consumer—the man in whose automobile the gas is used. It means to me, if I must decide without evidence, that these contracts are an almost necessary means to maintain this all-important competition for consumer business, in which it is admitted competition is keen. . . .

It does not seem to me inherently to lessen this real competition when an oil company tries to establish superior service by providing the consumer with a responsible dealer from which the public can purchase adequate and timely supplies of oil, gasoline and car accessories of some known and reliable standard of quality. No retailer, whether agent or independent, can long remain in business if he does not always, and not just intermittently, have gas to sell. Retailers' storage capacity usually is limited and they are in no position to accumulate large stocks. They can take gas only when and as they can sell it. The Government can hardly force someone to contract to stand by, ever ready to fill fluctuating demands of dealers who will not in turn undertake to buy from that supplier all their requirements. And it is important to the driving public to be able to rely on retailers to have gas to retail. It is equally important that the wholesaler have some incentive to carry the stocks and have the transport facilities to make the irregular deliveries caused by varied consumer demands.

*   *   *

If the courts are to apply the lash of the antitrust laws to the backs of businessmen to make them compete, we cannot in fairness also apply the lash whenever they hit upon a successful method of competing. That, insofar as I am permitted by the record to learn the facts, appears to be the case before us. I would reverse.

Questions and Comments

Let us put *Standard Stations,* as the case is often called, in context. In the early 1930s, in the throes and immediate aftermath of the Depression, national economic policy placed cooperation above competition. Then, following abandonment of the NIRA (see *Socony–Vacuum,* supra p. 296), there was, a "brief but spectacular" antitrust resurgence. See L. Schwartz Cycles of Antitrust Zeal: Predictability? (forthcoming in 1989 spring or summer edition of Antitrust Bull.) The resurgence came to a halt with World War II. But following the war, three cases—*Alcoa, Associated Press* and *Standard Stations*—seemed to strike an aggressive tone once again. See pp. 114, 432 and 630 supra.

In *Standard Stations,* as in *Standard Fashion,* the majority of the Court seemed content to discern the general Congressional intent and to do its judicial tasks without serious grappling with economics. Do you agree that Congress preferred competition to efficiency, and that therefore competition, not efficiency, must inform judicial construction? What does this mean?

Justice Douglas suggested that if enclusive dealing is efficient, the oil companies will achieve the same result through vertical integration. This, he thought, would both eliminate entrepreneurs and enhance the oil companies' market power. (Would it?) Should the Court have considered this possible effect of a judgment for plaintiffs? What difference would it make if the people who operated service stations were "independents" or worked for big integrated oil companies? Would downstream integration enhance the oil companies' market power? Would it facilitate cooperative arrangements among them? Or is Justice Jackson correct that the gas station is merely a conduit to the driver's tank?

The main concern of the Court seemed to be foreclosure. Independents competing at wholesale with the major oil companies were deprived of the chance to try to supply a substantial share of the retail market. Is this a competitive harm? Did the foreclosure tend to raise barriers to entry into wholesaling of gasoline? Into drilling and refining? If most existing gasoline stations were tied to one or another of the major oil companies by one-year exclusive contracts, what would be the probable response of the independent wholesalers? If the majors were charging supracompetitive prices to the retailers, what would be the effect on and probable response of the retailers? Could they pass on the overcharge to consumers?

Do you suppose that the Justice Department expected the case to lead to "open" or "split pump" stations at which independent dealers would buy and resell gasoline of two or more refiners? If not, did the Justice Department lawyers expect independently owned stations to shift more frequently between or among suppliers? For example, a station owner might sell Standard gas this year, and Gulf gas next year. In fact, practices in the industry remained rather constant even after the decision in *Standard Stations*. Split pump stations did not emerge. Shifting buyers did not emerge. Neither did the rush to vertical integration, feared by Justice Douglas, take place. What inferences can be drawn from this stability? Can we infer that refiners' offerings to dealers were already competitive? Or can we infer that refiners, having reinforced their market power by the foreclosure, were able to continue to "foreclose" potential entrants from needed outlets even without formal exclusive contracts or further integration?

Standard Stations spent little time on market definition. We turn now to a case that brought market definition to center stage.

TAMPA ELECTRIC CO. v. NASHVILLE COAL CO.
365 U.S. 320 (1961).

JUSTICE CLARK: * * * Petitioner Tampa Electric Company is a public utility located in Tampa, Florida. It produces and sells electric energy to a service area, including the city, extending from Tampa Bay eastward 60 miles to the center of the State, and some 30 miles in width. As of 1954 petitioner operated two electrical generating plants comprising a total of 11 individual generating units, all of which consumed oil in their burners. In 1955 Tampa Electric decided to expand its facilities by the construction of an additional generating plant to be comprised ultimately of six generating units, and to be known as the "Francis J. Gannon Station." Although every electrical generating plant in peninsular Florida burned oil at that time, Tampa Electric decided to try coal as boiler fuel in the first two units constructed at the Gannon Station. Accordingly, it contracted with the respondents to furnish the expected coal requirements for the units. The agreement, dated May 23, 1955, embraced Tampa Electric's "total requirements of fuel . . . for the operation of its first two units to be installed at the Gannon Station . . . not less than 225,000 tons of coal per unit per year," for a period of 20 years. The contract further provided that "if during the first 10 years of the term . . . the Buyer constructs additional units [at Gannon] in which coal is used as the fuel, it shall give the Seller notice thereof two years prior to the completion of such unit or units and upon completion of same the fuel requirements thereof shall be added to this contract." . . . The minimum price was set at $6.40 per ton delivered, subject to an escalation clause based on labor cost and other factors. . . .

In April 1957, soon before the first coal was actually to be delivered and after Tampa Electric, in order to equip its first two Gannon units for the use of coal, had expended some $3,000,000 more than the cost of constructing oil-burning units, and after respondents had expended approximately $7,500,000 readying themselves to perform the contract, the latter advised petitioner that the contract was illegal under the antitrust laws, would therefore not be performed, and no coal would be delivered. This turn of events required Tampa Electric to look elsewhere for its coal requirements. The first unit at Gannon began operating August 1, 1957, using coal purchased on a temporary basis, but on December 23, 1957, a purchase order contract for the total coal requirements of the Gannon Station was made with Love and Amos Coal Company. It was for an indefinite period cancellable on 12 months' notice by either party, or immediately upon tender of performance by respondents under the contract sued upon here. The maximum price was $8.80 per ton, depending upon the freight rate. . . .

The record indicates that the total consumption of coal in peninsular Florida, as of 1958, aside from Gannon Station, was approximately 700,000 tons annually. It further shows that there were some 700 coal suppliers in the producing area where respondents operated, and that Tampa Electric's anticipated maximum requirements at Gannon Station, *i.e.,* 2,250,000 tons annually, would approximate 1% of the total coal of the same type produced and marketed from respondents' producing area.

Petitioner brought this suit in the District Court pursuant to 28 U.S.C. § 2201, for a declaration that its contract with respondents was valid, and for enforcement according to its terms. In addition to its Clayton Act defense, respondents contended that the contract violated both §§ 1 and 2 of the Sherman Act which, it claimed, likewise precluded its enforcement. The District Court, however, granted respondents' motion for summary judgment on the sole ground that the undisputed facts, recited above, showed the contract to be a violation of § 3 of the Clayton Act. The Court of Appeals agreed. Neither court found it necessary to consider the applicability of the Sherman Act.

DECISIONS OF DISTRICT COURT AND COURT OF APPEALS

Both courts admitted that the contract "does not expressly contain the 'condition' " that Tampa Electric would not use or deal in the coal of respondents' competitors. Nonetheless, they reasoned, the "total requirements" provision had the same practical effect, for it prevented Tampa Electric for a period of 20 years from buying coal from any other source for use at that station. Each court cast aside as "irrelevant" arguments citing the use of oil as boiler fuel by Tampa Electric at its other stations, and by other utilities in peninsular Florida, because oil was not in fact used at Gannon Station, and the possibility of exercise by Tampa Electric of the option reserved to it to build oil-burning units at Gannon was too remote. Found to be equally remote was the possibility of Tampa's conversion of existing oil-burning units at its other stations to the use of coal which would not be covered by the contract with respondents. It followed, both courts found, that the "line of commerce" on which the restraint was to be tested was coal—not boiler fuels. Both courts compared the estimated coal tonnage as to which the contract pre-empted competition for 20 years, namely, 1,000,000 tons a year by 1961, with the previous annual consumption of peninsular Florida, 700,000 tons. Emphasizing that fact as well as the contract value of the coal covered by the

20–year term, *i.e.*, $128,000,000, they held that such volume was not "insignificant or insubstantial" and that the effect of the contract would "be to substantially lessen competition," in violation of the Act. Both courts were of the opinion that in view of the executory nature of the contract, judicial enforcement of any portion of it could not be granted without directing a violation of the Act itself, and enforcement was, therefore, denied.

APPLICATION OF § 3 OF THE CLAYTON ACT

*   *   *

In practical application, even though a contract is found to be an exclusive-dealing arrangement, it does not violate the section unless the court believes it probable that performance of the contract will foreclose competition in a substantial share of the line of commerce affected. Following the guidelines of earlier decisions, certain considerations must be taken. *First,* the line of commerce, *i.e.*, the type of goods, wares, or merchandise, etc., involved must be determined, where it is in controversy, on the basis of the facts peculiar to the case. *Second,* the area of effective competition in the known line of commerce must be charted by careful selection of the market area in which the seller operates, and to which the purchaser can practicably turn for supplies. In short, the threatened foreclosure of competition must be in relation to the market affected. . . .

Third, and last, the competition foreclosed by the contract must be found to constitute a substantial share of the relevant market. That is to say, the opportunities for other traders to enter into or remain in that market must be significantly limited as was pointed out in *Standard Oil Co. v. United States,* [337 U.S. 293 (1949)]. There the impact of the requirements contracts was studied in the setting of the large number of gasoline stations—5,937 or 16% of the retail outlets in the relevant market—and the large number of contracts, over 8,000, together with the great volume of products involved. This combination dictated a finding that "Standard's use of the contracts [created] just such a potential clog on competition as it was the purpose of § 3 to remove" where, as there, the affected proportion of retail sales was substantial. At p. 314. As we noted above, in *United States v. Columbia Steel Co.,* [334 U.S. 495 (1948); see 741–43 *infra*] substantiality was judged on a comparative basis, *i.e.*, Consolidated's use of rolled steel was "a small part" when weighed against the total volume of that product in the relevant market.

To determine substantiality in a given case, it is necessary to weigh the probable effect of the contract on the relevant area of effective competition, taking into account the relative strength of the parties, the proportionate volume of commerce involved in relation to the total volume of commerce in the relevant market area, and the probable immediate and future effects which pre-emption of that share of the market might have on effective competition therein. It follows that a mere showing that the contract itself involves a substantial number of dollars is ordinarily of little consequence.

The Application of § 3 Here.

In applying these considerations to the facts of the case before us, it appears clear that both the Court of Appeals and the District Court have not given the required effect to a controlling factor in the case—the relevant competitive market area. This omission, by itself, requires reversal, for, as we have pointed out, the relevant market is the prime factor in relation to which the ultimate question, whether the contract forecloses competition in a substantial share of the line of commerce involved, must be decided. For the purposes of this case, therefore, we need not decide two threshold questions pressed by Tampa Electric. They are whether the contract in fact satisfies the initial requirement of § 3, *i.e.*, whether it is truly an exclusive-dealing one, and, secondly, whether the line of commerce is boiler fuels, including coal, oil and gas, rather than coal alone. We, therefore, for the purposes of this case, assume, but do not decide, that the contract is an exclusive-dealing arrangement within the compass of § 3, and that the line of commerce is bituminous coal.

Relevant Market of Effective Competition.

. . . Respondents contend that the coal tonnage covered by the contract must be weighed against either the total consumption of coal in peninsular Florida, or all of Florida, or the Bituminous Coal Act area comprising peninsular Florida and the Georgia "finger," or, at most, all of Florida and Georgia. If the latter area were considered the relevant market, Tampa Electric's proposed requirements would be 18% of the tonnage sold therein. Tampa Electric says that both courts and respondents are in error, because the "700 coal producers who could serve" it, as recognized by the trial court and admitted by respondents, operated in the Appalachian coal area and that its contract requirements were less than 1% of the total marketed production of these producers; that the relevant effective area of competition was the area in which these producers operated, and in which they were willing to compete for the consumer potential.

We are persuaded that on the record in this case, neither peninsular Florida, nor the entire State of Florida, nor Florida and Georgia combined constituted the relevant market of effective competition. We do not believe that the pie will slice so thinly. By far the bulk of the overwhelming tonnage marketed from the same producing area as serves Tampa is sold outside of Georgia and Florida, and the producers were "eager" to sell more coal in those States. While the relevant competitive market is not ordinarily susceptible to a "metes and bounds" definition, it is of course the area in which respondents and the other 700 producers effectively compete. The record shows that, like the respondents, they sold bituminous coal "suitable for [Tampa's] requirements," mined in parts of Pennsylvania, Virginia, West Virginia, Kentucky, Tennessee, Alabama, Ohio and Illinois. . . . [I]t clearly appears that the proportionate volume of the total relevant coal product as to which the challenged contract preempted competition, less than 1%, is, conservatively speaking, quite insubstantial. . . .

EFFECT ON COMPETITION IN THE RELEVANT MARKET

* * *

The remaining determination . . . is whether the pre-emption of competition to the extent of the tonnage involved tends to substantially foreclose competition in the relevant coal market. We think not. That market sees an annual trade in excess of 250,000,000 tons of coal and over a billion dollars—multiplied by 20 years it runs into astronomical figures. There is here neither a seller with a dominant position in the market as in *Standard Fashions, supra;* nor myriad outlets with substantial sales volume, coupled with an industry-wide practice of relying upon exclusive contracts, as in *Standard Oil, supra;* nor a plainly restrictive tying arrangement as in *International Salt, supra.* On the contrary, we seem to have only that type of contract which "may well be of economic advantage to buyers as well as to sellers." *Standard Oil Co. v. United States, supra,* at p. 306. In the case of the buyer it "may assure supply," while on the part of the seller it "may make possible the substantial reduction of selling expenses, give protection against price fluctuations, and . . . offer the possibility of a predictable market." *Id.,* at 306–307. The 20–year period of the contract is singled out as the principal vice, but at least in the case of public utilities the assurance of a steady and ample supply of fuel is necessary in the public interest. Otherwise consumers are left unprotected against service failures owing to shutdowns; and increasingly unjustified costs might result in more burdensome rate structures eventually to be reflected in the consumer's bill. The compelling validity of such considerations has been recognized fully in the natural gas public utility field. This is not to say that utilities are immunized from Clayton Act proscriptions, but merely that, in judging the term of a requirements contract in relation to the substantiality of the foreclosure of competition, particularized considerations of the parties' operations are not irrelevant. In weighing the various factors, we have decided that in the competitive bituminous coal marketing area involved here the contract sued upon does not tend to foreclose a substantial volume of competition.

* * *

The judgment is reversed and the case remanded to the District Court for further proceedings not inconsistent with this opinion.

It is so ordered.

Questions and Comments

Does *Tampa Electric* modify *Standard Stations?* Does *GTE Sylvania* modify *Standard Stations?* Apply contemporary law and concepts to the facts of *Standard Stations.*

Suppose that demand in Florida and Georgia identified a proper economic coal-producing market; because of transportation expenses, all coal producers currently supplying Florida and Georgia could (if they formed a cartel) raise the price significantly before more distant producers would find it profitable to divert shipments into those states. All other facts of the case remain the same. Thus, Tampa Electric's need for coal represented 18% of the sales of coal in the geographic market.

You represent Nashville Coal. Market price has risen to $10.00 a ton, and your client wants to be relieved of its contractual obligations. Assume that Nashville Coal sells 23% of all coal sold in the area. The number two and three firms sell 20% each. Producers supplying the Florida–Georgia area seldom ship elsewhere because transportation costs are high and other coal-producing areas are closer to other consumers. In view of contemporary authorities, structure your case for illegality. Where you need additional facts, make assumptions that you think are plausible. Now outline the case for legality on behalf of Tampa Electric. Who prevails? Can Tampa credibly claim that Nashville will in no event suffer antitrust injury?

Where exclusive dealing blocks competitors from a substantial share of a market but exclusive dealing relationships are nonetheless dictated by the practical business needs of the parties, is legality a function of duration? An unnecessarily long term may influence a decision of illegality. (Should it?) See *FTC v. Motion Picture Advertising Service Co.*, 344 U.S. 392 (1953) (exclusive contracts to provide advertising films to movie theatres must be limited to one year). Compare, as to an exclusive franchise, *Twin City Sportservice v. Charles O. Finley & Co., Inc.*, 676 F.2d 1291 (9th Cir.1982), *cert. denied*, 459 U.S. 1009 (1982) (ten years was too long for a concessionaire's exclusive franchise with major league baseball owner).

Problem

Microchip X is a specialized microchip needed by the communications industry, which is comprised of numerous middle-sized firms. Five American companies—A through E—produce microchip X. Three Japanese firms—J, K and L—produce microchip X and sell it to American buyers among others. The Japanese have the leading edge in technology; they are constantly making improvements, which the Americans quickly adopt and sometimes surpass. There are increasing returns to scale; from the viewpoint of any one company, the larger the volume of its sales, the lower its costs per unit. In other words, there is a steep learning curve. Each company gets better and better with increased volume. While the Japanese are free to sell in the United States, the American firms cannot pierce the Japanese market, allegedly as a result of both visible and invisible trade barriers. Moreover, under Japanese Government auspices, the three Japanese firms share all of their knowledge with one another and work together on improvements. While the American firms have a research joint venture to share some of the results of their basic research, each of the American firms is so protective of its own trade secrets and has such a spirit of individualism that sharing is at best limited.

There are three major independent distributors of microchips in the United States—F, G and H. Each carries a full line of microchips, including microchip X. Each carries microchips made by more than one American producer. None carries microchips made by the Japanese. Each American producer of microchip X sells through one of the major independent distributors, all of whom have a high degree of technical expertise and who have well developed contacts with buyers. The Japanese have been selling to the U.S. market through small American independent distributors, but they are not satisfied with their market penetration. Each of the Japanese producers has asked each of the major American distributors if it will carry the Japanese product, and until recently each distributor—F, G and H—has refused.

Last month, independent distributor H agreed to carry the product of Japanese producer J. Last week, H informed J that it could not go forward with the deal; it would be unable to handle the line of J. When asked why, Hudson, H's vice president for marketing, said, "Look, we have been handling the product of A and B for several years. After we announced our new line, we had visits from A and then visits from B. They said (although in somewhat different words), 'Do you really want to help the Japanese? They won't let us into Japan. Who are you for? The Americans or the Japanese? It's either them or me.'" Ms. Hudson continued, "I know which side my bread is buttered on. So I dropped the Japanese."

You are a staff attorney in the Antitrust Division of the Department of Justice. Do you suspect that an antitrust violation has occurred?

Write a memorandum analyzing the problem. Because you do not yet know all of the facts and if you go forward you will need to ferret them out, make some alternative assumptions; e.g., that distributor H would, and would not, gain economies of scale from taking on the line of J. State what you think was probably happening and give the legal consequences of the alternative scenarios.

Be sure to combine your learning regarding horizontal restraints with your learning regarding vertical restraints. You will want to draw upon aspects of *Interstate Circuit, Matsushita, NCAA, Northwest Wholesale Stationers, Monsanto, Sharp Electronics* and *GTE Sylvania.*

If you think that there is probably, or plausibly, a violation, should the Justice Department investigate and sue? Is there any reason why the Justice Department should confer with the Commerce Department? With the State Department?

See Pollack, Big Chill on Asian Chips in U.S.—Import Distributors Feel Pressure From *American* Suppliers, New York Times, Sept. 6, 1988, D1, col. 3.

2. A NOTE ON FORECLOSING RESTRAINTS AND THE CONSUMER

The exclusive dealing and requirement cases you have seen, especially the earlier ones, do not focus primarily or perhaps even at all on consumers. They show concern with matters such as preserving competition as a process, assuring the opportunity for new or entering sellers to be evaluated on the merits by possible buyers, and preserving small business independence. Modern economic analysis focuses more sharply on consumers and offers a variety of possible views about restraints. Most commentators today recognize that there often are valid business reasons for using such restraints. It may be more efficient to sell two complementary articles together; a tie-in may reduce aggregate selling, packaging and delivery costs; tying and exclusive dealing may make production planning easier. Also, tying may (as we shall see) be used as a counting device to facilitate price discrimination, and thus to increase the sellers' aggregate return by charging heavy users more. Yet again, tying may be a means of protecting good will; if your calculating machines get jammed unless the cards fed into it meet certain specifications, perhaps it is wise to insist that the cards used be ones that you yourself have manufactured.

Commentators who regard output limitation as the only antitrust harm often regard antitrust concern with foreclosure as something close to nonsense. First, these commentators limit their focus to consumer price, and assert that consumers have no interest in who produces a product as long as they get it at the same or a lower price from someone else. (Thus, it is claimed, antitrust has no interest in protecting the opportunities of less well situated competitors.) Second, the claim is made that the foreclosing restraint cannot increase price to consumers, and might lower it, and that the restraint cannot be used as leverage to get an extra premium from the buyer or the dealer who is the subject of the restraint. Judge Bork, for example, might cite to the refiner who is contemplating exclusive contracts. If the refiner has market power, it can charge a supracompetitive price. It it does not have market power, it must charge a competitive price. In either case, it will not be able to persuade its independent dealer to accept an exclusive dealing or requirements provision in addition to the fees it must pay to be a dealer unless the refiner pays for the right to impose it; the refiner's monopoly return is a fixed sum that cannot be enlarged through leverage. See The Antitrust Paradox 299–309. Under this analysis, the perceived problem of limiting dealer independence or of exploiting dealers evaporates; the dealer makes only the deal she chooses to make. If the refiner "buys" the dealer's business in the form of a lower dealership fee, retail competition will assure that consumers receive an immediate benefit. The savings to the dealer will get passed on. Even if the refiner has power, its choice to impose exclusivity can only be made at the cost to it of otherwise higher dealer fees. (Unequal bargaining power and exploitation are a background fact of life whether or not a requirements contract or tie-in is a part of the bargain.) Given that the refiner that has market power will use it in one way or another, the refiner's choice to use vertical restraints is not adverse to the public interest. We will examine some of the limits of this fixed sum argument when we consider tying, infra pages 658–659.

Economists complement the fixed sum argument by a theoretical explanation of why vertical restraints tend to improve efficiency. Professor Oliver Williamson, for example, has greatly advanced thought on transaction costs. Williamson focuses attention on the transfer of goods or services across a technological or functional borderline. One activity (for example, refining or wholesaling gasoline) ends at some point, when another (for example, retailing) begins. When the functions are carried out by different firms, the interplay is not always harmonious. There may be misunderstandings and conflicts that lead to delays, breakdowns, exploitation, and other malfunctions. Williamson, Assessing Contract, 1 J. of Law, Econ. & Org. 177, 179 (1986). If the mutual welfare of sellers and buyers is not enhanced by a continuing relationship, they will deal on the open market, but otherwise they may consider some degree of integration. Requirements contracts or other devices by which the parties partially or loosely integrate their operations may effectively reduce risks and save costs. In short, sometimes efficiency explains the arrangement. See Williamson, Assessing Vertical Market Restraints: Antitrust Ramifications of the Transaction Cost Approach, 127 Pa.L.Rev. 953 (1979).

But vertical restraints can sometimes be explained as output-limiting. In some circumstances foreclosure restraints are used to raise rivals' costs relative to the actor's costs. In such cases the actor can reduce output by limiting the disadvantaged rivals' output. E.g., Krattenmaker & Salop, Anticompetitive Exclusion—Raising Rivals' Costs to Achieve Power Over Price, 96 Yale L.J. 209, 231–43 (1986). Also, foreclosing restraints can limit market output by significantly limiting competitors' access to necessary inputs or outlets so that a significant number of efficient competitors cannot survive. Where it is also the case that the disabled competitors cannot efficiently enter or contract for entry into the foreclosed adjacent market or do not have sufficient incentives to do so, the prime market can become oligopolized or monopolized. See F.M. Scherer, Industrial Market Structure and Economic Performance 89–91 (2d ed. 1980). However, the conditions necessary to sustain the output limitation story are not frequently present.

3. TYING AND RELATED ARRANGEMENTS

a. History and Status of the Per Se Rule

A tying arrangement involves two or more products or services. Buyers are eager to obtain one (the tying product), but the seller will supply it only if buyers agree to buy the other as well (the tied product). The Supreme Court's evolving treatment of tying provides a microcosm of today's evolving and conflicting antitrust attitudes.

KRAMER, THE SUPREME COURT AND TYING ARRANGEMENTS: ANTITRUST AS HISTORY
69 Minn.L.Rev. 1013 (1985).

I. THE EARLY HISTORY OF TYING ARRANGEMENTS, 1896–1914

The principal tool of antitrust enforcement is, of course, section 1 of the Sherman Act, which declares that "[e]very contract, combination in the form of trust or otherwise, or conspiracy, in restraint of trade or commerce among the several States, or with foreign nations, is [hereby] declared to be illegal."[13] Section 1 has rarely been read as broadly as its "every contract" language would suggest.[14] In the last decade of the nineteenth and the first decade of the twentieth centuries, the language was not thought adequate to prevent even those tying arrangements in which patentees sought to expand their legal monopolies by tying the patented products to nonpatented goods or services. In the germinal case of *Heaton–Peninsular Button–Fastener Co. v. Eureka Specialty Co.*,[15] the Sixth Circuit held in an opinion by Judge Horace Lurton that a patent carried with it the right to condition sale of the patented machine on the purchaser's agreement to use only the patentee's nonpatented goods with

13. Ch. 647, § 1, 26 Stat. 209 (codified at 15 U.S.C. § 1 (1982)) (brackets indicate language omitted from U.S.C.).

14. Strictly construed, § 1 could be interpreted to invalidate *all* contracts because all contracts "restrain" trade to a certain extent. Although enforcing the "plain mean-ing" of the statute received some early judicial support, *see* United States v. Trans-Missouri Freight Ass'n, 166 U.S. 290, 327–28 (1897), the Sherman Act has never been extended as far as its language would conceivably allow.

15. 77 F. 288 (6th Cir.1896).

the machine.[16] Although Judge Lurton recognized that the patentee's right to limit the use of the patented product was, like all property rights, subject to the general law of the land, the court never specified what such constraining laws might be and, significantly, never mentioned the six-year-old Sherman Act.

The first tying case to reach the Supreme Court[18] was *Henry v. A.B. Dick Co.,*[19] in which a manufacturer attached to its patented stencil-duplicating machine a "licensing restriction" that stated:

> This machine is sold by the A.B. Dick Co. with the licence restriction that it may be used only with the stencil paper, ink and other supplies made by A.B. Dick Company, Chicago, U.S.A.[20]

A.B. Dick brought a patent-infringement action against a subsequent seller of the machine, alleging that the defendant sold the machine with ink made by someone other than A.B. Dick.[21] Justice Lurton, by then sitting on the Supreme Court, wrote the majority opinion upholding this restriction under the reasoning of *Button–Fastener.*[22] The Sherman Act was mentioned only obliquely as not constituting a defense to the infringement action.[23]

16. *See id.* at 292. Coincidentally, the machine in question was used to fasten buttons to shoes. *See id.* at 295–96.

18. *See* L. Sullivan, [Law of Antitrust] § 151, at 433.

19. 224 U.S. 1 (1912).

20. *Id.* at 11.

21. *See id.* at 11–12.

22. *See id.* at 28; *supra* text accompanying notes 15–17. Chief Justice Edward White, writing for the dissent in *A.B. Dick,* called *Button–Fastener* "the leading one of the cases which all the others but follow and reiterate." *See id.* at 68 (White, C.J., joined by Hughes and Lamar, JJ., dissenting).

23. *See A.B. Dick,* 224 U.S. at 28–32. The Court relied on Bement v. National Harrow Co., 186 U.S. 70 (1902), which held that a provision in a licensing agreement, imposed by the holder of a patent, that fixed a price below which the patented articles could not be sold did not violate the Sherman Act. The *Bement* Court explained:

[T]he general rule is absolute freedom in the use or sale of rights under the patent laws of the United States. The very object of these laws is monopoly, and the rule is, with few exceptions, that any conditions that are not in their very nature illegal with regard to this kind of property, imposed by the patentee and agreed to by the licensee for the right to manufacture or use or sell the article, will be upheld by the courts. The fact that the conditions in the contracts keep up the monopoly or fix prices does not render them illegal.

. . . [W]e are brought back to the question whether the agreement between these parties with relation to these patented articles is valid within the [Sherman Act]. It is true that it has been held by this court that the act included any restraint of commerce, whether reasonable or unreasonable. . . . But that statute clearly does not refer to that kind of a restraint of interstate commerce which may arise from reasonable and legal conditions imposed upon the assignee or licensee of a patent by the owner thereof, restricting the terms upon which the article may be used and the price to be demanded therefor. Such a construction of the act we have no doubt was never contemplated by its framers.

Id. at 92–93; *see also A.B. Dick,* 224 U.S. at 29–30 (quoting *Bement*). The Court in *A.B. Dick* extended *Bement*'s analysis to tying arrangements, reasoning:

If the stipulation in an agreement between patentees and dealers in patented articles, which, among other things, fixed a price below which the patented articles should not be sold, would be a reasonable and valid condition, it must follow that any other reasonable stipulation, not inherently violative of some substantive law, imposed by a patentee as part of a sale of a patented machine, would be equally valid and enforceable.

A.B. Dick, 224 U.S. at 31. Even at this early date, the Court used economic arguments to supports its conclusions. For example, Justice Lurton addressed himself to the "leverage" argument that later became popular among economists opposed to tying arrangements. He wrote:

A.B. Dick, a four-to-three decision, was one of the relatively few decisions to seriously divide the Court in the early part of the century. A strong dissent was written by Chief Justice White and joined by Justices Hughes and Lamar, who feared that the doctrine on which the majority relied would permit such "evils" as a patentee's requiring that lumber from trees grown on a particular person's land or sawed by a particular mill be used with its patented carpenter's plane.[25] The minority overcame its "reluctance to dissent"[26] to "make it clear that if evils arise their continuance will not be caused by the interpretation now given to the statute, but will result from the inaction of the legislative department in failing to amend the statute so as to avoid such evils."[27]

Concern about the Sherman Act's apparent inability to reach tying arrangements was augmented by a general dissatisfaction about Supreme Court applications of the Act in other contexts.[28] The 1912 National Platform of the Democratic Party stated: "We regret that the Sherman Anti–Trust Law has received a judicial construction depriving it of much

But it has been very earnestly said that a condition restricting the buyer to use [the machine] only in connection with ink made by the patentee is one of a character which gives to a patentee the power to extend his monopoly so as to cause it to embrace any subject, not within the patent, which he chooses to require that the invention, shall be used in connection with. . . . If a patentee says, "I may suppress my patent if I will. I may make and have made devices under my patent, but I will neither sell nor permit anyone to use the patented things," he is within his right, and none can complain. But if he says, "I will sell with the right to use only with other things proper for using with the machines, and I will sell at the actual cost of the machines to me, provided you will agree to use only such articles as are made by me in connection therewith," if he chooses to take his profit in this way, instead of taking it by a higher price for the machines, has he exceeded his exclusive right to make, sell and use his patented machines? The market for the sale of such articles to the users of his machine, which, by such a condition, he takes to himself, was a market which he alone created by the making and selling of a new invention. Had he kept his invention to himself, no ink could have been sold by others for use upon machines embodying that invention. By selling it subject to the restriction he took nothing from others and in no wise restricted their legitimate market.

Id. at 31–32.

25. *See A.B. Dick,* 224 U.S. at 55 (White, C.J., joined by Hughes and Lamar, JJ., dissenting).

26. *See id.* at 49 (White, C.J., joined by Hughes and Lamar, JJ., dissenting).

27. *See id.* at 50 (White, C.J., joined by Hughes and Lamar, JJ., dissenting).

In United States v. Winslow, 227 U.S. 202 (1913), another pre-Clayton Act case, three separate groups of individuals, each controlling a different group of patented machines used in making shoes, formed into a combination, the United Shoe Machinery Co., that controlled between 70 and 80% of the market for their machines. *Id.* at 203 (argument for the United States); *id.* at 215–16 (opinion of the Court). The defendants then leased their machines on the condition that shoe manufacturers use only machines furnished by the combination. *Id.* at 216 (opinion of the Court). The defendants were charged with a criminal violation of the Sherman Act, *see id.,* and the Supreme Court, in an opinion by Justice Holmes, held that the combination was not unlawful, *see id.* at 216–17. Although the validity of the tying arrangements was not directly before the Court, Justice Holmes observed in passing that "[t]he machines are patented, making them is a monopoly in any case, the exclusion of competitors from the use of them is of the very essence of the right conferred by the patents, . . . and it may be assumed that the success of the several groups was due to their patents having been the best." *See id.* at 216 (citation omitted). The Court did not cite *A.B. Dick* or *Button–Fastener.*

28. In Standard Oil Co. v. United States, 221 U.S. 1 (1911), and United States v. American Tobacco Co., 221 U.S. 106 (1911), the Supreme Court interpreted the Sherman Act in "the light of reason." The Court's adoption of a rule of reason led some to decry the weakening of the Sherman Act and others to protest against its potentially broad scope. *See* Levy, *The Clayton Law— An Imperfect Supplement to the Sherman Law,* 3 Va.L.Rev. 411, 414–16 (1916).

of its efficiency, and we favor the enactment of legislation which will restore to the statute the strength of which it has been deprived by such interpretations." [29]   In the same year, the Democrats succeeded in having their candidate, Woodrow Wilson, elected President of the United States.

On January 20, 1914, President Wilson urged a joint session of Congress to adopt additional antitrust legislation.[30]   Wilson sought the establishment of a "trade commission" that would give "advice, . . . definite guidance and information" to businesses,[31] as well as the enactment of a statute designed to "explicitly" forbid, "item by item . . . in such terms as will practically eliminate uncertainty," [32] specified monopolistic practices not clearly unlawful under the Sherman Act.[33]   Within nine months of the address, Congress enacted both the Federal Trade Commission Act and the Clayton Act.[34]   Section 3 of the Clayton Act specifically applies to tying arrangements, stating:

> That it shall be unlawful for any person engaged in commerce, in the course of such commerce, to lease or make a sale or contract for sale of goods, wares, merchandise, machinery, supplies, or other commodities, whether patented or unpatented, for use, consumption or resale within the United States . . ., or fix a price charged therefor, or discount from, or rebate upon, such price, on the condition, agreement or understanding that the lessee or purchaser thereof shall not use or deal in the goods, wares, merchandise, machinery, supplies, or other commodities of a competitor or competitors of the lessor or seller, where the effect of such lease, sale, or contract for sale or such condition, agreement or understanding may be to substantially lessen competition or tend to create a monopoly in any line of commerce.[35]

Section 3 represented a late compromise between the opposing views of the Senate and the House of Representatives. As originally adopted by the House, section 4 of the bill criminalized all exclusive dealing, including tying arrangements, involving goods (as distinguished from services).[36] The Senate, however, struck section 4 from the bill.[37] The legislative history of the Clayton Act indicates that many senators objected to the section as unnecessary, apparently believing that the newly established

29. Levy, *supra* note 28, at 414–15.

30. President's Message to Congress of Jan. 20, 1914, 51 Cong.Rec. 1962, 1962 (1914).

31. *See id.* at 1963.

32. *See id.*

33. President Wilson's message outlined a number of provisions for inclusion in the statute, such as the prohibition of interlocking directorates, penalties for corporate officers who were responsible for antitrust law violations of their corporations, prohibition of holding companies, and tolling of the statute of limitations for the benefit of private antitrust plaintiffs. *See id.* at 1963–64. The President did not mention either exclusive dealing or tying arrangements.

34. The Federal Trade Commission Act was signed by the President on September 26, 1914. *See* Federal Trade Commission Act of 1914, Pub.L. No. 63–203, 38 Stat. 717 (codified as amended at 15 U.S.C. §§ 41–58 (1982)). The Clayton Act was signed on October 15, 1914. *See* Clayton Act of 1914, Pub.L. No. 63–212, 38 Stat. 730 (codified as amended in scattered sections of 15 U.S.C.).

35. Clayton Act, ch. 723, § 3, 38 Stat. 730, 731 (1914) (current version at 15 U.S.C § 14 (1982)).

36. *See* H.R. 15,657, § 4, 63d Cong., 2d Sess. (1914), *reprinted in* 2 The Legislative History of the Federal Antitrust Laws and Related Statutes 1729 (E. Kintner ed. 1978) [hereinafter cited as Legislative History].

37. *See* 51 Cong.Rec. 13,849 (1914) (deleting § 4); *id.* at 14,271–73 (amended version of § 4 deleted); H.R. 15,675, 63d Cong., 2d Sess. (1914) (as amended and passed by the Senate), *reprinted in* 3 Legislative History, *supra* note 36, at 2424–25.

Federal Trade Commission could better determine which exclusive dealing arrangements should be unlawful and could respond accordingly under section 5 of the Federal Trade Commission Act's [38] broad prohibition of "unfair methods of competition." [39] Other senators objected to the breadth of the bill. For example, during the debates, Senator Cummins remarked:

> If this section prohibited only the tying in of articles, I would be warmly and heartily for it, but it prohibits other transactions [as well].
> . . .
>
> . . . The manufacturer of Quaker Oats has acquired a great dominance in the trade. . . . The small competitor comes into the field desiring to introduce exactly the same thing . . . and calls it Rolled Oats. The only way in which he can make progress against his competitor is to secure a dealer . . . [to whom] he says, "If you will take my product, Rolled Oats, and agree not to sell the Quaker Oats . . . you shall have the exclusive privilege of selling it in this community, and you can make . . . a campaign for its introduction." I say that that transaction is not only an innocent one, but I think it is necessary in order to preserve competition among the manufacturers of the product. [40]

As indicated by Senator Cummins, some senators agreed with the House that certain tying arrangements should be prohibited outright and not left to the Trade Commission's discretion. The tying arrangements employed by the United Shoe Machinery Company received particular congressional condemnation. [41] United Shoe leased its patented shoe machinery on the condition that the lessee could not use the machinery to make shoes on which other work had been performed by a machine not leased from United Shoe. [42] In December 1911, the government had filed a Sherman Act suit attacking these lease provisions. [43] Barely three months later, the Supreme Court handed down its holding in *A.B. Dick*. [44]

Fear of *A.B. Dick*'s impact led some senators to urge reinstatement of the House provision outlawing tying arrangements. Senator Reed, for example, contended that *A.B. Dick* would "deprive the purchasing public of the advantages of . . . free use" of patented articles if not legislatively overruled. [45] He asserted that Chief Justice White's dissenting opinion in

38. Federal Trade Commission Act § 5, 38 Stat. 717, 719–21 (codified as amended at 15 U.S.C. § 45 (1982)).

39. *Id.* at 719; *see* Lockhart & Sacks, *The Relevance of Economic Factors in Determining Whether Exclusive Arrangements Violate Section 3 of the Clayton Act*, 65 Harv.L.Rev. 913, 934 (1952); McAllister, *Where the Effect May Be to Substantially Lessen Competition or Tend to Create a Monopoly*, 2 A.B.A. Sec. Antitrust L. 124, 125–26 (1953).

40. 51 Cong.Rec. 14,253 (1914) (statement of Sen. Cummins).

41. Reference to the tying arrangements of United Shoe Machinery during the congressional debates on the Clayton Act are extensive. *See, e.g.,* H.R.Rep. No. 627, 63d Cong., 2d Sess. 13 (1914), *reprinted in* 2 Legislative History, *supra* note 36, at 1089, 1094;

51 Cong.Rec. 15,990–91 (1914) (statement of Sen. Weeks); *id.* at 14,096–97 (statement of Sen. Reed); *id.* at 9408 (statement of Rep. Webb).

42. *See* United States v. United Shoe Mach. Co., 247 U.S. 32, 59–60 (1918).

43. *See* The Federal Antitrust Laws With Summary of Cases Instituted by the United States 1891–1951, at 92 (CCH 1952) (case 101) [hereinafter cited as Federal Antitrust Laws]. For a description of additional tying clauses in United Shoe's leases, see United States v. United Shoe Mach. Co., 247 U.S. 32, 61–63 (1918).

44. 224 U.S. 1 (1912); *see supra* notes 18–27 and accompanying text.

45. *See* 51 Cong.Rec. 14,091 (1914) (statement of Sen. Reed).

A.B. Dick was "a direct challenge to Congress to remedy this evil" [46] and that unless Congress acted, "it will be but a short time" until "every kind of restraint of trade will be protected by a [tying] clause." [47]

On August 26, 1914, the Senate agreed to an amendment prohibiting tying clauses in connection with patented products,[48] thus overruling the *A.B. Dick* decision.[49] Nevertheless, the legislation went to the conference committee with a wide difference of opinion between the House and the Senate on all other aspects of exclusive dealing. For nearly three weeks, the various factions battled over the section.[50] Finally, a compromise was reached, and both the Senate and the House adopted the new section 3, which made exclusive dealing arrangements unlawful when their effect "may be to substantially lessen competition." [51] The criminal sanctions were dropped entirely.[52]

In one respect, the congressional intent underlying section 3 seems reasonably clear: to condemn tying arrangements in which the tying product is patented.[53] Thus, section 3 was designed to ensure that United Shoe's tying arrangements would be unlawful under the Clayton Act regardless of the outcome of the pending Sherman Act challenge.[54] In other contexts, however, the compromise between the House and the

---

46. *See id.* at 14,092 (statement of Sen. Reed).

47. *See id.* at 14,095 (statement of Sen. Reed).

48. *See id.* at 14,273–76. Section 4, as adopted by the Senate, provided, in part:

> That it shall not be lawful to insert a condition in any contract relating to the sale or lease of or license to use any article or process protected by a patent or patents the effect of which will be to prohibit or restrict the purchaser, lessee, or licensee from using any article or class of articles, whether patented or not, or any patented process, supplied or owned by any person other than the seller, lessor, or licensor, or his nominees, or the effect of which will be to require the purchaser, lessee, or licensee to acquire from the seller, lessor, or licensor, or his nominees any article or class of articles not protected by the patent; and any such conditions, whether heretofore or hereafter made, shall be null and void, as being in restraint of trade and contrary to public policy. . . .

Id. at 14,275.

49. *See* Lockhart & Sacks, *supra* note 39, at 934 n. 63.

50. *See* 51 Cong.Rec. 16,273 (1914) (statement of Rep. Webb).

51. *See* H.R.Rep. No. 1168, 63d Cong., 2d Sess. 2 (1914), *reprinted in* 3 Legislative History, *supra* note 36, at 2456, 2457.

52. *See id.; supra* text accompanying note 35.

53. *See supra* notes 48–49 and accompanying text; *cf.* Jefferson Parish Hospital

Dist. No. 2 v. Hyde, 104 S.Ct. 1551, 1557 (1984) ("In enacting Section 3 of the Clayton Act, . . . Congress expressed great concern about the anticompetitive character of tying arrangements.") (citing H.R.Rep. No. 627, 63d Cong., 2d Sess. 10–13 (1914); Sen.Rep. No. 698, 63d Cong., 2d Sess. 6–9 (1914)). The accompanying footnote in *Hyde* contains numerous citations to the congressional debates in support of this proposition. *See Hyde*, 104 S.Ct. at 1557 n. 15; *see also* Lockhart & Sacks, *supra* note 39, at 934–35 (describing the competitive impact clause that was adopted by the conference committee as "undoubtedly the expression of the necessary compromise between the House and the Senate. This compromise was made necessary by the conviction of the majority of the Senate that not all exclusive arrangements adversely affect competition, and some should be permitted or even encouraged as helpful to competition. In the compromise, the Senate abandoned its insistence that only the FTC should exercise jurisdiction over exclusive arrangements, but by the competitive impact clause gained its point that discretion should be exercised by both the courts and the Commission in applying the Act.") (footnote omitted).

54. *See* McAllister, *supra* note 39, at 131–32 ("It is evident from the committee reports and debates on the floor that Congress was aiming this blow at the employment of exclusive dealing by established firms whose strength already verged on monopoly and not at smaller firms using it to cut down entrenched competitors.") (footnote omitted); *supra* notes 41–44 and accompanying text.

Senate did not clarify the law of tying arrangements, but instead dumped on the courts the responsibility for determining which arrangements were lawful and which were to be condemned because they "may . . . substantially lessen competition."[55] . . .

––––––––

The first post-Clayton Act tying case to reach the Supreme Court was *Motion Picture Patents,* decided in 1917 by a five-to-four majority.

MOTION PICTURE PATENTS CO. v. UNIVERSAL FILM MANUFACTURING COMPANY
243 U.S. 502 (1917).

JUSTICE CLARKE: ＊ ＊ ＊ [Motion Picture Patents Company owned a patent covering a mechanism used in motion picture exhibiting machines. Forty thousand of the plaintiff's machines were in use and the mechanism covered by the patent was the only one with which motion picture films could be used successfully. The company gave a license to the Precision Machine Company to manufacture and sell machines embodying the patent. The license stipulated that the machines made and sold by Precision were to be used solely for projecting films covered by other film patents licensed by Motion Picture Patents Company. The license also required Precision to attach a plate to each machine specifying that the sale and purchase of the machine gave the right to use it only with films utilizing those film patents.

Prague Amusement Company acquired one of the machines for its theater in New York City. It licensed and exhibited two films not covered by the film patents. When Motion Picture Patents Company sued for infringement, defendants pleaded that the restrictive conditions were void.]

[W]e are convinced that the exclusive right granted in every patent must be limited to the invention described in the claims of the patent and that it is not competent for the owner of a patent by notice attached to its machine to, in effect, extend the scope of its patent monopoly by restricting the use of it to materials necessary in its operation but which are no part of the patented invention, or to send its machines forth into the channels of trade of the country subject to conditions as to use or royalty to be paid to be imposed thereafter at the discretion of such patent owner. The patent law furnishes no warrant for such a practice and the cost, inconvenience and annoyance to the public which the opposite conclusion would occasion forbid it.

It is argued as a merit of this system of sale under a license notice that the public is benefited by the sale of the machine at what is practically its cost and by the fact that the owner of the patent makes its entire profit from the sale of the supplies with which it is operated. This fact, if it be a fact, instead of commending, is the clearest possible condemnation of, the practice adopted, for it proves that under color of its patent the owner intends to and does derive its profit, not from the

55. Clayton Act § 3, 15 U.S.C. § 14 (1982). . . .

invention on which the law gives it a monopoly but from the unpatented supplies with which it is used and which are wholly without the scope of the patent monopoly, thus in effect extending the power to the owner of the patent to fix the price to the public of the unpatented supplies as effectively as he may fix the price on the patented machine.

We are confirmed in the conclusion which we are announcing by the fact that since the decision of *Henry v. Dick Co.,* 224 U.S. 1, the Congress of the United States, the source of all rights under patents, as if in response to that decision, has enacted a law making it unlawful for any person engaged in interstate commerce "to lease or make a sale or contract for sale of goods . . . machinery, supplies or other commodities, *whether patented or unpatented,* for use, consumption or resale . . . or fix a price charged therefor . . . on the condition, agreement or under-standing that the lessee or purchaser thereof shall not use . . . the goods . . . . machinery, supplies or other commodities of a competitor or compet-itors of the lessor or seller, where the effect of such lease, sale, or contract for sale or such condition, agreement or understanding may be to substan-tially lessen competition or tend to create a monopoly in any line of commerce." 38 Stat. 730.

Our conclusion renders it unnecessary to make the application of this statute to the case at bar which the Circuit Court of Appeals made of it but it must be accepted by us as a most persuasive expression of the public policy of our country with respect to the question before us.

It is obvious that the conclusions arrived at in this opinion are such that the decision in *Henry v. Dick Co.,* 224 U.S. 1, must be regarded as overruled.

Coming now to the terms of the notice attached to the machine sold to the Seventy-second Street Amusement Company under the license of the plaintiff and to the first question as we have stated it.

This notice first provides that the machine, which was sold to and paid for by the Amusement Company may be used only with moving picture films containing the invention of reissued patent No. 12,192, so long as the plaintiff continues to own this reissued patent.

Such a restriction is invalid because such a film is obviously not any part of the invention of the patent in suit; because it is an attempt, without statutory warrant, to continue the patent monopoly in this particular character of film after it has expired, and because to enforce it would be to create a monopoly in the manufacture and use of moving picture films, wholly outside of the patent in suit and of the patent law as we have interpreted it.

The notice further provides that the machine shall be used only upon other terms (than those stated in the notice) to be fixed by the plaintiff, while it is in use and while the plaintiff "owns said patents." And it is stated at the bar that under this warrant a charge was imposed upon the purchaser graduated by the size of the theater in which the machine was to be used.

Assuming that the plaintiff has been paid an average royalty of $5 on each machine sold, prescribed in the license agreement, it has already received over $200,000 for the use of its patented improvement, which relates only to the method of using the films which another had invented, and yet it seeks by this device to collect during the life of the patent in suit what would doubtless aggregate many times this amount for the use of this same invention, after its machines have been sold and paid for.

A restriction which would give to the plaintiff such a potential power for evil over an industry which must be recognized as an important element in the amusement life of the nation, under the conclusions we have stated in this opinion, is plainly void, because wholly without the scope and purpose of our patent laws and because, if sustained, it would be gravely injurious to that public interest, which we have seen is more a favorite of the law than is the promotion of private fortunes.

* * *

JUSTICE HOLMES, dissenting: I suppose that a patentee has no less property in his patented machine than any other owner, and that in addition to keeping the machine to himself the patent gives him the further right to forbid the rest of the world from making others like it. In short, for whatever motive, he may keep his device wholly out of use. So much being undisputed, I cannot understand why he may not keep it out of use unless the licensee, or, for the matter of that, the buyer, will use some unpatented thing in connection with it. Generally speaking the measure of a condition is the consequence of a breach, and if that consequence is one that the owner may impose unconditionally, he may impose it conditionally upon a certain event. . . .

No doubt this principle might be limited or excluded in cases where the condition tends to bring about a state of things that there is a predominant public interest to prevent. But there is no predominant public interest to prevent a patented tea pot or film feeder from being kept from the public, because, as I have said, the patentee may keep them tied up at will while his patent lasts. Neither is there any such interest to prevent the purchase of the tea or films, that is made the condition of the use of the machine. The supposed contravention of public interest sometimes is stated as an attempt to extend the patent law to unpatented articles, which of course it is not, and more accurately as a possible domination to be established by such means. But the domination is one only to the extent of the desire for the tea pot or film feeder, and if the owner prefers to keep the pot or the feeder unless you will buy his tea or films, I cannot see in allowing him the right to do so anything more than an ordinary incident of ownership. . . .

Not only do I believe that the rule that I advocate is right * * *, but I think that it has become a rule of property that law and justice require to be retained. . . .

* * *

Questions and Comments

Motion Picture Patents, like *A.B. Dick,* involved contributory patent infringement. The court below based its decision on Clayton Act grounds. Justice Clarke's opinion sweeps more broadly. Although the opinion mentions Section 3 of the Clayton Act, it does so almost in passing. Overruling

A.B. Dick, the Court stated that using a patent in order to impose a tie is not sanctioned by the patent law and is against public policy. In the article excerpted above, Professor Kramer points out that when *Motion Picture Patents* was decided, the Supreme Court appeal was pending in *United States v. United Shoe Machinery,* 247 U.S. 32 (1918). That case, the first case brought by the government against *United Shoe,* was a Sherman Act Section 2 dissolution case. Among other things, it involved patent tying that dated back to 1899. As Justice Clarke knew, two Justices who voted with the majority in *Motion Picture Patents* had disqualified themselves from participating in *United Shoe.* Might Justice Clarke, by his broadly stated opinion in *Motion Picture Patents,* have been trying to affect the outcome in *United Shoe?*

If so, he failed. In 1918 the Court held all of the challenged conduct by United Shoe, including United Shoe's use of its patents for tying purposes, to be lawful. Justice Clarke dissented. What do you infer from the different outcomes in *Motion Picture Patents* and *United Shoe?* Did the two sets of tie ins have different market impacts? Or was the Court applying a different legal standard for tying offenses tested under the Clayton Act and those tested under the Sherman Act? Or was the Court applying a different legal philosophy? What is left of Justice Clarke's broad public policy analysis?

In *Motion Picture Patents,* what is the probable effect of the tying practice in the market for the tied product? Did the company imposing the tie have the power to secure a monopoly in the market for the tied product? Did it have the power to secure a monopoly in the market for the tied product? Does the Court's opinion condemn tying because it might yield a monopoly in the market for the tied product? If not, what evil did the Court mean to prevent?

The Court states, in effect, that use of a tie in for price discrimination (which may increase sales of the patented machine) condemns rather than commends the practice; it extends the patentee's power over price of the patented machine to power over price of unpatented supplies. Is this correct? Could A.B. Dick fix the price of the ink as effectively as it could fix the price of the patented mimeograph machine? Suppose that A.B. Dick's licensees used .01% of all ink sold; that the market price of ink was $1 per unit, and that A.D. Dick sold its machine at cost and charged its licenses $1.25 per unit of ink. Did A.B. Dick fix the price of ink? Did it gain power to cause the price of ink to rise? Would the tie in foreclose competitors from selling their ink on its merits, or would A.B. Dick be likely to buy (and resell) ink from the lowest-cost producer if other ink producers were more efficient than A.B. Dick? Is the same analysis applicable to the *Motion Picture Patents* situation?

Is it "bad" that A.B. Dick engaged in price discrimination through tying? Such discrimination could widen the deployment of the new technology. If A.B. Dick could not discriminate, thus charging heavy users more and light users less, its profit maximizing price for the mimeograph machine would be so high that some of the lighter users would be cut out of the market. Is there a counter argument? Allowing discrimination makes monopoly more profitable. Does the monopolist's increased ability to extract surplus from buyers induce more "rent chasing"—more investment and conduct aimed at getting or keeping monopoly? Should we worry about such incentives when the monopoly in question comes from a patent? When it comes from other sources?

In *Motion Picture Patents,* is it possible that the tie in had both of the following effects: (1) an increase in the average price of film used for motion pictures (net of the premium that was really a charge for the use of the feeding machine), and (2) an increase in the output of the machine? If so, and if analyzed under a contemporary rule of reason, would the tie in be lawful or unlawful?

Dissenting in *Motion Picture Patents,* Justice Holmes argued that a patentee cannot harm the public by a tie in because the patentee has the right to keep the product totally out of use, and a license on a stated condition is less restrictive than no license at all. Is this argument persuasive? If the argument prevailed, what would the emerging principle do to the law of vertical restraints generally?

The Department of Justice, undeterred by the loss of its 1918 Sherman Act suit against United Shoe, and perhaps heartened by intervening developments in the law, brought another case against the same company. Close in time to *Standard Fashion,* supra p. 627, which involved exclusive dealing, this was the first Supreme Court case in which tying was directly challenged under the Clayton Act. The opinion was written by Justice Day, who, like Justice Clarke, had dissented in the first *United Shoe* case in 1918.

UNITED SHOE MACHINERY CORP. v. UNITED STATES

258 U.S. 451 (1922).

JUSTICE DAY: This suit was brought by the United States against the defendants, United Shoe Machinery Company (of Maine), United Shoe Machinery Corporation, United Shoe Machinery Company (of New Jersey), and the officers and directors of these corporations, under the provisions of the Clayton Act of October 15, 1914, c. 323, 38 Stat. 731, 736, to enjoin them from making leases containing certain clauses, terms and conditions alleged to be violative of the act. Issues were made up, testimony taken, and a decree granted by the District Court enjoining the use of certain clauses in the leases. . . .

* * *

. . . The record discloses that the United Shoe Machinery Corporation, hereinafter called the United Company, controlled a very large portion of the business of supplying shoe machinery of the classes involved in this case. The court below found that it controlled more than 95% of such business in the United States. . . . It is evident from this record that the United Company occupies a dominant position in the production of such machinery and makes and supplies throughout the United States a very large percentage of such machinery used by manufacturers.

It may be conceded at the outset, and was so found in the court below, that the company did not act oppressively in the enforcement of the forfeiture clauses of the leases. It is established that it furnishes machines of excellent quality; that it renders valuable services in the installation of machines, instructions to operators, promptness in furnishing machines when desired by manufacturers, and is expeditious in making repairs and replacements when necessary so to do. The machines of the United Company are protected by patents granted prior to the passage of the Clayton Act, and the validity of none of them is called in question here.

* * *

Turning to the decree, it will be found that the court enjoined the use of (1) the restricted use clause, which provides that the leased machinery shall not, nor shall any part thereof, be used upon shoes, etc., or portions, thereof, upon which certain other operations have not been performed on other machines of the defendants; (2) the exclusive use clause, which provides that if the lessee fails to use exclusively machinery of certain kinds made by the lessor, the lessor shall have the right to cancel the right to use all such machinery so leased; (3) the supplies clause, which provides that the lessee shall purchase supplies exclusively from the lessor; (4) the patent insole clause, which provides that the lessee shall only use machinery leased on shoes which have had certain other operations performed upon them by the defendants' machines; (5) the additional machinery clause, which provides that the lessee shall take all additional machinery for certain kinds of work from the lessor or lose his right to retain the machines which he has already leased; (6) the factory output clause, which requires the payment of a royalty on shoes operated upon by machines made by competitors; (7) the discriminatory royalty clause, providing lower royalty for lessees who agree not to use certain machinery on shoes lasted on machines other than those leased from the lessor. The defendant's restrictive form of leases embraces the right of the lessor to cancel a lease for the breach of a provision in such lease, or in any other lease or license agreement between the lessor and the lessee. . . . The District Court held that the United Company had the right to cancel a lease for a violation of the terms of the particular lease, but could not, without violating the act reserve the right to cancel a lease because the lessee had violated the terms of some other lease. This part of the decree must be read in the light of the circumstances shown as to the necessity of procuring shoe machinery from the United Company, and the danger of a lessee losing his ability to continue business by a forfeiture incurred from the breach of a single covenant in one lease.

While the clauses enjoined do not contain specific agreements not to use the machinery of a competitor of the lessor, the practical effect of these drastic provisions is to prevent such use. We can entertain no doubt that such provisions as were enjoined are embraced in the broad terms of the Clayton Act which cover all conditions, agreements or understandings of this nature. That such restrictive and tying agreements must necessarily lessen competition and tend to monopoly is, we believe, equally apparent. When it is considered that the United Company occupies a dominating position in supplying shoe machinery of the classes involved, these covenants signed by the lessee and binding upon him effectually prevent him from acquiring the machinery of a competitor of the lessor except at the risk of forfeiting the right to use the machines furnished by the United Company which may be absolutely essential to the prosecution and success of his business.

This system of "tying" restrictions is quite as effective as express covenants could be and practically compels the use of the machinery of the lessor except upon risks which manufacturers will not willingly incur. . . .

[The Government was not estopped because of a decree in favor of United in a prior Sherman Act case] * * *

The Sherman Act suit had for its object the dissolution of the United Company, which had been formed by the union of other shoe machinery companies. It also attacked and sought to enjoin the use of the restrictive and tying clauses contained in the leases as being in themselves contracts in violation of the Sherman Act. The Sherman Act and the Clayton Act provide different tests of liability. This was determined in the recent case of *Standard Fashion Co. v. Magrane–Houston Co., ante,* 346. . . .

That the leases were attacked under the former bill as violative of the Sherman Act is true, but they were sustained as valid and binding agreements within the rights of holders of patents. The Clayton Act specifically applies to goods, wares, machinery, etc., whether "*patented or unpatented.*" This provision was inserted in the Clayton Act with the express purpose of preventing rights granted by letters patent from securing immunity from the inhibitions of the act. . . .

* * *

It is further insisted that the suit must fail because the parties were offered an alternative lease alleged to be free from the objectionable conditions complained of. But this lease was only granted upon the lessee making an initial payment in cash instead of paying the lessor royalties throughout the term. There is some conflict in the testimony as to whether the effect of such requirement was so onerous as to compel the lessee to choose the restricted form of leases. The issue involved here is whether leases with the restricted clauses in them, the enforcement of which has been enjoined by the District Court, were such as to make them violative of the provisions of the Clayton Act. The fact that a form of lease was offered which is not the subject of controversy is not a justification of the use of clauses in other leases which we find to be violative of the act.

* * *

Affirmed.

JUSTICE MCKENNA dissented.

JUSTICE BRANDEIS took no part in the consideration or decision of this case.

Questions and Comments

By use of tying, the Motion Picture Patents Company had threatened to extend monopoly from one market (film-feeding machines) to a complementary market (film for motion pictures). The conduct of A.B. Dick, on the other hand, did not threaten monopoly in the ink market, nor did it threaten increased monopoly power in the mimeograph machine market. Rather, for A.B. Dick, tying was a method for metering the intensities of demand of various buyers of the mimeograph machine and of extracting revenue according to the intensity of demand. Thus, it was a means of more fully exploiting existing power rather than of increasing power.

The lease clauses in *United Shoe Machinery II* reflect a number of purposes and effects of tying when used by a dominant firm. Consider each of the seven clauses. Which involves price discrimination? Which seems intended to impose additional costs on competitors? Would any clause foreclose markets for competitors to a degree that threatened to eliminate them or force them to scale back? Were any of the clauses likely to raise barriers to entry into the market of the tied product? Would they raise barriers to entry into the market of the tying product?

Evaluate the following propositions: United Shoe was dominant in the production of complex machines necessary to perform certain functions in shoe-making. It leased (rather than sold) machines to manufacturers of shoes, and required that the lessee not use its complex machines on any shoe as to which other functions were performed by the machine of a competitor. With its monopoly control over the complex machines, the restrictive clause forced its customers to use its simpler machines, also.

If a tied product (for example, a complementary machine) is always used in fixed proportions with the tying product, the possible adverse effects of tying are limited. At the extreme, think about shoe pairs. Shoe pairs are one product; there is no separate market for right shoes and for left shoes. But put that to one side. A shoe seller can never get more money for the sum of the parts then for the pair, even if the shoe seller is the only shoe seller in town; nor could it insinuate itself more deeply into the left shoe market by insisting that everyone who buys a right shoe must buy a left shoe. Customers are willing to spend a certain sum for a *pair* of shoes, say $50. It would make no difference if the shoe seller prices the "first" (let us say, right) shoe at $25, $20, or $30. For the tied shoe, the buyer would be willing to pay and would pay no more than $25, $30, and $20; moreover, the buyer would not buy more left shoes at the $20 price, nor fewer right shoes at the $30 price, for the package adds up to $50. The tie in cannot be used to exact an extra premium for the tied shoe, nor to obtain extra sales of the tied shoe.

So, too, if for every shoe partly manufactured on United's complex machine a fixed amount of use was needed on the complementary simple machines, United could not get additional revenue if it put a premium on the tied product (use of the simple machine) over what it could get if it put the premium on the tying (complex) machine. Given fixed proportions, there is one obtainable price for the package. Moreover, the allocation of price between tied and tying product does not influence the amount of the tied product that will be sold. Therefore, if this is all that is going on, the tie does not increase the seller's monopoly returns. Was this the case with United Shoe?

In a fixed proportions case (where no extra monopoly returns can be earned) is there any reason to object to the tie? It can result in a monopoly of the tied product, destroying suppliers that had invested in this market and were performing well. Might the second monopoly also result in less competitive pressure to innovate and otherwise to reduce costs in the tied product market? Might it also be the case that the destroyed suppliers were the most likely entrants into the market for the tying product and that the tie in eliminated potential competition and raised barriers to entry into the tying market, thus increasing United Shoe's available monopoly return?

(Fox & Sullivan) Antitrust ACB—23

The most formidable defense of tying comes from Chicago School theorists, most notably from Judge Bork. See The Antitrust Paradox 140–41, 213, 258, 290, 306, 366–67, 373–74. As Judge Bork sees the matter, even though United Shoe had monopoly power in the market for some machines, it would not be able to tie its machines that faced competition to the monopolized machines unless it gave buyers something (for example, a reduction in the price of the monopoly machine, or better service) sufficient to induce them to accept the reduction in their freedom to buy non-monopolized machines from others. United Shoe's monopoly profit is a fixed sum. The company cannot increase its monopoly profit by extending its monopoly from the machines on which it was dominant to those on which it was not, because to do so it would have to pay out part of its monopoly return to induce the buyer to accept the tie. To assume otherwise is to fall into "the fallacy of double counting." Id. at 140. See also H. Hovenkamp, Economics and Federal Antitrust Law 223–24 (1985), spelling out the double count argument.

Is Bork correct? Professors Louis Kaplow suggests not, or at least not entirely. Kaplow, Extension of Monopoly Power Through Leverage, 85 Colum.L.Rev. 515 (1985). Mindful of market failures and bounded rationality, Kaplow raises serious questions about the double count argument. In an unpublished paper sent to one of the editors, Professor Mark Roe, Columbia University School of Law, suggests these possibilities:

Lack of information, transaction costs, and bounded rationality: Suppose shoe manufacturers (relatively small firms, typically working on small, competitive mark-ups) accepted the tie and paid the full monopoly price for the monopolized machine without having investigated all of the alternatives they had for the non-monopolized machines. They dealt with United Shoe all of the time and knew they had to depend upon United Shoe. Why not just close the deal with United Shoe and get on with making shoes?

Free riding: Picture a shoe manufacturer who has just read Judge Bork's book and who is considering making a demand on United Shoe for a price concession on the tying product as a condition to agreeing to the tie. Would he not realize that United Shoe could, at small cost to itself, decline that request and simply cut the single manufacturer out entirely? Indeed, might he not fear a cut-off as a possible response, given that United Shoe might well suppose that granting such a concession to one shoe manufacturer might start a series of such demands from others? Since the shoe manufacturer needs United Shoe's monopoly machines, a risk that United Shoe will cut it off is not to be taken lightly. Thus, an aggressive strategy in dealing with the company would be feasible only if all or most shoe manufacturers acted concertedly (which would be unlawful?) or at least acted in the same way. None would have the incentive to get out in front to champion the cause of all, with others awaiting the outcome as free riders. Nor (even assuming that joint action would be lawful) is it likely that any one of them would incur the transaction costs of trying to organize all of them.

Passing on: Given the competitive structure of shoe manufacturing, as long as all shoe manufacturers paid United Shoe's "monopoly overcharge," it was likely that the overcharge would be passed on by shoe manufacturers to shoe buyers. The shoe manufacturers' own margin would not be reduced. If so, the single shoe manufacturer would have little incentive to take the risk of demanding a price reduction in return for accepting the tie.

Which perspective, that of Bork, or that of Roe, do you find most convincing? When a market functions like the Bork model, a tie will not be an effective way to increase monopoly returns. Might a tie in do so in markets that do not work so well? Is it feasible to investigate the market facts and make a judgment about the robustness of competition?

We have examined tie ins that have the effect of increasing output. What are the other possible explanations for tying? Under what structural circumstances might tying, and consequent foreclosure, be used to raise rivals' costs? Consider, for example, a variation of *Lorain Journal Company v. United States,* 342 U.S. 143 (1951). Lorain Journal knew that new entrant WEOL needed a certain level of advertising from the local businesses that placed ads in the Lorain Journal and that these businesses regarded Lorain Journal ads as a necessity. Suppose that Lorain Journal, instead of refusing to deal with advertisers who dealt with WEOL, told its customers that they could not buy space in its morning newspaper unless they bought space in its afternoon newspaper, and suppose that Lorain Journal knew that the tie in requirement would eat up the advertising budgets of its clients. Is this scenario virtually identical to the *Lorain Journal* case? But compare *Times-Picayune Publishing Co. v. United States,* 345 U.S. 594 (1953) (tying morning and afternoon space not illegal where there was no predatory purpose or effect).

Tying also may yield benefits. Judge Bork points out that tying may be a procompetitive response to competition in the tying product. The package may be a product consumers want. We have also mentioned that tying can facilitate price discrimination and that price discrimination could increase output (although price discrimination is by no means unambiguously efficient—it can exist only in the presence of, and increases the returns from, market power, and is sufficiently unfair to have provoked a law against certain forms of it).

When sellers in competitive markets sell their goods or services in packages one must suspect that the tie in is a way to compete, not exploit. Consider the following circumstances.

FTC v. SINCLAIR REFINING CO.
261 U.S. 463 (1923).

JUSTICE MCREYNOLDS: In separate proceedings against thirty or more refiners and wholesalers, the Federal Trade Commission condemned and ordered them to abandon the practice of leasing underground tanks with pumps to retail dealers at nominal prices and upon condition that the equipment should be used only with gasoline supplied by the lessor. Four of these orders were held invalid by the circuit courts of appeals for the third and seventh circuits in the above entitled causes; and like ones have been set aside by the circuit courts of appeals for the second and sixth circuits. The . . . four records now before us are so similar that it will suffice to consider No. 213, as typical of all.

July 18, 1919, the Commission issued a complaint charging that respondent, Sinclair Refining Company, was purchasing and selling refined oil and gasoline and leasing and loaning storage tanks and pumps as part of interstate commerce in competition with numerous other concerns similarly engaged; and that it was violating both the Federal Trade Commission Act, [§ 5], and the Clayton Act, [§ 3].

* * *

There is no covenant in the present contract which obligates the lessee not to sell the goods of another. . . . The lessee is free to buy wherever he chooses; he may freely accept and use as many pumps as he wishes and may discontinue any or all of them. He may carry on business as his judgment dictates and his means permit, save only that he cannot use the lessor's equipment for dispensing another's brand. By investing a comparatively small sum, he can buy an outfit and use it without hindrance. He can have respondent's gasoline, with the pump or without the pump, and many competitors seek to supply his needs.

* * *

. . . [The challenged practice] has been openly adopted by many competing concerns. Some dealers regard it as the best practical method of preserving the integrity of their brands and securing wide distribution. Some think it is undesirable. The devices are not expensive—$300 to $500—can be purchased readily of makers and, while convenient, they are not essential. The contract, open and fair upon its face, provides an unconstrained recipient with free receptacle and pump for storing, dispensing, advertising and protecting the lessor's brand. The stuff is highly inflammable and the method of handling it is important to the refiner. He is also vitally interested in putting his brand within easy reach of consumers with ample assurance of its genuineness. No purpose or power to acquire unlawful monopoly has been disclosed, and the record does not show that the probable effect of the practice will be unduly to lessen competition. Upon the contrary, it appears to have promoted the public convenience by inducing many small dealers to enter the business and put gasoline on sale at the crossroads.

The powers of the Commission are limited by the statutes. It has no general authority to compel competitors to a common level, to interfere with ordinary business methods or to prescribe arbitrary standards for those engaged in the conflict for advantage called competition. The great purpose of both statutes was to advance the public interest by securing fair opportunity for the play of the contending forces ordinarily engendered by an honest desire for gain. And to this end it is essential that those who adventure their time, skill and capital should have large freedom of action in the conduct of their own affairs.

The suggestion that the assailed practice is unfair because of its effect upon the sale of pumps by their makers is sterile and requires no serious discussion.

Questions and Comments

Ten years after *Sinclair* the Supreme Court decided the first private case challenging a tie-in under the Clayton Act. The case involved General Motors' franchise agreement, which required GM dealers to use only GM parts when they were doing repairs on GM cars. Although GM was a leading car maker, there was no evidence indicating the percentage of the repair market foreclosed. If a large volume of repairs of GM cars was done at independent garages and at non-GM dealerships (probably true at the time), the extent of the foreclosure was small. The court of appeals found the arrangement lawful, stressing (1) GM had an interest in assuring that repairs on its cars by its dealers were satisfactory, (2) the agreement protected expectations because consumers would expect a GM dealer to use GM parts in repairing a GM car, and (3) the restraint (which applied only to GM cars) was no broader that those two interests required. *Pick Manufacturing Co. v. General Motors Corp.*, 299 U.S. 3 (1936), *aff'ing per curiam* 80 F.2d 641 (7th Cir.1935).

Are *Sinclair* and *Pick* consistent with *United Shoe Machinery II?* Was the practice used by Sinclair consistent with efforts to sell more gasoline at a competitive price? Do you find credible the claim that Sinclair wanted to protect consumers from getting inferior gas that was passed off as Sinclair gas? Did the tie assure Sinclair that its product was handled and promoted properly?

What was the probable effect of the tie on manufacturers and sellers of gas pumps? Might the oil companies have bought their pumps from efficient independent manufacturers, notwithstanding the tie?

Sinclair presents another reason for the sale of two products in combination: an attractive package may be a way to wage competition.

A Note on the Development of the Law

Between the late 1930s and the late 1960s, the Supreme Court developed a strong rule against the use of tie ins by firms with market power. In *International Business Machines Corporation v. United States,* 298 U.S. 131 (1936), the Supreme Court held illegal IBM's lease of its tabulating machine on condition that lessees use only IBM-manufactured tabulating cards, despite IBM's claims that the condition was warranted by IBM's patents on both the machines and the cards and by IBM's interest in assuring quality so as not to undermine the performance of the machines. The Court held the first claim wrong as a matter of law. As to the second, the Court said:

> There is no contention that others than appellant cannot meet these requirements. It affirmatively appears, by stipulation, that others are capable of manufacturing cards suitable for use in appellant's machines, and that paper required for that purpose may be obtained from the manufacturers who supply appellant. . . . The Government, under the provisions of its lease, following its own methods, has made large quantities of the cards, which are in successful use with appellant's machines. The suggestion that without the tying clause an adequate supply of cards would not be forthcoming from competitive sources is not supported by the evidence. "The very existence of such restrictions suggests that in its absence a competing article of equal or better quality would be offered at the same or at a lower price." *Carbice Corporation v. American Patents Development Corp.* [283 U.S. 27], 32, Note 2, quoting Vaughan, Economics of Our Patent System, 125, 127. Appellant's sales of cards return a substantial profit and the Government's payment of 15% increase in rental to secure the privilege of making its own cards is profitable only if it produces the cards at a cost less than 55% of the price charged by appellant.

Appellant is not prevented from proclaiming the virtues of its own cards or warning against the danger of using, in its machines, cards which do not conform to the necessary specifications, or even from making its leases conditional upon the use of cards which conform to them. For aught that appears such measures would protect its good will, without the creation of monopoly or resort to the suppression of competition.

The Clayton Act names no exception to its prohibition of monopolistic tying clauses. Even if we are free to make an exception to its unambiguous command, we can perceive no tenable basis for an exception in favor of a condition whose substantial benefit to the lessor is the elimination of business competition and the creation of monopoly, rather than the protection of its good will, and where it does not appear that the latter can not be achieved by methods which do not tend to monopoly and are not otherwise unlawful. (298 U.S. at 139–40)

At first blush does the tie-in look benign—unless IBM has a duty to create a market for producers of IBM-compatible tabulating cards? Did the Court think IBM had such a duty?

The Court in the *IBM* case mentioned almost in passing that IBM and its only three rivals (one of which IBM proceeded to acquire and one of which failed) agreed that each manufacturer would impose the tabulating-card tie in on all of its lessees, and that none would try to sell its cards to lessees of the other. Does this give you a clue as to what was really happening? Were the producers, by agreement, charging less than the full monopoly price for their tabulating machines and putting a premium on each tabulating card (hence the enormous profit the Court observed), thus charging a hefty premium to heavy users and thereby maximizing their joint profits? If so, can you imagine IBM's anger when the market it "reserved" for the monopoly profit got skimmed by "knaves" who had invested nothing in inventing a tabulating machine? Would you be more sympathetic to IBM's cause if IBM had no rivals or at least had no agreement with rivals? If IBM was "merely" a monopolist price discriminating to reap its inventor's reward? Are you reminded of the contemporary controversies between IBM and the manufacturers of peripheral equipment?

Another landmark case—*International Salt Company v. United States,* 332 U.S. 392 (1947)—came down in 1947. The International Salt Company leased patented machines that injected salt into canned products during the canning process (the Saltomat)—and that dissolved rock salt into brine for industrial processes (the Lixator) on condition that the lessees bought the salt they would use in the leased machines from International Salt. But there were exceptions. Lessees of the Lixator were given the right to buy salt on the open market if there was a general reduction in market prices and if International Salt declined to meet the price reduction. Lessees of the Saltomat were given a most favored nation's clause on the price of salt; if International Salt generally reduced the price of salt tablets for use in its machine, the lessee would get the benefit of the reduction.

Like IBM, International Salt did not prove the necessity of a tie in to protect good will in its machines, and, despite the "exception" clauses, the Supreme Court ruled against the company. Thus:

Appellant contends, however, that summary judgment was unauthorized because it precluded trial of alleged issues of fact as to whether the restraint was unreasonable within the Sherman Act or substantially lessened competition or tended to create a monopoly in salt within the Clayton Act. We think the admitted facts left no genuine issue. Not only is price-fixing unreasonable, *per se, United States v. Socony–Vacuum Oil Co.,* 310 U.S. 150; *United States v. Trenton Potteries Co.,* 273 U.S. 392, but also it is unreasonable, *per se,* to foreclose competitors from any substantial market. *Fashion Originators Guild v. Federal Trade Commission,* 114 F.2d 80, affirmed, 312 U.S. 457. The volume of business affected by these contracts cannot be said to be insignificant or insubstantial and the tendency of the arrangement to accomplishment of monopoly seems obvious. Under the law, agreements are forbidden which "tend to create a monopoly," and it is immaterial that the tendency is a creeping one rather than one that proceeds at full gallop; nor does the law await arrival at the goal before condemning the direction of the movement. . . .

The "Lixator" provision does, of course, afford a measure of protection to the lessee, but it does not avoid the stifling effect of the agreement on competition. The appellant had at all times a priority on the business at equal prices. A competitor would have to undercut appellant's price to have any hope of capturing the market, while appellant could hold that market by merely meeting competition. We do not think this concession relieves the contract of being a restraint of trade, albeit a less harsh one than would result in the absence of such a provision. The "Saltomat" provision obviously has no effect of legal significance since it gives the lessee nothing more than a right to buy appellant's salt tablets at appellant's going price. (332 U.S. at 396–97)

Does the salt tie in look benign if your only concern is output limitation? Do the exception clauses seem to protect against output limitation? Don't the exception clauses even protect against price discrimination? Under the Lixator clause it was not possible for International Salt to profit maximize by charging salt users a premium over the market price, and thus to exploit the heavy users of salt.

How, then, can you explain International Salt's strategy? Would it surprise you to learn that International Salt's major competitors followed the same strategy? If so, might the Lixator clause have been a policing mechanism for a cartel? If any producers cheated from the cartel price, salt buyers would be the first to report the cheaters. Might the Saltomat clause have been another cartel clause? Cheating would be so expensive that it would probably not occur. Review the *Ethyl/du Pont* case, supra p. 490.

Suppose that *International Salt, IBM,* and *Dr. Miles,* supra p. 523, were really all producer cartel cases. If so, the Supreme Court did not understand this and it did not pursue clues that led to this inference; it formulated principles of law, indeed per se principles of law, based on a conception of freedom of trade and without regard to a cartel explanation. Does the existence of a cartel explanation strengthen or undercut the rule of law? Or is it totally irrelevant?

The broad principle and the economic philosophy of *International Salt* was underscored in the next decade by another landmark, *Northern Pacific Railway Company v. United States,* 356 U.S. 1 (1958). Congress had granted the predecessor of the Northern Pacific Railway 40 million acres of land to facilitate its construction of a railroad. In many of its sales contracts and most of its lease contracts, the railroad extracted preferential routing clauses, requiring the buyer or lessee to ship on the Northern Pacific line all goods produced on the land, provided that Northern Pacific's rates and in some cases its service were equal to those of competing carriers. The Court held the preferential routing clauses per se illegal under Section 1 of the Sherman Act. Justice Black wrote for the Court a much quoted opinion.

NORTHERN PACIFIC RAILROAD CO. V. UNITED STATES

356 U.S. 1 (1958).

Justice Black:

The Sherman Act was designed to be a comprehensive charter of economic liberty aimed at preserving free and unfettered competition as the rule of trade. It rests on the premise that the unrestrained interaction of competitive forces will yield the best allocation of our economic resources, the lowest prices, the highest quality and the greatest material progress, while at the same time providing an environment conducive to the preservation of our democratic political and social institutions. But even were that premise open to question, the policy unequivocally laid down by the Act is competition. . . .

. . . [T]here are certain agreements or practices which because of their pernicious effect on competition and lack of any redeeming virtue are conclusively presumed to be unreasonable and therefore illegal without elaborate inquiry as to the precise harm they have caused or the business excuse for their use. This principle of *per se* unreasonableness not only makes the type of restraints which are proscribed by the Sherman Act more certain to the benefit of everyone concerned, but it also avoids the necessity for an incredibly complicated and prolonged economic investigation into the entire history of the industry involved, as well as related industries, in an effort to determine at large whether a particular restraint has been unreasonable—an inquiry so often wholly fruitless when undertaken. Among the practices which the courts have heretofore deemed to be unlawful in and of themselves are price fixing, *United States v. Socony–Vacuum Oil Co.,* 310 U.S. 150, 210; division of markets, *United States v. Addyston Pipe & Steel Co.,* 85 F. 271, aff'd, 175 U.S. 211; group boycotts, *Fashion Originators' Guild v. Federal Trade Comm'n,* 312 U.S. 457; and tying arrangements, *International Salt Co. v. United States,* 332 U.S. 392.

. . . Indeed "tying agreements serve hardly any purpose beyond the suppression of competition." *Standard Oil Co. of California v. United States,* 337 U.S. 293, 305–306.[5] They deny competitors free access to the market for the tied product, not because the party imposing the tying requirements has a better product or a lower price but because of his power or leverage in another market. At the same time buyers are forced to forego their free choice between competing products. For these reasons

5. As this Court has previously pointed out such nonanticompetitive purposes as these arrangements have been asserted to possess can be adequately accomplished by other means much less inimical to competi-tion. *See, e.g., International Business Machines Corp. v. United States,* 298 U.S. 131; *International Salt Co. v. United States,* 332 U.S. 392.

"tying agreements fare harshly under the laws forbidding restraints of trade." *Times–Picayune Publishing Co. v. United States,* 345 U.S. 594, 606. They are unreasonable in and of themselves whenever a party has sufficient economic power with respect to the tying product to appreciably restrain free competition in the market for the tied product and a "not insubstantial" amount of interstate commerce is affected. *International Salt Co. v. United States,* 332 U.S. 392 [$500,000 not insubstantial]. Of course where the seller has no control or dominance over the tying product so that it does not represent an effectual weapon to pressure buyers into taking the tied item any restraint of trade attributable to such tying arrangements would obviously be insignificant at most. As a simple example, if one of a dozen food stores in a community were to refuse to sell flour unless the buyer also took sugar it would hardly tend to restrain competition in sugar if its competitors were ready and able to sell flour by itself.

In this case we believe the district judge was clearly correct in entering summary judgment declaring the defendant's "preferential routing" clauses unlawful restraints of trade. . . .

. . . The very existence of this host of tying arrangements is itself compelling evidence of the defendant's great power, at least where, as here, no other explanation has been offered for the existence of these restraints. The "preferential routing" clauses conferred no benefit on the purchasers or lessees. While they got the land they wanted by yielding their freedom to deal with competing carriers, the defendant makes no claim that it came any cheaper than if the restrictive clauses had been omitted. In fact any such price reduction in return for rail shipments would have quite plainly constituted an unlawful rebate to the shipper. So far as the Railroad was concerned its purpose obviously was to fence out competitors, to stifle competition. While this may have been exceedingly beneficial to its business, it is the very type of thing the Sherman Act condemns. . . .

* * *

After *Northern Pacific* it was clear that the country had a modified per se rule against tie ins. It was per se illegal for a firm with market power to condition the sale (or lease) of one product or service on the purchase (or lease) of another if a not insubstantial dollar amount of trade in the tied product was affected. In the 1960s, the reach of the principle was expanded. For one thing, "market power" and "conditioning" were generously defined.

Major motion picture producer/distributors developed a practice of block-booking (selling in packages) pre–1948 copyrighted motion picture feature films to television stations for television exhibition. Television stations complained that they had to accept "cabooses" with "engines." To get *Casablanca* they had to accept *Getting Gertie's Garter.* In fact, the movie companies offered packages that contained an array of films. Each package might include a small number of "A" films (outstanding quality), a large number of "B" films, perhaps 50 or 60, and a number of not very desirable or totally undesirable ("C") films, perhaps 20. The movie companies defended (in some cases) that the packages resulted from negotiation, not conditioning. Moreover, they argued that there was no tying product; there was no particularly unique product imbued with market power; rather, they said, old feature films were just a small part of television programming and were largely interchangeable with one another and with other types of television programming.

The Supreme Court rejected defendants' arguments and condemned block booking per se. It repeated the antitrust concerns regarding tie ins: "they may force buyers into giving up the purchase of substitutes for the tied product, . . . and they may destroy the free access of competing suppliers of the tied product to the consuming market." *United States v. Loew's Inc.,* 371 U.S. 38, 45 (1962). The Court then weakened the market power requirement, saying: "Even absent a showing of market dominance, the crucial economic power may be inferred from the tying product's desirability to consumers or from uniqueness of its attributes. . . . The requisite economic power is presumed when the tying product is patented or copyrighted." *Id.* (footnote omitted). The Court emphasized the public interest in limiting the rewards of a patent or copyright grant to the object of the grant.

Can the movie companies get more money for their films by block booking them? If *Getting Gertie's Garter* would command a $50 license fee if offered alone, or perhaps even 0, could the movie company successfully exact $100 for the film when it is licensed as part of the package with *Casablanca*? Or would the extra $50 or $100 commanded really be part of the premium that the station was willing to pay for *Casablanca*? If the latter is true, why should we care about block booking? Does the practice tend to foreclose producer/distributors that make only "B" films from making any sales to television at all? Should the law concern itself with such an effect? Did the Court in *Loew's*?

See Stigler, *United States v. Loew's Inc.*: A Note on Block–Booking, 1963 Supreme Court Review 152, explaining how package selling, with a single value placed on each package, can help the licensor extract from television stations the highest amount that they are willing to pay when the licensor does not know the relative values that stations in different regions place on different films.

A few years after *Loew's* in a patent tie in case, the Court clarified the concept of conditioning. Hazeltine Research, Inc. had a portfolio of some 500 U.S. patents relating to the manufacture of radios and television sets. Zenith wanted to license from Hazeltine nine of the patents for color TV. Hazeltine offered to grant a license for the nine color patents for $275,000 per year, or to grant a license for all of its present and future color and monochrome patents for $200,000 per year.

Zenith contracted for the entire package, and then sued. The district court held that Zenith was coerced to accept the package license. Finding patent misuse and an antitrust violation, the court enjoined Hazeltine from forcing acceptance of a package license by offering a much lower rate for the package than for the license of a few patents. The court of appeals, largely affirming, ordered the injunction modified so as to permit licensing of individual patents at rates the sum of which is greater than the package rate so long as the rates for individual patents are not so disproportionate to the package rate as to amount to economic coercion to force the taking of the package. . . .

Zenith Radio Corp. v. Hazeltine Research, Inc., 388 F.2d 25, 39 (7th Cir. 1967), *aff'd,* 395 U.S. 100 (1969).

Soon thereafter the saga of Fortner Enterprises and United States Steel unfolded. United States Steel Homes Credit Corporation was a subsidiary of United States Steel Corporation. It made secured loans to contractors to cover the purchase and subdivision of land and the purchase and construction on the land of prefabricated homes manufactured and sold by U.S. Steel. Fortner obtained such a loan for $2,000,000, purchased and subdivided land, purchased some U.S. Steel homes, and started building. Dissatisfied with the quality of U.S. Steel's houses, Fortner sued to enjoin U.S. Steel from enforcing the loan requirement that Fortner buy only U.S. Steel houses with the proceeds, and it sought treble damages. The district court entered summary judgment for U.S. Steel on the ground that neither U.S. Steel nor its subsidiary had sufficient market power over credit, the tying product, to foreclose a substantial volume of commerce in the tied product, prefabricated houses, and that the amount of commerce affected was insubstantial because only a small percentage of land was foreclosed to competing sellers of prefabricated houses.

In an opinion by Justice Black, the Supreme Court reversed. The Court held that the requirement that a "not insubstantial" amount of commerce be affected has reference to a dollar volume, not to a market percentage, and the volume allegedly foreclosed ($190,000) was substantial. The Court held, also, that the standard for "sufficient economic power" is not a demanding one; power may fall far short of dominance; power to impose a tie in on any appreciable number of buyers is sufficient; and Fortner should have his day in court to prove that the credit corporation had market power. *Fortner Enterprises, Inc. v. United States Steel Corp.,* 394 U.S. 495 (1969). The Court rejected the argument that credit terms are merely a part of price and therefore that credit cannot be a tying product. It said:

> The potential harm is also essentially the same when the tying product is credit. The buyer may have the choice of buying the tangible commodity separately, but as in other cases the seller can use his power over the tying product to win customers that would otherwise have constituted a market available to competing producers of the tied product. "[C]ompetition on the merits with respect to the tied product is inevitably curbed." *Northern Pacific,* 356 U.S., at 6.

Id. at 508. Justices White, Harlan, Fortas and Stewart dissented.

On remand and trial, the district court found for Fortner Enterprises. The court of appeals affirmed. Again certiorari was granted. In the interim, significant changes occurred on the Court. Justice Fortas, Chief Justice Warren, and Justices Black, Harlan and Douglas resigned or retired. Their seats were filled, respectively, by Harry A. Blackmun,

Warren E. Burger, William H. Rehnquist, Lewis F. Powell, Jr., and John Paul Stevens. The new Court handed down *Fortner II*.

UNITED STATES STEEL CORP. v. FORTNER ENTERPRISES, INC.

("Fortner II")

429 U.S. 610 (1977).

JUSTICE STEVENS: * * * [W]e disagree with the ultimate conclusion of the courts below. . . .

* * *

The impact of the agreement on the market for the tied product (prefabricated houses) is not in dispute. On the one hand, there is no claim—nor could there be—that the Home Division had any dominance in the prefabricated housing business. The record indicates that it was only moderately successful, and that its sales represented a small fraction of the industry total.[3] On the other hand, we have already held that the dollar value of the sales to respondent was sufficient to meet the "not insubstantial" test described in earlier cases. We therefore confine our attention to the source of the tying arrangement—petitioners' "economic power" in the credit market.

II

The evidence supporting the conclusion that the Credit Corp. had appreciable economic power in the credit market relates to four propositions: (1) petitioner Credit Corp. and the Home Division were owned by one of the Nation's largest corporations; (2) petitioners entered into tying arrangements with a significant number of customers in addition to Fortner; (3) the Home Division charged respondent a noncompetitive price for its prefabricated homes; and (4) the financing provided to Fortner was "unique," primarily because it covered 100% of Fortner's acquisition and development costs.

The Credit Corp. was established in 1954 to provide financing for customers of the Home Division. The United States Steel Corp. not only provided the equity capital, but also allowed the Credit Corp. to use its credit in order to borrow money from banks at the prime rate. Thus, although the Credit Corp. itself was not a particularly large company, it was supported by a corporate parent with great financial strength.

The Credit Corp.'s loan policies were primarily intended to help the Home Division sell its products. It extended credit only to customers of the Home Division, and over two-thirds of the Home Division customers obtained such financing. With few exceptions, all the loan agreements contained a tying clause comparable to the one challenged in this case. Petitioner's home sales in 1960 amounted to $6,747,353. Since over $4,600,000 of these sales were tied to financing provided by the Credit

---

3. In 1960, for example, the Home Division sold a total of 1,793 houses for $6,747,353. There were at least four larger prefabricated home manufacturers, the largest of which sold 16,804 homes in that year. In the following year the Home Division's sales declined while the sales of each of its four principal competitors remained steady or increased.

Corp., it is apparent that the tying arrangement was used with a number of customers in addition to Fortner.

The least expensive house package that Fortner purchased from the Home Division cost about $3,150. One witness testified that the Home Division's price was $455 higher than the price of comparable components in a conventional home; another witness, to whom the District Court made no reference in its findings, testified that the Home Division's price was $443 higher than a comparable prefabricated product. Whether the price differential was as great as 15% is not entirely clear, but the record does support the conclusion that the contract required Fortner to pay a noncompetitive price for the Home Division's houses.

The finding that the credit extended to Fortner was unique was based on factors emphasized in the testimony of Fortner's expert witness, Dr. Masten, a professor with special knowledge of lending practices in the Kentucky area. . . . It is a fair summary of his testimony, and of the District Court's findings, to say that the loan was unique because the lender accepted such a high risk and the borrower assumed such a low cost.

The District Court also found that banks and federally insured savings and loan associations generally were prohibited by law from making 100% land acquisition and development loans, and "that other conventional lenders would not have made such loans at the time in question since they were not prudent loans due to the risk involved."

Accordingly, the District Court concluded "that all of the required elements of an illegal tie-in agreement did exist since the tie-in itself was present, a not insubstantial amount of interstate commerce in the tied product was restrained and the Credit Corporation did possess sufficient economic power or leverage to effect such restraint."

III

Without the finding that the financing provided to Fortner was "unique," it is clear that the District Court's findings would be insufficient to support the conclusion that the Credit Corp. possessed any significant economic power in the credit market.

Although the Credit Corp. is owned by one of the Nation's largest manufacturing corporations, there is nothing in the record to indicate that this enabled it to borrow funds on terms more favorable than those available to competing lenders, or that it was able to operate more efficiently than other lending institutions. In short, the affiliation between the petitioners does not appear to have given the Credit Corp. any cost advantage over its competitors in the credit market. Instead, the affiliation was significant only because the Credit Corp. provided a source of funds to customers of the Home Division. That fact tells us nothing about the extent of petitioners' economic power in the credit market.

The same may be said about the fact that loans from the Credit Corp. were used to obtain house sales from Fortner and others. In some tying situations a disproportionately large volume of sales of the tied product resulting from only a few strategic sales of the tying product may reflect a form of economic "leverage" that is probative of power in the market for the tying product. If, as some economists have suggested, the purpose of a tie-in is often to facilitate price discrimination, such evidence would imply the existence of power that a free market would not tolerate.[7] But in this case Fortner was only required to purchase houses for the number of lots for which it received financing. The tying product produced no commitment from Fortner to purchase varying quantities of the tied product over an extended period of time. This record, therefore, does not describe the kind of "leverage" found in some of the Court's prior decisions condemning tying arrangements.[8]

The fact that Fortner—and presumably other Home Division customers as well—paid a noncompetitive price for houses also lends insufficient support to the judgment of the lower court. Proof that Fortner paid a higher price for the tied product is consistent with the possibility that the financing was unusually inexpensive and that the price for the entire package was equal to, or below, a competitive price. And this possibility is equally strong even though a number of Home Division customers made a package purchase of homes and financing.[10]

The most significant finding made by the District Court related to the unique character of the credit extended to Fortner. This finding is particularly important because the unique character of the tying product has provided critical support for the finding of illegality in prior cases. . . .

As the Court plainly stated in its prior opinion in this case, these decisions do not require that the defendant have a monopoly or even a dominant position throughout the market for a tying product. They do, however, focus attention on the question whether the seller has the power, within the market for the tying product, to raise prices or to require purchasers to accept burdensome terms that could not be exacted in a completely competitive market.[13] In short, the question is whether the

---

7. See Bowman, Tying Arrangements and the Leverage Problem, 67 Yale L.J. 19 (1957).

8. See *e.g., United Shoe Machinery v. United States*, 258 U.S. 451; *International Business Machines v. United States*, 298 U.S. 131; *International Salt Co. v. United States*, 332 U.S. 392. In his article in the 1969 Supreme Court Review 16, Professor Dam suggests that this kind of leverage may also have been present in *Northern Pacific R. Co. v. United States*, 356 U.S. 1.

10. Relying on *Advance Business Systems & Supply Co. v. SCM Corp.*, 415 F.2d 55 (CA4 1969), cert. denied, 397 U.S. 920, Fortner contends that acceptance of the package by a significant number of customers is itself sufficient to prove the seller's economic power. But this approach depends on the absence of other explanations for the willingness of buyers to purchase the package. . . .

• • • [T]his case differs from Northern Pacific because use of the tie-in in this case can be explained as a form of price competition in the tied product, whereas that expla-

nation was unavailable to the Northern Pacific Railway.

13. "Accordingly, the proper focus of concern is whether the seller has the power to raise prices, or impose other burdensome terms such as a tie-in, with respect to any appreciable number of buyers within the market." 394 U.S., at 504.

Professor Dam correctly analyzed the burden of proof imposed on Fortner by this language. In his article in the 1969 Supreme Court Review 25–26, he reasoned:

"One important question in interpreting the *Fortner* decision is the meaning of this language. Taken out of context, it might be thought to mean that, just as the 'host of tying arrangements' was 'compelling evidence' of 'great power' in *Northern Pacific*, so the inclusion of tie-in clauses in contracts with 'any appreciable numbers of buyers' establishes market power. But the passage read in context does not warrant this interpretation. For the immediately preceding sentence makes clear that market power in the sense of power over

seller has some advantage not shared by his competitors in the market for the tying product.

Without any such advantage differentiating his product from that of his competitors, the seller's product does not have the kind of uniqueness considered relevant in prior tying-clause cases. . . .

Quite clearly, if the evidence merely shows that credit terms are unique because the seller is willing to accept a lesser profit—or to incur greater risks—than its competitors, that kind of uniqueness will not give rise to any inference of economic power in the credit market. Yet this is, in substance, all that the record in this case indicates.

The unusual credit bargain offered to Fortner proves nothing more than a willingness to provide cheap financing in order to sell expensive houses. Without any evidence that the Credit Corp. had some cost advantage over its competitors—or could offer a form of financing that was significantly differentiated from that which other lenders could offer if they so elected—the unique character of its financing does not support the conclusion that petitioners had the kind of economic power which Fortner had the burden of proving in order to prevail in this litigation.

The judgment of the Court of Appeals is reversed.

CHIEF JUSTICE BURGER, with whom JUSTICE REHNQUIST joins, concurring.

I concur in the Court's opinion and write only to emphasize what the case before us does *not* involve; I join on the basis of my understanding of the scope of our holding. Today's decision does not implicate ordinary credit sales of only a single product and which therefore cannot constitute a tying arrangement subject to *per se* scrutiny under § 1 of the Sherman Act. In contrast to such transactions, we are dealing here with a peculiar arrangement expressly found by the Court in *Fortner I* to involve two separate products sold by two separate corporations. Consequently, I read the Court's assumption that a tie-in existed in this case, required as it is by the law of the case, to cast no doubt on the legality of credit financing by manufacturers or distributors.

Questions and Comments

Is *Fortner II* consistent with *Fortner I*? Does it undercut *Fortner I*? How would you formulate the law on tying after *Fortner II*?

Suppose these facts: Credit Corp. was in the business of "selling" credit in general and for a wide range of specific purposes. If, however, a borrower wished to use credit to buy prefabricated houses, Credit Corp. would offer the credit only on condition that the borrower buy from U.S. Steel. Otherwise, the terms of the credit were the same for tied and non-tied sales. Do these

price must still exist. If the price could have been raised but the tie-in was demanded in lieu of the higher price, then—and presumably only then—would the requisite economic power exist. Thus, despite the broad language available for quotation in later cases, the treatment of the law on market power is on close reading not only consonant with the precedents but in some ways less far-reaching than *Northern Pacific* and *Loew's,* which could be read to make actual market power irrelevant." (Footnotes omitted.)

changed facts make a difference? What can you infer from these facts about the profitability of the credit transaction, standing alone?

It was to be more than a decade before the Court would have another look at tying. During this decade, we would see growing support for the attitude that tie ins, when used, are usually procompetitive or trivial, and growing support for the idea that antitrust enforcement should be reserved for "inefficient" (output-limiting) transactions. Since the law on tie ins did not stem from the concern about output limitation, the tying law was a candidate for retrenchment.

JEFFERSON PARISH HOSPITAL DISTRICT NO. 2 v. HYDE

466 U.S. 2 (1984).

JUSTICE STEVENS: At issue in this case is the validity of an exclusive contract between a hospital and a firm of anesthesiologists. We must decide whether the contract gives rise to a *per se* violation of § 1 of the Sherman Act because every patient undergoing surgery at the hospital must use the services of one firm of anesthesiologists, and, if not, whether the contract is nevertheless illegal because it unreasonably restrains competition among anesthesiologists.

In July 1977, respondent Edwin G. Hyde, a board-certified anesthesiologist, applied for admission to the medical staff of East Jefferson Hospital. The credentials committee and the medical staff executive committee recommended approval, but the hospital board denied the application because the hospital was a party to a contract providing that all anesthesiological services required by the hospital's patients would be performed by Roux & Associates, a professional medical corporation. Respondent then commenced this action seeking a declaratory judgment that the contract is unlawful and an injunction ordering petitioners to appoint him to the hospital staff. After trial, the District Court denied relief, finding that the anticompetitive consequences of the Roux contract were minimal and outweighed by benefits in the form of improved patient care. The Court of Appeals reversed because it was persuaded that the contract was illegal *"per se."* We granted certiorari, and now reverse.

I

In February 1971, shortly before East Jefferson Hospital opened, it entered into an "Anesthesiology Agreement" with Roux & Associates (Roux), a firm that had recently been organized by Dr. Kermit Roux. The contract provided that any anesthesiologist designated by Roux would be admitted to the hospital's medical staff. The hospital agreed to provide the space, equipment, maintenance, and other supporting services necessary to operate the anesthesiology department. It also agreed to purchase all necessary drugs and other supplies. All nursing personnel required by the anesthesia department were to be supplied by the hospital, but Roux had the right to approve their selection and retention.[3] The hospital agreed to "restrict the use of its anesthesia department to Roux &

---

3. The contract required all of the physicians employed by Roux to confine their practice of anesthesiology to East Jefferson.

Associates and [that] no other persons, parties or entities shall perform such services within the Hospital for the ter[m] of this contract."[4]

The 1971 contract provided for a 1–year term automatically renewable for successive 1–year periods unless either party elected to terminate. In 1976, a second written contract was executed containing most of the provisions of the 1971 agreement. Its term was five years and the clause excluding other anesthesiologists from the hospital was deleted;[5] the hospital nevertheless continued to regard itself as committed to a closed anesthesiology department. Only Roux was permitted to practice anesthesiology at the hospital. At the time of trial the department included four anesthesiologists. The hospital usually employed 13 or 14 certified registered nurse anesthetists.

The exclusive contract had an impact on two different segments of the economy: consumers of medical services, and providers of anesthesiological services. Any consumer of medical services who elects to have an operation performed at East Jefferson Hospital may not employ any anesthesiologist not associated with Roux. No anesthesiologists except those employed by Roux may practice at East Jefferson.

There are at least 20 hospitals in the New Orleans metropolitan area and about 70 percent of the patients living in Jefferson Parish go to hospitals other than East Jefferson. Because it regarded the entire New Orleans metropolitan area as the relevant geographic market in which hospitals compete, this evidence convinced the District Court that East Jefferson does not possess any significant "market power"; therefore it concluded that petitioners could not use the Roux contract to anticompetitive ends. The same evidence led the Court of Appeals to draw a different conclusion. Noting that 30 percent of the residents of the parish go to East Jefferson Hospital, and that in fact "patients tend to choose hospitals by location rather than price or quality," the Court of Appeals concluded that the relevant geographic market was the East Bank of Jefferson Parish. The conclusion that East Jefferson Hospital possessed market power in that area was buttressed by the facts that the prevalence of health insurance eliminates a patient's incentive to compare costs, that the patient is not sufficiently informed to compare quality, and that family convenience tends to magnify the importance of location.[8]

---

4. Originally Roux agreed to provide at least two full-time anesthesiologists acceptable to the hospital's credentials committee. Roux agreed to furnish additional anesthesiologists as necessary. The contract also provided that Roux would designate one of its qualified anesthesiologists to serve as the head of the hospital's department of anesthesia.

The fees for anesthesiological services are billed separately to the patients by the hospital. They cover the hospital's costs and the professional services provided by Roux. After a deduction of eight percent to provide a reserve for uncollectible accounts, the fees are divided equally between Roux and the hospital.

5. "Roux testified that he requested the omission of the exclusive language in his 1976 contract because he believes a surgeon or patient is entitled to the services of the anesthesiologist of his choice. He admitted that he and others in his group did work outside East Jefferson following the 1976 contract but felt he was not in violation of the contract in light of the changes made in it." 513 F.Supp. 532, 537 (ED La.1981).

8. While the Court of Appeals did discuss the impact of the contract upon patients, it did not discuss its impact upon anesthesiologists. The District Court had referred to evidence that in the entire State of Louisiana there are 156 anesthesiologists and 345 hospitals with operating rooms. The record

The Court of Appeals held that the case involves a "tying arrangement" because the "users of the hospital's operating rooms (the tying product) are also compelled to purchase the hospital's chosen anesthesia service (the tied product)." [686 F.2d] at 289. Having defined the relevant geographic market for the tying product as the East Bank of Jefferson Parish, the court held that the hospital possessed "sufficient market power in the tying market to coerce purchasers of the tied product." *Id.*, at 291. Since the purchase of the tied product constituted a "not insubstantial amount of interstate commerce," under the Court of Appeals' reading of our decision in *Northern Pacific R. Co. v. United States*, 356 U.S. 1, 11 (1958), the tying arrangement was therefore illegal *"per se."*

II

Certain types of contractual arrangements are deemed unreasonable as a matter of law.[10] The character of the restraint produced by such an arrangement is considered a sufficient basis for presuming unreasonableness without the necessity of any analysis of the market context in which the arrangement may be found. A price-fixing agreement between competitors is the classic example of such an arrangement. *Arizona v. Maricopa County Medical Society*, 457 U.S. 332, 343–348 (1982). It is far too late in the history of our antitrust jurisprudence to question the proposition that certain tying arrangements pose an unacceptable risk of stifling competition and therefore are unreasonable *"per se."* The rule was first enunciated in *International Salt Co. v. United States*, 332 U.S. 392, 396 (1947), and has been endorsed by this Court many times since. The rule also reflects congressional policies underlying the antitrust laws. In enacting § 3 of the Clayton Act, Congress expressed great concern about the anti-competitive character of tying arrangements. See H.R. Rep. No. 627, 63d Cong., 2d Sess., 10–13 (1914); S.Rep. No. 698, 63d Cong., 2d Sess., 6–9 (1914).[15] While this case does not arise under the Clayton

does not tell us how many of the hospitals in the New Orleans metropolitan area have "open" anesthesiology departments and how many have closed departments. Respondent, for example, practices with two other anesthesiologists at a hospital which has an open department; he previously practiced for several years in a different New Orleans hospital and, prior to that, had practiced in Florida. The record does not tell us whether there is a shortage or a surplus of anesthesiologists in any part of the country, or whether they are thriving or starving.

10. "For example, where a complaint charges that the defendants have engaged in price fixing, or have concertedly refused to deal with non-members of an association, or have licensed a patented device on condition that unpatented materials be employed in conjunction with the patented device, then the amount of commerce involved is immaterial because such restraints are illegal *per se." United States v. Columbia Steel Co.*, 334 U.S. 495, 522–523 (1948) (footnotes omitted).

15. See also 51 Cong.Rec. 9072 (1914) (remarks of Rep. Webb); *id.*, at 9084 (remarks of Rep. Madden); *id.*, at 9090 (remarks of Rep. Mitchell); *id.*, at 9160–9164 (remarks of Rep. Floyd); *id.*, at 9184–9185 (remarks of Rep. Helvering); *id.*, at 9409 (remarks of Rep. Gardner); *id.*, at 9410 (remarks of Rep. Mitchell); *id.*, at 9553–9554 (remarks of Rep. Barkley); *id.*, at 14091–14097 (remarks of Sen. Reed); *id.*, at 14094 (remarks of Sen. Walsh); *id.*, at 14209 (remarks of Sen. Shields); *id.*, at 14226 (remarks of Sen. Reed); *id.*, at 14268 (remarks of Sen. Reed); *id.*, at 14599 (remarks of Sen. White); *id.*, at 15991 (remarks of Sen. Martine); *id.*, at 16146 (remarks of Sen. Walsh); Spivack, The Chicago School Approach to Single Firm Exercises of Monopoly Power: A Response, 52 Antitrust L.J. 651, 664–665 (1983). For example, the House Report on the Clayton Act stated:

"The public is compelled to pay a higher price and local customers are put to the inconvenience of securing many commodities in other communities or through mail-

Act, the congressional finding made therein concerning the competitive consequences of tying is illuminating, and must be respected.

It is clear, however, that not every refusal to sell two products separately can be said to restrain competition. If each of the products may be purchased separately in a competitive market, one seller's decision to sell the two in a single package imposes no unreasonable restraint on either market, particularly if competing suppliers are free to sell either the entire package or its several parts. For example, we have written that "if one of a dozen food stores in a community were to refuse to sell flour unless the buyer also took sugar it would hardly tend to restrain competition in sugar if its competitors were ready and able to sell flour by itself." *Northern Pacific R. Co. v. United States,* 356 U.S., at 7. Buyers often find package sales attractive; a seller's decision to offer such packages can merely be an attempt to compete effectively—conduct that is entirely consistent with the Sherman Act.

Our cases have concluded that the essential characteristic of an invalid tying arrangement lies in the seller's exploitation of its control over the tying product to force the buyer into the purchase of a tied product that the buyer either did not want at all, or might have preferred to purchase elsewhere on different terms. When such "forcing" is present, competition on the merits in the market for the tied item is restrained and the Sherman Act is violated.   *   *   *

order houses that can not be procured at their local stores. The price is raised as an inducement. This is the local effect. Where the concern making these contracts is already great and powerful, such as the United Shoe Machinery Co., the American Tobacco Co., and the General Film Co., the exclusive or 'tying' contract made with local dealers becomes one of the greatest agencies and instrumentalities of monopoly ever devised by the brain of man. It completely shuts out competitors, not only from trade in which they are already engaged, but from the opportunities to build up trade in any community where these great and powerful combinations are operating under this system and practice. By this method and practice the Shoe Machinery Co. has built up a monopoly that owns and controls the entire machinery now being used by all great shoe-manufacturing houses of the United States. No independent manufacturer of shoe machines has the slightest opportunity to build up any considerable trade in this country while this condition obtains. If a manufacturer who is using machines of the Shoe Machinery Co. were to purchase and place a machine manufactured by any independent company in his establishment, the Shoe Machinery Co. could under its contracts withdraw all their machinery from the establishment of the shoe manufacturer and thereby wreck the business of the manufacturer. The General Film Co., by the same method practiced by the Shoe Machinery Co. under the lease system, has practically destroyed all competition and acquired a virtual monopoly of all films manufactured and sold in the United States. When we consider contracts of sales made under this system, the result to the consumer, the general public, and the local dealer and his business is even worse than under the lease system." H.R.Rep. No. 627, 63d Cong., 2d Sess., 12–13 (1914).

Similarly, Representative Mitchell said: "[M]onopoly has been built up by these 'tying' contracts so that in order to get one machine one must take all of the essential machines, or practically all. Independent companies who have sought to enter the field have found that the markets have been preempted. . . . The manufacturers do not want to break their contracts with these giant monopolies, because, if they should attempt to install machinery, their business might be jeopardized and all of the machinery now leased by these giant monopolies would be removed from their places of business. No situation cries more urgently for relief than does this situation, and this bill seeks to prevent exclusive 'tying' contracts that have brought about a monopoly, alike injurious to the small dealers, to the manufacturers, and grossly unfair to those who seek to enter the field of competition and to the millions of consumers." 51 Cong.Rec. 9090 (1914).

Accordingly, we have condemned tying arrangements when the seller has some special ability—usually called "market power"—to force a purchaser to do something that he would not do in a competitive market. See *United States Steel Corp. v. Fortner Enterprises,* 429 U.S. 610, 620 (1977) *(Fortner II); Fortner I,* 394 U.S., at 503–504; *United States v. Loew's Inc.,* 371 U.S. 38, 45, 48, n. 5 (1962); *Northern Pacific R. Co. v. United States,* 356 U.S., at 6–7.[20] When "forcing" occurs, our cases have found the tying arrangement to be unlawful.

Thus, the law draws a distinction between the exploitation of market power by merely enhancing the price of the tying product, on the one hand, and by attempting to impose restraints on competition in the market for a tied product, on the other. When the seller's power is just used to maximize its return in the tying product market, where presumably its product enjoys some justifiable advantage over its competitors, the competitive ideal of the Sherman Act is not necessarily compromised. But if that power is used to impair competition on the merits in another market, a potentially inferior product may be insulated from competitive pressures.[21] This impairment could either harm existing competitors or create barriers to entry of new competitors in the market for the tied product, *Fortner I,* 394 U.S., at 509,[22] and can increase the social costs of market power by facilitating price discrimination, thereby increasing monopoly profits over what they would be absent the tie, *Fortner II,* 429 U.S., at 617.[23] And from the standpoint of the consumer—whose interests the statute was especially intended to serve—the freedom to select the best bargain in the second market is impaired by his need to purchase the tying product, and perhaps by an inability to evaluate the true cost of either product when they are available only as a package.[24] . . .

20. This type of market power has sometimes been referred to as "leverage." Professors Areeda and Turner provide a definition that suits present purposes. " 'Leverage' is loosely defined here as a supplier's power to induce his customer for one product to buy a second product from him that would not otherwise be purchased solely on the merit of that second product." 5 P. Areeda & D. Turner, Antitrust Law ¶ 1134a, p. 202 (1980).

21. See Report of the Attorney General's National Committee to Study the Antitrust Laws 145 (1955); Craswell, Tying Requirements in Competitive Markets: The Consumer Protection Issues, 62 B.U.L.Rev. 661, 666–668 (1982); Slawson, A Stronger, Simpler Tie–In Doctrine, 25 Antitrust Bull. 671, 676–684 (1980); Turner, The Validity of Tying Arrangements under the Antitrust Laws, 72 Harv.L.Rev. 50, 60–62 (1958).

22. See 3 Areeda & Turner, *supra* n. 20, ¶ 733e (1978); C. Kaysen & D. Turner, Antitrust Policy 157 (1959); L. Sullivan, Law of Antitrust § 156 (1977); O. Williamson, Markets and Hierarchies: Analysis and Antitrust Implications 111 (1975); Pearson, Tying Arrangements and Antitrust Policy, 60 Nw.U.L.Rev. 626, 637–638 (1965).

23. Sales of the tied item can be used to measure demand for the tying item; purchasers with greater needs for the tied item make larger purchases and in effect must pay a higher price to obtain the tying item. *See* P. Areeda, Antitrust Analysis ¶ 533 (2d ed. 1974); R. Posner, Antitrust Law 173–180 (1976); Sullivan, *supra* n. 22, § 156; Bowman, Tying Arrangements and the Leverage Problem, 67 Yale L.J. 19 (1957); Burstein, A Theory of Full–Line Forcing, 55 Nw.U.L. Rev. 62 (1960); Dam, Fortner Enterprises v. United States Steel: "Neither a Borrower, Nor a Lender Be," 1969 S.Ct.Rev. 1, 15–16; Ferguson, Tying Arrangements and Reciprocity: An Economic Analysis, 30 Law & Contemp.Prob. 552, 554–558 (1965); Markovits, Tie–Ins, Reciprocity, and the Leverage Theory, 76 Yale L.J. 1397 (1967); Pearson, *supra* n. 22, at 647–653; Sidak, Debunking Predatory Innovation, 83 Colum.L.Rev. 1121, 1127–1131 (1983); Stigler, United States v. Loew's Inc.: A Note on Block–Booking, 1963 S.Ct.Rev. 152.

24. Especially where market imperfections exist, purchasers may not be fully sensitive to the price or quality implications of a tying arrangement, and hence it may im-

Per se condemnation—condemnation without inquiry into actual market conditions—is only appropriate if the existence of forcing is probable.[25] Thus, application of the *per se* rule focuses on the probability of anticompetitive consequences. Of course, as a threshold matter there must be a substantial potential for impact on competition in order to justify *per se* condemnation. If only a single purchaser were "forced" with respect to the purchase of a tied item, the resultant impact on competition would not be sufficient to warrant the concern of antitrust law. It is for this reason that we have refused to condemn tying arrangements unless a substantial volume of commerce is foreclosed thereby. Similarly, when a purchaser is "forced" to buy a product he would not have otherwise bought even from another seller in the tied-product market, there can be no adverse impact on competition because no portion of the market which would otherwise have been available to other sellers has been foreclosed.

Once this threshold is surmounted, *per se* prohibition is appropriate if anticompetitive forcing is likely. For example, if the Government has granted the seller a patent or similar monopoly over a product, it is fair to presume that the inability to buy the product elsewhere gives the seller market power. *United States v. Loew's Inc.,* 371 U.S., at 45–47. Any effort to enlarge the scope of the patent monopoly by using the market power it confers to restrain competition in the market for a second product will undermine competition on the merits in that second market. Thus, the sale or lease of a patented item on condition that the buyer make all his purchases of a separate tied product from the patentee is unlawful. See *United States v. Paramount Pictures, Inc.,* 334 U.S. 131, 156–159 (1948); *International Salt,* 332 U.S., at 395–396; *International Business Machines Corp. v. United States,* 298 U.S. 131 (1936).

The same strict rule is appropriate in other situations in which the existence of market power is probable. When the seller's share of the market is high, see *Times–Picayune Publishing Co. v. United States,* 345 U.S., at 611–613, or when the seller offers a unique product that competitors are not able to offer, see *Fortner I,* 394 U.S., at 504–506, and n. 2, the Court has held that the likelihood that market power exists and is being used to restrain competition in a separate market is sufficient to make *per se* condemnation appropriate. Thus, in *Northern Pacific R. Co. v. United States,* 356 U.S. 1 (1958), we held that the railroad's control over vast tracts of western real estate, although not itself unlawful, gave the railroad a unique kind of bargaining power that enabled it to tie the sales of that land to exclusive, long-term commitments that fenced out competition in the transportation market over a protracted period. When, however, the seller does not have either the degree or the kind of market power that enables him to force customers to purchase a second, unwanted product in order to obtain the tying product, an antitrust violation can

pede competition on the merits. See Craswell, *supra* n. 21, at 675–679.

25. The rationale for *per se* rules in part is to avoid a burdensome inquiry into actual market conditions in situations where the likelihood of anticompetitive conduct is so great as to render unjustified the costs of determining whether the particular case at bar involves anticompetitive conduct. *See, e.g., Arizona v. Maricopa County Medical Society,* 457 U.S. 332, 350–351 (1982).

be established only by evidence of an unreasonable restraint on competition in the relevant market.

In sum, any inquiry into the validity of a tying arrangement must focus on the market or markets in which the two products are sold, for that is where the anticompetitive forcing has its impact. Thus, in this case our analysis of the tying issue must focus on the hospital's sale of services to its patients, rather than its contractual arrangements with the providers of anesthesiological services. In making that analysis, we must consider whether petitioners are selling two separate products that may be tied together, and, if so, whether they have used their market power to force their patients to accept the tying arrangement.

III

The hospital has provided its patients with a package that includes the range of facilities and services required for a variety of surgical operations. At East Jefferson Hospital the package includes the services of the anesthesiologist. Petitioners argue that the package does not involve a tying arrangement at all—that they are merely providing a functionally integrated package of services. Therefore, petitioners contend that it is inappropriate to apply principles concerning tying arrangements to this case.

Our cases indicate, however, that the answer to the question whether one or two products are involved turns not on the functional relation between them, but rather on the character of the demand for the two items.[30] . . .

* * *

Unquestionably, the anesthesiological component of the package offered by the hospital could be provided separately and could be selected either by the individual patient or by one of the patient's doctors if the hospital did not insist on including anesthesiological services in the package it offers to its customers. As a matter of actual practice, anesthesiological services are billed separately from the hospital services petitioners provide. There was ample and uncontroverted testimony that patients or surgeons often request specific anesthesiologists to come to a hospital and provide anesthesia, and that the choice of an individual

---

30. The fact that anesthesiological services are functionally linked to the other services provided by the hospital is not in itself sufficient to remove the Roux contract from the realm of tying arrangements. We have often found arrangements involving functionally linked products at least one of which is useless without the other to be prohibited tying devices. *See Mercoid Corp. v. Mid–Continent Co.,* 320 U.S. 661 (1944) (heating system and stoker switch); *Morton Salt Co. v. Suppiger Co.,* 314 U.S. 488 (1942) (salt machine and salt); *International Salt Co. v. United States,* 332 U.S. 392 (1947) (same); *Leitch Mfg. Co. v. Barber Co.,* 302 U.S. 458 (1938) (process patent and material used in the patented process); *International Business Machines Corp. v. United States,* 298 U.S. 131 (1936) (tabulators and tabulat-ing punch cards); *Carbice Corp. v. American Patents Development Corp.,* 283 U.S. 27 (1931) (ice cream transportation package and coolant); *FTC v. Sinclair Refining Co.,* 261 U.S. 463 (1923) (gasoline and underground tanks and pumps); *United Shoe Machinery Co. v. United States,* 258 U.S. 451 (1922) (shoe machinery and supplies, maintenance, and peripheral machinery); *United States v. Jerrold Electronics Corp.,* 187 F.Supp. 545, 558–560 (ED Pa.1960) (components of television antennas), aff'd, 365 U.S. 567 (1961) *(per curiam).* In fact, in some situations the functional link between the two items may enable the seller to maximize its monopoly return on the tying item as a means of charging a higher rent or purchase price to a larger user of the tying item. *See* n. 23, *supra.*

anesthesiologist separate from the choice of a hospital is particularly frequent in respondent's specialty, obstetric anesthesiology. The District Court found that "[t]he provision of anesthesia services is a medical service separate from the other services provided by the hospital." 513 F.Supp., at 540.[37] The record amply supports the conclusion that consumers differentiate between anesthesiological services and the other hospital services provided by petitioners.[39]

Thus, the hospital's requirement that its patients obtain necessary anesthesiological services from Roux combined the purchase of two distinguishable services in a single transaction. . . . .[41] The fact that petitioners' patients are required to purchase two separate items is only the beginning of the appropriate inquiry.[42]

37. Accordingly, in its conclusions of law the District Court treated the case as involving a tying arrangement. 513 F.Supp., at 542.

39. One of the most frequently cited statements on this subject was made by Judge Van Dusen in *United States v. Jerrold Electronics Corp.*, 187 F.Supp. 545 (ED Pa. 1960), aff'd, 365 U.S. 567 (1961) *(per curiam).* While this statement was specifically made with respect to § 3 of the Clayton Act, its analysis is also applicable to § 1 of the Sherman Act, since with respect to the definition of tying the standards used by the two statutes are the same. See *Times–Picayune,* 345 U.S., at 608–609.

"There are several facts presented in this record which tend to show that a community television antenna system cannot properly be characterized as a single product. Others who entered the community antenna field offered all of the equipment necessary for a complete system, but none of them sold their gear exclusively as a single package as did Jerrold. The record also establishes that the number of pieces in each system varied considerably so that hardly any two versions of the alleged product were the same. Furthermore, the customer was charged for each item of equipment and not a lump sum for the total system. Finally, while Jerrold had cable and antennas to sell which were manufactured by other concerns, it only required that the electronic equipment in the system be bought from it." 187 F.Supp., at 559.

The record here shows that other hospitals often permit anesthesiological services to be purchased separately, that anesthesiologists are not fungible in that the services provided by each are not precisely the same, that anesthesiological services are billed separately, and that the hospital required purchases from Roux even though other anesthesiologists were available and Roux had no objection to their receiving staff privileges at East Jefferson. Therefore, the *Jer-*

rold analysis indicates that there was a tying arrangement here. *Jerrold* also indicates that tying may be permissible when necessary to enable a new business to break into the market. Assuming this defense exists, and assuming it justified the 1971 Roux contract in order to give Roux an incentive to go to work at a new hospital with an uncertain future, that justification is inapplicable to the 1976 contract, since by then Roux was willing to continue to service the hospital without a tying arrangement.

41. * * * [W]e reject the view of the District Court that the legality of an arrangement of this kind turns on whether it was adopted for the purpose of improving patient care.

42. Petitioners argue and the District Court found that the exclusive contract had what it characterized as procompetitive justifications in that an exclusive contract ensures 24–hour anesthesiology coverage, enables flexible scheduling, and facilitates work routine, professional standards, and maintenance of equipment. The Court of Appeals held these findings to be clearly erroneous since the exclusive contract was not necessary to achieve these ends. Roux was willing to provide 24–hour coverage even without an exclusive contract and the credentials committee of the hospital could impose standards for staff privileges that would ensure staff would comply with the demands of scheduling, maintenance, and professional standards. In the past, we have refused to tolerate manifestly anticompetitive conduct simply because the health care industry is involved. We have also uniformly rejected similar "goodwill" defenses for tying arrangements, finding that the use of contractual quality specifications are generally sufficient to protect quality without the use of a tying arrangement. Since the District Court made no finding as to why contractual quality specifications would not protect the hospital, there is no basis for departing from our prior cases here.

IV

The question remains whether this arrangement involves the use of market power to force patients to buy services they would not otherwise purchase. Respondent's only basis for invoking the *per se* rule against tying and thereby avoiding analysis of actual market conditions is by relying on the preference of persons residing in Jefferson Parish to go to East Jefferson, the closest hospital. A preference of this kind, however, is not necessarily probative of significant market power.

Seventy percent of the patients residing in Jefferson Parish enter hospitals other than East Jefferson. Thus East Jefferson's "dominance" over persons residing in Jefferson Parish is far from overwhelming. The fact that a substantial majority of the parish's residents elect not to enter East Jefferson means that the geographic data do not establish the kind of dominant market position that obviates the need for further inquiry into actual competitive conditions. . . .

* * *

V

In order to prevail in the absence of *per se* liability, respondent has the burden of proving that the Roux contract violated the Sherman Act because it unreasonably restrained competition. That burden necessarily involves an inquiry into the actual effect of the exclusive contract on competition among anesthesiologists. This competition takes place in a market that has not been defined. The market is not necessarily the same as the market in which hospitals compete in offering services to patients; it may encompass competition among anesthesiologists for exclusive contracts such as the Roux contract and might be statewide or merely local. There is, however, insufficient evidence in this record to provide a basis for finding that the Roux contract, as it actually operates in the market, has unreasonably restrained competition. The record sheds little light on how this arrangement affected consumer demand for separate arrangements with a specific anesthesiologist. The evidence indicates that some surgeons and patients preferred respondent's services to those of Roux, but there is no evidence that any patient who was sophisticated enough to know the difference between two anesthesiologists was not also able to go to a hospital that would provide him with the anesthesiologist of his choice.

In sum, all that the record establishes is that the choice of anesthesiologists at East Jefferson has been limited to one of the four doctors who are associated with Roux and therefore have staff privileges.[51] Even if Roux did not have an exclusive contract, the range of alternatives open to the patient would be severely limited by the nature of the transaction and the hospital's unquestioned right to exercise some control over the identity and the number of doctors to whom it accords staff privileges. . . .

51. The effect of the contract, of course, has been to remove the East Jefferson Hospital from the market open to Roux's competitors. Like any exclusive-requirements contract, this contract could be unlawful if it foreclosed so much of the market from penetration by Roux's competitors as to unreasonably restrain competition in the affected market, the market for anesthesiological services. However, respondent has not attempted to make this showing.

VI

. . . There is no evidence that the price, the quality, or the supply or demand for either the "tying product" or the "tied product" involved in this case has been adversely affected by the exclusive contract between Roux and the hospital. It may well be true that the contract made it necessary for Dr. Hyde and others to practice elsewhere, rather than at East Jefferson. But there has been no showing that the market as a whole has been affected at all by the contract. . . . Accordingly, the judgment of the Court of Appeals is reversed, and the case is remanded to that court for further proceedings consistent with this opinion.

JUSTICE BRENNAN, with whom JUSTICE MARSHALL joins, concurring.

As the opinion for the Court demonstrates, we have long held that tying arrangements are subject to evaluation for *per se* illegality under § 1 of the Sherman Act. Whatever merit the policy arguments against this longstanding construction of the Act might have, Congress, presumably aware of our decisions, has never changed the rule by amending the Act. In such circumstances, our practice usually has been to stand by a settled statutory interpretation and leave the task of modifying the statute's reach to Congress. See *Monsanto Co. v. Spray–Rite Service Corp.,* 465 U.S. 752, 769 (1984) (Brennan, J., concurring). I see no reason to depart from that principle in this case and therefore join the opinion and judgment of the Court.

JUSTICE O'CONNOR, with whom CHIEF JUSTICE BURGER and JUSTICES POWELL and REHNQUIST join, concurring in the judgment.

. . . I concur in the Court's decision to reverse but write separately to explain why I believe the hospital-Roux contract, whether treated as effecting a tie between services provided to patients, or as an exclusive dealing arrangement between the hospital and certain anesthesiologists, is properly analyzed under the rule of reason.

I

Tying is a form of marketing in which a seller insists on selling two distinct products or services as a package. A supermarket that will sell flour to consumers only if they will also buy sugar is engaged in tying. Flour is referred to as the *tying* product, sugar as the *tied* product. In this case the allegation is that East Jefferson Hospital has unlawfully tied the sale of general hospital services and operating room facilities (the tying service) to the sale of anesthesiologists' services (the tied services). The Court has on occasion applied a *per se* rule of illegality in actions alleging tying in violation of § 1 of the Sherman Act.

Under the usual logic of the *per se* rule, a restraint on trade that rarely serves any purposes other than to restrain competition is illegal without proof of market power or anticompetitive effect. In deciding whether an economic restraint should be declared illegal *per se*, "[t]he probability that anticompetitive consequences will result from a practice and the severity of those consequences [is] balanced against its procompetitive consequences. Cases that do not fit the generalization may arise, but a *per se* rule reflects the judgment that such cases are not sufficiently common or important to justify the time and expense necessary to identify them." *Continental T.V., Inc. v. GTE Sylvania Inc.,* 433 U.S. 36, 50, n. 16 (1977). Only when there is very little loss to society from banning a restraint altogether is an inquiry into its costs in the individual case considered to be unnecessary.

Some of our earlier cases did indeed declare that tying arrangements serve "hardly any purpose beyond the suppression of competition." *Standard Oil Co. of California v. United States,* 337 U.S. 293, 305–306 (1949) (dictum). However, this declaration was not taken literally even by the cases that purported to rely upon it. In practice, a tie has been illegal only if the seller is shown to have "sufficient economic power with respect to the tying product to appreciably restrain free competition in the market for the tied product. . . ." *Northern Pacific R. Co.,* 356 U.S., at 6. Without "control or dominance over the tying product," the seller could not use the tying product as "an effectual weapon to pressure buyers into taking the tied item," so that any restraint of trade would be "insignificant." *Ibid.* The Court has never been willing to say of tying arrangements, as it has of price fixing, division of markets, and other agreements subject to *per se* analysis, that they are always illegal, without proof of market power or anticompetitive effect.

The *"per se"* doctrine in tying cases has thus always required an elaborate inquiry into the economic effects of the tying arrangement. As a result, tying doctrine incurs the costs of a rule-of-reason approach without achieving its benefits: the doctrine calls for the extensive and time-consuming economic analysis characteristic of the rule of reason, but then may be interpreted to prohibit arrangements that economic analysis would show to be beneficial. Moreover, the *per se* label in the tying context has generated more confusion than coherent law because it appears to invite lower courts to omit the analysis of economic circumstances of the tie that has always been a necessary element of tying analysis.

The time has therefore come to abandon the *"per se"* label and refocus the inquiry on the adverse economic effects, and the potential economic benefits, that the tie may have. The law of tie-ins will thus be brought into accord with the law applicable to all other allegedly anticompetitive economic arrangements, except those few horizontal or quasi-horizontal restraints that can be said to have no economic justification whatsoever. This change will rationalize rather than abandon tie-in doctrine as it is already applied.

II

Our prior opinions indicate that the purpose of tying law has been to identify and control those tie-ins that have a demonstrable exclusionary impact in the tied-product market, or that abet the harmful exercise of market power that the seller possesses in the tying product market. Under the rule of reason tying arrangements should be disapproved only in such instances.

Market power in the *tying* product may be acquired legitimately (*e.g.,* through the grant of a patent) or illegitimately (*e.g.,* as a result of unlawful monopolization). In either event, exploitation of consumers in the market for the tying product is a possibility that exists and that may be regulated under § 2 of the Sherman Act without reference to any tying arrangements that the seller may have developed. The existence of a tied product normally does not increase the profit that the seller with market power can extract from sales of the *tying* product. A seller with a monopoly on flour, for example, cannot increase the profit it can extract from flour consumers simply by forcing them to buy sugar along with their flour. Counterintuitive though that assertion may seem, it is easily demonstrated and widely accepted. See, *e.g.,* R. Bork, The Antitrust Paradox 372–374 (1978); P. Areeda, Antitrust Analysis 735 (3d ed. 1981).

Tying may be economically harmful primarily in the rare cases where power in the market for the tying product is used to create *additional* market power in the market for the *tied* product.[4] The antitrust law is properly concerned with tying when, for example, the flour monopolist threatens to use its market power to acquire additional power in the sugar market, perhaps by driving out competing sellers of sugar, or by making it more difficult for new sellers to enter the sugar market. But such extension of market power is unlikely, or poses no threat of economic harm, unless the two markets in question and the nature of the two products tied satisfy three threshold criteria.

First, the seller must have power in the tying-product market. . . .[7]

Second, there must be a substantial threat that the tying seller will acquire market power in the tied-product market. No such threat exists if the tied-product market is occupied by many stable sellers who are not likely to be driven out by the tying, or if entry barriers in the tied-product market are low. . . .

Third, there must be a coherent economic basis for treating the tying and tied products as distinct. All but the simplest products can be broken down into two or more components that are "tied together" in the final sale. Unless it is to be illegal to sell cars with engines or cameras with lenses, this analysis must be guided by some limiting principle. For products to be treated as distinct, the tied product must, at a minimum, be one that some consumers might wish to purchase separately *without also*

---

4. Tying might be undesirable in two other instances, but the hospital-Roux arrangement involves neither one.

In a regulated industry a firm with market power may be unable to extract a supercompetitive profit because it lacks control over the prices it charges for regulated products or services. Tying may then be used to extract that profit from sale of the unregulated, tied products or services.

Tying may also help the seller engage in price discrimination by "metering" the buyer's use of the tying product. Price discrimination may be independently unlawful, see 15 U.S.C. § 13. Price discrimination may, however, *decrease* rather than increase the economic costs of a seller's market power. See, *e.g.,* R. Bork, The Antitrust Paradox 398 (1978); P. Areeda, Antitrust Analysis 608–610 (3d ed. 1981); O. Williamson, Markets

and Hierarchies: Analysis and Antitrust Implications 11–13 (1975). . . .

7. A common misconception has been that a patent or copyright, a high market share, or a unique product that competitors are not able to offer suffices to demonstrate market power. While each of these three factors might help to give market power to a seller, it is also possible that a seller in these situations will have no market power: for example, a patent holder has no market power in any relevant sense if there are close substitutes for the patented product. Similarly, a high market share indicates market power only if the market is properly defined to include all reasonable substitutes for the product. See generally Landes & Posner, Market Power in Antitrust Cases, 94 Harv.L.Rev. 937 (1981). . . .

purchasing the tying product.[8] When the tied product has no use other than in conjunction with the tying product, a seller of the tying product can acquire no *additional* market power by selling the two products together. . . .

Even when the tied product does have a use separate from the tying product, it makes little sense to label a package as two products without also considering the economic justifications for the sale of the package as a unit. When the economic advantages of joint packaging are substantial the package is not appropriately viewed as two products, and that should be the end of the tying inquiry. The lower courts largely have adopted this approach.

These three conditions—market power in the tying product, a substantial threat of market power in the tied product, and a coherent economic basis for treating the products as distinct—are only threshold requirements. Under the rule of reason a tie-in may prove acceptable even when all three are met. Tie-ins may entail economic benefits as well as economic harms, and if the threshold requirements are met these benefits should enter the rule-of-reason balance.

*   *   *

The ultimate decision whether a tie-in is illegal under the antitrust laws should depend upon the demonstrated economic effects of the challenged agreement. . . . A tie-in should be condemned only when its anticompetitive impact outweighs its contribution to efficiency.

III

Application of these criteria to the case at hand is straightforward.

Although the issue is in doubt, we may assume that the hospital does have market power in the provision of hospital services in its area. . . .

Second, in light of the hospital's presumed market power, we may also assume that there is a substantial threat that East Jefferson will acquire market power over the provision of anesthesiological services in its market. . . .

But the third threshold condition for giving closer scrutiny to a tying arrangement is not satisfied here: there is no sound economic reason for treating surgery and anesthesia as separate services. Patients are interested in purchasing anesthesia only in conjunction with hospital services, so the hospital can acquire no *additional* market power by selling the two services together. Accordingly, the link between the hospital's services and anesthesia administered by Roux will affect neither the amount of anesthesia provided nor the combined price of anesthesia and surgery for those who choose to become the hospital's patients. In these circumstances, anesthesia and surgical services should probably not be characterized as distinct products for tying purposes.

---

8. Whether the tying product is one that consumers might wish to purchase without the tied product should be irrelevant. Once it is conceded that the seller has market power over the tying product it follows that the seller can sell the tying product on non-competitive terms. The injury to consumers does not depend on whether the seller chooses to charge a supercompetitive price, or charges a competitive price but insists that consumers also buy a product that they do not want.

Even if they are, the tying should not be considered a violation of § 1 of the Sherman Act because tying here cannot increase the seller's already absolute power over the volume of production of the tied product, which is an inevitable consequence of the fact that very few patients will choose to undergo surgery without receiving anesthesia. The hospital-Roux contract therefore has little potential to harm the patients. On the other side of the balance, . . . the tie-in conferred significant benefits upon the hospital and the patients that it served.

The tie-in improves patient care and permits more efficient hospital operation in a number of ways. From the viewpoint of hospital management, the tie-in ensures 24–hour anesthesiology coverage, aids in standardization of procedures and efficient use of equipment, facilitates flexible scheduling of operations, and permits the hospital more effectively to monitor the quality of anesthesiological services. . . .

IV

Whether or not the hospital-Roux contract is characterized as a tie between distinct products, the contract unquestionably does constitute exclusive dealing. Exclusive-dealing arrangements are independently subject to scrutiny under § 1 of the Sherman Act, and are also analyzed under the rule of reason.

The hospital-Roux arrangement could conceivably have an adverse effect on horizontal competition among anesthesiologists, or among hospitals. . . .

* * *

At issue here is an exclusive-dealing arrangement between a firm of four anesthesiologists and one relatively small hospital. There is no suggestion that East Jefferson Hospital is likely to create a "bottleneck" in the availability of anesthesiologists that might deprive other hospitals of access to needed anesthesiological services, or that the Roux associates have unreasonably narrowed the range of choices available to other anesthesiologists in search of a hospital or patients that will buy their services. A firm of four anesthesiologists represents only a very small fraction of the total number of anesthesiologists whose services are available for hire by other hospitals, and East Jefferson is one among numerous hospitals buying such services. Even without engaging in a detailed analysis of the size of the relevant markets we may readily conclude that there is no likelihood that the exclusive-dealing arrangement challenged here will either unreasonably enhance the hospital's market position relative to other hospitals, or unreasonably permit Roux to acquire power relative to other anesthesiologists. Accordingly, this exclusive-dealing arrangement must be sustained under the rule of reason.

V

For these reasons I conclude that the hospital-Roux contract does not violate § 1 of the Sherman Act. . . .

* * *

Questions and Comments

The members of the Court unanimously agreed that Dr. Hyde did not have a good claim against East Jefferson Hospital, but they disagreed on the grounds of decision. Is their disagreement major or trivial? Is it based on fact and different inferences drawn from basic facts? On procedure and disagreement about who has the burden of proof? On economics and differences in application of economics? Or on law and different conceptions about the importance of Congressional intent, of stare decisis, or "best policy" (including efficiency as best policy)? Does disagreement on one score drive disagreement in others? Bear these general questions in mind as we think more specifically about the plurality opinion of Justice Stevens and the concurring opinion of Justice O'Connor.

What is the applicable principle of law on tying, as reflected in the plurality opinion? What is the essence of an illegal tie in? To what extent does per se illegality depend upon competitors' being fenced out of the market for the tied product, or (which is the same thing) foreclosed from a portion of the market for the tied product and thus deprived of opportunities to sell their product on the merits? What are the dynamic potential losses to competition that may flow from such fencing out? (See the analysis by Justice White quoted in note 19 of the plurality opinion.)

Does the foreclosure also result in unfairness to the fenced out sellers? (Congress thought so; see note 15 of the plurality opinion.)

To what extent is per se illegality a function of defendant's forcing plaintiff to accept a product or service that plaintiff may not wish to buy or might otherwise buy from another seller? Is choice of buyers protected alone and in its own right? Or only in conjunction with a fencing out of defendant's competitors?

What does Justice Stevens mean when he says that there must be harm to competition? Does he use "harm to competition" in other than an output-limiting sense? To him and the plurality, does harm to competition include some mixture of foreclosure of opportunities, unfairness (limitations on freedom of trade for reasons other than the merits), and limitation on consumer choice? Does the plurality derive its concept from Congress? The prior case law? Their idea of "best" policy?

Having explored the roots of the law, did Stevens make a convincing case that "forcing" was not present? East Jefferson Hospital had some market power, as the Court notes. Should the Court have asked: Were patients for whom no other hospital was a good substitute required to accept Roux Associate anesthesiologists in order to get hospital care? Should the case have turned on good business justification rather than forcing? Did East Jefferson probably have a good business justification (substantial efficiencies in the delivery of health care)? If you were a Justice deciding *Jefferson Parish*, faced with the choices of holding closely to established law, narrowing the scope of "forcing," or expanding the scope of good business justifications, which would you do? Could you argue from cases such as *Aspen Skiing*, *NCAA*, and *Northwest Wholesale Stationers* that "the law" has already expanded to allow a limited efficiencies or good business justification defense, at least in cases where the conduct was intended to provide a better product for consumers and had a good chance of doing so?

Let us turn, now, to the opinion of Justice O'Connor. What is the principle of law by which she would judge the legality of tying? What does she mean by "harm to competition"? In her view, are harms to competition limited to provable output-limiting restraints not offset by productive efficiencies? From what source or sources does she derive her principle of law?

Who has the better of the argument in the one-product/two-products controversy? Does it depend upon whether output restraint not offset by productive efficiencies is your guiding principle?

Justice O'Connor says that a seller even with market power cannot increase profits by imposing a tie, and that this proposition is "easily demonstrated and widely accepted." In fact, this is a subject of lively controversy. Compare R. Bork, The Antitrust Paradox 372–74, with Kaplow, Extension of Monopoly Power Through Leverage, 85 Col.L.Rev. 515 (1985) and authorities cited by the plurality in note 23.

The history of the per se rule for tying may throw light on the value of per se responses in general. Does the per se rule outlaw restraints that, on fuller analysis, at least in almost all cases, would be unreasonable under the rule of reason? How does Justice Stevens answer this question? How does Justice O'Connor? Does the Supreme Court's opinion in *Business Electronics Corp. v. Sharp Electronics Corp.*, supra, p. 564 bear upon this question? Do you get guidance from the Supreme Court's opinion in *FTC v. Indiana Federation of Dentists*, 476 U.S. 447 (1986)? From the Court's opinion in *National Society of Professional Engineers v. United States*, 435 U.S. 679 (1978)? Does the answer depend on the kind of restraint in question and whether the case law has formulated a clear rule to govern analysis of the restraint? Does the answer depend upon the deciding jurists' assessment of the value of the dynamic qualities likely to emerge from open markets (i.e., freedom from the restraint) versus the value of the dynamic qualities likely to emerge from freedom of business choice (including freedom to impose the restraint)? Does the answer depend in part upon the deciding jurists' faith in courts versus faith in business to bring about the public good? See the dialogue between Judge Easterbrook and Dean Pitofsky in The Fall and Rise of Antitrust: Law and Policy in the Second Century (First, Fox & Pitofsky, eds., in publication, Greenwood Books 1989).

Problem 1

Kemper Insurance Company was negotiating with American Broadcasting Company to sponsor ABC's 15–minute news program, "Evening Report," one night a week for 24 weeks. Kemper offered to sponsor the program on 68 specified stations for a stated price. ABC counter-offered, adopting many of the same terms, proposing virtually the same price, but substituting its full 99–station lineup. ABC told Kemper that if it did not want sponsorship on all of the 99 stations, ABC would have to black out the program on the unwanted stations, and it noted that the cost of the black out would be exorbitant. Kemper proceeded to negotiate on other issues and concluded the deal on the basis of the 99 stations. Was Kemper coerced to take the 31 unwanted stations? Was this an illegal tie?

See *American Manufacturers Mutual Insurance Co. v. American Broadcasting–Paramount Theatres, Inc.*, 446 F.2d 1131 (2d Cir.1971), *cert. denied*, 404 U.S. 1063 (1972).

Problem 2

Data General Corporation manufactures computer systems. It produces a central processing unit called the NOVA, and copyrighted software designed for use with the NOVA, called RDOS. It faces many competitors, including IBM, Honeywell, Hewlett–Packard, Texas Instruments, Burroughs and NCR. RDOS might be thought unique for the following reasons: (1) RDOS has special characteristics that many users think make it superior, and (2) it can be used only with specially designed hardware. Once a user chooses RDOS and buys RDOS-based applications programs, she is "locked into" RDOS software because her original investment is large and only RDOS software will run with RDOS-based applications programs. However, Data General does not price discriminate so as to extract more revenue from locked-in customers; it faces considerable competition from software competitors and its share of all computer software is not large. A number of computer companies manufacture NOVA emulators—hardware modeled after the NO-VA which are compatible with RDOS.

Data General begins to tie most sales of its NOVA unit to the RDOS software. However, it has waived the tie and approved the use of its software with central processing units manufactured by ROLM and Nippon, whose computer products do not compete with the products offered by Data General.

The manufacturers of the NOVA emulators other than ROLM and Nippon sue for an injunction against the tie in and for treble damages. A not insubstantial amount of commerce is involved in the tied NOVA sales, and plaintiffs can prove that they have lost substantial sales because of the tie in.

Is there an unlawful tie? See *Digidyne Corp. v. Data General Corporation,* 734 F.2d 1336 (9th Cir.1984), *reh'g denied,* 473 U.S. 926 (1985).

If there is an unlawful tie, have plaintiffs suffered antitrust injury? In general, who suffers antitrust injury from a tie and thus has standing to challenge it? Foreclosed competitors? Customers who would have bought the tied product elsewhere and at a lower price? Both? What about a customer who would not have bought the tied product at all? Would only the government have standing on the theory that ties that do not produce monopoly do not injure competition and thus cannot cause antitrust injury to any private party?

A Note on Automobile Replacement Parts

The Mercedes–Benz automobile dealer agreement required dealers to purchase replacement parts from Mercedes–Benz or a source approved by it. Relying on the per se rule, the government challenged the clause. *United States v. Mercedes–Benz of North America, Inc.,* 517 F.Supp. 1369 (N.D.Cal. 1981). It noted that defendants' prices for many replacement parts were consistently higher than similar, non-Mercedes approved parts available from other sources. Both sides moved for summary judgment. The court denied both motions. It held that the Mercedes–Benz tie in was a plausible candidate for illegality; the Mercedes–Benz automobile and its trademark were a single tying product; the replacement parts were a separate tied product. While Mercedes–Benz was not one of the industry's largest firms, sufficient economic power was a question of fact. If the government proved sufficient power, Mercedes–Benz would have the opportunity to "demonstrate the necessity for its quality control procedures and the unavailability of comparable mechanically necessary replacement parts from non-[Mercedes–Benz] sources." *Id.* at 1390.

While suit was pending and after the government had moved for summary judgment, administrations changed and President Reagan appointed William F. Baxter to be Assistant Attorney General in Charge of the Antitrust Division. Baxter stated his belief that the antitrust laws should be enforced only if enforcement would prevent an increment in market power and thus prevent an inefficient transaction. Announcing that the government was dropping its suit against Mercedes–Benz, Baxter explained that the tie in was a way to allow Mercedes–Benz "to capture, in a particular way, the value of the customer preference for [its] . . . trade name." That "particular way" was price discrimination; a premium was put on replacement parts; those who needed replacement parts would not be price sensitive and would pay more. If Mercedes could not capture the value of the brand preference by a tie in, Baxter said, it would seek to do so in another less efficient way, such as increasing the price for the automobile and decreasing the price for the parts. "This rearrangement would be unlikely to yield any economic benefits" (*i.e.,* increased output). 42 Antitrust & Trade Reg. Rep. (BNA) No. 1056, at 587 (March 18, 1982) (quoting Department of Justice Press Release, March 15, 1982). See *United States v. Mercedes–Benz of North America,* 547 F.Supp. 399 (N.D.Cal.1982). (The Tunney Act requires a public hearing and judicial findings when the government agrees to end an antitrust suit by a consent decree; but this suit was withdrawn, not settled, so Baxter avoided a hearing.)

Do you agree with the decision to withdraw the suit? If you were Assistant Attorney General, even if you thought that society would be best off if antitrust suits were reserved for output-limiting transactions, what would you do? Should Baxter have filed a competitive impact statement and invited public comment as required by the Tunney Act even though the Tunney Act was probably not technically applicable?

Should the prosecutor seek to change the law when he thinks it is wrong? How? By talking to Congress? To the courts? By not bringing suits and announcing his policy not to bring them? By terminating suits?

b. Defenses and Justification

To make its case under the modified per se rule against tie ins, the plaintiff will want to prove: (1) that two (or more) products are involved, (2) that the seller has forced the buyer to accept a less desired tied product in order to obtain a desired (tying) product, (3) that the seller has economic power in the market for the tying product, and (4) that a not insubstantial amount of commerce in the tied product is affected.

If the seller establishes these four elements, the plaintiff has made its prima facie case of a per se violation. The defendant may nonetheless justify the tie in by showing that it is necessary to protect good will in the tying product. In *IBM,* supra p. 661, and in *International Salt,* supra p. 662, the Supreme Court narrowly confined this justification to cases in which the specifications necessary to assure the quality of the tied product cannot adequately be stated and there is no less restrictive alternative for protecting the integrity of the tying product. In the pre-*Jefferson Parish* era the courts also developed a new entry justification, *United States v.*

Jerrold Electronics Corp., 187 F.Supp. 545 (E.D.Pa.1960), *aff'd per curiam*, 365 U.S. 567 (1961); but since a new entrant would almost surely not have sufficient economic power, the defense would seem to be surplusage.

c. *Franchising*

Beginning in the 1950s, franchising burgeoned as a way of doing business. Fast food outlets, with uniform and limited menus, grew and flourished. The franchisor would develop a distinctive image or concept, associated with a trademark or trade name, such as Chock Full O'Nuts, Dairy Queen or McDonald's. It would develop plans for a chain of franchised stores, which would sell the product directly to the consumer. It would select individuals or entities—sometimes hundreds or thousands—to be its franchisees and to run the retail operations in the uniform style developed by the franchisor. The franchisor would license each franchisee for a period of years. Sometimes it charged a flat annual fee but usually it charged royalties based on the licensee's revenues. Sometimes the franchisor sought compensation in other ways as well—for example, by tying to the license the supplies that the franchisee would need and by placing a premium on those supplies, or by requiring the franchisee to lease real estate from the franchisor at higher than market rates.

Some franchisors would provide their franchisees with turn-key operations; when the franchisee arrived to begin operations, every table, chair and kitchen facility would be in place (usually in real estate owned by the franchisor and leased to the franchisee). Others would merely license the trade mark, name and logo and provide detailed descriptions of the required structure and design of building, content and quality of the offerings and manner and style of service. Some franchisors would own and operate some of the retail operations in their chain and franchise others; thus, they would be dual distributors. Others would franchise all of the retail operations.

Franchising offered new business opportunities. Entrepreneurial individuals who did not have enough capital, or perhaps imagination, to conceive of a viable business concept and start their own business could nonetheless become "independent" business people. The "independence," however, was sometimes illusory because the franchisees were contractually constrained by the franchisor through detailed requirements about business operations and style. Moreover, the profit opportunities, as well as the opportunity to capitalize on the success of their own investment, were limited by the terms of the franchise. Sometimes the franchisor, or extraneous circumstances, gave the franchisee unrealistic expectations of profit, and sometimes the franchisor opportunistically exploited the franchisee—for example, by terminating or squeezing out a franchisee who had invested substantial amounts of money and successfully developed the franchise to the point where its earnings and its capital value were high.

The result was and still is much litigation by franchisees against franchisors. Most of the litigation is for breach of contract, fraud, deception, or violation of the many state statutes or federal regulations adopted to protect franchisees from overreaching by franchisors. Also, the franchisee frequently alleges violations of the antitrust laws.

In some of the cases that arose prior to the recent surge of franchise regulation courts were concerned that smaller suppliers would be foreclosed from opportunities to sell and that franchisees were foreclosed from the right to negotiate their own deals. *E.g. Susser v. Carvel Corp.*, 332 F.2d 505 (2d Cir. 1964), *cert. denied*, 381 U.S. 125 (1965). Are these values to be protected in their own right after *GTE Sylvania* and *Jefferson Parish?* Suppose the franchisor buys supplies and resells to franchisees, requiring that they buy only from it. Are the franchisees better or worse off as a result of the franchisor's consolidating the bargaining power of all franchisees and dealing as one purchaser with suppliers?

In many franchise cases, concerns of equity and fairness arise. If the franchisees, by pooling their buying power, can buy at a lower price, who is entitled to benefit? Only the franchisees? Only the franchisor? Whoever does the pooling and negotiating? If the franchisor, having contracted with a franchisee to buy the necessary business items, uses that buying power for its own profit, has it unfairly exploited the franchisee? (What does it mean to "unfairly exploit"?) Should unfair exploitation influence antitrust outcomes?

Suppose franchisees are not satisfied with the price at which a franchisor sells to them products it has purchased from a supplier. The franchisees sue the franchisor for an unlawful tie, and a court holds that the franchisor does not have sufficient economic power in the tying market for the tied sales to be unlawful. The franchisees, however, want to capture the benefits of joint buying. Can they lawfully appoint an agent to bargain collectively on their behalf with the franchisor or its supplier? Would a finding that the franchisor lacks power in the tying market help or hurt the franchisees in a suit by the franchisor challenging their conduct as an illegal buyers' cartel?

SIEGEL v. CHICKEN DELIGHT, INC.

448 F.2d 43 (9th Cir.1971), cert. denied, 405 U.S. 955 (1972).

JUDGE MERRILL: This antitrust suit is a class action in which certain franchisees of Chicken Delight seek treble damages for injuries allegedly resulting from illegal restraints imposed by Chicken Delight's standard form franchise agreements. The restraints in question are Chicken Delight's contractual requirements that franchisees purchase certain essential cooking equipment, dry-mix food items, and trade-mark bearing packaging exclusively from Chicken Delight as a condition of obtaining a Chicken Delight trade-mark license. These requirements are asserted to constitute a tying arrangement, unlawful per se under § 1 of the Sherman Act.

After five weeks of trial to a jury in the District Court, plaintiffs moved for a directed verdict, requesting the court to rule upon four propositions of law: (1) That the contractual requirements constituted a tying arrangement as a matter of law; (2) that the alleged tying products—the Chicken Delight name, symbols, and system of operation—possessed sufficient economic power to condemn the tying arrangement as a matter of law; (3) that the tying arrangement had not, as a matter of law, been justified; and (4) that, as a matter of law, plaintiffs as a class had been injured by the arrangement.

The court ruled in favor of plaintiffs on all issues except part of the justification defense, which it submitted to the jury. On the questions submitted to it, the jury rendered special verdicts in favor of plaintiffs. . . .

I. FACTUAL BACKGROUND

Over its eighteen years existence, Chicken Delight has licensed several hundred franchisees to operate home delivery and pick-up food stores. It charged its franchisees no franchise fees or royalties. Instead, in exchange for the license granting the franchisees the right to assume its identity and adopt its business methods and to prepare and market certain food products under its trade-mark, Chicken Delight required its franchisees to purchase a specified number of cookers and fryers and to purchase certain packaging supplies and mixes exclusively from Chicken Delight. The prices fixed for these purchases were higher than, and included a percentage markup which exceeded that of, comparable products sold by competing suppliers.

II. THE EXISTENCE OF AN UNLAWFUL TYING ARRANGEMENT

* * *

A. Two Products

The District Court ruled that the license to use the Chicken Delight name, trade-mark, and method of operations was "a tying item in the traditional sense," 311 F.Supp. at 849, the tied items being the cookers and fryers, packaging products, and mixes.

* * *

The historical conception of a trade-mark as a strict emblem of source of the product to which it attaches has largely been abandoned. The burgeoning business of franchising has made trade-mark licensing a widespread commercial practice and has resulted in the development of a new rationale for trade-marks as representations of product quality. This is particularly true in the case of a franchise system set up not to distribute the trade-marked goods of the franchisor, but, as here, to conduct a certain business under a common trade-mark or trade name. Under such a type of franchise, the trade-mark simply reflects the goodwill and quality standards of the enterprise which it identifies. As long as the system of operation of the franchisees lives up to those quality standards and remains as represented by the mark so that the public is not misled, neither the protection afforded the trade-mark by law nor the value of the trade-mark to the licensee depends upon the source of the components.

This being so, it is apparent that the goodwill of the Chicken Delight trade-mark does not attach to the multitude of separate articles used in the operation of the licensed system or in the production of its end product. It is not what is used, but how it is used and what results that have given the system and its end product their entitlement to trade-mark protection. It is to the system and the end product that the public looks with the confidence that established goodwill has created.

Thus, sale of a franchise license, with the attendant rights to operate a business in the prescribed manner and to benefit from the goodwill of the trade name, in no way requires the forced sale by the franchisor of some or all of the component articles. Just as the quality of a copyrighted creation cannot by a tie-in be appropriated by a creation to which the copyright does not relate, United States v. Paramount Pictures, Inc., 334 U.S. 131, 158 (1948), so here attempts by tie-in to extend the trade-mark protection to common articles (which the public does not and has no reason to connect with the trade-mark) simply because they are said to be essential to production of that which is the subject of the trade-mark, cannot escape antitrust scrutiny.

* * *

We conclude that the District Court was not in error in ruling as matter of law that the arrangement involved distinct tying and tied products.

B. *Economic Power*

* * *

Chicken Delight points out that while it was an early pioneer in the fast food franchising field, the record establishes that there has recently been a dramatic expansion in this area, with the advent of numerous firms, including many chicken franchising systems, all competing vigorously with each other. Under the circumstances, it contends that the existence of the requisite market dominance remained a jury question.

The District Court ruled, however, that Chicken Delight's unique registered trade-mark, in combination with its demonstrated power to impose a tie-in, established as matter of law the existence of sufficient market power to bring the case within the Sherman Act.

We agree. . . .

* * *

C. *Justification*

Chicken Delight maintains that, even if its contractual arrangements are held to constitute a tying arrangement, it was not an unreasonable restraint under the Sherman Act. Three different bases for justification are urged.

First, Chicken Delight contends that the arrangement was a reasonable device for measuring and collecting revenue. There is no authority for justifying a tying arrangement on this ground. Unquestionably, there exist feasible alternative methods of compensation for the franchise licenses, including royalties based on sales volume or fees computed per unit of time, which would neither involve tie-ins nor have undesirable anticompetitive consequences.[8]

Second, Chicken Delight advances as justification the fact that when it first entered the fast food field in 1952 it was a new business and was the entitled to the protection afforded by United States v. Jerrold Electronics Corp., 187 F.Supp. 545. As to the period here involved—1963 to 1970—it contends that transition to a different arrangement would be difficult if not economically impossible.

---

8. It bears noting that Chicken Delight's competitors in the fast food franchising business did not find it necessary to use tie-ins.

We find no merit in this contention. Whatever claim Chicken Delight might have had to a new business defense in 1952—a question we need not decide—the defense cannot apply to the 1963–70 period. To accept Chicken Delight's argument would convert the new business justification into a perpetual license to operate in restraint of trade.

The third justification Chicken Delight offers is the "marketing identity" purpose, the franchisor's preservation of the distinctiveness, uniformity and quality of its product.

In the case of a trade-mark this purpose cannot be lightly dismissed. Not only protection of the franchisor's goodwill is involved. The licensor owes an affirmative duty to the public to assure that in the hands of his licensee the trade-mark continues to represent that which it purports to represent. For a licensor, through relaxation of quality control, to permit inferior products to be presented to the public under his licensed mark might well constitute a misuse of the mark. 15 U.S.C. §§ 1055, 1127.

However, to recognize that such a duty exists is not to say that every means of meeting it is justified. Restraint of trade can be justified only in the absence of less restrictive alternatives. In cases such as this, where the alternative of specification is available,[9] the language used in Standard Oil Co. v. United States, 337 U.S. at 306, in our view states the proper test, applicable in the case of trade-marks as well as in other cases:

> ". . . the protection of the good will of the manufacturer of the tying device—fails in the usual situation because specification of the type and quality of the product to be used in connection with the tying device is protection enough. * * * The only situation, indeed, in which the protection of good will may necessitate the use of tying clauses is where specifications for a substitute would be so detailed that they could not practicably be supplied."

The District Court found factual issues to exist as to whether effective quality control could be achieved by specification in the case of the cooking machinery and the dip and spice mixes. These questions were given to the jury under instructions [to determine whether specification was practicable]; and the jury, in response to special interrogatories, found against Chicken Delight.

As to the paper packaging, the court ruled as matter of law that no justification existed [because the packaging was easily specifiable]. . . .

We agree. . . .

We conclude that the District Court was not in error in holding as matter of law (and upon the limited jury verdict) that Chicken Delight's contractual requirements constituted a tying arrangement in violation of § 1 of the Sherman Act. Upon this aspect of the case, judgment is affirmed.

III. THE MEASURE OF DAMAGES

Section 4 of the Clayton Act provides that anyone "injured in his business or property" by reason of a violation of the antitrust laws "shall

---

9. There may, of course, be cases where some extraordinary condition forecloses specification, e.g., where it would divulge a trade secret.

recover threefold the damages by him sustained." In determining what damages plaintiffs incurred, the District Court noted that the contracts and all written representations by Chicken Delight stated that there were no franchise fees or royalty payments and from that fact concluded that the entire price paid by the franchisees was allocable to the tied items. Thus, the court ruled that the fact of damages equal in amount to the overcharge on the tied items (the amount by which the contract price exceeded the market price for comparable items) was established as a matter of law.

* * *

In this we feel the court erred.

It is by no means clear that any of the parties to the tying arrangements understood that the tying items were to be given free of charge. Indeed, the more reasonable reading of the contracts and of Chicken Delight's representations is that they stated simply that the contract prices for the tied items were to be the full compensation asked by Chicken Delight for both those items and the franchise licenses.

By its own terms, Clayton Act recovery is available only where actual injury has been suffered. The question here is whether the plaintiffs have suffered injury by virtue of the unlawful arrangement to which they were subjected. That arrangement of necessity involved both tying and tied products. To ascertain whether an unlawful arrangement for the sale of products has caused injury to the purchaser, the cost or value of the products involved, free from the unlawful arrangement, must first be ascertained.

Appellants contend that since the value of the tying items must be taken into account, as matter of law appellees have suffered no injury. They reason that the value of the tying items has been conclusively evidenced by what the franchisees were willing to pay (in overcharges for the tied items) in order to get them.

We cannot agree.[11] The franchisees' apparent willingness to pay the ultimate cost of the arrangement is clouded by the fact that they may well have been unaware of what that cost would come to in practice. Had the full amount of the over-charge on the tied items been openly specified as the cost of the tying items, agreement might not have been forthcoming. We can hardly rule as matter of law that it would have been.

We conclude that neither the existence of damage nor its lack of existence has been established as matter of law; that factual issues remain as to the value of both tying and tied products, free from the tying arrangement; that remand for the resolution of these issues is necessary.

Upon the issue of damages, judgment is reversed and the case remanded for limited new trial.

* * *

Questions and Comments

You represent Mr. and Mrs. Siegel. What is your theory of damages?

11. Were appellant's position correct, there could never be treble damage recovery by tie-in purchasers, since damage could never be demonstrated. . . .

Now suppose you represent Chicken Delight. Can you make a credible argument for dismissal based on lack of antitrust injury? Is the test of market power whether the seller could raise the price of the tying product or, instead, impose a burdensome tie (presumably putting the premium on the tied product rather than the tying product)? In the absence of the tie, would the franchisee pay virtually the same premium, in the form of a higher price or higher royalties for the franchise? Does damage (or antitrust injury) depend on proof that defendant was able to impose the tie without any reduction in the price for the tying product?

Does the *Chicken Delight* ruling on sufficiency of economic power withstand *Fortner II* and *Jefferson Parish*? How would you analyze the economic power question today? Some courts have held that sufficient economic power may be implied from strong and well established trademarks but not from weak ones. See *Capital Temporaries, Inc. of Hartford v. Olsten Corp.*, 506 F.2d 658 (2d Cir.1974). Do strong marks always (or presumptively) convey power? Suppose Bayer started to tie vitamins to its aspirin. How would you determine whether Bayer had the "sufficient power" required by the per se rule? Would you define the market (aspirin? analgesics? over the counter drugs?) and determine Bayer's share? Would evidence that Bayer has a very strong mark for aspirin be sufficient in itself?

What is the proper market for testing the economic power of a franchisor? The market for the sale of franchises? Fast food franchises? Hamburger franchises? Do prospective franchisees think of themselves as ice cream people? Pizza people? Chicken people? Do they shop for franchises only in their chosen line? Should we look to the market in which the franchisee shops, or to the market in which its customers shop? Does the competition from A & P supermarkets (nonfranchised) limit the price that 7–11 can get for its franchises?

Problem

McDonald's has a strong and well known trade name. New entrant, Burger Cheap, has a weak, little known name. Burger Cheap has considered charging franchisees for the right to use its name and style on the basis of a percentage of the franchisee's revenues. It is worried, however, that franchisees might not report their revenues accurately, and decides that if it, Burger Cheap, is the only source from which franchisees can get napkins, plates, and bags with the company logo, it will have a good device for measuring each franchisee's total revenues and will be able to keep its franchisees honest. Can Burger Cheap lawfully do business in this manner? Is there a principled basis on which Burger Cheap should be able to require its franchisees to buy their supplies from it, while McDonald's cannot?

Burger Cheap wants to associate its name with the slogan, "The 99¢-Burger." It asks you how it can achieve this image. It wants you to consider advertising, cooperative advertising with franchisees, logos, and restrictions in the franchise agreement. What do you advise? (Be sure to consider the vertical and horizontal price-fixing cases.)

PRINCIPE v. McDONALD'S CORP.

631 F.2d 303 (4th Cir.1980), cert. denied, 451 U.S. 970 (1981).

JUDGE PHILLIPS: This appeal presents the question of whether a fast food franchisor that requires its licensees to operate their franchises in premises leased from the franchisor is guilty of an illegal tying arrangement in violation of § 1 of the Sherman Act. On the facts of this case, we hold it does not and affirm the directed verdict for the defendants.

I

The appellants, Frank A. Principe, Ann Principe and Frankie, Inc., a family owned corporation, are franchisees of McDonald's System, Inc. The Principes acquired their first franchise, a McDonald's hamburger restaurant in Hopewell, Virginia, in 1970. At that time, they executed a twenty year franchise license agreement and a store lease of like duration. In consideration for their rights under these agreements, the Principes paid a $10,000 license fee and a $15,000 security deposit, and agreed to remit 2.2 per cent of their gross receipts as royalties under the franchise agreement and 8.0 per cent as rent under the lease. In 1974, Frank Principe and his son, Raymond, acquired a second franchise in Colonial Heights, Virginia, on similar terms. The Colonial Heights franchise subsequently was transferred to Frankie, Inc., a corporation owned jointly by Frank and Raymond Principe.

The Principes sought to purchase a third franchise in 1976 in Petersburg, Virginia. Robert Beavers, McDonald's regional manager, concluded the plaintiffs lacked sufficient management depth and capabilities to take on a third store without impairing the quality of their existing operations. During the next twenty months, the Principes obtained corporate review and reconsideration of the decision to deny them the franchise. They were notified in May 1978 that the Petersburg franchise was being offered to a new franchisee.

They filed this action a few days later alleging violations of federal and state antitrust and securities laws and state franchising laws. Courts I and II alleged McDonald's violated federal antitrust laws by tying store leases and $15,000 security deposit notes to the franchise rights at the Hopewell and Colonial Heights stores. Count XII alleged McDonald's denied the Principes a third franchise in retaliation for their refusal to follow McDonald's pricing guidelines. . . .

Following discovery the district court granted summary judgment for McDonald's on the security deposit note tie in claims. District Judge D. Dortch Warriner found the notes represented deposits against loss and do not constitute a product separate from the store leases to which they pertain.

The court directed a verdict for McDonald's on the store lease tie in counts at the close of all the evidence. . . . Judge Warriner held the Principes had failed to introduce any evidence of McDonald's power in the tying product market, which he held is the food retailing market. The court held, however, McDonald's sells only one product: the license contract and store lease are component parts of the overall package

McDonald's offers its prospective franchisees. Accordingly, Judge Warriner held as a matter of law there was no illegal tie in.

The remaining issue, whether McDonald's denied the Principes a third franchise in retaliation for their pricing independence, went to the jury which held for the defendants. The jury returned an unsolicited note stating they felt the Principes had been wronged, although price fixing was not the reason, and should be awarded the Petersburg franchise. The court disregarded the jury's note and entered judgment on the verdict for McDonald's.

The Principes appeal from the summary judgment for McDonald's on the security deposit tying claim, the directed verdict on the lease tying claim, various evidentiary rulings and the refusal of the district court to order a new trial. We affirm.

II

At the time this suit was filed, McDonald's consisted of at least four separate corporate entities. McDonald's Systems, Inc. controlled franchise rights and licensed franchisees to sell hamburgers under the McDonald's name. Franchise Realty Interstate Corporation (Franchise Realty) acquires real estate, either by purchase or long term lease, builds McDonald's hamburger restaurants, and leases them [4] either to franchisees or to a third corporation, McOpCo. McOpCo, which is not a party to this suit, operates about one-fourth of the McDonald's restaurants in the United States as company stores. Straddling this triad is McDonald's Corporation, the parent, who owns all the stock of the other defendants. Because the various defendants have substantially similar corporate hierarchies and operate in conjunction under the direction and control of the corporate parent, we shall refer to them collectively as McDonald's unless the context requires otherwise.

McDonald's is not primarily a fast food retailer. While it does operate over a thousand stores itself, the vast majority of the stores in its system are operated by franchisees. Nor does McDonald's sell equipment or supplies to its licensees. Instead its primary business is developing and collecting royalties from limited menu fast food restaurants operated by independent business people.

McDonald's develops new restaurants according to master plans that originate at the regional level and must be approved by upper management. Regional administrative staffs meet at least annually to consider new areas into which McDonald's can expand. Once the decision is made to expand into a particular geographic area, specialists begin to search for appropriate restaurant sites.

McDonald's uses demographic data generated by the most recent census and its own research in evaluating potential sites. McDonald's attempts to analyze and predict demographic trends in the geographic area. This process serves a two fold purpose: (1) by analyzing the demographic profile of a given market area, McDonald's hopes to determine whether the residents are likely to buy fast food in sufficient

---

4. The McDonald's system of restaurants included some 4465 stores in 1978, 99 per cent of which were owned by Franchise Realty.

quantities to justify locating a restaurant there; (2) by anticipating future growth, McDonald's seeks to plan its expansion to maximize the number of viable McDonald's restaurants within a given geographic area. Based on a comparison of data for various available sites, the regional staffs select what they believe is the best site in each geographic area. Occasionally no available site suits McDonald's requirements and expansion must be postponed.

* * *

After the specifics of each proposed new restaurant are approved, McDonald's decides whether the store will be company operated or franchised. If the decision is to franchise the store McDonald's begins the process of locating a franchisee. This involves offering the store either to an existing franchisee or to an applicant on the franchise waiting list. Applicants need not live near the store in order to be offered the franchise, and they need not accept the first franchise they are offered. The Principes lived in Kenosha, Wisconsin, and rejected eleven separate McDonald's restaurants before accepting their first franchise in Hopewell, Virginia. McDonald's often does not know who will operate a franchised store until it is nearly completed because a new restaurant may be offered to and rejected by several different applicants.

Meanwhile, Franchise Realty acquires the land, either by purchase or long term lease and constructs the store. Acquisition and development costs averaged over $450,000 per store in 1978. All McDonald's restaurants bear the same distinctive features with a few exceptions due to architectural restrictions: the golden arches motif, the brick and glass construction and the distinctive roofline. According to the defendants, these features identify the stores as a McDonald's even where zoning restrictions preclude other advertising or signs.

As constructed, McDonald's restaurants are finished shells; they contain no kitchen or dining room equipment. Furnishing store equipment is the responsibility of the operator, whether a franchisee or McOpCo. McDonald's does provide specifications such equipment must meet, but does not sell the equipment itself.

Having acquired the land, begun construction of the store and selected an operator, McDonald's enters into two contracts with the franchisee. Under the first, the franchise agreement, McDonald's grants the franchisee the rights to use McDonald's food preparation system and to sell food products under the McDonald's name. [Since 1970], [t]he franchisee pays a $12,500 franchise fee and agrees to remit three per cent of his gross sales as a royalty in return. Under the second contract, the lease, McDonald's grants the franchisee the right to use the particular store premises to which his franchise pertains. In return, the franchisee pays a $15,000 refundable security deposit (as evidence of which he receives a twenty year non-negotiable non-interest bearing note) and agrees to pay eight and one half per cent of his gross sales as rent. These payments under the franchise and lease agreements are McDonald's only sources of income from its franchised restaurants. The franchisee also assumes responsibility under the lease for building maintenance, improvements, property taxes and other costs associated with the premises. Both the franchise agreement and the lease generally have twenty year durations, both provide that termination of one terminates the other, and neither is available separately.

III

The Principes argue McDonald's is selling not one but three distinct products, the franchise, the lease and the security deposit note. The alleged antitrust violation stems from the fact that a prospective franchisee must buy all three in order to obtain the franchise.

As evidence that this is an illegal tying arrangement, the Principes point to the unfavorable terms on which franchisees are required to lease their stores. Not only are franchisees denied the opportunity to build equity and depreciate their property, but they must maintain the building, pay for improvements and taxes, and remit 8.5 per cent of their gross sales as rents. In 1978 the gross sales of the Hopewell store generated about $52,000 in rent. That figure nearly equalled Franchise Realty's original cost for the site and corresponds to more than a fourth of the original cost of the entire Hopewell restaurant complex. At that rate of return, the Principes argue, Franchise Realty will have recouped its entire investment in four years and the remainder of the lease payments will be pure profit. The Principes contend that the fact the store rents are so high proves that McDonald's cannot sell the leaseholds on their own merits.

Nor has McDonald's shown any need to forbid its licensees to own their own stores, the Principes say. Appellants contend that McDonald's is the only fast food franchisor that requires its licensees not only to pay royalties but to lease their stores from the franchisor. Before 1959 McDonald's itself permitted franchisees to own their own stores. McDonald's could maintain its desired level of uniformity by requiring franchisees to locate and construct stores according to company specifications. The Company could even provide planning and design assistance as it apparently does in connection with food purchasing and restaurant management. The Principes argue McDonald's has not shown that the success of its business or the integrity of its trademarks depends on company ownership of all store premises.

A separate tied product is the note that evidences the lessee's $15,000 security deposit, according to the appellants. The Principes argue the security deposit really is a mandatory contribution to McDonald's working capital, not security against damage to the store or breach of the lease contract. By tying the purchase of these $15,000 twenty year nonnegotiable non-interest bearing notes to that of the franchise, McDonald's allegedly has generated a capital fund that totalled over $45 million in 1978. It is argued that no one would purchase such notes on their own merits. The Principes assert that only by requiring franchisees to purchase the notes as a condition of obtaining a franchise has McDonald's been able to sell them at all.

McDonald's responds that it is not in the business of licensing use of its name, improving real estate for lease or selling long term notes. Its only business is developing a system of hamburger restaurants and collecting royalties from their sales. The allegedly tied products are but parts of the overall bundle of franchise benefits and obligations. According to McDonald's, the appellants are asking the court to invalidate the way McDonald's does business and to require it to adopt the licensing procedures of its less successful competitors. Federal antitrust laws do not compel such a result, McDonald's contends.

IV

"There is, at the outset of every tie-in case, including the familiar cases involving physical goods, the problem of determining whether two separate products are in fact involved." *Fortner Enterprises, Inc. v. United States Steel Corp.,* 394 U.S. 495, 507 (1969) (*Fortner I*). Because we agree with McDonald's that the lease, note and license are not separate products but component parts of the overall franchise package, we hold on the facts of this case there was no illegal tie in. Accordingly, we affirm the summary judgment and directed verdict for McDonald's on the tying claims.

As support for their position, the Principes rely primarily on the decision of the Ninth Circuit in *Siegel v. Chicken Delight, Inc.,* 448 F.2d 43 (9th Cir.1971), *cert. denied,* 405 U.S. 955 (1972), one of the first cases to address the problem of franchise tie-ins. Chicken Delight was what McDonald's characterizes as a "rent a name" franchisor: it licensed franchisees to sell chicken under the Chicken Delight name but did not own store premises or fixtures. The company did not even charge franchise fees or royalties. Instead, it required its franchisees to purchase a specified number of cookers and fryers and to purchase certain packaging supplies and mixes exclusively from Chicken Delight. These supplies were priced higher than comparable goods of competing sellers.

* * *

The Principes urge this court to apply the *Chicken Delight* reasoning to invalidate the McDonald's franchise lease note aggregation. They urge that McDonald's can protect the integrity of its trademarks by specifying how its franchisees shall operate, where they may locate their restaurants and what types of buildings they may erect. Customers do not and have no reason to connect the building's owner with the McDonald's operation conducted therein. Since company ownership of store premises is not an essential element of the trademark's goodwill, the Principes argue, the franchise, lease and note are separable products tied together in violation of the antitrust laws.

* * *

Without disagreeing with the result in *Chicken Delight,* we conclude that the court's emphasis in that case upon the trademark as the essence of a franchise is too restrictive. Far from merely licensing franchisees to sell products under its trade name, a modern franchisor such as McDonald's offers its franchisees a complete method of doing business. It takes people from all walks of life, sends them to its management school, and teaches them a variety of skills ranging from hamburger grilling to financial planning. It installs them in stores whose market has been researched and whose location has been selected by experts to maximize sales potential. It inspects every facet of every store several times a year and consults with each franchisee about his operation's strengths and weaknesses. Its regime pervades all facets of the business, from the design of the menu board to the amount of catsup on the hamburgers. Nothing is left to chance. This pervasive franchisor supervision and control benefits the franchisee in turn. His business is identified with a network of stores whose very uniformity and predictability attracts customers. In short, the modern franchisee pays not only for the right to use a trademark but for the right to become a part of a system whose business methods virtually guarantee his success. It is often unrealistic to view a franchise agreement as little more than a trademark license.

Given the realities of modern franchising, we think the proper inquiry is not whether the allegedly tied products are associated in the public mind with the franchisor's trademark, but whether they are integral components of the business method being franchised. Where the challenged aggregation is an essential ingredient of the franchised system's formula for success, there is but a single product and no tie in exists as a matter of law.

Applying this standard to the present case, we hold the lease is not separable from the McDonald's franchise to which it pertains. McDonald's practice of developing a system of company owned restaurants operated by franchisees has substantial advantages, both for the company and for franchisees. It is part of what makes a McDonald's franchise uniquely attractive to franchisees.

* * *

All of these factors [site selection, ownership of the restaurants by McDonald's, the building of the stores by McDonald's, and substantial investment by both McDonald and its franchisee] contribute significantly to the overall success of the McDonald's system. The formula that produced systemwide success, the formula that promises to make each new McDonald's store successful, that formula is what McDonald's sells its franchisees. To characterize the franchise as an unnecessary aggregation of separate products tied to the McDonald's name is to miss the point entirely. Among would be franchisees, the McDonald's name has come to stand for the formula, including all that it entails. We decline to find that it is an illegal tie in. . . .

* * *

Questions and Comments

Is *Principe v. McDonald's* simply about when an aggregation of items is one product? Or does the opinion chip away at antitrust as applied to franchising?

Analyze the one-product, two-product question under *Jefferson Parish* (first the plurality, then the concurrence). Did *Principe* involve one or two products?

Assume these to have been the facts: The Principes owned property in Petersburg, Virginia. On the basis of its own standard techniques of analysis, McDonald's thought the property ideal for a Petersburg location. It approached the Principes, offering to buy their land, build a store, and enter into a standard rental and franchise agreement with them. The Principes wanted to own the real estate, but they offered to take a franchise, build a store to McDonald's specifications, give McDonald's an option to buy the land at "fair market value" when their franchise terminated, and to negotiate a "fair and reasonable" franchise fee to compensate McDonald's in lieu of its usual rental revenue. Negotiations for the Petersburg franchise broke down when McDonald's insisted that the Principes sell the site to McDonald's and accept a lease back under the standard arrangement. Was ownership of the land by McDonald's an "essential ingredient of the franchised system's formula for success"? Was the land a separate product under Justice Stevens' analysis in *Jefferson Parish*? If the leasehold was a separate product, how would the case be analyzed?

In our notes above following *Chicken Delight* we assumed that McDonald's had sufficient economic power to bring it within the rule of *Chicken Delight* that a franchisor with market power cannot lawfully require its franchisees to purchase ingredients from it as a condition to getting a franchise. Now let us examine this assumption. It is correct? *Can* McDonald's lawfully require its franchisees to buy napkins, bags and cardboard containers with the McDonald's logo from McDonald's as a counting mechanism to double check the volume of sales reported by the franchisees and thus to police their honesty in the payment of royalties? Does contemporary law give McDonald's the opportunity to prove that it does not have economic power? That it cannot raise the price of its franchises to a supracompetitive level, in view of the hundreds, indeed thousands, of choices that buyers (franchisees) have and will take if price is too high? They can buy another franchise, they can form their own business, they can work for an established business. Why isn't the whole world of business and job opportunities the relevant market?

But suppose that the law presumes that McDonald's has sufficient economic power. (Does it? Should it?) Does *Jefferson Parish* give McDonald's another bite at the same apple by showing that no franchisee was coerced? Every one of them had the real opportunity to buy another franchise, to form their own business, to work for someone else. Surely they had more freedom of choice than an emergency patient in New Orleans who is taken by ambulance to Jefferson Parish Hospital and has to accept the "tied in" anesthetists.

Suppose the facts reveal sufficient coercion. Do *NCAA, Aspen Skiing* and *Northwest Wholesale Stationers* give McDonald's the opportunity to justify the tie in on the basis of efficiencies; indeed, efficiencies that will be passed on to the buyers? All franchisees profit from McDonald's effective policing of dishonesty. If even a quick rule of reason analysis is in order under *NCAA*, McDonald's can surely show that it has no power to limit output in the market for the sale of franchises; it cannot control entry; and as well, McDonald's can assert a quite credible efficiencies defense. Does McDonald's prevail? Has the new antitrust of the 1980s destroyed antitrust as a check on exploitative behavior of franchisors? Has the evaporation of the antitrust check led to the rise and expansion of state and federal regulation of franchising, much like blue sky securities regulation, which is costly for the government to run and costly for business to comply with? Professor John Flynn thinks that the retrenchment of antitrust has given rise to more intrusive regulation. Flynn, The "Is" and "Ought" of Vertical Restraints

After *Monsanto Co. v. Spray–Rite Service Corp.*, 71 Cornell L.Rev. 1095, 1148 (1986). Which way are we better off?

4. MISCELLANEOUS TECHNIQUES FOR SALES NOT SOLELY ON THE MERITS

a. *Promotional Techniques*

In the 1960s the Federal Trade Commission brought and won a series of cases under Section 5 of the Federal Trade Commission Act alleging that producers unfairly and anticompetitively pressured their dealers to carry products made or designated by the producers. One category was the TBA cases; major oil companies would induce their independent "authorized" gas stations to carry the tires, batteries and accessories of a specified major TBA company. The oil company would get commissions on the sales. Atlantic Richfield effectively required the Atlantic Richfield stations to carry only Goodyear TBA. See Atlantic Refining Co. v. FTC, 381 U.S. 357 (1965). Texaco, which had an arrangement with Goodrich, used somewhat gentler persuasion.

FTC v. TEXACO, INC.

393 U.S. 223 (1968).

JUSTICE BLACK: * * * That Texaco holds dominant economic power over its dealers is clearly shown by the record in this case. In fact, respondents do not contest the conclusion . . . that such power is "inherent in the structure and economics of the petroleum distribution system." Nearly 40% of the Texaco dealers lease their stations from Texaco. These dealers typically hold a one-year lease on their stations, and these leases are subject to termination at the end of any year on 10 days' notice. At any time during the year a man's lease on his service station may be immediately terminated by Texaco without advance notice if in Texaco's judgment any of the "housekeeping" provisions of the lease, relating to the use and appearance of the station, are not fulfilled. The contract under which Texaco dealers receive their vital supply of gasoline and other petroleum products also runs from year to year and is terminable on 30 days' notice under Texaco's standard form contract. The average dealer is a man of limited means who has what is for him a sizable investment in his station. He stands to lose much if he incurs the ill will of Texaco. . . .

* * *

. . . While the evidence in the present case fails to establish the kind of overt coercive acts shown in *Atlantic*, we think it clear nonetheless that Texaco's dominant economic power was used in a manner which tended to foreclose competition in the marketing of TBA. The sales-commission system for marketing TBA is inherently coercive. A service station dealer whose very livelihood depends upon the continuing good favor of a major oil company is constantly aware of the oil company's desire that he stock and sell the recommended brand of TBA. Through the constant reminder of the Texaco salesman, through demonstration projects and promotional materials, through all of the dealer's contacts with Texaco, he learns the lesson that Texaco wants him to purchase for his station the brand of TBA which pays Texaco 10% on every retail item the dealer buys. With the dealer's supply of gasoline, his lease on his station, and his Texaco identification subject to continuing review, we think it flies in the face of common sense to say, as Texaco asserts, that the dealer is "perfectly free" to reject Texaco's chosen brand of TBA. Equally applicable here is this Court's judgment in *Atlantic* that "[i]t is difficult to escape the conclusion that there would have been little point in paying substantial commissions to oil companies were it not for their ability to exert power over their wholesalers and dealers." 381 U.S., at 376.

We are similarly convinced that the Commission was correct in determining that this arrangement has an adverse effect on competition in the marketing of TBA. Service stations play an increasingly important role in the marketing of tires, batteries, and other automotive accessories. With five major companies supplying virtually all of the tires that come with new cars, only in the replacement market can the smaller companies hope to compete. Ideally, each service station dealer would stock the brands of TBA that in his judgment were most favored by customers for price and quality. To the extent that dealers are induced to select the sponsored brand in order to maintain the good favor of the oil company upon which they are dependent, the operation of the competitive market is adversely affected. As we noted in *Atlantic,* the essential anticompetitive vice of such an arrangement is "the utilization of economic power in one market to curtail competition in another." 381 U.S. 357, 369. Here the TBA manufacturer has purchased the oil company's economic power and used it as a partial substitute for competitive merit in gaining a major share of the TBA market. The nonsponsored brands do not compete on the even terms of price and quality competition; they must overcome, in addition, the influence of the dominant oil company that has been paid to induce its dealers to buy the recommended brand. While the success of this arrangement in foreclosing competitors from the TBA market has not matched that of the direct coercion employed by Atlantic, we feel that the anticompetitive tendencies of such a system are clear, and that the Commission was properly fulfilling the task that Congress assigned it in halting this practice in its incipiency. The Commission is not required to show that a practice it condemns has totally eliminated competition in the relevant market. It is enough that the Commission found that the practice in question unfairly burdened competition for a not insignificant volume of commerce. . . .

* * *

See also *FTC v. Brown Shoe Company,* 384 U.S. 316 (1966), holding illegal under the Federal Trade Commission Act the franchise store program of Brown Shoe Company (the old Buster Brown). Brown Shoe's program required independent retail stores to limit their purchases to the Brown lines. Dealers who chose this plan received special architectural, record keeping and insurance plan benefits in return.

Questions and Comments

Does *Texaco* survive contemporary antitrust analysis? What additional facts would you need for contemporary analysis? Even if the FTC could make out a prima facie case that the TBA arrangement was anticompetitive (could it?), would Texaco be likely to have a good business justification? Would single brand identification arguably enhance its image and desirability?

On the other hand, Texaco was getting a healthy commission for no effort. Why wouldn't this premium enhance the price of TBA at Texaco stations and make the stations less attractive to driver/customers? Could Texaco get away with this "exploitation" and not be outcompeted, unless: (1) Texaco reduced the price of the gas station lease, or (2) Texaco, Atlantic, etc. were facilitating a TBA cartel and getting paid for doing so. Which of the two latter possibilities seems more plausible?

b. Reciprocity

Reciprocity is the practice of buying from one's customers. It can take various forms. Mutual patronage reciprocity is reflected by the statement: "If you buy from me, I will buy from you." Coercive reciprocity, by contrast, reflects a threat (often implied) from a very important customer: "You must buy from me or I will stop placing my business with you." What is the functional difference between the two forms of reciprocity? Should the difference affect antitrust analysis?

In the 1950s and 1960s, with the growth of conglomerates, many large companies found themselves in a position in which reciprocity was possible and seemed to be a cheap and easy way of increasing sales. Many conglomerates were, in the context of one market, large and important customers of other conglomerates that bought products the first firm sold. These diversified companies set up "trade relations" departments to exploit opportunities to sell to their suppliers. Sometimes these departments merely provided information to sales people about customers or possible customers from whom the conglomerate was currently purchasing. Sometimes they developed and tried to implement more aggressive strategies; for example, selling on reciprocal terms. See generally Hausman, Reciprocal Dealing and the Antitrust Laws, 77 Harv.L.Rev. 873 (1964).

The Supreme Court has decided only one reciprocity case—a merger case. Consolidated Foods, a large purchaser of foods from food processors such as Swift, acquired Gentry, the second largest of the four firms that produced dehydrated onions and garlic, ingredients needed by firms such as Swift. Consolidated Foods had used reciprocal dealing in the past. The FTC found that reciprocal dealing was a probable result of the acquisition; that Gentry would thereby get special access to a quarter of the market for its product, and that the acquisition was therefore illegal under the merger law, Section 7 of the Clayton Act. The Court said, by Justice Douglas:

> We hold at the outset that the "reciprocity" made possible by such an acquisition is one of the congeries of anti-competitive practices at which the antitrust laws are aimed. The practice . . . [intrudes] into the

choice among competing products, creating at the least "a priority on the business at equal prices." *International Salt Co. v. United States,* 332 U.S. 392, 396–397; *Northern Pac. R. Co. v. United States,* 356 U.S. 1, 3, 6, 12. Reciprocal trading may ensure not from bludgeoning or coercion but from more subtle arrangements. A threatened withdrawal of orders if products of an affiliate cease being bought, as well as a conditioning of future purchases on the receipt of orders for products of that affiliate, is an anti-competitive practice.

FTC v. Consolidated Foods Corp., 380 U.S. 592, 594 (1965).

Meanwhile, the Justice Department sued General Dynamics Corporation for violating the Clayton Act and the Sherman Act by acquiring Liquid Carbonic Corporation, a major producer of carbon dioxide and other industrial gasses, and for violating the Sherman Act by the use of reciprocity.

UNITED STATES v. GENERAL DYNAMICS CORP.

258 F.Supp. 36 (S.D.N.Y.1966).

JUDGE CANNELLA: ＊ ＊ ＊ The legality of the use of reciprocity under Sherman § 1 is a question of first impression. The government contends that contracts made by the defendant with certain reciprocity accounts, as well as the merger agreement itself, are violative of the Section. These contentions will be considered separately.

While the general areas of inquiry are unique, the court is not without guidelines. Those who have had occasion to consider the use of reciprocity as an anti-competitive practice have invariably analogized it to "tying-in" agreements. The court finds, for reasons to be discussed shortly, that the analogy is sound. It therefore adopts for purposes of this case, the standards of decision delineated by the Supreme Court in those cases.

"Tying-in" occurs when the sale of one product (the tying product) is conditioned on agreement to purchase another (the tied product). "Where such conditions are successfully exacted competition on the merits with respect to the tied product is inevitably curbed. . . . They deny competitors free access to the market for the tied product, not because the party imposing the tying requirement has a better product of a lower price but because of his power or leverage in another market." *Northern Pacific Railroad Co. v. United States,* 356 U.S. 1, 6 (1958).

Similarly in the instant case General Dynamics, via the Special Sales Program, "ties" its purchases from a present or prospective vendor to that vendor's purchases of carbon dioxide from Liquid Carbonic. By so acting, the defendant manages to succeed in the carbon dioxide market, not because it has "a better product or a lower price" but because of its purchasing power as a defense contractor. This transference of purchasing power to inflate sales in other markets accomplishes the same result condemned in "tying-in" arrangements, viz., a frustration of competitive criteria in determining which firms receive which purchasing orders.

Few would dispute the above analogy with reference to coercive reciprocity. However, at least one prominent commentator in the antitrust field has questioned the analogy's applicability to mutual patronage reciprocity. For a "tying-in" arrangement to be consummated, there must be a strong demand for the tying product. If this is not the case, the would-be customer might well elect to purchase neither the tying nor tied product. In other words, without power in one market which can be transferred to interfere with a purchaser's freedom of choice in a second market, tying is impossible. With mutual patronage reciprocity, on the other hand, purchasing power is used by both parties as a sales generating device, although no force is exerted from any quarter.

If anti-trust legislation was designed primarily to insulate customers from abuse, the "tying-in" analogy would be without merit with reference to non-coercive reciprocity. However, this is not the case. The legislation is intended to preserve free competition. Reciprocity, whether mutual or coercive, serves to exclude competitors by the exercise of large scale purchasing power. This court concludes that the analogy of reciprocity to "tying-in" arrangements applies to both forms of reciprocity.

The Supreme Court has held that "tying-in" arrangements are *per se* violative of Section 1, if a not insubstantial amount of commerce is effected. . . .

Against this background, attention is now directed to the government's position regarding vendor contracts. The thrust of their argument is that reciprocity was systematically interjected into the sales presentations of Liquid Carbonic. It is pointed out that the statistics and statements of the defendant indicate that the program was effective. Therefore, the court is urged to infer the existence of contracts in restraint of trade.

Such a conclusion is not warranted. The Section's reference to contracts, combinations and conspiracies, is necessarily directed at bilateral arrangements. The statistics which the government mentions have been found by the court to be credible. Nonetheless, the business secured could be the result of the mere presence of the reciprocity power. Vendors of General Dynamics to curry favor or protect present sales to the defendant, might unilaterally decide to purchase the products of Liquid Carbonic. In such instances, no actual contacts would occur and thus no agreements would be present to serve as a predicate for a Sherman § 1 violation. This is true even though if a sufficient volume of trade was diverted in this fashion, a Clayton § 7 violation would be established.

To prove the presence of vendor contracts on condition, particular contracts with identifiable parties must be introduced into evidence, or legitimately inferred from the conduct of such identifiable parties. This was done by the government but the total amount of proven restrained trade totalled only $177,225. The $500,000 in *International Salt* has no magical significance; it merely was termed by the court as "not insubstantial". However, it is the lowest figure so designated by the court to date, in situations analogous to the present case. Since the government has proven the other prong of the Sherman § 1 case, viz., that the merger itself is violative of the statute, this aspect of this case is an inappropriate vehicle for finding an amount considerably less than $500,000 as "not insubstantial". Thus the government has failed to prove the illegality of the challenged vendor contracts.

The next subject for the court's considerations is the legality of the merger relative to Section 1. The court has found that both parties had the intent, at the time of merger, to employ the anti-competitive device of reciprocity to generate sales. The defendant's statistics and the statements of its officers clearly demonstrate, as indicated previously, that a "not insubstantial" amount of commerce was effected as a result of the merger agreement. The court therefore finds on this aspect of the case that the government has satisfactorily carried its burden of proof.

The final question concerns the appropriate relief to be ordered. As noted previously, the mere presence of reciprocity power may have significant anti-trust consequences. This fact alone indicates the need for divestiture. Moreover, in United States v. E.I. Du Pont De Nemours & Co., 366 U.S. 316, at 326, 328 (1961), it was noted that divestiture, "that most drastic, but most effective, of antitrust remedies" is "peculiarly appropriate in cases of stock acquisitions which violate § 7."

The court directs that the defendant divest itself of Liquid Carbonic by severing all common ties of ownership and management.

The defendant is also ordered to cease and desist, from the date of this decision, from using reciprocity to secure sales of carbon dioxide or other industrial gases.

*   *   *

Is reciprocity one of the congeries of anticompetitive practices that antitrust should prevent? Is it a practice that the law should view with skepticism, and condemn under certain circumstances; perhaps when the firm utilizing the practice has market (buying) power? Perhaps when the practice gives the utilizing firm preferred access to a significant percentage of sales in a concentrated market? Should defendant be able to defend by showing that no output limitation is possible or probable? Or should plaintiff's claim be dismissed out of hand on grounds that it is trivial? Are the Stevens and O'Connor opinions in *Jefferson Parish* germane? How would each, Justice Stevens and Justice O'Connor, analyze the reciprocity problem in *General Dynamics?*

As a result of law enforcement in the 1960s and early 1970s, the trade relations departments of the conglomerates disappeared. At least, they achieved a very low profile if not an underground posture. Can we expect the re-emergence of aggressive trade relations departments? Will they be justified on efficiency grounds (*i.e.*, on grounds that they save the costs of competition and are not output limiting)? If they re-emerge with a vengeance, will there be a new call for law to contain them? Will the new call for legal proscription be justified on fairness grounds? On grounds that unknowable efficiency benefits are likely to be achieved by opening the doors to competition on the merits?

We end, here, our treatment of contractual restraints that have the effect of foreclosing competitors from access to inputs or outlets, and we turn to corporate integration. If loose knit arrangements pose problems for competition, then tight-knit arrangements could be expected to aggravate the problems, for vertical integration is firmer, more permanent and harder to contract around. Yet, internal integration, the subject to which we turn, is normally driven by strong efficiency prospects. Most often, it is a natural response to market demands. Accordingly, even at the height of concern about trying and exclusive dealing, internal integration was treated with hospitality.

D. INTERNAL VERTICAL INTEGRATION

Thus far, as noted, we have talked about loose-knit vertical relationships; we have not focused on tight-knit or corporate integration. Firms may integrate vertically for various reasons and by various means. They may integrate to achieve efficiencies or to gain market power—a subject to which we return. They may integrate loosely, by contract, or more permanently by grass roots entry or merger. Mergers are normally tested under Section 7 of the Clayton Act; we discuss vertical mergers in Chapter 5.

Internal vertical integration (vertical integration by grass roots entry) can in theory be examined under the Sherman Act, although, as we shall see, it is seldom a subject that invokes scrutiny.

When a company enters a new vertical stage by internal expansion, it may be doing so in order to gain efficiencies and thus to reduce the cost of the end product. If significant efficiencies drive vertical integration, one would expect to see most firms in the industry vertically integrated. For example, if molding and stretching steel into rods is done at lower cost before molten steel hardens, one would expect the companies that make the steel to make the rods. Then we would think of the performance of the successive functions by one firm as natural and expected integration. Indeed, when the efficiencies are obvious enough, we do not think of the operations as separate stages at all. Pizza ovens could be operated in establishments separate from pizza restaurants, but they are not. We identify single vertical stages with the same intuition with which we identify single products for purposes of tying analysis. We think about efficiencies, observe what the market does, and use common sense.

Many kinds of efficiencies can result from vertical integration; we have referred to them above. In addition to the most obvious successive-stage efficiencies, a firm might hedge its risks by assuring stable outlets or a stable source of supply, or it might save transaction costs and assure a more tailored fit between the suppliers' product and its own, or it might gain important information to monitor its suppliers and prevent exploitation. Or, the firm might simply want to enter a new field, and it chooses a field that it knows something about. Or it chooses to imitate respected competitors.

The integration could also reflect anticompetitive potentials. First, a firm might invest at a vertically related level in order to increase, protect or exploit market power. If these are not the purposes, they might nevertheless be effects. Where a firm has market power at one horizontal level, vertical integration can, under certain conditions, raise, barriers to entry at the original level or transfer market power to the newly entered stage, and may tend to raise the price or lessen possibilities for lowering the price of the end product. Second, the integration might enable the firm to exploit market power through price discrimination. Third, the integration might foreclose rivals from an important and limited source of supply or a limited market outlet, with or without an end-price effect.

Nonetheless, vertical integration by internal growth rarely presents a serious Sherman Act problem. Problems are somewhat more likely to arise from conduct after entry; for example, a monopolist's refusal to supply necessary inputs to unintegrated competitors, or other strategies to impose costs on unintegrated competitors. Recall *Otter Tail,* supra p. 168, as an example. See also Williamson, Delimiting Antitrust, 76 Geo.L.J. 241 (1987).

The Supreme Court addressed internal vertical integration in *United States v. Paramount Pictures, Inc.,* 334 U.S. 131 (1948). *Paramount* involved also, a number of contracts and conspiracies among competing motion picture producers, distributors and exhibitors, and the Court found these agreements illegal. The Court declined to rule that single-firm integration of production, distribution and exhibition of motion pictures is illegal per se, but said rather, that the legality of vertical integration turns "on (1) the purpose or intent with which it was conceived, or (2) the power it creates and the attendant purpose of intent." Id. at 174. What does that mean? Contemporary discussion of vertical integration tends to be more permissive. See *Hiland Dairy, Inc. v. Kroger Co.,* 402 F.2d 968 (8th Cir. 1968); *Auburn News Co. v. Providence Journal Co.,* 659 F.2d 273 (1st Cir. 1981), cert. denied, 455 U.S. 921 (1982); *Paschall v. Kansas City Star Co.,* 727 F.2d 692 (8th Cir.1984), *cert. denied,* 469 U.S. 872 (1984).

Problem 1

Each of the three national television networks decides to enter the business of production of theatrical feature films. Each will produce about 15 films a year, license them for theater exhibition, and then televise them on prime time on its own network. Since prime time slots (by far the most desirable) are scarce, each network will have room for only about five other theatrical feature films a year and will want only blockbusters.

The major movie companies sue to enjoin the networks' production plans. The networks counter that the movie companies have been holding back on movie production and have been charging exorbitant license fees for their films, and that the networks can make equal-quality films for less than the price of a license.

Each network has entered into many contracts to facilitate its entry as a movie producer. Do these contracts satisfy the "contract" requirement of Section 1? Assume so, and analyze the problem under Section 1. Are the networks' plans anticompetitive or procompetitive, on balance? See *Columbia Pictures Industries, Inc. v. ABC,* 501 F.2d 894 (2d Cir.1974); *United States v. ABC,* 1981–1 CCH Trade Cas. ¶ 64,150 (consent decree C.D.Cal.1980).

Problem 2

By final judgment entered by consent in 1982, a United States District Court ordered American Telephone and Telegraph Company to spin off or divest itself of the local telephone exchange monopolies, all of which were and would remain regulated by the states. (The local exchanges are called "basic operating companies" or "BOCs".) AT & T would retain the long distance line business ("Long Lines"), where it was beginning to face competitors such as MCI and Sprint; and it would retain Western Electric Company, which manufactured telephones, lines, and other telecommunications equipment for the local exchange companies and for the long line business. See *United States v. American Telephone & Telegraph Co.*, 1982–2 CCH Trade Cas. ¶ 64,900 (D.D.C.1982).

The theory of the Justice Department's complaint and request for relief was that the combination of the potentially competitive long lines with the natural monopoly local exchanges was inherently inefficient; it encouraged cross-subsidization and the use of power in regulated monopoly markets to foreclose competition in potentially competitive markets. One possible scenario was that AT & T sold equipment to the BOCs at a monopoly price; and since the price would be a cost to the BOCs, which were subject to cost-plus regulation, the premium would get passed on the local telephone user. Another possible scenario cut in a different direction but nonetheless would exacerbate the market imperfections. State authorities put pressure on local exchanges to charge rates too low to cover costs. The Long Lines division made higher than competitive profits, and subsidized the local telephone service. Particularly because Long Lines needed the extra revenues in order to be able to subsidize local telephone calls, it tried to suppress competition in the long line business and (the United States contended) unreasonably suppressed competition by rivals offering new low-cost technologies, such as microwave.

Although Western Electric supplied equipment to Long Lines as well as to the BOCs, the government did not request and the court did not order separation of Long Lines from Western Electric. The government's reasons for this approach are stated in the following paragraphs of the Justice Department's Competitive Impact Statement:

UNITED STATES v. AMERICAN TELEPHONE & TELEGRAPH CO.

Proposed Consent Judgment
Feb. 10, 1982

Procurement of Equipment. The divestiture of the BOCs from AT & T will eliminate the incentives of the BOCs to buy from Western Electric regardless of the price or quality of Western's equipment. It will also remove AT & T's ability, through its control of the BOCs, to influence the purchasing decisions of the BOCs unfairly in favor of Western Electric. The injunctive provisions of Paragraph II(B) will reinforce this incentive structure by requiring the BOCs to treat all equipment manufacturers in an evenhanded, non-discriminatory manner. Finally, elimination of the license contracts between the BOCs and AT & T will eliminate the mandatory payments under those contracts as a source of subsidy to AT & T's equipment activities.

Given the divestiture of the operating companies, however, further divestiture of Western Electric or Long Lines is unnecessary to protect competition in equipment markets. While AT & T may retain the technical ability to cause purchases by the expanded Long Lines from Western Electric without regard to price or quality, its incentive to do so will be greatly reduced immediately and ultimately eliminated by divestiture of the BOCs. As explained earlier, because divestiture of the BOCs will remove AT & T's ability to disadvantage its interexchange competitors in access to essential facilities, AT & T will become subject to competition in all of its services. Because excessive transfer prices must be reflected in the cost of AT & T's intercity services, AT & T will have, as it becomes increasingly subject to competition, an incentive to procure inputs as efficiently as possible.

You represent a manufacturer of telecommunications equipment, useful principally for the long lines business. Your client is certain that AT & T will favor Western Electric, and that AT & T is likely to remain the dominant long-line firm in the United States. Your client asks you to file comments on its behalf for modification of the proposed judgment.

Draft modifying language that you would propose to the court. What authorities and what economic arguments support your proposal? If you were the judge, would you urge the parties to accept the proposed modification? [24]

You have now had a kaleidoscopic view of the possible competition problems that may arise from vertical contractual restraints and internal integration. While the law once broadly proscribed many such restraints, it does not any longer. Small dislocations to competitors are deemed not worth worrying about. Focus has shifted to concentrated markets, firms with market power, and serious foreclosures and barriers that have the potential to hurt consumers' interests. Even within this much-reduced range of concern, Chicagoans argue that vertical restraints have such strong efficiency properties, and law condemning them has such strong egalitarian implications that undercut efficiency, that purely vertical restraints should be beyond the reach of antitrust. Should they?

E. DISCRIMINATORY PRICING—SECONDARY LINE PRICE DISCRIMINATION—THE ROBINSON–PATMAN ACT

Before closing this chapter we treat pricing itself, not pursuant to contract, as a vertical restraint. In Chapter 2 we studied predatory pricing, and saw how pricing strategies can sometimes (although rarely) be predatorily monopolistic and offend Section 2 of the Sherman Act. We then looked briefly at the Robinson–Patman Act and saw how discriminatory pricing by a monopolist or near monopolist can lessen competition on the "primary line"—competition among the monopolist and its competitors—and can thereby run afoul of the Robinson–Patman Act.

---

24. The judge cannot rewrite the proposed consent judgment, but can find that the proposed judgment is not in the public interest without the modification, and can decline to enter the judgment unless modified. Judge Greene followed this procedure in the AT & T case, and prevailed upon the parties to accept certain modifications. See United States v. American Telephone & Telegraph Co., *aff'd sub nom.* Maryland v. United States, 460 U.S. 1001 (1983) (Rehnquist, Burger and White dissenting).

Price discrimination can also cause harm on the secondary line—the level of the disfavored buyer—and even on the tertiary line if there is yet another middleman in the process of distribution. Secondary line effects are thus downstream, or vertical, effects. The legislative history suggests that such effects, with their characteristic impact on small business, were the major concern of the Congress that passed the Robinson-Patman Act. See Hansen, *Robinson-Patman Law: A Review and Analysis*, 51 Fordham L.Rev. 1113 (1983). We look briefly at secondary line impacts in this section.

Downstream impacts, the major concern of Congress, may occur when the seller gives a lower price to one buyer than to other buyers and the disfavored buyer must compete with the favored one in the resale market. The secondary line concern is that large buyers—mainly chains—may use their size and power to extract from sellers prices lower than their small competitors can obtain, and that the discrimination will cause the smaller firms to lose so many sales that they will be hurt, they will be unable to operate effectively, and consumers generally will be hurt. The Robinson-Patman Act limits its proscriptions to price discriminations in interstate commerce. Thus, not only must interstate commerce be affected at the threshold level required by the Sherman Act, but the discriminatory sales must be in interstate commerce.

There are many critics of the Robinson–Patman Act. Critics challenge both of the basic premises of the act; namely, 1) that small business should be favored by the law, to be fair and to keep small business viable; and 2) that price discrimination threatens harm to downstream competition. See, e.g., Kintner & Bauer, The Robinson–Patman Act: A Look Backwards, A View Forward, 31 Antitrust Bull. 571 (1986). The criticism is not surprising, for the act was passed principally for political economy reasons (protection of small business) and for fairness. It does not fit into the output model; it would never have been passed if the goal of Congress had been to increase output; and law that does not fit into the output model naturally draws criticism from those who see antitrust through no other lens. As a result of their own ideological opposition, the Justice Department and the FTC practically never sue to enjoin Robinson–Patman Act violations. In Congressional oversight hearings, enforcers continually tell Congress that they will sue if they find the right case; but they virtually never find the right case. Nonetheless, the Robinson–Patman Act engages much attention from in-house counsel who review marketing programs for legal compliance, and it continues to generate private treble damage litigation.

Robinson–Patman cases, whether primary or secondary line, raise a wide range of issues. When is a sale "in commerce"? When is a discrimination "in commerce"? E.g., *Standard Oil v. FTC*, 340 U.S. 231 (1951). What is a "price"? Corn Products Refining Co. v. FTC, 324 U.S. 726 (1945). What is "discrimination"? *FTC v. Anheuser Busch, Inc.*, 363 U.S. 536 (1960). What is a "purchase"? *Naifeh v. Ronson Art Metal Works*, 218 F.2d 202 (10th Cir.1954). When and how must advertising and promotional benefits be made available to competing dealers? "Fred Meyer" Guides for Advertising Allowances and Other Merchandising

Payments and Services, 16 C.F.R. § 240 (1983) (in process of revision). Cases and commentary treat all of these issues. See, e.g., C. Oppenheim & G. Weston, Unfair Trade Practices and Consumer Protection, Ch. 10, (1974); Antitrust Law Developments (Second) Ch. 4 (1984) and supplements. We do not deal with these and other specific and sometimes technical questions; rather, we concentrate on the core conceptual issues of requisite anticompetitive effect and antitrust damages in secondary line cases.

Before turning to the cases we set forth relevant portions of the statute. In sum, Section 2(a) prohibits certain price discriminations by sellers, subject to a cost justification defense; Section 2(b) contains a meeting competition defense; and Section 2(f) prohibits buyers from knowingly inducing or receiving prohibited price discriminations.

Section 2(a)

It shall be unlawful for any person engaged in commerce, in the course of such commerce, either directly or indirectly, to discriminate in price between different purchasers of commodities of like grade and quality, where either or any of the purchases involved in such discrimination are in commerce, where such commodities are sold for use, consumption, or resale within the United States or any Territory thereof or the District of Columbia or any insular possession or other place under the jurisdiction of the United States, and where the effect of such discrimination may be substantially to lessen competition or tend to create a monopoly in any line of commerce, or to injure, destroy, or prevent competition or tend to create a monopoly in any line of commerce, or to injure, destroy, or prevent competition with any person who either grants or knowingly receives the benefit of such discrimination, or with customers of either of them[. N]othing herein contained shall prevent differentials which make only due allowance for differences in the cost of manufacture, sale, or delivery resulting from the differing methods or quantities in which such commodities are to such purchasers sold or delivered[.]

Section 2(b)

Upon proof being made, at any hearing on a complaint under this section, that there has been discrimination in price or services or facilities furnished, the burden of rebutting the prima-facie case thus made by showing justification shall be upon the person charged with a violation of this section, and unless justification shall be affirmatively shown, the Commission is authorized to issue an order terminating the discrimination: *Provided, however,* That nothing herein contained shall prevent a seller rebutting the prima-facie case thus made by showing that his lower price or the furnishing of services or facilities to any purchaser or purchasers was made in good faith to meet an equally low price of a competitor, or the services or facilities furnished by a competitor.

Section 2(f)

It shall be unlawful for any person engaged in commerce, in the course of such commerce, knowingly to induce or receive a discrimination in price which is prohibited by this section.

FEDERAL TRADE COMMISSION v. MORTON SALT CO.

334 U.S. 37 (1948).

JUSTICE BLACK: The Federal Trade Commission, after a hearing, found that the respondent, which manufactures and sells table salt in interstate commerce, had discriminated in price between different purchasers of like grades and qualities, and concluded that such discriminations were in violation of § 2 of the Clayton Act, as amended by the Robinson–Patman Act. It accordingly issued a cease and desist order. Upon petition of the respondent the Circuit Court of Appeals, with one judge dissenting, set aside the Commission's findings and order. . . . The Court's judgment rested on its construction of the Act, its holding that crucial findings of the Commission were either not supported by evidence or were contrary to the evidence, and its conclusion that the Commission's order was too broad. Since questions of importance in the construction and administration of the Act were presented, we granted certiorari. . . .

Respondent manufactures several different brands of table salt and sells them directly to (1) wholesalers or jobbers, who in turn resell to the retail trade, and (2) large retailers, including chain store retailers. Respondent sells its finest brand of table salt, known as Blue Label, on what it terms a standard quantity discount system available to all customers. Under this system the purchasers pay a delivered price and the cost to both wholesale and retail purchasers of this brand differs according to the quantities bought. These prices are as follows, after making allowance for rebates and discounts:

	Per case
Less-than-carload purchases	$1.60
Carload purchases	1.50
5,000–case purchases in any consecutive 12 months	1.40
50,000–case purchases in any consecutive 12 months	1.35

Only five companies have ever bought sufficient quantities of respondent's salt to obtain the $1.35 per case price. These companies could buy in such quantities because they operate large chains of retail stores in various parts of the country.[4] As a result of this low price these five companies have been able to sell Blue Label salt at retail cheaper than wholesale purchasers from respondent could reasonably sell the same brand of salt to independently operated retail stores, many of whom competed with the local outlets of the five chain stores.

Respondent's table salts, other than Blue Label, are also sold under a quantity discount system differing slightly from that used in selling Blue Label. Sales of these other brands in less-than-carload lots are made at list price plus freight from plant to destination. Carload purchasers are granted approximately a 5 per cent discount; approximately a 10 per cent discount is granted to purchasers who buy as much as $50,000 worth of all brands of salt in any consecutive twelve-month period. Respondent's

4. These chain stores are American Stores Company, National Tea Company, Kroger Grocery Co., Safeway Stores, Inc., and Great Atlantic & Pacific Tea Company.

quantity discounts on Blue Label and on other table salts were enjoyed by certain wholesalers and retailers who competed with other wholesalers and retailers to whom these discounts were refused.

In addition to these standard quantity discounts, special allowances were granted certain favored customers who competed with other customers to whom they were denied.

First. Respondent's basic contention, which it argues this case hinges upon, is that its "standard quantity discounts, available to all on equal terms, as contrasted, for example, to hidden or special rebates, allowances, prices or discounts, are not discriminatory within the meaning of the Robinson–Patman Act." Theoretically, these discounts are equally available to all, but functionally they are not. For as the record indicates (if reference to it on this point were necessary) no single independent retail grocery store, and probably no single wholesaler, bought as many as 50,000 cases or as much as $50,000 worth of table salt in one year. Furthermore, the record shows that, while certain purchasers were enjoying one or more of respondent's standard quantity discounts, some of their competitors made purchases in such small quantities that they could not qualify for any of respondent's discounts, even those based on carload shipments. The legislative history of the Robinson–Patman Act makes it abundantly clear that Congress considered it to be an evil that a large buyer could secure a competitive advantage over a small buyer solely because of the large buyer's quantity purchasing ability. The Robinson-Patman Act was passed to deprive a large buyer of such advantages except to the extent that a lower price could be justified by reason of a seller's diminished costs due to quantity manufacture, delivery or sale, or by reason of the seller's good faith effort to meet a competitor's equally low price.

Section 2 of the original Clayton Act had included a proviso that nothing contained in it should prevent "discrimination in price . . . on account of differences in the grade, quality, or quantity of the commodity sold, or that makes only due allowance for difference in the cost of selling or transportation. . . ." That section has been construed as permitting quantity discounts, such as those here, without regard to the amount of the seller's actual savings in cost attributable to quantity sales or quantity deliveries. The House Committee Report on the Robinson–Patman Act considered that the Clayton Act's proviso allowing quantity discounts so weakened § 2 "as to render it inadequate, if not almost a nullity." [6] The Committee considered the present Robinson–Patman amendment to § 2 "of great importance." Its purpose was to limit "the use of quantity price differentials to the sphere of actual cost differences. Otherwise," the report continued, "such differentials would become instruments of favor and privilege and weapons of competitive oppression." [7] The Senate Committee reporting the bill emphasized the same purpose, as did the Congressman in charge of the Conference Report when explaining it to the House just before final passage. And it was in furtherance of this avowed purpose—to protect competition from all price differentials except

6. H.R.Rep. No. 2287, 74th Cong., 2d   **7.** *Id.* at 9.
Sess. 7.

those based in full on cost savings—that § 2(a) of the amendment provided "That nothing herein contained shall prevent differentials which make only due allowance for differences in the cost of manufacture, sale, or delivery resulting from the differing methods or quantities in which such commodities are to such purchasers sold or delivered."

The foregoing references, without regard to others which could be mentioned, establish that respondent's standard quantity discounts are discriminatory within the meaning of the Act, and are prohibited by it whenever they have the defined effect on competition.

Second. The Government interprets the opinion of the Circuit Court of Appeals as having held that in order to establish "discrimination in price" under the Act the burden rested on the Commission to prove that respondent's quantity discount differentials were not justified by its cost savings. Respondent does not so understand the Court of Appeals decision, and furthermore admits that no such burden rests on the Commission. We agree that it does not. First, the general rule of statutory construction that the burden of proving justification or exemption under a special exception to the prohibitions of a statute generally rests on one who claims its benefits, requires that respondent undertake this proof under the proviso of § 2(a). Secondly, § 2(b) of the Act specifically imposes the burden of showing justification upon one who is shown to have discriminated in prices. And the Senate committee report on the bill explained that the provisos of § 2(a) throw "upon any who claim the benefit of those exceptions the burden of showing that their case falls within them." [12] We think that the language of the Act, and the legislative history just cited, show that Congress meant by using the words "discrimination in price" in § 2 that in a case involving competitive injury between a seller's customers the Commission need only prove that a seller had charged one purchaser a higher price for like goods than he had charged one or more of the purchaser's competitors. This construction is consistent with the first sentence of § 2(a) in which it is made unlawful "to discriminate in price between different purchasers of commodities of like grade and quality, where either or any of the purchases involved in such discrimination are in commerce . . . and where the effect of such discrimination may be . . . to injure, destroy, or prevent competition with any person who either grants or knowingly receives the benefit of such discrimination, or with customers of either of them: . . ."

Third. It is argued that the findings fail to show that respondent's discriminatory discounts had in fact caused injury to competition. There are specific findings that such injuries had resulted from respondent's discounts, although the statute does not require the Commission to find that injury has actually resulted. The statute requires no more than that the effect of the prohibited price discriminations "may be substantially to lessen competition . . . or to injure, destroy, or prevent competition." After a careful consideration of this provision of the Robinson–Patman Act, we have said that "the statute does not require that the discrimina-

---

12. Sen.Rep. No. 1502, 74th Cong., 2d Sess. 3. See also 80 Cong. Rec. 3599, 8241, 9418.

tions must in fact have harmed competition, but only that there is a reasonable possibility that they 'may' have such an effect." *Corn Products Co. v. Federal Trade Comm'n*, 324 U.S. 726, 742.[14] Here the Commission found what would appear to be obvious, that the competitive opportunities of certain merchants were injured when they had to pay respondent substantially more for their goods than their competitors had to pay. The findings are adequate.

Fourth. It is urged that the evidence is inadequate to support the Commission's findings of injury to competition. As we have pointed out, however, the Commission is authorized by the Act to bar discriminatory prices upon the "reasonable possibility" that different prices for like goods to competing purchasers may have the defined effect on competition. That respondent's quantity discounts did result in price differentials between competing purchasers sufficient in amount to influence their resale prices of salt was shown by evidence. This showing in itself is adequate to support the Commission's appropriate findings that the effect of such price discriminations "may be substantially to lessen competition . . . and to injure, destroy, and prevent competition."

The adequacy of the evidence to support the Commission's findings of reasonably possible injury to competition from respondent's price differentials between competing carload and less-than-carload purchasers is singled out for special attacks here. It is suggested that in considering the adequacy of the evidence to show injury to competition respondent's carload discounts and its other quantity discounts should not be treated alike. The argument is that there is an obvious saving to a seller who delivers goods in carload lots. Assuming this to be true, that fact would not tend to disprove injury to the merchant compelled to pay the less-than-carload price. For a ten-cent carload price differential against a merchant would injure him competitively just as much as a ten-cent differential under any other name. However relevant the separate carload argument might be to the question of justifying a differential by cost savings, it has no relevancy in determining whether the differential works an injury to a competitor. Since Congress has not seen fit to give carload discounts any favored classification we cannot do so. Such discounts, like all others, can be justified by a seller who proves that the full amount of

14. This language is to be read also in the light of the following statement in the same case, discussing the meaning of § 2(a), as contained in the Robinson–Patman Act, in relation to § 3 of the Clayton Act:

"It is to be observed that § 2(a) does not require a finding that the discriminations in price have in fact had an adverse effect on competition. The statute is designed to reach such discriminations 'in their incipiency,' before the harm to competition is effected. It is enough that they 'may' have the prescribed effect. *Cf. Standard Fashion Co. v. Magrane–Houston Co.*, 258 U.S. 346, 356–357. But as was held in the *Standard Fashion* case, *supra*, with respect to the like provisions of § 3 of the

Clayton Act, prohibiting tying clause agreements, the effect of which 'may be to substantially lessen competition,' the use of the word 'may' was not to prohibit discriminations having 'the mere possibility' of those consequences, but to reach those which would probably have the defined effect on competition." 324 U.S. at 738; see also *United States v. Lexington Mill Co.*, 232 U.S. 399, 411.

The Committee Reports and Congressional debate on this provision of the Robinson–Patman Act indicate that it was intended to have a broader scope than the corresponding provision of the old Clayton Act. *See* note 18 *infra*.

the discount is based on his actual savings in cost. The trouble with this phase of respondent's case is that it has thus far failed to make such proof.

It is also argued that respondent's less-than-carload sales are very small in comparison with the total volume of its business and for that reason we should reject the Commission's finding that the effect of the carload discrimination may substantially lessen competition and may injure competition between purchasers who are granted and those who are denied this discriminatory discount. To support this argument, reference is made to the fact that salt is a small item in most wholesale and retail businesses and in consumers' budgets. For several reasons we cannot accept this contention.

There are many articles in a grocery store that, considered separately, are comparatively small parts of a merchant's stock. Congress intended to protect a merchant from competitive injury attributable to discriminatory prices on any or all goods sold in interstate commerce, whether the particular goods constituted a major or minor portion of his stock. Since a grocery store consists of many comparatively small articles, there is no possible way effectively to protect a grocer from discriminatory prices except by applying the prohibitions of the Act to each individual article in the store.

Furthermore, in enacting the Robinson–Patman Act, Congress was especially concerned with protecting small businesses which were unable to buy in quantities, such as the merchants here who purchased in less-than-carload lots. To this end it undertook to strengthen this very phase of the old Clayton Act. The committee reports on the Robinson–Patman Act emphasized a belief that § 2 of the Clayton Act had "been too restrictive, in requiring a showing of general injury to competitive conditions. . . ." The new provision, here controlling, was intended to justify a finding of injury to competition by a showing of "injury to the competitor victimized by the discrimination." [18] Since there was evidence sufficient to show that the less-than-carload purchasers might have been handicapped in competing with the more favored carload purchasers by the differential in price established by respondent, the Commission was justified in finding that competition might have thereby been substantially lessened or have been injured within the meaning of the Act.

Apprehension is expressed in this Court that enforcement of the Commission's order against respondent's continued violations of the Robinson–Patman Act might lead respondent to raise table salt prices to its carload purchasers. Such a conceivable, though, we think, highly

18. In explaining this clause of the proposed Robinson–Patman Act, the Senate Judiciary Committee said:

"This clause represents a recommended addition to the bill as referred to your committee. It tends to exclude from the bill otherwise harmless violations of its letter, but accomplishes a substantial broadening of a similar clause now contained in section 2 of the Clayton Act. The latter has in practice been too restrictive, in requiring a showing of general injury to competitive conditions in the line of commerce concerned; whereas the more immediately important concern is in injury to the competitor victimized by the discrimination. Only through such injuries, in fact, can the larger general injury result, and to catch the weed in the seed will keep it from coming to flower." S.Rep. No. 1502, 74th Cong., 2d Sess. 4. See also H.R.Rep. No. 2287, 74th Cong., 2d Sess. 8; 80 Cong.Rec. 9417.

improbable, contingency, could afford us no reason for upsetting the Commission's findings and declining to direct compliance with a statute passed by Congress.

The Commission here went much further in receiving evidence than the statute requires. It heard testimony from many witnesses in various parts of the country to show that they had suffered actual financial losses on account of respondent's discriminatory prices. Experts were offered to prove the tendency of injury from such prices. The evidence covers about two thousand pages, largely devoted to this single issue—injury to competition. It would greatly handicap effective enforcement of the Act to require testimony to show that which we believe to be self-evident, namely, that there is a "reasonable possibility" that competition may be adversely affected by a practice under which manufacturers and producers sell their goods to some customers substantially cheaper than they sell like goods to the competitors of these customers. This showing in itself is sufficient to justify our conclusion that the Commission's findings of injury to competition were adequately supported by evidence.

* * *

Reversed, Justices Jackson and Frankfurter dissenting.

Questions and Comments

Why should the test be "reasonable possibility" of competitive injury, rather than "reasonable probability" as required under the usual Clayton Act incipiency approach? In view of *Morton Salt*, what must plaintiff prove to establish an illegal discrimination? How does the Court conceive of injury to competition? How does the Court relate harm to a small competitor to harm to competition? Is *Brunswick* relevant to contemporary consideration of injury to competition under the Robinson–Patman Act? Or should *Brunswick* be confined to injury under the Sherman Act and (as we shall see in *Cargill v. Monfort*) injury under the Clayton Act? Is there any principled way to distinguish Clayton Act (non Robinson–Patman) harm from Robinson–Patman harm?

Is the law as formulated in *Morton Salt* likely to produce higher prices? Was the Court correct that this result was doubtful? Is the availability of the cost justification defense sufficient to assure efficient pricing?

Consider whether "competitive opportunities" are injured simply because one merchant pays more for goods than another. How significant is the size of the discrimination, absolute and relative ($.10 can be 20% of a unit price; $10 can be 1%)? How significant is the relative importance of the product as an input into the downstream process, and the availability of substitutes? Suppose that widgits are an input into the productive process in which B and C compete, that gizmos are a somewhat less desirable substitute, and that widgits have been selling at $100 and gizmos at $85. If A cuts the price on widgits to $90 on sales to B, but keeps selling to C for $100, will competition be hurt? Or suppose that the product in question represents a very small part of the cost of the downstream activity. Morton sells salt to Canner A for $.90 and to Canner B for $1.00. Both introduce the salt into their competing canned goods. Salt represents less than .25% of the total direct costs of each canner. Is competition hurt?

To what extent does the competitive impact of a discrimination depend on how A, the favored buyer, uses the savings, and how B, the disfavored buyer, responds? If A neither lowers its price nor invests the cost savings in promotion but pockets the discrimination and pays it out in dividends, is competition hurt in the market for the output? What about the market for new capital? See *McCaskill v. Texaco Inc.*, 351 F.Supp. 1332 (S.D.Ala.1972), *aff'd sub nom. Harrelson v. Texaco Inc.*, 486 F.2d 1400 (5th Cir.1973).

Suppose A, maintaining a constant mark-up, uses the cost savings from the discrimination to cut its price, but that B responds with an equivalent price cut, thereby reducing its mark-up. Is competition in the output market injured? Suppose that following its reactive price cut (which reduced its profit margin) B looks around for ways to cut costs, thus to reestablish its old margin. It finds one. By using computers it can better control its inventory and it is able to reduce the amount of its capital that is tied up in inventory. Is competition injured? Suppose A doesn't cut prices but reinvests the benefit of the discrimination in promotion. Is competition injured? To what extent does injury depend on B's response? See *Foremost Dairies Inc. v. FTC*, 348 F.2d 674, 680 (5th Cir.), *cert. denied*, 382 U.S. 959 (1965).

We have focused on competitive injury. But assuming competition has been injured, how can the private plaintiff measure and prove its antitrust damages? For years many antitrust lawyers assumed that in secondary line cases the damage problem was easy. If defendant charged B $1 per unit more than A, and B purchased 1000 units, B's damages were $1000, the amount of the discrimination. Recently, the Supreme Court addressed that issue.

J. TRUETT PAYNE CO. v. CHRYSLER MOTORS CORP.

451 U.S. 557 (1981).

JUSTICE REHNQUIST: The question presented in this case is the appropriate measure of damages in a suit brought under § 2(a) of the Clayton Act, as amended by the Robinson–Patman Act.

Petitioner, for several decades a Chrysler–Plymouth dealer in Birmingham, Ala., went out of business in 1974. It subsequently brought suit against respondent in the United States District Court for the Northern District of Alabama, alleging that from January 1970 to May 1974 respondent's various "sales incentive" programs violated § 2(a). Under one type of program, respondent assigned to each participating dealer a sales objective and paid to the dealer a bonus on each car sold in excess of that objective. Under another type of program, respondent required each dealer to purchase from it a certain quota of automobiles before it would pay a bonus on the sale of automobiles sold at retail. The amount of the bonus depended on the number of retail sales (or wholesale purchases) made in excess of the dealer's objective, and could amount to several hundred dollars. Respondent set petitioner's objectives higher than those of its competitors, requiring it to sell (or purchase) more automobiles to obtain a bonus than its competitors. To the extent petitioner failed to meet those objectives and to the extent its competitors met their lower objectives, petitioner received fewer bonuses. The net effect of all this, according to petitioner, was that it paid more money for its automobiles than did its competitors. It contended that the amount of the price discrimination—the amount of the price difference multiplied by the number of petitioner's purchases—was $81,248. It also claimed that the going-concern value of the business as of May 1974 ranged between $50,000 and $170,000.

Respondent maintained that the sales incentive programs were non-discriminatory, and that they did not injure petitioner or adversely affect competition. The District Court denied respondent's motion for a directed verdict. The jury returned a verdict against respondent and awarded petitioner $111,247.48 in damages, which the District Court trebled.

The Court of Appeals for the Fifth Circuit reversed with instructions to dismiss the complaint. It found that in order to recover treble damages under § 4 of the Clayton Act, a plaintiff must prove (1) a violation of the antitrust laws, (2) cognizable injury attributable to the violation, and (3) at least the approximate amount of damage. It found it unnecessary to consider whether petitioner proved that respondent's incentive programs violated § 2(a) because, in its view, petitioner had "failed to introduce substantial evidence of injury attributable to the programs, much less substantial evidence of the amount of such injury." Rejecting petitioner's theory of "automatic damages," under which mere proof of discrimination establishes the fact and amount of injury, the court held that injury must be proved by more than mere "[c]onclusory statements by the plaintiff, without evidentiary support." [607 F.2d] at 1136–1137. The court concluded that the District Court erred in refusing respondent's motion for a directed verdict and in denying its motion for judgment notwithstanding the verdict. We granted certiorari to review the decision of the Court of Appeals.

I

Petitioner first contends that once it has proved a price discrimination in violation of § 2(a) it is entitled at a minimum to so-called "automatic damages" in the amount of the price discrimination. Petitioner concedes that in order to recover damages it must establish cognizable injury attributable to an antitrust violation and some approximation of damage. It insists, however, that the jury should be permitted to infer the requisite injury and damage from a showing of a substantial price discrimination. Petitioner notes that this Court has consistently permitted such injury to be inferred in injunctive actions brought to enforce § 2(a), e.g., FTC v. Morton Salt Co., 334 U.S. 37 (1948), and argues that private suits for damages under § 4 should be treated no differently. We disagree.

By its terms § 2(a) is a prophylactic statute which is violated merely upon a showing that "the effect of such discrimination *may be* substantially to lessen competition." (Emphasis supplied.) As our cases have recognized, the statute does not "require that the discriminations must in fact have harmed competition." *Corn Products Refining Co. v. FTC*, 324 U.S. 726, 742 (1945); *FTC v. Morton Salt Co., supra,* at 46 ("the statute does not require the Commission to find that injury has actually resulted"). Section 4 of the Clayton Act, in contrast, is essentially a remedial statute. It provides treble damages to "[a]ny person who *shall be injured* in his business or property by reason of anything forbidden in the antitrust laws. . . ." (Emphasis supplied.) To recover treble damages, then, a plaintiff must make some showing of actual injury attributable to something the antitrust laws were designed to prevent.

Our decision here is virtually governed by our reasoning in *Brunswick Corp. v. Pueblo Bowl–O–Mat, Inc.*, 429 U.S. 477 (1977). There we rejected the contention that the mere violation of § 7 of the Clayton Act, which prohibits mergers which *may* substantially lessen competition, gives rise to a damages claim under § 4. We explained that "to recover damages [under § 4] respondents must prove more than that the petitioner violated § 7, since such proof establishes only that injury may result." *Id.*, at 486. Likewise in this case, proof of a violation does not mean that a disfavored purchaser has been actually "injured" within the meaning of § 4.

The legislative history buttresses this view. Both the Patman bill, H.R. 8442, § 2(d), 74th Cong., 1st Sess. (1935), as introduced in the House, and the Robinson bill, S. 3154, § 2(d), 74th Cong., 2d Sess. (1935), as introduced in the Senate, provided that a plaintiff's damages for a violation of § 2(a) shall be presumed to be the amount of the price discrimination. The provision, however, encountered such strong opposition in both Houses that the House Committee eliminated it from its bill, H.R.Rep. No. 2287, 74th Cong., 2d Sess., 16 (1936), and the Senate Committee modified the provision to authorize presumptive damages in the amount of the discrimination only when plaintiff shows the "fact of damage." S.Rep. No. 1502, 74th Cong., 2d Sess., 8 (1936). The Conference Committee eliminated even that compromise, and § 2(a) was passed in its present form. Congress thus has rejected the very concept which petitioner seeks to have the Court judicially legislate.

II

Petitioner next contends that even though it may not be entitled to "automatic damages" upon a showing of a violation of § 2(a), it produced enough evidence of actual injury to survive a motion for a directed verdict. That evidence consisted primarily of the testimony of petitioner's owner, Mr. Payne, and an expert witness, a professor of economics. Payne testified that the price discrimination was one of the causes of the dealership going out of business. In support of that contention, he testified that his salesmen told him that the dealership lost sales to its competitors, and that its market share of retail Chrysler–Plymouth sales in the Birmingham area was 24% in 1970, 27% in 1971, 23% in 1972, and 25% in 1973. Payne contended that it was proper to infer that the 4% drop in 1972 was a result of the incentive programs. He also testified that the discrimination caused him to "force" business so that he could meet his assigned quotas. That is, his desire to make a sale induced him to "overallow" on trade-ins, thus reducing his profits on his used car operation. Payne adduced evidence showing that his average gross profit on used car sales was below that of his competitors, though that same evidence revealed that his average gross profit on new sales was higher.

Neither Payne nor petitioner's expert witness offered documentary evidence as to the effect of the discrimination on retail prices. Although Payne asserted that his salesmen and customers told him that the dealership was being undersold, he admitted he did not know if his competitors did in fact pass on their lower costs to their customers. Petitioner's expert witness took a somewhat different position. He believed that the discrimination would ultimately cause retail prices to be held at an artificially high level since petitioner's competitors would not reduce their retail prices as much as they would have done if petitioner received an equal bonus from respondent. He also testified that petitioner was harmed by the discrimination even if the favored purchasers did not lower their retail prices, since petitioner in that case would make less money per car.[4]

Even construed most favorably to petitioner, the evidence of injury is weak. Petitioner nevertheless asks us to consider the sufficiency of its evidence in light of our traditional rule excusing antitrust plaintiffs from an unduly rigorous standard of proving antitrust injury. In *Zenith Radio Corp. v. Hazeltine Research, Inc.*, 395 U.S. 100, 123–124 (1969), for example, the Court discussed at some length the fixing of damages in a case involving market exclusion. We accepted the proposition that damages could be awarded on the basis of plaintiff's estimate of sales it could have made absent the violation. . . .

In *Bigelow v. RKO Radio Pictures, Inc.*, 327 U.S. 251 (1946), relied on in *Zenith*, film distributors had conspired to deny the plaintiff theater access to first-run films. The jury awarded damages based on a comparison of plaintiff's actual profits with the contemporaneous profits of a competing theater with access to first-run films. Plaintiff had also adduced evidence comparing his actual profits during the conspiracy with his profits when he had been able to obtain first-runs. The lower court thought the evidence too imprecise to support the award, but we reversed because the evidence was sufficient to support a "just and reasonable inference" of damage. . . .

* * *

Applying the foregoing principles to this case is not without difficulty. In the first place, it is a close question whether petitioner's evidence

4. Respondent suggests that petitioner's inability to show that his favored competitors lowered their retail sales price should defeat recovery. That argument assumes that evidence of a lower retail price is the *sine qua non* of antitrust injury, that the disfavored purchaser is simply not "injured" unless the favored purchaser has lowered his price. If the favored purchaser has lowered his retail price, for example, the disfavored purchaser will lose sales to the extent it does not match that lower price. Similarly, if the disfavored purchaser matches the lower price, it will lose profits. Because petitioner has not shown that the favored purchasers have lowered their retail price, petitioner is arguably foreclosed from showing that it lost either sales or profits. Justice Cardozo seemingly adopted this position in *ICC v. United States*, 289 U.S. 385, 390–391 (1933), a case involving rate discrimination under the Interstate Commerce Act:

"If by reason of the discrimination, the preferred producers have been able to di-

vert business that would otherwise have gone to the disfavored shipper, damage has resulted to the extent of the diverted profits. If the effect of the discrimination has been to force the shipper to sell at a lowered price . . . damage has resulted to the extent of the reduction. But none of these consequences is a necessary inference from discrimination without more."

Petitioner argues that is an overly narrow view of antitrust injury. To the extent a disfavored purchaser must pay more for its goods than its competitors, it is less able to compete. It has fewer funds available with which to advertise, make capital expenditures, and the like. Although the inability of petitioner to show that the favored retailers lowered their retail price makes petitioner's argument particularly weak, we find it unnecessary to decide in this case whether such failure as a matter of law demonstrates no competitive injury.

would be sufficient to support a jury award even under our relaxed damages rules. In those cases where we have found sufficient evidence to permit a jury to infer antitrust injury and approximate the amount of damages, the evidence was more substantial than the evidence presented here. . . .

But a more fundamental difficulty confronts us in this case. The cases relied upon by petitioner all depend in greater or lesser part on the inequity of a wrongdoer defeating the recovery of damages against him by insisting upon a rigorous standard of proof. In this case, however, we cannot say with assurance that respondent is a "wrongdoer." Because the court below bypassed the issue of liability and went directly to the issue of damages, we simply do not have the benefit of its views as to whether respondent in fact violated § 2(a). Absent such a finding, we decline to apply to this case the lenient damages rules of our previous cases. Had the court below found a violation, we could more confidently consider the adequacy of petitioner's evidence.

Accordingly, we think the proper course is to remand the case so that the Court of Appeals may pass upon respondent's contention that the evidence adduced at trial was insufficient to support a finding of violation of the Robinson–Patman Act. We do not ordinarily address for the first time in this Court an issue which the Court of Appeals has not addressed, and we think this would be a poor case in which to depart from that practice. If the court determines on remand that respondent did violate the Act, the court should then consider the sufficiency of petitioner's evidence of injury in light of the cases discussed above. We, of course, intimate no views as to how that issue should be decided. We emphasize that even if there has been a violation of the Robinson–Patman Act, petitioner is not excused from its burden of proving antitrust injury and damages. It is simply that once a violation has been established, that burden is to some extent lightened.

*   *   *

JUSTICE POWELL, with whom JUSTICES BRENNAN, MARSHALL, and BLACKMUN join, dissenting in part:

I concur in Part I of the Court's opinion, but simply would affirm the judgment of the Court of Appeals.

*   *   *

Questions and Comments

What is the case for "automatic damages"? Should the Court have awarded damages on this basis? What is the probable effect, on pricing levels generally, of a rule that allows automatic damages?

Did the Court fairly distinguish *Truett Payne* from prior damages cases on grounds that in *Truett Payne* the liability issue was not finally determined? Did the Court leave open the possibility that, where a violation is proved, the discrimination *is* the injury as a matter of law? In spirit, did it leave this question open?

If the discrimination is not the measure of injury, what is? Is lost sales or profits caused by the discrimination, as suggested by the dissenters? How can the disfavored purchaser show that sales were lost because of the discrimination? More importantly, how do "mere" (even substantial) lost sales of a competitor equate with harm to competition in the marketplace and thus with antitrust injury? Is there a threat of output limitation in the ordinary Robinson–Patman case? Is substantial injury to a disfavored purchaser sufficient for Robinson–Patman harm even though (say) eight or ten viable competitors remain in the market in which the disfavored purchaser competes?

Truett Payne ends an era of "easy" litigation for disfavored buyers. Now plaintiff must gather more information and engage in complex analysis. But what must be proved?

M.R. Burns addresses this question in a new, as yet unpublished manuscript, The Analysis of Secondary–Line Injury and Damages From Price Discrimination Under Section 2 of the Robinson–Patman Act. Burns's microtheoretic study indicates that the favored buyer will normally reduce resale prices and may increase promotional expenditures. Harris & Sullivan, in Passing On the Monopoly Overcharge, 128 Pa.L.Rev. 269, 299–309 (1979), present a theoretical and institutional approach to show how a court might determine the extent to which a monopoly overcharge is passed on; similar analysis could be used to determine the extent to which a cost reduction is passed on. Would this help the plaintiff in its daunting task of proving how a cost reduction experienced by a competitor hurts competition?

Consider this sequence: A, selling to B and C at $100, drops its price to B alone to $90. B (using a 10% mark up) drops its resale price from $110 to $99. C, who also has been reselling at $110, cannot give up the product entirely because it is complementary to other things C sells; therefore, C drops its resale price to its cost, $100. Before the discrimination C sold 10,000 units a year at a gross profit of $100,000 and a net profit (given its own cost accounting methods) of $50,000. In the year after the discrimination its sales fell to $5,000, its gross was 0 and its net, on the same cost accounting methodology, was a loss of $20,000. Can you construct an argument, perhaps guided by *Jack Walters*, supra p. 599, that C has suffered no antitrust injury? *Has* C suffered antitrust injury? Has C suffered Robinson–Patman injury?

Consider whether the following case, which considers the problem of the dual distributor, throws light on these questions.

BOISE CASCADE CORP. v. FTC
837 F.2d 1127 (D.C.Cir.1988).

JUDGE STARR: This case comes before us on petition for review of a decision of the Federal Trade Commission holding Boise Cascade Corporation in violation of section 2(f) of the Robinson–Patman Act. The Commission determined that Boise's receipt of price discriminations, in the form of discounts on office products it purchased for resale to consumers, tended to cause competitive injury to dealers in the office products industry with whom Boise competes. In so concluding, the Commission relied upon the "inference" of competitive injury, articulated by the Supreme Court in *FTC v. Morton Salt*, 334 U.S. 37 (1948), that arises when a substantial price discrimination exists over time. For the reasons to be set forth, we grant the petition for review.

I

A

Before examining the facts in this case, we first pause briefly to describe the pertinent statutory framework. Section 2(f) of the Robinson–Patman Act makes it unlawful for any person "knowingly to induce or receive a discrimination in price which is prohibited [under the Robinson–Patman Act]." Since the Act directly proscribes only a *seller's* activities, the liability of a *buyer* under section 2(f) depends on whether the seller discriminated in the buyer's favor in violation of section 2(a) of the Act. See, e.g., *Great Atlantic & Pacific Tea Co. v. FTC,* 440 U.S. 69, 76–77 (1979); *Automatic Canteen Co. v. FTC,* 346 U.S. 61, 70–71 (1953). Section 2(a) prohibits price discrimination between different purchasers "where the effect of such discrimination may be substantially to lessen competition or tend to create a monopoly in any line of commerce, or to injure, destroy, or prevent competition with any person who either grants or knowingly receives the benefit of such discrimination, or with customers of either of them."

To establish a *prima facie* case under section 2(f), the Commission must establish two things: *first,* that the buyer received a lower price than its competitors, and *second,* that the price discrimination caused, or reasonably might cause, competitive injury.

The statute also specifies two defenses to a seller's (and therefore to a buyer's derivative) liability. No violation exists where the discount reflects the lower cost to the seller of selling to the favored customer (the "cost-justification" defense), nor where the seller granted the discount in good faith to meet a competing seller's price (the "meeting competition" defense). *Id.* § 13(a)–(b); see also *Automatic Canteen,* 346 U.S. 61 (interpreting "cost-justification" defense); *FTC v. Sun Oil Co.,* 371 U.S. 505 (1963) (interpreting "meeting competition" defense). In addition to these statutory defenses, the Commission recognizes a defense, or more precisely, finds an absence of competitive injury, where the discounts are generally and practically available to competitors of the favored customer (the "practical availability" defense). See, e.g., *FLM Collision Parts, Inc. v. Ford Motor Co.,* 543 F.2d 1019, 1025–26 (2d Cir.1976), cert. denied 429 U.S. 1097 (1977).

B

On April 23, 1980, the Commission issued a complaint, over vigorous dissent, charging that Boise, as a "dual distributor" (both wholesaler and retailer) of office products, had violated section 2(f) of the Robinson–Patman Act. The complaint alleged that Boise's receipt of *wholesale* discounts from manufacturers on products that it then resold in a *retail* capacity to consumers constituted price discrimination for purposes of section 2(a). (No charge as to wholesale discounts for products that Boise thereafter sold in a wholesale capacity was pursued). The complaint alleged that Boise received these discounts knowingly and that the effect of Boise's receipt of such favorable pricing (and the resulting differential in prices) "has been or may be substantially to lessen, injure, destroy, or prevent competition" with dealers that were ineligible for the wholesale discounts.

In issuing the complaint, the Commission directed the Administrative Law Judge to receive evidence and to make findings of fact sufficient for disposition of the case under the competing standards of two FTC cases, namely *Mueller Co.,* F.T.C. 120 (1962), aff'd, 323 F.2d 44 (7th Cir.1963), cert. denied, 377 U.S. 923 (1964), and an earlier FTC case that *Mueller* had overruled, *Doubleday & Co.,* 52 F.T.C. 169 (1955). *Doubleday,* in brief, had articulated an additional defense under section 2(f) when the amount of the price disparity was reasonably related to the buyer's cost (as distinguished from the seller's cost savings) of providing additional marketing services. As we shall presently see in fuller detail, *Mueller* rejected entirely *Doubleday's* rationale, but both cases nonetheless seemed to live on within FTC chambers as competing strains of Robinson–Patman thought.

II

* * *

B

In the office products industry, price is typically expressed in the form of a "manufacturer's suggested list price," less a discount, if any. To illustrate by way of a simple example, suppose the manufacturer's suggested list price for a product is $1.00. If the manufacturer offers a buyer a 50% discount, the list price is reduced by 50% and the product is thus sold to that buyer for 50 cents. If the manufacturer offers a 50–20% discount, the list price is reduced first by 50%. A 20% discount is then applied to that amount (50 cents), thus leaving 40 cents as the net price to the buyer.

Manufacturers' discounts take many forms. Perhaps best-known are quantity and volume discounts. . . . In addition, promotional discounts . . . are prevalent in the industry.

To a more limited extent, manufacturers also offer bid discounts . . . when large end-users—typically government entities—that need substantial quantities of office products solicit bids from marketing intermediaries. . . . Manufacturers offer the same "bid" discounts to all distributors submitting bids to these end-users. . . .

Most significant for purposes of this case, however, are functional and trade discounts. A trade discount is one given to purchasers on the basis of the level of trade at which they operate. The discount depends solely on to whom the purchaser resells; it is entirely independent of marketing functions performed by the purchaser. A functional discount, in contrast, is offered by a manufacturer to a purchaser for assuming and performing a function that would otherwise be performed by the manufacturer. The pure functional discount operates independently of the purchaser's level of trade. In other words, any purchaser that performs the required functions would be eligible for the discount regardless of whether it is nominally a wholesaler or retailer.

At issue in this case is the validity of a hybrid discount which partakes of both a trade and functional discount. This discount, which for purposes of clarity and consistency we will call a "wholesale discount," has existed, without change, for many years in the office products industry. Indeed, the wholesale discount has been extended by most manufacturers of office supplies since well before Boise entered the industry. Its purpose is to induce wholesalers to undertake distribution and marketing functions on behalf of manufacturers. Manufacturers therefore extend the discount to *any* company, regardless of size, that meets the objective criteria contained in their respective definitions of "wholesaler."

In defining "wholesaler," all manufacturers in this industry require that the candidate resell products to dealers. Significantly, however, manufacturers do not require that the candidate resell exclusively to dealers (or other non-end-users). Nor do manufacturers limit the availability of the discount to those goods that are resold to dealers. . . .

* * *

III

A

Boise is an integrated forest products company. It entered the office products industry in 1964 as a dual distributor through the acquisition of Associated Stationers Company. . . . Notwithstanding its considerable size, Boise's purchases typically account for less than 5% of any single manufacturer's total sales. . . .

* * *

Although in its capacity as a dealer Boise performs essentially the same marketing functions for manufacturers as do other dealers, Boise is, by virtue of being a dual distributor, able to obtain wholesale discounts unavailable to the 23 dealers selected by the Commission for review in this case. These discounts are received on goods of like grade and quality that Boise sells in competition with those dealers. As we previously indicated, all six manufacturers studied in this case extend to companies (including Boise) that qualify as wholesalers, wholesale discounts that represent reductions in list prices beyond those offered to dealers. As a result of the difference between dealer and wholesaler discounts, the 23 selected dealers pay between 5% and 33% more for their purchases from manufacturers than does Boise.

At the same time, Boise played no role in the adoption or formulation of the manufacturers' standards for offering wholesale discounts. And, although the Commission points to evidence of Boise's successful negotiation for the discounts, the Commission candidly admits that the ALJ did not find that Boise had in any way coerced or pressured the manufacturers into extending it the wholesale discounts.

* * *

C

In addition to this undisputed evidence of competitive health of the selected dealers and in the industry as a whole, there is another aspect of this case that is relevant to resolution of this controversy and unusual in the context of a Robinson–Patman proceeding—a virtually complete absence of sales lost to Boise by the selected dealers traceable to the price differential caused by wholesale discounts to Boise. Although the Commission aggregated 23 dealers, each of which carries hundreds, and in some cases thousands, of accounts, the record shows only 162 specific accounts identified by the dealers as lost to Boise. This stability of dealer accounts is of especial note in an industry where switching of accounts is common. Significantly, none of the selected dealers that lost accounts in whole or in part to Boise was able to conclude that the losses were due to the fact that Boise received a greater discount from the six manufacturers.

To be more specific, the Commission's selected dealers testified that they lost accounts to Boise, in whole or in part, due to Boise's lower prices, better service, or a combination of these factors. . . .

In addition to the small number of lost accounts, the record shows many instances where accounts shifted not because of price or service, but because sales representatives shifted. . . .

Further diluting the Commission's attempted showing of diverted sales, *Boise introduced considerable evidence of sales that it had lost to the selected dealers.* . . .

* * *

IV

Notwithstanding his findings (1) that the selected dealers were competitively healthy and (2) that "accounts lost to Boise were counterbalanced by accounts which Boise lost to the dealers," the ALJ concluded that that evidence went only to the price discrimination's lack of effect on market structure. By virtue of that characterization, the ALJ determined that market structure evidence was by its nature inadequate to rebut the inference of competitive injury raised by the sustained and substantial price discrimination that Boise received. The ALJ stated his position in the following way: "[I]t is inconceivable that the substantial and sustained price differences documented in this record can have had no substantial effect on the ability of the dealers to compete with Boise."

Having determined that a *prima facie* violation of section 2(f) existed, the ALJ went on to conclude that the discounts were not practically available to the selected dealers, and that Boise knew, or should have known, that the discriminations in price were neither cost-justified nor given in good faith to meet competition. In addition, the ALJ recommended that the Commission adhere to its decision in *Mueller.* On the possibility that the Commission would reembrace the *Doubleday* rule, the ALJ determined that, because Boise did not perform services not performed by the selected dealers, Boise did not qualify for that "defense."

The Commission issued its order and opinion adopting and affirming the ALJ's findings of fact and conclusions of law. In its opinion, the Commission expressly relied on *Morton Salt's* inference that substantial price discrimination between competing purchasers over time causes, or tends to cause, competitive injury. In doing so, the Commission expressly recognized that the inference " 'may be overcome by evidence breaking the causal connection between a price differential and lost sales or profits.' " *Id.* (quoting *Falls City Industries, Inc. v. Vanco Beverage, Inc.*, 460 U.S. 428, 435 (1983)). Specifically, the Commission suggested that the

Morton Salt inference could be overcome by a showing that market conditions unrelated to the price discrimination explained the lost accounts or shifted sales or the effects on the disfavored competitors (presumably lost profits or market share).

The Commission nonetheless determined that Boise's showing of dealer-specific and industry-wide competitive health, in conjunction with the relative absence of lost sales, "fails to rebut the 'self-evident' inference of causation." . . .

Having found the two essential elements to a *prima facie* case (price discrimination and resulting competitive injury), the Commission concluded that Boise did not satisfy any of the defenses, statutory or Commission-fashioned, to Robinson–Patman liability. In addition, for reasons that we will detail shortly, the Commission decided that *Doubleday* should not be revitalized and, accordingly, reaffirmed the anti-*Doubleday* holding of *Mueller*.

V

The Commission's decision confronts us with a difficult issue arising under a statute that does not represent the highwater mark of skillful draftsmanship. . . .

* * *

In recent years, the Supreme Court has reaffirmed the viability of the *Morton Salt* inference of competitive injury arising from a substantial price difference existing over time. It has, moreover, declined to cabin the *Morton Salt* inference to "cases involving 'large buyer preference or seller predation.'" *Falls City,* 460 U.S. at 436. To the contrary, the *Falls City* Court upheld application of *Morton Salt's* rule to a discriminatory pricing system based upon the geographical location of the buyer. (In that case, Indiana distributors of Falls City beer were charged higher prices than Kentucky beer distributors.)

The *Morton Salt* inference is thus alive and well in the law. The case before us, however, presents the Commission's modern-day invocation of that inference in the setting of a pricing system which is entirely different from quantity and regional discounts.[14] For as we have seen, the *Morton Salt* inference has been applied in the case at hand to a system of wholesale discounts. (The Commission uses the term "functional discount" generically to describe the wholesale discounts at issue here. We will therefore proceed to use these terms interchangeably.) Acting Chairman Calvani, in writing for the Commission, succinctly described the legislative landscape as to wholesale functional discounts: "The Act does not expressly address functional discounts, and the legislative history is inconclusive." Thus, the imprecise statutory language of which the Supreme Court has complained, beclouds the area of functional discounts as well.

---

14. With all respect, this is scarcely a paradigmatic Robinson–Patman Act case, contrary to what our colleague in dissent argues at such length. The Commission recognized at the creation of this long-lived proceeding that it was venturing into relatively new territory, namely into the area of dual distribution. This has been a hard fought venture by the Commission, with powerful and eloquent voices, such as that of now-Dean Pitofsky, railing against what some deem to be a quixotic application of Robinson–Patman. This case is simply not of the lineage of *Morton Salt*.

The rather chaotic state of the law as to functional discounts was aptly summarized by then-Professor Calvani who, as fate would have it, was destined in another capacity to author the decision now before us:

> [T]he uncertain status of functional discounting is primarily due to the failure of Congress, the Federal Trade Commission, and the courts to give explicit and independent recognition to the practice and to define with any modicum of specificity its permissible contours. The result of this failure of recognition has been a lack of focus upon the validity of the functional discount which, in turn, has left the law in a state of confusion, causing often legitimate practices to be condemned.

Calvani, Functional Discounts Under the Robinson–Patman Act, 17 Boston C.Indus. & Com.L.Rev. 543, 543–44 (1976).

Eloquent attestation as to the unsettled nature of the law of functional discounts is found in events surrounding the complaint that brought this case to life. In considering whether to issue a complaint, the Commission divided three to two in favor of sending the staff forward, with Commissioner Clanton and now-Dean Pitofsky in dissent. . . .

* * *

. . . *Mueller* and *Doubleday,* the two warring rules spawned almost a generation ago by the Commission, shared a salient characteristic with *Morton Salt.* . . . In each instance, a manufacturer or supplier's idiosyncratic, non-economically justified pricing regime favored certain identified distributors (big distributors in *Morton Salt, Doubleday* and *Mueller* . . .), with nothing but favoritism—the evil sought to be remedied through the Robinson–Patman Act—to explain the disparate treatment.

VI

This case loomed at the Commission as the test of whether *Mueller* or *Doubleday* would survive in the present generation. . . .

. . . [T]he Commission (affirming the ALJ) embraced *Mueller.* . . . But we see a preliminary difficulty that precludes our declaring in this case whether the champions of *Mueller* or those of *Doubleday* should be the ultimate winners in the long-lived struggle over the application of Robinson–Patman to dual distributors in modern-day distribution systems. And that has to do with the threshold question whether *in this case* competitive injury, even as expansively defined under Robinson–Patman, has been shown. Competitive injury, which no one disputes is the condition precedent for establishing violations of the Act, is a critical element. For, as we have seen, Robinson–Patman is directed to the preservation of competition. Indeed, the terms of the statute itself mandate that, in order for a price differential to be unlawful, it must tend "*to injure, destroy, or prevent competition.*" 15 U.S.C. § 13(a). Injury to competition is thus the name of the Robinson–Patman game.

In its opinion, the FTC waved aside substantial evidence (1) that competition among dealers generally was healthy, (2) that the selected dealers singled out for FTC examination were thriving, and (3) that this happy picture of prosperity was apparently unclouded by instances of diverted sales attributable to the challenged discounts. The Commission flatly concluded that this entire body of evidence was *irrelevant.* . . .

This cannot be. In our view, the Commission's conclusion that Boise's dealer-specific evidence was irrelevant to the inference of competitive injury is wrong as a matter of law.

It is clear that *Morton Salt's* inference of competitive injury "may be overcome by evidence breaking the causal connection between a price differential and lost sales or profits." *Falls City,* 460 U.S. at 435. In reason, *the inference can also be overcome by evidence showing an absence of competitive injury within the meaning of Robinson–Patman.* That is to say, a sustained and substantial price discrimination raises an inference, but it manifestly does not create an irrebuttable presumption of competitive injury. Specific, substantial evidence of absence of competitive injury is, in our view, sufficient to rebut what is, after all, only an inference. The Commission, in effect, employed the *Morton Salt* inference to presume competitive injury conclusively in this case, and would only treat as relevant evidence "breaking the causal connection" between that assumed injury and the price discrimination to rebut the inference. This approach defies both logic and the import of *Morton Salt* that the inference of injury is rebuttable; for if the respondent's evidence demonstrates that there is no competitive injury (or reasonable possibility of competitive injury) to begin with, then evidence breaking the causal connection is obviously impossible to adduce. There is, under those circumstances, no causal connection to break.

As a result of its interpretation of Robinson–Patman, the Commission found it unnecessary to sift and weigh Boise's evidence of absence of injury. All those days of trial before the ALJ were, it seems, largely for naught. In reaching this odd result, the Commission simply failed to determine whether Boise's evidence demonstrated that no injury or "reasonable possibility" of competitive injury existed.

First. Important among the salient facts that the Commission chose to ignore was the ALJ's finding that the selected dealers were not wallowing in a hopeless or deteriorating environment. Quite to the contrary, as we have already recounted, the ALJ found that all selected dealers for which data was available enjoyed an increase in sales and gross profits in excess of 22% annually during the period in question, despite the recessionary condition of the economy. . . .

* * *

In addition, the evidence, as found by the ALJ, failed to demonstrate "displaced sales," another form the *Falls City* Court indicated injury could take. The ALJ found that switches of accounts from one supplier to another were "not uncommon"; to the contrary, they were the order of the day. . . .

Second. To explain its refusal to consider Boise's evidence (and, indeed, the countervailing evidence) of absence of actual competitive injury, the Commission asserted that "the competitive injury requirement of Section 2(a) is satisfied by a showing of 'a reasonable possibility that a price difference may harm competition.'" *Commission Decision,* (quoting *Falls City,* 460 U.S. at 434–35). While true, that principle does not justify abdication of the duty to consider evidence indicating that a "reasonable possibility" of harm does not, in fact, exist in the particular industry.

Robinson–Patman has not ushered in a bizarre rule of law that exalts theory "no matter what" in the face of hard, cold facts. That curious rule, if it ever was a rule, has been scotched by *Falls City's* teaching. . . .

* * *

Third. In assuming, without analysis, the existence of competitive injury, we believe that the Commission erred in another way as well. It entirely failed to inform its application of *Morton Salt's* inference of injury with the purposes of the Robinson–Patman Act. As we have previously detailed, it is fairness, as Congress perceives it, that Robinson–Patman is all about. That Act, a legislative monument to smallness in a century which rewards bigness, is aimed at putting a halt to singling out the "Big Fives" and "Big Threes" of the world for disparately favorable treatment (unless, of course, a statutory defense lies).

This is not a case of the "Big Five" retailers (*Morton Salt*), the "Big Three" book distributors (*Doubleday*), the long-established, large jobbers who enjoyed manufacturer protection from uppity newcomers (*Mueller*) or the Hoosier beer distributor which happened to be on the "wrong" side of the Indiana–Kentucky state line (*Falls City*). Quite to the contrary, there is among the six manufacturers selected in this case no regime of favoritism towards Boise. There is not the slightest hint in the ALJ's opinion, or in the Commission's for that matter, that the manufacturers were singling out Boise (and other big fish) for disparately favorable treatment. Rather, in accordance with a practice prevalent well before Boise even entered the industry, *it is undisputed that the six manufacturers in question treated all wholesalers alike and provided the wholesale discount to Boise solely because it met their respective definitions of "wholesaler."* There is simply no cabal between Boise and the six manufacturers to give Boise an additional price break.

* * *

Fourth. We note, finally, the irony of the Commission's concept of Robinson–Patman liability, namely that these egalitarian-minded manufacturers with their long-settled commercial practices now stand condemned as price discriminators in violation of federal law. As the Supreme Court has made abundantly clear, a buyer's liability under section 2(f) is entirely derivative in nature. *Great A & P Tea Co.,* 440 U.S. at 76–77. For there to be a guilty buyer, there must be a guilty seller. And thus it cannot pass unnoticed that under the Commission's approach, Bates, Master Products, Boorum & Pease and the other three manufacturers have run afoul of Robinson–Patman even though they have followed neutral, objective criteria in determining what buyers are to be considered wholesalers. . . .

In sum, although the Commission (and the ALJ) correctly took the view that the *Morton Salt* inference is rebuttable, its rejection on relevancy grounds of Boise's evidence of the absence of competitive injury (or reasonable possibility of competitive injury) was in error. The petition for review is therefore granted, and the case is remanded for further proceedings consistent with this opinion.

JUDGE WILLIAMS concurred. JUDGE MIKVA dissented.

Questions and Comments

After *Boise Cascade* (if the law of the case is widely adopted), must plaintiff prove reasonable probability of competitive injury? How does the court define injury to competition? Has the Robinson–Patman Act now been brought almost into harmony with the Sherman Act? Can harmony be achieved without destroying the Robinson–Patman Act?

How would a judgment for the FTC have been likely to affect pricing levels?

We have now concluded our brief look at secondary line injury under the Robinson–Patman Act. Do not assume that you now have a good working knowledge of Robinson–Patman law; rather, you have a window into one of the principal tensions of antitrust—fairness to small business versus respect for the toughest possible price competition.

CONCLUSION

The history and development of the law on vertical restraints is one of convulsive change. Antitrust, when guided by concerns for the nonestablished and when based on the dynamic principle that open markets serve consumers' interests, treats with skepticism restraints that foreclose significant shares of concentrated markets as well as restraints that tightly bind resellers' discretion. At the other extreme, the minimalist version of antitrust is concerned not by private vertical restraints but by enforcement against them. In a middle ground, all agree that cartel-reproducing and monopolistic vertical restraints are anticompetitive; but minimalists, applying robust-market premises, find this to be a seldom plausible story. The 1980s have been an age of hospitality for vertical restraints; many vertical relationships that would have been suspect, or assumed to be anticompetitive, say, in 1960, will be explained on efficiency grounds, and found lawful today.

Chapter 5

MERGERS

A. HISTORICAL PERSPECTIVE

1. INTRODUCTION

You will recall from Chapter 1 that during the last quarter of the nineteenth century the Industrial Revolution expanded markets, triggered capital investment and technological change, and brought firms that had earlier enjoyed local market power into vigorous competition. Seeking relief, firms tried both cartelization and consolidation. When cartelization was chilled by early judicial interpretations of the Sherman Act, consolidation became the preferred recourse. At first consolidation was in the form of "trust"; a small group of trustees, typically dominated by one of the great American industrialists, held the stock of the consolidating companies and exercised control to the mutual advantage of the ostensible competitors.

State corporations laws, granting limited liability, paved the way for change. Initially corporations were created by the state to meet public needs, but as the century went on corporations were increasingly used as convenient agents for private ends. In 1890 New Jersey became the first state to allow a corporation to hold the stock of other corporations. Delaware followed suit nine years later. The holding company became a feasible and popular form of consolidation.

While many consolidations were undoubtedly a means to avoid competition, others were (or even the same ones were also) a way to achieve efficiencies through economies of scale or scope. John D. Rockefeller, founder of the great oil trust, exemplified the ambitious empire-builders who believed that consolidation of the hundreds of competing entrepreneurs was manifest destiny. He persuaded competitors to join his combination by prospect of profit or coerced them to join (or sell out) by threat of destruction. As we saw in Chapter 1, the Rockefeller oil trust used its power as a buyer to force down the prices at which it would buy, and its power as a seller to destroy remaining competitors by setting prices below what they could endure. The trust could not restrict output significantly, for new oil fields were constantly discovered, bringing new entry, new output and renewed pressure on prices. Nonetheless, the Rockefeller

trust made large profits through efficiency and power.[1] With Standard
Oil as a model, industrialists in other industries followed suit. The first
great consolidation movement began about 1849, intensified in 1890, and
continued to about 1893.[2] Another even bigger one began in 1895 and ran
until 1904.

2. EARLY MERGER CASES UNDER THE SHERMAN ACT

State common law on restraints and monopolies reached some consolidations, but before passage of the Sherman Act no federal law restricted
consolidation. With the passage of the Sherman Act, the law was federal-
ized. The first consolidation case to reach the Supreme Court was the
case of the sugar trust; the American Sugar Refinery Company had
acquired all of the competing sugar refineries in the United States except
for a two-percent firm in Boston. The Supreme Court affirmed dismissal
of the case. At most, said the Court, the American Sugar Refinery
Company had monopolized the *manufacture* of sugar; it had not monopolized trade or commerce. "[T]hat trade or commerce might be indirectly
affected was not enough to entitle complainants to a decree." *United
States v. E.C. Knight Co.*, 156 U.S. 1, 17 (1895).[3]

The decision in *E.C. Knight* was a defeat for antitrust. In its wake,
consolidations increased. Meanwhile, J. Pierpont Morgan controlled the
Northern Pacific Company and James J. Hill controlled its principal
competitor, the Great Northern Company. Morgan and Hill had a running battle with their third competitor Harriman, who controlled the
Union Pacific, the only other railroad to run across the Northwest. The
three railroad magnates settled their dispute by organizing Northern
Securities Company as a jointly-owned company to hold the stock of the
competing lines. During the presidency of Theodore Roosevelt, the great
"trust-buster," [4] the government sued. The Supreme Court held the
combination illegal. Justice John Harlan (grandfather of the John
Harlan who was later to serve as a Justice on the Warren Court) wrote
the plurality opinion. He applied Section 1 of the Sherman Act as it had
been interpreted in *Trans–Missouri* and *Joint–Traffic* (see pp. 37 and 51
supra): direct restraints imposed by combination were illegal. The combination of the three railroad competitors was a direct restraint. Therefore it was illegal. *Northern Securities Co. v. United States,* 193 U.S. 197,
330–31 (1904). Taken literally, Justice Harlan's opinion implied that all
combinations of competitors offended the law.

To the disappointment of the President who appointed him,[5] Justice
Holmes (and three other Justices) dissented.

1. See M. Josephson, The Robber Barons: The Great American Capitalists 1861–1901, 109–120 (1962).

2. See L. Sullivan, The Law of Antitrust § 193 (1977).

3. This narrow construction of the Sher-man Act's commerce clause would soon be-come obsolete.

4. The suits against Standard Oil and American Tobacco were also launched dur-ing the administration of Teddy Roosevelt. Roosevelt, you may recall, was not hostile to size. He believed that there were good trusts and bad trusts, and that the Sherman Act should be invoked only against the bad trusts. See T. Roosevelt, An Autobiography 431–33 (1921).

5. See L. Pfeffer, This Honorable Court 239 (1965).

NORTHERN SECURITIES CO. v. UNITED STATES
193 U.S. 197 (1904).

Justice Holmes, dissenting: This act is construed by the Government to affect the purchasers of shares in two railroad companies because of the effect it may have, or, if you like, is certain to have, upon the competition of these roads. If such a remote result of the exercise of an ordinary incident of property and personal freedom is enough to make that exercise unlawful, there is hardly any transaction concerning commerce between the States that may not be made a crime by the finding of a jury or a court. . . .

[The] meaning [of the words of the statute] seems to me plain on their face.

The first section makes "Every contract, combination in the form of trust or otherwise, or conspiracy in restraint of trade or commerce among the several States, or with foreign nations" a misdemeanor, punishable by fine, imprisonment or both. . . . The court below argued as if maintaining competition were the expressed object of the act. The act says nothing about competition. I stick to the exact words used. The words hit two classes of cases, and only two—Contracts in restraint of trade and combinations or conspiracies in restraint of trade, and we have to consider what these respectively are. Contracts in restraint of trade are dealt with and defined by the common law. They are contracts with a stranger to the contractor's business . . . which wholly or partially restrict the freedom of the contractor in carrying on that business as otherwise he would. The objection of the common law to them was primarily on the contractor's own account. . . . Of course this objection did not apply to partnerships or other forms, if there were any, of substituting a community of interest where there had been competition. There was no objection to such combinations merely as in restraint of trade, or otherwise unless they amounted to a monopoly. Contracts in restraint of trade, I repeat, were contracts with strangers to the contractor's business, and the trade restrained was the contractor's own.

Combinations or conspiracies in restraint of trade, on the other hand, were combinations to keep strangers to the agreement out of the business. The objection to them was not an objection to their effect upon the parties making the contract, the members of the combination or firm, but an objection to their intended effect upon strangers to the firm and their supposed consequent effect upon the public at large. In other words, they were regarded as contrary to public policy because they monopolized or attempted to monopolize some portion of the trade or commerce of the realm. . . . [Section 2] is more important as an aid to the construction of § 1 than it is on its own account. It shows that whatever is criminal when done by way of combination is equally criminal if done by a single man. That I am right in my interpretation of the words of § 1 is shown by the words "in the form of trust or otherwise." The prohibition was suggested by the trusts, the objection to which, as every one knows, was not the union of former competitors, but the sinister power exercised or supposed to be exercised by the combination in keeping rivals out of the

business and ruining those who already were in. It was the ferocious
extreme of competition with others, not the cessation of competition
among the partners, that was the evil feared. . . .

* * *

. . . [T]he act of Congress will not be construed to mean the
universal disintegration of society into single men, each at war with all
the rest, or even the prevention of all further combinations for a common
end.

* * *

In the years between 1904, when the Court decided *Northern Securities,* and 1911, when it handed down the landmark *Standard Oil* decision
(see p. 75 *supra*), the balance of the Court shifted. Justice Edward White,
who had dissented in *Trans–Missouri, Joint–Traffic* and *Northern Securities,* became the voice of a new majority when, as Chief Justice, he wrote
the opinion for the Court in *Standard Oil.* In *Standard Oil,* the Court
declared that only "unreasonable" restraints were illegal. Doing so, it left
open the question whether combinations could ever be found unreasonable
if they did not use power in sinister ways to ruin rivals. Subsequently,
three more railroad merger cases reached the Supreme Court, and the
Court followed the *Northern Securities* precedent. *United States v. Union
Pacific R.R. Co.,* 226 U.S. 61 (1912) (combination of two great alternate
transcontinental systems having a small competitive overlap); *United
States v. Reading Co.,* 253 U.S. 26 (1920) (combination of two great
competing railroad systems and two great competing coal companies that
shipped on the railroads), and *United States v. Southern Pacific Co.,* 259
U.S. 214 (1922) (combination of two great lines running from the West
Coast to Central U.S., with overlapping branches in California). But
apart from the railroad cases, even consolidations producing monopoly
survived Sherman Act challenge in the absence of "bad" behavior. E.g.,
United States v. United Shoe Machinery Co., 247 U.S. 32 (1918) (consolidation of virtually the entire shoe machinery business; see dissenting
opinion of Justice Clarke at 75–91).

In the years following *Standard Oil,* permissiveness and uncertainty
led to a search for new ways to control mergers. Addressing the concern
that holding companies tended to lessen competition, Congress passed
Section 7 of the Clayton Act in 1914. Section 7 provided:

> That no corporation engaged in commerce shall acquire, directly or
> indirectly, the whole or any part of the stock or other share capital of
> another corporation engaged also in commerce, where the effect of such
> acquisition may be to substantially lessen competition between the corporation whose stock is so acquired and the corporation making the acquisition, or to restrain such commerce in any section of the country, or tend
> to create a monopoly of any line of commerce. 38 Stat. 730 (1914).

The statutory proscription, however, was easily evaded. Companies
bought their competitors' assets. In ensuing litigation, the Supreme
Court construed Section 7 technically and narrowly, exacerbating the
assets loophole. See, e.g., *FTC v. Western Meat Co.,* 272 U.S. 554 (1926);
International Shoe Co. v. FTC, 280 U.S. 291 (1930). Accordingly, major

consolidation cases, if brought at all, continued to be prosecuted under Section 1 of the Sherman Act.

Meanwhile, two major steel cases ran their course to the Supreme Court: *United States v. United States Steel Corp.*, 251 U.S. 417 (1920), and *United States v. Columbia Steel Co.*, 334 U.S. 495 (1948). Both were brought under the Sherman Act; the first because the challenged combinations took place long before the passage of the Clayton Act; the second because the acquisition (like most large post-Clayton Act acquisitions) was an assets acquisition.

We examined the first case, *United States v. United States Steel Corp.*, 251 U.S. 417 (1920), in Chapter 1 (see p. 85 *supra*).

At trial, two hundred customers of U.S. Steel and a number of its competitors testified. Not one complained about conduct or performance of U.S. Steel. The trial court found that U.S. Steel did not have power over price and that "it resorted to none of the brutalities or tyrannies" of other combinations that were found illegal. See 251 U.S. at 437–41.

U.S. Steel is a period piece. It has now long been clear that acquisitions unaccompanied by brutalities are nonetheless illegal if their net effect is anticompetitive. The task is to ascertain when the effect is anticompetitive. The Court addressed this task in the next great merger landmark, *United States v. Columbia Steel Co.*, 334 U.S. 495 (1948).

Columbia Steel was a wholly owned subsidiary of United States Steel. The government sued to enjoin Columbia Steel from acquiring the assets of Consolidated Steel, the largest independent steel fabricator on the West Coast. In a five-to-four decision, the Court found no violation of the Sherman Act.

U.S. Steel was the largest producer of rolled steel. Consolidated was a substantial purchaser of that product, which it made into frameworks for buildings, bridges and pipes. The government asserted that the acquisition would bring about anticompetitive foreclosure. It argued that the acquisition would unreasonably restrain trade by excluding other producers of rolled steel from selling to Consolidated.

The Court observed that the combination would be illegal if the effect of the vertical integration was "to unreasonably restrict the opportunities of competitors to market their product." 334 U.S. at 524. But Consolidated represented only 3% of demand in the 11–state geographic market. In view of this small foreclosure, the Court held that the acquisition would not unreasonably restrict competitors' opportunities.

The case also had horizontal aspects. U.S. Steel competed with Consolidated in the sale of structural steel products in western states. The extent and significance of that competition was disputed. Although the Court assumed that U.S. Steel (which was the largest steel company) accounted for 13% of sales, and that Consolidated accounted for 11% of sales, it found that the combination did not create an unreasonable restraint in view of the conditions in the industry and the relationship between the merger partners. Transportation costs made it difficult for eastern fabricators to sell their product in the West at prices competitive with western fabricators, and U.S. Steel and Consolidated made different types of structural steel products; therefore U.S. Steel could not be considered a close or direct competitor.

Justice Douglas's dissenting opinion was a precursor to a legislative response:

> This is the most important antitrust case which has been before the Court in years. It is important because it reveals the way of growth of monopoly power—the precise phenomenon at which the Sherman Act was aimed. Here we have the pattern of the evolution of the great trusts. Little, independent units are gobbled up by bigger ones. At times the independent is driven to the wall and surrenders. At other times any number of "sound business reasons" appear why the sale to or merger with the trust should be made.[1] If the acquisition were the result of predatory practices or restraints of trade, the trust could be required to disgorge. But the impact on future competition and on the economy is the same though the trust was built in more gentlemanly ways.

> We have here the problem of bigness. Its lesson should by now have been burned into our memory by Brandeis. *The Curse of Bigness* shows how size can become a menace—both industrial and social. It can be an industrial menace because it creates gross inequalities against existing or putative competitors. It can be a social menace—because of its control of prices. Control of prices in the steel industry is powerful leverage on our economy. For the price of steel determines the price of hundreds of other

1. The most frequent reasons given for mergers are that they prevent waste and promote efficiency, reduce overhead, dilute sales and advertising costs, spread risks, etc. But that these advantages are largely illusory has long been recognized. The theory was never more forcefully exploded than by Brandeis in The Curse of Bigness:

"The only argument that has been seriously advanced in favor of private monopoly is that competition involves waste, while the monopoly prevents waste and leads to efficiency. This argument is essentially unsound. The wastes of competition are negligible. The economies of monopoly are superficial and delusive. The efficiency of monopoly is at the best temporary.

"Undoubtedly competition involves waste. What human activity does not? The wastes of democracy are among the greatest obvious wastes, but we have compensations in democracy which far outweigh that waste and make it more efficient than absolutism. So it is with competition. The waste is relatively insignificant. There are wastes of competition which do not develop, but kill. These the law can and should eliminate, by regulating competition.

"It is true that the unit in business may be too small to be efficient. It is also true that the unit may be too large to be efficient, and this is no uncommon incident of monopoly." P. 105.

". . . no monopoly in private industry in America has yet been attained by efficiency alone. No business has been so superior to its competitors in the processes of manufacture or of distribution as to enable it to control the market solely by reason of its superiority." Pp. 114–15.

"The Steel Trust, while apparently free from the coarser forms of suppressing competition, acquired control of the market not through greater efficiency, but by buying up existing plants and particularly ore supplies at fabulous prices, and by controlling strategic transportation systems." Pp. 115.

"But the efficiency of monopolies, even if established, would not justify their existence unless the community should reap benefit from the efficiency; experience teaches us that whenever trusts have developed efficiency, their fruits have been absorbed almost wholly by the trusts themselves. From such efficiency as they have developed the community has gained substantially nothing. For instance: . . . *The Steel Trust,* a corporation of reputed efficiency. The high prices maintained by it in the industry are matters of common knowledge. In less than ten years it accumulated for its shareholders or paid out as dividends on stock representing merely water, over $650,000,000." Pp. 120–121.

articles. Our price level determines in large measure whether we have prosperity or depression—an economy of abundance or scarcity. Size in steel should therefore be jealously watched. In final analysis, size in steel is the measure of the power of a handful of men over our economy. That power can be utilized with lightning speed. It can be benign or it can be dangerous. The philosophy of the Sherman Act is that it should not exist. For all power tends to develop into a government in itself. Power that controls the economy should be in the hands of elected representatives of the people, not in the hands of an industrial oligarchy. Industrial power should be decentralized. It should be scattered into many hands so that the fortunes of the people will not be dependent on the whim or caprice, the political prejudices, the emotional stability of a few self-appointed men. The fact that they are not vicious men but respectable and social-minded is irrelevant. That is the philosophy and the command of the Sherman Act. It is founded on a theory of hostility to the concentration in private hands of power so great that only a government of the people should have it. . . . (*Id.* at 534–36.)

Now, 40 years and hundreds of acquisitions later, the United States steel industry is laggard. Producers in Japan and Germany produce cheaper and better steel at least for some steel products, and they have made deep inroads into the American market. The big U.S. companies, pleading that they need more money to invest in modernizing their plants, repeatedly prevail upon the government for protective trade barriers, in the form of trigger pricing and quotas. See A. Lowenfeld, Public Controls on International Trade §§ 6.12–6.27 (2d ed. 1983). Having won protection, however, leaders of the industry use their extra revenues to diversify away from steel. In 1982, for example, United States Steel (now USX) bought Marathon Oil Company, the leading supplier of gasoline to independent service stations. As a response to the foreign competition, specialty mini-mills have taken root in the United States; they probably reflect the country's most effective response to the strong foreign competition.

3. THE 1950 AMENDMENT TO SECTION 7 OF THE CLAYTON ACT

We turn back to the decade before the *Columbia Steel* decision. In the late 1930s and early 1940s, with the ascendancy of Hitler supported by the German cartels, Americans became increasingly fearful of concentrated political power. A lively merger movement intensified the fear. In 1938 Franklin D. Roosevelt established the Temporary National Economic Committee (TNEC) to study the causes of and cures for industrial concentration. In the hearings and in the numerous resulting monographs, witnesses and writers expressed alarm that increasing industrial concentration was causing social and economic dislocations. Scholars and other observers saw the trend towards concentration as a threat to democratic institutions and to the tradition of entrepreneurial competition. See, e.g., W. Hamilton and I. Till, TNEC Monograph No. 16 (1940). In its Final Report, the TNEC recommended extending the merger law to acquisitions of assets and further recommended that planned mergers and

acquisitions be notified to the government. S.Doc. No. 35, 77th Cong., 1st
Sess. 38–40 (1941).

Under President Truman, the Federal Trade Commission made detailed studies and reports on the merger movement. It concluded in its
1948 report: "[T]here are few greater dangers to small business than the
continued growth of the conglomerate corporation." Report of the Federal Trade Commission on the Merger Movement: A Summary Report 59
(1948). The FTC, too, recommended that the merger law be strengthened.

Congress held hearings throughout most of the 1940s on the need for
a tougher merger law and on the form such a law should take. In 1948,
the Supreme Court's green light to U.S. Steel's acquisition of Consolidated
fueled the fire. Two years later Congress enacted the Celler–Kefauver
Amendment to Section 7 of the Clayton Act.

The language of the 1950 amendment reads in relevant part: [7]

> [N]o corporation engaged in commerce shall acquire, directly or indirect-
> ly, the whole or any part of the stock or other share capital and no
> corporation subject to the jurisdiction of the Federal Trade Commission
> shall acquire the whole or any part of the assets of another corporation
> engaged also in commerce, where in any line of commerce in any section
> of the country, the effect of such acquisition may be substantially to
> lessen competition, or to tend to create a monopoly. 38 Stat. 731 (1950).

This new merger law closed the assets loophole by extending the
proscriptions of the 1914 law to asset as well as stock transactions. Also,
it proscribed mergers and acquisitions that may lessen competition in any
market, not just those that may lessen competition between the merging
parties. As the legislative history makes clear, the new law was meant to
have a broad sweep; it was intended to nip concentration in the bud. It
was meant to apply to all mergers that may threaten competition,
whether horizontal, vertical or conglomerate. The legislative intent was
summarized at length by the Supreme Court in *Brown Shoe Co. v. United
States,* 370 U.S. 294 (1962), the first Supreme Court case to apply the
Celler–Kefauver Amendment. In the *Brown Shoe* case, the Court said:

> The dominant theme pervading congressional consideration of the
> 1950 amendments was a fear of what was considered to be a rising tide of
> economic concentration in the American economy. Apprehension in this
> regard was bolstered by the publication in 1948 of the Federal Trade
> Commission's study on corporate mergers. Statistics from this and other
> current studies were cited as evidence of the danger to the American
> economy in unchecked corporate expansions through mergers. Other
> considerations cited in support of the bill were the desirability of retain-
> ing "local control" over industry and the protection of small businesses.
> Throughout the recorded discussion may be found examples of Congress'
> fear not only of accelerated concentration of economic power on economic
> grounds, but also of the threat to other values a trend toward concentra-
> tion was thought to pose.

7. The statute was subsequently
amended to change "corporation" to "person" and to lower the threshold of the interstate commerce requirement. See App. A.

What were some of the factors, relevant to a judgment as to the validity of a given merger, specifically discussed by Congress in redrafting § 7?

First, there is no doubt that Congress did wish to "plug the loophole" and to include within the coverage of the Act the acquisition of assets no less than the acquisition of stock.

Second, by the deletion of the "acquiring-acquired" language in the original text, it hoped to make plain that § 7 applied not only to mergers between actual competitors, but also to vertical and conglomerate mergers whose effect may tend to lessen competition in any line of commerce in any section of the country.

Third, it is apparent that a keystone in the erection of a barrier to what Congress saw was the rising tide of economic concentration, was its provision of authority for arresting mergers at a time when the trend to a lessening of competition in a line of commerce was still in its incipiency. Congress saw the process of concentration in American business as a dynamic force; it sought to assure the Federal Trade Commission and the courts the power to brake this force at its outset and before it gathered momentum.[32]

Fourth, and closely related to the third, Congress rejected, as inappropriate to the problem it sought to remedy, the application to § 7 cases of the standards for judging the legality of business combinations adopted by the courts in dealing with cases arising under the Sherman Act, and which may have been applied to some early cases arising under original § 7.[33]

---

32. That § 7 of the Clayton Act was intended to reach incipient monopolies and trade restraints outside the scope of the Sherman Act was explicitly stated in the Senate Report on the original Act. S.Rep. No. 698, 63d Cong., 2d Sess. 1. This theme was reiterated in congressional consideration of the amendments adopted in 1950, and found expression in the final House and Senate Reports on the measure. H.R.Rep. No. 1191, 81st Cong., 1st Sess. 8 ("Acquisitions of stock or assets have a cumulative effect, and control of the market . . . may be achieved not in a single acquisition but as the result of a series of acquisitions. The bill is intended to permit intervention in such a cumulative process when the effect of an acquisition may be a significant reduction in the vigor of competition."); S.Rep. No. 1775, 81st Cong., 2d Sess. 4–5 ("The intent here . . . is to cope with monopolistic tendencies in their incipiency and well before they have attained such effects as would justify a Sherman Act proceeding.")

33. The Report of the House Judiciary Committee on H.R. 515 recommended the adoption of tests more stringent than those in the Sherman Act. H.R.Rep. No. 596, 80th Cong., 1st Sess. 7. A vigorous minority thought no new legislation was needed. Id., at 11–18. Between the issuance of this Report and the Committee's subsequent consid-

eration of H.R. 2734, this Court had decided *United States v. Columbia Steel Co.*, 334 U.S. 495, which some understood to indicate that existing law might be inadequate to prevent mergers that had substantially lessened competition in a section of the country, but which, nevertheless, had not risen to the level of those restraints of trade or monopoly prohibited by the Sherman Act. See 96 Cong.Rec. 16502 (remarks of Senator Kefauver); H.R.Rep. No. 1191, 81st Cong., 1st Sess. 10–11. Numerous other statements by Congressmen and Senators and by representatives of the Federal Trade Commission, the Department of Justice and the President's Council of Economic Advisors were made to the Congress suggesting that a standard of illegality stricter than that imposed by the Sherman Act was needed. . . . The Senate Report was explicit: "The committee wish to make it clear that the bill is not intended to revert to the Sherman Act test. The intent here . . . is to cope with monopolistic tendencies in their incipiency and well before they have attained such effects as would justify a Sherman Act proceeding. . . . [The] various additions and deletions—some strengthening and others weakening the bill—are not conflicting in purpose and effect. They merely are different steps toward the same objective, namely, that of framing a bill which, though drop-

Fifth, at the same time that it sought to create an effective tool for preventing all mergers having demonstrable anticompetitive effects, Congress recognized the stimulation to competition that might flow from particular mergers. When concern as to the Act's breadth was expressed, supporters of the amendments indicated that it would not impede, for example, a merger between two small companies to enable the combination to compete more effectively with larger corporations dominating the relevant market, nor a merger between a corporation which is financially healthy and a failing one which no longer can be a vital competitive factor in the market. The deletion of the word "community" in the original Act's description of the relevant geographic market is another illustration of Congress' desire to indicate that its concern was with the adverse effects of a given merger on competition only in an economically significant "section" of the country. Taken as a whole, the legislative history illuminates congressional concern with the protection of *competition*, not *competitors*, and its desire to restrain mergers only to the extent that such combinations may tend to lessen competition.

Sixth, Congress neither adopted nor rejected specifically any particular tests for measuring the relevant markets, either as defined in terms of product or in terms of geographic locus of competition, within which the anti-competitive effects of a merger were to be judged. Nor did it adopt a definition of the word "substantially," whether in quantitative terms of sales or assets or market shares or in designated qualitative terms, by which a merger's effects on competition were to be measured.[36]

Seventh, while providing no definite quantitative or qualitative tests by which enforcement agencies could gauge the effects of a given merger to determine whether it may "substantially" lessen competition or tend toward monopoly, Congress indicated plainly that a merger had to be functionally viewed, in the context of its particular industry.[37] That is, whether the consolidation was to take place in an industry that was fragmented rather than concentrated, that had seen a recent trend toward domination by a few leaders or had remained fairly consistent in its distribution of market shares among the participating companies, that had experienced easy access to markets by suppliers and easy access to

ping portions of the so-called Clayton Act test that have no economic significance [the reference would appear to be primarily to the "acquiring-acquired" standard of the original Act], reaches far beyond the Sherman Act." S.Rep. No. 1775, 81st Cong., 2d Sess. 4–5.

36. The House Report on H.R. 2734 stated that two tests of illegality were included in the proposed Act: whether the merger substantially lessened competition or tended to create a monopoly. It stated that such effects could be perceived through findings, for example, that a whole or material part of the competitive activity of an enterprise, which had been a substantial factor in competition, had been eliminated; that the relative size of the acquiring corporation had increased to such a point that its advantage over competitors threatened to be "decisive"; that an "undue" number of competing enterprises had been eliminated; or that buyers and sellers in the relevant market had established relationships depriving their rivals of a fair opportunity to compete. H.R.Rep. No. 1191, 81st Cong., 1st Sess. 8. Each of these standards, couched in general language, reflects a conscious avoidance of exclusively mathematical tests . . .

37. A number of the supporters of the amendments voiced their concern that passage of the bill would amount to locking the barn door after most of the horses had been stolen, but urged approval of the measure to prevent the theft of those still in the barn. Which was to say that, if particular industries had not yet been subject to the congressionally perceived trend toward concentration, adoption of the amendments was urged as a way of preventing the trend from reaching those industries as yet unaffected.

suppliers by buyers or had witnessed foreclosure of business, that had witnessed the ready entry of new competition or the erection of barriers to prospective entrants, all were aspects, varying in importance with the merger under consideration, which would properly be taken into account.[38]

Eighth, Congress used the words "*may be* substantially to lessen competition" (emphasis supplied), to indicate that its concern was with probabilities, not certainties.[39] Statutes existed for dealing with clear-cut menaces to competition; no statute was sought for dealing with ephemeral possibilities. Mergers with a probable anticompetitive effect were to be proscribed by this Act. . . .

Most commentators regard the Supreme Court's summary of the legislative history as accurate.[8] Judge Robert Bork, however, does not. In his influential book, The Antitrust Paradox: A Policy at War with Itself (1978) (hereafter the Antitrust Paradox), Judge Bork says:

Proponents of the [Clayton] bill discussed the alleged increase of overall concentration in the American economy, the increase in concentration in particular industries, the role of mergers in both types of concentration, the effects of big business on individuality and initiative, harm to civic responsibility, and so on, through a long catalog of the real and imagined economic and social consequences of mergers. Many commentators and courts rather uncritically assume that it is the duty of the courts in some way to reflect these woolly congressional concerns in deciding particular cases. In *Brown Shoe,* in fact, the Supreme Court went so far as to attribute to Congress a decision to prefer the interests of small, locally

---

38. Subsequent to the adoption of the 1950 amendments, both the Federal Trade Commission and the courts have, in the light of Congress' expressed intent, recognized the relevance and importance of economic data that places any given merger under consideration within an industry framework almost inevitably unique in every case. Statistics reflecting the shares of the market controlled by the industry leaders and the parties to the merger are, of course, the primary index of market power; but only a further examination of the particular market—its structure, history and probable future—can provide the appropriate setting for judging the probable anticompetitive effect of the merger.

39. In the course of both the Committee hearings and floor debate, attention was occasionally focused on the issue of whether "possible," "probable" or "certain" anticompetitive effects of a proposed merger would have to be proven to establish a violation of the Act. Language was quoted from prior decisions of the Court in antitrust cases in which each of these interpretations of the word "may" was suggested as appropriate. H.R. Hearings on H.R. 2734, at 74; S. Hearings on H.R. 2734, at 32, 33, 160–168; 96 Cong.Rec. 16453, 16502. The final Senate Report on the question was explicit on the point:

"The use of these words ["may be"] means that the bill, if enacted, would not apply to the mere possibility but only to the reasonable probability of the prescribed [*sic*] effect. . . . The words 'may be' have been in section 7 of the Clayton Act since 1914. The concept of reasonable probability conveyed by these words is a necessary element in any statute which seeks to arrest restraints of trade in their incipiency and before they develop into full-fledged restraints violative of the Sherman Act. A requirement of certainty and actuality of injury to competition is incompatible with any effort to supplement the Sherman Act by reaching incipient restraints." S.Rep. No. 1775, 81st Cong., 2d Sess. 6. See also 51 Cong. Rec. 14464 (remarks of Senator Reed).

Id. at 315–323.

8. E.g., C. Kaysen and D. Turner, Antitrust Policy, Ch. 3 (1959); Bok, Section 7 of the Clayton Act and the Merging of Law and Economics, 74 Harv.L.Rev. 226 (1960); Blake, Conglomerate Mergers and the Antitrust Laws, 73 Colum.L.Rev. 555 (1973); Brodley, Potential Competition Mergers: A Structural Synthesis, 87 Yale L.J. 1 (1977).

owned businesses to the interests of consumers. But to put the matter bluntly, there simply was no such congressional decision either in the legislative history or in the text of the statute. . . . The Warren Court was enforcing its own social preferences, not Congress's. Id. at 64–66.

4. LAW AND POLICY UNDER THE 1950 CELLER–KEFAUVER MERGER LAW

During the 1950s and 1960s, merger policy was an integral part of an antitrust tradition that valued competitive markets for their efficiencies, their distributional properties, and their tendency to disperse power. Although there were differences in the zeal of enforcers from one administration to another, a consensus that transcended party developed about mergers and the meaning of the new act. Throughout the Eisenhower, Kennedy, Johnson, Nixon, Ford and Carter years, the following conclusions or convictions defined merger policy: that high concentration led to inertia, that it produced x-inefficiencies and thus led to higher costs, that it reduced innovation and the ability to respond flexibly to market changes, and that higher prices resulted. Among the leading economic texts that informed policy were J. Bain, Industrial Organization (1959) and E. Mason, Economic Concentration and the Monopoly Problem (1959). These books advanced the thesis that market structure affects firm conduct, which in turn affects performance, and that concentrated market structure tends to produce anticompetitive conduct, noncompetitive behavior, and bad performance. During these decades, the structure-conduct-performance paradigm represented orthodoxy. So did the conviction that a merger policy with a bias against high concentration would also advance the other goals that lay behind the Celler–Kefauver Amendment.

In the 1960s a number of merger cases, some brought during Eisenhower's presidency, reached the Supreme Court. The Court's opinions during this period were responsive to then current enforcement attitudes and were faithful to the legislative spirit. They emphasized the danger of undue concentration and the goal of stopping concentration trends in their incipiency. They expressed the purpose of the law in social and political terms as well as in economic terms. In 1968, under the leadership of Donald Turner, Assistant Attorney General, the Department of Justice issued merger guidelines. The guidelines restated and made more specific the structural norms that the case law had been developing.[9]

The 1968 guidelines provided, in essence, as follows: A "market" is any distinct line of commerce and section of the country "in which each of the firms whose sales are included enjoys some advantage over firms whose sales are not included." Mergers of not insignificant competitors (e.g., each firm with 4% to 5% of the market or more) were probably in the danger zone. Also in the danger zone were mergers of substantial buyer-supplier pairs when there were barriers to entry, high concentration in the seller's or buyer's market, and either: (1) in the supplier market, the merger threatened to foreclose the supplier-partner's competitors from access to at least 6% to 10% of the market outlet, or (2) in

9. See C. Kaysen and D. Turner, supra. The guidelines are a statement of policy indicating when the government will probably challenge a merger.

relation to the market of the buyer partner, the relevant product was a scarce or complex input and the merger threatened to foreclose the buyer-partner's competitors from access to 10% to 20% of the supply of this input. Also, mergers that created a likelihood of reciprocal buying in 15% of a market were probably illegal; and acquisition by a leading firm of one of the most likely potential entrants into a concentrated market was probably illegal.[10]

By the mid–1970s, however, the Supreme Court had once again shifted course. The new majority deemphasized socio-political values as the guide to antitrust policy. Opinions became more economically based. At the same time, a "new economic learning" expressing Chicago School attitudes was coming into vogue. Advocates of the "new economics" tried to dislodge the structure-conduct-performance paradigm. The new economic thinking involved a return to neo-classicism and to deductive thinking from highly generalized economic models based on the assumptions that markets work well and private power is hard to get.

The vision behind Chicago School analysis differed fundamentally from the vision behind the earlier consensus. The new advocates became proponents *for* mergers. They asserted, and assert, that industry structure, as well as business decisions that will change it, reflect efficiency. If concentration is high, the argument goes, one should not infer the existence of market power but should infer the existence of economies of scale. If higher profits are observed in more highly concentrated markets, the argument continues, the relationship is evidence not of power but of success; the more efficient a firm is, the faster its share will grow; as less efficient smaller firms are driven out, concentration will naturally increase. If some power is acquired in the process, productive efficiency gains (leading to allocative gains) will offset the allocative efficiency losses. Several "new learning" studies purported to show that the relationship Bain had identified between structure and profitability is temporary—perhaps due to short-run disequilibrium. Drawing upon these studies, leading Chicago School antitrust scholars criticized and trivialized the merger cases of the Warren Court era, blamed antitrust for handicapping American business, and called for a change in direction.

In 1980, Ronald Reagan was elected President, in part on the basis of promises that the government would stop intrusive interventions into markets. President Reagan appointed William F. Baxter as Assistant Attorney General in charge of the Antitrust Division. Baxter articulated the view that the antitrust laws should be applied only to prevent inefficiency, and that inefficiency should be identified only by power to limit output. Thus, Baxter would apply the merger law only to mergers that gave the parties increased power to limit output and that provided no offsetting efficiency gains. Under the guidance of Baxter, the Justice Department issued new merger guidelines in 1982. These merger guidelines, slightly revised in 1984, are based on the output-limitation principle, which in turn is informed by a deep skepticism that private business can

10. See 1968 Merger Guidelines, reprinted in Fox and Fox, Corporate Acquisitions and Mergers, App. 11 (1988).

ever succeed in limiting output. The current (1984) guidelines are reproduced in Appendix B, *infra*. After Baxter stepped down as Assistant Attorney General, even mergers plainly exceeding the 1984 guideline thresholds were allowed.[11]

B. MERGERS OF COMPETITORS

1. SETTING THE STAGE FOR MERGER ANALYSIS

Merger analysis requires several exercises. The principal object is to determine the probable competitive impact of the merger. In order to make a prediction of competitive impact, a court doing traditional analysis defines the relevant market, measures the shares of the merging companies before and after the merger, measures market concentration before and after the merger, and draws inferences from these facts as well as from other factors such as barriers to entry, the dynamics of competition in the particular market, the strength of potential competition, and the competitive style and history of the merger participants.

Price theorists remind us that the above framework for analysis is not the only model. If adverse competitive impact is equated only with increased power to raise price over existing price, one wants to know the elasticity of demand facing the market before and after the merger. If demand becomes less elastic, pricing power increases. Market definition, market shares, concentration and change in concentration provide merely a rough way to approximate pricing power produced by the merger. Indeed, the same market share and concentration can reflect quite different levels of pricing power depending on the elasticity of demand facing the market. For example, if at current prices of copper, aluminum would be a reasonably good substitute for copper in all or most uses, merging copper companies, whatever their shares of copper sales, would gain no significant power over price; but if the next good substitute were distant, they would gain significant power.

Price theorists, however, had nothing to do with the passage of Section 7 of the Clayton Act, and little to do with the first two decades of its development. We will return to the economics of defining markets and assessing competitive effects. The first important guidance to the meaning of the law that proscribed mergers that "may . . . substantially . . . lessen competition" was provided not by economists but by the Supreme Court in *Brown Shoe Co. v. United States*.

BROWN SHOE CO. v. UNITED STATES
370 U.S. 294 (1962).

CHIEF JUSTICE WARREN: This suit was initiated in November 1955 when the Government filed a civil action in the United States District Court for the Eastern District of Missouri alleging that a contemplated

11. See, e.g., Fox and Sullivan, Antitrust—Retrospective and Prospective—Where Are We Coming From? Where Are We Going?, 62 N.Y.U.L.Rev. 936 (1987); Harris and Sullivan, Horizontal Merger Policy: Promoting Competition and American Competitiveness, 31 Antitrust Bull. 871 (1987). But compare Ginsburg, The Reagan Administration's Legislative Initiative in Antitrust, 31 Antitrust Bull. 851 (1987). (Judge Douglas Ginsburg was then head of the Antitrust Division.)

merger between the G.R. Kinney Company, Inc. (Kinney), and the Brown Shoe Company, Inc. (Brown), through an exchange of Kinney for Brown stock, would violate § 7 of the Clayton Act. The Act, as amended, provides in pertinent part:

> "No corporation engaged in commerce shall acquire, directly or indirectly, the whole or any part of the stock or other share capital . . . of another corporation engaged also in commerce, where in any line of commerce in any section of the country, the effect of such acquisition may be substantially to lessen competition, or to tend to create a monopoly."

The complaint sought injunctive relief under § 15 of the Clayton Act to restrain consummation of the merger.

A motion by the Government for a preliminary injunction *pendente lite* was denied, and the companies were permitted to merge provided, however, that their businesses be operated separately and that their assets be kept separately identifiable. The merger was then effected on May 1, 1956.

In the District Court, the Government contended that the effect of the merger of Brown—the third largest seller of shoes by dollar volume in the United States, a leading manufacturer of men's, women's, and children's shoes, and a retailer with over 1,230 owned, operated or controlled retail outlets—and Kinney—the eighth largest company, by dollar volume, among those primarily engaged in selling shoes, itself a large manufacturer of shoes, and a retailer with over 350 retail outlets—"may be substantially to lessen competition or to tend to create a monopoly" by eliminating actual or potential competition in the production of shoes for the national wholesale shoe market and in the sale of shoes at retail in the Nation, by foreclosing competition from "a market represented by Kinney's retail outlets whose annual sales exceed $42,000,000," and by enhancing Brown's competitive advantage over other producers, distributors and sellers of shoes. The Government argued that the "line of commerce" affected by this merger is "footwear," or alternatively, that the "line[s]" are "men's," "women's," and "children's" shoes, separately considered, and that the "section of the country," within which the anticompetitive effect of the merger is to be judged, is the Nation as a whole, or alternatively, each separate city or city and its immediate surrounding area in which the parties sell shoes at retail.

In the District Court, Brown contended that the merger would be shown not to endanger competition if the "line[s] of commerce" and the "section[s] of the country" were properly determined. Brown urged that not only were the age and sex of the intended customers to be considered in determining the relevant line of commerce, but that differences in grade of material, quality of workmanship, price, and customer use of shoes resulted in establishing different lines of commerce. While agreeing with the Government that, with regard to manufacturing, the relevant geographic market for assessing the effect of the merger upon competition is the country as a whole, Brown contended that with regard to retailing, the market must vary with economic reality from the central business district of a large city to a "standard metropolitan area" for a smaller community. Brown further contended that, both at the manufacturing level and at the retail level, the shoe industry enjoyed healthy competition and that the vigor of this competition would not, in any event, be diminished by the proposed merger because Kinney manufactured less than 0.5% and retailed less than 2% of the Nation's shoes.

The District Court rejected the broadest contentions of both parties. The District Court found that "there is one group of classifications which is understood and recognized by the entire industry and the public—the classification into 'men's,' 'women's' and 'children's' shoes separately and independently." On the other hand, "[t]o classify shoes as a whole could be unfair and unjust; to classify them further would be impractical, unwarranted and unrealistic."

Realizing that "the areas of effective competition for retailing purposes cannot be fixed with mathematical precision," the District Court found that "when determined by economic reality, for retailing, a 'section of the country' is a city of 10,000 or more population and its immediate and contiguous surrounding area, regardless of name designation, and in which a Kinney store and a Brown (operated, franchise, or plan) store are located."

The District Court rejected the Government's contention that the combining of the manufacturing facilities of Brown and Kinney would substantially lessen competition in the production of men's, women's, or children's shoes for the national wholesale market. However, the District Court did find that the likely foreclosure of other manufacturers from the market represented by Kinney's retail outlets may substantially lessen competition in the manufacturers' distribution of "men's," "women's," and "children's" shoes, considered separately, throughout the Nation. The District Court also found that the merger may substantially lessen competition in retailing alone in "men's," "women's," and "children's" shoes, considered separately, in every city of 10,000 or more population and its immediate surrounding area in which both a Kinney and a Brown store are located. . . .

THE INDUSTRY

The District Court found that although domestic shoe production was scattered among a large number of manufacturers, a small number of large companies occupied a commanding position. Thus, while the 24 largest manufacturers produced about 35% of the Nation's shoes, the top 4—International, Endicott–Johnson, Brown (including Kinney) and General Shoe—alone produced approximately 23% of the Nation's shoes or 65% of the production of the top 24. . . .

The District Court found a "definite trend" among shoe manufacturers to acquire retail outlets. For example, International Shoe Company had no retail outlets in 1945, but by 1956 had acquired 130; General Shoe Company had only 80 retail outlets in 1945 but had 526 by 1956; Shoe Corporation of America, in the same period, increased its retail holdings from 301 to 842; Melville Shoe Company from 536 to 947; and Endicott–Johnson from 488 to 540. Brown, itself, with no retail outlets of its own prior to 1951, had acquired 845 such outlets by 1956. Moreover, between 1950 and 1956 nine independent shoe store chains, operating 1,114 retail shoe stores, were found to have become subsidiaries of these large firms and to have ceased their independent operations.

And once the manufacturers acquired retail outlets, the District Court found there was a "definite trend" for the parent-manufacturers to supply an ever increasing percentage of the retail outlets' needs, thereby foreclosing other manufacturers from effectively competing for the retail accounts. Manufacturer-dominated stores were found to be "drying up" the available outlets for independent producers.

Another "definite trend" found to exist in the shoe industry was a decrease in the number of plants manufacturing shoes. And there appears to have been a concomitant decrease in the number of firms manufacturing shoes. In 1947, there were 1,077 independent manufacturers of shoes, but by 1954 their number had decreased about 10% to 970.

Brown Shoe

Brown Shoe was found not only to have been a participant, but also a moving factor, in these industry trends. Although Brown had experimented several times with operating its own retail outlets, by 1945 it had disposed of them all. However, in 1951, Brown again began to seek retail outlets by acquiring the Nation's largest operator of leased shoe departments, Wohl Shoe Company (Wohl), which operated 250 shoe departments in department stores throughout the United States. Between 1952 and 1955 Brown made a number of . . . acquisitions [of retail outlets]. . . .

The acquisition of these corporations was found to lead to increased sales by Brown to the acquired companies . . . During the same period of time, Brown also acquired the stock or assets of seven companies engaged solely in shoe manufacturing. As a result, in 1955, Brown was the fourth largest shoe manufacturer in the country, producing about 25.6 million pairs of shoes or about 4% of the Nation's total footwear production.

Kinney

Kinney is principally engaged in operating the largest family-style shoe store chain in the United States. At the time of trial, Kinney was found to be operating over 400 such stores in more than 270 cities. These stores were found to make about 1.2% of all national retail shoe sales by dollar volume. Moreover, in 1955 the Kinney stores sold approximately 8 million pairs of nonrubber shoes or about 1.6% of the national pairage sales of such shoes. Of these sales, approximately 1.1 million pairs were of men's shoes or about 1% of the national pairage sales of men's shoes; approximately 4.2 million pairs were of women's shoes or about 1.5% of the national pairage sales of women's shoes; and approximately 2.7 million pairs were of children's shoes or about 2% of the national pairage sales of children's shoes.

In addition to this extensive retail activity, Kinney owned and operated four plants which manufactured men's, women's, and children's shoes and whose combined output was 0.5% of the national shoe production in 1955, making Kinney the twelfth largest shoe manufacturer in the United States.

Kinney stores were found to obtain about 20% of their shoes from Kinney's own manufacturing plants. At the time of the merger, Kinney bought no shoes from Brown; however, in line with Brown's conceded reasons for acquiring Kinney, Brown had, by 1957, become the largest outside supplier of Kinney's shoes, supplying 7.9% of all Kinney's needs.

It is in this setting that the merger was considered and held to violate § 7 of the Clayton Act. The District Court ordered Brown to divest itself completely of all stock, share capital, assets or other interests it held in Kinney, to operate Kinney to the greatest degree possible as an independent concern pending complete divestiture, to refrain thereafter from acquiring or having any interest in Kinney's business or assets, and to file with the court within 90 days a plan for carrying into effect the divestiture decreed. . . . Brown filed a notice of appeal in the District Court. . . .

* * *

. . . [A]s we have previously noted,

"[d]etermination of the relevant market is a necessary predicate to a finding of a violation of the Clayton Act because the threatened monopoly must be one which will substantially lessen competition 'within the area of effective competition.' Substantiality can be determined only in terms of the market affected." [41]

The "area of effective competition" must be determined by reference to a product market (the "line of commerce") and a geographic market (the "section of the country").

The Product Market

The outer boundaries of a product market are determined by the reasonable interchangeability of use or the cross-elasticity of demand between the product itself and substitutes for it.[42] However, within this broad market, well-defined submarkets may exist which, in themselves, constitute product markets for antitrust purposes. The boundaries of such a submarket may be determined by examining such practical indicia as industry or public recognition of the submarket as a separate economic entity, the product's peculiar characteristics and uses, unique production facilities, distinct customers, distinct prices, sensitivity to price changes, and specialized vendors. Because § 7 of the Clayton Act prohibits any merger which may substantially lessen competition "in *any* line of commerce" (emphasis supplied), it is necessary to examine the effects of a merger in each such economically significant submarket to determine if there is a reasonable probability that the merger will substantially lessen competition. If such a probability is found to exist, the merger is proscribed.

41. *United States v. E.I. du Pont de Nemours & Co.*, 353 U.S. 586, 593.

42. The cross-elasticity of production facilities may also be an important factor in defining a product market within which a vertical merger is to be viewed. However, the District Court made but limited findings concerning the feasibility of interchanging equipment in the manufacture of nonrubber footwear. At the same time, the record supports the court's conclusion that individual plants generally produced shoes in only one of the product lines the court found relevant.

Applying these considerations to the present case, we conclude that the record supports the District Court's finding that the relevant lines of commerce are men's, women's, and children's shoes. These product lines are recognized by the public; each line is manufactured in separate plants; each has characteristics peculiar to itself rendering it generally noncompetitive with the others; and each is, of course, directed toward a distinct class of customers.

Appellant, however, contends that the District Court's definitions fail to recognize sufficiently "price/quality" . . . distinctions in shoes. Brown argues that the predominantly medium-priced shoes which it manufacturers occupy a product market different from the predominantly low-priced shoes which Kinney sells. But agreement with that argument would be equivalent to holding that medium-priced shoes do not compete with low-priced shoes. We think the District Court properly found the facts to be otherwise. It would be unrealistic to accept Brown's contention that, for example, men's shoes selling below $8.99 are in a different product market from those selling above $9.00.

This is not to say, however, that "price/quality" differences, where they exist, are unimportant in analyzing a merger; they may be of importance in determining the likely effect of a merger. But the boundaries of the relevant market must be drawn with sufficient breadth to include the competing products of each of the merging companies and to recognize competition where, in fact, competition exists. Thus we agree with the District Court that in this case a further division of product lines based on "price/quality" differences would be "unrealistic."

* * *

The Horizontal Aspects of the Merger

An economic arrangement between companies performing similar functions in the production or sale of comparable goods or services is characterized as "horizontal." The effect on competition of such an arrangement depends, of course, upon its character and scope. Thus, its validity in the face of the antitrust laws will depend upon such factors as: the relative size and number of the parties to the arrangement; whether it allocates shares of the market among the parties; whether it fixes prices at which the parties will sell their product; or whether it absorbs or insulates competitors. Where the arrangement effects a horizontal merger between companies occupying the same product and geographic market, whatever competition previously may have existed in that market between the parties to the merger is eliminated. Section 7 of the Clayton Act, prior to its amendment, focused upon this aspect of horizontal combinations by proscribing acquisitions which might result in a lessening of competition between the acquiring and the acquired companies. The 1950 amendments made plain Congress' intent that the validity of such combinations was to be gauged on a broader scale: their effect on competition generally in an economically significant market.

Thus, again, the proper definition of the market is a "necessary predicate" to an examination of the competition that may be affected by the horizontal aspects of the merger. The acquisition of Kinney by Brown resulted in a horizontal combination at both the manufacturing and retailing levels of their businesses. Although the District Court found that the merger of Brown's and Kinney's *manufacturing* facilities was economically too insignificant to come within the prohibitions of the Clayton Act, the Government has not appealed from this portion of the lower court's decision. Therefore, we have no occasion to express our views with respect to that finding. On the other hand, appellant does contest the District Court's finding that the merger of the companies' *retail* outlets may tend substantially to lessen competition.

The Product Market

Shoes are sold in the United States in retail shoe stores and in shoe departments of general stores. These outlets sell: (1) men's shoes, (2) women's shoes, (3) women's or children's shoes, or (4) men's, women's or children's shoes. Prior to the merger, both Brown and Kinney sold their shoes in competition with one another through the enumerated kinds of outlets characteristic of the industry.

In Part IV of this opinion we hold that the District Court correctly defined men's, women's, and children's shoes as the relevant lines of commerce in which to analyze the vertical aspects of the merger. For the reasons there stated we also hold that the same lines of commerce are appropriate for considering the horizontal aspects of the merger.

The Geographic Market

The criteria to be used in determining the appropriate geographic market are essentially similar to those used to determine the relevant product market. See S.Rep. No. 1775, 81st Cong., 2d Sess. 5–6; *United States v. E.I. du Pont de Nemours & Co.,* 353 U.S. 586, 593. Moreover, just as a product submarket may have § 7 significance as the proper "line of commerce," so may a geographic submarket be considered the appropriate "section of the country." *Erie Sand & Gravel Co. v. Federal Trade Comm'n,* 291 F.2d 279, 283 (C.A.3d Cir.); *United States v. Bethlehem Steel Corp.,* 168 F.Supp. 576, 595–603 (D.C.S.D.N.Y.). Congress prescribed a pragmatic, factual approach to the definition of the relevant market and not a formal, legalistic one. The geographic market selected must, therefore, both "correspond to the commercial realities" of the industry and be economically significant. Thus, although the geographic market in some instances may encompass the entire Nation, under other circumstances it may be as small as a single metropolitan area. The fact that two merging firms have competed directly on the horizontal level in but a fraction of the geographic markets in which either has operated, does not, in itself, place their merger outside the scope of § 7. That section speaks of "any . . . section of the country," and if anticompetitive effects of a merger are probable in "any" significant market, the merger—at least to that extent—is proscribed.[65]

* * *

65. To illustrate: If two retailers, one operating primarily in the eastern half of the Nation, and the other operating largely in the West, competed in but two mid-Western cities, the fact that the latter outlets represented but a small share of each company's business would not immunize the merger in those markets in which competition might be adversely affected. On the other hand, that fact would, of course, be properly considered in determining the equitable relief to be decreed.

The District Court found that the effects of this aspect of the merger must be analyzed in every city with a population exceeding 10,000 and its immediate contiguous surrounding territory in which both Brown and Kinney sold shoes at retail through stores they either owned or controlled. By this definition of the geographic market, less than one-half of all the cities in which either Brown or Kinney sold shoes through such outlets are represented. The appellant recognizes that if the District Court's characterization of the relevant market is proper, the number of markets in which both Brown and Kinney have outlets is sufficiently numerous so that the validity of the entire merger is properly judged by testing its effects in those markets. However, it is appellant's contention that the areas of effective competition in shoe retailing were improperly defined by the District Court. It claims that such areas should, in some cases, be defined so as to include only the central business districts of large cities, and in others, so as to encompass the "standard metropolitan areas" within which smaller communities are found. It argues that any test failing to distinguish between these competitive situations is improper.

We believe, however, that the record fully supports the District Court's findings that shoe stores in the out-skirts of cities compete effectively with stores in central downtown areas, and that while there is undoubtedly some commercial intercourse between smaller communities within a single "standard metropolitan area," the most intense and important competition in retail sales will be confined to stores within the particular communities in such an area and their immediate environs.

We therefore agree that the District Court properly defined the relevant geographic markets in which to analyze this merger as those cities with a population exceeding 10,000 and their environs in which both Brown and Kinney retailed shoes through their own outlets. Such markets are large enough to include the downtown shops and suburban shopping centers in areas contiguous to the city, which are the important competitive factors, and yet are small enough to exclude stores beyond the immediate environs of the city, which are of little competitive significance.

The Probable Effect of the Merger

Having delineated the product and geographic markets within which the effects of this merger are to be measured, we turn to an examination of the District Court's finding that as a result of the merger competition in the retailing of men's, women's and children's shoes may be lessened substantially in those cities in which both Brown and Kinney stores are located. . . . [The data show] that during 1955 in 32 separate cities, ranging in size and location from Topeka, Kansas, to Batavia, New York, and Hobbs, New Mexico, the combined share of Brown and Kinney sales of women's shoes (by unit volume) exceeded 20%. In 31 cities . . . the combined share of children's shoes sales exceeded 20%; in 6 cities their share exceeded 40%. In Dodge City, Kansas, their combined share of the market for women's shoes was over 57%; their share of the children's shoe market in that city was 49%. In the 7 cities in which Brown's and Kinney's combined shares of the market for women's shoes were greatest (ranging from 33% to 57%) each of the parties alone, prior to the merger, had captured substantial portions of those markets (ranging from 13% to 34%); the merger intensified this existing concentration. In 118 separate cities the combined shares of the market of Brown and Kinney in the sale of one of the relevant lines of commerce exceeded 5%. In 47 cities, their share exceeded 5% in all three lines.

The market share which companies may control by merging is one of the most important factors to be considered when determining the probable effects of the combination on effective competition in the relevant market. In an industry as fragmented as shoe retailing, the control of substantial shares of the trade in a city may have important effects on competition. If a merger achieving 5% control were now approved, we might be required to approve future merger efforts by Brown's competitors seeking similar market shares. The oligopoly Congress sought to avoid would then be furthered and it would be difficult to dissolve the combinations previously approved. Furthermore, in this fragmented industry, even if the combination controls but a small share of a particular market, the fact that this share is held by a large national chain can adversely affect competition. Testimony in the record from numerous independent retailers, based on their actual experience in the market, demonstrates that a strong, national chain of stores can insulate selected outlets from the vagaries of competition in particular locations and that the large chains can set and alter styles in footwear to an extent that renders the independents unable to maintain competitive inventories. A third significant aspect of this merger is that it creates a large national chain which is integrated with a manufacturing operation. The retail outlets of integrated companies, by eliminating wholesalers and by increasing the volume of purchases from the manufacturing division of the enterprise, can market their own brands at prices below those of competing independent retailers. Of course, some of the results of large integrated or chain operations are beneficial to consumers. Their expansion is not rendered unlawful by the mere fact that small independent stores may be adversely affected. It is competition, not competitors, which the Act protects. But we cannot fail to recognize Congress' desire to promote competition through the protection of viable, small, locally owned businesses. Congress appreciated that occasional higher costs and prices might result from the maintenance of fragmented industries and markets. It resolved these competing considerations in favor of decentralization. We must give effect to that decision.

Other factors to be considered in evaluating the probable effects of a merger in the relevant market lend additional support to the District Court's conclusion that this merger may substantially lessen competition. One such factor is the history of tendency toward concentration in the industry.[72] As we have previously pointed out, the shoe industry has, in

---

72. A company's history of expansion through mergers presents a different economic picture than a history of expansion through unilateral growth. Internal expansion is more likely to be the result of increased demand for the company's products and is more likely to provide increased investment in plants, more jobs and greater output. Conversely, expansion through merger is more likely to reduce available consumer choice while providing no increase in industry capacity, jobs or output. It was for these reasons, among others, Congress expressed its disapproval of successive acquisitions. Section 7 was enacted to prevent even small mergers that added to concentra-

recent years, been a prime example of such a trend. Most combinations have been between manufacturers and retailers, as each of the larger producers has sought to capture an increasing number of assured outlets for its wares. Although these mergers have been primarily vertical in their aim and effect, to the extent that they have brought even greater numbers of retail outlets within fewer and fewer hands, they have had an additional important impact on the horizontal plane. By the merger in this case, the largest single group of retail stores still independent of one of the large manufacturers was asorbed into an already substantial aggregation of more or less controlled retail outlets. As a result of this merger, Brown moved into second place nationally in terms of retail stores directly owned. Including the stores on its franchise plan, the merger placed under Brown's control almost 1,600 shoe outlets, or about 7.2% of the Nation's retail "shoe stores" as defined by the Census Bureau, and 2.3 of the Nation's total retail shoe outlets. We cannot avoid the mandate of Congress that tendencies toward concentration in industry are to be curbed in their incipiency, particularly when those tendencies are being accelerated through giant steps striding across a hundred cities at a time. In the light of the trends in this industry we agree with the Government and the court below that this is an appropriate place at which to call a halt.

At the same time appellant has presented no mitigating factors, such as the business failure or the inadequate resources of one of the parties that may have prevented it from maintaining its competitive position, nor a demonstrated need for combination to enable small companies to enter into a more meaningful competition with those dominating the relevant markets. On the basis of the record before us, we believe the Government sustained its burden of proof. We hold that the District Court was correct in concluding that this merger may tend to lessen competition substantially in the retail sale of men's, women's, and children's shoes in the overwhelming majority of those cities and their environs in which both Brown and Kinney sell through owned or controlled outlets.

The judgment is

Affirmed.

Questions and Comments

The economic literature commonly relied upon in the 1950s and 1960s offered the structure-conduct-performance paradigm. This literature displayed two alternative approaches. The work of Mason and his students favored systematic study of the competitive interaction of firms within a single industry. Bain, by contrast, went beyond the single industry to do investigations that yielded cross-industry generalizations about the probable effects on performance of particular levels of concentration. In *Brown Shoe* the Court spoke in Mason-like terms; it stressed the wide range of factors that may be relevant in evaluating the legality of a merger. But it also generalized extravagantly about concentration, and ultimately invalidated a relative-

tion in an industry. See S.Rep. No. 1775, 81st Cong., 2d Sess. 5.

ly small merger, largely on the basis of a trend towards concentration in view of Congress's social concerns.

How might the combination of the competing retail outlets have lessened competition? The Court says that even 5% control must be condemned. Does a shoe retailer's 5% of a market seem ominous? Could a retailer who sells 5% of all shoes sold in a local retail market raise prices to supracompetitive levels? Could one that sells 10%? 50%? What values other than consumer interests were, according to the Court, threatened by the levels of concentration achieved through the Brown–Kinney merger? What conception of competition would warrant a conclusion of threatened injury, on facts like these?

Did the merger confer efficiencies? Did it contain seeds of inefficiency? Do you suppose that the Court thought efficiencies were either gained or lost?

What does the Court mean when it says: "It is competition, not competitors, which the Act protects"? (370 U.S. at 344, at p. 746 supra.) How did the Court apply the distinction between protecting competition and protecting competitors? Remember the above-quoted sentence. It is cited frequently in contemporary antitrust jurisprudence. Reread the text in the context in which the sentence appears. If construed to mean that the law prohibits only mergers that increase market power and lessen output, does the text make sense?

Brown Shoe was the somewhat eccentric vehicle for the Court's first pronouncement on the scope of the new merger law. Perhaps in view of the criticism and Congressional mandate that followed *Consolidated Steel,* the Supreme Court felt obliged to announce a generous construction of the law. What should it have done? If you were a Justice, what different formulation would you have offered?

While in *Brown Shoe* the Court found a violation in spite of many sellers and low barriers to entry, the next important case involved few sellers and high government-imposed barriers.

UNITED STATES v. PHILADELPHIA NATIONAL BANK

374 U.S. 321 (1963).

JUSTICE BRENNAN: The United States, appellant here, brought this civil action in the United States District Court for the Eastern District of Pennsylvania under § 4 of the Sherman Act, 15 U.S.C. § 4, and § 15 of the Clayton Act, 15 U.S.C. § 25, to enjoin a proposed merger of The Philadelphia National Bank (PNB) and Girard Trust Corn Exchange Bank (Girard), appellees here. The complaint charged violations of § 1 of the Sherman Act, and § 7 of the Clayton Act. From a judgment for appellees after trial, the United States appealed. . . .

* * *

The Philadelphia National Bank and Girard Trust Corn Exchange Bank are, respectively, the second and third largest of the 42 commercial banks with head offices in the Philadelphia metropolitan area, which consists of the City of Philadelphia and its three contiguous counties in Pennsylvania. The home county of both banks is the city itself; Pennsylvania law, however, permits branching into the counties contiguous to the home county, and both banks have offices throughout the four-county area. PNB, a national bank, has assets of over $1,000,000,000, making it (as of 1959) the twenty-first largest bank in the Nation. Girard, a state bank, . . . has assets of about $750,000,000. Were the proposed merger to be consummated, the resulting bank would be the largest in the four-county area, with (approximately) 36% of the area banks' total assets. 36% of deposits, and 34% of net loans. It and the second largest (First Pennsylvania Bank and Trust Company, now the largest) would have between them 59% of the total assets, 58% of deposits, and 58% of the net loans, while after the merger the four largest banks in the area would have 78% of total assets, 77% of deposits, and 78% of net loans.

The present size of both PNB and Girard is in part the result of mergers. Indeed, the trend toward concentration is noticeable in the Philadelphia area generally, in which the number of commercial banks has declined from 108 in 1947 to the present 42. Since 1950, PNB has acquired nine formerly independent banks and Girard six; and these acquisitions have accounted for 59% and 85% of the respective banks' asset growth during the period, 63% and 91% of their deposit growth, and 12% and 37% of their loan growth. During this period, the seven largest banks in the area increased their combined share of the area's total commercial bank resources from about 61% to about 90%.

. . . [Pursuant to the Bank Merger Act of 1960, the Comptroller of the Currency] approved the merger. [H]e reasoned that "[s]ince there will remain an adequate number of alternative sources of banking service in Philadelphia, and in view of the beneficial effects of this consolidation upon international and national competition it was concluded that the over-all effect upon competition would not be unfavorable." He also stated that the consolidated bank "would be far better able to serve the convenience and needs of its community by being of material assistance to its city and state in their efforts to attract new industry and to retain existing industry." The day after the Comptroller approved the merger, the United States commenced the present action. . . .

The Government's case in the District Court relied chiefly on statistical evidence bearing upon market structure and on testimony by economists and bankers to the effect that, notwithstanding the intensive governmental regulation of banking, there was a substantial area for the free play of competitive forces; that concentration of commercial banking, which the proposed merger would increase, was inimical to that free play; that the principal anticompetitive effect of the merger would be felt in the area in which the banks had their offices, thus making the four-county metropolitan area the relevant geographical market; and that commercial banking was the relevant product market. The defendants, in addition to offering contrary evidence on these points, attempted to show business justifications for the merger. They conceded that both banks were economically strong and had sound management, but offered the testimony of bankers to show that the resulting bank, with its greater prestige and increased lending limit, would be better able to compete with large out-of-state (particulary New York) banks, would attract new business to Philadelphia, and in general would promote the economic development of the metropolitan area.

* * *

We have no difficulty in determining the "line of commerce" (relevant product or services market) and "section of the country" (relevant geographical market) in which to appraise the probable competitive effects of appellees' proposed merger. We agree with the District Court that the cluster of products (various kinds of credit) and services (such as checking accounts and trust administration) denoted by the term "commercial banking" composes a distinct line of commerce. Some commercial banking products or services are so distinctive that they are entirely free of effective competition from products or services of other financial institutions; the checking account is in this category. Others enjoy such cost advantages as to be insulated within a broad range from substitutes furnished by other institutions. For example, commercial banks compete with small-loan companies in the personal-loan market; but the small-loan companies' rates are invariably much higher than the banks', in part, it seems, because the companies' working capital consists in substantial part of bank loans. Finally, there are banking facilities which, although in terms of cost and price they are freely competitive with the facilities provided by other financial institutions, nevertheless enjoy a settled consumer preference, insulating them, to a marked degree, from competition; this seems to be the case with savings deposits.[34] In sum, it is clear that commercial banking is a market "sufficiently inclusive to be meaningful in terms of trade realities." *Crown Zellerbach Corp. v. Federal Trade Comm'n,* 296 F.2d 800, 811 (C.A. 9th Cir.1961).

We part company with the District Court on the determination of the appropriate "section of the country." The proper question to be asked in this case is not where the parties to the merger do business or even where they compete, but where, within the area of competitive overlap, the effect of the merger on competition will be direct and immediate. See Bock, Mergers and Markets (1960), 42. This depends upon "the geographic structure of supplier-customer relations." Kaysen and Turner, Antitrust Policy (1959), 102. In banking, as in most service industries, convenience of location is essential to effective competition. Individuals and corporations typically confer the bulk of their patronage on banks in their local community; they find it impractical to conduct their banking business at a distance. The factor of inconvenience localizes banking competition as effectively as high transportation costs in other industries. Therefore, since, as we recently said in a related context, the "area of effective

34. As one witness for the defendants testified:

"We have had in Philadelphia for 50 years or more the mutual savings banks offering ½ per cent and in some instances more than ½ per cent higher interest than the commercial banks. Nevertheless, the rate of increase in savings accounts in commercial banks has kept pace with and in many of the banks exceeded the rate of increase of the mutual banks paying 3½ per cent. . . .

"I have made some inquiries. There are four banks on the corner of Broad and Chestnut. Three of them are commercial banks all offering 3 per cent, and one is a mutual savings bank offering 3½. As far as I have been able to discover, there isn't anybody in Philadelphia who will take the trouble to walk across Broad Street to get ½ of 1 per cent more interest. If you ask me why, I will say I do not know. Habit, custom, personal relationships, convenience, doing all your banking under one roof appear to be factors superior to changes in the interest rate level."

competition in the known line of commerce must be charted by careful selection of the market area in which the seller operates, *and to which the purchaser can practicably turn for supplies,*" Tampa Elec. Co. v. Nashville Coal Co., 365 U.S. 320, 327 (emphasis supplied); see *Standard Oil Co. v. United States,* 337 U.S. 293, 299 and 300, n. 5, the four-county area in which appellees' offices are located would seem to be the relevant geographical market. Cf. *Brown Shoe Co., supra,* at 338–339. In fact, the vast bulk of appellees' business originates in the four-county area. Theoretically, we should be concerned with the possibility that bank offices on the perimeter of the area may be in effective competition with bank offices within; actually, this seems to be a factor of little significance.[37]

We recognize that the area in which appellees have their offices does not delineate with perfect accuracy an appropriate "section of the country" in which to appraise the effect of the merger upon competition. Large borrowers and large depositors, the record shows, may find it practical to do a large part of their banking business outside their home community; very small borrowers and depositors may, as a practical matter, be confined to bank offices in their immediate neighborhood; and customers of intermediate size, it would appear, deal with banks within an area intermediate between these extremes. See notes 35–37, *supra.* So also, some banking services are evidently more local in nature than others. But that in banking the relevant geographical market is a function of each separate customer's economic scale means simply that a workable compromise must be found: some fair intermediate delineation which avoids the indefensible extremes of drawing the market either so expansively as to make the effect of the merger upon competition seem insignificant, because only the very largest bank customers are taken into account in defining the market, or so narrowly as to place appellees in different markets, because only the smallest customers are considered. We think that the four-county Philadelphia metropolitan area, which state law apparently recognizes as a meaningful banking community in allowing Philadelphia banks to branch within it, and which would seem roughly to delineate the area in which bank customers that are neither very large nor very small find it practical to do their banking business, is a more appropriate "section of the country" in which to appraise the instant merger than any larger or smaller or different area. . . .

37. Appellees suggest not that bank offices skirting the four-county area provide meaningful alternatives to bank customers within the area, but that such alternatives are provided by large banks, from New York and elsewhere, which solicit business in the Philadelphia area. There is no evidence of the amount of business done in the area by banks with offices outside the area; it may be that such figures are unobtainable. In any event, it would seem from the local orientation of banking insofar as smaller customers are concerned, that competition from outside the area would only be important to the larger borrowers and depositors. If so, the four-county area remains a valid geographical market in which to assess the anticompetitive effect of the proposed merger upon the banking facilities available to the smaller customer—a perfectly good "line of commerce," in light of Congress' evident concern, in enacting the 1950 amendments to § 7, with preserving small business. See *Brown Shoe Co., supra,* at 315–316. As a practical matter the small businessman can only satisfy his credit needs at local banks. To be sure, there is still some artificiality in deeming the four-county area the relevant "section of the country" so far as businessmen located near the perimeter are concerned. But such fuzziness would seem inherent in any attempt to delineate the relevant geographical market. . . .

Having determined the relevant market, we come to the ultimate question under § 7: whether the effect of the merger "may be substantially to lessen competition" in the relevant market. Clearly, this is not the kind of question which is susceptible of a ready and precise answer in most cases. It requires not merely an appraisal of the immediate impact of the merger upon competition, but a prediction of its impact upon competitive conditions in the future; this is what is meant when it is said that the amended § 7 was intended to arrest anticompetitive tendencies in their "incipiency." See *Brown Shoe Co., supra,* at 317, 322. Such a prediction is sound only if it is based upon a firm understanding of the structure of the relevant market; yet the relevant economic data are both complex and elusive. And unless businessmen can assess the legal consequences of a merger with some confidence, sound business planning is retarded. So also, we must be alert to the danger of subverting congressional intent by permitting a too-broad economic investigation. *Standard Oil Co. v. United States,* 337 U.S. 293, 313. And so in any case in which it is possible, without doing violence to the congressional objective embodied in § 7, to simplify the test of illegality, the courts ought to do so in the interest of sound and practical judicial administration. This is such a case.

We noted in *Brown Shoe Co., supra,* at 315, that "[t]he dominant theme pervading congressional consideration of the 1950 amendments [to § 7] was a fear of what was considered to be a rising tide of economic concentration in the American economy." This intense congressional concern with the trend toward concentration warrants dispensing, in certain cases, with elaborate proof of market structure, market behavior, or probable anticompetitive effects. Specifically, we think that a merger which produces a firm controlling an undue percentage share of the relevant market, and results in a significant increase in the concentration of firms in that market, is so inherently likely to lessen competition substantially that it must be enjoined in the absence of evidence clearly showing that the merger is not likely to have such anticompetitive effects.

Such a test lightens the burden of proving illegality only with respect to mergers whose size makes them inherently suspect in light of Congress' design in § 7 to prevent undue concentration. Furthermore, the test is fully consonant with economic theory. That "[c]ompetition is likely to be greatest when there are many sellers, none of which has any significant market share," [39] is common ground among most economists, and was undoubtedly a premise of congressional reasoning about the antimerger statute.

The merger of appellees will result in a single bank's controlling at least 30% of the commercial banking business in the four-county Philadelphia metropolitan area. Without attempting to specify the smallest market share which would still be considered to threaten undue concentration, we are clear that 30% presents that threat. Further, whereas

39. Comment, "Substantially to Lessen Competition . . .": Current Problems of Horizontal Mergers, 68 Yale L.J. 1627, 1638–1639 (1959); see, *e.g.,* Machlup, The Economics of Sellers' Competition (1952), 84–93, 333–336; Bain, Barriers to New Competition (1956), 27. Cf. Mason, Market Power and Business Conduct: Some Comments, 46–2 Am.Econ.Rev. (1956), 471.

presently the two largest banks in the area (First Pennsylvania and PNB) control between them approximately 44% of the area's commercial banking business, the two largest after the merger (PNB–Girard and First Pennsylvania) will control 59%. Plainly, we think, this increase of more than 33% in concentration must be regarded as significant.[42]

Our conclusion that these percentages raise an inference that the effect of the contemplated merger of appellees may be substantially to lessen competition is not an arbitrary one, although neither the terms of § 7 nor the legislative history suggests that any particular percentage share was deemed critical. The House Report states that the tests of illegality under amended § 7 "are intended to be similar to those which the courts have applied in interpreting the same language as used in other sections of the Clayton Act." H.R.Rep. No. 1191, 81st Cong., 1st Sess. 8. Accordingly, we have relied upon decisions under these other sections in applying § 7. . . .

There is nothing in the record of this case to rebut the inherently anticompetitive tendency manifested by these percentages. There was, to be sure, testimony by bank officers to the effect that competition among banks in Philadelphia was vigorous and would continue to be vigorous after the merger. We think, however, that the District Court's reliance on such evidence was misplaced. This lay evidence on so complex an economic-legal problem as the substantiality of the effect of this merger upon competition was entitled to little weight, in view of the witnesses' failure to give concrete reasons for their conclusions.[43]

Of equally little value, we think, are the assurances offered by appellees' witnesses that customers dissatisfied with the services of the resulting bank may readily turn to the 40 other banks in the Philadelphia area. In every case short of outright monopoly, the disgruntled customer has alternatives; even in tightly oligopolistic markets, there may be small firms operating. A fundamental purpose of amending § 7 was to arrest the trend toward concentration, the *tendency* to monopoly, before the consumer's alternatives disappeared through merger, and that purpose would be ill-served if the law stayed its hand until 10, or 20, or 30 more Philadelphia banks were absorbed. This is not a fanciful eventuality, in view of the strong trend toward mergers evident in the area; and we might note also that entry of new competitors into the banking field is far from easy.[44]

42. . . . It is no answer that, among the three presently largest firms (First Pennsylvania, PNB, and Girard), there will be no increase in concentration. If this argument were valid, then once a market had become unduly concentrated, further concentration would be legally privileged. On the contrary, if concentration is already great, the importance of preventing even slight increases in concentration and so preserving the possibility of eventual deconcentration is correspondingly great.

43. The fact that some of the bank officers who testified represented small banks in competition with appellees does not substantially enhance the probative value of their testimony. The test of a competitive market is not only whether small competitors flourish but also whether consumers are well served. . . . In an oligopolistic market, small companies may be perfectly content to follow the high prices set by the dominant firms, yet the market may be profoundly anticompetitive.

44. Entry is, of course, wholly a matter of governmental grace. . . .

So also, we reject the position that commercial banking, because it is subject to a high degree of governmental regulation, or because it deals in the intangibles of credit and services rather than in the manufacture or sale of tangible commodities, is somehow immune from the anticompetitive effects of undue concentration. Competition among banks exists at every level—price, variety of credit arrangements, convenience of location, attractiveness of physical surroundings, credit information, investment advice, service charges, personal accommodations, advertising, miscellaneous special and extra services—and it is keen; on this appellees' own witnesses were emphatic. There is no reason to think that concentration is less inimical to the free play of competition in banking than in other service industries. On the contrary, it is in all probability more inimical. For example, banks compete to fill the credit needs of businessmen. Small businessmen especially are, as a practical matter, confined to their locality for the satisfaction of their credit needs. If the number of banks in the locality is reduced, the vigor of competition for filling the marginal small business borrower's needs is likely to diminish. At the same time, his concomitantly greater difficulty in obtaining credit is likely to put him at a disadvantage *vis-à-vis* larger businesses with which he competes. In this fashion, concentration in banking accelerates concentration generally.

We turn now to three affirmative justifications which appellees offer for the proposed merger. The first is that only through mergers can banks follow their customers to the suburbs and retain their business. This justification does not seem particularly related to the instant merger, but in any event it has no merit. There is an alternative to the merger route: the opening of new branches in the areas to which the customers have moved—so-called *de novo* branching. Appellees do not contend that they are unable to expand thus, by opening new offices rather than acquiring existing ones, and surely one premise of an antimerger statute such as § 7 is that corporate growth by internal expansion is socially preferable to growth by acquisition.

Second, it is suggested that the increased lending limit of the resulting bank will enable it to compete with the large out-of-state banks, particularly the New York banks, for very large loans. We reject this application of the concept of "countervailing power." Cf. *Kiefer–Stewart Co. v. Joseph E. Seagram & Sons*, 340 U.S. 211. If anti-competitive effects in one market could be justified by pro-competitive consequences in another, the logical upshot would be that every firm in an industry could, without violating § 7, embark on a series of mergers that would make it in the end as large as the industry leader. For if all the commercial banks in the Philadelphia area merged into one, it would be smaller than the largest bank in New York City. This is not a case, plainly, where two small firms in a market propose to merge in order to be able to compete more successfully with the leading firms in that market. Nor is it a case in which lack of adequate banking facilities is causing hardships to individuals or businesses in the community. The present two largest banks in Philadelphia have lending limits of $8,000,000 each. The only businesses located in the Philadelphia area which find such limits inadequate are large enough readily to obtain bank credit in other cities.

This brings us to appellees' final contention, that Philadelphia needs a bank larger than it now has in order to bring business to the area and stimulate its economic development. We are clear, however, that a merger the effect of which "may be substantially to lessen competition" is not saved because, on some ultimate reckoning of social or economic debits and credits, it may be deemed beneficial. A value choice of such magnitude is beyond the ordinary limits of judicial competence, and in any event has been made for us already, by Congress when it enacted the amended § 7. Congress determined to preserve our traditionally competitive economy. It therefore proscribed anticompetitive mergers, the benign and the malignant alike, fully aware, we must assume, that some price might have to be paid.

In holding as we do that the merger of appellees would violate § 7 and must therefore be enjoined, we reject appellees' pervasive suggestion that application of the procompetitive policy of § 7 to the banking industry will have dire, although unspecified, consequences for the national economy. Concededly, PNB and Girard are healthy and strong; they are not undercapitalized or overloaned; they have no management problems; the Philadelphia area is not overbanked; ruinous competition is not in the offing. Section 7 does not mandate cut-throat competition in the banking industry, and does not exclude defenses based on dangers to liquidity or solvency, if to avert them a merger is necessary.[46] It does require, however, that the forces of competition be allowed to operate within the broad framework of governmental regulation of the industry. The fact that banking is a highly regulated industry critical to the Nation's welfare makes the play of competition not less important but more so. At the price of some repetition, we note that if the businessman is denied credit because his banking alternatives have been eliminated by mergers, the whole edifice of an entrepreneurial system is threatened; if the costs of banking services and credit are allowed to become excessive by the absence of competitive pressures, virtually all costs, in our credit economy, will be affected; and unless competition is allowed to fulfill its role as an economic regulator in the banking industry, the result may well be even more governmental regulation. Subject to narrow qualifications, it is surely the case that competition is our fundamental national economic policy, offering as it does the only alternative to the cartelization or governmental regimentation of large portions of the economy. There is no warrant for declining to enforce it in the instant case.

The judgment of the District Court is reversed and the case remanded with direction to enter judgment enjoining the proposed merger.

Questions and Comments

What does *Philadelphia National Bank* add to the holding of *Brown Shoe?* What sources of learning or public policy support the Court's rule of presumptive illegality? Does the Court suggest that economic analysis supports an inference that a merger of the specified proportions producing the specified increase in concentration produces an increment in power over price?

46. Thus, arguably, the so-called failing-company defense, see *International Shoe Co. v. Federal Trade Comm'n*, 280 U.S. 291, 299–303, might have somewhat larger contours as applied to bank mergers because of the greater public impact of a bank failure compared with ordinary business failures. . . .

After the plaintiff has raised a presumption of illegality, could the defendants rebut that presumption by showing that they would gain no power over price (because, for example, competition from distant banks or local alternatives such as savings and loan associations, or government regulation, would frustrate any attempt to raise price)? What if defendants showed also that, before the merger, the leading banks had no power over price?

Would the merger be justified if it enabled Philadelphia banks to compete more effectively in national or international money markets? Was the Court's answer mandated by Congress? Would the Court give the same answer today? Is the Supreme Court's contemporary non-merger antitrust jurisprudence (e.g., *BMI, Aspen Skiing, Sharp Electronics* (see pp. 316, 252 and 564 *supra*) relevant?

Philadelphia National Bank gave infrastructure to the *Brown Shoe* jurisprudence. Then, in the following year, in a span of three months, the Supreme Court decided four more major merger cases—*El Paso, Lexington Bank, Alcoa (Rome),* and *Continental Can.* Two years later it decided *Von's Grocery.* All gave further breadth to the law.

In *United States v. El Paso Natural Gas Co.,* 376 U.S. 651 (1964), El Paso, which supplied more than 50% of all natural gas consumed in California, acquired Pacific Northwest Pipeline Corporation, an out-of-state firm that was trying to make sales to customers in the rapidly expanding California market. Pacific Northwest had engaged in negotiations to sell gas to Southern California Edison, the largest industrial user of natural gas in Southern California. Although El Paso won the bid, the competition by Pacific Northwest pressured El Paso to lower its price by 25%. Pacific Northwest continued its efforts to enter the California market. The Court said: "We would have to wear blinders not to see that the mere efforts of Pacific Northwest to get into the California market, though unsuccessful, had a powerful influence on El Paso's business attitudes within the state." Id. at 659. Holding the acquisition illegal, the Court observed: "Unsuccessful bidders are no less competitors than the successful one. The presence of two or more suppliers gives buyers a choice." Id. at 661. Reversing the district court, the Supreme Court directed it to "order divestiture without delay." Id. at 662.

On the same day the Supreme Court handed down *United States v. First National Bank and Trust Company of Lexington,* 376 U.S. 665 (1964). This action, challenging consolidation of the first and fourth largest of the six commercial banks in Fayette County, Kentucky, was tried under the Sherman Act because the case was initiated at a time when Section 7 was thought not to reach bank mergers. Together, the consolidating banks would have occupied more than half the market; the next largest bank was no more than one third of their size.

UNITED STATES v. FIRST NATIONAL BANK AND TRUST COMPANY OF LEXINGTON
376 U.S. 665 (1964).

JUSTICE DOUGLAS: * * *.

. . . There was here no "predatory" purpose. But we think it clear that significant competition will be eliminated by the consolidation. There is testimony in the record from three of the four remaining banks that the consolidation will seriously affect their ability to compete effectively over the years; that the "image" of "bigness" is a powerful attraction to customers, an advantage that increases progressively with disparity in size; and that the multiplicity of extra services in the trust field which the new company could offer tends to foreclose competition there.

We think it clear that the elimination of significant competition between First National and Security Trust constitutes an unreasonable restraint of trade in violation of § 1 of the Sherman Act. The case, we think, is governed by *Northern Securities Co. v. United States*, 193 U.S. 197, and its progeny. The Northern Pacific and the Great Northern operated parallel lines west of Chicago. A holding company acquired the controlling stock in each company. A violation of § 1 was adjudged without reference to or a determination of the extent to which the traffic of the combined roads was still subject to some competition. It was enough that the two roads competed, that their competition was not insubstantial, and that the combination put an end to it. Id., at 326–328.

* * *

. . . Where, as here, the merging companies are major competitive factors in a relevant market, the elimination of significant competition between them constitutes a violation of § 1 of the Sherman Act. . . . *Reversed.*

The third and fourth cases in the group similarly involved expansive readings of the merger law, particularly with regard to market definition:

UNITED STATES v. ALUMINUM CO. OF AMERICA
377 U.S. 271 (1964).

JUSTICE DOUGLAS: * * *

. . . Admittedly, there is competition between insulated aluminum conductor and its copper counterpart, as the District Court found. Thus in 1959 insulated copper conductor comprised 22.8% of the gross additions to insulated overhead distribution lines. This is enough to justify grouping aluminum and copper conductors together in a single product market. Yet we conclude, contrary to the District Court, that that degree of competitiveness does not preclude their division for purposes of § 7 into separate submarkets, just as the existence of broad product markets in *Brown Shoe Co. v. United States*, 370 U.S. 294, did not preclude lesser submarkets.

Insulated aluminum conductor is so intrinsically inferior to insulated copper conductor that in most applications it has little consumer acceptance. But in the field of overhead distribution it enjoys decisive advantages—its share of total annual installations increasing from 6.5% in 1950 to 77.2% in 1959. In the field of overhead distribution the competition of copper is rapidly decreasing. As the record shows, utilizing a high-cost metal, fabricators of insulated copper conductor are powerless to eliminate the price disadvantage under which they labor and thus can do little to make their product competitive, unless they enter the aluminum field.

The price of most insulated aluminum conductors is indeed only 50% to 65% of the price of their copper counterparts; and the comparative installed costs are also generally less. As the District Court found, aluminum and copper conductor prices do not respond to one another.

Separation of insulated aluminum conductor from insulated copper conductor and placing it in another submarket is, therefore, proper. It is not inseparable from its copper equivalent though the class of customers is the same. The choice between copper and aluminum for overhead distribution does not usually turn on the quality of the respective products, for each does the job equally well. The vital factors are economic considerations. It is said, however, that we should put price aside and *Brown Shoe, supra,* is cited as authority. There the contention of the industry was that the District Court had delineated too broadly the relevant submarkets—men's shoes, women's shoes, and children's shoes—and should have subdivided them further. It was argued, for example, that men's shoes selling below $8.99 were in a different product market from those selling above $9. We declined to make price, particularly such small price differentials, the determinative factor in that market. A purchaser of shoes buys with an eye to his budget, to style, and to quality as well as to price. But here, where insulated aluminum conductor pricewise stands so distinctly apart, to ignore price in determining the relevant line of commerce is to ignore the single, most important, practical factor in the business.

The combination of bare and insulated aluminum conductor products into one market or line of commerce seems to us proper. Both types are used for the purpose of conducting electricity and are sold to the same customers, electrical utilities. While the copper conductor does compete with aluminum conductor, each has developed distinctive end uses—aluminum as an overhead conductor and copper for underground and indoor wiring, applications in which aluminum's brittleness and larger size render it impractical. And, as we have seen, the price differential further sets them apart.

Thus, contrary to the District Court, we conclude (1) that aluminum conductor and copper conductor are separable for the purpose of analyzing the competitive effect of the merger and (2) that aluminum conductor (bare and insulated) is therefore a submarket and for purposes of § 7 a "line of commerce."

Taking aluminum conductor as an appropriate "line of commerce" we conclude that the merger violated § 7.

Alcoa is a leader in markets in which economic power is highly concentrated. . . .

* * *

The acquisition of Rome added, it is said, only 1.3% to Alcoa's control of the aluminum conductor market. But in this setting that seems to us reasonably likely to produce a substantial lessening of competition within the meaning of § 7. It is the basic premise of that law that competition will be most vital "when there are many sellers, none of which has any significant market share." *United States v. Philadelphia National Bank,* 374 U.S., at 363. It would seem that the situation in the aluminum industry may be oligopolistic. As that condition develops, the greater is the likelihood that parallel policies of mutual advantage, not competition, will emerge. That tendency may well be thwarted by the presence of small but significant competitors. Though percentagewise Rome may have seemed small in the year prior to the merger, it ranked ninth among all companies and fourth among independents in the aluminum conductor market; and in the insulated aluminum field it ranked eighth and fourth respectively. Furthermore, in the aluminum conductor market, no more than a dozen companies could account for as much as 1% of industry production in any one of the five years (1955–1959) for which statistics appear in the record. Rome's competition was therefore substantial. The record shows indeed that Rome was an aggressive competitor. It was a pioneer in aluminum insulation and developed one of the most widely used insulated conductors. Rome had a broad line of high-quality copper wire and cable products in addition to its aluminum conductor business, a special aptitude and skill in insulation, and an active and efficient research and sales organization. The effectiveness of its marketing organization is shown by the fact that after the merger Alcoa made Rome the distributor of its entire conductor line. Preservation of Rome, rather than its absorption by one of the giants, will keep it "as an important competitive factor," to use the words of S.Rep. No. 1775, . . . p. 3. Rome seems to us the prototype of the small independent that Congress aimed to preserve by § 7.

* * *

In *United States v. Continental Can Company,* Continental Can, the second largest producer of metal containers with 33% of that market, acquired Hazel–Atlas Glass Company, the third largest producer of glass containers with 9.6% of that market. Continental Can was the second largest seller of glass and metal containers in the United States, and Hazel–Atlas was number six. Here are excerpts:

UNITED STATES v. CONTINENTAL CAN CO.
378 U.S. 441 (1964).

JUSTICE WHITE: * * * Since the purpose of delineating a line of commerce is to provide an adequate basis for measuring the effects of a given acquisition, its contours must, as nearly as possible, conform to competitive reality. Where the area of effective competition cuts across industry lines, so must the relevant line of commerce; otherwise an adequate determination of the merger's true impact cannot be made.

Based on the evidence thus far revealed by this record we hold that the interindustry competition between glass and metal containers is sufficient to warrant treating as a relevant product market the combined glass and metal container industries and all end uses for which they compete. There may be some end uses for which glass and metal do not and could not compete, but complete inter-industry competitive overlap need not be shown. We would not be true to the purpose of the Clayton Act's line of commerce concept as a framework within which to measure the effect of mergers on competition were we to hold that the existence of noncompetitive segments within a proposed market area precludes its being treated as a line of commerce.

This line of commerce was not pressed upon the District Court. However, since it is coextensive with the two industries, which were held to be lines of commerce, and since it is composed largely, if not entirely, of the more particularized end-use lines urged in the District Court by the Government, we see nothing to preclude us from reaching the question of its prima facie existence at this stage of the case.

Nor are we concerned by the suggestion that if the product market is to be defined in these terms it must include plastic, paper, foil and any other materials competing for the same business. That there may be a broader product market made up of metal, glass and other competing containers does not necessarily negative the existence of submarkets of cans, glass, plastic or cans and glass together, for "within this broad market, well-defined submarkets may exist which, in themselves, constitute product markets for antitrust purposes." *Brown Shoe Co. v. United States,* 370 U.S., at 325.

*   *   *

The evidence so far presented leads us to conclude that the merger between Continental and Hazel–Atlas is in violation of § 7. The product market embracing the combined metal and glass container industries was dominated by six firms having a total of 70.1% of the business. Continental, with 21.9% of the shipments, ranked second within this product market, and Hazel–Atlas, with 3.1%, ranked sixth. Thus, of this vast market—amounting at the time of the merger to almost $3 billion in annual sales—a large percentage already belonged to Continental before the merger. By the acquisition of Hazel–Atlas stock Continental not only increased its own share more than 14% from 21.9% to 25%, but also reduced from five to four the most significant competitors who might have threatened its dominant position. The resulting percentage of the combined firms approaches that held presumptively bad in *United States v. Philadelphia National Bank,* and is almost the same as that involved in *United States v. Aluminum Co. of America.* The incremental addition to the acquiring firm's share is considerably larger than in *Aluminum Co.* The case falls squarely within the principle that where there has been a "history of tendency toward concentration in the industry" tendencies toward further concentration "are to be curbed in their incipiency." *Brown Shoe Co. v. United States,* 370 U.S., at 345, 346. Where "concentration is already great, the importance of preventing even slight increases in concentration and so preserving the possibility of eventual deconcentration is correspondingly great." *United States v. Philadelphia National Bank,* 374 U.S. 321, 365, n. 42; *United States v. Aluminum Co. of America, supra.*

*   *   *

. . . . A merger between the second and sixth largest competitors in a gigantic line of commerce is significant not only for its intrinsic effect on competition but also for its tendency to endanger a much broader anticompetitive effect by triggering other mergers by companies seeking the same competitive advantages sought by Continental in this case. . . . .

. . . It is not at all self-evident that the lack of current competition between Continental and Hazel–Atlas for some important end uses of metal and glass containers significantly diminished the adverse effect of the merger on competition. Continental might have concluded that it could effectively insulate itself from competition by acquiring a major firm not presently directing its market acquisition efforts toward the same end uses as Continental, but possessing the potential to do so. Two examples will illustrate. Both soft drinks and baby food are currently packed predominantly in glass, but Continental has engaged in vigorous and imaginative promotional activities attempting to overcome consumer preferences for glass and secure a larger share of these two markets for its tin cans. Hazel–Atlas was not at the time of the merger a significant producer of either of these containers, but with comparatively little difficulty, if it were an independent firm making independent business judgments, it could have developed its soft drink and baby food capacity. . . .

We think our holding is consonant with the purpose of § 7 to arrest anticompetitive arrangements in their incipiency. Some product lines are offered in both metal and glass containers by the same packer. In such areas the interchangeability of use and immediate interindustry sensitivity to price changes would approach that which exists between products of the same industry. In other lines, as where one packer's products move in one type container while his competitor's move in another, there are inherent deterrents to customer diversion of the same type that might occur between brands of cans or bottles. But the possibility of such transfers over the long run acts as a deterrent against attempts by the dominant members of either industry to reap the possible benefits of their position by raising prices above the competitive level or engaging in other comparable practices. And even though certain lines are today regarded as safely within the domain of one or the other of these industries, this pattern may be altered, as it has been in the past. From the point of view not only of the static competitive situation but also the dynamic long-run potential, we think that the Government has discharged its burden of proving prima facie anticompetitive effect. Accordingly the judgment is reversed and the case remanded for further proceedings consistent with this opinion.

———

Von's Grocery Company was the second largest retail grocery store in Los Angeles, accounting for 4.7% of sales. It was located in the southern and western portion of Los Angeles. Shopping Bag Food Stores ranked sixth in the Los Angeles market. Situated in the northern and eastern portion of the city, it accounted for about 4.2% of sales in the Los Angeles retail grocery market. The leading firm had 8% of sales; the eighth largest accounted for 40.9%. Von's acquired Shopping Bag. In the eleven-year period before the merger, the number of single-store grocery firms in Los Angeles decreased from 5365 to 3818. Both merger partners were family-owned stores. The president and principal owner of Shopping Bag was old and was concerned that he did not have qualified executives to succeed him.

The government brought suit to challenge the merger, the district court dismissed the case, and the Supreme Court reversed, directing the district court to grant divestiture. *United States v. Von's Grocery Co.,* 384 U.S. 270 (1966). Justice Black, writing the opinion, stressed the intent of Congress to prevent a decline in the number of small businesses and to avert, in its incipiency, a trend towards concentration. The Court treated as irrelevant defendants' primary argument that "the Los Angeles grocery market was competitive before the merger, has been since, and may continue to be in the future." Id. at 278.

Justice Stewart dissented. He said that the competition in the grocery market was at a "pugnacious level." He saw small business as "strong and secure," especially in view of the spectacular growth of buying cooperatives. He thought it clear that there were "no substantial barriers to market entry." Id. at 299, 300. As for the law, Justice Stewart said:

> Section 7 was never intended by Congress for use by the Court as a charter to roll back the supermarket revolution. Yet the Court's opinion is hardly more than a requiem for the so-called "Mom and Pop" grocery stores—the bakery and butcher shops, the vegetable and fish markets— that are now economically and technologically obsolete in many parts of the country. No action by this Court can resurrect the old single-line Los Angeles food stores that have been run over by the automobile or obliterated by the freeway. . . .
>
> . . . The sole consistency that I can find is that in litigation under § 7, the Government always wins. 384 U.S. at 288, 301.

Questions and Comments

The markets involved in these mid–1960s cases range from highly concentrated with high barriers to entry (*El Paso*) to fragmented with low barriers (*Von's*). The cases came on the heels of *Brown Shoe* and *Philadelphia National Bank,* which involved, respectively, low and high concentration and barriers.

In which of the cases, beginning with *Brown Shoe,* could you plausibly infer that the merger would give the merged firm power (or greater power) to raise price and lower output? Which would create a risk of interdependent conduct that would lower output and raise price? Which would make overt cartelization easier or more likely? Which mergers were part of a trend that, if it continued, would have any of the above monopoly or cartel effects? In each case, suppose that all other competitors of a similar size paired off (an express concern of the Court in *Brown Shoe*); would the cartelization hypothesis or the interdependent output-reduction hypothesis become plausible?

In any of these cases, was the concern of the Court quite distinct from a fear of higher prices? Was the Court afraid that defendants would lower their prices and make it more difficult for small business to compete? Did any of the 1960s decisions prevent a merger that probably would have resulted in lower prices or other advantages for consumers?

Alcoa (Rome) and *Continental Can* turned largely on market definition. In *Alcoa (Rome)*, if copper had been included in the market, the shares would have been too insignificant to support an inference that competition might be lessened. What is the principle on which insulated copper conductor was excluded from the submarket approved by the Court? In *Continental Can,* by what principle were glass containers included in the market with metal containers? By what principle were paper and plastic containers excluded? If Continental had merged with National Can, how would the Court have defined the market? How would you define it?

Analyzing competitive effect in *Continental Can,* the Court relied on a theory of oligopolistic coordination. The Court pointed out that there was intense competition by metal can makers for end uses traditionally served by glass container makers, and vice versa. If Continental Can and Hazel–Atlas lessened their efforts to invade the end-use markets of one another, what would you expect to happen? Would elimination of this competition promote oligopolistic coordination and tend to raise price?

In *Von's,* the Court had a different concern: protecting small business. Did the Court's ruling in fact protect small business? Did the acquisition and others like it tend to harm small business? What inference do you draw from the fact that, over a period of 11 years, the number of single-store grocery firms in Los Angeles declined by 29%, from 5365 to 3818? During this period of time, local pedestrian shopping patterns changed; driving to the grocery store became routine. Might the vitality of retail competition have increased in spite of declining atomism? Is there a minimum number, more or less, of grocery stores or supermarkets needed to assure healthy competition? Would the Von's merger have reduced the number of competitors in the Los Angeles market to a level of concern?

By 1987 Von's operated 183 supermarkets in Southern California. It then acquired 172 Safeway supermarkets in Southern California. This acquisition was approved by the FTC subject to the divestiture of overlapping stores. In 1988 American Stores, also a leading supermarket chain in California and in Los Angeles, with 240 Alpha Beta supermarkets in California, proposed to acquire Lucky Stores, owner of 340 California discount supermarkets. As a result of the acquisition, American/Lucky would become number one with almost 25% of the Los Angeles retail supermarket market, and the top four firms would have almost 75% of the market. The large grocery chains asserted that supermarketing was fiercely competitive and that the merger gave them efficiencies in warehousing which would be reflected in lower supermarket prices. Is an American/Lucky consolidation likely to increase or lessen competition? Assume that there are significant warehousing efficiencies. Would the consolidation be likely to lead to higher or lower prices? Does it depend upon the magnitude of the efficiencies? Does it depend upon whether the warehousing efficiencies are available to small competitors through joint ventures? Does it depend upon whether sites are available in particular neighborhoods (defined by convenient driving distances?) for other supermarkets to move in?

The Federal Trade Commission provisionally approved the American/Lucky acquisition, subject to minimal divestiture and the merger was consummated. The Attorney General of California, maintaining that the acquisition would confer market power and raise supermarket prices, sued in federal court for a violation of Section 7 (thus challenging the effectiveness of federal enforcement). The federal district court entered a preliminary injunction. *California v. American Stores Co.,* 697 F.Supp. 1125 (C.D.Cal.1988). On appeal, the Ninth Circuit held that California had established a prima facie violation of Clayton § 7 and that, had it sued before the merger was consummated it would have been entitled to preliminary relief; however, once the merger is effectuated private parties are not entitled to divestiture under

§ 16. 56 ATRR No. 1411 at 493 (Filed March 31, 1989). (Does the state have power to challenge (in effect) the FTC's evaluation of the merger? [12] How can it be that the expert analysts at the FTC thought prices would go down and the expert analysts at the California Attorney General's Office thought prices would go up?)

As you can see from *Brown Shoe* and *Von's,* and as you will see in *Procter and Gamble,* infra at 815, the Warren Court interpreted the merger law as incompatible with an efficiencies defense. Indeed, efficiencies were treated as a negative factor if they fueled a drive towards concentration and "bigness." There came a time when efficiencies would be affirmatively considered as a positive factor in merger analysis, at least if they did not create or aggravate market power and would be passed on to consumers. But long before that time the Court gave serious attention to a defense at the other end of the spectrum—the failing condition of the acquired firm.

a. The Failing Firm Defense

CITIZEN PUBLISHING COMPANY v. UNITED STATES

394 U.S. 131 (1969).

JUSTICE DOUGLAS: [In 1940, the Citizen and the Star, the only two daily newspapers in Tucson, entered into a joint operating agreement providing for joint sale of advertising, joint distribution of the newspapers, and pooling of profits. As extended, the agreement was to run for 50 years. Prior to the joint operating agreement, the Citizen had annual losses of about $23,500. It owed $79,000 to its stockholders for advances of working capital, and its liabilities exceeded its assets by more than $53,000. Some years after the agreement was renewed, Citizen's shareholders acquired the stock of the Star.

The Court held that the agreement involved price fixing and profit pooling illegal per se under Section 1 of the Sherman Act.] * * *

The only real defense of appellants was the "failing company" defense—a judicially created doctrine. The facts tendered were excluded on the § 1 charge but were admitted on the § 2 charge as well as on the § 7 charge under the Clayton Act. So whether or not the District Court was correct in excluding the evidence under the § 1 charge, it is now before us; and a consideration of it makes plain that the requirements of the failing company doctrine were not met. That defense was before the Court in *International Shoe Co. v. FTC,* 280 U.S. 291, where § 7 of the Clayton Act was in issue. The evidence showed that the resources of one company were so depleted and the prospect of rehabilitation so remote that "it faced the grave probability of a business failure." 280 U.S., at 302.

---

12. Dual federal/state enforcement raises complex preemption issues. In *Illinois Brick Co. v. Illinois,* 431 U.S. 720 (1977) the Court, in the interest of simplifying litigation, protecting defendants against duplicative damage awards, and enhancing deterrence, held that even when all or part of a cartelist's illegal overcharge is passed on to downstream buyers, the first purchaser may nevertheless recover treble damages and downstream buyers may not recover. Several states responded by passing statutes authorizing downstream buyers who could prove passing on to recover under state law. In *California v. ARC America,* ___ U.S. ___ (1989) the Court held that these state statutes were not preempted by the *Illinois Brick* rule even though a violator may now end up paying treble damages twice over, once under federal law to the first purchasers, once under state law to those to whom the overcharge was passed on.

There was, moreover, "no other prospective purchaser." *Ibid.* It was in that setting that the Court held that the acquisition of that company by another did not substantially lessen competition within the meaning of § 7. 280 U.S., at 302–303.

In the present case the District Court found:

"At the time Star Publishing and Citizen Publishing entered into the operating agreement, and at the time the agreement became effective, Citizen Publishing was not then on the verge of going out of business, nor was there a serious probability at that time that Citizen Publishing would terminate its business and liquidate its assets unless Star Publishing and Citizen Publishing entered into the operating agreement." 280 F.Supp., at 980.

The evidence sustains that finding. There is no indication that the owners of the Citizen were contemplating a liquidation. They never sought to sell the Citizen and there is no evidence that the joint operating agreement was the last straw at which the Citizen grasped. Indeed the Citizen continued to be a significant threat to the Star. How otherwise is one to explain the Star's willingness to enter into an agreement to share its profits with the Citizen? Would that be true if as now claimed the Citizen was on the brink of collapse?

The failing company doctrine plainly cannot be applied in a merger or in any other case unless it is established that the company that acquires the failing company or brings it under dominion is the only available purchaser. For if another person or group could be interested, a unit in the competitive system would be preserved and not lost to monopoly power. So even if we assume, *arguendo,* that in 1940 the then owners of the Citizen could not long keep the enterprise afloat, no effort was made to sell the Citizen; its properties and franchise were not put in the hands of a broker; and the record is silent on what the market, if any, for the Citizen might have been.

Moreover, we know from the broad experience of the business community since 1930, the year when the *International Shoe* case was decided, that companies reorganized through receivership, or through Chapter X or Chapter XI of the Bankruptcy Act often emerged as strong competitive companies. The prospects of reorganization of the Citizen in 1940 would have had to be dim or nonexistent to make the failing company doctrine applicable to this case.

The burden of proving that the conditions of the failing company doctrine have been satisfied is on those who seek refuge under it. That burden has not been satisfied in this case.

* * *

[The Court affirmed the district court's judgment requiring the Citizen to divest itself of the Star and to reestablish the Star as an independent competitor, while permitting continuance of the joint operating agreement without its illegal restrictions.] [13]

13. In 1970, Congress passed the Newspaper Preservation Act, 15 U.S.C. §§ 1801 et seq., authorizing the Attorney General of the United States to grant a limited exemption from the antitrust laws for a joint operating agreement between two newspapers, at least one of which is "in probable danger of financial failure," if approval would save failing newspapers whose editorial and reportorial independence can be maintained. For a recent and controversial exercise of such authority by Attorney General Edwin Meese,

Questions and Comments

Might a merger lessen competition even though the failing firm would otherwise disappear from the market? Consider the following situations. In each would a failing company defense be good for consumers? Would it otherwise be good for society?

1. Shopping Bag Food Stores is on the brink of bankruptcy. No firm but Von's is interested in acquiring it as a going concern, and successful reorganization through bankruptcy proceedings seems unlikely.

2. Chrysler is again on the brink of bankruptcy and General Motors is its only available savior. (This time the U.S. Government adamantly refuses to aid Chrysler with loans).

3. The same facts as in (2) except that, if General Motors does not buy Chrysler, the Japanese firm, Nissan, will bid for its more efficient plants; other Chrysler facilities will be withdrawn from auto production.

2. MID–1970S AND ONWARDS—IMPORTANT CHANGES

Merger law was by no means fixed in place by the mid 1960s. In 1974 the new antitrust majority emerged on the Supreme Court. The majority's style of analysis, and the law itself, began to change. The first acquiring firm to get the benefit of the change was General Dynamics. General Dynamics' case was a sympathetic one. United Electric, one of the acquired firms, was in financial straits (although not on the brink of bankruptcy); the coal industry was besieged by competition from other sources of energy, and the fact-finder had found that the challenged acquisitions would not lessen competition.

UNITED STATES v. GENERAL DYNAMICS CORPORATION

415 U.S. 486 (1974).

JUSTICE STEWART: [General Dynamics Corporation and its predecessor, Material Service, acquired the stock of two major Illinois coal producers, Freeman Coal Mining Corporation and United Electric Companies. In a suit by the Government charging that the acquisition violated Section 7 of the Clayton Act, the district court found no violation, and dismissed the case.]. . . .

* * *

The Government sought to prove a violation of § 7 of the Clayton Act principally through statistics showing that within certain geographic markets the coal industry was concentrated among a small number of large producers; that this concentration was increasing; and that the acquisition of United Electric would materially enlarge the market share

see In re Application by Detroit Free Press, 55 Antitrust & Trade Reg.Rep. (BNA) No. 257, Aug. 11, 1988. An application for exemption was submitted by the Detroit Free Press and The Detroit News, owned respectively by Gannett Company and Knight–Ridder, Inc., the country's first and second largest newspaper chains. Attorney General Meese approved the application despite negative recommendations by the Antitrust Division and by an administrative law judge. Michigan Citizens for an Independent Press challenged the Attorney General's authority in federal court, and the challenge is pending at the time this book goes to press.

of the acquiring company and thereby contribute to the trend toward concentration.

The concentration of the coal market in Illinois and, alternatively, in the Eastern Interior Coal Province [a group of eight states including Illinois and Indiana] was demonstrated by a table of the shares of the largest two, four, and 10 coal-producing firms in each of these areas for both 1957 and 1967 [the year in which the Government sued] that revealed the following:

	Eastern Interior Coal Province		Illinois	
	1957	1967	1957	1967
Top 2 firms	29.6	48.6	37.8	52.9
Top 4 firms	43.0	62.9	54.5	75.2
Top 10 firms	65.5	91.4	84.0	98.0

These statistics, the Government argued, showed not only that the coal industry was concentrated among a small number of leading producers, but that the trend had been toward increasing concentration. Furthermore, the undisputed fact that the number of coal-producing firms in Illinois decreased almost 73% during the period of 1957 to 1967 from 144 to 39 was claimed to be indicative of the same trend. The acquisition of United Electric by Material Service resulted in increased concentration of coal sales among the leading producers in the areas chosen by the Government, as shown by the following table:

	1959			1967		
	Share of top 2 but for merger	Share of top 2 given merger	Percent increase	Share of top 2 but for merger	Share of top 2 given merger	Percent increase
Province	33.1	37.9	14.5	45.0	48.6	8.0
Illinois	36.6	44.3	22.4	44.0	52.9	20.2

Finally, the Government's statistics indicated that the acquisition increased the share of the merged company in the Illinois and Eastern Interior Coal Province coal markets by significant degrees:

	Province		Illinois	
	Rank	Share (percent)	Rank	Share (percent)
1959				
Freeman	2	7.6	2	15.1
United Electric	6	4.8	5	8.1
Combined	2	12.4	1	23.2
1967				
Freeman	5	6.5	2	12.9
United Electric	9	4.4	6	8.9
Combined	2	10.9	2	21.8

In prior decisions involving horizontal mergers between competitors, this Court has found prima facie violations of § 7 of the Clayton Act from aggregate statistics of the sort relied on by the United States in this case. In *Brown Shoe Co. v. United States,* 370 U.S. 294, the Court reviewed the legislative history of the most recent amendments to the Act and found that "[t]he dominant theme pervading congressional consideration of the 1950 amendments was a fear of what was considered to be a rising tide of economic concentration in the American economy." *Id.,* at 315. A year later, in *United States v. Philadelphia National Bank,* 374 U.S. 321, the Court clarified the relevance of a statistical demonstration of concentration in a particular industry and of the effects thereupon of a merger or acquisition with the following language:

> "This intense congressional concern with the trend toward concentration warrants dispensing, in certain cases, with elaborate proof of market structure, market behavior, or probable anticompetitive effects. Specifically, we think that a merger which produces a firm controlling an undue percentage share of the relevant market, and results in a significant increase in the concentration of firms in that market, is so inherently likely to lessen competition substantially that it must be enjoined in the absence of evidence clearly showing that the merger is not likely to have such anticompetitive effects." *Id.,* at 363.

The effect of adopting this approach to a determination of a "substantial" lessening of competition is to allow the Government to rest its case on a showing of even small increases of market share or market concentration in those industries or markets where concentration is already great or has been recently increasing, since "if concentration is already great, the importance of preventing even slight increases in concentration and so preserving the possibility of eventual deconcentration is correspondingly great." *United States v. Aluminum Co. of America,* 377 U.S. 271, 279, citing *United States v. Philadelphia National Bank, supra,* at 365 n. 42.

While the statistical showing proffered by the Government in this case, the accuracy of which was not discredited by the District Court or contested by the appellees, would under this approach have sufficed to support a finding of "undue concentration" in the absence of other considerations, the question before us is whether the District Court was justified in finding that other pertinent factors affecting the coal industry and the business of the appellees mandated a conclusion that no substantial lessening of competition occurred or was threatened by the acquisition of United Electric. We are satisfied that the court's ultimate finding was not in error. . . .

Much of the District Court's opinion was devoted to a description of the changes that have affected the coal industry since World War II. On the basis of more than three weeks of testimony and a voluminous record, the court discerned a number of clear and significant developments in the industry. First, it found that coal had become increasingly less able to compete with other sources of energy in many segments of the energy market. Following the War the industry entirely lost its largest single purchaser of coal—the railroads—and faced increasingly stiffer competition from oil and natural gas as sources of energy for industrial and residential uses. Because of these changes in consumption patterns, coal's share of the energy resources consumed in this country fell from 78.4% in 1920 to 21.4% in 1968. The court reviewed evidence attributing this decline not only to the changing relative economics of alternative fuels and to new distribution and consumption patterns, but also to more recent concern with the effect of coal use on the environment and consequent regulation of the extent and means of such coal consumption.

Second, the court found that to a growing extent since 1954, the electric utility industry has become the mainstay of coal consumption. While electric utilities consumed only 15.76% of the coal produced nationally in 1947, their share of total consumption increased every year thereafter, and in 1968 amounted to more than 59% of all the coal consumed throughout the Nation.

Third, and most significantly, the court found that to an increasing degree, nearly all coal sold to utilities is transferred under long-term requirements contracts, under which coal producers promise to meet utilities' coal consumption requirements for a fixed period of time, and at predetermined prices. The court described the mutual benefits accruing to both producers and consumers of coal from such long-term contracts. . . .

These developments in the patterns of coal distribution and consumption, the District Court found, have limited the amounts of coal immediately available for "spot" purchases on the open market, since "[t]he growing practice by coal producers of expanding mine capacity only to meet long-term contractual commitments and the gradual disappearance of the small truck mines has tended to limit the production capacity available for spot sales." *Ibid.*

Because of these fundamental changes in the structure of the market for coal, the District Court was justified in viewing the statistics relied on by the Government as insufficient to sustain its case. Evidence of past production does not, as a matter of logic, necessarily give a proper picture of a company's future ability to compete. In most situations, of course, the unstated assumption is that a company that has maintained a certain share of a market in the recent past will be in a position to do so in the immediate future. Thus, companies that have controlled sufficiently large shares of a concentrated market are barred from merger by § 7, not because of their past acts, but because their past performances imply an ability to continue to dominate with at least equal vigor. In markets involving groceries or beer, as in *Von's Grocery*, [384 U.S. 270] and *Pabst*, [384 U.S. 546] statistics involving annual sales naturally indicate the power of each company to compete in the future. Evidence of the amount of annual sales is relevant as a prediction of future competitive strength, since in most markets distribution systems and brand recognition are such significant factors that one may reasonably suppose that a company which has attracted a given number of sales will retain that competitive strength.

In the coal market, as analyzed by the District Court, however, statistical evidence of coal *production* was of considerably less significance. The bulk of the coal produced is delivered under long-term requirements contracts, and such sales thus do not represent the exercise of competitive power but rather the obligation to fulfill previously negotiated contracts at a previously fixed price. The focus of competition in a given time frame is not on the disposition of coal already produced but on the procurement of new long-term supply contracts. In this situation, a company's past ability to produce is of limited significance, since it is in a position to offer for sale neither its past production nor the bulk of the coal it is presently capable of producing, which is typically already committed under a long-term supply contract. A more significant indicator of a company's power effectively to compete with other companies lies in the state of a company's uncommitted reserves of recoverable coal. A company with relatively large supplies of coal which are not already under contract to a consumer will have a more important influence upon competition in the contemporaneous negotiation of supply contracts than a firm with small reserves, even though the latter may presently produce a greater tonnage of coal. In a market where the availability and price of coal are set by long-term contracts rather than immediate or short-term purchases and sales, reserves rather than past production are the best measure of a company's ability to compete.

The testimony and exhibits in the District Court revealed that United Electric's coal reserve prospects were "unpromising." 341 F.Supp., at 559. United's relative position of strength in reserves was considerably weaker than its past and current ability to produce. While United ranked fifth among Illinois coal producers in terms of annual production, it was 10th in reserve holdings, and controlled less than 1% of the reserves held by coal producers in Illinois, Indiana, and western Kentucky. *Id.*, at 538. Many of the reserves held by United had already been depleted at the time of trial, forcing the closing of some of United's midwest mines. Even more significantly, the District Court found that of the 52,033,304 tons of currently mineable reserves in Illinois, Indiana, and Kentucky controlled by United, only four million tons had not already been committed under long-term contracts. United was found to be facing the future with relatively depleted resources at its disposal, and with the vast majority of those resources already committed under contracts allowing no further adjustment in price. In addition, the District Court found that "United Electric has neither the possibility of acquiring more [reserves] nor the ability to develop deep coal reserves," and thus was not in a position to increase its reserves to replace those already depleted or committed. *Id.*, at 560.

Viewed in terms of present and future reserve prospects—and thus in terms of probable future ability to compete—rather than in terms of past production, the District Court held that United Electric was a far less significant factor in the coal market than the Government contended or the production statistics seemed to indicate. While the company had been and remained a "highly profitable" and efficient producer of relatively large amounts of coal, its current and future power to compete for subsequent long-term contracts was severely limited by its scarce uncommitted resources. Irrespective of the company's size when viewed as a producer, its weakness as a competitor was properly analyzed by the District Court and fully substantiated that court's conclusion that its acquisition by Material Service would not "substantially . . . lessen competition. . . ."

JUSTICE DOUGLAS, joined by JUSTICES BRENNAN, WHITE and MARSHALL, dissented. They said: "[T]he judgment may not be affirmed except on a deep-seated judicial bias against § 7 of the Clayton Act."

Questions and Comments

What is the holding of *General Dynamics*? Does the Court apply the law as previously formulated by the Supreme Court? Note that the Court not only reaffirmed *Philadelphia National Bank*'s presumptive rule but also indicated that concentration figures of the level presented by the government in *General Dynamics* were normally adequate to invoke that rule.

The Court was swayed by United Electric's weak reserve position. Did the Court accept a watered-down "failing company" defense? Or was the Court merely unconvinced by the reliability of the plaintiff's statistics as proxies for future performance?

After *General Dynamics,* Supreme Court decisions in other areas of antitrust law began to reflect a more skeptical approach to antitrust. The Court expressed a heightened and more narrowly focused concern with market impact, often defined in terms of output limitation. Recall, for example *Continental T.V., Inc. v. GTE Sylvania Inc.,* 433 U.S. 36 (1977), *Broadcast Music, Inc. v. Columbia Broadcasting System, Inc.,* 441 U.S. 1 (1979), and *NCAA v. Board of Regents,* 468 U.S. 85 (1984), *supra* pp. 606, 316 and 334. Do these cases help you predict future Supreme Court merger law? In view of *GTE Sylvania* and *BMI,* would merging defendants overcome a presumption of illegality by proof that the merger would not give defendants power over price? Even if a merger would increase market power, would defendant prevail by proving that the merger would also increase productive efficiency and would result in a net resource savings? Would defendant prevail by proving that the merger would result in cost-savings that would make the merger partners better able to wage competition? Does the language or legislative history of Section 7 stand in the way of any of these defenses?

3. CURRENT MERGER ENFORCEMENT

a. The Justice Department Guidelines

We mentioned above the Reagan administration's 1982 and 1984 merger guidelines. The 1984 version appears in Appendix B.[14] The key to the Justice Department's merger guidelines is market definition. We begin with a discussion of market definition, and then proceed to discuss how, under the guidelines, one assesses whether the merger lessens competition in the relevant market.

To define the product or service market, begin, as a hypothesis, with the smallest plausible market. Thus, in a hypothetical merger of Clorox and Purex (both household liquid bleach companies), one would begin with

14. For an analysis of the Justice Department guidelines and a somewhat similar FTC statement on horizontal mergers, see 2 Fox and Fox, Corporate Acquisitions & Mergers, Ch. 22 (1988). For a number of excellent critiques and analyses of the guidelines, see Symposium, 1982 Merger Guidelines, 71 Calif.L.Rev. 280 (1983).

household liquid bleach as a provisional product market and hypothesize only one producer of household liquid bleach. Are there any other products (say, powdered bleach) that, at current prices, consumers regard as a good substitute for liquid bleach? If so, add these to the market. Next, assume that the sole producer of the provisional relevant product (household bleach) tests its market power by raising price 5% or 10% above current price.[15] Now, include in the product market not only household liquid bleach and products that consumers find to be good substitutes at the current price, but also those products that become good substitutes at the new elevated price. (In the hypothetical, if powdered bleach is not perceived as a good substitute at current prices, it may become a good substitute as the price of liquid bleach rises). Next, identify all firms that produce the relevant product. Also identify all firms whose production and distribution facilities can easily be adjusted to do so (perhaps, makers of industrial bleaches). All of these firms will be included in the market. Those making the relevant product and good substitutes at current prices are normally counted in terms of their sales or capacity. Firms that would have to adjust facilities or methods to enter the market would be counted in terms of the amount of relevant product they are likely to add to the market if price should rise by the hypothesized increment, or the capacity likely to be used for producing the product in the event of the assumed price rise.

Geographic market is similarly delineated. Begin with the locations of each merging firm. Identify the geographic area that delimits the firms with whom they now compete. Assume a monopolist in this area, and then assume a hypothetical 5% to 10% price rise. Will so many buyers shift to producers selling from other locations in response to the price rise? If so, include those other locations. Also, will firms now distributing outside the area start distributing in the area? If so, include them. In our case of household bleach, we will quickly reach the boundaries of the United States. The guidelines state that foreign locations may be included, and indeed some markets may in theory be international markets. However, especially in view of trade barriers and the reality that there are few free international markets, it is more common to measure foreign competition by accepting the geographic limits of the United States and counting as within the U.S. market all product that flows into the United States and all product likely to do so in response to the hypothesized price increase.

After the market has been defined and a market share has been assigned to each firm therein, one must measure concentration. Prior to 1982, concentration was normally measured by taking, for example, the top 2, 4 or 8 firms in the market and observing what percentage of the market they accounted for. This resulted in 2–firm, 4–firm, and 8–firm concentration ratios. If the top four firms accounted for 75% of the market and upwards, we said that the market was concentrated. The

15. The guidelines state that 5% will normally be used as the hypothetical price rise. However, by the end of the Reagan administration the current practice of the Justice Department was to use 10%. As you can see, the higher the percentage, the larger will be the market and the lower will be the market shares of merging competitors, because more potential competition will be counted in the market.

1982 and 1984 guidelines measure concentration, instead, by use of an index called the Herfindahl–Hirshman Index. The index is computed by squaring the market share of each firm and then adding up the resulting numbers. As a result of squaring each firm's share, the index reflects the relative size of each firm in the market. An HHI of 1000 or less, which is the HHI for 10 equal-sized firms ($10 \times 10 = 100$; 100 ten times = 1000) is regarded by the guidelines as describing a market too fragmented to worry about. A merger producing an HHI of 1000 would thus be ignored by the enforcement authorities. (Should it be, necessarily? Would such a merger be trivial if your only concern was whether the remaining firms could successfully cartelize? Might you need to know more industry-specific facts? Would it be relevant in analyzing an oil merger, for example, that there are "honeycombs" of joint venture relationships between and among the oil companies?)

The guidelines call "moderately concentrated" a market having an HHI of 1000 to 1800. They state that the Department is likely to challenge a merger that yields concentration in this range if the merger increases the HHI by more than 100 points, unless the Department concludes that the merger is not likely to lessen competition in view of obstacles to collusion,[16] ease of entry, and efficiencies. (A merger of a 7% and 8% firm would produce an increase in the HHI of more than 100. The increase resulting from a merger can be calculated by multiplying the shares of the two firms and multiplying the product by 2; thus, $7 \times 8 \times 2 = 112$.)

The guidelines call "highly concentrated" a market having an HHI of more than 1800. (Five equal-sized firms have an HHI of 2000; six equal-sized firms have an HHI of 1666.6.) The guidelines state that the Department is likely to challenge a merger that yields concentration of more than 1800 if the merger produces an increase of more than 50 points (a merger of two 5% firms increases the HHI by 50 points; $5 \times 5 \times 2$), unless it concludes that the merger is not likely to lessen competition. The guidelines further state that if the increase is more than 100 points and the post merger HHI substantially exceeds 1800, "only in extraordinary cases" will other factors establish that the merger is not likely substantially to lessen competition.

The guidelines have a "leading firm" proviso, stating that the Department is likely to challenge a merger involving a leading firm that has 35% or more of the market and is at least twice as large as the next largest firm, and a partner with at least 1% or more of the market. This proviso is meant to address the monopoly model; the other portions relate largely to the oligopoly-collusion model.

---

16. In determining likelihood of collusion (or of more effective collusion), the Department will consider all factors that make collusion easier or more profitable, or that make cheating more detectable (*e.g.*, homogeneous product, available detailed information about specific transactions, a large gap between the relevant product and the next best substitute). It will consider, also, factors that make collusion harder or less profitable (*e.g.*, significant foreign producers, big buyers) and all factors that make cheating from a cartel more tempting (*e.g.*, big buyers) and more easily concealed (*e.g.*, little available information about specific transactions).

The guidelines state that the guideline thresholds generally allow firms to realize all available efficiencies. Indeed, the policy behind the guidelines would encourage efficiency-producing mergers. To recognize this policy but to guard against "soft" justifications of anticompetitive mergers, the Department states that it will consider efficiencies "[i]f the parties to the merger establish by clear and convincing evidence that a merger will achieve such efficiencies" and "equivalent or comparable savings can[not] reasonably be achieved by the parties through other means."

While the Reagan Justice Department seldom found an efficiency justification, it also seldom found an anticompetitive merger. At least in the Reagan years, the Department almost never challenged a merger unless the HHI was well above 2000; and even then it rarely found that entry barriers were sufficiently high to "worry" about market failures serious enough to justify government intervention.

We suggest that you study the guidelines themselves; see Appendix B. Among other things, they explain the Herfindahl–Hirshman Index (HHI) and how to use it. The following notations on the mechanics of applying the index may reinforce what the guidelines teach about the HHI:

1. Computing the HHI: Assume a four-firm market with firm shares of 40%, 30%, 20%, and 10%. The 20% and 10% firms merge.

    a. Post-merger HHI:

$$
\begin{aligned}
40^2 &= 1600 \\
30^2 &= 900 \\
30^2 &= \underline{900} \\
\text{HHI} \quad &\;\; 3400
\end{aligned}
$$

    b. The increase in the HHI as a result of the merger:

Either compute the premerger HHI and subtract this figure from the post-merger HHI:

$$
\begin{aligned}
40^2 &= 1600 \\
30^2 &= 900 \\
20^2 &= 400 \\
10^2 &= \underline{100} \\
\text{HHI} \quad &\;\; 3000
\end{aligned}
$$

$$
\begin{aligned}
3400 &\text{ post merger HHI} \\
\underline{-3000} &\text{ premerger HHI} \\
400 &\text{ increase}
\end{aligned}
$$

Or, multiply the shares of the merging firms and multiply the product by 2:

$$20 \times 10 \times 2 = 400$$

Note the limiting cases:

    a. The highest possible HHI is the monopoly situation:

Single firm market: $100^2 = 10,000$ HHI

    b. A highly fragmented market has an insignificant HHI:

Assume a 200–firm market, each firm with .5%:

      i. $.5^2 = .25 \times 200 = 50$ HHI

      ii. Because the square of any number less than one is always lower than the number being squared, if no firm in a market has one or more percent, the HHI will be less than 100.

3. Note that the HHI differs from the 4–, 8–, or 10–firm concentration ratio in that the HHI gives significance to the way size is distributed in the market.

    a. The following three markets all yield a four-firm concentration ratio of 85%:

        i. A 65% firm, a 10% firm, two 5% firms and a scattering of very small firms;

        ii. A 40% firm, three 15% firms, and a scattering of very small ones;

        iii. A 25% firm, three 20% firms, and a scattering of very small ones.

    b. However, they yield very different HHI's:

        i. $65^2 = 4225$

          $10^2 = 100$

          $5^2 = 25$

          $5^2 = \underline{25}$

        HHI 4375

        ii. $40^2 = 1600$

          $15^2 = 225$

          $15^2 = 225$

          $15^2 = \underline{225}$

        HHI 2275

        iii. $25^2 = 625$

          $20^2 = 400$

          $20^2 = 400$

          $20^2 = \underline{400}$

        HHI 1825

Very small firms are normally not reflected in the calculations because they yield insignificant numbers. One squared is only one.

Questions and Comments

The 1984 Justice Department guidelines on market definition and on horizontal merger standards are not wholly consistent with the case law. What are the major differences? Are the guidelines consistent with your view of appropriate policy?

Suppose there are three major copper producers, each having 30% of the market. They are pricing at supracompetitive levels but just below the point that would trigger a massive invasion by aluminum sellers. There are 19 aluminum producers, each equal in size to the three copper producers. Two of the copper producers propose to merge. Can they do so under the guidelines? Can they do so under the case law? Is there any sound economic reason to prevent their merger? Would there be a sound economic basis to ban the merger if we do not know whether the copper producers are pricing at supracompetitive levels?

Making some educated guesses about facts, which of the following mergers would probably be objectionable under the guidelines:

Brown Shoe–Kinney (horizontal aspects)
Philadelphia National Bank–Girard Bank
El Paso–Pacific Northwest
Alcoa–Rome
Continental Can–Hazel Atlas
Von's Grocery–Shopping Bag?

If any one of these mergers is probably objectionable under the guidelines, why? As to those that appear competitively beneficial or neutral under the guidelines, explain.

The guidelines define markets in terms of how trade would flow if the merging parties and their current competitors were to raise prices and sustain the increase for a significant period. Many jurists, however, continue to take "snapshots" of markets; they look at trade patterns as they are. Even using the snapshot approach, one may, and courts normally do, take into account market forces that would put a lid on price if price were to be artifically raised. Thus, whether you use one, the other, or both models for market definition, you can take account of potential competition.

Contrary to the approach of cases such as *Von's* and *Brown Shoe,* contemporary cases give importance to facts tending to show that competition is dynamic and is likely to remain so, despite high concentration. The continuing dynamism of competition is sometimes a function of foreign competition, and it is sometimes a function of low entry barriers. See, e.g., *United States v. Waste Management, Inc.,* 743 F.2d 976 (2d Cir. 1984); *Stroh Brewery Co. v. Malmgren,* 1982–1 Trade Cas. (CCH) ¶ 64,670 (W.D.Wis.1982).

b. *Proposals for Legislative Change*

Introduction of guidelines was one way in which Reagan administration officials attempted to change the law. The administration was active also in Congress. It introduced legislation to amend Section 7 of the Clayton Act. The present language forbids a merger the effect of which "may be substantially to lessen competition, or to tend to create a monopoly." The "Merger Modernization" bill would substitute language making an acquisition unlawful only if "there is a significant probability" that it will "increase the ability to exercise market power." According to Judge Ginsburg (then head of the Antitrust Division), the purpose of this change was "to make explicit . . . the distinction between procompetitive, efficiency-enhancing mergers on the one hand, and mergers that create a significant probability of increasing prices to consumers on the other." Ginsburg, The Reagan Administration's Legislative Initiative in Antitrust, 31 Antitrust Bull. 851, 853 (1987). Is there such a clear dichotomy? Would such a change be a move in the right direction? Would the language of the bill accomplish the result envisaged?

c. Policing the Current Merger Movement

In the decade of the 1980s, the number of mergers has increased dramatically. In 1984 there were 21,543 mergers aggregating $122.2 billion in value. Mergers of firms valued at greater than $100 million increased from 94 in 1980 to 200 in 1984. Despite this surge, the federal government has challenged only a handful of mergers each year. The mammoth LTV–Republic steel merger was challenged but the case was immediately settled on terms that required a partial spin off. See *United States v. LTV Corp.,* 1984–1 Trade Cas. (CCH) ¶ 66,133 (D.D.C.1984). The GM–Toyota joint venture was approved by the FTC on conditions that the joint venture welcomed. See p. 1174 infra. Major airline mergers such as Northwest–Republic, although opposed by the Department of Justice, were cleared by the Department of Transportation. See Fox and Sullivan, supra note 10, 62 N.Y.U.L.Rev. at 950. Large horizontal oil mergers were virtually ignored by the enforcement agencies. See Pertschuk Report, for Subcommittee on Oversight and Investigations of the Committee on Energy and Commerce, H.Rep., 98th Cong., 2d Sess. (Sept.1984). In consequence, there is very little current case law.

In addition to slowing down the pace of enforcement, the government, as amicus, has challenged the standing of competitors who sue. It has done so with some success. Private plaintiffs, the one time safety valve, now have a difficult time proving antitrust injury sufficient to give them standing to stay in court. See *Cargill Inc. v. Monfort of Colorado,* 479 U.S. 104 (1986), infra at 859.

Nonetheless, here are two recent horizontal merger cases in which one of the enforcement agencies challenged a merger and prevailed. One victory was in view of "moderate" Chicago School economics; [17] the other victory was in spite of Chicago School economics.

HOSPITAL CORP. OF AMERICA v. FTC
807 F.2d 1381 (7th Cir.1986), *cert. denied,* 481 U.S. 1038 (1987).

JUDGE POSNER: Hospital Corporation of America, the largest proprietary hospital chain in the United States, asks us to set aside the decision by the Federal Trade Commission that it violated section 7 of the Clayton Act by the acquisition in 1981 and 1982 of two corporations, Hospital Affiliates International, Inc. and Health Care Corporation. Before these acquisitions (which cost Hospital Corporation almost $700 million), Hospital Corporation had owned one hospital in Chattanooga, Tennessee. The acquisitions gave it ownership of two more. In addition, pursuant to the terms of the acquisitions it assumed contracts, both with four-year terms, that Hospital Affiliates International had made to manage two other Chattanooga-area hospitals. So after the acquisitions Hospital Corporation owned or managed 5 of the 11 hospitals in the area. Later one of the management contracts was cancelled; and one of the lesser issues raised by Hospital Corporation, which we might as well dispose of right now, is whether the Commission should have disregarded the assumption of that

---

17. In a more extreme form of Chicago School economics, such as that reflected by Judge Bork and Professor Harold Demsetz, the analyst is so skeptical of the collusion hypothesis that he or she draws no negative inference from high concentration.

contract. We agree with the Commission that it was not required to take account of a post-acquisition transaction that may have been made to improve Hospital Corporation's litigating position. The contract was cancelled after the Commission began investigating Hospital Corporation's acquisition of Hospital Affiliates, and while the initiative in cancelling was taken by the managed hospital, Hospital Corporation reacted with unaccustomed mildness by allowing the hospital to withdraw from the contract. For it had sued three other hospitals that tried to get out of their management contracts with Hospital Affiliates when Hospital Corporation assumed the contracts—only none of these hospitals was in a market where Hospital Corporation's acquisition of Hospital Affiliates was likely to be challenged. Post-acquisition evidence that is subject to manipulation by the party seeking to use it is entitled to little or no weight. The Commission was entitled to give it no weight in this case, both to simplify the adjudication of merger cases generally and because excluding this one hospital would not have altered the market share figures significantly.

If all the hospitals brought under common ownership or control by the two challenged acquisitions are treated as a single entity, the acquisitions raised Hospital Corporation's market share in the Chattanooga area from 14 percent to 26 percent. This made it the second largest provider of hospital services in a highly concentrated market where the four largest firms together had a 91 percent market share compared to 79 percent before the acquisitions. These are the FTC's figures, and Hospital Corporation thinks they are slightly too high (quite apart from the question what to do with either or both management contracts); but the discrepancy is too slight to make a legal difference. Nor would expressing the market shares in terms of the Herfindahl index alter the impression of a highly concentrated market.

The administrative law judge concluded that the acquisitions violated section 7 because of their probable anticompetitive effects in the Chattanooga hospital market. While modifying some of his findings, the Commission agreed that the acquisitions were unlawful and ordered Hospital Corporation to divest the hospitals acquired in Chattanooga and to notify the Commission, in advance, of any similar acquisitions planned for anywhere in the country. The Clayton Act allows Hospital Corporation to seek judicial review of the Commission's order in any circuit in which it does business, see 15 U.S.C. § 21(c), and for unexplained reasons it has chosen this circuit. It makes three arguments to us: there is no reasonable probability that its acquisitions in Chattanooga will lessen competition substantially; anyway the Federal Trade Commission has no constitutional power to bring an enforcement action, because the members of the Commission do not serve at the pleasure of the President; failing all else, Hospital Corporation should at least not be required to give the Commission advance notice of all future acquisitions.

The first 79 pages of Hospital Corporation's 85–page opening brief are devoted to the first argument, yet they make no mention of the standard of judicial review of the Federal Trade Commission's findings of fact and no effort to show that the findings are vulnerable under it. The standard is the familiar substantial-evidence standard: findings of fact that are supported by substantial evidence on the record considered as a whole bind the reviewing court. When the FTC pointed out this omission Hospital Corporation replied: "The decisive question on this appeal is . . . whether Chattanooga hospitals are likely to collude because of these acquisitions. This is a matter of economic analysis, not a dispute of underlying facts." The first sentence is wrong: the issue for this court is not whether the acquisitions create a danger of collusion but whether the Commission's conclusion that they do is supported by substantial evidence on the record as a whole. The second sentence is irrelevant, because the substantial evidence rule applies to ultimate as well as underlying facts, including economic judgments. This is implicit in the many cases that hold that the ultimate question under the Clayton Act—whether the challenged transaction may substantially lessen competition—is governed by the substantial evidence rule. . . .

The Commission's detailed analysis of those effects fills most of a 117–page opinion that, whatever its substantive merits or demerits, is a model of lucidity. The Commission may have made its task harder (and opinion longer) than strictly necessary, however, by studiously avoiding reliance on any of the Supreme Court's section 7 decisions from the 1960s except *United States v. Philadelphia Nat'l Bank,* 374 U.S. 321 (1963), which took an explicitly economic approach to the interpretation of the statute. The other decisions in that decade—in particular *Brown Shoe Co. v. United States,* 370 U.S. 294 (1962); *United States v. Aluminum Co. of America,* 377 U.S. 271 (1964); *United States v. Von's Grocery Co.,* 384 U.S. 270 (1966), and *United States v. Pabst Brewing Co.,* 384 U.S. 546 (1966)— seemed, taken as a group, to establish the illegality of any nontrivial acquisition of a competitor, whether or not the acquisition was likely either to bring about or shore up collusive or oligopoly pricing. The elimination of a significant rival was thought by itself to infringe the complex of social and economic values conceived by a majority of the Court to inform the statutory words "may . . . substantially . . . lessen competition."

None of these decisions has been overruled. Although both *United States v. General Dynamics Corp.,* 415 U.S. 486 (1974), and *United States v. Citizens & Southern Nat'l Bank,* 422 U.S. 86 (1975) (both discussed in our recent decision in *Ball Memorial Hospital, Inc. v. Mutual Hospital Ins., Inc.,* 784 F.2d 1325, 1336–37 (7th Cir.1986)), refused to equate the possession of a significant market share with a significant threat to competition, these cases involved highly unusual facts, having no counterpart in this case, that required discounting large market shares. In *General Dynamics* the shares were of current sales (of coal) made pursuant to long-term contracts entered into a long time ago; future sales would depend on uncommitted reserves, and one of the acquired firms had no uncommitted reserves. In *Citizens & Southern* the acquired banks were already under the effective control of the acquirer (they were its "de facto branches"), so that the formal merger had little competitive significance.

These cases show that market share figures are not always decisive in a section 7 case, but it can be argued that the cases themselves carve only

limited exceptions to the broad holdings of some of the merger decisions of
the 1960s. *General Dynamics* was like a failing-company case; in *Citizens
& Southern* the merger was a mere formality—like a marriage ceremony
between common law spouses. The most important developments that
cast doubt on the continued vitality of such cases as *Brown Shoe and
Von's* are found in other cases, where the Supreme Court, echoed by the
lower courts, has said repeatedly that the economic concept of competition, rather than any desire to preserve rivals as such, is the lodestar that
shall guide the contemporary application of the antitrust laws, not excluding the Clayton Act. For recent discussions of this point, citing the
relevant precedents, see *Fishman v. Estate of Wirtz*, 807 F.2d 520, 535–536
(7th Cir.1986); *id.* at 565–567 (separate opinion); *Morrison v. Murray
Biscuit Co.*, 797 F.2d 1430, 1437 (7th Cir.1986). See also *Cargill, Inc. v.
Montfort of Colorado, Inc.*, 479 U.S. 104, (1986). Applied to cases brought
under section 7, this principle requires the district court (in this case, the
Commission) to make a judgment whether the challenged acquisition is
likely to hurt consumers, as by making it easier for the firms in the
market to collude, expressly or tacitly, and thereby force price above or
farther above the competitive level. So it was prudent for the Commission, rather than resting on the very strict merger decisions of the 1960s,
to inquire into the probability of harm to consumers. . . .

When an economic approach is taken in a section 7 case, the ultimate
issue is whether the challenged acquisition is likely to facilitate collusion.
In this perspective the acquisition of a competitor has no economic
significance in itself; the worry is that it may enable the acquiring firm to
cooperate (or cooperate better) with other leading competitors on reducing
or limiting output, thereby pushing up the market price. Hospital Corporation calls the issue whether an acquisition is likely to have such an
effect "economic," which of course it is. But for purposes of judicial
review, as we have said, it is a factual issue subject to the substantial
evidence rule, not a legal issue on which review usually is plenary and
invariably is much less deferential than is the review of findings of
fact. . . . In the present case the underlying facts are, as Hospital
Corporation asserts, largely undisputed. The dispute is over the inferences of competitive consequence to be drawn from them. But the
drawing of those inferences is a matter within the Commission's primary
responsibility too. There is plenty of evidence to support the Commission's prediction of adverse competitive effect in this case; whether we
might have come up with a different prediction on our own is irrelevant.

The acquisitions reduced the number of competing hospitals in the
Chattanooga market from 11 to 7. True, this calculation assumes that the
hospitals that came under the management although not ownership of
Hospital Corporation should be considered allies rather than competitors
of Hospital Corporation; but the Commission was entitled to so conclude.
The manager (Hospital Corporation) sets the prices charged by the managed hospitals, just as it sets its own prices. Although the pricing and
other decisions that it makes in its management role are subject to the
ultimate control of the board of directors of the managed hospital, there is
substantial evidence that the board usually defers to the manager's
decisions. . . .

The reduction in the number of competitors is significant in assessing the competitive vitality of the Chattanooga hospital market. The fewer competitors there are in a market, the easier it is for them to coordinate their pricing without committing detectable violations of section 1 of the Sherman Act, which forbids price fixing. This would not be very important if the four competitors eliminated by the acquisitions in this case had been insignificant, but they were not; they accounted in the aggregate for 12 percent of the sales of the market. As a result of the acquisitions the four largest firms came to control virtually the whole market, and the problem of coordination was therefore reduced to one of coordination among these four.

Moreover, both the ability of the remaining firms to expand their output should the big four reduce their own output in order to raise the market price (and, by expanding, to offset the leading firms' restriction of their own output), and the ability of outsiders to come in and build completely new hospitals, are reduced by Tennessee's certificate-of-need law. Any addition to hospital capacity must be approved by a state agency. . . .

All this would be of little moment if, in the event that hospital prices in Chattanooga rose above the competitive level, persons desiring hospital services in Chattanooga would switch to hospitals in other cities, or to nonhospital providers of medical care. But this would mean that the Chattanooga hospital market, which is to say the set of hospital-services providers to which consumers in Chattanooga can feasibly turn, see *United States v. Philadelphia Nat'l Bank, supra,* 374 U.S. at 358–61; *Tampa Elec. Co. v. Nashville Coal Co.,* 365 U.S. 320, 327–28 (1961), includes hospitals in other cities plus nonhospital providers both in Chattanooga and elsewhere; and we do not understand Hospital Corporation to be challenging the Commission's market definition, which is limited to hospital providers in Chattanooga. Anyway, these competitive alternatives are not important enough to deprive the market shares statistics of competitive significance. Going to another city is out of the question in medical emergencies; and even when an operation or some other hospital service can be deferred, the patient's doctor will not (at least not for reasons of price) send the patient to another city, where the doctor is unlikely to have hospital privileges. . . .

In showing that the challenged acquisitions gave four firms control over an entire market so that they would have little reason to fear a competitive reaction if they raised prices above the competitive level, the Commission went far to justify its prediction of probable anticompetitive effects. Maybe it need have gone no further. See *United States v. Philadelphia Nat'l Bank, supra,* 374 U.S. at 362–63; *Monfort of Colorado, Inc. v. Cargill, Inc.,* 761 F.2d 570, 580 (10th Cir.1985), rev'd on other grounds, 479 U.S. 104 (1986). But it did. First it pointed out that the demand for hospital services by patients and their doctors is highly inelastic under competitive conditions. This is not only because people place a high value on their safety and comfort and because many of their treatment decisions are made for them by their doctor, who doesn't pay their hospital bills; it is also because most hospital bills are paid largely by insurance companies or the federal government rather than by the patient. The less elastic the demand for a good or service is, the greater are the profits that providers can make by raising price through collusion. A low elasticity of demand means that raising price will cause a relatively slight fall in demand, with the result that total revenues will rise sharply. For example, if the price elasticity of demand throughout the relevant portion of the demand curve is $-.2$, meaning that within that area every 1 percent increase in price will result in a two-tenths of 1 percent decrease in the quantity demanded, then a 10 percent increase in price will cause only a 2 percent reduction in quantity sold, and hence an almost 8 percent increase in total revenue. And since less is being produced, costs will fall at the same time that revenue is rising, resulting in an even greater percentage increase in profit than in revenue.

Second, there is a tradition, well documented in the Commission's opinion, of cooperation between competing hospitals in Chattanooga. Of course, not all forms of cooperation between competitors are bad. See, e.g., *Broadcast Music, Inc. v. Columbia Broadcasting System, Inc.,* 441 U.S. 1 (1979). But a market in which competitors are unusually disposed to cooperate is a market prone to collusion. . . .

* * *

Third, hospitals are under great pressure from the federal government and the insurance companies to cut costs. One way of resisting this pressure is by presenting a united front in negotiations with the third-party payors—which indeed, as we have just said, hospitals in Chattanooga have done. The fewer the independent competitors in a hospital market, the easier they will find it, by presenting an unbroken phalanx of representations and requests, to frustrate efforts to control hospital costs. . . .

All these considerations, taken together, supported—we do not say they compelled—the Commission's conclusion that the challenged acquisitions are likely to foster collusive practices, harmful to consumers, in the Chattanooga hospital market. Section 7 does not require proof that a merger or other acquisition has caused higher prices in the affected market. All that is necessary is that the merger create an appreciable danger of such consequences in the future. A predictive judgment, necessarily probabilistic and judgmental rather than demonstrable (see *United States v. Philadelphia Nat'l Bank, supra,* 374 U.S. at 362), is called for. Considering the concentration of the market, the absence of competitive alternatives, the regulatory barrier to entry (the certificate of need law), the low elasticity of demand, the exceptionally severe cost pressures under which American hospitals labor today, the history of collusion in the industry, and the sharp reduction in the number of substantial competitors in this market brought about by the acquisition of four hospitals in a city with only eleven (one already owned by Hospital Corporation), we cannot say that the Commission's prediction is not supported by substantial evidence.

But of course we cannot just consider the evidence that supports the Commission's prediction. We must consider all the evidence in the record. We must therefore consider the significance of the facts, pressed on us by Hospital Corporation, that hospital services are complex and heterogeneous, that the sellers in this market are themselves heterogeneous because of differences in the services provided by the different hospitals and differences in the corporate character of the hospitals (some are publicly owned, some are proprietary, and some are private but nonprofit), that the hospital industry is undergoing rapid technological and economic change, that the payors for most hospital services (Blue Cross and other insurance companies, and the federal government) are large and knowledgeable, and that the FTC's investigation which led to this proceeding was touched off by a complaint from a competitor of Hospital Corporation. Most of these facts do detract from a conclusion that collusion in this market is a serious danger, but it was for the Commission—it is not for us—to determine their weight.

* * *

Questions and Comments

If Judge Posner were deciding the questions on which he deferred to the FTC, would he have found that the acquisition threatened to enhance collusion?

Suppose the findings made by the FTC had been made by a district court. Would this court of appeals have been equally deferential?

Which of the mergers found illegal in the Supreme Court cases you have read would have survived a Posnerian review?

What political consideration did Judge Posner bring to bear in considering the merger's legality? Would Judge Bork have entertained this argument? Would you?

Judge Bork has written that output restriction falls off greatly from a monopoly market to a two-firm market, and that a merger that would concentrate a market to only two firms of roughly equal size might well create efficiencies. In his view mergers creating firms that have up to 60% or 70% of a market should be allowed. However, given the existence of Section 7 of the Clayton Act, which was clearly intended to tighten up the Sherman Act, Bork suggests that all mergers that leave at least three significant companies in the market should be presumptively lawful. Thus, if there were six companies, all having about 15% to 17% of the market, a merger of any pair would be presumptively lawful. The Antitrust Paradox 221–22. Is this view derived from law? From economics? From what?

In 1986, Pepsi Cola announced its intention to buy Seven–Up. Coca–Cola, not to be outdone, announced its plan to buy Dr. Pepper. The FTC opened investigations. Both acquiring firms argued that the acquisitions could not lessen output because Coke and Pepsi were such fierce rivals against one another. Unconvinced, the FTC decided to sue. Pepsi abandoned its plans to buy Seven–Up (but it proceeded to buy the foreign assets of Seven–Up). Coca–Cola decided to fight.

FTC v. COCA–COLA CO.

641 F.Supp. 1128 (D.D.C.1986).

JUDGE GESELL: By its complaint filed June 24, 1986, the Federal Trade Commission ("FTC") seeks a preliminary injunction pursuant to Section

13(b) of the Federal Trade Commission Act to enjoin The Coca–Cola Company from consummating its proposed acquisition of Dr. Pepper Company, which sponsors a carbonated soft drink called Dr. Pepper, pending FTC administrative hearings to determine whether the acquisition violates Section 7 of the Clayton Act. Dr. Pepper Company is being offered for sale by DP Holdings, Inc., which owns and controls all its outstanding shares.

* * *

The Proposed Acquisition

The Coca–Cola Company is primarily a carbonated soft drink company. It is also a major producer and distributor of motion pictures and television programs and one of the world's largest citrus marketers. Founded a century ago, it operates throughout the United States and internationally. It reported in its most recent Letter to Shareholders that "one of every two colas and one of every three soft drinks consumed by the American public is a Coca–Cola branded product." It is forming by acquisition and otherwise the world's largest bottling system in aid of its marketing strategies, thus increasing its power over the principal channel of distribution. It is an aggressive, flexible, creative marketer. It has been and is a highly successful, well-managed, profitable enterprise, with 1985 revenues of approximately $7.9 billion.

Dr Pepper Company is also an old, well-established carbonated soft drink company that is principally involved in marketing its Dr Pepper brand, a soft drink which is sold nationally in direct competition with Coca–Cola Company brands. The Dr Pepper brand has a distinctive "spicy-cherry" or "pepper" taste and the company has developed significant sales, particularly in the South and Southwest United States. Dr Pepper Company was offered for sale through Goldman Sachs & Co., an investment banking firm, which caused Coca–Cola Company to initiate discussions leading to an agreement to buy the entire stock for $470,000,000.

Coca–Cola Company was motivated by a variety of somewhat divergent considerations in agreeing to acquire Dr Pepper Company. As a strictly business matter, the acquisition would be profitable for Coca–Cola Company's shareholders. Essentially, Coca–Cola Company is buying the company for its trademark and existing market. It would give the Dr Pepper brand new life by absorbing it into its multiproduct line of carbonated soft drinks. Dr Pepper's debts would be paid off, expenses would be greatly reduced, and Coca–Cola Company's marketing skills, research ability, resources and position in the overall market would assure greater sales of the Dr Pepper brand at wider per-unit profit margins.

Another special factor played a role in the bid for Dr Pepper Company. Coca–Cola Company had been expanding without acquisition, but when PepsiCo, Inc., its principal competitor, sought to make a major acquisition of Seven–Up Company, Coca–Cola Company apparently felt it should have the same privilege, if the rules permitted. The Seven–Up acquisition was abandoned domestically under threat of FTC suit but Coca–Cola Company decided to press on.

* * *

The Position of the Parties

FTC challenges Coca–Cola Company's acquisition of Dr Pepper Company on two major grounds. It claims that Dr Pepper is a carbonated soft drink concern competing both nationally and regionally directly with Coca–Cola Company's products, particularly its cherry Coke and Mr. PiBB brands, and that such competition will be eliminated. It further contends that the acquisition will increase concentration in the market and encourage tacit price collusion and other parallel policies of mutual advantage between Coca–Cola Company and PepsiCo, the other major seller in the carbonated soft drink business, thus encouraging if not resulting in a lessening of competition.

Coca–Cola Company, while admitting that the carbonated soft drink market is concentrated, contends that any threat to competition posed by concentration will not significantly change if Dr Pepper is acquired. It says it is locked in an all-out competitive rivalry with PepsiCo which has been and will remain so intense that the possibility of collusion simply does not exist. Any relaxation of the existing competition, it suggests, would, moreover, simply fortify the existing smaller competitors and encourage entry by larger concerns now exploring entry on a full scale. Since it believes entry is otherwise relatively easy, Coca–Cola Company argues that competition will continue should the vigor of the struggle between the two principal companies diminish. Thus it suggests the acquisition of Dr Pepper is basically irrelevant in considering the objectives of Section 7. Moreover, Coca–Cola Company contends that, if anything, the acquisition will actually promote competition by making the Dr Pepper brand a more effective competitor in the market nationwide.

II. THE LINE OF COMMERCE INVOLVED

The Market is Carbonated Soft Drinks

Both Coca–Cola Company and Dr Pepper Company manufacture and sell soft drink concentrate and syrup as their primary business. In order to appraise the probable effects of the proposed acquisition, it is necessary at the outset to understand the forces at work in the market where the buyers and sellers of concentrate and syrup principally compete.

Proper market analysis directs attention to the nature of the products that the acquirer and the acquired company principally sell, the channels of distribution they primarily use, the outlets they employ to distribute their products to the ultimate consumer, and the geographic areas they mutually serve. Factors affecting price and interchangeability of products must be considered. Analysis of the market is a matter of business reality—a matter of how the market is perceived by those who strive for profit in it. Moreover, under Section 7 market forces must be analyzed as they operate in "any section of the country"—any geographic submarket possessing its own economically significant attributes.

The Court is persuaded that the appropriate "line of commerce" for measuring the probable effects of this acquisition is the carbonated soft drink market and that such effects must be appraised both nationally and, as will be noted, in a seven-state area in the South and Southwest United States.

Carbonated soft drinks are produced by adding carbonated water to a syrup consisting of a "concentrate" flavoring and a sweetener. The carbonated soft drink market is guided primarily by "concentrate companies" like Coca–Cola Company and Dr Pepper Company that develop, test, market and promote a variety of concentrate flavorings to appeal to the consumer. Concentrate is normally purchased by "bottlers" alone or in syrup form; the bottlers then mix the flavoring with carbonated water and package the mixture in bottles and cans. Bottlers normally are also largely responsible for distributing the final product directly to retailers through a variety of channels to consumers. Food stores and similar retail outlets are the primary channel, accounting for approximately 63 percent of carbonated soft drink retail sales. "Fountain" distribution of carbonated soft drinks in restaurants and other outlets for immediate consumption is responsible for about 25 percent of sales, while sales through vending machines account for about 12 percent.

Concentrate companies are faced with keen competition for the limited shelf space in stores and for placement among the few products featured in the typical fountain or vending machine. Bottlers are key participants in this competition. Concentrate companies normally grant bottlers exclusive franchises to produce and distribute the company's products, to stores and vending accounts, within a defined territory. In return for these perpetual franchises, bottlers are obliged to use their best efforts to promote the company's product line, and are typically barred from dealing in same-flavored products of other concentrate companies. Although most bottlers are not owned by the concentrate companies, the companies provide substantial marketing assistance, research data and a variety of short- and long-term promotional benefits.

In view of the structure and operation of this industry, the relevant line of commerce in evaluating the acquisition is assuredly not what Coca–Cola Company suggests—"all . . . beverages including tap water"—even though it is true that other beverages quench thirst and that "[t]he human stomach can consume only a finite amount of liquid in any given period of time." The market or submarkets delineated need not be this broad (anything potable) nor as unduly narrow (concentrate flavoring) as lawyers or economists may choose to suggest.

Although other beverages could be viewed as within the "outer boundaries of a product market . . . determined by the reasonable interchangeability of use or the cross-elasticity of demand between [carbonated soft drinks] and substitutes" for them, carbonated soft drinks represent at minimum a well-defined and the major beverage submarket sufficient to "constitute [a] product market[ ] for antitrust purposes." The Court is guided here by *Brown Shoe Co. v. United States,* from which this quotation is adopted, where the Supreme Court counsels reliance on "such practical indicia as industry or public recognition of the submarket as a separate economic entity, the product's peculiar characteristics and uses, unique production facilities, distinct consumers, distinct prices, sensitivity to price changes, and specialized vendors" as guides for defining the appropriate market.

Such indicia are present here. . . .

* * *

The Market Is Highly Concentrated

There is general agreement that the market for carbonated soft drinks is already highly concentrated. It consists of a few major concentrate companies and a number of minor concerns, not all of which do business nationally. The major concerns, their 1985 national market shares and their principal soft drink products are approximately as follows:

Company	Co./Cumulative	Principal Products
1. Coca–Cola Company	37.4 / 37.4	Coca–Cola Classic, Coke, diet Coke, cherry Coke, Tab, Sprite, Minute Maid orange and lemon-lime flavors, Fanta flavors, Mellow Yellow, Fresca and Mr. PiBB
2. PepsiCo, Inc.	28.9 / 66.3	Pepsi–Cola, Diet Pepsi, Mountain Dew and Slice lemon-lime, apple and cherry flavors
3. Philip Morris	5.7 / 72.0	7–Up, Diet 7–Up, Like Cola
4. Dr Pepper Company	4.6 / 76.6	Dr Pepper, Diet Dr Pepper
5. R.J. Reynolds	3.0 / 79.6	Sunkist Orange Soda, Canada Dry flavor line
6. Royal Crown	2.9 / 82.5	RC Cola, Diet RC, Diet Rite, assorted other flavors
7. Procter & Gamble	1.3 / 83.8	Orange and other Crush flavors, Hires Root Beer

As the above table illustrates, there are only a few companies presently of any competitive significance. Coca–Cola Company and PepsiCo dominate. . . .

* * *

Distribution Channels are Controlled by Dominant Concerns

. . . To ensure effective distribution, the major concentrate companies grant exclusive territorial marketing rights to their bottlers, provide substantial marketing assistance and promotional funds, and generally prohibit their bottlers from distributing competing flavors of other companies. This strategy strengthens the ability of the dominant firms to move their product lines to the store shelves, vending machines and fountain outlets by leveraging a variety of products together through one committed seller directly to retailers. . . .

. . . In the carbonated soft drink industry, a bottler generally cannot be an effective distribution and marketing force in a local market unless it has a market share of at least 15 to 20 percent of total distribution. There is considerable indication that absent such a presence in the market, the bottler will be unable to command sufficient sales volume to convince retailers to carry its promotional activities rather than those of the dominant companies.

As Dr Pepper Company's experience demonstrates, the strongest and preferred bottlers are those primarily affiliated with Coca–Cola Company and PepsiCo. Of its approximately 450 bottlers, 208 carry Coca–Cola Company products as their main brand line; they distribute 39 percent of Dr Pepper volume. Another 166 bottlers, with 31 percent of Dr Pepper sales, are affiliated with PepsiCo. The remaining 30 percent of Dr Pepper volume is distributed by about 75 "independent" bottlers that do not bottle for the dominant companies. Typically, the independents are affiliated with Seven–Up Company or Royal Crown or both, along with other smaller brands.

It is the combination of several popular brands that enables these independent bottlers to compete against the dominant companies by moving enough volume to serve as effective distributors. For this reason they are often referred to as the "third bottler" within a given territory; rarely do the smaller brands have enough volume to support a fourth bottler of effective size in a local market. The Dr Pepper business of these independents strengthens their ability to offer a line of products that can collectively compete for retail space and that can "piggyback" new entrants into the retail outlets.

Dr Pepper Company, however, is in an enviable position because it enjoys access to the bottlers of the dominant companies. Other companies seeking to seriously challenge the dominance of Coca–Cola Company and PepsiCo by entering in the major flavor segments would probably have serious difficulty finding effective distribution.[18] To equal Dr Pepper's distribution success, they would have to convince the affiliated bottlers to abandon their currently successful flavors for a new brand with no track record. Moreover, even if the new brand promises to be successful, affiliated bottlers have strong incentives to carry the dominant company's brand to reap the substantial marketing advantages conferred by a full line of highly promoted flavors, and to maintain a good relationship with their main supplier.[19]

* * *

. . . [E]ffective access to bottlers is likely to become even more difficult in the future as dominant companies increasingly focus their energies on controlling their distribution network even more tightly. Coca–Cola Company, for example, has long moved toward this goal by acquiring its bottlers, often subsequently selling them to stronger and more congenial management. Earlier this year, it announced a new effort to "strengthen further [its] U.S. distribution system and accelerate volume

---

18. Of course, it is conceivable that an entrant could challenge existing companies with a successful new flavor not barred by existing restrictions. In all likelihood, however, such an entrant would face severe challenge from the dominant companies' present practice of expanding their flavor lines to fill new "niches." Dr Pepper has survived this challenge largely because it enjoyed several decades as the sole occupant of its niche, enabling it to build up a substantial consumer franchise.

19. For example, Seven–Up Company was able to secure bottling for its Like Cola (introduced in 1982) in only half the country at the height of the brand's popularity because bottlers, including many affiliated with the company, refused to drop their established cola flavors.

growth" by consolidating its present bottling operations with those of its largest bottling franchise, JTL Corporation, to form "the world's largest independent bottling operation." This decision was part of its "strategy to achieve a stronger, more efficient bottler network by investing more aggressively in bottler operations through minority interests and joint ventures, when appropriate." . . .

. . . Post-acquisition, a substantial portion of Coca–Cola Company's Dr Pepper sales would be bottled by independent bottlers. This situation would conflict with its firm and long-standing practice of selling all its products in a given territory through a single bottler. To the extent Coca–Cola Company chooses to vigorously promote independent bottlers' sales of the Dr Pepper brand, it will be placed in the position of directly competing in marketing against its own bottlers. . . .

. . . [I]t is likely that Coca–Cola Company would gradually shift Dr Pepper bottling either to existing Coca–Cola Company bottlers or to its own bottling concern, as part of its usual practice of transferring owner-ship of bottling franchises to ensure efficient distribution. Of course, the company has assured the independent bottlers that it will not unfairly seek to terminate their franchises. Indeed, it has every reason, if it is to expand sales of the Dr Pepper brand, to promote good relations with Dr Pepper bottlers at least temporarily. But with the substantial incentives involved, it is more than likely that Dr Pepper bottling will gradually find its way into the Coca–Cola Company system one way or another.

* * *

Other Barriers to Entry are Significant

The lack of adequate distribution channels enhances the market power of the dominant companies. Other difficulties facing companies seeking to enter the carbonated soft drink market on a substantial scale also tend to leave that power unchallenged. These barriers to entry include the substantial time and expense required to build a brand name that may overcome existing consumer preferences; the large sums needed for frequent promotions to secure the brand a place in retail outlets already dominated by companies with a full line of flavors; and the inability promptly to recoup the substantial investments involved. Thus, regardless of the ease of entering solely at the concentrate company level, what cannot be doubted from the record is that entry on a scale sufficient to challenge the major companies is exceedingly difficult, requiring enor-mous sums of money and years of effort.

* * *

Finally, it has been the experience of the industry that effective entry against the dominant companies is likely to require years of sustained effort for any continuing success, thus making the prospects of profitable investment in new brands remote. For example, Procter & Gamble, an enormously successful consumer products company that entered the mar-ket in 1980 through acquisition of Crush International, Inc., with its Crush and Hires Root Beer brand lines, has been able to expand sales only marginally. . . .

III. AN OVERVIEW OF THE ACQUISITION'S EFFECTS

The record contains much speculation as to the effects the obvious increase in concentration caused by the proposed acquisition may have upon market performance. FTC presents as its major concern the possibility that the dominant competitors may choose to relax competition and enjoy larger, more uncontested profits. No tendency in that direction has yet been evidenced and there is no proof that the mere addition of Dr Pepper to Coca–Cola Company's line, standing alone, will trigger a foreseeable development of this kind. The present intensity of competition between Coca–Cola Company and PepsiCo does not seem likely to diminish in the immediate future. But the fact remains that if the proposed acquisition is consummated there will be one less independent factor in the market to challenge the dominance of Coca–Cola Company.

At the preliminary injunction hearing economists, drawing on experience in this multi-faceted discipline, flatly disagreed as to the significance of the proposed acquisition upon competition in the market. These sincere professionals are theoreticians in an imprecise field. They have never sold a can of carbonated soft drink and indeed the principal economist for Coca–Cola Company frankly admitted he had little knowledge of the underlying facts.

The Court should not, in any event, rely on the economic testimony in reaching a conclusion about the probable effects of the proposed acquisition given the concentrated nature of the market just outlined. Section 7 of the Clayton Act was not designed to support a particular economic theory; it was directed at what Congress in the exercise of its own common sense perceived. Congress desired to outlaw substantial increases in concentration through acquisition by a dominant concern in an already concentrated industry by placing a heavy burden of proof upon anyone seeking to justify growth by purchase under such circumstances. Section 7 was founded on a "fear of what was considered to be a rising tide of economic concentration in the American economy." *Brown Shoe Co. v. United States,* 370 U.S. 294, 315 (1962). This compelling concern, the Supreme Court has "observed many times," led Congress to design Section 7 as "a prophylactic measure, intended 'primarily to arrest apprehended consequences of intercorporate relationships before those relationships could work their evil. . . .' " [21]

Given this dominant legislative desire to curb the economic concentration of power, it is unnecessary to speculate about the economic effect of the proposed acquisition. Without more, substantial mergers of this kind in heavily concentrated industries are presumed illegal. In such cases, as the Supreme Court made clear in *United States v. Philadelphia National Bank,* 374 U.S. 321, 363 (1963), "elaborate proof of market structure, market behavior, or probable anticompetitive effects" can even be dispensed with. Instead, a court must be guided by the view that "a merger which produces a firm controlling an undue percentage share of the relevant market, and results in a significant increase in the concentration of firms in that market, is so inherently likely to lessen competition

---

21. *Brunswick Corp. v. Pueblo Bowl–O–Mat, Inc.,* 429 U.S. 477, 485 (1977) (quoting *United States v. E.I. du Pont de Nemours & Co.,* 353 U.S. 586, 597 (1957)).

substantially that it must be enjoined in the absence of evidence clearly showing that the merger is not likely to have such anticompetitive effects." *Id.*

The Supreme Court has made clear that once the government has established a prima facie case of a Section 7 violation based on a significant increase in market concentration, as the FTC has done here, it is "incumbent upon [the acquiring company] to show that the market-share statistics give an inaccurate account of the acquisitions' probable effects on competition." *United States v. Citizens & Southern National Bank,* 422 U.S. 86, 120 (1975). Thus, in *Philadelphia National Bank,* the Court enjoined a bank merger which would have given the defendant bank a market share of at least 30 percent, increasing the market share of the two largest banks by more than one-third, from 44 percent to 59 percent. In doing so the Court rejected the argument that the merger was acceptable because it would not alter the underlying dynamics of the already highly concentrated market, stating that "if concentration is already great, the importance of preventing even slight increases in concentration and so preserving the possibility of eventual deconcentration is correspondingly great." *Id.* 374 U.S. at 365 n. 42, 83 S.Ct. at 1742 n. 42.

The same rationale applies to the questioned acquisition. . . .

Use of bare market statistics alone to invalidate this particular acquisition, quite apart from evidence of the control of distribution channels and other barriers to entry already shown, is presumptively justified. Evidence suggesting otherwise must be clear and specific.

Such evidence is not present in this case. . . .

*   *   *

Conclusion

*   *   *

Any federal judge considering regulatory aims such as those laid down by Congress in Section 7 of the Clayton Act should hesitate before grafting onto the Act an untried economic theory such as the wealth-maximization and efficiency-through-acquisition doctrine expounded by Coca–Cola Company. Congress never made such a choice nor has the FTC, a specialized agency to which Congress entrusted part of the Section 7 enforcement task. Surely Congress had a variety of considerations in mind when it enacted the major public policy enunciated by this Section. There were concerns about size as such, about opportunity for small business, about concentration trends; there was also a belief that a diversified competitive market assures a healthy economy and encourages innovation. To be sure, efficiencies that benefit consumers were recognized as desirable but they were to be developed by dominant concerns using their brains, not their money by buying out troubling competitors. The Court has no authority to move in a direction neither the Congress nor the Supreme Court has accepted.

A preliminary injunction in the form attached shall issue forthwith.

Questions and Comments

Did the FTC prove what it set out to prove? What would have happened if Coke and Pepsi relaxed their competition against one another? If output limitation is our sole concern, does it matter whether Coke would continue to compete intensely against Dr. Pepper as long as Coke would continue to compete intensely against Pepsi? Would a Coke/Dr. Pepper merger have reduced the nation's consumption of carbonated soft drinks? If not, was there anything for the antitrust laws to protect? Under Chicago School theory? Under the court's theory? How would Judge Posner have decided the case?

Note Coca–Cola's suggestion that the acquisition would result in a consumer benefit—Dr. Pepper soda would be more widely available when marketed through the Coca–Cola network, and sales would increase. Is this a consumer benefit? Should the court have weighed it? How? Indeed, if Coke proved that after the acquisition Coke/Dr. Pepper would expand, not contract, would Coca–Cola thereby disprove the FTC's output-limitation theory?

Was this acquisition unfair to Royal Crown and other independents who sought access to bottlers affiliated with Coca–Cola? Would the worsening of the odds for the independents such as Royal Crown hurt consumers? Or would it only hurt smaller competitors?

Is the court's decision based on socio-political values or economics? Can you make a strong economic case for condemning the acquisition? For supporting it? We have seen that there are various ways to engage in economic thinking. Is the economics applied by this court harmonious or at odds with the non-economic values that produced the statute?

Note the court's use of presumptions regarding the burden of proof. What is the basis for these presumptions? After applying the presumptions, the court will be guided only by consumers' interests. Does the bearer of the burden of proof lose?

The Pepsi/Seven Up and Coke/Dr. Pepper merger proposals would have been unthinkable in the 1960s. Is the new antitrust world, in which they are clearly thinkable and perhaps worth litigating about, a better antitrust world than the one in which the Von's/Shopping Bag merger was condemned?

It is sometimes argued that we should maintain a free market for corporate control; that a free market for control will tend to assure that corporate assets are in the most productive hands. Moreover, entry is encouraged by the existence of a robust market for exit. Is a permissive stance on mergers, even horizontal mergers, desirable to assure an adequate market for corporate control?

4. PRODUCTION JOINT VENTURES

Frequently, combinations of competitors take the form of a joint venture. Two firms that normally compete pool talents, risks and profits in some specific phase of their operations. When the partners form a new corporation and acquire the stock of that corporation, the transaction is normally analyzed under the law of mergers and acquisitions. Sometimes the joint venture is a partnership rather than a corporation, and there is technically no acquisition; however, the legal question is the same: Is the transaction, on balance, anticompetitive?

As we move through this era of high technology, joint ventures of competitors have become common. Each firm has somewhat different advantages, and a combination may promise synergies. Often these ventures involve major competitors, however, and anticompetitive risks can be greater than probable procompetitive gains. But this is a fact-specific question.

In the 1960s General Motors was the leading automobile producer in the world. It accounted for some 50% of U.S. purchases of cars. Ford, Chrysler and American Motors were all financially strong firms, and together the four companies occupied almost all of the American market. In the 1970s the fortune of the American automobile companies turned. After General Motors made a major commitment to manufacturing more big cars, a serious oil shortage struck and buyers began to shift in large numbers from big "gas guzzlers" to fuel efficient foreign cars. Meanwhile the Japanese came into their own as a major world force. By the 1980s, because of cheaper labor costs, a favorable exchange rate, uniquely successful quality controls, the high-quality of worker performance, and other successful business methods, Japanese firms were able to produce cars at nearly $2000 per car less than American firms.

Japanese autos began to gain a strong position in the U.S. market. All of the major American auto companies suffered economic reverses. Chrysler was saved from bankruptcy only by a government bailout. Political pressures led the U.S. Government to induce the Japanese Government to initiate a system of voluntary import quotas. "Local content" bills were introduced in Congress; they were designed to limit the extent to which automobiles and their parts can be produced abroad and imported into the United States. See A. Lowenfeld, Public Controls on International Trade § 8.46 (2d ed. 1983).

In 1982 General Motors, still the world's largest automobile maker (accounting for about 44% of car sales in the United States and Canada, 27% of small cars, and 14% of subcompacts), concluded that it needed the help of the Japanese to make a successful small car. General Motors' aim was to reduce its production costs to the Japanese level and to raise its quality control to the Japanese standard. In turn, Toyota, the world's third largest auto maker with a 6.7% and rising share of the U.S.–Canada market, was eager to expand its market position in the United States. Given the establishment of quotas and the threat of further protectionist measures, Toyota wanted to produce cars in America.

GM and Toyota formed a joint venture to make a new small car—the TVX (now, the Nova)—based on the Toyota Corolla. Toyota would make the engines and transmissions in Japan and the joint venture would make some parts and assemble the cars in GM's idle facility in Fremont, California. Management personnel would be largely from Toyota, with a few GM managers available to learn Toyota methods in a hands-on situation. The Americans would supply know-how for identifying and negotiating with suppliers and working with organized labor and government. The cars would be sold to GM. Production plans called for approximately 200,000 joint venture cars per year, which would account for approximately 5% of all sales of small cars in the United States.

The FTC conducted an intensive investigation. Its officials then conferred with General Motors and Toyota and they negotiated certain limitations on the joint venture. The FTC and the joint venturers entered into a consent order in the shadow of Congressional oversight hearings, during which Lee Iacocca, President of Chrysler, tried to convince Congress (having failed to convince the FTC) that a joint venture between the number one U.S. automaker and the number one Japanese automaker was bad for America.

IN THE MATTER OF GENERAL MOTORS CORP.
103 FTC 374 (1984).

* * *

ORDER

I.

It is ordered, That for the purposes of this Order the following definitions shall apply:

* * *

4. The term *Module* means an integrated manufacturing facility, comprising, at a minimum, body, paint and final assembly functions, capable of producing not more than approximately 250,000 New Automobiles per year.

* * *

II.

It is further ordered, That respondents shall not, without the prior approval of the Commission, form any Joint Venture except a single Joint Venture that is limited to the manufacture for or sale to GM of New Automobiles derived from the Toyota Sprinter and produced by a single Module. Nothing in this paragraph is intended to or is to be construed to prohibit this single Joint Venture from manufacturing or selling additional products to Toyota.

III.

It is further ordered, That respondents shall not form any Joint Venture that is not limited in duration to a maximum of twelve years after the start of production or that continues in operation beyond the earlier of twelve years after the start of production or December 31, 1997. . . .

IV.

It is further ordered, That respondents shall not exchange or discuss between themselves, or with any Joint Venture, non-public information in connection with New Automobiles relating to current or future:

1. Prices of GM or Toyota New Automobiles or component parts of New Automobiles, except pursuant to a supplier-customer relationship entered into in the ordinary course of business;

2. Costs of GM or Toyota products, except as provided in Paragraph V of this order;

3. Sales or production forecasts or plans for any product other than the product of the Joint Venture; or

4. Marketing plans for any product.

V.

It is further ordered, That respondents shall not, except as may be necessary to accomplish, and solely in connection with, the legitimate purposes or functioning of any Joint Venture, exchange or discuss between themselves, or with any Joint Venture, non-public information in connection with New Automobiles relating to current or future:

1. Model changes, design changes, product designs, or development or engineering activities relating to the product of the Joint Venture;

2. Sales or production forecasts or plans as they relate to the product of the Joint Venture; or

3. Costs of GM or Toyota products supplied to the Joint Venture.

VI.

It is further ordered, That each respondent shall, and respondents shall cause any Joint Venture to:

1. Maintain complete files and records of all correspondence and other communications, whether in the United States or elsewhere, between and among GM, Toyota and the Joint Venture concerning information described in Paragraph V;

2. Maintain logs of all meetings and nonwritten communications, whether in the United States or elsewhere, between and among GM, Toyota, and the Joint Venture concerning information described in Paragraph V, including in such logs the names and corporate positions of all participants, the dates and locations of the meetings or other communications and a summary or description of such information;

3. For a period of six years, retain and make available to the Federal Trade Commission on request the complete files, records and logs required by subparagraphs 1 and 2; and

4. Annually, on the anniversary date of this Order, furnish a copy of this Order to each management employee of the Joint Venture and each management employee of GM and Toyota with responsibilities for the Joint Venture, and furnish to the Federal Trade Commission a signed statement provided by each such employee affirming that he or she has read a copy of this Order, understands it, and intends to comply fully with its provisions.

VII.

It is further ordered, That each respondent shall, within sixty days from the date of issuance of this Order, and annually thereafter, submit in writing to the Commission a report setting forth in detail the manner and form in which it intends to comply, is complying and has complied with the terms of this Order, and such additional information relating thereto as may from time to time reasonably be required.

* * *

STATEMENT OF CHAIRMAN JAMES C. MILLER III

On December 22, 1983, the Federal Trade Commission provisionally accepted for public comment a consent agreement concerning the proposed joint venture between General Motors Corporation and Toyota Motor Corporation ("the venture"). Under that consent agreement, which was accepted after one of the most thorough and intensive antitrust reviews in Commission history, GM and Toyota may only undertake the joint venture subject to safeguards limiting the venture's scope and preventing the exchange of competitively sensitive information not required to achieve the legitimate objectives of the venture.

* * *

In analyzing the joint venture, it is important to separate reality from rhetoric. The Fremont venture is a limited production joint venture, not a merger of GM and Toyota. The extent of continuing competition between the companies dwarfs the limited area of cooperation represented by the venture. The FTC's approval of the joint venture, subject to the safeguards of the consent order, does not, as some have charged, ignore the antitrust laws, nor does it turn them upside down. Rather, it represents a careful application of antitrust principles to the specific facts at hand. The goal of the Commission's antitrust review has been to protect competition, and hence consumers. We've also been very sensitive to the substantial gains to competition and consumers projected by the venture under the safeguards incorporated in the consent agreement.

In evaluating the proposed consent agreement, the Commission weighed a number of possible competitive concerns. These included the effect of the joint venture pricing formula, the possibility of tacit or explicit collusion resulting from the venture, and the venture's effect on Toyota's incentives to enter into production in the United States. Nothing in the comments received alters my preliminary assessment that with the safeguards incorporated in the consent these possibilities do not represent significant antitrust dangers. Let me explain.

Without the restraints incorporated in the consent agreement, the Fremont venture does raise two potentially troubling issues: the venture's effect on GM's incentives to continue alternative production of small cars, and the possibility of anticompetitive information exchanges that are unnecessary to achieve the legitimate purposes of the joint venture. To address these concerns, the Commission has incorporated certain safeguards in the consent agreement. The joint venture's production at the Fremont plant has been restricted to ensure that GM would retain incentives to fill the remainder of its small car needs from other sources. Expansion of the venture would be permitted only if approved in advance by the Commission.

To ensure that the joint venture were not used to facilitate the exchange of competitively sensitive information unnecessary to its operation, the exchange of certain information was prohibited, and record-keeping and reporting requirements concerning exchanges of other information were imposed to ensure continued, close monitoring of the venture's future operations.

As a result of the public comments received and our further analysis, the Commission has determined to broaden slightly both the scope of prohibited information exchanges and the record-keeping requirements by adding product development and engineering activities to the other categories of restricted information. . . .

Against these concerns, it is important to weigh the three major procompetitive benefits that are likely to result from the joint venture. First, the Fremont venture will increase the total number of small cars available in America, thus allowing consumers a greater choice at lower prices, despite present restrictions on Japanese imports. Second, the joint venture car will cost less to produce than if GM were forced to rely immediately on some other production source. Finally, the joint venture offers a valuable opportunity for GM to complete its learning of more efficient Japanese manufacturing and management techniques. Moreover, to the extent the Fremont venture demonstrates the Japanese system can be successfully adapted to the United States, the venture should lead to the development of a more efficient and competitive U.S. industry. . . .

* * *

DISSENTING STATEMENT OF COMMISSIONER PERTSCHUK

The Commission's final acceptance of this consent agreement is a gift from the American public to GM and Toyota's shareholders and Toyota's workers. Based on highly speculative "learning efficiencies," which—if they exist to any degree—are obtainable in less anticompetitive ways, the Commission has approved an arrangement whereby GM and Toyota will cooperate in setting price levels as well as sharing information about the most sensitive commercial subjects. Aside from setting a new antitrust standard—one which allows virtually any automobile production joint venture imaginable—the most likely result is upward pressure on GM and Toyota automobile prices, with other manufacturers' prices following along.

GM can accomplish any legitimate objectives of the joint venture through less harmful ways. . . . The question—why Toyota rather than a smaller Japanese partner—remains unanswered. The Bureau of Economics provides speculative estimates of the marginal gain from GM's joining hands with Toyota, as opposed to Isuzu or others, but these estimates deserve the healthiest of skepticism. They are based on the highly unrealistic assumption that Toyota's lower cost structure can be transferred intact to U.S. assembly.

* * *

The key role of the import quotas is also reconfirmed in staff's latest analysis. The voluntary restraint agreement prevents other Japanese manufacturers from offsetting price increases which stem from any price coordination between GM and Toyota and helps protect the American oligopoly from more vigorous price competition. This buffer against competition is a major reason Toyota dealers are able to charge a premium of $2,000 to $4,000 above list price. Further, staff predicts that import restraints are unlikely to disappear quickly. . . .

But, aside from the fact that the VRA increases the anticompetitive potential of the joint venture, what is its relevance to antitrust analysis? The staff continues to justify the joint venture, in part, because it *evades* the VRA: ". . . the joint venture *does* increase the mix of small cars available to the American public by circumventing existing, and probable future, import limitations." I cannot accept this line of reasoning, which amounts to elevating the evasion of national policy to an antitrust defense.

* * *

The Modification

The prospective futility of the consent agreement is highlighted by the modification to the order. All the Commissioners, I believe, agree that the risks to competition from the joint venture stem primarily from information exchanges, involving price, output decisions, product innovation, marketing plans, etc. In recognition of the fact that sensitive information is *inherent* in the venture, the consent agreement does not—and logically cannot if the venture is allowed to proceed—prevent this type of information exchange. Consequently, the agreement requires GM and Toyota to keep records of communications about model changes, design changes, product designs, sales or production forecasts or plans, and costs of GM or Toyota products supplied to the joint venture. (*See* paragraph V and VI of the order)

The modification approved by the Commission adds "development or engineering activities" to this list of types of communications for which records must be kept. The fact is, however, we could ask GM and Toyota to keep records on *all* communications about *any* subject and the result would be file cabinets of documentation of information exchange that is likely to reduce competition between the two companies but which will not be prohibited under the order because they are part and parcel of the joint venture. . . .

* * *

Commissioner Bailey filed a separate dissenting statement.

Statements of Commissioners Calvani and Douglas in favor of the consent order are omitted.

Questions and Comments

To evaluate any joint venture you will want to know the purpose of the joint venturers because purpose tends to indicate effect. You will want to know the structure of the market and to understand the dynamic forces in the market to determine whether the joint venturers have market power and whether the joint venture might augment this market power. For example, does the joint venture provide a forum for collusion? Does it bring into existence a new institution that facilitates non-rivalrous behavior, such as information exchanges? Does each venture partner gain a significant interest in the profits of the other and is that interest sufficient to dampen the incentive to compete? In general, you will also want to assess the efficiency, progressiveness and procompetitive effects of the joint venture, and the extent to which any restrictive aspects of the venture are necessary or important to achieve the positive effects.

Focus now on GM–Toyota. As always, one must define markets. There may be more than one market. In the automobile industry is there a small car market? The FTC concluded in the affirmative. Within that market, would the venture deaden GM's and Toyota's incentives to compete against one another? Could they afford to lessen their competitive vigor in view of the other competition?

Is there also a broader "car market"? Would General Motors and Toyota have the incentive and the power to stabilize the price at which cars in the United States are sold?

The analyst must consider also whether Toyota was on the brink of building a plant in the United States, from which it could wage yet fiercer competition against GM and others. By the joint venture, was General Motors "paying off" Toyota not to build its own plant in the United States by providing it with a comfortable joint entry and a way to jump the hurdle of the VRA? Or would Toyota's prospects of profit from eventual independent plant facilities be so great that the pay-off hypothesis is unrealistic? (Indeed, is it unrealistic even to think of Japanese firm strategy in accordance with American profit-maximizing models?)

What do you make of the apparent "war" between American competition policy, as expressed in the antitrust laws, and protectionist trade policy, as expressed in the "voluntary" quotas? For Toyota, the venture was a way to skirt the quota policy. Does getting more subcompact cars into the American market count as a benefit, even though specific government policy counts it as a detriment?

Today, the joint venture—New American Motors—is operative. The Nova car is not a best seller and its costs are higher than anticipated. But GM asserts that it is learning high-quality worker performance from the Japanese, and that it uses performance in the Fremont plant as a goad and a yardstick to spur better performance in its other American plants. See Holusha, G.M.'s Big Burden in Toyota Venture, New York Times, May 7, 1987, at D1, col. 3.

5. RESEARCH AND DEVELOPMENT JOINT VENTURES

There was a time when joint ventures between competitors were regarded with grave suspicion. That time has long since passed, as the GM–Toyota analysis suggests. Nonetheless, some analysts continued to fear rigid applications of the law. This fear was particularly strong in the late 1970s and early 1980s when progressive technological development became so important to American business, and businesses—often leading firms—wished to share and jointly develop basic research in order to help regain their competitive edge in world competition. Some policymakers, business people and others sought an antitrust exemption for R & D collaboration. Proponents pointed out that collaboration on basic research is likely to aid progressiveness and is not likely to lessen competition if (1) the collaborators do not engage in joint production (thus, they cannot limit output), (2) a sufficient number of research centers remain, and (3) each joint venturer continues independent research activities. In response to the call for a new law, Congress, in 1984, passed the National Cooperative Research Act. 15 U.S.C. §§ 4301–05. The act declares that all research and development joint ventures will be judged under a rule of reason, and that if venturers file their plans for a research and development joint venture with the government, they will not be subject to treble damage liability in a subsequent antitrust suit. See the statutory language in Appendix A.

How are research ventures to be evaluated under the rule of reason? How does one define a market? (Consider the approach outlined in the statute.) How should we evaluate claims of scale economies? Suppose that there are six important U.S. firms in the market and four important Japanese firms. How can we determine whether a concentrated, collaborative effort at research by the six U.S. firms will yield more progressiveness than independent research of all competing firms? Or whether two or three U.S. research joint ventures are better than one? How should we balance potential for anticompetitive harms against potential for technological gains?

Where does R & D end and production begin? Suppose the joint venture is to work out detailed production techniques for a known process, and then to educate the participants so they can produce in more efficient ways. Would there then be greater concerns than there would be about more basic research?

Problem

The dynamic random access memory ("DRAM") microchip is a widely used staple; it is one of the least complex of all microchips. In the last five years, Japanese firms have captured an overwhelming share of world and U.S. DRAM markets, markets previously dominated by American producers. In early 1987 the Semiconductor Industry Association ("SIA") announced formation of Sematech, a venture including a large majority of American chip manufacturers aimed at producing production-ready technology for DRAM microchips. The goal of Sematech, and its justification, is to respond to the erosion of the American market share for this basic chip.

Assume that Sematech includes Texas Instruments, Motorola, National Semiconductor, Intel, and Advanced Micro Devices, the five largest U.S. chip manufacturers, as well as IBM, Digital Equipment and Hewlett–Packard, three very important U.S. computer manufacturers that make some of their own chips. We want to consider the legality of the Sematech joint venture; that is, whether on balance it is procompetitive or anticompetitive. Consider the following factual circumstances:

(1) In recent years most American firms have withdrawn from DRAM production because they have not been able to meet prices offered by Japanese firms. Before withdrawing, many American firms experienced large losses. Of the few American firms still producing DRAMs, only one is currently covering its costs at a comfortable level.

(2) American firms routinely meet or beat Japanese competition both as to price and quality in the production of other more complex microchips. These more complex chips represent about 70% to 80% of aggregate revenues in the semiconductor market. In general, the more complex and specialized the chip, the greater the American advantage.

(3) American firms generally (including those that have withdrawn from DRAM production) are financially sound and highly profitable.

(4) DRAM production might be useful as a "technology-driver"; cost-cutting production techniques learned in this activity might be applied to producing more complex chips.

(5) The Defense Department endorses and encourages Sematech. It does not want American weapons systems to be solely reliant on foreign DRAM production.

(6) The semiconductor industry is very dynamic. Innovation is rapid; most products go through rapid "generational" development and, before long, are phased out entirely. As this occurs, market shares rapidly change.

Taking these facts and others available to you into account as you analyze the Sematech joint venture, consider the following legal and policy issues:

(1) How do we define the market? Do we define it in terms of DRAM production? Chip production? DRAM-relevant research? Chip-relevant research? Is the market national? International? If it is a research market, what is its configuration? Do we focus only on research aimed at DRAM or chip applications, or on all research that might prove relevant to DRAMs or chips? Do we focus only on research directly relevant to production or do we include research focused primarily on design? Do we try to identify firms not now operating in the relevant research arena but that might enter if the potential research pay-off should increase?

(2) Consider whether the facts in each of the above factual statements would count for or against approval of the joint venture. How much weight should each be given?

(3) Must we learn whether Sematech will tend to increase or decrease the total amount of money spent annually on DRAM (or DRAM production, or chip or chip production) research in America (or worldwide)? If so, how can we estimate these probable expenditures? Must we learn whether more research paths will be pursued with or without Sematech? How can we get the data to make this prediction? Should we learn whether there are scale economies for pursuit of some research paths, and perhaps not for others?

(4) Might Sematech have socially advantageous or disadvantageous spillover effects on the behavior of participating firms? Explain.

On balance, is this joint venture procompetitive or anticompetitive? Is it good for America? If you were Assistant Attorney General, would you sue to enjoin the joint venture? Would you refrain from bringing suit if the parties made certain revisions and imposed certain safeguards? What conditions would you seek?

6. TAKEOVERS

While joint ventures reflect friendly activity, much litigation and debate arises from unfriendly activity—corporate takeovers, usually in the form of tender offers. In recent years individuals associated with the Chicago School and other theorists have argued that a free market in takeovers is likely to produce such substantial efficiencies that takeovers should be encouraged and that neither public regulation nor private acts should stand in their path. These theorists stress that managements tend to become entrenched and, not being adequately policed by boards of directors (who are often cronies of management, or uninformed, or who react to negative information about management by selling rather than voting), may act in self-serving or simply inefficient ways. See, e.g., Jensen & Ruback, The Market for Corporate Control: The Scientific Evidence, 11 J. of Fin.Econ. 5 (1983). The theory asserts that normally only inefficient firms are attractive takeover targets. After takeover, the incumbent managements can be replaced and efficiency restored, and share values will increase. The ongoing risk of takeover activity is seen as an important incentive to management efficiency.

Reagan administration antitrust enforcers endorsed this "free-market-for-control" analysis. Submitting comments to the Securities Exchange Commission's Advisory Committee on Tender Offers, the Antitrust Division said: "[Takeovers] generally perform socially beneficial functions by moving assets from lower to higher-valued uses." Comments of Antitrust Division, May 2, 1983, 44 Antitrust Trade Reg.Rep. (BNA) No. 1114, at 971 (May 12, 1983).

How sound is the free-market-for-control theory? Is it realistic to assume that managements of publicly held corporations normally have friendly, uncritical or inadequately informed boards of directors? Is it realistic to assume that managers tend to act in self-regarding ways and not in the effort to serve stockholder interests? Is it realistic to assume that, while takeover targets behave inefficiently, the corporate raider (another publicly-held firm) is managed by people who are both efficient and are committed to increasing their stockholders' wealth?

Some scholars and observers point out that takeovers create incentives for inefficiency as well as efficiency. They induce managements to spend time and money unproductively. Managers and their lawyers have devised a great variety of techniques to reduce the risks of hostile takeovers: golden parachutes, poison pills, leveraged buy-outs by management, for example. Also, takeover activity may lead managements to discount future income flows for the corporation at the same discount rate that "typical" investors (or possible raiders) would currently use. For example, investment in research and development that promises a much later expected payout is not highly valued. The priority is profits now. Managements seeking to reduce takeover risks emphasize short-term corporate goals and not long-term investment. Moreover, when takeovers occur the resulting very large entity often suffers from inefficiencies of size; the bidder cannot digest its prey; or if the bidder was a liquidator to begin with, it often sells off viable parts of the organism for the short term gain. J. Coffee, Jr., L. Lowenstein and S. Rose–Ackerman, eds., Knights, Raiders, and Targets: The Impact of the Hostile Takeover (1988); Lipton, Corporate Governance in the Age of Finance Corporatism, 136 U.Pa.L. Rev. 1 (1988).

Many of the litigated merger antitrust cases involve attempted takeovers. When a company is a target of an unwanted takeover, its management has a strong incentive to cause the company to sue, and to do so quickly, if a suit has any credible legal basis. The target might get an injunction against the takeover. Or it might merely cause enough delay to abort the deal. (Is it ethical to bring an action and a motion to abort a takeover? Does it matter whether the antitrust claim is strong or weak?)

Currently, enforcers in the Justice Department and some courts view suits by targets skeptically because the target's management has an interest in self-perpetuation and not an interest in increased competition. Indeed, usually the theory of the violation is that the merged firm will have greater market power at the expense of the consumer. Therefore the target might be a beneficiary, not a victim, of the violation. Moreover, as noted, timing is of the essence in takeovers; a preliminary injunction can kill the deal. Should the target firm have standing to challenge the takeover? Is the target ever (or often) likely to be hurt by a merger that hurts competition? It is likely to suffer antitrust injury? See *Cargill, Inc. v. Monfont of Colorado, Inc.,* 479 U.S. 104 (1986), infra at p. 859. Do your answers depend upon whether you view takeovers as generally productive or unproductive for our economy?

C. MERGERS OF POTENTIAL COMPETITORS

1. NON–HORIZONTAL ACQUISITION

We have looked thus far at mergers and joint ventures between competitors. These are called horizontal combinations; they eliminate actual competition between the parties involved, and sometimes they harm the competitive process. Mergers may also eliminate potential competition and may sometimes thereby harm the competitive process. The most likely potential competitors of firms in a market are firms closely related to that market. Consider the U.S. market for widgits. A firm not now in that market may be closely related. It may sell widgits in a different geographic market; it may sell a product or service in the United States that can be produced with the same facilities or technology or marketed through the same distribution system as are widgits; or it may operate in an adjacent upstream or downstream U.S. product market, either selling supplies to widget makers or using widgits as an input to some further production process. Firms with links of this kind will tend to know more about the U.S. widget market than will firms without such links. They will be aware of what is going on in the market and will have some sense of profit opportunities there. Mergers that involve expansion into a related product or service or into a new geographic area are called market-extension mergers.

We looked at *United States v. El Paso Natural Gas Company* (supra p. 768) in our discussion of horizontal mergers. *El Paso* may be classified either as an actual or a potential competition case; Pacific Northwest, although making active efforts to sell natural gas in California, was not located there and had not as yet made any sales there. We now examine *Procter & Gamble,* the Supreme Court's first look at a non-horizontal acquisition.

FTC v. PROCTER & GAMBLE CO.
386 U.S. 568 (1967).

JUSTICE DOUGLAS: This is a proceeding initiated by the Federal Trade Commission charging that respondent, Procter & Gamble Co., had acquired the assets of Clorox Chemical Co. in violation of § 7 of the Clayton Act. . . .

* * *

At the time of the merger, in 1957, Clorox was the leading manufacturer in the heavily concentrated household liquid bleach industry. It is agreed that household liquid bleach is the relevant line of commerce. The product is used in the home as a germicide and disinfectant, and, more importantly, as a whitening agent in washing clothes and fabrics. It is a distinctive product with no close substitutes. Liquid bleach is a low-price, high-turnover consumer product sold mainly through grocery stores and supermarkets. The relevant geographical market is the Nation and a series of regional markets. Because of high shipping costs and low sales price, it is not feasible to ship the product more than 300 miles from its point of manufacture. Most manufacturers are limited to competition within a single region since they have but one plant. Clorox is the only firm selling nationally; it has 13 plants distributed throughout the Nation. Purex, Clorox's closest competitor in size, does not distribute its bleach in the northeast or mid-Atlantic States; in 1957, Purex's bleach was available in less than 50% of the national market.

At the time of the acquisition, Clorox was the leading manufacturer of household liquid bleach, with 48.8% of the national sales—annual sales of slightly less than $40,000,000. Its market share had been steadily increasing for the five years prior to the merger. . . . Purex accounted for 15.7% of the household liquid bleach market. The industry is highly concentrated; in 1957, Clorox and Purex accounted for almost 65% of the Nation's household liquid bleach sales, and, together with four other firms, for almost 80%. The remaining 20% was divided among over 200 small producers. . . .

In light of the territorial limitations on distribution, national figures do not give an accurate picture of Clorox's dominance in the various regions. Thus, Clorox's seven principal competitors did no business in New England, the mid-Atlantic States, or metropolitan New York. Clorox's share of the sales in those areas was 56%, 72%, and 64% respectively. . . .

Since all liquid bleach is chemically identical, advertising and sales promotion are vital. In 1957 Clorox spent almost $3,700,000 on advertising, imprinting the value of its bleach in the mind of the consumer. In addition, it spent $1,700,000 for other promotional activities. The Commission found that these heavy expenditures went far to explain why Clorox maintained so high a market share despite the fact that its brand, though chemically indistinguishable from rival brands, retailed for a price equal to or, in many instances, higher than its competitors.

Procter is a large, diversified manufacturer of low-price, high-turnover household products sold through grocery, drug, and department stores. Prior to its acquisition of Clorox, it did not produce household liquid bleach. Its 1957 sales were in excess of $1,100,000,000 from which it realized profits of more than $67,000,000; its assets were over $500,000,000. Procter has been marked by rapid growth and diversification. It has successfully developed and introduced a number of new products. Its primary activity is in the general area of soaps, detergents, and cleansers; in 1957, of total domestic sales, more than one-half (over $500,000,000) were in this field. Procter was the dominant factor in this area. It accounted for 54.4% of all packaged detergent sales. The industry is heavily concentrated—Procter and its nearest competitors, Colgate–Palmolive and Lever Brothers, account for 80% of the market.

In the marketing of soaps, detergents, and cleansers, as in the marketing of household liquid bleach, advertising and sales promotion are vital. In 1957, Procter was the Nation's largest advertiser, spending more than $80,000,000 on advertising and an additional $47,000,000 on sales promotion. Due to its tremendous volume, Procter receives substantial discounts from the media. As a multiproduct producer Procter enjoys substantial advantages in advertising and sales promotion. Thus, it can and does feature several products in its promotions, reducing the printing, mailing, and other costs for each product. It also purchases network programs on behalf of several products, enabling it to give each product network exposure at a fraction of the cost per product that a firm with only one product to advertise would incur.

Prior to the acquisition, Procter was in the course of diversifying into product lines related to its basic detergent-soap-cleanser business. Liquid bleach was a distinct possibility since packaged detergents—Procter's primary product line—and liquid bleach are used complementarily in washing clothes and fabrics, and in general household cleaning. . . .

The decision to acquire Clorox was the result of a study conducted by Procter's promotion department designed to determine the advisability of entering the liquid bleach industry. The initial report noted the ascendancy of liquid bleach in the large and expanding household bleach market, and recommended that Procter purchase Clorox rather than enter independently. Since a large investment would be needed to obtain a satisfactory market share, acquisition of the industry's leading firm was attractive. "Taking over the Clorox business . . . could be a way of achieving a dominant position in the liquid bleach market quickly, which would pay out reasonably well." . . .

The Commission found that the acquisition might substantially lessen competition. . . .

The Court of Appeals said that the Commission's finding of illegality had been based on "treacherous conjecture," mere possibility and suspicion. 358 F.2d 74, 83. It [reversed]. . . .

* * *

The anticompetitive effects with which this product-extension merger is fraught can easily be seen: (1) the substitution of the powerful acquiring firm for the smaller, but already dominant, firm may substantially reduce the competitive structure of the industry by raising entry barriers and by dissuading the smaller firms from aggressively competing; (2) the acquisition eliminates the potential competition of the acquiring firm.

The liquid bleach industry was already oligopolistic before the acquisition, and price competition was certainly not as vigorous as it would have been if the industry were competitive. Clorox enjoyed a dominant posi-

(Fox & Sullivan) Antitrust ACB—28

tion nationally, and its position approached monopoly proportions in certain areas. The existence of some 200 fringe firms certainly does not belie that fact. Nor does the fact, relied upon by the court below, that, after the merger, producers other than Clorox "were selling more bleach for more money than ever before." 358 F.2d, at 80. In the same period, Clorox increased its share from 48.8% to 52%. The interjection of Procter into the market considerably changed the situation. There is every reason to assume that the smaller firms would become more cautious in competing due to their fear of retaliation by Procter. It is probable that Procter would become the price leader and that oligopoly would become more rigid.

The acquisition may also have the tendency of raising the barriers to new entry. The major competitive weapon in the successful marketing of bleach is advertising. Clorox was limited in this area by its relatively small budget and its inability to obtain substantial discounts. By contrast, Procter's budget was much larger; and, although it would not devote its entire budget to advertising Clorox, it could divert a large portion to meet the short-term threat of a new entrant. Procter would be able to use its volume discounts to advantage in advertising Clorox. Thus, a new entrant would be much more reluctant to face the giant Procter than it would have been to face the smaller Clorox.[3]

Possible economies cannot be used as a defense to illegality. Congress was aware that some mergers which lessen competition may also result in economies but it struck the balance in favor of protecting competition. See *Brown Shoe Co. v. United States,* [370 U.S. 294 (1962)] at 344.

The Commission also found that the acquisition of Clorox by Procter eliminated Procter as a potential competitor. The Court of Appeals declared that this finding was not supported by evidence because there was no evidence that Procter's management had ever intended to enter the industry independently and that Procter had never attempted to enter. The evidence, however, clearly shows that Procter was the most likely entrant. Procter had recently launched a new abrasive cleaner in an industry similar to the liquid bleach industry, and had wrested leadership from a brand that had enjoyed even a larger market share than had Clorox. Procter was engaged in a vigorous program of diversifying into product lines closely related to its basic products. Liquid bleach was a natural avenue of diversification. . . .

It is clear that the existence of Procter at the edge of the industry exerted considerable influence on the market. First, the market behavior of the liquid bleach industry was influenced by each firm's predictions of

3. The barriers to entry have been raised both for entry by new firms and for entry into new geographical markets by established firms. The latter aspect is demonstrated by Purex's lesson in Erie, Pennsylvania. In October 1957, Purex selected Erie, Pennsylvania—where it had not sold previously—as an area in which to test the salability, under competitive conditions, of a new bleach. The leading brands in Erie were Clorox, with 52%, and the "101" brand, sold by Gardner Manufacturing Company, with 29% of the market. Purex launched an advertising and promotional campaign to obtain a broad distribution in a short time, and in five months captured 33% of the Erie market. Clorox's share dropped to 35% and 101's to 17%. Clorox responded by offering its bleach at reduced prices, and then added an offer of a $1-value ironing board cover for 50¢ with each purchase of Clorox at the reduced price. It also increased its advertising with television spots. The result was to restore Clorox's lost market share and, indeed, to increase it slightly. Purex's share fell to 7%. . . .

the market behavior of its competitors, actual and potential. Second, the barriers to entry by a firm of Procter's size and with its advantages were not significant. There is no indication that the barriers were so high that the price Procter would have to charge would be above the price that would maximize the profits of the existing firms. Third, the number of potential entrants was not so large that the elimination of one would be insignificant. Few firms would have the temerity to challenge a firm as solidly entrenched as Clorox. Fourth, Procter was found by the Commission to be the most likely entrant. These findings of the Commission were amply supported by the evidence.

The judgment of the Court of Appeals is reversed and remanded with instructions to affirm and enforce the Commission's order.

It is so ordered.

The concurring opinion of Justice Harlan is omitted.

Questions and Comments

Prior to *Procter & Gamble,* the mergers we examined involved elimination of actual competition between the merging firms. Courts sometimes found that elimination of competition between the partners also lessened competition in the marketplace, either by facilitating collusion, as in *Hospital Corporation of America,* chilling an important competitive dynamic, as in *Coca–Cola,* or depriving customers of important options, as in *Philadelphia National Bank.*

Procter & Gamble, by its acquisition of Clorox, did not eliminate actual competition; the firms were not competitors. Instead, the theory of the case involved two other concepts: entrenchment of Clorox's dominance, and elimination of Procter's potential competition. Let us look separately at each ground.

Consider, first, "entrenchment" of a dominant firm. Was Clorox a dominant firm—a possessor of market power along lines of the monopoly model? Does entrenchment of Clorox mean that Clorox gained greater market power? Did it build a larger moat, or reinforce a moat, insulating itself from competitive inroads of others?

A firm can increase its dominance in one of two ways. It can lower its own costs relative to those of its competitors (or it can raise quality at a given cost—which is treated as the same thing), or it can raise barriers to entry or expansion. The Court examined both routes to entrenched dominance.

The Court noted that Procter spent enormous sums on advertising and got volume advertising discounts apparently not previously available to Clorox and not available to its competitors. Post acquisition, Clorox would have access to these discounts. What would be the effect of the discounts on Clorox's competitors? Was advertising as a competitive strategy equally important to Clorox and to Purex? Was it equally important to Clorox and to its hundreds of small competitors?

Suppose that the discounts were cost-justified and thus reflected an efficiency. On that assumption should they weigh for or against the acquisition? What if Procter realized cost-savings because it could advertise Clorox's liquid bleach with a group of its other products in a single space? Should that efficiency weigh for or against the acquisition? What is Justice Harlan's view? Suppose the discounts were not cost-justified, but were due to Procter's monopsony power as a buyer of advertising. Is it clear, then, that the discounts should weigh against the merger? Did the Court think the discounts were cost-justified? Did it care?

Another way that a firm can lower its costs relative to those of its rivals is to raise its rivals' costs. Similarly, a firm might threaten rivals with increased costs if they should dare to compete; not wishing to provoke a giant predator, the smaller firms might forsake competition. The Court noted one incident in which Clorox "attacked" an expanding competitor—by selective low prices, promotional offers and increased advertising. Clorox not only responded to Purex's entry into Erie but regained its lost market share and reduced Purex's share in Erie from 33% to 7%. See Court's footnote 3. (Is this predation in violation of Section 2?)

The Court assumed that the small firms in the market and possible unknown entrants would be much more reluctant to compete against the colossal Procter/Clorox than they were to compete against the "merely" giant Clorox. Is this a fair assumption? Justice Harlan did not think so. As plaintiff, is it enough to show that the acquiring firm is a giant entering a market of pygmies? Must the giant have engaged elsewhere in "anticompetitive attacks" on rivals? Must it have a reputation for doing so? Do the facts suggest that smaller firms would lessen their competitive efforts for fear of predatory reprisals?

In addition to entrenchment, the Court feared negative effects from the elimination of Procter's potential competition. The Court concluded that Procter was the most likely potential entrant. (On what basis?) The Court further concluded that Procter, as a potential entrant, must have "exerted considerable influence on the market."

Was the Court suggesting that Procter was a present force in the relevant market, in the same sense that Pacific Northwest was a market force in *El Paso?* Is there evidence to support such a conclusion? Is there reason to suppose that Clorox (and Purex?) would have charged higher prices but for their awareness of Procter as a potential entrant? Why was Justice Harlan, the most skeptical Justice, willing to assume that Procter's presence constrained Clorox?

The Court thought that Procter removed its potential competition by removing its moderating effect on Clorox's price. If this was so, and if no other potential entrant exerted an equally strong force, then price would rise and output would probably fall after the acquisition. In other words, removal of significant, perceived potential competition from a market lacking sufficiently robust actual competition and lacking other equally significant potential competition can have an output effect. The effect is sometimes referred to as a "water's edge" or "wings" effect. (There was no such effect after this acquisition, but, as the Court observed, the new firm had the incentive to restrain itself in order to build a good litigation record.)

There is another and alternative conception of potential competition. Suppose no firm making bleach was aware of Procter as a possible entrant but that (as the FTC alleged but failed to prove) Procter had a well-developed plan to enter the market; it would acquire Clorox if it could get away with it; but if not it would either acquire and then expand a small firm or it would enter the market *de novo*. What would probably have happened to price and output if Procter had pursued the path of independent (or toe-hold) entry? Could you say, on the assumed facts, that Procter's acquisition of Clorox would have eliminated Procter's own future, deconcentrating independent entry; a route that would have increased output? Is elimination of this prospect of "shaking things up" a violation? See *United States v. Marine Bancorporation, Inc.,* infra, p. 824.

The Court decided *Procter & Gamble* in 1967. The Court was then concerned with stifling effects of bigness, and it stressed those concerns. Later, potential competition cases began to deal more directly, and eventually more technically, with the economic effects of eliminating the potential competition of the acquiring firm. *Falstaff Brewing Company* was the next important case. It was also the last case decided before the emergence of the new antitrust majority on the Supreme Court. As you will see from Justice Douglas' concurrence in *Falstaff,* the days of "impassioned" antitrust had not yet ended.

UNITED STATES v. FALSTAFF BREWING CORP.
410 U.S. 526 (1973).

JUSTICE WHITE: [Falstaff was the fourth largest beer producer in the country, with 5.9% of the nation's production. It was the largest U.S. beer seller that did not sell in New England. To penetrate the New England market, it acquired Narrangansett, the largest seller of beer in New England, with a 20% market share. In New England the top 8 firms had 81.2%.]

* * *

Falstaff met increasingly strong competition in the 1960's from four brewers who sold in all of the significant markets. National brewers possess competitive advantages since they are able to advertise on a nationwide basis, their beers have greater prestige than regional or local beers, and they are less affected by the weather or labor problems in a particular region. Thus Falstaff concluded that it must convert from "regional" to "national" status, if it was to compete effectively with the national producers. For several years Falstaff publicly expressed its desire for national distribution and after making several efforts in the early 1960's to enter the Northeast by acquisition, agreed to acquire Narragansett in 1965.

Before the acquisition was accomplished, the United States brought suit alleging that the acquisition would violate § 7 because its effect may be to substantially lessen competition in the production and sale of beer in the New England market. This contention was based on two grounds: because Falstaff was a potential entrant and because the acquisition eliminated competition that would have existed had Falstaff entered the market *de novo* or by acquisition and expansion of a smaller firm, a so-called "toe-hold" acquisition.[10] The acquisition was completed after the Government's motions for injunctive relief were denied, and Falstaff agreed to operate Narragansett as a separate subsidiary until otherwise ordered by the court.

After a trial on the merits, the District Court found that the geographic market was highly competitive; that Falstaff was desirous of becoming a national brewer by entering the Northeast; that its manage-

---

10. Hereinafter, reference to *de novo* entry includes "toe-hold" acquisition as well.

ment was committed against *de novo* entry; and that competition had not diminished since the acquisition. The District Court then held:

> "The Government's contentions that Falstaff at the time of said acquisition was a potential entrant into said New England market, and that said acquisition deprived the New England market of additional competition are not supported by the evidence. On the contrary, the credible evidence establishes beyond a reasonable doubt that the executive management of Falstaff had consistently decided not to attempt to enter said market unless it could acquire a brewery with a strong and viable distribution system such as that possessed by Narragansett. Said executives had carefully considered such possible alternatives as (1) acquisition of a small brewery on the east coast, (2) the shipping of beer from its existing breweries, the nearest of which was located in Ft. Wayne, Indiana, (3) the building of a new brewery on the east coast and other possible alternatives, but concluded that none of said alternatives would have effected a reasonable probability of a profitable entry for it in said New England market. In my considered opinion the plaintiff has failed to establish by a fair preponderance of the evidence that Falstaff was a potential competitor in said New England market at the time it acquired Narragansett. The credible evidence establishes that it was not a potential entrant into said market by any means or way other than by said acquisition. Consequently it cannot be said that its acquisition of Narragansett eliminated it as a potential competitor therein." 332 F.Supp., at 972.

Also finding that the Government had failed to establish that the acquisition would result in a substantial lessening of competition, the District Court entered judgment for Falstaff and dismissed the complaint.

* * *

The District Court erred as a matter of law. The error lay in the assumption that because Falstaff, as a matter of fact, would never have entered the market *de novo,* it could in no sense be considered a potential competitor. More specifically, the District Court failed to give separate consideration to whether Falstaff was a potential competitor in the sense that it was so positioned on the edge of the market that it exerted beneficial influence on competitive conditions in that market.

* * *

The specific question with respect to this phase of the case is not what Falstaff's internal company decisions were but whether, given its financial capabilities and conditions in the New England market, it would be reasonable to consider it a potential entrant into that market. Surely, it could not be said on this record that Falstaff's general interest in the New England market was unknown; and if it would appear to rational beer merchants in New England that Falstaff might well build a new brewery to supply the northeastern market then its entry by merger becomes suspect under § 7. The District Court should therefore have appraised the economic facts about Falstaff and the New England market in order to determine whether in any realistic sense Falstaff could be said to be a potential competitor on the fringe of the market with likely influence on existing competition. . . .

Since it appears that the District Court entertained too narrow a view of Falstaff as a potential competitor and since it appears that the District Court's conclusion that the merger posed no probable threat to competition followed automatically from the finding that Falstaff had no intent to enter *de novo,* we remand this case for the District Court to make the proper assessment of Falstaff as a potential competitor.

. . . We leave for another day the question of the applicability of § 7 to a merger that will leave competition in the marketplace exactly as it was, neither hurt nor helped, and that is challengeable under § 7 only on grounds that the company could, but did not, enter *de novo* or through "toe-hold" acquisition and that there is less competition than there would have been had entry been in such a manner. . . .

* * *

JUSTICE DOUGLAS, concurring in part: . . . I offer the following observations with respect to the question which the Court does not reach.

There can be no question that it would be sufficient for the Government to prove its case to show that Falstaff would have made a *de novo* entry but for the acquisition of Narragansett or that Falstaff was a potential competitor exercising present influence on the market. . . .

* * *

I conclude that there is "reasonable likelihood" that the acquisition in question "may be substantially to lessen competition." Accordingly, I would be inclined to reverse and direct the District Judge to enter judgment for the Government and afford appropriate relief. Nevertheless, since the Court will not reach this question and I agree with the legal principles set forth in . . . its opinion, I join the judgment remanding the case for further proceedings.

JUSTICE MARSHALL, concurring in the result: I share the majority's view that the District Judge erred as a matter of law and that the case must be remanded for further proceedings. I cannot agree, however, with the theory upon which the majority bases the remand.

The majority accuses the District Judge of neglecting to assess the present procompetitive effect which Falstaff exerted by remaining on the fringe of the market. The explanation for this failing is rather simple. The Government never alleged in its complaint that Falstaff was exerting a present procompetitive influence, it introduced not a scrap of evidence to support this view, and even at this stage of the proceedings, it seemingly disclaims reliance on this theory.

* * *

Inasmuch as the District Court grounded its dismissal on these conclusions [that Falstaff would not enter the market unless it could acquire a strong brewery such as Narragansett], I think we have a responsibility to assess the validity of the legal standard from which they are derived. I would hold that where, as here, strong objective evidence indicates that a firm is a potential entrant into a market, it is error for the trial judge to rely solely on the firm's subjective prediction of its own future conduct. While such subjective evidence is probative on the issue of potential entry, it is inherently unreliable and must be used with great care. Ordinarily, the district court should presume that objectively measurable market forces will govern a firm's future conduct. Only when there is a compelling demonstration that a firm will not follow its economic self-interest may the district court consider subjective evidence in predicting that conduct. Even then, subjective evidence should be preferred only when the objective evidence is weak or contradictory. Because the District Court failed to apply these standards, I would remand the case for further consideration.

* * *

Question and Comments

Falstaff arose as an "actual" potential competition case. By acquiring Narragansett, the government alleged, Falstaff eliminated Narragansett's future independent, deconcentrating entry. Why do you think Falstaff acquired Narragansett? Do you suspect that Narragansett would probably have entered *de novo*, but for Falstaff's offer? Soon? Eventually? Who proposes the better legal standard, Justice White or Justice Douglas? Who proposes the better rule of evidence and draws sounder inferences from the basic facts, Justice White or Justice Marshall?

Justices Rehnquist and Stewart dissented on grounds that the government had failed to introduce evidence to support the one theory it had initially advanced—elimination of procompetitive entry. Within a year after *Falstaff* was decided, Justices Rehnquist and Stewart, along with Chief Justice Burger and Justices Powell and Blackmun, were to form the new majority—deferent to business interests and needs, tolerant of bigness and industrial concentration, and demanding of plaintiffs in their proof that a challenged acquisition would lessen competition.

UNITED STATES v. MARINE BANCORPORATION, INC.

418 U.S. 602 (1974).

JUSTICE POWELL: [National Bank of Commerce (NBC), a subsidiary of Marine Bancorporation, was the second largest bank headquartered in the State of Washington. NBC proposed to acquire Washington Trust Bank (WTB), the third largest bank in Spokane. The top three banks in Spokane held 42.1%, 31.6% and 18.6% of deposits, respectively. NBC did not operate in Spokane. The government sued on potential competition theories. The district court dismissed the complaint.]

* * *

II

THE RELEVANT MARKETS

* * *

Prior to trial the Government stipulated that the Spokane area is a relevant geographic market in the instant case, and there is no dispute that it is the only banking market in which WTB is a significant participant. Nevertheless, the Government contends that the entire State is also an appropriate "section of the country" in this case. It is conceded that the State is not a banking market. But the Government asserts that the State is an economically differentiated region, because its boundaries delineate an area within which Washington banks are insulated from most forms of competition by out-of-state banking organizations. The Government further argues that this merger, and others it allegedly will trigger, may lead eventually to the domination of all banking in the State by a few large banks, facing each other in a network of local, oligopolistic banking markets. This assumed eventual statewide linkage of local markets, it is argued, will enhance statewide the possibility of parallel, standardized, anticompetitive behavior. This concern for the possible statewide consequences of geographic market extension mergers by commercial banks appears to be an important reason for the Government's recent efforts to block such mergers through an application of the potential-competition doctrine under § 7.

The Government's proposed reading of the "any section of the country" phrase of § 7 is at variance with this Court's § 7 cases, and we reject it. Without exception the Court has treated "section of the country" and "relevant geographic market" as identical, and it has defined the latter concept as the area in which the goods or services at issue are marketed to a significant degree by the acquired firm. *E.g., Philadelphia National Bank*, [374 U.S. 321 (1963)] at 357–362. In cases in which the acquired firm markets its products or services on a local, regional, and national basis, the Court has acknowledged the existence of more than one relevant geographic market. But in no previous § 7 case has the Court determined the legality of a merger by measuring its effects on areas where the acquired firm is not a direct competitor. . . . We hold that in a potential-competition case like this one, the relevant geographic market or appropriate section of the country is the area in which the acquired firm is an actual, direct competitor.

Apart from the fact that the Government's statewide approach is not supported by the precedents, it is simply too speculative on this record. . . . [I]t is to be remembered that § 7 deals in "probabilities," not "ephemeral possibilities." *Brown Shoe Co.*, [370 U.S. 294 (1962)] at 323. The Government's underlying concern for a linkage or network of statewide oligopolistic banking markets is, on this record at least, considerably closer to "ephemeral possibilities" than to "probabilities." To assume, on the basis of essentially no evidence, that the challenged merger will tend to produce a statewide linkage of oligopolies is to espouse a *per se* rule against geographic market extension mergers like the one at issue here. No § 7 case from this Court has gone that far,[23] and we do not do so today. For the purpose of this case, the appropriate "section of the country" and the "relevant geographic market" are the same—the Spokane metropolitan area.

---

23. We put aside cases where an acquiring firm's market power, existing capabilities, and proposed merger partner are such that the merger would produce an enterprise likely to dominate the target market (a concept known as entrenchment). See *FTC v.* *Procter & Gamble Co.*, 386 U.S. 568 (1967). Cf. *Falstaff Brewing Corp.*, [410 U.S. 526 (1973)] at 531. There is no allegation that the instant merger would produce entrenchment in the Spokane market.

III

POTENTIAL COMPETITION DOCTRINE

The term "potential competitor" appeared for the first time in a § 7 opinion of this Court in *United States v. El Paso Natural Gas Co.*, 376 U.S. 651, 659 (1964). *El Paso* was in reality, however, an actual-competition rather than a potential-competition case. The potential-competition doctrine has been defined in major part by subsequent cases, particularly *United States v. Falstaff Brewing Corp.*, 410 U.S. 526 (1973). Unequivocal proof that an acquiring firm actually would have entered *de novo* but for a merger is rarely available. Thus, as *Falstaff* indicates, the principal focus of the doctrine is on the likely effects of the premerger position of the acquiring firm on the fringe of the target market. In developing and applying the doctrine, the Court has recognized that a market extension merger may be unlawful if the target market is substantially concentrated, if the acquiring firm has the characteristics, capabilities, and economic incentive to render it a perceived potential *de novo* entrant, and if the acquiring firm's premerger presence on the fringe of the target market in fact tempered oligopolistic behavior on the part of existing participants in that market. In other words, the Court has interpreted § 7 as encompassing what is commonly known as the "wings effect"—the probability that the acquiring firm prompted premerger procompetitive effects within the target market by being perceived by the existing firms in that market as likely to enter *de novo*. *Falstaff, supra,* at 531–537. The elimination of such present procompetitive effects may render a merger unlawful under § 7.

Although the concept of perceived potential entry has been accepted in the Court's prior § 7 cases, the potential-competition theory upon which the Government places principal reliance in the instant case has not. The Court has not previously resolved whether the potential-competition doctrine proscribes a market extension merger solely on the ground that such a merger eliminates the prospect for long-term deconcentration of an oligopolistic market that in theory might result if the acquiring firm were forbidden to enter except through a *de novo* undertaking or through the acquisition of a small existing entrant (a so-called foothold or toehold acquisition). *Falstaff* expressly reserved this issue.

* * *

C. Potential De Novo or Foothold Entry

. . . The Government contends that the challenged merger violates § 7 because it eliminates the alleged likelihood that, but for the merger, NBC would enter Spokane *de novo* or through a foothold acquisition. Utilization of one of these methods of entry, it is argued, would be likely to produce deconcentration of the Spokane market over the long run or other procompetitive effects, because NBC would be required to compete vigorously to expand its initially insignificant market share.

Two essential preconditions must exist before it is possible to resolve whether the Government's theory, if proved, establishes a violation of § 7. It must be determined: (i) that in fact NBC has available feasible means for entering the Spokane market other than by acquiring WTB; and (ii) that those means offer a substantial likelihood of ultimately producing deconcentration of that market or other significant procompetitive effects. The parties are in sharp disagreement over the existence of each of these preconditions in this case. There is no dispute that NBC possesses the financial capability and incentive to enter. The controversy turns on what methods of entry are realistically possible and on the likely effect of various methods on the characteristics of the Spokane commercial banking market.

It is undisputed that under state law NBC cannot establish *de novo* branches in Spokane and that its parent holding company cannot hold more than 25% of the stock of any other bank. Entry for NBC into Spokane therefore must be by acquisition of an existing bank. The Government contends that NBC has two distinct alternatives for acquisition of banks smaller than WTB and that either alternative would be likely to benefit the Spokane commercial banking market.

First, the Government contends that NBC could arrange for the formation of a new bank (a concept known as "sponsorship"), insure that the stock for such a new bank is placed in friendly hands, and then ultimately acquire that bank. Appellees respond that this approach would violate the spirit if not the letter of state-law restrictions on bank branching. . . .

[W]e will assume, *arguendo,* that NBC conceivably could succeed in sponsoring and then acquiring a new bank in Spokane at some indefinite time in the future. It does not follow from this assumption, however, that this method of entry would be reasonably likely to produce any significant procompetitive benefits in the Spokane commercial banking market. To the contrary, it appears likely that such a method of entry would not significantly affect that market.

State law would not allow NBC to branch from a sponsored bank after it was acquired. NBC's entry into Spokane therefore would be frozen at the level of its initial acquisition. Thus, if NBC were to enter Spokane by sponsoring and acquiring a small bank, it would be trapped into a position of operating a single branch office in a large metropolitan area with no reasonable likelihood of developing a significant share of that market. This assumed method of entry therefore would offer little realistic hope of ultimately producing deconcentration of the Spokane market. Moreover, it is unlikely that a single new bank in Spokane with a small market share, and forbidden to branch, would have any other significant procompetitive effect on that market. . . .

As a second alternative method of entry, the Government proposed that NBC could enter by a foothold acquisition of one of two small, state-chartered commercial banks that operate in the Spokane metropolitan area. . . .

Granting the Government the benefit of the doubt that these two small banks were available merger partners for NBC, or were available at some not too distant time, it again does not follow that an acquisition of either would produce the long-term market-structure benefits predicted by the Government. Once NBC acquired either of these banks, it could not branch from the acquired bank. This limitation strongly suggests that

NBC would not develop into a significant participant in the Spokane market. . . .

In sum, with regard to either of its proposed alternative methods of entry, the Government has offered an unpersuasive case on the first precondition of the question reserved in *Falstaff*—that feasible alternative methods of entry in fact existed. Putting these difficulties aside, the Government simply did not establish the second precondition. It failed to demonstrate that the alternative means offer a reasonable prospect of long-term structural improvement or other benefits in the target market. In fact, insofar as competitive benefits are concerned, the Government is in the anomalous position of opposing a geographic market extension merger that will introduce a third full-service banking organization to the Spokane market, where only two are now operating, in reliance on alternative means of entry that appear unlikely to have any significant procompetitive effect. Accordingly, we cannot hold for the Government on its principal potential-competition theory. Indeed, since the preconditions for that theory are not present, we do not reach it, and therefore we express no view on the appropriate resolution of the question reserved in *Falstaff*. We reiterate that this case concerns an industry in which new entry is extensively regulated by the State and Federal Governments.

D. Perceived Potential Entry.

The Government's failure to establish that NBC has alternative methods of entry that offer a reasonable likelihood of producing procompetitive effects is determinative of the fourth step of its argument. Rational commercial bankers in Spokane, it must be assumed, are aware of the regulatory barriers that render NBC an unlikely or an insignificant potential entrant except by merger with WTB. In light of those barriers, it is improbable that NBC exerts any meaningful procompetitive influence over Spokane banks by "standing in the wings."

Moreover, the District Court found as a fact that "the threat of entry by NBC into the Spokane market by any means other than the consummation of the merger, to the extent any such threat exists, does not have any significant effect on the competitive practices of commercial banks in that market nor any significant effect on the level of competition therein." . . . Our review of the record indicates that the court's finding was not in error. The Government's only hard evidence of any "wings effect" was a memorandum written in 1962 by an officer of NBC expressing the view that Spokane banks were likely to engage in price competition as NBC approached their market. Evidence of an expression of opinion by an officer of the acquiring bank, not an official of a bank operating in the target market, in a memorandum written a decade prior to the challenged merger does not establish a violation of § 7.

* * *

IV

CONCLUSION

In applying the doctrine of potential competition to commercial banking, courts must, as we have noted, take into account the extensive federal and state regulation of banks. Our affirmance of the District

Court's judgment in this case rests primarily on state statutory barriers to *de novo* entry and to expansion following entry into a new geographic market. In States where such stringent barriers exist and in the absence of a likelihood of entrenchment, the potential-competition doctrine— grounded as it is on relative freedom of entry on the part of the acquiring firm—will seldom bar a geographic market extension merger by a commercial bank. In States that permit free branching or multibank holding companies, courts hearing cases involving such mergers should take into account all relevant factors, including the barriers to entry created by state and federal control over the issuance of new bank charters. Testimony by responsible regulatory officials that they will not grant new charters in the target market is entitled to great weight, although it is not determinative. To avoid the danger of subjecting the enforcement of the antitrust laws to the policies of a particular bank regulatory official or agency, courts should look also to the size and growth prospects of the target market, the size and number of banking organizations participating in it, and past practices of regulatory agencies in granting charters. If regulatory restraints are not determinative, courts should consider the factors that are pertinent to any potential-competition case, including the economic feasibility and likelihood of *de novo* entry, the capabilities and expansion history of the acquiring firm, and the performance as well as the structural characteristics of the target market.

The judgment is

Affirmed.

JUSTICE WHITE, joined by JUSTICES BRENNAN and MARSHALL, dissenting: For the second time this Term, the Court's new anti-trust majority has chipped away at the policies of § 7 of the Clayton Act. In *United States v. General Dynamics Corp.*, 415 U.S. 486 (1974), the majority sustained the failing-company defense in a new guise. Here, it redefines the elements of potential competition and dramatically escalates the burden of proving that a merger "may be substantially to lessen competition" within the meaning of § 7.

*   *   *

Questions and Comments

In *United States v. Connecticut National Bank*, 418 U.S. 656 (1974), a companion case to *Marine Bancorporation*, the Court dealt largely with market definition. It held that the government had the burden "to come forward with evidence delineating the rough approximation of localized banking markets," and that the government could not rely solely on either Standard Metropolitan Statistical Areas or on town borders since neither delineation presumptively corresponds with the "areas of significant competitive influence" wherein each of the consolidating banks maintains its offices. Id. at 669–71.

While *Connecticut National Bank* rebuffs attempts to define markets so broadly that firms appear never to have market power, *Marine Bancorporation* places weighty burdens on plaintiffs seeking to prove significant loss of potential competition. Are the burdens of *Marine Bancorporation* surmountable? Is it likely that a plaintiff could prove that Procter & Gamble caused

Clorox to charge a lower price because Clorox foresaw Procter's strategy to make a grass roots or toe-hold entry? How would you go about trying to prove this hypothesis if you represented the plaintiff? Could a firm in the posture of Procter & Gamble frustrate a plaintiff's attempt to prove probable de novo entry by testimony of its executives that it would not enter the market de novo? Could it do so by documents to that effect prepared by the firm's executives or by its planning staff? Will plaintiff's failure to prove probable de novo entry also defeat its attempt to prove edge effect?

Predictably, in the wake of *Marine Bancorporation,* potential entry problems became far less significant an obstacle to mergers. Today, plaintiffs challenging mergers on potential competition grounds virtually always fail to carry their burden. See e.g., *Tenneco, Inc. v. FTC,* 689 F.2d 346 (2d Cir.1982), and *BOC Intern. Ltd. v. FTC,* 557 F.2d 24 (2d Cir.1977), both setting aside FTC divestiture orders. For a suggested formulation of presumptions that would ease plaintiffs' burdens and, in the authors' view, be more realistic, see Brodley, Potential Competition under the Merger Guidelines, 71 Calif.L.Rev. 376 (1983).

The paragraph above addresses a question of fact: Did a merger eliminate significant potential competition? Recall that the Court reserved judgment on a question of law: Can elimination of the acquiring firm's own procompetitive grass roots or toe-hold entry ever be grounds for a violation of Section 7? The FTC has answered the reserved question in the affirmative—an acquirer's elimination of its own procompetitive entry into a noncompetitive market may result in a violation. E.g., *Yamaha Motor Co. v. FTC,* 657 F.2d 971 (8th Cir.1981), *cert. denied sub nom. Brunswick Corp. v. FTC,* 657 F.2d 971 (1981), *cert. denied,* 456 U.S. 915 (1982); *In re British Oxygen Co.,* 86 FTC 1241 (1975), *rev'd on other grounds,* 557 F.2d 24 (2d Cir.1977). In its 1982 and 1984 merger guidelines, the Department of Justice has likewise taken this position. Why would an otherwise minimalist administration adopt this view?

The 1984 guidelines state the following standards for mergers that may eliminate potential competition, whether in the form of actual potential competition (elimination of future deconcentrating entry) or of perceived potential competition (elimination of edge or wings effect):

The Department will consider the following factors to determine whether the acquisition is likely to increase market power through monopolization or collusion:

(1) Market concentration must normally be more than 1800 on the Herfindahl–Hirshman Index.

(2) Entry must not be easy; it must require a specific entry advantage.

(3) The acquiring firm's entry advantage must not be shared by more than two other firms. This condition may be relaxed if probable actual entry is particularly strong.

(4) The market share of the acquired firm must be more than 5%. The Department is likely to sue if the acquired firm's share is 20% or more and all other conditions are met.

2. JOINT VENTURES AND POTENTIAL COMPETITION

Two firms might jointly form a new entity to engage in a line of business in which only one is currently engaged and the other is a potential entrant, or in which neither is currently engaged but both are potential entrants. By eliminating important potential competition, the joint venture might offend the law.

In 1964 the Supreme Court heard a potential competition joint venture case, *United States v. Penn–Olin Chemical Company,* 378 U.S. 158 (1964). Pennsalt Chemicals Corporation produced sodium chlorate (a chemical used principally by the pulp and paper industry) in Portland, Oregon. It accounted for 57.8% of all sales west of the Rocky Mountains. Olin Mathieson Chemical Corporation was a leading producer of chemicals and owned a patent on a process for bleaching pulp that required sodium chlorate. Pennsalt and Olin Mathieson formed a new company, Penn–Olin, and each acquired 50% of its stock.

Penn–Olin was formed to produce and sell sodium chlorate in the Southeast. At the time of the formation of the joint venture, Hooker Chemical Corporation accounted for 49.5% of sales in the southeast market, American Potash & Chemical Corporation accounted for 41.6%, and Pennsalt, using Olin as its marketing agent, accounted for 8.9%. Both of the joint venturers had extensive financial resources, both had the know-how for making sodium chlorate, and both had demonstrated a strong interest in entering the southeast market. Neither had completely rejected the possibility of individual entry into the southeast market when they decided to enter by joint venture.

At trial, the district court determined that the joint venture would not violate Section 1 of the Sherman Act or Section 7 of the Clayton Act unless, but for the joint venture, both companies would have entered the market independently. Finding that the government had not proved that both would have entered, the court dismissed the complaint. The government appealed to the Supreme Court, which reversed. It held that if, but for the venture, either (1) both Pennsalt and Olin would have built plants in the Southeast, or (2) one would have done so and the other would have continued to remain at the edge, continually threatening to enter, important potential competition may have been eliminated and Section 7 may have been violated. It remanded for findings on these issues.

In *Penn–Olin,* did the Supreme Court actually (by necessary implication) decide the question it later reserved in *Marine Bancorporation*— whether Section 7 can ever be violated by an acquisition that does nothing more than deprive the market of the benefits from a more competitive route that would otherwise have been taken?

Problem

Brunswick Corporation, through its subsidiary Mariner, bought a half interest in Sanshin, a subsidiary of a Japanese company, Yamaha Motor Company. Brunswick was the second largest producer of outboard motors for the U.S. market. Outboard Marine Corporation, the number one firm, and Brunswick accounted for 72.9% of sales in the U.S. market. The top four firms accounted for 98.6% of sales. Yamaha manufactured outboard motors but had not yet been successful in selling to the U.S. market.

The joint venture, Sanshin, was to produce a new line of outboard motors and to sell its production to Yamaha. Yamaha was to sell a portion of the motors under its own brand name, and to resell the rest to Mariner. The parties contracted (1) to give Brunswick the exclusive right to sell Sanshin-made outboard motors in North America, and (2) to give Yamaha the exclusive right to sell Sanshin-made outboard motors in Japan. (3) Yamaha agreed not to make or buy for resale *any* outboard motors except for sale in Japan. Yamaha was an actual potential entrant into the U.S. market and probably the most important potential entrant. Despite its prior unsuccessful attempts, it had available means for entering the market and those means offered a substantial likelihood of deconcentrating the U.S. market or producing other significant procompetitive effects. The companies argued that the joint venture was procompetitive because it facilitated introduction of a new line of outboard motors in the United States, and that each of the covenants was important to facilitate the joint venture. As judge, how would you rule?

See *Yamaha Motor Co. v. FTC,* 657 F.2d 971 (8th Cir.1981), *cert. denied sub nom. Brunswick Corp. v. FTC,* 456 U.S. 915 (1982).

D. VERTICAL AND OTHER MERGERS WITH FORECLOSURE EFFECTS

In an earlier time, a major, recognized purpose of the antitrust laws was to protect small and middle-sized firms from foreclosure of substantial opportunities to compete on the merits, even when consumers were not hurt by the foreclosure and sometimes in spite of the fact that the challenged restraint might help consumers. The law has changed, as such cases as *GTE Sylvania* and *BMI* signify; case law from the mid–1970s forward suggests that antitrust enforcement should not harm consumers.

Also (as we studied in Chapter 4), vertical integration tends to benefit consumers when lower costs can be achieved through hierarchical decision-making than through markets. A vertical merger, one between a buyer and a seller, may often (some would say, will almost always) have attributes that help consumers. See O. Williamson, Vertical Merger Guidelines: Interpreting the 1982 Reforms, 71 Calif.L.Rev. 604 (1983).

Accordingly, facilitating market access and protecting efficiency are potentially conflicting objectives. To explore ways in which this conflict can be resolved, we present excerpts from two vertical acquisition cases and from a reciprocity case. (Bear in mind as you study them that they are cases from the 1950s and 1960s and are not reliable predictors of the law.) We then summarize a contemporary vertical acquisition case, and the Justice Department's Guidelines on Vertical Mergers.

The first vertical acquisition that reached the Supreme Court after enactment of the Celler–Kefauver Amendment to Section 7 was not a full-blown merger; it was du Pont's acquisition of a large block of General Motors' stock. (Although the case reached the Court in 1957, the challenged stock acquisition pre-dated the 1950 amendment.) The stock ownership gave du Pont an advantage not based on merits in competing for the opportunity to supply automotive fabrics and finishes to General Motors. Partially as a result of its stock interest, du Pont won the right to supply half of General Motors' needs for fabrics and finishes; General Motors' needs comprised half of all automobile company needs. The

Court held the acquisition illegal under the original (1914) version of Section 7 (supra p. 740).

UNITED STATES v. E.I. DU PONT DE NEMOURS & CO.

353 U.S. 586 (1957).

JUSTICE REED: * * * The fact that sticks out in this voluminous record is that the bulk of du Pont's production has always supplied the largest part of the requirements of the one customer in the automobile industry connected to du Pont by a stock interest. The inference is overwhelming that du Pont's commanding position was promoted by its stock interest and was not gained solely on competitive merit.

We agree with the trial court that considerations of price, quality and service were not overlooked by either du Pont or General Motors. Pride in its products and its high financial stake in General Motors' success would naturally lead du Pont to try to supply the best. But the wisdom of this business judgment cannot obscure the fact, plainly revealed by the record, that du Pont purposely employed its stock to pry open the General Motors market to entrench itself as the primary supplier of General Motors' requirements for automotive finishes and fabrics.

Similarly, the fact that all concerned in high executive posts in both companies acted honorably and fairly, each in the honest conviction that his actions were in the best interests of his own company and without any design to overreach anyone, including du Pont's competitors, does not defeat the Government's right to relief. It is not requisite to the proof of a violation of § 7 to show that restraint or monopoly was intended.

The statutory policy of fostering free competition is obviously furthered when no supplier has an advantage over his competitors from an acquisition of his customer's stock likely to have the effects condemned by the statute. . . .

* * *

Questions and Comments

Du Pont apparently obtained a "foot-in-the-door" advantage from the acquisition when selling fabrics and finishes to GM. Is that an "efficiency," since it reduced du Pont's selling expenses and, perhaps, yielded more sales?

The Court thought du Pont's foot-in-the-door advantage weighed against the merger. Why? Was anyone hurt, other than competitors who were "foreclosed"? From what were competitors foreclosed? Could such a foreclosure affect market structure in a way that might reduce competition and lead to output reduction? Under what circumstances might that happen? Were those circumstances present here?

Is a foreclosure by a foot-in-the-door acquisition unfair to the foreclosed competitors? Seriously so? Should such acquisitions be illegal? Should they be illegal if no efficiencies are claimed and proved? Should they be proscribed when the acquisition yields preferred access to the business of one of the largest corporations in the world? Should such an acquisition be illegal when it gives preferred access to more than half of the purchases of the relevant product? Does the case for illegality of a foreclosure-producing acquisition become weaker when the integration is "tighter" (not a mere minority interest), and thus where claims of resulting efficiencies are more plausible?

Brown Shoe Co. v. United States, 370 U.S. 294 (1962), was the second vertical merger case to come before the Supreme Court. We treated the horizontal aspects of the case above. See p. 750 supra. We treat the vertical aspects here.

In *Brown Shoe,* four firms produced 25% of all pairs of shoes sold in the United States. Brown, the acquiring company, was the fourth largest shoe manufacturer, manufacturing about 4% of the nation's shoes. Kinney, the acquired firm (which produced about 0.5% of the nation's shoes), sold about 1.6% of all pairs of shoes and accounted for about 1.2% of all sales of shoes in the nation. Kinney was the largest family-style shoe store chain.

BROWN SHOE CO. v. UNITED STATES
370 U.S. 294 (1962).

CHIEF JUSTICE WARREN: * * *

THE VERTICAL ASPECTS OF THE MERGER.

Economic arrangements between companies standing in a supplier-customer relationship are characterized as "vertical." The primary vice of a vertical merger or other arrangement tying a customer to a supplier is that, by foreclosing the competitors of either party from a segment of the market otherwise open to them, the arrangement may act as a "clog on competition," *Standard Oil Co. of California v. United States,* 337 U.S. 293, 314, which "deprive[s] . . . rivals of a fair opportunity to compete." [40] H.R.Rep. No. 1191, 81st Cong., 1st Sess. 8. Every extended vertical arrangement by its very nature, for at least a time, denies to competitors of the supplier the opportunity to compete for part or all of the trade of the customer-party to the vertical arrangement. However, the Clayton Act does not render unlawful all such vertical arrangements, but forbids only those whose effect "may be substantially to lessen competition, or to tend to create a monopoly" "in any line of commerce in any section of the country." . . .

* * *

Since the diminution of the vigor of competition which may stem from a vertical arrangement results primarily from a foreclosure of a share of the market otherwise open to competitors, an important consideration in determining whether the effect of a vertical arrangement "may be substantially to lessen competition, or to tend to create a monopoly" is the size of the share of the market foreclosed. However, this factor will seldom be determinative. If the share of the market foreclosed is so large that it approaches monopoly proportions, the Clayton Act will, of course, have been violated; but the arrangement will also have run afoul of the Sherman Act. And the legislative history of § 7 indicates clearly that the tests for measuring the legality of any particular economic arrangement

---

40. In addition, a vertical merger may disrupt and injure competition when those independent customers of the supplier who are in competition with the merging customer, are forced either to stop handling the supplier's lines, thereby jeopardizing the goodwill they have developed, or to retain the supplier's lines, thereby forcing them into competition with their own supplier.

under the Clayton Act are to be less stringent than those used in applying the Sherman Act. On the other hand, foreclosure of a *de minimis* share of the market will not tend "substantially to lessen competition."

Between these extremes, in cases such as the one before us, in which the foreclosure is neither of monopoly nor *de minimis* proportions, the percentage of the market foreclosed by the vertical arrangement cannot itself be decisive. In such cases, it becomes necessary to undertake an examination of various economic and historical factors in order to determine whether the arrangement under review is of the type Congress sought to proscribe.

A most important such factor to examine is the very nature and purpose of the arrangement. Congress not only indicated that "the tests of illegality [under § 7] are intended to be similar to those which the courts have applied in interpreting the same language as used in other sections of the Clayton Act," but also chose for § 7 language virtually identical to that of § 3 of the Clayton Act, 15 U.S.C. § 14, which had been interpreted by this Court to require an examination of the interdependence of the market share foreclosed by, and the economic purpose of, the vertical arrangement. . . .

* * *

The present merger involved neither small companies nor failing companies. In 1955, the date of this merger, Brown was the fourth largest manufacturer in the shoe industry with sales of approximately 25 million pairs of shoes and assets of over $72,000,000 while Kinney had sales of about 8 million pairs of shoes and assets of about $18,000,000. Not only was Brown one of the leading manufacturers of men's, women's, and children's shoes, but Kinney, with over 350 retail outlets, owned and operated the largest independent chain of family shoe stores in the Nation. Thus, in this industry, no merger between a manufacturer and an independent retailer could involve a larger potential market foreclosure. Moreover, it is apparent both from past behavior of Brown and from the testimony of Brown's President, that Brown would use its ownership of Kinney to force Brown shoes into Kinney stores. Thus, in operation this vertical arrangement would be quite analogous to one involving a tying clause.

Another important factor to consider is the trend toward concentration in the industry. It is true, of course, that the statute prohibits a given merger only if the effect of *that* merger may be substantially to lessen competition. But the very wording of § 7 requires a prognosis of the probable *future* effect of the merger.

The existence of a trend toward vertical integration, which the District Court found, is well substantiated by the record. Moreover, the court found a tendency of the acquiring manufacturers to become increasingly important sources of supply for their acquired outlets. The necessary corollary of these trends is the foreclosure of independent manufacturers from markets otherwise open to them. And because these trends are not the product of accident but are rather the result of deliberate policies of Brown and other leading shoe manufacturers, account must be taken of these facts in order to predict the probable future consequences of this merger. It is against this background of continuing concentration that the present merger must be viewed.

Brown argues, however, that the shoe industry is at present composed of a large number of manufacturers and retailers, and that the industry is dynamically competitive. But remaining vigor cannot immunize a merger if the trend in that industry is toward oligopoly. See *Pillsbury Mills, Inc.,* 50 F.T.C. 555, 573. It is the probable effect of the merger upon the future as well as the present which the Clayton Act commands the courts and the Commission to examine.

Moreover, as we have remarked above, not only must we consider the probable effects of the merger upon the economics of the particular markets affected but also we must consider its probable effects upon the economic way of life sought to be preserved by Congress. Congress was desirous of preventing the formation of further oligopolies with their attendant adverse effects upon local control of industry and upon small business. Where an industry was composed of numerous independent units, Congress appeared anxious to preserve this structure. The Senate Report, quoting with approval from the Federal Trade Commission's 1948 report on the merger movement, states explicitly that amended § 7 is addressed, *inter alia,* to the following problem:

> "Under the Sherman Act, an acquisition is unlawful if it creates a monopoly or constitutes an attempt to monopolize. Imminent monopoly may appear when one large concern acquires another, but it is unlikely to be perceived in a small acquisition by a large enterprise. As a large concern grows through a series of such small acquisitions, its accretions of power are individually so minute as to make it difficult to use the Sherman Act test against them. . . .

> "Where several large enterprises are extending their power by successive small acquisitions, the cumulative effect of their purchases may be to convert an industry from one of intense competition among many enterprises to one in which three or four large concerns produce the entire supply." S.Rep. No. 1775, 81st Cong., 2d Sess. 5. And see H.R.Rep. No. 1191, 81st Cong., 1st Sess. 8.

The District Court's findings, and the record facts, many of them set forth in Part I of this opinion, convince us that the shoe industry is being subjected to just such a cumulative series of vertical mergers which, if left unchecked, will be likely "substantially to lessen competition."

We reach this conclusion because the trend toward vertical integration in the shoe industry, when combined with Brown's avowed policy of forcing its own shoes upon its retail subsidiaries, may foreclose competition from a substantial share of the markets for men's, women's, and children's shoes, without producing any countervailing competitive, economic, or social advantages.

* * *

. . . [Another] significant aspect of this merger is that it creates a large national chain which is integrated with a manufacturing operation. The retail outlets of integrated companies, by eliminating wholesalers and by increasing the volume of purchases from the manufacturing division of the enterprise, can market their own brands at prices below those of competing independent retailers. Of course, some of the results of large integrated or chain operations are beneficial to consumers. Their expansion is not rendered unlawful by the mere fact that small independent stores may be adversely affected. It is competition, not competitors, which the Act protects. But we cannot fail to recognize Congress' desire to promote competition through the protection of viable, small, locally owned business. Congress appreciated that occasional higher costs and prices might result from the maintenance of fragmented industries and markets. It resolved these competing considerations in favor of decentralization. We must give effect to that decision. . . .

* * *

Questions and Comments

Who was hurt by the fact that Brown Shoe, a manufacturer, acquired Kinney, a retailer? Is it plausible that before the merger Brown Shoe's manufacturing rivals had sufficient outlets but after the merger they did not? If so, could they cure their problem by market moves of their own? Suppose there were two or three manufacturers that had sold all of their output to Kinney and that after the merger Kinney would not buy from them; being unable to adjust rapidly enough in the ensuing game of "musical chairs," they failed. Should such a result, or its likelihood, invalidate a merger? Is it plausible that before the merger Kinney's retailing competitors had sufficient sources of supply but after the merger did not? Where might they turn if they could not get Brown shoes? Might their sources include not only the hundreds of U.S. manufacturers but also Italian, Korean, and other foreign manufacturers?

Were consumers hurt by the acquisition? Were they hurt if Brown–Kinney had—as the Court feared—the ability to change styles quickly in response to consumer demand? Were they (and was Kinney) hurt by the acquisition because, as the Court also feared, Brown would "force" Kinney to carry its shoes? Is it plausible that Brown got market power as a result of this vertical integration? Is it plausible that Kinney was a valuable outlet needed by other shoe manufacturers?

Were consumers helped by this acquisition? Is there basis for inferring that an ownership link between manufacturer and retailer was more efficient than an open market relationship? If so, could either or both firms have attained the available efficiencies without merging? How?

Three years after *Brown Shoe* another foreclosure case came before the Court. This was a reciprocity-inducing merger, rather than a vertical merger. While we briefly mentioned this case in Chapter IV on vertical restraints, we describe it here in the merger context.

The acquired firm, Gentry, sold its product, dehydrated onions and garlic, to customers (food processors, such as Swift and Armour), who sold their product to the acquiring firm, Consolidated Foods. Consolidated Foods was a very big purchaser and a cherished customer of the food processors. The dehydrated onion and garlic market was highly concentrated, and Gentry was number two with about 32%. The Justice Department feared that Consolidated Foods would use its reciprocity power ("I'll buy from you only if you buy from me") to steer the food processors' purchases of dehydrated onions and garlic to Gentry, thus foreclosing Gentry's competitors' opportunity to com-

pete for that business on the merits. Indeed, Consolidated Foods had successfully used such selling tactics in the past. The Justice Department sued,
alleging the illegality of an acquisition that created a market structure
conducive to substantial reciprocity, and it won.

FTC v. CONSOLIDATED FOODS CORP.

380 U.S. 592 (1965).

JUSTICE DOUGLAS: The question presented involves an important construction and application of § 7 of the Clayton Act. Consolidated Foods
Corp.—which owns food processing plants and a network of wholesale and
retail food stores—acquired Gentry, Inc., in 1951. Gentry manufactures
principally dehydrated onion and garlic. The Federal Trade Commission
held that the acquisition violated § 7 because it gave respondent the
advantage of a mixed threat and lure of reciprocal buying in its competition for business and "the power to foreclose competition from a substantial share of the markets for dehydrated onion and garlic." It concluded,
in other words, that the effect of the acquisition "may be substantially to
lessen competition" within the meaning of § 7, and it ordered divestiture
and gave other relief. The Court of Appeals, relying mainly on 10 years
of post-acquisition experience, held that the Commission had failed to
show a probability that the acquisition would substantially lessen competition. The case is here on certiorari.

We hold at the outset that the "reciprocity" made possible by such an
acquisition is one of the congeries of anticompetitive practices at which
the antitrust laws are aimed. The practice results in "an irrelevant and
alien factor," intruding into the choice among competing products, creating at the least "a priority on the business at equal prices." *International
Salt Co. v. United States*, 332 U.S. 392, 396–397; *Northern Pac. R. Co. v.
United States*, 356 U.S. 1, 3, 6, 12. Reciprocal trading may ensue not from
bludgeoning or coercion but from more subtle arrangements. A threatened withdrawal of orders if products of an affiliate cease being bought, as
well as a conditioning of future purchases on the receipt of orders for
products of that affiliate, is an anticompetitive practice. . . .

* * *

. . . [T]he Commission was surely on safe ground in reaching the
following conclusion:

"If reciprocal buying creates for Gentry a protected market, which others
cannot penetrate despite superiority of price, quality, or service, competition is lessened whether or not Gentry can expand its market share. It is
for this reason that we reject respondent's argument that the decline in
its share of the garlic market proves the ineffectiveness of reciprocity.
We do not know that its share would not have fallen still farther, had it
not been for the influence of reciprocal buying. This loss of sales fails to
refute the likelihood that Consolidated's reciprocity power, which it has
shown a willingness to exploit to the full, will not immunize a substantial
segment of the garlic market from normal quality, price, and service
competition." . . .

* * *

We do not go so far as to say that any acquisition, no matter how small, violates § 7 if there is a probability of reciprocal buying. Some situations may amount only to *de minimis*. But where, as here, the acquisition is of a company that commands a substantial share of a market, a finding of probability of reciprocal buying by the Commission, whose expertise the Congress trusts, should be honored, if there is substantial evidence to support it.

* * *

Questions and Comments

Are the economic issues here more like those in *du Pont–GM* or more like those in *Brown Shoe?* Consolidated Foods said it was merely dealing with friends. Selling to "built-in" friends may reduce selling expense. Should that cost-saving be treated as an efficiency? If the market is otherwise competitive, the cost-saving will result in lower prices to consumers. Was this market otherwise competitive? Is a reciprocity-inducing merger likely to produce any technical efficiencies? Any marketing efficiencies other than the savings from not having to compete for sales?

Can foreclosure through reciprocity harm market structure in a way that may lead to output reduction and price enhancement? Under what circumstances? Can you fashion an illustration of reciprocal dealing that produces a price rise? Is the Consolidated Foods merger such a case?

Above we asked if vertical foreclosures are unfair to less-well-situated competitors. Is the use of reciprocity unfair? Is it unfair when the "friends" whose good will is curried represent a large part of the buying market in which the defendant and its competitors sell? Would it be wise to ignore reciprocity effects of mergers and (if desired) police reciprocity directly? Would it be wiser to ignore all reciprocity effects whether or not the practice is facilitated by merger? Are mergers that are driven by reciprocity gains both less likely to increase competition and less likely to harm competition than are vertical mergers? Do your answers to the above questions, then, depend on whether you worry about the underdog or whether you worry only about optimum output?

During the same period when these vertical and reciprocity mergers were held illegal by the Supreme Court, a number of vertical mergers were held illegal by federal district and appellate courts. Often illegality was linked with the share of the market foreclosed, which was frequently calculated in terms of the share of all purchases represented by the buying partner that could and probably would be supplied to it by the supplying partner. See cases cited at 1 Fox and Fox, Corporate Acquisitions and Mergers, Ch. 9, chart, § 9.2[3] (1988).

1. VERTICAL MERGERS AND EFFICIENCY

There are conflicting views among antitrust analysts, including economists, about the values and dangers of vertical acquisitions. Until the early 1970s the dominant view was that vertical mergers are almost always unnecessary to realize available efficiencies and that their dominant effect is to foreclose rivals and thereby deprive them of opportunities to compete on the merits. It was thought that available efficiencies from vertical relationships could be realized by contract or internal growth.

There seemed to be consensus that rivalry among a number of unintegrated firms at each vertical stage adds to the vitality of competition and yields optimal competitive alternatives to buyers. See, e.g., Markham, Merger Policy Under the New Section 7: A Six–Year Appraisal, 43 Va.L. Rev. 489, 497 (1957). Moreover, while an individual firm might, by integration, reduce its own vulnerability to market fluctuations by acquiring its supplier, that very acquisition might impose on the unintegrated competitors higher risks from the same market fluctuations, thus imposing higher costs on the competitors. See 4 Areeda & Turner, Antitrust Law ¶ 10.09 (1980).

Today, however, the dominant "learning" is that vertical integration, whether by merger or otherwise, is almost always efficient. (Reciprocity is treated as trivial. Indeed, it is not treated at all.) Vertical integration can produce substantial production economies of integration and can enable the integrating firm to save substantial transaction costs. Partial vertical integration can produce cost-savings through better monitoring of the performance of independent suppliers and less dependence on them. Thus, the integrated firm can avoid the opportunism of and the exploitation by its suppliers. See, e.g., Williamson, Vertical Merger Guidelines: Interpreting the 1982 Reforms, 71 Calif.L.Rev. 604, 611–614 (1983). Moreover, since mere vertical integration does not combine competitors and increase strength on a horizontal plane, it does not normally facilitate collusion. Those individuals who worry only about output restraint and believe that vertical integration is presumptively efficient would almost never condemn a vertical merger.

From at least the mid–1960s forward, there has been little enforcement against vertical mergers. For one of the few contemporary vertical cases, see *Fruehauf Corporation v. FTC*, 603 F.2d 345 (2d Cir.1979). Fruehauf Corporation, the nation's largest manufacturer of truck trailers, with 25% of the truck trailer market, acquired Kelsey Hayes Company, a major manufacturer of components for motor vehicles and the third largest supplier of heavy duty wheels (HDW). Kelsey accounted for 15% sales of HDW. The top four firms accounted for 65% or more of sales, and the top eight firms had nearly 95%. Fruehauf bought 5.8% of HDW production. The Federal Trade Commission found the acquisition illegal, but the Court of Appeals reversed. Despite high concentration and high barriers to entry, the court said, the foreclosed share of the market was small and suppliers and buyers could reshuffle their allegiances. There was no evidence that competitors in the buying market would be unable to get their needs from Kelsey or its competitors at competitive prices, nor that removal of Fruehauf's needs from the open market would preclude any HDW seller from continuing to operate economically or preclude any potential HWD seller from entering the market.

In 1982 the Justice Department Merger Guidelines outlined the circumstances under which it would challenge a vertical merger. The guidelines, as slightly revised in 1984, express three possible concerns regarding vertical mergers, although as a practical matter the Department is favorably disposed toward vertical mergers and concerns are unlikely to materialize. The stated concerns are:

(1) Raising barriers to entry. Three conditions are necessary, but not sufficient, for a competitive problem in this regard:

   (a) Integration must be so extensive that entrants into one market would have to enter the other at the same time.

   (b) The need to enter the second market simultaneously must make entry into the first significantly more difficult and less likely to occur.

   (c) The first market must be so conducive to noncompetitive performance that the increased difficulty of entry would probably make it worse. The first market must be very highly concentrated.

(2) Facilitating collusion.

   (a) Vertical integration to the retail level can make it easier for upstream sellers to monitor a cartel price. The integration is unlikely to be a problem unless the upstream market is very highly concentrated and a large percentage of the upstream product would be sold through vertically integrated retail outlets.

   (b) Vertical integration that eliminates a particularly disruptive buyer in a downstream market may facilitate collusion in the upstream market if the upstream market is very highly concentrated.

(3) Evading rate regulation. For example, a regulated utility that acquires a supplier would have the incentive to inflate prices of products it sells to itself. Under a cost-plus regime, the utility would show the high price as a "cost," and the regulators would normally authorize a percentage profit above that cost. But substantial economies of integration could counsel against suit.

Are the guidelines helpful? Do they, at least, pinpoint conditions under which output restraint would be likely to occur? Would you add any other conditions, or delete any of the "necessary" conditions? What has become of the concept of unfair exclusion from inputs or outlets, as in *du Pont–General Motors* and in *Consolidated Foods?*

Enforcement against vertical mergers continues to be infrequent. Lip service is some times paid to *Brown Shoe,* but "foreclosure of a [significant] share of the market otherwise open to competitors" is no longer assumed to result in "diminution of the vigor of competition"; and foreclosure of the nearly de minimis market share present in *Brown Shoe* is treated as inconsequential. In this a predictable counterpart to developments in the law with respect to exclusive dealing, tying and other contractual foreclosures?

2. JOINT VENTURES AND VERTICAL EFFECTS

Joint ventures may, of course, have vertical implications: unintegrated rivals may lose a needed source of supply or outlet. As in the case of other joint ventures, if an acquisition is involved, the transaction may be tested under both the Sherman and Clayton Acts; otherwise, the Sherman Act controls. In any event one must ask: Is the joint venture, on balance, anticompetitive?

One joint venture case with horizontal and vertical implications is *United States v. Columbia Pictures Industries, Inc.,* 507 F.Supp. 412 (S.D.

N.Y.1980), *aff'd without opinion* (2d Cir.1981). After films are shown in movie theatres, motion picture producers license them for cable TV distribution. Home Box Office (HBO) dominated the cable TV market, and the movie companies were unhappy with the price they could command from HBO. Four of the major movie companies decided to form a joint venture, Premiere, to engage in cable TV distribution of movies. Their purpose, allegedly, was to bypass HBO and/or to force a better price from it. The four venturers, who accounted for about half of all "hit" movies—the most desirable film fare for cable TV—agreed that they would grant to Premiere the exclusive cable rights to their films for the first nine months of their cable showings. The first nine months are the period of highest demand.

The government sued to enjoin the formation of Premiere. A federal district court granted its motion for a preliminary injunction.

Should the court have granted the preliminary injunction? What were the anticompetitive properties of the transaction? (Note that you must examine at least two markets: cable distribution and movie production. Are there any important submarkets? Is cable distribution of movies a market?) If movies are so important to HBO, couldn't it make its own movies or contract for the production of movies? Could it contract for the production of potential hit movies? Should it have been required to invest in movie making before (or instead of) complaining that it was foreclosed from an important source of supply? Would the Justice Department Guidelines require it to do so? Even if HBO itself did not make this investment, would "the market" come forth with more movies if cable TV needed more movies? Does Chicago School predict that the market will work and that therefore (among other reasons) vertical integration is not a problem? Do you so predict? Starting about 1981 HBO did integrate backwards into film production, and it did so on a significant scale, perhaps to the consternation of the major movie makers).

Note that the joint venture was a new entrant into concentrated market. Was the entry necessarily procompetitive? Can even new entry be predominately anticompetitive? Under what circumstances?

In the 1940s and 1950s, the government attacked the big motion picture producer-distributors' ownership of theatres as anticompetitive, and secured decrees against the major firms in the industry. The decrees forbade vertical integration, with selective exceptions requiring court approval. See *United States v. Paramount Pictures,* 334 U.S. 131 (1948) (also involving horizontal conspiracy); *United States v. Paramount Pictures,* 1948–1949 Trade Cas. (CCH) ¶ 62,335 (S.D.N.Y.1948); *United States v. Paramount Pictures,* 1948–1949 Trade Cas. (CCH) ¶ 62,377 (S.D.N.Y. 1949). In the 1980s, the government reviewed the decrees, observed that they may be anticompetitive, and suggested that they should be vacated. See Antitrust Division is close to Lifting Restrictions on Distribution of Movies, 45 Antitrust Trade Reg.Rep. (BNA) No. 1129, at 296 (August 25, 1983).

E. AGGREGATE CONCENTRATION, MEGA– MERGERS, AND PUBLIC POLICY

The 1960s, when horizontal and vertical merger policy was very aggressive, were the years of the go-go conglomerates. See J. Brooks, The Go–Go Years (1973). Companies and entrepreneurs set out to win their place in the corporate sun. Success was symbolized by a high rank on the list of Fortune's 500.

"Synergy" was the watchword; two and two made five, or so it was thought. Midnight takeovers were a common means to the glorious end until Congress passed the Williams Act in 1968. 15 U.S.C. § 78(1–n), as amended. "Dirty pooling" was a common device for showing paper profits, until the Accounting Principles Board of the American Institute of Certified Public Accountants adopted new rules of accountancy in 1970. See Fox and Fox, Corporate Acquisitions & Mergers § 27.01 (1988).

While corporate and financial tycoons were gobbling up thousands of enterprises, numerous citizens and policymakers became concerned. The economic assets of the country were falling into fewer and fewer hands. People feared that greater concentration of corporate assets meant greater economic power, and that economic power meant political power. As conglomerates swallowed entrepreneurial firms, some people feared the loss of autonomy, and with it the loss of the pioneering spirit that produced the country's industrial greatness. See R. Nader and M. Green, Taming the Giant Corporation (1976); M. Mintz and J. Cohen, America, Inc. (1971). The reactions to all of this at executive and congressional levels was most interesting.

1. AGGREGATE CONCENTRATION AND THE NIXON ADMINIS-TRATION

a. The McLaren Challenges to the ITT Acquisitions

Richard Nixon was President and Richard W. McLaren was Assistant Attorney General in Charge of the Antitrust Division. Alarmed by the brash young conglomerateurs who took over established businesses and ousted their managements, McLaren compared takeovers to mushroom-growing. First, he said in a speech to the Antitrust Section of the American Bar Association, they pour manure over you. Next, they keep you in the dark. Then they can you. (Was this an irony? The brash young conglomerateurs did not arise from the ranks of power. Were they not pioneers? Did it take a challenge to the establishment to spur the attack on concentration?)

Between April and August 1969, McLaren initiated three major law suits against ITT, the twelfth largest industrial company in the United States. One suit challenged ITT's merger with Canteen Corporation, one of few nation-wide food vending organizations; one challenged its pro-posed acquisition of Grinnell Corporation, the largest U.S. manufacturer of automatic fire protection systems, and one challenged its proposed merger with the Hartford Fire Insurance Company, the sixth largest domestic property and liability insurer. Hartford had $400 million in excess of its required surplus, and this "extra" money could be used for further acquisitions.[18]

At least initially, McLaren had the backing of Attorney General John N. Mitchell. In June 1969, after some but not all of the ITT cases had been initiated, Mitchell spoke out against increasing concentration in America. In an address to the Georgia Bar Association he announced that the Department of Justice "may well oppose any merger among the top 200 manufacturing firms," and "will probably oppose any merger by one of the top 200 manufacturing firms with any leading producer in any concentrated industry." [19]

There were, at the time, three conventional bases that might have been available to challenge conglomerate acquisitions: that the merger facilitated reciprocal dealing, that it entrenched a leading firm, and that it reduced potential competition. In all of the *ITT* cases, the government could point to a potential for reciprocal dealing. In *Grinnell* the government alleged that Grinnell was dominant in the fire and burglar alarm markets and that the acquisitions would entrench its dominance. But in *Grinnell* and *Canteen,* the government also alleged a novel theory of Section 7 liability: that the acquisitions would increase the concentration of manufacturing and mining assets (sometimes called "aggregate industrial concentration," as opposed to concentration within a particular economic market); and in the case of *Hartford,* which was not an industrial company, the government alleged that the merger was part of a movement that "has substantially increased aggregate concentration and eliminated the independent existence of a rising number of very large firms . . . reduc[ing] the number of firms likely to enter many of the nation's concentrated industries, the number of sources of competitive innovation, and the centers of decision making upon important industrial and commercial matters." [20]

By 1970, theories for aggressive enforcement against big mergers had caught the fancy of many enforcers and public citizens. As of that time, all three of the conventional bases for enforcement seemed legally credible although the reciprocity allegations included concerns about remote and merely potential reciprocity claims, raising questions of first impression. How strong were the novel "aggregate concentration" theories? Was a proscription of mergers that substantially increased aggregate concentration inherent in the legislative history and spirit of Section 7?

The trial courts denied the government's requested preliminary injunctions in *Hartford* and *Grinnell* (*United States v. ITT Corp.,* 306 F.Supp. 766 (D.Conn.1969)), and dismissed *Canteen* and *Grinnell* after trial. *United States v. ITT Corp.,* 1971 Trade Cas. (CCH) ¶ 73,619 (D.Ill. 1971), 324 F.Supp. 19 (D.Conn.1970). In all of these cases, the courts said, the government had failed to prove a lessening of competition in any traditional sense, and it had not shown how asserted increases in aggre-

18. For a detailed description of the cases, see Fox, The ITT Antimerger Cases, 9 Conference Board Record 34 (June 1972).

19. Address, June 6, 1969, Antitrust & Trade Reg.Rep. (BNA) No. 413, at A–2, X–9–

11 (June 10, 1969). See 2 Fox and Fox, Corporate Acquisitions & Mergers § 14.02 (1988).

20. See Fox, supra, 9 Conference Board Record at 36.

gate concentration would lessen competition in any defined market. (Was this a failure of proof or rejection of a theory? If you were counsel for the government, what would you have undertaken to prove in order to convince the court that the acquisitions unduly increased aggregate concentration?) [21]

In 1971 the Justice Department filed a notice of appeal to the Supreme Court from the judgment dismissing the *Grinnell* complaint, and it contemplated an appeal from the *Canteen* dismissal. McLaren announced that appeal in the *ITT* cases was a matter of principle. . . . But in the spring and summer of 1971, there were rumors of ITT's political contributions to President Nixon and then of a secret deal between ITT and President Nixon.[22] On July 31, 1971, the Justice Department announced that it and ITT had reached agreement in principle to settle the three lawsuits, thus eliminating the need (and opportunity) for Supreme Court review.

Pursuant to the settlement, ITT agreed to divest itself of Canteen, the Fire Protection Division of Grinnell, and either Hartford or specified companies of nearly equal assets. ITT agreed that for 10 years it would not use reciprocity power and it would make no acquisitions without government consent or court approval. 1971 Trade Cas. (CCH) ¶ 73,665 (D.Conn.1971), 1971 Trade Cas. (CCH) ¶ 73,667 (D.Ill.1971). In turn, ITT escaped the scrutiny of the Supreme Court at a time when the Court was at the peak of its receptivity to argument that the merger law prohibited undue increases in aggregate concentration.

In view of the losses in the district court, the state of the proof, and the untested government theory, the settlement was not necessarily unfavorable to the government. Nevertheless, a popular view at the time was that the Nixon Administration had "sold out" the antitrust laws to do a favor for a political friend.

b. Antitrust and Political Influence

Those participating in the enforcement process obviously have a range of prosecutorial discretion. Government guidelines—such as the merger guidelines—constitute an effort to articulate how this discretion is being used. We do not suppose that antitrust enforcement is more politicized than any other area of law enforcement. Nonetheless, the financial significance to firms of some enforcement decisions may make it tempting for them to seek to influence outcomes, and the complexity of the facts and the generality of norms might make it difficult for outside

21. Showing an increase in aggregate concentration would have been a difficult task. Dr. Betty Bock conducted statistical studies over many years. Her studies show no increases and some decreases in aggregate concentration. Companies sell as well as buy other companies, and smaller firms, through internal growth or merger, rise into the ranks of large firms. See Bock, Statistical Games and the "200 Largest" Industrials: 1954 and 1968, Conference Board, Studies in Business Economics (1970).

22. See Blake, Beyond the ITT Case, Harpers' June 19, 1972, p. 74. A scandal erupted when columnist Jack Anderson disclosed a memorandum written by ITT's chief lobbyist, Dita Beard, linking the antitrust settlement to an ITT subsidiary's pledge to help finance the 1972 Republican Convention. See Alleged Memo Ties I.T.T. Trust Action to G.O.P. Funding, N.Y. Times, March 1, 1972, § 1, at 1, col. 4.

observers to know whether a decision not to challenge particular conduct (say, a merger) is other than routine.

We have little hard information about the extent to which political considerations influence prosecutorial decisions in this or other areas of national life. When information of political influence does come to light in a particular situation, it is worth having a look at the circumstances. Information of that sort bearing on the settlement of the ITT cases was revealed in the course of the Watergate inquiry and is collected in teaching materials prepared by Judge John T. Noonan, Jr., entitled: The Lawyer: Personal and Professional Responsibility.[23] Here is a summary of the materials gathered by Judge Noonan.

August 1970: Being unable to settle the *Grinnell* case with McLaren, lawyers for ITT took several steps during early August 1970: "Ned" Garrity met, lunched with, and wrote a letter and memorandum to Vice President Agnew (to "Ted" from "Ned"). He told Agnew that other ITT lawyers had had "a friendly session with John [Attorney General Mitchell] . . . [who] made plain . . . that the President was not opposed to mergers per se [and did not think that] 'bigness is bad.'" He also told Agnew that ITT lawyers had met with Chuck Colson and John Ehrlichman (both presidential advisors) and were told by Ehrlichman "that the President was not enforcing a bigness-is-bad policy and . . . had [so] instructed the Justice Department." He also informed the Vice President that an ITT trial lawyer

> had [met] with McLaren and his trial people . . ., [that] Justice really had no case, . . . that all that was alleged was that ITT was getting too big . . ., [but that] McLaren, ignoring the evidence, said that ITT must be stopped, that the merger movement must be stopped, etc., in effect saying he was running a campaign based on his own beliefs and he intended to prosecute diligently [which made it] . . . plain that McLaren's views were not and are not consistent with those of the Attorney General and the White House [and that ITT was] being pursued . . . not on law but on theory bordering on the fanatic.

In light of these problems, Garrity asked the Vice President for advice about whether to "get this development back to John [Mitchell] so he is aware" and about "how [to] do it? What is the best way?"

September 1970: On September 17 Ehrlichman wrote a memorandum to Attorney General Mitchell as follows:

> I was disappointed to learn that the ITT case had gone to trial with apparently no further effort on the part of Mr. McLaren to settle this case with ITT on the basis of our understanding that largeness was not really an issue in the case.

> ITT has passed word to us that the gravamen of the case remains largeness which is contrary to the understanding that I believe you and I had during the time that we each talked to [ITT Chairman] Geneen.

23. Materials published by Boalt Hall for the use of Judge Noonan's students in his course on Professional Responsibility. See Part I–B of the materials, Client and Political Superior, pp. 64–114. Sources include the settlement in the ITT case and a Statement of Information, Hearing on H.R.Res. 803 Before the Judiciary Committee, 93rd Cong., 2d Sess. (1974), Book V, pts. 1 & 2.

I think we are in a rather awkward position with ITT in view of the assurances that both you and I must have given Geneen on this subject.

I'll be out of touch for about two weeks, but I would appreciate your reexamining our position in the case in view of these conversations. Geneen is, of course, entitled to assume the Administration meant what it said to him.

October 1970: On October 1, Colson sent a memorandum to Ehrlichman, reading as follows:

I am enclosing a copy of the speech which Mr. McLaren gave on September 17th. He does not, as you will see, defend the proposition that under the existing anti-trust laws a case can be brought on the grounds of bigness per se. What he does argue is that bigness is not good, and that the thrust of the anti-trust laws should be directed to economic concentration and bigness. He points out that while legislation might be needed, Justice can and is doing things, short of obtaining new legislation (note the last paragraph in particular).

In sum, I think that we still have a problem here, which is a serious one and which is manifesting itself in Mr. McLaren's conduct of the ITT case.

April 1971: After the cases were lost by the government and while one petition was pending in the Supreme Court, ITT lawyers continued to try to dispose of the cases by agreement. ITT's efforts included their preparation of a "Memorandum for the Department of Justice in Support of A Comprehensive Review of the Administration Policy Toward Diversification by Merger." The memorandum, submitted over the name of a distinguished attorney, leader of the bar, and chair of the Judiciary Committee of the American Bar Association, Lawrence E. Walsh, argued that conglomerate mergers yielded efficiencies. After the memo was prepared, Mr. Walsh telephoned Richard G. Kleindienst and then wrote to him enclosing a copy of the memo. Attorney General Mitchell had disqualified himself, and Kleindienst was acting Attorney General in respect of the *ITT* cases.

In the letter to Kleindienst ("Dear Dick"; Walsh had a relationship with Kleindienst through Walsh's ABA committee work) dated April 16, Walsh wrote that "Mr. Harold S. Geneen, Chairman and President of ITT, asked me to prepare a presentation to you . . . and, through you, to the national administration [about] . . . diversification mergers . . . and, more specifically, [to urge] that the Department of Justice not advocate any position before the Supreme Court . . . without a full study of the economic consequences. . . ." The letter went on to say that "[o]rdinarily I would first have seen Dick McLaren, but I understand that you, as Acting Attorney General, have already been consulted. . . ." The letter closed with an expression of the "hope that after reading the enclosed memorandum . . . you and Dick McLaren and the Solicitor General would be willing to delay the submission [to the Supreme Court] of the jurisdictional statement in the . . . case long enough to permit us to make a more adequate presentation. . . ."

On April 19 the *ITT–Grinnell* case was discussed at a meeting between President Nixon, John Ehrlichman and George Shultz. The transcript prepared by the House Judiciary Committee Impeachment Inquiry staff reads, in part, as follows:

EHRLICHMAN: Richard Kleindienst, uh, uh, has been supervising Mc-Laren's work. It's the Grinnell case. It involves an attack on, uh, conglomerates, on a theory which specifically had been contemplated by the Johnson Administration and laid aside as too anti-business.

PRESIDENT: Kleindienst is in this? [Picks up telephone.]

EHRLICHMAN: Yes.

PRESIDENT: [To telephone operator] Dick Kleindienst. [Hangs up.]

EHRLICHMAN: And—

PRESIDENT: How long before that [unintelligible] do you expect a moratorium?

EHRLICHMAN: Well, they filed a notice of appeal. If

PRESIDENT: Who did?

EHRLICHMAN: [If] We do not file a statement of jurisdiction by tomorrow the case is dead, and, uh,

PRESIDENT: Who?

EHRLICHMAN: uh—the Justice Department.

PRESIDENT: They're not going to file.

EHRLICHMAN: Well, I thought that was your position.

PRESIDENT: Oh, hell.

EHRLICHMAN: I've been trying to give, I've been trying to give them signals on this, and, uh, they've been horsing us pretty steadily. Uh, uh, Geneen—

PRESIDENT: Statement of jurisdiction.

EHRLICHMAN: Right.

PRESIDENT: I don't want to know anything about the case. Don't tell me a . . .

EHRLICHMAN: Yeah, I won't.

PRESIDENT: . . . thing about it. I don't want to know about Geneen. I've met him and I don't know—I don't know whether ITT is bad, good, or indifferent. But there is not going to be any more antitrust actions as long as I am in this chair.

EHRLICHMAN: Well, there's one—

PRESIDENT: God damn it, we're going to stop it.

                              . . .

PRESIDENT: [Picks up telephone.] Yeah.

Hi, Dick, how are you?

Fine, fine. I'm going to talk to John [Mitchell] tomorrow about my general attitude on antitrust . . . and in the meantime, I know that he has left with you, uh, the IT&T thing because apparently he says he had something to do with them once.

Well, I have, I have nothing to do with them, and I want something clearly understood, and, if it is not understood, McLaren's ass is to be out within one hour. The IT&T thing—stay the hell out of it. Is that clear? That's an order.

The order is to leave the God damned thing alone. Now, I've said this, Dick, a number of times, and you fellows apparently don't get the me—the message over there. I do not want McLaren to run around prosecuting people, raising hell about conglomerates, stirring things up at this point. Now, you keep him the hell out of that. Is that clear?

Or either he resigns. I'd rather have him out anyway. I don't like the son-of-a-bitch.

The question is, I know, that the jurisdiction—I know all the legal things, Dick, you don't have to spell out the legal—

That's right.

That's right. Don't file the brief.

Your—my order is to drop the God damn thing. Is that clear?

Okay. [Hangs up.]

PRESIDENT: This is, this is the problem. The problem is McLaren's a nice little fellow who's a good little antitrust lawyer out in Chicago. Now he comes in and all these bright little bastards that worked for the Antitrust Department for years and years and years and who hate business with a passion—any business—have taken him over. They haven't taken him over. Then of course McLaren is the man. They go into—Kleindienst is busy appointing judges; Mitchell is busy doing other things, so they're afraid to overrule him. By God they're not going to do it. I mean the point is that on this antitrust they had deliberately gone into a number of areas which have no relationship with each other, to—whether it's a question of operating more, more efficiently than the rest. There's simply a question of tactically, they've gone off on a kick, that'll make them big God damn trust busters. That was all right fifty years ago. Fifty years ago maybe it was a good thing for the country. It's not a good thing for the country today. That's my views about it, and I am not—We've been, been through this crap. They've done several of them already about—They have raised holy hell with the people that we, uh, uh—Well, Geneen, hell, he's no contributor. He's nothing to us. I don't care about him. So you can—I've only met him once, twice—uh, we've, I'm just, uh—I can't understand what the trouble is.

EHRLICHMAN: Well,

PRESIDENT: It's McLaren, isn't it?

EHRLICHMAN: McLaren has a very strong sense of mission here.

PRESIDENT: Good—Jesus, he's—Get him out. In one hour, . . .

EHRLICHMAN: He's got a . . .

PRESIDENT: . . . one hour.

EHRLICHMAN: very strong. . . .

PRESIDENT: And he's not going to be a judge, either. He is out of the God damn government. . . .

          . . .

Soon, thereafter, the settlement described supra p. 845 was reached. Not long after that McLaren was "out," but he was appointed to the federal district court bench in his home city of Chicago.

Questions and Comments

The events summarized above raise problems that are not easily or comfortably answered. One issue concerns prosecutorial discretion. Neither the language nor the legislative history of the 1950 merger act strongly favors the conclusion that conglomerate mergers like ITT–Grinnell are within its prohibitions. Yet in the late 1960s and early 1970s there was considerable concern about aggregate concentration, about the loss of pluralism, and about the deployment of managerial resources for acquisitions rather than production. (Some of the letter concern is with us again today in response to unprecedented takeover activity.) At the time it seemed plausible that a majority of the Warren Court would have been persuaded to adopt aggregate concentration theory and to invalidate the ITT mergers.

Where does prosecutorial discretion properly repose? Should the head of the Antitrust Division have the last word on the administration's enforcement program? Should the Attorney General? The President's staff?

Why shouldn't the President or his or her principal policy advisors be the ones to decide whether to press a suit asserting a novel, politically significant theory about the meaning of an important law? On what basis might one argue against the propriety or wisdom of exercising prosecutorial discretion about specific pending cases at such high political levels? On the ground that high political officials are not likely to know the relevant facts, or that they are not likely to be adequately informed about the relevant legal and policy issues? On the ground that their very involvement in such particularities gives a hint of corruption?

Consider, also, accessibility of justice. Ideally, a litigant's financial resources would be irrelevant or at least not profoundly important to litigation results; there would be no "entry barriers" excluding some from access to justice. But in the antitrust field and many others, the resources of the litigant and the skill and learning of the advocates and experts do influence outcomes. Does "political interference" tip the balance even further? Would ITT have been able to achieve the same settlement if it or the attorneys representing it did not have congenial access to Messrs. Mitchell, Agnew, Colson and Ehrlichman? Should this consideration have any weight in evaluating who should exercise prosecutorial discretion, and at what stage?

We might contrast questions of prosecutorial discretion that arose during the Nixon years and those that arose during the Reagan years. We have noted that Congress thought the Reagan Justice Department was in some sense overreaching in promulgating the Vertical Restraints Guidelines and in urging the Court to overrule *Dr. Miles,* supra p. 587 and 556. There was also criticism of the Reagan Justice Department's merger guidelines (supra Appendix B), of the Department's withdrawal of the *IBM* monopolization case, and of its abandonment of the *Mercedes–Benz* tying case after it was all but won. See, e.g., Sullivan, Judicial Oversight of Antitrust Enforcement: Questions of Power; Questions of Wisdom, 52 Antitrust L.J. 943 (1983). But despite such criticisms, the Reagan era antitrust decisions did not leave suspicion of corruption. All critical decisions about terminating particular cases were apparently made by the administration's antitrust officials or by these officials after discussion with Commerce Department officials at comparable levels of responsibility. Criticism focused on policies adopted, but not on the claim that policy was ignored to favor friends.

2. MEGA–MERGERS, TAKEOVERS, AND CONGRESS

In any event, the 1971 ITT settlements marked the end of efforts to persuade the courts that Section 7 prohibits very big mergers, virtually per se. After the *ITT* cases, those concerned with conglomerates and aggregate concentration turned their efforts from the courts to Congress. In the 1970s bills that would proscribe or limit very large mergers, subject to procompetition or efficiencies defenses, were introduced. E.g., S. 600 (96th Cong. 1st Sess.1979).

The issue reappeared, but in a different form, in the 1980s. With a relaxed government approach to merger enforcement, economic conditions favorable to mergers, and get-rich-quick takeovers on the rise, takeover battles and leveraged management buyouts have engulfed the board rooms and enlivened the stock exchanges. Some assert that takeover fever was one of the artificial stimulants that brought stock prices to "unrealistic" levels and set the stage for Black Monday in October 1987.

Numerous companies became caught up in the takeover frenzy. Seagram and Mobil waged war for control of Conoco, which escaped by fleeing to du Pont, its "white knight." Mobil then bid for Marathon, which fled into the arms of U.S. Steel, now USX. Perhaps the most lively (or lurid) battle was that between Bendix Corporation and Martin Marietta. Bendix sought to take over Martin Marietta, after selling divisions and accumulating $500 million in cash. Martin Marietta responded with the "Pac Man defense"—the target's own tender offer for controlling shares of the aggressor, which is predicated on taking on an enormous amount of new debt. When it appeared that Martin Marietta's Pac Man offer would not give it control of Bendix, Martin Marietta induced United Technologies (its "grey knight") to make a back-up tender offer for Bendix that would become effective upon failure of the Martin Marietta offer; if United Technologies' offer prevailed, United Technologies and Martin Marietta would split up the Bendix divisions. Sensing skepticism of the market towards its offer, Martin Marietta engaged its "doomsday weapon"; it amended its offer for Bendix shares by dropping most of the escape clauses, and it took on the look of a firm that would be compelled to take tendered Bendix shares, even at the cost of being drastically undercapitalized when the strategic game ended. Not daunted by the clouds of doom, Bendix bought the Martin Marietta shares that were tendered to it, which ultimately totaled 70% of the company.

Failing to enjoin Martin Marietta's purchases, Bendix arranged to merge with a white knight, Allied Corporation. Martin Marietta nevertheless purchased all of the Bendix shares that were tendered in response to its offer. It traded to Allied all of the Bendix shares it had acquired, in return for the Martin Marietta shares first acquired by Bendix and then transferred to Allied. After $20 million or so was paid by both parties to investment bankers and lawyers, Martin Marietta was "free," if financially bent, Bendix was in the hands of Allied, and Bendix executives were either employed by Allied or floated to soft landings in golden parachutes. See K.M. Davidson, Mega–Mergers: Corporate America's Billion Dollar Takeovers 86–100 (1985).

Martin Marietta was one of many stories not atypical of the mid– 1980s. As the decade progressed, yet a new scenario emerged: the staggering takeover—for upwards of $20 billion—accomplished by leveraged buyout, wherein the raider borrows heavily to buy the target stock from public shareholders. Since the debt burden incurred by the raider is normally more than it can bear, after the buyout it must sell assets of the target to reduce the debt. Often, it announces layoffs of tens of thousands of employees to reduce expenses. Meanwhile, the target has been bought for its short-term break-up value and the assets of the target retained by the raider are used to produce the largest possible short-term wealth for the shareholders. Within a few years, perhaps five, the raider may sell off the remains of the target.

The raider may be Wall Street investment bankers, as in Kohlberg, Kravis, Roberts & Company, which, in 1988, made a $20.3 billion bid for RJR Nabisco, triggering even more lucrative bids by other investment groups; or the raider may be another industrial company, as in Philip Morris' $11.5 billion bid for Kraft, and Grand Metropolitan's $5.23 billion bid for Pillsbury. These deals of the late 1980s are heralded as the biggest "corporate restructurings" in Wall Street history, since break-up and dispersion follows the buyout. One article reported: "The result is a market more and more driven by the prospect of a quick killing"—a killing that yields billions in short-term value to the buyers, the selling shareholders of the target, the golden-parachuted executives of the target, the lawyers, and the investment bankers. See Wallace, Takeover Spree Starts a Speculative Frenzy, New York Times, Oct. 25, 1988, D1, col. 3. These high-debt quick killings have dour implications for the economy. Federal Reserve Board Chairman Alan Greenspan warned that the resulting debt-equity ratios may cause the economic collapse of the whole American economy if the country should slip into a recession. See Silk, Debt in Buyouts Causing Anxiety, New York Times, Oct. 28, 1988, D2, col. 1. The buyouts also have implications for efficiency, progressiveness, and competitiveness. Leonard Silk observed: "The takeover wave also appears to be causing a widespread misallocation of corporate resources, especially of managerial talent, time and energy." Referring to recent failures of savings-and-loan banks, he said: "[This] is only the latest reminder that folly can affect wide classes of institutions and that the marketplace is not always efficient or rational." Id.

What implications do these gigantic buyouts have for antitrust? Do they, at least, counsel against the presumption that mergers are efficient? Might they lead an observer to join issue with the Easterbrook thesis that, since mergers are efficient and an injunction deprives markets of a merger's efficiency gains, high costs attend erroneously-granted merger injunctions and courts should therefore err on the side of non-intervention? See Easterbrook, The Limits of Antitrust, 63 Tex.L.Rev. 1 (1984). Beyond weakening or undermining the presumptive-efficiency hypothesis, does takeover frenzy have relevance to antitrust? Or should concerns, if any, be channelled elsewhere? Consider this editorial that appeared in the *New York Times:*

SMOKE CLOUDS A MEGA–MERGER
The New York Times, Nov. 14, 1988, A18, col. 1.[*]

Velveeta, Parkay, Breyers, Sealtest, Miracle Whip, Frusen Glädjé: meet Maxwell House, Birds Eye, Kool–Aid, Jell–O, Oscar Meyer, Post, Ronzoni and Miller Lite. The prospective merger of the Philip Morris Companies and Kraft Inc. will marry the formidable marketing skills of two packaged-goods giants, creating the largest food company in the world.

Not long ago such a mega-merger would have triggered instant opposition from Government antitrust lawyers inclined to equate bigness with badness. If, on the other hand, this merger is examined in fashionably pure economic terms, it is big but benign, unlikely to reduce competition. In the Kraft case, however, non-economic considerations shouldn't be so casually dismissed.

Philip Morris is the largest cigarette company in America. Arguably, the more the company enlarges its economic base, the more it will enlarge its already substantial power to influence public policy on smoking.

That's why Senator Howard Metzenbaum of Ohio is asking the Federal Trade Commission to condition approval of the merger on a commitment from Philip Morris not to use its economic power to inhibit public debate on tobacco use. That's a worthy goal, but there's a better way to achieve it: for Philip Morris to pledge such restraint voluntarily.

. . .

Kraft sells $5 billion in packaged edibles; Philip Morris's General Foods division has revenues of $10 billion. Even so, the merger wouldn't much increase market concentration. Kraft's muscle is in dairy foods, Philip Morris's elsewhere in the supermarket. Though the merged company would be larger than any competitor, its share of the packaged-food market wouldn't exceed 7 percent.

Some theorists believe that big business is, at best, a necessary evil that concentrates power and threatens democracy. They argue that

[*] Reprinted with permission of the *New York Times.*

merging giants should be required to show substantial efficiency gains to offset the intangible social and political costs of greater economic concentration.

But even accepting the premise, relative size seems a crude measure of relative power or of conflict with the public interest. Sometimes bigness can dilute a company's clout by diversifying its interests. The Exxon Corporation, which must worry about everything from gasoline pump emissions to keeping the Saudi royal family happy, probably has less influence in Congress than Texas wildcatters.

The troubling question in the Philip Morris–Kraft case is whether the merged company would wield its increased power as a lobbyist, employer, purchaser of supplies and advertiser to protect the market for cigarettes.

RJR Nabisco Inc., another tobacco-food conglomerate, fired the ad agency for one of its cracker divisions after the agency made antismoking commercials for Northwest Airlines. Might Philip Morris act similarly? Would it discourage its Kraft division from subsidizing employee attendance at smoking clinics? Would it try to influence the internal smoking policies of companies that sell it jars, cellophane or health insurance?

Most worrisome, would Philip Morris use Kraft's $400 million to $500 million ad budget as leverage to discourage magazines and newspapers from printing material critical of tobacco? Just last week, US magazine admitted that it had turned down an ad for an antismoking product for fear of offending cigarette advertisers.

Senator Metzenbaum believes the F.T.C. should examine this potential chilling effect on the smoking debate and decide whether it is an "unfair act or practice." That would put welcome pressure on Philip Morris. But so broad an interpretation of the law would inevitably provoke a court challenge and invite Congressional interference.

Philip Morris could short-circuit the controversy by pledging to keep hands off the internal smoking policies of its food divisions and to keep tobacco politics out of its advertising decisions. If Kraft is really worth $11 billion, surely it is worth such a demonstration of good will.

————

Do you agree with Senator Metzenbaum? Do you agree with the *New York Times*? Can you structure a legitimate antitrust challenge to the Philip Morris–Kraft takeover, based, perhaps, on the *Clorox* case? If Philip Morris plans a massive dismembering of Kraft, does this plan defeat your tentative antitrust theory of the case?

Even before the leveraged buyout frenzy, some members of Congress responded to the surge in takeovers. Congressman Peter Rodino, then Chairman of the House Judiciary Committee, introduced the big-firm merger bill of 1983. Its purpose, said Rodino, was to send a "clear signal to corporate America that we will no longer tolerate unrestrained warfare between top managements," and we will discourage companies from "raiding other firms at the expense of the public, stockholders, and other diligent company managements." 45 Antitrust & Trade Reg.Rep. (BNA) No. 1124, at 83 (July 21, 1983); 129 Cong.Rec.H. 5128 (July 13, 1983). Was Rodino helping entrenched managements, or helping the public?

The Rodino bill—H.R. 3561 98th Cong., 1st Sess. (1983)—declared that acquisitions that result in the acquirer's having more than $5 billion of assets in the United States may not be consummated "if it is unlikely that such acquisition would serve the public interest." In determining whether a proposed acquisition would serve the public interest, the Assistant Attorney General or the Federal Trade Commission (the sole enforcers) could consider all relevant matters, including whether it is likely that the acquisition would:

(A) maintain and promote existing or potential competition in the market for any good or service within the United States;

(B) result in the effective and productive management of corporate assets, the offering of new goods or services, the enhancement of the quality or reliability of existing goods or services, or the reduction in price of such goods and services;

(C) unduly disrupt management or employees; and

(D) in light of the probable benefits, result in excessive fees and other transactional costs.

In 1987 Congressman Byron Dorgan introduced another form of a big-merger act. The Dorgan Bill—H.R. 3090, 100th Cong., 1st Sess. (1987)—would prohibit acquisition of more than 10% of a company worth $1 billion or more unless one of the enforcement agencies granted a certificate. To obtain a certificate, the acquirer would have to persuade the Antitrust Division or the FTC that the acquisition "would not substantially reduce competition, would enhance operating efficiency and international competitiveness, and would promote the welfare of the affected employees and local communities." 53 Antitrust & Trade Reg.Rep. (BNA) No. 1330, at 365–366 (Aug. 27, 1987). See 133 Cong.Rec. E3242 (remarks of Rep. Dorgan).

Note that in both of these bills the usual burdens are reversed. The proponent of the acquisition must prove that, as a result of the acquisition, competition is maintained or increased, or not reduced. (Which is the better formulation?)

Should the burdens be reversed in the case of very large mergers? Should other public interest factors be considered? More concretely, should we have a law that, absent an available justification, would prohibit ITT from acquiring Hartford? That would prohibit Exxon from acquiring ITT–Hartford? That would prohibit a five-way merger of General Motors, Royal Dutch/Shell, IBM, Hitachi, and Daewoo?

F. PROCEDURE AND ENFORCEMENT

1. INTRODUCTION

In the 1960s and 1970s the legality of a merger was often determined in a court, often on a motion for preliminary injunction; sometimes after trial. During the earlier part of this period, the law was made largely in Justice Department suits or through FTC proceedings. Later, suits by private plaintiffs became common also. Sometimes, after the government announced an intention to sue, merger parties dropped their deal or agreed to relief that satisfied the government, entering into a consent decree on the same day as the filing of the complaint; but very often the cases proceeded directly to court. And when competitors or takeover targets sued, the fight was on, often with heated and quick litigation as the parties tried their cases on extended motions for preliminary relief.

In the 1980s, the landscape for merger enforcement changed. First, merger practice became more regulatory and less judicial. This shift resulted in part from enactment in 1976 of the Hart–Scott–Rodino Antitrust Improvements Act, 15 U.S.C. § 18a. The 1976 statute requires premerger notification and contemplates a greater administrative role for the government in overseeing mergers. Government lawyers who scrutinize merger plans often give pre-litigation advice about how to cure problems they identify. For that reason, and because of the government's assumption that mergers are efficient and help competition, only a trickle of government merger cases now reach the courts.

Second, there has been a change in the role of private and state enforcement. Pursuant to Supreme Court decisions of the 1980s, both competitors and takeover targets face serious hurdles in establishing standing to challenge a merger. Courthouse doors, wide open in the 1960s and 1970s, are not open today. And since consumers are usually too numerous and dispersed to muster their troops to sue, there are often no private attorneys general to challenge anticompetitive mergers, even at a time when the government's standards are more lax than the substantive law. In the face of lax federal enforcement and suppressed private enforcement, state attorneys general have stepped into the breach, challenging potentially anticompetitive mergers that have a distinct intrastate impact. Thus, California attempted to enjoin Texaco's acquisition of Getty's oil assets, and Pennsylvania obtained partial divestiture in the May Department Stores/Associated Dry Goods merger. See Abrams (Attorney General of the State of New York), Developments in State Antitrust Enforcement, 62 N.Y.U.L.Rev. 989, 992 (1987). Meanwhile, questions have been raised regarding the preemptive effect of federal law over state law where the merger has substantial interstate effects and the state threshold for violation is arguably different from the federal threshold for violation. Is the state law preempted? Can the State of California enjoin an oil merger that would (let us assume), in the opinion of the Justice Department, improve the efficiency of Texaco and increase its competitiveness in world markets? Compare *CTS Corp. v. Dynamics Corp.*, 481 U.S. 69 (1987).

Hereafter, we briefly describe the premerger notification law, and then we present a recent Supreme Court opinion on standing.

2. PREMERGER NOTIFICATION

Until 1976 the government had no ready source of information regarding mergers that were about to be consummated. Staff members clipped articles from the Wall Street Journal. Sometimes an important merger would be consummated before antitrust authorities caught wind of its prospect and the merged company then typically argued that the Court should leave it alone; it would be too difficult and costly to "unscramble the eggs." [24] Other times the government had such short notice before the scheduled closing that it could not obtain the necessary facts and adequately prepare for motions for preliminary relief.

These circumstances led Congress to pass the Hart–Scott–Rodino Antitrust Improvements Act. In Title II of the Hart–Scott–Rodino Act, which is Section 7A of the Clayton Act, Congress adopted a plan for premerger notification of mergers above a certain threshold size. If the merger is reportable, the parties must file a notification form along with the information requested by the form; then they must wait 30 days (15 days for cash tender offers). Within the waiting period the government may require further information and if it does the waiting period is extended for 20 days from the time of compliance (10 days for cash tender offers). If within the waiting period the government sues and moves for preliminary relief, its motion is entitled to expedited treatment in the courts.

The size thresholds for filing premerger notification forms are governed by the following three rules:

First, one part to the transaction must have net sales or total assets of $100 million or more, and the other must have net sales or total assets of $10 million or more. Where, however, the acquired company is a non-manufacturing firm, it must have total assets of at least $10 million; its net sales are not a part of the threshold test.

Second, as a result of the acquisition the acquirer must hold either:

1) 15% or more of the voting securities or assets of the acquired person, or

2) voting securities and assets of the acquired person in excess of $15 million.

Third, if the transaction would fall within (1) above but not (2), the transaction is not reportable unless, as a result of the acquisition, the acquirer would also hold: (a) assets of the acquired person valued at more than $15 million, or (b) voting securities that confer control of an issuer with annual net sales or total assets of $25 million or more.[25]

Partially as a result of the 1976 statute, much of the activity and sparring in merger analysis takes place at the reporting and waiting stage of the merger, with the parties' lawyers and economists visiting with and making presentations to the FTC or Justice Department staff to convince them that problems do not exist (e.g., foreign competition is so robust that even large American firms in concentrated markets cannot hope to exercise market power), or to resolve differences.

24. While these factors have never constituted a defense to an antitrust violation, equities including shareholder and worker equities can influence enforcement, liability and relief decisions in marginal cases.

porate Acquisitions & Mergers, Apps. 13 & 14. The statute and regulations are outlined and analyzed in 2 Fox and Fox, Chapter 20B.

25. The statute and supporting FTC regulations are printed in 1 Fox and Fox, Cor-

3. PRIVATE STANDING TO SUE

Sections 4 and 16 of the Clayton Act created an enforcement role for private attorneys general. Private persons injured by or threatened with injury from antitrust violations are empowered to sue. Under Section 4 they can get treble damages. Under Section 16 they can get injunctive relief.

In *Brunswick v. Pueblo Bowl–O–Mat, Inc.,* 429 U.S. 477 (1977), a small operator of bowling alleys challenged Brunswick's acquisition of several failing bowling alleys, some of which competed directly with plaintiff. Plaintiff alleged that the acquisitions were anticompetitive and that it was injured by the antitrust violation; but for the acquisitions the acquired alleys would have failed and the plaintiff would have won the "extra" business available. The Supreme Court took the opportunity to clarify the limits of Section 4 of the Clayton Act. A damage claimant must prove "antitrust injury"—injury by reason of that which the antitrust laws forbid. Pueblo Bowl–O–Mat was injured not by restrained competition, which the law forbids, but by competition itself. Brunswick had kept alive the faltering alleys; as a result of its acquisitions they were competitive factors in the marketplace. Injury from competition itself cannot be antitrust injury.

Of course, most private antimerger actions were not damage actions at all. Private plaintiffs—usually competitors or targets—wanted to prevent a merger or takeover from happening. For many years, in most cases, these plaintiffs were accorded standing without challenge. Occasionally standing was challenged, with mixed results.

In the early 1980s the Justice Department embarked on an effort, through speeches and amicus briefs, to stop private competitor and target lawsuits. For competitor lawsuits, the Justice Department presented a simple paradigm: If a merger is anticompetitive, that is because it is price-raising and output-limiting. If a merger raises price the competitors will come under the price umbrella and stand to profit. They will be happy and they will not sue. But if the merger is efficiency creating the merged firm is likely to become a fierce rival. The competitors will be unhappy and will try to block the merger. Therefore if competitors sue the merger must be efficient and good. Does this make sense? Are there holes in the logic? Does your answer depend upon whether you worry about strategic behavior and believe that strategic behavior can hurt both targeted competitors and consumers? See Williamson, Delimiting Antitrust, 76 Geo.L.J. 271 (1988), for an economic argument that merging competitors can threaten antitrust injury to smaller rivals as well as to consumers.

In the mid–1980s, Monfort of Colorado, a beef packer, challenged the merger of two of its big competitors, Cargill (Excel) and Spencer. The district court found a violation and ordered divestiture. When the case reached the Supreme Court the Justice Department filed an amicus brief, arguing among other things that Monfort did not have standing to sue. The Supreme Court dealt only with the standing question.

CARGILL, INC. v. MONFORT OF COLORADO, INC.

479 U.S. 104 (1986).

JUSTICE BRENNAN: Under § 16 of the Clayton Act, private parties "threatened [with] loss or damage by a violation of the antitrust laws" may seek injunctive relief. This case presents two questions: whether a plaintiff seeking relief under § 16 must prove a threat of antitrust injury, and, if so, whether loss or damage due to increased competition constitutes such injury.

I

Respondent Monfort of Colorado, Inc. (Monfort), the plaintiff below, owns and operates three integrated beef-packing plants, that is, plants for both the slaughter of cattle and the fabrication of beef.[1] Monfort operates in both the market for fed cattle (the input market) and the market for fabricated beef (the output market). These markets are highly competitive, and the profit margins of the major beef packers are low. The current markets are a product of two decades of intense competition, during which time packers with modern integrated plants have gradually displaced packers with separate slaughter and fabrication plants.

Monfort is the country's fifth-largest beef packer. Petitioner Excel Corporation (Excel), one of the two defendants below, is the second-largest packer. Excel operates five integrated plants and one fabrication plant. It is a wholly owned subsidiary of Cargill, Inc., the other defendant below, a large privately owned corporation with more than 150 subsidiaries in at least 35 countries.

On June 17, 1983, Excel signed an agreement to acquire the third-largest packer in the market, Spencer Beef, a division of the Land O'Lakes agricultural cooperative. Spencer Beef owned two integrated plants and one slaughtering plant. After the acquisition, Excel would still be the second-largest packer, but would command a market share almost equal to that of the largest packer, IBP, Inc. (IBP).[2]

Monfort brought an action under § 16 of the Clayton Act, 15 U.S.C. § 26, to enjoin the prospective merger. Its complaint alleged that the acquisition would "violat[e] Section 7 of the Clayton Act because the effect of the proposed acquisition may be substantially to lessen competition or tend to create a monopoly in several different ways. . . ." 1 App. 19. Monfort described the injury that it allegedly would suffer in this way:

"(f) *Impairment of plaintiff's ability to compete.* The proposed acquisition will result in a concentration of economic power in the relevant

---

1. As the District Court explained, " '[f]abrication' is the process whereby the carcass is broken down into either whole cuts (referred to as 'primals', 'subprimals' and 'portions') or ground beef." 591 F.Supp. 683, 690 (Colo.1983). Whole cuts that are then vacuum-packed before shipment are called "boxed beef"; the District Court found that "80% of all beef received at the retail supermarket level and at the hotel, restau-rant, and institutional ('HRI') level" is boxed beef. *Ibid.*

2. . . . According to the testimony, Monfort's share of the cattle slaughter market was 5.5%, Excel's share was 13.3%, and IBP's was 24.4%. Monfort's share of the production market was 5.7%, Excel's share was 14.1%, and IBP's share was 27.3%. After the merger, Excel's share of each market would increase to 20.4%.

markets which threatens Monfort's supply of fed cattle and its ability to compete in the boxed beef market." *Id.,* at 20.

. . . After the trial, the court entered a memorandum opinion and order enjoining the proposed merger. The court held that Monfort's allegation of "price-cost 'squeeze'" that would "severely narro[w]" Monfort's profit margins constituted an allegation of antitrust injury. It also held that Monfort had shown that the proposed merger would cause this profit-squeeze to occur, and that the merger violated § 7 of the Clayton Act.

On appeal, Excel argued that an allegation of lost profits due to a "price-cost squeeze" was nothing more than an allegation of losses due to vigorous competition, and that losses from competition do not constitute antitrust injury. It also argued that the District Court erred in analyzing the facts relevant to the § 7 inquiry. The Court of Appeals affirmed the judgment in all respects. It held that Monfort's allegation of a "price-cost squeeze" was not simply an allegation of injury from competition; in its view, the alleged "price-cost squeeze" was a claim that Monfort would be injured by what the Court of Appeals "consider[ed] to be a form of predatory pricing in which Excel will drive other companies out of the market by paying more to its cattle suppliers and charging less for boxed beef that it sells to institutional buyers and consumers." 761 F.2d 570, 575 (CA10 1985). On the § 7 issue, the Court of Appeals held that the District Court's decision was not clearly erroneous. We granted certiorari.

II

This case requires us to decide, at the outset, a question we have not previously addressed: whether a private plaintiff seeking an injunction under § 16 of the Clayton Act must show a threat of antitrust injury. To decide the question, we must look first to the source of the antitrust injury requirement, which lies in a related provision of the Clayton Act, § 4, 15 U.S.C. § 15.

Like § 16, § 4 provides a vehicle for private enforcement of the antitrust laws. Under § 4, "any person who shall be injured in his business or property by reason of anything forbidden in the antitrust laws may sue therefor in any district court of the United States . . ., and shall recover threefold the damages by him sustained, and the cost of suit, including a reasonable attorney's fee." 15 U.S.C. § 15. In *Brunswick Corp. v. Pueblo Bowl–O–Mat, Inc.,* [429 U.S. 477 (1977)] we held that plaintiffs seeking treble damages under § 4 must show more than simply an "injury causally linked" to a particular merger; instead, "plaintiffs must prove *antitrust* injury, which is to say injury of the type the antitrust laws were intended to prevent and that flows from that which makes the defendants' acts unlawful." *Id.,* at 489 (emphasis in original). The plaintiffs in *Brunswick* did not prove such injury. The plaintiffs were 3 of the 10 bowling centers owned by a relatively small bowling chain. The defendant, one of the two largest bowling chains in the country, acquired several bowling centers located in the plaintiffs' market that would have gone out of business but for the acquisition. The plaintiffs sought treble damages under § 4, alleging as injury "the loss of income that would have accrued had the acquired centers gone bankrupt" and had competition in their markets consequently been reduced. *Id.,* at 487. We held that this injury, although causally related to a merger alleged to violate § 7, was not an antitrust injury, since "[i]t is inimical to [the antitrust] laws to award damages" for losses stemming from continued competition. *Id.,* at 488. This reasoning in *Brunswick* was consistent with the principle that "the antitrust laws . . . were enacted for 'the protection of *competition,* not *competitors.*' " *Ibid.,* quoting *Brown Shoe Co. v. United States,* 370 U.S. 294, 320 (1962) (emphasis in original).

Subsequent decisions confirmed the importance of showing antitrust injury under § 4. In *Blue Shield of Virginia v. McCready,* 457 U.S. 465 (1982), we found that a health-plan subscriber suffered antitrust injury as a result of the plan's "purposefully *anticompetitive scheme* " to reduce competition for psychotherapeutic services by reimbursing subscribers for services provided by psychiatrists but not for services provided by psychologists. *Id.,* at 483. We noted that antitrust injury, "as analyzed in *Brunswick,* is one factor to be considered in determining the redressability of a particular form of injury under § 4," *id.,* at 483, n. 19, and found it "plain that McCready's injury was of a type that Congress sought to redress in providing a private remedy for violations of the antitrust laws." *Id.,* at 483. Similarly, in *Associated General Contractors of California, Inc. v. Carpenters,* 459 U.S. 519 (1983), we applied "the *Brunswick* test," and found that the petitioner had failed to allege antitrust injury. *Id.,* at 539–540.[5]

Section 16 of the Clayton Act provides in part that "[a]ny person, firm, corporation, or association shall be entitled to sue for and have injunctive relief . . . against threatened loss or damage by a violation of the antitrust laws. . . ." 15 U.S.C. § 26. It is plain that § 16 and § 4 do differ in various ways. For example, § 4 requires a plaintiff to show actual injury, but § 16 requires a showing only of "threatened" loss or damage; similarly, § 4 requires a showing of injury to "business or property," cf. *Hawaii v. Standard Oil Co.,* 405 U.S. 251 (1972), while § 16 contains no such limitation.[6] Although these differences do affect the

5. A showing of antitrust injury is necessary, but not always sufficient, to establish standing under § 4, because a party may have suffered antitrust injury but may not be a proper plaintiff under § 4 for other reasons. . . . Thus, in *Associated General Contractors* we considered other factors in addition to antitrust injury to determine whether the petitioner was a proper plaintiff under § 4. 459 U.S., at 540. As we explain *infra,* n. 6, however, many of these other factors are not relevant to the standing inquiry under § 16.

6. Standing analysis under § 16 will not always be identical to standing analysis under § 4. For example, the difference in the remedy each section provides means that certain considerations relevant to a determination of standing under § 4 are not relevant under § 16. The treble-damages remedy, if afforded to "every person tangentially

affected by an antitrust violation," *Blue Shield of Virginia v. McCready,* 457 U.S. 465, 476–477 (1982), or for "all injuries that might conceivably be traced to an antitrust violation," *Hawaii v. Standard Oil Co.,* 405 U.S., at 263, n. 14, would "open the door to duplicative recoveries," *id.,* at 264, and to multiple lawsuits. In order to protect against multiple lawsuits and duplicative recoveries, courts should examine other factors in addition to antitrust injury, such as the potential for duplicative recovery, the complexity of apportioning damages, and the existence of other parties that have been more directly harmed, to determine whether a party is a proper plaintiff under § 4. See *Associated General Contractors,* 459 U.S, at 544–545; *Illinois Brick Co. v. Illinois,* 431 U.S. 720 (1977). Conversely, under § 16, the only remedy available is equitable in nature, and, as we recognized in *Hawaii v. Standard*

nature of the injury cognizable under each section, the lower courts, including the courts below, have found that under both § 16 and § 4 the plaintiff must still allege an injury of the type the antitrust laws were designed to prevent. We agree.

The wording concerning the relationship of the injury to the violation of the antitrust laws in each section is comparable. Section 4 requires proof of injury "by reason of anything forbidden in the antitrust laws"; § 16 requires proof of "threatened loss or damage by a violation of the antitrust laws." It would be anomalous, we think, to read the Clayton Act to authorize a private plaintiff to secure an injunction against a threatened injury for which he would not be entitled to compensation if the injury actually occurred.

There is no indication that Congress intended such a result. Indeed, the legislative history of § 16 is consistent with the view that § 16 affords private plaintiffs injunctive relief only for those injuries cognizable under § 4. . . .[8] Sections 4 and 16 are thus best understood as providing complementary remedies for a single set of injuries. Accordingly, we conclude that in order to seek injunctive relief under § 16, a private plaintiff must allege threatened loss or damage "of the type the antitrust laws were designed to prevent and that flows from that which makes defendants' acts unlawful." *Brunswick*, 429 U.S., at 489. We therefore turn to the question of whether the proposed merger in this case threatened respondent with antitrust injury.

III

. . . Monfort did present testimony and other evidence that helped define the threatened loss. Monfort alleged that after the merger, Excel would attempt to increase its market share at the expense of smaller rivals, such as Monfort. To that end, Monfort claimed, Excel would bid up the price it would pay for cattle, and reduce the price at which it sold boxed beef. Although such a strategy, which Monfort labeled a "cost-price squeeze," would reduce Excel's profits, Excel's parent corporation had the financial reserves to enable Excel to pursue such a strategy. Eventually, according to Monfort, smaller competitors lacking significant reserves and unable to match Excel's prices would be driven from the market; at this point Excel would raise the price of its boxed beef to

Oil Co., "the fact is that one injunction is as effective as 100, and, concomitantly, that 100 injunctions are no more effective than one." 405 U.S., at 261. Thus, because standing under § 16 raises no threat of multiple lawsuits or duplicative recoveries, some of the factors other than antitrust injury that are appropriate to a determination of standing under § 4 are not relevant under § 16.

8. See also S.Rep. No. 698, 63d Cong., 2d Sess., 17–18, 50 (1914). Although the references to § 16 in the debates on the passage of the Clayton Act are scarce, those that were made are consistent with the House and Senate Reports. For example, in this excerpt from a provision-by-provision description of the bill, Representative McGil-

licuddy (a member of the House Judiciary Committee) stated:

"Under the present law any person injured in his business or property by acts in violation of the Sherman antitrust law may recover his damage. In fact, under the provisions of the law he is entitled to recover threefold damage whenever he is able to prove his case. There is no provision under the present law, however, to prevent threatened loss or damage even though it be irreparable. The practical effect of this is that a man would have to sit by and see his business ruined before he could take advantage of his remedy. In what condition is such a man to take up a long and costly lawsuit to defend his rights? . . .

supracompetitive levels, and would more than recoup the profits it lost during the initial phase.

From this scenario two theories of injury to Monfort emerge: (1) a threat of a loss of profits stemming from the possibility that Excel, after the merger, would lower its prices to a level at or only slightly above its costs; (2) a threat of being driven out of business by the possibility that Excel, after the merger, would lower its prices to a level below its costs. We discuss each theory in turn.

A

Monfort's first claim is that after the merger, Excel would lower its prices to some level at or slightly above its costs in order to compete with other packers for market share. Excel would be in a position to do this because of the multiplant efficiencies its acquisition of Spencer would provide. To remain competitive, Monfort would have to lower its prices; as a result, Monfort would suffer a loss in profitability, but would not be driven out of business.[10] The question is whether Monfort's loss of profits in such circumstances constitutes antitrust injury.

To resolve the question, we look again to *Brunswick v. Pueblo Bowl-O-Mat, supra.* In *Brunswick,* we evaluated the antitrust significance of several competitors' loss of profits resulting from the entry of a large firm into its market. We concluded:

> "[T]he antitrust laws are not merely indifferent to the injury claimed here. At base, respondents complain that by acquiring the failing centers petitioner preserved competition, thereby depriving respondents of the benefits of increased concentration. The damages respondents obtained are designed to provide them with the profits they would have realized had competition been reduced. The antitrust laws, however, were enacted for 'the protection of *competition,* not *competitors,*' *Brown Shoe Co. v. United States,* 370 U.S., at 320. It is inimical to the purposes of these laws to award damages for the type of injury claimed here." *Id.,* at 488.

The loss of profits to the competitors in *Brunswick* was not of concern under the antitrust laws, since it resulted only from continued competition. Respondent argues that the losses in *Brunswick* can be distinguished from the losses alleged here, since the latter will result from an increase, rather than from a mere continuation, of competition. The range of actions unlawful under § 7 of the Clayton Act is broad enough, respondent claims, to support a finding of antitrust injury whenever a competitor is faced with a threat of losses from increased competition. We find respondent's proposed construction of § 7 too broad, for reasons that *Brunswick* illustrates. *Brunswick* holds that the antitrust laws do not require the courts to protect small businesses from the loss of profits due to continued competition, but only against the loss of profits from practices forbidden by the antitrust laws. The kind of competition that Monfort alleges here, competition for increased market share, is not activity forbidden by the antitrust laws. It is simply, as petitioners claim, vigorous competition. To hold that the antitrust laws protect competitors

---

10. In this case, Monfort has conceded that its viability would not be threatened by Excel's decision to lower prices: "Because Monfort's operations were as efficient as those of Excel, only below-cost pricing could remove Monfort as an obstacle."

from the loss of profits due to such price competition would, in effect, render illegal any decision by a firm to cut prices in order to increase market share. The antitrust laws require no such perverse result. . . . The logic of *Brunswick* compels the conclusion that the threat of loss of profits due to possible price competition following a merger does not constitute a threat of antitrust injury.

B

The second theory of injury argued here is that after the merger Excel would attempt to drive Monfort out of business by engaging in sustained predatory pricing. Predatory pricing may be defined as pricing below an appropriate measure of cost for the purpose of eliminating competitors in the short run and reducing competition in the long run.[12] It is a practice that harms both competitors *and* competition. In contrast to price cutting aimed simply at increasing market share, predatory pricing has as its aim the elimination of competition. Predatory pricing is thus a practice "inimical to the purposes of [the antitrust] laws," *Brunswick*, 429 U.S., at 488, and one capable of inflicting antitrust injury.[13]

The Court of Appeals held that Monfort had alleged "what we consider to be a form of predatory pricing. . . ." 761 F.2d, at 575. The court also found that Monfort "could only be harmed by sustained predatory pricing," and that "it is impossible to tell in advance of the acquisition" whether Excel would in fact engage in such a course of conduct; because it could not rule out the possibility that Excel would engage in predatory pricing, it found that Monfort was threatened with antitrust injury. *Id.*, at 576.

12. Most commentators reserve the term predatory pricing for pricing below some measure of cost, although they differ on the appropriate measure. See, *e.g.*, Areeda & Turner, Predatory Pricing and Related Practices under Section 2 of the Sherman Act, 88 Harv.L.Rev. 697 (1975); McGee, Predatory Pricing Revisited, 23 J. Law & Econ. 289 (1980) (reviewing various proposed definitions). No consensus has yet been reached on the proper definition of predatory pricing in the antitrust context, however. For purposes of decision in *Matsushita Electric Industrial Co. v. Zenith Radio Corp.*, 475 U.S. 574 (1986), for example, we defined predatory pricing as either "(i) pricing below the level necessary to sell their products, or (ii) pricing below some appropriate measure of cost." *Id.*, at 585, n. 8. Definitions of predatory pricing also vary among the Circuits. Compare *Arthur S. Langenderfer, Inc. v. S.E. Johnson Co.*, 729 F.2d 1050, 1056–1057 (CA6) (pricing below marginal or average variable cost presumptively illegal, pricing above such cost presumptively legal), cert. denied, 469 U.S. 1036 (1984), with *Transamerica Computer Co. v. International Business Machines Corp.*, 698 F.2d 1377 (CA9) (pricing above average total costs may be deemed predatory upon showing of predatory intent), cert. denied, 464 U.S. 955 (1983).

Although neither the District Court nor the Court of Appeals explicitly defined the term predatory pricing, their use of the term is consistent with a definition of pricing below cost. Such a definition is sufficient for purposes of this decision, because only below-cost pricing would threaten to drive Monfort from the market, and because Monfort made no allegation that Excel would act with predatory intent. Thus, in this case, as in *Matsushita Electric Industrial Co. v. Zenith Radio Corp., supra*, we find it unnecessary to "consider whether recovery should *ever* be available . . . when the pricing in question is above some measure of incremental cost," 475 U.S., at 585, n. 9, or whether above-cost pricing coupled with predatory intent is ever sufficient to state a claim of predation.

13. See also *Brunswick*, 429 U.S., at 489, n. 14 ("The short-term effect of certain anticompetitive behavior—predatory below-cost pricing, for example—may be to stimulate price competition. But competitors may be able to prove antitrust injury before they actually are driven from the market and competition is thereby lessened").

Although the Court of Appeals did not explicitly define what it meant by predatory pricing, two interpretations are plausible. First, the court can be understood to mean that Monfort's allegation of losses from the above-cost "cost-price squeeze" was equivalent to an allegation of injury from predatory conduct. If this is the proper interpretation, then the court's judgment is clearly erroneous because (a) Monfort made no allegation that Excel would act with predatory intent after the merger, and (b) price competition is not predatory activity.

Second, the Court of Appeals can be understood to mean that Monfort had shown a credible threat of injury from below-cost pricing. To the extent the judgment rests on this ground, however, it must also be reversed, because Monfort did not allege injury from below-cost pricing before the District Court. The District Court twice noted that Monfort had made no assertion that Excel would engage in predatory pricing. Monfort argues that there is evidence in the record to support its view that it did raise a claim of predatory pricing below. This evidence, however, consists only of four passing references, three in deposition testimony, to the possibility that Excel's prices might dip below costs. Such references fall far short of establishing an allegation of injury from predatory pricing. We conclude that Monfort neither raised nor proved any claim of predatory pricing before the District Court.[15]

15. Even had Monfort actually advanced a claim of predatory pricing, we doubt whether the facts as found by the District Court would have supported it. Although Excel may have had the financial resources to absorb losses over an extended period, other factors, such as Excel's share of market capacity and the barriers to entry after competitors have been driven from the market, must also be considered.

In order to succeed in a sustained campaign of predatory pricing, a predator must be able to absorb the market shares of its rivals once prices have been cut. If it cannot do so, its attempt at predation will presumably fail, because there will remain in the market sufficient demand for the competitors' goods at a higher price, and the competitors will not be driven out of business. In this case, Excel's 21% market share after the merger suggests it would lack sufficient market power to engage in predatory pricing. See Williamson, Predatory Pricing: A Strategic and Welfare Analysis, 87 Yale L.J. 284, 292 (1977) (60% share necessary); Areeda & Turner, Williamson on Predatory Pricing, 87 Yale L.J. 1337, 1348 (1978) (60% share not enough). It is possible that a firm with a low market share might nevertheless have sufficient excess capacity to enable it rapidly to expand its output and absorb the market shares of its rivals. According to Monfort's expert witness, however, Excel's postmerger share of market capacity would be only 28.4%. Moreover, it appears that Excel, like the other large beef packers, operates at over 85% of capacity.

Thus Excel acting alone would clearly lack sufficient capacity after the merger to satisfy all or most of the demand for boxed beef. Although it is conceivable that Excel could act collusively with other large packers, such as IBP, in order to make the scheme work, the District Court found that Monfort did not "assert that Excel and IBP would act in collusion with each other in an effort to drive others out of the market," 591 F.Supp., at 692. With only a 28.4% share of market capacity and lacking a plan to collude, Excel would harm only itself by embarking on a sustained campaign of predatory pricing. Courts should not find allegations of predatory pricing credible when the alleged predator is incapable of successfully pursuing a predatory scheme.

It is also important to examine the barriers to entry into the market, because "without barriers to entry it would presumably be impossible to maintain supracompetitive prices for an extended time." *Matsushita, supra*, at 591, n. 15. In discussing the potential for oligopoly pricing in the beef-packing business following the merger, the District Court found significant barriers to entry due to the "costs and delays" of building new plants, and "the lack of [available] facilities and the cost [$20–40 million] associated with refurbishing old facilities." 591 F.Supp., at 707–708. Although the District Court concluded that these barriers would restrict entry following the merger, the court's analysis was premised on market conditions during the premerger period of competitive pricing. *Ibid.* In evaluating entry barriers in the

IV

In its *amicus* brief, the United States argues that the "danger of allowing a competitor to challenge an acquisition on the basis of necessarily speculative claims of post-acquisition predatory pricing far outweighs the danger that any anticompetitive merger will go unchallenged." On this basis, the United States invites the Court to adopt in effect a *per se* rule "denying competitors standing to challenge acquisitions on the basis of predatory pricing theories."

We decline the invitation. As the foregoing discussion makes plain, predatory pricing is an anticompetitive practice forbidden by the antitrust laws. While firms may engage in the practice only infrequently, there is ample evidence suggesting that the practice does occur.[16] It would be novel indeed for a court to deny standing to a party seeking an injunction against threatened injury merely because such injuries rarely occur.[17] In any case, nothing in the language or legislative history of the Clayton Act suggests that Congress intended this Court to ignore injuries caused by such anticompetitive practices as predatory pricing.

V

We hold that a plaintiff seeking injunctive relief under § 16 of the Clayton Act must show a threat of antitrust injury, and that a showing of

context of a predatory-pricing claim, however, a court should focus on whether significant entry barriers would exist *after* the merged firm had eliminated some of its rivals, because at that point the remaining firms would begin to charge supracompetitive prices, and the barriers that existed during competitive conditions might well prove insignificant. In this case, for example, although costs of entry into the current competitive market may be high, if Excel and others in fact succeeded in driving competitors out of the market, the facilities of the bankrupt competitors would then be available, and the record shows, without apparent contradiction, that shut-down plants could be producing efficiently in a matter of months and that equipment and a labor force could readily be obtained. Similarly, although the District Court determined that the high costs of building new plants and refurbishing old plants created a "formidable" barrier to entry given "the low profit margins in the beef industry," 591 F.Supp., at 707, this finding speaks neither to the likelihood of entry during a period of supracompetitive profitability nor to the potential return on investment in such a period.

16. See Koller, The Myth of Predatory Pricing: An Empirical Study, 4 Antitrust Law & Econ.Rev. 105 (1971); Miller, Comments on Baumol and Ordover, 28 J. Law & Econ. 267 (1985).

17. Claims of threatened injury from predatory pricing must, of course, be evaluated with care. As we discussed in *Matsu-*

shita Electric Industrial Co. v. Zenith Radio Corp., the likelihood that predatory pricing will benefit the predator is "inherently uncertain: the short-run loss [from pricing below cost] is definite, but the long-run gain depends on successfully neutralizing the competition. . . . [and] on maintaining monopoly power for long enough both to recoup the predator's losses and to harvest some additional gain." 475 U.S., at 589. Although the commentators disagree as to whether it is ever rational for a firm to engage in such conduct, it is plain that the obstacles to the successful execution of a strategy of predation are manifold, and that the disincentives to engage in such a strategy are accordingly numerous. See, *e.g., id.,* at 588–593 (discussing obstacles to successful predatory pricing conspiracy); R. Bork, The Antitrust Paradox 144–159 (1978); McGee, Predatory Pricing Revisited, 23 J. Law & Econ., at 291–300; Posner, The Chicago School of Antitrust Analysis, 127 U.Pa.L. Rev. 925, 939–940 (1979). As we stated in *Matsushita*, "predatory pricing schemes are rarely tried, and even more rarely successful." 475 U.S., at 589. Moreover, the mechanism by which a firm engages in predatory pricing—lowering prices—is the same mechanism by which a firm stimulates competition; because "cutting prices in order to increase business often is the very essence of competition . . .[;] mistaken inferences . . . are especially costly, because they chill the very conduct the antitrust laws are designed to protect." *Id.,* at 594.

loss or damage due merely to increased competition does not constitute such injury. The record below does not support a finding of antitrust injury, but only of threatened loss from increased competition. Because respondent has therefore failed to make the showing § 16 requires, we need not reach the question of whether the proposed merger violates § 7. The judgment of the Court of Appeals is reversed, and the case is remanded for further proceedings consistent with this opinion.

JUSTICE STEVENS, joined by JUSTICE WHITE, dissenting: This case presents the question whether the antitrust laws provide a remedy for a private party that challenges a horizontal merger between two of its largest competitors. The issue may be approached along two fundamentally different paths. First, the Court might focus its attention entirely on the postmerger conduct of the merging firms and deny relief unless the plaintiff can prove a violation of the Sherman Act. Second, the Court might concentrate on the merger itself and grant relief if there is a significant probability that the merger will adversely affect competition in the market in which the plaintiff must compete. Today the Court takes a step down the former path; I believe that Congress has directed us to follow the latter path.

In this case, one of the major firms in the beef-packing market has proved to the satisfaction of the District Court and the Court of Appeals that the merger between Excel and Spencer Beef is illegal. This Court holds, however, that the merger should not be set aside because the adverse impact of the merger on respondent's profit margins does not constitute the kind of "antitrust injury" that the Court described in *Brunswick Corp. v. Pueblo Bowl–O–Mat, Inc.*, 429 U.S. 477 (1977). . . . *Brunswick* merely rejected a "novel damages theory," *id.*, at 490; the Court's implicit determination that *Brunswick* forecloses the appropriate line of inquiry in this quite different case is therefore misguided. In my view, a competitor in Monfort's position has standing to seek an injunction against the merger. Because Monfort must compete in the relevant market, proof establishing that the merger will have a sufficient probability of an adverse effect on competition to violate § 7 is also sufficient to authorize equitable relief.

* * *

Questions and Comments

Consider the three sources of law from which the Court might have derived its conclusion: (1) the statute, (2) decisional law, and (3) public policy. Who has the better side of the argument as to each—the majority or the dissent?

Would it be fair to think about the Court's argumentation as follows: Monfort must have been worried only about defendants' low pricing, because only low pricing would hurt it. Since it did not (pre-merger) prove defendant's post-merger intent to engage in illegal (below-cost) low pricing, Monfort must have been worried only about pricing at competitively low levels—that is, about competition itself. Harm from competition itself is not protected by the antitrust laws. Therefore Monfort is not threatened with antitrust injury and has no standing to sue.

Is this argument sound? Does it miss something about Monfort's claim? Can you make out a claim of threatened injury by strategic behavior, through a price squeeze? But does the claim of strategic behavior require proof of ability to monopolize or oligopolize the input market, while excluding Monfort from entering that market on a scale sufficient to satisfy its own needs? Why else would Spencer/Excel find it profitable to bid up the price of feed cattle, since they must pay the higher price, too?

The Court says that predatory pricing by Spencer/Excel would not have made economic sense because barriers were too low and Spencer/Excel was too small. What if barriers were high and Spencer/Excel had 90% of the industry's capacity? Could Spencer/Excel still defeat Monfort's standing by asserting that it was a law-abiding company and would not violate Section 2 and that the penalties for predation are so high that they would deter a rational profit maximizer from doing so?

Has the Court made the burdens for proving probable predation so high that virtually no competitor plaintiff can meet them? See *R.C. Bigelow, Inc. v. Unilever N.V.*, (No. 88–7502, 2d Cir., Jan. 1, 1989), 56 ATRR 160 (small competitor may challenge acquisition by dominant firm yielding post acquisition share of 84%). Does the Court view predatory pricing as the only possible antitrust injury to a competitor resulting from an anticompetitive merger?

At a minimum, the Court's majority is saying: a competitor must show harm to itself other than harm resulting from increased competition facilitated by the merger. Justice Steven's approach is quite different: "When the proof discloses a reasonable probability that competition will be harmed as a result of a merger, . . . there is a reasonable probability that a competitor of the merging firms will suffer some corresponding harm in due course." Which approach is sounder?

We present below four problems of antitrust standing, in view of *Monfort*.

1. In Mobil–Marathon,[26] Marathon was the largest, most dependable supplier to cut-rate gas sellers. It sold non-branded gas to the discount market. Mobil, the number two supplier, sold only Mobil-branded gasoline and had a policy against selling non-branded gas. Mobil made a hostile bid for Marathon. If the takeover had succeeded, would Marathon have suffered antitrust injury? Would antitrust injury to Marathon have resulted if an effect of the acquisition would have been to cut back output and raise the price of gasoline? What if a combined Mobil/Marathon would have had no power to limit output but the merged firm's management would have taken Marathon out of the non-branded gas market in order to continue Mobil's policy of refusing to sell non-branded gas?

2. Would (did) Chrysler have standing to challenge the joint venture between General Motors and Toyota? (See pp. 805–811 supra). Would Chrysler have had standing if the only alleged anticompetitive consequence of the joint venture was to facilitate cooperative behavior? If the joint venture saved General Motors the costs of a small car design while Chrysler was obliged to continue to incur these costs, would Chrysler thereby suffer antitrust injury? Or would it merely suffer injury from more efficient competi-

26. See Marathon Oil Co. v. Mobil Corp., 669 F.2d 378 (6th Cir.1981), *cert. denied*, 445 U.S. 982 (1982).

tion? As lawyer for Chrysler, could you articulate probable strategic behavior of GM–Toyota that would produce antitrust injury to Chrysler?[27]

3. If Royal Crown sued Coca–Cola to enjoin its acquisition of Dr Pepper (see FTC v. Coca–Cola Co., supra p. 795), could Coca–Cola win on a motion to dismiss for lack of standing? If Royal Crown reasonably feared loss of access to the business of bottlers affiliated with Coca–Cola, would it be able to show threatened antitrust injury? Does the answer depend on whether output of soda would be reduced?

4. Recall the Premiere joint venture of movie companies to enter cable TV distribution, supra p. 841. Suppose HBO had challenged the joint venture on grounds of foreclosure from necessary inputs (hit films). The movie companies, in turn, assert that HBO was merely complaining about the fierce competition Premiere would offer; that HBO would be hurt by competition, not by a lessening of competition. The movie companies move to dismiss for lack of standing. Do they win?

In view of *Monfort,* can a non-competitor takeover target ever show standing to sue for a violation of Section 7 of the Clayton Act?

Must the plaintiff whose standing is challenged prove a credible case on the merits as a first step in proof of antitrust injury? Does a challenge to standing quickly involve the court in a mini-trial of the merits?

In the aftermath of *Cargill v. Monfort,* Senator Metzenbaum introduced a bill that would grant competitors standing to sue to enjoin anticompetitive mergers. (S. 1407, 100th Cong., 1st Sess. 1987) What is the biggest benefit of such a bill? What is its biggest cost? If you were a senator, would you support or oppose it?

G. END PROBLEM

The Z–RAM microchip has just been invented by a research consortium of American universities, called RECAU. The Z–RAM is a complex memory microchip that has 500% greater memory and can perform a multitude more functions than any chip previously developed. It promises to revolutionize the data industry.

After conversations with IBM and AT & T, who provided generous research grants, RECAU announced that it will license U.S. producers immediately and will license non-U.S. producers after the lapse of one year. The availability of the Z–RAM technology leads to several American merger plans; but before we state these plans we will describe the market.

The six largest producers of memory chips are Japanese; namely, Toshiba, NEC, Hitachi, Fujitsu, Mitsubishi and Oki Electric. The American industry has been overtaken by the Japanese, who were selling D–RAMs (dynamic random access memory chips) to American buyers at prices below the American producers' costs. The American producers sought trade relief from the U.S. Government. In response, the U.S. Government negotiated the 1986 semiconductor trade agreement with Japan. The agreement set floor prices for imported computer chips,

---

27. See Chrysler Corp. v. General Motors Corp., 589 F.Supp. 1182 (D.D.C.1984).

pushing up the market price of chips in the United States and giving the Japanese extra profits, which they invested in more R & D and new facilities.

While the price umbrella might have encouraged the American companies to expand their chip operations and increase their R & D investments, it did not. The size of the Japanese investment generally discouraged American investment. Nevertheless, three American chip makers continued to be leaders in the market: Texas Instruments, recently purchased by a Japanese firm, which makes most of its D–RAMs in Japan; IBM, the dominant computer company, which makes chips and sells them to itself; and AT & T, the dominant telecommunications firm, which is a recent entrant into both memory chips and computers (the biggest market for memory chips). Three other American chip producers have held their own, more or less: Micron Technology, which makes chips in small quantities; Motorola, which holds its own proprietary microprocessor designs and has formed a joint venture with Toshiba to manufacture chips in Japan; and Intel, which, like Motorola, holds proprietary microprocessor designs. The two other significant U.S. chip producers, National Semiconductor and Advanced Micro Devices, have been experiencing serious losses.

A few years ago the U.S. chip producers formed an R & D consortium, Sematech, whose mission is to advance chip technology. Sematech is subsidized by the Federal Government. Some of the U.S. chip producers have been lobbying for a separate U.S. Government-organized and supported consortium to manufacture memories, accompanied by an antitrust exemption; and some have been lobbying to replace the 1986 trade agreement with tariffs, so that the U.S. Government rather than the Japanese would profit from the Japanese producers' low prices.

The memory chip market is international. There are no significant transportation costs or duties; to make an advantageous purchase, buyers will purchase chips in the country of the producer. At present the Japanese account for 90% of the world memory chip market, for 90% of U.S. open market purchases (thus excluding IBM's sales to itself), and for 90% of sales in Japan—the largest national market for chips in the world.

The computer industry will probably account for 80% of all Z–RAM uses; the telecommunications market will account for nearly 20%. The market for large (main-frame) computers is concentrated, with shares of U.S. sales as follows:

IBM	40%
Digital Equipment	12%
Hewlett–Packard	10%
Fujitsu	8%
Burroughs-Honeywell	8%
Sun Micro–Systems	8%
Control Data	7%
Small firms	7%.

The announced availability of the Z–RAM technology led to the following plans: Texas Instruments and Advanced Micro Devices wish to merge. They plan to use their joint capabilities as chip manufacturers to develop applications and to market the chips. Intel and Micron Technologies (chip makers) wish to merge with Digital Equipment, a leading U.S. computer manufacturer, in order to combine their capabilities, have a ready outlet for their Z–RAM production, and experiment on applications with greatest facility and least cost. Motorola and National Semiconductor (chip manufacturers) and Hewlett–Packard (computer manufacturer) likewise plan to merge; they will concentrate on exploitation of horizontal and vertical economies of integration and scale. IBM, AT & T and each group above will, individually, take a license to make the Z–RAM.

These merger plans and other initiatives (described below) have been influenced by the expectation of a steep learning curve for production of Z–RAMS. Whichever firms get there first and establish a large market share fast will gain significant efficiencies and will have most of the market for themselves. The Americans (including the Defense Department) hope it will be the Americans and not the Japanese. Moreover, they know that the Japanese are investing billions of dollars in research and new facilities, and hope that the Japanese will not surpass the new American technology before the Americans get to market.

The U.S. firms that expect to get licenses to make the Z–RAM have just formed a Z–RAM trade association, ZRAMTA. Under the aegis of ZRAMTA they have discussed in general terms the advantages of being out in front first and the value of strategic pricing of the first generation of Z–RAMs. At a ZRAMTA meeting a professor, the author of a book on strategic planning, lectured. She told ZRAMTA members that if they price below initial marginal cost they will get larger markets at home and abroad, that they will get more experience, that the experience will produce significantly lower costs per Z–RAM, that they will recoup their foregone profits within five years, and they will continue to produce more and more Z–RAMs. After this meeting members agreed that each firm will set its prices independently.

Toshiba, NEC, Hitachi, Fujitsu, Mitsubishi and Oki sue for violations of the Sherman and Clayton Acts. State their claims with greater specificity. Do they have standing to sue? Analyze their claims.

* * *

Four years have passed. The Japanese chip producers have lost their case. The American firms have carried out their plans. The mergers have taken place; the low-price strategies are in process. While the Japanese have advanced their technology they have not yet been able to duplicate or approach the Z–RAM. The six Japanese producers obtained Z–RAM licenses, but only after one year of American Z–RAM production. Meanwhile, their American memory chip customers switched to Z–RAMs, for all but incidental purposes. The Japanese have been unable to make substantial inroads into the American Z–RAM market.

The Japanese buyers bought Z–RAMs from the Americans for the first year of Z–RAM production, but immediately thereafter they switched 100% of their Z–RAM business to Japanese producers. Thereupon, the members of ZRAMTA refused to sell IBM and other desired computers and AT & T and other desired telecommunications services to Japanese customers until such time as the Japanese should open their market to American Z–RAM sellers. The Japanese chip producers, computer buyers, and telecommunications service users sue. Also, the unintegrated American computer companies sue, alleging imminent monopolization of the chip market and thus higher prices for chips. Can plaintiffs successfully prosecute their cases? Analyze the claims.

* * *

You have been summoned to a meeting of the Attorney General of the United States, the Secretary of Commerce, the U.S. Trade Representative, and the Secretary of Defense. Rumour has it that the Japanese have just surpassed the Z–RAM technology. The subject is: The chip crisis and what to do about it.

Write a "transcript" of the meeting. After each official has spoken, you are asked your opinion of the best strategy for the United States. What is it?

CONCLUSION

We have come full circle. We began our odyssey through antitrust with a sense of the outrage of the American people, who distrusted bigness, cherished individualism, and wished to condemn monarchs of trade. Congress passed a law against the trusts. It established a system of public enforcement and private enforcement to protect consumers and to tear down barriers to market participation that fenced out the powerless. As early as the late nineteenth century, the Supreme Court interpreted the law to condemn cartel agreements outright. As the twentieth century began to unfold, the law continued its inhospitality to cartels, and it took a harsh stance also towards industrial empires that rose to power by bullying their small competitors. The law developed a moralistic approach, which the Court applied to Standard Oil's paradigmatic empire, making it possible, for a time, to entertain the distinction between good trusts and bad ones. In the early 1900s enthusiasm for antitrust declined, first during a period of great prosperity, and later, during the depression, when cooperation was seen as the key to recovery. But before mid-century, as political events unfolded, there was a reemergence of distrust of bigness. In the 1950s and 1960s, Congress and the courts responded to the societal desire to retain pluralism, and diversity, and to provide economic opportunity to the less-well-established.

In the last quarter century, the old moral and socio-political bases of the law have again been eroded. Law—antitrust, environmental, tort law—is seen as handicapping American business in its battles against foreign competitors who seek the patronage of American buyers. Americans' nostalgia for their lost hegemony has opened the door to the seemingly clean and simple paradigms of Chicago School economics, which offers laissez faire as the prescription for restored efficiency, and which is unsympathetic to positive law.

Economists like to say that antitrust law is simply a matter of economic learning; that as the science of economics develops, we will better understand antitrust; economics will lead the law. If history holds lessons, however, the path of the law will not be economics in the service of aggregate national efficiency. More likely, in the twenty-first century, the antitrust vehicle—having absorbed insights from Chicago and elsewhere—will take another turn. It will adapt to the currents of society and to the changing needs and expectations as the American people adapt to an increasingly interdependent world.

Appendix A

THE STATUTES

THE SHERMAN ACT

Section 1. Every contract, combination in the form of trust or otherwise, or conspiracy, in restraint of trade or commerce among the several States, or with foreign nations, is declared to be illegal. Every person who shall make any contract or engage in any combination or conspiracy hereby declared to be illegal shall be deemed guilty of a felony, and, on conviction thereof, shall be punished by fine not exceeding one million dollars if a corporation, or, if any other person, one hundred thousand dollars, or by imprisonment not exceeding three years, or by both said punishments, in the discretion of the court.*

Section 2. Every person who shall monopolize, or attempt to monopolize, or combine or conspire with any other person or persons, to monopolize any part of the trade or commerce among the several States, or with foreign nations, shall be deemed guilty of a felony, and, on conviction thereof, shall be punished by fine not exceeding one million dollars if a corporation, or, if any other person, one hundred thousand dollars, or by imprisonment not exceeding three years, or by both said punishments, in the discretion of the court.*

Section 3. Every contract, combination in form of trust or otherwise, or conspiracy, in restraint of trade or commerce in any Territory of the United States or of the District of Columbia, or in restraint of trade or commerce between any such Territory and another, or between any such Territory or Territories and any State or States or the District of Columbia, or with foreign nations, or between the District of Columbia and any State or States or foreign nations, is declared illegal. Every person who shall make any such contract or engage in any such combination or conspiracy, shall be deemed guilty of a felony, and, on conviction thereof, shall be punished by fine not exceeding one million dollars if a corporation, or, if any other person, one hundred thousand dollars, or by imprisonment not exceeding three years, or by both said punishments, in the discretion of the court.

* The Sentencing Reform Act of 1984, 18 U.S.C. § 3571, increases the maximum fine for individuals to $250,000 and allows for an alternative fine (which may be imposed on individuals or entities) of not more than the greater of twice the gain made or loss caused by the violation.

Section 4. The several district courts of the United States are invested with jurisdiction to prevent and restrain violations of [this Act]; and it shall be the duty of the several United States attorneys, in their respective districts, under the direction of the Attorney General, to institute proceedings in equity to prevent and restrain such violations. Such proceedings may be by way of petition setting forth the case and praying that such violation shall be enjoined or otherwise prohibited. When the parties complained of shall have been duly notified of such petition the court shall proceed, as soon as may be, to the hearing and determination of the case; and pending such petition and before final decree, the court may at any time make such temporary restraining order or prohibition as shall be deemed just in the premises.

* * *

Section 6. Any property owned under any contract or by any combination, or pursuant to any conspiracy (and being the subject thereof) mentioned in section [one of this Act], and being in the course of transportation from one State to another, or to a foreign country, shall be forfeited to the United States, and may be seized and condemned by like proceedings as those provided by law for the forfeiture, seizure, and condemnation of property imported into the United States contrary to law.

Section 7. [This Act] shall not apply to conduct involving trade or commerce (other than import trade or import commerce) with foreign nations unless—

(1) such conduct has a direct, substantial, and reasonably foreseeable effect—

(A) on trade or commerce which is not trade or commerce with foreign nations, or on import trade or import commerce with foreign nations; or

(B) on export trade or export commerce with foreign nations, of a person engaged in such trade or commerce in the United States; and

(2) such effect gives rise to a claim under the provisions of [this Act], other than this section.

If sections 1 to 7 of this title apply to such conduct only because of the operation of paragraph (1)(B), then sections 1 to 7 of this title shall apply to such conduct only for injury to export business in the United States.

THE CLAYTON ACT

Section 1. (a) "Antitrust laws," as used herein, includes the Act entitled "An Act to protect trade and commerce against unlawful restraints and monopolies," approved July second, eighteen hundred and ninety; sections [of Wilson Tariff Act amendments, prohibiting combinations in import trade]; and also this Act.

"Commerce," as used herein, means trade or commerce among the several States and with foreign nations, or between the District of Columbia or any Territory of the United States and any State, Territory, or foreign nation, or between any insular possessions or other places under the jurisdiction of the United States, or between any such possession or place and any State or Territory of the United States or the District of Columbia or any foreign nation, or within the District of Columbia or any Territory or any insular possession or other place under the jurisdiction of the United States: *Provided,* That nothing in this Act contained shall apply to the Philippine Islands.

The word "person" or "persons" wherever used in this Act shall be deemed to include corporations and associations existing under or authorized by the laws of either the United States, the laws of any of the Territories, the laws of any State, or the laws of any foreign country.

(b) This Act may be cited as the "Clayton Act".

Section 2. [See Robinson–Patman Act, Section 1, infra.]

Section 3. It shall be unlawful for any person engaged in commerce, in the course of such commerce, to lease or make a sale or contract for sale of goods, wares, merchandise, machinery, supplies, or other commodities, whether patented or unpatented, for use, consumption, or resale within the United States or any Territory thereof or the District of Columbia or any insular possession or other place under the jurisdiction of the United States, or fix a price charged therefor, or discount from, or rebate upon, such price, on the condition, agreement, or understanding that the lessee or purchaser thereof shall not use or deal in the goods, wares, merchandise, machinery, supplies, or other commodities of a competitor or competitors of the lessor or seller, where the effect of such lease, sale, or contract for sale or such condition, agreement, or understanding may be to substantially lessen competition or tend to create a monopoly in any line of commerce.

Section 4. (a) Except as provided in subsection (b) of this section, any person who shall be injured in his business or property by reason of anything forbidden in the antitrust laws may sue therefor in any district court of the United States in the district in which the defendant resides or is found or has an agent, without respect to the amount in controversy, and shall recover threefold the damages by him sustained, and the cost of suit, including a reasonable attorney's fee. . . .

(b)(1) Except as provided in paragraph (2), any person who is a foreign state may not recover under subsection (a) of this section an amount in excess of the actual damages sustained by it and the cost of suit, including a reasonable attorney's fee.

(2) Paragraph (1) shall not apply to a foreign state if—

(A) such foreign state would be denied, under section 1605(a)(2) of Title 28, immunity in a case in which the action is based upon a commercial activity, or an act, that is the subject matter of its claim under this section;

(B) such foreign state waives all defenses based upon or arising out of its status as a foreign state, to any claims brought against it in the same action;

(C) such foreign state engages primarily in commercial activities; and

(D) such foreign state does not function, with respect to the commercial activity, or the act, that is the subject matter of its claim under this section as a procurement entity for itself or for another foreign state.

(c) For purposes of this section—

(1) the term "commercial activity" shall have the meaning given it in section 1603(d) of Title 28, and

(2) the term "foreign state" shall have the meaning given it in section 1603(a) of Title 28.

Section 4A. Whenever the United States is hereafter injured in its business or property by reason of anything forbidden in the antitrust laws it may sue therefor in the United States district court for the district in which the defendant resides or is found or has an agent, without respect to the amount in controversy, and shall recover actual damages by it sustained and the cost of suit. . . .

Section 4B. Any action to enforce any cause of action under section [4, 4A or 4C of this Act] shall be forever barred unless commenced within four years after the cause of action accrued. No cause of action barred under existing law on the effective date of this Act shall be revived by this Act.

Section 4C. (a)(1) Any attorney general of a State may bring a civil action in the name of such State, as parens patriae on behalf of natural persons residing in such State, in any district court of the United States having jurisdiction of the defendant, to secure monetary relief as provided in this section for injury sustained by such natural persons to their property by reason of any violation of the Sherman Act. The court shall exclude from the amount of monetary relief awarded in such action any amount of monetary relief (A) which duplicates amounts which have been awarded for the same injury, or (B) which is properly allocable to (i) natural persons who have excluded their claims pursuant to subsection (b)(2) of this section, and (ii) any business entity.

(2) The court shall award the State as monetary relief threefold the total damage sustained as described in paragraph (1) of this subsection, and the cost of suit, including a reasonable attorney's fee. . . .

* * *

Section 6. The labor of a human being is not a commodity or article of commerce. Nothing contained in the antitrust laws shall be construed to forbid the existence and operation of labor, agricultural, or horticultural organizations, instituted for the purposes of mutual help, and not having capital stock or conducted for profit, or to forbid or restrain individual members of such organizations from lawfully carrying out the legitimate objects thereof; nor shall such organizations, or the members thereof, be held or construed to be illegal combinations or conspiracies in restraint of trade, under the antitrust laws.

Section 7. No person engaged in commerce or in any activity affecting commerce shall acquire, directly or indirectly, the whole or any part of the stock or other share capital and no person subject to the jurisdiction of the Federal Trade Commission shall acquire the whole or any part of the assets of another person engaged also in commerce or in any activity affecting commerce, where in any line of commerce or in any activity affecting commerce in any section of the country, the effect of such acquisition may be substantially to lessen competition, or to tend to create a monopoly.

No person shall acquire, directly or indirectly, the whole or any part of the stock or other share capital and no person subject to the jurisdiction of the Federal Trade Commission shall acquire the whole or any part of the assets of one or more persons engaged in commerce or in any activity affecting commerce, where in any line of commerce or in any activity affecting commerce in any section of the country, the effect of such acquisition, of such stocks or assets, or of the use of such stock by the voting or granting of proxies or otherwise, may be substantially to lessen competition, or to tend to create a monopoly.

This section shall not apply to persons purchasing such stock solely for investment and not using the same by voting or otherwise to bring about, or in attempting to bring about, the substantial lessening of competition. Nor shall anything contained in this section prevent a corporation engaged in commerce or in any activity affecting commerce from causing the formation of subsidiary corporations for the actual carrying on of their immediate lawful business, or the natural and legitimate branches or extensions thereof, or from owning and holding all or a part of the stock of such subsidiary corporations, when the effect of such formation is not to substantially lessen competition.

Nor shall anything herein contained be construed to prohibit any common carrier subject to the laws to regulate commerce from aiding in the construction of branches or short lines so located as to become feeders to the main line of the company so aiding in such construction or from acquiring or owning all or any part of the stock of such branch lines, nor to prevent any such common carrier from acquiring and owning all or any part of the stock of a branch or short line constructed by an independent company where there is no substantial competition between the company owning the branch line so constructed and the company owning the main line acquiring the property or an interest therein, nor to prevent such common carrier from extending any of its lines through the medium of the acquisition of stock or otherwise of any other common carrier where there is no substantial competition between the company extending its lines and the company whose stock, property, or an interest therein is so acquired.

Nothing contained in this section shall be held to affect or impair any right heretofore legally acquired: *Provided,* That nothing in this section shall be held or construed to authorize or make lawful anything heretofore prohibited or made illegal by the antitrust laws, nor to exempt any person from the penal provisions thereof or the civil remedies therein provided.

Nothing contained in this section shall apply to transactions duly consummated pursuant to authority given by the Civil Aeronautics Board, Federal Communications Commission, Federal Power Commission, Interstate Commerce Commission, the Securities and Exchange Commission in the exercise of its jurisdiction under section 79j of this title, the United States Maritime Commission, or the Secretary of Agriculture under any statutory provision vesting such power in such Commission, Secretary, or Board.

* * *

Section 7A. (a) Except as exempted pursuant to subsection (c) of this section, no person shall acquire, directly or indirectly, any voting securities or assets of any other person, unless both persons (or in the case of a tender offer, the acquiring person) file notification pursuant to rules under subsection (d)(1) of this section and the waiting period described in subsection (b)(1) of this section has expired, if—

(1) the acquiring person, or the person whose voting securities or assets are being acquired, is engaged in commerce or in any activity affecting commerce;

(2)(A) any voting securities or assets of a person engaged in manufacturing which has annual net sales or total assets of $10,000,000 or more are being acquired by any person which has total assets or annual net sales of $100,000,000 or more;

(B) any voting securities or assets of a person not engaged in manufacturing which has total assets of $10,000,000 or more are being acquired by any person which has total assets or annual net sales of $100,000,000 or more; or

(C) any voting securities or assets of a person with annual net sales or total assets of $100,000,000 or more are being acquired by any person with total assets or annual net sales of $10,000,000 or more; and

(3) as a result of such acquisition, the acquiring person would hold—

(A) 15 per centum or more of the voting securities or assets of the acquired person, or

(B) an aggregate total amount of the voting securities and assets of the acquired person in excess of $15,000,000.

In the case of a tender offer, the person whose voting securities are sought to be acquired by a person required to file notification under this subsection shall file notification pursuant to rules under subsection (d) of this section.

(b)(1) The waiting period required under subsection (a) of this section shall—

(A) begin on the date of the receipt by the Federal Trade Commission and the Assistant Attorney General in charge of the Antitrust Division of the Department of Justice (hereinafter referred to in this section as the "Assistant Attorney General") of—

(i) the completed notification required under subsection (a) of this section, or

(ii) if such notification is not completed, the notification to the extent completed and a statement of the reasons for such noncompliance, from both persons, or, in the case of a tender offer, the acquiring person; and

   (B) end on the thirtieth day after the date of such receipt (or in the case of a cash tender offer, the fifteenth day), or on such later date as may be set under subsection (e)(2) or (g)(2) of this section.

(2) The Federal Trade Commission and the Assistant Attorney General may, in individual cases, terminate the waiting period specified in paragraph (1) and allow any person to proceed with any acquisition subject to this section, and promptly shall

   (A) define the terms used in this section;

   (B) exempt, from the requirements of this section, classes of persons, acquisitions, transfers, or transactions which are not likely to violate the antitrust laws; and

   (C) prescribe such other rules as may be necessary and appropriate to carry out the purposes of this section.

                              *   *   *

   (e)(1) The Federal Trade Commission or the Assistant Attorney General may, prior to the expiration of the 30–day waiting period (or in the case of a cash tender offer, the 15–day waiting period) specified in subsection (b)(1) of this section, require the submission of additional information or documentary material relevant to the proposed acquisition, from a person required to file notification with respect to such acquisition under subsection (a) of this section prior to the expiration of the waiting period specified in subsection (b)(1) of this section, or from any officer, director, partner, agent, or employee of such person.

   (2) The Federal Trade Commission or the Assistant Attorney General, in its or his discretion, may extend the 30–day waiting period (or in the case of a cash tender offer, the 15–day waiting period) specified in subsection (b)(1) of this section for an additional period of not more than 20 days (or in the case of a cash tender offer, 10 days) after the date on which the Federal Trade Commission or the Assistant Attorney General, as the case may be, receives from any person to whom a request is made under paragraph (1), or in the case of tender offers, the acquiring person, (A) all the information and documentary material required to be submitted pursuant to such a request, or (B) if such request is not fully complied with, the information and documentary material submitted and a statement of the reasons for such noncompliance. Such additional period may be further extended only by the United States district court, upon an application by the Federal Trade Commission or the Assistant Attorney General pursuant to subsection (g)(2) of this section.

   (f) If a proceeding is instituted or an action is filed by the Federal Trade Commission, alleging that a proposed acquisition violates section [7 of this Act or section 5 of the Federal Trade Commission Act], or an action is filed by the United States, alleging that a proposed acquisition violates such section [7 or section 1 or 2 of the Sherman Act], and the Federal Trade Commission or the Assistant Attorney General (1) files a motion for a preliminary injunction against consummation of such acquisition pendente lite, and (2) certifies the United States district court for the judicial district within which the respondent resides or carries on business, or in which the action is brought, that it or he believes that the public interest requires relief pendente lite pursuant to this subsection, then upon the filing of such motion and certification, the chief judge of such district court shall immediately notify the chief judge of the United States court of appeals for the circuit in which such district court is located, who shall designate a United States district judge to whom such action shall be assigned for all purposes.

(g)(1) Any person, or any officer, director, or partner thereof, who fails to comply with any provision of this section shall be liable to the United States for a civil penalty of not more than $10,000 for each day during which such person is in violation of this section. Such penalty may be recovered in a civil action brought by the United States.

(2) If any person, or any officer, director, partner, agent, or employee thereof, fails substantially to comply with the notification requirement under subsection (a) of this section or any request for the submission of additional information or documentary material under subsection (e)(1) of this section within the waiting period specified in subsection (b)(1) of this section and as may be extended under subsection (e)(2) of this section, the United States district court—

(A) may order compliance;

(B) shall extend the waiting period specified in subsection (b)(1) of this section and as may have been extended under subsection (e)(2) of this section until there has been substantial compliance, except that, in the case of a tender offer, the court may not extend such waiting period on the basis of a failure, by the person whose stock is sought to be acquired, to comply substantially with such notification requirement or any such request; and

(C) may grant such other equitable relief as the court in its discretion determines necessary or appropriate,

upon application of the Federal Trade Commission or the Assistant Attorney General.

* * *

Section 8. No private banker or director, officer, or employee of any member bank of the Federal Reserve System or any branch thereof shall be at the same time a director, officer, or employee of any other bank, banking association, savings bank, or trust company organized under the National Bank Act or organized under the laws of any State or of the District of Columbia, or any branch thereof, except that the Board of Governors of the Federal Reserve System may by regulation permit such service as a director, officer, or employee of not more than one other such institution or branch thereof; but the foregoing prohibition shall not apply in the case of any one or more of the following or any branch thereof:

(1) A bank, banking association, savings bank, or trust company, more than 90 per centum of the stock of which is owned directly or indirectly by the United States or by any corporation of which the

United States directly or indirectly owns more than 90 per centum of the stock.

(2) A bank, banking association, savings bank, or trust company which has been placed formally in liquidation or which is in the hands of a receiver, conservator, or other official exercising similar functions.

(3) A corporation, principally engaged in international or foreign banking or banking in a dependency or insular possession of the United States which has entered into an agreement with the Board of Governors of the Federal Reserve System pursuant to section [25 of the Federal Reserve Act].

(4) A bank, banking association, savings bank, or trust company, more than 50 per centum of the common stock of which is owned directly or indirectly by persons who own directly or indirectly more than 50 per centum of the common stock of such member bank.

(5) A bank, banking association, savings bank, or trust company not located and having no branch in the same city, town, or village as that in which such member bank or any branch thereof is located, or in any city, town, or village contiguous or adjacent thereto.

(6) A bank, banking association, savings bank, or trust company not engaged in a class or classes of business in which such member bank is engaged.

(7) A mutual savings bank having no capital stock.

*   *   *

Section 12. Any suit, action, or proceeding under the antitrust laws against a corporation may be brought not only in the judicial district whereof it is an inhabitant, but also in any district wherein it may be found or transacts business; and all process in such cases may be served in the district of which it is an inhabitant, or wherever it may be found.

*   *   *

Section 14. Whenever a corporation shall violate any of the penal provisions of the antitrust laws, such violation shall be deemed to be also that of the individual directors, officers, or agents of such corporation who shall have authorized, ordered, or done any of the acts constituting in whole or in part such violation, and such violation shall be deemed a misdemeanor, and upon conviction therefor of any such director, officer, or agent he shall be punished by a fine of not exceeding $5,000 or by imprisonment for not exceeding one year, or by both, in the discretion of the court.

Section 15. The several district courts of the United States are invested with jurisdiction to prevent and restrain violations of this Act, and it shall be the duty of the several United States attorneys, in their respective districts, under the direction of the Attorney General, to institute proceedings in equity to prevent and restrain such violations. . . .

Section 16. Any person, firm, corporation, or association shall be entitled to sue for and have injunctive relief, in any court of the United States having jurisdiction over the parties, against threatened loss or damage by a violation of the antitrust laws, including sections [two, three, seven and eight of this Act], when and under the same conditions and principles as injunctive relief against threatened conduct that will cause loss or damage is granted by courts of equity, under the rules governing such proceedings, and upon the execution of proper bond against damages for an injunction improvidently granted and a showing that the danger of irreparable loss or damage is immediate, a preliminary injunction may issue: *Provided,* That nothing herein contained shall be construed to entitle any person, firm, corporation, or association, except the United States, to bring suit in equity for injunctive relief against any common carrier subject to the provisions of [the Act to regulate commerce, approved February fourth, eighteen hundred and eighty-seven], in respect of any matter subject to the regulation, supervision, or other jurisdiction of the Interstate Commerce Commission. In any action under this section in which the plaintiff substantially prevails, the court shall award the cost of suit, including a reasonable attorney's fee, to such plaintiff.

* * *

THE FEDERAL TRADE COMMISSION ACT

* * *

Section 5. (a)(1) Unfair methods of competition in or affecting commerce, and unfair or deceptive acts or practices in or affecting commerce, are declared unlawful.

(2) The Commission is empowered and directed to prevent persons, partnerships, or corporations, except banks, savings and loan institutions described in section [18(f)(3) of this Act], common carriers subject to the Acts to regulate commerce, air carriers and foreign air carriers subject to the Federal Aviation Act of 1958, and persons, partnerships, or corporations insofar as they are subject to the Packers and Stockyards Act, 1921, as amended, except as provided in section 406(b) of said Act, from using unfair methods of competition in or affecting commerce and unfair or deceptive acts or practices in or affecting commerce.

(3) This subsection shall not apply to unfair methods of competition involving commerce with foreign nations (other than import commerce) unless—

(A) such methods of competition have a direct, substantial, and reasonably foreseeable effect—

(i) on commerce which is not commerce with foreign nations, or on import commerce with foreign nations; or

(ii) on export commerce with foreign nations, of a person engaged in such commerce in the United States; and

(B) such effect gives rise to a claim under the provisions of this subsection, other than this paragraph.

If this subsection applies to such methods of competition only because of the operation of subparagraph (A)(ii), this subsection shall apply to such conduct only for injury to export business in the United States.

* * *

Section 6.   The Commission shall also have power—

(a) To gather and compile information concerning, and to investigate from time to time the organization, business, conduct, practices, and management of any person, partnership, or corporation engaged in or whose business affects commerce, excepting banks, savings and loan institutions described in section [18(f)(3) of this Act], and common carriers subject to the Act to regulate commerce, and its relation to other persons, partnerships, and corporations.

(b) To require, by general or special orders, persons, partnerships, and corporations, engaged in or whose business affects commerce, excepting banks, savings and loan institutions described in section [18(f)(3) of this Act], and common carriers subject to the Act to regulate commerce, or any class of them, or any of them, respectively, to file with the Commission in such form as the Commission may prescribe annual or special, or both annual and special, reports or answers in writing to specific questions, furnishing to the Commission such information as it may require as to the organization, business, conduct, practices, management, and relation to other corporations, partnerships, and individuals of the respective persons, partnerships, and corporations filing such reports or answers in writing.   Such reports and answers shall be made under oath, or otherwise, as the Commission may prescribe, and shall be filed with the Commission within such reasonable period as the Commission may prescribe, unless additional time be granted in any case by the Commission.

(c) Whenever a final decree has been entered against any defendant corporation in any suit brought by the United States to prevent and restrain any violation of the antitrust Acts, to make investigation, upon its own initiative, of the manner in which the decree has been or is being carried out, and upon the application of the Attorney General it shall be its duty to make such investigation.   It shall transmit to the Attorney General a report embodying its findings and recommendations as a result of any such investigation, and the report shall be made public in the discretion of the Commission.

(d) Upon the direction of the President or either House of Congress to investigate and report the facts relating to any alleged violations of the antitrust Acts by any corporation.

(e) Upon the application of the Attorney General to investigate and make recommendations for the readjustment of the business of any corporation alleged to be violating the antitrust Acts in order that the corporation may thereafter maintain its organization, management, and conduct of business in accordance with law.

(f) To make public from time to time such portions of the information obtained by it hereunder as are in the public interest; and to make annual and special reports to the Congress and to submit therewith recommendations for additional legislation; and to provide for the publication of its reports and decisions in such form and manner as may be best adapted for public information and use: *Provided,* That the Commission shall not have any authority to make public any trade secret or any commercial or financial information which is obtained from any person and which is privileged or confidential, except that the Commission may disclose such information to officers and employees of appropriate Federal law enforcement agencies or to any officer or employee of any State law enforcement agency upon the prior certification of an officer of any such Federal or State law enforcement agency that such information will be maintained in confidence and will be used only for official law enforcement purposes.

(g) From time to time to classify corporations and (except as provided in section [18(a)(2) of this Act] to make rules and regulations for the purpose of carrying out the provisions of [this Act].

* * *

THE ROBINSON-PATMAN ACT

Section 2. (a) It shall be unlawful for any person engaged in commerce, in the course of such commerce, either directly or indirectly, to discriminate in price between different purchasers of commodities of like grade and quality, where either or any of the purchases involved in such discrimination are in commerce, where such commodities are sold for use, consumption, or resale within the United States or any Territory thereof or the District of Columbia or any insular possession or other place under the jurisdiction of the United States, and where the effect of such discrimination may be substantially to lessen competition or tend to create a monopoly in any line of commerce, or to injure, destroy, or prevent competition with any person who either grants or knowingly receives the benefit of such discrimination, or with customers of either of them: *Provided,* That nothing herein contained shall prevent differentials which make only due allowance for differences in the cost of manufacture, sale, or delivery resulting from the differing methods or quantities in which such commodities are to such purchasers sold or delivered: *Provided, however,* That the Federal Trade Commission may, after due investigation and hearing to all interested parties, fix and establish quantity limits, and revise the same as it finds necessary, as to particular commodities or classes of commodities, where it finds that available purchasers in greater quantities are so few as to render differentials on account thereof unjustly discriminatory or promotive of monopoly in any line of commerce; and the foregoing shall then not be construed to permit differentials based on differences in quantities greater than those so fixed and established: *And provided further,* That nothing herein contained shall prevent persons engaged in selling goods, wares, or merchandise in commerce from selecting their own customers in bona fide transactions and not in restraint of trade: *And provided further,* That nothing herein contained shall prevent price changes from time to time where in response to changing conditions affecting the market for or the marketability of the goods concerned, such as but not limited to actual or imminent deterioration of perishable goods, obsolescence of seasonal goods, distress sales under court process, or sales in good faith in discontinuance of business in the goods concerned.

(b) Upon proof being made, at any hearing on a complaint under this section, that there has been discrimination in price or services or facilities furnished, the burden of rebutting the prima-facie case thus made by showing justification shall be upon the person charged with a violation of this section, and unless justification shall be affirmatively shown, the Commission is authorized to issue an order terminating the discrimination: *Provided, however,* That nothing herein contained shall prevent a seller rebutting the prima-facie case thus made by showing that his lower price or the furnishing of services or facilities to any purchaser or purchasers was made in good faith to meet an equally low price of a competitor, or the services or facilities furnished by a competitor.

(c) It shall be unlawful for any person engaged in commerce, in the course of such commerce, to pay or grant, or to receive or accept, anything of value as a commission, brokerage, or other compensation, or any allowance or discount in lieu thereof, except for services rendered in connection with the sale or purchase of goods, wares, or merchandise, either to the other party to such transaction or to an agent, representative, or other intermediary therein where such intermediary is acting in fact for or in behalf, or is subject to the direct or indirect control, of any party to such transaction other than the person by whom such compensation is so granted or paid.

(d) It shall be unlawful for any person engaged in commerce to pay or contract for the payment of anything of value to or for the benefit of a customer of such person in the course of such commerce as compensation or in consideration for any services or facilities furnished by or through such customer in connection with the processing, handling, sale, or offering for sale of any products or commodities manufactured, sold, or offered for sale by such person, unless such payment or consideration is available on proportionally equal terms to all other customers competing in the distribution of such products or commodities.

(e) It shall be unlawful for any person to discriminate in favor of one purchaser against another purchaser or purchasers of a commodity bought for resale, with or without processing, by contracting to furnish or furnishing, or by contributing to the furnishing of, any services or facilities connected with the processing, handling, sale, or offering for sale of such commodity so purchased upon terms not accorded to all purchasers on proportionally equal terms.

(f) It shall be unlawful for any person engaged in commerce, in the course of such commerce, knowingly to induce or receive a discrimination in price which is prohibited by this section.

Section 3.   It shall be unlawful for any person engaged in commerce, in the course of such commerce, to be a party to, or assist in, any transaction of sale, or contract to sell, which discriminates to his knowledge against competitors of the purchaser, in that, any discount, rebate, allowance, or advertising service charge is granted to the purchaser over and above any discount, rebate, allowance, or advertising service charge available at the time of such transaction to said competitors in respect of a sale of goods of like grade, quality, and quantity; to sell, or contract to sell, goods in any part of the United States at prices lower than those exacted by said person elsewhere in the United States for the purpose of destroying competition, or eliminating a competitor in such part of the United States; or, to sell, or contract to sell, goods at unreasonably low prices for the purpose of destroying competition or eliminating a competitor.

Any person violating any of the provisions of this section shall, upon conviction thereof, be fined not more than $5,000 or imprisoned not more than one year, or both.

Section 4. Nothing in [this Act], shall apply to purchases of their supplies for their own use by schools, colleges, universities, public libraries, churches, hospitals, and charitable institutions not operated for profit.

THE EXPORT TRADING COMPANY ACT OF 1982

Section 102. (a) The Congress finds that—

(1) United States exports are responsible for creating and maintaining one out of every nine manufacturing jobs in the United States and for generating one out of every seven dollars of total United States goods produced;

(2) the rapidly growing service-related industries are vital to the well-being of the United States economy inasmuch as they create jobs for seven out of every ten Americans, provide 65 per centum of the Nation's gross national product, and offer the greatest potential for significantly increased industrial trade involving finished products;

(3) trade deficits contribute to the decline of the dollar on international currency markets and have an inflationary impact on the United States economy;

(4) tens of thousands of small- and medium-sized United States businesses produce exportable goods or services but do not engage in exporting;

(5) although the United States is the world's leading agricultural exporting nation, many farm products are not marketed as widely and effectively abroad as they could be through export trading companies;

(6) export trade services in the United States are fragmented into a multitude of separate functions, and companies attempting to offer export trade services lack financial leverage to reach a significant number of potential United States exporters;

(7) the United States needs well-developed export trade intermediaries which can achieve economies of scale and acquire expertise enabling them to export goods and services profitably, at low per unit cost to producers;

(8) the development of export trading companies in the United States has been hampered by business attitudes and by Government regulations;

(9) those activities of State and local governmental authorities which initiate, facilitate, or expand exports of goods and services can be an important source for expansion of total United States exports,

as well as for experimentation in the development of innovative export programs keyed to local, State, and regional economic needs;

(10) if United States trading companies are to be successful in promoting United States exports and in competing with foreign trading companies, they should be able to draw on the resources, expertise, and knowledge of the United States banking system, both in the United States and abroad; and

(11) the Department of Commerce is responsible for the development and promotion of United States exports, and especially for facilitating the export of finished products by United States manufacturers.

(b) It is the purpose of this chapter to increase United States exports of products and services by encouraging more efficient provision of export trade services to United States producers and suppliers, in particular by establishing an office within the Department of Commerce to promote the formation of export trade associations and export trading companies, by permitting bank holding companies, bankers' banks, and Edge Act corporations and agreement corporations that are subsidiaries of bank holding companies to invest in export trading companies, by reducing restrictions on trade financing provided by financial institutions, and by modifying the application of the antitrust laws to certain export trade.

Section 103.   (a) For purposes of this subchapter—

(1) the term "export trade" means trade or commerce in goods or services produced in the United States which are exported, or in the course of being exported, from the United States to any other country;

(2) the term "services" includes, but is not limited to, accounting, amusement, architectural, automatic data processing, business, communications, construction franchising and licensing, consulting, engineering, financial, insurance, legal, management, repair, tourism, training, and transportation services;

(3) the term "export trade services" includes, but is not limited to, consulting, international market research, advertising, marketing, insurance, product research and design, legal assistance, transportation, including trade documentation and freight forwarding, communication and processing of foreign orders to and for exporters and foreign purchasers, warehousing, foreign exchange, financing, and taking title to goods, when provided in order to facilitate the export of goods or services produced in the United States;

(4) the term "export trading company" means a person, partnership, association, or similar organization, whether operated for profit or as a nonprofit organization, which does business under the laws of the United States or any State and which is organized and operated principally for purposes of—

(A) exporting goods or services produced in the United States; or

(B) facilitating the exportation of goods or services produced in the United States by unaffiliated persons by providing one or more export trade services;

(5) the term "State" means any of the several States of the United States, the District of Columbia, the Commonwealth of Puerto Rico, the Virgin Islands, American Samoa, Guam, the Commonwealth of the Northern Mariana Islands, and the Trust Territory of the Pacific Islands;

(6) the term "United States" means the several States of the United States, the District of Columbia, the Commonwealth of Puerto Rico, the Virgin Islands, American Samoa, Guam, the Commonwealth of the Northern Mariana Islands, and the Trust Territory of the Pacific Islands; and

(7) the term "antitrust laws" means the antitrust laws as defined in section [(a) of the first section of the Clayton Act, section 5 of the Federal Trade Commission Act to the extent that section 5] applies to unfair methods of competition, and any State antitrust or unfair competition law.

(b) The Secretary of Commerce may by regulation further define any term defined in subsection (a) of this section, in order to carry out this subchapter.

Section 104. The Secretary of Commerce shall establish within the Department of Commerce an office to promote and encourage to the greatest extent feasible the formation of export trade associations and export trading companies. Such office shall provide information and advice to interested persons and shall provide a referral service to facilitate contact between producers of exportable goods and services and firms offering export trade services.

* * *

Section 301. To promote and encourage export trade, the Secretary may issue certificates of review and advise and assist any person with respect to applying for certificates of review.

Section 302. (a) To apply for a certificate of review, a person shall submit to the Secretary a written application which—

(1) specifies conduct limited to export trade, and

(2) is in a form and contains any information, including information pertaining to the overall market in which the applicant operates, required by rule or regulation promulgated under section [310 of this Act].

* * *

Section 303. (a) A certificate of review shall be issued to any applicant that establishes that its specified export trade, export trade activities, and methods of operation will—

(1) result in neither a substantial lessening of competition or restraint of trade within the United States nor a substantial restraint of the export trade of any competitor of the applicant,

(2) not unreasonably enhance, stabilize, or depress prices within the United States of the goods, wares, merchandise, or services of the class exported by the applicant,

(3) not constitute unfair methods of competition against competitors engaged in the export of goods, wares, merchandise, or services of the class exported by the applicant; and

(4) not include any act that may reasonably be expected to result in the sale for consumption or resale within the United States of the goods, wares, merchandise, or services exported by the applicant.

(b) Within ninety days after the Secretary receives an application for a certificate of review, the Secretary shall determine whether the applicant's export trade, export trade activities, and methods of operation meet the standards of subsection (a) of this section. If the Secretary, with the concurrence of the Attorney General, determines that such standards are met, the Secretary shall issue to the applicant a certificate of review. The certificate of review shall specify—

(1) the export trade, export trade activities, and methods of operation to which the certificate applies,

(2) the person to whom the certificate of review is issued, and

(3) any terms and conditions the Secretary or the Attorney General deems necessary to assure compliance with the standards of subsection (a) of this section.

* * *

Section 306. (a) Except as provided in subsection (b) of this section, no criminal or civil action may be brought under the antitrust laws against a person to whom a certificate of review is issued which is based on conduct which is specified in, and complies with the terms of, a certificate issued under section 4013 of this title which certificate was in effect when the conduct occurred.

(b)(1) Any person who has been injured as a result of conduct engaged in under a certificate of review may bring a civil action for injunctive relief, actual damages, the loss of interest on actual damages, and the cost of suit (including a reasonable attorney's fee) for the failure to comply with the standards of section [303(a) of this Act]. Any action commenced under this subchapter shall proceed as if it were an action commenced under section 4 or section 16 of the Clayton Act, except that the standards of section [303(a) of this Act] and the remedies provided in this paragraph shall be the exclusive standards and remedies applicable to such action.

(2) Any action brought under paragraph (1) shall be filed within two years of the date the plaintiff has notice of the failure to comply with the standards of section 4013(a) of this title but in any event within four years after the cause of action accrues.

(3) In any action brought under paragraph (1), there shall be a presumption that conduct which is specified in and complies with a certificate of review does comply with the standards of section [303(a) of this Act].

(4) In any action brought under paragraph (1), if the court finds that the conduct does comply with the standards of section [303(a) of this Act], the court shall award to the person against whom the claim is brought the cost of suit attributable to defending against the claim (including a reasonable attorney's fee).

(5) The Attorney General may file suit pursuant to section 15 of the Clayton Act (15 U.S.C. 25) to enjoin conduct threatening clear and irreparable harm to the national interest.

* * *

Section 310. The Secretary, with the concurrence of the Attorney General, shall promulgate such rules and regulations as are necessary to carry out the purposes of this chapter.

THE NATIONAL COOPERATIVE RESEARCH ACT OF 1984

Section 2. (a) For purposes of this chapter:

(1) The term "antitrust laws" has the meaning given it in subsection (a) of [the first section of the Clayton Act], except that such term includes section [5 of the Federal Trade Commission Act] to the extent that such section 5 applies to unfair methods of competition.

(2) The term "Attorney General" means the Attorney General of the United States.

(3) The term "Commission" means the Federal Trade Commission.

(4) The term "person" has the meaning given it in subsection (a) of section 12 of this title.

(5) The term "State" has the meaning given it in section 15g(2) of this title.

(6) The term "joint research and development venture" means any group of activities, including attempting to make, making, or performing a contract, by two or more persons for the purpose of—

(A) theoretical analysis, experimentation, or systematic study of phenomena or observable facts,

(B) the development or testing of basic engineering techniques,

(C) the extension of investigative findings or theory of a scientific or technical nature into practical application for experimental and demonstration purposes, including the experimental production and testing of models, prototypes, equipment, materials, and processes,

(D) the collection, exchange, and analysis of research information, or

(E) any combination of the purposes specified in subparagraphs (A), (B), (C), and (D),

and may include the establishment and operation of facilities for the conducting of research, the conducting of such venture on a protected and proprietary basis, and the prosecuting of applications for patents and the granting of licenses for the results of such venture, but does not include any activity specified in subsection (b) of this section.

(b) The term "joint research and development venture" excludes the following activities involving two or more persons:

(1) exchanging information among competitors relating to costs, sales, profitability, prices, marketing, or distribution of any product, process, or service that is not reasonably required to conduct the research and development that is the purpose of such venture,

(2) entering into any agreement or engaging in any other conduct restricting, requiring, or otherwise involving the production or marketing by any person who is a party to such venture of any product, process, or service, other than the production or marketing of proprietary information developed through such venture, such as patents and trade secrets, and

(3) entering into any agreement or engaging in any other conduct—

(A) to restrict or require the sale, licensing, or sharing of inventions or developments not developed through such venture, or

(B) to restrict or require participation by such party in other research and development activities,

that is not reasonably required to prevent misappropriation of proprietary information contributed by any person who is a party to such venture or of the results of such venture.

Section 3.   In any action under the antitrust laws, or under any State law similar to the antitrust laws, the conduct of any person in making or performing a contract to carry out a joint research and development venture shall not be deemed illegal per se; such conduct shall be judged on the basis of its reasonableness, taking into account all relevant factors affecting competition, including, but not limited to, effects on competition in properly defined, relevant research and development markets.

Section 4.   (a) Notwithstanding section [4 of the Clayton Act] and in lieu of the relief specified in such section, any person who is entitled to recovery on a claim under such section shall recover the actual damages sustained by such person, interest calculated at the rate specified in section 1961 of Title 28 on such actual damages as specified in subsection (d) of this section, and the cost of suit attributable to such claim, including a reasonable attorney's fee pursuant to section [5 of this Act] if such claim—

(1) results from conduct that is within the scope of a notification that has been filed under section [6(a) of this Act] for a joint research and development venture, and

(2) is filed after such notification becomes effective pursuant to section [6(c) of this Act].

(b) Notwithstanding section [4c of the Clayton Act], and in lieu of the relief specified in such section, any State that is entitled to monetary relief on a claim under such section shall recover the total damage sustained as described in subsection (a)(1) of such section, interest calculated at the rate specified in section 1961 of Title 28 on such total damage as specified in subsection (d) of this section, and the cost of suit attributable to such claim, including a reasonable attorney's fee pursuant to section 15c of this title if such claim—

(1) results from conduct that is within the scope of a notification that has been filed under section [6(a) of this Act] for a joint research and development venture, and

(2) is filed after such notification becomes effective pursuant to section [6(c) of this Act].

(c) Notwithstanding any provision of any State law providing damages for conduct similar to that forbidden by the antitrust laws, any person who is entitled to recovery on a claim under such provision shall not recover in excess of the actual damages sustained by such person, interest calculated at the rate specified in section 1961 of Title 28 on such actual damages as specified in subsection (d) of this section, and the cost of suit attributable to such claim, including a reasonable attorney's fee pursuant to section [5 of this Act] if such claim—

(1) results from conduct that is within the scope of a notification that has been filed under section [6(a) of this Act] for a joint research and development venture, and

(2) is filed after notification has become effective pursuant to section [6(c) of this Act].

(d) Interest shall be awarded on the damages involved for the period beginning on the earliest date for which injury can be established and ending on the date of judgment, unless the court finds that the award of all or part of such interest is unjust in the circumstances.

(e) This section shall be applicable only if the challenged conduct of a person defending against a claim is not in violation of any decree or order, entered or issued after October 11, 1984, in any case or proceeding under the antitrust laws or any State law similar to the antitrust laws challenging such conduct as part of a joint research and development venture.

Section 5. (a) Notwithstanding sections [4 and 16 of the Clayton Act], in any claim under the antitrust laws, or any State law similar to the antitrust laws, based on the conducting of a joint research and development venture, the court shall, at the conclusion of the action—

(1) award to a substantially prevailing claimant the cost of suit attributable to such claim, including a reasonable attorney's fee, or

(2) award to a substantially prevailing party defending against any such claim the cost of suit attributable to such claim, including a reasonable attorney's fee, if the claim, or the claimant's conduct during the litigation of the claim, was frivolous, unreasonable, without foundation, or in bad faith.

(b) The award made under subsection (a) of this section may be offset in whole or in part by an award in favor of any other party for any part of the cost of suit, including a reasonable attorney's fee, attributable to conduct during the litigation by any prevailing party that the court finds to be frivolous, unreasonable, without foundation, or in bad faith.

Section 6. (a) Any party to a joint research and development venture, acting on such venture's behalf, may, not later than 90 days after entering into a written agreement to form such venture or not later than 90 days after October 11, 1984, whichever is later, file simultaneously with the Attorney General and the Commission a written notification disclosing—

(1) the identities of the parties to such venture, and

(2) the nature and objectives of such venture.

Any party to such venture, acting on such venture's behalf, may file additional disclosure notifications pursuant to this section as are appropriate to extend the protections of section 4303 of this title. In order to maintain the protections of section 4303 of this title, such venture shall, not later than 90 days after a change in its membership, file simultaneously with the Attorney General and the Commission a written notification disclosing such change.

(b) Except as provided in subsection (e) of this section, not later than 30 days after receiving a notification filed under subsection (a) of this section, the Attorney General or the Commission shall publish in the Federal Register a notice with respect to such venture that identifies the parties to such venture and that describes in general terms the area of planned activity of such venture. Prior to its publication, the contents of such notice shall be made available to the parties to such venture.

(c) If with respect to a notification filed under subsection (a) of this section, notice is published in the Federal Register, then such notification shall operate to convey the protections of section 4303 of this title as of the earlier of—

(1) the date of publication of notice under subsection (b) of this section, or

(2) if such notice is not so published within the time required by subsection (b) of this section, after the expiration of the 30-day period beginning on the date the Attorney General or the Commission receives the applicable information described in subsection (a) of this section.

(d) Except with respect to the information published pursuant to subsection (b) of this section—

(1) all information and documentary material submitted as part of a notification filed pursuant to this section, and

(2) all other information obtained by the Attorney General or the Commission in the course of any investigation, administrative proceeding, or case, with respect to a potential violation of the antitrust laws by the joint research and development venture with respect to which such notification was filed.

shall be exempt from disclosure under section 552 of Title 5 and shall not be made publicly available by any agency of the United States to which such section applies except in a judicial or administrative proceeding in which such information and material is subject to any protective order.

(e) Any person who files a notification pursuant to this section may withdraw such notification before notice of the joint research and development venture involved is published under subsection (b) of this section. Any notification so withdrawn shall not be subject to subsection (b) of this section and shall not confer the protections of section [4 of this Act] on any person with respect to whom such notification was filed.

(f) Any action taken or not taken by the Attorney General or the Commission with respect to notifications filed pursuant to this section shall not be subject to judicial review.

(g)(1) Except as provided in paragraph (2), for the sole purpose of establishing that a person is entitled to the protections of section [4 of this Act], the fact of disclosure of conduct under subsection (a) of this section and the fact of publication of a notice under subsection (b) of this section shall be admissible into evidence in any judicial or administrative proceeding.

(2) No action by the Attorney General or the Commission taken pursuant to this section shall be admissible into evidence in any such proceeding for the purpose of supporting or answering any claim under the antitrust laws or under any State law similar to the antitrust laws.

Appendix B

MERGER GUIDELINES, UNITED STATES DEPARTMENT OF JUSTICE 1984

Table of Contents

1. PURPOSE AND UNDERLYING POLICY ASSUMPTIONS

These Guidelines state in outline form the present enforcement policy of the U.S. Department of Justice ("Department") concerning acquisitions and mergers ("mergers") subject to section 7 of the Clayton Act [1] or to section 1 of the Sherman Act.[2] They describe the general principles and specific standards normally used by the Department in analyzing mergers.[3] By stating its policy as simply and clearly as possible, the Depart-

---

1. 15 U.S.C. § 18 (1982). Mergers subject to section 7 are prohibited if their effect "may be substantially to lessen competition, or to tend to create a monopoly."

2. 15 U.S.C. § 1 (1982). Mergers subject to section 1 are prohibited if they constitute a "contract, combination . . ., or conspiracy in restraint of trade."

3. They update the Guidelines issued by the Department in 1982. The Department may from time to time revise the Merger Guidelines as necessary to reflect any signif-

ment hopes to reduce the uncertainty associated with enforcement of the antitrust laws in this area.

Although the Guidelines should improve the predictability of the Department's merger enforcement policy, it is not possible to remove the exercise of judgment from the evaluation of mergers under the antitrust laws. Because the specific standards set forth in the Guidelines must be applied to a broad range of possible factual circumstances, strict application of those standards may provide misleading answers to the economic questions raised under the antitrust laws. Moreover, the picture of competitive conditions that develops from historical evidence may provide an incomplete answer to the forward-looking inquiry of the Guidelines. Therefore, the Department will apply the standards of the Guidelines reasonably and flexibly to the particular facts and circumstances of each proposed merger.

The Guidelines are designed primarily to indicate when the Department is likely to challenge mergers, not how it will conduct the litigation of cases that it decides to bring. Although relevant in the latter context, the factors contemplated in the standards do not exhaust the range of evidence that the Department may introduce in court.[4]

The unifying theme of the Guidelines is that mergers should not be permitted to create or enhance "market power" or to facilitate its exercise. A sole seller (a "monopolist") of a product with no good substitutes can maintain a selling price that is above the level that would prevail if the market were competitive. Where only a few firms account for most of the sales of a product, those firms can in some circumstances either explicitly or implicitly coordinate their actions in order to approximate the performance of a monopolist. This ability of one or more firms profitably to maintain prices above competitive levels for a significant period of time is termed "market power." Sellers with market power also may eliminate rivalry on variables other than price. In either case, the result is a transfer of wealth from buyers to sellers and a misallocation of resources.

"Market power" also encompasses the ability of a single buyer or group of buyers to depress the price paid for a product to a level that is below the competitive price. The exercise of market power by buyers has wealth transfer and resource misallocation effects analogous to those associated with the exercise of market power by sellers.

Although they sometimes harm competition, mergers generally play an important role in a free enterprise economy. They can penalize ineffective management and facilitate the efficient flow of investment capital and the redeployment of existing productive assets. While challenging competitively harmful mergers, the Department seeks to avoid unnecessary interference with that larger universe of mergers that are either competitively beneficial or neutral. In attempting to mediate between these dual concerns, however, the Guidelines reflect the congres-

icant changes in enforcement policy or to clarify aspects of existing policy.

4. Parties seeking more specific advance guidance concerning the Department's en-

forcement intentions with respect to any particular merger should consider using the Business Review Procedure. 28 C.F.R. § 50.6.

sional intent that merger enforcement should interdict competitive problems in their incipiency.

2. MARKET DEFINITION AND MEASUREMENT

2.0 Using the standards stated below, the Department will define and measure the market for each product or service (hereinafter "product") of each of the merging firms. The standards in the Guidelines are designed to ensure that the Department analyzes the likely competitive impact of a merger within economically meaningful markets—i.e., markets that could be subject to the exercise of market power. Accordingly, for each product of each merging firm, the Department seeks to define a market in which firms could effectively exercise market power if they were able to coordinate their actions. Formally, a market is defined as a product or group of products and a geographic area in which it is sold such that a hypothetical, profit-maximizing firm, not subject to price regulation, that was the only present and future seller of those products in that area would impose a "small but significant and nontransitory" increase in price above prevailing or likely future levels. The group of products and geographic area that comprise a market will be referred to respectively as the "product market" and the "geographic market."

In determining whether one or more firms would be in a position to exercise market power, it is necessary to evaluate both the probable demand responses of consumers and the probable supply responses of other firms. A price increase could be made unprofitable by any of four types of demand or supply responses: 1) consumers switching to other products; 2) consumers switching to the same product produced by firms in other areas; 3) producers of other products switching existing facilities to the production of the product; or 4) producers entering into the production of the product by substantially modifying existing facilities or by constructing new facilities. Each type of response is considered under the Guidelines.

In determining whether any of these responses are probable, the Department usually must rely on historical market information as the best, and sometimes the only, indicator of how the market will function in the future. It is important to note, however, that the Guidelines are fundamentally concerned with probable future demand or supply responses. Sections 2.1 through 2.4 describe how product and geographic markets will be defined under these Guidelines and how market shares will be calculated.

2.1 Product Market Definition

2.11 General Approach

The Department will first determine the relevant product market with respect to each of the products of each of the merging firms. In general, the Department will include in the product market a group of products such that a hypothetical firm that was the only present and future seller of those products ("monopolist") could profitably impose a "small but significant and nontransitory" increase in price. That is, assuming that buyers could respond to an increase in price for a tentatively identified product group only by shifting to other products, what would happen? If readily available alternatives were, in the aggregate, sufficiently attractive to enough buyers, an attempt to raise price would not prove profitable, and the tentatively identified product group would prove to be too narrow.

Specifically, the Department will begin with each product (narrowly defined) produced or sold by each merging firm and ask what would happen if a hypothetical monopolist of that product imposed a "small but significant and nontransitory" increase in price.[5] If the price increase would cause so many buyers to shift to other products that a hypothetical monopolist would not find it profitable to impose such an increase in price, then the Department will add to the product group the product that is the next-best substitute for the merging firm's product and ask the same question again. This process will continue until a group of products is identified for which a hypothetical monopolist could profitably impose a "small but significant and nontransitory" increase in price. The Department generally will consider the relevant product market to be the smallest group of products that satisfies this test.

In the above analysis, the Department will use prevailing prices of the products of the merging firms and possible substitutes for such products. However, the Department may use likely future prices when changes in the prevailing prices can be predicted with reasonable reliability. Changes in price may be predicted on the basis of, for example, expected changes in costs or demand caused by changes in environmental regulations or expected changes in regulations that directly affect price.

In general, the price for which an increase will be postulated will be whatever is considered to be the price of the product at the stage of the industry being examined.[6] In attempting to determine objectively the effect of a "small but significant and nontransitory" increase in price, the Department in most contexts will use a price increase of five percent lasting one year. However, what constitutes a "small but significant and nontransitory" increase in price will depend on the nature of the industry, and the Department at times may use a price increase that is larger or smaller than five percent.[7] For the purposes of its analysis, the Department will assume that the buyers and sellers immediately become aware of the price increase.

2.12 Relevant Evidence

Although direct evidence of the likely effect of a future price increase may sometimes be available, it usually will be necessary for the Depart-

5. Although discussed separately, product market definition and geographic market definition are interrelated. In particular, the extent to which buyers of a particular product would shift to other products in the event of a "small but significant and nontransitory" increase in price must be evaluated in the context of the relevant geographic market.

6. For example, in a merger between retailers, the relevant price would be the retail price of a product to consumers. In the case of a merger among oil pipelines, the relevant price would be the tariff—the price of the transportation service.

7. For example, a larger increase may be appropriate if the "price" to be increased is a tariff or commission that constitutes a small fraction of the price of the product being transported or sold.

ment to infer the likely effects of a price increase from various types of reliable, circumstantial evidence. The postulated "small but significant and nontransitory" price increase provides an objective standard by which to analyze the available evidence. Thus, in evaluating product substitutability, the Department will consider all relevant evidence but will give particular weight to the following factors:

1) Evidence of buyers' perceptions that the products are or are not substitutes, particularly if those buyers have actually considered shifting purchases between the products in response to changes in relative price or other competitive variables;

2) Differences in the price movements of the products or similarities in price movements over a period of years that are not explainable by common or parallel changes in factors such as costs of inputs, income, or other variables;

3) Similarities or differences between the products in customary usage, design, physical composition, and other technical characteristics; and

4) Evidence of sellers' perceptions that the products are or are not substitutes, particularly if business decisions have been based on those perceptions.

2.13 Price Discrimination

The analysis of product market definition to this point has assumed that price discrimination—charging different buyers different prices for products having the same cost, for example—would not be possible after the merger. Existing buyers sometimes will differ significantly in their assessment of the adequacy of a particular substitute and the ease with which they could substitute it for the product of the merging firm. Even though a general increase in price might cause such significant substitution that it would not be profitable, sellers who can price discriminate could raise price only to groups of buyers who cannot easily substitute away.[8] If such price discrimination is possible, the Department will consider defining additional, narrower relevant product markets consisting of particular uses of the product for which a hypothetical monopolist could profitably impose a "small but significant and nontransitory" increase in price.

2.2 Identification of Firms that Produce the Relevant Product

In most cases, the Department's evaluation of a merger will focus primarily on firms that currently produce and sell the relevant product. In addition, the Department may include other firms in the market if their inclusion would more accurately reflect probable supply responses. The following are examples of circumstances in which such additional firms would be included in the market.

---

8. Price discrimination requires that sellers be able to identify those buyers and that other buyers be unable profitably to purchase and resell to them.

2.21 Production Substitution

The same productive and distributive facilities can sometimes be used to produce and sell two or more products that buyers do not regard as good substitutes. Production substitution refers to the shift by a firm in the use of facilities from producing and selling one product to producing and selling another. Depending upon the cost and speed of that shift, production substitution may allow firms that do not currently produce the relevant product to respond effectively to an increase in the price of that product.[9]

If a firm has existing productive and distributive facilities that could easily and economically be used to produce and sell the relevant product within one year in response to a "small but significant and nontransitory" increase in price, the Department will include that firm in the market.[10] In this context, a "small but significant and nontransitory" increase in price will be determined in the same way in which it is determined in product market definition. In many cases, a firm that could readily convert its facilities from the production of one product to another would have significant difficulty distributing or marketing the new product or for some other reason would find the substitution unprofitable. Such firms will not be included in the market. The competitive significance of such firms, as well as those that will not be included in the market because they must construct significant new productive and distributive facilities, will be considered in evaluating entry conditions generally. See Section 3.3 (Ease of Entry).

2.22 Durable Products

Some long-lived products may continue to exert competitive influence after the time of original sale. If, under the standards stated in Section 2.1, recycled or reconditioned products represent good substitutes for new products, the Department will include in the market firms that recycle or recondition those products.

2.23 Internal Consumption

Captive production and consumption of the relevant product by vertically integrated firms are part of the overall market supply and demand. Such firms may respond to an increase in the price of the relevant product in either of two ways. They may begin selling the relevant product, or alternatively, they may continue to consume all of their production but increase their production of both the relevant product and products in which the relevant product is embodied. Either kind of supply response

9. Under other analytical approaches, production substitution sometimes has been reflected in the description of the product market. For example, the product market for stamped metal products such as automobile hub caps might be described as "light metal stamping," a production process rather than a product. The Department believes that the approach described in the text provides a more clearly focused method of incorporating this factor in merger analysis. If production substitution among a group of products is nearly universal among the firms selling one or more of those products, however, the Department may use an aggregate description of those markets as a matter of convenience.

10. The amount of sales or capacity to be included in the market is a separate question discussed in Section 2.4, below.

could frustrate collusion by firms currently selling the relevant product. If a firm would be likely to respond either way to a "small but significant and nontransitory" increase in price, the Department will include that firm in the market. In this context, a "small but significant and nontransitory" increase in price will be determined in the same way in which it is determined in product market definition.

2.3 Geographic Market Definition

2.31 General Approach

For each product market of each merging firm, the Department will determine the geographic market or markets in which that firm sells. The purpose of geographic market definition is to establish a geographic boundary that roughly separates firms that are important factors in the competitive analysis of a merger from those that are not. Depending on the nature of the product and the competitive circumstances, the geographic market may be as small as part of a city or as large as the entire world. Also, a single firm may operate in a number of economically discrete geographic markets.

In general, the Department seeks to identify a geographic area such that a hypothetical firm that was the only present or future producer or seller of the relevant product in that area could profitably impose a "small but significant and nontransitory" increase in price. That is, assuming that buyers could respond to a price increase within a tentatively identified area only by shifting to firms located outside the area, what would happen? If firms located elsewhere readily could provide the relevant product to the hypothetical firm's buyers in sufficient quantity at a comparable price, an attempt to raise price would not prove profitable, and the tentatively identified geographic area would prove to be too narrow.

In defining the geographic market or markets affected by a merger, the Department will begin with the location of each merging firm (or each plant of a multiplant firm) and ask what would happen if a hypothetical monopolist of the relevant product at that point imposed a "small but significant and nontransitory" increase in price. If this increase in price would cause so many buyers to shift to products produced in other areas that a hypothetical monopolist producing or selling the relevant product at the merging firm's location would not find it profitable to impose such an increase in price, then the Department will add the location from which production is next-best substitute for production at the merging firm's location and ask the same question again. This process will be repeated until the Department identifies an area in which a hypothetical monopolist could profitably impose a "small but significant and nontransitory" increase in price. The "smallest market" principle will be applied as it is in product market definition. Both the price in which an increase will be postulated and what constitutes a "small but significant and nontransitory" increase in price will be determined in the same way in which it is determined in product market definition.

2.32 Relevant Evidence

Although direct evidence of the likely effect of a future price increase may sometimes be available, it usually will be necessary for the Department to infer the likely effects of a price increase from various types of reliable, circumstantial evidence. The postulated "small but significant and nontransitory" increase in price provides an objective standard by which to analyze the available evidence. Thus, in evaluating geographic substitutability, the Department will consider all relevant evidence but will give particular weight to the following factors:

1) The shipment patterns of the merging firm and of those firms with which it actually competes for sales;

2) Evidence of buyers having actually considered shifting their purchases among sellers at different geographic locations, especially if the shifts corresponded to changes in relative price or other competitive variables;

3) Differences in the price movements of the relevant product or similarities in price movements over a period of years that are not explainable by common or parallel changes in factors such as the cost of inputs, income, or other variables in different geographic areas;

4) Transportation costs;

5) Costs of local distribution; and

6) Excess capacity of firms outside the location of the merging firm.

2.33 Price Discrimination

The analysis of geographic market definition to this point has assumed that geographic price discrimination—charging different prices net of transportation costs for the same product to buyers in different locations, for example—would not be possible after the merger. As in the case of product market definition, however, where price discrimination is possible,[11] the Department will consider defining additional, narrower geographic markets consisting of particular locations in which a hypothetical monopolist could profitably impose a "small but significant and nontransitory" increase in price.

2.34 Foreign Competition

In general, the foregoing standards will govern market definition, whether domestic or international. Although voluntary or involuntary quotas may prevent foreign competitors from increasing their imports into the United States in response to a domestic price increase, the Department will not exclude foreign competitors from the relevant market solely on the basis of the quotas. This is primarily because it frequently is difficult to determine and measure the effectiveness and longevity of a particular quota or any offsetting supply response from firms in countries not subject to the quota. The Department will consider the effects of a

---

11. Geographic price discrimination against a group of buyers is more likely when other buyers cannot easily purchase and resell the relevant product to them. Such arbitrage is particularly difficult where the product is sold on a delivered basis and where transportation costs are a significant percentage of the final cost.

quota as a separate factor in interpreting the significance of market shares and market concentration. See Section 3.23 (Special Factors Affecting Foreign Firms).

2.4 Calculating Market Shares

The Department normally will include in the market the total sales or capacity of all domestic firms (or plants) that are identified as being in the market under Sections 2.2 and 2.3. Market shares can be expressed either in dollar terms through measurement of sales, shipments, or production, or in physical terms through measurement of sales, shipments, production, capacity, or reserves. As a practical matter, the availability of data often will determine the measurement basis. When the availability of data allows a choice, dollar sales or shipments generally will be used if branded or relatively differentiated are involved, and physical capacity, reserves, or dollar production generally will be used if relatively homogeneous, undifferentiated products are involved.

In some cases, however, total sales or capacity may overstate the competitive significance of a firm. The Department will include only those sales likely to be made or capacity likely to be used in the market in response to a "small but significant and nontransitory" increase in price, for example, with respect to firms included in the market under Sections 2.21 (Production Substitution) and 2.23 (Internal Consumption). Similarly, a firm's capacity may be so committed elsewhere that it would not be available to respond to an increase in price in the market. In such cases, the Department also may include a smaller part of the firm's sales or capacity. To the extent available information permits, market shares will be assigned to foreign competitors in the same way in which they are assigned to domestic competitors. If dollar sales or shipments are used to measure shares of domestic firms, the market shares of foreign firms will be measured using dollar sales in, or shipments to, the relevant market.[12] If physical capacity, reserves, or dollar production is used for domestic firms, the shares of foreign firms will be measured in terms of the capacity or reserves likely to be used to supply, or production that is likely to be shipped to, the relevant market in response to a "small but significant and nontransitory" price increase. If shipments from a particular country to the United States are subject to a quota, the market shares assigned to firms in that country will not exceed the amount of shipments by such firms allowed under the quota. Current shipments rather than capacity or reserves may be used for foreign firms if it is impossible reliably to quantify the proportion of the firms' capacity, reserves, or production that would be devoted to the relevant market in response to a "small but significant and nontransitory" increase in price because of, for example, the lack of available data regarding foreign capacity or the commitment of such capacity to other markets. Finally, a single market share may be assigned to a country or group of countries if firms in that country or group of countries act in coordination or if necessitated by data limitations.

12. If exchange rates fluctuate significantly, making comparable dollar calculations for different firms difficult, then the volume of unit sales may be a better measure of market share than dollar sales and may be used instead.

3. HORIZONTAL MERGERS

3.0 Where the merging firms are in the same product and geographic market, the merger is horizontal. In such cases, the Department will focus first on the post-merger concentration of the market and the increase in concentration caused by the merger. For mergers that result in low market concentration or a relatively slight increase in concentration, the Department will be able to determine without a detailed examination of other factors that the merger poses no significant threat to competition. In other cases, however, the Department will proceed to examine a variety of other factors relevant to that question.

3.1 Concentration and Market Shares

Market concentration is a function of the number of firms in a market and their respective market shares.[13] Other things being equal, concentration affects the likelihood that one firm, or a small group of firms, could successfully exercise market power. The smaller the percentage of total supply that a firm controls, the more severely it must restrict its own output in order to produce a given price increase, and the less likely it is that an output restriction will be profitable. If collective action is necessary, an additional constraint applies. As the number of firms necessary to control a given percentage of total supply increases, the difficulties and costs of reaching and enforcing consensus with respect to the control of that supply also increase.

As an aid to the interpretation of market data, the Department will use the Herfindahl–Hirschman Index ("HHI") of market concentration. The HHI is calculated by summing the squares of the individual market shares of all the firms included in the market under the standards in Section 2 of these Guidelines.[14] Unlike the traditional four-firm concentration ratio, the HHI reflects both the distribution of the market shares of the top four firms and the composition of the market outside the top four firms. It also gives proportionately greater weight to the market shares of the larger firms, which probably accords with their relative importance in any collusive interaction.

The Department divides the spectrum of market concentration as measured by the HHI into three regions that can be broadly characterized as unconcentrated (HHI below 1000), moderately concentrated (HHI between 1000 and 1800), and highly concentrated (HHI above 1800). An empirical study by the Department of the size dispersion of firms within

13. Markets can range from atomistic, where very large numbers of firms that are small relative to the overall size of the market compete with one another, to monopolistic, where one firm controls the entire market. Far more common, and more difficult analytically, is the large middle range of instances where a relatively small number of firms accounts for most of the sales in the market.

14. For example, a market consisting of four firms with market shares of 30 percent, 30 percent, 20 percent and 20 percent has an HHI of 2600 ($30^2 + 30^2 + 20^2 + 20^2 = 2600$). The HHI ranges from 10,000 (in the case of a pure monopoly) to a number approaching zero (in the case of an atomistic market). Although it is desirable to include all firms in the calculation, lack of information about small fringe firms is not critical because such firms do not affect the HHI significantly.

markets indicates that the critical HHI thresholds at 1000 and 1800 correspond roughly to four-firm concentration ratios of 50 percent and 70 percent, respectively. Although the resulting regions provide a useful format for merger analysis, the numerical divisions suggest greater precision than is possible with the available economic tools and information. Other things being equal, cases falling just above and just below a threshold present comparable competitive concerns. Moreover, because concentration and market share data present a historical picture of the market, the Department must interpret such data in light of the relevant circumstances and the forward-looking objective of the Guidelines—to determine likely future effects of a given merger.

3.11 General Standards

In evaluating horizontal mergers, the Department will consider both the post-merger market concentration and the increase in concentration resulting from the merger.[15] The link between concentration and market power is explained above. The increase in concentration is relevant to several key issues. Although mergers among small firms increase concentration, they are less likely to have anticompetitive consequences. Moreover, even in concentrated markets, it is desirable to allow firms some scope for merger activity in order to achieve economies of scale and to permit exit from the market. However, market share and concentration data provide only the starting point for analyzing the competitive impact of a merger. Before determining whether to challenge a merger, the Department will consider all other relevant factors that pertain to its competitive impact.

The general standards for horizontal mergers are as follows:

a) Post–Merger HHI Below 1000. Markets in this region generally would be considered to be unconcentrated. Because implicit coordination among firms is likely to be difficult and because the prohibitions of section 1 of the Sherman Act are usually an adequate response to any explicit collusion that might occur, the Department will not challenge mergers falling in this region, except in extraordinary circumstances.

b) Post–Merger HHI Between 1000 and 1800. Because this region extends from the point at which the competitive concerns associated with concentration are raised to the point at which they become quite serious, generalization is particularly difficult. The Department, however, is unlikely to challenge a merger producing an increase in the HHI of less than 100 points.[16] The Department is likely to challenge mergers in this

---

15. The increase in concentration as measured by the HHI can be calculated independently of the overall market concentration by doubling the product of the market shares of the merging firms. For example, the merger of firms with shares of 5 percent and 10 percent of the market would increase the HHI by 100 $(5 \times 10 \times 2 = 100)$. The explanation for this technique is as follows: In calculating the HHI before the merger, the market shares of the merging firms are squared individually: $(a)2 + (b)2$. After the merger,

the sum of those shares would be squared: $(a + b)2$, which equals $a2 + 2ab + b2$. The increase in the HHI therefore is represented by $2ab$.

16. Mergers producing increases in concentration close to the 100 point threshold include those between firms with market shares of 25 percent and 2 percent, 16 percent and 3 percent, 12 percent and 4 percent, 10 percent and 5 percent, 8 percent and 6 percent, and 7 percent and 7 percent.

region that produce an increase in the HHI of more than 100 points, unless the Department concludes, on the basis of the post-merger HHI, the increase in the HHI, and the presence or absence of the factors discussed in Sections 3.2, 3.3, 3.4, and 3.5 that the merger is not likely substantially to lessen competition.

c) Post–Merger HHI Above 1800. Markets in this region generally are considered to be highly concentrated. Additional concentration resulting from mergers is a matter of significant competitive concern. The Department is unlikely, however, to challenge mergers producing an increase in the HHI of less than 50 points.[17] The Department is likely to challenge mergers in this region that produce an increase in the HHI of more than 50 points, unless the Department concludes, on the basis of the post-merger HHI, the increase in the HHI, and the presence or absence of the factors discussed in Sections 3.2, 3.3, 3.4, and 3.5 that the merger is not likely substantially to lessen competition. However, if the increase in the HHI exceeds 100 and the post-merger HHI substantially exceeds 1800, only in extraordinary cases will such factors establish that the merger is not likely substantially to lessen competition.

3.12 Leading Firm Proviso

In some cases, typically where one of the merging firms is small, mergers that may create or enhance the market power of a single dominant firm could pass scrutiny under the standards stated in Section 3.11. Notwithstanding those standards, the Department is likely to challenge the merger of any firm with a market share of at least one percent with the leading firm in the market, provided the leading firm has a market share that is at least 35 percent. Because the ease and profitability of collusion are of little relevance to the ability of a single dominant firm to exercise market power, the Department will not consider the presence or absence of the factors discussed in Section 3.4 because they relate to the likelihood of collusion. The Department will consider, however, the factors in Sections 3.2, 3.3, and 3.5 because they are relevant to the competitive concerns associated with a leading-firm merger.

3.2 Factors Affecting the Significance of Market Shares and Concentration

In a variety of situations, market share and market concentration data may either understate or overstate the likely future competitive significance of a firm or firms in the market. The following are examples of such situations.

3.21 Changing Market Conditions

Market concentration and market share data of necessity are based on historical evidence. However, recent or on-going changes in the market may indicate that the current market share of a particular firm either understates or overstates the firm's future competitive significance. For example, if a new technology that is important to long-term competi-

---

17. Mergers producing increases in concentration close to the 50 point threshold include those between firms with market shares of 12 percent and 2 percent, 8 percent and 3 percent, 6 percent and 4 percent, and 5 percent and 5 percent.

tive viability is not available to a particular firm, the Department may conclude that the historical market share of the firm overstates the firm's future competitive significance. The Department will consider reasonably predictable effects of recent or on-going changes in market conditions in interpreting market concentration and market share data.

3.22 Financial Condition of Firms in the Relevant Market

The Department will consider the financial condition of a merging firm or any firm in the relevant market, to the extent that it is relevant to an analysis of the firm's likely future competitive significance.[18] If the financial difficulties of a firm cannot be explained as phenomena of, for example, the business cycle but clearly reflect an underlying structural weakness of the firm, the firm's current market share may overstate its likely future competitive significance. For example, a firm's current market share may overstate its future competitive significance if that firm has chronic financial difficulties resulting from obsolete productive facilities in a market experiencing a long-term decline in demand.

3.23 Special Factors Affecting Foreign Firms

Actual import sales, shipment data, or capacity in some cases may tend to overstate the relative competitive significance of foreign firms. This will be the case, for example, if foreign firms are subject to quotas (imposed either by the United States or by their own country) that effectively limit the volume of their imports into this country. Foreign firms that are subject to such quotas generally cannot increase imports into the United States in response to a domestic price increase. In the case of restraints that limit imports to some percentage of the total amount of the product sold in the United States (i.e., percentage quotas), a domestic price increase that reduces domestic consumption would actually reduce the volume of imports into the United States. Thus, actual import sales and shipment data will tend to overstate the competitive significance of firms in countries subject to binding quotas.[19] Less significant, but still important factors, such as other types of trade restraints and changes in exchange rates, also may cause actual import sales and shipment data to overstate the future competitive significance of foreign firms. To the extent that the relative competitive significance of imports is overstated by the current market shares of foreign firms, the relative competitive significance of domestic firms concomitantly will be understated.

In addition, limitations on available data concerning the amount of foreign capacity that could be devoted to the United States in response to a "small but significant and nontransitory" increase in price may require the Department to use market share data that understate the true competitive significance of foreign competitors. Despite the inability to

18. This factor is distinguished from the failing company doctrine, which is an affirmative defense to an otherwise unlawful merger and which, as noted in Section 5.1, the Department will construe strictly.

19. For example, in the extreme situation where there is an effective trade restraint that places a fixed or percentage limitation on the quantity of goods that can be imported into the United States from all or almost all foreign sources, market shares of foreign sources would usually be accorded little, if any, weight.

obtain data to quantify precisely the supply response of foreign competitors, the Department will consider strong qualitative evidence that, for example, there is significant worldwide excess capacity that could readily be devoted to the United States. To the extent market shares based on the best available evidence tend to understate the competitive significance of foreign competitors, the relative competitive significance of domestic firms may be overstated. In all cases addressed by this section of the Guidelines (Section 3.23), the Department will make appropriate adjustments in its analysis of the available data to reflect more accurately actual competitive concerns.

3.3 Ease of Entry

If entry into a market is so easy that existing competitors could not succeed in raising price for any significant period of time, the Department is unlikely to challenge mergers in that market. Under the standards in Section 2.21, firms that do not currently sell the relevant product, but that could easily and economically sell it using existing facilities, are included in the market and are assigned a market share. This section considers the additional competitive effects of 1) production substitution requiring significant modifications of existing facilities and 2) entry through the construction of new facilities.[20]

In assessing the ease of entry into a market, the Department will consider the likelihood and probable magnitude of entry in response to a "small but significant and nontransitory" increase in price.[21] Both the price to be increased and what constitutes a "small but significant and nontransitory" increase in price will be determined as they are in product market definition, except that a two-year time period generally will be used.[22] The more difficult entry into the market is, the more likely the Department is to challenge the merger.

3.4 Other Factors

A variety of other factors affect the likelihood that a merger will create, enhance, or facilitate the exercise of market power. In evaluating mergers, the Department will consider the following factors, among others, as they relate to the ease and profitability of collusion. Where relevant, the factors are most likely to be important where the Department's decision whether to challenge a merger is otherwise close.

---

20. "Entry" may occur as firms outside the market enter for the first time or as fringe firms currently in the market greatly expand their current capacity.

21. In general, entry is more likely to occur when the additional assets necessary to produce the relevant product are short-lived or widely used outside the particular market. Conversely, entry is less likely to occur when those assets are long-lived and highly specialized to the particular application. Entry is generally facilitated by the growth of the market and hindered by its stagnation or decline. Entry also is hindered by the need for scarce special skills or resources, or the need to achieve a substantial market share in order to realize important economies of scale. See also Section 4.212 (Increased Difficulty of Simultaneous Entry to Both Markets).

22. Although this type of supply response may take longer to materialize than those considered under Section 2.21, its prospect may have a greater deterrent effect on the exercise of market power by present sellers. Where new entry involves the dedication of long-lived assets to a market, the resulting capacity and its adverse effects on profitability will be present in the market until those assets are economically depreciated.

3.41 Nature of the Product and Terms of Sale

3.411 Homogeneity–Heterogeneity of the Relevant Product

Generally, in a market with a homogeneous and undifferentiated product, a cartel need establish only a single price—a circumstance that facilitates reaching consensus and detecting deviation. As the products which constitute the relevant product market become more numerous, heterogeneous, or differentiated, however, the problems facing a cartel become more complex. Instead of a single price, it may be necessary to establish and enforce a complex schedule of prices corresponding to gradations in actual or perceived quality attributes among the competing products.[23]

Product variation is arguably relevant in all cases, but practical considerations dictate a more limited use of the factor. There is neither an objective index of product variation nor an empirical basis for its use in drawing fine distinctions among cases. As a result, this factor will be taken into account only in relatively extreme cases where both identification and effect are more certain. For example, when the relevant product is completely homogeneous and undifferentiated, the Department is more likely to challenge the merger. Conversely, when the relevant product is very heterogeneous or sold subject to complex configuration options or customized production, the Department is less likely to challenge the merger.[24] Over a significant middle range of the spectrum of product variation, this factor is less likely to affect the Department's analysis.

3.412 Degree of Difference Between the Products and Locations in the Market and the Next–Best Substitutes

The market definition standards stated in Section 2 of these Guidelines require drawing relatively bright lines in order to determine the products and sellers to be considered in evaluating a merger. For example, in defining the relevant product, all "good substitutes" in demand are included. The profitability of any collusion that might occur will depend in part, however, on the quality of the next-best substitute. That is, it matters whether the next-best substitute is only slightly or significantly inferior to the last product included in the relevant product. Similarly, it matters whether the next-most-distant seller is only slightly or significantly farther away than the last seller included in the geographic market. The larger the "gap" at the edge of the product and geographic markets, the more likely the Department is to challenge the merger.

3.413 Similarities and Differences in the Products and Locations of the Merging Firms

There also may be relevant comparisons among the products or sellers included in the market. Where products in a relevant market are differentiated or sellers are spatially dispersed, individual sellers usually

---

23. A similar situation may exist where there is rapid technological change or where supply arrangements consist of many complicated terms in addition to price.

24. This conclusion would not apply, however, where the significance of heterogeneity is substantially reduced through detailed specifications that are provided by the buyer and that form the basis for all firms' bids.

compete more directly with some rivals than with others. In markets with highly differentiated products, the Department will consider the extent to which consumers perceive the products of the merging firms to be relatively better or worse substitutes for one another than for other products in the market. In markets with spatially dispersed sellers and significant transportation costs, the Department will consider the relative proximity of the merging firms. If the products or plants of the merging firms are particularly good substitutes for one another, the Department is more likely to challenge the merger.

3.42 Information About Specific Transactions and Buyer Characteristics

Collusive agreements are more likely to persist if participating firms can quickly detect and retaliate against deviations from the agreed prices or other conditions. Such deviations are easiest to detect, and therefore least likely to occur, in markets where detailed information about specific transactions or individual price or output levels is readily available to competitors. The Department is more likely to challenge a merger if such detailed information is available to competitors, whether the information comes from an exchange among sellers, public disclosure by buyers, reporting by the press or a government agency, or some other source.

Certain buyer market characteristics also may facilitate detection of deviation from collusive agreements. If orders for the relevant product are frequent, regular and small relative to the total output of a typical firm in the market, collusion is more likely to succeed because the benefits of departing from the collusive agreement in any single transaction are likely to be small relative to the potential costs. In order to increase its sales significantly in such circumstances, a seller would have to depart from the collusive agreement on a large number of orders. Each such sale takes customers away from other parties to the agreement, a fact that is particularly evident when demand is stable or declining. As a result, the chances of detection and effective response by other sellers increase with the number of such sales. The Department is more likely to challenge a merger where such buyer market characteristics exist.

3.43 Ability of Small or Fringe Sellers to Increase Sales

Collusion is less likely to occur if small or fringe sellers in the market are able profitably to increase output substantially in response to a "small but significant and nontransitory" increase in price and thus to undermine a cartel. The Department is less likely to challenge a merger if small or fringe firms currently are able to expand significantly their sales at incremental costs that are approximately equal to their incremental costs experienced at current levels of output.

3.44 Conduct of Firms in the Market

The Department is more likely to challenge a merger in the following circumstances:

a) Firms in the market previously have been found to have engaged in horizontal collusion regarding price, territories, or customers, and the characteristics of the market have not changed appreciably since the most recent finding. The additional concentration resulting from the merger could make explicit collusion more difficult to detect or tacit collusion more feasible.

b) One or more of the following types of practices are adopted by substantially all of the firms in the market: 1) mandatory delivered pricing; 2) exchange of price or output information in a form that could assist firms in setting or enforcing an agreed price; 3) collective standardization of product variables on which the firms could compete; and 4) price protection clauses. Although not objectionable under all circumstances, these types of practices tend to make collusion easier, and their widespread adoption by the firms in the market raises some concern that collusion may already exist.

c) The firm to be acquired has been an unusually disruptive and competitive influence in the market. Before invoking this factor, the Department will determine whether the market is one in which performance might plausibly deteriorate because of the elimination of one disruptive firm.

3.45 Market Performance

When the market in which the proposed merger would occur is currently performing noncompetitively, the Department is more likely to challenge the merger. Noncompetitive performance suggests that the firms in the market already have succeeded in overcoming, at least to some extent, the obstacles to effective collusion. Increased concentration of such a market through merger could further facilitate the collusion that already exists. When the market in which the proposed merger would occur is currently performing competitively, however, the Department will apply its ordinary standards of review. The fact that the market is currently competitive casts little light on the likely effect of the merger.

In evaluating the performance of a market, the Department will consider any relevant evidence, but will give particular weight to the following evidence of possible noncompetitive performance when the factors are found in conjunction:

a) Stable relative market shares of the leading firms in recent years;

b) Declining combined market share of the leading firms in recent years; and

c) Profitability of the leading firms over substantial periods of time that significantly exceeds that of firms in industries comparable in capital intensity and risk.

3.5 Efficiencies

The primary benefit of mergers to the economy is their efficiency-enhancing potential, which can increase the competitiveness of firms and result in lower prices to consumers. Because the antitrust laws, and thus the standards of the Guidelines, are designed to proscribe only mergers that present a significant danger to competition, they do not present an obstacle to most mergers. As a consequence, in the majority of cases, the Guidelines will allow firms to achieve available efficiencies through mergers without interference from the Department.

Some mergers that the Department otherwise might challenge may be reasonably necessary to achieve significant net efficiencies. If the parties to the merger establish by clear and convincing evidence that a merger will achieve such efficiencies, the Department will consider those efficiencies in deciding whether to challenge the merger. Cognizable efficiencies include, but are not limited to, achieving economies of scale, better integration of production facilities, plant specialization, lower transportation costs, and similar efficiencies relating to specific manufacturing, servicing, or distribution operations of the merging firms. The Department may also consider claimed efficiencies resulting from reductions in general selling, administrative, and overhead expenses, or that otherwise do not relate to specific manufacturing, servicing, or distribution operations of the merging firms, although, as a practical matter, these types of efficiencies may be difficult to demonstrate. In addition, the Department will reject claims of efficiencies if equivalent or comparable savings can reasonably be achieved by the parties through other means. The more parties must establish a greater level of expected net efficiencies the more significant are the competitive risks identified in Section 3.

4. HORIZONTAL EFFECT FROM NON-HORIZONTAL MERGERS

4.0 By definition, non-horizontal mergers involve firms that do not operate in the same market. It necessarily follows that such mergers produce no immediate change in the level of concentration in any relevant market as defined in Section 2 of these Guidelines. Although non-horizontal mergers are less likely than horizontal mergers to create competitive problems, they are not invariably innocuous. This section describes the principal theories under which the Department is likely to challenge non-horizontal mergers.

4.1 Elimination of Specific Potential Entrants

4.11 The Theory of Potential Competition

In some circumstances, the non-horizontal merger [25] of a firm already in a market (the "acquired firm") with a potential entrant to that market (the "acquiring firm") [26] may adversely affect competition in the market. If the merger effectively removes the acquiring firm from the edge of the market, it could have either of the following effects:

25. Under traditional usage, such a merger could be characterized as either "vertical" or "conglomerate," but the label adds nothing to the analysis.

the market of interest, not to the way the particular transaction is formally structured.

26. The terms "acquired" and "acquiring" refer to the relationship of the firms to

4.111 Harm to "Perceived Potential Competition"

By eliminating a significant present competitive threat that constrains the behavior of the firms already in the market, the merger could result in an immediate deterioration in market performance. The economic theory of limit pricing suggests that monopolists and groups of colluding firms may find it profitable to restrain their pricing in order to deter new entry that is likely to push prices even lower by adding capacity to the market. If the acquiring firm had unique advantages in entering the market, the firms in the market might be able to set a new and higher price after the threat of entry by the acquiring firm was eliminated by the merger.

4.112 Harm to "Actual Potential Competition"

By eliminating the possibility of entry by the acquiring firm in a more procompetitive manner, the merger could result in a lost opportunity for improvement in market performance resulting from the addition of a significant competitor. The more procompetitive alternatives include both new entry and entry through a "toehold" acquisition of a present small competitor.

4.12 Relation Between Perceived and Actual Competition

If it were always profit-maximizing for incumbent firms to set price in such a way that all entry was deterred and if information and coordination were sufficient to implement this strategy, harm to perceived potential competition would be the only competitive problem to address. In practice, however, actual potential competition has independent importance. Firms already in the market may not find it optimal to set price low enough to deter all entry; moreover, those firms may misjudge the entry advantages of a particular firm and, therefore, the price necessary to deter its entry.[27]

4.13 Enforcement Standards

Because of the close relationship between perceived potential competition and actual potential competition, the Department will evaluate mergers that raise either type of potential competition concern under a single structural analysis analogous to that applied to horizontal mergers. The Department first will consider a set of objective factors designed to identify cases in which harmful effects are plausible. In such cases, the Department then will conduct a more focused inquiry to determine whether the likelihood and magnitude of the possible harm justify a challenge to the merger. In this context, the Department will consider any specific evidence presented by the merging parties to show that the inferences of competitive harm drawn from the objective factors are unreliable.

The factors that the Department will consider are as follows:

27. When collusion is only tacit, the problem of arriving at and enforcing the correct limit price is likely to be particularly difficult.

4.131 Market Concentration

Barriers to entry are unlikely to affect market performance if the structure of the market is otherwise not conducive to monopolization or collusion. Adverse competitive effects are likely only if overall concentration, or the largest firm's market share, is high. The Department is unlikely to challenge a potential competition merger unless overall concentration of the acquired firm's market is above 1800 HHI (a somewhat lower concentration will suffice if one or more of the factors discussed in Section 3.4 indicate that effective collusion in the market is particularly likely). Other things being equal, the Department is increasingly likely to challenge a merger as this threshold is exceeded.

4.132 Conditions of Entry Generally

If entry to the market is generally easy, the fact that entry is marginally easier for one or more firms is unlikely to affect the behavior of the firms in the market. The Department is unlikely to challenge a potential competition merger when new entry into the acquired firm's market can be accomplished by firms without any specific entry advantages under the conditions stated in Section 3.3. Other things being equal, the Department is increasingly likely to challenge a merger as the difficulty of entry increases above that threshold.

4.133 The Acquiring Firm's Entry Advantage

If more than a few firms have the same or a comparable advantage in entering the acquired firm's market, the elimination of one firm is unlikely to have any adverse competitive effect. The other similarly situated firm(s) would continue to exert a present restraining influence, or, if entry would be profitable, would recognize the opportunity and enter. The Department is unlikely to challenge a potential competition merger if the entry advantage ascribed to the acquiring firm (or another advantage of comparable importance) is also possessed by three or more other firms. Other things being equal, the Department is increasingly likely to challenge a merger as the number of other similarly situated firms decreases below three and as the extent of the entry advantage over non-advantaged firms increases.

If the evidence of likely actual entry by the acquiring firm is particularly strong,[28] however, the Department may challenge a potential competition merger, notwithstanding the presence of three or more firms that are objectively similarly situated. In such cases, the Department will determine the likely scale of entry, using either the firm's own documents or the minimum efficient scale in the industry. The Department will then evaluate the merger much as it would a horizontal merger between a firm the size of the likely scale of entry and the acquired firm.

4.134 The Market Share of the Acquired Firm

Entry through the acquisition of a relatively small firm in the market may have a competitive effect comparable to new entry. Small firms

---

28. For example, the firm already may have moved beyond the stage of considera- tion and have made significant investments demonstrating an actual decision to enter.

frequently play peripheral roles in collusive interactions, and the particular advantages of the acquiring firm may convert a fringe firm into a significant factor in the market.[29] The Department is unlikely to challenge a potential competition merger when the acquired firm has a market share of five percent or less. Other things being equal, the Department is increasingly likely to challenge a merger as the market share of the acquired firm increases above that threshold. The Department is likely to challenge any merger satisfying the other conditions in which the acquired firm has a market share of 20 percent or more.

4.135 Efficiencies

As in the case of horizontal mergers, the Department will consider expected efficiencies in determining whether to challenge a potential competition merger. See Section 3.5 (Efficiencies).

4.2 Competitive Problems from Vertical Mergers

4.21 Barriers to Entry from Vertical Mergers

In certain circumstances, the vertical integration resulting from vertical mergers could create competitively objectionable barriers to entry. Stated generally, three conditions are necessary (but not sufficient) for this problem to exist. First, the degree of vertical integration between the two markets must be so extensive that entrants to one market (the "primary market") also would have to enter the other market (the "secondary market")[30] simultaneously. Second, the requirement of entry at the secondary level must make entry at the primary level significantly more difficult and less likely to occur. Finally, the structure and other characteristics of the primary market must be otherwise so conducive to non-competitive performance that the increased difficulty of entry is likely to affect its performance. The following standards state the criteria by which the Department will determine whether these conditions are satisfied.

4.211 Need for Two–Level Entry

If there is sufficient unintegrated capacity[31] in the secondary market, new entrants to the primary market would not have to enter both

---

29. Although a similar effect is possible with the acquisition of larger firms, there is an increased danger that the acquiring firm will choose to acquiesce in monopolization or collusion because of the enhanced profits that would result from its own disappearance from the edge of the market.

30. This competitive problem could result from either upstream or downstream integration, and could affect competition in either the upstream market or the downstream market. In the text, the term "primary market" refers to the market in which the competitive concerns are being considered, and the term "secondary market" refers to the adjacent market.

31. Ownership integration does not necessarily mandate two-level entry by new en-

trants to the primary market. Such entry is most likely to be necessary where the primary and secondary markets are completely integrated by ownership and each firm in the primary market uses all of the capacity of its associated firm in the secondary market. In many cases of ownership integration, however, the functional fit between vertically integrated firms is not perfect, and an outside market exists for the sales (purchases) of the firms in the secondary market. If that market is sufficiently large and diverse, new entrants to the primary market may be able to participate without simultaneous entry to the secondary market. In considering the adequacy of this alternative, the Department will consider the likelihood of predatory price or supply "squeezes"

markets simultaneously. The Department is unlikely to challenge a merger on this ground where post-merger sales (purchases) by unintegrated firms in the secondary market would be sufficient to service two minimum-efficient-scale plants in the primary market. When the other conditions are satisfied, the Department is increasingly likely to challenge a merger as the unintegrated capacity declines below this level.

4.212 Increased Difficulty of Simultaneous Entry to Both Markets

The relevant question is whether the need for simultaneous entry to the secondary market gives rise to a substantial incremental difficulty as compared to entry into the primary market alone. If entry at the secondary level is easy in absolute terms, the requirement of simultaneous entry to that market is unlikely adversely to affect entry to the primary market. Whatever the difficulties of entry into the primary market may be, the Department is unlikely to challenge a merger on this ground if new entry into the secondary market can be accomplished under the conditions stated in Section 3.3.[32] When entry is not possible under those conditions, the Department is increasingly concerned about vertical mergers as the difficulty of entering the secondary market increases. The Department, however, will invoke this theory only where the need for secondary market entry significantly increases the costs (which may take the form of risks) of primary market entry.

More capital is necessary to enter two markets than to enter one. Standing alone, however, this additional capital requirement does not constitute a barrier to entry to the primary market. If the necessary funds were available at a cost commensurate with the level of risk in the secondary market, there would be no adverse effect. In some cases, however, lenders may doubt that would-be entrants to the primary market have the necessary skills and knowledge to succeed in the secondary market and, therefore, in the primary market. In order to compensate for this risk of failure, lenders might charge a higher rate for the necessary capital. This problem becomes increasingly significant as a higher percentage of the capital assets in the secondary market are long-lived and specialized to that market and, therefore, the Department will consider both the degree of similarity in the essential skills in the primary and secondary markets and the economic life and degree of specialization of the capital assets in the secondary market.

Economies of scale in the secondary market may constitute an additional barrier to entry to the primary market in some situations requiring two-level entry. The problem could arise if the capacities of minimum-efficient-scale plants in the primary and secondary markets differ significantly. For example, if the capacity of a minimum-efficient-scale plant in the secondary market were significantly greater than the needs of a minimum-efficient-scale plant in the primary market, entrants would have to choose between inefficient operation at the secondary level (be-

by the integrated firms against their unintegrated rivals.

32. Entry into the secondary market may be greatly facilitated in that an assured sup-

plier (customer) is provided by the primary market entry.

cause of operating an efficient plant at an inefficient output or because of operating an inefficiently small plant) or a larger than necessary scale at the primary level. Either of these effects could cause a significant increase in the operating costs of the entering firm.[33]

4.213 Structure and Performance of the Primary Market

Barriers to entry are unlikely to affect performance if the structure of the primary market is otherwise not conducive to monopolization or collusion.[34] The Department is unlikely to challenge a merger on this ground unless overall concentration of the primary market is above 1800 HHI (a somewhat lower concentration will suffice if one or more of the factors discussed in Section 3.4 indicate that effective collusion is particularly likely). Above that threshold, the Department is increasingly likely to challenge a merger that meets the other criteria set forth above as the concentration increases.

4.22 Facilitating Collusion Through Vertical Mergers

* * *

4.221 Vertical Integration to the Retail Level

A high level of vertical integration by upstream firms into the associated retail market may facilitate collusion in the upstream market by making it easier to monitor price. Retail prices are generally more visible than prices in upstream markets, and vertical mergers may increase the level of vertical integration to the point at which the monitoring effect becomes significant. Adverse competitive consequences are unlikely unless the upstream market is generally conducive to collusion and a large percentage of the products produced there are sold through vertically integrated retail outlets.

The Department is unlikely to challenge a merger on this ground unless 1) overall concentration of the upstream market is above 1800 HHI (a somewhat lower concentration will suffice if one or more of the factors discussed in Section 3.4 indicate that effective collusion is particularly likely), and 2) a large percentage of the upstream product would be sold through vertically-integrated retail outlets after the merger. Where the stated thresholds are met or exceeded, the Department's decision whether to challenge a merger on this ground will depend upon an individual evaluation of its likely competitive effect.

4.222 Elimination of a Disruptive Buyer

The elimination by vertical merger of a particularly disruptive buyer in a downstream market may facilitate collusion in the upstream market. If upstream firms view sales to a particular buyer as sufficiently important, they may deviate from the terms of a collusive agreement in an effort to secure that business, thereby disrupting the operation of the

---

33. It is important to note, however, that this problem would not exist if a significant outside market exists at the secondary level. In that case, entrants could enter with the appropriately scaled plants at both levels, and sell or buy in the market as necessary.

34. For example, a market with 100 firms of equal size would perform competitively despite a significant increase in entry barriers.

agreement. The merger of such a buyer with an upstream firm may eliminate that rivalry, making it easier for the upstream firms to collude effectively. Adverse competitive consequences are unlikely unless the upstream market is generally conducive to collusion and the disruptive firm is significantly more attractive to sellers than the other firms in its market.

The Department is unlikely to challenge a merger on this ground unless 1) overall concentration of the upstream market is 1800 HHI or above (a somewhat lower concentration will suffice if one or more of the factors discussed in Section 3.4 indicate that effective collusion is particularly likely), and 2) the allegedly disruptive firm differs substantially in volume of purchases or other relevant characteristics from the other firms in its market. Where the stated thresholds are met or exceeded, the Department's decision whether to challenge a merger on this ground will depend upon an individual evaluation of its likely competitive effect.

4.23 Evasion of Rate Regulation

Non-horizontal mergers may be used by monopoly public utilities subject to rate regulation as a tool for circumventing that regulation. The clearest example is the acquisition by a regulated utility of a supplier of its fixed or variable inputs. After the merger, the utility would be selling to itself and might be able arbitrarily to inflate the prices of internal transactions. Regulators may have great difficulty in policing these practices, particularly if there is no independent market for the product (or service) purchased from the affiliate.[35] As a result, inflated prices could be passed along to consumers as "legitimate" costs. In extreme cases, the regulated firm may effectively preempt the adjacent market, perhaps for the purpose of suppressing observable market transactions, and may distort resource allocation in that adjacent market as well as in the regulated market. In such cases, however, the Department recognizes that genuine economies of integration may be involved. The Department will consider challenging mergers that create substantial opportunities for such abuses.[36]

4.24 Efficiencies

As in the case of horizontal mergers, the Department will consider expected efficiencies in determining whether to challenge a vertical merger. See Section 3.5 (Efficiencies). An extensive pattern of vertical integration may constitute evidence that substantial economies are afforded by vertical integration. Therefore, the Department will give relatively more weight to expected efficiencies in determining whether to challenge a vertical merger than in determining whether to challenge a horizontal merger.

35. A less severe, but nevertheless serious, problem can arise when a regulated utility acquires a firm that is not vertically related. The use of common facilities and managers may create an insoluble cost allocation problem and provide the opportunity to charge utility customers for non-utility costs, consequently distorting resource allocation in the adjacent as well as the regulated market.

36. Where a regulatory agency has the responsibility for approving such mergers, the Department may express its concerns to that agency in its role as competition advocate.

5. DEFENSES

5.1 Failing Firm

The "failing firm defense" is a long-established, but ambiguous, doctrine under which an anticompetitive merger may be allowed because one of the merging firms is "failing." Because the defense can immunize significantly anticompetitive mergers, the Department will construe its elements strictly.

The Department is unlikely to challenge an anticompetitive merger in which one of the merging firms is allegedly failing when: 1) the allegedly failing firm probably would be unable to meet its financial obligations in the near future; 2) it probably would not be able to reorganize successfully under Chapter 11 of the Bankruptcy Act,[37] and 3) it has made unsuccessful good faith efforts to elicit reasonable alternative offers of acquisition of the failing firm [38] that would both keep it in the market and pose a less severe danger to competition than does the proposed merger.

5.2 Failing Division

A similar argument can be made for "failing" divisions as for failing firms. A multidivisional firm may decide to leave a particular line of business by selling or liquidating a division. If the specific conditions set out below are met, the Department will consider the "failure" of the division as an important factor affecting the likely competitive effect of the merger. First, the proponents of a merger involving a "failing" division must establish, not based solely on management plans, which could be prepared simply for the purpose of creating evidence of intent, that the division would be liquidated in the near future if not sold. Second, the proponents of the merger also must demonstrate compliance with the competitively preferable purchaser requirement of the "failing firm" defense.

U.S. DEPARTMENT OF JUSTICE STATEMENT ACCOMPANYING RELEASE OF REVISED MERGER GUIDELINES, June 14, 1984

The U.S. Department of Justice ("Department") today issued revisions to its 1982 Merger Guidelines. The revisions reflect the Department's experience in applying the 1982 Guidelines during the past two years and, in addition, incorporate numerous suggestions made by various knowledgeable observers, both inside and outside the government. Although the revisions make some important refinements and clarifications, the Department believes that the 1982 Merger Guidelines provide a sound framework for applying the antitrust laws to mergers and do not require extensive modification.

---

37. 11 U.S.C. ¶¶ 1101–1174 (1982).

38. The fact that an offer is less than the proposed transaction does not make it unreasonable.

During the 14 years following the original publication of the Merger Guidelines in 1968, antitrust enforcers and the courts made great strides in improving and refining the way they analyzed mergers. Over time, the Department's merger policy changed so much that there was little similarity between that policy and the policy described in 1968 Guidelines. The 1982 revisions eliminated the resulting confusion by accurately describing the Department's actual merger enforcement policy.

The 1982 Guidelines did not simply clarify the Department's merger policy, however; they also represented an important advance in merger analysis. The 1982 Guidelines recognized that most mergers do not threaten competition and that many are in fact pro-competitive and benefit consumers. Moreover, the 1982 Guidelines reflected for the first time the important role that foreign competition plays in the Department's merger analysis. They thus provided a flexible analysis that proscribed only those mergers that—on the basis of sound economic and legal analysis—threaten competition. At the same time, the Guidelines set out clear standards enabling businesses to avoid antitrust problems when planning mergers.

The Department's experience in applying the Guidelines during the last two years has reaffirmed the soundness of their underlying principles. Nevertheless, the Department recognizes that unless its analysis is as dynamic and vital as the economy to which it is applied, that analysis may unnecessarily impede the efficiency of the economy, restrict the efforts of American businesses to compete internationally, and, thus, reduce the well-being of American consumers. Thus, over the past two years, the Department has continued to refine its merger analysis to incorporate new insights and to ensure the continued relevance of that analysis to a changing economic environment. The Department also has discovered that certain aspects of the 1982 Guidelines either are ambiguous or have been interpreted by observers in ways that are not fully consistent with the Department's actual policy. With today's revisions, the Department intends to refine further its merger analysis at the same time it clears up any misunderstanding about those aspects that remain unchanged.

Today's revisions principally address five key areas: (1) market definition and measurement; (2) factors that may affect the significance of concentration and market share data in evaluating horizontal mergers; (3) the treatment of foreign competition; (4) the treatment of efficiencies; and (5) the treatment of failing divisions of healthy firms. Generally, the revisions are intended to correct any misperception that the Guidelines are a set of rigid mathematical formulas that ignore market realities and rely solely on a static view of the marketplace. The revisions also make a number of stylistic and technical changes. Many important points have been moved from footnotes to the text to emphasize their importance, and other footnotes have been deleted because they were redundant or potentially confusing. However, no change in policy should be inferred from the deletion of a footnote.

The following is an explanation of the revisions made in the five key areas listed above.

1. Market Definition and Measurement

Perhaps the single most important contribution of the 1982 Guidelines was the development of a clear, economically sound framework for defining markets within which to analyze mergers. Market definition has historically played a crucial role in merger analysis; however, before the 1982 Guidelines, markets often were defined largely on an ad hoc basis. The 1982 Guidelines developed a general framework for market definition that can be objectively applied to a myriad of factual circumstances.

The Guidelines define a market as a group of products and a geographic area such that a hypothetical firm that is the only present and future seller of those products in that area would possess market power—the power profitably to restrict output and to raise prices. A firm that is the only present seller of those products in that area would not be able to exercise market power, if its attempt to impose a small but significant and nontransitory price increase would cause buyers to switch to other products or to products in other areas or would induce other firms to begin selling the particular products. Firms that sell products to which consumers would switch and that would begin selling the particular products would prevent the exercise of market power and should be included in the market.

The Guidelines translate these principles of market power into a market-definition standard that has become known as the "five-percent test". Markets are delineated by postulating a "small but significant and nontransitory" price increase—generally an increase of five percent for one year—for each product of each merging firm at that firm's location and examining the likely responses of buyers, sellers of other products, and sellers in other areas. If these competitive responses would cause the price increase to be unprofitable, then the area and group of products are expanded to include additional products and areas until the price increase would be profitable to impose. At that point—when it would be profitable for a hypothetical firm that was the only seller of the products in that area to impose a "small but significant and nontransitory" increase in price—the group of products and the area are considered to be a market.

Many apparently have attributed an unwarranted rigidity to the "five-percent test." Today's revisions clarify that the "five-percent test" is not an inflexible standard that will be used regardless of the circumstances of a given case. Rather, it is an analytical tool with which to analyze traditional types of probative evidence, such as those listed in the Guidelines. In addition, although in most contexts it will be appropriate to use five percent as a "small but significant" increase in price, in other contexts using five percent may result in markets that are defined either too narrowly or too broadly for the purpose of evaluating the potential exercise of market power. Therefore, the Department may at times postulate a price increase that is much larger or smaller than five percent, depending on the nature of the industry involved. (See Guidelines Section 2.11)

The 1982 Guidelines did not define the "price" for which an increase would be postulated. Today's revisions clearly state that the Department will consider the relevant price to be whatever is considered to be the price of the product at the stage of the industry being examined. For example, the relevant price at the retailing stage of an industry is generally the retail price. On the other hand, in certain transportation industries in which products are transported for a fee, the price is the price of the transportation services sold, or the tariff.

The Guidelines also clarify a number of other points relating to market definition:

—The Department generally will consider the relevant market to be the smallest group of products and geographic area that could be subjected to the exercise of market power. (See Guidelines Section 2.11)

—In defining markets the Department generally will use prevailing prices. However, likely future prices may be used instead of prevailing prices when changes in the prevailing price can be predicted with reasonable reliability. (See Guidelines Sections 2.12, 2.32)

—If all the necessary data were available, evidence of similarities or differences in price movements would be the best evidence that products are good substitutes for one another. However, similarities in price movements often occur for reasons that do not reflect substitutability. Therefore, the Department will deem relevant only those similarities in price movements that are not explainable by common or parallel changes in factors such as costs of common inputs, income, or other variables. (See Guidelines Section 2.11)

—The best base for measuring market shares often will depend on the availability of data. Assuming the relevant data are available, the Department generally will prefer to use dollar sales or shipments if branded or relatively differentiated products are involved and physical capacity, reserves, or dollar production if relatively homogeneous, undifferentiated products are involved. This rule-of-thumb reflects the fact that, if a product is relatively homogeneous and undifferentiated, the capacity to produce and distribute the product generally provides the best indication of a firm's likely supply response. On the other hand, if the relevant product is branded or differentiated, the firm's supply response will depend on factors other than capacity. For example, even if other perfume manufacturers raised their prices, a manufacturer of a different brand of perfume with a great deal of excess capacity may nevertheless be unable to utilize that capacity because it cannot sell the additional output of perfume. (See Guidelines Section 2.4)

—The period for determining whether production substitution by other firms is likely to occur in response to a "small but significant and nontransitory" increase in price has been changed from six months to one year to conform with the time period that is used to identify firms that are in the relevant geographic market. (See Guidelines Sections 2.2, 2.3)

2. Factors Affecting the Significance of Concentration and Market Share Data

Several revisions have been made in the Guidelines' discussion of horizontal mergers to clarify the degree to which factors other than simple concentration and market share data influence the Department's consideration of mergers. The 1982 Guidelines may have created the perception that they were a set of strict mathematical rules—that the Department collects historical data, plugs this data into a series of formulas, and then slavishly adheres to resulting answers without regard to qualitative factors that may affect the significance of the concentration and market share data. The following changes were made to correct any such misperception.

First, the discussion of the HHI thresholds has been modified to clarify that the Department will not challenge mergers solely on the basis of concentration and market share data without considering other relevant factors. The revisions make it clear that the Department will not challenge mergers with a post-merger HHI of less than 1000 points, except in extraordinary circumstances.

For mergers resulting in an HHI of between 1000 to 1800, the Department is unlikely to sue if the increase in the HHI is less than 100 points. The Department is likely to challenge mergers in this region that produce an increase in the HHI of more than 100 points, unless the Department concludes on the basis of the post-merger HHI, the increase in the HHI, and the presence or absence of the factors discussed in Sections 3.2, 3.3, 3.4, and 3.5 of the Guidelines that the merger is not likely substantially to lessen competition. For mergers resulting in an HHI of more than 1800, the Department is unlikely to sue if the increase in the HHI is less than 50 points. The Department is likely to challenge mergers in this region that produce an increase in the HHI of more than 50 points, unless the Department concludes, on the basis of the post-merger HHI, the increase in the HHI, and the presence or absence of the factors discussed in Sections 3.2, 3.3, 3.4, and 3.5 that the merger is not likely substantially to lessen competition. However, if the increase in the HHI exceeds 100 and the post-merger HHI substantially exceeds 1800, only in extraordinary cases will such factors establish that the merger is not likely substantially to lessen competition. Despite this fact, the Department will never ignore other factors when they are relevant. (See Guidelines Section 3.11)

Second, a new section has been added that discusses several factors that will be taken into account in interpreting concentration and market share data. The new subsection indicates that the Department will consider a number of factors that may indicate that a firm's current market share either understates or overstates its future competitive significance. One such factor is a recent or ongoing change in market-conditions. For example, if a new technology that is important to long-term competitive viability is not available to a particular firm, the Department may conclude that the historical market share of that firm overstates its future competitive significance. The Department will consider the reasonably predictable effects of such recent or ongoing changes in market conditions in interpreting market concentration and market share data. (See Guidelines Section 3.2)

Another consideration is the financial condition of a merging firm or any firm in the relevant market, to the extent that the firm's financial condition reflects underlying structural weaknesses of the firm and is not explainable as a phenomenon of, for example, the business cycle. In such a case, the firm's chronic financial weakness may indicate that its current market share overstates its future competitive significance. The 1982 Guidelines indicated in footnote 54 that the Department would consider the financial condition of a firm to the extent it was relevant to the competitive analysis. The revisions explain in greater detail the circumstances under which the Department will consider the financial condition of a firm to be a reliable indicator of that firm's future competitive significance. (See Guidelines Section 3.22) It is important to distinguish consideration of a firm's financial condition under Section 3.22 from the Guidelines' treatment of failing firms and failing divisions, however. Those doctrines will continue to be interpreted very strictly.

A third consideration is factors that may affect the competitive importance of foreign firms. These factors are discussed below in connection with the general discussion of foreign competition.

The revisions also add a new "other factor" to Section 3.4 relating to the ability of small or fringe firms to increase sales in response to a "small but significant and nontransitory" increase in price. (See Guidelines Section 3.43) The ability of fringe firms with excess capacity to expand output quickly and easily can substantially reduce the likelihood of collusion. Therefore, the Department is less likely to challenge a merger if small or fringe firms are currently able to expand significantly their sales at incremental costs that are approximately equal to their incremental costs at current levels of output.

Finally, the section on ease of entry has been revised to clarify how the Department considers this factor. For example, the revisions recognize that "entry" may occur as firms outside the market enter or as fringe firms currently in the market significantly expand their current capacity. (See Guidelines Section 3.3)

3. Treatment of Foreign Competition

One of the important advances of the 1982 Guidelines was their explicit recognition of foreign competition and world markets. The presence of foreign firms frequently makes it impossible for American firms to collude because any attempt to fix prices will attract increased imports. Although the 1982 Guidelines recognized the importance of foreign competition, they were somewhat unclear as to how imports and foreign capacity would actually be treated in specific circumstances.

Today's revisions clarify that, in general, the Guidelines' standards relating to the definition of markets and the calculation of market shares will apply equally to foreign and domestic firms. Moreover, no foreign firm will be excluded from the market solely because its sales in the United States are subject to import quotas. This is due to the fact that it is generally difficult to assess the effectiveness and longevity of a particular quota or to measure the likely offsetting supply response from firms in countries that are not subject to a quota. A quota that applies to only some countries and not others may have only a limited effect on the foreign competition that domestic firms face, because a country subject to a quota may divert its exports to a country that is not subject to the quota and that country in turn may divert an equivalent quantity of the product to the United States. Given the limitations on available data, the problems associated with trying to quantify the effects of such trade restraints often are insuperable.

To the extent permitted by available data, market shares generally will be assigned to foreign firms in the same way they are assigned to domestic firms. When dollar sales or shipments are used to measure the shares of domestic firms, the market shares of foreign firms will be measured using dollar sales in, or shipments to, the relevant market. If physical capacity, reserves, or dollar production is used for domestic firms, the market shares of foreign firms will be measured in terms of the capacity, reserves, or production that is likely to be devoted to the relevant United States market in response to a "small but significant and nontransitory" increase in price. If a quota would prevent a foreign competitor from increasing the amount of its shipments to the United States in response to such a price increase, the market shares assigned to the foreign competitor will not exceed the amount of imports permitted to be shipped to the United States under the quota. Although shares ordinarily will be assigned on a firm-by-firm basis, a single market share may be assigned to a country or to a group of countries if firms in the country or group of countries act in coordination, or if necessitated by the lack of relevant data. (See Guidelines Section 2.4)

Because of limitations on data, market shares of foreign firms may inaccurately reflect the firms' competitive significance. As noted above, foreign firms may be included in the market even though their U.S. imports are subject to quotas. In such cases, as well as others, the resulting market shares may overstate the competitive significance of the firms. Conversely, the Department may use shipment data because it may be impossible to measure foreign capacity that would be devoted to the United States in response to a "small but significant and nontransitory" increase in price. In such cases, the foreign firm's market share may understate its competitive significance. In general then, the Department will consider, where appropriate, qualitative evidence relating to the competitive significance of foreign firms in interpreting market share and concentration data. (See Guidelines Section 3.23)

4. Efficiencies

One of the important advances of the 1982 Guidelines was the increased freedom they gave to American industries to enhance efficiency through mergers. Implicit throughout the Guidelines is the recognition that the efficiency-enhancing potential of mergers can increase the competitiveness of firms and result in lower prices to consumers.

The language of the 1982 Guidelines, however, had a restrictive, somewhat misleading tone and indicated that the Department would explicitly consider efficiency claims only in "extraordinary cases." In practice, the Department never ignores efficiency claims. Rather, as the revisions now make clear, the Department considers and gives appropriate weight to efficiency claims in all cases in which they are established by clear and convincing evidence. In addition, the revisions clarify that efficiencies do not constitute a defense to an otherwise anticompetitive merger but are one of many factors that will be considered by the Department in determining whether to challenge a merger.

The revisions are intended not only to correct any misimpressions as to when the Department will consider efficiencies but also to provide guidance as to how efficiencies will be evaluated. The Guidelines indicate that the Department will consider various types of efficiencies including economies of scale, better integration of production facilities, plant specialization, and lower transportation costs. The Department also will consider general selling, administrative and overhead expenses; however, as a practical matter, these types of efficiencies may be difficult to demonstrate. In addition, the Department will reject claimed efficiencies if equivalent or comparable savings can reasonably be achieved by the parties by other means. Moreover, the greater the competitive concerns that the merger raises under the other standards of Section 3 of the Guidelines, the greater will be the level of expected efficiencies that the parties must establish. (See Guidelines Section 3.5)

5. Failing Divisions of Healthy Firms

The dynamic nature of our economy underscores the necessity of a merger policy that facilitates the ability of firms to respond to structural changes in the economy. The Department has considered several suggestions that the Guidelines should contain a declining industries defense or that the failing firm defense should be relaxed. However, the Department has concluded that, as revised, the basic framework of the Guidelines provides firms with adequate leeway for any needed restructuring. For example, the Department will consider the financial condition of firms in evaluating the competitive significance of their market shares. (See Guidelines Section 3.22) In addition, if the acquisition of a failing firm significantly increases efficiency, that fact will be considered. (See Guidelines Section 3.5)

Although the Department did not relax the failing firm defense or create a declining industries defense, the Department did conclude that it was appropriate to clarify the Guidelines' analysis of mergers involving a "failing division" of an otherwise healthy firm. The 1982 Guidelines stated only that although the standards applicable to failing firms are more difficult to apply to an unincorporated part of a larger parent firm, the Department would recognize the defense "in appropriate cases of that type." The revisions clarify that, in general, a division will be considered to be "failing" only if it would be sold or liquidated in the near future and if there is no competitively preferable purchaser available. (See Guidelines Section 5.2)

*

Index

FREE RIDER
Definition of problem, 605–606

GARY DINNERS
Steel industry consolidation, 86–87, 91

GEORGE, H.
Social commentary on "the promised land," 30

HARDING, WARREN
Term of abated antitrust activism, 97–98

**HART–SCOTT–RODINO ANTITRUST IM-
PROVEMENTS ACT**
See also Clayton Act
Premerger notification, 856–857

**HEALTH CARE QUALITY IMPROVEMENTS
ACT OF 1986**
Provisions, 416

HERFINDAHL–HIRSHMAN INDEX
See Mergers

HOOVER, HERBERT
Association movement champion, as, 355
Secretary of Commerce, under Harding and
Coolidge, 355

HORIZONTAL RESTRAINTS
See also Boycotts, Joint Action, Mergers,
Monopolies, Vertical Restraints
Concerted refusal to deal on certain terms,
see Federal Trade Commission Act, this
index
Doctrinal stability in mid-twentieth century,
307–308
Joint Venture, this index
Market Division, this index
Patents and, 350–354
Per se rules and rule of reason,
1920's and 1930's, pp. 282–307
Recent complex relationship, 308–343
Political Action, this index
Price restraints,
Direct exchange of information among
competitors, 367–375
Inference of price fixing, 375–381
Formative years of antitrust, 283–307
Recent cases, 309–343
Trade associations, 355–367
Product standardization, 381–383
Professional Self-regulation, this index
Rule of reason,
Recent complex relationship with per se
rule, 308–343
Trade associations and dissemination of in-
formation, 355–367
Historical note, 354–355

INTERSTATE COMMERCE ACT
Enacted, 44

INTERSTATE COMMERCE COMMISSION
Railroad rate regulation by, 52

JOINT ACTION
See also Boycotts, Horizontal Restraints,
Mergers, Vertical Restraints
Characterization of collaboration, 426
"Contract, combination, or conspiracy" un-
der Sherman Act, 450–481
Inference of agreement, 450–480
Existence of interdependent coordination
as support for inference, 480–484
Intra-enterprise conspiracy, note, 497–506
Joint Venture, this index
Parallel conduct, 484–497
Price signalling, 484–489
"Rimless wheel," 456
Sherman on, 504

JOINT VENTURE
Access to and exclusion from, 427–438
Analysis questions, 426–427
Anticompetitive essence, 448–450
See also Mergers, this index
Contractual restraints, 438–448
Definition, 295
Merger analysis applicable, 804
National Cooperative Research Act, this in-
dex
Potential competition, 830–832
Production by competitors, 804–811
Research and development by competitors,
811–813
Vertical effects, 841–842

JOSEPHSON, MATTHEW
On background of Standard Oil "Trust," 70–
75

JUSTICE DEPARTMENT GUIDELINES
See Mergers

KIRKLAND, E.C.
On rise of corporate structure, 26

KRAMER
On early history of tying arrangements,
644–650

LAW OF DEMAND
Derivation, 101

LETWIN, L.
On prosecution of *Northern Securities* railroad combination, 63

LOCAL GOVERNMENT ACTION
Not per se immune, 419

**LOCAL GOVERNMENT ANTITRUST ACT OF
1984**
Limited liability, 419

MARKET DIVISION
Horizontal restraints, 344–350
"Specialization agreements" allowed under
law of European Economic Community,
350
Variations, 344

MARKET POWER
Defined, 122

McGUIRE ACT
Extension of Sherman Act immunity, 533
Repeal, 533

McLAREN, RICHARD W.
Antitrust Division Assistant Attorney General under Nixon, 843–845
Speech to ABA Antitrust Section, 843

MERGERS
Accounting Principles Board of American Institute of Certified Public Accountants, new rules of accountancy, 843
Aggregate concentration, 843–851
Conventional bases to challenge, 844–845
Analysis, traditional and other models, 750, 778–783
Current enforcement, 789–804
Early consolidation movement, 737–738
Enforcement changes, in 1980's, p. 856
Failing firm defense, 776–778
Herfindahl–Hirshman Index, 784–787
Horizontal acquisition, 815–832
Joint Venture, this index
Justice Department Guidelines,
Market definition as key, 783–788
Potential competition, text concerning, 830
Text, 896–927
Legislative change, proposals, 788
Market definition, expansive readings of law, 769–776
Market-extension mergers, definition, 815
Mega-mergers, 843, 851–855
Dorgan bill, 855
Premerger notification, 856–857
"Merger Modernization" bill, 788
Newspaper Preservation Act, this index
Non-horizontal acquisition, 815–830
"Pac Man" defense, 851
Policy and practice in 1960's, p. 843
Potential competitors, 815–832
Reciprocity, 837–839
Sherman Act, early cases under, 738–743
Standing to challenge, 856
Private standing, 858–869
Supreme Court, new antitrust majority, 821, 824
Takeovers,
Attempts, 814–815
Free-market-for-control theory, 813–814
Leveraged buyout, 852–853
Relaxed government approach to enforcement, 851
Rodino bill, 854–855
Temporary National Economic Committee, this index
Vertical acquisitions, 832–837
Comments on efficiency, 839–841

MILLER–TYDINGS AMENDMENT
Purpose, 530–531
Repeal, 533

MITCHELL, JOHN N.
Address to Georgia Bar Association, 844

MONOPOLIES
See also Mergers
Attempts, 161–162, 269–280
Monopolization conduct standards distinguished, 269–270
Relevant market, 163–164
Combinations and conspiracies, 162–163
Relevant market, 163–164
Common Laws, this index
Conduct test, development, 143–164
Dominant firm conduct, 164–269
Anticompetitive strategies, 280–281
Predatory strategies, 206–244
Duty to continue dealing,
Cooperation with competitor, 244, 251–269
Vertical integration of distribution, 244–251
Elements of, 160
Exclusionary conduct, 146–159
Fraud on Patent Office, 200
Market definition predicate to evaluation of power, 114–122
Modern laws,
Development, 99–281
Distinguished from preceding cases, 175
New technologies, issues, 175–205
"New wave" cases, 175–206
Political Action, this index
Post-World War II attitudes, 175–176
Power as lever in other markets, 182–191
Predatory conduct by non-dominant firms, 269–280
Predatory strategies,
Design Conduct, this index
Dominant firms, strategies of, 206–244
Pricing, see Predatory Pricing, this index
Pricing considerations, 122–124
Refusal to deal, 164–175
See also Resale Price Maintenance, this index
Relevant market definition, 128–143
Structural consensus, this index
Submarkets, 141–143

NATIONAL COOPERATIVE RESEARCH ACT
Rule of reason applied to research and development joint ventures, 811–812
Text, 891–895

NATIONAL INDUSTRIAL RECOVERY ACT
Petroleum shipments under, 297
Provision unconstitutional, 298
Termination, 306

NATIONAL RECOVERY ACT
Cartelization of industry under governmental aegis contemplated, 99

"NEW FREEDOM"
Address to Congress, 96
Wilson's 1912 campaign, 93

VERTICAL RESTRAINTS
See also Boycotts, Horizontal Restraints, Joint Action, Mergers, Monopolies
Discriminatory Pricing, this index
Distribution Restraints, this index
Exclusive selling, see Foreclosing Restraints
Foreclosing Restraints, this index
Guidelines published by Justice Department, 587–588
Historical note, 522, 736
Internal corporate integration, 710–713
Joint Venture, this index
Maximum resale prices, 588–599
Standing to challenge, 599–601
Nonprice restraints and rule of reason, 564–582

VERTICAL RESTRAINTS—Cont'd
Price restraints illegal per se, 564–582
Tying Arrangements, this index

VERTICALITY
Definition, 522

WALSH, LAWRENCE E.
Memorandum in ITT case, 847

WILSON, WOODROW
Antitrust legislative program under, 94
Campaign of 1912, pp. 92–94
Election as expression of national sentiment for antitrust legislation, 92
"New freedom," 93, 96

†